XML

How to Program

Deitel™ Books, Cyber Classrooms, Complete Training Courses and Web-Based Training Courses published by Prentice Hall

How to Program Series

Advanced Java™ 2 Platform How to Program
C How to Program, 3/E
C++ How to Program, 3/E
C# How to Program
e-Business and e-Commerce How to Program
Internet and World Wide Web How to Program, 2/E
Java™ How to Program, 4/E
Perl How to Program
Python How to Program
Visual Basic® 6 How to Program
Visual Basic® .NET How to Program, 2/E
Visual C++® .NET How to Program (2002)
Wireless Internet & Mobile Business How to Program
XML How to Program

Multimedia Cyber Classroom and Web-Based Training Series

(for information regarding Deitel™ Web-based training visit **www.ptgtraining.com**)
Advanced Java™ 2 Platform Multimedia Cyber Classroom
C++ Multimedia Cyber Classroom, 3/E
C# Multimedia Cyber Classroom
e-Business and e-Commerce Multimedia Cyber Classroom
Internet and World Wide Web Multimedia Cyber Classroom, 2/E
Java™ 2 Multimedia Cyber Classroom, 4/E
Perl Multimedia Cyber Classroom
Python Multimedia Cyber Classroom
Visual Basic® 6 Multimedia Cyber Classroom
Visual Basic® .NET Multimedia Cyber Classroom, 2/E
Visual C++® .NET M/M Cyber Classroom (2002)
Wireless Internet & Mobile Business Programming Multimedia Cyber Classroom
XML Multimedia Cyber Classroom

The Complete Training Course Series

The Complete Advanced Java™ 2 Platform Training Course
The Complete C++ Training Course, 3/E
The Complete C# Training Course
The Complete e-Business and e-Commerce Programming Training Course
The Complete Internet and World Wide Web Programming Training Course, 2/E
The Complete Java™ 2 Training Course, 4/E
The Complete Perl Training Course
The Complete Python Training Course
The Complete Visual Basic® 6 Training Course
The Complete Visual Basic® .NET Training Course, 2/E
The Complete Visual C++® .NET Training Course (2002)
The Complete Wireless Internet & Mobile Business Programming Training Course
The Complete XML Training Course

.NET Series

C# How to Program
Visual Basic® .NET How to Program, 2/E
Visual C++® .NET How to Program (2002)

Visual Studio® Series

Getting Started with Microsoft® Visual C++™ 6 with an Introduction to MFC
Visual Basic® 6 How to Program
C# How to Program
Visual Basic® .NET How to Program, 2/E
Visual C++® .NET How to Program (2002)

For Managers Series

e-Business and e-Commerce for Managers

Coming Soon

e-books and e-whitepapers
Course Compass, WebCT and Blackboard Multimedia Cyber Classrooms versions

To communicate with the authors, send e-mail to:

deitel@deitel.com

For information on corporate on-site seminars and public seminars offered by Deitel & Associates, Inc. worldwide and to register for the *Deitel Buzz* e-mail newsletter, visit:

www.deitel.com

For continuing updates on Prentice Hall and Deitel & Associates, Inc. publications visit the Prentice Hall Deitel Web site or the InformIT Deitel kiosk:

XML
HOW TO PROGRAM

H. M. Deitel
Deitel & Associates, Inc.

P. J. Deitel
Deitel & Associates, Inc.

T. R. Nieto
Deitel & Associates, Inc.

T. M. Lin

P. Sadhu

Prentice
Hall

PRENTICE HALL, Upper Saddle River, New Jersey 07458

Library of Congress Cataloging-in-Publication Data
on File

Vice President and Editorial Director: *Marcia Horton*
Acquisitions Editor: *Petra J. Recter*
Assistant Editor: *Sarah Burrows*
Project Manager: *Crissy Statuto*
Editorial Assistant: *Karen Schultz*
Production Editor: *Camille Trentacoste*
Managing Editor: *David A. George*
Executive Managing Editor: *Vince O'Brien*
Chapter Opener and Cover Designer: *Tamara Newnam Cavallo*
Art Director: *Heather Scott*
Marketing Manager: *Jennie Burger*
Manufacturing Buyer: *Pat Brown*
Manufacturing Manager: *Trudy Pisciotti*
Assistant Vice President of Production and Manufacturing: *David W. Riccardi*

© 2001 by Prentice-Hall, Inc.
Upper Saddle River, New Jersey 07458

Printed in the United States of America

10 9 8 7 6 5 4 3 2

ISBN 0-13-028417-3

Prentice-Hall International (UK) Limited, *London*
Prentice-Hall of Australia Pty. Limited, *Sydney*
Prentice-Hall Canada Inc., *Toronto*
Prentice-Hall Hispanoamericana, S.A., *Mexico*
Prentice-Hall of India Private Limited, *New Delhi*
Prentice-Hall of Japan, Inc., *Tokyo*
Pearson Education Asia Pte. Ltd., *Singapore*
Editora Prentice-Hall do Brasil, Ltda., *Rio de Janeiro*

In loving memory of Morris and Lena Deitel.
Harvey, Barbara, Paul, and Abbey Deitel

To Frank L. Nieto
  Thanks, big brother, for always being there when I needed you.
  Tem R. Nieto

To the people who supported me—KC, Angie, the Moore's and Dennis.
  Ted M. Lin

To my parents for their support, encouragement, love,
affection, and understanding.
  Praveen Sadhu

Contents

7   Schemas   165

8   Document Object Model (DOM™)   192

9   Simple API for XML (SAX)   232

Illustrations

5   Creating Markup with XML

6   Document Type Definition (DTD)

13   XSL: Extensible Stylesheet Language Formatting Objects

14   XLink, XPointer, XInclude and XBase

15   Case Study: Message Forum with Active Server Pages

16   Server-side Java Programming

17   Perl and XML: A Web-based Message Forums Application

18   Accessibility

19   XHTML and XForms

20   Custom Markup Languages: Part I

21   Custom Markup Languages: Part II

25   Bonus Chapter: Introduction to Active Server Pages (ASP)

26   Bonus Chapter: Introduction to Perl Programming

27   Bonus Chapter: Introduction to Java 2 Programming

A   HTML Special Characters

B   HTML Colors

C   ASCII Character Set

D   Operator Precedence Charts

E   Number Systems

Preface

Live in fragments no longer. Only connect.
Edward Morgan Forster

Welcome to the exciting world of XML! This book is by an old guy and four young guys. The old guy (HMD; Massachusetts Institute of Technology 1967) has been programming and/or teaching programming for 40 years. The four young guys (PJD; MIT 1991, TRN; MIT 1992, TML; Carnegie Mellon 2001, PS; Northeastern 2000) have each been programming and/or teaching programming for many years. The old guy programs and teaches from experience; the young guys do so from an inexhaustible reserve of energy. The old guy wants clarity; the young guys want performance. The old guy seeks elegance and beauty; the young guys want results. We got together to produce a book we hope you will find informative, challenging and entertaining.

Why We Wrote XML How to Program

Today, XML is arguably the hottest technology in the computer industry. Therefore, university professors are eager to incorporate XML into their undergraduate and graduate Internet, Web, e-business and e-commerce curricula. Professionals are eager to use XML in their industrial-strength information-technology applications. Students are highly motivated by the fact that they are learning a leading-edge technology (XML) that will be immediately useful to them as they leave the university environment and head into a world where the Internet and World Wide Web have a massive prominence.

After mastering the material in this book, students will be well prepared to take advantage of the Internet and the Web as they take upper-level courses and venture into the rapidly changing programming world.

XML How to Program is the latest book in the Deitel/Prentice Hall *How to Program* series. It is distinguished by its focus on XML-based application development using programming languages such as Java, VBScript and Perl.

We have syntax-colored the code throughout the book. The key focus of this book is applications development with XML. Our audiences care about XML processing on the client, XML processing on the server, using XML encoded data as a database, etc.

Many XML books are reference manuals with exhaustive listings of features. That is not our style. We concentrate on creating real, working applications. We provide the live-code™ examples on the CD accompanying this book (and on **www.deitel.com**) so that you can run the applications and see the results.

We are excited about the enormous range of possibilities XML has to offer. We performed extensive research for this book and located hundreds of Internet and Web resources (which we provide as live links on the CD-ROM that accompanies this book and on **www.deitel.com**) to help you learn about XML and its related technologies. These links include general information, tutorials and demonstrations. Please read the tour of the book in Chapter 1 to familiarize yourself with the XML technologies we present.

A cutting-edge technology, XML is constantly evolving. This creates tremendous challenges for us as authors, for our publisher—Prentice Hall, for instructors, and for students and professional people.

We have worked hard to create useful live-code™ examples to help you master XML quickly and effectively. All of the code examples are on the accompanying disk and are available for free download from our Web sites:

> **www.deitel.com**
> **www.prenhall.com/deitel**

Teaching Approach

XML How to Program contains a rich collection of examples and exercises drawn from many fields to provide the student with a chance to solve interesting real-world problems. The book concentrates on the principles of good software engineering and stresses clarity. We avoid arcane terminology and syntax specifications in favor of teaching by example. The book is written by educators who spend most of their time writing about and teaching edge-of-the-practice programming topics.

Live-Code™ Teaching Approach

The book is loaded with live-code™ examples. This is the focus of the way we teach and write about programming, and the focus of our multimedia *Cyber Classrooms* and *Web-Based Training Courses* as well. Each new concept is presented in the context of a complete, working program immediately followed by one or more windows showing the program's input/output dialog. We call this style of teaching and writing our *live-code™ approach. We use programming languages to teach programming languages.* Reading these programs is much like entering and running them on a computer.

XML How to Program shows how to create Web sites starting with HTML programming, then rapidly proceeding to programming in XML. HTML and XML are considered to be markup languages rather than programming languages, but many of our examples use XML in the context of Java, VBScript, Active Server Pages, Perl and JavaScript. For those readers who wish to review these programming technologies, we include full-chapter introductions to VBScript, Active Server Pages, Perl and Java. The Java treatment is especially substantial.

World Wide Web Access

All of the code for *XML How to Program* (and our other publications) is on the Internet free for download at the Deitel & Associates, Inc. Web site

www.deitel.com

Please download all the code and run each program as you read the text. Make changes to the code examples and immediately see the effects of those changes. It is a great way to learn programming. [*Note:* You must respect the fact that this is copyrighted material. Feel free to use it as you study, but you may not republish any portion of it in any form without explicit permission from Prentice Hall and the authors.]

Objectives

Each chapter begins with a statement of *Objectives.* This tells students what to expect and gives them an opportunity, after reading the chapter, to determine if they have met these objectives. It is a confidence builder and a source of positive reinforcement.

Quotations

The learning objectives are followed by quotations. Some are humorous, some are philosophical, and some offer interesting insights. Our students enjoy relating the quotations to the chapter material. Many of the quotations are worth a "second look" *after* you read each chapter.

Outline

The chapter *Outline* helps students approach the material in top-down fashion. This, too, helps students anticipate what is to come and set a comfortable and effective learning pace.

Example XML documents (with Program Outputs)

We present features in the context of complete, working XML documents. This is the focus of our teaching and our writing. We call it our live-code™ approach. Each Web document is followed by the outputs produced when the document is rendered in a Web browser (We use both Microsoft's Internet Explorer 5 and Netscape 6) and its scripts are executed. This enables students to confirm that the Web pages are rendered as expected. Reading the book carefully is much like entering the code and rendering these documents on a computer. The documents range from just a few lines of code to substantial examples with several hundred lines of code. Students should download all the code for the book from our Web site, and run each program while studying that program in the text.

Illustrations/Figures

An abundance of charts, line drawings and program outputs is included.

Programming Tips

We have included programming tips to help students focus on important aspects of program development. We highlight these tips in the form of *Good Programming Practices, Common Programming Errors, Testing and Debugging Tips, Performance Tips, Portability Tips, Software Engineering Observations* and *Look-and-Feel Observations.* These tips and practices represent the best we have gleaned from a total of almost eight decades of programming and teaching experience. One of our students—a mathematics major—told us that she feels this approach is like the highlighting of axioms, theorems and corollaries in mathematics books; it provides a foundation on which to build good software.

Good Programming Practices

Good Programming Practices are highlighted in the text. They call the students attention to techniques that help produce better programs. When we teach introductory courses to non-programmers, we state that the "buzzword" of each course is "clarity," and we tell the students that we will highlight (in these Good Programming Practices) techniques for writing programs that are clearer, more understandable and more maintainable.

Common Programming Error

Students learning a language—especially in their first programming course—tend to make certain kinds of errors frequently. Focusing on these Common Programming Errors helps students avoid making the same errors. It also helps reduce long lines outside instructors' offices during office hours!

Performance Tips

In our experience, teaching students to write clear and understandable programs is by far the most important goal for a first programming course. But students want to write the programs that run the fastest, use the least memory, require the smallest number of keystrokes, or dazzle in other nifty ways. Students really care about performance. They want to know what they can do to "turbo charge" their programs. So we have include Performance Tips to highlight opportunities for improving program performance.

Portability Tips

Software development is a complex and expensive activity. Organizations that develop software must often produce versions customized to a variety of computers and operating systems. So there is a strong emphasis today on portability, i.e., on producing software that will run on a variety of computer systems with few, if any, changes. Achieving portability requires careful and cautious design. There are many pitfalls. We include Portability Tips to help students write portable code.

Software Engineering Observations

The Software Engineering Observations highlight techniques, architectural issues and design issues, etc. that affect the architecture and construction of software systems, especially large-scale systems. Much of what the student learns here will be useful in upper-level courses and in industry as the student begins to work with large, complex real-world systems.

Testing and Debugging Tips

This "tip type" may be misnamed. When we first decided to incorporate Testing and Debugging Tips, we thought these tips would be suggestions for testing programs to expose bugs and suggestions for removing those bugs. In fact, most of these tips tend to be observations about programming capabilities and features that prevent bugs from getting into programs in the first place.

Look-and-Feel Observations

We provide Look-and-Feel Observations to highlight graphical user interface (GUI) conventions. These observations help students design their own graphical user interfaces to conform with industry norms.

Summary

Each chapter ends with additional pedagogical devices. We present a thorough, bullet-list-style *Summary* of the chapter. This helps the students review and reinforce key concepts.

Terminology

We include in a *Terminology* section an alphabetized list of the important terms defined in the chapter—again, further reinforcement.

Self-Review Exercises and Answers

Extensive self-review exercises and answers are included for self-study. This gives the student a chance to build confidence with the material and prepare for the regular exercises. Students should attempt all the self-review exercises and check their answers.

Exercises (Solutions in Instructor's Manual)

Each chapter concludes with a set of exercises including simple recall of important terminology and concepts; writing individual statements; writing small portions of XML documents and program; and writing complete XML documents. Instructors can use these exercises to form homework assignments, short quizzes and major examinations. The solutions for most of the exercises are included in the *Instructor's Manual* and the *Instructor's CD **available only to instructors*** through their Prentice-Hall representatives. [*NOTE*: **Please do not write to us requesting the instructor's manual. Distribution of this publication is strictly limited to college professors teaching from the book. Instructors may obtain the solutions manual only from their regular Prentice Hall representatives. We regret that we cannot provide the solutions to professionals**.] Solutions to approximately half of the exercises are included on the *XML Multimedia Cyber Classroom* CD (available in bookstores and computer stores; please see the last few pages of this book or visit our Web site at **www.deitel.com** for ordering instructions). If you purchased this book as part of *The Complete XML Training Course*, you should have also received the *XML Multimedia Cyber Classroom CD*. If you purchased only the book, you can purchase the Cyber Classroom CD separately—please see the ordering instructions at the end of the book.

Index Entries

We have included an extensive *Index* at the back of the book. This helps the student find any term or concept by keyword. The *Index* is useful to people reading the book for the first time and is especially useful to practicing programmers who use the book as a reference. The terms in the *Terminology* sections generally appear in the *Index* (along with many more index items from each chapter). Students can use the *Index* in conjunction with the *Terminology* sections to be sure they have covered the key material of each chapter.

"Double Indexing" of Live-Code™ Examples and Exercises

XML How to Program has many live-code™ examples. We have "double indexed" each of the live-code™ examples. For every source-code program in the book, we took the figure caption and indexed it both alphabetically and as a subindex item under "Examples." This makes it easier to find examples using particular features.

Bibliography

An extensive bibliography of books, articles and online documentation is included to encourage further reading.

Software Included with XML How to Program

The CD-ROM at the end of this book contains a variety of software, including Microsoft Internet Explorer 5, Apache Xalan (for Java), FOP and Xerces, W3C Amaya Web browser and Sun Microsystems' JAXP. The CD also contains the book's code examples and an HTML Web page with links to the Deitel & Associates, Inc. Web site, the Prentice Hall Web site and the many Web sites listed in the Web resources sections of the chapters. If you have access to the Internet, the Web page on the CD can be loaded into your World Wide Web browser to give you quick access to all the resources.

If you have any questions about using this software, please read the introductory documentation on the CD-ROM. Additional information is available at our Web site: **www.deitel.com. We do not provide technical support for the software application programs. However, if you have any technical questions about the installation of the CD, please email media.support@pearsoned.com. They will respond promptly.**

XML Programming Multimedia Cyber Classroom and The Complete XML Programming Training Course

We have prepared an optional interactive, CD-ROM-based, software version of *XML How to Program* called the *XML Multimedia Cyber Classroom*. It is loaded with features for learning and reference. The *Cyber Classroom* is wrapped with the textbook at a discount in *The Complete XML Training Course*. If you already have the book and would like to purchase the *XML Multimedia Cyber Classroom* separately, please call 1-800-811-0912 and ask for ISBN# 0-13-089555-5.

The CD has an introduction with the authors overviewing the *Cyber Classroom*'s features. The live-code™ example Web documents in the textbook truly "come alive" in the *Cyber Classroom*. With many of the examples, you can simply click the lightning bolt icon and the document will be loaded into a Web browser and rendered. You will immediately see the program's outputs. If you want to modify a document and see the effects of your changes, simply click the floppy-disk icon that causes the source code to be "lifted off" the CD and "dropped into" one of your own directories so that you can edit the document and try out your new version. Click the speaker icon for an audio that talks about the document and walks you through the code.

The *Cyber Classroom* also provides navigational aids including extensive hyperlinking. The *Cyber Classroom* remembers in a "history list" recent sections you have visited and allows you to move forward or backward in that history list. The thousands of index entries are hyperlinked to their text occurrences. You can key in a term using the "find" feature and the *Cyber Classroom* will locate occurrences of that term throughout the text. The *Table of Contents* entries are "hot," so clicking a chapter name takes you to that chapter.

Students like the solved problems from the textbook that are included with the *Cyber Classroom*. Studying and running these extra programs is a nice way for students to enhance their learning experience.

Students and professional users of our *Cyber Classrooms* tell us they like the interactivity and that the *Cyber Classroom* is an effective reference because of the extensive hyperlinking and other navigational features. We recently had an e-mail from a person who said that he lives "in the boonies" and cannot take a live course at a university, so the *Cyber Classroom* was a good solution to his educational needs.

Professors tell us that their students enjoy using the *Cyber Classroom*, spend more time on the course and master more of the material than in textbook-only courses. Also, the *Cyber Classroom* helps shrink lines outside professors' offices during office hours. We have also published the *C++ Multimedia Cyber Classroom (3/e)*, the *Visual Basic 6 Multimedia Cyber Classroom, the Java 2 Multimedia Cyber Classroom 3/e, the Internet and World Wide Web Programming Multimedia Cyber Classroom, e-Business and e-Commerce Multimedia Cyber Classroom* and *the Perl Multimedia Cyber Classroom*.

Acknowledgments

One of the great pleasures of writing a textbook is acknowledging the efforts of the many people whose names may not appear on the cover, but whose hard work, cooperation, friendship and understanding were crucial to the production of the book.

Many other people at Deitel & Associates, Inc. devoted long hours to this book.

- Barbara Deitel managed the preparation of the manuscript. She did all this in parallel with handling her extensive financial and administrative responsibilities at Deitel & Associates, Inc.

- Sean Santry revised Chapters 2 through 4 and verified the technical accuracy of the entire book.

- Kate Steinbuhler co-authored Appendix F and handled the permissions for the book.

- Matthew Kowalewski created illustrations for Chapter 21 and contributed to the terminology sections. Matthew also performed the vast majority of indexing for the book.

- Peter Brandano created several illustrations.

The Deitel & Associates, Inc. *College Internship Program* offers a limited number of paid positions to Boston-area college students majoring in Computer Science, Information Technology, Marketing or English. Students work at our corporate headquarters in Sudbury, Massachusetts full-time in the summers and/or part-time during the academic year. Full-time positions are available to college graduates. For more information about this competitive program, please contact Abbey Deitel at **deitel@deitel.com** and check our Web site, **www.deitel.com**. Deitel & Associates, Inc. student interns who worked on this book include:

- Audrey Lee, a junior majoring in mathematics and computer science at Wellesley College, wrote major portions of Chapter 10's Java-based XML messenger case study and Chapter 16's Java-based wireless bookstore case study.

- Joshua Gould a graduate of Clark University wrote major portions of Chapter 16's Java-based wireless bookstore case study.

- Rudolf Faust, a freshman at Stanford University, co-authored Chapter 1. Rudolf also wrote portions of Chapters 20, 21 and 22.

- Blake Perdue, a junior majoring in computer science at Vanderbilt University, contributed to Chapters 5, 11 and 15.

- Ben Wiedermann, a senior majoring in computer science at Boston University, contributed to Chapters 5, 20, 21 and 22.

- Jacob Ellis, a freshman at University of Pennsylvania, contributed to the self-review exercises and Web resources, checked Chapters 2, 3 and 4 for accuracy and contributed to Chapters 20 and 21.

- Melissa Jordan, a senior majoring in graphic design at Boston University, created most of the illustrations.

- Carlo Garcia, a senior majoring in computer science at Boston University, contributed to Chapter 5 and helped edit Chapter 6.

- Jeni Jefferson, a graduate of Boston College, researched the quotes.

- Gary Grinev, a senior at Framingham High School, contributed to the bibliography and the Web resources.

- Rioa MacMaster, a graduate of Tufts University, contributed to the terminology sections.

We would also like to acknowledge contributions related to the book's bonus chapters:

- Robin Trudell, an independent consultant, co-authored Chapter 26 "Active Server Pages" in our *Internet and World Wide Web How to Program* book. It is from this chapter that our Chapter 25 evolved. We would also like to acknowledge Hani Hamandi, a graduate student at Boston University, who contributed to Chapter 25.

- Chris Poirer, a senior at the University of Rhode Island, co-authored Chapter 27 "Perl and CGI" in our *Internet and World Wide Web How to Program* book. It is from this chapter that our Chapter 26 evolved. We would also like to acknowledge David McPhie, a graduate of Harvard, Andrew Jones, a senior at Dartmouth College, Jeff Listfield, a Junior at Harvard and Justin Gordon, a Junior at Brandeis University who made many contributions to Chapter 26.

- Jacob Ellis—a freshman at the University of Pennsylvania, and David Gusovsky—a freshman at Berkeley, co-authored Chapters 3, 4 and 14 in our *Internet and World Wide Web How to Program* book. It is from these chapters that our Chapters 2, 3 and 4 evolved.

We are fortunate to have been able to work on this project with the talented and dedicated team of publishing professionals at Prentice Hall. We especially appreciate the extraordinary efforts of our computer science editor, Petra Recter, our project manager, Crissy Statuto, our assistant editor, Sarah Burrows, and their boss—our mentor in publishing—Marcia Horton, Editor-in-Chief of Prentice-Hall's Engineering and Computer Science Division. Vince O'Brien and Camille Trentacoste did a marvelous job managing production.

The *XML Multimedia Cyber Classroom* was developed in parallel with *XML How to Program*. We sincerely appreciate the new-media insight, savvy and technical expertise of our multimedia, computer-based training and Web-based training editors, Mark Taub and Karen McLean. They did a remarkable job bringing the *XML Multimedia Cyber Classroom* to publication under a tight schedule.

We owe special thanks to the creativity of Tamara Newnam Cavallo (`smart_art@earthlink.net`) who did the art work for our programming tips icons and the cover. She created the delightful bug creature who shares with you the book's programming tips.

We wish to acknowledge the efforts of our 21 reviewers and to give a special note of thanks to Crissy Statuto of Prentice Hall who managed this extraordinary review effort:

- Charles McCathieNevile (W3C)
- Ian Jacobs (W3C)
- Scott Woodgate (Microsoft)
- Michael Corning (Microsoft)
- Scott Tsao (Boeing)
- Simon North (Synopsys)
- Dave Peterson (SGML Works!)
- Simon St. Laurent
- Devan Shepherd (Shepherd Consulting Services)
- Steven Livingstone
- M.C. Shraefel (Dept. of Computer Science, University of Toronto)
- Paul Foote (California State University–Fullerton)
- Andrew Watt
- Maxim Loukianov (Broadvision)
- Steve Smith (Software Architects, Inc.)
- Darrin Bishop (Levi, Ray and Shoup, Inc.)
- Jonathan Earl (Technical Training and Consulting)
- Jesse Wilkins (Metalinear Media)
- Jim Kurtz (Visible Systems)
- Carl Burnham
- Irina Golfman (Inera Incorporated)

Under a tight time schedule, these reviewers scrutinized the text and made countless suggestions for improving the accuracy and completeness of the presentation.

We would sincerely appreciate your comments, criticisms, corrections and suggestions for improving the text. Please address all correspondence to our email address:

`deitel@deitel.com`

We will respond immediately. Well, that's it for now. Welcome to the exciting world of XML programming. We hope you enjoy this look at leading-edge computer applications development. Our best wishes to you.

Dr. Harvey M. Deitel
Paul J. Deitel
Tem R. Nieto
Ted Lin
Praveen Sadhu

About the Authors

Dr. Harvey M. Deitel, CEO of Deitel & Associates, Inc., has 40 years experience in the computing field including extensive industry and academic experience. He is one of the world's leading computer science instructors and seminar presenters. Dr. Deitel earned B.S. and M.S. degrees from the Massachusetts Institute of Technology and a Ph.D. from Boston University. He worked on the pioneering virtual memory operating systems projects at IBM and MIT that developed techniques widely implemented today in systems like UNIX, Linux and Windows NT. He has 20 years of college teaching experience including earning tenure and serving as the Chairman of the Computer Science Department at Boston College before founding Deitel & Associates, Inc. with Paul J. Deitel. He is author or co-author of several dozen books and multimedia packages and is currently writing many more. With translations published in Japanese, Russian, Spanish, Elementary Chinese, Advanced Chinese, Korean, French, Polish, Portuguese and Italian, Dr. Deitel's texts have earned international recognition. Dr. Deitel has delivered professional seminars internationally to major corporations, government organizations and various branches of the military.

Paul J. Deitel, Executive Vice President of Deitel & Associates, Inc., is a graduate of the Massachusetts Institute of Technology's Sloan School of Management where he studied Information Technology. Through Deitel & Associates, Inc. he has delivered Java, C, C++ and Internet and World Wide Web courses for industry clients including Compaq, Sun Microsystems, White Sands Missile Range, Rogue Wave Software, Computervision, Stratus, Fidelity, Cambridge Technology Partners, Boeing, Lucent Technologies, Adra Systems, Entergy, CableData Systems, NASA at the Kennedy Space Center, the National Severe Storm Laboratory, IBM and many other organizations. He has lectured on C++ and Java for the Boston Chapter of the Association for Computing Machinery, and has taught satellite-based Java courses through a cooperative venture of Deitel & Associates, Inc., Prentice Hall and the Technology Education Network. He and his father, Dr. Harvey M. Deitel, are the world's best-selling Computer Science textbook authors.

Tem R. Nieto, Director of Product Development with Deitel & Associates, Inc., is a graduate of the Massachusetts Institute of Technology where he studied engineering and computing. Through Deitel & Associates, Inc. he has delivered courses for industry clients including Sun Microsystems, Compaq, EMC, Stratus, Fidelity, Art Technology, Progress Software, Toys "R" Us, Operational Support Facility of the National Oceanographic and Atmospheric Administration, Jet Propulsion Laboratory, Nynex, Motorola, Federal Reserve Bank of Chicago, Banyan, Schlumberger, University of Notre Dame, NASA, various military installations and many others. He has co-authored several books and multimedia packages with the Deitels and has contributed to virtually every Deitel & Associates, Inc. publication.

Ted M. Lin is a senior at Carnegie Mellon University where he is double majoring in computer science and electrical/computer engineering. He enjoys building Web sites and internet applications involving leading-edge technologies.

Praveen Sadhu is a graduate student at Northeastern University majoring in engineering software design. He received his bachelor's degree in Electrical Engineering from Hyderabad, India.

The Deitels are co-authors of the best-selling introductory college computer-science programming language textbooks, *C How to Program: Third Edition*, *C++ How to Program: Third Edition* and *Java How to Program: Third Edition*. With Tem R. Nieto, they have co-authored *Visual Basic 6 How to Program, Internet and World Wide Web How to Program, e-Business and e-Commerce How to Program, XML How to Program* and *Perl How to Program*. The Deitels are also co-authors of the *C++ Multimedia Cyber Classroom: Third Edition*—the third edition of Prentice Hall's first multimedia-based computer science textbook and the *Java 2 Multimedia Cyber Classroom: Third Edition*. Tem R. Nieto joined them as a co-author on the *Visual Basic 6 Multimedia Cyber Classroom,* the *Internet and World Wide Web Multimedia Cyber Classroom,* the *e-Business and e-Commerce Multimedia Cyber Classroom,* the *XML Multimedia Cyber Classroom* and the *Perl Multimedia Cyber Classroom*.

The Deitels are also co-authors of *The Complete C++ Training Course: Third Edition, The Complete Visual Basic 6 Training Course (with Tem R. Nieto), The Complete Java 2 Training Course: Third Edition, The Complete Internet and World Wide Web Training Course (with Tem R. Nieto), The Complete e-Business and e-Commerce Training Course (with Tem R. Nieto), The Complete XML Training Course (with Tem R. Nieto, Ted M. Lin and Praveen Sadhu)* and *The Complete Perl Training Course (with Tem R. Nieto and David McPhie)*—these products each contain the corresponding *How to Program Series* textbook and the corresponding *Multimedia Cyber Classroom*.

About Deitel & Associates, Inc.

Deitel & Associates, Inc. is an internationally recognized corporate-training and content-creation organization specializing in programming languages, Internet/World Wide Web, e-business/e-commerce and object technology education. Deitel & Associates, Inc. is a member of the World Wide Web Consortium. The company provides elementary through advanced courses on Java™, C++, Visual Basic®, C, C#, Perl, Python, XML™, Internet and World Wide Web programming, e-business and e-commerce programming and object technology. The principals of Deitel & Associates, Inc. are Dr. Harvey M. Deitel and Paul J. Deitel. The company's clients include many of the world's largest computer companies, government agencies, branches of the military and business organizations. Through its publishing partnership with Prentice Hall, Deitel & Associates, Inc. publishes leading-edge programming textbooks, professional books, interactive CD-ROM-based multimedia *Cyber Classrooms* and Web-based training courses. Deitel & Associates, Inc. and the authors can be reached via email at

> `deitel@deitel.com`

To learn more about Deitel & Associates, Inc., its publications and its worldwide corporate on-site training curriculum, see the last few pages of this book and visit:

> `www.deitel.com`

Deitel & Associates, Inc. has competitive opportunities in its College Internship Program for students in the Boston area. For information, please contact Abbey Deitel at `deitel@deitel.com`.

Individuals wishing to purchase Deitel books and *Complete Training Courses* can do so through popular online booksellers at

> `www.deitel.com`

Bulk orders by corporations and academic institutions should be placed directly with Prentice Hall—please see the last few pages of this book for worldwide ordering details.

The World Wide Web Consortium (W3C)

W3C® Deitel & Associates, Inc. is a member of the *World Wide Web Consortium* **MEMBER** *(W3C)*. The W3C was founded in 1994 "to develop common protocols for the evolution of the World Wide Web." As a W3C member, we hold a seat on the W3C Advisory Committee (our Advisory Committee representative is our Chief Technology Officer, Paul Deitel). Advisory Committee members help provide "strategic direction" to the W3C through meetings around the world (the Spring 2000 meeting was held in Amsterdam). Member organizations also help develop standards recommendations for Web technologies (such as HTML, XML and many others) through participation in W3C activities and groups. Membership in the W3C is intended for companies and large organizations. For information on becoming a member of the W3C visit **www.w3.org/Consortium/Prospectus/Joining**.

1

Introduction to the Internet and World Wide Web

Objectives

- To become familiar with the World Wide Web Consortium.
- To become familiar with the history of the Internet and World Wide Web.
- To become familiar with the history of the Standard Generalized Markup Language (SGML).
- To become familiar with the history of the Extensible Markup Language (XML).

Our life is frittered away by detail ... Simplify, simplify.
Henry Thoreau

High thoughts must have high language.
Aristophanes

The chief merit of language is clearness.
Galen

He had a wonderful talent for packing thought close, and rendering it portable.
Thomas Babington Macaulay

1.1 Introduction

Welcome to the world of XML! We have worked hard to create what we hope will be an informative, entertaining and challenging learning experience for you. As you read this book, you may want to refer to our Web site

```
www.deitel.com
```

for updates and additional information on each subject.

The technologies you will learn in this book are intended for experienced professionals building substantial systems. Perhaps most important, the book uses working programs and shows the outputs produced when those programs are run on a computer. We present all programming concepts in the context of complete working programs. We call this the *live-code*™ approach. These examples are available from three locations—they are on the CD-ROM inside the back cover of this book, they may be downloaded from our Web site **www.deitel.com** and they are available on our interactive CD-ROM product, the *XML Multimedia Cyber Classroom*. The *Cyber Classroom*'s features and ordering information appear in the last few pages of this book. The *Cyber Classroom* also contains answers to approximately half the exercises in this book, including short answers and small programs. If you purchased our boxed product *The Complete XML Training Course*, you already have the *Cyber Classroom*.

1.2 World Wide Web Consortium (W3C)

In October 1994, Tim Berners-Lee founded an organization—called the *World Wide Web Consortium (W3C)*—devoted to developing non-proprietary, interoperable technologies for the World Wide Web. One of the W3C's primary goals is to make the Web universally accessible—regardless of disabilities, language, culture, etc.

The W3C is also a standardization organization. Web technologies standardized by the W3C are called *Recommendations*. Current W3C Recommendations include HyperText Markup Language (HTML), Cascading Style Sheets (CSS) and the Extensible Markup

Language (XML). Recommendations are not actual software products, but documents that specify the role, syntax, rules, etc. of a technology. Before becoming a W3C Recommendation, a document primarily passes through three major phases: *Working Draft*—which, as its name implies, specifies an evolving draft, *Candidate Recommendation*—a stable version of the document that industry may begin implementing and *Proposed Recommendation*—a Candidate Recommendation that is considered mature (i.e., has been implemented and tested over a period of time) and is ready to be considered for W3C Recommendation status. For detailed information about the W3C Recommendation track, see "6.2 The W3C Recommendation track" at

```
www.w3.org/Consortium/Process/Process-19991111/
process.html#RecsCR
```

The W3C is comprised of three *hosts*—the Massachusetts Institute of Technology (MIT), INRIA (Institut National de Recherche en Informatique et Automatique) and Keio University of Japan—and over 400 *members*, including Deitel & Associates, Inc. Members provide the primary financing for the W3C and help provide the strategic direction of the Consortium. To learn more about the W3C visit **www.w3.org**.

1.3 History of the Internet

In the late 1960s, one of the authors (HMD) was a graduate student at MIT. His research at MIT's Project Mac (now the Laboratory for Computer Science—the home of the World Wide Web Consortium) was funded by ARPA—the Advanced Research Projects Agency of the Department of Defense. ARPA sponsored a conference at which several dozen ARPA-funded graduate students were brought together at the University of Illinois at Urbana-Champaign to meet and share ideas. During this conference, ARPA rolled out the blueprints for networking the main computer systems of about a dozen ARPA-funded universities and research institutions. They were to be connected with communications lines operating at a then-stunning 56 Kbps (i.e., 56,000 bits per second), at a time when most people (of the few who could be) were connecting over telephone lines to computers at a rate of 110 bits per second. HMD vividly recalls the excitement at that conference. Researchers at Harvard talked about communication with the Univac 1108 "supercomputer" across the country at the University of Utah to handle calculations related to their computer graphics research. Many other intriguing possibilities were raised. Academic research was about to take a giant leap forward. Shortly after this conference, ARPA proceeded to implement what quickly became called the *ARPAnet*, the grandparent of today's *Internet*.

Things worked out differently than originally planned. Although the ARPAnet did enable researchers to share each others' computers, its chief benefit proved to be the capability of quick and easy communication via what came to be known as *electronic mail (e-mail)*. This is true even today on the Internet, with e-mail facilitating communications of all kinds among millions of people worldwide.

One of ARPA's primary goals for the network was to allow multiple users to send and receive information at the same time over the same communications paths (such as phone lines). The network operated with a technique called *packet switching* in which digital data was sent in small packages called *packets*. The packets contained data, address information, error-control information and sequencing information. The address information was used to route the packets of data to their destination, and the sequencing information was used to help reassemble the packets (which—because of complex routing mechanisms—could actually arrive out of order) into their original order for presentation to the recipient. This packet-switching technique greatly reduced transmission costs from those of dedicated communications lines.

The network was designed to operate without centralized control. This meant that if a portion of the network should fail, the remaining working portions would still be able to route packets from senders to receivers over alternate paths.

The protocols for communicating over the ARPAnet became known as *TCP—the Transmission Control Protocol*. TCP ensured that messages were properly routed from sender to receiver and that those messages arrived intact.

In parallel with the early evolution of the Internet, organizations worldwide were implementing their own networks for both intra-organization (i.e., within the organization) and inter-organization (i.e., between organizations) communication. A huge variety of networking hardware and software appeared. One challenge was to get these to intercommunicate. ARPA accomplished this with the development of *IP—the Internet Protocol*), truly creating a "network of networks," the current architecture of the Internet. The combined set of protocols is now commonly called *TCP/IP*.

Initially, use of the Internet was limited to universities and research institutions; then the military became a big user. Eventually, the government decided to allow access to the Internet for commercial purposes. Initially there was resentment among the research and military communities—it was felt that response times would become poor as "the net" became saturated with so many users.

In fact, the exact opposite has occurred. Businesses rapidly realized that, by making effective use of the Internet, they could tune their operations and offer new and better services to their clients. So, they started spending vast amounts of money to develop and enhance the Internet. This generated fierce competition among the communications carriers and hardware and software suppliers to meet this demand. The result is that *bandwidth* (i.e., the information carrying capacity of communications lines) on the Internet has increased tremendously and costs have plummeted. It is widely believed that the Internet has played a significant role in the economic prosperity that the United States and many other industrialized nations have enjoyed over the last decade and are likely to continue enjoying for many years.

1.4 History of the World Wide Web

The *World Wide Web* allows computer users to locate and view multimedia-based documents (i.e., documents with text, graphics, animations, audios and/or videos) on almost any subject. Even though the Internet was developed more than three decades ago, the introduction of the *World Wide Web* was a relatively recent event. In 1989, *Tim Berners-Lee* of CERN (the European Laboratory for Particle Physics) began to develop a technology for sharing information by using hyperlinked text documents. He based his new language on the well-established *Standard Generalized Markup Language (SGML)*—a standard for business data interchange that we discuss in Section 1.6—and called it the *HyperText Markup Language* (HTML). He also wrote communication protocols to form the backbone of his new hypertext information system, which he termed the *World Wide Web*.

The Internet and the World Wide Web will surely be listed among the most important and profound creations of humankind. In the past, most computer applications ran on "stand-alone" computers, i.e., computers that were not connected to one another. Today's applications can be written to communicate among the world's hundreds of millions of computers. The Internet mixes computing and communications technologies. It makes our work easier. It makes information instantly and conveniently accessible worldwide. It makes it possible for individuals and small businesses to get worldwide exposure. It is changing the nature of the way business is done. People can search for the best prices on virtually any product or service. Special-interest communities can stay in touch with one another. Researchers can be made instantly aware of the latest breakthroughs worldwide.

1.5 Future of Computing

Most people are familiar with the exciting things computers do. It is *software* (i.e., the instructions that command the computer to perform *actions* and make *decisions*) that controls computers (often referred to as *hardware*). Computer use is increasing in almost every field of endeavor. In an era of steadily rising costs, computing costs have been decreasing dramatically because of the rapid developments in both hardware and software technology. Computers that might have filled large rooms and cost millions of dollars just two decades ago can now be inscribed on the surfaces of silicon chips smaller than a fingernail, costing perhaps a few dollars each. Ironically, silicon is one of the most abundant materials on earth—it is an ingredient in common sand. Silicon chip technology has made computing so economical that hundreds of millions of general-purpose computers are in use worldwide, helping people in business, industry, government and in their personal lives. That number could easily double in a few years.

Advances in hardware and software have led to the explosion of the Internet and World Wide Web. Propelling the wave of innovation is a constant demand for new and improved technology. People want to transmit pictures and they want those pictures to be in color. They want to transmit voices, sounds and audio clips. They want to transmit full-motion color video. And at some point, they will insist on three-dimensional, moving-image transmission. Our current flat, two-dimensional televisions will eventually be replaced with three-dimensional versions that turn our living rooms into "theaters-in-the-round" or sports stadiums. Our business offices will enable video conferencing among colleagues half a world apart as if they were sitting around one conference table. Consumers who want to buy products from electronic storefronts will be able to see perfect 3D images of them beforehand. The possibilities are intriguing and the Internet is sure to play a key role in making many of these possibilities become reality.

There have been predictions that the Internet will eventually replace the telephone system. Why stop there? It could also replace radio and television as we know them today. It's not hard to imagine the Internet and the World Wide Web replacing newspapers with completely electronic news media. Many newspapers and magazines already offer Web-based versions, some fee based and some free. Over 95 percent of printed material is currently not online, but in the future it may be. The e-book, an electronic text that is encryption-protected by the publisher, is on the rise and could well supplant the paper book. With a chemistry e-book, students could watch animations of chemical reactions, and a history e-book could be updated to include current events. Increased bandwidth is making it possible to stream audio and video over the Web. Companies and even individuals already run their own Web-based radio and television stations. Just a few decades ago, there were only a few television stations. Today, standard cable boxes accommodate about 100 stations. In a few more years, we will have access to thousands of stations broadcasting over the Web worldwide. This textbook you are reading may someday appear in a museum alongside radios, TVs and newspapers in an "early media of ancient civilization" exhibit.

The Internet has enabled people worldwide to communicate easily with one another. Online communities have been, are being and will be formed to bring together people of similar backgrounds, lifestyles, professions and interests. These communities provide resources for their members as well as forums in which their members can meet and chat. Professionals such as lawyers, doctors and scientists have online communities that offer a wealth of readily accessible information and an ideal environment for exchanging ideas. The number of online communities is proliferating and will continue to do so.

People with disabilities form one of the largest online communities, as the Internet and Web have enabled them to take advantage of computing and communication to perform tasks of which they were not previously able. Things that were once difficult for people with disabilities, such as buying goods at a store, will be made easy by e-commerce technologies. However, at the time of this writing, 95 to 99 percent of all Web sites are inaccessible to the visually, hearing or mobility impaired. In this regard, the World Wide Web Consortium (W3C) is pursuing its *Web Accessibility Initiative*. Information about the Web Accessibility Initiative is available at **www.w3.org/WAI**.

To enable people with disabilities to author their own Web sites, the WAI is instituting the *ATAG (Authoring Tools Accessibility Guidelines)*, which contains specifications for software developers to follow. The goal of the WAI is to transform the Web into a medium in which all people are able to access and use the technology and information available. In the future, their aim will undoubtedly be achieved.

1.6 History of SGML

In the late 1960's, Charles Goldfarb, Edward Mosher and Raymond Lorie of IBM tackled the problem of building a powerful yet portable system for the interchange and manipulation of legal documents. At the time, communication between computer systems at IBM was hindered by a profusion of different file formats. The three researchers realized that communication would be best facilitated by a system-independent common format which was specific to legal documents. They decided to use a markup language at the center of their system. Markup, which identifies structures in a document, was a mainstay of text processing and thus compatible across many platforms. The IBM team's prototype language marked up structural elements that specified the abstract nature rather than the formatting of the information they contained. The formatting information itself would be kept in separate files called *style sheets*, with which computers could format the elements and render a finished document. This method of structuring data made it possible for computers to automatically process documents in many new ways. Documents could only be processed reliably, the IBM team realized, if they adhered to a standard, so that a system would be able to recognize and reject *invalid documents* (i.e., documents with missing information, extra information, etc.). The structure of each document type, therefore, was strictly defined in a file called a *document type definition (DTD)*. This separation of presentation and validation provided great flexibility, because DTDs and style sheets could easily be modified without directly affecting the marked up data.

By 1969, the team of researchers had developed a language with all of these capabilities and called it the *Generalized Markup Language (GML)*. In 1974, Goldfarb proved that a *parser* (i.e., software capable of analyzing the structure and syntax of a document) could validate a document without actually processing it. This opened the door to further development, which culminated in the 1986 adoption of the *Standard Generalized Markup Language (SGML)* as an international standard. It quickly became the business standard for data storage and interchange throughout the world. Processing of SGML documents is defined by the *Document Style Semantics and Specification Language (DSSSL)*, another international standard. Six years after SGML became an International Organization for Standards (ISO) standard, it was followed by the *Hypermedia/Time-based Structuring Language (HyTime)*, which was designed for SGML representation of hypermedia and multimedia and has powerful linking capabilities.

1.7 XML and *XML How to Program*

With the explosion of the Web, the limitations of HTML eventually became apparent. Its lack of extensibility frustrated developers and its ambiguous definition allowed erroneous HTML to proliferate. Platform-specific formatting commands were created as HTML extensions by browser vendors attempting to gain market share. In response to this threat to the interoperability and scalability of the Web, the W3C created a stylesheet technology for HTML, *Cascading Style Sheets (CSS)*, that could be used in place of the proprietary markup. The W3C also added limited extensibility to HTML. These were, however, only stopgap solutions. The need for a new, standardized, fully extensible, structurally strict language was apparent. As a result, the *Extensible Markup Language (XML)* was born. XML combines the power and extensibility of its parent language, SGML, with the simplicity demanded by the Web community. The W3C also began to develop XML-based standards for stylesheets and advanced hyperlinking. *Extensible Stylesheet Language (XSL)* incorporates the elements of both CSS and Document Style and Semantics Specification Language (DSSSL). The *Extensible Linking Language (XLink)* combines ideas from HyTime and the *Text Encoding Initiative (TEI)*, which provides SGML guidelines for the academic community.

HTML documents are human-readable but are not optimized for computer manipulation, whereas most forms of data storage are optimized for computer manipulation and not for human viewing. XML is the first language that makes documents both human-readable and computer-manipulable, a result of a tag set that is more powerful, flexible and extensible than HTML's. It is the language of the intelligent document, a step ahead of conventional methods of document representation that rely on format rather than structure.

Data independence, the separation of content and its presentation, is the essential characteristic of XML. Because an XML document describes data, it can conceivably be processed by any application. The absence of formatting instructions makes it easy to parse. This makes XML an ideal framework for data exchange. Recognizing this fact, software developers across the world are integrating XML into their applications in order to gain Web functionality and interoperability. For the same reason, XML is becoming the language of choice to implement the middle tier of client/server interfaces. Its flexibility and power make it perfect for middleware, which must be maximally interoperable in order to be effective. Because XML's semantic and structural information enables it to be manipulated by any application, much of the processing that was once limited to servers will be performed by clients. This will reduce server load and network traffic, resulting in a faster, more efficient Web. However, XML is not limited to Web applications. It is increasingly being used in databases, as the structured yet unformatted nature of an XML document enables it to be manipulated by database applications. In the future, as the Web continues to expand, it seems likely that XML will become the universal language for representing data. Then, all applications would be able to communicate provided they could understand each others' XML markup or *vocabularies.*

XML, though it has many advanced capabilities, is accessible to all levels of programmers because of its inherent simplicity. It is text-based, so anybody can create an XML document with even the most primitive text processing tools. However, XML is not limited to describing only textual data, but also can describe images, vector graphics, animation or any other data type to which it is extended. It enables a nonprogrammer to do things that would have previously required extensive knowledge of scripting languages or thousands of dollars worth of custom software. Because XML is an open standard, there is a wide selection of tools for implementing it, so a user can pick whatever fits their needs without fear of being tied to a specific platform.

What XML did for marking up data, XSL and XLink will do for presenting and linking it. Like XML, they will be accessible to nonprogrammers yet powerful enough to handle industrial tasks. With XSL, the same XML document can be published in different formats depending, for instance, on the user to whom it is served. XLink will provide the ability to link between different types of resources. A link could be made, for instance, between the tenth second of a song and the fourth second of a video. In addition, links will contain information on the resources to which they are linking, or *metadata.* This will make it easier to search for and find information on the Web.

The business community is rushing to get on the XML bandwagon. Faced with the shortcomings of *Electronic Document Interchange (EDI),* the standard method of information transfer in the business world, business is implementing XML to accomplish their goal of *Enterprise Application Integration (EAI)* for interoperability both within and between organizations. XML provides the perfect vehicle for moving EDI and other such technologies onto the Internet and into the hands of the smaller business that previously did not have the resources to implement EDI.

XML's metadata infrastructure provides a foundation for data interchange technologies to thrive. The *Resource Definition Framework (RDF),* developed by the W3C, adds to XML's metadata capabilities, defining entire categories of data. This makes it possible for businesses to create a metadata layer that is uniform throughout an enterprise or even between enterprises. Thus, an application can understand data without knowing where it came from; it just has to absorb the self-describing XML document. XML/RDF gives the different computer systems of different organizations and companies a common language in which to talk. With XML/RDF, businesses have the capability to communicate with each other as never before in terms of interoperability, simplicity and speed. All that is necessary to open these doors is a standard metadata vocabulary. Many vocabularies are being developed and are already in use in major sectors such as the automotive and airline industries. In the future, it is quite possible that most business transactions will be carried out using the XML/RDF framework for information interchange.

RDF will also make it easier to find information on the Internet. No longer will a search engine query produce a random list of predominantly useless links. Instead, a *bot* program (autonomous software that acts on the user's behalf) that searches the Internet will finally be able to deal with intelligent data that it can make sense of, resulting in accuracy unimaginable to today's Web surfers.

The *Universal Description, Discovery and Integration (UDDI) Project*, an initiative backed by a coalition of leading technology companies such as Microsoft, IBM and Ariba, is currently developing a framework for automated integration of all e-commerce transactions and Web services. At its heart, this framework will have an XML-based language used in a directory of businesses and their services.

The medical community is also adopting XML. *HL7*, the international medical informatics standard, is being retooled to work with SGML and XML. This will enable disparate medical computer systems to easily communicate and transfer information, meaning that a doctor will have all of his patients' information at his fingertips, or that the results of lab tests will be sent back to hospitals in real time. In addition, the information will be readable to systems that follow other medical standards because it is in the common language of XML.

Chess enthusiasts around the world are tapping into the power of XML. *CaXML*, a markup language for chess data, will allow sophisticated handling of chess data. It will be used not only to display chess data, but also to make chess computer games and mark up tournament or player information. Because of XML's inherent simplicity, it will be possible to translate from CaXML to other formats that describe chess data.

Another application of XML is *OnStar, Inc*. OnStar is a service that delivers information to drivers as they are on the road. To access the service, a driver simply has to push a button on their dashboard to access an automated voice system. The driver asks a question, which is translated by voice-recognition software into a tagged XML data request, which is then matched to an existing user profile. Then, the request is processed and forwarded to a partner Web service provider, which returns data marked up as XML that is converted to a *VoiceXML* document. The computer system then reads the VoiceXML to the user, answering the question. Without XML serving as a common language, this data exchange would have been extremely difficult, if not impossible. With XML, OnStar also gained the ability to present its content on other devices such as cellular phones and personal digital assistants (PDAs), which speak the XML-based *Wireless Markup Language (WML)*.

Although XML is rapidly making inroads in all fields of endeavor, it is by no means displacing older technologies. Because XML data is easy for computers to read and convert between formats, it can be used as middleware to integrate legacy systems with other applications and networks.

To make the possibilities of XML data interchange a reality, it will be necessary for businesses, software developers and other major users of XML to work with and not against each other. Otherwise, an assortment of different markup languages and even proprietary extensions to XML will result. Though there are definitely tensions between competing businesses and countries, it appears that the community of XML users is moving toward global cooperation.

Already, there is a host of software tools that use XML to facilitate the development of high level content and systems. Some are for Web authoring, such as Apache's Cocoon framework, which we will discuss in Chapter 16. Others integrate XML in order to create more efficient, interoperable, Web-friendly applications.

The possible uses for XML are endless. Information can be transmitted in simple, small files without XML, but with XML, the information is described precisely, so applications such as browsers can work with the information more intelligently. The beauty of smart data—a combination of simplicity, extensibility, and power—will propel XML to a place as the universal medium of communication on the Web and beyond.

Because XML is the future of the Internet, we had to write a book that would give a thorough grounding in the language and many of the related technologies on which future innovation will be based. The book offers a solid one- or two-semester upper-level elective. The book is also intended for professional programmers in corporate training programs or doing self-study. We will publish fresh editions of this book promptly in response to rapidly evolving Internet and Web technologies. [*Note:* Our publishing plans are updated regularly at our Web site **www.deitel.com**. The contents and publication dates of our forth-coming publications are always subject to change. If you need more specific information, please email us at **deitel@deitel.com**.]

1.8 A Tour of the Book

In this section, we take a tour of the subjects you will study in *XML How to Program*. Many of the chapters end with an Internet and World Wide Web Resources section that provides a listing of resources through which you can enhance your knowledge of XML and its re-lated topics. These Web resources are particularly valuable for such a dynamic technology as XML. In addition, you may want to visit our Web site to stay informed of the latest in-formation and corrections.

Chapter 1—Introduction to the Internet and the World Wide Web
In Chapter 1, we present some historical information about the Internet, the World Wide Web and XML. In this Tour of the Book, we also present an overview of the concepts you will learn in the remaining chapters.

Chapter 2—Introduction to HyperText Markup Language 4: Part I
In this chapter, we begin unlocking the power of the Web with *HTML*—the *Hypertext Markup Language*. HTML is a *markup language* for describing the elements of an HTML document (Web page) so that a browser, such as Microsoft's Internet Explorer or Netscape's Communicator, can render (i.e., display) that page.

We introduce the basics of creating Web pages in HTML using our *live-code*™ approach. Every concept is presented in the context of a complete working HTML docu-ment (or Web page) that is immediately followed by the screen output produced when that HTML document is rendered. We write many simple Web pages. The next chapter intro-duces more sophisticated HTML techniques, such as tables, which are particularly useful for presenting and manipulating information from databases.

We introduce basic HTML *tags* and *attributes*. A key issue when using HTML is the separation of the *presentation of a document* (i.e., how the document is rendered on the screen by a browser) from the *structure of that document*. This chapter begins our in-depth discussion of this issue. As the book proceeds, you will be able to create increasingly appealing and powerful Web pages.

Some key topics covered in this chapter include: incorporating text and images in an HTML document, linking to other HTML documents on the Web, incorporating special characters (such as copyright and trademark symbols) into an HTML document and sepa-rating parts of an HTML document with horizontal lines (called *horizontal rules*).

Chapter 3—Introduction to HyperText Markup Language 4: Part II
In this chapter, we discuss more substantial HTML elements and features. We demonstrate how to present information in *lists* and *tables*. We discuss how to collect information from

people browsing a site. We explain how to use *internal linking* and *image maps* to make Web pages easier to navigate. We also discuss how to use *frames* to make attractive Web sites. By the end of this chapter, we will have covered most commonly used HTML tags and features and will then be able to create more complex and visually appealing Web sites.

Chapter 4—Cascading Style Sheets (CSS)

In earlier versions of HTML, Web browsers controlled the appearance (i.e., the rendering) of every Web page. For example, if a document author placed an **h1** (i.e., a large heading) element in a document, the browser rendered the element in its own manner. With the advent of *Cascading Style Sheets*, the document author can specify the way the browser renders the page.

Applying Cascading Style Sheets to Web pages can give major portions of a Web site (or the entire Web site for that matter) a distinctive look and feel. Cascading Style Sheets technology allows document authors to specify the style of their page elements (spacing, margins, etc.) separately from the structure of their document (section headers, body text, links, etc.). This *separation of structure from content* allows greater manageability and makes changing the style of the document easier and faster.

Chapter 5—Creating Markup With XML

Having presented HTML and CSS, we now discuss the fundamentals of XML, setting the stage for the remainder of the book. Unlike HTML, which formats information for display, XML structures information. Therefore, it does not have a fixed set of tags as HTML does, but instead enables the document author to create new ones. We discuss the properties of the XML character set, which is *Unicode*—the standard aimed at expanding the boundaries of character representation. A brief overview of *parsers*—programs that process XML documents and their data—is given, as are the requirements for a *well-formed document* (i.e., a document that is syntactically correct). *Namespaces*, which differentiate elements with the same name, are introduced, and the chapter concludes with a case study for a day planner that we will enhance in subsequent chapters.

Chapter 6—Document Type Definition (DTD)

A *Document Type Definition (DTD)* is a structural definition for an XML document, specifying the type, order, number and attributes of the elements in an XML document as well as other information. By defining the structure of an XML document, a DTD reduces the validation and error-checking work of the application using the document. Well-formed and valid documents (i.e., documents that conform to the DTD) are discussed. This chapter shows how to specify different element and attribute types, values and defaults that describe the structure of the XML document. At the end of the chapter, we enhance the day-planner case study introduced in Chapter 5 by writing a DTD for it.

Chapter 7—Schemas

Schemas are an emerging technology that serves a similar purpose to DTDs. Schemas have several advantages over DTDs and may eventually replace DTDs entirely. Schemas use XML syntax, which enables them to be manipulated by XML tools; thus, the creation of elements and attributes in schema is similar to that in XML. In DTDs, all text data is just text, but by using schema data types, text can be given more meaning.

Two major types of schema models exist, one created by Microsoft and the other by the W3C. We examine each of them, but we concentrate on Microsoft Schema because

W3C Schema is not as widely supported yet. To validate our documents against a Microsoft schema, we use Microsoft's XML Validator. We enhance the day-planner case-study application introduced in Chapter 5 by writing a Microsoft schema for it.

Chapter 8—Document Object Model (DOM)

The W3C *Document Object Model (DOM)* is a Application Programming Interface (API) for XML that is platform and language neutral. The DOM API provides a standard set of interfaces (i.e., methods, objects, etc.) for manipulating an XML document's contents. Different industry vendors (e.g., Sun Microsystems, Microsoft, IBM, etc.) provide implementations of the DOM in their parsers. Because XML documents are hierarchically structured, they are represented in the DOM as a tree structure. Using DOM, scripts and programs can dynamically modify the content, structure and formatting of documents.

This chapter examines several important DOM capabilities, including the ability to retrieve data, insert data and replace data. It also demonstrates how to create and traverse documents using the DOM.

Because portions of the DOM are still being developed, we demonstrate some Microsoft extensions to the DOM. These extensions include the ability to load an XML document from disk. We use Microsoft's implementation of the DOM with JavaScript for our first DOM example, and then use Java applications and Sun Microsystem's implementation of the DOM for the remaining examples. At the end of the chapter, we enhance the day-planner case study to use the DOM. [*Note*: We provide a highly condensed introduction to Java in Chapter 27 for those readers who want a short review or introduction to Java.]

Chapter 9—Simple API for XML (SAX)

Simple API for XML (SAX) is another XML API. Unlike DOM which builds a tree structure in memory, SAX calls specific methods when a start tag, end tag, attribute, etc., are encountered in a document. For this reason, SAX is often referred to as an *event-based API*. SAX does not have all the features of DOM, but is complementary to DOM because it does not have some of DOM's shortcomings—such as memory requirements. Instead of storing an entire document in memory, it receives small pieces of data with the event model, a more efficient though sometimes less convenient approach.

We provide information on several SAX parsers and the setup of Sun Microsystem's Java-based JAXP parser, which we use for the chapter examples. We demonstrate the important classes, interfaces and methods related to SAX. We enhance the day-planner case-study application so that it uses SAX instead of DOM. This provides the reader with a nice opportunity to compare SAX and DOM. Both SAX 1.0 and the recently released SAX 2.0 are discussed. [*Note*: This is another Java-based chapter. Some readers may wish to read Chapter 27 before studying this chapter.]

Chapter 10—Case Study: XmlMessenger Program

In this chapter, we implement an instant messaging program, written in Java, that marks up client/server communication in XML. Instant messaging programs enable people to send text messages to each other in real time.

This case study makes extensive use of Java 2's networking capabilities for sending messages marked up as XML between clients. We use the DOM to manipulate the XML-based messages. We use Sun Microsystem's DOM extensions to read XML from and write XML to streams. We overview and implement first the server then the client side of the program.

Chapter 11—XML Path Language (XPath)

XML provides a way of describing data in a rich, flexible and efficient way by marking up data with descriptive tags. However, XML does not provide a way to locate specific pieces of structured data in a given document. For example, an XML document containing data about books published by Deitel & Associates, Inc., would need to be parsed then searched through element by element to find a specific book. For large documents, this process could be inefficient and error prone.

The *XML Path Language (XPath)* provides a syntax for locating specific parts (e.g., attribute values) of an XML document effectively and efficiently. XPath is not a structural language like XML; rather, it is a string-based language of expressions used by other XML technologies, such as *Extensible Stylesheet Language Transformations (XSLT)*, which converts (or transforms) XML documents to other formats (e.g., HTML), and the *XML Pointer Language (XPointer)*, which provides a means to "point" to information inside another XML document.

This chapter introduces the basics of XPath. We cover the most common high-level expression in XPath the *location path*—which specifies how to navigate the XPath tree.

Chapter 12—XSL: Extensible Stylesheet Language Transformations (XSLT)

XSL was designed to manipulate the rich and sophisticated data contained in an XML document, and is considerably more powerful than CSS. XSL has two major functions: formatting XML documents and transforming them into other data formats such as HTML, Rich Text Format (RTF), etc. In this chapter, we discuss the subset of XSL called XSLT. XSLT uses XPath to match nodes for transforming an XML document into another text document. We use the Java version of Apache's Xalan XSLT processor in our examples.

An XSL stylesheet contains *templates* with which elements and attributes can be matched. New elements and attributes can be created to facilitate a transformation. XSL allows iteration through node sets and thus sorting, which we demonstrate. We use XSL's conditional operators **if** and **choose**. We demonstrate how to copy nodes, combine stylesheets using **import** and store data in variables.

Chapter 13—XSL: Extensible Stylesheet Language Formatting Objects

This chapter covers the other half of XSL—formatting. We use Apache's FOP Formatting Object processor to render XSL formatting object's into Adobe Portable Document Format (PDF). Most of the formatting objects in XSL are based on CSS.

Throughout the chapter, important formatting object elements and attributes are discussed. We demonstrate how to create a formatting object, how to format text, how to format lists and tables and how to render XSL documents that contain formatting objects.

Chapter 14—XLink, XPointer, XInclude and XBase

One of the major contributing factors to the Web's popularity is hyperlinks, which provide a simple, yet powerful, means of linking documents. In this chapter, we introduce several emerging XML-related technologies that promise to go significantly beyond what is currently possible with HTML hyperlinks. We introduce the *XML Linking Language (XLink)* for describing links between resources (e.g., documents), the *XML Pointer Language (XPointer)* for "pointing" to a document's contents, *XML Inclusion (XInclude)* for including existing XML documents or portions of XML documents into another XML document and *XML Base (XBase)* for specifying a "base" URL for relative URLs. We demonstrate

XLink *simple links* (i.e., links similar to those written in HTML) and *extended links* (i.e., links that can be bi-directional and link to multiple resources). To demonstrate simple linking, we use Netscape Communicator 6. To demonstrate extended linking, we use Fujitsu's XLink processor.

Chapter 15—Case Study: Message Forum with Active Server Pages

In this chapter we create an online message forum using Microsoft's Active Server Pages (ASP), the first of the three server-side software development paradigms the book presents. We also use DOM, CSS, XSL, HTML and of course XML. Active Server Pages can be programmed in a variety of languages, but by far the most popular of these is Microsoft's *Visual Basic Scripting Edition (VBScript)*.

In a typical *multitiered Web-based application*, the *top tier* contains the code that interacts directly with the user. This tier, called the *client*, is usually the browser (such as Internet Explorer 5 or Netscape Communicator) rendering the Web page. The *bottom tier* is the database containing the organization's information. The *middle tier*, called the *server*, contains the *business logic*. It receives client requests from the top tier, references the data stored in the database in the bottom tier, and responds to the client by creating a new XML page and sending the page to the client to be rendered by the browser.

ASP is Microsoft's technology for implementing middle-tier business logic. In our online message forum, Active Server Pages are used to send messages and create new forums, and XML documents are used to store the forums. After we present all of the Active Server Pages in the program, we discuss the XML documents created by the program and their transformation with XSL and formatting with CSS. [*Note*: In Chapters 24 and 25 we provide introductions to VBScript and Active Server Pages, respectively.]

Chapter 16—Server-side Java Programming

In this chapter, we introduce three technologies that take advantage of XML to deliver Web content. We first introduce the Apache Group's Web publishing framework *Cocoon*. In our first example, we use Cocoon's XSL capabilities to dynamically deliver Web content to different types of clients, including Web browsers, such as Netscape Communicator and Internet Explorer, and wireless devices, such as digital cellular phones. In our second example, we use Cocoon's XML-based scripting technology—*Extensible Server Pages (XSP)*—to perform a user survey.

Also included in this chapter is a case study in which we build a wireless online bookstore using Java servlets, XML, XSL and *wireless markup language (WML)*—which is part of the *wireless applications protocol (WAP)* and is used to deliver Web content to cellular phones and other wireless devices. The case study demonstrates how these technologies can be used to build an integrated application in which presentation logic is separate from application logic.

Java servlets represent a popular way of building the server side of Web-based applications. In Chapters 15 and 17, we explore other server-side paradigms such as Microsoft's Active Server Pages and Perl/CGI.

Servlets are written in full-scale Java (not JavaScript), which requires a substantial book-length treatment to learn. We provide a highly condensed introduction to Java in Chapter 27, which includes servlets.

Chapter 17—Perl and XML: A Web-based Message Forums Application

There are a variety of popular server-side technologies for developing Web-based applications. Historically, the most widely used (and the third such technology we cover in this book) has been Perl/CGI.

Despite newer technologies from Microsoft and Sun—Active Server Pages (ASP) and JavaServer Pages, respectively—Perl/CGI is well entrenched and growing rapidly. Chapter 17 presents a case study where Perl is used along with XML to implement an online message forum. This message forum is a Perl implementation of the ASP message forum presented in Chapter 15.

Chapter 18—Accessibility

Currently, the World Wide Web presents a challenge to people with disabilities. Multimedia-rich Web sites often present difficulty to text readers and other programs designed to help the vision impaired and the increasing amount of audio on the Web is inaccessible to the deaf. The World Wide Web Consortium's Web Accessibility Initiative (WAI) provides guidelines on making the Web accessible to people with disabilities. This chapter provides a description of these methods, such as use of the **<headers>** tag to make tables more accessible to page readers, use of the **alt** attribute of the **<img>** tag to describe images, and proper use of HTML, CSS and XSL to ensure that a page can be viewed on any type of display or reader.

VoiceXML, which is presently supported only on the Windows platform, can be used to increase accessibility with speech synthesis and speech recognition. We examine a VoiceXML home page and how it generates a speech dialog with the user. The chapter concludes with an extensive list of Web resources related to accessibility.

Chapter 19—XHTML and XForms

XHTML (Extensible HyperText Markup Language) is the W3C's proposed successor to HTML. It corrects many of the problems that HTML has in dealing with complex data by making the markup conform to XML's strict syntax rules. XHTML's design is better equipped than HTML's to represent complex data on the Internet.

The majority of existing HTML code is not well formed because browsers do not explicitly check the markup. Browsers can treat poorly written HTML documents differently, requiring browser vendors to write additional features to handle the problem. With the emergence of the wireless Web and Web-enabled appliances, smaller devices such as PDAs (personal digital assistants) have a limited amount of memory far below that of today's desktops and cannot provide the extra resources required to process poorly written HTML. Documents intended for these devices must be well formed to guarantee uniform processing.

XHTML is HTML marked up as XML. We discuss the three DTDs that XHTML documents must conform to—strict, transitional and frameset—and provide examples of each type. Like many XML technologies, XHTML related technologies are still evolving.

We also introduce *XForms*, an XML technology that attempts to address the problems of HTML forms by dividing the form into three distinct parts: *data*, *logic* and *presentation*.

Chapter 20—Custom Markup Languages (Part I)

This chapter and Chapter 21 present many of the most popular and promising XML-based custom markup languages being developed.

The extensibility of XML provides ample opportunity for any individual or community to create a language that marks up data according to their specific needs. In this chapter, we discuss XML-based markup languages (or vocabularies) for mathematics, chemicals, wireless communication, multimedia/graphics and others.

Mathematical Markup Language (MathML) was created so mathematical information could be exchanged in an application independent manner. *Chemical Markup Language (CML)* is used by chemists for marking up molecules. Applications that process MathML and CML use their data as they see fit. For example, a mathematical equation may be graphed and a molecule might be rendered in three dimensions.

Wireless Markup Language (WML) is one of the most important markup languages that has arisen from XML, as it is a foundation of the wireless Web, allowing people to surf the Internet on cell phones and personal digital assistants (PDAs). In Chapter 16 we presented a substantial case study that used WML. Some readers may want to read the discussion of the WML presented in this chapter before studying Chapter 16.

To facilitate processing and integration of multimedia, *Synchronized Multimedia Integration Language (SMIL)* was created. SMIL has the potential to become the standard means of presenting multimedia content over the Web. *Scalable Vector Graphics (SVG)* is a language for describing graphics in a more efficient, Web friendly way.

The *Extensible 3D (X3D) Language* is the result of the combined efforts of the World Wide Web Consortium and the Web3D Consortium to extend the Virtual Reality Modelling Language (VRML) with XML. X3D is the next generation of VRML. We create an example that marks up a rocket.

Chapter 21—Custom Markup Languages (Part II)

Chapter 21 continues our study of custom markup languages. The first half of the chapter discusses markup languages related to e-business/e-commerce—one area of industry profoundly affected by XML. The second half of the chapter discusses markup languages related to law, publishing and graphical user interfaces.

The first markup language we introduce is the *Extensible Business Reporting Language (XBRL)*, which marks up financial reports and data. Other e-business/e-commerce markup languages discussed are the *Bank Internet Payment System (BIPS)*—which facilitates secure electronic transactions over the Internet, *Electronic Business XML (ebXML)*—which is designed to facilitate e-commerce between organizations, Visa XML Invoice Specification—which exchanges VISA credit-card purchase information between businesses over the Internet, and *Commerce XML (cXML)*—an XML-based framework for describing catalog data and performing business-to-business (B2B) electronic transactions that use the data.

LegalXML is a markup language for marking up court documents. *NewsML* marks up news content (e.g., text, audio, images, video, etc.). The chapter concludes with a discussion of the *XML Open eBook Publication Structure*—a standard for describing publishable electronic content and the *Extensible User Interface Language (XUL)*—which is designed to mark up graphical user interfaces.

Because most of the markup languages introduced in this chapter are in the early stages of development, we provide several Web resources for each markup language.

Chapter 22—XML Technologies and Applications

In this chapter, we discuss XML-based technologies and applications that represent the future of the Web. Many of these technologies are emerging technologies that promise to bring profound changes to the Web. However, many of these technologies have not as of yet been implemented in industry. Each section provides a brief introduction to the technology and a list of resources that contains more information. When possible, we use our live-code™ approach to illustrate a given technology.

Technologies discussed include: *XML Query*—a language for searching and retrieving data from XML documents, the *Resource Definition Format (RDF)*—which enables document authors to describe the data in an XML document, the *Channel Definition Format (CDF)*—a Microsoft technology for providing dynamic content to subscribers, *Rich Site Summary (RSS)*—a Netscape technology which provides dynamic content to channel subscribers, the *Platform for Privacy Preferences (P3P)*—a specification for describing a Web site's privacy policy so that visitors can make informed choices about how their information is being used on the Internet, the *Blocks Extensible Exchange Protocol (BXXP)*—an emerging technology for transferring data over the Internet. This chapter also introduces *XML Topic Maps (XTM)*—a technology for mapping information. For the XTM example, we use a Python implementation that is freely available.

Chapter 23—Simple Object Access Protocol (SOAP) and Microsoft Biztalk™

In this chapter, we present two emerging XML-based technologies for distributed communication over a network. Both of them enable applications without a common platform or communication protocol to exchange information.

The *Simple Object Access Protocol (SOAP)* is a new technology developed primarily by Microsoft and DevelopMentor for distributing objects (marked up as XML) over the Internet. SOAP provides a framework for expressing application semantics, encoding that data and packaging it in modules. We cover the three parts of SOAP: the *envelope*, which describes the content and intended recipient of a SOAP message; the SOAP *encoding rules*; and the SOAP *Remote Procedure Call (RPC) representation* for commanding other computers to perform a task.

Microsoft's BizTalk technology, which supports SOAP, is a messaging framework for business transactions designed to overcome barriers to *Enterprise Application Integration (EAI)*—the networking of diverse software systems both within and between organizations. BizTalk supports a standard set of schema (available at **BizTalk.org**) which can be used for loosely coupled messaging between different applications and systems. We examine the BizTalk Library of these schema, and demonstrate the applications of the BizTalk Framework and the workings of Microsoft BizTalk Server 2000.

Chapter 24—Bonus Chapter: An Introduction to VBScript

This chapter provides an introduction to VBScript to support the Active Server Pages used in Chapters 15 and 25. Many of our readers will be familiar with JavaScript, but not VBScript. When possible, we compare VBScript features to their equivalent JavaScript features. Key topics covered include control structures, functions, arrays and data types.

Chapter 25—Bonus Chapter: Introduction to Active Server Pages

This chapter provides an introduction to Active Server Pages to support the ASP case study introduced in Chapter 15. Before reading this chapter, readers are strongly encouraged to read Chapter 24. Key topics covered include session tracking, cookies, ActiveX Data Objects (ADO), file processing and Structured Query Language (SQL).

Chapter 26—Bonus Chapter: Introduction to Perl Programming

This chapter provides an introduction to Perl programming and the Common Gateway Interface (CGI) to support the case study introduced in Chapter 17. Key topics covered include data types, control structures, regular expressions, cookies, server-side includes and database access.

Chapter 27—Introduction to Java 2 Programming

This chapter provides an introduction to Java programming to support the Java code used in Chapters 8–10, 13, 16, 20 and 23. Key topics covered include data types, control structures, keywords, multithreading, database access using Java Database Connectivity (JDBC) and servlets.

Appendix A—HTML Special Characters

A table shows many commonly used HTML special characters, called *character entity references* by the World Wide Web Consortium (W3C).

Appendix B—HTML Colors

An explanation of how to create any color using either color names or hexadecimal RGB value is provided, along with a table that matches colors to values.

Appendix C—ASCII Character Set

This appendix contains a table of the 128 ASCII alphanumeric symbols.

Appendix D—Operator Precedence Chart

A series of tables show the precedence of the operators in JavaScript/JScript/ECMAScript, VBScript, Perl and Java.

Appendix E—Number Systems

This appendix explains the binary, octal, decimal and hexadecimal number systems. It explains how to convert between bases and perform mathematical operations in each base.

Appendix F—Career Resources

This appendix provides a listing of URLs and other resources related to careers in XML and its related technologies.

Appendix G—ActiveState Perl Installation [CD-ROM]

This appendix walks the reader through the installation of ActiveState's implementation of Perl for Windows (used in Chapter 17 and 26).

Appendix H—Setting Up an ODBC Data Source Name (DSN) [CD-ROM]

This appendix walks the user through the creation of a Windows DSN, which is used in Chapters 15 and 25–27 that access databases.

Appendix I—Installing a Windows Web Server [CD-ROM]

This appendix walks the reader through the installation of Microsoft's Personal Web Server (PWS), which is used in Chapters 15, 25 and 26 to serve Web documents to client Web browsers.

Well, there you have it! We have worked hard to create this book and its optional interactive multimedia *Cyber Classroom* version. The book is loaded with working, live-code™ examples, programming tips, self-review exercises and answers, challenging exercises that help you master the material. The technologies we introduce will help you write Web-based applications quickly and effectively. As you read the book, if something is not clear, or if you find an error, please write to us at **deitel@deitel.com**. When contacting us, provide as much information as possible—including the name and edition of the book. We will respond promptly, and we will post corrections and clarifications on our Web site

www.deitel.com

Prentice Hall maintains **www.prenhall.com/deitel** a Web site dedicated to our Prentice Hall textbooks, multimedia packages and Web-based training products. The site contains "Companion Web Sites" for each of our books that include frequently asked questions (FAQs), example downloads, errata, updates, additional self-test questions and other resources.

You are about to start on a challenging and rewarding path. We hope you enjoy learning with *XML How to Program* as much as we enjoyed writing it!

1.9 W3C XML Resources

The W3C homepage is a comprehensive description of the Web and where it is headed. The World Wide Web Consortium is an international joint effort with the goal of overseeing the development of the World Wide Web. The goals of the W3C are divided into categories: User Interface Domain, Technology and Society Domain, Architecture Domain and Web Accessibility Initiatives. For each Internet technology with which the W3C is involved, the site provides a description of the technology and its benefits to Web designers, the history of the technology and the future goals of the W3C in developing the technology.

The W3C Web site is the single best XML resource on the Internet, containing information on all of the important XML technologies. Updated daily to reflect the latest developments in the XML world, it also has complete archives dating back to the inception of XML. Every major XML technology has its own Web page which can be accessed from the XML home page, **www.w3.org/XML**. Each of these pages has a large list of links to various resources including the latest specifications, events, publications, developer discussions, software, tutorials, recommended reading and research notes. A brief explanation of XML can be found at **www.w3.org/XML/1999/XML-in-10-points**, and a description of the W3C's work on XML can be found at **www.w3.org/XML/Activity.html**.

1.10 Internet and World Wide Web Resources

www.deitel.com
Please check this site for daily updates, corrections and additional resources for all Deitel & Associates, Inc. publications.

www.learnthenet.com/english/index.html
Learn the Net is a Web site containing a complete overview of the Internet, the World Wide Web and the underlying technologies. The site contains information that can help novices get started with the Internet and Web.

www.xml.com
This Web site contains information, resources, tutorials and links related to any aspect and application of XML.

www.xml.org
This Web site is the industry portal for XML and contains many useful resources.

www.oasis-open.org/cover
This Web site is a portal to an extensive listing of articles and links concerning various XML technologies.

SUMMARY

[Note: Because this chapter is primarily a summary of the rest of the book, we have not provided a summary section. In the remaining chapters we provide, where appropriate, a detailed summary of the points covered in that chapter.]

TERMINOLOGY

Active Server Pages (ASP)
Application Programming Interface (API)
attribute
bandwidth
BizTalk
BizTalk Server 2000
bottom tier
browser
Cascading Style Sheets (CSS)
Channel Definition Format (CDF)
Chemical Markup Language (CML)
Commerce XML (cXML)
Document Object Model (DOM)
Document Style and Semantics Specification
    Language (DSSSL)
Document Type Definition (DTD)
e-book
e-business
e-commerce
Electronic Data Interchange (EDI)
Enterprise Application Integration (EAI)
Extensible 3D Language (X3D)
Extensible HyperText Markup Language
    (XHTML)
Extensible Linking Language (XLink)
Extensible Markup Language (XML)
Extensible Path Language (XPath)
Extensible Server Pages (XSP)
Extensible Stylesheet Language (XSL)
Extensible Stylesheet Language
    Transformations (XSLT)
frame
Generalized Markup Language (GML)

Hypertext Markup Language (HTML)
HyTime
Internet
Internet Protocol (IP)
invalid document
Java
JavaScript
live-code™ approach
markup language
metadata
middle tier
middleware
multimedia
Namespace
parser
Perl
Platform for Privacy Preferences (P3P)
presentation of a document
Resource Definition Format (RDF)
Rich Site Summary (RSS)
Scalable Vector Graphics (SVG)
semantics
separation of structure from content
servlet
Simple API for XML (SAX)
Simple Object Access Protocol (SOAP)
speech
Standard Generalized Markup Language (SGML)
structured documents
style sheets
Synchronized Multimedia Integration
    Language (SMIL)
tags

Text Encoding Initiative (TEI)
top tier
Transmission Control Protocol (TCP)
Unicode
Universal Description, Discovery and
    Integration (UDDI) Project
valid document
VBScript
W3C Candidate Recommendation

W3C host
W3C member
W3C Proposed Recommendation
W3C Recommendation
W3C Working Draft
well-formed document
Wireless Markup Language (WML)
World Wide Web Consortium (W3C)
XML Topic Maps (XTM)

SELF-REVIEW EXERCISES

1.1 Fill in the blanks in each of the following.
   a) The acronym W3C stands for _____.
   b) W3C standards are called _____.
   c) The acronym XML stands for _____.
   d) _____ incorporates the elements of both CSS and DSSSL.
   e) _____ combines ideas from HyTime and the Text Encoding Initiative (TEI).
   f) The acronym SGML stands for _____.

1.2 Fill in the blanks in each of the following sentences.
   a) _____ is the information carrying capacity of communications lines.
   b) The W3C is pursuing its _____ to help individuals with disabilities utilize the Web.
   c) The _____ is the grandparent of what is today called the Internet.
   d) The information carrying capacity of a communications medium like the Internet is called _____.
   e) The acronym TCP/IP stands for _____.

1.3 Fill in the blanks in each of the following statements.
   a) The _____ allows computer users to locate and view multimedia-based documents on almost any subject over the Internet.
   b) _____ of CERN developed the World Wide Web and several of the communications protocols that form the backbone of the Web.
   c) The acronym SOAP stands for _____.
   d) _____, developed by the W3C, adds to XML's metadata capabilities, defining entire categories of data.
   e) The acronym SVG stands for _____.

ANSWERS TO SELF-REVIEW EXERCISES

1.1   a) World Wide Web Consortium. b) Recommendations. c) Extensible Markup Language. d) Extensible Stylesheet Language (XSL). e) Extensible Linking Language (XLink). f) Standardized General Markup Language.

1.2   a) bandwidth. b) Web Accessibility Initiative. c) ARPAnet. d) bandwidth. e) Transmission Control Protocol/Internet Protocol.

1.3   a) World Wide Web. b) Tim Berners-Lee. c) Simple Object Access Protocol. d) *Resource Description Framework (RDF)*. e) Scalable Vector Graphics.

EXERCISES

1.4 State whether the following are *true* or *false*. If *false*, explain why.
   a) In 1994, Bill Gates founded the W3C.

     b) XML is a subset of HTML used to format data.
     c) MathML is one of many markup languages created with XML.
     d) HTML is a W3C Recommendation.
     e) The W3C has three hosts.
     f) XSL consists of transformations, formatting objects and SOAP.
     g) XHTML is an acronym for Extended HyperText Markup Language.

1.5 State whether the following are *true* or *false*. If *false*, explain why.
     a) HTML is an acronym for HyperText Markup Language.
     b) SAX is an acronym for Simple API for XML.
     c) HyTime is a markup language created with XML.
     d) XHTML is the proposed successor to HTML.
     e) Tim Berners-Lee and two other individuals created SGML.
     f) Parsers are software programs that process XML documents.
     g) Cascading Style Sheets technology allows you to specify the style of your page elements (spacing, margins, etc.) separately from the structure of your document (section headers, body text, links, etc.).

2

Introduction to HyperText Markup Language 4: Part I

Objectives

- To understand the key components of an HTML document.
- To be able to use basic HTML elements to create World Wide Web pages.
- To be able to add images to your Web pages.
- To understand how to create and use hyperlinks to traverse Web pages.
- To be able to create lists of information.

To read between the lines was easier than to follow the text.
Henry James

Mere colour, unspoiled by meaning, and annulled with definite form, can speak to the soul in a thousand different ways.
Oscar Wilde

High thoughts must have high language.
Aristophanes

I've gradually risen from lower-class background to lower-class foreground.
Marvin Cohen

2.1 Introduction

Welcome to the wonderful world of opportunities being created by the World Wide Web. The Internet is now three decades old, but it was not until the World Wide Web became popular in the 1990s that this current explosion of opportunities began. It seems that exciting new developments occur almost daily—a pace of innovation unlike what we have seen with any other technology. In this chapter, you will begin developing your own Web pages. As the book proceeds, you will be able to create increasingly appealing and powerful Web pages. In the last portion of the book you will learn how to create complete Web-based applications.

We begin unlocking the power of the Web in this chapter with *HTML*—the *Hypertext Markup Language*. HTML is not a procedural programming language like C, Fortran, Cobol or Pascal. Rather it is a *markup language* for identifying the elements of a page so that a browser, such as Microsoft's Internet Explorer or Netscape's Communicator, can render that page on your computer screen.

In this chapter we introduce the basics of creating Web pages in HTML. We write many simple Web pages. In later chapters we introduce more sophisticated HTML techniques, such as *tables*, which are particularly useful for structuring information from databases. We will also introduce Cascading Style Sheets, which are used to make Web pages more visually appealing.

We begin *XML How to Program* with these chapters on HTML in order to provide a foundation for structuring data with markup. In this chapter we introduce basic HTML *elements* and *attributes*. A key issue when using HTML (and, as we will see, when using XML) is the separation of the *presentation of a document* (i.e., how the document is rendered on the screen by a browser) from the *structure of that document*. Over the next several chapters, we discuss this issue in depth. In later chapters, we will show how XML provides a richer vocabulary for building structured documents.

2.2 Markup Languages

HTML is a *markup language*. It is used to format text and information. This "marking up" of information is different from the intent of traditional programming languages, which is to perform actions in a designated order. In the next several chapters, we discuss HTML markup in detail.

In HTML, text is marked up with *elements*, delineated by *tags* that are keywords contained in pairs of angle brackets. For example, the HTML *element* itself, which indicates that we are writing a Web page to be rendered by a browser, begins with a start tag of **<html>** and terminates with an end tag of **</html>**. These elements format your page in a specified way. Over the course of the next two chapters, we introduce many of the commonly used tags and how to use them.

Good Programming Practice 2.1

HTML tags are not case sensitive. However, keeping all the letters in one case improves program readability. Although the choice of case is up to you, we recommend that you write all of your code in lowercase. Writing in lowercase ensures greater compatibility with future markup languages that are designed to be written with only lowercase tags and elements.

Common Programming Error 2.1

Forgetting to include end tags for elements that require them is a syntax error and can grossly affect the formatting and look of your page. Unlike conventional programming languages, a syntax error in HTML does not usually cause page display in browsers to fail completely.

2.3 Editing HTML

In this chapter we show how to write HTML in its *source-code form*. We create *HTML documents* using a text editor and store them in files with either the **.html** or **.htm** file name extension. A wide variety of text editors exist. We recommend that you initially use a text editor called Notepad, which is built into Windows. Notepad can be found inside the **Accessories** panel of your **Program** list, inside the **Start** menu. You can also download a free HTML source-code editor called HTML-Kit at **www.chami.com/html-kit**. Unix users can use popular text editors like *vi* or *emacs*.

Good Programming Practice 2.2

*Assign names to your files that describe their functionality. This practice can help you identify documents faster. It also helps people who want to link to your page, by giving them an easier-to-remember name for the file. For example, if you are writing an HTML document that will display your products, you might want to call it **products.html**.*

As mentioned previously, errors in conventional programming languages like C, C++ and Java often prevent the program from running. Errors in HTML markup are usually not fatal. The browser will make its best effort at rendering the page, but will probably not display the page as you intended.

The file name of your *home page* (the first of your HTML pages that a user sees when browsing your Web site) should be **index.html**, because when a browser does not request a specific file in a directory, the normal default Web server response is to return **index.html** (this may be different for your server) if it exists in that directory. For example, if you direct your browser to **www.deitel.com**, the server actually sends the file **www.deitel.com/index.html** to your browser.

2.4 Common Elements

Throughout these HTML chapters we will present both HTML source code and a sample screen capture of the rendering of that HTML in Internet Explorer 5. Figure 2.1 shows an HTML file that displays one line of text.

Lines 1 and 2

```
<!DOCTYPE HTML PUBLIC "-//W3C//DTD HTML 4.01//EN"
            "http://www.w3.org/TR/html4/strict.dtd">
```

are required in every HTML document and are used to specify the *document type*. The document type specifies which version of HTML is used in the document and can be used with a validation tool, such as the W3C's **validator.w3.org**, to ensure an HTML document conforms to the HTML recommendation. In these examples we create HTML version 4.01 documents. All of the examples in these chapters have been validated through the Web site **validator.w3.org**.

The HTML document begins with the opening **<html>** tag (line 3) and ends with the closing **</html>** tag (line 17).

```
1   <!DOCTYPE HTML PUBLIC "-//W3C//DTD HTML 4.01//EN"
2               "http://www.w3.org/TR/html4/strict.dtd">
3   <html>
4
5   <!-- Fig. 2.1: main.html -->
6   <!-- Our first Web page   -->
7
8   <head>
9      <title>XML How to Program - Welcome</title>
10  </head>
11
12  <body>
13
14     <p>Welcome to Our Web Site!</p>
15
16  </body>
17  </html>
```

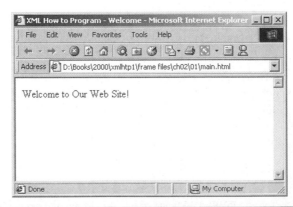

Fig. 2.1   Basic HTML file.

Good Programming Practice 2.3

Always include the **`<html>`**...**`</html>`** *tags in the beginning and end of your HTML document.*

Good Programming Practice 2.4

Place comments throughout your code. Comments in HTML are placed inside the **`<!--`**...**`-->`** *tags. Comments help other programmers understand the code, assist in debugging and list other useful information that you do not want the browser to render. Comments also help you understand your own code, especially if you have not looked at it for a while.*

We see our first *comments* (i.e., text that documents or describes the HTML markup) on lines 5 and 6.

```
<!-- Fig. 2.1: main.html -->
<!-- Our first Web page   -->
```

Comments in HTML always begin with **`<!--`** and end with **`-->`**. The browser ignores any text and/or tags inside a comment. We place comments at the top of each HTML document giving the figure number, the file name and a brief description of the purpose of the example. In subsequent examples, we also include comments in the markup, especially when we introduce new features.

Every HTML document contains a ***head*** element, which generally contains information about the document, and a **body** element, which contains the page content. Information in the **head** element is not generally rendered in the display window but may be made available to the user through other means.

Lines 8–10

```
<head>
    <title>XML How to Program - Welcome</title>
</head>
```

show the **head** element section of our Web page. Including a **`title`** element is required for every HTML document. To include a title in your Web page, enclose your chosen title between the pair of tags **`<title>`**...**`</title>`** in the **head** element.

Good Programming Practice 2.5

Use a consistent title naming convention for all pages on your site. For example, if your site is called "Al's Web Site," then the title of your links page might best be "Al's Web Site - Links," etc. This practice presents a clearer picture to those browsing your site.

The **`title`** element names your Web page. The title usually appears on the colored bar at the top of the browser window, and will also appear as the text identifying your page if a user adds your page to their list of **Favorites** or **Bookmarks**. The title is also used by search engines for cataloging purposes, so picking a meaningful title can help search engines direct a more focused group of people to your site.

Line 12

```
<body>
```

opens the ***body*** element. The body of an HTML document is the area where you place the content of your document. This includes text, images, links, forms, etc. We discuss many elements that can be inserted in the **body** element later in this chapter. Remember to include the end **</body>** tag before the closing **</html>** tag.

Various elements enable you to place text in your HTML document. We see the *paragraph element* on line 14

```
<p>Welcome to Our Web Site!</p>
```

All text placed between the **<p>**...**</p>** tags forms one paragraph. Most Web browsers render paragraphs as set apart from all other material on the page by a line of vertical space both before and after the paragraph. The HTML in line 12 causes Internet Explorer to render the enclosed text as shown in Fig. 2.1.

Our code example ends on lines 16 and 17 with

```
</body>
</html>
```

These two tags close the body and HTML sections of the document, respectively. As discussed earlier, the last tag in any HTML document should be **</html>**, which tells the browser that all HTML coding is complete. The closing **</body>** tag is placed before the **</html>** tag because the body section of the document is entirely enclosed by the HTML section. Therefore, the body section must be closed before the HTML section.

2.5 Headers

The six *headers* are used to delineate new sections and subsections of a page. Figure 2.2 shows how these elements (**h1** through **h6**) are used. Note that the actual size of the text of each header element is selected by the browser and can vary significantly between browsers. In Chapter 4, we discuss how you can "take control" of specifying these text sizes and other text attributes as well.

```
1   <!DOCTYPE HTML PUBLIC "-//W3C//DTD HTML 4.01//EN"
2            "http://www.w3.org/TR/html4/strict.dtd">
3   <html>
4
5   <!-- Fig. 2.2: header.html -->
6   <!-- HTML headers          -->
7
8   <head>
9      <title>XML How to Program - Headers</title>
10  </head>
11
12  <body>
13
14      <h1>Level 1 Header</h1>     <!-- Level 1 header -->
15      <h2>Level 2 header</h2>     <!-- Level 2 header -->
16      <h3>Level 3 header</h3>     <!-- Level 3 header -->
17      <h4>Level 4 header</h4>     <!-- Level 4 header -->
18      <h5>Level 5 header</h5>     <!-- Level 5 header -->
19      <h6>Level 6 header</h6>     <!-- Level 6 header -->
```

Fig. 2.2   Header elements **h1** through **h6** (part 1 of 2).

```
20
21   </body>
22   </html>
```

Fig. 2.2   Header elements **h1** through **h6** (part 2 of 2).

Good Programming Practice 2.6

Adding comments to the right of short HTML lines is a clean-looking way to comment code.

Line 14

```
<h1>Level 1 Header</h1>
```

introduces the **h1** *header element*, with its start tag **<h1>** and its end tag **</h1>**. Any text to be displayed is placed between the two tags. All six header elements, **h1** through **h6**, follow the same pattern.

Look-and-Feel Observation 2.1

Putting a header at the top of every Web page helps those viewing your pages understand what the purpose of each page is.

2.6 Linking

The most important capability of HTML is its ability to create hyperlinks to other documents, making possible a world-wide network of linked documents and information. In HTML, both text and images can act as *anchors* to *link* to other pages on the Web. We introduce anchors and links in Fig. 2.3.

```
1   <!DOCTYPE HTML PUBLIC "-//W3C//DTD HTML 4.01//EN"
2              "http://www.w3.org/TR/html4/strict.dtd">
3   <html>
4
5   <!-- Fig. 2.3: links.html        -->
6   <!-- Introduction to hyperlinks -->
7
8   <head>
9      <title>XML How to Program - Links</title>
10  </head>
11
12  <body>
13
14     <h1>Here are my favorite Internet Search Engines</h1>
15
16     <p><strong>Click on the Search Engine address to go to that
17        page.</strong></p>
18
19     <p><a href = "http://www.yahoo.com">Yahoo</a></p>
20
21     <p><a href = "http://www.altavista.com">AltaVista</a></p>
22
23     <p><a href = "http://www.askjeeves.com">Ask Jeeves</a></p>
24
25     <p><a href = "http://www.webcrawler.com">WebCrawler</a></p>
26
27  </body>
28  </html>
```

Fig. 2.3   Linking to other Web pages.

The first link can be found on line 19

```
<p><a href = "http://www.yahoo.com">Yahoo</a></p>
```

Links are inserted using the **a** *(anchor) element.* The anchor element is unlike the elements we have seen thus far in that it requires certain *attributes* (i.e., markup that provides information about the element) to specify the hyperlink. Attributes are placed inside an element's start tag and consist of a name and a value. The most important attribute for the **a** element is the location to which you would like the anchoring object to be linked. This location can be any resource on the Web, including pages, files and email addresses. To specify the address to link to, add the **href** *attribute* to the anchor element as follows: **<a href = "***address***">**. In this case, the address we are linking to is **http://www.yahoo.com**. The hyperlink (line 19) makes the text **Yahoo** a link to the address specified in **href**.

Anchors can use **mailto** URLs to provide links to email addresses. When someone selects this type of anchored link, most browsers launch the default email program to initiate an email message to the linked address. This type of anchor is demonstrated in Fig. 2.4.

```
 1   <!DOCTYPE HTML PUBLIC "-//W3C//DTD HTML 4.01//EN"
 2               "http://www.w3.org/TR/html4/strict.dtd">
 3   <html>
 4
 5   <!-- Fig. 2.4: contact.html   -->
 6   <!-- Adding email hyperlinks -->
 7
 8   <head>
 9      <title>XML How to Program - Contact Page</title>
10   </head>
11
12   <body>
13
14      <p>My email address is <a href = "mailto:deitel@deitel.com">
15      deitel@deitel.com</a>. Click on the address and your browser
16      will open an email message and address it to me.</p>
17
18   </body>
19   </html>
```

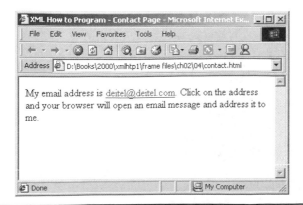

Fig. 2.4   Linking to an email address.

We see an email link on lines 14 and 15

```
<p>My email address is <a href = "mailto:deitel@deitel.com">
deitel@deitel.com</a>. Click on the address and your browser
```

The form of an email anchor is **<a href = "mailto:***emailaddress***">...</a>**. It is important that this whole attribute, including the **mailto:**, be placed in quotation marks.

2.7 Images

We have thus far dealt exclusively with text. We now show how to incorporate images into Web pages (Fig. 2.5).

```
1   <!DOCTYPE HTML PUBLIC "-//W3C//DTD HTML 4.01//EN"
2            "http://www.w3.org/TR/html4/strict.dtd">
3   <html>
4
5   <!-- Fig. 2.5: picture.html   -->
6   <!-- Adding images with HTML -->
7
8   <head>
9      <title>XML How to Program - Welcome</title>
10  </head>
11
12  <body>
13
14     <p><img src = "xmlhtp.jpg" height = "238" width = "183"
15        alt = "Demonstration of the alt attribute"></p>
16
17  </body>
18  </html>
```

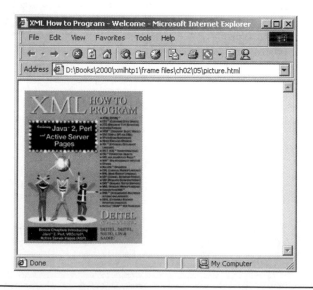

Fig. 2.5   Placing images in HTML files.

The image in this code example is inserted in lines 14 and 15

```
<p><img src = "xmlhtp.jpg" height = "238" width = "183"
    alt = "Demonstration of the alt attribute"></p>
```

You specify the location of the image file in the *img* element. This is done by adding the **src** = "*location*" attribute. You can also specify the **height** and **width** of an image, measured in pixels. The term pixel stands for "picture element." Each pixel represents one dot of color on the screen. This image is 183 pixels wide and 238 pixels high.

Good Programming Practice 2.7

*Always include the **height** and the **width** of an image inside the **img** tag. When the browser loads the HTML file, it will know immediately how much screen space to give the image and will therefore lay out the page properly, even before it downloads the image.*

Common Programming Error 2.2

Entering new dimensions for an image that change its inherent width-to-height ratio distorts the appearance of the image. For example, if your image is 200 pixels wide and 100 pixels high, you should always make sure that any new dimensions have a 2:1 width-to-height ratio.

The **alt** attribute is required for every **img** element. In Fig. 2.5, the value of this attribute is

```
alt = "Demonstration of the alt attribute"
```

Attribute **alt** is provided for browsers that have images turned off, or that cannot view images (e.g., text-based browsers). The value of the **alt** attribute will appear on-screen in place of the image, giving the user an idea of what was in the image. The **alt** attribute is especially important for making Web pages *accessible* to users with disabilities, as we will see in Chapter 18, Accessibility.

Good Programming Practice 2.8

*Include a description of the purpose of every image using the **alt** attribute in the **img** tag.*

Now that we have discussed placing images on your Web page, we will show you how to transform images into anchors to provide links to other sites on the Internet (Fig. 2.6).

```
1   <!DOCTYPE HTML PUBLIC "-//W3C//DTD HTML 4.01//EN"
2               "http://www.w3.org/TR/html4/strict.dtd">
3   <html>
4
5   <!-- Fig. 2.6: nav.html           -->
6   <!-- Using images as link anchors -->
7
8   <head>
9      <title>XML How to Program - Navigation Bar</title>
10  </head>
11
```

Fig. 2.6   Using images as link anchors (part 1 of 2).

```
12   <body>
13
14      <p>
15         <a href = "links.html">
16         <img src = "buttons/links.jpg" width = "65" height = "50"
17            alt = "Links Page"></a><br>
18
19         <a href = "list.html">
20         <img src = "buttons/list.jpg" width = "65" height = "50"
21            alt = "List Example Page"></a><br>
22
23         <a href = "contact.html">
24         <img src = "buttons/contact.jpg" width = "65" height = "50"
25            alt = "Contact Page"></a><br>
26
27         <a href = "header.html">
28         <img src = "buttons/header.jpg" width = "65" height = "50"
29            alt = "Header Page"></a><br>
30
31         <a href = "table.html">
32         <img src = "buttons/table.jpg" width = "65" height = "50"
33            alt = "Table Page"></a><br>
34
35         <a href = "form.html">
36         <img src = "buttons/form.jpg" width = "65" height = "50"
37            alt = "Feedback Form"></a><br>
38      </p>
39
40   </body>
41   </html>
```

Fig. 2.6   Using images as link anchors (part 2 of 2).

We see an image hyperlink in lines 15–17

```
<a href = "links.html">
<img src = "buttons/links.jpg" width = "65" height = "50"
    alt = "Links Page"></a><br>
```

Here we use the **a** element and the **img** element. The anchor works the same way as when it surrounds text; the image becomes an active hyperlink to a location somewhere on the Internet, indicated by the **href** attribute inside the **<a>** tag. Remember to close the anchor element when you want the hyperlink to end.

If you direct your attention to the **src** attribute of the **img** element,

```
src = "buttons/links.jpg"
```

you will see that it is not in the same form as that of the image in the previous example. This is because the image we are using here, **links.jpg**, resides in a subdirectory called **buttons**, which is in the main directory for our site. We have done this so that we can keep all our button graphics in the same place, making them easier to find and edit.

You can always refer to files in different directories simply by putting the directory name in the correct format in the **src** attribute. If, for example, there was a directory inside the **buttons** directory called **images**, and we wanted to put a graphic from that directory onto our page, we would just have to make the source attribute reflect the location of the image: **src = "buttons/images/filename"**.

You can even insert an image from a different Web site into your site (after obtaining permission from the site's owner, of course). Just make the **src** attribute reflect the location and name of the image file.

On line 17

```
alt = "Links Page"></a><br>
```

we introduce the **br** *element* in line 17, which causes a *line break* to be rendered in most browsers.

2.8 Special Characters and More Line Breaks

In HTML, the old QWERTY typewriter setup no longer suffices for all our textual needs. HTML 4.01 has a provision for inserting special characters and symbols (Fig. 2.7).

```
1  <!DOCTYPE HTML PUBLIC "-//W3C//DTD HTML 4.01//EN"
2              "http://www.w3.org/TR/html4/strict.dtd">
3  <html>
4
5  <!-- Fig. 2.7: contact.html      -->
6  <!-- Inserting special characters -->
7
8  <head>
9     <title>XML How to Program - Contact Page</title>
10 </head>
11
```

Fig. 2.7   Inserting special characters into HTML (part 1 of 2).

```
12   <body>
13
14      <!-- Special characters are entered using the form &code; -->
15      <p>My email address is <a href = "mailto:deitel@deitel.com">
16      deitel@deitel.com</a>. Click on the address and your browser
17      will automatically open an email message and address it to my
18      address.</p>
19
20      <hr> <!-- Inserts a horizontal rule -->
21
22      <p>All information on this site is <strong>&copy;</strong>
23      Deitel <strong>&amp;</strong> Associates, 1999.</p>
24
25      <!-- Text can be struck out with a set of <del>...</del>   -->
26      <!-- tags, it can be set in subscript with <sub>...</sub>, -->
27      <!-- and it can be set into superscript with <sup...</sup> -->
28      <p><del>You may copy up to 3.14 x 10<sup>2</sup> characters
29      worth of information from this site.</del> Just make sure
30      you <sub>do not copy more information</sub> than is allowable.
31      </p>
32
33      <p>No permission is needed if you only need to use <strong>
34      &lt; &frac14;</strong> of the information presented here.</p>
35
36   </body>
37   </html>
```

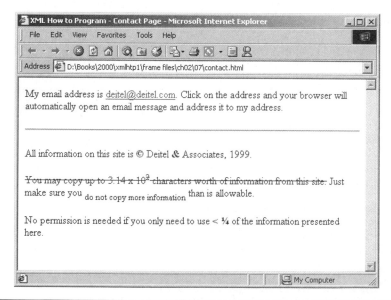

Fig. 2.7   Inserting special characters into HTML (part 2 of 2).

There are some *special characters* inserted into the text of lines 22 and 23

```
<p>All information on this site is <strong>&copy;</strong>
Deitel <strong>&amp;</strong> Associates, 1999.</p>
```

All special characters are inserted in their code form. The format of the code is always &*code*;. An example of this is **&**, which inserts an ampersand. Codes are often abbreviated forms of the character (like **amp** for ampersand and **copy** for copyright) and can also be in the form of *hex codes*. (For example, the hex code for an ampersand is 38, so another method of inserting an ampersand is to use **&**.) Please refer to the chart in Appendix A for a listing of special characters and their respective codes.

In lines 28–31, we introduce three new styles.

```
<p><del>You may copy up to 3.14 x 10<sup>2</sup> characters
worth of information from this site.</del> Just make sure
you <sub>do not copy more information</sub> than is allow-
able.
</p>
```

You can indicate text that has been deleted from a document by including it in a ***del*** element. This could be used as an easy way to communicate revisions of an online document. Many browsers render the **del** element as strike-through text. To turn text into *superscript* (i.e., raised vertically to the top of the line and made smaller) or to turn text into *subscript* (the opposite of superscript, lowers text on a line and makes it smaller), use the ***sup*** and ***sub*** elements, respectively.

Line 20

```
<hr> <!-- Inserts a horizontal rule -->
```

inserts a horizontal rule, indicated by the ***<hr>*** tag. A horizontal rule is rendered by most browsers as a straight line going across the screen horizontally. The **hr** element also inserts a line break directly below it.

2.9 Unordered Lists

Figure 2.8 demonstrates displaying text in an *unordered list*. Here we reuse the HTML file from Fig. 2.3, adding an unordered list to enhance the structure of the page. The *unordered list element* **ul** creates a list in which every line begins with a bullet mark in most Web browsers.

```
1   <!DOCTYPE HTML PUBLIC "-//W3C//DTD HTML 4.01//EN"
2           "http://www.w3.org/TR/html4/strict.dtd">
3   <html>
4
5   <!-- Fig. 2.8: links.html              -->
6   <!-- Unordered list containing hyperlinks -->
7
8   <head>
9      <title>XML How to Program - Links</title>
10  </head>
11
12  <body>
13
14     <h1>Here are my favorite Internet Search Engines</h1>
```

Fig. 2.8   Unordered lists in HTML (part 1 of 2).

```
15
16
17      <p><strong>Click on the Search Engine address to go to that
18         page.</strong></p>
19
20      <ul>
21         <li><a href = "http://www.yahoo.com">Yahoo</a></li>
22
23         <li><a href = "http://www.altavista.com">AltaVista</a></li>
24
25         <li><a href = "http://www.askjeeves.com">Ask Jeeves</a></li>
26
27         <li><a href = "http://www.webcrawler.com">WebCrawler</a></li>
28      </ul>
29
30   </body>
31   </html>
```

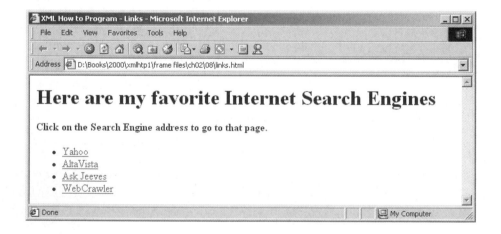

Fig. 2.8   Unordered lists in HTML (part 2 of 2).

The first list item appears on line 21

```
<li><a href = "http://www.yahoo.com">Yahoo</a></li>
```

Each entry in an unordered list is a *li* (*list item*) element. Most Web browsers render these elements with a line break and a bullet mark at the beginning of the line.

2.10 Nested and Ordered Lists

Figure 2.9 demonstrates *nested lists* (i.e., one list inside another list). This feature is useful for displaying information in outline form.

```
1   <!DOCTYPE HTML PUBLIC "-//W3C//DTD HTML 4.01//EN"
2           "http://www.w3.org/TR/html4/strict.dtd">
3   <html>
4
5   <!-- Fig. 2.9: list.html              -->
6   <!-- Advanced Lists: nested and ordered -->
7
8   <head>
9      <title>XML How to Program - Lists</title>
10  </head>
11
12  <body>
13
14     <h1>The Best Features of the Internet</h1>
15
16     <ul>
17        <li>You can meet new people from countries around
18           the world.</li>
19        <li>You have access to new media as it becomes public:
20
21           <!-- This starts a nested list, which uses a modified  -->
22           <!-- bullet. The list ends when you close the <ul> tag -->
23           <ul>
24              <li>New games</li>
25              <li>New applications
26
27                 <!-- Another nested list -->
28                 <ul>
29                    <li>For business</li>
30                    <li>For pleasure</li>
31                 </ul> <!-- This ends the double nested list -->
32              </li>
33
34              <li>Around the clock news</li>
35              <li>Search engines</li>
36              <li>Shopping</li>
37              <li>Programming
38
39                 <ul>
40                    <li>XML</li>
41                    <li>Java</li>
42                    <li>HTML</li>
43                    <li>Scripts</li>
44                    <li>New languages</li>
45                 </ul>
46
47              </li>
48
49           </ul> <!-- This ends the first level nested list -->
50        </li>
51
52        <li>Links</li>
```

Fig. 2.9   Nested and ordered lists in HTML (part 1 of 2).

```
53          <li>Keeping in touch with old friends</li>
54          <li>It is the technology of the future!</li>
55
56      </ul>   <!-- This ends the primary unordered list -->
57
58      <h1>My 3 Favorite <em>CEOs</em></h1>
59
60      <!-- Ordered lists are constructed in the same way as   -->
61      <!-- unordered lists, except their starting tag is <ol> -->
62      <ol>
63          <li>Bill Gates</li>
64          <li>Steve Jobs</li>
65          <li>Michael Dell</li>
66      </ol>
67
68  </body>
69  </html>
```

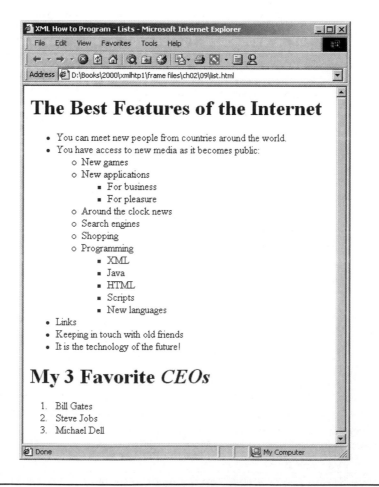

Fig. 2.9   Nested and ordered lists in HTML (part 2 of 2).

Our first nested list begins on line 23, with its first element on 24

```
<ul>
    <li>New games</li>
```

A nested list is created in the same way as the list in Fig. 2.8, except that the nested list is itself contained in a list element. Most Web browsers render nested lists by indenting the list one level and changing the bullet type for the list elements.

 Good Programming Practice 2.9

Indenting each level of a nested list in your code makes the code easier to edit and debug.

In Fig. 2.9, lines 16–56 show a list with three levels of nesting. When nesting lists, be sure to insert the closing **</ul>** tags in the appropriate places. Lines 62–66

```
<ol>
    <li>Bill Gates</li>
    <li>Steve Jobs</li>
    <li>Michael Dell</li>
</ol>
```

define an *ordered list* element with the tags **<ol>**...**</ol>**. Most browsers render ordered lists with a sequence number for each list element instead of a bullet. By default, ordered lists use decimal sequence numbers (1, 2, 3, ...).

2.11 Internet and World Wide Web Resources

There are many resources available on the World Wide Web that go into more depth on the topics we cover. Visit the following sites for additional information on this chapter's topics.

www.w3.org
The *World Wide Web Consortium* (W3C), is the group that makes HTML recommendations. This Web site holds a variety of information about HTML—both its history and its present status.

www.w3.org/TR/html401
The *HTML 4.01 Specification* contains all the nuances and fine points in HTML 4.01.

www.w3schools.com/html
The HTMl School. This site contains a complete guide to HTML, starting with an introduction to the WWW and ending with advanced HTML features. This site also has a good reference for the features of HTML.

www2.utep.edu/~kross/tutorial
This University of Texas at El Paso site contains another guide for simple HTML programming. The site is helpful for beginners, because it focuses on teaching and gives specific examples.

www.astentech.com/tutorials/HTML.html
This site contains links and rates over 40 HTML tutorials located all over the Web.

www.w3scripts.com/html
This site, an offshoot of *W3Schools*, is a repository for code examples exhibiting all of the features of HTML, from beginner to advanced.

SUMMARY

- HTML is not a procedural programming language like C, Fortran, Cobol or Pascal. It is a markup language that identifies the elements of a page so a browser can render that page on the screen.

- HTML is used to format text and information. This "marking up" of information is different from the intent of traditional programming languages, which is to perform actions in a designated order.

- In HTML, text is marked up with elements, delineated by tags that are keywords contained in pairs of angle brackets.

- HTML documents are created using text editors.

- All HTML documents stored in files require either the `.htm` or the `.html` file name extension.

- Making errors while coding in conventional programming languages like C, C++ and Java often produces a fatal error, preventing the program from running. Errors in HTML code are usually not fatal. The browser will make its best effort at rendering the page but will probably not display the page as you intended. In our Common Programming Errors and Testing and Debugging Tips we highlight common HTML errors and how to detect and correct them.

- For most Web servers, the filename of your home page should be `index.html`. When a browser requests a directory, the default Web server response is to return `index.html`, if it exists in that directory.

- The document type specifies which version of HTML is used in the document and can be used with a validation tool, such as the W3C's `validator.w3.org`, to ensure an HTML document conforms to the HTML specification.

- `<html>` tells the browser that everything contained between the opening `<html>` tag and the closing `</html>` tag is HTML.

- Comments in HTML always begin with `<!--` and end with `-->` and can span across several source lines. The browser ignores any text and/or tags placed inside a comment.

- Every HTML file is separated into a header section and a body.

- Including a title is mandatory for every HTML document. Use the `<title>`...`</title>` tags to do so. They are placed inside the header.

- `<body>` opens the `body` element. The body of an HTML document is the area where you place all content you would like browsers to display.

- All text between the `<p>`...`</p>` tags forms one paragraph. Most browsers render paragraphs as set apart from all other material on the page by a line of vertical space both before and after the paragraph.

- Headers are a simple form of text formatting that typically increase text size based on the header's "level" (`h1` through `h6`). They are often used to delineate new sections and subsections of a page.

- The purpose of HTML is to mark up text; the question of how it is presented is left to the browser itself.

- People who have difficulty seeing can use special browsers that read the text on the screen aloud. These browsers (which are text based and do not show images, colors or graphics) might read `strong` and `em` with different inflections to convey the impact of the styled text to the user.

- You should close tags in the reverse order from that in which they were started to ensure proper nesting.

- The most important capability of HTML is creating hyperlinks to documents on any server to form a world-wide network of linked documents and information.

- Links are inserted using the `a` (anchor) element. To specify the address you would like to link to, add the `href` attribute to the anchor element, with the address as the value of `href`.

- Anchors can link to email addresses. When someone clicks this type of anchored link, their default email program initiates an email message to the linked address.
- The term pixel stands for "picture element". Each pixel represents one dot of color on the screen.
- You specify the location of the image file with the **src = "**location**"** attribute in the **<img>** tag. You can specify the **height** and **width** of an image, measured in pixels.
- **alt** is provided for browsers that cannot view pictures or that have images turned off (text-based browsers, for example). The value of the **alt** attribute will appear on-screen in place of the image, giving the user an idea of what was in the image.
- You can refer to files in different directories by including the directory name in the correct format in the **src** attribute. You can insert an image from a different Web site onto your site (after obtaining permission from the site's owner). Just make the **src** attribute reflects the location and name of the image file.
- The **br** element forces a line break. If the **br** element is placed inside a text area, the text begins a new line at the place of the **
** tag.
- HTML 4.01 has a provision for inserting special characters and symbols. All special characters are inserted in the format of the code, always **&**code**;**. An example of this is **&**, which inserts an ampersand. Codes are often abbreviated forms of the character (like **amp** for ampersand and **copy** for copyright) and can also be in the form of hex codes. (For example, the hex code for an ampersand is 38, so another method of inserting an ampersand is to use **&**.)
- The **del** element marks text as deleted, which is rendered with a strike through by most browsers. To turn text into superscript or subscript, use the **sup** and **sub** elements respectively.
- Most visual Web browsers place a bullet mark at the beginning of each element in an unordered list. All entries in an unordered list must be enclosed within **<ul>**...**</ul>** tags, which open and close the unordered list element.
- Each entry in an unordered list is contained in an **li** element. You then insert and format any text.
- Nested lists display information in outline form. A nested list is a list that is contained in an **li** element. Most visual Web browsers indent nested lists one level and change the bullet type to reflect the nesting.
- An ordered list (**<ol>**...**</ol>**) is rendered by most browsers with a sequence number instead of a bullet at the beginning of each list element. By default, ordered lists use decimal sequence numbers (1,2,3, ...).

TERMINOLOGY

&	content of an HTML element
.htm	**del** element
.html	**em** element (****...****)
<!--...--> (comment)	emphasis
<body>...**</body>**	**h1** element (**<h1>**...**</h1>**)
<hr> element (horizontal rule)	**h2** element (**<h2>**...**</h2>**)
a element (anchor; **<a>**...**</a>**)	**h3** element (**<h3>**...**</h3>**)
alt	**h4** element (**<h4>**...**</h4>**)
anchor	**h5** element (**<h5>**...**</h5>**)
attributes of an HTML tag	**h6** element (**<h6>**...**</h6>**)
clear = "all" in ** **	**head** element (**<head>**...**</head>**)
closing tag	height
color	horizontal rule
comments	**href** attribute of **<a>** element

HTML (HyperText Markup Language)
HTML document
html element (**<html>...</html>**)
HTML file
HTML tags
html-kit
hyperlink
hypertext
image
img element
index.html
line break element (**
**)
link
link attribute of **body** element
mailto:
Markup Language
opening tag
p element (paragraph; **<p>...</p>**)
presentation of a Web Page

RGB colors
size = in **<font>**
source-code form
special characters
src attribute in **img** element
strong element (**...**)
structure of a Web page
sub (subscript)
sup (superscript)
tags in HTML
text in **body**
text-based browser
title element (**<title>...</title>**)
unordered list (**<ul>...</ul>**)
Web site
width attribute
width by percentage
width by pixel
World Wide Web

SELF-REVIEW EXERCISES

2.1   State whether the following are *true* or *false*. If *false*, explain why.
  a) The document type for an HTML document is optional.
  b) The use of the **em** and **strong** elements is deprecated.
  c) The name of your site's home page should always be **homepage.html**.
  d) It is a good programming practice to insert comments into your HTML document that explain what you are doing.
  e) A hyperlink is inserted around text with the **link** element.

2.2   Fill in the blanks in each of the following:
  a) The _____ element is used to insert a horizontal rule.
  b) Superscript is formatted with the _____ element and subscript is formatted with the _____ element.
  c) The _____ element is located within the **<head>...</head>** tags.
  d) The least important header is the _____ element and the most important text header is _____.
  e) The _____ element is used to create an unordered list.

2.3   Identify each of the following as either an element or attribute:
  a) **html**
  b) **width**
  c) **href**
  d) **br**
  e) **h3**
  f) **a**
  g) **src**

ANSWERS TO SELF-REVIEW EXERCISES

2.1   a) False. The document type is required for HTMl documents. b) False. The use of the **i** and **b** elements is deprecated. Elements **em** and **strong** may be used instead. c) False. The name of your home page should always be **index.html**. d) True. e) False. A hyperlink is inserted around text with the **a** (anchor) element.

2.2   a) **hr**. b) **sup**, **sub**. c) **title**. d) **h6**, **h1**. e) **ul**.

2.3   a) Tag. b) Attribute. c) Attribute. d) Tag. e) Tag. f) Tag. g) Attribute.

EXERCISES

2.4   Use HTML to mark up the first paragraph of this chapter. Use **h1** for the section header, **p** for text, **strong** for the first word of every sentence, and **em** for all capital letters.

2.5   Why is this code valid? (*Hint*: you can find the W3C specification for the **p** element at **www.w3.org/TR/html4**)

```
<p>Here's some text...
<hr>
<p>And some more text...</p>
```

2.6   Why is this code invalid? [*Hint*: you can find the W3C specification for the **br** element at the same URL given in Exercise 2.5.]

```
<p>Here's some text...<br></br>
And some more text...</p>
```

2.7   We have an image named **deitel.gif** that is 200 pixels wide and 150 pixels high. Use the **width** and **height** attributes of the **img** tag to a) increase image size by 100%; b) increase image size by 50%; c) change the width-to-height ratio to 2:1, keeping the width attained in a).

2.8   Create a link to each of the following: a) **index.html**, located in the **files** directory; b) **index.html**, located in the **text** subdirectory of the **files** directory; c) **index.html**, located in the **other** directory in your *parent directory* [*Hint*: **..** signifies parent directory.]; d) A link to the President of the United States' email address (**president@whitehouse.gov**); e) An **FTP** link to the file named **README** in the **pub** directory of **ftp.cdrom.com** [*Hint*: remember to use **ftp://**].

3

Introduction to HyperText Markup Language 4: Part II

Objectives

- To be able to create tables with rows and columns of data.
- To be able to control the display and formatting of tables.
- To be able to create and use forms.
- To be able to create and use image maps to aid hyperlinking.
- To be able to make Web pages accessible to search engines.
- To be able to use the **frameset** element to create more interesting Web pages.

Yea, from the table of my memory
I'll wipe away all trivial fond records.
William Shakespeare

Outline

3.1 Introduction

In the previous chapter, we discussed some basic HTML features. We built several complete Web pages featuring text, hyperlinks, images and such formatting tools as horizontal rules and line breaks.

In this chapter, we discuss more substantial HTML elements and features. We will see how to present information in *tables*. We discuss how to use forms to collect information from people browsing a site. We explain how to use *internal linking* and *image maps* to make pages more navigable. We also discuss how to use *frames* to make navigating Web sites easier.

By the end of this chapter, you will be familiar with most commonly used HTML tags and features. You will then be able to create more complex Web sites. In the next chapter, Cascading Style Sheets (CSS), we will show you how to make your Web sites more visually appealing.

3.2 Basic HTML Tables

HTML 4.0 *tables* are used to mark up tabular data, such as data stored in a database. The table in Fig. 3.1 organizes data into rows and columns.

```
1    <!DOCTYPE HTML PUBLIC "-//W3C//DTD HTML 4.01//EN"
2               "http://www.w3.org/TR/html4/strict.dtd">
3    <html>
4
5    <!-- Fig. 3.1: table.html -->
6    <!-- Basic table design   -->
7
```

Fig. 3.1   HTML table (part 1 of 2).

```
8   <head>
9      <title>XML How to Program - Tables</title>
10  </head>
11
12  <body>
13
14     <h1>Table Example Page</h1>
15
16     <!-- The <table> tag opens a new table and lets you put in -->
17     <!-- design options and instructions                       -->
18     <table border = "1" width = "40%">
19
20     <!-- Use the <caption> tag to summarize the table's contents -->
21     <!-- (this helps the visually impaired)                      -->
22     <caption>Here is a small sample table.</caption>
23
24     <!-- The <thead> is the first (non-scrolling) horizontal   -->
25     <!-- section. Use it to format the table header area.       -->
26     <!-- <th> inserts a header cell and displays bold text      -->
27     <thead>
28        <tr><th>This is the head.</th></tr>
29     </thead>
30
31     <!-- All of your important content goes in the <tbody>. -->
32     <!-- Use this tag to format the entire section           -->
33     <!-- <td> inserts a data cell, with regular text         -->
34     <tbody>
35        <tr><td>This is the body.</td></tr>
36     </tbody>
37
38     </table>
39
40  </body>
41  </html>
```

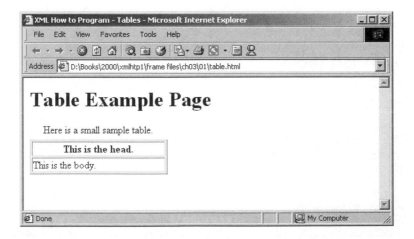

Fig. 3.1   HTML table (part 2 of 2).

All tags and text that apply to the table go inside the **<table>** element, which begins on line 18

```
<table border = "1" width = "40%">
```

The **border** *attribute* lets you set the width of the table's border in pixels. If you want the border to be invisible, you can specify **border = "0"**. In the table shown in Fig. 3.1, the value of the border attribute is set to **1**. The **width** attribute sets the width of the table as either a number of pixels or a percentage of the screen width.

Line 22

```
<caption>Here is a small sample table.</caption>
```

inserts a **caption** element into the table. The text inside the **caption** element is inserted directly above the table in most visual browsers. The caption text is also used to help *text-based browsers* interpret the table data.

Tables can be split into distinct horizontal and vertical sections. The first of these sections, the head area, appears in lines 27–29

```
<thead>
   <tr><th>This is the head.</th></tr>
</thead>
```

Put all header information (for example, the titles of the table and column headers) inside the **thead** element. The **tr**, or *table row element*, is used to create rows of table cells. All of the cells in a row belong in the **<tr>** element for that row.

The smallest unit of the table is the *data cell*. There are two types of data cells, one type—the **th** element—is located in the table header. The other type—the **td** element—is located in the table body. The code example in Fig. 3.1 inserts a header cell using the **th** element. Header cells, which are placed in the **<thead>** element, are suitable for column headings.

The second grouping section, the **tbody** element, appears in lines 34–36

```
<tbody>
   <tr><td>This is the body.</td></tr>
</tbody>
```

Like **thead**, the **tbody** element is used for formatting and grouping purposes. Although there is only one row and one cell (line 35) in the above example, most tables will use **tbody** to group the majority of their content in multiple rows and multiple cells.

Look-and-Feel Observation 3.1

Use tables in your HTML pages to mark up tabular data.

Common Programming Error 3.1

Forgetting to close any of the elements inside the **table** *element is an error and can distort the table format. Be sure to check that every element is opened and closed in its proper place to make sure that the table is structured as intended.*

3.3 Intermediate HTML Tables and Formatting

In the previous section and code example, we explored the structure of a basic table. In Fig. 3.2, we extend our table example with more structural elements and attributes.

The table begins on line 16. The *colgroup* element, used for grouping columns, is shown on lines 22–25

```
1   <!DOCTYPE HTML PUBLIC "-//W3C//DTD HTML 4.01//EN"
2           "http://www.w3.org/TR/html4/strict.dtd">
3   <html>
4
5   <!-- Fig. 3.2: table.html     -->
6   <!-- Intermediate table design -->
7
8   <head>
9       <title>XML How to Program - Tables</title>
10  </head>
11
12  <body>
13
14      <h1>Table Example Page</h1>
15
16      <table border = "1">
17          <caption>Here is a more complex sample table.</caption>
18
19      <!-- <colgroup> and <col> are used to format entire   -->
20      <!-- columns at once. SPAN determines how many columns -->
21      <!-- the col tag effects.                              -->
22      <colgroup>
23          <col align = "right">
24          <col span = "4">
25      </colgroup>
26
27      <thead>
28
29          <!-- rowspans and colspans combine the indicated number -->
30          <!-- of cells vertically or horizontally                -->
31          <tr>
32              <th rowspan = "2">
33                  <img src = "camel.gif" width = "205" height = "167"
34                      alt = "Picture of a camel">
35              </th>
36              <th colspan = "4" valign = "top">
37                  <h1>Camelid comparison</h1><br>
38                  <p>Approximate as of 8/99</p>
39              </th>
40          </tr>
41
42          <tr valign = "bottom">
43              <th># of Humps</th>
44              <th>Indigenous region</th>
45              <th>Spits?</th>
```

Fig. 3.2   Complex HTML table (part 1 of 2).

```
46              <th>Produces Wool?</th>
47          </tr>
48
49      </thead>
50
51      <tbody>
52
53          <tr>
54              <th>Camels (bactrian)</th>
55              <td>2</td>
56              <td>Africa/Asia</td>
57              <td rowspan = "2">Llama</td>
58              <td rowspan = "2">Llama</td>
59          </tr>
60
61          <tr>
62              <th>Llamas</th>
63              <td>1</td>
64              <td>Andes Mountains</td>
65          </tr>
66
67      </tbody>
68
69      </table>
70
71  </body>
72  </html>
```

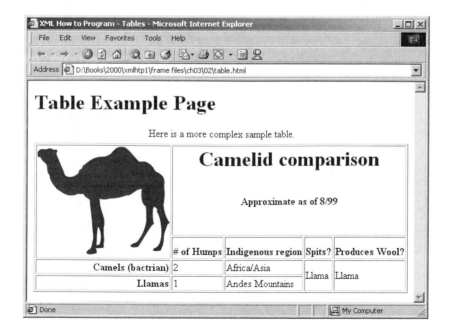

Fig. 3.2   Complex HTML table (part 2 of 2).

```
<colgroup>
   <col align = "right">
   <col span = "4">
</colgroup>
```

The **colgroup** element can be used to group and format columns. Each *col* element in the **<colgroup>...</colgroup>** tags can format any number of columns (specified with the **span** attribute). Any formatting to be applied to a column or group of columns can be specified in both the **colgroup** and **col** tags. In this case, we align the text inside the leftmost column to the right. Another useful attribute to use here is **width**, which specifies the width of the column.

Most visual Web browsers automatically format data cells to fit the data they contain. However, it is possible to make some data cells larger than others. This effect is accomplished with the *rowspan* and *colspan* attributes, which can be placed inside any data cell element. The value of the attribute specifies the number of rows or columns to be occupied by the cell, respectively. For example, **rowspan = "2"** tells the browser that this data cell will span the area of two vertically adjacent cells. These cells will be joined vertically (and will thus span over two rows). An example of **colspan** appears in line 36

```
<th colspan = "4" valign = "top">
```

where the header cell is widened to span four cells.

We also see here an example of vertical alignment formatting. The *valign* attribute accepts the following values: **"top"**, **"middle"**, **"bottom"** and **"baseline"**. All cells in a row whose **valign** attribute is set to **"baseline"** will have the first text line occur on a common baseline. The default vertical alignment in all data and header cells is **valign = "middle"**.

The remaining code in Fig. 3.2 demonstrates other uses of the **table** attributes and elements outlined above.

 Common Programming Error 3.2

When using ***colspan*** *and* ***rowspan*** *in table data cells, consider that the modified cells will cover the areas of other cells. Compensate for this in your code by reducing the number of cells in that row or column. If you do not, the formatting of your table will be distorted, and you may inadvertently create more columns and/or rows than you originally intended.*

3.4 Basic HTML Forms

HTML provides several mechanisms to collect information from people viewing your site; one is the *form* (Fig. 3.3).

```
1   <!DOCTYPE HTML PUBLIC "-//W3C//DTD HTML 4.01//EN"
2              "http://www.w3.org/TR/html4/strict.dtd">
3   <html>
4
5   <!-- Fig. 3.3: form.html    -->
6   <!-- Form Design Example 1 -->
7
```

Fig. 3.3   Simple form with hidden fields and a text box (part 1 of 2).

```
8   <head>
9       <title>XML How to Program - Forms</title>
10  </head>
11
12  <body>
13
14      <h1>Feedback Form</h1>
15
16      <p>Please fill out this form to help us improve our site.</p>
17
18      <!-- This tag starts the form, gives the method of sending -->
19      <!-- information and the location of form scripts.         -->
20      <!-- Hidden inputs give the server non-visual information  -->
21      <form method = "post" action = "/cgi-bin/formmail">
22
23      <p>
24          <input type = "hidden" name = "recipient"
25              value = "deitel@deitel.com">
26          <input type = "hidden" name = "subject"
27              value = "Feedback Form">
28          <input type = "hidden" name = "redirect"
29              value = "main.html">
30      </p>
31
32      <!-- <input type = "text"> inserts a text box -->
33      <p><label>Name:
34          <input name = "name" type = "text" size = "25">
35      </label></p>
36
37      <p>
38          <!-- Input types "submit" and "reset" insert buttons -->
39          <!-- for submitting or clearing the form's contents  -->
40          <input type = "submit" value = "Submit Your Entries">
41          <input type = "reset" value = "Clear Your Entries">
42      </p>
43
44      </form>
45
46  </body>
47  </html>
```

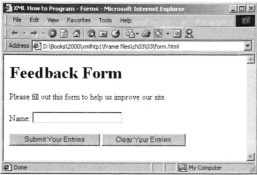

Fig. 3.3   Simple form with hidden fields and a text box (part 2 of 2).

The form begins on line 21

```
<form method = "post" action = "/cgi-bin/formmail">
```

with the *form* element. The *method* attribute indicates the way the information gathered in the form will be sent to the *Web server* for processing. Use *method = "post"* in a form that causes changes to server data, for example when updating a database. The form data will be sent to the server as an *environment variable,* which scripts are able to access. The other possible value, **method = "get"**, should be used when your form does not cause any changes in server-side data, for example when making a database request. The form data from **method = "get"** is appended to the end of the URL (for example, **/cgi-bin/formmail?name=bob&order=5**). Also be aware that **method = "get"** is limited to standard characters, and cannot submit any special characters.

A *Web server* is a machine that runs a software package such as Microsoft's PWS (Personal Web Server), Microsoft's IIS (Internet Information Server), Apache, etc. Web servers handle browser requests. When a browser requests a page or file somewhere on a server, the server processes the request and returns an answer to the browser. In this example, the data from the form goes to a CGI (Common Gateway Interface) script, which is a means of interfacing an HTML page with a script (i.e., a program) written in Perl, C, Tcl or other languages. The script then handles the data fed to it by the server and typically returns some information for the user. The **action** attribute in the **form** tag is the URL for this script; in this case, it is a simple script that emails form data to an address. Most Internet Service Providers (ISPs) will have a script like this on their site, so you can ask your system administrator how to set up your HTML to use the script correctly.

For this particular script, there are several pieces of information (not seen by the user) needed in the form. Lines 24–29

```
<input type = "hidden" name = "recipient"
   value = "deitel@deitel.com">
<input type = "hidden" name = "subject"
   value = "Feedback Form">
<input type = "hidden" name = "redirect"
   value = "main.html">
```

specify this information using *hidden input elements*. The **input** element is common in forms and always requires the *type* attribute. Two other attributes are *name*, which provides a unique identifier for the **input** element, and *value*, which indicates the value that the *input* element sends to the server upon submission.

As shown above, hidden inputs always have the attribute *type = "hidden"*. The three hidden inputs shown are typical for this kind of CGI script: An email address to which the data will be sent, the subject line of the email and a URL to which the user is redirected after submitting the form.

Good Programming Practice 3.1

Place hidden **input** *elements in the beginning of a form, right after the opening* **<form>** *tag. This makes these elements easier to find and identify.*

The usage of an **input** element is defined by the value of its **type** attribute. We introduce another of these options in lines 33–35

```
<p><label>Name:
   <input name = "name" type = "text" size = "25">
</label></p>
```

The input **type = "text"** inserts a one-line text box into the form (line 34). A good use of the textual input element is for names or other one-line pieces of information. The **label** element on lines 33–35 provide a description for the **input** element on line 34.

We also use the **size** attribute of the **input** element to specify the width of the text input, measured in characters. You can also set a maximum number of characters that the text input will accept using the **maxlength** attribute.

Good Programming Practice 3.2

*When using **input** elements in forms, be sure to leave enough space with the **maxlength** attribute for users to input the pertinent information.*

Common Programming Error 3.3

*Forgetting to include a **label** element for each form element is a design error. Without these labels, users will have no way of knowing what the function of individual form elements is.*

There are two types of **input** elements in lines 40 and 41

```
<input type = "submit" value = "Submit Your Entries">
<input type = "reset" value = "Clear Your Entries">
```

that should be inserted into every form. The **type = "submit"** input element allows the user to submit the data entered in the form to the server for processing. Most visual Web browsers place a button in the form that submits the data when clicked. The **value** attribute changes the text displayed on the button (the default value is **"submit"**). The input element **type = "reset"** allows a user to reset all form elements to the default values. This can help the user correct mistakes or simply start over. As with the **submit** input, the **value** attribute of the **reset input** element affects the text of the button on the screen, but does not affect its functionality.

Common Programming Error 3.4

*Be sure to close your form code with the **</form>** tag. Neglecting to do so is an error and can affect the functionality of other forms on the same page.*

3.5 More Complex HTML Forms

We introduce additional form input options in Fig. 3.4.

```
1   <!DOCTYPE HTML PUBLIC "-//W3C//DTD HTML 4.01//EN"
2              "http://www.w3.org/TR/html4/strict.dtd">
3   <html>
4
5   <!-- Fig. 3.4: form.html    -->
6   <!-- Form Design Example 2 -->
7
```

Fig. 3.4   Form including textareas, password boxes and checkboxes (part 1 of 3).

```
 8   <head>
 9      <title>XML How to Program - Forms</title>
10   </head>
11
12   <body>
13
14      <h1>Feedback Form</h1>
15
16      <p>Please fill out this form to help us improve our site.</p>
17
18      <form method = "post" action = "/cgi-bin/formmail">
19
20      <p>
21         <input type = "hidden" name = "recipient"
22            value = "deitel@deitel.com">
23         <input type = "hidden" name = "subject"
24            value = "Feedback Form">
25         <input type = "hidden" name = "redirect"
26            value = "main.html">
27      </p>
28
29      <p><label>Name:
30         <input name = "name" type = "text" size = "25">
31      </label></p>
32
33      <!-- <textarea> creates a textbox of the size given -->
34      <p><label>Comments:
35         <textarea name = "comments" rows = "4" cols = "36">
36         </textarea>
37      </label></p>
38
39      <!-- <input type = "password"> inserts a textbox whose    -->
40      <!-- readout will be in *** instead of regular characters -->
41      <p><label>Email Address:
42         <input name = "email" type = "password" size = "25">
43      </label></p>
44
45      <p>
46         <strong>Things you liked:</strong><br>
47
48         <label>Site design
49         <input name = "thingsliked" type = "checkbox"
50            value = "Design"></label>
51
52         <label>Links
53         <input name = "thingsliked" type = "checkbox"
54            value = "Links"></label>
55
56         <label>Ease of use
57         <input name = "thingsliked" type = "checkbox"
58            value = "Ease"></label>
59
60         <label>Images
```

Fig. 3.4   Form including textareas, password boxes and checkboxes (part 2 of 3).

```
61            <input name = "thingsliked" type = "checkbox"
62               value = "Images"></label>
63
64         <label>Source code
65         <input name = "thingsliked" type = "checkbox"
66            value = "Code"></label>
67      </p>
68
69      <p>
70         <input type = "submit" value = "Submit Your Entries">
71         <input type = "reset" value = "Clear Your Entries">
72      </p>
73
74      </form>
75
76   </body>
77   </html>
```

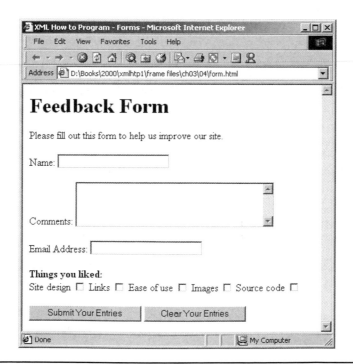

Fig. 3.4   Form including textareas, password boxes and checkboxes (part 3 of 3).

Lines 35 and 36

```
<textarea name = "comments" rows = "4" cols = "36"></textarea>
```

introduces the **textarea** element. The **textarea** element inserts a text box into the form. You specify the size of the box with the **rows** *attribute*, which sets the number of rows that will appear in the **textarea**. With the **cols** *attribute*, you specify how wide the **textarea** should be. This **textarea** is four rows of characters tall and 36 characters wide. Any default text that you want to place inside the **textarea** should be contained in the **textarea** element.

The input **type = "password"** (line 42)

```
<input name = "email" type = "password" size = "25">
```

inserts a text box with the indicated size. The password input field provides a way for users to enter information that the user would not want others to be able to read on the screen. In visual browsers, the data the user types into a password input field is shown as asterisks. However, the actual value the user enters is sent to the server. Non-visual browsers may render this type of input field differently.

Lines 48–66 introduce another type of form element, the checkbox. Every **input** element with **type = "checkbox"** creates a new checkbox item in the form. Checkboxes can be used individually or in groups. Each checkbox in a group should have the same **name** (in this case, **name = "thingsliked"**). This notifies the script handling the form that all of the checkboxes are related to one another.

Common Programming Error 3.5

*When your form has several checkboxes with the same **name**, you must make sure that they have different **value**s, or else the script will have no way of distinguishing between them.*

Additional form elements are introduced in Fig. 3.5. In this form example, we introduce two new types of input options. The first of these is the *radio button*, introduced (lines 71–89). Inserted into forms with the **input** attribute **type = "radio"**, radio buttons are similar in function and usage to checkboxes. Radio buttons are different in that only one element in the group may be selected at any time. All of the **name** attributes of a group of radio inputs must be the same and all of the **value** attributes different. Insert the attribute **checked** to indicate which radio button you would like selected initially. The **checked** attribute can also be applied to checkboxes.

Common Programming Error 3.6

*When you are using a group of radio inputs in a form, forgetting to set the **name** values to the same name will let the user select all the radio buttons at the same time: an undesired result.*

```
1    <!DOCTYPE HTML PUBLIC "-//W3C//DTD HTML 4.01//EN"
2               "http://www.w3.org/TR/html4/strict.dtd">
3    <html>
4
5    <!-- Fig. 3.5: form.html    -->
6    <!-- Form Design Example 3 -->
7
8    <head>
9       <title>XML How to Program - Forms</title>
10   </head>
11
12   <body>
13
```

Fig. 3.5   Form including radio buttons and pulldown lists (part 1 of 4).

```
14        <h1>Feedback Form</h1>
15
16        <p>Please fill out this form to help us improve our site.</p>
17
18        <form method = "post" action = "/cgi-bin/formmail">
19
20        <p>
21           <input type = "hidden" name = "recipient"
22              value = "deitel@deitel.com">
23           <input type = "hidden" name = "subject"
24              value = "Feedback Form">
25           <input type = "hidden" name = "redirect"
26              value = "main.html">
27        </p>
28
29        <p><label>Name:
30           <input name = "name" type = "text" size = "25">
31        </label></p>
32
33        <p><label>Comments:
34           <textarea name = "comments" rows = "4" cols = "36"></textarea>
35        </label></p>
36
37        <p><label>Email Address:
38           <input name = "email" type = "password" size = "25">
39        </label></p>
40
41        <p>
42           <strong>Things you liked:</strong><br>
43
44           <label>Site design
45           <input name = "things" type = "checkbox" value = "Design">
46           </label>
47
48           <label>Links
49           <input name = "things" type = "checkbox" value = "Links">
50           </label>
51
52           <label>Ease of use
53           <input name = "things" type = "checkbox" value = "Ease">
54           </label>
55
56           <label>Images
57           <input name = "things" type = "checkbox" value = "Images">
58           </label>
59
60           <label>Source code
61           <input name = "things" type = "checkbox" value = "Code">
62           </label>
63        </p>
64
65        <!-- <input type = "radio"> creates a radio button. The      -->
66        <!-- difference between radio buttons and checkboxes is       -->
```

Fig. 3.5   Form including radio buttons and pulldown lists (part 2 of 4).

```
67       <!-- that only one radio button in a group can be selected   -->
68       <p>
69          <strong>How did you get to our site?:</strong><br>
70
71          <label>Search engine
72          <input name = "how get to site" type = "radio"
73             value = "search engine" checked></label>
74
75          <label>Links from another site
76          <input name = "how get to site" type = "radio"
77             value = "link"></label>
78
79          <label>Deitel.com Web site
80          <input name = "how get to site" type = "radio"
81             value = "deitel.com"></label>
82
83          <label>Reference in a book
84          <input name = "how get to site" type = "radio"
85             value = "book"></label>
86
87          <label>Other
88          <input name = "how get to site" type = "radio"
89             value = "other"></label>
90
91       </p>
92
93       <!-- The <select> tag presents a drop down menu with -->
94       <!-- choices indicated by the <option> tags          -->
95       <p>
96          <label>Rate our site:
97
98          <select name = "rating">
99             <option selected>Amazing:-)</option>
100            <option>10</option>
101            <option>9</option>
102            <option>8</option>
103            <option>7</option>
104            <option>6</option>
105            <option>5</option>
106            <option>4</option>
107            <option>3</option>
108            <option>2</option>
109            <option>1</option>
110            <option>The Pits:-(</option>
111         </select>
112
113         </label>
114      </p>
115
116      <p>
117         <input type = "submit" value = "Submit Your Entries">
118         <input type = "reset" value = "Clear Your Entries">
119      </p>
```

Fig. 3.5   Form including radio buttons and pulldown lists (part 3 of 4).

```
120
121      </form>
122
123  </body>
124  </html>
```

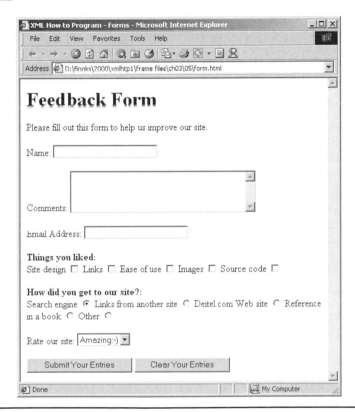

Fig. 3.5   Form including radio buttons and pulldown lists (part 4 of 4).

The last type of form input that we introduce here is the ***select*** element (lines 98–111). This will place a selectable list of items inside your form.

```
<select name = "rating">
   <option selected>Amazing:-)</option>
   <option>10</option>
   <option>9</option>
   <option>8</option>
   <option>7</option>
   <option>6</option>
   <option>5</option>
   <option>4</option>
   <option>3</option>
   <option>2</option>
   <option>1</option>
   <option>The Pits:-(</option>
</select>
```

This type of form input is created using a **select** element. Inside the opening *\<select\>* tag, be sure to include the **name** attribute.

To add an item to the list, add to the **select** element an *option* element containing the text to be displayed. The **selected** attribute, like the **checked** attribute for radio buttons and checkboxes, applies a default selection to your list.

The preceding code will generate a pull-down list of options in most visual browsers, as shown in Fig. 3.5. You can change the number of list options visible at one time using the *size* attribute of the **select** element. Use this attribute if you prefer an expanded version of the list to the one-line expandable list.

3.6 Internal Linking

In Chapter 2, we discussed how to link one Web page to another using text and image anchors. Figure 3.6 introduces *internal linking*, which lets you create named anchors for hyperlinks to particular parts of an HTML document.

```
1   <!DOCTYPE HTML PUBLIC "-//W3C//DTD HTML 4.01//EN"
2             "http://www.w3.org/TR/html4/strict.dtd">
3   <html>
4
5   <!-- Fig. 3.6: links.html   -->
6   <!-- Internal Linking       -->
7
8   <head>
9      <title>XML How to Program - List</title>
10  </head>
11
12  <body>
13
14     <!-- <a name = ".."></a> makes an internal hyperlink -->
15     <p><a name = "features"></a></p>
16     <h1>The Best Features of the Internet</h1>
17
18     <!-- An internal link's address is "xx.html#linkname" -->
19     <p><a href = "#ceos">Go to <em>Favorite CEOs</em></a></p>
20
21     <ul>
22       <li>You can meet people from countries around the world.</li>
23
24       <li>You have access to new media as it becomes public:
25          <ul>
26             <li>New games</li>
27             <li>New applications
28                <ul>
29                   <li>For Business</li>
30                   <li>For Pleasure</li>
31                </ul>
32             </li>
33
```

Fig. 3.6   Using internal hyperlinks to make your pages more navigable (part 1 of 3).

```
34                    <li>Around the Clock news</li>
35                    <li>Search Engines</li>
36                    <li>Shopping</li>
37                    <li>Programming
38                        <ul>
39                            <li>HTML</li>
40                            <li>Java</li>
41                            <li>Dynamic HTML</li>
42                            <li>Scripts</li>
43                            <li>New languages</li>
44                        </ul>
45                    </li>
46                </ul>
47            </li>
48
49            <li>Links</li>
50            <li>Keeping In touch with old friends</li>
51            <li>It is the technology of the future!</li>
52        </ul>
53
54
55        <p><a name = "ceos"></a></p>
56        <h1>My 3 Favorite <em>CEOs</em></h1>
57
58        <p>
59            <a href = "#features">Go to <em>Favorite Features</em></a>
60        </p>
61
62        <ol>
63            <li>Bill Gates</li>
64            <li>Steve Jobs</li>
65            <li>Michael Dell</li>
66        </ol>
67
68    </body>
69    </html>
```

Fig. 3.6   Using internal hyperlinks to make your pages more navigable (part 2 of 3).

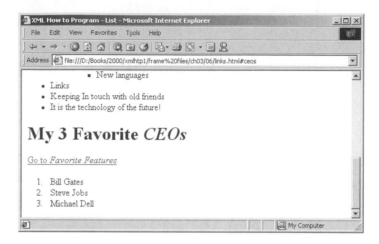

Fig. 3.6   Using internal hyperlinks to make your pages more navigable (part 3 of 3).

Line 15

```
<p><a name = "features"></a></p>
```

shows a named anchor for an internal hyperlink. A named anchor is created using an **a** element with a **name** attribute. Line 15 creates an anchor named **features**. Because the name of the page is **list.html**, the URL of this anchor in the Web page is **list.html#features**. Line 59

```
<a href = "#features">Go to <em>Favorite Features</em></a>
```

shows a hyperlink with the anchor **features** as its target. Selecting this hyperlink in a visual browser would scroll the browser window to the **features** anchor (line 15). Examples of this occur in Fig 3.6, which shows two different screen captures from the same page, each at a different anchor. You can also link to an anchor in another page using the URL of that location (using the format **href = "page.html#name"**).

Look-and-Feel Observation 3.2

Internal hyperlinks are most useful in large HTML files with lots of information. You can link to various points on the page to save the user from having to scroll down and find a specific location.

3.7 Creating and Using Image Maps

We have seen that images can be used as links to other places on your site or elsewhere on the Internet. We now discuss how to create *image maps* (Fig. 3.7), which allow you to designate certain sections of the image as *hotspots* and then use these hotspots as links.

All elements of an image map are contained inside the **<map>...</map>** tags. The required attribute for the *map* element is **name** (line 17)

```
<map name = "picture">
```

As we will see, this attribute is needed for referencing purposes. A hotspot on the image is designated with the **area** element. Every **area** element has the following attributes: **href** sets the target for the link on that spot, **shape** and **coords** set the characteristics of the area and **alt** functions just as it does in the **img** element.

```
1   <!DOCTYPE HTML PUBLIC "-//W3C//DTD HTML 4.01//EN"
2              "http://www.w3.org/TR/html4/strict.dtd">
3   <html>
4
5   <!-- Fig. 3.7: picture.html       -->
6   <!-- Creating and Using Imape Maps -->
7
8   <head>
9      <title>XML How to Program - Image Map</title>
10  </head>
11
12  <body>
13
14     <p>
15     <!-- <map> opens and names an image map formatting area -->
16     <!-- and to be referenced later -->
17     <map name = "picture">
18
19        <!-- The "shape = rect" indicates a rectangular area, with -->
20        <!-- coordinates of the upper-left and lower-right corners -->
21         <area href = "form.html" shape = "rect"
22           coords = "3, 122, 73, 143" alt = "Go to the feedback form">
23         <area href = "contact.html" shape = "rect"
24           coords = "109, 123, 199, 142" alt = "Go to the contact page">
25         <area href = "main.html" shape = "rect"
26           coords = "1, 2, 72, 17" alt = "Go to the homepage">
27         <area href = "links.html" shape = "rect"
28           coords = "155, 0, 199, 18" alt = "Go to the links page">
29
30        <!-- The "shape = polygon" indicates an area of cusotmizable -->
31        <!-- shape, with the coordinates of every vertex listed -->
32         <area href = "mailto:deitel@deitel.com" shape = "poly"
33           coords = "28, 22, 24, 68, 46, 114, 84, 111, 99, 56, 86, 13"
34           alt = "Email the Deitels">
35
36        <!-- The "shape = circle" indicates a circular area with -->
37        <!-- center and radius listed -->
38         <area href = "mailto:deitel@deitel.com" shape = "circle"
39           coords = "146, 66, 42" alt = "Email the Deitels">
40     </map>
41
42     <!-- <img src=... usemap = "#name"> says that the indicated -->
43     <!-- image map will be used with this image -->
44     <img src = "deitel.gif" width = "200" height = "144"
45        alt = "Harvey and Paul Deitel" usemap = "#picture">
46     </p>
47
```

Fig. 3.7   Picture with links anchored to an image map (part 1 of 2).

```
48    </body>
49    </html>
```

Fig. 3.7   Picture with links anchored to an image map (part 2 of 2).

The markup on lines 21 and 22

```
<area href = "form.html" shape = "rect"
   coords = "3, 122, 73, 143" alt = "Go to the feedback form">
```

causes a *rectangular hotspot* to be drawn around the *coordinates* given in the **coords** element. A coordinate pair consists of two numbers, which are the locations of the point on the *x* and *y* axes. The *x* axis extends horizontally from the upper-left corner and the *y* axis vertically. Every point on an image has a unique *x–y* coordinate. In the case of a rectangular hotspot, the required coordinates are those of the upper-left and lower-right corners of the rectangle. In this case, the upper-left corner of the rectangle is located at 3 on the *x* axis and 122 on the *y* axis, annotated as (*3, 122*). The lower-right corner of the rectangle is at (*73, 143*).

Another map area is in lines 32–34

```
<area href = "mailto:deitel@deitel.com" shape = "poly"
   coords = "28, 22, 24, 68, 46, 114, 84, 111, 99, 56, 86, 13
   alt = "Email the Deitels">
```

In this case, we use the value **poly** for the **shape** attribute. This creates a hotspot in the shape of a polygon using the coordinates in the **coords** attribute. These coordinates represent each vertex, or corner, of the polygon. The browser will automatically connect these points with lines to form the area of the hotspot.

shape = "circle" is the last shape attribute that is commonly used in image maps. It creates a *circular hotspot*, and requires both the coordinates of the center of the circle and the radius of the circle, in pixels.

To use the image map with an **img** element, you must insert the **usemap = "#***name*" attribute into the **img** element, where *name* is the value of the **name** attribute in the **map** element. Lines 44 and 45

```
<img src = "deitel.gif" width = "200" height= "144" alt =
"Harvey and Paul Deitel" usemap = "#picture">
```

show how the image map **name = "picture"** is applied to the **img** element.

3.8 <meta> Tags

People use search engines to find interesting Web sites. Search engines usually catalog sites by following links from page to page and saving identification and classification information for each page visited. The main HTML element that search engines use to catalog pages is the **meta** tag (Fig. 3.8).

A **meta** tag contains two attributes that should always be used. The first of these, **name**, identifies the type of **meta** tag you are including. The **content** attribute provides information the search engine will catalog about your site.

```
1   <!DOCTYPE HTML PUBLIC "-//W3C//DTD HTML 4.01//EN"
2            "http://www.w3.org/TR/html4/strict.dtd">
3   <html>
4
5   <!-- Fig. 3.8: main.html        -->
6   <!-- <meta> and <!doctype> tags -->
7
8   <head>
9      <!-- <meta> tags give search engines information they need -->
10     <!-- to catalog your site                                  -->
11     <meta name = "keywords" content = "Webpage, design, HTML,
12        tutorial, personal, help, index, form, contact, feedback,
13        list, links, frame, deitel">
14
15     <meta name = "description" content = "This Web site will help
16        you learn the basics of HTML and Webpage design through the
17        use of interactive examples and instruction.">
18
19     <title>XML How to Program - Welcome</title>
20  </head>
21
22  <body>
23
24     <h1>Welcome to Our Web Site!</h1>
25
26     <p>We have designed this site to teach about the wonders of
27     <em>HTML</em>. We have been using <em>HTML</em> since version
28     <strong>2.0</strong>, and we enjoy the features that have been
29     added recently. It seems only a short time ago that we read
30     our first <em>HTML</em> book. Soon you will know about many of
31     the great new features of HTML 4.01.</p>
32
33     <p>Have Fun With the Site!</p>
34
35  </body>
36  </html>
```

Fig. 3.8   Using **meta** to provide keywords and a description.

Lines 11–13 demonstrate the **meta** tag.

```
<meta name = "keywords" content = "Webpage, design, HTML,
   tutorial, personal, help, index, form, contact, feedback,
   list, links, frame, deitel">
```

The **content** of a **meta** tag with *name = "keywords"* provides search engines with a list of words that describe key aspects of your site. These words are used to match with searches—if someone searches for some of the terms in your **keywords meta** tag, they have a better chance of being informed about your site in the search engine output. Thus, including **meta** tags and their **content** information will draw more viewers to your site.

The *description* attribute value (lines 15–17)

```
<meta name = "description" content = "This Web site will help
   you learn the basics of HTML and Webpage design through the
   use of interactive examples and instruction.">
```

is quite similar to the **keywords** value. Instead of giving a list of words describing your page, the **content**s of the keywords **meta** element should be a readable 3-to-4 line description of your site, written in sentence form. This description is also used by search engines to catalog and display your site.

Software Engineering Observation 3.1

meta elements are not visible to users of the site and must be placed inside the header section of your HTML document.

3.9 frameset Element

All of the Web pages we have designed so far have the ability to link to other pages but can display only one page at a time. Figure 3.9 introduces *frames*, which can help you display more than one HTML file at a time. Frames, when used properly, can make your site more readable and usable for your users.

```
1   <!DOCTYPE HTML PUBLIC "-//W3C//DTD HTML 4.01 Frameset//EN"
2            "http://www.w3.org/TR/html4/frameset.dtd">
3   <html>
4
5   <!-- Fig. 3.9: index.html  -->
6   <!-- HTML Frames I         -->
7
8   <head>
9      <meta name = "keywords" content = "Webpage, design, HTML,
10        tutorial, personal, help, index, form, contact, feedback,
11        list, links, frame, deitel">
12
13     <meta name = "description" content = "This Web site will help
14        you learn the basics of HTML and Webpage design through the
15        use of interactive examples and instruction.">
16
17     <title>XML How to Program - Main</title>
```

Fig. 3.9   Web site using two frames—navigation and content (part 1 of 2).

```
18   </head>
19
20   <!-- The <frameset> tag gives the dimensions of your frame -->
21   <frameset cols = "110,*">
22
23      <!-- The individual frame elements specify which pages -->
24      <!-- appear in the given frames                        -->
25      <frame name = "nav" src = "nav.html">
26      <frame name = "main" src = "main.html">
27
28      <noframes>
29         <p>This page uses frames, but your browser does not support
30         them.</p>
31
32         <p>Please, <a href = "nav.html">follow this link to browse our
33         site without frames</a>.</p>
34      </noframes>
35
36   </frameset>
37   </html>
```

Fig. 3.9   Web site using two frames—navigation and content (part 2 of 2).

On lines 1 and 2

```
<!DOCTYPE HTML PUBLIC "-//W3C//DTD HTML 4.01 Frameset//EN"
         "http://www.w3.org/TR/html14/frameset.dtd">
```

we encounter a new document type. The document type specified here indicates that this HTML document uses frames. You should use this document type whenever you use frames in your HTML document.

The framed page begins with the opening **frameset** tag, on line 21

```
<frameset cols = "110,*">
```

This tag tells the browser that the page contains frames. The **cols** attribute of the opening **frameset** tag gives the layout of the frameset. The value of **cols** (or **rows**, if you will be writing a frameset with a horizontal layout) gives the width of each frame, either in pixels or as a percentage of the screen. In this case, the attribute **cols = "110,*"** tells the browser that there are two frames. The first one extends 110 pixels from the left edge of the screen, and the second frame fills the remainder of the screen (as indicated by the asterisk).

Now that we have defined the page layout, we have to specify what files will make up the frameset. We do this with the **frame** element in lines 25 and 26

```
<frame name = "nav" src = "nav.html">
<frame name = "main" src = "main.html">
```

In each **frame** element, the **src** attribute gives the URL of the page that will be displayed in the frame. In the preceding example, the first frame (which covers 110 pixels on the left side of the **frameset**) will display the page **nav.html** and has the attribute **name = "nav"**. The second frame will display the page **main.html** and has the attribute **name = "main"**.

The purpose of a **name** attribute in the **frame** element is to identify the frame, enabling hyperlinks in a **frameset** to load in their intended target **frame**. For example,

```
<a href = "links.html" target = "main">
```

would load **links.html** in the frame whose **name** attribute is **"main"**.

A target in an anchor element can also be set to a number of preset values: **target="_blank"** loads the page in a new blank browser window, **target="_self"** loads the page into the same window as the anchor element, **target="_parent"** loads it in the parent **frameset** (i.e., the **frameset** which contains the current frame) and **target="_top"** loads the page into the full browser window (the page loads over the **frameset**).

In lines 28–34 of the code example in Fig. 3.9, the **noframes** element displays HTML in those browsers that do not support frames.

Portability Tip 3.1

*Not everyone uses a browser that supports frames. Use the **noframes** element inside the **frameset** to direct users to a non-framed version of your site.*

Look-and-Feel Observation 3.3

Frames are capable of enhancing your page, but are often misused. Never use frames to accomplish what you could with other, simpler HTML formatting.

3.10 Nested **framesets**

You can use the **frameset** element to create more complex layouts in a framed Web site by nesting **frameset** areas as in Fig. 3.10.

The first level of **frameset** tags is on lines 21 and 22

```
<frameset cols = "110,*">
    <frame name = "nav"src = "nav.html">
```

The **frameset** and **frame** elements here are constructed in the same manner as in Fig. 3.9. We have one frame that extends over the first 110 pixels starting at the left edge.

The second (nested) level of the **frameset** element covers only the remaining **frame** area that was not included in the primary **frameset**. Thus, any frames included in the second **frameset** will not include the left-most 110 pixels of the screen. Lines 26–29 show the second level of **frameset** tags.

```
1   <!DOCTYPE HTML PUBLIC "-//W3C//DTD HTML 4.01 Frameset//EN"
2              "http://www.w3.org/TR/html4/frameset.dtd">
3   <html>
4
5   <!-- Fig. 3.10: index.html -->
6   <!-- HTML Frames II         -->
7
8   <head>
9
10  <meta name = "keywords" content = "Webpage, design, HTML,
11     tutorial, personal, help, index, form, contact, feedback,
12     list, links, frame, deitel">
13
14  <meta name = "description" content = "This Web site will help
15     you learn the basics of HTML and Webpage design through the
16     use of interactive examples and instruction.">
17
18  <title>XML How to Program - Main</title>
19  </head>
20
21  <frameset cols = "110,*">
22     <frame name = "nav" src = "nav.html">
23
24     <!-- Nested framesets are used to change the formatting -->
25     <!-- and spacing of the frameset as a whole            -->
26     <frameset rows = "175,*">
27        <frame name = "picture" src = "picture.html">
28        <frame name = "main" src = "main.html">
29     </frameset>
30
31     <noframes>
32        <p>This page uses frames, but your browser does not support
33        them.</p>
34
35       <p>Please, <a href = "nav.html">follow this link to browse our
36        site without frames</a>.</p>
37     </noframes>
38
39  </frameset>
40  </html>
```

Fig. 3.10   Framed Web site with a nested frameset (part 1 of 2).

Fig. 3.10   Framed Web site with a nested frameset (part 2 of 2).

```
<frameset rows = "175,*">
   <frame name = "picture" src = "picture.html">
   <frame name = "main" src = "main.html">
</frameset>
```

In this **frameset** area, the first frame extends 175 pixels from the top of the screen, as indicated by the **rows = "175,*"**. Be sure to include the correct number of **frame** elements inside the second **frameset** area. Also, be sure to include a **noframes** element and to close both of the **frameset** areas at the end of the Web page.

Testing and Debugging Tip 3.1

*When using nested **frameset** elements, indent every level of **frame** tag. This makes the page clearer and easier to debug.*

Look-and-Feel Observation 3.4

*Nested **frameset**s can help you create visually pleasing, easy-to-navigate Web sites.*

3.11 Internet and World Wide Web Resources

There are many Web sites that cover the more advanced and difficult features of HTML. Several of these sites are featured here.

www.geocities.com/SiliconValley/Orchard/5212
Adam's Advanced HTML Page is geared to those looking to master the more advanced techniques of HTML. It includes instructions for creating tables, frames and marquees and other advanced topics.

www.w3scripts.com/html
This site, an offshoot of *W3Schools*, is a repository for code examples exhibiting all of the features of HTML, from beginner to advanced.

www.blooberry.com/indexdot/html
Index Dot HTML, The Advance HTML Reference... The name speaks for itself. This site has a great directory and tree-based index of all HTML elements plus more.

www.markradcliffe.co.uk/html/advancedhtml.htm
The *Advanced HTML Guide* gives insights into improving your site using HTML in ways you might not have thought possible.

SUMMARY

- HTML tables organize data into rows and columns. All tags and text that apply to a table go inside the **<table>**...**</table>** tags. The **border** attribute lets you set the width of the table's border in pixels. The **width** attribute sets the width of the table—you specify either a number of pixels or a percentage of the screen width.

- The text inside the **<caption>**...**</caption>** tags is inserted directly above the table in the browser window. The caption text is also used to help text-based browsers interpret the table data.

- Tables can be split into distinct horizontal and vertical sections. Put all header information (such as table titles and column headers) inside the **<thead>**...**</thead>** tags. The **tr** (table row) element is used for formatting the cells of individual rows. All of the cells in a row belong within the **<tr>**...**</tr>** tags of that row.

- The smallest area of the table that we are able to format is the data cell. There are two types of data cells: ones located in the header (**<th>**...**</th>**) and ones located in the table body (**<td>**...**</td>**). Header cells, usually placed in the **<thead>** area, are suitable for titles and column headings.

- Like **thead**, the **tbody** is used for formatting and grouping purposes. Most tables use **tbody** to house the majority of their content.

- **td** table data cells are left aligned by default. **th** cells are centered by default.

- Just as you can use the **thead** and **tbody** elements to format groups of table rows, you can use the **colgroup** element to group and format columns. **colgroup** is used by setting in its opening tag the number of columns it affects and the formatting it imposes on that group of columns.

- Each **col** element contained inside the **<colgroup>**...**</colgroup>** tags can in turn format a specified number of columns.

- It is possible to make some table data cells larger than others by using the **rowspan** and **colspan** attributes. The attribute value extends the data cell to span the specified number of cells.

- The **valign** (vertical alignment) attribute of a table data cell accepts the following values: **"top"**, **"middle"**, **"bottom"** and **"baseline"**.

- All cells in a table row whose **valign** attribute is set to **"baseline"** will have the first text line on a common baseline.

- The default vertical alignment in all data and header cells is **valign="middle"**.

- HTML provides several mechanisms—including the **form**—to collect information from people viewing your site.

- Use **method = "post"** in a form that causes changes to server data, for example when updating a database. The form data will be sent to the server as an environment variable, which scripts are able to access. The other possible value, **method = "get"**, should be used when your form does not cause any changes in server-side data, for example when making a database request. The form data from **method = "get"** is appended to the end of the URL. Also be aware that **method = "get"** is limited to standard characters, and cannot submit any special characters.

- A Web server is a machine that runs a software package such as Apache or IIS; servers are designed to handle browser requests. When a user uses a browser to request a page or file somewhere on the server, the server processes this request and returns an answer to the browser.

- The **action** attribute in the **form** tag is the path to a script that processes the form data.

- The input element is common in forms, and always requires the **type** attribute. Two other attributes are **name**, which provides a unique identification for the **input**, and **value**, which indicates the value that the **input** element sends to the server upon submission.

- The input **type="text"** inserts a one-line text bar into the form. The value of this **input** element and the information that the server sends to you from this **input** is the text that the user types into the bar. The **size** attribute determines the width of the text input, measured in characters. You can also set a maximum number of characters that the text input will accept by inserting the **maxlength="**_length_**"** attribute.

- You must make sure to include a **label** element for each form element to indicate the function of the element.

- The **type="submit" input** element places a button in the form that submits data to the server when clicked. The **value** attribute of the **submit** input changes the text displayed on the button.

- The **type="reset"** input element places a button on the form that, when clicked, will clear all entries the user has entered into the form.

- The **textarea** element inserts a box into the form. You specify the size of the box (which is scrollable) inside the opening **<textarea>** tag with the **rows** attribute and the **cols** attribute.

- Data entered in a **type="password"** input appears on the screen as asterisks. The password is used for submitting sensitive information that the user would not want others to be able to read. It is just the browser that displays asterisks—the real form data is still submitted to the server.

- Every **input** element with **type="checkbox"** creates a new checkbox in the form. Checkboxes can be used individually or in groups. Each checkbox in a group should have the same **name** (in this case, **name="things"**).

- Inserted into forms by means of the **input** attribute **type="radio"**, radio buttons are different from checkboxes in that only one in the group may be selected at any time. All of the **name** attributes of a group of radio inputs must be the same and all of the **value** attributes different.

- Insert the attribute **checked** to indicate which radio button you would like selected initially.

- The **select** element places a selectable list of items inside your form. To add an item to the list, insert an **option** element in the **<select>...</select>** area and type what you want the list item to display on the same line. You can change the number of list options visible at one time by including the **size="**_size_**"** attribute inside the **<select>** tag. Use this attribute if you prefer an expanded version of the list to the one-line expandable list.

- A location on a page is marked by including a **name** attribute in an **a** element. Clicking this hyperlink in a browser would scroll the browser window to that point on the page.

- An image map allows you to designate certain sections of the image as hotspots and then use these hotspots as anchors for linking.

- All elements of an image map are contained inside the **<map>**...**</map>** tags. The required attribute for the **map** element is **name**.
- A hotspot on the image is designated with the ***area*** element. Every ***<area>*** tag has the following attributes: **href** sets the target for the link on that spot, **shape** and **coords** set the characteristics of the area and **alt** function just as it does in **<img>** tags.
- **shape="rect"** creates a rectangular hotspot around the coordinates of a **coords** element.
- A coordinate pair consists of two numbers, which are the locations of the point on the x and y axes. The x axis extends horizontally from the upper-left corner and the y axis vertically. Every point on an image has a unique x-y coordinate, annotated as (x, y).
- In the case of a rectangular hotspot, the required coordinates are those of the upper-left and lower-right corners of the rectangle.
- The **shape="poly"** creates a hotspot of no preset shape—you specify the shape of the hotspot in the **coords** attribute by listing the coordinates of every vertex, or corner of the hotspot.
- **shape="circle"** creates a circular hotspot; it requires both the coordinates of the center of the circle and the length of the radius, in pixels.
- To use an image map with a graphic on your page, you must insert the **usemap="#*name*"** attribute into the **img** element, where "name" is the value of the **name** attribute in the **map** element.
- The main element that interacts with search engines is the **meta** element.
- **meta** tags contain two attributes that should always be used. The first of these, **name**, is an identification of the type of **meta** tag you are including. The **content** attribute gives the information the search engine will be cataloging.
- The **content** of a **meta** tag with **name="keywords"** provides the search engines with a list of words that describe the key aspects of your site. By including **meta** tags and their content information, you can give precise information about your site to search engines. This will help you draw a more focused audience to your site.
- The **description** value of the **name** attribute in the **meta** tag should be a 3-to-4 line description of your site, written in sentence form. This description is used by the search engine to catalog and display your site.
- **meta** elements are not visible to users of the site and should be placed inside the header section of your HTML document.
- The **frameset** tag tells the browser that the page contains frames.
- **cols** or **rows** gives the width of each frame in pixels or as a percentage of the screen.
- In each **frame** element, the **src** attribute gives the URL of the page that will be displayed in the specified frame.
- The purpose of a **name** attribute in the **frame** element is to give an identity to that specific frame, in order to enable hyperlinks in a **frameset** to load their intended **frame**. The **target** attribute in an anchor element is set to the **name** of the **frame** in which the new page should load.
- A target in an anchor element can be set to a number of preset values: **target="_blank"** loads the page in a new blank browser window, **target="self"** loads the page into the same window as the anchor element, **target="_parent"** loads the page into the parent **frameset** and **target="_top"** loads the page into the full browser window.
- Not everyone viewing a page has a browser that can handle frames. You therefore need to include a **noframes** element inside of the **frameset**. You should include regular HTML tags and elements within the **<noframes>**...**</noframes>** tags. Use this area to direct the user to a non-framed version of the site.
- By nesting **frameset** elements, you can create more complex layouts.

TERMINOLOGY

`<!doctype...>`
`<meta>` tag
`<option>`
ACTION attribute in **form** element
area
border property of **table** element
caption element
cell of a table
CGI script
checked
circular hotspot
col element
colgroup element
cols attribute of **table** element
colspan attribute of **td** element
column of a table
coords attribute inside **area** element
data cell
environment variable
form
frame element (`<frame>...</frame>`)
frameset element
header cell
hotspot
image map
indenting lists
input element (`<input>...</input>`)
input type="button"
input type="checkbox"
input type="password"
input type="radio"
input type="reset"
input type="submit"
input type="text"
input type="textarea"
internal linking
list
map element
maxlength="#"

method="get"
method="post"
name attribute in **input** element
name="recipient" in **input** element
name="redirect" in **input** element
name="subject" in **input** element
nested lists
noframes
noresize attribute in **frame**
ol (ordered list) element (`<ol>...</ol>`)
rectangular hotspot
row of a table
rowspan attribute of **td** element
scrolling attribute in **frame**
select element (`<select>...</select>`)
shape attribute inside **area** element
size attribute in **select**
src attribute of **frame** element
table
table element (`<table>...</table>`)
target="_blank"
target="_parent"
target="_top"
tbody
td (table data) element (`<td>...</td>`)
text-based browser
th (header cell) element (`<th>...</th>`)
thead element (`<thead>...</thead>`)
tr (table row) element (`<tr>...</tr>`)
type=1 attribute of `<ol>`
type=a attribute of `<ol>`
type=A attribute of `<ol>`
type=i attribute of `<ol>`
type=I attribute of `<ol>`
ul (unordered list) element (`<ul>...</ul>`)
usemap="name" attribute in **img**
value attribute of **input** element
Web server

SELF-REVIEW EXERCISES

3.1   State whether the following are *true* or *false*. If *false*, explain why.

a) The width of all data cells in a table must be the same.

b) The **thead** element is mandatory in a **table**.

c) You are limited to a maximum of 100 internal links per page.

d) All browsers can render **frameset**s.

3.2   Fill in the blanks in each of the following statements:

    a) The _____ attribute in an **input** element inserts a button that, when clicked, will clear the contents of the form.

    b) The spacing of a **frameset** is set by including the _____ attribute or the _____ attribute inside of the **<frameset>** tag.

    c) The _____ element inserts a new item in a list.

    d) The _____ element tells the browser what version of HTML is included on the page. Two types of this element are _____ and _____.

    e) The common shapes used in image maps are _____, _____ and _____.

3.3   Write HTML tags to accomplish the following:

    a) Insert a framed Web page with the first frame extending 300 pixels across the page from the left side.

    b) Insert an ordered list that will have numbering by lowercase Roman numerals.

    c) Insert a scrollable list (in a form) that will always display four entries of the list.

    d) Insert an image map onto a page using **deitel.gif** as an image and **map** with **name="hello"** as the image map, and have "**hello**" be the **alt** text.

ANSWERS TO SELF-REVIEW EXERCISES

3.1   a) False. You can specify the width of any column either in pixels or as a percentage of the total width of the table. b) False. The **thead** element is used only for formatting purposes and is optional (but it is recommended that you include it). c) False. You can have an unlimited number of hyperlink locations on any page. d) False. Text-based browsers are unable to render a **frameset** and must therefore rely on the information that you include inside the **<noframes>...</noframes>** tag.

3.2   a) **type = "reset"**. b) **cols, rows**. c) **li**. d) **<!doctype...>, transitional, frameset**. e) **poly, circle, rect**.

3.3   a) **<frameset cols = "300,*">...</frameset>** b) **<ol type = "i">...</ol>** c)**<select size = "4">...</select>** d)**<img src = "deitel.gif" alt = "hello" usemap = "#hello">**

EXERCISES

3.4   Categorize each of the following as an element or an attribute:

    a) width

    b) td

    c) th

    d) frame

    e) name

    f) select

    g) type

3.5   What will the **frameset** produced by the following code look like? Assume that the pages being imported are blank with white backgrounds and that the dimensions of the screen are 800 by 600. Sketch the layout, approximating the dimensions.

```
<frameset rows = "20%,*">
<frame src = "hello.html" name = "hello">
   <frameset cols = "150,*">
   <frame src = "nav.html" name = "nav">
   <frame src = "deitel.html" name = "deitel">
   </frameset>
</frameset>
```

3.6   Assume that you have a document with many subsections. Write the HTML markup to create a frame with a table of contents on the left side of the window, and have each entry in the table of contents use internal linking to scroll down the document frame to the appropriate subsection.

Cascading Style Sheets™ (CSS)

Objectives

- To take control of the appearance of a Web site by creating stylesheets.
- To use a stylesheet to give all the pages of a Web site the same look and feel.
- To use the **class** attribute to apply styles.
- To specify the precise font, size, color and other properties of displayed text.
- To specify element backgrounds and colors.
- To understand the box model and be able to control the margins, borders and padding.
- To use stylesheets to separate presentation from content.

Fashions fade, style is eternal.
Yves Saint Laurent

A style does not go out of style as long as it adapts itself to its period. When there is an incompatibility between the style and a certain state of mind, it is never the style that triumphs.
Coco Chanel

How liberating to work in the margins, outside a central perception.
Don DeLillo

Our words have wings, but fly not where we would.
George Eliot

4.1 Introduction

Cascading Style Sheets (*CSS*) allow you to specify the style of your page elements (spacing, margins, etc.) separately from the structure of your document (section headers, body text, links, etc.). This *separation of structure from presentation* allows greater manageability and makes changing the style of your document easier.

4.2 Inline Styles

There are many ways to declare styles for a document. Figure 4.1 presents *inline styles* in which an individual element's style is declared using the **style** attribute.

```
1   <!DOCTYPE HTML PUBLIC "-//W3C//DTD HTML 4.01//EN"
2           "http://www.w3.org/TR/html4/strict.dtd">
3   <html>
4
5   <!-- Fig. 4.1: inline.html -->
6   <!-- Using inline styles   -->
7
8   <head>
9      <title>XML How to Program - Inline Styles</title>
10  </head>
11
12  <body>
13
14     <p>This text does not have any style applied to it.</p>
15
16     <!-- The style attribute allows you to declare inline   -->
17     <!-- styles. Separate multiple styles with a semicolon. -->
```

Fig. 4.1   Inline styles (part 1 of 2).

```
18      <p style = "font-size: 20pt">This text has the <em>font-size</em>
19      style applied to it, making it 20pt.</p>
20
21      <p style = "font-size: 20pt; color: #0000ff">This text has the
22      <em>font-size</em> and <em>color</em> styles applied to it,
23      making it 20pt. and blue.</p>
24
25   </body>
26   </html>
```

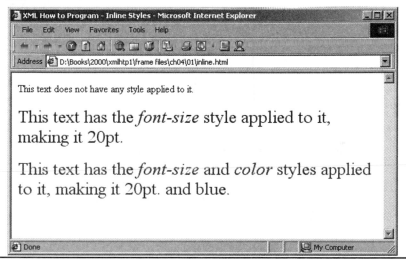

Fig. 4.1   Inline styles (part 2 of 2).

Our first inline style declaration appears on line 18

```
<p style = "font-size: 20pt">This text has the <em>font-size</em>
```

The **style** *attribute* allows you to specify a style for an element. Each *CSS property* (in this case, **font-size**) is followed by a colon then by the value of the property. On line 18 we declare the **p** element to have 20-point text size.

Line 21

```
<p style = "font-size: 20pt; color: #0000ff">This text has the
```

specifies two properties separated by a semicolon. In this line we also set the **color** of the text to blue using the hex code **#0000ff**. Color names may be used in place of hex codes as we will see in the next example. Note that inline styles override any other styles applied by the methods we cover later in this chapter.

4.3 Creating Style Sheets with the **style** Element

In Fig. 4.2 we declare styles in the **head** of the document. These styles may be applied to the entire document.

The **style** element on line 12

```
<style type = "text/css">
```

begins the *style sheet*. Styles that are placed here apply to matching elements in the entire document, not just a single element as with inline styles. The **type** attribute specifies the *MIME type* of the stylesheet. MIME is a standard for specifying the format of content—some other MIME types are **text/html**, **image/gif**, and **text/javascript**. Regular text style sheets always use the MIME type **text/css**.

```
1    <!DOCTYPE HTML PUBLIC "-//W3C//DTD HTML 4.01//EN"
2             "http://www.w3.org/TR/html4/strict.dtd">
3    <html>
4
5    <!-- Fig. 4.2: declared.html                         -->
6    <!-- Declaring a style sheet in the header section. -->
7
8    <head>
9       <title>XML How to Program - Style Sheets</title>
10
11      <!-- This begins the style sheet section. -->
12      <style type = "text/css">
13
14         em        { background-color: #8000ff;
15                     color: white }
16
17         h1        { font-family: arial, sans-serif }
18
19         p         { font-size: 14pt }
20
21         .special { color: blue }
22
23      </style>
24   </head>
25
26   <body>
27
28      <!-- This class attribute applies the .blue style -->
29      <h1 class = "special">Deitel & Associates, Inc.</h1>
30
31      <p>Deitel & Associates, Inc. is an internationally recognized
32      corporate training and publishing organization specializing
33      in programming languages, Internet/World Wide Web technology
34      and object technology education. Deitel & Associates, Inc. is
35      a member of the World Wide Web Consortium. The company
36      provides courses on Java, C++, Visual Basic, C, Internet and
37      World Wide Web programming, and Object Technology.</p>
38
39      <h1>Clients</h1>
40      <p class = "special"> The company's clients include many
41      <em>Fortune 1000 companies</em>, government agencies, branches
42      of the military and business organizations. Through its
43      publishing partnership with Prentice Hall, Deitel & Associates,
44      Inc. publishes leading-edge programming textbooks, professional
45      books, interactive CD-ROM-based multimedia Cyber Classrooms,
46      satellite courses and World Wide Web courses.</p>
```

Fig. 4.2   Declaring styles in the **head** of a document (part 1 of 2).

```
47
48    </body>
49    </html>
```

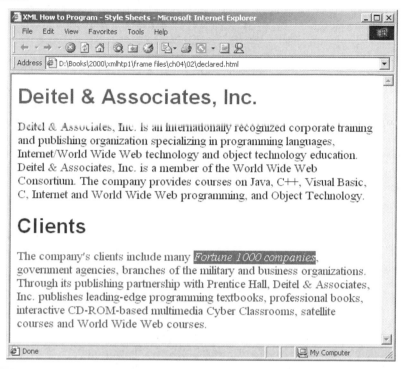

Fig. 4.2   Declaring styles in the **head** of a document (part 2 of 2).

The body of the stylesheet on lines 13–22

```
em      { background-color: #8000ff;
          color: white }

h1      { font-family: arial, sans-serif }

p       { font-size: 14pt }

.special { color: blue }
```

declares the *CSS rules* for this style sheet. We declare rules for the **em, h1** and **p** elements. All **em, h1** and **p** elements in this document will be modified with the specified properties. Notice that each rule body begins and ends with a curly brace (**{** and **}**). We also declare a *style class* named **special** on line 21. Class declarations are preceded with a period and are applied to elements only of that specific class (as we will see momentarily).

The CSS rules in a style sheet use the same syntax as inline styles—the property is followed by a colon (**:**) and the value of that property. Multiple properties are separated with a semicolon (**;**). The **color** property specifies the color of text in an element. Property **background-color** specifies the background color of the element.

The **font-family** property (line 17) specifies the name of the font that should be displayed. In this case, we use the **arial** font. The second value, **sans-serif**, is a *generic font family*. Generic font families allow you to specify a general type of font instead of a specific font. This allows much greater flexibility since not every client will have the same specific fonts installed. In this example, if the **arial** font is not found on the system, the browser will instead display another **sans-serif** font (such as **helvetica** or **verdana**). Other generic font families are **serif** (e.g., **times new roman** or **Georgia**), **cursive** (e.g., **script**), **fantasy** (e.g., **critter**) and **monospace** (e.g., **courier** or **fixedsys**).

The **font-size** property specifies the size to use to render the font—in this case we use 14 points. Other possible measurements besides **pt** are covered later in the chapter. You can also use the relative values **xx-small**, **x-small**, **small**, **smaller**, **medium**, **large**, **larger**, **x-large** and **xx-large**. In general, relative values for **font-size** are preferred because, as an author, you do not know the specific measurements of the display for each different client. For example, someone may wish to view your page on a handheld computer with a small screen. Specifying an 18pt font size in your stylesheet will prevent such a user from seeing more than one or two characters at a time. However, if you specify a relative font size, such as **large** or **larger**, the actual size will be determined by the user's browser and will therefore be displayed properly.

On line 29

```
<h1 class = "special">Deitel & Associates, Inc.</h1>
```

the **class** attribute applies a style class, in this case **special** (this was declared as **.special** in the stylesheet). Note that the text appears on screen with *both* the properties of an **h1** element (i.e., **arial** or **sans-serif** font) and the properties of the **.special** style class applied (i.e., **color** blue).

The **p** element and the **.special** class style are applied to the text on lines 40–46. All styles applied to an element (the *parent*, or *ancestor element*) also apply to elements contained in that element (*descendant elements*). The **em** element *inherits* the style from the **p** element (namely, the 14-point font size on line 19). However, because the **em** element has its own **color** property, this overrides the **color** property of the **special** class. We discuss the rules for resolving these kinds of conflicts in Section 4.4.

4.4 Conflicting Styles

CSS stylesheets are *cascading* because styles may defined by a user, an author and a *user agent* (e.g., a Web browser). Styles defined by authors take precedence over styles defined by the user, and styles defined by the user take precedence over styles defined by the user agent. Styles defined for parent and ancestor elements are also inherited by child and descendant elements. In this section we discuss the rules for resolving conflicts between styles defined for elements and those inherited from parent and ancestor elements.

We showed an example of inheritance in Fig. 4.2, in which a child **em** element inherited the **font-size** property from its parent **p** element. However, in Fig. 4.2 the child **em** element also had a **color** property that conflicted with (i.e., had a different value than) the **color** property of its parent **p** element. Properties defined for child and descendant elements have a greater *specificity* than properties defined for parent and ancestor elements.

According to the CSS specification, conflicts are resolved in favor properties with a higher specificity. Figure 4.3 has more examples of inheritance and specificity.

```
1   <!DOCTYPE HTML PUBLIC "-//W3C//DTD HTML 4.01//EN"
2             "http://www.w3.org/TR/html4/strict.dtd">
3   <html>
4
5   <!-- Fig 4.3: advanced.html      -->
6   <!-- More advanced style sheets -->
7
8   <head>
9      <title>XML How to Program - More Styles</title>
10
11     <style type = "text/css">
12
13        a.nodec  { text-decoration: none }
14
15        a:hover  { text-decoration: underline;
16                   color: red;
17                   background-color: #ccffcc }
18
19        li em    { color: red;
20                   font-weight: bold }
21
22        ul       { margin-left: 75px }
23
24        ul ul    { text-decoration: underline;
25                   margin-left: 15px }
26
27     </style>
28  </head>
29
30  <body>
31
32     <h1>Shopping list for <em>Monday</em>:</h1>
33
34     <ul>
35        <li>Milk</li>
36        <li>Bread
37           <ul>
38              <li>White bread</li>
39              <li>Rye bread</li>
40              <li>Whole wheat bread</li>
41           </ul>
42        </li>
43        <li>Rice</li>
44        <li>Potatoes</li>
45        <li>Pizza <em>with mushrooms</em></li>
46     </ul>
47
48     <p><a class = "nodec" href = "http://food.com">Go to the Grocery
49     store</a></p>
50
```

Fig. 4.3   Inheritance in style sheets (part 1 of 2).

```
51    </body>
52    </html>
```

Fig. 4.3   Inheritance in style sheets (part 2 of 2).

Line 13

```
a.nodec   { text-decoration: none }
```

applies the **text-decoration** property to all **a** elements whose **class** attribute is set to **nodec**. The default browser rendering of an **a** element is to underline, but here we set it to **none**. The **text-decoration** property applies *decorations* to text within an element. Other possible values are **overline**, **line-through** and **blink**. The **.nodec** appended to **a** is an extension of class styles—this style will apply only to **a** elements that specify **nodec** as their class.

Lines 15–17

```
a:hover   { text-decoration: underline;
            color: red;
            background-color: #ccffcc }
```

specify a style for **hover**, which is a *pseudo-class*. Pseudo-classes give the author access to content not specifically declared in the document. The **hover** pseudo-class is dynamically activated when the user moves the mouse cursor over an **a** element.

Portability Tip 4.1

Always test stylesheets on all intended client Web browsers to ensure that the display is reasonable.

Lines 19 and 20

```
li em    { color: red;
            font-weight: bold }
```

declare a style for all **em** elements that are descendants of **li** elements. In the screen output of Fig. 4.3 notice that **Monday** is not made red and bold because it is not contained in an **li** element. However, **with mushrooms** (line 45) is contained in an **li** element and therefore is made red and bold.

The syntax for applying rules to multiple elements is similar. For example, to apply the rule on lines 19 and 20 to both **li** and **em** elements, you would separate the elements with commas, as follows:

```
li, em   { color: red;
            font-weight: bold }
```

Lines 24 and 25

```
ul ul    { text-decoration: underline;
            margin-left: 15px }
```

specify that all nested lists (**ul** elements that are descendants of **ul** elements) will be underlined and have a left-hand margin of 15 pixels (margins and the box model will be covered in Section 4.9).

A pixel is a *relative-length* measurement—it varies in size based on screen resolution. Other relative lengths are **em** (the size of the font), **ex** (the so-called "x-height" of the font, which is usually set to the height of a lowercase x) and percentages (e.g., **margin-left: 10%**). To set an element to display text at 150% of its normal size, you could use the syntax

```
font-size: 1.5em
```

The other units of measurement available in CSS are *absolute-length* measurements, i.e., units that do not vary in size based on the system. These are **in** (inches), **cm** (centimeters), **mm** (millimeters), **pt** (points—1 **pt**=1/72 **in**) and **pc** (picas—1 **pc** = 12 **pt**).

Good Programming Practice 4.1

Whenever possible, use relative length measurements. If you use absolute length measurements, your document may not be readable on some client browsers (e.g, wireless phones).

Software Engineering Observation 4.1

*There are three possible sources for styles sheets—browser defaults, preset user styles and author styles (e.g., in the **style** section). Author styles have a greater precedence than most preset user styles, so most conflicts are resolved in favor of the author styles.*

In Fig. 4.3, the whole list is indented because of the 75-pixel left-hand margin for top-level **ul** elements, but the nested list is indented only 15 pixels (not another 75 pixels) because the child **ul** element's **margin-left** property overrides the parent **ul** element's **margin-left** property.

4.5 Linking External Style Sheets

As we have seen, style sheets are an efficient way to give a document a uniform theme. With *external linking*, you can give your whole Web site a uniform look—separate pages on your site can all use the same style sheet, and you only need to modify only a single file to make changes to styles across your whole Web site. Figure 4.4 shows an external style sheet, and Fig. 4.5 shows the syntax for including an external style sheet in an HTML document (line 11).

```
1   /* Fig. 4.4: styles.css    */
2   /* An external stylesheet */
3
4   a         { text-decoration: none }
5
6   a:hover { text-decoration: underline;
7                 color: red;
8                 background-color: #ccffcc }
9
10  li em    { color: red;
11                 font-weight: bold}
12
13  ul       { margin-left: 2cm }
14
15  ul ul    { text-decoration: underline;
16                 margin-left: .5cm }
```

Fig. 4.4   An external style sheet (**styles.css**).

```
1   <!DOCTYPE HTML PUBLIC "-//W3C//DTD HTML 4.01//EN"
2              "http://www.w3.org/TR/html4/strict.dtd">
3   <html>
4
5
6   <!-- Fig. 4.5: imported.html      -->
7   <!-- Linking external style sheets  -->
8
9   <head>
10     <title>XML How to Program - Importing Style Sheets</title>
11     <link rel = "stylesheet" type = "text/css" href = "styles.css">
12  </head>
13
14  <body>
15
16     <h1>Shopping list for <em>Monday</em>:</h1>
17     <ul>
18        <li>Milk</li>
19        <li>Bread
20           <ul>
21              <li>White bread</li>
22              <li>Rye bread</li>
23              <li>Whole wheat bread</li>
24           </ul>
25        </li>
26        <li>Rice</li>
27        <li>Potatoes</li>
28        <li>Pizza <em>with mushrooms</em></li>
29     </ul>
```

Fig. 4.5   Linking an external style sheet (part 1 of 2).

```
30
31     <p>
32     <a href = "http://food.com">Go to the Grocery store</a>
33     </p>
34
35  </body>
36  </html>
```

Fig. 4.5   Linking an external style sheet (part 2 of 2).

Line 11 (Fig. 4.5) shows a **link** element, which specifies a *relationship* between the current document and another document using the **rel** attribute. In this case, we declare the linked document to be a **stylesheet** for this document. We use the **type** attribute to specify the MIME type as **text/css** and provide the URL for the stylesheet with the **href** attribute.

Software Engineering Observation 4.2

Stylesheets are reusable. Creating them once and reusing them reduces programming effort.

Software Engineering Observation 4.3

*The **link** element can be placed only in the **head** element. Other relationships you can specify between documents are **next** and **previous**, which would allow you to link a whole series of documents. This could let browsers print a large collection of related documents at once (in Internet Explorer, select **Print all linked documents** in the **Print...** submenu of the **File** menu).*

4.6 Positioning Elements

In the past, controlling the positioning of elements in an HTML document was difficult; positioning was basically up to the browser. CSS introduces the **position** property and a capability called *absolute positioning*, which gives authors greater control over how documents are displayed (Fig. 4.6).

```
1   <!DOCTYPE HTML PUBLIC "-//W3C//DTD HTML 4.01//EN"
2             "http://www.w3.org/TR/html4/strict.dtd">
3   <html>
4
5   <!-- Fig 4.6: positioning.html          -->
6   <!-- Absolute positioning of elements -->
7
8   <head>
9      <title>XML How to Program - Absolute Positioning</title>
10  </head>
11
12  <body>
13
14     <p><img src = "i.gif" style = "position: absolute; top: 0px;
15        left: 0px; z-index: 1" alt = "First positioned image"></p>
16     <p style = "position: absolute; top: 50px; left: 50px;
17        z-index: 3; font-size: 20pt;">Positioned Text</p>
18     <p><img src = "circle.gif" style = "position: absolute; top: 25px;
19        left: 100px; z-index: 2" alt = "Second positioned image"></p>
20
21  </body>
22  </html>
```

Fig. 4.6   Positioning elements with CSS.

Lines 14 and 15

```
<p><img src = "i.gif" style = "position: absolute; top: 0px;
   left: 0px; z-index: 1" alt = "First positioned image"></p>
```

position the first **img** element (**i.gif**) on the page. Specifying an element's **position** as **absolute** removes it from the normal flow of elements on the page and instead, positions the element according to distance from the **top**, **left**, **right** or **bottom** margins of its *containing block* (i.e., an element such as **body** or **p**). Here we position the element to be **0** pixels away from both the **top** and **left** margins of the **body** element.

The **z-index** attribute allows you to properly layer overlapping elements. Elements that have higher **z-index** values are displayed in front of elements with lower **z-index** values. In this example, **i.gif**, with a **z-index** of 1, is displayed at the back; **circle.gif**, with a **z-index** of 2, is displayed in front of that; the **h1** element ("Positioned Text"), with a **z-index** of 3, is displayed in front of both of the others. If you do not specify **z-index**, the elements that occur later in the document are displayed in front of those that occur earlier.

Absolute positioning is not the only way to specify page layout—*relative positioning* is shown in Fig. 4.7.

```
1   <!DOCTYPE HTML PUBLIC "-//W3C//DTD HTML 4.01//EN"
2              "http://www.w3.org/TR/html4/strict.dtd">
3   <html>
4
5   <!-- Fig. 4.7: positioning2.html      -->
6   <!-- Relative positioning of elements -->
7
8   <head>
9      <title>XML How to Program - Relative Positioning</title>
10
11     <style type = "text/css">
12
13        p              { font-size: 1.3em;
14                         font-family: verdana, arial, sans-serif }
15
16        span           { color: red;
17                         font-size: .6em;
18                         height: 1em }
19
20        .super         { position: relative;
21                         top: -1ex }
22
23        .sub           { position: relative;
24                         bottom: -1ex }
25
26        .shiftleft     { position: relative;
27                         left: -1ex }
28
29        .shiftright    { position: relative;
30                         right: -1ex }
31
32     </style>
33   </head>
34
35   <body>
36
37      <p>The text at the end of this sentence
38      <span class = "super">is in superscript</span>.</p>
39
40      <p>The text at the end of this sentence
41      <span class = "sub">is in subscript</span>.</p>
```

Fig. 4.7   Relative positioning of elements (part 1 of 2).

```
42
43       <p>The text at the end of this sentence
44       <span class = "shiftleft">is shifted left</span>.</p>
45
46       <p>The text at the end of this sentence
47       <span class = "shiftright">is shifted right</span>.</p>
48
49   </body>
50   </html>
```

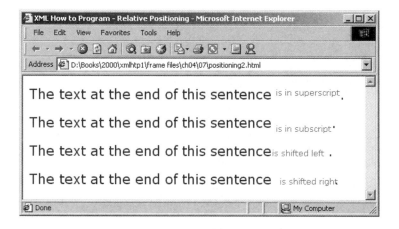

Fig. 4.7   Relative positioning of elements (part 2 of 2).

Setting the **position** property to **relative**, as in lines 20 and 21,

```
.super    { position: relative;
            top: -1ex }
```

will first lay out the element on the page, then offset the element by the specified **top**, **bottom**, **left** or **right** values. Unlike absolute positioning, relative positioning keeps elements in the general flow of elements on the page.

 Common Programming Error 4.1

Because relative positioning keeps elements in the flow of text in your documents, be careful to avoid overlapping text unintentionally.

4.7 Backgrounds

CSS also gives you control over the backgrounds of elements. We have used the **background-color** property in previous examples. You can also add background images to your documents using CSS. In Fig. 4.8, we add a corporate logo to the bottom-right corner of the document—this logo stays fixed in the corner, even when the user scrolls up or down the screen.

The code that adds the background image in the bottom-right corner of the window is on lines 13–16

```
body   { background-image: url(logo.gif);
         background-position: bottom right;
         background-repeat: no-repeat;
         background-attachment: fixed; }
```

The **background-image** property (line 13) specifies the URL of the image to use, in the format **url(fileLocation)**. You can also specify **background-color** to use in case the image is not found.

The **background-position** property (line 14) positions the image on the page. You can use the keywords **top**, **bottom**, **center**, **left** and **right** individually or in combination for vertical and horizontal positioning. You can also position using lengths, specifying the horizontal length followed by the vertical length. For example, to position the image centered vertically (positioned at 50% of the distance across the screen) and 30 pixels from the top, you would use

```
1   <!DOCTYPE HTML PUBLIC "-//W3C//DTD HTML 4.01//EN"
2            "http://www.w3.org/TR/html4/strict.dtd">
3   <html>
4
5   <!-- Fig. 4.8: background.html              -->
6   <!-- Adding background images and indentation -->
7
8   <head>
9      <title>XML How to Program - Background Images</title>
10
11     <style type = "text/css">
12
13        body   { background-image: url(logo.gif);
14                 background-position: bottom right;
15                 background-repeat: no-repeat;
16                 background-attachment: fixed; }
17
18        p      { font-size: 18pt;
19                 color: #aa5588;
20                 text-indent: 1em;
21                 font-family: arial, sans-serif; }
22
23        .dark { font-weight: bold; }
24
25     </style>
26  </head>
27
28  <body>
29
30     <p>
31     This example uses the background-image,
32     background-position and background-attachment
33     styles to place the <span class = "dark">Deitel
34     & Associates, Inc.</span> logo in the bottom,
35     right corner of the page. Notice how the logo
36     stays in the proper position when you resize the
```

Fig. 4.8   Adding a background image with CSS (part 1 of 2).

```
37        browser window.
38        </p>
39
40    </body>
41    </html>
```

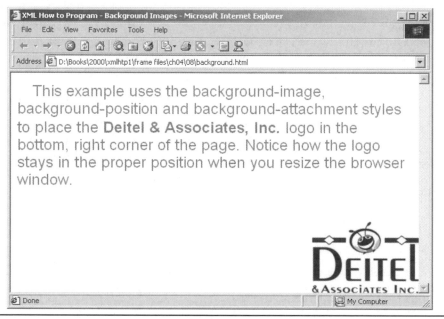

Fig. 4.8   Adding a background image with CSS (part 2 of 2).

```
background-position: 50% 30px;
```

The ***background-repeat*** *property* (line 15) controls the *tiling* of the background image. Tiling places multiple copies of the image next to each other to fill the background. Here we set the tiling to **no-repeat** so that only one copy of the background image is placed on screen. The **background-repeat** property can be set to **repeat** (the default) to tile the image vertically and horizontally, **repeat-x** to tile the image only horizontally or **repeat-y** to tile the image only vertically.

The final property setting, **background-attachment: fixed** (line 16), fixes the image in the position specified by **background-position**. Scrolling the browser window will not move the image from its set position. The default value, **scroll**, moves the image as the user scrolls the browser window down.

Line 20

```
text-indent: 1em;
```

indents the first line of text in the element by the specified amount. You might use this to make your Web page read more like a novel, in which the first line of every paragraph is indented.

Line 23

```
.dark { font-weight: bold }
```

uses the **font-weight** *property* to specify the "boldness" of text. Values besides **bold** and **normal** (the default) are **bolder** (bolder than **bold** text) and **lighter** (lighter than **normal** text). You can also specify the value using multiples of 100 from 100 to 900 (i.e., **100**, **200**, ..., **900**). Text specified as **normal** is equivalent to **400** and **bold** text is equivalent to **700**. Most systems do not have fonts that can be scaled this finely so using the **100**...**900** values might not display the desired effect.

Another CSS property you can use to format text is the **font-style** property, which allows you to set text to **none**, **italic** or **oblique** (**oblique** will default to **italic** if the system does not have a separate font file for oblique text).

We introduce the **span** element on lines 33 and 34

```
<span class = "dark">Deitel & Associates, Inc.</span>
```

Element **span** is a grouping element—it does not apply any inherent formatting to its contents. Its main use is to apply styles or **ID** attributes to a block of text. It is displayed inline (a so-called *inline-level element*) with other text, with no line breaks. A similar element is the **div** element, which also applies no inherent styles, but is displayed on its own line, with margins above and below (a so-called *block-level element*).

4.8 Element Dimensions

The dimensions of each element on the page can be specified using CSS (Fig. 4.9).

```
1   <!DOCTYPE HTML PUBLIC "-//W3C//DTD HTML 4.01//EN"
2              "http://www.w3.org/TR/html4/strict.dtd">
3   <html>
4
5   <!-- Fig. 4.9: width.html                     -->
6   <!-- Setting box dimensions and aligning text -->
7
8   <head>
9      <title>XML How to Program - Box Dimensions</title>
10
11     <style type = "text/css">
12
13        div { background-color: #ffccff;
14              margin-bottom: .5em }
15     </style>
16
17  </head>
18
19  <body>
20
21     <div style = "width: 20%">Here is some
22     text that goes in a box which is
23     set to stretch across twenty precent
24     of the width of the screen.</div>
25
26     <div style = "width: 80%; text-align: center">
27     Here is some CENTERED text that goes in a box
```

Fig. 4.9   Setting box dimensions and aligning text (part 1 of 2).

```
28        which is set to stretch across eighty precent of
29        the width of the screen.</div>
30
31        <div style = "width: 20%; height: 30%; overflow: scroll">
32        This box is only twenty percent of
33        the width and thirty percent of the height.
34        What do we do if it overflows? Set the
35        overflow property to scroll!</div>
36
37   </body>
38   </html>
```

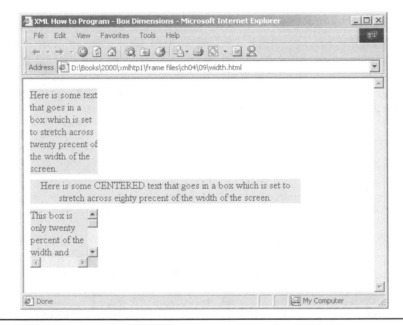

Fig. 4.9   Setting box dimensions and aligning text (part 2 of 2).

The inline style on line 21

```
<div style = "width: 20%">Here is some
```

shows how to set the **width** of an element on screen; here we indicate that this **div** element should occupy 20% of the screen width (which 20% of the screen depends on how the element is aligned, most elements are left-aligned by default). The height of an element can be set similarly, using the **height** property. Relative lengths and absolute lengths may also be used to specify **height** and **width**. For example, you could set the width of an element using

```
width: 10em
```

to have the element's width be equal to 10 times the size of the font.
    Line 26

```
<div style = "width: 80%; text-align: center">
```

shows that text within an element can be aligned to the **center**—other values for the **text-align** property are **left**, **right** and justify.

One problem with setting both element dimensions is that content inside might sometimes exceed the set boundaries, in which case the element is simply made large enough for all the content to fit. However, on line 31

```
<div style = "width: 20%; height: 30%; overflow: scroll">
```

we can set the **overflow** property to **scroll**; this adds scrollbars if the text overflows the boundaries.

4.9 Text Flow and the Box Model

A browser normally places text and elements on screen in the order they appear in the HTML document. However, as we saw with absolute positioning, it is possible to remove elements from the normal flow of text. *Floating* allows you to move an element to one side of the screen—other content in the document will then flow around the floated element. In addition, each block-level element has a box drawn around it, known as the *box model*— the properties of this box are easily adjusted (Fig. 4.10).

In addition to text, whole elements can be *floated* to the left or right of a document. This means that any nearby text will wrap around the floated element. For example, in lines 29 and 30

```
<div style = "float: right; margin: .5em; text-align: right">
    Corporate Training and Publishing</div>
```

we float a **div** element to the **right** side of the screen. As you can see, the text from lines 32–38 flows cleanly to the left and underneath this **div** element.

The second property we set in line 29, **margin**, specifies the distance between the edge of the element and any other element on the page. When elements are rendered on the screen using the box model, the content of each element is surrounded by *padding*, a *border* and a *margin* (Fig. 4.10).

Margins for individual sides of an element can be specified by using **margin-top**, **margin-right**, **margin-left** and **margin-bottom**.

A related property, **padding**, is set for the **div** element on lines 40 and 41

```
<div style = "float: right; padding: .5em; text-align:
right"> Leading-edge Programming Textbooks</div>
```

The *padding* is the distance between the content inside an element and the edge of the element. Like the margin, the padding can be set for each side of the box with **padding-top**, **padding-right**, **padding-left** and **padding-bottom**.

A portion of lines 49 and 50

```
<span style = "clear: right">Here is some unflowing text.
Here is some unflowing text.</span>
```

shows that you can interrupt the flow of text around a **float**ed element by setting the **clear** *property* to the same direction the element is **float**ed—**right** or **left**. Setting the **clear** property to **all** interrupts the flow on both sides of the document.

```
1   <!DOCTYPE HTML PUBLIC "-//W3C//DTD HTML 4.01//EN"
2              "http://www.w3.org/TR/html4/strict.dtd">
3   <html>
4
5   <!-- Fig. 4.10: floating.html              -->
6   <!-- Floating elements and element boxes -->
7
8   <head>
9      <title>XML How to Program - Flowing Text Around
10        Floating Elements</title>
11
12     <style type = "text/css">
13
14        div { background-color: #ffccff;
15              margin-bottom: .5em;
16              font-size: 1.5em;
17              width: 50% }
18
19        p    { text-align: justify; }
20
21     </style>
22
23  </head>
24
25  <body>
26
27     <div style = "text-align: center">Deitel & Associates, Inc.</div>
28
29     <div style = "float: right; margin: .5em; text-align: right">
30        Corporate Training and Publishing</div>
31
32     <p>Deitel & Associates, Inc. is an internationally recognized
33     corporate training and publishing organization specializing
34     in programming languages, Internet/World Wide Web technology
35     and object technology education. Deitel & Associates,
36     Inc. is a member of the World Wide Web Consortium. The company
37     provides courses on Java, C++, Visual Basic, C, Internet and
38     World Wide Web programming, and Object Technology.</p>
39
40     <div style = "float: right; padding: .5em; text-align: right">
41        Leading-edge Programming Textbooks</div>
42
43     <p>The company's clients include many Fortune 1000 companies,
44     government agencies, branches of the military and business
45     organizations. Through its publishing partnership with Prentice
46     Hall, Deitel & Associates, Inc. publishes leading-edge
47     programming textbooks, professional books, interactive
48     CD-ROM-based multimedia Cyber Classrooms, satellite courses
49     and World Wide Web courses.<span style = "clear: right">Here
50     is some unflowing text. Here is some unflowing text.</span></p>
51
52  </body>
53  </html>
```

Fig. 4.10   Floating elements, aligning text and setting box dimensions (part 1 of 2).

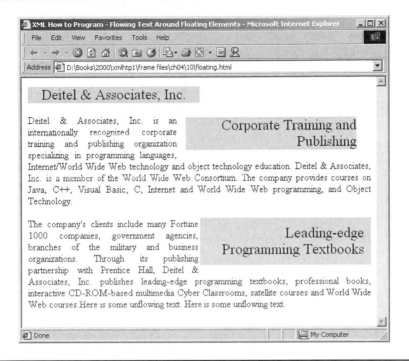

Fig. 4.10 Floating elements, aligning text and setting box dimensions (part 2 of 2).

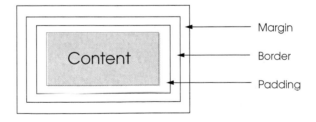

Fig. 4.11 Box model for block-level elements.

Another property of every block-level element on screen is the border. The border lies between the padding space and the margin space, and has numerous properties to adjust its appearance (Fig. 4.12).

In this example, we set three properties: the **border-width**, **border-style** and **border-color**. The **border-width** property may be set to any of the CSS lengths, or the predefined values of **thin**, **medium** or **thick**. The **border-color** sets the color used for the border (this has different meanings for different borders).

As with padding and margins, each of the border properties may be set for individual sides of the box (e.g., **border-top-style** or **border-left-color**). Also, as shown on line 40

```
<div class = "thick groove">This text has a border</div>
```

it is possible to assign more than one class to an HTML element using the **class** attribute.

The **border-style**s are **none**, **hidden**, **dotted**, **dashed**, **solid**, **double**, **groove**, **ridge**, **inset** and **outset**. Figure 4.13 illustrates these border styles.

As you can see, the **groove** and **ridge border-style**s have opposite effects, as do **inset** and **outset**.

```
1   <!DOCTYPE HTML PUBLIC "-//W3C//DTD HTML 4.01//EN"
2           "http://www.w3.org/TR/html4/strict.dtd">
3   <html>
4
5   <!-- Fig. 4.12: borders.html      -->
6   <!-- Setting borders of an element -->
7
8   <head>
9      <title>XML How to Program - Borders</title>
10
11     <style type = "text/css">
12
13        body    { background-color: #ccffcc }
14
15        div     { text-align: center;
16                  margin-bottom: 1em;
17                  padding: .5em }
18
19        .thick  { border-width: thick }
20
21        .medium { border-width: medium }
22
23        .thin   { border-width: thin }
24
25        .groove { border-style: groove }
26
27        .inset  { border-style: inset }
28
29        .outset { border-style: outset }
30
31        .red    { border-color: red }
32
33        .blue   { border-color: blue }
34
35     </style>
36  </head>
37
38  <body>
39
40     <div class = "thick groove">This text has a border</div>
41     <div class = "medium groove">This text has a border</div>
42     <div class = "thin groove">This text has a border</div>
43
44     <p class = "thin red inset">A thin red line...</p>
45     <p class = "medium blue outset">And a thicker blue line</p>
46
```

Fig. 4.12   Applying borders to elements (part 1 of 2).

```
47   </body>
48   </html>
```

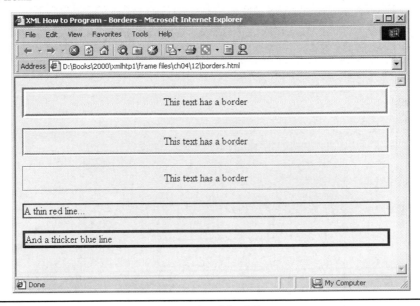

Fig. 4.12 Applying borders to elements (part 2 of 2).

```
1    <!DOCTYPE HTML PUBLIC "-//W3C//DTD HTML 4.01//EN"
2              "http://www.w3.org/TR/html4/strict.dtd">
3    <html>
4
5    <!-- Fig. 4.13: borders2.html    -->
6    <!-- Various border-styles       -->
7
8    <head>
9       <title>XML How to Program - Borders</title>
10
11      <style type = "text/css">
12
13         body    { background-color: #ccffcc }
14
15         div     { text-align: center;
16                   margin-bottom: .3em;
17                   width: 50%;
18                   position: relative;
19                   left: 25%;
20                   padding: .3em }
21      </style>
22
23   </head>
24
```

Fig. 4.13 Various **border-style**s (part 1 of 2).

```
25    <body>
26
27        <div style = "border-style: solid">Solid border</div>
28        <div style = "border-style: double">Double border</div>
29        <div style = "border-style: groove">Groove border</div>
30        <div style = "border-style: ridge">Ridge border</div>
31        <div style = "border-style: inset">Inset border</div>
32        <div style = "border-style: outset">Outset border</div>
33
34    </body>
35    </html>
```

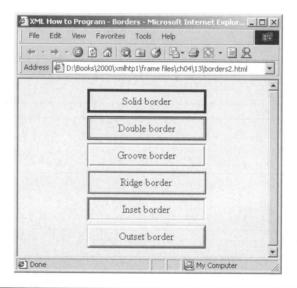

Fig. 4.13   Various **border-style**s (part 2 of 2).

4.10 User Style Sheets

An important issue to keep in mind when adding style sheets to your site is what kind of users will be viewing your site. Users have the option to define their own *user style sheets* to format pages based on their own preferences—for example, visually impaired people might want to increase the text size on all pages they view. As a Web-page author, if you are not careful, you might inadvertently override user preferences with the styles defined on your Web pages. This section explores possible conflicts between *user styles* and *author styles*. Figure 4.14 is a simple example of a Web page using the **em** measurement for the **font-size** property to increase text size on the page.

```
1    <!DOCTYPE HTML PUBLIC "-//W3C//DTD HTML 4.01//EN"
2              "http://www.w3.org/TR/html4/strict.dtd">
3    <html>
4
```

Fig. 4.14   Modifying text size with the **em** measurement (part 1 of 2).

```
5    <!-- Fig. 4.14: user.html    -->
6    <!-- User styles             -->
7
8    <head>
9       <title>XML How to Program - User Styles</title>
10
11      <style type = "text/css">
12
13         .note { font-size: 1.5em }
14
15      </style>
16   </head>
17
18   <body>
19
20      <p>Thanks for visiting my Web site. I hope you enjoy it.</p>
21      <p class = "note">Please Note: This site will be moving soon.
22      Please check periodically for updates.</p>
23
24   </body>
25   </html>
```

Fig. 4.14   Modifying text size with the **em** measurement (part 2 of 2).

In line 13

```
.note { font-size: 1.5em }
```

we multiply by 1.5 the font size of all elements with **class = "note"** (see lines 20 and 21). Assuming the default browser font size of 12 points, this same text size increase could also have been accomplished by specifying

```
.note { font-size:   18pt }
```

However, what if the user had defined their own **font-size** in a user style sheet? Because the CSS specification gives precedence to author styles over user styles, this conflict would be resolved with the author style overriding the user style. This can be avoided by using relative measurements (such as **em** or **ex**) instead of absolute measurements (such as **pt**).

Adding a user style sheet (Fig. 4.15) in Internet Explorer 5 is done by selecting **Internet Options...** located in the **Tools** menu. In the dialog box that appears, click **Accessibility...**, check the **Format documents using my style sheet** check box and type in the location of your user style sheet. Note that you also have the option of overriding colors, font styles, and font sizes specified on Web pages with your own user styles.

User style sheets are created in the same format as the linked external style sheet shown in Fig. 4.4. A sample user style sheet is shown in Fig. 4.16.

The Web page shown in Fig. 4.14 is re-rendered in Fig. 4.17, this time with the user style sheet from 4.16 applied.

Because the code for this page uses a relative **font-size** measurement of **1.5em**, it multiplies the original size of the affected text (**20pt**) by **1.5** times, giving it an effective size of **30pt**.

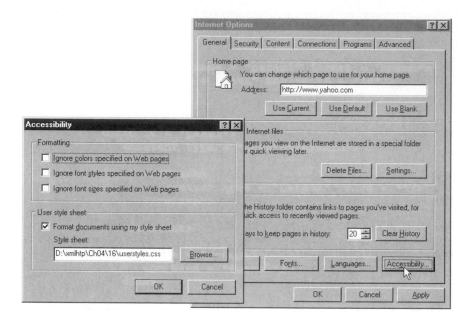

Fig. 4.15 Adding a user style sheet in Internet Explorer 5.

```
1   /* Fig. 4.16: userstyles.css */
2   /* A user stylesheet          */
3
4   body      { font-size: 20pt;
5               background-color: #ccffcc }
6
7   a         { color: red }
```

Fig. 4.16 A sample user style sheet.

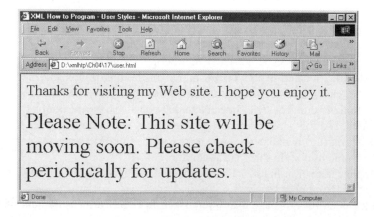

Fig. 4.17 A Web page with user styles enabled.

4.11 Internet and World Wide Web Resources

www.w3.org/Style/CSS
The W3C Cascading Style Sheets Homepage contains the CSS links and resources deemed most important by the people in charge of the Web.

www.w3.org/TR/REC-CSS2
The W3C *Cascading Style Sheets, Level 2* specification contains a list of all the CSS properties. The specification is also filled with helpful examples detailing the use of many of the properties.

www.w3.org/TR/REC-CSS1
This site contains the W3C *Cascading Style Sheets, Level 1* specification.

style.webreview.com
This site has several charts of CSS properties, including a listing of which browsers support which attributes, and to what extent.

www.blooberry.com/indexdot/css/index.html
Index Dot CSS is a good reference source for CSS properties, syntax and more.

www.w3schools.com/css
The *W3Schools CSS site* has a good CSS tutorial and script repository.

SUMMARY

- The inline style allows you to declare a style for an individual element using the **style** attribute in that element's opening HTML tag.
- Each CSS property is followed by a colon, then the value of that attribute.
- The **color** property sets the color of text. Color names and hex codes may be used as the value.
- Styles that are placed in the **<style>** section apply to the whole document.
- **style** element attribute **type** specifies the MIME type (the specific encoding format) of the style sheet. Regular text style sheets always use **text/css**.
- Each rule body begins and ends with a curly brace (**{** and **}**).
- Style class declarations are preceded with a period and are applied to elements of that specific class.
- The CSS rules in a style sheet use the same format as inline styles—the property is followed by a colon (**:**) and the value of that property. Multiple properties are separated with a semicolon (**;**).
- The **background-color** attribute specifies the background color of the element.
- The **font-family** attribute specifies the name of the font that should be displayed. Generic font families allow you to specify a type of font instead of a specific font for greater display flexibility. The **font-size** property specifies the size to use to render the font.
- The **class** attribute applies a style class to an element.
- All styles applied to a parent element also apply to child elements inside that element.
- Pseudo-classes give the author access to content not specifically declared in the document. The **hover** pseudo-class is activated when the user moves the mouse cursor over an **a** element.
- The **text-decoration** property applies decorations to text within an element, such as **underline**, **overline**, **line-through** and **blink**
- To apply rules to multiple elements separate the elements with commas in the stylesheet.
- A pixel is a relative-length measurement—it varies in size based on screen resolution. Other relative lengths are **em** (font size), **ex** ("x-height" of the font—the height of a lowercase x) and percentages.

- The other units of measurement available in CSS are absolute-length measurements, i.e., units that do not vary in size based on the system. These are **in** (inches), **cm** (centimeters), **mm** (millimeters), **pt** (points—1 **pt**=1/72 **in**) and **pc** (picas—1 **pc** = 12 **pt**).

- External linking can help give a Web site a uniform look—separate pages on a site can all use the same styles. Modifying a single file can then make changes to styles across an entire Web site.

- **link**'s **rel** attribute specifies a relationship between a document and another document.

- The CSS **position** property allows absolute positioning, which gives us greater control over how documents are displayed. Specifying an element's **position** as **absolute** removes it from the normal flow of elements on the page, and positions it according to distance from the **top**, **left**, **right** or **bottom** margins of its parent element.

- The **z-index** property allows you to properly layer overlapping elements. Elements that have higher **z-index** values are displayed in front of elements with lower **z-index** values.

- Unlike absolute positioning, relative positioning keeps elements in the general flow of elements on the page, and offsets them by the specified **top**, **left**, **right** or **bottom** values.

- Property **background-image** specifies the URL of the image to use, in the format **url** (*file-Location*). Specify the **background-color** to use if the image is not found. The property **background-position** positions the image on the page using the values **top**, **bottom**, **center**, **left** and **right** individually or in combination for vertical and horizontal positioning. You can also position using lengths.

- The **background-repeat** property controls the tiling of the background image. Setting the tiling to **no-repeat** displays one copy of the background image on screen. The **background-repeat** property can be set to **repeat** (the default) to tile the image vertically and horizontally, to **repeat-x** to tile the image only horizontally or **repeat-y** to tile the image only vertically.

- The property setting **background-attachment: fixed** fixes the image in the position specified by **background-position**. Scrolling the browser window will not move the image from its set position. The default value, **scroll**, moves the image as the user scrolls the window.

- The **text-indent** property indents the first line of text in the element by the specified amount.

- The **font-weight** property specifies the "boldness" of text. Values besides **bold** and **normal** (the default) are **bolder** (bolder than **bold** text) and **lighter** (lighter than **normal** text). You can also specify the value using multiples of 100 from 100 to 900 (i.e., **100**, **200**, ..., **900**). Text specified as **normal** is equivalent to **400** and **bold** text is equivalent to **700**.

- The **font-style** property allows you to set text to **none**, **italic** or **oblique** (**oblique** will default to **italic** if the system does not have a separate font file for oblique text, which is normally the case).

- **span** is a generic grouping element—it does not apply any inherent formatting to its contents. Its main use is to apply styles or **ID** attributes to a block of text. It is displayed inline (a so-called in-line element) with other text, with no line breaks. A similar element is the **div** element, which also applies no inherent styles, but is displayed on a separate line, with margins above and below (a so-called block-level element).

- The dimensions of page elements can be set using CSS using the **height** and **width** properties.

- Text within an element can be **center**ed using **text-align**—other values for the **text-align** property are **left** and **right**.

- One problem with setting both element dimensions is that content inside might sometimes exceed the set boundaries, in which case the element is simply made large enough for all the content to fit. However, you can set the **overflow** property to **scroll**; this adds scroll bars if the text overflows the boundaries we have set for it.

- Browsers normally place text and elements on screen in the order they appear in the HTML file. Elements can be removed from the normal flow of text. Floating allows you to move an element to one side of the screen—other content in the document will then flow around the floated element.

- Each block-level element has a box drawn around it, known as the box model—the properties of this box are easily adjusted.

- The **margin** property determines the distance between the element's edge and any outside text.

- CSS uses a box model to render elements on screen—the content of each element is surrounded by padding, a border and margins

- Margins for individual sides of an element can be specified by using **margin-top**, **margin-right**, **margin-left** and **margin-bottom**.

- The padding, as opposed to the margin, is the distance between the content inside an element and the edge of the element. Padding can be set for each side of the box with **padding-top**, **padding-right**, **padding-left** and **padding-bottom**.

- You can interrupt the flow of text around a **float**ed element by setting the **clear** property to the same direction the element is **float**ed—**right** or **left**. Setting the **clear** property to **all** interrupts the flow on both sides of the document.

- A property of every block-level element on screen is its border. The border lies between the padding space and the margin space and has numerous properties to adjust its appearance.

- The **border-width** property may be set to any of the CSS lengths, or the predefined values of **thin**, **medium** or **thick**.

- The **border-style**s available are **none**, **hidden**, **dotted**, **dashed**, **solid**, **double**, **groove**, **ridge**, **inset** and **outset**. Keep in mind that the **dotted** and **dashed** styles are available only for Macintosh systems.

- The **border-color** property sets the color used for the border.

- It is possible to assign more than one class to an HTML element using the **class** attribute.

TERMINOLOGY

<link> element	**class** attribute of an element
absolute positioning	**clear: all**
absolute-length measurement	**clear: left**
arial font	**clear: right**
background	**cm** (centimeters)
background-attachment	colon (**:**) in a CSS rule
background-color	**color**
background-image	CSS rule
background-position	**cursive** generic font family
background-repeat	**dashed** border style
blink	**dotted** border style
block-level element	**double** border style
border	**em** (size of font)
border-color	embedded style sheet
border-style	**ex** (x-height of font)
border-width	**float** property
box model	**font-style** property
Cascading Style Sheet (CSS) specification	generic font family
child element	**groove** border style

hidden border style
hover pseudo-class
href attribute of **\<link\>** element
importing a style sheet
in (inches)
inline styles
inline-level element
inset border style
large font size
larger font size
left
line-through text decoration
linking to an external style sheet
margin
margin-bottom property
margin-left property
margin-right property
margin-top property
medium border width
medium font size
mm (millimeters)
monospace generic font family
none border style
outset border style
overflow property
overline text decoration
padding
parent element
pc (picas)
position: absolute
position: relative
pseudo-class
pt (points)

rel attribute of **\<link\>** element
relative positioning
relative-length measurement
repeat-x
repeat-y
ridge border style
right
rule in CSS
sans-serif generic font family
scroll
separation of structure from content
serif generic font family
small font size
smaller font size
solid border style
style
style attribute
style class
style in header of document
style sheet (CSS rules separate text file)
text flow
text/css MIME type
text-align
text-decoration
text-indent
thick border width
thin border width
user style sheet
x-large font size
x-small font size
xx-large font size
xx-small font size
z-index

SELF-REVIEW EXERCISES

4.1   Assume that the size of the base font on a system is 12 points.
   a) How big is 36 point font in ems?
   b) How big is 8 point font in ems?
   c) How big is 24 point font in picas?
   d) How big is 12 point font in inches?
   e) How big is 1 inch font in picas?

4.2   Fill in the blanks in the following questions:
   a) Using the _____ element allows you to use external style sheets in your pages.
   b) To apply a CSS rule to more than one element at a time, separate the element names with a _____.
   c) Pixels are a _____ length measurement unit.
   d) The **hover** _____-_____ is activated when the user moves the mouse cursor over the specified element.

e) Setting the **overflow** property to _____ provides a mechanism for containing inner content without compromising specified box dimensions.

f) While _____ is a generic inline element that applies no inherent formatting, the _____ is a generic block-level element that applies no inherent formatting.

g) Setting the **background-repeat** property to _____ will tile the specified **background-image** only vertically.

h) If you **float** an element, you can stop the flowing text by using the _____ property.

i) The _____ property allows you to indent the first line of text in an element.

j) Three components of the box model are the _____, _____ and _____.

ANSWERS TO SELF-REVIEW EXERCISES

4.1   a) 3 ems. b) .75 ems. c) 2 picas. d) 1/6 inch. e) 6 picas.

4.2   a) **link**. b) comma. c) relative. d) pseudo-element. e) **scroll**. f) **span**, **div**. g) **y-repeat**. h) **clear**. i) **text-indent**. j) content, padding, border or margin.

EXERCISES

4.3   Write a CSS rule that makes all text 1.5 times larger than the base font of the system and colors it red.

4.4   Write a CSS rule that removes the underline from all links inside list items (**li**) and shifts them left by 3 **em**s.

4.5   Write a CSS rule that places a background image halfway down the page, tiling horizontally. The image should remain in place when the user scrolls up or down.

4.6   Write a CSS rule that gives all **h1** and **h2** elements a padding of .5 **em**s, a **groove**d border style and a margin of .5 **em**s.

4.7   Write a CSS rule that changes the color of all elements with attribute **class="green-Move"** to green and shifts them down 25 pixels and right 15 pixels.

Creating Markup with XML

Objectives

- To create custom markup using XML.
- To understand the concept of an XML parser.
- To use elements and attributes to mark up data.
- To understand the difference between markup text and character data.
- To be able to use Unicode in an XML document.
- To be able to use **CDATA** sections.
- To understand the concept of a well-formed XML document.
- To understand the concept of an XML namespace.

The chief merit of language is clearness, and we know that nothing detracts so much from this as do unfamiliar terms.
Galen

Every country has its own language, yet the subjects of which the untutored soul speaks are the same everywhere.
Tertullian

The historian, essentially, wants more documents than he can really use; the dramatist only wants more liberties than he can really take.
Henry James

Entities should not be multiplied unnecessarily.
William of Occam

5.1 Introduction

In Chapters 2 and 3, we discussed HTML, a markup language that is used to structure documents for delivery on the Web. HTML is an application of the *Standard Generalized Markup Language (SGML)*. SGML is a meta language (i.e., a language for creating other languages) that is used to create markup languages, such as HTML. XML is a subset of SGML and, although XML's basic syntax is similar to HTML's, the purpose of XML is different.

XML is a technology for creating markup languages to describe data of virtually any type in a structured manner. Unlike HTML, which limits the document author to a fixed set of tags, XML allows document authors to describe data more precisely by creating new tags. XML can be used to create markup languages for describing data in almost any field. In Chapters 20 through 22, we discuss several of these XML-based markup languages that mark up data such as mathematical formulas, chemical molecular structures, graphics, financial data, etc. In this chapter, we introduce the basics of XML.

5.2 Introduction to XML Markup

Consider a simple XML document (**intro.xml**) that marks up a message as XML (Fig. 5.1). Note that line numbers are not part of an XML document, but are included for reference purposes. We discuss rendering XML documents in the next section.

XML documents are commonly stored in text files that end in the extension **.xml**, although this is not a requirement of XML. Any text editor can be used to create an XML document. Many software packages also allow data to be saved as XML documents.

```
1   <?xml version = "1.0"?>
2
3   <!-- Fig. 5.1 : intro.xml              -->
4   <!-- Simple introduction to XML markup -->
5
6   <myMessage>
7       <message>Welcome to XML!</message>
8   </myMessage>
```

Fig. 5.1   Simple XML document containing a message.

The document in Fig. 5.1 begins with an XML *declaration* in line 1. This declaration specifies the **version** of XML to which the document conforms—in this case, version **1.0**, which is currently the only version. Lines 3 and 4 contain comments. XML uses the same comment syntax as HTML.

Good Programming Practice 5.1

Although the XML declaration is optional, it should be used to identify the XML version to which the document conforms. Otherwise, in the future, a document without an XML declaration might be assumed to conform to the latest version of XML. Errors or other serious problems may result.

All XML documents must contain exactly one *root element* (e.g., **myMessage** in lines 6–8). The root element contains all other elements in the XML document. Lines preceding the root element are the *prolog* of the XML document. Element **message** (line 7) is called a *child element* of element **myMessage** because it is nested inside element **myMessage**. This child element contains the text **Welcome to XML!**.

Common Programming Error 5.1

Attempting to create more than one root element in an XML document is an error.

Common Programming Error 5.2

Improperly nesting XML elements is an error. For example, **<x><y>hello</x><y>** *is an error; here the nested* **y** *element must end before the* **x** *element.*

5.3 Parsers and Well-formed XML Documents

A software program called an *XML parser* (or an *XML processor*) is required to process an XML document. The XML parser reads the XML document, checks its syntax, reports any errors and allows programmatic access to the document's contents. An XML document is considered *well formed* if it is syntactically correct. XML syntax requires a single root element, a start tag and end tag for each element, properly-nested tags and attribute values in quotes. Furthermore, XML is case sensitive, so the proper capitalization must be used in element and attribute names. A document that properly conforms to this syntax is a well-formed XML document.

Parsers can support the *Document Object Model (DOM)* and/or the *Simple API for XML (SAX)* for accessing a document's content programmatically using languages such as Java™, Python, C, etc. A DOM-based parser builds a tree structure containing the XML document's data in memory. A SAX-based parser processes the document and generates events (i.e., notifications to the application) when tags, text, comments, etc. are encountered. These events return data from the XML document. In Chapters 8 and 9, we provide detailed discussions of DOM and SAX, respectively.

Common Programming Error 5.3

XML tags are case sensitive. Using the wrong mixture of case is an error. For example, using the start tag `<message>` *and end tag* `</Message>` *is an error.*

Most XML parsers can be downloaded at no charge. Some applications, such as Microsoft Internet Explorer 5 (IE5), have built-in XML parsers. In this chapter, we will use IE5's XML parser—*msxml*. In later chapters, we will use msxml, the Apache XML Project's parser *Xerces*, Sun Microsystem's *Java API for XML Parsing (JAXP)* and IBM's parser *XML for Java (XML4J)*.

5.4 Parsing an XML Document with msxml

An XML document contains data, not formatting information. When an XML document (e.g., **intro.xml** in Fig. 5.1) is loaded into IE5, the document is parsed by msxml. If the document is well formed, the parser makes the document's data available to the application (i.e., IE5), using the XML document. The application can format and render the data and perform other processing. IE5 renders the data as shown in the top screen image in Fig. 5.2 by applying a *stylesheet* that formats and colors the markup almost identically to the original document (in this case, Fig. 5.1). The stylesheet could have done virtually any type of formatting for presentation, but this formatting is the default chosen by Microsoft.

Fig. 5.2   XML document shown in IE5.

Notice the minus sign (-) and the plus sign (+) in the left margins of Fig. 5.2. These are not part of the XML document. IE5 places either a plus sign or minus sign next to all elements that contain one or more child elements. Because these elements store other elements, they are called *container elements*. A *minus sign* indicates that all child elements are visible. When a minus sign is clicked, it becomes a *plus sign*—which collapses the container element and hides all its children. When a plus sign is clicked, it becomes a minus sign—which expands the container element and displays all its children.

This behavior is similar to viewing a disk's directory structure using a program such as Windows Explorer or File Manager. In fact, a directory structure is often modelled as a series of tree structures, with one folder (e.g., **C:**, **/**, etc.) representing the root of the directory tree. Each folder (that contains at least one folder inside it) is a *node* in the tree. XML documents (when they are parsed by a DOM-based parser) have their data placed into a tree structure. We discuss how to retrieve data items from a parsed XML document using the Document Object Model (DOM) in Chapter 8.

We provide screen captures later in the chapter that show some formatting possibilities for XML documents using CSS (Chapter 4). In Chapter 12, you will learn about a related-XML technology called the *Extensible Stylesheet Language (XSL)* that provides more powerful features than CSS for creating stylesheets. Starting with Chapter 12, we will use XSL capabilities to format XML documents for display.

If an XML document is not well formed, the parser generates an error. For example, if we omit the end tag (line 8) in Fig. 5.1, mxsml produces the error message shown in Fig. 5.3.

5.5 Characters

In this section, we discuss the *character set* used in XML documents and some of its properties. A character set consists of the characters that may be represented in a document. For example, the *ASCII (American Standard Code for Information Interchange)* character set contains the letters of the English alphabet, the numbers 0–9 and punctuation characters, such as **!**, **-** and **?**.

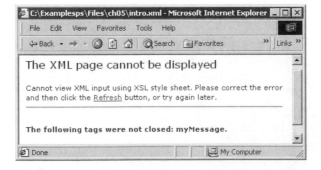

Fig. 5.3   Error message for a missing end tag.

5.5.1 Character Set

XML documents may contain the following characters: carriage returns, line feeds and *Unicode®* characters. Unicode is a standard of the Unicode consortium. Its goal is to enable computers to process the characters for most of the world's major languages. In Section 5.5.4, we demonstrate how to use Unicode in an XML document. Visit **www.unicode.org** for more information about the Unicode standard.

5.5.2 Characters vs. Markup

Once a parser determines that all characters in a document are legal, it must differentiate between *markup text* and *character data*. Markup text is enclosed in angle brackets (**<** and **>**). Character data is the *text* between a start tag and an end tag. Child elements are considered markup—not character data. Lines 1, 3–4 and 6–8 in Fig. 5.1 contain markup text. In line 7, tags **<message>** and **</message>** are the markup text and the text **Welcome to XML!** is the character data.

5.5.3 White Space, Entity References and Built-in Entities

Spaces, tabs, line feeds and carriage returns are characters commonly called *whitespace characters*. An XML parser is required to pass all characters in a document, including whitespace characters, to the application using the XML document. An application may consider whitespace characters either *significant* (i.e., preserved by the application) or *insignificant* (i.e., not preserved by the application). Depending on the application, insignificant whitespace characters may be collapsed into a single whitespace character or even removed entirely. This process is called *normalization*. For example,

```
<markup>This is character        data</markup>
```

contains three significant whitespace characters in the character data. When this character data is normalized, the five spaces between **character** and **data** are collapsed into a single significant space. We discuss whitespace characters in greater detail in Chapter 6.

Good Programming Practice 5.2

When creating an XML document, add whitespace to emphasize the document's hierarchical structure. This makes documents more readable to humans.

Almost any character can be used in an XML document, but the characters *ampersand* (**&**), *left-angle bracket* (**<**), *right-angle bracket* (**>**), *apostrophe* (**'**) and *double quote* (**"**) are reserved in XML and may not be used in character data. To use these characters in the content of an element or attribute we must use *entity references*, which begin with an ampersand (**&**) and end with a *semicolon* (**;**). Using entity references prevents XML processors from misinterpreting character data as XML markup. For example, angle brackets are reserved for delimiting markup tags. If angle brackets were found in a the content of an element or attribute, the XML parser would interpret these as XML markup and would incorrectly parse the document. In the next section, we demonstrate how to use entity references to represent Unicode characters in an XML document. The apostrophe and double quote characters are reserved for delimiting attribute values. We discuss attributes and their values in Section 5.6.

Common Programming Error 5.4

Attempting to use either the left-angle bracket (`<`), right-angle bracket (`>`), apostrophe (`'`) or double quote (`"`) in character data is an error.

Common Programming Error 5.5

Attempting to use the ampersand (`&`)—other than in an entity reference—in character data is an error.

XML provides *built-in entities* for ampersand (`&amp;`), left-angle bracket (`&lt;`), right-angle bracket (`&gt;`), apostrophe (`&apos;`) and quotation mark (`&quot;`). For example, to mark up the characters "`<>&`" in element **message** we would write

```
<message>&lt;&gt;&amp;</message>
```

Using these entities instead of the `<`, `>` and `&` characters prevents the XML processor from mistaking these characters for XML markup.

5.5.4 Using Unicode in an XML Document

This section demonstrates XML's Unicode support. Figure 5.4 lists an XML document that displays Arabic words. Each Arabic character is represented by an entity reference for a Unicode character. Each line that contains a series of entity references represents one Arabic word. When translated to English, element **from** (line 9–17) contains **Deitel and Associates** and element **subject** (lines 19–29) contains **Welcome to the world of Unicode**.

```
1   <?xml version = "1.0"?>
2
3   <!-- Fig. 5.4 : lang.xml     -->
4   <!-- Demonstrating Unicode   -->
5
6   <!DOCTYPE welcome SYSTEM "lang.dtd">
7
8   <welcome>
9      <from>
10
11        <!-- Deitel and Associates -->
12        &#1583;&#1575;&#1610;&#1578;&#1614;&#1604;
13        &#1571;&#1606;&#1583;
14
15        <!-- entity -->
16        &assoc;
17     </from>
18
19     <subject>
20
21        <!-- Welcome to the world of Unicode -->
22        &#1571;&#1607;&#1604;&#1575;&#1611;
23        &#1576;&#1603;&#1605;
```

Fig. 5.4   XML document that contains Arabic words (part 1 of 2).

```
24              &#1601;&#1610;&#1616;
25              &#1593;&#1575;&#1604;&#1605;
26
27              <!-- entity -->
28              &text;
29          </subject>
30      </welcome>
```

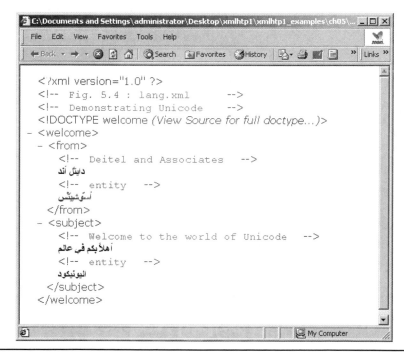

Fig. 5.4   XML document that contains Arabic words (part 2 of 2).

The document begins with the XML declaration in line 1. Line 6

```
<!DOCTYPE welcome SYSTEM "lang.dtd">
```

specifies the file—called a *document type definition (DTD)* file—that defines the structure (i.e., what elements the XML document must contain, what order the elements must have, etc.) of this document and the entities used by the document. This tag contains four items: the **DOCTYPE**, the name of the root element (**welcome**), the **SYSTEM** flag—which indicates that the DTD is located in an external file rather than the document itself and the name of the file (**lang.dtd**) containing the DTD. We discuss DTDs in detail in Chapter 6.

Root element **welcome** contains two elements: **from** (lines 9–17) and **subject** (lines 19–29). Both elements contain entity references for Unicode characters. Element **from** also contains two comments. Lines 12, 13 and 22–25 contain a sequence of entity references for Unicode characters in the Arabic alphabet.

New entity references may also be created by the author of a document. In the DTD for this document, we defined two new entities, **assoc** and **text**. The entity reference **&assoc;** (line 16) is replaced with the value

أسّوشِيَ
تْس

and the entity reference **&text;** (line 28) is replaced with the value

اليونيكو
د

These values are defined inside the file **lang.dtd** (referenced on line 6). We will examine this DTD in detail in Chapter 6.

5.6 Markup

This section elaborates on elements and their attributes as well as how they are used to construct proper XML markup. XML element markup consists of a start tag, content and an end tag. Unlike HTML, all XML start tags must have a corresponding end tag. For example,

```
<img src = "img.gif">
```

is correct HTML, but in XML, the ending tag must also be supplied, as in

```
<img src = "img.gif"></img>
```

This type of element is called an *empty element,* because it does not contain content (i.e., character data). Alternatively, an empty tag may be written more concisely as

```
<img src = "img.gif"/>
```

which uses the *forward slash* (**/**) for termination.

Elements define structure. An element may or may not contain content (i.e., child elements or character data). Attributes describe elements. An element may have zero, one or more attributes associated with it. Attributes are placed within the element's start tag. Attribute values are enclosed in quotes—either single or double. For example, element **car**

```
<car doors = "4"/>
```

contains attribute **doors**, whose value is **"4"**.

XML element and attribute names can be of any length and may contain letters, digits, underscores, hyphens and periods; they must begin with a letter or an underscore.

Common Programming Error 5.6

Not placing the value of an attribute in single or double quotes is a syntax error.

Good Programming Practice 5.3

*XML elements and attribute names should be meaningful. For example, use **<address>** instead of **<adr>**.*

Common Programming Error 5.7

Using spaces in an XML element name or attribute name is an error.

Figure 5.5 contains XML markup for a book. The elements in Fig. 5.5 structure the document such that a **book** element contains a **title** element, **author** element, **chapter** element and **media** element. The output shown is the result of applying an XSL stylesheet to the XML document (**usage.xml**). [*Note*: We will discuss this stylesheet in Chapter 12, where we formally present XSL.]

```
1   <?xml version = "1.0"?>
2
3   <!-- Fig. 5.5 : usage.xml              -->
4   <!-- Usage of elements and attributes -->
5
6   <?xml:stylesheet type = "text/xsl" href = "usage.xsl"?>
7
8   <book isbn = "999-99999-9-X">
9       <title>Deitel&apos;s XML Primer</title>
10
11      <author>
12          <firstName>Paul</firstName>
13          <lastName>Deitel</lastName>
14      </author>
15
16      <chapters>
17          <preface num = "1" pages = "2">Welcome</preface>
18          <chapter num = "1" pages = "4">Easy XML</chapter>
19          <chapter num = "2" pages = "2">XML Elements?</chapter>
20          <appendix num = "1" pages = "9">Entities</appendix>
21      </chapters>
22
23      <media type = "CD"/>
24  </book>
```

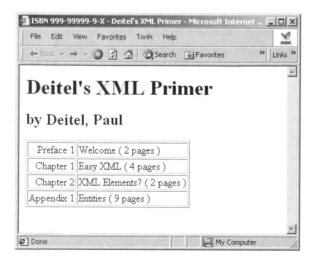

Line 6

```
<?xml:stylesheet type = "text/xsl" href = "usage.xsl"?>
```

is an example of a *processing instruction (PI)*. The information contained in a PI is passed to the application using the XML document and provides additional application-specific information about the document. Processing instructions are delimited by **<?** and **?>** and consist of a *PI target* and a *PI value*. This PI references an XSL stylesheet, as indicated by the PI target **xml:stylesheet**. The PI value is **type = "text/xsl" href = "usage.xsl"**. We will discuss this PI in detail later in the book when we discuss XSL.

Document authors may create their own processing instructions. Almost any name may be used for a PI target, except the reserved word *xml* (also **XML**, **Xml**, etc.). Processing instructions provide a convenient syntax to allow document authors to embed application-specific data within an XML document. Processing instructions have no effect on a document if the application processing the document does not use them.

Line 8 contains the root element **book**. Attribute **isbn** is associated with this element and has the value **"99-99999-9-X"**. Element **book** contains four child elements: **title**, **author**, **chapters** and **media**. Empty element **media** contains attribute **type** with the value **"CD"**.

Element **author** contains two child elements: **firstName** and **lastName**. Element **chapters** contains four child elements: **preface**, two **chapter** elements and **appendix**. Each of these elements has two attributes: **num** and **pages**. These attributes describe the chapter, preface or appendix number and their page count.

Figure 5.6 lists a more substantial XML document that contains a marked-up letter. The output shown is the result of applying an XSL stylesheet to this XML document (**letter.xml**). [*Note:* We will discuss this stylesheet in Chapter 13 where we formally present XSL formatting objects.

```
1   <?xml version = "1.0"?>
2
3   <!-- Fig. 5.6: letter.xml                -->
4   <!-- Business letter formatted with XML -->
5
6   <letter>
7
8      <contact type = "from">
9         <name>Jane Doe</name>
10        <address1>Box 12345</address1>
11        <address2>15 Any Ave.</address2>
12        <city>Othertown</city>
13        <state>Otherstate</state>
14        <zip>67890</zip>
15        <phone>555-4321</phone>
16        <flag gender = "F"/>
17     </contact>
18
19     <contact type = "to">
20        <name>John Doe</name>
```

Fig. 5.6   XML document that marks up a letter (part 1 of 2).

```
21          <address1>123 Main St.</address1>
22          <address2></address2>
23          <city>Anytown</city>
24          <state>Anystate</state>
25          <zip>12345</zip>
26          <phone>555-1234</phone>
27          <flag gender = "M"/>
28      </contact>
29
30      <salutation>Dear Sir:</salutation>
31
32      <paragraph>It is our privilege to inform you about our new
33          database managed with <bold>XML</bold>. This new system
34          allows you to reduce the load on your inventory list
35          server by having the client machine perform the work of
36          sorting and filtering the data.</paragraph>
37
38      <paragraph>The data in an XML element is normalized, so
39          plain-text diagrams such as
40              /---\
41              |   |
42              \---/
43          will become gibberish.</paragraph>
44
45      <closing>Sincerely</closing>
46      <signature>Ms. Doe</signature>
47
48  </letter>
```

```
                                    Jane Doe
                                    Box 12345
                                    15 Any Ave.
                                    Othertown, Otherstate 67890
                                    555-4321



        John Doe
        123 Main St.
        Anytown, Anystate 12345
        555-1234

        Dear Sir:

        It is our privilege to inform you about our new
        database managed with XML. This new system allows you
        to reduce the load on your inventory list server by
        having the client machine perform the work of sorting
        and filtering the data.

        The data in an XML element is normalized, so plain-text
        diagrams such as /---\ | | \---/ will become gibberish.

        Sincerely,
        Ms. Doe
```

Fig. 5.6   XML document that marks up a letter (part 2 of 2).

Line 6 contains the root element **letter**. This element contains six child elements which represent the different parts of the letter. This letter contains the recipient, the sender, a salutation, the letter body, a closing remark and a signature. These parts are represented by the **letter** element's six child elements: two **contact** elements (the sender and the recipient), **salutation**, **paragraph** (the letter body), **closing** and **signature**.

Each **contact** element contains one attribute named **type** and eight child elements. Empty element **flag** (lines 16 and 27) contains one attribute **gender**. The **paragraph** element's (line 38) content is normalized by IE5, removing the whitespace formatting.

5.7 CDATA Sections

In the previous section, we discussed markup. In this section, we discuss sections of an XML document—called **CDATA** *sections*—that may contain text, reserved characters (e.g., <) and whitespace characters. Character data in a **CDATA** section is not processed by the XML parser. A common use of a **CDATA** section is for scripting code (e.g., JavaScript or VBScript), which often include the characters **&**, **<**, **>**, **'** and **"**. Figure 5.7 lists an XML document that compares text in a **CDATA** section to character data.

The first **sample** element (lines 8–12) contains C++ code as character data. Each occurrence of **<**, **>** and **&** must be replaced by an entity reference in order prevent syntax errors. Lines 15–20 use a **CDATA** section to indicate a block of text that the parser should not treat as character data or markup. **CDATA** sections begin with **<![CDATA[** and terminate with **]]>**. Notice that **<**, **>** and **&** characters (lines 18 and 19) do not need to be replaced by entity references. IE5 also preserves whitespace in the **CDATA** section, although this is not a requirement of XML processors.

```
1   <?xml version = "1.0"?>
2
3   <!-- Fig. 5.7 : cdata.xml              -->
4   <!-- CDATA section containing C++ code   -->
5
6   <book title = "C++ How to Program" edition = "3">
7
8      <sample>
9           // C++ comment
10          if ( this-&gt;getX() &lt; 5 &amp;&amp; value[ 0 ] != 3 )
11             cerr &lt;&lt; this-&gt;displayError();
12      </sample>
13
14      <sample>
15        <![CDATA[
16
17          // C++ comment
18          if ( this->getX() < 5 && value[ 0 ] != 3 )
19             cerr << this->displayError();
20        ]]>
21      </sample>
22
23      C++ How to Program by Deitel &amp; Deitel
24   </book>
```

Fig. 5.7   Using a **CDATA** section (part 1 of 2).

```
D:\Books\2000\xmlhtp1\frame files\ch05examples\cdata.xml - Microsoft Internet Explorer    _□×
←  ·  →  ·  ⊗  🗋  🏠  |  Q  🖹  ⊗  |  🗈·  🖨  🖷  🗐  🖳        File  Edit  View  Favorites  Tools  He  »
Address  🖳 D:\Books\2000\xmlhtp1\frame files\ch05examples\cdata.xml                                ▼

  <?xml version="1.0" ?>
  <!-- Fig. 5.7 : cdata.xml                 -->
  <!-- CDATA section containing C++ code    -->
- <book title="C++ How to Program" edition="3">
    <sample>// C++ comment if ( this->getX() < 5 && value[ 0 ] != 3 ) cerr <<
      this->displayError();</sample>
  - <sample>
    - <![CDATA[

                  // C++ comment
                  if ( this->getX() < 5 && value[ 0 ] != 3 )
                     cerr << this->displayError();

        ]]>
    </sample>
    C++ How to Program by Deitel & Deitel
  </book>

🖹 Done                                                          🖳 My Computer
```

Fig. 5.7   Using a **CDATA** section (part 2 of 2).

Common Programming Error 5.8

*Placing one or more spaces inside the opening **< ! [CDATA [** or closing **]] >** is an error.*

Because a **CDATA** section is not parsed, it can contain almost any text, including characters normally reserved for XML syntax, such as **<**, **>** and **&**. However, **CDATA** sections cannot contain the text **]] >**, because this is used to terminate a **CDATA** section. For example,

```
<![CDATA[
    The following characters cause an error: ]]>
]]>
```

is an error because the character data in the **CDATA** section contains **]] >**.

5.8 XML Namespaces

Because XML allows document authors to create their own tags, *naming collisions* (i.e., two different elements that have the same name) can occur. For example, we may use the element **book** to mark up data about one of our publications. A stamp collector may also create an element **book** to mark up data about a book of stamps. If both of these elements were used in the same document there would be a naming collision and it would be difficult to determine which kind of data each element contained.

Namespaces provide a means for document authors to prevent collisions. For example,

```
<subject>Math</subject>
```

and

```
<subject>Thrombosis</subject>
```

use a **subject** element to mark up a piece of data. However, in the first case the subject is something one studies in school, whereas in the second case the subject is in the field of medicine. These two **subject** elements can be differentiated using namespaces. For example

```
<school:subject>Math</school:subject>
```

and

```
<medical:subject>Thrombosis</medical:subject>
```

Both **school** and **medical** are *namespace prefixes*. Namespace prefixes are prepended to element and attribute names in order to specify the namespace in which the element or attribute can be found. Each namespace prefix is tied to a *uniform resource identifier (URI)* that uniquely identifies the namespace. Document authors can create their own namespace prefixes as shown in Fig. 5.8 (lines 6 and 7). Virtually any name may be used for a namespace, except the reserved namespace **xml**. We will discuss namespace **xml**, which was introduced in Fig. 5.5 later in the book.

Figure 5.8 demonstrates how to create namespaces. In this document, two distinct **file** elements are differentiated using namespaces.

Lines 6 and 7

```
<text:directory xmlns:text = "urn:deitel:textInfo"
                xmlns:image = "urn:deitel:imageInfo">
```

use the XML namespace keyword *xmlns* to create two namespace prefixes: **text** and **image**. The values assigned to attributes **xmlns:text** and **xmlns:image** are called *Uniform Resource Identifiers (URIs)*. By definition, a URI is a series of characters used to differentiate names.

```
1   <?xml version = "1.0"?>
2
3   <!-- Fig. 5.8 : namespace.xml -->
4   <!-- Namespaces                -->
5
6   <text:directory xmlns:text = "urn:deitel:textInfo"
7                   xmlns:image = "urn:deitel:imageInfo">
8
9      <text:file filename = "book.xml">
10        <text:description>A book list</text:description>
11     </text:file>
12
13     <image:file filename = "funny.jpg">
14        <image:description>A funny picture</image:description>
15        <image:size width = "200" height = "100"/>
16     </image:file>
17
18  </text:directory>
```

Fig. 5.8   Listing for **namespace.xml**.

In order to ensure that a namespace is unique, the document author must provide a unique URI. Here, we use the text **urn:deitel:textInfo** and **urn:deitel:imageInfo** as URIs. A common practice is to use *Universal Resource Locators (URLs)* for URIs, because the domain names (e.g., **deitel.com**) used in URLs are guaranteed to be unique. For example, lines 6 and 7 could have been written as

```
<text:directory xmlns:text="http://www.deitel.com/xmlns-text"
                xmlns:image = "http://www.deitel.com/xmlns-image">
```

where we use URLs related to the Deitel & Associates, Inc. domain name (**www.deitel.com**). These URLs are never visited by the parser—they only represent a series of characters for differentiating names and nothing more. The URLs need not even exist or be properly formed.

Lines 9–11

```
<text:file filename = "book.xml">
    <text:description>A book list</text:description>
</text:file>
```

use the namespace prefix **text** to describe elements **file** and **description**. Notice that end tags have the namespace prefix **text** applied to them as well. Lines 13–16 apply namespace prefix **image** to elements **file**, **description** and **size**.

In order to eliminate the need to place a namespace prefix in each element, authors may specify a *default namespace* for an element and all of its child elements. Fig. 5.9 demonstrates using default namespaces.

We declare a default namespace using the **xmlns** attribute with a URI as its value (line 6). Once this default namespace is in place, child elements that are part of this namespace do not need a namespace prefix. Element **file** (line 9) is in the namespace corresponding to the URI **urn:deitel:textInfo**. Compare this to Fig. 5.8, where we prefixed the **file** and **description** elements with the namespace prefix **text** (lines 9–11).

```
1   <?xml version = "1.0"?>
2
3   <!-- Fig. 5.9 : defaultnamespace.xml -->
4   <!-- Using Default Namespaces        -->
5
6   <directory xmlns = "urn:deitel:textInfo"
7              xmlns:image = "urn:deitel:imageInfo">
8
9       <file filename = "book.xml">
10          <description>A book list</description>
11      </file>
12
13      <image:file filename = "funny.jpg">
14          <image:description>A funny picture</image:description>
15          <image:size width = "200" height = "100"/>
16      </image:file>
17
18  </directory>
```

Fig. 5.9   Using default namespaces.

The default namespace applies to all elements contained in the **directory** element. However, we may use a namespace prefix in order to specify a different namespace for particular elements. For example, the **file** element on line 13 uses the prefix **image** to indicate it is in the namespace corresponding to the URI **urn:deitel:imageInfo**.

5.9 Case Study: A Day Planner Application

In this section, we discuss markup used by a day planner application for scheduling appointments. This case study will be enhanced in later chapters.

When scheduling appointments and tasks, the date, time and appointment type are required. An XML document that marks up appointments is shown in Fig. 5.10.

Line 6 is the root element **planner**, which holds all of the appointments. Within element **planner**, we have a **year** element, which has attribute **value** for storing the year being planned. If we make appointments for the year **2001**, a new **year** element with value of **2001** is created before the **planner** end tag.

```
1   <?xml version = "1.0"?>
2
3   <!-- Fig. 5.10 : planner.xml    -->
4   <!-- Day Planner XML document   -->
5
6   <planner>
7
8      <year value = "2000">
9
10        <date month = "7" day = "15">
11           <note time = "1430">Doctor&apos;s appointment</note>
12           <note time = "1620">Physics class at BH291C</note>
13        </date>
14
15        <date month = "7" day = "4">
16           <note>Independence Day</note>
17        </date>
18
19        <date month = "7" day = "20">
20           <note time = "0900">General Meeting in room 32-A</note>
21        </date>
22
23        <date month = "7" day = "20">
24           <note time = "1900">Party at Joe&apos;s</note>
25        </date>
26
27        <date month = "7" day = "20">
28           <note time = "1300">Financial Meeting in room 14-C</note>
29        </date>
30
31     </year>
32
33  </planner>
```

Fig. 5.10   Day planner XML document **planner.xml**.

Line 10 shows element **date**, which is used to store a specific date. Element **date** has two attributes, **month** and **day**, which store the month and day of the appointment, respectively.

Line 11

```
<note time = "1430">Doctor&apos;s appointment</note>
```

marks up an appointment for July 15, 2000, at 1430 military time (i.e., 2:30 pm). A **date** element may contain many **note** elements, each for a specific time. A **note** element does not have to contain a **time** attribute, such as on line 16

```
<note>Independence Day</note>
```

which denotes an event for an entire day—July 4, Independence Day.

Figure 5.11 shows a screen capture of an application that we present in Chapters 8 and 9 for querying the day-planner XML document.

5.10 Internet and World Wide Web Resources

XML Reference Sites

www.w3.org/XML
Worldwide Web Consortium Extensible Markup Language homepage. Contains links to related XML technologies (e.g., XSL), recommended books, working drafts in progress, time line for publications, developer discussions, translations, software, etc.

www.w3.org/Addressing
Worldwide Web Consortium addressing homepage. Contains information on URIs and links to other resources.

www.xml.com
This is one of the most popular XML sites on the Web. It has resources and links relating to all aspects of XML, including articles, news, seminar information, tools, Frequently Asked Questions (FAQs), etc.

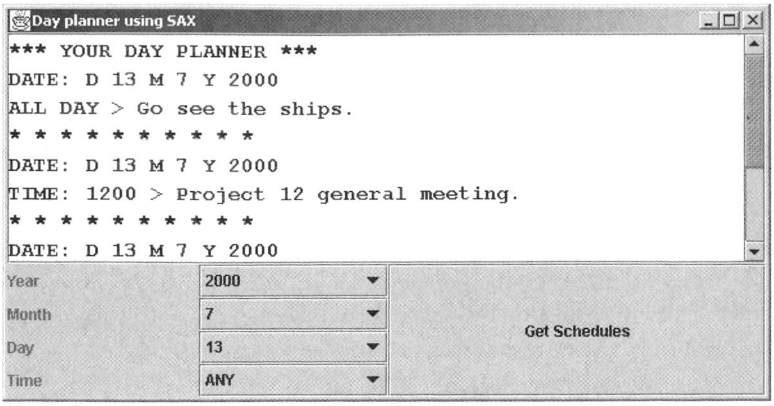

Fig. 5.11 Application that uses the day planner.

www.xml.org
"The XML Industry Portal," is another popular XML site that includes links to many different XML resources.

www.oasis-open.org/cover
Oasis XML Cover Pages home page is a comprehensive reference for many aspects of XML and its related technologies.

xml.about.com
Contains XML-related information.

msdn.microsoft.com/xml
The Microsoft Developers Network XML homepage. It is a good XML reference source and includes information about msxml.

XML Tutorial Sites

www.w3schools.com/xml
Contains a tutorial that introduces the reader to the major aspects of XML. The tutorial contains many examples.

Unicode Sites

www.unicode.org
Unicode Web site that includes general information, versions, character charts, FAQs, etc.

home.att.net/~jameskass
Contains downloadable Unicode charts.

XML Parsers

xml.apache.org
Home page of the Apache XML Project. Contains information about the Xerces XML parser.

www.alphaworks.ibm.com/tech/xml
Home page of IBM's XML4J parser.

technet.oracle.com/tech/xml
Home page of Oracle's XML development kit.

java.sun.com/xml
Home page of the Sun's JAXP and parser technology.

SUMMARY

- XML is a technology for creating markup languages to describe data of virtually any type in a structured manner.

- XML allows document authors to describe data precisely by creating their own tags. Markup languages can be created using XML for describing almost anything.

- XML documents are commonly stored in text files that end in the extension **.xml**. Any text editor can be used to create an XML document. Many software packages allow data to be saved as XML documents.

- The XML declaration specifies the version to which the document conforms.

- XML uses the same syntax for comments as HTML.

- All XML documents must contain exactly one root element that contains all of the other elements. Markup preceding the root element are collectively called the *prolog*.

- In order to process an XML document, a software program called an *XML parser* is required. The XML parser reads the XML document, checks its syntax, reports any errors and allows access to the document's contents.

- An XML document is considered well formed if it is syntactically correct (i.e., the parser did not report any errors due to missing tags, overlapping tags, etc.). Every XML document must be well formed.

- Parsers may or may not support the *Document Object Model (DOM)* and/or the *Simple API for XML (SAX)* for accessing a document's content programmatically by using languages such as Java, Python, C, etc.

- A related XML technology is the *Extensible Stylesheet Language (XSL),* which provides more powerful features than CSS for creating stylesheets.

- XML documents may contain the following characters: carriage return, the line feed and Unicode characters. Unicode is a standard that was released by the Unicode Consortium in 1991 to expand character representation for most of the world's major languages. American Standard Code for Information Interchange (ASCII) is a subset of Unicode.

- Markup text is enclosed in angle brackets (i.e., < and >). Character data is the *text* between a start tag and an end tag. Child elements are considered markup—not character data.

- Spaces, tabs, line feeds and carriage returns are whitespace *characters*. In an XML document, the parser considers whitespace characters to be either *significant* (i.e., preserved by the parser) or *insignificant* (i.e., not preserved by the parser). Depending on the parser and the XML document's structure, insignificant whitespace characters may be collapsed into a single whitespace character or even removed by the parser. This process is called *normalization*.

- Almost any character may be used in an XML document. However, the characters ampersand (**&**), left-angle bracket (**<**), right-angle bracket (**>**), *apostrophe* (**'**) and double quote (**"**) are reserved in XML and may not be used in character data, except in **CDATA** sections. Angle brackets are reserved for delimiting markup tags. The ampersand is reserved for delimiting hexadecimal values that refer to a specific Unicode character. These expressions are terminated with a *semicolon* (**;**) and are called *entity references*. The apostrophe and double-quote characters are reserved for delimiting attribute values.

- XML provides *built-in* entities for ampersand (**&**), left-angle bracket (**<**), right-angle bracket (**>**), apostrophe (**'**) and quotation mark (**"**).

- A *document type definition (DTD)* file defines the structure (i.e., what elements the XML must contain, what order the elements must have, etc.) of an XML document and the entities used by the document.

- All XML start tags must have a corresponding end tag and all start- and end tags must be properly nested. XML is case sensitive, therefore start tags and end tags must have matching capitalization.

- Elements define structure. An element may or may not contain content (i.e., child elements or character data). Attributes describe elements. An element may have zero, one or more attributes associated with it. Attributes are nested within the element's start tag. Attribute values are enclosed in quotes—either single or double.

- XML element and attribute names can be of any length and may contain letters, digits, underscores, hyphens and periods; and they must begin with either a letter or an underscore.

- A processing instruction's (PI's) information is passed by the parser to the application using the XML document. Document authors may create their own processing instructions. Almost any name may be used for a PI target except the reserved word **xml** (also **XML**, **Xml**, etc.). Processing instructions allow document authors to embed application-specific data within an XML document. This data is not intended to be readable by humans, but application readable.

- *CDATA sections* may contain text, reserved characters (e.g., **<**), words and whitespace characters. XML parsers do not process the text in **CDATA** sections. **CDATA** sections allow the document author to include data that is not intended to be parsed. **CDATA** sections cannot contain the text **]] >**.

- Because document authors can create their own tags, naming *collisions* (e.g., when document authors use the same names for elements) can occur. Namespaces provide a means for document authors to prevent naming collisions. Document authors create their own namespaces. Virtually any name may be used for a namespace, except the reserved namespace **xml**.

- A Universal Resource Identifier (URI) is a series of characters used to differentiate names. URIs are used with namespaces.

TERMINOLOGY

<! [CDATA [and **]] >** to delimit a **CDATA** section

<? and **?>** to delimit a processing instruction

American Standard Code for Information Interchange (ASCII)

ampersand (**&**)

angle brackets (**<** and **>**)

Apache XML Project

apostrophe (**'**)

application

ASCII (American Standard Code for Information Interchange)

attributes

built-in entities

case-sensitive XML tags

CDATA section

CDATA section for scripting code

character data

child

child element

comment

container element

content

Document Object Model (DOM)

document type definition (DTD)

DOM-based parser

element

empty element

end tag

entity references

Extensible Stylesheet Language (XSL)

insignificant whitespace characters

Java API for XML Parsing (JAXP)

left-angle bracket (**<**)

markup language

markup text

msxml

namespace

namespace prefixes

namespace **xml**

naming collision

node

normalization

parser

parser in IE5

PI target

PI value

processing instruction (PI)

prolog

quotation mark (**"**)

reserved characters

reserved keyword

reserved namespace

right-angle bracket (**>**)

root element

SAX-based parser

Standard Generalized Markup Language (SGML)

significant whitespace characters

Simple API for XML (SAX)

start tag

structured data

subelement

tag

tree structure of an XML document

Unicode

Unicode consortium

Universal Resource Identifier (URI)

XML

XML declaration

XML document

.xml extension

XML namespace

XML parser

XML processor

XML version

SELF-REVIEW EXERCISES

5.1   State whether the following are *true* or *false*. If *false*, explain why.

a) XML is a technology for creating markup languages.

b) XML markup text is delimited by forward and backward slashes (**/** and ****).

c) Arabic characters can only be placed in to an XML document using an Arabic language keyboard.

d) Unlike HTML, all XML start tags must have corresponding end tags.

e) Parsers check an XML document's syntax and may support the Document Object Model and/or the Simple API for XML.

f) An XML document is considered well formed if the XML document contains whitespace characters.

g) URIs are strings that identify resources such as files, images, services, electronic mailboxes and more.

h) When creating new XML tags, document authors must use the set of XML tags provided by the W3C.

i) The pound character (**#**), the dollar sign (**$**), ampersand (**&**), greater-than (**>**) and less-than (**<**) are examples of XML reserved characters.

j) Any text file is automatically considered to be an XML document by a parser.

5.2   Fill in the blanks in each of the following statements.

a) A/An _____ processes an XML document.

b) Valid characters that can be used in an XML document are the carriage return, the line feed and _____ characters.

c) An entity reference must be proceeded by a/an _____ character.

d) A/An _____ is delimited by **<?** and **?>**.

e) Text in a/an _____ section is not parsed.

f) An XML document is considered _____ if it is syntactically correct.

g) _____ help document authors prevent element naming collisions.

h) Lines proceeding the root element in an XML document are collectively called the _____.

i) A/An _____ tag does not contain character data.

j) XML documents commonly have the file extension _____.

5.3   Identify and correct the error(s) in each of the following:

```
a) <my Tag>This is my custom markup<my Tag>
b) <!PI value!>    <!-- a sample processing instruction -->
c) <myXML>I know XML!!!</MyXML>
d) <CDATA>This is a CDATA section.</CDATA>
e) <xml>x < 5 && x > y</xml>  <!-- mark up a Java condition **>
```

ANSWERS TO SELF-REVIEW EXERCISES

5.1   a) True. b) False. In an XML document, markup text is any text delimited by angle brackets (**<** and **>**) with a forward slash being used in the end tag. c) False. Arabic characters are placed into an XML document as Unicode character entity references. d) True. e) True. f) False. An XML document is considered well formed if it is parsed successfully. g) True. h) False. When creating new tags, programmers may use any valid name except the reserved word **xml** (also **XML**, **Xml**, etc.). i) False. XML reserved characters include the ampersand (**&**), the left-angle bracket (**<**) and the right-angle bracket (**>**) but not **#** and **$**. j) False. The text file must be parsable by an XML parser. If parsing fails, the document cannot be considered an XML document.

5.2   a) parser. b) Unicode. c) ampersand (**&**). d) processing instruction. e) **CDATA**. f) well formed. g) Namespaces. h) prolog. i) empty. j) **.xml**.

5.4
- a) Element name **my tag** contains a space. The forward slash, **/** is missing in the end tag. Corrected markup is: **<myTag>This is my custom markup</myTag>**
- b) Incorrect delimiters for a processing instruction. Corrected markup is
  <?PI value?>   <!-- a sample processing instruction -->
- c) Incorrect mixture of case in end tag. Corrected markup is
  <myXML>I know XML!!!</myXML> or **<MyXML>I know XML!!!</MyXML>**
- d) Incorrect syntax for a **CDATA** section. Corrected markup is
  <![CDATA[This is a CDATA section.]]>
- e) The name **xml** is reserved and cannot be used as an element. The characters **<**, **&** and **>** must be represented using entities. The closing comment delimiter should be two hyphens—not two stars. Corrected markup is
  <someName>x < 5 && x > y</someName>
  <!-- mark up a Java condition -->

EXERCISES

5.5   Create an XML document that marks up the nutrition facts for a package of Grandma Deitel's Cookies. A package of Grandma Deitel's Cookies has a serving size of 1 package and the following nutritional value per serving: 260 calories, 100 fat calories, 11 grams of fat, 2 grams of saturated fat, 5 milligrams of cholesterol, 210 milligrams of sodium, 36 grams of total carbohydrates, 2 grams of fiber, 15 grams of sugars and 5 grams of protein.Render the XML documents in Internet Explorer 5. [*Hint*: Your markup should contain elements describing the product name, serving size/amount, calories, sodium, cholesterol, proteins, etc. Mark up each nutrition fact/ingredient listed above. Use nested elements as necessary.]

5.6   Markup the Java code listed in Fig. 5.12 using XML. Represent the **if** statement with element **if**—which contains one or more **condition** elements and one or more **statement** elements. Element **condition** contains the condition (e.g., **m == month && d == day**) and element **statement** contains the statements (e.g., **resultDay = "DATE: D " + d + " M " + m**). We have provided comments to the right of conditions and statements for easy identification. Element **else** represents an **else** statement in Java and contains one or more **statement** elements. Render the XML document in IE5.

5.7   Modify your solution to Exercise 5.5 by placing the Java code (Fig. 5.12) inside a **CDATA** section. Then render the document in IE5. Other than the syntax coloring, the Java code should be displayed exactly as shown in Fig. 5.12.

```
1   if ( ( m == month && d == day ) ||      // m == month && d == day
2          ( month == -1 && d == day ) ||    // month == -1 && d == day
3          ( m == month && day == -1 ) ||    // m == month && day == -1
4          ( month > -1 && day <= -1 ) ) {   // month > -1 && day <= -1
5       resultDay = "DATE: D " + d + " M " + m;       // a statement
6       processChildNodes(dateElement.getChildNodes());// a statement
7   }
8   else          // else statement
9       return;    // a statement
```

Fig. 5.12   Java code to markup.

5.8   Rewrite the XML document in Fig. 5.10 such that each **note** element has **year**, **month**, **day** and **time** attributes rather than child elements. The solution should contain only the root element and **note** child elements.

5.9   Write a CSS stylesheet for Fig. 5.1 that results in the text **Welcome to XML!** being displayed in blue Times 20 pt.

6

Document Type Definition (DTD)

Objectives

- To understand what a DTD is.
- To be able to write DTDs.
- To be able to declare elements and attributes in a DTD.
- To understand the difference between general entities and parameter entities.
- To be able to use conditional sections with entities.
- To be able to use **NOTATION**s.
- To understand how an XML document's whitespace is processed.

To whom nothing is given, of him can nothing be required.
Henry Fielding

Like everything metaphysical, the harmony between thought and reality is to be found in the grammar of the language.
Ludwig Wittgenstein

Grammar, which knows how to control even kings.
Molière

6.1 Introduction

In this chapter, we discuss *Document Type Definitions* (*DTD*s) that define an XML document's structure (e.g., what elements, attributes, etc. are permitted in the document). An XML document is not required to have a corresponding DTD. However, DTDs are often recommended to ensure document conformity, especially in *business-to-business (B2B) transactions,* where XML documents are exchanged. DTDs specify an XML document's structure and are themselves defined using *EBNF (Extended Backus-Naur Form) grammar*—not the XML syntax introduced in Chapter 5.

 Software Engineering Observation 6.1

A transition is underway in the XML community from DTDs to Schema (Chapter 7), which improve upon DTDs. Schema use XML syntax, not EBNF grammar.

6.2 Parsers, Well-formed and Valid XML Documents

Parsers are generally classified as *validating* or *nonvalidating*. A validating parser is able to read the DTD and determine whether or not the XML document conforms to it. If the document conforms to the DTD, it is referred to as *valid*. If the document fails to conform to the DTD but is syntactically correct, it is well formed but not valid. By definition, a valid document is well formed.

A nonvalidating parser is able to read the DTD, but cannot check the document against the DTD for conformity. If the document is syntactically correct, it is well formed.

We will discuss validating and nonvalidating parsers in greater depth in Chapters 8 and 9. In this chapter, we use Microsoft's *XML Validator* to check for document conformance to a DTD. XML Validator is available at no charge from

```
msdn.microsoft.com/downloads/samples/Internet/xml/
xml_validator/sample.asp
```

6.3 Document Type Declaration

DTDs are introduced into XML documents using the *document type declaration* (i.e., **DOCTYPE**). A document type declaration is placed in the XML document's prolog and begins with **<!DOCTYPE** and ends with **>**. The document type declaration can point to declarations that are outside the XML document (called the *external subset*) or can contain the declaration inside the document (called *internal subset*). For example, an internal subset might look like

```
<!DOCTYPE myMessage [
    <!ELEMENT myMessage ( #PCDATA )>
]>
```

The first **myMessage** is the name of the document type declaration. Anything inside the *square brackets* (**[ ]**) constitutes the internal subset. As we will see momentarily, **ELEMENT** and **#PCDATA** are used in "element declarations."

External subsets physically exist in a different file that typically ends with the **.dtd** *extension*, although this file extension is not required. External subsets are specified using either keyword **SYSTEM** or **PUBLIC**. For example, the **DOCTYPE** external subset might look like

```
<!DOCTYPE myMessage SYSTEM "myDTD.dtd">
```

which points to the **myDTD.dtd** document. Using the **PUBLIC** keyword indicates that the DTD is widely used (e.g., the DTD for HTML documents). The DTD may be made available in well-known locations for more efficient downloading. We used such a DTD in Chapters 2 and 3 when we created HTML documents. The **DOCTYPE**

```
<!DOCTYPE HTML PUBLIC "-//W3C//DTD HTML 4.01//EN"
           "http://www.w3.org/TR/html4/strict.dtd">
```

uses the **PUBLIC** keyword to reference the well-known DTD for HTML version 4.01. XML parsers that do not have a local copy of the DTD may use the URL provided to download the DTD to perform validation.

Both the internal and external subset may be specified at the same time. For example, the **DOCTYPE**

```
<!DOCTYPE myMessage SYSTEM "myDTD.dtd" [
    <!ELEMENT myElement ( #PCDATA )>
]>
```

contains declarations from the **myDTD.dtd** document as well as an internal declaration.

Software Engineering Observation 6.2

The document type declaration's internal subset plus its external subset form the DTD.

Software Engineering Observation 6.3

The internal subset is visible only within the document in which it resides. Other external documents cannot be validated against it. DTDs that are used by many documents should be placed in the external subset.

6.4 Element Type Declarations

Elements are the primary building block used in XML documents and are declared in a DTD with *element type declarations (ELEMENTs)*. For example, to declare element **myMessage**, we might write

```
<!ELEMENT myElement ( #PCDATA )>
```

The element name (e.g., **myElement**) that follows **ELEMENT** is often called a *generic identifier*. The set of parentheses that follow the element name specify the element's allowed content and is called the *content specification*. *Keyword PCDATA* specifies that the element must contain *parsable character data*. This data will be parsed by the XML parser, therefore any markup text (i.e., **<**, **>**, **&**, etc.) will be treated as markup. We will discuss the content specification in detail momentarily.

Common Programming Error 6.1

Attempting to use the same element name in multiple element type declarations is an error.

Figure 6.1 lists an XML document that contains a reference to an external DTD in the **DOCTYPE**. We use Microsoft's XML Validator to check the document's conformity against its DTD. [*Note*: To use XML Validator, Internet Explorer 5 is required. In Chapters 8 and 9, we introduce parsers XML4J and Xerces, which can be used to check a document's validity against a DTD programmatically. Using Java and one of these parsers provides a platform-independent way to validate XML documents.]

The document type declaration (line 6) is named **myMessage**—the name of the root element. The element **myMessage** (lines 8–10) contains a single child element named **message** (line 9).

```
1   <?xml version = "1.0"?>
2
3   <!-- Fig. 6.1: intro.xml      -->
4   <!-- Using an external subset -->
5
6   <!DOCTYPE myMessage SYSTEM "intro.dtd">
7
8   <myMessage>
9      <message>Welcome to XML!</message>
10  </myMessage>
```

Fig. 6.1 XML document declaring its associated DTD.

```
1   <!-- Fig. 6.2: intro.dtd   -->
2   <!-- External declarations -->
3
4   <!ELEMENT myMessage ( message )>
5   <!ELEMENT message ( #PCDATA )>
```

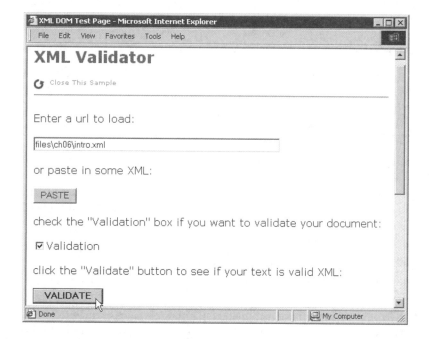

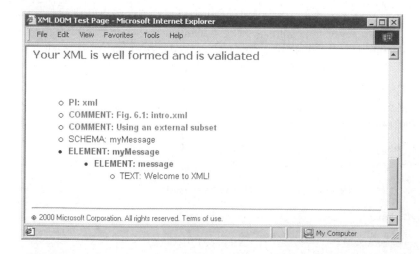

Fig. 6.2   Validation with using an external DTD.

Line 4 of the DTD (Fig. 6.2) declares element **myMessage**. Notice that the content specification contains the name **message**. This indicates that element **myMessage** contains exactly one child element named **message**. Because **myMessage** can only have an element as its content, it is said to have *element content*. Line 5 declares element **message** whose content is of type **PCDATA**. [*Note*: Many XML Validator screen captures contain the term **SCHEMA**. The XML Validator is capable of validating an XML document against both DTDs and documents—called *Schemas*—that also define an XML document's structure. In Chapter 7, we will discuss Schema in Chapter 7 and how they differ from DTDs.]

Common Programming Error 6.2

Having a root element name other than the name specified in the document type declaration is an error.

If an XML document's structure is inconsistent with its corresponding DTD but is syntactically correct, it is only well formed—not valid. Figure 6.3 shows the messages generated by Microsoft's XML Validator when the required **message** element is omitted.

6.4.1 Sequences, Pipe Characters and Occurrence Indicators

DTDs allow the document author to define the order and frequency of child elements. The *comma* (**,**)—called a *sequence*—specifies the order in which the elements must occur. For example,

```
<!ELEMENT classroom ( teacher, student )>
```

```
1   <?xml version = "1.0"?>
2
3   <!-- Fig. 6.3 : intro-invalid.xml      -->
4   <!-- Simple introduction to XML markup -->
5
6   <!DOCTYPE myMessage SYSTEM "intro.dtd">
7
8   <!-- Root element missing child element message -->
9   <myMessage>
10  </myMessage>
```

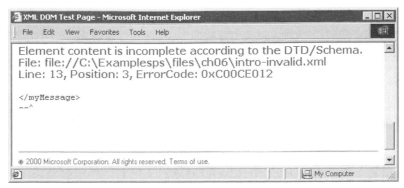

Fig. 6.3   Non-valid XML document.

specifies that element **classroom** must contain exactly one **teacher** element followed by exactly one **student** element. The content specification can contain any number of items in sequence.

Similarly, choices are specified using the *pipe character* (|), as in

```
<!ELEMENT dessert ( iceCream | pastry )>
```

which specifies that element **dessert** must contain either one **iceCream** element or one **pastry** element, but not both. The content specification may contain any number of pipe character-separated choices.

An element's frequency (i.e., number of occurrences) is specified by using either the *plus sign* (**+**), *asterisk* (*****) or *question mark* (**?**) *occurrence indicator* (Fig. 6.4).

A plus sign indicates one or more occurrences. For example,

```
<!ELEMENT album ( song+ )>
```

specifies that element **album** contains one or more **song** elements.

The frequency of an *element group* (i.e., two or more elements that occur in some combination) is specified by enclosing the element names inside the content specification with parentheses, followed by either the plus sign, asterisk or question mark. For example,

```
<!ELEMENT album ( title, ( songTitle, duration )+ )>
```

indicates that element **album** contains one **title** element followed by any number of **songTitle**/**duration** element groups. At least one **songTitle**/**duration** group must follow **title**, and in each of these element groups, the **songTitle** must precede the **duration**. An example of markup that conforms to this is

```
<album>
    <title>XML Classical Hits</title>

    <songTitle>XML Overture</songTitle>
    <duration>10</duration>

    <songTitle>XML Symphony 1.0</songTitle>
    <duration>54</duration>
</album>
```

which contains one **title** element followed by two **songTitle**/**duration** groups.

Occurrence Indicator	Description
Plus sign (**+**)	An element can appear any number of times, but must be appear at least once (i.e., the element appears one or more times).
Asterisk (*****)	An element is optional and if used, the element can appear any number of times (i.e., the element appears zero or more times).
Question mark (**?**)	An element is optional, and if used, the element can appear only once (i.e., the element appears zero or one times).

Fig. 6.4   Occurrence indicators.

The asterisk (*) character indicates an optional element that, if used, can occur any number of times. For example,

```
<!ELEMENT library ( book* )>
```

indicates that element **library** contains any number of **book** elements, including the possibility of none at all. Markup examples that conform to this are

```
<library>
    <book>The Wealth of Nations</book>
    <book>The Iliad</book>
    <book>The Jungle</book>
</library>
```

and

```
<library></library>
```

Optional elements that, if used, may occur only once are followed by a question mark (**?**). For example,

```
<!ELEMENT seat ( person? )>
```

indicates that element **seat** contains at most one **person** element. Examples of markup that conform to this are

```
<seat>
    <person>Jane Doe</person>
</seat>
```

and

```
<seat></seat>
```

Now we consider three more complicated element type declarations and provide a declaration for each. The declaration

```
<!ELEMENT class ( number, ( instructor | assistant+ ),
                  ( credit | noCredit ) )>
```

specifies that a **class** element must contain a **number** element, either one **instructor** element or any number of **assistant** elements and either one **credit** element or one **noCredit** element. Markup examples that conform to this are

```
<class>
    <number>123</number>
    <instructor>Dr. Harvey Deitel</instructor>
    <credit>4</credit>
</class>
```

and

```
<class>
   <number>456</number>
   <assistant>Tem Nieto</assistant>
   <assistant>Paul Deitel</assistant>
   <credit>3</credit>
</class>
```

The declaration

```
<!ELEMENT donutBox ( jelly?, lemon*,
                     ( ( creme | sugar )+ | glazed ) )>
```

specifies that element **donutBox** can have zero or one **jelly** elements, followed by zero or more **lemon** elements, followed by one or more **creme** or **sugar** elements or exactly one **glazed** element. Markup examples that conform to this are

```
<donutBox>
   <jelly>grape</jelly>
   <lemon>half-sour</lemon>
   <lemon>sour</lemon>
   <lemon>half-sour</lemon>
   <glazed>chocolate</glazed>
</donutBox>
```

and

```
<donutBox>
   <sugar>semi-sweet</sugar>
   <creme>whipped</creme>
   <sugar>sweet</sugar>
</donutBox>
```

The declaration

```
<!ELEMENT farm ( farmer+, ( dog* | cat? ), pig*,
                 ( goat | cow )?,( chicken+ | duck* ) )>
```

indicates that element **farm** can have one or more **farmer** elements, any number of optional **dog** elements or an optional **cat** element, any number of optional **pig** elements, an optional **goat** or **cow** element and one or more **chicken** elements or any number of optional **duck** elements. Examples of markup that conform to this are

```
<farm>
   <farmer>Jane Doe</farmer>
   <farmer>John Doe</farmer>
   <cat>Lucy</cat>
   <pig>Bo</pig>
   <chicken>Jill</chicken>
</farm>
```

and

```
<farm>
   <farmer>Red Green</farmer>
   <duck>Billy</duck>
   <duck>Sue</duck>
</farm>
```

6.4.2 EMPTY, Mixed Content and ANY

Elements must be further refined by specifying the types of content they contain. In the last section, we introduced element content, indicating that an element can contain one or more child elements as its content. In this section, we introduce *content specification types* for describing non-element content.

In addition to element content, three other types of content exist: **EMPTY**, *mixed content* and **ANY**. Keyword **EMPTY** declares empty elements. Empty elements do not contain character data or child elements. For example,

```
<!ELEMENT oven EMPTY>
```

declares element **oven** to be an empty element. The markup for an **oven** element would appear as

```
<oven/>
```

in an XML document conforming to this declaration.

An element can also be declared as having mixed content. Such elements may contain any combination of elements and **PCDATA**. For example, the declaration

```
<!ELEMENT myMessage ( #PCDATA | message )*>
```

indicates that element **myMessage** contains mixed content. Markup conforming to this declaration might look like

```
<myMessage>Here is some text, some
   <message>other text</message>and
   <message>even more text</message>.
</myMessage>
```

Element **myMessage** contains two **message** elements and three instances of character data. Because of the *****, element **myMessage** could have contained nothing.

Figure 6.5 specifies a DTD as an internal subset (lines 6–10) as opposed to an external subset (Fig. 6.1). In the prolog (line 1) we use the *standalone* attribute with a value of **yes**. *An XML document is **standalone** if it does not reference an external subset.* This DTD defines three elements: one that contains mixed content and two that contain parsed character data.

```
1   <?xml version = "1.0" standalone = "yes"?>
2
```

Fig. 6.5 Example of a mixed-content element (part 1 of 2).

```
3   <!-- Fig. 6.5 : mixed.xml         -->
4   <!-- Mixed content type elements -->
5
6   <!DOCTYPE format [
7      <!ELEMENT format ( #PCDATA | bold | italic )*>
8      <!ELEMENT bold ( #PCDATA )>
9      <!ELEMENT italic ( #PCDATA )>
10  ]>
11
12  <format>
13     This is a simple formatted sentence.
14     <bold>I have tried bold.</bold>
15     <italic>I have tried italic.</italic>
16     Now what?
17  </format>
```

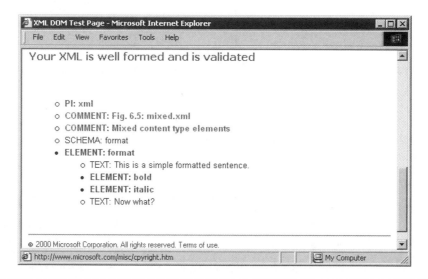

Fig. 6.5   Example of a mixed-content element (part 2 of 2).

Line 7 declares element **format** as a mixed content element. According to the declaration, the **format** element may contain either parsed character data (**PCDATA**), element **bold** or element **italic**. The asterisk indicates that the content can occur zero or more times. Lines 8 and 9 specify that **bold** and **italic** elements have **PCDATA** only for their content specification—they cannot contain child elements. Despite the fact that elements with **PCDATA** content specification cannot contain child elements, they are still considered to have mixed content. The comma (**,**), plus sign (**+**) and question mark (**?**) occurrence indicators cannot be used with mixed content elements that contain only **PCDATA**.

Figure 6.6 shows the results of changing the first pipe character in line 7 of Fig. 6.5 to a comma and the result of removing the asterisk. Both of these are illegal DTD syntax.

 Common Programming Error 6.3

*When declaring mixed content, not listing **PCDATA** as the first item is an error.*

Fig. 6.6   Illegal mixed-content element syntax.

An element declared as type **ANY** can contain any content, including **PCDATA**, elements or a combination of elements and **PCDATA**. Elements with **ANY** content can also be empty elements.

Common Programming Error 6.4

*Child elements of an element declared as type **ANY** must have their own element type declarations.*

Software Engineering Observation 6.4

*Elements with **ANY** content are commonly used in the early stages of DTD development. Document authors typically replace **ANY** content with more specific content as the DTD evolves.*

6.5 Attribute Declarations

In this section, we discuss *attribute declarations*. An attribute declaration specifies an *attribute list* for an element by using the **ATTLIST** *attribute list declaration*. An element can have any number of attributes. For example,

```
<!ELEMENT x EMPTY>
<!ATTLIST x y CDATA #REQUIRED>
```

declares **EMPTY** element **x**. The attribute declaration specifies that **y** is an attribute of **x**. Keyword **CDATA** indicates that **y** can contain any character text except for the **<, >, &, '** and **"** characters. Note that the **CDATA** keyword in an attribute declaration has a different meaning than the **CDATA** section in an XML document we introduced in Chapter 5. Recall that in a **CDATA** section all characters are legal except the **]]>** end tag. *Keyword **#RE-QUIRED*** specifies that the attribute must be provided for element **x**. We will say more about other keywords momentarily.

Figure 6.7 demonstrates how to specify attribute declarations for an element. Line 9 declares attribute **id** for element **message**. Attribute **id** contains required **CDATA**. Attribute values are normalized (i.e., consecutive whitespace characters are combined into one whitespace character). We discuss normalization in detail in Section 6.8. Line 13 assigns attribute **id** the value **"445"**.

```
1    <?xml version = "1.0"?>
2
3    <!-- Fig. 6.7: intro2.xml -->
4    <!-- Declaring attributes -->
5
6    <!DOCTYPE myMessage [
7       <!ELEMENT myMessage ( message )>
8       <!ELEMENT message ( #PCDATA )>
9       <!ATTLIST message id CDATA #REQUIRED>
10   ]>
11
12   <myMessage>
13
14      <message id = "445">
15         Welcome to XML!
16      </message>
17
18   </myMessage>
```

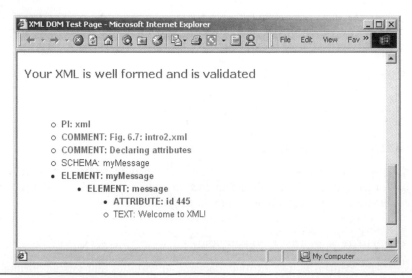

Fig. 6.7   Declaring attributes.

6.5.1 Attribute Defaults (#REQUIRED, #IMPLIED, #FIXED)

DTDs allow document authors to specify an attribute's default value using *attribute defaults*, which we briefly touched upon in the last section. Keywords **#IMPLIED**, **#REQUIRED** and **#FIXED** are attribute defaults. Keyword **#IMPLIED** specifies that if the attribute does not appear in the element, then the application using the XML document can use whatever value (if any) it chooses.

Keyword **#REQUIRED** indicates that the attribute must appear in the element. The XML document is not valid if the attribute is missing. For example, the markup

```
<message>number</message>
```

when checked against the DTD attribute list declaration

```
<!ATTLIST message number CDATA #REQUIRED>
```

does not conform because attribute **number** is missing from element **message**.

An attribute declaration with default value **#FIXED** specifies that the attribute value is constant and cannot be different in the XML document. For example,

```
<!ATTLIST address zip #FIXED "02115">
```

indicates that the value **"02115"** is the only value attribute **zip** can have. The XML document is not valid if attribute **zip** contains a value different from **"02115"**. If element **address** does not contain attribute **zip**, the default value **"02115"** is passed to the application using the XML document's data.

6.6 Attribute Types

Attribute types are classified as either *strings* (**CDATA**), *tokenized* or *enumerated*. String attribute types do not impose any constraints on attribute values—other than disallowing the **<, >, &, '** and **"** characters. Entity references (e.g., **<**, **>**, etc.) must be used for these characters. *Tokenized attributes* impose constraints on attribute values—such as which characters are permitted in an attribute name. We discuss tokenized attributes in the next section. *Enumerated attributes* are the most restrictive of the three types. They can take only one of the values listed in the attribute declaration. We will discuss enumerated attribute types in Section 6.6.2.

6.6.1 Tokenized Attribute Type (ID, IDREF, ENTITY, NMTOKEN)

Tokenized attribute types allow a DTD author to restrict the values used for attributes. For example, an author may want to have a unique ID for each element or only allow an attribute to have one or two different values. Four different tokenized attribute types exist: **ID**, **IDREF**, **ENTITY** and **NMTOKEN**.

Tokenized attribute type **ID** uniquely identifies an element. Attributes with type **IDREF** point to elements with an **ID** attribute. A validating parser verifies that every **ID** attribute type referenced by **IDREF** is in the XML document.

Common Programming Error 6.5

*Using the same value for multiple **ID** attributes is a logic error—the document validated against the DTD is not valid.*

Figure 6.8 lists an XML document that uses **ID** and **IDREF** attribute types. Element **bookstore** consists of element **shipping** and element **book**. Each **shipping** element describes a shipping method.

Line 9 declares attribute **shipID** as an **ID** type attribute (i.e., each **shipping** element has a unique identifier). Lines 24–34 declare **book** elements with attribute **shippedBy** (line 11) of type **IDREF**. Attribute **shippedBy** points to one of the **shipping** elements by matching its **shipID** attribute.

If we assign **shippedBy** (line 28) the value **"s3"**, an error occurs when we use Microsoft's Validator (Fig. 6.9). No **shipID** attribute has a value **"s3"**, which results in a non-valid XML document.

Common Programming Error 6.6

*Not beginning a type attribute **ID**'s value with a letter, underscore (_) or a colon (:) is an error.*

Common Programming Error 6.7

*Providing more than one **ID** attribute type for an element is an error.*

```
1    <?xml version = "1.0"?>
2
3    <!-- Fig. 6.8: IDExample.xml                         -->
4    <!-- Example for ID and IDREF values of attributes -->
5
6    <!DOCTYPE bookstore [
7       <!ELEMENT bookstore ( shipping+, book+ )>
8       <!ELEMENT shipping ( duration )>
9       <!ATTLIST shipping shipID ID #REQUIRED>
10      <!ELEMENT book ( #PCDATA )>
11      <!ATTLIST book shippedBy IDREF #IMPLIED>
12      <!ELEMENT duration ( #PCDATA )>
13   ]>
14
15   <bookstore>
16      <shipping shipID = "s1">
17         <duration>2 to 4 days</duration>
18      </shipping>
19
20      <shipping shipID = "s2">
21         <duration>1 day</duration>
22      </shipping>
23
24      <book shippedBy = "s2">
25         Java How to Program 3rd edition.
26      </book>
27
28      <book shippedBy = "s2">
29         C How to Program 3rd edition.
30      </book>
31
```

Fig. 6.8   XML document with **ID** and **IDREF** attribute types (part 1 of 2).

```
32      <book shippedBy = "s1">
33          C++ How to Program 3rd edition.
34      </book>
35   </bookstore>
```

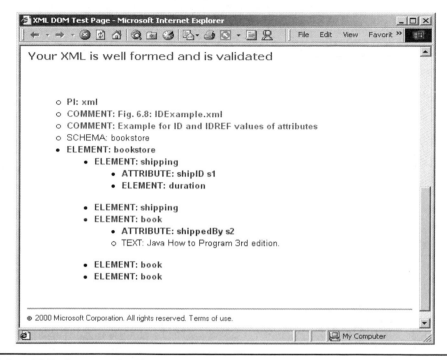

Fig. 6.8   XML document with **ID** and **IDREF** attribute types (part 2 of 2).

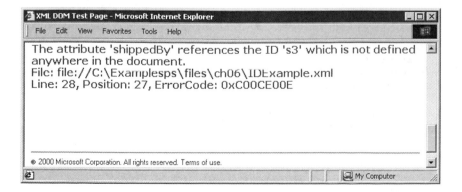

Fig. 6.9   Error displayed by XML Validator when an invalid **ID** is referenced.

Common Programming Error 6.8

*Declaring attributes of type **ID** as **#FIXED** is an error.*

In Chapter 5, we briefly introduced the concept of DTDs and entities. Figure 5.4 (**lang.xml**) referenced **lang.dtd**, which contained the values for the entity references **&assoc;** and **&text;**. External subset **lang.dtd** contains the two *entity declarations*

```
<!ENTITY assoc
"&#1571;&#1587;&#1617;&#1608;&#1588;&#1616;&#1610;&#1614;&#15
78;&#1618;&#1587;">
```

and

```
<!ENTITY text
"&#1575;&#1604;&#1610;&#1608;&#1606;&#1610;&#1603;&#1608;&#15
83;">
```

for entities **assoc** and **text**. A parser replaces the entity references with their values. For example, consider the following entity declaration

```
<!ENTITY digits "0123456789">
```

for **digits**. This entity might be used as follows

```
<useAnEntity>&digits;</useAnEntity>
```

The entity reference **&digits;** is replaced by its value, resulting in

```
<useAnEntity>0123456789</useAnEntity>
```

the value **0123456789** being placed inside the tags. These entities are called *general entities*. Related to entities are *entity attributes,* which indicate that an attribute has an entity for its value. These entity attributes are specified by using tokenized attribute type **ENTITY**. The primary constraint placed on **ENTITY** attribute types is that they must refer to *external unparsed entities*. An external unparsed entity is defined in the external subset of a DTD and consists of character data that will not be parsed by the XML parser.

Figure 6.10 lists an XML document that demonstrates the use of entities and entity attribute types.

```
1   <?xml version = "1.0"?>
2
3   <!-- Fig. 6.10: entityExample.xml       -->
4   <!-- ENTITY and ENTITY attribute types  -->
5
6   <!DOCTYPE database [
7      <!NOTATION html SYSTEM "iexplorer">
8      <!ENTITY city SYSTEM "tour.html" NDATA html>
9      <!ELEMENT database ( company+ )>
10     <!ELEMENT company ( name )>
```

Fig. 6.10 XML document that contains an **ENTITY** attribute type (part 1 of 2).

```
11        <!ATTLIST company tour ENTITY #REQUIRED>
12        <!ELEMENT name ( #PCDATA )>
13    ]>
14
15    <database>
16        <company tour = "city">
17            <name>Deitel &amp; Associates, Inc.</name>
18        </company>
19    </database>
```

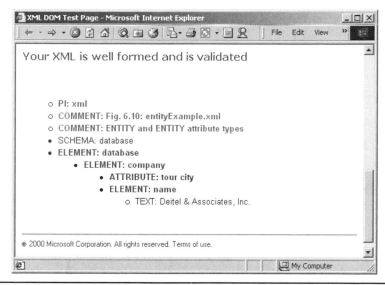

Fig. 6.10   XML document that contains an **ENTITY** attribute type (part 2 of 2).

Line 7

```
<!NOTATION html SYSTEM "iexplorer">
```

declares a *notation* named **html** that refers to a **SYSTEM** identifier named **"iexplorer"**. Notations provide information that an application using the XML document can use to handle unparsed entities. For example, the application using this document may choose to open Internet Explorer and load the document **tour.html** (line 8).

Line 8

```
<!ENTITY city SYSTEM "tour.html" NDATA html>
```

declares an entity named **city** that refers to an external document (**tour.html**). *Keyword **NDATA*** indicates that the content of this external entity is not XML. The name of the notation (e.g., **html**) that handles this unparsed entity is placed to the right of **NDATA**.

Line 11

```
<!ATTLIST company tour ENTITY #REQUIRED>
```

declares attribute **tour** for element **company**. Attribute **tour** specifies a required **ENTITY** attribute type. Line 16

```
<company tour = "city">
```

assigns entity **city** to attribute **tour**. If we replaced line 16 with

```
<company tour = "country">
```

the document fails to conform to the DTD because entity **country** does not exist. Figure 6.11 shows the message generated by XML Validator if **country** is used.

Common Programming Error 6.9

*Not assigning an unparsed external entity to an attribute with attribute type **ENTITY** results in a non-valid XML document.*

Attribute type ***ENTITIES*** may also be used in a DTD to indicate that an attribute has multiple entities for its value. Each entity is separated by a space. For example

```
<!ATTLIST directory file ENTITIES #REQUIRED>
```

specifies that attribute **file** is required to contain multiple entities. An example of markup that conforms to this might look like

```
<directory file = "animations graph1 graph2">
```

where **animations**, **graph1** and **graph2** are entities declared in a DTD.

A more restrictive attribute type is attribute type ***NMTOKEN*** (*name token*), whose value consists of letters, digits, periods, underscores, hyphens and colon characters. For example, consider the declaration

```
<!ATTLIST sportsClub phone NMTOKEN #REQUIRED>
```

which indicates **sportsClub** contains a required **NMTOKEN phone** attribute. An example of markup that conforms to this is

```
<sportsClub phone = "555-111-2222">
```

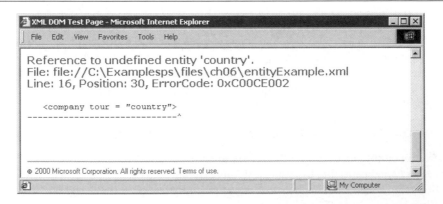

Fig. 6.11 Error generated by XML Validator when a DTD contains a reference to an undefined entity.

An example that does not conform to this is

```
<sportsClub phone = "555 555 4902">
```

because spaces are not allowed in an **NMTOKEN** attribute.

Similarly, when an **NMTOKENS** attribute type is declared, the attribute may contain multiple string tokens separated by spaces.

6.6.2 Enumerated Attribute Types

In this section, we discuss *enumerated attribute types*, which declare a list of possible values an attribute can have. The attribute must be assigned a value from this list to conform to the DTD. Enumerated type values are separated by pipe characters (|). For example, the declaration

```
<!ATTLIST person gender ( M | F ) "F">
```

contains an enumerated attribute type declaration that allows attribute **gender** to have either the value **M** or **F**. A default value of **"F"** is specified to the right of the element attribute type. Alternatively, a declaration such as

```
<!ATTLIST person gender ( M | F ) #IMPLIED>
```

does not provide a default value for **gender**. This type of declaration might be used to validate a marked up mailing list that contains first names, last names, addresses, etc. The application that uses this mailing list may want to precede each name by either Mr., Ms. or Mrs. However, some first names are gender neutral (e.g., Chris, Sam, etc.), and the application may not know the **person**'s gender. In this case, the application has the flexibility to process the name in a gender neutral way.

NOTATION is also an enumerated attribute type. For example,

```
<!ATTLIST book reference NOTATION ( JAVA | C ) "C">
```

the declaration indicates that **reference** must be assigned either **JAVA** or **C**. If a value is not assigned, **C** is specified as the default. The notation for **C** might be declared as

```
<!NOTATION C SYSTEM
    "http://www.deitel.com/books/2000/chtp3/chtp3_toc.htm">
```

6.7 Conditional Sections

DTDs provide the ability to include or exclude declarations using conditional sections. Keyword *INCLUDE* specifies that declarations are included, while keyword *IGNORE* specifies that declarations are excluded. For example, the conditional section

```
<![INCLUDE[
<!ELEMENT name ( #PCDATA )>
]]>
```

directs the parser to include the declaration of element **name**.

Similarly, the conditional section

```
<![IGNORE[
<!ELEMENT message ( #PCDATA )>
]]>
```

directs the parser to exclude the declaration of element **message**.

Conditional sections are often used with entities, as demonstrated in Fig 6.12. Lines 4 and 5

```
<!ENTITY % reject "IGNORE">
<!ENTITY % accept "INCLUDE">
```

declare entities **reject** and **accept**, with the values **IGNORE** and **INCLUDE**, respectively. Because each of these entities is preceded by a *percent (%) character*, they can be used only inside the DTD in which they are declared. These types of entities—called *parameter entities*—allow document authors to create entities specific to a DTD—not an XML document. [*Note:* Recall that the DTD is the combination of the internal subset and external subset. Parameter entities may only be placed in the external subset.]

Lines 7–13 use the entities **accept** and **reject**, which represent the strings **INCLUDE** and **IGNORE**, respectively. Notice that the parameter entity references are preceded by **%**, where as normal entity references are preceded by **&**. Line 7

```
<![ %accept; [
```

represents the beginning tag of an **IGNORE** section (the value of the **accept** entity is **IGNORE**), while line 11 represents the start tag of an **INCLUDE** section. By changing the values of the entities, we can easily choose which **message** element declaration to allow.

Figure 6.13 shows the XML document that conforms to the DTD in Fig. 6.12.

```
1   <!-- Fig. 6.12: conditional.dtd        -->
2   <!-- DTD for conditional section example -->
3
4   <!ENTITY % reject "IGNORE">
5   <!ENTITY % accept "INCLUDE">
6
7   <![ %accept; [
8      <!ELEMENT message ( approved, signature )>
9   ]]>
10
11  <![ %reject; [
12     <!ELEMENT message ( approved, reason, signature )>
13  ]]>
14
15  <!ELEMENT approved EMPTY>
16  <!ATTLIST approved flag ( true | false ) "false">
17
18  <!ELEMENT reason ( #PCDATA )>
19  <!ELEMENT signature ( #PCDATA )>
```

Fig. 6.12 Conditional sections in a DTD.

```
 1   <?xml version = "1.0" standalone = "no"?>
 2
 3   <!-- Fig. 6.13: conditional.xml -->
 4   <!-- Using conditional sections -->
 5
 6   <!DOCTYPE message SYSTEM "conditional.dtd">
 7
 8   <message>
 9      <approved flag = "true"/>
10      <signature>Chairman</signature>
11   </message>
```

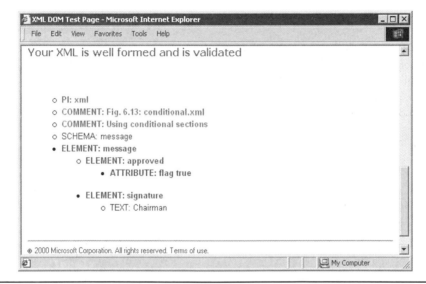

Fig. 6.13   XML document that conforms to **conditional.dtd**.

Software Engineering Observation 6.5

Parameter entities allows document authors to use entity names in DTDs without conflicting with entities used in an XML document.

6.8 Whitespace Characters

In Chapter 5, we briefly discussed whitespace characters and normalization. In this section, we discuss how whitespace characters and normalization relate to DTDs. Whitespace is either preserved or normalized, depending on the context in which it is used.

Figure 6.14 contains a DTD and markup that conforms to the DTD. The output shown is generated by a Java application presented in Chapter 9.

```
 1   <?xml version = "1.0"?>
 2
```

Fig. 6.14   Processing whitespace in an XML document (part 1 of 3).

```
3    <!-- Fig. 6.14 : whitespace.xml        -->
4    <!-- Demonstrating whitespace parsing -->
5
6    <!DOCTYPE whitespace [
7       <!ELEMENT whitespace ( hasCDATA,
8          hasID, hasNMTOKEN, hasEnumeration, hasMixed )>
9
10      <!ELEMENT hasCDATA EMPTY>
11      <!ATTLIST hasCDATA cdata CDATA #REQUIRED>
12
13      <!ELEMENT hasID EMPTY>
14      <!ATTLIST hasID id ID #REQUIRED>
15
16      <!ELEMENT hasNMTOKEN EMPTY>
17      <!ATTLIST hasNMTOKEN nmtoken NMTOKEN #REQUIRED>
18
19      <!ELEMENT hasEnumeration EMPTY>
20      <!ATTLIST hasEnumeration enumeration ( true | false )
21                  #REQUIRED>
22
23      <!ELEMENT hasMixed ( #PCDATA | hasCDATA )*>
24   ]>
25
26   <whitespace>
27
28      <hasCDATA cdata = "  simple cdata  "/>
29
30      <hasID id = "  i20"/>
31
32      <hasNMTOKEN nmtoken = "   hello"/>
33
34      <hasEnumeration enumeration = "   true"/>
35
36      <hasMixed>
37         This is text.
38         <hasCDATA cdata = " simple    cdata"/>
39         This is some additional text.
40      </hasMixed>
41
42   </whitespace>
```

```
>java Tree yes whitespace.xml
URL: file:C:/Examplesps/Files/deleted/ch09/Tree/whitespace.xml
[ document root ]
+-[ element : whitespace ]
  +-[ ignorable ]
  +-[ ignorable ]
  +-[ ignorable ]
  +-[ element : hasCDATA ]
    +-[ attribute : cdata ] "  simple cdata  "
  +-[ ignorable ]
  +-[ ignorable ]
  +-[ ignorable ]
                                                    Continued
```

Fig. 6.14   Processing whitespace in an XML document (part 2 of 3).

Continued

```
  +-[ element : hasID ]
    +-[ attribute : id ] "i20"
  +-[ ignorable ]
  +-[ ignorable ]
  +-[ ignorable ]
  +-[ element : hasNMTOKEN ]
    +-[ attribute : nmtoken ] "hello"
  +-[ ignorable ]
  +-[ ignorable ]
  +-[ ignorable ]
  +-[ element : hasEnumeration ]
    +-[ attribute : enumeration ] "true"
  +-[ ignorable ]
  +-[ ignorable ]
  +-[ ignorable ]
  +-[ element : hasMixed ]
    +-[ text ] "
"
    +-[ text ] "        This is text."
    +-[ text ] "
"
    +-[ text ] "        "
  +-[ element : hasCDATA ]
      +-[ attribute : cdata ] " simple    cdata"
    +-[ text ] "
"
    +-[ text ] "        This is some additional text."
    +-[ text ] "
"
    +-[ text ] "    "
  +-[ ignorable ]
  +-[ ignorable ]
[ document end ]
```

Fig. 6.14 Processing whitespace in an XML document (part 3 of 3).

Line 28

```
<hasCDATA cdata = "   simple cdata   "/>
```

assigns a value containing multiple whitespace characters to attribute **cdata**. Attribute **cdata** (declared in line 11) is required and must contain **CDATA**. As mentioned earlier, **CDATA** can contain almost any text, including whitespace. As the output illustrates, spaces in **CDATA** are preserved and passed on to the application using the XML document.

Line 30 assigns a value to attribute **id** that contains leading whitespace. Attribute **id** is declared on line 14 with tokenized attribute type **ID**. Because this is not **CDATA**, it is normalized and the leading whitespace characters are removed. Similarly, lines 32 and 34 assign values that contain leading whitespace to attributes **nmtoken** and **enumeration**—which are declared in the DTD as an **NMTOKEN** and an enumeration, respectively. Both these attributes are normalized by the parser. [*Note*: We discuss the **ignorable** and **text** portions of the output in Chapter 9.]

6.9 Case Study: Writing a DTD for the Day Planner Application

In this section, we build upon the case study introduced in Chapter 5. Figure 6.15 lists the external subset of the DTD for the day planner XML document, **planner.xml**. The following document type declaration is inserted into the day planner XML document

```
<!DOCTYPE planner SYSTEM "planner.dtd">
```

```
1  <!-- Fig. 6.15: planner.dtd   -->
2  <!-- DTD for day planner      -->
3
4  <!ELEMENT planner ( year* )>
5
6  <!ELEMENT year ( date+ )>
7  <!ATTLIST year value CDATA #REQUIRED>
8
9  <!ELEMENT date ( note+ )>
10 <!ATTLIST date month CDATA #REQUIRED>
11 <!ATTLIST date day CDATA #REQUIRED>
12
13 <!ELEMENT note ( #PCDATA )>
14 <!ATTLIST note time CDATA #IMPLIED>
```

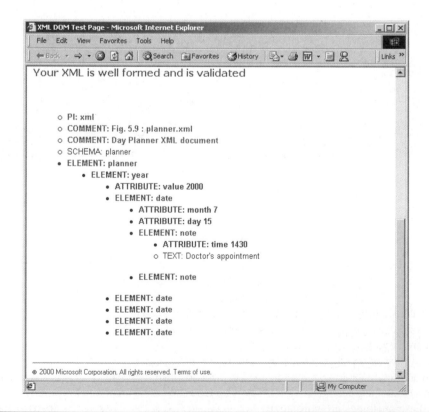

Fig. 6.15   DTD for **planner.xml**.

Software Engineering Observation 6.6

When an attribute's value is normalized, consecutive carriage returns/line feeds are collapsed into a single carriage return/line feed that is replaced by a space character.

Element **planner** is the root element of the document, which contains any number of optional **year** elements. The declarations (lines 6 and 7) specify that **year** element must contain one or more **date** elements and must contain an attribute **value** that has character data.

Line 9 indicates that a **date** element contains one or more **note** elements. Element **date** is required to have two attributes: **month** and **day**. Element **note** contains parsed character data and an optional attribute **time**.

6.10 Internet and World Wide Web Resources

www.wdvl.com/Authoring/HTML/Validation/DTD.html
Contains a description of the historical uses of DTDs, including a description of SGML and the HTML DTD.

www.dtd.com
A repository of DTDs for XML documents.

www.xml101.com/dtd
Contains tutorials and explanations on creating DTDs.

wdvl.internet.com/Authoring/Languages/XML/Tutorials/Intro/index3.html
A DTD tutorial.

www.w3schools.com/dtd
Contains DTD tutorials and examples.

www.schema.net
A DTD repository with XML links and resources.

msdn.microsoft.com/downloads/samples/Internet/xml/xml_validator/sample.asp
Download page for Microsoft's XML Validator.

www.networking.ibm.com/xml/XmlValidatorForm.html
IBM's DOMit XML Validator.

SUMMARY

- Document Type Definitions (DTDs) define an XML document's structure (e.g., what elements, attributes, etc. are permitted in the XML document). An XML document is not required to have a corresponding DTD. DTDs use EBNF (Extended Backus-Naur Form) grammar.

- Parsers are generally classified as validating or nonvalidating. A validating parser is able to read the DTD and determine whether or not the XML document conforms to it. If the document conforms to the DTD, it is referred to as valid. If the document fails to conform to the DTD but is syntactically correct, it is well formed but not valid. By definition, a valid document is well formed.

- A nonvalidating parser is able to read a DTD, but cannot check the document against the DTD for conformity. If the document is syntactically correct, it is well formed.

- DTDs are introduced into XML documents by using the document type declaration (i.e., **DOC-TYPE**). The document type declaration can point to declarations that are outside the XML document (called the external subset) or can contain the declaration inside the document (called internal subset).

- External subsets physically exist in a different file that typically ends with the **.dtd** extension, although this file extension is not required. External subsets are specified using keyword **SYSTEM**. Both the internal and external subset may be specified at the same time.

- Elements are the primary building block used in XML documents and are declared in a DTD with element type declarations (**ELEMENT**s).

- The element name that follows **ELEMENT** is often called a generic identifier. The set of parentheses that follow the element name specify the element's allowed content and is called the content specification.

- Keyword **PCDATA** specifies that the element must contain parsable character data—that is, any text except the characters less-than (**<**), greater-than (**>**), ampersand (**&**), quote (**'**) and double quote (**"**).

- An XML document is a **standalone** XML document if it does not reference an external DTD.

- An XML element that can only have another element for content, it is said to have element content.

- DTDs allow the document author to define the order and frequency of child elements. The comma (,)—called a sequence—specifies the order in which the elements must occur. Choices are specified using the pipe character (|). The content specification may contain any number of pipe-character-separated choices.

- An element's frequency (i.e., number of occurrences) is specified by using either the plus sign (+), asterisk (*) or question mark (?) occurrence indicator.

- The frequency of an element group (i.e., two or more elements that occur in some combination) is specified by enclosing the element names inside the content specification followed by an occurrence indicator.

- Elements can be further refined by describing the content types they may contain. Content specification types (e.g., **EMPTY**, mixed content, **ANY**, etc.) describe nonelement content.

- An element can be declared as having mixed content (i.e., a combination of elements and **PCDATA**). The comma (**,**), plus sign (**+**) and question mark (**?**) occurrence indicators cannot be used with mixed content elements.

- An element declared as type **ANY** can contain any content including **PCDATA**, elements, or a combination of elements and **PCDATA**. Elements with **ANY** content can also be empty elements.

- An attribute list for an element is declared using the **ATTLIST** element type declaration.

- Attribute values are normalized (i.e., consecutive whitespace characters are combined into one whitespace character).

- DTDs allow document authors to specify an attribute's default value using attribute defaults. Keywords **#IMPLIED**, **#REQUIRED** and **#FIXED** are attribute defaults.

- Keyword **#IMPLIED** specifies that if the attribute does not appear in the element, then the application using the XML document can apply whatever value (if any) it chooses.

- Keyword **#REQUIRED** indicates that the attribute must appear in the element. The XML document is not valid if the attribute is missing.

- An attribute declaration with default value **#FIXED** specifies that the attribute value is constant and cannot be different in the XML document.

- Attribute types are classified as either strings (**CDATA**), tokenized or enumerated. String attribute types do not impose any constraints on attribute values—other than disallowing the **<**, **>**, **&**, **'** and **"** characters. Entity references (e.g., **<**, **>**, etc.) must be used for these characters. Tokenized attributes impose constraints on attribute values—such as which characters are permitted in an attribute name. Enumerated attributes are the most restrictive of the three types. They can take only one of the values listed in the attribute declaration.

- Four different tokenized attribute types exist: **ID**, **IDREF**, **ENTITY** and **NMTOKEN**. Tokenized attribute type **ID** uniquely identifies an element. Attributes with type **IDREF** point to elements with an **ID** attribute. A validating parser verifies that every **ID** attribute type referenced by **IDREF** is in the XML document.

- Entity attributes indicate that an attribute has an entity for its value and are specified using tokenized attribute type **ENTITY**. The primary constraint placed on **ENTITY** attribute types is that they must refer to external unparsed entities.

- Attribute type **ENTITIES** may also be used in a DTD to indicate that an attribute has multiple entities for its value. Each entity is separated by a space.

- A more restrictive attribute type is attribute type **NMTOKEN** (name token), whose value consists of letters, digits, periods, underscores, hyphens and colon characters.

- Attribute type **NMTOKENS** may contain multiple string tokens separated by spaces.

- Enumerated attribute types declare a list of possible values an attribute can have. The attribute must be assigned a value from this list to conform to the DTD. Enumerated type values are separated by pipe characters (**|**).

- **NOTATION** is also an enumerated attribute type. Notations provide information that an application using the XML document can use to handle unparsed entities.

- Keyword **NDATA** indicates that the content of this external entity is not XML. The name of the notation that handles this unparsed entity is placed to the right of **NDATA**.

- DTDs provide the ability to include or exclude declarations using conditional sections. Keyword **INCLUDE** specifies that declarations are included, while keyword **IGNORE** specifies that declarations are excluded. Conditional sections are often used with entities.

- Parameter entities are preceded by percent (**%**) characters and can be used only inside the DTD in which they are declared. Parameter entities allow document authors to create entities specific to a DTD—not an XML document.

- Whitespace is either preserved or normalized, depending on the context in which it is used. Spaces in CDATA are preserved. Attributes values with tokenized attribute types **ID**, **NMTOKEN** and enumeration are normalized.

TERMINOLOGY

ANY	**CDATA**
application	character data type
ATTLIST statement	child elements
attribute	comma character
attribute content	conditional section
attribute declaration	content specification
attribute default	content specification type
attribute list	declaration
attribute name	default value of an attribute
attribute value	**DOCTYPE** (document type declaration)
asterisk (*****)	document type declaration

Document Type Definition (DTD)
double quote (**"**)
DTD (Document Type Definition)
EBNF (Extended Backus-Naur Form) grammar
.dtd extension
ELEMENT statement
element
element content
element name
element type declaration (**!ELEMENT**)
EMPTY
empty element
ENTITIES
entity attributes
ENTITY tokenized attribute type
enumerated attribute type
Extended Backus-Naur Form (EBNF) grammar
external subset
external unparsed entity
#FIXED
fixed value
general entity
generic identifier
hyphen (**-**)
type
ID tokenized attribute type
IDREF tokenized attribute type
IGNORE
#IMPLIED
INCLUDE
internal subset
mixed content
mixed content element
mixed content type
NDATA

NMTOKEN tokenized attribute type (name token)
non-valid document
nonvalidating parser
normalization
NOTATION
notation type
occurrence indicator
optional elements
parameter entity
parsed character data
parser
#PCDATA
percent sign (**%**)
period
pipe character (**|**)
plus sign (**+**)
question mark (**?**)
quote (**'**)
#REQUIRED
schema
sequence (**,**)
standalone XML document
string attribute type
string token
structural definition
syntax
SYSTEM
text
tokenized attribute type
valid document
validating parser
validation
well-formed document
whitespace character

SELF-REVIEW EXERCISES

6.1   State whether the following are *true* or *false*. If the answer is *false*, explain why.

a) The document type declaration, **DOCTYPE**, introduces DTDs in XML documents.

b) External DTDs are specified by using the keyword **EXTERNAL**.

c) A DTD can contain either internal or external subsets of declarations, but not both.

d) Child elements are declared in parentheses, inside an element type declaration.

e) An element that appears any number of times is followed by an exclamation point (**!**).

f) A mixed content element can contain text as well as other declared elements.

g) An attribute declared as type **CDATA** can contain all characters except for the asterisk (*****) and pound sign (**#**) characters.

h) Each element attribute of type **ID** must have a unique value.

i) Enumerated attribute types are the most restrictive category of attribute types.

j) An enumerated attribute type requires a default value.

6.2   Fill in the blanks in each of the following statements:

a) The set of document type declarations inside an XML document is called the _____.

b) Elements are declared with the _____ type declaration.

c) Keyword _____ indicates that an element contains parsable character data.

d) In an element type declaration, the pipe character (|) indicates that the element can contain _____ of the elements indicated.

e) Attributes are declared by using the _____ type.

f) Keyword _____ specifies that the attribute can only take a specific value that has been defined in the DTD.

g) **ID**, **IDREF**, _____ and **NMTOKEN** are all types of tokenized attributes.

h) The **%** character is used to declare a/an _____.

i) DTD is an acronym for _____.

j) Conditional sections of DTDs are often used with _____.

ANSWERS TO SELF-REVIEW EXERCISES

6.1   a) True. b) False. External DTDs are specified using keyword **SYSTEM**. c) False. A DTD contains both the internal and external subsets. d) True. e) False. An element that appears one or zero times is specified by a question mark (**?**). f) True. g) False. An attribute declared as type **CDATA** can contain all characters except for ampersand (**&**), less than (**<**), greater than (**>**), quote (**'**) and double quotes (**"**). h) True. i) True. j) False. A default value is not required.

6.2   a) internal subset. b) **ELEMENT**. c) **PCDATA**. d) one. e) **ATTLIST**. f) **#FIXED**. g) **ENTITY**. h) parameter entity. i) Document Type Definition. j) entities.

EXERCISES

6.3   Create a DTD for Fig. 5.6 (**letter.xml**).

6.4   Create a DTD (**products.dtd**) for a retailer with the following specifications: The XML document that conforms to the DTD must contain a list of products and manufacturers. Each product should be represented by a **product** element and each manufacturer should be represented by a **manufacturer** element. Each manufacturer has a unique **ID**. Represent details like name, address, etc., as child elements of a **manufacturer** element. Each product has attributes such as product code (which is always unique), unit price, etc. Each product is classified into one of four categories: electronics, household, furniture and groceries. Each product should be related to a manufacturer described in the XML document and should be represented as an element. The product can have a model name and description as elements. [*Hint*: Relate products to manufacturers using the **IDREF** type attribute.]

6.5   Use the DTD shown in Fig. 6.16 to construct an XML document. Use the declared entities for the **authors** element. Validate your XML document against the DTD using Microsoft's XML Validator (or a similar validation program).

```
1   <!-- ex06_15.dtd: Database containing books -->
2
3   <!ELEMENT database ( book+ )>
4
5   <!ENTITY HD "Harvey Deitel">
6   <!ENTITY PD "Paul Deitel">
```

Fig. 6.16   DTD for a book database (part 1 of 2).

```
 7   <!ENTITY TN "Tem Nieto">
 8
 9   <!ENTITY % CH "( chapter, description )">
10
11   <!ELEMENT book ( author+, image*, content+, newchapters* )>
12   <!ATTLIST book bookID ID #REQUIRED>
13
14   <!ELEMENT author ( #PCDATA )>
15
16   <!ELEMENT image ( #PCDATA )>
17
18   <!ELEMENT content %CH; >
19
20   <!ELEMENT newchapters %CH; >
21   <!ATTLIST newchapters added ( true | false ) "false">
22
23   <!ELEMENT chapter ( #PCDATA )>
24   <!ATTLIST chapter number CDATA #REQUIRED>
25
26   <!ELEMENT description ( section*, resources*, summary? )>
27
28   <!ELEMENT section ( #PCDATA )>
29
30   <!ELEMENT resources ( #PCDATA )>
31
32   <!ELEMENT summary ( #PCDATA )>
```

Fig. 6.16 DTD for a book database (part 2 of 2).

6.6   Write an XML document that declares an address book containing contacts. Each contact has a name and address. An address should contain attributes for street name, state and phone number. The attribute value for state should not contain spaces. For example, **"New York"** would invalidate the XML document. The attribute value for a phone number must contain hyphens and no spaces (e.g., **978-555-1212**). Use entities for states names. [*Hint*: use **NMTOKEN**s]

6.7   Write an XML document for the DTD created in Exercise 6.6 and validate it.

6.8   Write a DTD for an XML document that stores company profiles. Each company is represented by a **company** element. Profiles must contain a **name** element and a **tour** element. Element **tour** points to a **.jpg** image or to an HTML page that relates to the company. Element **tour** should specify the type of image or document to which it points. [*Note*: The type of image should be specified by a **NOTATION** type attribute.]. Also write an XML document and validate it against this DTD.

6.9   For the preceding exercise, write an internal subset of declarations that declare the **type** attribute as enumerated. Make corresponding changes in the XML document. Observe that the internal subset overrides the external subset when declarations collide.

6.10   Briefly describe each element type declaration:
   a) `<!ELEMENT name ( firstName, middleName?, lastName )>`
   b) `<!ELEMENT test ( question, answer )*>`
   c) `<!ELEMENT discussion ( agenda, ( issues, solutions )* )>`

7

Schemas

Objectives

- To understand what a schema is.
- To understand the basic differences between DTDs and schema.
- To be able to create Microsoft XML Schema.
- To become familiar with both Microsoft XML Schema and W3C XML Schema.
- To use schema to describe elements and attributes.
- To use schema data types.

It is hard to be truly excellent, four-square in hand and foot and mind, formed without blemish.
Simonides

If you describe things as better than they are, you are considered to be romantic; if you describe things as worse than they are, you will be called a realist; and if you describe things exactly as they are, you will be thought of as a satirist.
Quentin Crisp

7.1 Introduction

In Chapter 6, we studied Document Type Definitions (DTDs). These describe an XML document's structure. DTDs are inherited from SGML. Many developers in the XML community feel DTDs are not flexible enough to meet today's programming needs. For example, DTDs cannot be manipulated (e.g., searched, transformed into different representation such as HTML, etc.) in the same manner as XML documents can because DTDs are not XML documents.

In this chapter, we introduce an alternative to DTDs—called *schemas*—for validating XML documents. Like DTDs, schemas must be used with validating parsers. Schemas are expected to replace DTDs as the primary means of describing document structure.

Two major schema models exist: *W3C XML Schema* and *Microsoft XML Schema*. Because W3C XML Schema technology is still in the early stages of development, we focus primarily on the well-developed Microsoft XML Schema in this chapter. [*Note*: New schema models (e.g., *RELAX*—**www.xml.gr.jp/relax**) are beginning to emerge.]

At the end of this chapter, we continue enhancing the day-planner case study by writing a Microsoft XML Schema for it.

Software Engineering Observation 7.1

Schema documents use XML syntax and are therefore XML documents.

Software Engineering Observation 7.2

Schemas are XML documents that conform to DTDs, which define the structure of a schema. These DTDs are bundled with the parser and are used to validate the schemas that authors create.

Software Engineering Observation 7.3

Many organizations and individuals are creating DTDs and schemas for a broad range of categories (e.g., financial transactions, medical prescriptions, etc.). These collections—called repositories—*are often available free for download from the Web (see Section 7.8, Internet and World Wide Web Resources).*

7.2 Schema vs. DTDs

In this section, we highlight a few major differences between XML Schema and DTDs. A DTD describes an XML document's structure—not its element content. For example,

```
<quantity>5</quantity>
```

contains character data. Element **quantity** can be validated to confirm that it does indeed contain content (e.g., **PCDATA**), but its content cannot be validated to confirm that it is numeric; DTDs do not provide such a capability. So, unfortunately, markup such as

```
<quantity>hello</quantity>
```

is also considered valid. The application using the XML document containing this markup would need to test if **quantity** is numeric and take appropriate action if it is not.

With XML Schema, element **quantity**'s data can indeed be described as numeric. When the preceding markup examples are validated against an XML Schema that specifies element **quantity**'s data must be numeric, **5** conforms and **hello** fails. An XML document that conforms to a schema document is *schema valid* and a document that does not conform is *invalid*.

Software Engineering Observation 7.4

Because schema are XML documents that conform to DTDs, they must be valid.

Unlike DTDs, schema do not use the Extended Backus-Naur Form (EBNF) grammar. Instead, schema use XML syntax. Because schema are XML documents, they can be manipulated (e.g., elements added, elements removed, etc.) like any other XML document. In Chapter 8, we discuss how to manipulate XML documents programmatically.

In the next section, we begin our discussion of Microsoft XML Schema. We discuss several key schema elements and attributes, which are used in the chapter examples. We also present our first Microsoft XML Schema document and use *Microsoft's XML Validator* to check it for validity. XML Validator also validates documents against DTDs as well as schema.

7.3 Microsoft XML Schema: Describing Elements

Elements are the primary building blocks used to create XML documents. In Microsoft XML Schema, element **ElementType** defines an element. **ElementType** contains attributes that describe the element's content, data type, name, etc.

Portability Tip 7.1

To use Microsoft XML Schema, Microsoft's XML parser (msxml) is required; this parser is part of Internet Explorer 5.

Fig. 7.1 presents a complete schema. This schema describes the structure for an XML document that marks up messages passed between users. We name the schema **intro-schema.xml**. In Fig. 7.2, we show a document that conforms to this schema.

```
1    <?xml version = "1.0"?>
2
3    <!-- Fig. 7.2 : intro-schema.xml              -->
4    <!-- Microsoft XML Schema showing the ElementType -->
5    <!-- element and element element               -->
6
7    <Schema xmlns = "urn:schemas-microsoft-com:xml-data">
8       <ElementType name = "message" content = "textOnly"
9          model = "closed">
10          <description>Text messages</description>
11       </ElementType>
12
13       <ElementType name = "greeting" model = "closed"
14          content = "mixed" order = "many">
15          <element type = "message"/>
16       </ElementType>
17
18       <ElementType name = "myMessage" model = "closed"
19          content = "eltOnly" order = "seq">
20
21          <element type = "greeting" minOccurs = "0"
22             maxOccurs = "1"/>
23          <element type = "message" minOccurs = "1"
24             maxOccurs = "*"/>
25
26       </ElementType>
27    </Schema>
```

Fig. 7.1   Microsoft XML Schema document.

Line 7

```
<Schema xmlns = "urn:schemas-microsoft-com:xml-data">
```

declares the Microsoft XML Schema root element. Element **Schema** is the root element for every Microsoft XML Schema document. The **xmlns** attribute specifies the default namespace for the Schema element and the elements it contains. The attribute value **urn:schemas-microsoft-com:xml-data** specifies the URI for this namespace. Microsoft Schema documents always use this URI because it is recognized by msxml. Microsoft's XML parser recognizes element **Schema** and this particular namespace URI and validates the schema. Element **Schema** can contain only elements **ElementType**—for defining elements, **AttributeType**—for defining attributes and **description**—for describing the **Schema** element. We will discuss each of these elements momentarily.
    Lines 8–11

```
<ElementType name = "message" content = "textOnly"
   model = "closed">
   <description>Text messages</description>
</ElementType>
```

define element **message**, which can contain only text, because attribute **content** is *textOnly*. Attribute *model* has the value **closed** (line 9)—indicating that only elements declared in this schema are permitted in a conforming XML document. Any elements not defined in this schema would invalidate the document. We will elaborate on this when we discuss an XML document that conforms to the schema (Fig. 7.2). Element **description** contains text that describe this schema. In this particular case (line 10), we indicate in the **description** element that the **message** element we define is intended to contain **Text messages**.

Software Engineering Observation 7.5

*Element **description** provides a means for the schema author to provide information about a schema to a parser or application using the schema.*

Lines 13–16

```
<ElementType name = "greeting" model = "closed"
    content = "mixed" order = "many">
    <element type = "message"/>
</ElementType>
```

define element **greeting**. Because attribute **content** has the value **mixed**, this element can contain both elements and character data. The **order** attribute specifies the number and order of child elements a **greeting** element may contain. The value **many** indicates that any number of **message** elements and text can be contained in the **greeting** element in any order. The **element** element on line 15 indicates **message** elements (defined on lines 8–11) may be included in a **greeting** element.

Lines 18 and 19

```
<ElementType name = "myMessage" model = "closed"
    content = "eltOnly" order = "seq">
```

define element **myMessage**. The **content** attribute's value *eltOnly* specifies that the **myMessage** element can only contain elements. Attribute **order** has the value *seq*, indicating that **myMessage** child elements must occur in the sequence defined in the schema. Lines 21–24

```
<element type = "greeting" minOccurs = "0"
    maxOccurs = "1"/>
<element type = "message" minOccurs = "1"
    maxOccurs = "*"/>
```

indicate that element **myMessage** contains child elements **greeting** and **message**. These elements are **myMessage** child elements, because the **element** elements that reference them are nested inside element **myMessage**. Because the element order in element **myMessage** is set as sequential, the **greeting** element (if used) must precede all **message** elements. Attributes **minOccurs** and **maxOccurs** specify the minimum and maximum number of times the element may appear in the **myMessage** element, respectively. The value **1** for the **minOccurs** attribute (line 23) indicates that element **myMessage** must contain at least one **message** element. The value ***** for the **maxOccurs** attribute (line 24) indicates that there is no limit on the maximum number of **message** elements that may appear in **myMessage**.

Figure 7.2 shows an XML document that conforms to the schema shown in Fig. 7.1. We use Microsoft's XML Validator to check the document's conformity. It is available as a free download at

**msdn.microsoft.com/downloads/samples/internet/xml/
xml_validator/sample.asp**

Line 6

```
<myMessage xmlns = "x-schema:intro-schema.xml">
```

references the schema (Fig. 7.1) through the namespace declaration. A document using a Microsoft XML Schema uses attribute **xmlns** to reference its schema through a URI which begins with *x-schema* followed by a colon (**:**) and the name of the schema document.

```
1   <?xml version = "1.0"?>
2
3   <!-- Fig. 7.2 : intro.xml              -->
4   <!-- Introduction to Microsoft XML Schema -->
5
6   <myMessage xmlns = "x-schema:intro-schema.xml">
7
8      <greeting>Welcome to XML Schema!
9         <message>This is the first message.</message>
10     </greeting>
11
12     <message>This is the second message.</message>
13  </myMessage>
```

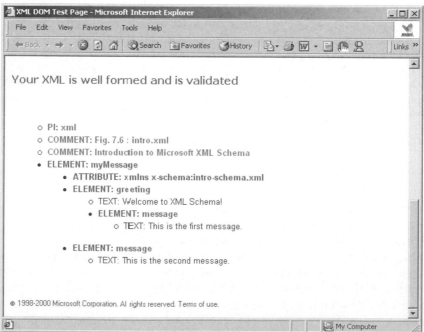

Fig. 7.2   XML document that conforms to **intro-schema.xml**.

Lines 8–10

```
<greeting>Welcome to XML Schema!
   <message>This is the first message.</message>
</greeting>
```

use element **greeting** to mark up text and a **message** element. Recall that in Fig. 7.1, element **greeting** (lines 13–16) may contain **mixed content**. Line 12

```
<message>This is the second message.</message>
```

marks up text in a **message** element. Line 8 in Fig. 7.1 specifies that element **message** can contain only text.

In the discussion of Fig. 7.1, we mentioned that a **closed model** allows an XML document to contain only those elements defined in its schema. For example, the markup

```
<greeting>Welcome to XML Schema!
   <message>This is the first message.</message>
   <newElement>A new element.</newElement>
</greeting>
```

uses element **newElement**, which is not defined in the schema. With a **closed model**, the document containing **newElement** is invalid. However, with an **open model**, the document is valid.

Software Engineering Observation 7.6

*The **open model** makes Microsoft XML Schema documents extensible by allowing authors to add elements to documents without invalidating a document.*

Figure 7.3 shows a well-formed document that fails to conform to the schema shown in Fig. 7.1, because element **message** cannot contain child elements.

Figure 7.4 lists the available attributes for the **ElementType** element. Schema authors use these attributes to specify the properties of an element, such as its content, data type, name, etc.

```
1   <?xml version = "1.0"?>
2
3   <!-- Fig. 7.3 : intro2.xml -->
4   <!-- An invalid document    -->
5
6   <myMessage xmlns = "x-schema:intro-schema.xml">
7
8      <greeting>Welcome to XML Schema!</greeting>
9
10     <message>This is a message that contains another message.
11         <message>This is the inner message.</message>
12     </message>
13
14  </myMessage>
```

Fig. 7.3   Well-formed, but invalid XML document (part 1 of 2).

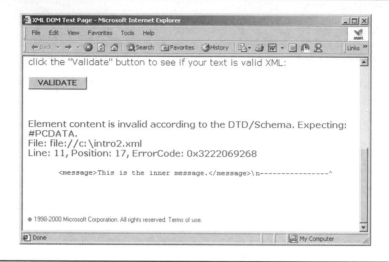

Fig. 7.3   Well-formed, but invalid XML document (part 2 of 2).

If the **content** attribute for an **ElementType** element has the value **eltOnly** or **mixed content**, the **ElementType** may only contain the elements listed in Fig. 7.5.

Attribute Name	Description
content	Describes the element's content. The valid values for this attribute are **empty** (an empty element), **eltOnly** (may contain only elements), **textOnly** (may contain only text) and **mixed** (may contain both elements and text). The default value for this attribute is **mixed**.
dt:type	Defines the element's data type. Data types exist for real numbers, integers, booleans, etc. Namespace prefix **dt** qualifies data types. We discuss data types in detail in Section 7.5.
name	The element's name. This is a required attribute.
model	Specifies whether elements not defined in the schema are permitted in the element. Valid values are **open** (the default, which permits the inclusion of elements defined outside the schema) and **closed** (only elements defined inside the schema are permitted). We use only **closed model**s.
order	Specifies the order in which child elements must occur. The valid values for this attribute are *one* (exactly one child element is permitted), **seq** (child elements must appear in the order in which they are defined) and **many** (child elements can appear in any order, any number of times). The default value is **many** if attribute **content** is **mixed** and is **seq** if attribute **content** has the value **eltOnly**.

Fig. 7.4   **ElementType** element attributes.

Element Name	Description
description	Provides a description of the **ElementType**.
datatype	Specifies the data type for the **ElementType** element. We will discuss data types in Section 7.5.
element	Specifies a child element by **name**.
group	Groups related **element** elements and defines their order and frequency.
AttributeType	Defines an attribute.
attribute	Specifies an **AttributeType** for an element.

Fig. 7.5   Element **ElementType**'s child elements.

Good Programming Practice 7.1

*Although the **ElementType** attributes have default values, explicitly writing the attribute and its value improves the schema's readability.*

The element **element** does not define an element, but rather refers to an element defined by an **ElementType**. This allows the schema author to define an element once and refer to it from many places inside the schema document. The attributes of the **element** element are listed in Fig. 7.6.

Good Programming Practice 7.2

*Although **1** is the default value for attributes **minOccurs** and **maxOccurs**, explicitly writing the attribute and its value improves the schema's readability.*

As mentioned in Fig. 7.5, element **group** creates groups of **element** elements. Groups define the order and frequency in which elements appear using the attributes listed in Fig. 7.7.

Attribute Name	Description
type	A required attribute that specifies a child element's **name** (i.e., the **name** defined in the **ElementType**).
minOccurs	Specifies the minimum number of occurrences an element can have. The valid values are **0** (the element is optional) and **1** (the element must occur one or more times). The default value is **1**.
maxOccurs	Specifies the maximum number of occurrences an element can have. The valid values are **1** (the element occurs at most once) and ***** (the element can occur any number of times). The default value is **1** unless the **ElementType**'s **content** attribute is **mixed**.

Fig. 7.6   Element **element** attributes.

Attribute Name	Description
order	Specifies the order in which the **element**s occur. The valid values are **one** (contains exactly one child element from the **group**), **seq** (all child elements must appear in the sequential order in which they are listed) and **many** (the child elements can appear in any order, any number of times).
minOccurs	Specifies the minimum number of occurrences an element can have. The valid values are **0** (the element is optional) and **1** (the element must occur at least once). The default value is **1**.
maxOccurs	Specifies the maximum number of occurrences an element can have. The valid values are **1** (the element occurs at most once) and ***** (the element can occur any number of times). The default value is **1** unless the **ElementType**'s **content** attribute is **mixed**.

Fig. 7.7 Element **group**'s attributes.

7.4 Microsoft XML Schema: Describing Attributes

XML elements can contain attributes that describe elements. In Microsoft XML Schema, element **AttributeType** defines attributes. Figure 7.8 lists **AttributeType** element attributes.

Like element **ElementType** element, element **AttributeType** may contain **description** elements and **datatype** elements.

To indicate that an element has an **AttributeType**, element **attribute** is used. The attributes of the **attribute** element are shown in Fig. 7.9.

Figure 7.10 is a schema for a contact list document that contains a person's name, address and phone number(s).

Attribute Name	Description
default	Specifies the attribute's default value.
dt:type	Defines the element's data type. Data types exist for real numbers, integers, booleans, *enumerations* (i.e., a series of values from which one can be selected), etc. Namespace prefix **dt** qualifies data types. We discuss data types in detail in Section 7.5.
dt:values	Contains an enumeration data type's values. We discuss the enumeration data type in Section 7.5.
name	The attribute name. This is a required attribute.
required	Indicates whether the attribute is required. The valid values for this attribute are **yes** and **no**. The default value is **no**.

Fig. 7.8 Element **AttributeType**'s attributes.

Attribute Name	Description
default	Specifies the attribute's default value. This value overrides the value defined in the **AttributeType** element.
type	Specifies the name of the **AttributeType** for the attribute. This is a required attribute.
required	Indicates whether the attribute is required. Valid values for this attribute are **yes** and **no**. The default value is **no**.

Fig. 7.9   Element **attribute**'s attributes.

```
1   <?xml version = "1.0"?>
2
3   <!-- Fig. 7.10 : contact-schema.xml   -->
4   <!-- Defining attributes              -->
5
6   <Schema xmlns = "urn:schemas-microsoft-com:xml-data">
7
8      <ElementType name = "contact" content = "eltOnly" order = "seq"
9         model = "closed">
10
11         <AttributeType name = "owner" required = "yes"/>
12         <attribute type = "owner"/>
13
14         <element type = "name"/>
15         <element type = "address1"/>
16         <element type = "address2" minOccurs = "0" maxOccurs = "1"/>
17         <element type = "city"/>
18         <element type = "state"/>
19         <element type = "zip"/>
20         <element type = "phone" minOccurs = "0" maxOccurs = "*"/>
21      </ElementType>
22
23      <ElementType name = "name" content = "textOnly"
24         model = "closed"/>
25
26      <ElementType name = "address1" content = "textOnly"
27         model = "closed"/>
28
29      <ElementType name = "address2" content = "textOnly"
30         model = "closed"/>
31
32      <ElementType name = "city" content = "textOnly"
33         model = "closed"/>
34
35      <ElementType name = "state" content = "textOnly"
36          model = "closed"/>
```

Fig. 7.10   Demonstrating **AttributeType** and **attribute** (part 1 of 2).

```
37
38      <ElementType name = "zip" content = "textOnly" model = "closed"/>
39
40      <ElementType name = "phone" content = "textOnly" model = "closed">
41         <AttributeType name = "location" default = "home"/>
42         <attribute type = "location"/>
43      </ElementType>
44
45   </Schema>
```

Fig. 7.10 Demonstrating **AttributeType** and **attribute** (part 2 of 2).

Line 6

```
<Schema xmlns = "urn:schemas-microsoft-com:xml-data">
```

specifies the default namespace for the URI.
Lines 11 and 12

```
<AttributeType name = "owner" required = "yes"/>
<attribute type = "owner"/>
```

define the **contact** element attribute **owner**. The **AttributeType** element (line 11) defines the properties of the attribute (e.g., its **name**). An **attribute** element creates an attribute with a specific **AttributeType** for an element. The name of the **AttributeType** is referenced in the **type** attribute of the **attribute** element (line 12). In this particular case, line 12 indicates that element **contact** has an **owner** attribute.
Lines 40–43

```
<ElementType name = "phone" content = "textOnly" model =
"closed">
   <AttributeType name = "location" default = "home"/>
   <attribute type = "location"/>
</ElementType>
```

define element **phone**, which can contain **textOnly** and has one attribute named **location**. If **location** is omitted, **"home"** is the **default**.
An XML document that conforms to the contact list schema (Fig. 7.10) is shown in Fig. 7.11.

```
1   <?xml version = "1.0"?>
2
3   <!-- Fig. 7.11 : contact.xml          -->
4   <!-- A contact list marked up as XML -->
5
6   <contact owner = "Bob Smith" xmlns = "x-schema:contact-schema.xml">
7      <name>Jane Doe</name>
8      <address1>123 Main St.</address1>
9      <city>Sometown</city>
```

Fig. 7.11 Contact list that conforms to **contact-schema.xml** (part 1 of 2).

```
10      <state>Somestate</state>
11      <zip>12345</zip>
12      <phone>617-555-1234</phone>
13      <phone location = "work">978-555-4321</phone>
14   </contact>
```

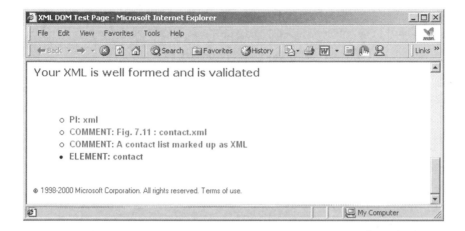

Fig. 7.11   Contact list that conforms to **contact-schema.xml** (part 2 of 2).

7.5 Microsoft XML Schema: Data Types

One important schema feature is the ability to indicate the type of content an element or attribute contains—something not possible with DTDs, which treat element and attribute content as text.

To use data types, namespace prefix **dt** is defined (by the document author) and assigned the URI ***urn:schemas-microsoft-com:datatypes***. A wide variety of data types exists, some of which are listed in Fig. 7.12. For a complete list of data types visit

      msdn.microsoft.com/xml/reference/schema/datatypes.asp

Good Programming Practice 7.3

*By convention, Microsoft XML Schema authors use namespace prefix **dt** when referring to the URI **urn:schemas-microsoft-com:datatypes**.*

Data Type	Description
boolean	**0** (false) or **1** (true).
char	A single character (e.g., **"D"**).
string	A series of characters (e.g., **"Deitel"**).

Fig. 7.12   Some Microsoft XML Schema data types (part 1 of 2).

Data Type	Description
`float`	A real number (e.g., **123.4567890**).
`int`	A whole number (e.g., **5**).
`date`	A date formatted as **YYYY-MM-DD** (e.g., **2000-04-25**).
`time`	A time formatted as **HH-MM-SS** (e.g., **14:30:00**).
`id`	Text that uniquely identifies an element or attribute.
`idref`	A reference to an **id**.
`enumeration`	A series of values from which only one may be chosen.

Fig. 7.12   Some Microsoft XML Schema data types (part 2 of 2).

Figure 7.13 is a schema for an XML document containing book shipping information.

```
1    <?xml version = "1.0"?>
2
3    <!-- Fig. 7.13 : id-schema.xml    -->
4    <!-- Using datatype ID            -->
5
6    <Schema xmlns = "urn:schemas-microsoft-com:xml-data"s
7            xmlns:dt = "urn:schemas-microsoft-com:datatypes">
8
9       <ElementType name = "bookstore" content = "eltOnly"
10         order = "many" model = "closed">
11
12         <element type = "shipping"/>
13         <element type = "book"/>
14      </ElementType>
15
16      <ElementType name = "shipping" content = "eltOnly" order = "seq"
17         model = "closed">
18
19         <AttributeType name = "shipID" dt:type = "id"
20            required = "yes"/>
21         <attribute type = "shipID"/>
22
23         <element type = "duration"/>
24      </ElementType>
25
26      <ElementType name = "duration" content = "textOnly"
27         model = "closed" dt:type = "date"/>
28
29      <ElementType name = "book" content = "textOnly" model = "closed"
30         dt:type = "string">
31
```

Fig. 7.13   Using Microsoft XML Schema data types (part 1 of 2).

```
32              <AttributeType name = "shippedBy" dt:type = "idref"/>
33              <attribute type = "shippedBy"/>
34          </ElementType>
35
36     </Schema>
```

Fig. 7.13   Using Microsoft XML Schema data types (part 2 of 2).

Lines 19 and 20

```
<AttributeType name = "shipID" dt:type = "id"
    required = "yes"/>
```

assigns attribute **dt:type** the value **id**. This defines attribute **shipID** as the unique identifier for element **shipping**.

Lines 29 and 30

```
<ElementType name = "book" content = "textOnly" model = "closed"
    dt:type = "string">
```

define **element book**, which can contain only text. This element's **content** has data type **string**. Line 32

```
<AttributeType name = "shippedBy" dt:type = "idref"/>
```

specifies attribute **shippedBy**'s data type as **idref**—which indicates that attribute **shippedBy** must be assigned an attribute declared with type **id**.

Figure 7.14 shows an XML document that conforms to Fig. 7.13's schema.

```
1   <?xml version = "1.0"?>
2
3   <!-- Fig. 7.14 : id.xml            -->
4   <!-- Demonstrating ID and IDREF    -->
5
6   <bookstore xmlns = "x-schema:id-schema.xml">
7      <shipping shipID = "s1">
8         <duration>2000-08-01</duration>
9      </shipping>
10
11     <shipping shipID = "s2">
12        <duration>2000-08-20</duration>
13     </shipping>
14
15     <book shippedBy = "s1">
16        Java How to Program 3rd edition.
17     </book>
18
19     <book shippedBy = "s2">
20        C How to Program 3rd edition.
21     </book>
```

Fig. 7.14   XML document conforming to **id-schema.xml** (part 1 of 2).

```
22
23      <book shippedBy = "s2">
24         C++ How to Program 3rd edition.
25      </book>
26   </bookstore>
```

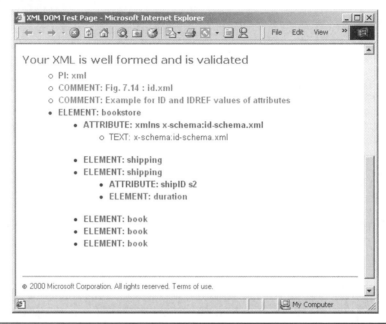

Fig. 7.14   XML document conforming to **id-schema.xml** (part 2 of 2).

Lines 7–13 contain two **shipping** elements with the unique identifiers **s1** and **s2**.
Each of these elements contains a **duration** element that marks up a date. The **book** elements (lines 15–25) use the **shippedBy** attribute to reference the unique identifiers **s1**
and **s2**. Recall that the schema requires attribute **shippedBy** to have an **idref** data type.

Figure 7.15 shows the result of validating the XML document of Fig. 7.14 when
shippedBy is assigned a value other than **s1** or **s2**.

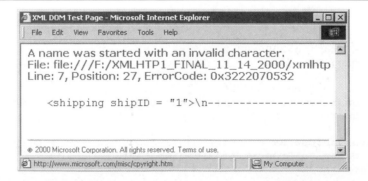

Fig. 7.15   Invalid XML document.

Figure 7.16 presents another schema that might be used to validate a document that marks up a book retailer's inventory. In this example, every element (e.g., **name**, **price**, etc.) that contains character data has a data type. Element **book** (line 14) has attributes **isbn** and **inStock**. Attribute **inStock** (line 21) is an **enumeration**, which is assigned either **yes** or **no**. The value **no** is the **default**.

```
1   <?xml version = "1.0"?>
2
3   <!-- Fig. 7.16 : inventory-schema.xml   -->
4   <!-- Data type example                  -->
5
6   <Schema xmlns = "urn:schemas-microsoft-com:xml-data"
7           xmlns:dt = "urn:schemas-microsoft-com:datatypes">
8
9      <ElementType name = "inventory" content = "eltOnly"
10        model = "closed">
11        <element type = "book" minOccurs = "0" maxOccurs = "*"/>
12     </ElementType>
13
14     <ElementType name = "book" content = "eltOnly" order = "seq"
15        model = "closed">
16
17        <AttributeType name = "isbn" dt:type = "string"
18           required = "yes"/>
19        <attribute type = "isbn"/>
20
21        <AttributeType name = "inStock" dt:type = "enumeration"
22           dt:values = "yes no" default = "no"/>
23        <attribute type = "inStock"/>
24
25        <element type = "name"/>
26        <element type = "price"/>
27
28        <group order = "one">
29           <element type = "quantity"/>
30           <element type = "available"/>
31        </group>
32     </ElementType>
33
34     <ElementType name = "name" content = "textOnly" model = "closed"
35        dt:type = "string"/>
36
37     <ElementType name = "price" content = "textOnly" model = "closed"
38        dt:type = "float"/>
39
40     <ElementType name = "quantity" content = "textOnly"
41        dt:type = "int" model = "closed"/>
42
43     <ElementType name = "available" content = "textOnly"
44        dt:type = "date" model = "closed"/>
45  </Schema>
```

Fig. 7.16   Schema for an inventory document.

Lines 28–31

```
<group order = "one">
   <element type = "quantity"/>
   <element type = "available"/>
</group>
```

group elements **quantity** and **available**. Only **one** of these two elements can be used in a **book** element—not both. A **book** element must contain either **quantity** or **available**, indicating that books are either in stock or available on a certain date.

Figure 7.17 shows an XML document that conforms to the schema shown in Fig. 7.16.

```
1   <?xml version = "1.0"?>
2
3   <!-- Fig. 7.17 : inventory.xml   -->
4   <!-- Data type example           -->
5
6   <inventory xmlns = "x-schema:inventory-schema.xml">
7      <book isbn = "0-13-012507-5" inStock = "yes">
8         <name>Java How to Program 3/e</name>
9         <price>68.00</price>
10        <quantity>200</quantity>
11     </book>
12
13     <book isbn = "0-13-028418-1" inStock = "no">
14        <name>Perl How to Program</name>
15        <price>68.00</price>
16        <available>2000-12-15</available>
17     </book>
18  </inventory>
```

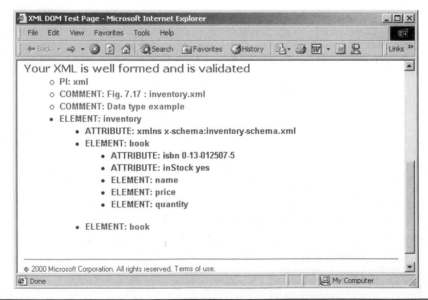

Fig. 7.17 XML document conforming to **inventory-schema.xml**.

The first **book** (lines 7–11) in the **inventory** has **200** books in stock. The second **book** (lines 13–17) is not in stock, but will be **available** on December 15, 2000.

For additional information about Microsoft XML Schema, visit

msdn.microsoft.com/xml/reference/schema/start.asp

7.6 W3C XML Schema

The W3C is developing an XML Schema specification, which is a *Candidate Recommendation* (i.e., the last step in the recommendation process) at the time of this writing. For the latest specification of W3C XML Schema, visit **www.w3.org/XML/Schema**. [*Note*: Because W3C XML Schema was only a Candidate Recommendation at the time of this writing, the syntax presented here is subject to change.]

Figure 7.18 shows the equivalent W3C XML Schema (i.e., **xml-schema.xsd**) of the Microsoft XML Schema (i.e., **intro-schema.xml**) in Fig. 7.5. Although virtually any filename extension may be used, Microsoft XML Schema documents commonly use the **.xml** extension and W3C XML Schema commonly use the **.xsd** extension.

W3C XML Schema use the URI **http://www.w3.org/2000/10/XMLSchema** and *namespace prefix **xsd***. Root element **schema** contains the document definitions.

In W3C XML Schema, element **element** (line 7) defines elements. Attributes **name** and **type** specify the **element**'s name and data type, respectively. Attribute **ref** (line 12) references the existing element definition for **message**. This indicates that **greeting** can have element **message** as a child element.

```
1    <?xml version = "1.0"?>
2
3    <!-- Figure 7.20 : xml-schema.xsd -->
4    <!-- Example W3C XML Schema        -->
5
6    <xsd:schema xmlns:xsd = "http://www.w3.org/2000/10/XMLSchema">
7       <xsd:element name = "message" type = "xsd:string"/>
8
9       <xsd:element name = "greeting" type = "greetingType"/>
10
11      <xsd:complexType name = "greetingType" content = "mixed">
12         <xsd:element ref = "message"/>
13      </xsd:complexType>
14
15      <xsd:element name = "myMessage" type = "myMessageType"/>
16
17      <xsd:complexType name = "myMessageType">
18         <xsd:element ref = "greeting" minOccurs = "0"
19            maxOccurs = "1"/>
20         <xsd:element ref = "message" minOccurs = "1"
21            maxOccurs = "unbounded"/>
22      </xsd:complexType>
23   </xsd:schema>
```

Fig. 7.18   W3C XML Schema document.

When an element has a type such as **string**, it is prohibited from containing attributes and child elements. Any element (e.g., **greeting** in line 9) that contains attributes or child elements, must define a type—called a *complex type*—that defines each attribute and child element. Lines 11–13 use element **complexType** to define an element type that has **mixed content**. The **element** named **greeting** (line 9) specifies the **name** of this **complexType** in its **type** attribute to indicate element **greeting** contains mixed content.

Lines 17–22 use element **complexType** to create an element that contains an optional **greeting** element followed by one or more **message** elements. Attribute **maxOccurs** with the value **unbounded** (line 21) indicates that there is no limit on the maximum number of **message** elements contained in a **myMessage** element.

Figure 7.19 shows an XML document that conforms to Fig. 7.18's schema. We use Icon Information-Systems' XML development environment (*XML Spy 3.0*) for validation.

```
1   <?xml version = "1.0"?>
2
3   <!-- Fig. 7.19 : intro3.xml            -->
4   <!-- Introduction to W3C XML Schema    -->
5
6   <myMessage
7      xmlns:xsd   = "http://www.w3.org/2000/10/XMLSchema-instance"
8      xsd:noNamespaceSchemaLocation = "xml-schema.xsd">
9
10     <greeting>Welcome to W3C XML Schema!</greeting>
11     <message>This is a message.</message>
12     <message>This is another message.</message>
13
14  </myMessage>
```

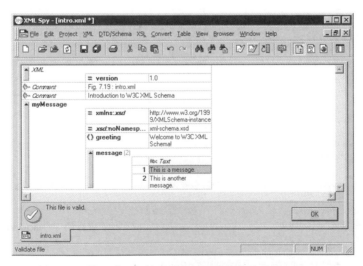

(Courtesy of Icon Information Systems.)

Fig. 7.19 Document that conforms to **xml-schema.xsd**

A 30-day trial version of XML Spy 3.0 is available at no charge from **www.xmlspy.com/download.html**. [*Note*: In Chapter 8, we introduce Apache's *Xerces parser,* which also validates an XML document against a W3C Schema.]

Software Engineering Observation 7.7

Independent Software Venders (ISVs) such as Oracle, Apache Foundation Organization, etc. are beginning to provide parsers that support W3C XML Schema.

Good Programming Practice 7.4

*By convention, W3C XML Schema authors use namespace prefix **xsd** when referring to the URI **http://www.w3.org/2000/10/XMLSchema.***

7.7 Case Study: Writing a Microsoft XML Schema for the Day Planner Application

Figure 7.20 is a Microsoft XML Schema for the day planner introduced in Chapter 5.

```
1   <?xml version = "1.0"?>
2
3   <!-- Fig. 7.20 : planner-schema.xml      -->
4   <!-- Microsoft XML Schema for day planner -->
5
6   <Schema xmlns = "urn:schemas-microsoft-com:xml-data"
7           xmlns:dt = "urn:schemas-microsoft-com:datatypes">
8
9      <ElementType name = "planner" content = "eltOnly"
10        model = "closed">
11        <element type = "year" minOccurs = "0" maxOccurs = "*"/>
12     </ElementType>
13
14     <ElementType name = "year" content = "eltOnly" model = "closed">
15        <AttributeType name = "value" dt:type = "int"/>
16        <attribute type = "value"/>
17        <element type = "date" minOccurs = "0" maxOccurs = "*"/>
18     </ElementType>
19
20     <ElementType name = "date" content = "eltOnly" model = "closed">
21        <AttributeType name = "month" dt:type = "int"/>
22        <attribute type = "month"/>
23
24        <AttributeType name = "day" dt:type = "int"/>
25        <attribute type = "day"/>
26
27        <element type = "note" minOccurs = "0" maxOccurs = "*"/>
28     </ElementType>
29
30     <ElementType name = "note" content = "textOnly" model = "closed"
31        dt:type = "string">
32
33        <AttributeType name = "time" dt:type = "int"/>
34        <attribute type = "time"/>
35     </ElementType>
```

Fig. 7.20 Microsoft XML Schema for **dayplanner.xml** (part 1 of 2).

```
36
37   </Schema>
```

Fig. 7.20   Microsoft XML Schema for **dayplanner.xml** (part 2 of 2).

Because years, months and days are whole number values, they are defined as **int**s in lines 15, 21 and 24, respectively. We also define **time** (line 33), which stores the time as an **int**. We do not use the **date** or **time** data types because we use our own format (i.e., **int**) for dates and times.

Figure 7.21 shows an XML document that conforms to the Microsoft XML Schema of Fig. 7.20.

7.8 Internet and World Wide Web Resources

msdn.microsoft.com/xml/xmlguide/schema-overview.asp
The *Microsoft Schema Developer's Guide* provides an extensive coverage of schemas from a basic introduction to advanced definitions and uses.

msdn.microsoft.com/xml/reference/schema/start.asp
The *Microsoft XML Schema Reference* contains an introduction to schema.

```
1    <?xml version = "1.0"?>
2
3    <!-- Fig. 7.21 : planner.xml    -->
4    <!-- Day Planner XML document   -->
5
6    <planner xmlns = "x-schema:planner-schema.xml">
7       <year value = "2000">
8          <date month = "7" day = "15">
9             <note time = "1430">Doctor&apos;s appointment</note>
10            <note time = "1620">Physics class at BH291C</note>
11         </date>
12
13         <date month = "7" day = "4">
14            <note>Independance Day</note>
15         </date>
16
17         <date month = "7" day = "20">
18            <note time = "0900">General Meeting in room 32-A</note>
19         </date>
20
21         <date month = "7" day = "20">
22            <note time = "1900">Party at Joe&apos;s</note>
23         </date>
24
25         <date month = "7" day = "20">
26            <note time = "1300">Financial Meeting in room 14-C</note>
27         </date>
28      </year>
29   </planner>
```

Fig. 7.21   Day planner XML document that conforms to Fig. 7.20 (part 1 of 2).

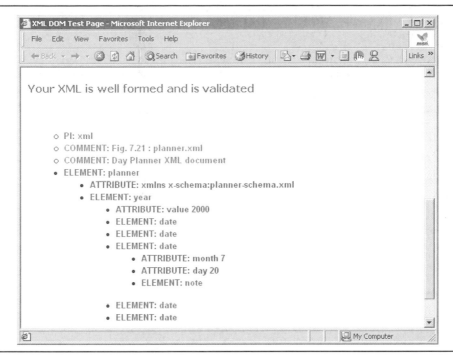

Fig. 7.21   Day planner XML document that conforms to Fig. 7.20 (part 2 of 2).

**msdn.microsoft.com/downloads/samples/internet/xml/xml_validator/
sample.asp**
The *Microsoft XML Schema Validator* can be used with both schemas and DTDs.

msdn.microsoft.com/xml/reference/schema/datatypes.asp
Provides a list of Microsoft XML Schema data types.

www.w3.org/XML/Schema
The *W3C XML Schema Primer* provides a succinct introduction to W3C XML Schemas.

www.DTD.com
Provides a schema/DTD repository for a wide range of technologies. Provides a Web-based program named *DTDFactory* from which DTDs can be created, edited and saved to disk. DTDFactory allows DTD authors to submit DTDs they create to the repository. In the future, a Web-based program named *SchemaFactory* will be implemented for creating and editing W3C Schema.

www.xmlspy.com/download.html
Download for XML Spy 3.0 development environment. A 30-day trial version is available at this site.

www.extensibility.com
Home page for the *XML Authority* W3C Schema and DTD editor.

www.xmlschema.com
Provides various resources for creating and validating W3C schema.

SUMMARY

- A DTD cannot be manipulated (e.g., searched, transformed into a different representation such as HTML, etc.) in the same manner as an XML document—because it is not an XML document.

- XML schemas are an alternative for validating XML documents. DTDs and schemas need validating parsers. Schemas are an emerging technology that is expected to eventually replace DTDs as the primary means of describing XML document structure.

- Two major schema models exist: W3C XML Schema and Microsoft XML Schema. W3C XML Schema is still in the early stages of development; Microsoft XML Schema is well defined.

- An XML document that conforms to a schema document is schema valid; a document that does not conform is *invalid*.

- Schema do not use the Extended Backus-Naur Form (EBNF) grammar, but use XML syntax and can be manipulated (e.g., elements can be added, removed, etc.) as with any other XML document.

- Elements are the primary building blocks used to create XML documents. In Microsoft XML Schema, element **ElementType** defines elements. Because it is an element, **ElementType** may contain attributes that describe the element's content, data type, name, etc.

- Element **element** does not define an element, but rather refers to an element defined by **ElementType**. This allows the schema author to define an element once and refer to it from potentially many places inside the schema document.

- Element **Schema** is the root element for every Microsoft XML Schema document. Keyword **xmlns** specifies the namespace (i.e., **urn:schemas-microsoft-com:xml-data**) used by **Schema** and its child elements.

- Microsoft's XML parser automatically recognizes element **Schema** and its namespace URI, and validates the schema. Element **Schema** can contain elements **ElementType**—for defining elements, **AttributeType**—for defining attributes and **description**—for describing the **Schema** element.

- Attribute **content** specifies the content allowed in an element or attribute.

- Attribute **model** specifies whether elements can contain elements not defined in the schema. Any elements not defined in the schema invalidate the document. Assigning **model** a value of **open** indicates that definitions not defined in the schema are permitted. Assigning **model** a value of **closed** specifies that elements defined only in the schema are permitted.

- Element **description** contains any text the document author chooses to describe the schema document.

- When attribute **content** is **mixed**, an element can contain both elements and character data.

- When attribute **order** is assigned **many**, any number of child elements and text can be combined—in any order.

- When attribute **order** is assigned **seq**, child elements must occur in sequential order.

- A document using a Microsoft XML Schema references the schema through a URI that begins with *x-schema*, followed by a colon (**:**) and the name of the schema document.

- XML elements can contain attributes that provide additional information for describing elements. In Microsoft XML Schema, element **AttributeType** defines attributes.

- Element **AttributeType** can contain **description** elements and **datatype** elements.

- To indicate that an element has an **AttributeType**, element **attribute** is used.

- One important schema feature is the ability to indicate the type of content an element or attribute has—something not possible with DTDs, which treat content as text.

- To use data types in Microsoft XML Schema, namespace prefix **dt** is defined and assigned the URI **urn:schemas-microsoft-com:datatypes**. A wide variety of data types exists.

- The W3C is developing an XML Schema specification, which is at the time of this writing a W3C Candidate Recommendation.

- Although virtually any extension may be used, Microsoft XML Schema documents commonly use the **.xml** extension and W3C XML Schema documents commonly use the **.xsd** extension.

- W3C XML Schema use the URI **http://www.w3.org/2000/10/XMLSchema** and namespace prefix **xsd**. Root element **schema** contains the document definitions.

- In W3C XML Schema documents, element **element** defines elements. Attributes **name** and **type** specify the **element**'s name and data type, respectively. Attribute **ref** references an existing element definition.

- When an element has a type such as string (in W3C XML Schema), it is prohibited from containing attributes and child elements. Any element that contains attributes or child elements, must define a type—called a complex type—that defines each attribute and child element.

TERMINOLOGY

attribute
attribute element
AttributeType element
boolean
char
character
character string
child element
closed
complexType element
content order
contents
data types
default namespace
default value
description element
document type definition (DTD)
dt namespace prefix
dt:type
dt:values
element element
element type
ElementType element
eltOnly
empty
empty element
enumeration
group
http://www.w3.org/2000/10/
   XMLSchema URI
id
idref
int
integer

invalid
many
maximum occurrence
maxOccurs
Microsoft XML Schema
Microsoft XML Validator
minimum occurrence
minOccurs
mixed
model
name attribute of **ElementType** element
notation
NOTATION type
real number
repositories
required attribute
root element
Schema element in Microsoft XML Schema
schema element in W3C XML Schema
schema valid
seq
string
text data
textOnly
time
type
urn:schemas-microsoft-
   com:datatypes
urn:schemas-microsoft-com:xml-
   data
W3C Candidate Recommendation
x-schema URI prefix
.xsd filename extension
xsd namespace prefix

SELF-REVIEW EXERCISES

7.1   State whether the following are *true* or *false*. If *false*, explain why.
   a) Web site authors can define data types and constraints for the contents of an element using schemas.
   b) An application can use a schema to validate a document's contents, but not its structure.
   c) Microsoft XML Schema provide a means for defining the structure of HTML documents.
   d) The element **ElementType** is used to define elements using a Microsoft XML Schema.
   e) The **collect** element is used to group a set of **element** elements together.
   f) The **AttributeType** element defines an attribute type, which is referred to by the **attribute** element.
   g) An enumeration is a list of possible values for an attribute.
   h) Element **AttributeType** is identical to element **ElementType**, except for the fact that it cannot contain **description** elements and **datatype** elements.
   i) The **dt:type** attribute and the **datatype** element are each designed for use in specific locations in an XML document.
   j) Any parser can be used to validate an XML document against a Microsoft W3C Schema.

7.2   Fill in the blanks in each of the following statements.
   a) If the content of a document conforms to a schema, then the document is said to be _____.
   b) The root element of a Microsoft XML Schema document is the _____ element.
   c) Element **Schema** can contain **ElementType**, **AttributeType** and _____ elements.
   d) Valid values for **ElementType**'s **content** attribute include **empty**, **eltOnly**, _____ and _____.
   e) Element _____ is the root element for all W3C Schema documents.
   f) Element **element**'s _____ attribute specifies the maximum occurrences a child element can have.
   g) Attributes can be created in Microsoft XML schema using the _____ element.
   h) In Microsoft Schema documents, namespace prefix **dt** is defined with the URI **uri:schemas-microsoft-com:**_____.
   i) Data type _____ indicates a real number, like 5.3672887.
   j) Element **AttributeType**'s _____ attribute contains enumeration values.

ANSWERS TO SELF-REVIEW EXERCISES

7.1   a) True. b) False. An application can use a schema to validate the contents of an XML document, in addition to the document's structure. c) False. Microsoft XML Schema provide a means for defining the structure of XML documents. d) True. e) False. The **group** element is used to group a set of **element** elements together. f) True. g) True. h) False. Element **AttributeType** is similar to element **ElementType** in that they can both contain the **description** and **datatype** elements. i) False. The **dt:type** attribute and the **datatype** element can be used interchangeably in an element type of attribute type. j) False. Only msxml can be used.

7.2   a) schema valid. b) **Schema**. c) **description**. d) **textOnly**, **mixed**. e) **schema**. f) **maxOccurs**. g) **AttributeType**. h) **datatypes**. i) **float**. j) **dt:values**.

EXERCISES

7.3   Write a Microsoft XML Schema document for the XML document in Fig. 7.2 that would allow element **note** to be a child element of element **myMessage**. Element **note** can contain only text. Validate your document using Microsoft XML Validator.

7.4   Write a schema to validate the XML document shown in Fig. 7.22. This XML document contains information about products in a grocery store. Each product is represented by a **product** element that contains the name, manufacturer, quantity and price of the product. Each product has a unique ID and is categorized as either perishable or nonperishable. If the product is perishable, it contains a **food** element. Element **food** contains the expiration date and nutrition facts. Nutrition facts describe the amount of proteins, fats and calcium in the food. If the product is nonperishable, it contains details of the stock available in one or more warehouses. A warehouse element has a unique ID and contains a description of the warehouse, along with product stock available at the warehouse.

```
1   <?xml version = "1.0"?>
2
3   <!-- Exercise 7.4 : exer07_4.xml -->
4
5   <products xmlns = "x-schema:exer07_4-schema.xml">
6
7      <product id = "p12" perishable = "yes">
8         <name>Ice cream</name>
9         <manufacturer>xsz Co.</manufacturer>
10        <quantity>25</quantity>
11        <price>2</price>
12
13        <food>
14           <nutrition>
15              <calcium>10.30</calcium>
16              <proteins>35.5</proteins>
17              <fat>10</fat>
18           </nutrition>
19
20           <expirationDate>2000-09-12</expirationDate>
21        </food>
22     </product>
23
24     <product id = "p13" perishable = "no">
25        <name>AA Battries</name>
26        <manufacturer>DCells</manufacturer>
27        <quantity>100</quantity>
28        <price>4</price>
29
30        <stock>
31           <warehouse id = "w12">
32              xsz warehouse
33              <stock>25000</stock>
34           </warehouse>
35
36           <warehouse id = "w13">
37              rza warehouse
38              <stock>5000</stock>
39           </warehouse>
40        </stock>
41
42     </product>
43  </products>
```

Fig. 7.22 XML document containing food product information.

Document Object Model (DOM™)

Objectives

- To understand what the Document Object Model is.
- To understand and be able to use the major DOM features.
- To use JavaScript to manipulate an XML document.
- To use Java to manipulate an XML document.
- To become familiar with DOM-based parsers.

Knowing trees, I understand the meaning of patience.
Knowing grass, I can appreciate persistence.
Hal Borland

There was a child went forth every day,
And the first object he look'd upon, that object he became.
Walt Whitman

I think that I shall never see
A poem lovely as a tree.
Joyce Kilmer

8.1 Introduction

In previous chapters, we concentrated on basic XML markup and documents (e.g., DTDs and schema) for validating XML documents. In this chapter, we focus on manipulating the contents of an XML document.

XML documents, when parsed, are represented as a hierarchical tree structure in memory. This tree structure contains the document's elements, attributes, content, etc. XML was designed to be a live, dynamic technology—a programmer can modify the contents of the tree structure, which essentially allows the programmer to add data, remove data, query for data, etc. in a manner similar to a database.

The W3C provides a standard recommendation for building a tree structure in memory for XML documents called the *XML Document Object Model (DOM)*. Any parser that adheres to this recommendation is called a *DOM-based parser*. Each element, attribute, **CDATA** section, etc., in an XML document is represented by a *node* in the DOM tree. For example, the simple XML document

```
<?xml version = "1.0"?>
<message from = "Paul" to = "Tem">
   <body>Hi, Tem!</body>
</message>
```

results in a DOM tree with several nodes. One node is created for the **message** element. This node has a *child node* that corresponds to the **body** element. The **body** element also has a child node that corresponds to the text **Hi, Tem!**. The **from** and **to** attributes of the **message** element also have corresponding nodes in the DOM tree.

A DOM-based parser *exposes* (i.e., makes available) a programmatic library—called the *DOM Application Programming Interface (API)*—that allows data in an XML document to be accessed and modified by manipulating the nodes in a DOM tree.

 Portability Tip 8.1

The DOM interfaces for creating and manipulating XML documents are platform and language independent. DOM parsers exist for many different languages, including Java, C, C++, Python and Perl.

Another API—JDOM—provides a higher-level API than the W3C DOM for working with XML documents in Java. Because JDOM is an API that is specific to the Java programming language, it can take advantage of features in Java that make it easier to program. JDOM is still in the early stages of development, therefore we do not discuss it in this Chapter. Visit **www.jdom.org** for more information on the JDOM API.

In order to use the DOM API, programming experience is required. Although the DOM API is available in many languages (e.g., C, Java, VBScript, etc.), we use JavaScript and Java in this chapter. [*Note*: Chapter 27 provides a concise introduction to Java.]

8.2 DOM Implementations

DOM-based parsers are written in a variety of programming languages and are usually available for download at no charge. Many applications (such as Internet Explorer 5) have built-in parsers. Figure 8.1 lists six different DOM-based parsers that are available at no charge. In this chapter, we use Microsoft's msxml and Sun Microsystem's JAXP parsers.

8.3 DOM with JavaScript

To introduce document manipulation with the XML Document Object Model, we begin with a simple scripting example that uses JavaScript and Microsoft's msxml parser. This example takes an XML document (Fig. 8.2) that marks up an article and uses the DOM API to display the document's element names and values. Figure 8.3 lists the JavaScript code that manipulates this XML document and displays its content in an HTML page.

Line 15

```
<script type = "text/javascript" language = "JavaScript">
```

Parser	Description
JAXP	Sun Microsystem's *Java API for XML Parsing (JAXP)* is available at no charge from **java.sun.com/xml**.
XML4J	IBM's *XML Parser for Java (XML4J)* is available at no charge from **www.alphaworks.ibm.com/tech/xml4j**.
Xerces	Apache's *Xerces Java Parser* is available at no charge from **xml.apache.org/xerces**.
msxml	Microsoft's XML parser (*msxml*) version 2.0 is built-into Internet Explorer 5.5. Version 3.0 is also available at no charge from **msdn.microsoft.com/xml**.
4DOM	4DOM is a parser for the Python programming language and is available at no charge from **fourthought.com/4Suite/4DOM**.
XML::DOM	XML::DOM is a Perl module that we use in Chapter 17 to manipulate XML documents using Perl. For additional information, visit **www-4.ibm.com/software/developer/library/xml-perl2**.

Fig. 8.1   Some DOM-based parsers.

```
1    <?xml version = "1.0"?>
2
3    <!-- Fig. 8.2: article.xml        -->
4    <!-- Article formatted with XML  -->
5
6    <article>
7
8       <title>Simple XML</title>
9
10      <date>December 6, 2000</date>
11
12      <author>
13         <fname>Tem</fname>
14         <lname>Nieto</lname>
15      </author>
16
17      <summary>XML is pretty easy.</summary>
18
19      <content>Once you have mastered HTML, XML is easily
20         learned. You must remember that XML is not for
21         displaying information but for managing information.
22      </content>
23
24   </article>
```

Fig. 8.2   Article marked up with XML tags.

is the opening ***script*** tag, which allows the document author to include scripting code. Attribute **type** indicates that the **script** element is of media type ***text/javascript***. JavaScript is the most popular client-side (e.g., browser) scripting language used in industry. If the browser does not support JavaScript, **script**'s contents are treated as text. Attribute ***language*** indicates to the browser that the script is written in the ***JavaScript*** scripting language.

```
1    <!DOCTYPE html PUBLIC "-//W3C//DTD HTML 4.01//EN"
2       "http://www.w3.org/TR/html4/strict.dtd">
3
4    <html>
5
6    <!-- Fig. 8.3 : DOMExample.html -->
7    <!-- DOM with JavaScript        -->
8
9    <head>
10      <title>A DOM Example</title>
11   </head>
12
13   <body>
14
15   <script type = "text/javascript" language = "JavaScript">
16
```

Fig. 8.3   Traversing **article.xml** with JavaScript (part 1 of 3).

```
17      var xmlDocument = new ActiveXObject( "Microsoft.XMLDOM" );
18
19      xmlDocument.load( "article.xml" );
20
21      // get the root element
22      var element = xmlDocument.documentElement;
23
24      document.writeln(
25         "<p>Here is the root node of the document:" );
26      document.writeln( "<strong>" + element.nodeName
27         + "</strong>" );
28
29      document.writeln(
30         "<br>The following are its child elements:" );
31      document.writeln( "</p><ul>" );
32
33      // traverse all child nodes of root element
34      for ( i = 0; i < element.childNodes.length; i++ ) {
35         var curNode = element.childNodes.item( i );
36
37         // print node name of each child element
38         document.writeln( "<li><strong>" + curNode.nodeName
39            + "</strong></li>" );
40      }
41
42      document.writeln( "</ul>" );
43
44      // get the first child node of root element
45      var currentNode = element.firstChild;
46
47      document.writeln( "<p>The first child of root node is:" );
48      document.writeln( "<strong>" + currentNode.nodeName
49         + "</strong>" );
50      document.writeln( "<br>whose next sibling is:" );
51
52      // get the next sibling of first child
53      var nextSib = currentNode.nextSibling;
54
55      document.writeln( "<strong>" + nextSib.nodeName
56         + "</strong>." );
57      document.writeln( "<br>Value of <strong>" + nextSib.nodeName
58         + "</strong> element is:" );
59
60      var value = nextSib.firstChild;
61
62      // print the text value of the sibling
63      document.writeln( "<em>" + value.nodeValue + "</em>" );
64      document.writeln( "<br>Parent node of " );
65      document.writeln( "<strong>" + nextSib.nodeName
66         + "</strong> is:" );
67      document.writeln( "<strong>" + nextSib.parentNode.nodeName
68         + "</strong>.</p>" );
69
```

Fig. 8.3   Traversing **article.xml** with JavaScript (part 2 of 3).

```
70    </script>
71
72    </body>
73    </html>
```

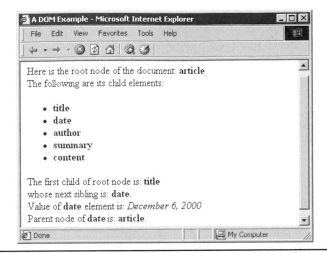

Fig. 8.3   Traversing **article.xml** with JavaScript (part 3 of 3).

Line 17

```
var xmlDocument = new ActiveXObject( "Microsoft.XMLDOM" );
```

instantiates a Microsoft XML Document Object Model object and assigns it to reference **xmlDocument**. This object represents an XML document (in memory) and provides methods for manipulating its data. The statement simply creates the object, which does not yet refer to any specific XML document.

Line 19

```
xmlDocument.load( "article.xml" );
```

calls method *load* to load **article.xml** (Fig. 8.2) into memory. This XML document is parsed by msxml and stored in memory as a tree structure.

Line 22

```
var element = xmlDocument.documentElement;
```

assigns the root element (i.e., **article**) to variable **element**. Property *documentElement* corresponds to the document's root element. The root element is important because it is used as a reference point for retrieving child elements, text, etc.

Lines 26 and 27

```
document.writeln( "<strong>" + element.nodeName
    + "</strong>" );
```

place the name of the root element in a **strong** element and write it to the browser where it is rendered. Property *nodeName* corresponds to the name of an attribute, element, etc.

which are collectively called nodes. In this particular case, **element** refers to the root node named **article**.
Line 34

```
for ( i = 0; i < element.childNodes.length; i++ ) {
```

uses a **for** loop to iterate through the root node's child nodes (accessed using property *childNodes*). Property *length* is used to get the number of child nodes of the document element.

Individual child nodes are accessed using the *item* method. Each node is given an integer index (starting at zero) based on the order in which they occur in the XML document. For example in Fig. 8.2, **title** is given the index 0, **date** is given the index 1, etc. Line 35

```
var curNode = element.childNodes.item( i );
```

calls method **item** to return the child node identified by the index **i**. This node is assigned to variable **curNode**.
Line 45

```
var currentNode = element.firstChild;
```

retrieves the root node's first child node (i.e., **title**) using property *firstChild*. This expression is a more concise alternative to

```
var currentNode = element.childNodes.item( 0 );
```

Nodes at the same level in a document (i.e., that have the same parent node) are called *siblings*. For example, **title**, **date**, **author**, **summary** and **content** are all sibling nodes. Property *nextSibling* returns a node's next sibling. Line 60

```
var nextSib = currentNode.nextSibling;
```

assigns **currentNode**'s (i.e., **title** from line 45) next sibling (i.e., **date**) to **nextSib**.

In addition to elements and attributes, text (e.g., **Simple XML** in line 8 of Fig. 8.2) is also a node. Line 60

```
var value = nextSib.firstChild;
```

assigns **nextSib**'s (i.e., **date**) first child node to **value**. In this case, the first child node is a text node. On line 63 the *nodeValue* method retrieves the value of this text node. The value of a text node's value is the text it contains. Element nodes have a value of *null* (i.e., the absence of a value).
Lines 67 and 68

```
document.writeln( "<strong>" + nextSib.parentNode.nodeName
    + "</strong>.</p>" );
```

retrieve and display **nextSib**'s (i.e., **date**) parent node (i.e., **article**). Property *parentNode* returns a node's parent node.

8.4 Setup

In successive sections, we will be using Java applications to illustrate the DOM API. This section describes the software needed to run these Java applications. To be able to compile and execute the examples, you will need to do the following:

1. Download and install the Java 2 Standard Edition from

2. **www.java.sun.com/j2se**

3. For step-by-step installation instructions, visit

4. **www.deitel.com/faq/java3install.htm**

5. Download and install JAXP from **java.sun.com/xml/download.html**. Installation instructions are provided at the Web site and HTML files are included with the download.

6. Copy the Chapter 8 examples from the CD-ROM that accompanies this book to your hard drive. These examples are also available for download free of charge from **www.deitel.com**.

As we present an example, we will discuss the steps necessary to execute it. However the steps outlined in this section must be followed before attempting to execute any example.

8.5 DOM Components

In this section, we will use Java, JAXP and the XML-related Java packages described in Fig. 8.4 to manipulate an XML document. Before discussing our first Java-based example, we summarize several important DOM classes, interfaces and methods. Due to the number of DOM objects and methods available, we provide only a partial list of these objects and methods.

For a complete list of DOM classes and interfaces, browse the HTML documentation (**index.html** in the **api** folder) included with JAXP.

Interface	Description
Document interface	Represents the XML document's top-level node, which provides access to all the document's nodes—including the root element.
Node interface	Represents an XML document node.
NodeList interface	Represents a read-only list of **Node** objects.
Element interface	Represents an element node. Derives from **Node**.
Attr interface	Represents an attribute node. Derives from **Node**.
CharacterData interface	Represents character data. Derives from **Node**.
Text interface	Represents a text node. Derives from **CharacterData**.

Fig. 8.4   DOM classes and interfaces (part 1 of 2).

Interface	Description
Comment interface	Represents a comment node. Derives from **CharacterData**.
ProcessingInstruction interface	Represents a processing instruction node. Derives from **Node**.
CDATASection interface	Represents a **CDATA** section. Derives from **Text**.

Fig. 8.4   DOM classes and interfaces (part 2 of 2).

The **Document** interface represents the top-level node of an XML document in memory and provides a means of creating nodes and retrieving nodes. Figure 8.5 lists some **Document** methods.

Figure 8.6 lists the methods of class **XmlDocument**, including the methods inherited from **Document**. Class **XmlDocument** is part of the JAXP internal APIs and its methods are not part of the W3C DOM recommendation.

Interface **Node** represents an XML document node. Figure 8.7 lists the methods of interface **Node**.

Method Name	Description
createElement	Creates an element node.
createAttribute	Creates an attribute node.
createTextNode	Creates a text node.
createComment	Creates a comment node.
createProcessingInstruction	Creates a processing instruction node.
createCDATASection	Creates a **CDATA** section node.
getDocumentElement	Returns the document's root element.
appendChild	Appends a child node.
getChildNodes	Returns the child nodes.

Fig. 8.5   Some **Document** methods.

Method Name	Description
createXmlDocument	Parses an XML document.
write	Outputs the XML document.

Fig. 8.6   **XmlDocument** methods.

Method Name	Description
appendChild	Appends a child node.
cloneNode	Duplicates the node.
getAttributes	Returns the node's attributes.
getChildNodes	Returns the node's child nodes.
getNodeName	Returns the node's name.
getNodeType	Returns the node's type (e.g., element, attribute, text, etc.). Node types are described in greater detail in Fig. 8.9.
getNodeValue	Returns the node's value.
getParentNode	Returns the node's parent.
hasChildNodes	Returns **true** if the node has child nodes.
removeChild	Removes a child node from the node.
replaceChild	Replaces a child node with another node.
setNodeValue	Sets the node's value.
insertBefore	Appends a child node in front of a child node.

Fig. 8.7   **Node** methods.

Figure 8.8 lists some node types that may be returned by method **getNodeType**. Each type in Fig. 8.8 is a **static final** (i.e., constant) member of class **Node**.

Element represents an element node. Figure 8.9 lists some **Element** methods.

Node Type	Description
Node.ELEMENT_NODE	Represents an element node.
Node.ATTRIBUTE_NODE	Represents an attribute node.
Node.TEXT_NODE	Represents a text node.
Node.COMMENT_NODE	Represents a comment node.
Node.PROCESSING_INSTRUCTION_NODE	Represents a processing instruction node.
Node.CDATA_SECTION_NODE	Represents a **CDATA** section node.

Fig. 8.8   Some node types.

Method Name	Description
getAttribute	Returns an attribute's value.

Fig. 8.9   **Element** methods (part 1 of 2).

Method Name	Description
`getTagName`	Returns an element's name.
`removeAttribute`	Removes an element's attribute.
`setAttribute`	Sets an attribute's value.

Fig. 8.9   Element methods (part 2 of 2).

We are now ready to present our first Java-based example. Figure 8.10 lists a Java application that validates **intro.xml** (Fig. 8.12) and replaces the text in its **message** element with **New Changed Message!!**. The output box at the end of the listing shows the steps necessary to compile and execute the program. We discuss these after presenting the program.

```
1   // Fig 8.10 : ReplaceText.java
2   // Reads intro.xml and replaces a text node.
3
4   import java.io.*;
5   import org.w3c.dom.*;
6   import javax.xml.parsers.*;
7   import com.sun.xml.tree.XmlDocument;
8   import org.xml.sax.*;
9
10  public class ReplaceText {
11      private Document document;
12
13      public ReplaceText()
14      {
15         try {
16
17            // obtain the default parser
18            DocumentBuilderFactory factory =
19               DocumentBuilderFactory.newInstance();
20
21            // set the parser to validating
22            factory.setValidating( true );
23
24            DocumentBuilder builder = factory.newDocumentBuilder();
25
26            // set error handler for validation errors
27            builder.setErrorHandler( new MyErrorHandler() );
28
29            // obtain document object from XML document
30            document = builder.parse( new File( "intro.xml" ) );
31
32            // fetch the root node
33            Node root = document.getDocumentElement();
34
```

Fig. 8.10   Simple example to replace an existing text node (part 1 of 2).

```
35              if ( root.getNodeType() == Node.ELEMENT_NODE ) {
36                 Element myMessageNode = ( Element ) root;
37                 NodeList messageNodes =
38                    myMessageNode.getElementsByTagName( "message" );
39
40                 if ( messageNodes.getLength() != 0 ) {
41                    Node message = messageNodes.item( 0 );
42
43                    // create a text node
44                    Text newText = document.createTextNode(
45                                      "New Changed Message!!" );
46
47                    // get the old text node
48                    Text oldText =
49                       ( Text ) message.getChildNodes().item( 0 );
50
51                    // replace the text
52                    message.replaceChild( newText, oldText );
53                 }
54              }
55
56              ( (XmlDocument) document).write( new FileOutputStream(
57                 "intro1.xml" ) );
58           }
59           catch ( SAXParseException spe ) {
60              System.err.println( "Parse error: " +
61                 spe.getMessage() );
62              System.exit( 1 );
63           }
64           catch ( SAXException se ) {
65              se.printStackTrace();
66           }
67           catch ( FileNotFoundException fne ) {
68              System.err.println( "File \'intro.xml\' not found. " );
69              System.exit( 1 );
70           }
71           catch ( Exception e ) {
72              e.printStackTrace();
73           }
74        }
75
76        public static void main( String args[] )
77        {
78           ReplaceText d = new ReplaceText();
79        }
80     }
```

```
set PATH=%PATH%;C:\jdk1.3\bin\
set CLASSPATH=%CLASSPATH%;C:\jaxp\jaxp.jar;C:\jaxp\parser.jar;.
javac ReplaceText.java MyErrorHandler.java
java ReplaceText
```

Fig. 8.10 Simple example to replace an existing text node (part 2 of 2).

Lines 4–8

```
import java.io.*;
import org.w3c.dom.*;
import javax.xml.parsers.*;
import com.sun.xml.tree.XmlDocument;
import org.xml.sax.*;
```

import (i.e., specify the location of) the classes needed by the program. The Java programming language provides a feature—called *packages*—that groups a series of related Java files (e.g., compiled **.class** files). For example, the first **import** statement indicates that our program uses some classes from the package **java.io**. Sun Microsystems, the creator of Java, provides several packages related to XML. Package *org.w3c.dom* provides the DOM-API programmatic interface (i.e., classes, methods, etc.). Package *javax.xml.parsers* provides classes related to parsing an XML document.

Package *com.sun.xml.tree* contains classes and interfaces from Sun Microsystem's internal XML API, which provides features currently not available in the XML 1.0 recommendation (e.g., saving an XML document). Documentation for Sun's internal APIs can be found at

java.sun.com/xml/docs/api

[*Note*: The documentation at this site specifies that the internal APIs are subject to change.]
A DOM-based parser may use an event-based implementation (i.e., as the document is parsed events are raised when starting tags, attributes, etc. are encountered) to help create the tree structure in memory. A popular event-based implementation is called the *Simple API for XML (SAX),* which we present in Chapter 9. The main SAX features we discuss in this chapter are exceptions thrown by the default parser used by JAXP. An exception occurs when an error is encountered in a program. The error may be caught by an exception handler and processed, ensuring the program does not terminate abnormally. Package *org.xml.sax* provides the SAX programmatic interface.
Line 11

```
    private Document document;
```

declares **Document** reference **document**. This reference is assigned an object (in line 30) that represents the document root.

JAXP uses the *DocumentBuilderFactory* class to create a *Document-Builder* object. Class **DocumentBuilder** provides a standard interface to an XML parser. JAXP can be configured to use many different XML parsers, such as the Apache Group's Xerces and IBM's XML4J. JAXP also has its own parser built in, which is used by default. The **DocumentBuilderFactory** produces an appropriate **Document-Builder** object for the currently-configured XML parser.
Lines 18 and 19

```
    DocumentBuilderFactory factory =
        DocumentBuilderFactory.newInstance();
```

create and assign a **DocumentBuilderFactory** object to reference **factory**.

Line 22

```
factory.setValidating( true );
```

indicates that a validating parser is being used by passing the value **true** as an argument to method *setValidating*.

Line 24

```
DocumentBuilder builder = factory.newDocumentBuilder();
```

creates a new **DocumentBuilder** object and assigns it to reference **builder**. This object provides an interface for loading and parsing XML documents.

Line 27

```
builder.setErrorHandler( new MyErrorHandler() );
```

specifies that a **MyErrorHandler** (Fig. 8.11) object provides methods for handling exceptions related to parsing.

Line 30

```
document = builder.parse( new File( "intro.xml" ) );
```

calls method *parse* to load and parse the XML document stored in the file **intro.xml**. If parsing is successful, a **Document** object is returned that contains nodes representing each part of the **intro.xml** document. If parsing fails, a *SAXException* is thrown.

Line 33

```
Node root = document.getDocumentElement();
```

calls method *getDocumentElement* to get the **Document**'s root node and assign it to **Node** reference **root**. Line 35

```
if ( root.getNodeType() == Node.ELEMENT_NODE ) {
```

tests if the root element is an element node. Method **getNodeType** is called to retrieve the node's type.

Line 36

```
Element myMessageNode = ( Element ) root;
```

down casts **root** from a superclass **Node** type to an **Element** derived type. As mentioned earlier, class **Element** inherits from class **Node**. By down casting, this allows **Element myMessageNode** to be assigned the object referenced by **root**. Methods specific to class **Element** can now be called on the object using the **myMessageNode** reference.

Lines 37 and 38

```
NodeList messageNodes =
    myMessageNode.getElementsByTagName( "message" );
```

get a list of all the **message** elements in the XML document using method **getElementsByTagName**. Each element is stored as an item (i.e., a **Node**) in a **NodeList**. The first item added is stored at index 0, the next at index 1, and so forth. This index is used to access an individual item in the **NodeList**.

Line 40

```
if ( messageNodes.getLength() != 0 ) {
```

determines if the **NodeList** contains at least one item by calling method **getLength** and testing the value returned from it against zero.

If there are items in the **NodeList**, line 41

```
Node message = messageNodes.item( 0 );
```

assigns the first **NodeList** node (i.e., element **message**) to **Node** reference **message**. Method **item** returns an individual **Node** from the **NodeList**. In this case, the first **Node** is returned.

Lines 44 and 45

```
Text newText = document.createTextNode(
                "New Changed Message!!" );
```

use the **createTextNode** method to create a text node that contains the text **New Changed Message!!**. This node exists in memory independent of the XML document—i.e., it has not been inserted into the document yet. Interface *Text* represents an element or attribute's character data.

Lines 48 and 49

```
Text oldText =
    ( Text ) message.getChildNodes().item( 0 );
```

get the first child node of the **message** element (referenced by **Node message** in line 33), which is a text node containing the text **Welcome to XML!**. Because **item** returns an object of superclass type **Object**, a downcast to **Text** is performed. Line 52

```
message.replaceChild( newText, oldText );
```

calls method **replaceChild** to replace the **Node** referenced by the second argument with the **Node** referenced by the first argument. The XML document has now been modified—element message now contains the text **New Changed Message!!**.

Lines 56 and 57

```
( (XmlDocument) document).write( new FileOutputStream(
    "intro1.xml" ) );
```

create a **FileOutputStream** (package **java.io**) object for the file **intro1.xml** and write the XML document to it using method **write**. Method **write** is a member of **XmlDocument**, which requires casting **document** to **XmlDocument**. We need to use this internal API class because the **Document** interface does not provide a method for saving an XML document to a file.

Lines 59 and 64 begin **catch** blocks for a *SAXParseException* and a *SAXException*. These exceptions contain information about errors and warnings thrown by the parser. Class **SAXParseException** is a subclass of **SAXException** and includes methods for locating the error.

Figure 8.11 presents **MyErrorHandler.java**, which provides the implementation for handling errors thrown by the parser in **ReplaceText.java**. By default, JAXP does not throw any exceptions when a document fails to conform to a DTD. The programmer must provide an error handler, which is registered using method **setErrorHandler** (line 27 in Fig. 8.10).

Lines 4–6

```
import org.xml.sax.ErrorHandler;
import org.xml.sax.SAXException;
import org.xml.sax.SAXParseException;
```

import ErrorHandler, SAXException and **SAXParseException**. Interface **ErrorHandler** provides methods *fatalError*, *error* and *warning* for fatal errors (i.e., errors that violate the XML 1.0 specification; parsing is halted), errors (e.g., validity constraints that do not stop the parsing process) and warnings (i.e., not classified as fatal errors or errors and that do not stop the parsing process), respectively. These methods are overridden in lines 12, 18 and 25. Fatal errors and errors are rethrown and warnings are output to the standard error device (**System.err**).

Three steps (beyond the setup in Section 8.4) are required to run this Java application. First the **CLASSPATH** (i.e., the path a Java compiler and interpreter use to locate **.class** files) is set to the location where **jaxp.jar** and **parser.jar** reside as well as the current directory (**.**). On our Windows machine, we installed these on the **C:** drive. [*Note*: in successive examples, we will assume that the **CLASSPATH** is already set.] Next, we compiled Fig. 8.10 and Fig. 8.11 together, using the Java compiler, **javac**. Finally, we execute the application, using the **java** interpreter.

```
1    // Fig 8.11  : MyErrorHandler.java
2    // Error Handler for validation errors.
3
4    import org.xml.sax.ErrorHandler;
5    import org.xml.sax.SAXException;
6    import org.xml.sax.SAXParseException;
7
8    public class MyErrorHandler implements ErrorHandler
9    {
10
11       // throw SAXException for fatal errors
12       public void fatalError( SAXParseException exception )
13          throws SAXException
14       {
15          throw exception;
16       }
17
18       public void error( SAXParseException e )
19          throws SAXParseException
20       {
21         throw e;
22       }
```

Fig. 8.11 Class definition for **MyErrorHandler** (part 1 of 2).

```
23
24        // print any warnings
25        public void warning( SAXParseException err )
26           throws SAXParseException
27        {
28           System.err.println( "Warning: " + err.getMessage() );
29        }
30   }
```

Fig. 8.11   Class definition for **MyErrorHandler** (part 2 of 2).

Figure 8.12 lists the XML document manipulated by the Java application in Fig. 8.10. Figure 8.13 lists the document after it is modified.

Notice that in Fig. 8.13 the **message** element's text has been changed and the comments are missing. The DTD is preserved, because we are using a validating parser—otherwise the DTD would not be included in the file. Figure 8.13 also introduces an *encoding* in the XML declaration. The **encoding** specifies the character set used in the document. Recall from Chapter 5 that XML uses the Unicode character set. Unicode provides characters in most of the worlds major languages. Use an **encoding** (e.g., **UTF-8**) to specify a subset of the characters in Unicode will be used in a document.

```
1    <?xml version = "1.0"?>
2
3    <!-- Fig. 8.12 : intro.xml              -->
4    <!-- Simple introduction to XML markup -->
5
6    <!DOCTYPE myMessage [
7       <!ELEMENT myMessage ( message )>
8       <!ELEMENT message ( #PCDATA )>
9    ]>
10
11   <myMessage>
12      <message>Welcome to XML!</message>
13   </myMessage>
```

Fig. 8.12   Input document (**intro.xml**).

```
1    <?xml version = "1.0" encoding = "UTF-8"?>
2
3    <!-- Fig. 8.12 : intro.xml              -->
4    <!-- Simple introduction to XML markup -->
5
6    <!DOCTYPE myMessage [
7       <!ELEMENT myMessage ( message )>
8       <!ELEMENT message ( #PCDATA )>
9    ]>
10
```

Fig. 8.13   Ouput of **replaceText.java**, which is stored in **intro1.xml** (part 1 of 2).

```
11    <myMessage>
12        <message>New Changed Message!!</message>
13    </myMessage>
```

Fig. 8.13   Ouput of `replaceText.java`, which is stored in `intro1.xml` (part 2 of 2).

8.6 Creating Nodes

The majority of XML markup presented up to this point has been "hand coded" (i.e., typed into an editor by a document author). Using the DOM, XML documents can be created in an automated way through programming.

Figure 8.14 lists a Java application that creates an XML document for a contact list. This application is compiled and executed in the same manner as the last Java application.

```
1    // Fig. 8.14 : BuildXml.java
2    // Creates element node, attribute node, comment node,
3    // processing instruction and a CDATA section.
4
5    import java.io.*;
6    import org.w3c.dom.*;
7    import org.xml.sax.*;
8    import javax.xml.parsers.*;
9    import com.sun.xml.tree.XmlDocument;
10
11   public class BuildXml {
12       private Document document;
13
14       public BuildXml()
15       {
16
17           DocumentBuilderFactory factory =
18                   DocumentBuilderFactory.newInstance();
19
20           try {
21
22               // get DocumentBuilder
23               DocumentBuilder builder =
24                   factory.newDocumentBuilder();
25
26               // create root node
27               document = builder.newDocument();
28           }
29           catch ( ParserConfigurationException pce ) {
30               pce.printStackTrace();
31           }
32
33           Element root = document.createElement( "root" );
34           document.appendChild( root );
35
36           // add a comment to XML document
```

Fig. 8.14   Building an XML document with the DOM (part 1 of 3).

```
37          Comment simpleComment = document.createComment(
38             "This is a simple contact list" );
39          root.appendChild( simpleComment );
40
41          // add a child element
42          Node contactNode = createContactNode( document );
43          root.appendChild( contactNode );
44
45          // add a processing instruction
46          ProcessingInstruction pi =
47             document.createProcessingInstruction(
48                "myInstruction", "action silent" );
49          root.appendChild( pi );
50
51          // add a CDATA section
52          CDATASection cdata = document.createCDATASection(
53             "I can add <, >, and ?" );
54          root.appendChild( cdata );
55
56          try {
57
58             // write the XML document to a file
59             ( (XmlDocument) document).write( new FileOutputStream(
60                "myDocument.xml" ) );
61          }
62          catch ( IOException ioe ) {
63             ioe.printStackTrace();
64          }
65       }
66
67       public Node createContactNode( Document document )
68       {
69
70          // create FirstName and LastName elements
71          Element firstName = document.createElement( "FirstName" );
72          Element lastName = document.createElement( "LastName" );
73
74          firstName.appendChild( document.createTextNode( "Sue" ) );
75          lastName.appendChild( document.createTextNode( "Green" ) );
76
77          // create contact element
78          Element contact = document.createElement( "contact" );
79
80          // create an attribute
81          Attr genderAttribute = document.createAttribute( "gender" );
82          genderAttribute.setValue( "F" );
83
84          // append attribute to contact element
85          contact.setAttributeNode( genderAttribute );
86          contact.appendChild( firstName );
87          contact.appendChild( lastName );
88          return contact;
89       }
```

Fig. 8.14   Building an XML document with the DOM (part 2 of 3).

```
90
91      public static void main( String args[] )
92      {
93         BuildXml buildXml = new BuildXml();
94      }
95   }
```

```
javac BuildXml.java
java BuildXml
```

Fig. 8.14   Building an XML document with the DOM (part 3 of 3).

Lines 17 and 18

```
DocumentBuilderFactory factory =
        DocumentBuilderFactory.newInstance();
```

create and assign a **DocumentBuilderFactory** object to reference **factory**. Class **DocumentBuilderFactory** is used to obtain an instance of a parser—in this particular case, the default JAXP parser.

Lines 23 and 24

```
DocumentBuilder builder =
    factory.newDocumentBuilder();
```

create a new **DocumentBuilder** object and assign it to reference **builder**. This object provides facilities for loading and parsing XML documents.

Line 27

```
document = builder.newDocument();
```

calls method *newDocument* to create a new **Document** object. We will use the **Document** object returned by **newDocument** to build an XML document in memory.

Lines 33 and 34

```
Element root = document.createElement( "root" );
document.appendChild( root );
```

create an element named **root** and append it to the document root. Because this is the first element appended, it is the root element of the document.

Lines 37–39

```
Comment simpleComment = document.createComment(
    "This is a simple contact list" );
root.appendChild( simpleComment );
```

create a comment node using method **createComment** and append the node as a child of element **root**.

Line 42

```
Node contactNode = createContactNode( document );
```

calls programmer-defined method **createContactNode** (line 67) to create the **contact** element. We will discuss this method momentarily.

Lines 46–48

```
ProcessingInstruction pi =
    document.createProcessingInstruction(
        "myInstruction", "action silent" );
```

create a processing instruction node. The first argument passed to **createProcessingInstruction** is the target **myInstruction** and the second argument passed is the value **action silent**. Line 49 appends the processing instruction to the root element.

Lines 52 and 53

```
CDATASection cdata = document.createCDATASection(
    "I can add <, >, and ?" );
```

create a **CDATA** section, which is appended to element **root** in line 54.

Line 67

```
public Node createContactNode( Document document )
```

defines method **createContactNode** that returns a **Node** object. This method creates a **contact** element node and returns it. The returned **Node** is appended to the **root** element in line 43.

Lines 71 and 72

```
Element firstName = document.createElement( "FirstName" );
Element lastName = document.createElement( "LastName" );
```

create elements **FirstName** and **LastName**, which have their text values set on lines 74 and 75

```
firstName.appendChild( document.createTextNode( "Sue" ) );
lastName.appendChild( document.createTextNode( "Green" ) );
```

Lines 81 and 82

```
Attr genderAttribute = document.createAttribute( "gender" );
genderAttribute.setValue( "F" );
```

create attribute **gender** using method **createAttribute** and assign it a value using **Attr** method **setValue**. Line 85

```
contact.setAttributeNode( genderAttribute );
```

assigns the attribute to the **contact** element node using method **setAttributeNode**.

The XML document is written to disk in lines 59 and 60. Figure 8.15 lists the XML document (**myDocument.xml**) created by Fig. 8.14's **buildXml.java**.

```
1   <?xml version = "1.0" encoding = "UTF-8"?>
2
3   <root>
4      <!--This is a simple contact list-->
5      <contact gender = "F">
6         <FirstName>Sue</FirstName>
7         <LastName>Green</LastName>
8      </contact>
9      <?myInstruction action silent?>
10     <![CDATA[I can add <, >, and ?]]>
11  </root>
```

Fig. 8.15 Output for **buildXml.java**.

8.7 Traversing the DOM

In this section, we demonstrate how to use the DOM to traverse an XML document. In Fig. 8.16, we present a Java application that outputs element nodes, attribute nodes and text nodes. This application takes the name of an XML document (e.g., **simpleContact.xml** in Fig. 8.17) from the *command line* (i.e., a window—such as a DOS prompt or shell window—where commands are entered into a computer).

```
1    // Fig. 8.16 : TraverseDOM.java
2    // Traverses DOM and prints various nodes.
3
4    import java.io.*;
5    import org.w3c.dom.*;
6    import org.xml.sax.*;
7    import javax.xml.parsers.*;
8    import com.sun.xml.tree.XmlDocument;
9
10   public class TraverseDOM {
11      private Document document;
12
13      public TraverseDOM( String file )
14      {
15         try {
16
17            // obtain the default parser
18            DocumentBuilderFactory factory =
19               DocumentBuilderFactory.newInstance();
20            factory.setValidating( true );
21            DocumentBuilder builder = factory.newDocumentBuilder();
22
23            // set error handler for validation errors
24            builder.setErrorHandler( new MyErrorHandler() );
25
26            // obtain document object from XML document
27            document = builder.parse( new File( file ) );
28            processNode( document );
29         }
```

Fig. 8.16 Traversing the DOM (part 1 of 3).

```
30            catch ( SAXParseException spe ) {
31               System.err.println(
32                  "Parse error: " + spe.getMessage() );
33               System.exit( 1 );
34            }
35            catch ( SAXException se ) {
36               se.printStackTrace();
37            }
38            catch ( FileNotFoundException fne ) {
39               System.err.println( "File \'"
40                  + file + "\' not found. " );
41               System.exit( 1 );
42            }
43            catch ( Exception e ) {
44               e.printStackTrace();
45            }
46         }
47
48         public void processNode( Node currentNode )
49         {
50            switch ( currentNode.getNodeType() ) {
51
52               // process a Document node
53               case Node.DOCUMENT_NODE:
54                  Document doc = ( Document ) currentNode;
55
56                  System.out.println(
57                     "Document node: " + doc.getNodeName() +
58                     "\nRoot element: " +
59                     doc.getDocumentElement().getNodeName() );
60                  processChildNodes( doc.getChildNodes() );
61                  break;
62
63               // process an Element node
64               case Node.ELEMENT_NODE:
65                  System.out.println( "\nElement node: " +
66                                      currentNode.getNodeName() );
67                  NamedNodeMap attributeNodes =
68                     currentNode.getAttributes();
69
70                  for ( int i = 0; i < attributeNodes.getLength(); i++){
71                     Attr attribute = ( Attr ) attributeNodes.item( i );
72
73                     System.out.println( "\tAttribute: " +
74                        attribute.getNodeName() + " ; Value = " +
75                        attribute.getNodeValue() );
76                  }
77
78                  processChildNodes( currentNode.getChildNodes() );
79                  break;
80
81               // process a text node and a CDATA section
82               case Node.CDATA_SECTION_NODE:
```

Fig. 8.16 Traversing the DOM (part 2 of 3).

```
83                    case Node.TEXT_NODE:
84                       Text text = ( Text ) currentNode;
85
86                       if ( !text.getNodeValue().trim().equals( "" ) )
87                          System.out.println( "\tText: " +
88                                               text.getNodeValue() );
89                       break;
90                 }
91           }
92
93           public void processChildNodes( NodeList children )
94           {
95              if ( children.getLength() != 0 )
96
97                 for ( int i = 0; i < children.getLength(); i++)
98                    processNode( children.item( i ) );
99           }
100
101          public static void main( String args[] )
102          {
103             if ( args.length < 1 ) {
104                System.err.println(
105                   "Usage: java TraverseDOM <filename>" );
106                System.exit( 1 );
107             }
108
109             TraverseDOM traverseDOM = new TraverseDOM( args[ 0 ] );
110          }
111    }
```

Fig. 8.16   Traversing the DOM (part 3 of 3).

Lines 13–46 define the class constructor for **TraverseDOM**, which takes the name of the file (i.e., **simpleContact.xml**) specified at the command line, loads and parses the XML document before passing it to programmer-defined method **processNode**.

Lines 48–91 define method **processNode**, which takes one **Node** argument and outputs information about the **Node** and its child elements. This method uses a **switch** structure (line 50) to determine the **Node** type.

Line 53

```
case Node.DOCUMENT_NODE:
```

matches a document node. This **case** outputs the document node and processes its child nodes by calling method **processChildNodes** (lines 93–99). We will discuss method **processchildNodes** momentarily.

Line 64

```
case Node.ELEMENT_NODE:
```

matches an element node. This **case** outputs the element's attributes and then processes its child nodes in **processChildNodes**.

Lines 82 and 83

```
case Node.CDATA_SECTION_NODE:
case Node.TEXT_NODE:
```

match **CDATA** section nodes and text nodes. These **case**s output the node's text content (lines 87–88).

Lines 93–99 define method **processChildNodes**, which takes one **NodeList** argument and calls **processNode** on a node's child nodes. Each child node is retrieved by calling **NodeList** method **item** (line 98).

In Java, command-line arguments are accessible by using **String** array **args** passed to the **main** method (line 93). The command line used to execute this example is

```
java TraverseDOM simpleContact.xml
```

where **java** is the Java interpreter, **TraverseDOM** is the program being executed and **simpleContact.xml** is the command-line argument stored in array **args**. More precisely, **args[0]** contains the string **simpleContact.xml**.

Figure 8.17 lists the contents **simpleContact.xml**—the XML document used by **TraverseDOM.java**.

8.8 Case Study: Modifying the Day Planner Application to Use the DOM

In this section, we continue enhancing our day planner application—by creating a Java graphical user interface (GUI) for it and by creating a Java class that uses the DOM to query the day planner XML document (Fig. 5.10) for specific days, months, years or times.

We begin by presenting the Java class **DOMPlanner** (Fig. 8.18), which queries the XML document.

```
1   <?xml version = "1.0"?>
2
3   <!-- Fig 8.17 : simpleContact.xml    -->
4   <!-- Input file for traverseDOM.java -->
5
6   <!DOCTYPE contacts [
7      <!ELEMENT contacts ( contact+ )>
8      <!ELEMENT contact ( FirstName, LastName )>
9      <!ATTLIST contact gender ( M | F ) "M">
10     <!ELEMENT FirstName ( #PCDATA )>
11     <!ELEMENT LastName ( #PCDATA )>
12  ]>
13
14  <contacts>
15     <contact gender = "M">
16        <FirstName>John</FirstName>
17        <LastName>Black</LastName>
18     </contact>
19  </contacts>
```

Fig. 8.17 Sample execution for **TraverseDOM.java** (part 1 of 2).

```
javac TraverseDOM.java
java TraverseDOM simpleContact.xml

Document node: #document
Root element: contacts

Element node: contacts

Element node: contact
        Attribute: gender ; Value = M

Element node: FirstName
        Text: John

Element node: LastName
        Text: Black
```

Fig. 8.17 Sample execution for **TraverseDOM.java** (part 2 of 2).

```
1   // Fig. 8.18 : DOMPlanner.java
2   // A day planner application using DOM.
3   // The following program uses Sun's validating parser.
4
5   import java.io.*;
6   import java.awt.*;
7   import java.util.*;
8   import javax.swing.*;
9
10  import org.w3c.dom.*;
11  import org.xml.sax.*;
12  import javax.xml.parsers.*;
13  import com.sun.xml.tree.XmlDocument;
14
15  public class DOMPlanner {
16
17     private JTextArea display;      // for displaying output
18     private InputSource input;      // for reading the XML document
19     private Document document;      // document node object
20
21     // variables to store the query parameters and the result
22     private int year, month, day, timePeriod;
23     private String resultYear, resultDay;
24
25     public DOMPlanner( JTextArea output )
26     {
27        year = month = day = timePeriod = -1;
28        display = output;
29
30        try {
31
```

Fig. 8.18 Day planner using DOM (part 1 of 6).

```
32              // obtain the default parser
33              DocumentBuilderFactory factory =
34                 DocumentBuilderFactory.newInstance();
35              factory.setValidating( true );
36              DocumentBuilder builder = factory.newDocumentBuilder();
37
38              // set error handler for validation errors
39              builder.setErrorHandler( new MyErrorHandler() );
40
41              // obtain document object from XML document
42              document = builder.parse( new File( "planner.xml" ) );
43           }
44        catch ( SAXParseException spe ) {
45           System.err.println( "Parse error: " +
46              spe.getMessage() );
47           System.exit( 1 );
48        }
49        catch ( SAXException se ) {
50           se.printStackTrace();
51        }
52        catch ( FileNotFoundException fne ) {
53           System.err.println( "File \"planner.xml\" not found." );
54           System.exit( 1 );
55        }
56        catch ( Exception e ) {
57           e.printStackTrace();
58        }
59     }
60
61     // method to get the available years from the XML file
62     public String[] getYears()
63     {
64        String availableYears[];
65        StringTokenizer tokens;
66        String str = " ";
67        int i = 0;
68
69        Element root = document.getDocumentElement();
70        NodeList yearNodes =
71           root.getElementsByTagName( "year" );
72
73        // get value of attribute 'value' for each 'year' node
74        for ( i = 0; i < yearNodes.getLength(); i++ ) {
75           NamedNodeMap yearAttributes =
76              yearNodes.item( i ).getAttributes();
77
78           str += " " + yearAttributes.item( 0 ).getNodeValue();
79        }
80
81        tokens = new StringTokenizer( str );
82        availableYears = new String[ tokens.countTokens() + 1 ];
83        availableYears[ 0 ] = "ANY";
84        i = 1;
```

Fig. 8.18   Day planner using DOM (part 2 of 6).

```
85
86          // form an array of strings containing available years
87          while ( tokens.hasMoreTokens() )
88              availableYears[ i++ ] = tokens.nextToken();
89
90          return availableYears;
91      }
92
93      // method to initialize the query
94      public void getQueryResult( int y, int m, int d, int t )
95      {
96          year = y;
97          month = m;
98          day = d;
99          resultYear = "";
100         resultDay = "";
101         timePeriod = t;
102         display.setText( "*** YOUR DAY PLANNER ***" );
103         getResult( document );
104     }
105
106     // method to output the result of query
107     public void getResult( Node node )
108     {
109         // process each type of node
110         // if the node contains child nodes,
111         // process it recursively
112         switch ( node.getNodeType() ) {
113
114             // if it is a Document node process its children
115             case Node.DOCUMENT_NODE:
116                 Document doc = ( Document ) node;
117
118                 getResult( doc.getDocumentElement() );
119                 break;
120
121             // process element node according to its tag name
122             case Node.ELEMENT_NODE:
123
124                 if ( node.getNodeName().equals( "planner" ) )
125                     processChildNodes( node.getChildNodes() );
126                 else if ( node.getNodeName().equals( "year" ) ) {
127
128                     // find the attribute value for year and
129                     // check if it matches the query
130                     NamedNodeMap yearAttributes =
131                         node.getAttributes();
132                     Node value = yearAttributes.item( 0 );
133
134                     if ( Integer.parseInt( value.getNodeValue() )
135                         == year || year == -1 ) {
136                         resultYear = " Y " +
137                             Integer.parseInt( value.getNodeValue() );
```

Fig. 8.18   Day planner using DOM (part 3 of 6).

```
138                        processChildNodes( node.getChildNodes() );
139                    }
140                    else
141                        return;
142
143                }
144                else if ( node.getNodeName().equals( "date" ) ) {
145                    Element dateElement = ( Element ) node;
146                    int m = Integer.parseInt(
147                            dateElement.getAttribute( "month" ) );
148                    int d = Integer.parseInt(
149                            dateElement.getAttribute( "day" ) );
150
151                    // check if the current 'date' node satisfies query
152                    if ( ( m == month && d == day ) ||
153                         ( month == -1 && d == day ) ||
154                         ( m == month && day == -1 ) ||
155                         ( month == -1 && day == -1 ) ) {
156                        resultDay = "DATE: D " + d + " M " + m ;
157                        processChildNodes(
158                            dateElement.getChildNodes() );
159                    }
160                    else
161                        return;
162
163                }
164                else if ( node.getNodeName().equals( "note" ) ) {
165
166                    // fetch attributes for the note node and
167                    // verify its attribute values with the query
168                    NamedNodeMap noteAttributes =
169                        node.getAttributes();
170
171                    int scheduleTime;
172
173                    if ( noteAttributes.getLength() != 0 ) {
174                        Node nodeTime = noteAttributes.item( 0 );
175
176                        scheduleTime =
177                            Integer.parseInt( nodeTime.getNodeValue() );
178                    }
179                    else
180                        scheduleTime = -1;
181
182                    // if the time lies between the periods of the
183                    // day display the value of node 'note'
184                    if ( isBetween( scheduleTime ) )  {
185                        Node child =
186                            ( node.getChildNodes() ).item( 0 );
187                        String s =
188                            child.getNodeValue().trim();
189
190                        display.append( "\n" + resultDay +
```

Fig. 8.18   Day planner using DOM (part 4 of 6).

```
191                                            resultYear );
192
193                    if ( scheduleTime != -1 )
194                        display.append( "\nTIME: " +
195                            scheduleTime +" > " + s );
196                    else
197                        display.append( "\nALL DAY > " + s );
198
199                    display.append( "\n* * * * * * * * *" );
200                }
201                else
202                    return;
203            }
204          break;
205      }
206    }
207
208    // method to process child nodes
209    public void processChildNodes( NodeList children )
210    {
211       if ( children.getLength() != 0 )
212
213          for ( int i = 0; i < children.getLength(); i++ )
214             getResult( children.item( i ) );
215
216       return;
217    }
218
219    // method to compare the time with various periods
220    // of the day
221    public boolean isBetween( int time )
222    {
223       switch ( timePeriod ) {
224
225          case -1:        // all day
226             return true;
227
228          case 0:         // morning
229
230             if ( time >= 500 && time < 1200 )
231                return true;
232
233             break;
234
235          case 1:         // afternoon
236
237             if ( time >= 1200 && time < 1800 )
238                return true;
239
240             break;
241
242          case 2:         // evening
243
```

Fig. 8.18   Day planner using DOM (part 5 of 6).

```
244                    if ( time >= 1800 && time < 2100 )
245                        return true;
246
247                    break;
248
249              case 3:             // night
250
251                    if ( time >= 2100 || time < 500 )
252                        return true;
253
254                    break;
255
256              default:
257                    System.out.println( "Illegal time in XML file" );
258          }
259
260          return false;
261      }
262  }
```

Fig. 8.18   Day planner using DOM (part 6 of 6).

Lines 25–59 define the constructor that initializes the application and loads and parses the day planner XML document (i.e., **planner.xml**). Line 28 assigns the **JTextArea** reference **display** (line 17), which allows a **DOMPlanner** object to display text in the GUI of the object that created it. We will discuss the GUI in Fig. 8.19.

Lines 62–91 define method **getYears**, which returns a **String** array containing the day planner document's years. Line 69

```
Element root = document.getDocumentElement();
```

retrieves the **planner** document element and assigns it to reference **root**. Lines 70 and 71

```
NodeList yearNodes =
    root.getElementsByTagName( "year" );
```

retrieve all the **year** elements in the document and places them in a **NodeList** object referenced by **yearNodes**. This **NodeList** is then processed using a **for** loop (lines 74–79) to create a string containing the years—each separated by a space character. Method **getNodeValue** is called to retrieve each **year**'s value.

Lines 81–83

```
tokens = new StringTokenizer( str );
availableYears = new String[ tokens.countTokens() + 1 ];
availableYears[ 0 ] = "ANY";
```

construct a **StringTokenizer** (**java.util** package) object to split the space-delimited **String** into individual *tokens* (i.e., **String**s). By default, the class **StringTokenizer** uses whitespace characters as delimiters. Method **countTokens** is called to get the number of strings in **tokens**. We initialize the first item of the array to **ANY** to query any year.

Lines 87 and 88

```
while ( tokens.hasMoreTokens() )
    availableYears[ i++ ] = tokens.nextToken();
```

take the **String**s contained in **tokens** and place them in array **availableYears**. This array is returned in line 90.

Lines 94–104 define method **getQueryResult**, which initializes the variables (e.g., **year**, **month**, etc.) used in the query. Programmer-defined method **getResult** is called in line 103 to output the results of the query.

Lines 107–206 define method **getResult**, which processes the XML document. A **switch** structure (line 112) determines the **Node**'s type.

The **case** on lines 115–119 matches the document's root node and calls method **getResult** to process the document's nodes, beginning with the root element. *Recursion* (i.e., the process by which a method—such as **getResult**—calls itself repeatedly until some condition is met) is often used with tree structures for efficient traversal.

Lines 122–204 are the **Node.ELEMENT_NODE case** for element nodes. Lines 124 and 125

```
if ( node.getNodeName().equals( "planner" ) )
    processChildNodes( node.getChildNodes() );
```

check for the root element (i.e., **planner**) and process them if the condition is true.

Line 126 checks for **year** elements. We get the first **year** element's attribute (i.e., **value** in **planner.xml**) and reference it using **Node value** in lines 130–132. Next, (lines 134 and 135), we determine if the **Node** referenced by **value** matches the value of the **year** (declared in line 22) for which we are searching. If it matches, lines 136 and 137

```
resultYear = " Y " +
    Integer.parseInt( value.getNodeValue() );
```

concatenate the string **" Y "** to the year in variable **resultYear**. The element's child nodes are passed to method **processChildNodes** in line 138.

Line 144 tests for **date** elements. We get attribute **month**'s (lines 146 and 147) value and attribute **day**'s (lines 148 and 149) value. Using these values, we check the query and if they match, we store the month and day in variable **resultDay** and process the element's child nodes.

Line 164 tests for **note** elements. If an appointment time was specified (i.e., attribute **time** is present), we get the appointment time (lines 173–178). Otherwise, we set the appointment time as the entire day by setting **scheduleTime** to **-1**.

Line 184's condition

```
isBetween( scheduleTime )
```

calls programmer-defined method **isBetween** (lines 221–261) to check the time against the query. If they match, the date, time and appointment information are displayed in the **JTextArea** object referenced by **display**.

Lines 209–217 define **processChildNodes**, which iterates through a **NodeList** (i.e., an element's child nodes) and processes them using method **getResult**.

Lines 221–261 define method **isBetween**, which checks the time value of an appointment against the query. We define five periods of the day: all day, morning, afternoon, evening and night.

Figure 8.19 shows the Java application that creates the GUI. Class **DayPlanner** **extends JFrame** to create the user interface.

```
1   // Fig. 8.19 : DayPlanner.java
2   // Program for GUI interface for the day planner application.
3
4   import java.awt.*;
5   import java.awt.event.*;
6   import javax.swing.*;
7   import javax.swing.event.*;
8
9   public class DayPlanner extends JFrame
10     implements ActionListener {
11
12     // GUI components
13     private JTextArea display;
14     private JComboBox year, month, day, time;
15     private JButton query;
16     private JPanel panel1, panel2;
17     private DOMPlanner handler;
18
19     public DayPlanner()
20     {
21        super( "Day planner using DOM" );
22
23        // set the output font
24        Font font = new Font( "Monospaced",
25                              java.awt.Font.BOLD, 16 );
26        display = new JTextArea();
27        display.setFont( font );
28        display.setEditable( false );
29
30        handler = new DOMPlanner( display );
31
32        // initialize the user interface components
33        year = new JComboBox( handler.getYears() );
34
35        String months[] = new String[ 13 ];
36        months[ 0 ] = "ANY";
37
38        for ( int i = 1; i < 13; i++ )
39           months[ i ] = Integer.toString( i );
40
41        month = new JComboBox( months );
42
43        String days[] = new String[ 32 ];
44        days[ 0 ] = "ANY";
45
```

Fig. 8.19 Interface for day planner (part 1 of 3).

```
46              for ( int i = 1; i < 32; i++ )
47                  days[ i ] = Integer.toString( i );
48
49              day = new JComboBox( days );
50
51              String times[] = { "ANY", "Morning", "Afternoon",
52                                  "Evening", "Night" };
53              time = new JComboBox( times );
54
55              query = new JButton( "Get Schedules" );
56              query.addActionListener( this );
57
58              // panel containing components for querying
59              panel1 = new JPanel();
60              panel1.setLayout( new GridLayout( 4, 2 ) );
61              panel1.add( new JLabel( "Year" ) );
62              panel1.add( year );
63              panel1.add( new JLabel( "Month" ) );
64              panel1.add( month );
65              panel1.add( new JLabel( "Day" ) );
66              panel1.add( day );
67              panel1.add( new JLabel("Time") );
68              panel1.add( time );
69
70              // panel containing text area for output
71              // and panel2 containing other GUI components.
72              panel2 = new JPanel();
73              panel2.setLayout( new GridLayout( 1, 2 ) );
74              panel2.add( panel1 );
75              panel2.add( query );
76
77              Container c = getContentPane();
78              c.setLayout( new BorderLayout() );
79              c.add( new JScrollPane( display ), BorderLayout.CENTER );
80              c.add( panel2, BorderLayout.SOUTH );
81              setSize( 600, 450 );
82              show();
83          }
84
85          // method executed when query button is pressed
86          public void actionPerformed( ActionEvent e )
87          {
88              if ( e.getSource() == query ) {
89                  int yearIndex, monthIndex, dayIndex, timeIndex;
90
91                  // get the integer values of all the query parameters
92                  yearIndex =
93                      getIntegerValue( ( String ) year.getSelectedItem() );
94                  monthIndex =
95                      getIntegerValue( ( String ) month.getSelectedItem() );
96                  dayIndex =
97                      getIntegerValue( ( String ) day.getSelectedItem() );
98                  timeIndex = time.getSelectedIndex() - 1;
```

Fig. 8.19 Interface for day planner (part 2 of 3).

```
99
100            // get the result of query
101            handler.getQueryResult( yearIndex, monthIndex,
102                                     dayIndex, timeIndex );
103        }
104    }
105
106    // method to convert the string value to integer
107    public int getIntegerValue( String str )
108    {
109        // if the value 'ANY' is selected, return -1
110        if ( str.equals( "ANY" ) )
111            return -1;
112        else
113            return Integer.parseInt( str );
114    }
115
116    public static void main( String s[] )
117    {
118        DayPlanner d = new DayPlanner();
119
120        d.addWindowListener(
121            new WindowAdapter()
122            {
123                public void windowClosing( WindowEvent e )
124                {
125                    System.exit( 0 );
126                }
127            }
128        );
129    }
130 }
```

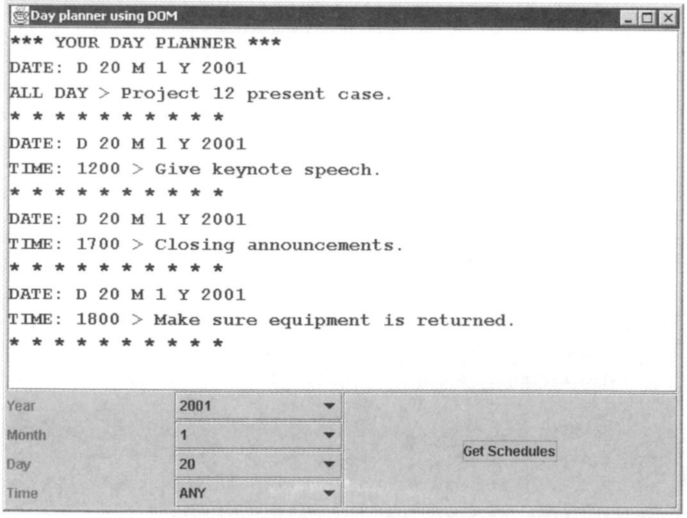

Fig. 8.19   Interface for day planner (part 3 of 3).

Line 30

```
handler = new DOMPlanner( display );
```

instantiates a **DOMPlanner** object and assigns it to reference **handler**. The **JTextArea** object referenced by display is passed to the **DOMPlanner** constructor. This allows the **DOMPlanner** object to write text to the **JTextArea**.

Line 33

```
year = new JComboBox( handler.getYears() );
```

instantiates a **JComboBox** object and populates it with the **String** array values returned from method **getYears** (line 62 in Fig. 8.18). Lines 35–53 create the other **JComboBox** objects and populate them with the month, day and time, respectively.

Method **actionPerformed** (lines 86–104) is invoked when **Get Schedules** is pressed. The four **JComboBox** values are passed to **getQueryResult** (line 94 in Fig. 8.18), which calls **getResult** to perform the query.

Lines 107–114 define method **getIntegerValue**, which converts the **JComboBox** values. A value of **ANY** is results in **-1** being returned. Other **String**s are converted into integers using **parseInt**.

8.9 Internet and World Wide Web Resources

www.w3.org/DOM
W3C DOM home page.

www.w3schools.com/dom
The W3Schools DOM introduction, tutorial and links site.

www.oasis-open.org/cover/dom.html
The Oasis-Open DOM page contains a comprehensive overview of the Document Object Model with references and links.

dmoz.org/Computers/Programming/Internet/W3C_DOM
This is a useful set of DOM links to different locations and instructional matter.

www.w3.org/DOM/faq.html
Answers to Frequently Asked DOM Questions.

www.jdom.org
Home page for the JDOM XML API in Java.

SUMMARY

- XML documents, when parsed, are represented as a hierarchal tree structure in memory. This tree structure contains the document's elements, attributes, text, etc. XML was designed to be a live, dynamic technology—the contents of the tree structure can be modified by a programmer. This essentially allows the programmer to add data, remove data, query for data, etc., in a manner similar to a database.

- The W3C provides a standard recommendation for building a tree structure in memory for XML documents called the XML Document Object Model (DOM). Any parser that adheres to this recommendation is called a DOM-based parser.

- A DOM-based parser exposes (i.e., makes available) a programmatic library—called the DOM Application Programming Interface (API)—that allows data in an XML document to be accessed and manipulated. This API is available for many different programming languages.

- DOM-based parsers are written in a variety of programming languages and are usually available for download at no charge. Many applications (such as Internet Explorer 5) have built-in parsers.

- A Microsoft XML Document Object Model object (i.e., **Microsoft.XMLDOM**) represents an XML document (in memory) and provides methods for manipulating its data.

- Property **documentElement** returns a document's root element. The root element is important because it is used as a reference point for retrieving child elements, text, etc.

- Property **nodeName** returns the name of an attribute, element, etc.—which are collectively called *nodes*.

- Property **childNodes** contains a node's child nodes. Property **length** returns the number of child nodes.

- Individual child nodes are accessed using the **item** method. Each node is given an integer value (starting at zero) based on the order in which they occur in the XML document.

- Property **firstChild** retrieves the root node's first child node.

- Nodes at the same level in a document (i.e., that have the same parent node) are called *siblings*. Property **nextSibling** returns a node's next sibling.

- A text node's value is its text, an element node's value is **null** (which indicates the absence of a value) and an attribute node's value is the attribute's value.

- Property **parentNode** returns a node's parent node.

- The **Document** object represents the top-level node of an XML document in memory and provides a means of creating nodes and retrieving nodes.

- Interface **Node** represents an XML document node.

- **Element** represents an element node.

- Sun Microsystems, the creator of Java, provides several packages related to XML. Package **org.w3c.dom** provides the DOM-API programmatic interface (i.e., classes, methods, etc.). Package **javax.xml.parsers** provides classes related to parsing an XML document. Package **com.sun.xml.tree** contains classes and interfaces from Sun Microsystem's internal API, which provides features (e.g., saving an XML document) currently not available in the DOM recommendation.

- A DOM-based parser may use an event-based implementation (i.e., as the document is parsed events are raised when starting tags, attributes, etc. are encountered) to help create the tree structure in memory. A popular event-based implementation is called the Simple API for XML (SAX). Package **org.xml.sax** provides the SAX programmatic interface.

- Class **DocumentBuilderFactory** (package **javax.xml.parsers**) obtains an instance of a parser.

- Method **setValidating** specifies whether a parser is validating or nonvalidating.

- Method **parse** loads and parses XML documents. If parsing is successful, a **Document** object is returned. Otherwise, a **SAXException** is thrown.

- Method **getDocumentElement** returns the **Document**'s root node. The **Document**'s root node represents the entire document—not the root element node.

- Method **getNodeType** retrieves the node's type.

- Elements in the XML document are retrieved by calling method **getElementsByTagName**. Each element is stored as an item (i.e., a **Node**) in a **NodeList**. The first item added is stored at index 0, the next at index 1, and so forth. This index is used to access an individual item in the **NodeList**.

- Interface *Text* represents an element or attribute's character data.

- Method **replaceChild** replaces a **Node**.

- Method **write** is a member of **XmlDocument**, which requires casting a **Document** to **Xml-Document**. This internal API class is used because **Document** does not provide a method for saving an XML document.

- *SAXParseException* and *SAXException* contain information about errors and warnings thrown by the parser. Class **SAXParseException** is a subclass of **SAXException** and includes methods for locating the location of the error.

- By default, JAXP does not throw any exceptions when a document fails to conform to a DTD. The programmer must provide their own implementation, which is registered using method **setErrorHandler**.

- Interface **ErrorHandler** provides methods **fatalError**, **error** and **warning** for fatal errors (i.e., errors that violate the XML 1.0 recommendation; parsing is halted), errors (e.g., such as validity constraints that do not stop the parsing process) and warnings (i.e., not classified as fatal errors or errors and that do not stop the parsing process), respectively.

- Method **newDocument** creates a new **Document** object, which can be used to build an XML document in memory.

- Method **createComment** creates a comment.

- Method **createProcessingInstruction** creates a processing instruction and method **createCDATASection** creates a **CDATA** section.

TERMINOLOGY

API
appendChild
Attr
CDATA section
childNodes
cloneNode
Comment
comment node
createAttribute
createCDATASection
createComment
createElement
createProcessingInstruction
createTextNode
createXmlDocument
Document
documentElement
document root
DOM
Element
encoding attribute
firstChild
getAttribute

getChildNodes
getDocumentElement
getNodeName
getNodeType
getNodeValue
getParentNode
getTagName
hasChildNodes
item method
Java API for XML Parsing (JAXP)
length property
msxml
nextSibling
Node
Node.ATTRIBUTE_NODE
Node.CDATA_SECTION_NODE
Node.COMMENT_NODE
Node.ELEMENT_NODE
Node.PROCESSING_INSTRUCTION_NODE
Node.TEXT_NODE
NodeList
nodeName
nodeValue

parentNode	setNodeValue
processing instruction node	setValue method of Attr
ProcessingInstruction	Text
removeAttribute	write
removeChild	Xerces
replaceChild	XML::DOM
root element node	XML4J
script element	XmlDocument
setAttribute	

SELF-REVIEW EXERCISES

8.1   State whether each of the following are *true* or *false*. If *false*, explain why.
   a) Class **XmlDocument** is a Sun Microsystem's internal API class.
   b) Text in XML document is not represented as a node.
   c) A **NodeList** contains a list of **Node**s.
   d) Interface **CDATASection** extends interface **CharacterData**.
   e) Interface **Attr** extends interface **Element**.
   f) Method **parse** loads and parses an XML document.
   g) Interface **ErrorHandler** defines methods **fatalError**, **error** and **warning**.
   h) Method **getElementByTagName** of class **Element** returns the first element in the XML document that matches the specified name.
   i) The **replaceChild** method of **XmlDocument** can be used to replace a processing instruction with a comment inside an element.
   j) An element's node value is text (i.e., character data).

8.2   Fill in the blanks in each of the following statements:
   a) DOM is an acronym for _____.
   b) DOM-based parsers represent an XML document's data as a _____ structure.
   c) The number of **Node**s in a **NodeList** is determined by calling method _____.
   d) Method _____ replaces one child node with another.
   e) Method _____ creates a text node.
   f) Method _____ returns a **NodeList** containing every occurrence of a particular element.
   g) _____ represents the root of an XML document.
   h) _____ is a **static Node** constant that represents an element.
   i) _____ method _____ outputs an XML document.

ANSWERS TO SELF-REVIEW EXERCISES

8.1 a) True. b) False. Text is represented as a node. c) True. d) True. e) False. Interface **Attr** is derived from interface **Node**. f) True. g) True. h) False. Method **getElementByTagName** returns a **NodeList** containing all the element nodes that match the specified name. i) True. j) False. An element's node value is **null**.

8.2   a) Document Object Model. b) tree. c) **getLength**. d) **replaceChild**. e) **createTextNode**. f) **getElementsByTagName**. g) **Document**. h) **NODE.ELEMENT_NODE**. i) **XmlDocument, write**.

EXERCISES

8.3   Using JavaScript, add to **article.xml**'s (Fig. 8.2) root element

```
<rating>*****</rating>
```

Display the result as shown in Fig. 8.3.

8.4   Using JavaScript, create an XML document. The document should have a root element named **message** that contains the child element **myMessage**—which contains a text node. Render the document using Internet Explorer. [*Hint*: Use the HTML **innerText** property to display the XML. Also use the **xml** property of **DOMDocument** object.]

8.5   Enhance the day planner case study (Figs. 8.18 and 8.19) to allow the user to add a **note** as a child node of **date**. Use graphical user interface components to accept year, month, day, time and notes from the user. If no existing **date** node matches the date entered by the user, create a new **date** node within the appropriate **year** node and append a new **note** node. If no **year** node matches, create both the **year** node and the **date** node and append a new **note** node to it. View the new nodes by query.

8.6   Write a Java application that loads an XML document that contains the DTD in Fig. 8.20 as part of its internal subset. Use the XML document's data to draw rectangles and circles with text inside them. Attributes **x** and **y** represent the top-left coordinates. Assume a circle is bounded by an imaginary rectangle. Attributes **width** and **height** represent the rectangle's width and height and attribute **radius** is the circle's radius. Validate your XML document(s) against the DTD.

8.7   *(Validator)* Write a Web page that uses JavaScript and msxml to validate XML documents. Display either a message indicating the document is valid or an error message indicating that the document does not conform to its DTD/schema. Error messages should include line numbers as well as a description. [*Hint*: Use Microsoft's **XMLDOMParseError** object to check for parse errors and property **reason** to get a description of why a document failed validation.]

```
1   <!DOCTYPE figure [
2      <!ELEMENT figure ( rectangle*, circle* )>
3      <!ELEMENT rectangle (#PCDATA)>
4      <!ATTLIST rectangle x CDATA #REQUIRED
5                          y CDATA #REQUIRED
6                          width CDATA #REQUIRED
7                          height CDATA #REQUIRED>
8
9      <!ELEMENT circle ( #PCDATA )>
10     <!ATTLIST circle x CDATA #REQUIRED
11                      y CDATA #REQUIRED
12                      radius CDATA #REQUIRED>
13  ]>
```

Fig. 8.20   DTD for Exercise 8.6.

Simple API for XML (SAX)

Objectives

- To be able to use the Simple API for XML (SAX).
- To understand the differences between the Document Object Model (DOM) and SAX.
- To be able to use JAXP's SAX implementation to parse a document.
- To understand fundamental differences between SAX 1.0 and SAX 2.0.
- To be able to use Xerces' SAX implementation to parse a document.

Tis one thing to show a man that he is in an error, and another to put him in possession of truth.
John Locke

An error is the more dangerous in proportion to the degree of truth which it contains.
Henri-Frédéric Amiel

I claim not to have controlled events, but confess plainly that events have controlled me.
Abraham Lincoln

9.1 Introduction

In Chapter 8, we discussed the Document Object Model (DOM) for programmatically manipulating an XML document. This chapter will discuss another method for accessing an XML document's contents, called the *Simple API for XML*, or *SAX*.

SAX was developed by the members of the *XML-DEV mailing list* and was released in May of 1998. SAX is an alternate method for parsing XML documents that uses an *event-based model*—notifications called events are raised as the document is parsed. In this chapter, we discuss how to use SAX. We also program the day planner case study using SAX instead of the DOM.

9.2 DOM vs. SAX

SAX and DOM are dramatically different APIs for accessing information in XML documents. DOM is a tree-based model that stores the document's data in a hierarchy of nodes. Because all the document's data is in memory, data can be quickly accessed. DOM also provides facilities for adding or removing nodes (i.e., modifying the document).

SAX-based parsers invoke methods when markup (e.g., a start tag, end tag, etc.) is encountered. With this event-based model, no tree structure is created by the SAX-based parser to store the XML document's data—data is passed to the application from the XML document as it is found. This results in greater performance and less memory overhead than with the DOM. In fact, Many DOM parsers use a SAX parser to retrieve data from a document for building the DOM tree. However, many programmers find it easier to traverse and manipulate XML documents using the DOM tree structure. As a result, SAX parsers are typically used for reading XML documents that will not be modified.

Performance Tip 9.1

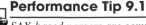

SAX-based parsers are commonly used in situations where memory must be conserved.

Software Engineering Observation 9.1

SAX was developed independently of the W3C and has been widely supported by industry. DOM is the official W3C recommendation.

9.3 SAX-based Parsers

SAX-based parsers are available for a variety of programming languages (e.g., Java, Python, etc.). Several SAX-based parsers are available for free download (Fig. 9.1). We use Sun Microsystem's JAXP with its default parser for the majority of the examples.

9.4 Setup

In successive sections, we will be using Java applications to illustrate the SAX API. This section describes the software needed to run these Java applications. To be able to compile and execute the examples you will need to

1. Download and install the Java 2 Standard Edition from

2. **www.java.sun.com/j2se**.

3. Visit **www.deitel.com/faq/java3install.htm**,

4. to receive step-by-step installation instructions.

5. Download and install JAXP from **java.sun.com/xml/download.html**. Installation instructions are provided at this Web site and as HTML documents included with the download.

6. Copy the Chapter 9 examples from the CD-ROM that accompanies this book to your hard drive. These examples are also available for download free of charge from **www.deitel.com**.

As we present an example, we will discuss the steps necessary to execute it. The steps outlined in this section must be followed before attempting to execute any example.

9.5 Events

The SAX parser invokes certain methods (Fig. 9.2) when events occur. Programmers override these methods to process the data in an XML document. Other SAX implementations may invoke additional methods on events.

Product	Description
JAXP	Sun's JAXP is available from **java.sun.com/xml**. JAXP supports both SAX and DOM.
Xerces	Apache's Xerces parser is available at **www.apache.org**. Xerces supports both SAX and DOM.
MSXML 3.0	Microsoft's msxml parser available at **msdn.microsoft.com/xml**. This parser supports both SAX and DOM.

Fig. 9.1   Some SAX-based parsers.

Method Name	Description
setDocumentLocator	Invoked at the beginning of parsing.
startDocument	Invoked when the parser encounters the start of an XML document.
endDocument	Invoked when the parser encounters the end of an XML document.
startElement	Invoked when the start tag of an element is encountered.
endElement	Invoked when the end tag of an element is encountered.
characters	Invoked when text characters are encountered.
ignorableWhitespace	Invoked when whitespace that can be safely ignored is encountered.
processingInstruction	Invoked when a processing instruction is encountered.

Fig. 9.2 Methods invoked by the SAX parser.

9.6 Example: Tree Diagram

Figure 9.3 is a program that parses an XML document with a SAX-based parser and outputs the document's data as a tree diagram.

```
1   // Fig. 9.3 : Tree.java
2   // Using the SAX Parser to generate a tree diagram.
3
4   import java.io.*;
5   import org.xml.sax.*;   // for HandlerBase class
6   import javax.xml.parsers.SAXParserFactory;
7   import javax.xml.parsers.ParserConfigurationException;
8   import javax.xml.parsers.SAXParser;
9
10  public class Tree extends HandlerBase {
11     private int indent = 0;   // indentation counter
12
13     // returns the spaces needed for indenting
14     private String spacer( int count )
15     {
16        String temp = "";
17
18        for ( int i = 0; i < count; i++ )
19           temp += "  ";
20
21        return temp;
22     }
23
24     // method called before parsing
25     // it provides the document location
```

Fig. 9.3 Application to create a tree diagram for an XML document (part 1 of 4).

```
26      public void setDocumentLocator( Locator loc )
27      {
28          System.out.println( "URL: " + loc.getSystemId() );
29      }
30
31      // method called at the beginning of a document
32      public void startDocument() throws SAXException
33      {
34          System.out.println( "[ document root ]" );
35      }
36
37      // method called at the end of the document
38      public void endDocument() throws SAXException
39      {
40          System.out.println( "[ document end ]" );
41      }
42
43      // method called at the start tag of an element
44      public void startElement( String name,
45          AttributeList attributes ) throws SAXException
46      {
47          System.out.println( spacer( indent++ ) +
48                             "+-[ element : " + name + " ]");
49
50          if ( attributes != null )
51
52              for ( int i = 0; i < attributes.getLength(); i++ )
53                  System.out.println( spacer( indent ) +
54                      "+-[ attribute : " + attributes.getName( i ) +
55                      " ] \"" + attributes.getValue( i ) + "\"" );
56      }
57
58      // method called at the end tag of an element
59      public void endElement( String name ) throws SAXException
60      {
61          indent--;
62      }
63
64      // method called when a processing instruction is found
65      public void processingInstruction( String target,
66          String value ) throws SAXException
67      {
68          System.out.println( spacer( indent ) +
69              "+-[ proc-inst : " + target + " ] \"" + value + "\"" );
70      }
71
72      // method called when characters are found
73      public void characters( char buffer[], int offset,
74          int length ) throws SAXException
75      {
76          if ( length > 0 ) {
77              String temp = new String( buffer, offset, length );
78
```

Fig. 9.3   Application to create a tree diagram for an XML document (part 2 of 4).

```
79                    System.out.println( spacer( indent ) +
80                                "+-[ text ] \"" + temp + "\"" );
81          }
82       }
83
84       // method called when ignorable whitespace is found
85       public void ignorableWhitespace( char buffer[],
86          int offset, int length )
87       {
88          if ( length > 0 ) {
89             System.out.println( spacer( indent ) + "+-[ ignorable ]" );
90          }
91       }
92
93       // method called on a non-fatal (validation) error
94       public void error( SAXParseException spe )
95          throws SAXParseException
96       {
97          // treat non-fatal errors as fatal errors
98          throw spe;
99       }
100
101      // method called on a parsing warning
102      public void warning( SAXParseException spe )
103         throws SAXParseException
104      {
105         System.err.println( "Warning: " + spe.getMessage() );
106      }
107
108      // main method
109      public static void main( String args[] )
110      {
111         boolean validate = false;
112
113         if ( args.length != 2 ) {
114            System.err.println( "Usage: java Tree [validate] " +
115                               "[filename]\n" );
116            System.err.println( "Options:" );
117            System.err.println( "   validate [yes|no] : " +
118                               "DTD validation" );
119            System.exit( 1 );
120         }
121
122         if ( args[ 0 ].equals( "yes" ) )
123            validate = true;
124
125         SAXParserFactory saxFactory =
126            SAXParserFactory.newInstance();
127
128         saxFactory.setValidating( validate );
129
130         try {
131            SAXParser saxParser = saxFactory.newSAXParser();
```

Fig. 9.3   Application to create a tree diagram for an XML document (part 3 of 4).

```
132                 saxParser.parse( new File( args[ 1 ] ), new Tree() );
133           }
134           catch ( SAXParseException spe ) {
135              System.err.println( "Parse Error: " + spe.getMessage() );
136           }
137           catch ( SAXException se ) {
138              se.printStackTrace();
139           }
140           catch ( ParserConfigurationException pce ) {
141              pce.printStackTrace();
142           }
143           catch ( IOException ioe ) {
144              ioe.printStackTrace();
145           }
146
147           System.exit( 0 );
148      }
149 }
```

Fig. 9.3   Application to create a tree diagram for an XML document (part 4 of 4).

Lines 4–8 **import** classes and interfaces used by the program. Package **org.xml.sax** provides the SAX programmatic interface (i.e., classes and interfaces) required by a SAX parser. JAXP package **javax.xml.parsers** provides classes for instantiating DOM and SAX parsers. We will discuss classes **SAXParserFactory**, **ParserConfigurationException** and **SAXParser** momentarily.

On line 10, we create class **Tree**, which **extends** class **HandlerBase** (package **org.xml.sax**). Class **HandlerBase** implements four interfaces: *EntityResolver*—for handling external entities, *DTDHandler*—for handling notations and unparsed entities, *DocumentHandler*—for handling parsing events and *ErrorHandler*—for error handling. Because we do not want **HandlerBase**'s default implementation, we inherit from it and override (i.e., provide a different implementation) several methods. We discuss each overridden method below.

Programmer-defined method **spacer** (lines 14–22) returns a **String** of spaces that is used to emphasize the hierarchal relationship of the data output by indenting each part of the document. We use two spaces per tree level.

Lines 26–29

```
public void setDocumentLocator( Locator loc )
{
    System.out.println( "URL: " + loc.getSystemId() );
}
```

override **HandlerBase** method *setDocumentLocator* to output the parsed document's URL. Using reference **loc**, the document's URL is retrieved by calling method *getSystemId*. Lines 32–35

```
public void startDocument() throws SAXException
{
    System.out.println( "[ document root ]" );
}
```

override **HandlerBase** method ***startDocument***, which is called when the document's root node is encountered. This method is called exactly once. We output the text **[document root]** to indicate that the root node was encountered.

There are a few specialized exceptions for SAX parsing, consisting of *fatal errors*, *nonfatal errors* and *warnings*. Fatal errors most often occur because the XML document is not well formed. Nonfatal errors typically occur due to validation errors, and warnings usually occur because of DTD inconsistencies (e.g., duplicate or unused declarations). The exceptions that are thrown by the SAX parser are ***SAXException*** (thrown when an error occurs), ***SAXParseException*** (a subclass of **SAXException** that is thrown when a parsing error occurs) and ***ParserConfigurationException*** (thrown if the parser could not be instantiated).

Lines 38–41

```
public void endDocument() throws SAXException
{
    System.out.println( "[ document end ]" );
}
```

override **HandlerBase** method ***endDocument***, which is called when the end of the document is encountered. This method is called last and exactly once. We output the text **[document end]** to indicate that the end of the document was encountered. Method **endDocument** is also called when a fatal error occurs.

Lines 44–56 override **HandlerBase** method ***startElement***, which is called when a start tag is encountered. Method **startElement** takes two arguments: the element name (referenced by **name**) and the element's attributes (referenced by **attributes**). Lines 47 and 48 output the element's **name** with the appropriate indenting returned by method **spacer**.

Lines 50–55

```
if ( attributes != null )

    for ( int i = 0; i < attributes.getLength(); i++ )
       System.out.println( spacer( indent ) +
          "+-[ attribute : " + attributes.getName( i ) +
          " ] \"" + attributes.getValue( i ) + "\"" );
```

determine whether the element contains attributes. If the element does not contain attributes, **attributes** has the value **null**, and the **for** loop is not executed. Otherwise, we output each attribute's name and value. To retrieve the number of attributes, we call **AttributeList** method ***getLength***. Methods ***getName*** and ***getValue*** each take an integer argument, which represents the position of the attribute, and return the name and value of the attribute, respectively. The first attribute is at position zero.

Software Engineering Observation 9.2

*Method **startElement**'s second argument contains only attributes with explicit values. Attributes with **#IMPLIED** are not placed in the attribute list.*

Lines 59–62 override **HandlerBase** method ***endElement***, which is called when the end of an element—including an empty element—is encountered. On line 61, we decrement the value of **indent** because we are moving up one level in the tree.

Lines 65–70 override **HandlerBase** method *processingInstruction*, which is called when a processing instruction is encountered. This method takes two **String** arguments representing the processing instruction's target and value. For example, the processing instruction

```
<?test this is a test?>
```

contains target **test** and value **this is a test**. On lines 68–69, we output the processing instruction node. [*Note*: A SAX parser does not invoke **processingInstruction** for an XML declaration (e.g., line 1).]

Lines 73–82 override **HandlerBase** method *characters*, which is invoked when character data is encountered. We declare variables **buffer**, **offset** and **length** of type **char []**, **int** and **int**, respectively. Variable **buffer** contains the element's character data, starting at **offset** and containing **length** number of characters. In preparation for output, we convert the character array to a **String** in line 77.

Lines 85–91 override **HandlerBase** method *ignorableWhitespace*, which is invoked when ignorable whitespace characters are encountered. If a DTD is not present for an XML document, all text is considered important and cannot be ignored. Method **ignorableWhitespace** takes three arguments, similar to method **characters**.

When a DTD is present, some whitespace characters are ignorable. For example, whitespace characters between an element's child elements are ignored—if the parent element does not contain mixed content (i.e., character data and elements). When ignorable whitespace characters are encountered, method **ignorableWhitespace** is invoked instead of method **characters**.

Lines 94–99

```
public void error( SAXParseException spe )
   throws SAXParseException
{
   // Treat non-fatal errors as fatal errors.
   throw spe;
}
```

override **HandlerBase** method *error*, which is usually invoked when a validation error occurs. Because we do not want to continue parsing if the document fails validation, we re**throw** the **SAXParseException**.

Lines 102–106 override **HandlerBase** method **warning**. This method is invoked when problems are detected that are not considered errors, according to the XML 1.0 recommendation.

Lines 109–148 define method **main** where we check for correct program initialization and start the parsing of an XML document. Line 111

```
boolean validate = false;
```

will be used to specify whether or not to use a validating parser. If the user specifies a validating parser from the command line (by typing **yes**), we change **validate** to **true** (lines 122 and 123). Lines 125 and 126

```
SAXParserFactory saxFactory =
   SAXParserFactory.newInstance();
```

instantiate a ***SAXParserFactory*** (package **javax.xml.parsers**) object from which a SAX-based parser can be obtained. Line 128

```
saxFactory.setValidating( validate );
```

configures the **SAXParserFactory** object for a validating parser if **validate** is **true** or a nonvalidating parser if **validate** is **false**.
Lines 131 and 132

```
SAXParser saxParser = saxFactory.newSAXParser();
saxParser.parse( new File( args[ 1 ] ), new Tree() );
```

instantiate a SAX-based parser object by calling method ***newSAXParser*** and passes the parser an XML document and an instance of our **Tree** class. The parser reads the XML document and invokes the appropriate methods. If the parser throws any exceptions, we **catch** them on lines 134–145.

To compile **Tree**, either the **CLASSPATH** environment variable must be set or the compiler option **classpath** must be used to include the appropriate classes for JAXP. For example, to compile the application on a Windows machine, type the following at the command line:

```
set CLASSPATH=c:\jaxp\jaxp.jar;c:\jaxp\parser.jar;.
javac Tree.java
```

Note that this assumes JAXP was installed in the **jaxp** folder on the **C:** drive. We will defer the discussion of executing the application until we have presented our first XML document.

Figure 9.4 shows an XML document that contains elements **test**, **example** and **object**. Root element **test** contains one attribute **name** that is assigned the value **"   spacing 1   "**. Element **object**, which contains the character data **World**, is a child element of **example**. This document does not reference a DTD. To load this document into the program shown in Fig. 9.3, type

```
java Tree no spacing1.xml
```

The output generated by class **Tree** is displayed in Fig. 9.4.

```
1   <?xml version = "1.0"?>
2
3   <!-- Fig. 9.4 : spacing1.xml                   -->
4   <!-- Whitespaces in nonvalidating parsing -->
5   <!-- XML document without DTD                 -->
6
7   <test name = "   spacing 1   ">
8      <example><object>World</object></example>
9   </test>
```

Fig. 9.4   XML document **spacing1.xml** (part 1 of 2).

```
URL: file:C:/Tree/spacing1.xml
[ document root ]
+-[ element : test ]
  +-[ attribute : name ] "  spacing 1  "
  +-[ text ] "                                  ◄─────── Output of line 7's
"                                                         line feed (this line
  +-[ text ] "    "                                       and the next).
  +-[ element : example ]
    +-[ element : object ]
      +-[ text ] "World"
  +-[ text ] "                                  ◄─────── Output of line 8's
"                                                         line feed (this line
[ document end ]                                          and the next).
```

Fig. 9.4   XML document **spacing1.xml** (part 2 of 2).

Notice that whitespace characters are preserved. The attribute value (line 7) is not normalized. The line feed (at the end of line 7) is passed to our application and is shown in the output. The indentation in line 8 is also preserved and displayed as text. The line feed at end of line 8 is also output.

Figure 9.5 shows an XML document that contains elements **test**, **example** and **object**. Root element **test** contains one attribute **name** that is assigned the value **" spacing 2 "**. Element **object**, which contains the character data **World**, is a child element of **example**. This document references a DTD (lines 7–12). To load the document into the program of Fig. 9.3, type

      java Tree no spacing2.xml

the output generated by **Tree.java** is displayed in Fig. 9.5. Even though we are not validating the XML document, the DTD is used to check the XML document's characters—so any whitespace that can be removed is set as ignorable.

```
1   <?xml version = "1.0"?>
2
3   <!-- Fig. 9.5 : spacing2.xml            -->
4   <!-- Whitespace and nonvalidated parsing -->
5   <!-- XML document with DTD              -->
6
7   <!DOCTYPE test [
8   <!ELEMENT test (example)>
9   <!ATTLIST test name CDATA #IMPLIED>
10  <!ELEMENT example (object*)>
11  <!ELEMENT object (#PCDATA)>
12  ]>
13
14  <test name = "  spacing 2  ">
15     <example><object>World</object></example>
16  </test>
```

Fig. 9.5   XML document **spacing2.xml** (part 1 of 2).

```
URL: file:C:/Tree/spacing2.xml
[ document root ]
+-[ element : test ]
  +-[ attribute : name ] "  spacing 2  "
  +-[ ignorable ]
  +-[ ignorable ]
  +-[ element : example ]
    +-[ element : object ]
      +-[ text ] "World"
  +-[ ignorable ]
[ document end ]
```

Fig. 9.5   XML document **spacing2.xml** (part 2 of 2).

The three **ignorable**s in the output are the line feed at the end of line 14, the spaces at the beginning of line 15 and the line feed at the end of line 15.

Consider the XML document shown in Fig. 9.6. This document contains a DTD (lines 6–9), root element **test**, which contains a processing instruction (line 12) and an **example** element. Element **example** contains an **item** element, which contains a **CDATA** section.

The first output shows the result when

> **java Tree no notvalid.xml**

is typed at the command line. The DTD is not used to validate the document. The second output shows the result when

> **java Tree yes notvalid.xml**

is typed at the command line.

This document is well formed, but not valid, because element **example** cannot contain an **item** element. In the first output, validation was disabled and the document was successfully parsed. When a **CDATA** section is encountered, the parser does not process the text—it simply returns the character data. Because validation is enabled in the second output, a fatal error occurs when element **item** is encountered inside element **example**. Parsing terminates when the fatal error occurs. Recall that in Fig. 9.3 (lines 94–99) the **error** method was overridden to re**throw** the **SAXParseException**.

```
1   <?xml version = "1.0"?>
2
3   <!-- Fig. 9.6 : notvalid.xml      -->
4   <!-- Validation and non-validation -->
5
6   <!DOCTYPE test [
7   <!ELEMENT test (example)>
8   <!ELEMENT example (#PCDATA)>
9   ]>
10
```

Fig. 9.6   Well-formed XML document (part 1 of 2).

```
11   <test>
12      <?test message?>
13      <example><item><![CDATA[Hello & Welcome!]]></item></example>
14   </test>
```

```
URL: file:C:/Tree/notvalid.xml
[ document root ]
+-[ element : test ]
  +-[ ignorable ]
  +-[ ignorable ]
  +-[ proc-inst : test ] "message"
  +-[ ignorable ]
  +-[ ignorable ]
  +-[ element : example ]
    +-[ element : item ]
      +-[ text ] "Hello & Welcome!"
  +-[ ignorable ]
[ document end ]
```

```
URL: file:C:/Tree/notvalid.xml
[ document root ]
+-[ element : test ]
  +-[ ignorable ]
  +-[ ignorable ]
  +-[ proc-inst : test ] "message"
  +-[ ignorable ]
  +-[ ignorable ]
  +-[ element : example ]
Parse Error: Element "example" does not allow "item"
```

Fig. 9.6   Well-formed XML document (part 2 of 2).

Figure 9.7 presents an XML document containing root element **test**, which contains element **example**. This document does not contain a DTD. The first output shows the result when

        java Tree no valid.xml

is typed at the command line. The second output shows the result when

        java Tree yes valid.xml

is typed at the command line.

The first output shows a successful parse. Notice that the ampersand (**&**) character is placed in its own text node. When an entity is encountered, the parser replaces the entity with its associated character in its own text node. By doing so, the current text node is terminated, and a new one is started for the entity. Any remaining characters are placed in another text node.

The second output shows the result when validation is attempted. The second execution fails because a DTD is required for an XML document to be valid. Before failing due

```
1   <?xml version = "1.0"?>
2
3   <!-- Fig. 9.7 : valid.xml   -->
4   <!-- DTD-less document       -->
5
6   <test>
7       <example>Hello &amp; Welcome!</example>
8   </test>
```

```
URL: file:C:/Tree/valid.xml
[ document root ]
+-[ element : test ]
  +-[ text ] "
"
  +-[ text ] "    "
  +-[ element : example ]
    +-[ text ] "Hello "
    +-[ text ] "&"
    +-[ text ] " Welcome!"
  +-[ text ] "
"
[ document end ]
```

```
URL: file:C:/Tree/valid.xml
[ document root ]
Warning: Valid documents must have a <!DOCTYPE declaration.
Parse Error: Element type "test" is not declared.
```

Fig. 9.7   Checking an XML document without a DTD for validity.

to a fatal error, method **warning** (Fig. 9.3 line 102) is invoked, indicating the **DOCTYPE** is missing from this document.

9.7 Case Study: Using SAX with the Day Planner Application

In this section, we implement the day planner application from Chapter 8 using SAX. Recall that unlike the DOM, SAX does not store data in a tree structure. For this application, we have to either create one ourselves or parse the XML document multiple times. For simplicity, we have chosen to re-parse the document (e.g., **planner.xml**) each time a query is performed. Figure 9.8 shows the GUI for the appointment query application. The only change made to **dayPlanner.java** from the version in Chapter 8 is to use **SAXPlanner** (Fig. 9.9) instead of **DOMPlanner** in line 17 and 30.

```
1   // Fig. 9.8: DayPlanner.java
2   // Program for GUI interface for day planner.
3
```

Fig. 9.8   User interface for a day-planning application (part 1 of 4).

```
4    import java.awt.*;
5    import java.awt.event.*;
6    import javax.swing.*;
7    import javax.swing.event.*;
8
9    public class DayPlanner extends JFrame
10       implements ActionListener {
11
12       // GUI components
13       private JTextArea display;
14       private JComboBox year, month, day, time;
15       private JButton query;
16       private JPanel panel1, panel2;
17       private SAXPlanner handler;
18
19       public DayPlanner()
20       {
21          super( "Day planner using SAX" );
22
23          // set the output font
24          Font font = new Font( "Monospaced",
25                                 java.awt.Font.BOLD, 16 );
26          display = new JTextArea();
27          display.setFont( font );
28          display.setEditable( false );
29
30          handler = new SAXPlanner( display );
31
32          // initialize the user interface components
33          year = new JComboBox( handler.getYears() );
34
35          String months[] = new String[ 13 ];
36          months[ 0 ] = "ANY";
37
38          for ( int i = 1; i < 13; i++ )
39             months[ i ] = "" + ( i );
40
41          month = new JComboBox( months );
42
43          String days[] = new String[ 32 ];
44          days[ 0 ] = "ANY";
45
46          for ( int i = 1; i < 32; i++ )
47             days[ i ] = "" + ( i );
48
49          day = new JComboBox( days );
50
51          String times[] = { "ANY", "Morning", "Afternoon",
52                             "Evening", "Night" };
53          time = new JComboBox( times );
54
55          query = new JButton( "Get Schedules" );
56          query.addActionListener( this );
```

Fig. 9.8   User interface for a day-planning application (part 2 of 4).

```
57
58          // panel containing components for querying
59          panel1 = new JPanel();
60          panel1.setLayout( new GridLayout( 4, 2 ) );
61          panel1.add( new JLabel( "Year" ) );
62          panel1.add( year );
63          panel1.add( new JLabel( "Month" ) );
64          panel1.add( month );
65          panel1.add( new JLabel( "Day" ) );
66          panel1.add( day );
67          panel1.add( new JLabel("Time") );
68          panel1.add( time );
69
70          // panel containing text area for output
71          // and panel2 containing other GUI components
72          panel2 = new JPanel();
73          panel2.setLayout( new GridLayout( 1, 2 ) );
74          panel2.add( panel1 );
75          panel2.add( query );
76
77          Container c = getContentPane();
78          c.setLayout( new BorderLayout() );
79          c.add( new JScrollPane( display ), BorderLayout.CENTER );
80          c.add( panel2, BorderLayout.SOUTH );
81          setSize( 600, 450 );
82          show();
83       }
84
85       // method executed when query button is pressed
86       public void actionPerformed( ActionEvent e )
87       {
88          if ( e.getSource() == query ) {
89             int yearIndex, monthIndex, dayIndex, timeIndex;
90
91             // get the integer values of all the query parameters
92             yearIndex =
93                getIntegerValue( ( String ) year.getSelectedItem() );
94             monthIndex =
95                getIntegerValue( ( String ) month.getSelectedItem() );
96             dayIndex =
97                getIntegerValue( ( String ) day.getSelectedItem() );
98             timeIndex = time.getSelectedIndex() - 1;
99
100            // get the result of query
101            handler.getQueryResult( yearIndex, monthIndex,
102                                    dayIndex, timeIndex );
103         }
104      }
105
106      // method to convert the string value to integer
107      public int getIntegerValue( String str )
108      {
109
```

Fig. 9.8   User interface for a day-planning application (part 3 of 4).

```
110        // if ANY value is selected, return -1
111        if ( str.equals( "ANY" ) )
112           return -1;
113        else
114           return Integer.parseInt( str );
115     }
116
117     public static void main( String s[] )
118     {
119        DayPlanner d = new DayPlanner();
120        d.addWindowListener(
121
122           new WindowAdapter()
123           {
124              public void windowClosing( WindowEvent e )
125              {
126                 System.exit( 0 );
127              }
128           }
129        );
130     }
131  }
```

Fig. 9.8   User interface for a day-planning application (part 4 of 4).

Figure 9.9 shows the SAX implementation (i.e., **SAXPlanner**) of the day planner.

```
132  // Fig. 9.9 : SAXPlanner.java
133  // Using the JAXP Parser to retrieve schedules
134
135  import java.io.*;
136  import java.util.*;
137  import javax.swing.*;
138  import org.xml.sax.*;
139  import javax.xml.parsers.SAXParserFactory;
140  import javax.xml.parsers.ParserConfigurationException;
141  import javax.xml.parsers.SAXParser;
142
143  public class SAXPlanner extends HandlerBase {
144
145     // variables used for parsing
146     private File fileXML;
147     private SAXParserFactory saxFactory;
148
149     // variables used for returning data
150     private static String strYear, strOutput;
151
152     // variables used for querying
153     private static int queryYear = -1;
154     private static int queryMonth = -1;
155     private static int queryDay = -1;
156     private static int queryTime = -1;
```

Fig. 9.9   Day-planning application with SAX (part 1 of 6).

```
157
158     // variables used for node state
159     private boolean boolYear, boolDate, boolNote;
160
161     // variables used for information state
162     private int currYear, currMonth, currDay, currTime;
163
164     // variable for display
165     private JTextArea display;
166
167     public SAXPlanner(){}
168
169     public SAXPlanner( JTextArea output )
170     {
171        display = output;
172
173        // the XML document needed is "planner.xml"
174        init( "planner.xml" );
175     }
176
177     public void startDocument() throws SAXException
178     {
179        strYear = "";
180        strOutput = "";
181     }
182
183     public void startElement( String name,
184        AttributeList attributes ) throws SAXException
185     {
186        if ( name.equals( "year" ) ) {
187           currYear =
188              Integer.parseInt( attributes.getValue( 0 ) );
189
190           strYear += attributes.getValue( 0 ) + " ";
191
192           boolYear = false;
193           boolDate = false;
194           boolNote = false;
195
196           // check the elements within this year
197           if ( queryYear == -1 || queryYear == currYear )
198              boolYear = true;
199
200        }
201        else if ( boolYear && name.equals( "date" ) ) {
202           currMonth =
203              Integer.parseInt( attributes.getValue( 0 ) );
204           currDay =
205              Integer.parseInt( attributes.getValue( 1 ) );
206
207           boolDate = false;
208           boolNote = false;
209
```

Fig. 9.9   Day-planning application with SAX (part 2 of 6).

```
210          if ( ( queryMonth == -1 || queryMonth == currMonth ) &&
211                 ( queryDay == -1 || queryDay == currDay ) ) {
212
213             // check the elements within this date
214             boolDate = true;
215          }
216       }
217       else if ( boolDate && name.equals( "note" ) ) {
218
219          if ( attributes.getValue( 0 ) != null )
220             currTime =
221                Integer.parseInt( attributes.getValue( 0 ) );
222          else
223             currTime = -1;
224
225          boolNote = false;
226
227          switch ( queryTime ) {
228
229             case 0:
230
231                if ( currTime >= 500 && currTime < 1200 )
232                   boolNote = true;
233
234                break;
235
236             case 1:
237
238                if ( currTime >= 1200 && currTime < 1800 )
239                   boolNote = true;
240
241                break;
242
243             case 2:
244
245                if ( currTime >= 1800 && currTime < 2100 )
246                   boolNote = true;
247
248                break;
249
250             case 3:
251
252                if ( currTime >= 2100 && currTime < 500 )
253                   boolNote = true;
254
255                break;
256
257             default:
258                boolNote = true;
259          }
260
261          if ( currTime == -1 )
262             boolNote = true;
```

Fig. 9.9   Day-planning application with SAX (part 3 of 6).

```
263          }
264      }
265
266      public void characters( char buffer[], int offset,
267          int length ) throws SAXException
268      {
269          if ( boolNote ) {
270              String value = new String( buffer, offset, length );
271              value = value.trim();
272
273              if ( !value.equals( "" ) ) {
274                  strOutput += "\nDATE: D " + currDay + " M " +
275                              currMonth + " Y " + currYear + "\n";
276
277                  if ( currTime != -1 )
278                      strOutput += "TIME: " + currTime + " > " +
279                                  value + "\n";
280                  else
281                      strOutput += "ALL DAY > " + value + "\n";
282
283                  strOutput += "* * * * * * * * *";
284              }
285          }
286      }
287
288      public void error( SAXParseException spe )
289          throws SAXParseException
290      {
291          throw spe;
292      }
293
294      public void warning( SAXParseException spe )
295          throws SAXParseException
296      {
297          System.err.println( "Warning: " + spe.getMessage() );
298      }
299
300      public void init( String filename )
301      {
302          fileXML = new File( filename );
303          saxFactory = SAXParserFactory.newInstance();
304          saxFactory.setValidating( true );
305      }
306
307      public String[] getYears()
308      {
309          String buffer[];
310          StringTokenizer tokens;
311          int i;
312
313          try {
314
315              // parse the file
```

Fig. 9.9   Day-planning application with SAX (part 4 of 6).

```
316              SAXParser saxParser = saxFactory.newSAXParser();
317              saxParser.parse( fileXML, new SAXPlanner() );
318           }
319        catch ( SAXParseException spe ) {
320
321              // parser error
322              System.out.println( "Parse Error: " +
323                                      spe.getMessage() );
324           }
325        catch ( Exception e ) {
326              e.printStackTrace();
327           }
328
329        tokens = new StringTokenizer( strYear );
330
331        buffer = new String[ tokens.countTokens() + 1 ];
332        buffer[ 0 ] = "ANY";
333        i = 1;
334
335        while ( tokens.hasMoreTokens() )
336           buffer[ i++ ] = tokens.nextToken();
337
338        return buffer;
339     }
340
341     public void getQueryResult( int year, int month,
342                                 int day, int time )
343     {
344        queryYear = year;
345        queryMonth = month;
346        queryDay = day;
347        queryTime = time;
348        display.setText( "*** YOUR DAY PLANNER ***" );
349        display.append( getResult() );
350     }
351
352     public String getResult()
353     {
354        try {
355
356           // parse the file
357           SAXParser saxParser = saxFactory.newSAXParser();
358
359           saxParser.parse( fileXML, new SAXPlanner() );
360        }
361        catch( SAXParseException spe ) {
362
363           // parser error
364           System.err.println( "Parse Error: " +
365                                   spe.getMessage() );
366           spe.printStackTrace();
367
368        }
```

Fig. 9.9   Day-planning application with SAX (part 5 of 6).

```
369                 catch ( Exception e ) {
370                     e.printStackTrace();
371                 }
372
373                 return strOutput;
374         }
375     }
```

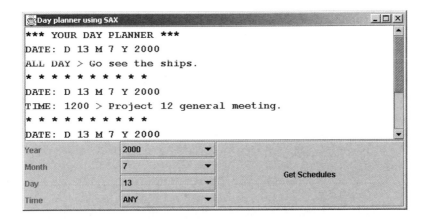

Fig. 9.9   Day-planning application with SAX (part 6 of 6).

Lines 146–165 declare the references and instance variables used to process the XML document. References **strYear** and **strOutput** store the processed data. Variables **queryYear**, **queryMonth**, **queryDay** and **queryTime** store the search data. Variables **boolYear**, **boolDate** and **boolNote** keep track of the current location within the XML document. Variables **currYear**, **currMonth**, **currDay** and **currTime** store the current date and time.

Class **SAXPlanner**'s constructor is defined in line 169 and associates the user interface with the document processor and then sets **planner.xml** as the XML document to be parsed by passing it to programmer-defined method **init** (defined in line 300).

Method **startDocument** (lines 177) initializes variables **strYear** and **strOutput** to the empty string. We do this to ensure that these variables are "cleared out" on each successive parse.

Method **startElement** (line 183) processes the document's elements. Lines 190–205 process **year** elements. We retrieve the **year** element's **value** attribute and append it to **strYear** (lines 187–190), which stores the years that are available in the document. The state variables are reset (lines 192–194), and if the year matches the query, we set **boolYear** to **true**, thus allowing any **date** elements within this **year** element to be processed.

Lines 201–216 process **date** elements. The **month** and **day** attributes are retrieved (lines 202–205) and then checked against the query. If they match, **boolDate** is set to **true** (line 214), which allows processing of **note** elements.

Lines 217–263 process **note** elements. Attribute **time** is retrieved in line 221. If it does not exist, it is assigned **-1**, which denotes "any" time. If the query matches, then we set **boolNote** to **true** inside the **switch** structure (line 227), which allows processing of the text in the **note** element.

Method **characters** (line 266) processes the character data only if **boolNote** is **true**. Using the current date and time information, we create the output string and append it to **strOutput**, which is eventually displayed in the GUI.

Method **init** (line 300) sets the file to be parsed; and creates a **SAXParserFactory** object and configures it for validation.

Method **getYears** (line 307) is called from class **DayPlanner** (line 33 of **Day-Planner.java**) to populate a combo box. This method returns the years in the XML document as an array of **String**s and creates a SAX-based parser object (line 316) that parses the XML document. After parsing, we tokenize the **String** object referenced by **strYear** and return the resulting array.

Method **getQueryResult** (line 341) is called from class **DayPlanner** (line 101 of **DayPlanner.java**). This method queries the XML document with the date arguments, with the assistance of method **getResult** (line 352), and displays the result.

Method **getResult** (lines 352) creates a SAX parser object that parses the XML document. The result is retrieved from **strOutput** and returned. Method **getResult** is called each time a query is made.

Comparing our SAX implementation with the DOM implementation in Chapter 8, we find that the total lines of code in each is about the same. The SAX implementation has to store its own state to determine the current location in the XML document—in the DOM implementation this is handled automatically. Programming of the SAX application was easier because recursion was not needed, but requerying the XML document requires parsing the document again.

For a large planner XML document, the SAX implementation would make more efficient use of memory than the DOM implementation, because the overhead of storing the document in memory is eliminated. However, in the SAX implementation each query requires time to parse the document.

9.8 SAX 2.0

The examples we have studied up to this point use the SAX Version 1.0 API. SAX Version 2.0 was recently released. Although eagerly anticipated, industry is slow to adapt to rapidly changing technologies. Code based on SAX 1.0 is widely used in industry and it will take some time for this code to be upgraded to SAX 2.0. Many parsers either do not support SAX 2.0 or are just beginning to support it. In this section, we provide an example of SAX 2.0 and contrast it with SAX 1.0.

In previous sections, we used JAXP to demonstrate some SAX 1.0 features. Because JAXP does not support SAX 2.0, we use Apache's Xerces Java Parser Version 1.1.3, which does. The Xerces parser can be downloaded from **xml.apache.org/xerces**.

The methods used to process an XML document are mostly the same. Some of the major changes between SAX 1.0 and SAX 2.0 are class **HandlerBase** being replaced with class **DefaultHandler**; element and attribute processing has been expanded to support namespaces; and the process of loading and parsing an XML document has changed. SAX 2.0 also provides methods for retrieving and setting parser properties and features, such as whether the parser performs validation.

Figure 9.10 shows a Java application that uses SAX 2.0 to output the document's data in a hierarchical format. This Java application is based upon the code in Fig. 9.3.
Line 11

```
public class PrintXML extends DefaultHandler {
```

```
1   // Fig. 9.10 : printXML.java
2   // Using the SAX Parser to indent an XML document.
3
4   import java.io.*;
5   import org.xml.sax.*;
6   import org.xml.sax.helpers.*;
7   import javax.xml.parsers.SAXParserFactory;
8   import javax.xml.parsers.ParserConfigurationException;
9   import javax.xml.parsers.SAXParser;
10
11  public class PrintXML extends DefaultHandler {
12     private int indent = 0;   // indention counter
13
14     // returns the spaces needed for indenting
15     private String spacer( int count )
16     {
17        String temp = "";
18
19        for ( int i = 0; i < count; i++ )
20           temp += " ";
21
22        return temp;
23     }
24
25     // method called at the beginning of a document
26     public void startDocument() throws SAXException
27     {
28        System.out.println( "<?xml version = \"1.0\"?>" );
29     }
30
31     // method called at the end of the document
32     public void endDocument() throws SAXException
33     {
34        System.out.println( "---[ document end ]---" );
35     }
36
37     // method called at the start tag of an element
38     public void startElement( String uri, String eleName,
39        String raw, Attributes attributes ) throws SAXException
40     {
41
42        System.out.print( spacer( indent ) + "<" + eleName );
43
44        if ( attributes != null )
45
```

Fig. 9.10   Java application that indents an XML document (part 1 of 3).

```
46                    for ( int i = 0; i < attributes.getLength(); i++ )
47                        System.out.print( " "+ attributes.getLocalName( i ) +
48                                    " = " + "\"" +
49                                    attributes.getValue( i ) + "\"" );
50               System.out.println( ">" );
51               indent += 3;
52         }
53
54         // method called at the end tag of an element
55         public void endElement( String uri, String eleName,
56             String raw ) throws SAXException
57         {
58             indent -= 3;
59             System.out.println( spacer(indent) + "</" + eleName + ">");
60         }
61
62         // method called when characters are found
63         public void characters( char buffer[], int offset,
64             int length ) throws SAXException
65         {
66             if ( length > 0 ) {
67                 String temp = new String( buffer, offset, length );
68
69                 if ( !temp.trim().equals( "" ) )
70                     System.out.println( spacer(indent) + temp.trim() );
71             }
72         }
73
74         // method called when a processing instruction is found
75         public void processingInstruction( String target,
76             String value ) throws SAXException
77         {
78             System.out.println( spacer( indent ) +
79                 "<?" + target + "  " + value + "?>");
80         }
81
82         // main method
83         public static void main( String args[] )
84         {
85
86           try {
87               XMLReader saxParser = ( XMLReader ) Class.forName(
88                   "org.apache.xerces.parsers.SAXParser" ).newInstance();
89
90               saxParser.setContentHandler( new PrintXML() );
91               FileReader reader = new FileReader( args[ 0 ] );
92               saxParser.parse( new InputSource( reader ) );
93           }
94           catch ( SAXParseException spe ) {
95               System.err.println( "Parse Error: " + spe.getMessage() );
96           }
97           catch ( SAXException se ) {
98               se.printStackTrace();
```

Fig. 9.10   Java application that indents an XML document (part 2 of 3).

```
99          }
100         catch ( Exception e ) {
101             e.printStackTrace();
102         }
103
104         System.exit( 0 );
105     }
106 }
```

Fig. 9.10   Java application that indents an XML document (part 3 of 3).

defines class **PrintXML**, which **extends** class *DefaultHandler* (instead of **HandlerBase**). Class **DefaultHandler** provides essentially the same interface as class **HandlerBase**. In SAX 2.0, class **HandlerBase** is deprecated (i.e., obsolete).

Lines 26–29 override **DefaultHandler** method **startDocument**, lines 32–35 override method **endDocument**, lines 63–72 override method **characters** and lines 75–80 override method **processingInstruction**. All these methods provide the same services they did in SAX 1.0.

Lines 38–52 override method **startElement**, which now has four arguments, the namespace URI, the element name, the qualified element name and the element attributes. Element attributes are now stored in an object of type *Attributes* and support retrieval of URIs, attribute names and qualified attribute names.

Lines 55–60 override method **endElement**, which now has three arguments, the namespace URI, the element name and the qualified element name.

Lines 87 and 88

```
XMLReader saxParser = ( XMLReader ) Class.forName(
    "org.apache.xerces.parsers.SAXParser" ).newInstance();
```

create a SAX-based parser object and assign it to reference **saxParser**. Method **forName** is called to load the class definition for Xerces. Method **newInstance** creates the instance that is downcast from **Object** to **XMLReader**.

Line 90

```
saxParser.setContentHandler( new PrintXML() );
```

specifies that an object of type **PrintXML** (which **extends DefaultHandler**) contains the event methods (e.g., **startElement**, etc.) that the parser will call.

Lines 91 and 92

```
FileReader reader = new FileReader( args[ 0 ] );
saxParser.parse( new InputSource( reader ) );
```

create an **InputSource** using the filename passed to the application and parses it. To compile this example, we type

```
set CLASSPATH=c:\xerces\xerces.jar;.
javac PrintXML.java
```

at the command line.

Figure 9.11 lists an XML document that contains a processing instruction that links to a stylesheet in line 5. The root element **test** (lines 7–13) contains **example** and **a** child elements. Element **example** contains attribute **value** and the character data **Hello and Welcome!**. Element **a** contains element **b**, which contains the character data **12345**. To pass this XML document to the program of Fig. 9.10, type

```
java PrintXML test.xml
```

at the command line.

9.9 Internet and World Wide Web Resources

www.megginson.com/SAX
The *SAX 2.0 home page* features various SAX specifications and resources.

www.whatis.com/sax.htm
Definition of SAX and links on the **Whatis.com** site.

xarch.tu-graz.ac.at/publ/tutorial/java/tutorials/5120/Java826.htm
Provides the tutorial "XML to Objects and Objects to XML using SAX."

SUMMARY

- SAX was developed by the members of the XML-DEV mailing list and is an alternative model for parsing XML documents that uses an *event-based model*—notifications called events are raised as the document is parsed.

- DOM is a tree-based model, which stores the document's data in a hierarchy of nodes. Because all the document's data is in memory, data can be quickly accessed. DOM also provides facilities for adding or removing nodes (i.e., modifying the document).

- SAX-based parsers invoke methods when markup (e.g., a start tag, end tag, etc.) is encountered. With this event-based model, no object (e.g., a tree structure) is created by the SAX-based parser to store the XML document's data—data is passed to the application using the XML document as it is encountered.

- SAX-based parsers are available for a variety of programming languages (e.g., Java, Python, etc.). Several SAX-based parsers (e.g., JAXP, Xerces and msxml) are available for free download.

```
1    <?xml version = "1.0"?>
2
3    <!-- Fig. 9.11 : test.xml -->
4
5    <?xml:stylesheet type = "text/xsl" href = "something.xsl"?>
6
7    <test>
8       <example value = "100">Hello and Welcome!</example>
9
10      <a>
11         <b>12345</b>
12      </a>
13   </test>
```

Fig. 9.11   Sample execution of **printXML.java** (part 1 of 2).

```
<?xml version = "1.0"?>
<?xml:stylesheet type = "text/xsl" href = "something.xsl"?>
<test>
    <example value = "100">
       Hello and Welcome!
    </example>
    <a>
       <b>
          12345
       </b>
    </a>
</test>
---[ document end ]---
```

Fig. 9.11 Sample execution of **printXML.java** (part 2 of 2).

- Package *org.xml.sax* provides the SAX programmatic interface (i.e., classes and interfaces) required by a SAX parser. JAXP package **javax.xml.parsers** provides classes for instantiating DOM and SAX parsers.

- Class **HandlerBase** implements four interfaces: *EntityResolver*—for handling external entities, *DTDHandler*—for handling notations and unparsed entities, *DocumentHandler*—for handling parsing events and *ErrorHandler*—for error handling.

- **HandlerBase** method *setDocumentLocator* provides access to the parsed document's URL. Calling method *getSystemID* retrieves a document's URL.

- **HandlerBase** method *startDocument* is called when the document's root node is encountered. This method is called exactly once.

- When a fatal error occurs, the XML document is usually not well formed. Nonfatal errors typically occur due to validation errors, and warnings usually occur because of DTD inconsistencies (e.g., duplicate or unused declarations).

- The exceptions that are thrown by the SAX parser are *SAXException* (thrown when an error occurs), *SAXParseException* (a subclass of **SAXException** that is thrown when a parsing error occurs) and *ParserConfigurationException* (thrown if the parser could not be instantiated).

- **HandlerBase** method *endDocument* is called when the end of the document is reached. This method is called last and exactly once. It is also called when a fatal error occurs.

- **HandlerBase** method *startElement* is called when a start tag is encountered. Method **startElement** takes two arguments: the element name and the element's attributes.

- **AttributeList** method *getLength* returns the number of attributes an element has. Methods *getName* and *getValue* each take an integer argument, which represents the position of the attribute, and return the name and value of the attribute, respectively. The first attribute is at position zero.

- **HandlerBase** method *endElement* is called when the end of an element—including an empty element—is encountered.

- **HandlerBase** method *processingInstruction* is called when a processing instruction is encountered. This method takes two **String** arguments representing the processing instruction's target and value. A SAX parser does not invoke **processingInstruction** for an XML declaration.

- **HandlerBase** method ***characters*** is invoked when character data is encountered.

- **HandlerBase** method ***ignorableWhitespace*** is invoked when ignorable whitespace characters are encountered. If a DTD is not present for an XML document, all text is considered important and cannot be ignored. Method **ignorableWhitespace** takes three arguments, similar to method **characters**.

- When a DTD is present, some whitespace characters are ignorable. When ignorable whitespace characters are encountered, method **ignorableWhitespace** is invoked instead of method **characters**.

- **HandlerBase** method ***error*** is usually invoked when a validation error occurs.

- **HandlerBase** method **warning** is invoked when problems are detected that are not considered errors according to the XML 1.0 recommendation.

- A SAX-based parser can be obtained from a ***SAXParserFactory*** object.

- A **SAXParserFactory** object is configured for a validating parser by passing method **validate true**. Passing **validate false** indicates that a nonvalidating parser is being used.

- A SAX-based parser object is obtained by calling method ***newSAXParser***.

- Some of the major changes between SAX 1.0 and SAX 2.0 are class **HandlerBase** being replaced with class **DefaultHandler**, element and attribute processing has been expanded to support namespaces; and the process of loading and parsing an XML document has changed.

- Class **DefaultHandler** provides essentially the same interface as class **HandlerBase**. In SAX 2.0, class **HandlerBase** is deprecated (i.e., obsolete).

TERMINOLOGY

AttributeList interface	**ParserConfigurationException**
document root node	processing instruction node
DOM	**processingInstruction**
endDocument method of HandlerBase	SAX (Simple API for XML)
endElement method of **HandlerBase**	SAX parser
error method of **HandlerBase**	SAX Version 2.0
getLength method of **AttributeList**	**SAXException**
getName method of class **AttributeList**	**SAXParseException**
getSystemId method of class **Locator**	**setDocumentLocator** method
getValue method of **AttributeList**	of **HandlerBase**
ignorableWhitespace	**startDocument** method of **HandlerBase**
JAXP parser	**startElement** method of **HandlerBase**
name	**warning** method of **HandlerBase**

SELF-REVIEW EXERCISES

9.1   State whether the following are *true* or *false*. If *false*, explain why.
   a) SAX is an alternate model for parsing XML documents that uses a tree-based model, unlike DOM, which is event-based.
   b) SAX is a W3C recommendation.
   c) JAXP utilizes the DTD for element definitions, even if document validation is not performed.
   d) Method **characters** throws a **SAXException**.
   e) Because SAX dynamically builds an object to store the information in an XML document, processing the document depends on the methods that are automatically built into that object for handling events.

f) When SAX is used, any data that is not stored upon parsing is lost to the application, unless the document is parsed again.

g) When a DTD is present, some whitespace is ignorable.

h) SAX is an event-based model, so a parser will invoke methods when certain objects are encountered.

i) JAXP supports SAX 2.0.

j) SAX 2.0 provides class **HandlerBase**, which deprecates class **DefaultHandler**.

9.2 Fill in the blanks in each of the following statements:

a) SAX is an acronym for _____.

b) The JAXP package that provides all the interfaces for the SAX parser is _____.

c) Method _____ is called when the end of the document is reached.

d) During parsing, if a _____ section is encountered, the parser will not process the text, but will simply return the character data.

e) Method _____ is called when a element is encountered.

f) Both SAX and _____ are APIs for accessing information in XML documents.

g) SAX method _____ is invoked when the end tag of an element is encountered.

h) Method _____ is invoked when a nonfatal error occurs.

i) Method _____ is invoked when a processing instruction is encountered.

j) Method _____ is invoked when the end of an element is encountered.

ANSWERS TO SELF-REVIEW EXERCISES

9.1   a) False. SAX is an alternate model for parsing XML documents using an event-based system, unlike DOM, which is tree based. b) False. DOM is a W3C recommendation. c) True. d) True. e) False. Because SAX does not build an object to store the information in an XML document, processing the document depends only on the methods that the programmer writes for handling events. f) True. g) True. h) True. i) False. JAXP supports SAX 1.0. j) False. Class **DefaultHandler** deprecates **HandlerBase**.

9.2   a) Simple API for XML. b) **org.xml.sax**. c) **endDocument**. d) **CDATA**. e) **method**. f) DOM. g) **endElement**. h) **error**. i) **processingInstruction**. j) **endElement**.

EXERCISES

9.3   Modify the code of Fig. 9.3 (**Tree.java**) to replace the JAXP default parser with the Xerces SAX 2.0 parser.

9.4   Using the JAXP default parser, write an application to process the document in Fig. 9.12 and output it as shown at the end of the code document. Also write a DTD for the application to validate the document.

```
1   <?xml version = "1.0"?>
2
3   <!DOCTYPE community SYSTEM "community.dtd">
4
5   <community>
6
7      <family>
8         <parent>
9
```

Fig. 9.12   Input XML document (part 1 of 2).

```
10              John
11              <child>Sue</child>
12              <child>Bob</child>
13              <child>Mary</child>
14          </parent>
15      </family>
16
17      <family>
18          <parent>
19              Mike
20
21              <child>
22                  Bill
23                  <grandchild>Jane</grandchild>
24              </child>
25
26              <child>Gary</child>
27          </parent>
28      </family>
29  </community>
```

```
OUTPUT:
Head of Family: John
John's Children:
        1. Sue
        2. Bob
        3. Mary
-------------------------------------------------
Head of Family: Mike
Mike's Children:
        1. Bill
        Bill's Children:
                1.Jane
        2. Gary
-------------------------------------------------
```

Fig. 9.12   Input XML document (part 2 of 2).

10

Case Study: XmlMessenger Program

Objectives

- To understand how XML can be used with Java to achieve powerful results.
- To manipulate and traverse the DOM from within a Java application.
- To understand the advantage of using XML to communicate between the client and the server.
- To understand the advantage of using XML to store data.
- To know when it is appropriate to use XML instead of a Java class.

Friends share all things.
Pythagorus

Mr. Watson, come here, I want you.
Alexander Graham Bell

What networks of railroads, highways and canals were in another age, the networks of telecommunications, information and computerization...are today.
Bruno Kreisky, Austrian Chancellor

10.1 Introduction

Instant messaging is one of the fastest growing communications media in history. According to America Online, the pioneer of instant messaging, its instant messaging services grew from 0 to 50 million users in less than three years, and it now has over 64 million users. There are predictions that over 175 million users will be instant messaging by 2002. *Instant-messaging applications* enable users to instantly send text messages to other users on the Internet. They combine the immediacy of a phone call with the functionality of a e-mail-based application. Currently, there are number of instant-messaging services provided by software giants such as Microsoft, Yahoo, AOL and Infoseek. Some of these services also provide more sophisticated instant-messaging features that allow voice communication, file transfer and Internet conferencing. Once, instant messaging was thought of as the province of teenagers, but that perception has changed. Lawyers, doctors, scientists and all other types of professionals are on-line. Instant messaging is becoming standard operating procedure at businesses worldwide. It is integrated into the next generation of Web browsers. It is spreading rapidly to other platforms and is already available for cellular phones, personal digital assistants (PDAs) and even televisions.

This chapter implements a Java-based instant-messenger application that uses XML. There are two main components in the system: the *server* and the *client/user*. Figure 10.1 shows the architecture of our application. Clients, or users of the system, are the people who need to communicate with other users in the system. Consider a case where user 1 needs to communicate with user 2. For communication to be established, both users need to be logged on to the server. The instant-messenger application used by user 1 and user 2 displays all the users who are currently logged on to the server. User 1 can then choose to send messages to user 2. When user 1 types in a message for user 2, the message is tagged with XML and sent to the server. The XML message also contains the destination (user 2) of the message and its source (user 1). The server then reroutes the message to the respective user based on the destination information provided in the message.

The client-side application has two main functions. First, it registers the user with the server by sending an XML document that contains the user's name and ID. It then updates its current list of logged-on users with the new information it receives from the server. During the session, that is, the period during which the user is logged on, it has to update this list whenever a new user logs in. All such information is exchanged in the form of XML. The second function of the client is to convert the text typed in by the user into XML-based messages, tagging them appropriately to identify the source and destination of each message, and to send them to the server. The client also has to parse the XML messages received from the server and display them to the user.

This messaging system demonstrates how to incorporate XML into all the tiers of a client/server interface. It can be expanded to include many more advanced capabilities, but for our purposes, the system we implement provides ample illustration of XML. Because the **XmlMessenger** uses Sun's Java implementation of the **org.w3c.dom** package, Chapter 8 is a prerequisite for this chapter.

10.2 Setup

To run the **XmlMessenger**, implement the following steps:

1. Make sure the following are installed: J2SDK and JAXP from Sun.

2. Copy the **XmlMessenger** directory from the Chapter 10 examples directory on the CD included with this book onto your computer. This set of steps assumes that you will copy it onto your C drive; if you install it into a different directory, be sure to change the paths in the steps.

3. To execute the server, start MS-DOS (or a command window), change to the **XmlMessenger** directory (**cd XmlMessenger**) and type the command

   ```
   java MessengerServer
   ```

4. For each client, start MS-DOS (or, in Windows 2000, open a command window), change to the **XmlMessenger** directory and type the command

   ```
   java MessengerClient
   ```

5. The server application must be running before you run any client applications.

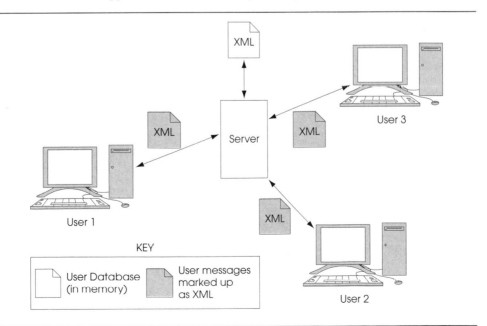

Fig. 10.1 XmlMessenger architecture.

10.3 Overview: Server Side of **XmlMessenger**

Using a **ServerSocket**, a **MessengerServer** object waits for clients to connect. When a client connects, the server creates a new **UserThread** object to manage the client's socket and streams. The **MessengerServer** object uses a **Vector** to store all **UserThread** instances.

The **MessengerServer** also uses a **Document** object **users**, consisting of the names of on-line users stored in individual **user** elements. For example, after **User1** and **User2** have logged in, the server's **Document users** is

```
<users>
    <user>User1</user>
    <user>User2</user>
</users>
```

When a user first logs in, an XML document is sent to the **MessengerServer** object's corresponding **UserThread** object as

```
<user>username</user>
```

The **UserThread** object processes all incoming messages; when it receives this message, it tests if *username* has already been taken by another user. If so, the **UserThread** object sends the client an XML document containing

```
<nameInUse />
```

If *username* is not in use, the **UserThread** object sends the client the **MessengerServer** object's **Document users**. The **MessengerServer** then notifies all other users of this new user's login by sending them the XML document

```
<update type = "login">
    <user>username</user>
</update>
```

If the user sends a message to another user, the corresponding **UserThread** object receives an XML document with root element **message**. For example, if **User1** sends "hello" to **User2**, the following XML is received by the **UserThread** corresponding to **User1**

```
<message to = "User2" from = "User1">hello</message>
```

When the **UserThread** object receives the XML, it relays it to the **MessengerServer** for appropriate routing. The **MessengerServer** object then sends the above XML to the user referenced in the **to** attribute.

The last XML document the **UserThread** object receives from the client is sent when the user disconnects. This XML document contains

```
<disconnect/>
```

When this XML message is received, the **MessengerServer** object notifies all other users that this user has logged out by sending them the following:

```
<update type = "logout">
   <user>username</user>
</update>
```

The **MessengerServer** object then removes the user from its **Vector onlineUsers** and its **Document users**. The GUI for the **MessengerServer** is updated as the above processes occur (Fig. 10.2).

10.4 Implementation: Server Side of **XmlMessenger**

In this section, we discuss the server-side Java files. Figure 10.3 contains the source code for **MessengerServer.java**, which implements the server, and Fig. 10.4 contains the source code for **UserThread.java**, which implements the thread used to manage each client.

Fig. 10.2 MessengerServer graphical user interface.

```
1    // Fig. 10.3: MessengerServer.java
2    // This program provides implementation for the
3    // messenger server.
4
5    import java.awt.*;
6    import java.awt.event.*;
7    import java.net.*;
8    import java.io.*;
9    import javax.swing.*;
10   import java.util.*;
11
12   import org.w3c.dom.*;
13   import org.xml.sax.*;
14   import javax.xml.parsers.*;
15   import com.sun.xml.tree.XmlDocument;
16
```

Fig. 10.3 MessengerServer.java (part 1 of 6).

```
17   public class MessengerServer extends JFrame {
18      private JLabel status;
19      private JTextArea display;
20      private Vector onlineUsers;
21      private DocumentBuilderFactory factory;
22      private DocumentBuilder builder;
23      private Document users;
24
25      public MessengerServer()
26      {
27         // create GUI
28         super ( "Messenger Server" );
29
30         try {
31
32            // obtain the default parser
33            factory = DocumentBuilderFactory.newInstance();
34
35            // get DocumentBuilder
36            builder = factory.newDocumentBuilder();
37         }
38         catch ( ParserConfigurationException pce ) {
39            pce.printStackTrace();
40         }
41
42         Container c = getContentPane();
43
44         status = new JLabel( "Status" );
45         c.add( status, BorderLayout.NORTH );
46
47         display = new JTextArea();
48         display.setLineWrap( true );
49         display.setEditable( false );
50         c.add( new JScrollPane( display ), BorderLayout.CENTER );
51         display.append( "Server waiting for connections\n" );
52
53         setSize( 300, 300 );
54         show();
55
56         // initialize variables
57         onlineUsers = new Vector();
58         users = initUsers();
59      }
60
61      public void runServer()
62      {
63         ServerSocket server;
64
65         try {
66            // create a ServerSocket
67            server = new ServerSocket( 5000, 100 );
68
```

Fig. 10.3 MessengerServer.java (part 2 of 6).

```
69              // wait for connections
70              while ( true ) {
71                 Socket clientSocket = server.accept();
72
73                 display.append( "\nConnection received from: " +
74                    clientSocket.getInetAddress().getHostName() );
75
76                 UserThread newUser =
77                    new UserThread( clientSocket, this );
78
79                 newUser.start();
80              }
81           }
82           catch ( IOException e ) {
83              e.printStackTrace();
84              System.exit( 1 );
85           }
86        }
87
88        private Document initUsers()
89        {
90           // initialize users xml document with root element users
91           Document init = builder.newDocument();
92
93           init.appendChild( init.createElement( "users" ) );
94           return init;
95        }
96
97        public void updateGUI( String s )
98        {
99           display.append( "\n" + s );
100       }
101
102       public Document getUsers()
103       {
104          return users;
105       }
106
107       public void addUser( UserThread newUserThread )
108       {
109          // get new user's name
110          String userName = newUserThread.getUsername();
111
112          updateGUI( "Received new user: " + userName );
113
114          // notify all users of user's login
115          updateUsers( userName, "login" );
116
117          // add new user element to Document users
118          Element usersRoot = users.getDocumentElement();
119          Element newUser = users.createElement( "user" );
120
```

Fig. 10.3 MessengerServer.java (part 3 of 6).

```
121        newUser.appendChild(
122           users.createTextNode( userName ) );
123        usersRoot.appendChild( newUser );
124
125        updateGUI( "Added user: " + userName );
126
127        // add to Vector onlineUsers
128        onlineUsers.addElement( newUserThread );
129     }
130
131     public void sendMessage( Document message )
132     {
133        // transfer message to specified receiver
134        Element root = message.getDocumentElement();
135        String from = root.getAttribute( "from" );
136        String to = root.getAttribute( "to" );
137        int index = findUserIndex( to );
138
139      updateGUI( "Received message To: " + to + ",  From: " + from );
140
141        // send message to corresponding user
142        UserThread receiver =
143           ( UserThread ) onlineUsers.elementAt( index );
144        receiver.send( message );
145        updateGUI( "Sent message To: " + to +
146           ",  From: " + from );
147     }
148
149     public void updateUsers( String userName, String type )
150     {
151        // create xml update document
152        Document doc = builder.newDocument();
153        Element root = doc.createElement( "update" );
154        Element userElt = doc.createElement( "user" );
155
156        doc.appendChild( root );
157        root.setAttribute( "type", type );
158        root.appendChild( userElt );
159        userElt.appendChild( doc.createTextNode( userName ) );
160
161        // send to all users
162        for ( int i = 0; i < onlineUsers.size(); i++ ) {
163           UserThread receiver =
164              ( UserThread ) onlineUsers.elementAt( i );
165           receiver.send( doc );
166        }
167
168        updateGUI( "Notified online users of " +
169           userName + "'s " + type );
170     }
171
```

Fig. 10.3   MessengerServer.java (part 4 of 6).

```
172     public int findUserIndex( String userName )
173     {
174        // find index of specified UserThread in Vector onlineUsers
175        // return -1 if no corresponding UserThread is found
176        for ( int i = 0; i < onlineUsers.size(); i++ ) {
177           UserThread current =
178              ( UserThread ) onlineUsers.elementAt( i );
179
180           if ( current.getUsername().equals( userName ) )
181              return i;
182        }
183
184        return -1;
185     }
186
187     public void removeUser( String userName )
188     {
189        // remove user from Vector onlineUsers
190        int index = findUserIndex( userName );
191
192        onlineUsers.removeElementAt( index );
193
194        // remove this user's element from Document users
195        NodeList userElements =
196           users.getDocumentElement().getElementsByTagName(
197           "user" );
198
199        for ( int i = 0; i < userElements.getLength(); i++ ) {
200           String str =
201              userElements.item( i ).getFirstChild().getNodeValue();
202
203           if ( str.equals( userName ) )
204              users.getDocumentElement().removeChild(
205                 userElements.item( i ) );
206
207        }
208
209        updateGUI( "Removed user: " + userName );
210
211        // update all users of user's logout
212        updateUsers( userName, "logout" );
213     }
214
215     public static void main( String args[] )
216     {
217        MessengerServer ms = new MessengerServer();
218
219        ms.addWindowListener(
220           new WindowAdapter() {
221              public void windowClosing( WindowEvent e ) {
222                 System.exit( 0 );
223              }
224           }
```

Fig. 10.3 MessengerServer.java (part 5 of 6).

```
225        );
226
227        ms.runServer();
228    }
229 }
```

Fig. 10.3 MessengerServer.java (part 6 of 6).

Class **MessengerServer** (Fig. 10.3) implements the server for the **XmlMessenger** application. Lines 5–15 **import** the packages necessary for this class; these include Java networking and I/O packages as well as packages for manipulating the DOM. **Vector onlineUsers** stores the individual **UserThread** objects, which represent the individual users. The names of all users are stored in the **Document** object referenced by **users**. Each user is stored in a separate **user** element, as in

```
<users>
    <user>username1</user>
    <user>username2</user>
    ...
</users>
```

This **Document** is sent to every new user that logs in and is updated whenever a user logs in or out.

The constructor creates the GUI; note that class **MessengerServer extends** class **JFrame**. It also initializes the instance variables; when initializing the **Document users**, it invokes the **private** method **initUsers** (line 88), which creates a new **Document**. We then create the root element **users** and append it as the child of the **Document** object referenced by **init** (line 93). Note that a **Document** object can have only one child—its root element.

Method **runServer** (line 61) is invoked by method **main** (line 227). It creates a new **ServerSocket server**, which waits for clients to connect. When **server** receives a connection, method **accept** returns a **Socket** object specific to the client. This **Socket** object is then passed **UserThread**'s constructor. Class **UserThread** (Fig. 10.4) **extend**s class **Thread**. By managing each client as a separate thread, the server can handle more than one client at a time.

When a new user successfully logs in, method **addUser** is invoked (lines 107–129). We notify all users of this user's login using **MessengerServer** method **updateUsers** (discussed momentarily). Lines 119–123 add the user to the **users Document** by creating a new **user** element and setting its contents to the specified *username*. Finally, we add the passed **UserThread** object to the **Vector onlineUsers**; note that we do not want to add it until a successful login has occurred, since the user is not officially online until that point.

Lines 131–147 define method **sendMessage**, which is invoked when a message from one user to another is received by the sender's **UserThread**. Parameter **message** references a **Document** object containing the message in the form

```
<message to = "receiver" from = "sender">
    message text
</message>
```

We traverse the DOM to access attributes **to** and **from** to determine the receiver and sender of this message, respectively. Local variable **index** stores the index of the **User-Thread** corresponding to the receiver in the **Vector onlineUsers**. To initialize **index**, we call helper method **findUserIndex** (line 137). This method searches the **Vector onlineUsers** for the **userName**. When a match is found, the index is returned; if there is no match, **-1** is returned. Using **index**, **sendMessage** sends the message to the receiving client using the receiver's **UserThread** method **send**. Finally, method **sendMessage** calls method **updateGUI**, updating the server's GUI to reflect the message transfer.

Method **updateUsers** is invoked when a user either successfully logs in or logs out. It is used to notify all other users of the login or logout. Line 152 creates a **Document** object. Lines 153 and 154 create the **root** element **update** and element **user**. After the **root** element is appended as the child of **Document doc**, attribute **type** is created, and its value is set to "**login**" or "**logout**," depending on the passed **String** parameter **type**. Then element **user** is appended as a child to the **root** element (line 158). Finally, a text node containing the passed **String userName** is added to element **user**. This step creates the XML document

```
<update type = "type">
    <user>userName</user>
</update>
```

The **for** loop (lines 162–166) iterates through the **UserThread** instances stored in the **Vector onlineUsers**, sending each the newly created XML document. The method **updateGUI** is called to update the GUI.

When a user logs out, method **removeUser** is invoked. We remove the specified **UserThread** from the **Vector onlineUsers**. We must also remove the user from the **Document users**. To do this, we retrieve all **user** elements with **Element** method **getElementsByTagName**. We iterate through the resulting **NodeList** until we find the **user** element corresponding to this user. Using **Node** method **removeChild**, we remove this element from the root element **users**.

Class **UserThread** (Fig. 10.4) **extends** class **Thread**. A **UserThread** class object is created for each client that connects to the server. Variable **connection** references the **Socket** for this particular client; **input** and **output** reference the input and output streams, respectively. Variable **server** references the **MessengerServer** that instantiated this **UserThread** object. The client's username is stored in **String username**. Finally, **boolean keepListening** is used in a **while** loop (line 351); the **UserThread** object listens for communication from the client until **keepListening** is set to **false** (line 318) in response to the user's logout.

```
230  // Fig. 10.4: UserThread.java
231  // This program provides implementation on the server side
232  // for threads which are created for each of the clients who
233  // have connected.
234
235  import java.net.*;
236  import java.io.*;
```

Fig. 10.4 UserThread.java (part 1 of 4).

```
237
238  import org.w3c.dom.*;
239  import org.xml.sax.*;
240  import javax.xml.parsers.*;
241  import com.sun.xml.tree.XmlDocument;
242
243  public class UserThread extends Thread {
244     private Socket connection;
245     private InputStream input;
246     private OutputStream output;
247     private MessengerServer server;
248     private String username = "";
249     private boolean keepListening;
250     private DocumentBuilderFactory factory;
251     private DocumentBuilder builder;
252
253     public UserThread( Socket s, MessengerServer ms )
254     {
255        try
256        {
257           // obtain the default parser
258           factory = DocumentBuilderFactory.newInstance();
259
260           // get DocumentBuilder
261           builder = factory.newDocumentBuilder();
262        }
263        catch ( ParserConfigurationException pce ) {
264           pce.printStackTrace();
265           System.exit( 1 );
266        }
267
268        // initialize variables
269        connection = s;
270        server = ms;
271        keepListening = true;
272
273        // get input and output streams
274        try {
275           input = connection.getInputStream();
276           output = connection.getOutputStream();
277        }
278        catch ( IOException e ) {
279           e.printStackTrace();
280           System.exit( 1 );
281        }
282     }
283
284     public String getUsername()
285     {
286        return username;
287     }
288
```

Fig. 10.4 UserThread.java (part 2 of 4).

```
289    public void messageReceived( Document message )
290    {
291        Element root = message.getDocumentElement();
292
293        if ( root.getTagName().equals( "user" ) ) {
294
295            // if initial login, root element is "user"
296            // add user element to server's user document
297
298            // test if user entered unique name
299            String enteredName = root.getFirstChild().getNodeValue();
300
301            if ( server.findUserIndex( enteredName ) != -1 )
302                nameInUse(); // not a unique name
303            else {
304
305                // unique name
306                // send server's Document users
307                send( server.getUsers() );
308
309                username = enteredName; // update username variable
310
311                // add user to server
312                server.addUser( this );
313            }
314        }
315        else if ( root.getTagName().equals( "message" ) )
316            server.sendMessage( message );
317        else if ( root.getTagName().equals( "disconnect" ) ) {
318            keepListening = false;
319
320            // remove user from server
321            server.removeUser( username );
322        }
323    }
324
325    private void nameInUse()
326    {
327        Document enterUniqueName = builder.newDocument();
328
329        enterUniqueName.appendChild(
330            enterUniqueName.createElement( "nameInUse" ) );
331
332        send( enterUniqueName );
333    }
334
335    public void send( Document message )
336    {
337        try {
338            // write to output stream
339            ( ( XmlDocument )message).write( output );
340        }
```

Fig. 10.4 UserThread.java (part 3 of 4).

```
341              catch ( IOException e ) {
342                 e.printStackTrace();
343              }
344           }
345
346           public void run()
347           {
348              try {
349                 int bufferSize = 0;
350
351                 while ( keepListening ) {
352                    bufferSize = input.available();
353
354                    if ( bufferSize > 0 ) {
355                       byte buf[] = new byte[ bufferSize ];
356
357                       input.read( buf );
358
359                       InputSource source = new InputSource(
360                          new ByteArrayInputStream( buf ) );
361                       Document message = builder.parse( source );
362
363                       if ( message != null )
364                          messageReceived( message );
365                    }
366                 }
367
368                 input.close();
369                 output.close();
370                 connection.close();
371              }
372              catch ( SAXException e ) {
373                 e.printStackTrace();
374              }
375              catch ( IOException e ) {
376                 e.printStackTrace();
377              }
378           }
379        }
```

Fig. 10.4 `UserThread.java` (part 4 of 4).

Method **messageReceived** (line 289) is invoked by method **run** and is used to process incoming XML from the client. It references the XML through parameter **Document message**. Line 291 uses **Document** method **getDocumentElement** to retrieve the **root** element. If the **root** element is **user**, then this message indicates that the user is attempting to log in. Recall that the XML sent looks like

> **<user>**username**</user>**

To access *username*, we must first access the **root**'s first child and then obtain the **String** *username* with **Node** method **getNodeValue**. We then check to see if the submitted name is already in use by another user (line 301).

If it is, we call method **nameInUse**, which is defined on line 325. This method creates a **Document** object **enterUniqueName**. It then creates and appends element **nameInUse**, resulting in the XML

    <nameInUse/>

The **Document** is then sent to the client by invoking method **send** (discussed shortly).

If the name is not in use, then we send the **server**'s **users Document** to the client using method **send** (discussed momentarily). Instance variable **name** is updated to reflect the submitted *username*. We call **MessengerServer** method **addUser** to add this user to the server.

If the **root** element is not **user**, line 315 tests if it is **message**. If so, it passes the **Document** as a parameter to the **MessengerServer** method **sendMessage** (discussed in Fig. 10.3).

If the **root** element is **disconnect**, then the user is logging off. Line 318 sets **boolean keepListening** to **false** to exit the **while** loop. We invoke **MessengerServer** method **removeUser** to remove this user from the server.

Method **send** (lines 335–344) accepts a **Document** object as its parameter. We cast the **Document** object to an **XmlDocument** and invoke the **XmlDocument**'s **write** method to send the XML to the client, using the specified **output** stream.

Finally, method **run**, which is executed when the **UserThread** object receives **Thread** method **start**, is defined in lines 346–378. Using **boolean keepListening**, which is set to **true** by the constructor, we create a **while** loop (lines 351–366) to continuously listen for messages. The **UserThread** object listens for incoming messages from the client. Line 355 creates a buffer to hold the current XML data. Using a **byteArrayInputStream**, we instantiate an **InputSource** from this buffer. Line 361 then uses this **InputSource** to create a **Document** object, which is passed as a parameter to method **messageReceived** (defined in line 289). This **while** loop terminates when the client disconnects, at which point **messageReceived** sets **boolean keepListening** to **false**. Once the loop has been exited, the **Socket** and streams are closed, terminating the server's connection with the client.

10.5 Overview: Client Side of **XmlMessenger**

On the client side, a **MessengerClient** object connects to the server, establishing a socket. Once a connection has been made, the **MessengerClient** object gets the input and output streams. The user attempts to login by entering a *username* and clicking on **Submit** (Fig. 10.5); the *username* entered is sent to the server in the following XML document

    <user>*username***</user>**

If *username* is already taken by another user, the server sends back the XML

    <nameInUse/>

When the **MessengerClient** processes this message, it displays an alert dialog to the user, asking for a unique name (Fig. 10.5).

Fig. 10.5 `MessengerClient` GUI and alert dialog box.

Once the user has entered a unique name, the server sends back an XML document containing the names of all users currently on-line. For example, if **User2** and **User3** are the only other users on-line, the client receives

```
<users>
   <user>User2</user>
   <user>User3</user>
</users>
```

The **MessengerClient** object stores this XML document as a **Document** object for use by the **ClientStatus** object it creates. The **ClientStatus** GUI displays all users, as in Fig. 10.6, by traversing the DOM. Because the user has successfully logged on, the **Messenger Client** window (Fig. 10.5) is hidden. The main window for the user is now the **ClientStatus** window (i.e., **Messenger Status**). When the user double clicks a name in this window, a new **Conversation** object is created. The **Conversation** object is stored in the **MessengerClient**'s **conversations Vector**, allowing the **MessengerClient** to access it as needed.

For instance, if **User1** double clicks **User2**, a window pops up, created by a new **Conversation** object. When **User1** types "**hello**" and clicks **Enter** (Fig. 10.7), a new **Document** is created, containing

Fig. 10.6 `ClientStatus` GUI.

```
<message to = "User2" from = "User1">hello</message>
```

This message is sent to the server through the **MessengerClient**'s **output** stream.

Now suppose **User2** replies with "**hi**." The server sends **User1**'s **MessengerClient** the XML

```
<message to = "User1" from = "User2">hi</message>
```

After retrieving the **from** attribute, the **MessengerClient** then accesses the **Conversation** with **User2** and displays **User2**'s "**hi**" message, as demonstrated in Fig. 10.7.

If **User2** then logs out, **User1**'s **MessengerClient** receives XML from the server

```
<update type = "logout">
   <user>User2</user>
</update>
```

User1's **ClientStatus** updates its **onlineUsers Vector** and GUI to reflect **User2**'s logout, then checks for an open **Conversation** with **User2**; if so, it informs **User1** that **User2** has logged out and disables the **Conversation**'s GUI components (Fig. 10.7).

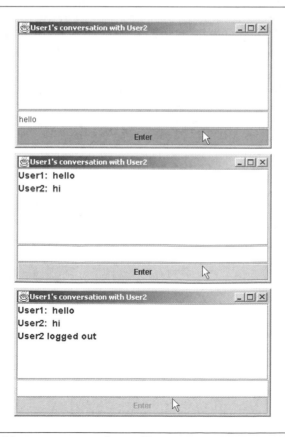

Fig. 10.7   **User1**'s **Conversation** with **User2**.

If **User4** logs in, a similar process occurs. First, **User1**'s **MessengerClient** receives the XML update message

```
<update type = "login">
    <user>User4</user>
</update>
```

User1's **ClientStatus** then updates its **onlineUsers Vector** and GUI to indicate that **User4** is now on-line (Fig. 10.8).

User1 can disconnect by clicking the **Disconnect** button in the **ClientStatus** window. This action creates and sends the XML

```
<disconnect/>
```

to the server. The server terminates the connection to this client, and the client's application closes.

10.6 Implementation: Client Side of **XmlMessenger**

In this section, we discuss the client-side of **XmlMessenger**. Figure 10.9 contains the source code for **MessengerClient.java**, which manages the connection with the server; Fig. 10.10 contains the source code for **ClientStatus.java**, which creates the status window for the user after login, and Fig. 10.11 contains the source code for **Conversation.java**, which implements an individual conversation with another user.

Fig. 10.8 **User1**'s updated GUI after **User4** logs in.

```
380  // Fig. 10.9: MessengerClient.java
381  // This program provides implementation for user login
382  // and client connection with server.
383
```

Fig. 10.9 **MessengerClient.java** (part 1 of 7).

```
384  import java.awt.*;
385  import java.awt.event.*;
386  import javax.swing.*;
387  import java.io.*;
388  import java.net.*;
389  import java.util.*;
390
391  import org.w3c.dom.*;
392  import org.xml.sax.*;
393  import javax.xml.parsers.*;
394  import com.sun.xml.tree.XmlDocument;
395
396  public class MessengerClient extends JFrame {
397      private JPanel centerPanel, namePanel;
398      private JLabel status, nameLab;
399      private JTextField name;
400      private ImageIcon bug;
401      private JButton submit;
402      private Socket clientSocket;
403      private OutputStream output;
404      private InputStream input;
405      private boolean keepListening;
406      private ClientStatus clientStatus;
407      private Document users;
408      private Vector conversations;
409      private DocumentBuilderFactory factory;
410      private DocumentBuilder builder;
411
412      public MessengerClient()
413      {
414          // create GUI
415          super ( "Messenger Client" );
416
417          try
418          {
419              // obtain the default parser
420              factory = DocumentBuilderFactory.newInstance();
421
422              // get DocumentBuilder
423              builder = factory.newDocumentBuilder();
424          }
425          catch ( ParserConfigurationException pce ) {
426              pce.printStackTrace();
427          }
428
429          Container c = getContentPane();
430
431          centerPanel = new JPanel( new GridLayout( 2, 1 ) );
432
433          namePanel = new JPanel();
434
435          nameLab = new JLabel( "Please enter your name: " );
436          namePanel.add( nameLab );
```

Fig. 10.9 MessengerClient.java (part 2 of 7).

```
437
438          name = new JTextField( 15 );
439          namePanel.add( name );
440
441          centerPanel.add( namePanel );
442
443          bug = new ImageIcon( "travelbug.jpg" );
444          submit = new JButton( "Submit", bug );
445          submit.setEnabled( false );
446          centerPanel.add( submit );
447
448          submit.addActionListener(
449             new ActionListener() {
450                public void actionPerformed( ActionEvent e ) {
451                   loginUser();
452                }
453             }
454          );
455
456          c.add( centerPanel, BorderLayout.CENTER );
457
458          status = new JLabel( "Status: Not connected" );
459          c.add( status, BorderLayout.SOUTH );
460
461          addWindowListener(
462             new WindowAdapter() {
463                public void windowClosing( WindowEvent e ) {
464                   System.exit( 0 );
465                }
466             }
467          );
468
469          setSize( 200, 200 );
470          show();
471       }
472
473       public void runMessengerClient()
474       {
475          try {
476             clientSocket = new Socket(
477                InetAddress.getByName( "127.0.0.1" ), 5000 );
478             status.setText( "Status: Connected to " +
479                clientSocket.getInetAddress().getHostName() );
480
481             // get input and output streams
482             output = clientSocket.getOutputStream();
483             input = clientSocket.getInputStream();
484
485             submit.setEnabled( true );
486             keepListening = true;
487
488             int bufferSize = 0;
489
```

Fig. 10.9 MessengerClient.java (part 3 of 7).

```
490              while ( keepListening ) {
491
492                 bufferSize = input.available();
493
494                 if ( bufferSize > 0 ) {
495                    byte buf[] = new byte[ bufferSize ];
496
497                    input.read( buf );
498
499                    InputSource source = new InputSource(
500                       new ByteArrayInputStream( buf ) );
501                    Document message;
502
503                    try {
504
505                       // obtain document object from XML document
506                       message = builder.parse( source );
507
508                       if ( message != null )
509                          messageReceived( message );
510
511                    }
512                    catch ( SAXException se ) {
513                       se.printStackTrace();
514                    }
515                    catch ( Exception e ) {
516                       e.printStackTrace();
517                    }
518                 }
519              }
520
521           input.close();
522           output.close();
523           clientSocket.close();
524           System.exit( 0 );
525        }
526        catch ( IOException e ) {
527           e.printStackTrace();
528           System.exit( 1 );
529        }
530     }
531
532     public void loginUser()
533     {
534        // create Document with user login
535        Document submitName = builder.newDocument();
536        Element root = submitName.createElement( "user" );
537
538        submitName.appendChild( root );
539        root.appendChild(
540           submitName.createTextNode( name.getText() ) );
541
```

Fig. 10.9 MessengerClient.java (part 4 of 7).

```
542            send( submitName );
543        }
544
545        public Document getUsers()
546        {
547            return users;
548        }
549
550        public void stopListening()
551        {
552            keepListening = false;
553        }
554
555        public void messageReceived( Document message )
556        {
557            Element root = message.getDocumentElement();
558
559            if ( root.getTagName().equals( "nameInUse" ) )
560                // did not enter a unique name
561                JOptionPane.showMessageDialog( this,
562                    "That name is already in use." +
563                    "\nPlease enter a unique name." );
564            else if ( root.getTagName().equals( "users" ) ) {
565                // entered a unique name for login
566                users = message;
567                clientStatus = new ClientStatus( name.getText(), this );
568                conversations = new Vector();
569                hide();
570            }
571            else if ( root.getTagName().equals( "update" ) ) {
572
573                // either a new user login or a user logout
574                String type = root.getAttribute( "type" );
575                NodeList userElt = root.getElementsByTagName( "user" );
576                String updatedUser =
577                    userElt.item( 0 ).getFirstChild().getNodeValue();
578
579                // test for login or logout
580                if ( type.equals( "login" ) )
581                    // login
582                    // add user to onlineUsers Vector
583                    // and update usersList
584                    clientStatus.add( updatedUser );
585                else {
586                    // logout
587                    // remove user from onlineUsers Vector
588                    // and update usersList
589                    clientStatus.remove( updatedUser );
590
591                    // if there is an open conversation, inform user
592                    int index = findConversationIndex( updatedUser );
593
```

Fig. 10.9 `MessengerClient.java` (part 5 of 7).

```
594                    if ( index != -1 ) {
595                        Conversation receiver =
596                          ( Conversation ) conversations.elementAt( index );
597
598                        receiver.updateGUI( updatedUser + " logged out" );
599                        receiver.disableConversation();
600                    }
601                }
602            }
603            else if ( root.getTagName().equals( "message" ) ) {
604                String from = root.getAttribute( "from" );
605                String messageText = root.getFirstChild().getNodeValue();
606
607                // test if conversation already exists
608                int index = findConversationIndex( from );
609
610                if ( index != -1 ) {
611                    // conversation exists
612                    Conversation receiver =
613                        ( Conversation ) conversations.elementAt( index );
614                    receiver.updateGUI( from + ":   " + messageText );
615                }
616                else {
617                    // conversation does not exist
618                    Conversation newConv =
619                        new Conversation( from, clientStatus, this );
620                    newConv.updateGUI( from + ":   " + messageText );
621                }
622            }
623        }
624
625        public int findConversationIndex( String userName )
626        {
627            // find index of specified Conversation
628            // in Vector conversations
629            // if no corresponding Conversation is found, return -1
630            for ( int i = 0; i < conversations.size(); i++ ) {
631                Conversation current =
632                    ( Conversation ) conversations.elementAt( i );
633
634                if ( current.getTarget().equals( userName ) )
635                    return i;
636            }
637
638            return -1;
639        }
640
641        public void addConversation( Conversation newConversation )
642        {
643            conversations.add( newConversation );
644        }
645
```

Fig. 10.9 MessengerClient.java (part 6 of 7).

```
646       public void removeConversation( String userName )
647       {
648          conversations.removeElementAt(
649             findConversationIndex( userName ) );
650       }
651
652       public void send( Document message )
653       {
654          try {
655             // write to output stream
656             ( ( XmlDocument ) message).write( output );
657          }
658          catch ( IOException e ) {
659             e.printStackTrace();
660          }
661       }
662
663       public static void main( String args [] )
664       {
665          MessengerClient cm = new MessengerClient();
666
667          cm.runMessengerClient();
668       }
669    }
```

Fig. 10.9 MessengerClient.java (part 7 of 7).

Class **MessengerClient** (Fig. 10.9) establishes and maintains the client's connection to the server. We **import** packages in lines 384–394, including the Java networking and I/O packages as well as the DOM and SAX packages. As with class **UserThread** (Fig. 10.4), **boolean keepListening** is used in a **while** loop (line 490); this allows the client to listen continually for communication from the server until the user disconnects. Variable **clientStatus** references the **ClientStatus** object that is created when a successful login occurs. We store the server's response to a successful login in the **Document** object **users**. Finally, every class **Conversation** object (discussed in Fig. 10.11) that is affiliated with this user is stored in **Vector conversations**.

Lines 412–471 define the constructor, setting up the GUI for the **Messenger-Client**. Note that we disable **JButton submit** in line 445; it is enabled in line 485 if a successful connection to the server has been established.

Method **runMessengerClient** is called by method **main** (line 667). It attempts to establish a connection with the server (lines 476 and 477). We set up the **output** and **input** streams in lines 482 and 483. Once a successful connection has been made, we enable the **Submit** button in line 485 and set **boolean keepListening** to **true**. Lines 490–519 create a **while** loop, in which the **MessengerClient** object listens for communication from the server. As with the loop in the **UserThread** class, we create a buffer to hold the incoming XML. We then instantiate a new **InputSource** object from this buffer, using a **byteArrayInputStream**. By invoking **XmlDocument** method **createXmlDocument**, we create a **Document** object from this **InputSource** (line 506). If this object is not **null**, it is passed to method **messageReceived** (discussed momentarily) for processing. When the user disconnects, the **while** loop is exited, and the client's application terminates (line 524).

When the user clicks the **Submit** button, method **loginUser** (lines 532–543) is invoked. This method creates a new **Document** object. In line 536, we create a new element **user**, to which a new text node is appended containing **JTextField name**'s text. This step creates the XML

```
<user>username</user>
```

Using method **send** (discussed momentarily), we send the XML to the server.

When an XML message is received, method **runMessengerClient** passes the **Document** to **messageReceived**. Lines 555–623 define method **messageReceived**, which processes the XML from the server. First, we retrieve the **root** element in line 557. Then we test if it is **nameInUse**; if it is, then the server is responding to an attempted login by indicating that the submitted name is already in use by another user. We inform the user by displaying a dialog box asking the user to enter a unique name (Fig. 10.5).

If the **root** is **users**, then the server is responding to a successful login by sending XML containing the name of all the users. We initialize reference **users** with the **Document** object for later use. Then, in line 567, a new **ClientStatus** (discussed in Fig. 10.10) object is created. Finally, we initialize the **conversations Vector** to a new **Vector** and hide the window for the **MessengerClient class**. Note that creating a new **ClientStatus** object displays a different window; the current login window is no longer relevant.

The server could also send XML with root **update**, indicating that another user has either logged in or logged out. Recall that this XML takes the form

```
<update type = "login or logout">
    <user>username</user>
</update>
```

We retrieve the contents of attribute **type** and element **user** in lines 574–577. Then we test if the **type** attribute is **login** (line 580). If so, we invoke **ClientStatus** method **add**, which will be discussed in Fig. 10.10. Otherwise, the **type** attribute must be "**logout**," and we invoke **ClientStatus** method **remove** (also discussed in Fig. 10.10). We also check if a **Conversation** with the specified user exists; if so, we inform the user that the other user has logged out and disable various GUI components of the **Conversation** object.

Finally, the **root** element could be **message**, indicating that the user is receiving an instant message from another user. We retrieve the sender's username in line 604 and the of the text message in line 605. Then we initialize local variable **index** using helper method **findConversationIndex**. Lines 625–639 define method **findConversationIndex**. We iterate through the **conversations Vector**, testing if the **Conversation** instance variable **target** equals **userName**. If no **Conversation** matching **userName** is found, **findConversationIndex** returns −1. Line 594 of method **messageReceived** tests if **index** is not −1 (i.e., a **Conversation** with the sender already exists); if it is not −1, we access the **Conversation** with the sender and display the message text. If **index** is **-1** (line 594), we create a new **Conversation** object with the sender and display the message text.

Methods **addConversation** and **removeConversation** (lines 641–650) add and remove the specified **Conversation** object from **Vector conversations**, respectively.

In lines 652–661, we define method **send**. This method accepts a **Document** object as its parameter. We send the XML to the server via the **output** stream by using **Xml-Document** method **write**

```
670  // Fig. 10.10: ClientStatus.java
671  // This program provides implementation for
672  // displaying all current users on the client side.
673
674  import java.awt.*;
675  import java.awt.event.*;
676  import javax.swing.*;
677  import java.util.*;
678
679  import org.w3c.dom.*;
680  import org.xml.sax.*;
681  import javax.xml.parsers.*;
682  import com.sun.xml.tree.XmlDocument;
683
684  public class ClientStatus extends JFrame {
685      private MessengerClient client;
686      private JLabel statusLabel;
687      private JList usersList;
688      private JButton disconnectButton;
689      private String user;
690      private Vector onlineUsers;
691
692      public ClientStatus( String name, MessengerClient mc )
693      {
694          // create GUI
695          super( name + "'s Messenger Status" );
696
697          client = mc;
698          user = name;
699
700          Container c = getContentPane();
701
702          statusLabel = new JLabel( "Available users:" );
703          c.add( statusLabel, BorderLayout.NORTH );
704
705          // determine how many users are online
706          NodeList userElts =
707             client.getUsers().getDocumentElement().
708                getElementsByTagName( "user" );
709          int numberOfUsers = userElts.getLength();
710
711          // initialize Vector onlineUsers
712          onlineUsers = new Vector( numberOfUsers );
```

Fig. 10.10 ClientStatus.java (part 1 of 4).

```
713
714        for ( int i = 0; i < numberOfUsers; i++) {
715           String currentUser =
716              userElts.item( i ).getFirstChild().getNodeValue();
717           onlineUsers.addElement( currentUser );
718        }
719
720        usersList = new JList( onlineUsers );
721        usersList.setSelectionMode(
722           ListSelectionModel.SINGLE_SELECTION );
723
724        MouseListener usersListener = new MouseAdapter() {
725           public void mouseClicked( MouseEvent e ) {
726              int selectedIndex = usersList.getSelectedIndex();
727
728              if ( e.getClickCount() == 2 && selectedIndex >= 0 )
729                 initiateMessage( selectedIndex );
730           }
731        };
732        usersList.addMouseListener( usersListener );
733        c.add( new JScrollPane( usersList ), BorderLayout.CENTER );
734
735        disconnectButton = new JButton( "Disconnect" );
736        disconnectButton.addActionListener(
737           new ActionListener() {
738              public void actionPerformed( ActionEvent e ) {
739                 disconnectUser();
740              }
741           }
742        );
743        c.add( disconnectButton, BorderLayout.SOUTH );
744        addWindowListener(
745           new WindowAdapter() {
746              public void windowClosing( WindowEvent e ) {
747                 disconnectUser();
748              }
749           }
750        );
751
752        setSize( 250, 300 );
753        show();
754     }
755
756     public String getUser()
757     {
758        return user;
759     }
760
761     public void initiateMessage( int index )
762     {
763        String target = ( String ) onlineUsers.elementAt( index );
764
```

Fig. 10.10 ClientStatus.java (part 2 of 4).

```
765            // only open a new Conversation
766            // if there is not an already open one
767            if ( client.findConversationIndex( target ) == -1 )
768               new Conversation( target, this, client );
769         }
770
771         public void add( String userToAdd )
772         {
773            // add user to Vector onlineUsers
774            onlineUsers.addElement( userToAdd );
775
776            // update JList usersList
777            usersList.setListData( onlineUsers );
778         }
779
780         public void remove( String userToRemove )
781         {
782            // remove user from Vector onlineUsers
783            onlineUsers.removeElementAt(
784               findOnlineUsersIndex( userToRemove ) );
785
786            // update JList usersList
787            usersList.setListData( onlineUsers );
788         }
789
790         public int findOnlineUsersIndex( String onlineUserName )
791         {
792           for ( int i = 0; i < onlineUsers.size(); i++ ) {
793              String currentUserName =
794                 ( String ) onlineUsers.elementAt( i );
795
796              if ( currentUserName.equals( onlineUserName ) )
797                 return i;
798           }
799
800           return -1;
801         }
802
803         public void disconnectUser()
804         {
805            DocumentBuilderFactory factory =
806               DocumentBuilderFactory.newInstance();
807            Document disconnectUser;
808            try {
809
810               // get DocumentBuilder
811               DocumentBuilder builder =
812                  factory.newDocumentBuilder();
813
814               // create root node
815               disconnectUser = builder.newDocument();
816
```

Fig. 10.10 `ClientStatus.java` (part 3 of 4).

```
817                disconnectUser.appendChild(
818                   disconnectUser.createElement( "disconnect" ) );
819
820             client.send( disconnectUser );
821             client.stopListening();
822          }
823          catch ( ParserConfigurationException pce ) {
824             pce.printStackTrace();
825          }
826       }
827    }
```

Fig. 10.10 `ClientStatus.java` (part 4 of 4).

Class **ClientStatus** (Fig. 10.10) creates the status window for the user after a successful login has occurred. Variable **client** references the **MessengerClient** object that created this **ClientStatus** object. We store the user's username in **String name**. **Vector onlineUsers** is used to create and update the **usersList**.

The constructor (lines 692–754) creates the GUI for the **ClientStatus** window. When initializing **Vector onlineUsers** (used as the basis for **JList usersList**), we access the **client**'s **users Document**. Using **Element** method **getElements-ByTagName**, we retrieve all the **user** elements. The **for** loop (lines 714–718) iterates through the **user** elements, accessing the content of each and adding it to the **onlineUsers Vector**. We use this **Vector** to initialize **JList usersList** in line 720. In lines 724–731, we create a new **MouseAdapter** object to respond when the user double clicks a name in the **usersList** component. In line 728, we check to see if the user double clicked a username. If so, we call method **initiateMessage** (discussed momentarily). We also create an event handler for **JButton disconnect**; when the user clicks the **Disconnect** button, method **disconnectUser** (also discussed momentarily) is invoked.

Method **initiateMessage** first determines the name the user selected (lines 761–769). We then test to see if a **Conversation** with the targeted user already exists by using **ClientMessenger** method **findConversationIndex** (discussed in Fig. 10.9). If no **Conversation** exists, we create a new **Conversation** object (discussed in Fig. 10.11).

Lines 771–778 define method **add**, which is invoked in response to the server informing the client that a new user is logging in. We add the specified user to the **onlineUsers Vector** and update the **JList usersList** so that the user knows that a new user is on-line.

When the server notifies the client that a user has logged out, method **remove** is invoked. We first remove the specified user from the **onlineUsers Vector**. To find the index of the element that we want to remove, method **findOnlineUsersIndex** (defined in lines 790–801) is invoked. Method **findOnlineUsersIndex** iterates through the **onlineUsers Vector**, returning the index corresponding to parameter **onlineUserName**; it returns **-1** otherwise. Once the corresponding element has been removed, we update the **usersList**.

We define method **disconnectUser** in lines 803–826. This method is invoked in response to the user clicking the **Disconnect** button. To inform the server that this user is disconnecting, we create a new **Document** object. We then create and append element **disconnect**. Using the **MessengerClient** method **send** (discussed in Fig. 10.9), we send the XML to the server. Finally, we invoke **MessengerClient** method **stopListening**, which results in the termination of the client's application.

```
828  // Fig. 10.11: Conversation.java
829  // This program provides implementation on the client side
830  // for exchanging messages between users.
831
832  import java.awt.*;
833  import java.awt.event.*;
834  import javax.swing.*;
835
836  import org.w3c.dom.*;
837  import org.xml.sax.*;
838  import javax.xml.parsers.*;
839
840  public class Conversation extends JFrame {
841     private ClientStatus clientStatus;
842     private MessengerClient client;
843     private JTextArea display;
844     private JTextField message;
845     private JButton enter;
846     private JPanel messageArea;
847     private GridLayout messageAreaLayout;
848     private String target;
849
850     public Conversation( String contact, ClientStatus cs,
851                          MessengerClient mc )
852     {
853        // create GUI and initialize variables
854        super( cs.getUser() + "'s conversation with " + contact );
855        target = contact;
856        clientStatus = cs;
857        client = mc;
858
859        Container c = getContentPane();
860        Font font = new Font( "SansSerif",
861                              java.awt.Font.BOLD, 14 );
862
863        display = new JTextArea();
864        display.setLineWrap( true );
865        display.setEditable( false );
866        display.setFont( font );
867        c.add( new JScrollPane( display ), BorderLayout.CENTER );
868
869        messageArea = new JPanel();
870        messageArea.setLayout( new GridLayout( 2, 1 ) );
871
872        message = new JTextField( 20 );
873        message.setText( "" );
874        messageArea.add( message );
```

Fig. 10.11 `Conversation.java` (part 1 of 3).

```
875
876          message.addActionListener (
877             new ActionListener () {
878                public void actionPerformed ( ActionEvent e ) {
879                   submitMessage();
880                }
881             }
882          );
883
884          enter = new JButton( "Enter" );
885          messageArea.add( enter );
886          c.add( messageArea, BorderLayout.SOUTH );
887
888          enter.addActionListener (
889             new ActionListener () {
890                public void actionPerformed ( ActionEvent e ) {
891                   submitMessage();
892                }
893             }
894          );
895
896          addWindowListener(
897             new WindowAdapter() {
898                public void windowClosing( WindowEvent e ) {
899                   // remove conversation from client's
900                   // conversations Vector
901                   client.removeConversation( target );
902                }
903             }
904          );
905
906          setSize( 400, 200 );
907          show();
908
909          // add this Conversation object to conversations Vector
910          client.addConversation( this );
911       }
912
913       public String getTarget()
914       {
915          return target;
916       }
917
918       public void disableConversation()
919       {
920          message.setEnabled( false );
921          enter.setEnabled( false );
922       }
923
924       public void updateGUI( String dialog )
925       {
926          display.append( dialog + "\n" );
927       }
```

Fig. 10.11 Conversation.java (part 2 of 3)

```
928
929    public void submitMessage()
930    {
931       String messageToSend = message.getText();
932
933       // do nothing if the user has not typed a message
934       if ( !messageToSend.equals( "" ) ) {
935
936          Document sendMessage;
937          DocumentBuilderFactory factory =
938             DocumentBuilderFactory.newInstance();
939
940          try {
941
942             // get DocumentBuilder
943             DocumentBuilder builder =
944                factory.newDocumentBuilder();
945
946             // create xml message
947             sendMessage = builder.newDocument();
948             Element root = sendMessage.createElement( "message" );
949
950             root.setAttribute( "to", target );
951             root.setAttribute( "from", clientStatus.getUser() );
952             root.appendChild(
953                sendMessage.createTextNode( messageToSend ) );
954             sendMessage.appendChild( root );
955
956             client.send( sendMessage );
957
958             updateGUI( clientStatus.getUser() +
959                ":  " + messageToSend );
960             message.setText( "" );
961          }
962          catch ( ParserConfigurationException pce ) {
963             pce.printStackTrace();
964          }
965       }
966    }
967 }
```

Fig. 10.11 Conversation.java (part 3 of 3).

Every **Conversation** object (Fig. 10.11) manages an instant-message conversation between this user and another user. The **clientStatus** and **client** variables reference the **ClientStatus** object that created this **Conversation** object and the **Client-Messenger** object associated with it, respectively. **String target** contains the name of the user with whom this user is conversing.

The constructor (lines 850–911) creates the GUI and initializes the instance variables. In lines 896–904, we specify that when the window is closed, this **Conversation** object should be removed from the **client**'s **conversations Vector**. We add this **Conversation** object to the **client**'s **conversations Vector** in line 910.

When the user hits the *Enter* key or clicks the **Enter** button, method **submitMessage** is invoked. We define **submitMessage** in lines 929–966. First, we retrieve the text contained in the **JTextField message** (line 931). Then, line 934 tests if the user actually entered text. If so, we create XML to send to the server; recall that it takes the form

```
<message to = "receiver" from = "sender">
    message text
</message>
```

We create a new **Document** object in lines 936–938; then we create the **root** element **message**. Lines 950 and 951 set the attributes **to** and **from** to **target** and the **clientStatus**'s instance variable **user**, respectively. We create and append a text node containing the message text in lines 952 and 953. Using the **MessengerClient** method **send**, we send the XML to the server (line 956). Finally, we update the **Conversation** GUI to display the entered message and clear the **message JTextField**.

TERMINOLOGY

class **JFrame**

class **Thread**

client

client connection to a server

clients handled by separate threads

Document interface of **org.w3c.dom**
　　package

DOM

graphical user interface (GUI)

InputSource

instant messaging

J2SDK

JAXP parser

networking

org.w3c.dom package

SAX

SAX package

server

ServerSocket class

Socket class

streams

terminate connection to a client

Vector class

write method of class **XmlDocument**

XmlDocument class

SELF-REVIEW EXERCISES

10.1　What is the significance of **XmlDocument** object **users** (Fig 10.3, line 23)? How does class **UserThread** use it?

10.2　Explain the significance of class **UserThread** and its role in the application.

10.3　Explain briefly the sequence of steps that take place between the server and a client before the client can start a conversation. Mention the relevant methods and classes involved.

ANSWERS TO SELF-REVIEW EXERCISES

10.1　Object **users** is used to store the information of all on-line users in an XML document. It acts as a database on the server side. Class **UserThread** retrieves the list of current users from object **users** using **MessengerServer** method **getUsers**. It also uses object **users** to update the list of users whenever a new user logs in or logs out of the system. The content of object **users** is written to the output stream to update the client.

10.2　Class **UserThread** acts as an interface between server and client. Each client has a **UserThread** object created for it on the server side. The server communicates with the client through this **UserThread** object. A **UserThread** object continuously listens to the client. Upon receiving a message from the client, it parses the message and identifies the type of message. It then passes the message to the server for further processing.

10.3   An instant-messenger user logs on to the system by typing in their username or ID. The username is tagged with XML by method **loginUser**. It is then sent to the server by method **send**. This message is received by **UserThread** object method **run**. The message is parsed here, and method **messageReceived** is invoked to identify the type of message. If the user is a valid user, the user is updated using method **addUser** of **MessengerServer**. The list of current users is retrieved using method **getUsers** of **MessengerServer** and sent to the client using method **send** of **UserThread**. The list of users is received by the client using **runMessengerClient**. A new object of **ClientStatus** is instantiated by method **messageReceived** of **MessengerClient** to display the list of users.

EXERCISES

10.4   Modify the **XmlMessenger** application so that the server holds an XML file of registered users with passwords. This file should be stored on the server and should contain every user ever to register (i.e., not just those who log in to the current server session). When a user logs in, their name and password should be checked against this document for validity. If the name is registered with a different password, indicate so to the user and ask for the correct password or a unique user name.

10.5   Modify your solution to Exercise 10.4 so that a user can create a list of on-line friends to be displayed instead of displaying all on-line users. The user should be able to add to the list of friends; if the new friend is currently on-line, the friend's name should be added to the list of on-line friends. If the friend is not logged in, nothing should be added to the display; however, if the friend logs in later, the friend's username should then be added to the list.

11

XML Path Language (XPath)

Objectives

- To understand why XML Path Language (XPath) is useful for information processing.
- To be able to write XPath expressions.
- To understand the usage of XPath for locating parts of an XML document.
- To be able to use axes and predicates to locate information in multiple nodes.

Attempt the end, and never stand to doubt;
Nothing's so hard, but search will find it out.
Robert Herrick

It is an immutable law in business that words are words,
explanations are explanations, promises are promises—but
only performance is reality.
Harold S. Green

I read part of it all the way through.
Samual Goldwyn

11.1 Introduction

XML provides a way of describing data in a rich, flexible and efficient way by marking up data with descriptive tags. However, XML does not provide a way to locate specific pieces of structured data within a given document. For example, an XML document containing data about books published by Deitel & Associates, Inc., would need to be parsed and then searched through element by element in order to find a specific book. For large documents, this process could be inefficient and error prone.

The *XML Path Language (XPath)* provides a syntax for locating specific parts (e.g., attribute values) of an XML document effectively and efficiently. XPath is not a structural language like XML; rather, it is a string-based language of expressions used by other XML technologies, such as *Extensible Stylesheet Language Transformations (XSLT)*, which converts or transforms XML documents to other formats (e.g., HTML), and the *XML Pointer Language (XPointer)*, which provides a means to "point" to information inside an XML document. In this chapter, we discuss XPath. In Chapters 12 and 14, we discuss XSLT and XPointer, respectively. At the time of this writing, XPath Version 1.0 was the current W3C Recommendation.

11.2 Nodes

In XPath, an XML document is viewed conceptually as a tree in which each part of the document is represented as a *node*. Recall that a tree is much like the structure of files and folders on a computer's hard drive; nodes are much like the individual files and folders. Just as folders may contain files and other folders, some nodes may contain other nodes. In XPath, the result is a hierarchy of nodes that represent the elements of an XML document in a searchable structure.

XPath has seven node types: *root, element, attribute, text, comment, processing instruction* and *namespace*. The nodes in this tree are similar to those in the DOM we presented in Chapter 8. The first two examples illustrate each of these seven node types.

The XPath tree has a single root node, which contains all other nodes in the tree. The root node and element nodes contain ordered lists of child nodes. Each node except the root node has a parent node, and parent nodes may have any number of child, or descendant, nodes. The only node types that may be child nodes are the element, comment, text and processing node types. Note that although an attribute or namespace node has a parent node that is either an element or root node, the attribute or namespace node is not considered a child of its parent node. The relationship between a parent node and a child node is containment, that is, a parent node contains a child node. Attribute nodes and namespace nodes describe their parent nodes. A namespace node, for example, describes the namespace in which its parent node can be found. Therefore attribute and namespace nodes are not child nodes because they are not contained in a parent node, but are used to provide descriptive information about their parent node.

Software Engineering Observation 11.1

Namespace and attribute nodes have parent nodes, but are not children of those parent nodes.

Figure 11.1 shows a simple XML document that marks up a description for a Deitel & Associates, Inc., textbook. Figure 11.2 shows a graphical representation of the XPath tree for this document. The root node contains two child nodes (i.e., a comment—lines 3 and 4—and an element—**book**). Element node **book** (lines 6–18) contains a child-element node **sample** (lines 8–15) and a child-text node (lines 16 and 17) that includes the whitespace on line 16. The element node **book** is the parent of the attribute nodes **title** and **edition** (line 6), but the attribute nodes **title** and **edition** are not children of the element node **book**. The element node **sample** contains a text node (lines 9–14) that consists of a single attribute **CDATA** section.

Each XPath tree node has a string representation—called a *string-value*—that XPath uses to compare nodes. Let us discuss the string-value for each node in the tree, starting with the text node on lines 9–14. The string-value of a text node consists of the character data contained in the node. Because the character data in lines 9–14 are contained within a **CDATA** section, the **&**, **<** and **>** characters are permitted and are part of the character data in the text node that will be used to determine the string-value. However, **<![CDATA[** and **]]>** are not part of the character data and are therefore not part of the string-value. The string-value for the text node on lines 9–14 is therefore

```
1   <?xml version = "1.0"?>
2
3   <!-- Fig. 11.1 : simple.xml -->
4   <!-- Simple XML document     -->
5
6   <book title = "C++ How to Program" edition = "3">
7
8      <sample>
9         <![CDATA[
10
11            // C++ comment
12            if ( this->getX() < 5 && value[ 0 ] != 3 )
13               cerr << this->displayError();
14         ]]>
15      </sample>
16
17      C++ How to Program by Deitel &amp; Deitel
18   </book>
```

Fig. 11.1 Simple XML document.

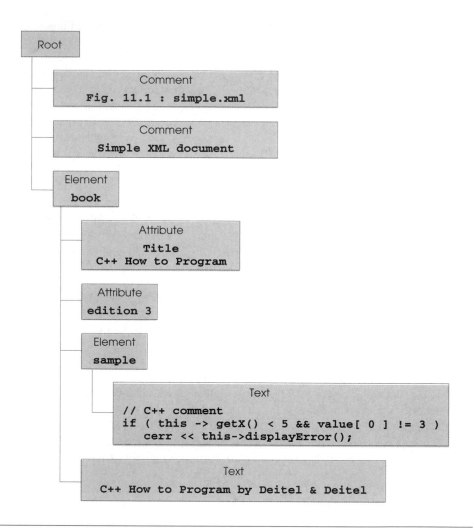

Fig. 11.2 XPath tree for Fig. 11.1.

```
// C++ comment
if ( this->getX() < 5 && value[ 0 ] != 3 )
    cerr << this->displayError();
```

The string-value for the **sample** element node is determined by concatenating the string-values for all of its *descendant text nodes* (i.e., all text nodes that follow the node) in *document order*. Nodes in an XPath tree have an ordering—called document order—that is determined by the order in which the nodes appear in the original XML document. The *reverse document order* is the reverse ordering of the nodes in a document. In this case, the **sample** element node has as its only descendent the text node on lines 9–14. Therefore, the string-value for the **sample** element node is the same as the string-value for the text node on lines 8–13.

The **book** element node (lines 6–18) has two descendent text nodes. The first is the text node shown on lines 16 and 17. The second is the text node on lines 9–14. The string-value for the **book** element node therefore consists of the concatenation of these two text nodes in document order. Thus, the resulting string-value is

```
// C++ comment
if ( this->getX() < 5 && value[ 0 ] != 3 )
   cerr << this->displayError();
C++ How to Program by Deitel & Deitel
```

Because the text node on lines 16 and 17 is not contained within a **CDATA** section, it is normalized (i.e., whitespace is either removed or combined into a single whitespace character). For the root node of the document, the string-value is also determined by concatenating the string-values of its text-node descendents in document order. The string-value of the root node is therefore identical to the string-value calculated for the **book** element node.

The attribute node **title** (line 6) has a string-value that consists of the normalized value of the attribute (i.e., **C++ How to Program**). The string-value for the **edition** attribute node consists of its value as well, which is **3**. The string-value for a comment node consists only of the comment's text, excluding **<!--** and **-->**. The string-value for the comment node on line 4 is therefore: **simple XML document**.

The XML document in Fig. 11.3 includes processing instruction and namespace nodes. Figure 11.4 shows a graphical representation of the document's XPath tree. In this document, the root node contains two comment nodes (lines 3–4) and one element node, **html** (lines 6–23). The namespace node's parent is **html**. This namespace node is not a child of the **html** element node, because namespace nodes cannot be child nodes. The element node **html** has three child nodes, including the element node **head** (lines 8–10), the processing-instruction node (line 12) and the element node **body** (lines 14–21).

```
1    <?xml version = "1.0"?>
2
3    <!-- Fig. 11.3 : simple2.xml                        -->
4    <!-- Processing instructions and namespacess        -->
5
6    <html xmlns = "http://www.w3.org/TR/REC-htm140">
7
8       <head>
9          <title>Processing Instruction and Namespace Nodes</title>
10      </head>
11
12      <?deitelprocessor example = "fig11_03.xml"?>
13
14      <body>
15
16          <deitel:book deitel:edition = "1"
17             xmlns:deitel = "http://www.deitel.com/xmlhtp1">
18             <deitel:title>XML How to Program</deitel:title>
19          </deitel:book>
20
21      </body>
22
23   </html>
```

Fig. 11.3 XML document with processing-instruction and namespace nodes.

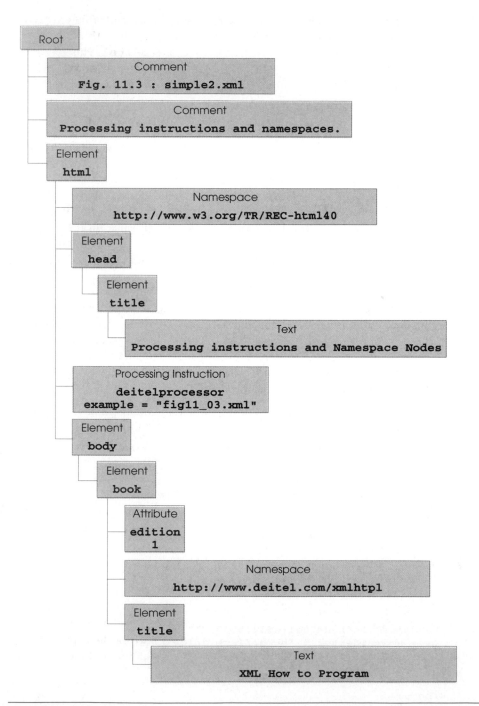

Fig. 11.4 Tree diagram of an XML document with a processing-instruction node.

The element node **head** contains the element node **title** (line 9) as its only child. In turn, the element node **title** contains a text node as its only child (line 9). The element node **body** (lines 14–21) contains one element node, **deitel:book** (lines 16–19). In element node **deitel:book**, we introduce a new namespace (line 17) with the URI **http://www.deitel.com/xmlhtp1** bound to the prefix **deitel**. This code results in a namespace node in the XPath tree whose parent is the element node **deitel:book**. The element node **deitel:title** (line 18), which is in the **deitel** namespace, is the only child of element node **deitel:book** and has a single text-node child.

The string-values for the nodes in this tree are determined exactly as they were for the nodes in Fig. 11.1. For the element node **html**, the string-value is the concatenation of the string-values of all its text-node descendents in document order. In the document in Fig. 11.3, there are only two text nodes (lines 9 and 18), and both are descendents of the element node **html**. The string-value for element node **html** is

Processing Instruction and Namespace NodesXML How to Program

Because all whitespace is removed when the text nodes are normalized, there is no space in the concatenation.

For processing instructions, the string-value consists of the remainder of the processing instruction after the target, including whitespace, but excluding the ending **?>**. The string-value for the processing instruction on line 12 is

```
example = "fig11_03.xml"
```

Namespace-node string-values consist of the URI for the namespace. The string-value for the namespace declaration on line 17 is

```
http://www.deitel.com/xmlhtp1
```

Certain nodes (i.e., element, attribute, processing instruction and namespace) also have a name—called an *expanded-name*—that can be used to locate specific nodes in the XPath tree. We will see how we can use the expanded-name in Section 11.4. Let us now determine the expanded-names for each of the nodes in Fig. 11.3. Expanded-names consist of both a *local part* and a *namespace URI*. For element nodes, the local part of the expanded-name corresponds to the name of the element in the XML document. The local part for the element node **html** (line 6) is therefore **html**. For each of the element nodes **head**, **title**, **body**, **book** and **title** and the attribute node **edition**, the local part of the expanded-name is **head**, **title**, **body**, **book**, **title** and **edition**, respectively.

If there is a prefix for the element node, the namespace URI of the expanded-name is the URI to which the prefix is bound. If there is no prefix for the element node, the namespace URI of the expanded name is the URI for the default namespace. The **html**, **head**, **title** and **body** element nodes on lines 6, 8, 9 and 14, respectively, do not have a prefix, but are in a default namespace, which is bound to the URI on line 6. This URI (i.e., **http://www.w3.org/TR/REC-html40**) is the namespace URI for the expanded-name of these nodes. Element nodes **book** and **title** (lines 16 and 18) have the namespace prefix **deitel**, which is bound to the URI

```
http://www.deitel.com/xmlhtp1
```

on line 17. This URI is the namespace URI for the expanded-name of these element nodes. The local part of the expanded name for an attribute node is the name of the attribute. The local part of the expanded name for the **edition** attribute node is **edition**.

The local part of the expanded name for a processing instruction node corresponds to the target of the processing instruction in the XML document. Therefore, the local part of the expanded-name for the processing instruction on line 12 is the string **deitelpro-cessor**. For processing instructions, the namespace URI of the expanded-name is *null* (i.e., it has no value).

The local part of the expanded-name for a namespace node corresponds to the prefix for the namespace, if one exists; or, if it is a default namespace, the local part is empty (i.e., the empty string). The namespace URI of the expanded-name for a namespace node is always null.

For reference purposes, we provide a summary of the node types in Fig. 11.5.

Node Type	string-value	expanded-name	Description
root	Determined by concatenating the string-values of all text-node descendents in document order.	None.	Represents the root of an XML document. This node exists only at the top of the tree and may contain element, comment or processor-instruction children.
element	Determined by concatenating the string-values of all text-node descendents in document order.	The element tag, including the namespace prefix (if applicable).	Represents an XML element and may contain element, text, comment or processor-instruction children.
attribute	The normalized value of the attribute.	The name of the attribute, including the namespace prefix (if applicable).	Represents an attribute of an element.
text	The character data contained in the text node.	None.	Represents the character data content of an element.
comment	The content of the comment (not including `<!--` and `-->`).	None.	Represents an XML comment.
processing instruction	The part of the processing instruction that follows the target and any whitespace.	The target of the processing instruction.	Represents an XML processing instruction.
namespace	The URI of the namespace.	The namespace prefix.	Represents an XML namespace.

Fig. 11.5 XPath node types.

11.3 Location Paths

Now that we have seen the structure of an XML document in XPath, we examine how we can use this structure to locate particular parts of a document. A *location path* is an expression that specifies how to navigate an XPath tree from one node to another. A location path is composed of *location steps*, each of which is composed of an "axis," a "node test" and an optional "predicate." We show several examples of location steps and location paths in Section 11.3.3. To locate a specific node in an XML document, we put together multiple location steps, each of which refines the search. The following sections introduce each part of a location step.

11.3.1 Axes

Searching through an XML document begins at a *context node* in the XPath tree. Searches through the XPath tree are made relative to this context node. For example, the XML document in Fig. 11.3 contains a **head** element (lines 8–10). The **head** element contains a single child element named **title** (line 9). In XPath, the **head** element would be represented as an element node whose parent is the **html** element node (lines 6–23). The **head** element node would have a single child element node corresponding to the **title** element. Suppose we have an XPath expression that returns the first child element node of the context node. Using the **head** element node as the context node, this expression would return the **title** element node. However, if we use the **html** element node as the context node, this expression would return the **head** element node.

　An *axis* indicates which nodes, relative to the context node, should be included in the search. The axis also dictates the ordering of the nodes in the set. Axes that select nodes that follow the context node in document order are called *forward axes*. Axes that select nodes that precede the context node in document order are called *reverse axes*. Figure 11.6 summarizes the 13 XPath axes and their ordering and provides a description of each.

Axis Name	Ordering	Description
self	none	The context node itself.
parent	reverse	The context node's parent, if one exists.
child	forward	The context node's children, if they exist.
ancestor	reverse	The context node's ancestors, if they exist.
ancestor-or-self	reverse	The context node's ancestors and also itself.
descendant	forward	The context node's descendants.
descendant-or-self	forward	The context node's descendants and also itself.
following	forward	The nodes in the XML document following the context node, not including descendants.
following-sibling	forward	The sibling nodes following the context node.

Fig. 11.6　XPath axes (part 1 of 2).

Axis Name	Ordering	Description
`preceding`	reverse	The nodes in the XML document preceding the context node, not including ancestors.
`preceding-sibling`	reverse	The sibling nodes preceding the context node.
`attribute`	forward	The attribute nodes of the context node.
`namespace`	forward	The namespace nodes of the context node.

Fig. 11.6   XPath axes (part 2 of 2).

An axis has a *principal node type* that corresponds to the type of node the axis may select. For attribute axes, the principal node type is **attribute**. For namespace axes, the principal node type is **namespace**. All other axes have a **element** principal node type.

11.3.2 Node Tests

An axis selects a set of nodes from the document tree. The set of selected nodes is refined with *node tests*. In Section 11.3.4 we will use these node tests to select nodes from the document tree. As we will see, node tests rely upon the principal node type of an axis for selecting nodes in a location path. Figure 11.7 lists some node tests and provides a description of each.

11.3.3 Location Paths Using Axes and Node Tests

Location paths are composed of sequences of location steps. A location step contains an axis and a node test separated by a *double-colon* (`::`) and, optionally, a "predicate" enclosed in *square brackets* (`[ ]`). We discuss predicates in Section 11.4. Let us now introduce example location paths for locating particular elements in an XML document. For the upcoming examples, we will use the XML document presented in Fig. 11.3 and its corresponding tree representation in Fig. 11.4. The location step

Node Test	Description
`*`	Selects all nodes of the same principal node type.
`node()`	Selects all nodes, regardless of their type.
`text()`	Selects all text nodes.
`comment()`	Selects all comment nodes.
`processing-instruction()`	Selects all processing-instruction nodes.
node name	Selects all nodes with the specified *node name*.

Fig. 11.7   Some XPath node tests.

```
child::*
```

selects all element-node children of the context node, because the principal node type for the **child** axis is element. If we use the **html** element node from line 6 in Fig. 11.3 as our context node, the **head** and **body** element nodes will be selected. The location step

```
child::text()
```

uses the axis **child** and the node test **text()** to select all text-node children of the context node. We can combine these two location steps to form the location path

```
child::*/child::text()
```

which selects all text-node grandchildren of the context node. There are two steps in this location path. The first step, **child::***, selects all element-node children of the context node. The second step, **child::text()**, selects all the child-text nodes contained in the set of nodes selected in the first step. If we again use the **html** element node from line 6 of Fig. 11.3 as our context node, there will be no nodes selected by this location path, because the **html** element node does not have any text-node grandchildren. If element node **head** had a text-node child, it would be selected by this location path.

Some location paths can also be abbreviated, as shown in Fig. 11.8. The child axis, for example, may be omitted, as it is considered the default axis. The location path

```
body
```

is therefore equivalent to the location path

```
child::body
```

and will select all element-node **body** children of the context node. In order to select all **body** element nodes in an entire document, the abbreviation

```
//body
```

may be used in place of the location path

```
/descendent-or-self::node()/child::body
```

Location Path	Description
`child::`	This location path is used by default if no axis is supplied and may therefore be omitted.
`attribute::`	The attribute axis may be abbreviated as **@**.
`/descendant-or-self::node()/`	This location path is abbreviated as two slashes (**//**).
`self::node()`	The context node is abbreviated with a period (**.**).
`parent::node()`	The context node's parent is abbreviated with two periods (**..**).

Fig. 11.8 Some location-path abbreviations.

In Fig. 11.9, we show an XML document that marks up some book translations. [*Note:* In Chapter 12, we will discuss the stylesheet used to render this document.] We show the XPath tree for the first **book** element node in Fig. 11.10.

```
1   <?xml version = "1.0"?>
2
3   <!-- Fig. 11.9 : books.xml -->
4   <!-- XML book list        -->
5
6   <books>
7
8      <book>
9         <title>Java How to Program</title>
10        <translation edition = "1">Spanish</translation>
11        <translation edition = "1">Chinese</translation>
12        <translation edition = "1">Japanese</translation>
13        <translation edition = "2">French</translation>
14        <translation edition = "2">Japanese</translation>
15     </book>
16
17     <book>
18        <title>C++ How to Program</title>
19        <translation edition = "1">Korean</translation>
20        <translation edition = "2">French</translation>
21        <translation edition = "2">Spanish</translation>
22        <translation edition = "3">Italian</translation>
23        <translation edition = "3">Japanese</translation>
24     </book>
25
26  </books>
```

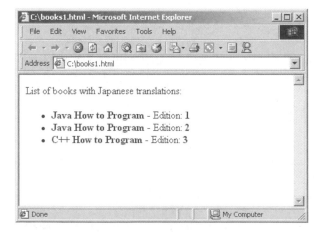

Fig. 11.9   XML document that marks up book translations.

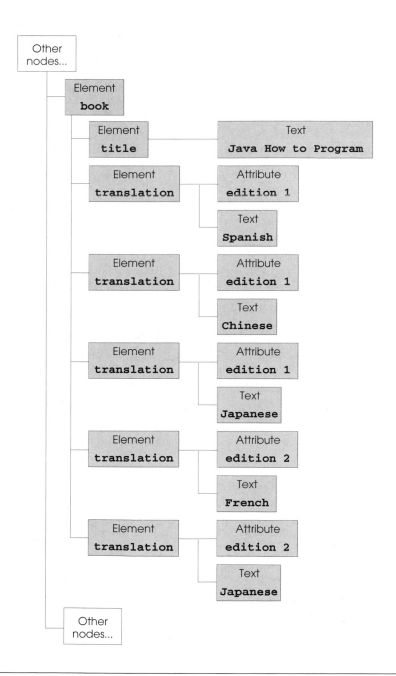

Fig. 11.10 XPath tree for **books.xml**.

Suppose we want to know which books have Japanese translations available in one or more editions, so that we can send a copy to a client who reads Japanese. Using the root node of the XPath tree as the context node, we could use the location path

```
/books/book/translation[. = 'Japanese']/../title
```

to select the **title** element node for each book that has a Japanese translation. This location path uses a simple *predicate* that compares the string value of the current node to the string **'Japanese'**. A predicate is a boolean expression used as part of a location path to filter nodes from the search. We discuss predicates further in Section 11.4. We could use the location path

```
/books/book/translation[. = 'Japanese']/@edition
```

to select the **edition** attribute node for books with Japanese translations. In the case study in Chapter 12, we study XPath in further detail. In particular, we use many of the axes listed in Fig. 11.6.

11.4 Node-set Operators and Functions

In the previous section, we discussed how we can select sets of nodes from a document tree using location paths. *Node-set operators* (Fig. 11.11) allow us to manipulate these node sets to form other node sets. We will show examples of how node-set operators are used momentarily.

XPath also provides *node-set functions* that perform an action on a node-set returned by a location path (Fig. 11.12).

Node-set Operators	Description
pipe (|)	Performs the union of two node-sets.
slash (**/**)	Separates location steps.
double-slash (**//**)	Abbreviation for the location path **/descendant-or-self::node()/**

Fig. 11.11 Node-set operators.

Node-set Functions	Description
last()	Returns the number of nodes in the node-set.
position()	Returns the position number of the current node in the node-set being tested.
count(*node-set* **)**	Returns the number of nodes in *node-set*.
id(*string* **)**	Returns the element node whose ID attribute matches the value specified by argument *string*.

Fig. 11.12 Some node-set functions (part 1 of 2).

Node-set Functions	Description
local-name (*node-set*)	Returns the local part of the expanded-name for the first node in *node-set*.
namespace-uri (*node-set*)	Returns the namespace URI of the expanded-name for the first node in *node-set*.
name (*node-set*)	Returns the qualified name for the first node in *node-set*.

Fig. 11.12 Some node-set functions (part 2 of 2).

Node-set operators and functions can be combined to form location-path expressions. For example, the location

```
head | body
```

selects all **head** and **body** children element nodes of the context node. If we use the **html** element node on line 6 of Fig. 11.3 as our context node, the above location path will result in the set of nodes containing the **head** element node on lines 8–10 and the **body** element node on lines 14–21. The location path

```
head/title[ last() ]
```

uses the *predicate **last*** to select the last **title** element node contained in the **head** element node. Predicates are expressions used as criteria for inclusion in the set of nodes selected. For each node in a node set, the predicate expression is tested with that node as the context node. In Fig. 11.3, the above location path and predicate would select the **title** element node on line 9. The location path

```
book[ position() = 3 ]
```

and the abbreviated location path

```
bold[ 3 ]
```

would each select the third **book** element of the context node. The location path

```
count( * )
```

would return the total number of element-node children of the context node. For our example, the result would be 2. The location path

```
//book
```

selects all **book** element nodes in the document.

Figure 11.13 is an XML document that contains stock information for several companies. In Fig. 11.14 we use XPath *string functions* in an XSL stylesheet to locate certain nodes in this document. We discuss XSL in greater detail in Chapter 12 and Chapter 13. String functions allow us to manipulate the strings of characters. For example, string function ***concat*** takes two string arguments and concatenates them into a single string.

```
 1   <?xml version = "1.0"?>
 2
 3   <!-- Fig. 11.13 : stocks.xml -->
 4   <!-- Stock list              -->
 5
 6   <stocks>
 7
 8      <stock symbol = "INTC">
 9         <name>Intel Corporation</name>
10      </stock>
11
12      <stock symbol = "CSCO">
13         <name>Cisco Systems, Inc.</name>
14      </stock>
15
16      <stock symbol = "DELL">
17         <name>Dell Computer Corporation</name>
18      </stock>
19
20      <stock symbol = "MSFT">
21         <name>Microsoft Corporation</name>
22      </stock>
23
24      <stock symbol = "SUNW">
25         <name>Sun Microsystems, Inc.</name>
26      </stock>
27
28      <stock symbol = "CMGI">
29         <name>CMGI, Inc.</name>
30      </stock>
31
32   </stocks>
```

Fig. 11.13 List of companies with stock symbols.

Figure 11.14 is an XSLT stylesheet that uses string functions in XPath expressions. We discuss XSLT in detail in Chapter 12. This XSLT stylesheet selects particular elements from an XML document and builds an HTML page containing an unordered list.

```
 1   <?xml version = "1.0"?>
 2
 3   <!-- Fig. 11.14 : stocks.xsl -->
 4   <!-- string function usage   -->
 5
 6   <xsl:stylesheet version = "1.0"
 7      xmlns:xsl = "http://www.w3.org/1999/XSL/Transform">
 8
 9      <xsl:template match = "/stocks">
10         <html>
11            <body>
12               <ul>
13
```

Fig. 11.14 Demonstrating some String functions (part 1 of 2).

```
14                          <xsl:for-each select = "stock">
15
16                              <xsl:if test =
17                                  "starts-with(@symbol, 'C')">
18
19                                  <li>
20                                      <xsl:value-of select =
21                                          "concat(@symbol,' - ', name)"/>
22                                  </li>
23                              </xsl:if>
24
25                          </xsl:for-each>
26                      </ul>
27                  </body>
28              </html>
29          </xsl:template>
30      </xsl:stylesheet>
```

Fig. 11.14 Demonstrating some String functions (part 2 of 2).

Line 17 of Fig. 11.14

```
"starts-with(@symbol, 'C')"
```

uses the XPath string function ***starts-with***, which takes two string arguments. The function returns the boolean value **true** if the string passed in the second argument matches the beginning of the string passed in the first argument. In this example, we retrieve the value of the **symbol** attribute using **@symbol** and compare it to the string **'C'**. If the string returned by **@symbol** begins with the letter **C**, **starts-with** returns **true**; otherwise, **starts-with** returns **false**. Line 21

```
"concat(@symbol,' - ', name)"
```

uses the XPath string function **concat**. The XPath expression **@** symbol again returns the value of the symbol attribute. The XPath expression **name** returns the string-value of the **name** element node. Recall that the string-value of an element node is the text that it contains. In Fig. 11.13, the **name** elements contain the names of companies listed in a stock exchange. In this case, the **concat** function returns the concatenation of the value of the symbol attribute, the string **' - '** and the name of the company.

The result of applying the XSLT stylesheet in Fig. 11.14 to the XML document in Fig. 11.13 is shown in Fig. 11.14. The XPath expression on line 17 matched only those element nodes in the document whose stock symbols began with the letter **'C'** (i.e., **CSCO** and **CMGI**). The XPath expression on line 21 then concatenated the stock symbol with the string **' - '** and the name of the company.

11.5 Internet and World Wide Web Resources

www.w3.org/TR/xpath
The World Wide Web Consortium's *XML Path Language Recommendation.*

www.vbxml.com/xsl/XPathRef.asp
The *XPath Reference Page* on the **vbxml.com** Web site.

SUMMARY

- In XPath, an XML document is viewed conceptually as a tree in which each XML construct is represented as a node.

- For each node, there is a corresponding string-value, which is determined differently for each node type.

- Some node types have a corresponding expanded-name, which has both a local part and a namespace URI.

- Nodes in an XPath tree have an ordering, called document order, which is determined by the order in which the nodes appear in the original XML document. The reverse document order is simply the reverse ordering of the nodes in a document.

- Each node, except the root node, has a parent node, and parent nodes may have any number of child, or descendant, nodes.

- The only node types that may be child nodes are the element, comment, text and processing-instruction node types.

- Namespace and attribute nodes have parent nodes, but are not children of those parent nodes.

- The string-value of a text node consists of the character data contained in the node.

- The string-value of an element node is determined by concatenating the string-values for all of its descendent text nodes in document order.

- An attribute node has a string-value that consists of the normalized value of the attribute.

- For processing instructions the string-value consists of the remainder of the processing instruction after the target, including whitespace, but excluding the ending **?>**.

- Namespace-node string-values consist of the URI for the namespace.

- Expanded-names consist of both a local part and a namespace URI.

- For element nodes, the local part of the expanded-name corresponds to the name of the element in the XML document.

- The local part of the expanded name for a processing-instruction node corresponds to the target of the processing instruction in the XML document.

- The local part of the expanded-name for a namespace node corresponds to the prefix for the namespace, if one exists; or, if it is a default namespace, the local part is empty.

- The namespace URI of the expanded-name for a namespace node is always null.

- Searching through an XML document begins at a context node in the XPath tree.

- An axis indicates which nodes, relative to the context node, are included in the search.

- An axis has a principal node type that corresponds to the type of node the axis may select.

- Predicates are expressions used as criteria for inclusion in the set of nodes selected.

- Location paths are composed of sequences of location steps.

- A location step contains an axis and node test separated by a double-colon (**::**) and, optionally, a predicate enclosed in square brackets (**[ ]**).

- The child axis may be omitted, as it is considered the default axis.
- XPath provides node-set functions that perform an action on a node-set returned by a location path.
- Node-set operators and functions can be combined to form location-path expressions.
- The boolean comparison operations can also be performed on numerical values.

TERMINOLOGY

ancestor axis
ancestor-or-self axis
asterisk (*****)
attribute axis
attribute node
axis
brackets (**[ ]**)
child axis
comment node
context node
default namespace node
descendant axis
descendent-or-self axis
document order
double-colon (**: :**)
double-slash (**/ /**)
expanded-name
following axis
following-sibling axis
forward-slash character (**/**)
id function
last function
local part
location path

location step
namespace axis
namespace node
namespace URI
node
node test
node type
parent axis
period (**.**)
pipe (**|**)
position function
preceding axis
preceding-sibling axis
predicate
processing-instruction node
reverse document order
root node
self axis
slash (**/**)
string-value
text node
two periods (**. .**)
XML Path Language (XPath)
XPath (XML Path Language)

SELF-REVIEW EXERCISES

11.1   State whether the following are *true* or *false*. If *false*, explain why.
a) XML Path Language (XPath) is used to locate specific parts of an XML document.
b) XPath views an XML document as a SAX document containing different elements.
c) There are seven different types of nodes that are found in the constructs of XML documents.
d) Attribute nodes have parent nodes and are also children of those parent nodes.
e) An axis indicates which nodes to search for and is defined relative to the context node.
f) Axes, node tests and predicates can be combined to form a location path.
g) Node-set operators perform actions on a node-set returned by a location path.
h) Predicates are used to refine a node-set based on certain criteria.
i) A step in a location path always contains a predicate.

11.2   Fill in the blanks in each of the following statements.
a) According to XPath, every node in an XML document, except for the root node, has a _____ node, each of which may have any number of _____ nodes.
b) In an XML document, the _____ node exists only at the top of the tree.
c) Each XML element has a set of _____ automatically associated with it.

    d) The node where an XPath search begins is called a _____ node.

    e) Node _____ specify a subset of nodes that are specified by an axis.

    f) A _____ path consists of location _____ separated by the forward-slash character.

    g) Node-set _____ perform an action on a node-set returned by a location path.

    h) The node-set function _____ returns the number of nodes in the argument node-set.

    i) The _____ value associated with a comment node includes the _____ of the comment, with leading and trailing whitespace removed.

ANSWERS TO SELF-REVIEW EXERCISES

11.1   a) True. b) False. XPath views an XML document as a tree, with each XML construct represented by a node. c) True. d) False. Attribute nodes have parent nodes, but are not children of those parent nodes. e) True. f) True. g) False. Node-set operators are used to perform operations on a node-set returned by a location path. h) True. i) False. A step in a location path sometimes contains a predicate.

11.2   a) parent, child. b) root. c) namespaces. d) context. e) tests. f) location, steps. g) functions. h) **count** (or **last**). i) string, contents.

EXERCISES

11.3   From the XML document in Fig. 11.15, answer the following questions.

    a) What is the XPath expression that selects all **transaction** elements with attribute **date** having values between **06/01/2000** and **07/30/2000**, inclusive?

    b) What is the XPath expression that selects all **transaction** elements that have an **amount** of U.S. dollars (**USD**) with a value greater than **200**?

    c) What is the XPath expression that selects all **transaction** elements from **account 100392**?

    d) What is the XPath expression that calculates the total value of transactions in **account 203921**?

    e) What is the XPath expression to determine the average amount transferred to **account 203921**?

    f) What is the XPath expression that selects all transactions dated **09/03/2000**?

    g) What is the XPath expression that selects all **amount** elements with a **currency** of **NTD** whose transaction date is after **09/01/2000**?

    h) What is the XPath expression to get all **transaction** elements from part (a) with **account** value **100392**?

```
1   <?xml version = "1.0"?>
2
3   <transactions>
4
5      <transaction date = "05/22/2000" id = "0122">
6         <from account = "100392"/>
7         <to account = "203921"/>
8         <amount currency = "USD">15</amount>
9      </transaction>
```

Fig. 11.15 Account transaction XML document (part 1 of 2).

```
10
11        <transaction date = "06/01/2000" id = "0129">
12           <from account = "203921"/>
13           <to account = "877521"/>
14           <amount currency = "USD">4800</amount>
15        </transaction>
16
17        <transaction date = "06/01/2000" id = "0130">
18           <from account = "100392"/>
19           <to account = "992031"/>
20           <amount currency = "YEN">7000</amount>
21        </transaction>
22
23        <transaction date = "06/10/2000" id = "0152">
24           <from account = "992031"/>
25           <to account = "100392"/>
26           <amount currency = "USD">402.53</amount>
27        </transaction>
28
29        <transaction date = "06/22/2000" id = "0188">
30           <from account = "100392"/>
31           <to account = "203921"/>
32           <amount currency = "USD">10000</amount>
33        </transaction>
34
35        <transaction date = "07/12/2000" id = "0200">
36           <from account = "100392"/>
37           <to account = "039211"/>
38           <amount currency = "NTD">3000</amount>
39        </transaction>
40
41        <transaction date = "07/26/2000" id = "0211">
42           <from account = "203921"/>
43           <to account = "100392"/>
44           <amount currency = "USD">400</amount>
45        </transaction>
46
47        <transaction date = "08/05/2000" id = "0225">
48           <from account = "039211"/>
49           <to account = "203921"/>
50           <amount currency = "USD">150</amount>
51        </transaction>
52
53        <transaction date = "09/03/2000" id = "0293">
54           <from account = "100392"/>
55           <to account = "039211"/>
56           <amount currency = "NTD">200000</amount>
57        </transaction>
58
59   </transactions>
```

Fig. 11.15 Account transaction XML document (part 2 of 2).

11.4   From the XPath expressions and results in Fig. 11.16, generate the XML document.

Expression	Result
`count( //* )`	7
`count( //@* )`	6
`count( //argument )`	2
`count( //description )`	1
`count( //class )`	1
`count( //function )`	2
`count( //return )`	1
`count( //text() )`	1
`count( //processing-instruction() )`	0
`count( //function/return )`	1
`count( //function/argument )`	2
`count( //class/* )`	3
`count( //description/* )`	0
`//class/description`	{ "This class handles input" }
`//@name`	{ "input", "text", "number" }
`//@type`	{ "string", "int", "string" }
`//return/@type`	{ "int" }
`//argument/@type`	{ "string", "string" }
`boolean( //function/@name )`	true
`boolean( //class/@name )`	true

Fig. 11.16 XPath expressions.

12

XSL: Extensible Stylesheet Language Transformations (XSLT)

Objectives

- To understand what Extensible Stylesheet Language is and how it relates to XML.
- To understand what an Extensible Stylesheet Language Transformation (XSLT) is.
- To be able to write XSLT documents.
- To be able to write templates.
- To be able to iterate through a node set returned by an XPath expression.
- To be able to sort.
- To be able to perform conditional processing.
- To be able to copy nodes.
- To be able to declare variables.

Guess if you can, choose if you dare.
Pierre Corneille

A Mighty Maze! but not without a plan.
Alexander Pope

Behind the outside pattern
the dim shapes get clearer every day.
It is always the same shape, only very numerous.
Charlotte Perkins Gilman

12.1 Introduction

The last chapter discussed XML Path Language (XPath) for locating specific nodes in an XML document. *Extensible Stylesheet Language (XSL)* is used to format XML documents and consists of two parts. This chapter presents the first part of XSL—the *XSL Transformation Language (XSLT)*. XSLT transforms an XML document from one form to another. XSLT uses XPath to match nodes for transforming an XML document into a different document. The resulting document may be XML, HTML, plain text or any other text-based document. The second part of XSL is XSL *formatting objects*, which provide an alternative to CSS for formatting and styling an XML document. We discuss formatting objects in Chapter 13. The following sections describe the use of XSLT and present many code examples.

12.2 Setup

To process XSLT documents, you will need an *XSLT processor*. In the following sections, we will provide examples using *Microsoft Internet Explorer 5* and *Apache's Xalan*.

Internet Explorer 5 has the ability to process XML and XSLT documents, providing an easy method to view XML documents as HTML documents via a transformation. In order to execute the examples in this chapter, you will need to download and install version 3.0 of msxml—the XML processor used by IE5. For instructions on downloading and installing msxml, visit the Deitel & Associates, Inc. Web site at **www.deitel.com**.

Apache has created the *Xalan XSLT processor for Java and C++*. In this chapter, we run a Java version of this application from the command line to perform the transformations. To use Xalan, you will need to perform the following steps:

1. Install the Java 2 SDK. For instructions, please visit **www.deitel.com**.

2. Get Apache Xalan from **xml.apache.org/xalan**. The Xalan distribution comes with Apache's XML parser, Xerces. In this chapter, we will assume that you have installed Xalan in **C:\xalan**.

3. Add the Xalan and Xerces JAR files to your **CLASSPATH** environment variable.

12.3 Templates

An XSLT document is an XML document with a root element **stylesheet**. The namespace for an XSLT document is **http://www.w3.org/1999/XSL/Transform**. The XSLT document shown in Fig. 12.1 transforms **intro.xml** (Fig. 12.2) into a simple HTML document (Fig 12.3). XSLT uses XPath expressions (discussed in Chapter 11) to locate nodes in an XML document. In an XSL transformation, there are two trees of nodes. The first node tree is the *source tree*. The nodes in this tree correspond to the original XML document to which the transformation is applied. The second node tree is the *result tree*. The result tree contains all of the nodes produced by the XSL transformation. This result tree represents the document produced by the transformation.

Lines 6 and 7

```
<xsl:stylesheet version = "1.0"
        xmlns:xsl = "http://www.w3.org/1999/XSL/Transform">
```

show the XSLT document's root element (i.e., **xsl:stylesheet**) and its attributes. Attribute **version** defines the XSLT specification used. Namespace prefix **xsl** is defined and assigned the URI *"http://www.w3.org/1999/XSL/Transform"*.

Line 9

```
<xsl:template match = "myMessage">
```

shows a **template** *element*. This element matches specific XML document nodes by using an XPath expression in attribute **match**. In this case, we **match** any **myMessage** element nodes.

Lines 10–12

```
<html>
    <body><xsl:value-of select = "message"/></body>
</html>
```

```
1   <?xml version = "1.0"?>
2
3   <!-- Fig. 12.1 : intro.xsl              -->
4   <!-- Simple XSLT document for intro.xml -->
5
6   <xsl:stylesheet version = "1.0"
7           xmlns:xsl = "http://www.w3.org/1999/XSL/Transform">
8
9       <xsl:template match = "myMessage">
10          <html>
11              <body><xsl:value-of select = "message"/></body>
12          </html>
13      </xsl:template>
14
15  </xsl:stylesheet>
```

Fig. 12.1 Simple template.

are the contents of the **template** element in line 9. When a **myMessage** element node is matched in the source tree, the contents of the **template** element are placed in the result tree. By using element *value-of* and an XPath expression in attribute *select*, the text contents of the node-set returned by the XPath expression are placed in the result tree.

We will be using Internet Explorer 5 to process the XML and XSLT documents. By viewing the XML document, IE5 will automatically apply the XSLT document.

Figure 12.2 lists the input XML document and Fig. 12.3 lists the result of the transformation.

Line 6

```
<?xml:stylesheet type = "text/xsl" href = "intro.xsl"?>
```

uses element **stylesheet** to attach a style sheet to an XML document. Attribute **type** defines the type of file being attached. The two valid values are **text/xsl**, which denotes an XSL document, and **text/css**, which denotes a CSS document. Attribute **href** holds the file being attached.

12.4 Creating Elements and Attributes

In the previous section, we demonstrated the use of XSLT for simple element matching. This section discuss the creation of new elements and attributes within an XSLT document.

Figure 12.4 lists an XML document that marks up various sports.

```
1   <?xml version = "1.0"?>
2
3   <!-- Fig. 12.2 : intro.xml         -->
4   <!-- Simple introduction to XML markup -->
5
6   <?xml:stylesheet type = "text/xsl" href = "intro.xsl"?>
7
8   <myMessage>
9      <message>Welcome to XSLT!</message>
10  </myMessage>
```

Fig. 12.2   Input XML document.

```
1   <html><body>Welcome to XSLT!</body></html>
```

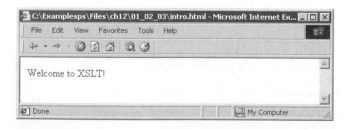

Fig. 12.3   Internet Explorer 5 displaying the results of an XSL transformation.

```
1   <?xml version = "1.0"?>
2
3   <!-- Fig. 12.4 : games.xml -->
4   <!-- Sports Database       -->
5
6   <sports>
7
8      <game title = "cricket">
9         <id>243</id>
10
11        <para>
12           More popular among commonwealth nations.
13        </para>
14     </game>
15
16     <game title = "baseball">
17        <id>431</id>
18
19        <para>
20           More popular in America.
21        </para>
22     </game>
23
24     <game title = "soccer">
25        <id>123</id>
26
27        <para>
28           Most popular sport in the world.
29        </para>
30     </game>
31
32  </sports>
```

Fig. 12.4 XML document containing a list of sports.

Figure 12.5 lists the XSLT document that transforms the XML document of Fig. 12.4 into another XML document.

```
1   <?xml version = "1.0"?>
2
3   <!-- Fig. 12.5 : elements.xsl         -->
4   <!-- Using xsl:element and xsl:attribute -->
5
6   <xsl:stylesheet version = "1.0"
7           xmlns:xsl = "http://www.w3.org/1999/XSL/Transform">
8
9      <xsl:template match = "/">
10        <xsl:apply-templates/>
11     </xsl:template>
12
```

Fig. 12.5 Using XSLT to create elements and attributes (part 1 of 2).

```
13   <xsl:template match = "sports">
14      <sports>
15         <xsl:apply-templates/>
16      </sports>
17   </xsl:template>
18
19   <xsl:template match = "game">
20      <xsl:element name = "{@title}">
21
22         <xsl:attribute name = "id">
23            <xsl:value-of select = "id"/>
24         </xsl:attribute>
25
26         <comment>
27            <xsl:value-of select = "para"/>
28         </comment>
29
30      </xsl:element>
31   </xsl:template>
32
33 </xsl:stylesheet>
```

Fig. 12.5   Using XSLT to create elements and attributes (part 2 of 2).

Lines 9–11

```
<xsl:template match = "/">
   <xsl:apply-templates/>
</xsl:template>
```

use the **match** attribute to select the document root of an XML document. Recall from Chapter 11 that the **/** character in an XPath expression selects the root element of an XML document. Element **apply-templates** is used to apply the templates of the XSLT document to specific nodes of an element. In this case, we have not specified any particular nodes. By default, element **apply-templates** will match all the child nodes of an element to templates. In Fig. 12.4, the child nodes of the document root are two comment nodes and the **sports** element node.

The XSLT recommendation defines default templates for the nodes of an XML document. If a programmer does not specify a template that matches a particular element, the default XSLT template will be applied. These templates are described in Fig. 12.6.

Lines 13–17

```
<xsl:template match = "sports">
   <sports>
      <xsl:apply-templates/>
   </sports>
</xsl:template>
```

match element **sports**. We output the **sports** element and apply templates to the child nodes of the **sports** element.

Template / Description

```
<xsl:template match = "/ | *">
   <xsl:apply-templates/>
</xsl:template>
```
This template matches the document root node (**/**) and any element nodes (*****) of an XML document and applies templates to their child nodes.

```
<xsl:template match = "text() | @*">
   <xsl:value-of select = "."/>
</xsl:template>
```
This template matches text nodes (**text()**) and attribute nodes (**@**) and outputs their values.

```
<xsl:template match = "processing-instruction() | comment()"/>
```
This template matches processing-instruction nodes (**processing-instruction()**) and comment nodes (**comment()**), but does not perform any actions with them.

Fig. 12.6 Default XSLT templates.

Line 19

```
<xsl:template match = "game">
```

matches element **game**. In the input XML document, element **game** contains the name of a sport, its unique identifier and a description.

Line 20

```
<xsl:element name = "{@title}">
```

shows the element **element**, which is used to create an element, with the element name specified in attribute **name**. An XPath expression in XSL is specified using curly braces (**{}**). Therefore, the name of this XML element will be the name of the sport contained in attribute **title** of element **game**.

Lines 22–24

```
<xsl:attribute name = "id">
   <xsl:value-of select = "id"/>
</xsl:attribute>
```

show element **attribute**, which is used to create an attribute for an element. Element **attribute** can be contained only within an **element** element. Attribute **name** provides the name of the attribute. The text contained in **element** attribute will result in the value of the attribute. The result of this statement will create attribute **id** for the new element, which contains the text in element **id** of element **game**.

Lines 26–28

```
<comment>
   <xsl:value-of select = "para"/>
</comment>
```

create element **comment** with the contents of element **para**.

The Apache Group has produced the Xalan XSLT processor. In the following examples, we use Xalan with Java to perform XSL transformations on XML documents. To use Apache Xalan to transform XML documents, set the **CLASSPATH** variable to point to **xalan.jar** and **xerces.jar**. For example, assuming that Xalan and Xerces are installed on the **C:** drive on a Windows machine, type

```
set CLASSPATH=C:\xalan\xalan.jar;C:\xalan\xerces.jar;.
```

From the command line, type

```
java org.apache.xalan.xslt.Process -INDENT 3 -IN games.xml
-XSL elements.xsl -OUT output.xml
```

Figure 12.7 lists the output of the transformation. Your output may not look exactly like that in the figure, because we have modified the output in the figure for presentation.

As you can see, the original XML document has been transformed into a new XML document with sport names as elements (instead of attributes, as in the original document). By using XSLT, you can easily convert XML documents from one form to another.

```
1  <?xml version = "1.0" encoding = "UTF-8"?>
2  <sports>
3
4     <cricket id = "243">
5        <comment>
6           More popular among commonwealth nations.
7        </comment>
8     </cricket>
9
10    <baseball id = "431">
11       <comment>
12          More popular in America.
13       </comment>
14    </baseball>
15
16    <soccer id = "123">
17       <comment>
18          Most popular sport in the world.
19       </comment>
20    </soccer>
21
22 </sports>
```

Fig. 12.7 Output of transformation.

12.5 Iteration and Sorting

XSLT also allows for iteration through a node set returned by an XPath expression. The node set can also be sorted. Figure 12.8 shows an XML document we introduced in Chapter 5. At the time we introduced this XML document, we briefly introduced the concept of an XSL stylesheet. Figure 12.9 shows the XML stylesheet used to render the document.

Figure 12.9 lists an XSLT document for transforming this XML document into an HTML document.

```
1   <?xml version = "1.0"?>
2
3   <!-- Fig. 12.8 : usage.xml            -->
4   <!-- Usage of elements and attributes -->
5
6   <?xml:stylesheet type = "text/xsl" href = "usage.xsl"?>
7
8   <book isbn = "999-99999-9-X">
9      <title>Deitel&apos;s XML Primer</title>
10
11     <author>
12        <firstName>Paul</firstName>
13        <lastName>Deitel</lastName>
14     </author>
15
16     <chapters>
17        <preface num = "1" pages = "2">Welcome</preface>
18        <chapter num = "1" pages = "4">Easy XML</chapter>
19        <chapter num = "2" pages = "2">XML Elements?</chapter>
20        <appendix num = "1" pages = "9">Entities</appendix>
21     </chapters>
22
23     <media type = "CD"/>
24  </book>
```

Fig. 12.8 Book table of contents as XML.

```
1   <?xml version = "1.0"?>
2
3   <!-- Fig. 12.9 : usage.xsl                      -->
4   <!-- Transformation of Book information into HTML -->
5
6   <xsl:stylesheet version = "1.0"
7      xmlns:xsl = "http://www.w3.org/1999/XSL/Transform">
8
9      <xsl:template match = "/">
10        <html>
11           <xsl:apply-templates/>
12        </html>
13     </xsl:template>
14
```

Fig. 12.9 Transforming XML data into HTML (part 1 of 3).

```
15    <xsl:template match = "book">
16       <head>
17          <title>ISBN <xsl:value-of select = "@isbn"/> -
18             <xsl:value-of select = "title"/></title>
19       </head>
20
21       <body bgcolor = "white">
22          <h1><xsl:value-of select = "title"/></h1>
23
24          <h2>by <xsl:value-of select = "author/lastName"/>,
25             <xsl:value-of select = "author/firstName"/></h2>
26
27          <table border = "1">
28             <xsl:for-each select = "chapters/preface">
29                <xsl:sort select = "@num" order = "ascending"/>
30                <tr>
31                   <td align = "right">
32                      Preface <xsl:value-of select = "@num"/>
33                   </td>
34
35                   <td>
36                      <xsl:value-of select = "."/> (
37                      <xsl:value-of select = "@pages"/> pages )
38                   </td>
39                </tr>
40             </xsl:for-each>
41
42             <xsl:for-each select = "chapters/chapter">
43                <xsl:sort select = "@num" order = "ascending"/>
44                <tr>
45                   <td align = "right">
46                      Chapter <xsl:value-of select = "@num"/>
47                   </td>
48
49                   <td>
50                      <xsl:value-of select = "."/> (
51                      <xsl:value-of select = "@pages"/> pages )
52                   </td>
53                </tr>
54             </xsl:for-each>
55
56             <xsl:for-each select = "chapters/appendix">
57                <xsl:sort select = "@num" order = "ascending"/>
58                <tr>
59                   <td align = "right">
60                      Appendix <xsl:value-of select = "@num"/>
61                   </td>
62
63                   <td>
64                      <xsl:value-of select = "."/> (
65                      <xsl:value-of select = "@pages"/> pages )
66                   </td>
67                </tr>
```

Fig. 12.9 Transforming XML data into HTML (part 2 of 3).

```
68                    </xsl:for-each>
69                </table>
70            </body>
71        </xsl:template>
72
73  </xsl:stylesheet>
```

Fig. 12.9 Transforming XML data into HTML (part 3 of 3).

Line 15

```
<xsl:template match = "book">
```

is an XSLT template that matches the **book** element. In this template, we construct the body of the HTML document.

Lines 17 and 18

```
<title>ISBN <xsl:value-of select = "@isbn"/> -
    <xsl:value-of select = "title"/></title>
```

create the title for the HTML document. We use the ISBN of the book from attribute **isbn** and also the contents of element **title** to create the title string, resulting in **ISBN 999-99999-9-X - Deitel's XML Primer**.

Line 22

```
<h1><xsl:value-of select = "title"/></h1>
```

creates a header element with the title of the book, selected from element **title**.

Lines 24 and 25

```
<h2>by <xsl:value-of select = "author/lastName"/>,
    <xsl:value-of select = "author/firstName"/></h2>
```

create another header element, displaying the author of the book. The XPath expression **author/lastName** is used to select the author's last name, and the expression **author/firstName** selects the author's first name.

Line 28

```
<xsl:for-each select = "chapters/preface">
```

shows XSLT element **for-each**, which applies the contents of the element to each of the nodes selected by attribute **select**. In this case, we select all **preface** elements of the **chapters** element.

Line 29

```
<xsl:sort select = "@num" order = "ascending"/>
```

shows XSLT element **sort**, which sorts the nodes selected by the **for-each** element by the field in attribute **select**, in the order specified in attribute **order**. Attribute **order** has values **ascending** (i.e., A–Z) and **descending** (i.e., Z–A). For this **for-each** element, we sort the nodes by attribute **num**, in ascending order.

Lines 30–39 output a table row displaying the preface number, the title of the preface and the number of pages in that preface for each **preface** element.

Similarly, lines 40–51 output the **chapter** elements, and lines 56–68 output the **appendix** elements.

We can use Xalan or IE 5 to output the resulting transformation, shown in Fig. 12.10. Your output may look different though, because we have modified ours for presentation.

```
1   <html>
2      <head>
3         <title>ISBN 999-99999-9-X - Deitel's XML Primer</title>
4      </head>
5
6      <body bgcolor = "white">
7         <h1>Deitel's XML Primer</h1>
8         <h2>by Deitel, Paul</h2>
9
10        <table border = "1">
11           <tr>
12              <td align = "right">Preface 1</td>
13              <td>Welcome ( 2 pages )</td>
14           </tr>
15
16           <tr>
17              <td align = "right">Chapter 1</td>
18              <td>Easy XML ( 4 pages )</td>
19           </tr>
20
21           <tr>
22              <td align = "right">Chapter 2</td>
23              <td>XML Elements? ( 2 pages )</td>
24           </tr>
25
26           <tr>
27              <td align = "right">Appendix 1</td>
28              <td>Entities ( 9 pages )</td>
29           </tr>
30        </table>
31     </body>
32
33  </html>
```

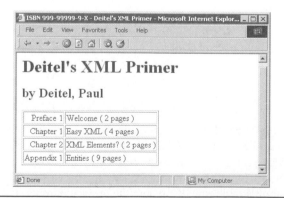

Fig. 12.10 Output of the transformation.

12.6 Conditional Processing

In the previous section, we discussed iteration of a node set. XSLT also provides elements to perform conditional processing, such as **if** statements. Figure 12.11 provides an XSLT document used to transform the day planner created in previous chapters into an HTML document.

```
1   <?xml version = "1.0"?>
2
3   <!-- Fig. 12.11 : conditional.xsl          -->
4   <!-- xsl:choose, xsl:when, and xsl:otherwise -->
5
6   <xsl:stylesheet version = "1.0"
7      xmlns:xsl = "http://www.w3.org/1999/XSL/Transform">
8
9      <xsl:template match = "/">
10         <html>
11
12         <body>
13            Appointments
14            <br/>
15            <xsl:apply-templates select = "planner/year"/>
16         </body>
17
18         </html>
19      </xsl:template>
20
21      <xsl:template match = "year">
22         <strong>Year:</strong>
23         <xsl:value-of select = "@value"/>
24         <br/>
25         <xsl:for-each select = "date/note">
26            <xsl:sort select = "../@day" order = "ascending"
27               data-type = "number"/>
28            <strong>
29               Day:
30               <xsl:value-of select = "../@day"/>/
31               <xsl:value-of select = "../@month"/>
32            </strong>
33
34            <xsl:choose>
35
36               <xsl:when test =
37                  "@time &gt;= '0500' and @time &lt; '1200'">
38                  Morning (<xsl:value-of select = "@time"/>):
39               </xsl:when>
40
41               <xsl:when test =
42                  "@time &gt;= '1200' and @time &lt; '1700'">
43                  Afternoon (<xsl:value-of select = "@time"/>):
44               </xsl:when>
45
```

Fig. 12.11 Using conditional elements (part 1 of 2).

```
46                    <xsl:when test =
47                       "@time &gt;= '1700' and @time &lt;= '2359'">
48                       Evening (<xsl:value-of select = "@time"/>):
49                    </xsl:when>
50
51                    <xsl:when test =
52                       "@time &gt;= '0100' and @time &lt; '0500'">
53                       Night (<xsl:value-of select = "@time"/>):
54                    </xsl:when>
55
56                    <xsl:otherwise>
57                       Entire day:
58                    </xsl:otherwise>
59
60             </xsl:choose>
61
62             <xsl:value-of select = "."/>
63
64             <xsl:if test = ". = ''">
65                n/a
66             </xsl:if>
67
68             <br/>
69          </xsl:for-each>
70
71       </xsl:template>
72
73    </xsl:stylesheet>
```

Fig. 12.11 Using conditional elements (part 2 of 2).

XSLT provides the **choose** element (lines 34–60) to allow alternate conditional statements, similar to a **switch** statement in C++ or Java. Element **choose** allows child elements **when** and **otherwise**.

Lines 36–39

```
<xsl:when test =
    "@time &gt; '0500' and @time &lt; '1200'">
    Morning (<xsl:value-of select = "@time"/>):
</xsl:when>
```

show one **when** conditional of the **choose** element. Attribute **test** provides the conditional statement to be tested. The **when** element stops after the first **true** result. The contents of element **when** are used if the condition is met. In this element, we test if attribute **time** of element **note** has a value greater than **0500** and less than **1200**.

Lines 56–58

```
<xsl:otherwise>
    Entire day:
</xsl:otherwise>
```

show the **otherwise** condition of the **choose** element. Element **otherwise** is optional, but if included, it must occur only once, after all **when** elements. This element is used if no **when** elements have been matched.

Lines 64–66

```
<xsl:if test = ". = ''">
    n/a
</xsl:if>
```

show the **if** conditional statement. Unlike element **choose**, element **if** is used to provide a single conditional test, in attribute **test**.

12.7 Copying Nodes

Instead of providing a template for each element of an XML document, XSLT provides an element to duplicate nodes from the source tree into the result tree. The XSLT element **copy** is used to produce a copy of the context node and place it in the result tree. An example using element **copy** is provided in Fig. 12.12.

```
1   <?xml version = "1.0"?>
2
3   <!-- Fig. 12.12: copyIntro.xsl        -->
4   <!-- xsl:copy example using Intro.xml -->
5
6   <xsl:stylesheet version = "1.0"
7      xmlns:xsl = "http://www.w3.org/1999/XSL/Transform">
8
9      <xsl:template match = "myMessage">
10
11         <xsl:copy>
12            <xsl:apply-templates/>
13         </xsl:copy>
14
```

Fig. 12.12 Using the XSLT element **copy** (part 1 of 2).

```
15        </xsl:template>
16
17        <xsl:template match = "message">
18
19            <xsl:copy>
20                How about &apos;Hi World&apos; for a change!
21            </xsl:copy>
22
23        </xsl:template>
24
25    </xsl:stylesheet>
```

Fig. 12.12 Using the XSLT element **copy** (part 2 of 2).

Lines 11–13

```
<xsl:copy>
   <xsl:apply-templates/>
</xsl:copy>
```

show element **copy**. Element **copy** produces a duplicate of the context node in the result tree. Any child nodes or attributes are not duplicated. If element **copy** contains children, they are processed after the copy has been performed. In this case, we apply templates to the child nodes of the element.

Lines 19–21

```
<xsl:copy>
   How about 'Hi World' for a change!
</xsl:copy>
```

show element **copy**, but in this case we replace the content of the element with text.

The result of the transformation on **intro.xml** from Fig. 12.2 is shown in Fig. 12.13. If lines 19–21 of Fig. 12.12 were changed to

```
<xsl:copy/>
```

the transformation would result in an empty **message** element, because this uses an empty **xsl:copy** element.

Figure 12.14 demonstrates element *copy-of*, which performs a copy of the subtree, starting with the selected node.

```
1    <?xml version = "1.0" encoding = "UTF-8"?>
2    <myMessage>
3       <message>
4          How about 'Hi World' for a change!
5       </message>
6    </myMessage>
```

Fig. 12.13 Resulting transformation.

```
1   <?xml version = "1.0"?>
2
3   <!-- Fig. 12.14 : usingCopyOf.xsl        -->
4   <!-- xsl:copy-of example using intro.xml -->
5
6   <xsl:stylesheet version = "1.0"
7      xmlns:xsl = "http://www.w3.org/1999/XSL/Transform">
8
9      <xsl:template match = "myMessage">
10
11         <xsl:comment>
12            The following XML tree has been copied into output.
13         </xsl:comment>
14
15         <xsl:copy-of select = "."/>
16      </xsl:template>
17
18   </xsl:stylesheet>
```

Fig. 12.14 xsl:copy-of element.

Lines 11–13

```
<xsl:comment>
   The following XML tree has been copied into output.
</xsl:comment>
```

create a comment in the resulting XML document.
Line 15

```
<xsl:copy-of select = "."/>
```

duplicates the nodes selected by attribute **select** into the output. Unlike element **copy**, element **copy-of** duplicates all children (i.e., text, processing instructions, comments, etc.) and attributes of the node.

Figure 12.15 shows the output of the transformation applied to **intro.xml** from Fig. 12.2.

12.8 Combining Stylesheets

XSLT allows for modularity in stylesheets. This feature enables XSLT documents to import other XSLT documents. Figure 12.16 lists an XSLT document that is imported into the XSLT document in Fig. 12.17 using element **import**.

```
1   <?xml version = "1.0" encoding = "UTF-8"?>
2   <!-- The following XML tree has been copied into output. -->
3   <myMessage>
4      <message>Welcome to XSLT!</message>
5   </myMessage>
```

Fig. 12.15 Ouput of the **copy-of** transformation.

```
1   <?xml version = "1.0"?>
2
3   <!-- Fig. 12.16 : usage2.xsl    -->
4   <!-- xsl:import example         -->
5
6   <xsl:stylesheet version = "1.0"
7         xmlns:xsl = "http://www.w3.org/1999/XSL/Transform">
8
9      <xsl:template match = "book">
10        <html>
11
12           <body>
13              <xsl:apply-templates/>
14           </body>
15        </html>
16
17     </xsl:template>
18
19     <xsl:template match = "title">
20        <xsl:value-of select = "."/>
21     </xsl:template>
22
23     <xsl:template match = "author">
24        <br/>
25
26        <p>Author:
27           <xsl:value-of select = "lastName"/>,
28           <xsl:value-of select = "firstName"/>
29        </p>
30
31     </xsl:template>
32
33     <xsl:template match = "*|text()"/>
34
35  </xsl:stylesheet>
```

Fig. 12.16 XSLT document being imported.

Line 33

```
<xsl:template match = "*|text()"/>
```

provides a template to match any text and leftover element nodes.

```
1   <?xml version = "1.0"?>
2
3   <!-- Fig. 12.17 : usage1.xsl             -->
4   <!-- xsl:import example using usage.xml -->
5
6   <xsl:stylesheet version = "1.0"
7      xmlns:xsl = "http://www.w3.org/1999/XSL/Transform">
8
```

Fig. 12.17 Importing another XSLT document (part 1 of 2).

```
 9      <xsl:import href = "usage2.xsl"/>
10
11      <!-- This template has higher precedence over the
12           templates being imported  -->
13      <xsl:template match = "title">
14
15         <h2>
16            <xsl:value-of select = "."/>
17         </h2>
18
19      </xsl:template>
20
21   </xsl:stylesheet>
```

Fig. 12.17 Importing another XSLT document (part 2 of 2).

Line 9

```
<xsl:import href = "usage2.xsl"/>
```

uses element **import** to use the templates defined in the XSLT document referenced by attribute **href**.

Common Programming Error 12.1

*The value of the **href** attribute in an **import** element must reference a local XSL document. Referencing a remote XSL document is an error.*

Line 13 provides a template for element **title**, which has already been defined in the XSLT document being imported. This local template has higher precedence than the imported template, so it is used instead of the imported template.

Figure 12.18 shows the transformed document **usage.xml** (Fig. 12.8). Figure 12.19 shows an example of the XSLT element **include**, which includes other XSLT documents in the current XSLT document. Lines 28 and 29

```
<xsl:include href = "author.xsl"/>
<xsl:include href = "chapters.xsl"/>
```

show element **include**, which includes the files referenced by attribute **href**. The difference between element **include** and element **import** is that templates included using element **include** have the same precedence as the local templates. Therefore, if any templates are duplicated, the template that occurs last is used.

```
1   <html>
2      <body>
3         <h2>Deitel's XML Primer</h2>
4         <br>
5         <p>
6            Author: Deitel, Paul
7         </p>
8      </body>
9   </html>
```

Fig. 12.18 Resulting HTML document using XSLT **import**.

```
1   <?xml version = "1.0"?>
2
3   <!-- Fig. 12.19 : book.xsl              -->
4   <!-- xsl:include example using usage.xml -->
5
6   <xsl:stylesheet version = "1.0"
7      xmlns:xsl = "http://www.w3.org/1999/XSL/Transform">
8
9      <xsl:template match = "/">
10
11     <html>
12        <body>
13           <xsl:apply-templates select = "book"/>
14        </body>
15     </html>
16
17     </xsl:template>
18
19     <xsl:template match = "book">
20
21        <h2>
22           <xsl:value-of select = "title"/>
23        </h2>
24
25        <xsl:apply-templates/>
26     </xsl:template>
27
28     <xsl:include href = "author.xsl"/>
29     <xsl:include href = "chapters.xsl"/>
30
31     <xsl:template match = "*|text()"/>
32
33  </xsl:stylesheet>
```

Fig. 12.19 Combining stylesheets using `xsl:include`.

Figure 12.20 and 12.21 list the XSLT documents being included by Fig. 12.19.

```
1   <?xml version = "1.0"?>
2
3   <!-- Fig. 12.20 : author.xsl              -->
4   <!-- xsl:include example using usage.xml -->
5
6   <xsl:stylesheet version = "1.0"
7           xmlns:xsl = "http://www.w3.org/1999/XSL/Transform">
8
9      <xsl:template match = "author">
10
11        <p>Author:
12           <xsl:value-of select = "lastName"/>,
13           <xsl:value-of select = "firstName"/>
14        </p>
```

Fig. 12.20 XSLT document for rendering the author's name (part 1 of 2).

```
15
16        </xsl:template>
17
18    </xsl:stylesheet>
```

Fig. 12.20 XSLT document for rendering the author's name (part 2 of 2).

```
1     <?xml version = "1.0"?>
2
3     <!-- Fig. 12.21 : chapters.xsl           -->
4     <!-- xsl:include example using usage.xml -->
5
6     <xsl:stylesheet version = "1.0"
7             xmlns:xsl = "http://www.w3.org/1999/XSL/Transform">
8
9         <xsl:template match = "chapters">
10           Chapters:
11
12           <ul>
13               <xsl:apply-templates select = "chapter"/>
14           </ul>
15        </xsl:template>
16
17        <xsl:template match = "chapter">
18
19           <li>
20               <xsl:value-of select = "."/>
21           </li>
22
23        </xsl:template>
24
25    </xsl:stylesheet>
```

Fig. 12.21 XSLT document for rendering chapter names.

The result of the XSLT document (Fig. 12.19) applied to the XML document describing a book (Fig. 12.8) is shown in Fig. 12.22.

```
1     <html>
2         <body>
3             <h2>Deitel's XML Primer</h2>
4             <p>Author:
5               Deitel, Paul</p>
6
7             Chapters:
8             <ul>
9                 <li>Easy XML</li>
10                <li>XML Elements?</li>
11            </ul>
12        </body>
13    </html>
```

Fig. 12.22 Output of an XSLT document using element **include** (part 1 of 2).

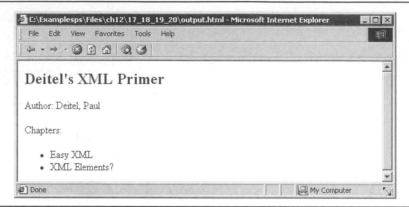

Fig. 12.22 Output of an XSLT document using element **include** (part 2 of 2).

12.9 Variables

XSLT also provides the ability to keep variables for the processing of information. Figure 12.23 provides an example of an XSLT document using element **variable**.

Lines 13 and 14

```
<xsl:variable name = "sum"
    select = "sum(book/chapters/*/@pages)"/>
```

create element **variable** with attribute **name** of **sum**, for storing the sum of the number of pages in the book. Attribute **select** has value   **sum(book/chapters/*/@pages)**, which is an XPath expression summing up the number of **pages** attributes of the elements in element **chapters**.

```
1   <?xml version = "1.0"?>
2
3   <!-- Fig. 12.23 : variables.xsl -->
4   <!-- using xsl:variables       -->
5
6   <xsl:stylesheet version = "1.0"
7           xmlns:xsl = "http://www.w3.org/1999/XSL/Transform">
8
9   <xsl:template match = "/">
10
11      <total>
12         Number of pages =
13         <xsl:variable name = "sum"
14             select = "sum(book/chapters/*/@pages)"/>
15         <xsl:value-of select = "$sum"/>
16      </total>
17
18   </xsl:template>
19
20   </xsl:stylesheet>
```

Fig. 12.23 Example for **xsl:variable**.

Line 15

```
<xsl:value-of select = "$sum"/>
```

uses element **value-of** to output the variable **sum** by using the dollar sign (**$**) to reference the variable. The **value-of** element can also be used to output the value of an element or attribute.

Figure 12.24 shows the output of the XSLT document in Fig. 12.23 applied to the book XML document in Fig. 12.8.

The XPath expression calculated the sum of the number of pages in each preface, chapter and appendix, which is 17 for the document in Fig. 12.8.

12.10 Case Study: XSLT and XPath

XPath and XSL are intimately related. The examples in this chapter used simple XPath expressions to locate elements, attributes and text in XML documents. In this section, we present a more substantial example that uses more complex XPath expressions.

Figure 12.25 marks up information about Deitel & Associates, Inc.'s complete training course and Web-based training products. The document contains root element **product**, which has three child elements: **completeTrainingCourses**, **books** and **webBasedTraining**. Each **completeTrainingCourse** element contains a **title**, **book** and **cd**. Element **books** contains **book** elements, and **webBasedTraining** contains **subject** elements.

```
1    <?xml version = "1.0" encoding = "UTF-8"?>
2    <total>Number of pages = 17</total>
```

Fig. 12.24 Ouput of transformation.

```
1    <?xml version = "1.0"?>
2
3    <!-- Fig. 12.25: axes.xml -->
4
5    <product>
6
7       <completeTrainingCourses>
8
9          <completeTrainingCourse>
10
11            <title>
12               The Complete C++ Training Course: Third Edition
13            </title>
14
15            <book>
16               C++ How to Program: Third Edition
17            </book>
18
```

Fig. 12.25 XML document containing information about complete training courses and Web-based training (part 1 of 2).

```
19              <cd>
20                  C++ Multimedia Cyber Classroom: Third Edition
21              </cd>
22
23          </completeTrainingCourse>
24
25          <completeTrainingCourse>
26
27              <title>
28                  The Complete Java 2 Training Course: Third Edition
29              </title>
30
31              <book>
32                  Java How to Program: Third Edition
33              </book>
34
35              <cd>
36                  Java Multimedia Cyber Classroom: Third Edition
37              </cd>
38
39          </completeTrainingCourse>
40
41          <completeTrainingCourse>
42              <title>The Complete XML Training Course</title>
43              <book>XML How to Program</book>
44              <cd>XML Multimedia Cyber Classroom</cd>
45          </completeTrainingCourse>
46
47      </completeTrainingCourses>
48
49      <books>
50
51          <book>
52              Getting Started with Microsoft Visual C++
53              6 with an Introduction to MFC
54          </book>
55
56          <book>C How to Program</book>
57      </books>
58
59      <webBasedTraining>
60          <subject>Introduction to Java programming</subject>
61          <subject>Advanced C++ programming</subject>
62          <subject>Programming COM+ with Visual Basic</subject>
63      </webBasedTraining>
64
65  </product>
```

Fig. 12.25 XML document containing information about complete training courses and Web-based training (part 2 of 2).

The XSL stylesheet in Fig. 12.26 uses a number of different XPath expressions to locate parts of the original XML document. The result of applying this stylesheet to the XML document in Fig. 12.25 is shown in Fig. 12.27.

```
1   <?xml version = "1.0"?>
2
3   <!-- Fig. 12.26 : axes.xsl      -->
4   <!-- XSLT document using XPath -->
5
6   <xsl:stylesheet version = "1.0"
7              xmlns:xsl = "http://www.w3.org/1999/XSL/Transform">
8
9       <xsl:template match = "/product">
10
11          <html>
12
13              <head>
14                  <title>Axes example</title>
15
16                  <style type = "text/css">
17                      .node { font-family: monospace;
18                              font-weight: bold; }
19                  </style>
20              </head>
21
22              <body>
23                  Decendents of
24
25                 <span class = "node">completeTrainingCourse</span> are:
26
27                  <xsl:apply-templates select =
28                      "completeTrainingCourses//node()"/>
29                  <br /><br />
30
31                  Self for
32                  <span class = "node">webBasedTraining</span> is
33
34                  <xsl:apply-templates
35                      select = "webBasedTraining"/>
36                  <br /><br />
37
38                  Parent of
39                  <strong>C How to Program</strong> is
40
41                  <em>
42                     <!-- returns the name of the parent element -->
43                     <xsl:value-of select =
44                    "name(//parent::node()[. = 'C How to Program'])"/>
45                  </em>
46
47                  <br /><br />
48
49                  Child of
50                  <span class = "node">title</span>
51                  element for the second
52
```

Fig. 12.26 XSL stylesheet for transforming **axes.xml** into HTML. (part 1 of 3).

```
53                    <span class = "node">completeTrainingCourse</span> is
54
55                 <em>
56                    <xsl:value-of select =
57                    "//child::completeTrainingCourse[ 2 ]/title"/>
58                 </em>
59
60                 <br /><br />
61
62                 Is <span class = "node">product</span>
63
64                 the ancestor of
65                 <span class = "node">XML How to Program</span>?
66
67                 <xsl:if test = "name(//node()[. =
68              'XML How to Program']/ancestor::product) = 'product'">
69                    <em>Yes</em>
70                 </xsl:if>
71
72                 <br /><br />
73
74                 First <span class = "node">subject</span> preceding
75
76                 <strong>
77                    Programming COM+ with Visual Basic
78                 </strong> is
79
80                 <em>
81                    <xsl:value-of select =
82                  "//subject[. = 'Programming COM+ with Visual Basic'
83                    ]/preceding-sibling::subject[ 1 ]"/>
84                 </em>
85
86                 <br /><br />
87
88                 First <span class = "node">subject</span> following
89
90                 <strong>
91                    Introduction to Java programming
92                 </strong> is
93
94                 <em>
95                    <xsl:value-of select =
96                    "//subject[. = 'Introduction to Java programming'
97                    ]/following-sibling::subject[ 1 ]"/>
98                 </em>
99
100            </body>
101
102         </html>
103
104    </xsl:template>
105
```

Fig. 12.26 XSL stylesheet for transforming **axes.xml** into HTML. (part 2 of 3).

```
106     <xsl:template match = "completeTrainingCourse">
107        <br /><br />
108        <em><xsl:value-of select = "title"/></em>
109        <li><em><xsl:value-of select = "book"/></em></li>
110        <li><em><xsl:value-of select = "cd"/></em></li>
111     </xsl:template>
112
113     <xsl:template match = "webBasedTraining">
114        <em><xsl:value-of select = "subject"/></em>
115     </xsl:template>
116
117     <xsl:template match = "*  |  text()"/>
118
119  </xsl:stylesheet>
```

Fig. 12.26 XSL stylesheet for transforming **axes.xml** into HTML. (part 3 of 3).

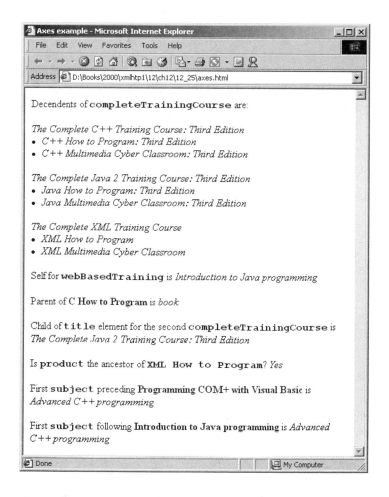

Fig. 12.27 HTML page generated by transforming **axes.xml** with **axes.xsl.**

On line 9, we use the location path **/product** to select all **product** children of the root node. In this case, this location path selects the **product** element node on lines 5–65 of **axes.xml** (Fig. 12.25). On line 27, there is an XSL element named **xsl:apply-templates**. This XSL element contains the location path **completeTraining-Courses//node()** in its **select** attribute (line 28). This location path selects the set of all nodes that are descendents of **completeTrainingCourses** elements. This set of nodes matches the location path defined in the **match** attribute of the **xsl:template** element on line 106–111. When the **xsl:apply-templates** element selects a set of nodes that match the location path of the **xsl:template** element's **match** attribute, the contents of the **xsl:template** element are applied to each node in the selected set in document order. In this case, lines 108–110 retrieve the string-values for the **title**, **book** and **cd** elements, respectively, and add them to an HTML unordered list. The elements of this unordered list then become elements in the resulting HTML document. On lines 34 and 35, we have another **xsl:apply-templates** element, with the location path **web-BasedTraining**. This matches the **xsl:template** on lines 113–115. This template adds the string-values for **webBasedTraining** nodes to the resulting HTML document.

On lines 43 and 44, the **xsl:value-of** element with the location path

```
name(//parent::node()[. = 'C How to Program'])
```

retrieves the parent node of any node in the XML document whose string-value equals the string **'C How to Program'**. The **xsl:value-of** element then adds the string-value of the resulting node to the HTML document. On lines 56 and 57, the **xsl:value-of** element uses the location path

```
//child::completeTrainingCourse[ 2 ]/title
```

which selects the **title** element node of the second **completeTrainingCourse** element in the document and adds its string-value to the resulting HTML document.

On lines 67–70, we use an **xsl:if** element with the XPath expression

```
name(//node()[. = 'XML How to Program']/ancestor::product) =
'product'
```

to determine if the **product** element is an ancestor of the node whose string-value is **XML How to Program**. If this XPath expression evaluates to **true**, then the HTML element on line 69 is included in the resulting HTML document.

The **xsl:value-of** element on lines 81–83 uses the location path

```
//subject[. = 'Programming COM+ with Visual Basic']/preced-
ing-sibling::subject[ 1 ]
```

to add the string-value of the **subject** element on line 61 of **axes.xml** to the resulting HTML document. The first location step of this location path selects the **subject** element with the string-value **Programming COM+ with Visual Basic**. The second step uses the **preceding-sibling** axis to select the **subject** element from the first sibling. Recall that the **preceding-sibling** axis is a reverse axis, so the nodes it selects are in reverse document order. Therefore this location path selects the **subject** node that corresponds to line 61 of **axes.xml**.

Lines 95–97 use another **xsl:value-of** element, with the location path

```
//subject[. = 'Introduction to Java programming']/following-
sibling::subject[ 1 ]
```

The first location step of this location path selects the **subject** element node whose string-value is **Introduction to Java programming**. The second location step selects the first **subject** element in document order on the **following-sibling** axis. The resulting HTML page is shown in Fig. 12.27.

12.11 Internet and World Wide Web Resources

www.w3.org/Style/XSL
The *W3C Extensible Style Language Web site.*

www.w3.org/TR/xsl
The most current *W3C XSL Specification.*

www.w3schools.com/xsl
This site features an XSL tutorial, along with a list of links and resources.

www.dpawson.freeserve.co.uk/xsl/xslfaq.html
A comprehensive collection of *XSL FAQs.*

www.xml101.com/examples/default.asp
A collection of *XSL examples*, located on **XML101.com** (IE5+ required).

www.bayes.co.uk/xml/index.xml
A portal site written entirely using XML and XSL.

msdn.microsoft.com/xml
Microsoft Developer Network XML Home page, which provides information on XML and XML-related technologies, such as XSL/XSLT.

xml.apache.org/xalan
Home page for Apache's XSLT processor Xalan.

www.jclark.com/xml/xt.html
Home page for XT, an implementation of XSLT in Java.

SUMMARY

- The Extensible Stylesheet Language (XSL) is used to format XML documents and consists of two parts—XSLT and XSL formatting objects.

- XSL Transformation Language (XSLT) transforms XML documents into other text-based documents using XSL format instructions. XSLT uses XPath to match nodes when transforming an XML document into a different document. The resulting document may be XML, HTML, plain text or any other text-based document.

- To process XSLT documents, an *XSLT processor is required.* Examples of XSLT processors include msxml in *Microsoft Internet Explorer 5* and *Apache's Xalan.*

- An XSLT document is an XML document with a root element **xsl:stylesheet**. Attribute **version** defines the XSLT specification used.

- An XSLT document's namespace URI is **http://www.w3.org/1999/XSL/Transform**.

- A **template** element matches specific XML document nodes by using an XPath expression in attribute *match*.

- Element **stylesheet** associates a stylesheet to an XML document. Attribute **type** defines the file type (i.e., **text/xsl**, which denotes an XSL document, and **text/css**, which denotes a CSS document). Attribute **href** specifies the file.

- Element **apply-templates** applies an XSLT document's templates to specific element nodes. By default, element **apply-templates** matches all element child nodes.

- The XSLT specification defines default templates for an XML document's nodes. The template

```
<xsl:template match = "/ | *">
    <xsl:apply-templates/>
</xsl:template>
```

matches the document root node and any element nodes of an XML document and applies templates to their child nodes. The template

```
<xsl:template match = "text() | @*">
    <xsl:value-of select = "."/>
</xsl:template>
```

matches text nodes and attribute nodes and outputs their values.

```
<xsl:template match ="processing-instruction() | comment()"/>
```

- This template matches processing-instruction nodes and comment nodes, but does not perform any actions with them.

- Element **element** creates an element with the name specified in attribute **name**.

- An XPath expression is specified using curly braces (**{}**).

- Element **attribute** creates an attribute for an element and can be contained only within an **element** element. Attribute **name** provides the name of the attribute.

- XSLT provides the capability to iterate through a node set returned by an XPath expression. XSLT also provides the capability to sort a node set.

- XSLT element **for-each** applies the element's contents to each of the nodes specified by attribute **select**.

- Element **sort** sorts (in the order specified by attribute **order**) the nodes specified in attribute **select**. Attribute **order** has values **ascending** (i.e., A–Z) and **descending** (i.e., Z–A).

- XSLT provides elements to perform conditional processing.

- Element **choose** allows alternate conditional statements to be processed. Element **choose** allows child elements **when** and **otherwise**. Attribute **test** provides the conditional statement to be tested. The contents of element **when** are used if the condition is met. Element **otherwise** is optional, but, if included, must occur only once, after all **when** elements. This element is used when no **when** elements have been matched.

- Instead of providing a template for each element of an XML document, XSLT provides an element to duplicate nodes. The XSLT element **copy** is used to copy only the context node.

- Children and attributes are not duplicated. If element **copy** has content, the content is processed after the copy has been performed.

- Element **copy-of** duplicates all children (i.e., text, processing instructions, comments, etc.) and attributes of the node.

- XSLT allows for modularity in stylesheets. This feature allows XSLT documents to import other XSLT documents by using element **import**. Other XSLT document are referenced using attribute **href**.

- Local templates have higher precedence than imported templates. XSLT element **include** includes other XSLT documents in the current XSLT document.

- The difference between element **include** and element **import** is that templates included using element **include** have the same precedence as the local templates. Therefore, if any templates are duplicated, the template that occurs last is used.

TERMINOLOGY

alternate conditional statements
ascending
attribute **href**
attribute **match**
attribute **name**
attribute **num**
attribute **order**
attribute **select**
attribute **test**
attribute **type**
attribute **version**
Cascading Style Sheets (CSS)
choose element
CLASSPATH environment variable
conditional processing
descending
element **apply-templates**
element **attribute**
element **comment**
element **copy**
element **copy-of**
element **element**
element **for-each**
element **if**

element **import**
element **include**
element **otherwise**
element **sort**
element **value-of**
element **variable**
element **when**
Extensible Stylesheet Language (XSL)
http://www.w3.org/1999/XSL/
    Transform URI
if conditional statement
otherwise condition
root element **stylesheet**
template element
text/css
text/xsl
text-based document
when conditional
XSL (Extensible Stylesheet Language)
XSL document
XSL Transformation Language (XSLT)
XSLT (XSL Transformation Language)
XSLT processor

SELF-REVIEW EXERCISES

12.1 State whether the following are *true* or *false*. If *false*, explain why.
   a) XSLT uses XLink to match nodes for transforming an XML document into a different document.
   b) In its most current specification, XSLT does not allow for iteration through a node set returned by an XPath expression.
   c) By using XSLT, XML documents can easily be converted between formats.
   d) Like element **choose**, element **if** is used to provide a single conditional test.
   e) XSLT allows for modularity in style sheets, which enables XSLT documents to import other XSLT documents.
   f) The document resulting from an XSLT transformation may be in the format of an XML document, HTML/plain text or any other text-based document.
   g) Instead of providing a template for each element of an XML document, XSLT provides an element to duplicate nodes.
   h) XSLT provides no default templates for the nodes of an XML document; all templates must be custom built by the programmer.
   i) XSLT provides elements to perform conditional processing, such as **if** statements.
   j) One of the shortcomings of XSLT is that it does not provide variables.

12.2   Fill in the blanks in each of the following statements.
   a) Attribute _____ is used to define the XSLT specification that is being used.
   b) An XSLT document is an XML document with a root element _____.
   c) XSLT provides the _____ element to allow alternate conditional statements.
   d) The XSLT element **copy** is used to copy only the _____ node, not duplicate nodes.
   e) XSLT stands for the XSL _____ Language.
   f) Templates of an XSLT document can be applied to specific nodes of an element by using element _____.
   g) The **template** element is used to match specific _____ of an XML document.
   h) The two valid values for attribute **type** are _____ and _____.
   i) Attribute _____ has values **ascending** and **descending**.
   j) Element _____ includes other XSLT documents in the current XSLT document.

ANSWERS TO SELF-REVIEW EXERCISES

12.1   a) False. XSLT uses XPath to match nodes for transforming an XML document into a different document. b) False. XSLT allows for iteration through a node set returned by an XPath expression. c) True. d) False. Unlike element **choose**, element **if** is used to provide a single conditional test. e) True. f) True. g) True. h) False. XSLT provides several default templates for the nodes of an XML document. i) True. j) False. XSLT provides the ability to keep variables for the processing of information.

12.2   a) **version**. b) **stylesheet**. c) **choose**. d) context. e) Transformation.
f) **apply-templates**. g) nodes. h) **text/xsl**, **text/css**. i) **order**. j) **include**.

EXERCISES

12.3   Write an XSLT document that would transform the XML document in Fig. 12.28 into the XML document Fig. 12.29.

```
1   <?xml version = "1.0"?>
2
3   <!-- Fig 12.28: xmlProducts.xml -->
4
5   <products>
6      <product unitPrice = "100" id = "A12">
7         <name>XML parser</name>
8      </product>
9
10     <product unitPrice = "50" id = "A14">
11        <name>XML editor</name>
12     </product>
13
14     <product unitPrice = "200" id = "A15">
15        <name>XML toolkit</name>
16     </product>
17  </products>
```

Fig. 12.28 XML document listing products.

```
1   <?xml version = "1.0" encoding = "UTF-8"?>
2
3   <!-- Fig 12.29 : xmlProducts2.xml -->
4
5   <products>
6      <product>
7         <unitPrice>100</unitPrice>
8         <id>A12</id>
9         <name>XML parser</name>
10     </product>
11
12     <product>
13        <unitPrice>50</unitPrice>
14        <id>A14</id>
15        <name>XML editor</name>
16     </product>
17
18     <product>
19        <unitPrice>200</unitPrice>
20        <id>A15</id>
21        <name>XML toolkit</name>
22     </product>
23  </products>
```

Fig. 12.29 Transformed XML document.

12.3   Write an XSLT document that transforms the XML document in Fig. 12.29 back to the XML document in Fig. 12.28.

12.4   For **planner.xml** in Chapter 6, write an XSLT document that would sort **year** elements by attribute **value** (ascending), **date** elements by attribute **month** (ascending) and attribute **day** (ascending) and **note** elements by attribute **time** (ascending). The output should have the same structure as the original document.

12.5   Write an XSLT document that transforms **games.xml** (Fig. 12.4) by adding attribute **index** for each **game** element. The value of attribute **index** should be its position among **game** elements. [*Hint:* Use XSLT element **number**, which outputs the position of the node that is specified in attribute **count**.]

12.6   Write an XSLT document to transform **planner.xml** from Chapter 5 into an HTML document that displays the schedules in a table. Each row should consist of a year, month, date and time. Sort the columns as in Exercise 12.5.

12.7   Write an XSLT document to transform **planner.xml** from Chapter 5 into the structure shown in Fig. 12.30.

```
1   <?xml version = "1.0" encoding = "UTF-8" ?>
2   <planner>
3
4      <note year = "2001" month = "5" day = "15" time = "1620">
5         Physics class at BH291C
6      </note>
7
```

Fig. 12.30 Document for Exercise 12.8 (part 1 of 2).

```
 8    <note year = "2001" month = "5" day = "15" time = "1430">
 9       Doctor's appointment
10    </note>
11
12    <note year = "2001" month = "7" day = "4">
13       Independance Day
14    </note>
15
16    <note year = "2001" month = "8" day = "20" time = "0900">
17       General Meeting in room 32-A
18    </note>
19
20    </planner>
```

Fig. 12.30 Document for Exercise 12.8 (part 2 of 2).

13

XSL: Extensible Stylesheet Language Formatting Objects

Objectives

- To become familiar with XSL formatting objects.
- To be able to use XSL Transformations to generate XSL documents.
- To be able to mark up a document with XSL formatting objects.
- To be able to use Apache's FOP processor to transform XSL documents.

Vigorous writing is concise. A sentence should contain no unnecessary words, a paragraph no unnecessary sentences.
William Strunk, Jr.

I have made this letter longer than usual, because I lack the time to make it short.
Blaise Pascal

Outline

13.1 Introduction

An XSL stylesheet can be used to transform an XML document into a variety of formats (Fig. 13.1). In Chapter 12, we used XSLT to transform XML documents into HTML, which is perhaps the most common use of XSLT. In this chapter, we introduce another aspect of XSL—called *formatting objects*—used to format XML documents for presentation. Formatting objects constitute the vast majority of XSL features. We present only a small subset of formatting-object features in this chapter. The latest XSL Working Draft can be found at **www.w3.org/TR/xsl**.

Formatting objects are typically used when the result of a transformation is for *print media* (e.g., books, magazines, etc.). An XML document is transformed into an XSL document that marks up the data using formatting objects. This XSL document can then be transformed into other formats, including *Portable Document Format (PDF)*, a portable, proprietary format created by Adobe; a Microsoft Word document; etc.

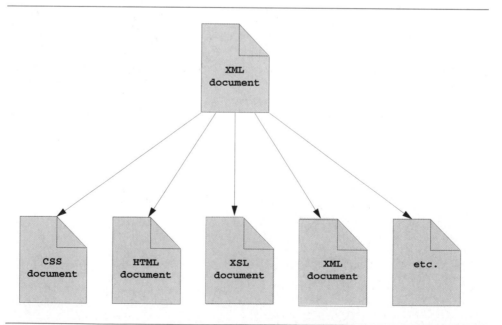

Fig. 13.1   Using XSL to transform XML into a variety of formats.

In this chapter, we present several examples that use Apache's Java-based tool *FOP* to transform XSL documents containing formatting objects (which we call "XSL formatting-object documents") into PDF documents. Apache FOP implements only a small subset of the available formatting-object elements, but full support for the Working Draft is expected in the near future. [*Note*: RenderX's *XEP* is another major tool (or processor) for transforming XSL documents containing formatting objects. A trial version of XEP can be downloaded from **www.renderx.com**.]

13.2 Setup

In this section, we describe the software necessary to execute the chapter examples. The following software is required:

1. Java 2 Standard Edition. Download and install the Java 2 Standard Edition from **www.java.sun.com/j2se**.

2. FOP requires a Java parser. In this chapter we use Apache's Xerces parser to run FOP. Apache's Xerces parser for Java can be downloaded from **xml.apache.org/xerces-j**.

3. Apache Xalan XSLT processor. Xalan can be downloaded free of charge from **xml.apache.org/xalan**.

4. Apache FOP. We use the Java-based version available at **xml.apache.org/fop**.

5. Chapter 13 examples. Copy them from the CD-ROM that accompanies this book to your machine. Our convention is to give XSL formatting objects documents the file extension **.fo**. Because these files are XML documents, they can have other extension (e.g., **.xsl**, **.xml**, etc.) as well.

13.3 Examples of XSL Formatting-object Documents

Figure 13.2 shows an XSL document that contains a formatted description of Deitel & Associates, Inc. Formatting objects describe the physical page dimensions, fonts, etc. Apache's FOP is used to transform the document into PDF form. [*Note*: This XSL formatting-object document typically would not be written by a document author, but would be created from an XSL transformation. For simplicity, we simply show the document.]

To generate a PDF document from this XSL formatting-object document, type

```
java org.apache.fop.apps.CommandLine welcome.fo welcome.pdf
```

at the command line to transform **welcome.fo** (Fig. 13.2) to PDF form (**welcome.pdf**). The **CLASSPATH** variable must be set for the *CommandLine* application (i.e., FOP) and Xalan. In case you do not wish to execute this example, we have provided **welcome.pdf** in the Chapter 13 examples directory. To open the PDF file created for viewing, Adobe® Acrobat Reader™ is required. Adobe Acrobat Reader is available for download free of charge from **www.adobe.com**.

Apache FOP also provides an alternative to Acrobat Reader—*Apache's FO viewer application*—for viewing the XSL formatting object-document. To view the results of the transformation, type

```
java org.apache.fop.apps.AWTCommandLine welcome.fo
```

at the command line. The **CLASSPATH** for *AWTCommandLine* (i.e., Apache's FO viewer) must be set. Line 6

```
<fo:root xmlns:fo = "http://www.w3.org/1999/XSL/Format">
```

defines root element *fo:root* and namespace prefix *fo* with the URI *http://www.w3.org/1999/XSL/Format*. Element **fo:root** is a container element only; it does not affect the document's format.

In publishing, *page masters* define a page's layout (e.g., its margins, headers, footers, etc.). Page masters provide the document author with the flexibility of changing the document's format on a page-by-page basis. Lines 8–11

```
<fo:layout-master-set>

    <fo:simple-page-master master-name = "layout1"
        page-height = "4in">
```

use container element *fo:layout-master-set* to group the document's page masters (i.e., *page templates*). To create a page master, element *fo:simple-page-master* is used. Attributes *master-name* and *page-height* specify the page name (i.e., **layout1**) and page height (i.e., **4in**), respectively. XSL formatting objects also provide attribute *page-width*, for specifying a page's width. Although a document may contain any number of page masters, we use only one page master. In a **simple-page-master** page master, the document is divided into the five regions shown in Fig. 13.3. The header, body, footer, start and end are represented by XSL formatting elements *fo:region-before*, *fo:region-body*, *fo:region-after*, *fo:region-start* and **fo:region-end**, respectively.

```
1   <?xml version = "1.0"?>
2
3   <!-- Fig. 13.2 : welcome.fo -->
4   <!-- Simple FO example      -->
5
6   <fo:root xmlns:fo = "http://www.w3.org/1999/XSL/Format">
7
8      <fo:layout-master-set>
9
10         <fo:simple-page-master master-name = "layout1"
11            page-height = "4in">
12
13            <fo:region-body margin-top = "1in"
14               margin-bottom = "1in" margin-left = "1.5in"
15               margin-right = "1.5in"/>
16
17            <fo:region-before extent = "1in" margin-top = "0.2in"
18               margin-bottom = "0.2in" margin-left = "0.2in"
19               margin-right = "0.2in"/>
20
21         </fo:simple-page-master>
```

Fig. 13.2 Simple FO example (part 1 of 3).

```
22
23          <fo:page-sequence-master master-name = "run">
24             <fo:repeatable-page-master-reference
25                master-name = "layout1"/>
26          </fo:page-sequence-master>
27
28      </fo:layout-master-set>
29
30      <fo:page-sequence master-name = "run">
31
32          <fo:static-content flow-name = "xsl-region-before">
33
34             <fo:block font-size = "10pt" line-height = "12pt"
35                font-family = "sans-serif">
36                page <fo:page-number/>
37             </fo:block>
38
39          </fo:static-content>
40
41          <fo:flow flow-name = "xsl-body">
42
43             <fo:block font-size = "36pt"
44                font-family = "sans-serif" font-weight = "bold"
45                space-after.optimum = "24pt" color = "blue"
46                text-align = "center">Welcome!
47             </fo:block>
48
49             <fo:block font-size = "12pt"
50                font-family = "sans-serif" line-height = "14pt"
51                space-after.optimum = "12pt">Deitel &amp; Associates,
52                Inc. is an internationally recognized corporate
53                training and publishing organization specializing in
54                programming languages, Internet/World Wide Web
55                technology and object technology education.
56             </fo:block>
57
58             <fo:block font-size = "12pt"
59                font-family = "sans-serif" line-height = "14pt"
60                space-after.optimum = "12pt">Deitel &amp; Associates,
61                Inc. is a member of the
62                <fo:inline-sequence font-weight = "bold">World
63                Wide Web</fo:inline-sequence>
64                Consortium.
65             </fo:block>
66
67             <fo:block font-size = "12pt"
68                font-family = "sans-serif" line-height = "14pt"
69                space-after.optimum = "12pt">The company&apos;s
70                clients include some of the world&apos;s largest
71                computer companies, government agencies, branches
72                of the military and business organizations.
73             </fo:block>
74
```

Fig. 13.2   Simple FO example (part 2 of 3).

```
75          </fo:flow>
76
77      </fo:page-sequence>
78
79  </fo:root>
```

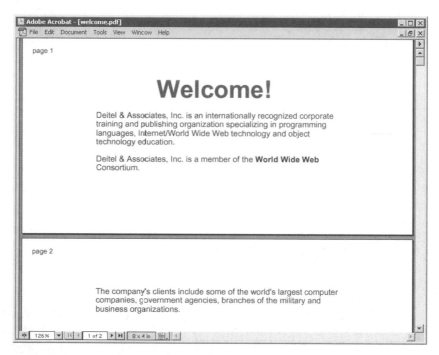

Adobe Acrobat displaying **welcome.pdf**. (Adobe and Acrobat Reader are either registered trademarks or trademarks of Adobe Systems Incorporated in the United States and/or other countries.)

Fig. 13.2   Simple FO example (part 3 of 3).

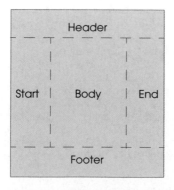

Fig. 13.3   Regions in a **simple-page-master** document.

Lines 13–15

```
<fo:region-body margin-top = "1in"
    margin-bottom = "1in" margin-left = "1.5in"
    margin-right = "1.5in"/>
```

use element **fo:region-body** to define the document's body size as having top and bottom margins of 1 inch, and left and right margins of 1.5 inches. Attributes ***margin-top***, ***margin-bottom***, ***margin-left*** and ***margin-right*** represent the top, bottom, left and right values, respectively.

Lines 17–19

```
<fo:region-before extent = "1in" margin-top = "0.2in"
    margin-bottom = "0.2in" margin-left = "0.2in"
    margin-right = "0.2in"/>
```

use element **fo:region-before** to set the page header's margins to 1 inch in height, with a 0.2-inch margin on all sides. The page header is contained within the top margin of the body.

Lines 23–26

```
<fo:page-sequence-master master-name = "run">
    <fo:repeatable-page-master-reference
        master-name = "layout1"/>
</fo:page-sequence-master>
```

use element ***fo:page-sequence-master*** to specify the order in which master pages will be created for the ***master-name*** **run**. We use element ***repeatable-page-master-reference*** to indicate that the **simple-page-master layout1** can be repeated as many times as necessary to contain the document's content. Notice that the second page (in Fig. 13.2) has the same format as the first page.

Lines 30–77 define the pages of the document. Lines 32–39

```
<fo:static-content flow-name = "xsl-region-before">

    <fo:block font-size = "10pt" line-height = "12pt"
        font-family = "sans-serif">
        page <fo:page-number/>
    </fo:block>

</fo:static-content>
```

use element ***fo:static-content*** to specify text that appears on each document page. Attribute ***flow-name*** is assigned the value ***xsl-region-before***, indicating that text will appear in each document page's "header." The text (i.e., the page number) is formatted using an ***fo:block*** element. Attribute ***line-height*** sets the line height to 12 points, and attribute ***font-family*** sets the text's font to ***sans-serif***. When the document is transformed, empty element ***fo:page-number*** is replaced with the page number. Page numbers begin at 1 by default.

Lines 41–75 denote the contents of the pages, with the text being placed in the region set by **fo:region-body**.

The first block, on lines 43–47

```
<fo:block font-size = "36pt"
   font-family = "sans-serif" font-weight = "bold"
   space-after.optimum = "24pt" color = "blue"
   text-align = "centered">Welcome!
</fo:block>
```

marks up blue, bold text that has a font size of 36 points and is centered in the page. We also set to 24 points the optimal amount of space that should follow the text by using attribute **space-after.optimum**. XSL formatting objects also provide attribute **space-before.optimum**, to specify the optimum amount of space preceding the text.

The three blocks of text on lines 49–73 each have a font size of 12 points, a line height of 14 points and an optimal spacing of 12 points following each block of text.

Lines 62 and 63

```
<fo:inline-sequence font-weight = "bold">World
Wide Web</fo:inline-sequence>
```

use element **inline-sequence** to change the format of **World Wide Web** to bold.

We present an XSL document (Fig. 13.5) for transforming Chapter 5's XML business letter (Fig. 5.6) into an XSL formatted-object document. We then transform the document to PDF format (Fig. 13.6) using Apache FOP. To generate a PDF document from this XSL formatting-object document, type (on a single line)

```
java -classpath C:\xalan\xerces.jar;C:\xalan\xalan.jar
   org.apache.xalan.xslt.Process -IN letter.xml
   -XSL letter.xsl -OUT letter.fo
```

Courtesy of XML project of the Apache Software Foundation; **xml.apache.org**.

Fig. 13.4   Viewing with Apache's FO viewer application.

to transform the document using Xalan to an XSL formatted-object document. Next, type

java org.apache.fop.apps.CommandLine letter.fo welcome.pdf

at the command line to transform **letter.fo** (Fig. 13.2) to PDF format (**welcome.pdf**). [*Note*: the Apache FOP JAR file must be in the **CLASSPATH**.] For more information about the PDF, visit the Web site **www.adobe.com/products/acrobat**.

```
1   <?xml version = "1.0"?>
2
3   <!-- Fig. 13.5 : letter.xsl      -->
4   <!-- Formatting a business letter -->
5
6   <xsl:stylesheet version = "1.0"
7      xmlns:xsl = "http://www.w3.org/1999/XSL/Transform"
8      xmlns:fo = "http://www.w3.org/1999/XSL/Format">
9
10     <xsl:template match = "/">
11
12        <fo:root xmlns:fo = "http://www.w3.org/1999/XSL/Format">
13
14           <fo:layout-master-set>
15
16              <fo:simple-page-master master-name = "first">
17
18                 <fo:region-body margin-top = "1.75in"
19                    margin-bottom = "1in" margin-left = "1.25in"
20                    margin-right = "1.25in"/>
21
22                 <fo:region-before extent = "1.5in"
23                    margin-top = "0.5in" margin-bottom = "0.2in"
24                    margin-left = "4.25in"
25                    margin-right = "1.25in"/>
26
27              </fo:simple-page-master>
28
29              <fo:simple-page-master master-name = "other">
30
31                 <fo:region-body margin-top = "1in"
32                    margin-bottom = "1in" margin-left = "1.25in"
33                    margin-right = "1.25in"/>
34
35              </fo:simple-page-master>
36
37              <fo:page-sequence-master master-name = "run1">
38
39                 <fo:single-page-master-reference
40                    master-name = "first"/>
41
42                 <fo:repeatable-page-master-reference
43                    master-name = "other"/>
44
```

Fig. 13.5 XSLT document for transforming an XML document into an XSL formatted-object document (part 1 of 4).

```
45              </fo:page-sequence-master>
46
47          </fo:layout-master-set>
48
49          <fo:page-sequence master-name = "run1">
50              <xsl:apply-templates/>
51          </fo:page-sequence>
52
53      </fo:root>
54
55  </xsl:template>
56
57  <xsl:template match = "letter">
58
59      <fo:static-content flow-name = "xsl-region-before">
60
61          <xsl:apply-templates
62              select = "contact[@type = 'from']"/>
63
64      </fo:static-content>
65
66      <fo:flow flow-name = "xsl-body">
67
68          <fo:block font-size = "10pt"
69              font-family = "monospace" line-height = "10pt">
70
71              <xsl:apply-templates
72                  select = "contact[@type = 'to']"/>
73
74          </fo:block>
75
76          <fo:block font-size = "12pt"
77              font-family = "monospace" line-height = "14pt"
78              space-before.optimum = "18pt"
79              space-after.optimum = "18pt">
80              <xsl:value-of select = "salutation"/>
81          </fo:block>
82
83          <xsl:apply-templates select = "paragraph"/>
84
85          <fo:block font-size = "12pt"
86              font-family = "monospace" line-height = "14pt">
87              <xsl:value-of select = "closing"/>,
88          </fo:block>
89
90          <fo:block font-size = "12pt"
91              font-family = "monospace" line-height = "14pt">
92              <xsl:value-of select = "signature"/>
93          </fo:block>
94
95      </fo:flow>
96
```

Fig. 13.5 XSLT document for transforming an XML document into an XSL formatted-object document (part 2 of 4).

```
 97      </xsl:template>
 98
 99      <xsl:template match = "contact[@type = 'from']">
100
101         <fo:block font-size = "10pt"
102            font-family = "monospace" line-height = "12pt">
103            <xsl:value-of select = "name"/>
104         </fo:block>
105
106         <fo:block font-size = "10pt"
107            font-family = "monospace" line-height = "12pt">
108            <xsl:value-of select = "address1"/>
109         </fo:block>
110
111         <fo:block font-size = "10pt"
112            font-family = "monospace" line-height = "12pt">
113            <xsl:value-of select = "address2"/>
114         </fo:block>
115
116         <fo:block font-size = "10pt"
117            font-family = "monospace" line-height = "12pt">
118            <xsl:value-of select = "city"/>,
119            <xsl:value-of select = "state"/>
120            <xsl:text> </xsl:text>
121            <xsl:value-of select = "zip"/>
122         </fo:block>
123
124         <fo:block font-size = "10pt"
125            font-family = "monospace" line-height = "12pt">
126            <xsl:value-of select = "phone"/>
127         </fo:block>
128
129      </xsl:template>
130
131      <xsl:template match = "contact[@type = 'to']">
132
133         <fo:block font-size = "12pt"
134            font-family = "monospace" line-height = "14pt">
135            <xsl:value-of select = "name"/>
136         </fo:block>
137
138         <fo:block font-size = "12pt"
139            font-family = "monospace" line-height = "14pt">
140            <xsl:value-of select = "address1"/>
141         </fo:block>
142
143         <fo:block font-size = "12pt"
144            font-family = "monospace" line-height = "14pt">
145            <xsl:value-of select = "address2"/>
146         </fo:block>
147
```

Fig. 13.5   XSLT document for transforming an XML document into an XSL formatted-object document (part 3 of 4).

```
148          <fo:block font-size = "12pt"
149             font-family = "monospace" line-height = "14pt">
150             <xsl:value-of select = "city"/>,
151             <xsl:value-of select = "state"/>
152             <xsl:text> </xsl:text>
153             <xsl:value-of select = "zip"/>
154          </fo:block>
155
156          <fo:block font-size = "12pt"
157             font-family = "monospace" line-height = "14pt">
158             <xsl:value-of select = "phone"/>
159          </fo:block>
160
161    </xsl:template>
162
163    <xsl:template match = "paragraph">
164
165          <fo:block font-size = "12pt" font-family = "monospace"
166             line-height = "14pt" space-after.optimum = "18pt">
167             <xsl:apply-templates/>
168          </fo:block>
169
170    </xsl:template>
171
172    <xsl:template match = "bold">
173
174          <fo:inline-sequence font-weight = "bold">
175             <xsl:value-of select = "."/>
176          </fo:inline-sequence>
177
178    </xsl:template>
179
180  </xsl:stylesheet>
```

Fig. 13.5   XSLT document for transforming an XML document into an XSL formatted-
object document (part 4 of 4).

Lines 16–27 create a page master named **first** that contains two regions. The first
region (lines 18–20) is the document's body, while the second region (lines 22–25) is the
document's header that contains the letter's return address. Attribute **extent** specifies the
size of a region (i.e., **fo:region-before**, **fo:region-after**, **fo:region-
start** and **fo:region-end**). Region **fo:region-body** does not have an **extent**
attribute and is given the remaining area after the other four regions are sized.

Lines 29–35 create a second page master named **other** that will define the layout for
successive pages (after the first). Lines 37–45

```
<fo:page-sequence-master master-name = "run1">

   <fo:single-page-master-reference
      master-name = "first"/>

   <fo:repeatable-page-master-reference
      master-name = "other"/>

</fo:page-sequence-master>
```

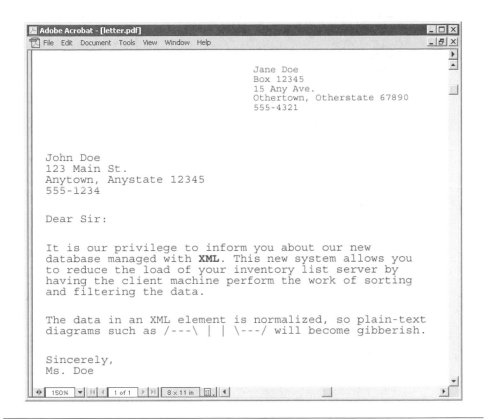

Fig. 13.6 PDF output of the business letter. (Adobe and Acrobat Reader are either registered trademarks or trademarks of Adobe Systems Incorporated in the United States and/or other countries.)

uses element **fo:page-sequence-master** to set the order in which the page masters occur. Page master **first** (line 16) occurs first and can occur only once, because it is marked up as *fo:single-page-master-reference*. Page master **other** (line 29) follows the **first** page master and can occur any number of times. Lines 59–64

```
<fo:static-content flow-name = "xsl-region-before">

    <xsl:apply-templates
        select = "contact[@type = 'from']"/>

</fo:static-content>
```

place the letter's return address in the document's header (i.e., **xsl-region-before**). The remainder of the document uses templates to match the text for the document's body.

13.4 Lists

XSL formatting objects also provide the capabilities to format lists of items. Apache FOP provides support for *lists* and *tables*. In this section, we provide an example (Fig. 13.7) that formats data into a list. The rendered output is shown in Fig. 13.8.

```
1    <?xml version = "1.0"?>
2
3    <!-- Fig. 13.7 : topic_list.fo -->
4    <!-- List example              -->
5
6    <fo:root xmlns:fo = "http://www.w3.org/1999/XSL/Format">
7
8        <fo:layout-master-set>
9
10           <fo:simple-page-master master-name = "layout1">
11
12               <fo:region-body margin-top = "1in"
13               margin-bottom = "1in" margin-left = "1.5in"
14               margin-right = "1.5in"/>
15           </fo:simple-page-master>
16
17           <fo:page-sequence-master master-name = "run">
18               <fo:repeatable-page-master-reference
19                   master-name = "layout1"/>
20           </fo:page-sequence-master>
21
22       </fo:layout-master-set>
23
24       <fo:page-sequence master-name = "run">
25
26           <fo:flow>
27
28               <fo:block font-size = "36pt"
29                   font-family = "sans-serif" font-weight = "bold"
30                   space-after.optimum = "12pt" color = "yellow"
31                   background-color = "black"
32                   text-align = "center" line-height = "42pt">
33                   Deitel Book Topics
34               </fo:block>
35
36               <fo:block font-size = "12pt"
37                   font-family = "sans-serif" line-height = "14pt"
38                   space-after.optimum = "12pt">Here are some topics
39                   that have been covered:
40               </fo:block>
41
42               <fo:list-block>
43
44                   <fo:list-item>
45
46                       <fo:list-item-label>
47                           <fo:block>-</fo:block>
48                       </fo:list-item-label>
49
50                       <fo:list-item-body>
51                           <fo:block>Java</fo:block>
52                       </fo:list-item-body>
53
```

Fig. 13.7   List supported by Apache's FOP (part 1 of 2).

```
54              </fo:list-item>
55
56              <fo:list-item>
57
58                  <fo:list-item-label>
59                      <fo:block>-</fo:block>
60                  </fo:list-item-label>
61
62                  <fo:list-item-body>
63                      <fo:block>C / C++</fo:block>
64                  </fo:list-item-body>
65
66              </fo:list-item>
67
68              <fo:list-item>
69
70                  <fo:list-item-label>
71                      <fo:block>-</fo:block>
72                  </fo:list-item-label>
73
74                  <fo:list-item-body>
75                      <fo:block>HTML</fo:block>
76                  </fo:list-item-body>
77
78              </fo:list-item>
79
80              <fo:list-item>
81
82                  <fo:list-item-label>
83                      <fo:block>-</fo:block>
84                  </fo:list-item-label>
85
86                  <fo:list-item-body>
87                      <fo:block>XML</fo:block>
88                  </fo:list-item-body>
89
90              </fo:list-item>
91
92          </fo:list-block>
93
94      </fo:flow>
95
96  </fo:page-sequence>
97
98 </fo:root>
```

Fig. 13.7 List supported by Apache's FOP (part 2 of 2).

Element **fo:flow** (line 26) specifies content that can flow from one page to the next. A common example of **fo:flow** is text on a book's page that naturally flows to the next page. The primary difference between **fo:flow** and **fo:static-content** is that **fo:static-content** is duplicated on each page. For example, a book title and page number (e.g., **fo:static-content**) generally appear on every page in a book. However, the text of a paragraph (e.g., **fo:flow**) in a novel is not duplicated on every page.

Lines 28–34 define a block that formats the text **Deitel Book Topics**. Attribute ***background-color*** sets the background color to black. Attribute ***text-align*** aligns the text. In this particular case, we **center** the text.

Lines 42–92 set the ***fo:list-block*** element, which contains the list items. Lines 46–48

```
<fo:list-item-label>
    <fo:block>-</fo:block>
</fo:list-item-label>
```

use element ***fo:list-item-label*** to mark up the text that precedes each item in the list. In this particular case, we mark up a hyphen, **-**.

Lines 50–52

```
<fo:list-item-body>
    <fo:block>Java</fo:block>
</fo:list-item-body>
```

use element ***fo:list-item-body*** to mark up an individual list item's text (i.e., **Java**). The remaining list items are marked up in a similar manner.

13.5 Internet and World Wide Web Resources

www.xml.com/pub/Guide/XSL_FO's
XSL Formatting Object vocabulary links.

www.renderx.com/Tests/validator/fo2000.dtd.html
DTD for the last version of XSL FO.

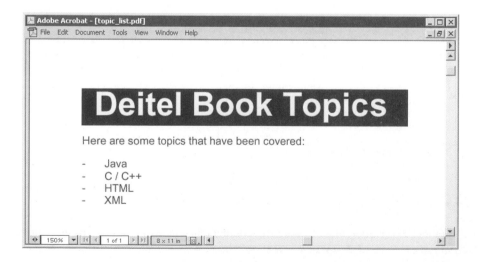

Fig. 13.8   Adobe Acrobat displaying **topic_list.pdf**. (Adobe and Acrobat Reader are either registered trademarks or trademarks of Adobe Systems Incorporated in the United States and/or other countries.)

`xml.apache.org/fop`
Home page of FOP, an open-source XSL formatter-renderer, from Apache.

`www.renderx.com`
Provides XEP, a commercial XSL FO processor.

`www.arbortext.com`
Arbortext Web site where a commercial XSL FO processor is available.

`www.xmlsoftware.com`
Provides links to many different XML-related pieces of software—including XSL processors.

SUMMARY

- XSL formatting objects format XML documents for presentation. Formatting objects constitute the vast majority of XSL features.

- Formatting objects are typically used when the result of a transformation is for print media (e.g., books, magazines, etc.).

- Apache's Java-based tool, FOP, transforms XSL documents containing formatting objects into PDF documents.

- XSL formatting object documents have root element **fo:root** and namespace prefix **fo**. Namespace URI **http://www.w3.org/1999/XSL/Format** is used with formatting objects. Element **fo:root** is a container element only; it does not affect the document's format.

- In publishing, page masters define a page's layout (e.g., its margins, headers, footers, etc.). Page masters provide the document author with the flexibility of changing the document's format on a page-by-page basis.

- Element **fo:layout-master-set** groups the document's page masters (i.e., *page templates*). To create a page master, element **fo:simple-page-master** is used. Attributes **master-name** and **page-height** specify the page name and page height, respectively. XSL formatting objects also provide attribute **page-width**, for specifying a page's width.

- In a **simple-page-master** page master, the document is divided into five regions: header, body, footer, start and end. Each of these regions are represented by XSL formatting elements **fo:region-before**, **fo:region-body**, **fo:region-after**, **fo:region-start** and **fo:region-end**, respectively.

- Attributes **margin-top**, **margin-bottom**, **margin-left** and **margin-right** represent the top, bottom, left and right margin values, respectively.

- Element **fo:page-sequence-master** specifies the order in which master pages are created for a page master. Element **repeatable-page-master-reference** indicates that a **simple-page-master** can be repeated as many times as necessary in order to contain the document's content.

- Element **fo:static-content** specifies text that appears on each document page. Attribute **flow-name**, when assigned the value **xsl-region-before**, indicates that text will appear in each document page's header.

- Attribute **line-height** sets the line height, and attribute **font-family** sets the text's font. Empty element **fo:page-number** represents the page number.

- XSL formatting objects provide attributes **space-before.optimum** and **space-after.optimum** to specify the optimum amount of space preceding and following the text, respectively.

- Element **inline-sequence** changes the format of text inside a block.

- Attribute **extent** specifies the size of a region (i.e., **fo:region-before**, **fo:region-af-ter**, **fo:region-start** and **fo:region-end**). Region **fo:region-body** does not have an **extent** attribute and is given the remaining area after the other four regions are sized.

- A page master occurs first and can occur only once when it is marked up as **fo:single-page-master-reference**.

- XSL formatting objects also provide the capabilities to format lists of items.

- Element **fo:flow** specifies content that can flow from one page to the next. The primary difference between **fo:flow** and **fo:static-content** is that **fo:static-content** is duplicated on each page.

- Attribute **background-color** sets the background color of text. Attribute **text-align** aligns text.

- Element **fo:list-block** marks up a list of items.

- Element **fo:list-item-label** marks up the text that precedes an item in a list.

- Element **fo:list-item-body** mark ups an individual list item's text.

TERMINOLOGY

Adobe Portable Document Format (PDF)
Apache FOP
Apache Xalan
background-color attribute
color attribute
document
document layout scheme
document pages
extent attribute
.fo filename extension
fo namespace prefix
fo:block element
fo:flow element
fo:layout-master-set element
fo:list-block element
fo:list-item element
fo:list-item-body element
fo:list-item-label element
fo:page-sequence-master element
fo:region-after element
fo:region-before element
fo:region-body element
fo:region-end element
fo:region-start element

fo:repeatable-page-master-refer ence element
fo:root element
fo:simple-page-master element
fo:single-page-master-reference element
fo:static-content element
font-family attribute
font-size attribute
formatting object
line-height attribute
margin-bottom attribute
margin-left attribute
margin-right attribute
margin-top attribute
master-name attribute
page masters
page-height attribute
page-width attribute
space-after.optimum attribute
space-before.optimum attribute
text-align attribute
XSL formatting-object document

SELF-REVIEW EXERCISES

13.1   State whether the following are *true* or *false*. If *false*, explain why.
   a) Apache's FOP provides support for lists and tables.
   b) Extensible Stylesheet Language was created to provide formatting for CSS documents.
   c) Element **fo:root** is the root element for an XSL formatting-object document.
   d) Attribute **text-align** specifies how text is aligned.

e) Each page sequence in a styled XML document is defined using element **fo:sequence-specification**, which contains elements **fo:static-content** and **fo:flow**.

f) If multiple single-page specifiers are used in sequence definitions, then each page of content is mapped to a page master.

g) The **fo:block** element is usually used to format paragraphs, titles, captions and other textual objects.

h) The set of page masters for a page sequence is defined using the element **fo:page-order**.

i) The **fo:static-content** element must precede any **fo:flow** elements.

j) The repeating page specifier does not allow for setting the page master for the first page. Another page master must be used to do this.

13.2   Fill in the blanks in each of the following statements.

a) XSL formatting objects are usually given the _____ namespace prefix.

b) Element **fo:page-sequence** defines a sequence of pages that use a specific _____.

c) Attribute _____ defines a region's width or height.

d) A single-page _____ instantiates a single-page master.

e) The _____ page specifier sets the page masters for _____ and odd pages.

f) Element **fo:_____** is used to define static content for a page region in the pages of a page _____.

g) Element **fo:flow** is used to hold the content for a _____ of a page, which can _____ multiple pages.

h) Element _____ is used within elements **fo:static-content** and **fo:flow**.

i) Element **fo:inline-_____** formats inline objects.

j) **fo:list-block** formats _____ and contains elements **fo:list-_____**.

ANSWERS TO SELF-REVIEW EXERCISES

13.1   a) True. b) False. The Extensible Stylesheet Language was created to provide formatting for XML documents. c) True. d) True. e) False. Each page sequence is defined using element **fo:page-sequence**, which contains element **fo:sequence-specification**, **fo:static-content** and **fo:flow**. f) True. g) True. h) False. The set of page masters for a page sequence is defined using the element **fo:sequence-specification**. i) True. j) False. The repeating page specifier allows for setting the page master for the first page and another page master for all pages following the first.

13.2   a) **fo**. b) page master. c) **extent**. d) specifier. e) **alternating**, even. f) **static-content**, sequence. g) region, span. h) **fo:block**. i) **sequence**. j) lists, **item**.

EXERCISES

13.3   Write a simple XSLT document that would transform **intro.xml** (Fig. 5.1) into an FO document. Process the FO document to obtain a PDF document by using Apache's FOP. Render the message element in different colors and font sizes. Each page in the PDF document should contain a page number on its top-right corner.

13.4   Write code that would create a PDF document using **usage.xml** (Fig. 5.5). The PDF document generated should contain the title of the book, appearing in bold fonts, followed by the author of the book. It should also contain a table with two columns, consisting of page numbers and corresponding titles (preface, chapter and appendix). [*Hint:* Tables can be drawn using the **fo:table** element. Columns are declared with the **fo:table-column** element. Rows are represented by the **fo:table-row** element that contains the **fo:table-cell** element.]

14

XLink, XPointer, XInclude and XBase

Objectives

- To become familiar with XML Linking Language (XLink).
- To become familiar with XML Pointer Language (XPointer).
- To become familiar with XML Inclusions (XInclude).
- To become familiar with XML Base (XBase).

I feel
The link of nature draw me: flesh of flesh,
Bone of my bone thou art, and from thy state
Mine never shall be parted, bliss or woe.
John Milton

14.1 Introduction

One of the major contributing factors to the Web's popularity is hyperlinks, which provide a simple, yet powerful, means of linking documents. In this chapter, we introduce several emerging XML-related technologies that promise to go significantly beyond what is currently possible with HTML hyperlinks. We introduce the *XML Linking Language (XLink)* for describing links between resources (e.g., documents), the *XML Pointer Language (XPointer)* for "pointing" to a document's contents, *XML Inclusions (XInclude)* for including existing XML documents or portions of XML documents into another XML document and *XML Base (XBase)* for specifying a "base" URL for relative URLs.

[*Note*: The technologies presented in this chapter are still evolving and subject to change. Although some of the technologies presented in this chapter have not yet been implemented in industry, the technologies are critical to XML and will have a profound impact on the Web. When possible, we have provided sample markup to illustrate the technologies.]

14.2 XML Linking Language (XLink)

In Chapter 2, we discussed HTML's **a** element and **href** attribute for linking to documents on the Web. The W3C has been actively developing a specification, called the *XML Linking Language (XLink)*, for linking to "resources" from an XML document. As we will soon discover, XLink goes far beyond HTML linking. XLink is currently a W3C Candidate Recommendation (i.e., one step away from becoming a W3C Recommendation). XLink was designed using ideas from other linking standards; HTML, HyTime and the Text Encoding Initiative (TEI) were the most influential. Visit **www.w3.org/TR/xlink** for the latest version of the XLink specification.

XLink is capable of linking more than just documents; XLink links *resources*, which include documents, audio, video, database data, etc. For example, a movie could be linked to its corresponding sound track, or a song could be linked to corresponding information—

about it. When the song begins to play, the link could be activated, allowing the user to view the lyrics, find out information about the songwriter, etc. With XLink, the song resource need not be accessed through a single link, but can be accessed through multiple links. One link might provide the lyrics; another link might provide the songwriter's biography and a third link might provide the sheet music. This type of link is quite different from HTML's **a** element, which links only one document.

Web browsers will eventually support XLink. However, XLink is intended for a broader base of applications than just Web browsers. As industry begins to implement XLink, it will become more obvious what these *XLink-aware applications* might be.

14.2.1 Simple Links

With XLink, resources can be linked in a variety of ways. The most basic type of link specified by XLink is a *simple link*, which links one resource to another in the same way that an HTML link does. Figure 14.1 illustrates a simple link, which is represented by the arrow between **document1** and **document2**.

XLink elements that specify linking information are called *linking elements*. For example, the linking element **book** in **document1** might look like

```
<book xlink:type = "simple"
        xlink:href = "/textbooks/xmlHowToProgram.xml">
```

where **document2** is referenced using the URI **/textbooks/xmlHowToProgram.xml**. We will explain the linking element's attributes momentarily. In this particular scenario, the linking element (i.e., **book**) that references **document2** is called a *local resource*. The resource referenced is called the *remote resource*.

In XLink terminology, the markup that specifies how to traverse between resources is called an *arc*. More precisely, Fig. 14.1 illustrates an *outbound arc*, which is named as such because the starting resource (i.e., **book**) is a local resource and the ending resource (i.e., **xmlHowToProgram.xml**) is a remote resource.

Figure 14.2 shows an XML document that contains a simple link.

On line 6, we introduce the **xlink** namespace prefix bound to the URI **http://www.w3.org/1999/xlink**. Lines 18–22

```
<contact
    xlink:type = "simple"
    xlink:href = "about.xml"
    xlink:role = "http://www.deitel.com/xlink/contact"
    xlink:title = "Read about Harvey Deitel">
```

create an XLink link in element **contact**. Line 19 uses required attribute **type** to specify the type of linking—in this case, a *simple* link. The **href**, **role** and **title** attributes describe the link. Attribute **href** defines the remote resource's URI (i.e., **about.xml**, shown in Fig. 14.3) and is required. Attribute **role** is a URI that references a resource that describes the link, and attribute **title** is a descriptive title for the link. Both **role** and **title** are optional.

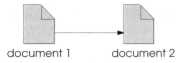

document 1   document 2

Fig. 14.1 Illustrating a simple link.

XLink provides attributes ***show*** and ***actuate*** for specifying how to display a resource when it is loaded and for specifying when the resource should be retrieved, respectively. Figure 14.4 is a variation of Fig. 14.2 that includes attributes **show** and **actuate**.

Software Engineering Observation 14.1

*Attribute **title** provides a human-readable description of the link, and attribute **role** provides a machine-readable description of the link.*

```
1   <?xml version = "1.0"?>
2
3   <!-- Fig. 14.2 : simpleLinks1.xml        -->
4   <!-- XML file that shows simple linking    -->
5
6   <contacts xmlns:xlink = "http://www.w3.org/1999/xlink">
7
8   Deitel &amp; Associates, Inc. is an internationally recognized
9   corporate training and content creation organization specializing
10  in programming languages, Internet/World Wide Web technology and
11  object technology education. Deitel &amp; Associates, Inc. is a
12  member of the World Wide Web Consortium. The company provides
13  elementary through advanced courses on Java, C++, Visual Basic,
14  C, Perl, Python, XML, Internet and World Wide Web programming,
15  e-business and e-commerce programming and Object Technology.
16  The principals of Deitel &amp; Associates, Inc. are
17
18     <contact
19        xlink:type = "simple"
20        xlink:href = "about.xml"
21        xlink:role = "http://www.deitel.com/xlink/contact"
22        xlink:title = "Read about Harvey Deitel">
23
24        Dr. Harvey Deitel
25     </contact>
26
27  and Paul J. Deitel. The company&apos;s clients include many of
28  the world&apos;s largest computer companies, government agencies,
29  branches of the military and business organizations. Through its
30  publishing partnership with Prentice Hall, Deitel &amp; Associates,
31  Inc. publishes leading-edge programming textbooks, professional
32  books, interactive CD-ROM-based multimedia Cyber Classrooms,
33  satellite courses and Web-based training courses.
34  </contacts>
```

Fig. 14.2 XML document with a simple link (part 1 of 2).

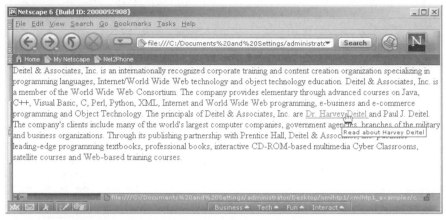

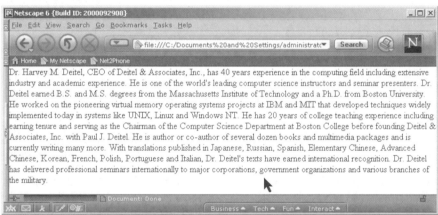

Netscape Communicator browser window© 1999 Netscape Communications
Corporation. Used with permission. Netscape Communications has not authorized,
sponsored, endorsed, or approved this publication and is not responsible for its
content.

Fig. 14.2   XML document with a simple link (part 2 of 2).

```
1   <?xml version = "1.0" ?>
2
3   <!-- Fig. 14.3 : about.xml   -->
4   <!-- About Harvey Deitel      -->
5
6   <about>
7   Dr. Harvey M. Deitel, CEO of Deitel &amp; Associates, Inc., has
8   40 years experience in the computing field including extensive
9   industry and academic experience. He is one of the world&apos;s
10  leading computer science instructors and seminar presenters.
11  Dr. Deitel earned B.S. and M.S. degrees from the Massachusetts
```

Fig. 14.3   Listing for **about.xml** (part 1 of 2).

```
12   Institute of Technology and a Ph.D. from Boston University.
13   He worked on the pioneering virtual memory operating systems
14   projects at IBM and MIT that developed techniques widely
15   implemented today in systems like UNIX, Linux and Windows NT.
16   He has 20 years of college teaching experience including earning
17   tenure and serving as the Chairman of the Computer Science
18   Department at Boston College before founding Deitel &amp;
19   Associates, Inc. with Paul J. Deitel. He is author or co-author
20   of several dozen books and multimedia packages and is currently
21   writing many more. With translations published in Japanese,
22   Russian, Spanish, Elementary Chinese, Advanced Chinese, Korean,
23   French, Polish, Portuguese and Italian, Dr. Deitel&apos;s texts have
24   earned international recognition. Dr. Deitel has delivered
25   professional seminars internationally to major corporations,
26   government organizations and various branches of the military.
27   </about>
```

Fig. 14.3   Listing for **about.xml** (part 2 of 2).

Line 13

```
xlink:show = "new"
```

assigns attribute **show** the value **new**, which indicates that the resource should be displayed in a new window (or equivalent, based on the XLink-aware application). Attribute **show** can also be assigned **replace**, for replacing the current resource with the linked resource; **embed**, for combining the current element with the linked resource, and **other** or **none**, which allows the XLink-aware application to decide how to display the link.

Line 14

```
xlink:actuate = "onRequest"
```

```
1    <?xml version = "1.0"?>
2
3    <!-- Fig. 14.4 : simpleLinks2.xml      -->
4    <!-- XML file that shows simple linking  -->
5
6    <contacts xmlns:xlink = "http://www.w3.org/1999/xlink">
7
8       <contact
9          xlink:type = "simple"
10         xlink:href = "about.xml"
11         xlink:role = "http://www.deitel.com/xlink/contact"
12         xlink:title = "About Harvey Deitel"
13         xlink:show = "new"
14         xlink:actuate = "onRequest">
15
16         Dr. Harvey Deitel
17      </contact>
18
19   </contacts>
```

Fig. 14.4   Attributes **show** and **actuate** (part 1 of 2).

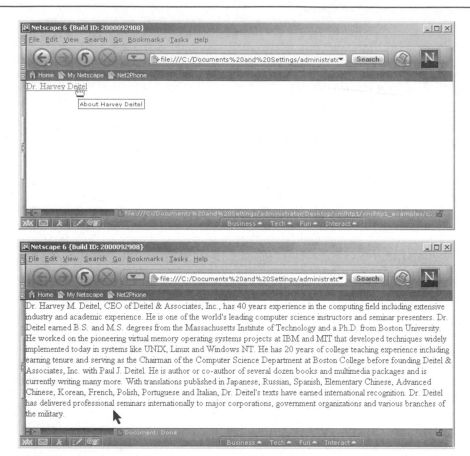

Netscape Communicator browser window© 1999 Netscape Communications Corporation. Used with permission. Netscape Communications has not authorized, sponsored, endorsed, or approved this publication and is not responsible for its content.

Fig. 14.4   Attributes **show** and **actuate** (part 2 of 2).

assigns attribute **actuate** the value **onRequest**, which indicates that the resource should not be retrieved until the user requests it (e.g., by clicking on the link). Attribute **actuate** can also be assigned the value **onLoad**, which indicates that the document should be retrieved as soon as it is loaded, the value **other**, which allows the XLink-aware application to decide when to load the resource based on other markup in the document and the value **none**, which provides no information on when to load the resource.

14.2.2 Extended Links

XLink's capabilities go well beyond simple links. XLink also provides *extended links*, for linking multiple combinations of local and remote resources. In Fig. 14.1, the illustration of a simple link shows a *unidirectional link* (i.e., a link that can only be traversed in one direction) between two resources. The remote resource (i.e., **xmlHowToProgram.xml**) has no knowledge of the local resource. If these two resources are documents in a Web browser, the back button can be clicked on to return to the local resource. This function is not linking, but simply browser functionality. Recall that XLink-aware applications are not necessarily browsers and may not provide such a feature. Consider Fig. 14.5, which modifies Fig. 14.1 by adding a link from **document2** to **document1**. Although this link might appear to provide the remote resource with knowledge of the local resource, it does not. All we have done is add another unidirectional link.

Software Engineering Observation 14.2

One of the greatest benefits of XLink is that it allows authors to create links between documents that they do not own.

With XLink, we can create multidirectional links for traversing between resources (Fig. 14.6). The user (or an application) can start at either end and traverse to the other. Multidirectional links are not limited to just two resources, but can link any number of resources (Fig. 14.7). The links need not be traversed sequentially. For example, the linking element in **document1** could be used to traverse to **document4** without going through **document2** and **document3**.

Figure 14.8 is an XML document that contains extended links that link a book, author, publisher and warehouse. Figure 14.9 shows the rendering of **booklinks.xml** in the Fujitsu XLink Processor.

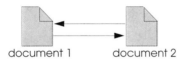

Fig. 14.5 Two unidirectional links.

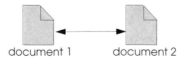

Fig. 14.6 Multidirectional link.

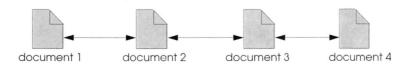

Fig. 14.7 Multidirectional linking between four resources.

```
1   <?xml version = "1.0"?>
2
3   <!-- Fig. 14.8 : booklinks.xml              -->
4   <!-- XML document containing extended links  -->
5
6   <books xmlns:xlink = "http://www.w3.org/1999/xlink"
7      xlink:type = "extended"
8      xlink:title = "Book Inventory">
9
10     <author xlink:label = "authorDeitel"
11        xlink:type = "locator"
12        xlink:href = "authors/deitel.xml"
13        xlink:role = "http://deitel.com/xlink/author"
14        xlink:title = "Deitel &amp; Associates, Inc.">
15        <persons id = "authors">
16           <person>Deitel, Harvey</person>
17           <person>Deitel, Paul</person>
18        </persons>
19     </author>
20
21     <publisher xlink:label = "publisherPrenticeHall"
22        xlink:type = "locator"
23        xlink:href = "/publisher/prenticehall.xml"
24        xlink:role = "http://deitel.com/xlink/publisher"
25        xlink:title = "Prentice Hall"/>
26
27     <warehouse xlink:label = "warehouseXYZ"
28        xlink:type = "locator"
29        xlink:href = "/warehouse/xyz.xml"
30        xlink:role = "http://deitel.com/xlink/warehouse"
31        xlink:title = "X.Y.Z. Books"/>
32
33     <book xlink:label = "JavaBook"
34        xlink:type = "resource"
35        xlink:role = "http://deitel.com/xlink/author"
36        xlink:title = "Textbook on Java">
37        Java How to Program: Third edition
38     </book>
39
40     <arcElement xlink:type = "arc"
41        xlink:from = "JavaBook"
42        xlink:arcrole = "http://deitel.com/xlink/info"
43        xlink:to = "authorDeitel"
44        xlink:show = "new"
45        xlink:actuate = "onRequest"
46        xlink:title = "About the author"/>
47
48     <arcElement xlink:type = "arc"
49        xlink:from = "JavaBook"
50        xlink:arcrole = "http://deitel.com/xlink/info"
51        xlink:to = "publisherPrenticeHall"
52        xlink:show = "new"
```

Fig. 14.8 XML document containing extended links (part 1 of 2).

```
53          xlink:actuate = "onRequest"
54          xlink:title = "About the publisher"/>
55
56      <arcElement xlink:type = "arc"
57          xlink:from = "warehouseXYZ"
58          xlink:arcrole = "http://deitel.com/xlink/info"
59          xlink:to = "JavaBook"
60          xlink:show = "new"
61          xlink:actuate = "onRequest"
62          xlink:title = "Information about this book"/>
63
64      <arcElement xlink:type = "arc"
65          xlink:from = "publisherPrenticeHall"
66          xlink:arcrole = "http://deitel.com/xlink/stock"
67          xlink:to = "warehouseXYZ"
68          xlink:show = "embed"
69          xlink:actuate = "onLoad"
70          xlink:title = "Publisher&apos;s inventory"/>
71
72  </books>
```

Fig. 14.8   XML document containing extended links (part 2 of 2).

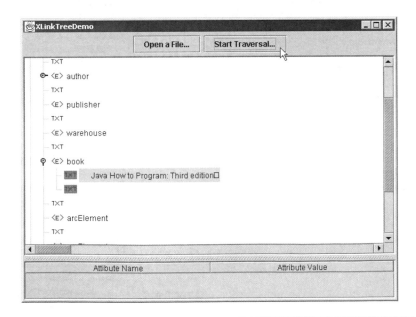

Fig. 14.9   XLink tree browser rendering of `booklinks.xml`.

Lines 6–8

```
<books xmlns:xlink = "http://www.w3.org/1999/xlink"
    xlink:type = "extended"
    xlink:title = "Book Inventory">
```

define root element **books**. This element defines the namespace prefix **xlink** and binds it to the URI **http://www.w3.org/1999/xlink**. The link **type** of *extended* indicates that the XLink being declared is an extended link. Attribute **title** is assigned **"Book Inventory"**.

Lines 10–19

```
<author xlink:label = "authorDeitel"
    xlink:type = "locator"
    xlink:href = "authors/deitel.xml"
    xlink:role = "http://deitel.com/xlink/author"
    xlink:title = "Deitel &amp; Associates, Inc.">
    <persons id = "authors">
        <person>Deitel, Harvey</person>
        <person>Deitel, Paul</person>
    </persons>
</author>
```

mark up a link to the book's authors with information located at **/authors/deitel.xml**. Attribute *label* is assigned a value that identifies the resource—in this case, **authorDeitel**. A **label**'s value is used to link one resource to another. We will discuss how this linking is done momentarily. Element **author** has **type** *locator*, which specifies a remote resource. Child element **persons** contains **person** elements that mark up individual authors. In this case, when either **Deitel, Harvey** or **Deitel, Paul** is selected, the document **deitel.xml** will be retrieved.

Lines 21–25

```
<publisher xlink:label = "publisherPrenticeHall"
    xlink:type = "locator"
    xlink:href = "/publisher/prenticehall.xml"
    xlink:role = "http://deitel.com/xlink/publisher"
    xlink:title = "Prentice Hall"/>
```

mark up the publisher. This resource is given the identifier **publisherPrenticeHall**. Attribute value **locator** indicates that this remote resource is located at **/publisher/prenticeHall.xml**.

Lines 27–31

```
<warehouse xlink:label = "warehouseXYZ"
    xlink:type = "locator"
    xlink:href = "/warehouse/xyz.xml"
    xlink:role = "http://deitel.com/xlink/warehouse"
    xlink:title = "X.Y.Z. Books"/>
```

mark up the warehouse. This remote resource is given the identifier **warehouseXYZ** and is located at **/warehouse/xyz.xml**.

Lines 33–38

```
<book xlink:label = "JavaBook"
    xlink:type = "resource"
    xlink:role = "http://deitel.com/xlink/author"
    xlink:title = "Textbook on Java">
    Java How to Program: Third edition
</book>
```

create a local resource labeled **JavaBook**. This resource represents a book, which can be linked to (or from) an author or publisher. We will discuss how this linking occurs momentarily.

Lines 40–46

```
<arcElement xlink:type = "arc"
    xlink:from = "JavaBook"
    xlink:arcrole = "http://deitel.com/xlink/info"
    xlink:to = "authorDeitel"
    xlink:show = "new"
    xlink:actuate = "onRequest"
    xlink:title = "About the author"/>
```

create an outbound arc between the book local resource (i.e., **JavaBook**) and the author remote resource (i.e., **authorDeitel**) using attributes *from* and *to*. Attribute *arcrole*, which describes the relationship between the resources, is assigned **http://deitel.com/xlink/info**. In this case, the arc's role is to provide information about the book's author. Attribute **show** is assigned **new**, so when the link is activated, the ending resource (the author resource) is loaded in a new window. Attribute **actuate** has value **onRequest**, so an application will traverse the link when a user requests it.

Lines 48–54

```
<arcElement xlink:type = "arc"
    xlink:from = "JavaBook"
    xlink:arcrole = "http://deitel.com/xlink/info"
    xlink:to = "publisherPrenticeHall"
    xlink:show = "new"
    xlink:actuate = "onRequest"
    xlink:title = "About the publisher"/>
```

create an outbound arc between the book local resource and the publisher remote resource.

Figure 14.10 shows the traversal of the link defined in lines 33–38. This link is the starting resource of two different arcs. The title of the first arc (lines 40–46) is **About the author** and links to the **authorDeitel** resource (lines 10–19). The title of the second arc (lines 48–54) is **About the publisher** and links to the **publisherPrenticeHall** resource (lines 21–25).

Figure 14.11 shows the result of following the **About the author** link. The link's title—**Deitel & Associates, Inc.**— is shown with an option to traverse the link.

Figure 14.12 shows the result of traversing the **authorDeitel** link. The ending resource of the link is displayed in a new window because the **xlink:show** attribute (line 44) of the **arcElement** (line 40) has the value **new**.

Lines 56–62

```
<arcElement xlink:type = "arc"
    xlink:from = "warehouseXYZ"
    xlink:arcrole = "http://deitel.com/xlink/info"
    xlink:to = "JavaBook"
    xlink:show = "new"
    xlink:actuate = "onRequest"
    xlink:title = "Information about this book"/>
```

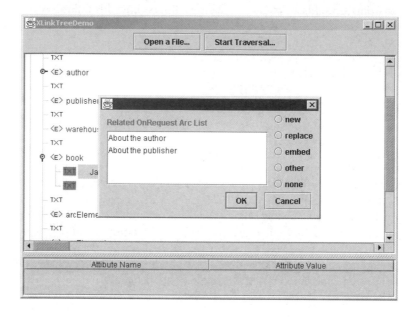

Fig. 14.10 Traversing on outbound link. (©Fujitsu Laboratories Ltd.)

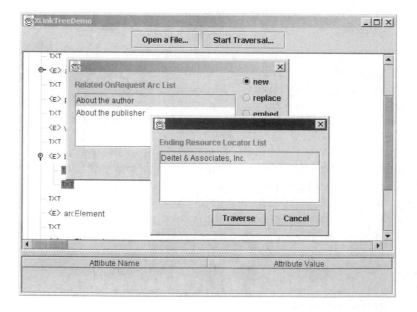

Fig. 14.11 Traversing an outbound link. (©Fujitsu Laboratories Ltd.)

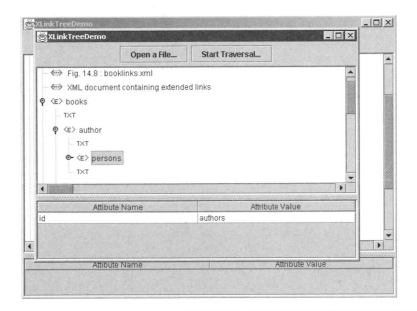

Fig. 14.12 Ending resource shown in a new window. (©Fujitsu Laboratories Ltd.)

create an arc, called an *inbound arc*, that has a starting resource that is remote (i.e., **ware-houseXYZ**) and an ending resource that is local (i.e., **JavaBook**).

Lines 64–70

```
<arcElement xlink:type = "arc"
    xlink:from = "publisherPrenticeHall"
    xlink:arcrole = "http://deitel.com/xlink/stock"
    xlink:to = "warehouseXYZ"
    xlink:show = "embed"
    xlink:actuate = "onLoad"
    xlink:title = "Publisher&apos;s inventory"/>
```

create an arc, called a *third-party arc*, that has starting and ending resources that are both remote. In this case, the arc is between resources **publisherPrenticeHall** and **warehouseXYZ**. Attribute **show** has value **embed**, which indicates that the ending resource should replace the starting resource when the link is traversed (Fig. 14.10). Attribute **actuate** has value **onLoad**, so upon loading the XML document, the link is traversed. Because we consider the relationship between the publisher and warehouse as being different than the previous three arcs, we provide a different **arcrole** value for this link.

14.3 XLink and DTDs

DTDs are often used with documents that use XLink for validation and to reduce the number of XLink attributes appearing in an XML document. For example, the linking element

```
<car xmlns:xlink = "http://www.w3.org/1999/xlink"
    xlink:type = "simple" xlink:role = "MT4606"
    xlink:title = "The Latest Model">
```

contains a namespace declaration and three attributes. By providing default values in the DTD, we could "hide" some of these attributes and the namespace declaration. The linking element might then look like

```
<car xlink:role = "MT4606" xlink:title = "The Latest Model">
```

where the namespace declaration and **type** attribute have **#FIXED** values in the DTD.
    Figure 14.13 shows the DTD to which the example in Fig. 14.8 would conform.

Common Programming Error 14.1

Forgetting to declare XLink attributes in a DTD can result in an invalid document.

```
1   <!-- Fig. 14.13 : booklinks.dtd -->
2   <!-- DTD for extended Links      -->
3
4   <!ELEMENT books (author, publisher, warehouse, book, arcElement*)>
5   <!ATTLIST books
6      xmlns:xlink CDATA #FIXED "http://www.w3.org/1999/xlink"
7      xlink:type (extended) #FIXED "extended"
8      xlink:role CDATA #IMPLIED
9      xlink:title CDATA #IMPLIED>
10
11  <!ELEMENT book (#PCDATA)>
12  <!ATTLIST book
13     xlink:type (resource) #FIXED "resource"
14     xlink:role CDATA #FIXED "http://deitel.com/xlink/book"
15     xlink:title CDATA #IMPLIED
16     xlink:label NMTOKEN #IMPLIED>
17
18  <!ELEMENT author (person*)>
19  <!ATTLIST author
20     xlink:type (locator) #FIXED "locator"
21     xlink:href CDATA #REQUIRED
22     xlink:role CDATA #FIXED "http://deitel.com/xlink/author"
23     xlink:title CDATA #IMPLIED
24     xlink:label NMTOKEN #IMPLIED>
25
26  <!ELEMENT publisher EMPTY>
27  <!ATTLIST publisher
28     xlink:type (locator) #FIXED "locator"
29     xlink:href CDATA #REQUIRED
30     xlink:role CDATA #FIXED "http://deitel.com/xlink/publisher"
31     xlink:title CDATA #IMPLIED
32     xlink:label NMTOKEN #IMPLIED>
33
34  <!ELEMENT warehouse EMPTY>
35  <!ATTLIST warehouse
36     xlink:type (locator) #FIXED "locator"
37     xlink:href CDATA #REQUIRED
38     xlink:role CDATA #FIXED "http://deitel.com/xlink/warehouse"
```

Fig. 14.13 DTD for extended XLink example (part 1 of 2).

```
39      xlink:title CDATA #IMPLIED
40      xlink:label NMTOKEN #IMPLIED>
41
42   <!ELEMENT arcElement EMPTY>
43   <!ATTLIST arcElement
44      xlink:type (arc) #FIXED "arc"
45      xlink:arcrole CDATA #IMPLIED
46      xlink:title CDATA #IMPLIED
47      xlink:from NMTOKEN #IMPLIED
48      xlink:to NMTOKEN #IMPLIED
49      xlink:show (new | replace | embed | undefined) #IMPLIED
50      xlink:actuate (onLoad | onRequest | undefined) #IMPLIED>
51
52   <!ELEMENT persons (person+)>
53   <!ATTLIST persons id ID #REQUIRED>
54
55   <!ELEMENT person (#PCDATA)>
```

Fig. 14.13 DTD for extended XLink example (part 2 of 2).

Line 4

```
<!ELEMENT books (author, publisher, book, arcElement*)>
```

defines element **books**, which contains elements **author**, **publisher**, **book** and **arcElement**. Lines 5–9

```
<!ATTLIST books
   xmlns:xlink CDATA #FIXED "http://www.w3.org/1999/xlink"
   xlink:type (extended) #FIXED "extended"
   xlink:role CDATA #IMPLIED
   xlink:title CDATA #IMPLIED>
```

define the attributes for element **books**. We set the namespace prefix **xlink** to the URI **http://www.w3.org/1999/xlink**, and we set attribute **type** to **extended**, which specifies an extended link. Because the namespace prefix is bound to a URI and attribute **type** is assigned a value in the DTD, we do not need to explicitly provide these attributes and their values in the XML document that conforms to this DTD.

Lines 11–16

```
<!ELEMENT book (#PCDATA)>
<!ATTLIST book
   xlink:type (resource) #FIXED "resource"
   xlink:role CDATA #FIXED "http://deitel.com/xlink/book"
   xlink:title CDATA #IMPLIED
   xlink:label NMTOKEN #IMPLIED>
```

define element **book** and its attributes. Element **book** references a local resource, because **type** is assigned **resource**. The element's **role** is **http://deitel.com/xlink/book**, which describes the element.

Lines 18–24

```
<!ELEMENT author (persons)>
<!ATTLIST author
   xlink:type (locator) #FIXED "locator"
   xlink:href CDATA #REQUIRED
   xlink:role CDATA #FIXED "http://deitel.com/xlink/author"
   xlink:title CDATA #IMPLIED
   xlink:label NMTOKEN #IMPLIED>
```

define element **author** and its attributes. This element can contain a **persons** element. Attribute **type** has value **locator**, which indicates that the element references remote resources.

Lines 26–32 define element **publisher**, and lines 34–40 define element **warehouse**. Each element's **type** attribute references a remote resource, because it is assigned **locator**.

Lines 42–50

```
<!ELEMENT arcElement EMPTY>
<!ATTLIST arcElement
   xlink:type (arc) #FIXED "arc"
   xlink:arcrole CDATA #IMPLIED
   xlink:title CDATA #IMPLIED
   xlink:from NMTOKEN #IMPLIED
   xlink:to NMTOKEN #IMPLIED
   xlink:show (new | replace | embed | undefined) #IMPLIED
   xlink:actuate (onLoad | onRequest | undefined) #IMPLIED>
```

define element **arcElement** and its attributes. Attribute **show** takes one of the values **new**, **replace**, **embed** or **undefined**. Attribute **actuate** is assigned either **onLoad**, **onRequest** or **undefined**.

14.4 XML Pointer Language (XPointer)

The XML Pointer Language (XPointer) is used to reference fragments of an XML document via a URI. In Chapter 11, we discussed XPath, which allowed for selecting specific nodes in an XML document. XPointer uses XPath expressions to provide a means for referencing an XML document's nodes from a URI. The XPointer specification is currently a W3C Candidate Recommendation. For the latest XPointer specification, visit **www.w3.org/TR/xptr**.

In Section 14.2, we discussed XLink, which links resources. By using XPointer with XLink, we can link to specific parts of a resource, instead of linking to the entire resource. XPointer can link to specific *locations* (i.e., nodes in an XPath tree), or even ranges of locations, in an XML document. XPointer also adds the ability to search XML documents by using string matching.

Software Engineering Observation 14.3

XPointer provides the ability to reference locations at a much finer level of granularity than does XPath. For example, XPointer is capable of referencing the location of a single character.

Figure 14.14 is an example XML contact list that contains **id**s for three authors. XPointer has not been implemented as of the time of this writing. We use this XML document as a basis for writing a few simple XPointer expressions.

Assume that the contact list has the relative URI **/contacts.xml**. With XLink, we can reference the entire contact list with the URI

```
xlink:href = "/contacts.xml"
```

We can use the XPointer expression

```
xlink:href =
    "/contacts.xml#xpointer(//contact[@id = 'author02'])"
```

to reference the **contact** element with an **id** of **author02**. The name **xpointer**—called a *scheme*—expresses the full XPointer form.

XPointer also provides abbreviations for expressions that use attribute **id**. For example, if a document's unique identifier is referenced in an expression such as

```
xlink:href = "/contacts.xml#xpointer(id('author01'))"
```

the expression can be simplified by writing

```
xlink:href = "/contacts.xml#author01"
```

which is a *bare-name XPointer address*. This simplified syntax is provided to encourage document authors to use **ID**s for elements.

XPointer also provides extensions to XPath, such as the ability to select ranges of locations and perform string searches in an XML document. For information about the XPointer extensions of XPath, please refer to the XPointer specification.

14.5 XML Inclusions (XInclude)

The XML 1.0 specification does not provide a method to reuse XML documents by including one or more documents within other XML documents. To provide this feature, the W3C has begun development of the XML Inclusions (XInclude) specification (currently a W3C Working Draft). The latest XInclude specification is available at **www.w3.org/TR/xinclude**.

```
1   <?xml version = "1.0"?>
2   <!-- Fig. 14.14 : contacts.xml -->
3   <!-- contact list document     -->
4
5   <contacts>
6      <contact id = "author01">Deitel, Harvey</contact>
7      <contact id = "author02">Deitel, Paul</contact>
8      <contact id = "author03">Nieto, Tem</contact>
9   </contacts>
```

Fig. 14.14 Example contact list.

Software Engineering Observation 14.4

XInclude differs from **xlink:show = "embed"** *in that it merges the tree structures of the two documents into a single tree.*

In object-oriented languages, such as Java and C++, methods and data are encapsulated in reusable components called classes. Entire programs can then be built by simply piecing together instances of these classes. Similarly, XInclude provides a framework for reusing existing XML documents.

To add one XML document inside another, an *include element* is used. An include element is any XML element that has particular attributes from the namespace **http://www.w3.org/1999/XML/xinclude**. For example,

```
<includer
    xmlns:xinclude = "http://www.w3.org/1999/XML/xinclude"
    xinclude:href = "test.xml"
    xinclude:parse = "xml"/>
```

includes the XML document **test.xml** in the current XML document. Element **includer** is an include element, with the required XInclude **href** attribute for referencing an XML document. To include portions of another XML document, XPointer can be used in the **xinclude** attribute **href**. The optional XInclude attribute *parse* can have value **xml** or **text**. The default value, **xml**, parses the XML document as XML for inclusion; thus, any entities, include elements and other parsable items are processed before being embedded into the XML document. Using the value **text** in the **parse** attribute incorporates the document referenced in the **href** attribute as plain-text character data, which is not parsed.

14.6 XML Base (XBase)

The W3C is currently working on a specification (currently a W3C Candidate Recommendation) to provide base URIs for relative links, similar to the HTML element **base**. XBase allows a document author to change the base URI for relative links in a document. For the latest specification, visit **www.w3.org/TR/xmlbase**.

In Section 14.4, we used the relative link **/contacts.xml** to reference a resource. If the base URI were **http://deitel.com**, then the complete URI for the resource would be **http://deitel.com/contacts.xml**.

By using the XML attribute *xml:base*, a document author can provide a new base URI. For example,

```
<contact
    xml:base = "http://deitel.net/"
    xlink:type = "simple"
    xlink:href = "/authors/author01biography.xml"
    xlink:role = "http://deitel.com/xlink/contact"
    xlink:title = "About this author">
```

uses attribute **xml:base** to provide the base URI **http://deitel.net/** for attribute **href**. The complete URI referenced by **href** is therefore

```
http://deitel.net/authors/author01biography.xml
```

14.7 Internet and World Wide Web Resources

www.w3.org/TR/xlink
The most recent *W3C XLink Recommendation*.

www.w3.org/TR/xmlbase
The most recent *XMLBase specification* from the W3C.

www.w3.org/TR/xptr
The most recent W3C *XML Pointer Language Recommendation*.

www.oasis-open.org/cover/xll.html
Oasis's *XML Linking and Addressing Languages Cover Page* provides a good introduction to XLink and XPath, accompanied by references and links.

www.consistencycheck.com
This site provides an introductory discussion of XLink and contains several examples.

www.simonstl.com/projects/xlinkfilter/resources.html
This site provides links to resources on XLink and XPointer.

www.thefaactory.com/xlink2html
Home page for XLink2HTML, which creates HTML representations of XLink elements.

SUMMARY

- The W3C has been actively developing a specification, called the XML Linking Language (XLink), for linking to "resources" from an XML document. XLink goes far beyond HTML linking and is currently a W3C Candidate Recommendation. XLink was designed using ideas from other linking standards; HTML, HyTime and Text Encoding Initiative (TEI) were the most influential.

- XLink is capable of linking more than just documents; XLink links resources, which include documents, audio, video, database data, etc. Web browsers will eventually support XLink. However, XLink is intended for a broader base of applications, not just Web browsers. As industry begins to implement XLink, it will become more obvious what these XLink-aware applications will be.

- With XLink, resources can be linked in a variety of ways. The most basic type of link specified by XLink is a simple link, which links one resource to another the same way that an HTML link does. Simple links are also called inline links, because the link's content is a resource.

- XLink elements that specify linking information are called linking elements.

- A local resource is contained in the linking element, and a remote resource is external to the linking element.

- In XLink terminology, the markup that specifies how to traverse between resources is called an arc. An outbound arc has a starting resource that is local and an ending resource that is remote.

- The **xlink** namespace prefix is bound to the URI **http://www.w3.org/1999/xlink**.

- Attribute **type** specifies the type of linking—either simple or extended. Attribute **href** defines the remote resource's URI and is required. Attribute **role** is a URI that references a resource that describes the link, and attribute **title** is a descriptive title for the link.

- XLink provides attributes **show** and **actuate** for specifying how to display a resource when it is loaded and for specifying when the resource should be retrieved, respectively.

- Attribute **show** can be assigned the value **new**, which indicates that the resource should be displayed in a new window (or equivalent, based on the XLink-aware application); **replace**, for replacing the current resource with the linked resource; **embed**, for replacing the current element with the linked resource, and **other** or **none**, which allows the XLink-aware application to decide how to display the link.

- Attribute **actuate** can be assigned the value **onRequest**, which indicates that the resource should not be retrieved until the user requests it (e.g., by clicking on the link); **onLoad**, which indicates that the document should be retrieved as soon as it is loaded; **other**, which allows the XLink-aware application to decide when to load the resource based on other markup in the document and the value **none**, which provides no information on when to load the resource.

- XLink's capabilities go well beyond simple links. XLink also provides *extended links* for linking multiple combinations of local and remote resources. With XLink, we can create multidirectional links for traversing between resources. The user (or an application) can start at either end and traverse to the other. Multidirectional links are not limited to just two resources, but can link any number of resources. The links need not be traversed sequentially.

- Attribute **type** is assigned **extended** for extended links.

- Attribute *label* is assigned a value that identifies the resource. A **label**'s value is used to link one resource to another.

- Attribute **type** is assigned *locator* for remote resources.

- Attribute **arcrole** describes the relationship between resources.

- An inbound arc has a starting resource that is remote and an ending resource that is local.

- A third-party arc has starting and ending resources that are both remote.

- DTDs are often used with documents that use XLink for validation and to reduce the number of XLink attributes appearing in a linking element.

- The XML Pointer Language (XPointer) is used to reference fragments of an XML document via a URI. XPointer uses XPath expressions to provide a means for referencing an XML document's nodes from a URI. The XPointer specification is currently a W3C Candidate Recommendation.

- By using XPointer with XLink, we can link to specific parts of a resource, instead of linking to the entire resource. XPointer can link to specific *locations*, or even ranges of locations, in an XML document. XPointer also adds the ability to search XML documents by using string matching.

- The XML 1.0 specification does not provide a method to reuse XML documents by including one or more documents within other XML documents. To provide this feature, the W3C has begun development of the XML Inclusion (XInclude) specification (currently a W3C Working Draft).

- To add one XML document inside another, an include element is used. An include element is any XML element that has particular attributes from the *namespace* **http://www.w3.org/1999/XML/xinclude**.

- To include portions of another XML document, XPointer can be used in the **xinclude** attribute **href**. The optional XInclude attribute **parse** can have value **xml** or **text**. The default value, **xml**, parses the XML document as XML for inclusion; thus, any entities, include elements and other parsable items are processed before being embedded into the XML document. Using the value **text** in the **parse** attribute incorporates the document referenced in the **href** attribute as plain-text character data, which is not parsed.

- XBase allows a document author to change the base URI for any relative links in a document, similar to the HTML element **base**. XBase is currently a W3C Candidate Recommendation. By using the XML attribute **xml:base**, a document author can provide a new base URI.

TERMINOLOGY

actuate attribute   arc
arc   **arcrole attribute**

bare-name XPointer address
base URI
Candidate Recommendation
embed attribute value
ending resource
extended attribute value
extended link
from attribute
href attribute
**http://www.w3.org/1999/XML/xin-
    clude**
hyperlink
inbound arc
include element
inline link
label attribute
link
local resource
locator attribute value
new attribute value
onLoad attribute value
onRequest attribute value
outbound arc
relative link
remote resource
replace
resource
resource

role attribute
show attribute
simple attribute value
simple link
text attribute
Text Encoding Initiative (TEI)
starting resource
third-party arc
title attribute
to attribute
traverse a link
type attribute
undefined attribute value
unidirectional link
XBase (XML Base)
XInclude (XML Inclusions)
XInclude attribute **href**
XInclude attribute **parse**
XLink (XML Linking Language)
xlink namespace prefix
XML Base
xml:base attribute
XML Inclusion
XML Linking Language
XML Pointer Language
XPointer (XML Pointer)
xpointer scheme

SELF-REVIEW EXERCISES

14.1   State whether the following are *true* or *false*. If *false*, explain why.
    a) XLink links resources.
    b) Simple links provide multiple links between resources.
    c) Extended links can contain any combination of inbound, outbound or third-party arcs.
    d) XPointer expressions always reference entire resources.
    e) An arc describes how to traverse between two resources.
    f) XLink attribute **actuate** specifies the meaning between an ending resource and a starting resource.
    g) A simple linking element can contain **href**, **role**, **arcrole**, **title**, **show** and **actuate** attributes.
    h) XLink adds the ability to search XML documents by using string matching.
    i) XPath extends XPointer.
    j) A simple link requires attribute **type** to have the value **simple**.

14.2   Fill in the blanks in each of the following statements:
    a) The two types of XLink links are _____ and _____.
    b) A/An _____ link can contain any number of links between local and/or remote resources.
    c) XLink attribute **type="_____"** defines an element for addressing a remote resource.
    d) The XML _____ Language references a resource or a fragment of a resource.

e) A _____ XPointer address simplifies expressions that use **id**s.
f) An XPath node is called a _____ in XPointer.
g) _____ was developed to provide a method for including XML documents within other XML documents.
h) An XML element that has XInclude attributes is called an _____ element.
i) XLink attribute _____ contains a human-readable description of a link.
j) Links between remote resources and local resources are known as _____ links.

ANSWERS TO SELF-REVIEW EXERCISES

14.1   a) True. b) False. Simple links provide a single outbound link between two resources. c) True. d) False. XPointer can reference resource fragments as well as the entire resource. e) True. f) False. XML attribute **actuate** specifies when to initiate traversal. g) True. h) False. XPointer adds the ability to search XML documents using string matching. i) False. XPointer extends XPath. j) True.

14.2   a) extended, simple. b) extended. c) **locator**. d) Pointer. e) bare-name. f) locations. g) XML Inclusions (XInclude). h) include. i) **title**. j) inbound.

EXERCISES

14.3   Construct a DTD and a corresponding XML document for the following scenario: Consider a video store that maintains a record (as an XML document) of every cassette it has. Each cassette is marked up by a **movie** element, which contains a simple link whose local resource is the document itself and whose remote resource is the movie's Web site. Element **movie** further contains element **stock**, which specifies the number of cassettes available, and element **dealer**, which describes the dealer who supplies the cassette. Element **dealer** also contains a simple link whose remote resource is the dealer's Web page. Specify all of the attributes required for each simple link.

14.4   A search engine needs to display all of the links related to an XML store. The store sells products such as XML browsers and parsers. The search engine provides information about customers and manufacturers related to the store. It also provides information about the manufacturers' franchises. Write an XML document with an extended link that would help the search engine. Product descriptions should be local resources. Customer data, manufacturer data and franchise data should be remote resources. Each product has inbound arcs from the customer database as well as from the manufacturer database. The document should also describe a third-party arc from a manufacturer to its franchise. Also, create a DTD for the XML document.

15

Case Study: Message Forum with Active Server Pages

Objectives

- To create a Web-based message forum using Active Server Pages.
- To use XML with Active Server Pages.
- To be able to add new forums.
- To be able to post messages to the message forum.
- To use Microsoft's DOM to manipulate an XML document.
- To use XSLT to transform XML documents.

If any man will draw up his case, and put his name at the foot of the first page, I will give him an immediate reply. Where he compels me to turn over the sheet, he must wait my leisure.
Lord Sandwich

They also serve who only stand and wait.
John Milton

A fair request should be followed by a deed in silence.
Dante Alighieri

Outline

15.1 Introduction

In this chapter, we use XML and many of the technologies presented in the first 14 chapters to create one of the most popular types of Web sites—a *message forum*. Message forums are "virtual" bulletin boards where various topics are discussed. Common features of message forum include discussion groups, questions and answers and general comments. Many Web sites host message forums. For example,

```
www.egroups.com
web.eesite.com/forums
www.deja.com
```

are popular message forums.

The message forum we create in this chapter uses Microsoft's *Active Server Pages (ASP)* technology. [*Note*: If you are not familiar with ASP or need a review, we have provided an introduction to ASP in Chapter 25.] In the case study presented in this chapter, users can post messages and start new forums. We leave the removal of a forum as an exercise for the reader.

15.2 Setup and Message Forum Documents

In this section, we provide the setup instructions for executing the case study. The case study requires the following software:

1. Microsoft Personal Web Server (PWS), Microsoft Internet Information Services or Microsoft Internet Information Server (IIS).

2. Internet Explorer 5.5 (for XML and XSLT processing).

Copy the files from the Chapter 15 examples directory (on the CD-ROM that accompanies this book) to the Web directory (e.g., `c:\inetpub\wwwroot`). [*Note*: Either PWS or IIS must be installed; otherwise, the Web directory will not exist. This directory must also have `Write` permissions to allow users to post messages and add forums.] Each of these files and documents is summarized in Fig. 15.1. We will discuss each of these files later in the chapter.

File Name	Description
forums.xml	XML document listing all available forums and their filenames.
default.asp	Main page, providing navigational links to the forums.
template.xml	Template for a message forum XML document.
addForum.asp	Adds a forum.
forum1.xml	Sample message forum.
formatting.xsl	Document for transforming message forums into HTML.
addPost.asp	Adds a message to a forum.
invalid.html	Used to display an error message.
site.css	Stylesheet for formatting HTML documents.

Fig. 15.1 Message forum documents.

The main page, **default.asp**, displays the list of available message forums, which is stored in the XML document **forums.xml**. Hyperlinks are provided to each XML message forum document and also to **addForum.asp**, which adds a forum to **forums.xml** and creates a new XML message forum (e.g., **forum2.xml**) using the message forum template **template.xml**.

Each XML message forum document (e.g., **forum1.xml**) is transformed into an HTML document using the XSLT document **formatting.xsl**. The CSS document **site.css** formats the HTML for display. New messages are posted to a forum by **addPost.asp**. If errors occur when the document is processed, **invalid.html** is displayed. Some of these key interactions between documents are illustrated in Fig. 15.2.

15.3 Forum Navigation

This section introduces the documents used for organizing and displaying the message forums. Figure 15.3 lists the XML document (**forums.xml**) that marks up each message forum.

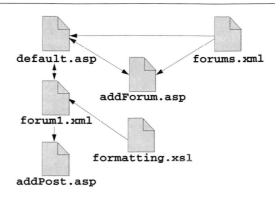

Fig. 15.2 Key interactions between message forum documents.

```
1    <?xml version = "1.0"?>
2
3    <!-- Fig. 15.3 : forums.xml -->
4
5    <forums>
6
7       <forum filename = "forum1.xml">
8          <name>Forum 1 Name</name>
9       </forum>
10
11   </forums>
```

Fig. 15.3   XML document that marks up the message forums.

Root element **forums** can hold any number of message forums. We provide an initial forum named **forum1.xml**. An individual message forum is marked up using element **forum**. Attribute **filename** stores the name of the XML document that contains the forum's markup. Child element **name** marks up the name of the forum, which is used as a hyperlink descriptor in **default.asp**. We will discuss how this XML document is manipulated momentarily.

Figure 15.4 shows the Active Server Page (**default.asp**) that displays the list of message forums contained in **forums.xml**. CSS document **site.css** is applied to the HTML sent to the Web browser. On line 1 we set the scripting language for the ASP page to **VBScript**. Although other languages may be used (e.g., JavaScript, Perl, etc.), VBScript is the most common language for ASP scripting.

```
1    <% @LANGUAGE = "VBScript" %>
2    <% Option Explicit %>
3
4    <% ' Fig. 15.4 : default.asp %>
5
6    <!DOCTYPE html
7       PUBLIC "-//W3C//DTD HTML 4.0//EN"
8       "http://www.w3.org/TR/REC-html40/strict.dtd">
9
10   <html>
11
12   <head>
13      <title>Deitel Message Forums</title>
14      <link rel = "stylesheet" type = "text/css" href = "site.css">
15   </head>
16
17   <body>
18      <h1>Deitel Message Forums</h1>
19      <p><strong>Available Forums</strong></p>
20      <ul>
21   <%
22      Dim xmlFile, xmlNodes, xmlItem
23      Dim strPath, strTitle, strFileName
```

Fig. 15.4   Message forums main page (part 1 of 2).

```
24
25        strPath = Server.MapPath( "forums.xml" )
26
27        Set xmlFile = Server.CreateObject( "Microsoft.XMLDOM" )
28        xmlFile.Async = False
29
30        If Not xmlFile.Load( strPath ) Then
31            Call Response.Redirect( "invalid.html" )
32        End If
33
34        Set xmlNodes = xmlFile.DocumentElement.ChildNodes
35
36        For Each xmlItem In xmlNodes
37            strFileName = xmlItem.getAttribute( "filename" )
38            strTitle = xmlItem.text
39    %>
40        <li>
41            <a href = "<% =strFileName %>"><% =strTitle %></a>
42        </li>
43    <%
44        Next
45    %>
46        </ul>
47
48        <p><strong>Forum Management</strong></p>
49
50        <ul>
51            <li><a href = "addForum.asp">Add a Forum</a></li>
52            <li>Delete a Forum</li>
53        </ul>
54
55    </body>
56
57    </html>
```

Fig. 15.4 Message forums main page (part 2 of 2).

Line 25

```
strPath = Server.MapPath( "forums.xml" )
```

gets the absolute path for the file **forums.xml** and stores it in variable **strPath**. Microsoft's XML parser (i.e., msxml) requires an absolute path.

Line 27

```
Set xmlFile = Server.CreateObject( "Microsoft.XMLDOM" )
```

calls the **Server** object's **CreateObject** method to instantiate a *DOMDocument* object (**Microsoft.XMLDOM**) and assigns the object to **xmlFile**. The **DOMDocument** object is the document root of an XML document.

Line 28

```
xmlFile.Async = False
```

sets the object referenced by **xmlFile** to behave *synchronously* (i.e., when a method is called, it must finish executing before any other method is allowed to execute). We will explain the significance of setting **Async** to **False** momentarily.

Lines 30–32

```
If Not xmlFile.Load( strPath ) Then
    Call Response.Redirect( "invalid.html" )
End If
```

call method *Load* to parse the XML document (e.g., **forums.xml**). If parsing succeeded, **True** is returned; otherwise, **False** is returned. Because **xmlFile** is synchronous, execution does not continue until method **Load** completes. If method calls are not synchronous (i.e., they are *asynchronous*), execution continues despite the fact that the method may not have finished executing, which could result in *logic errors* (i.e., the code does not execute as intended). If parsing fails, we redirect the browser to **invalid.html**, which is discussed in Section 15.7.

Line 34

```
Set xmlNodes = xmlFile.DocumentElement.ChildNodes
```

uses property **DocumentElement** to get the root element's child nodes. Element nodes have property **ChildNodes**, which returns a *collection* (e.g., a list) of the element node's child nodes.

Lines 36–44 contain a **For Each** loop that iterates through all the nodes in the collection of child nodes stored in **xmlNodes**. Line 36

```
For Each xmlItem In xmlNodes
```

uses a **For Each** loop to iterate through each node referenced by **xmlNodes** and sets variable **xmlItem** to that node.

Line 37

```
strFileName = xmlItem.getAttribute( "filename" )
```

calls method **getAttribute** to get a forum's filename. This method returns the value of the node's **filename** attribute and assigns it to **strFileName**.
Line 38

```
strTitle = xmlItem.text
```

uses property **text** to return the node's text content, which is the forum's name.
Line 41

```
<a href = "<% =strFileName %>"><% =strTitle %></a>
```

writes, as an anchor, the value of **strFileName** and writes the value of **strTitle** to describe the anchor.

Line 51 provides a hyperlink to **addForum.asp**, which adds a new forum and is discussed in the next section. Line 52 is a placeholder for a link to delete forums, the process of which is left to the reader as an exercise.

15.4 Adding Forums

In this section, we discuss the documents used to add new forums. Each new forum created is based upon a template XML document named **template.xml** (Fig. 15.5).

This template document contains the bare components for a message forum. It contains a **stylesheet** element that references **formatting.xsl** (discussed in Fig. 15.8) and the root element **forum**. The Active Server Page (**addForum.asp**) that modifies the template document is presented in Fig. 15.6. [*Note:* Actually, the copy of the template document loaded into memory is modified and saved to disk with a different name.]

This Active Server Page performs two tasks: First, it displays the form that gets the new forum's information (lines 104–146). Second, it provides the script for creating the forum (lines 1–102). We will discuss the form for getting information first.
Line 115

```
<p><% =strError %></p>
```

writes **strError**'s content to the Web browser. Error messages, if they exist, are stored in **strError**.

Lines 117–154 create a form to post information back to **addForum.asp**. The form has fields for the forum name, forum filename, user name, first message title and first message text. The **Request** object is used to retrieve the submitted form's value.

```
1   <?xml version = "1.0"?>
2
3   <!-- Fig. 15.5 : template.xml -->
4   <?xml:stylesheet type = "text/xsl" href = "formatting.xsl"?>
5
6   <forum>
7   </forum>
```

Fig. 15.5 Template for message forum XML documents.

```
1   <% @LANGUAGE = "VBScript" %>
2   <% Option Explicit %>
3
4   <% ' Fig. 15.6 : addForum.asp %>
5
6   <%
7       Dim xmlFile, xmlRoot, xmlNode
8       Dim strTitle, strError, strPath
9
10      If Request( "submit" ) <> Empty Then
11
12          If Request( "name" ) <> Empty And _
13              Request( "filename" ) <> Empty And _
14              Request( "user" ) <> Empty And _
15              Request( "title" ) <> Empty And _
16              Request( "text" ) <> Empty Then
17
18              ' Lock application. No modifications but ours.
19              Call Application.Lock()
20
21              ' Creating a new XML file.
22              strPath = Server.MapPath( Request( "filename" ) )
23
24              Set xmlFile = Server.CreateObject( "Microsoft.XMLDOM" )
25              xmlFile.Async = False
26
27              If xmlFile.Load( strPath ) Then
28                  Call Application.Unlock()
29                  Call Response.Redirect( "invalid.html" )
30              End If
31
32              ' Set up the file.
33              Call xmlFile.Load( Server.MapPath( "template.xml" ) )
34
35              ' Get the root node.
36              Set xmlRoot = xmlFile.DocumentElement
37
38              ' Set the filename.
39              Call xmlRoot.SetAttribute( "filename", _
40                  Request( "filename" ) )
41
42              ' Create Name node.
43              Set xmlNode = xmlFile.CreateElement( "name" )
44              xmlNode.Text = Request( "name" )
45              Call xmlRoot.AppendChild( xmlNode )
46
47              ' Create first message.
48              Set xmlNode = xmlFile.CreateElement( "message" )
49              Call xmlNode.SetAttribute( "timestamp", Now & " EST" )
50              Call xmlRoot.AppendChild( xmlNode )
51
52              Set xmlRoot = xmlNode
53
```

Fig. 15.6   Page to add a forum (part 1 of 4).

```
54              ' Create user node.
55              Set xmlNode = xmlFile.CreateElement( "user" )
56              xmlNode.Text = Request( "user" )
57              Call xmlRoot.AppendChild( xmlNode )
58
59              ' Create title node.
60              Set xmlNode = xmlFile.CreateElement( "title" )
61              xmlNode.Text = Request( "title" )
62              Call xmlRoot.AppendChild( xmlNode )
63
64              ' Create text node.
65              Set xmlNode = xmlFile.CreateElement( "text" )
66              xmlNode.Text = Request( "text" )
67              Call xmlRoot.AppendChild( xmlNode )
68
69              Call xmlFile.Save( strPath ) ' Save the file.
70
71              ' Load XML file.
72              strPath = Server.MapPath( "forums.xml" )
73
74              Set xmlFile = Server.CreateObject( "Microsoft.XMLDOM" )
75              xmlFile.Async = False
76
77              If Not xmlFile.Load( strPath ) Then
78                 Call Application.Unlock()
79                 Call Response.Redirect( "invalid.html" )
80              End If
81
82              ' Get the root node.
83              Set xmlRoot = xmlFile.DocumentElement
84
85              ' Create Nodes.
86              Set xmlNode = xmlFile.CreateElement( "forum" )
87              Call xmlNode.SetAttribute( "filename", _
88                 Request( "filename" ) )
89              xmlNode.Text = Request( "name" )
90              Call xmlRoot.AppendChild( xmlNode )
91
92              Call xmlFile.Save( strPath ) ' Save the file.
93
94              ' Finished processing.
95              Call Application.Unlock()
96              Call Response.Redirect( "default.asp" )
97           Else
98              strError = "ERROR: Invalid input."
99           End If
100
101       End If
102   %>
103
104   <!DOCTYPE html
105       PUBLIC "-//W3C//DTD HTML 4.0//EN"
106       "http://www.w3.org/TR/REC-html40/strict.dtd">
```

Fig. 15.6 Page to add a forum (part 2 of 4).

```
107
108  <html>
109  <head>
110     <title>Add a Forum</title>
111     <link rel = "stylesheet" TYPE = "text/css" href = "site.css">
112  </head>
113
114  <body>
115     <p><% =strError %></p>
116
117     <form method = "POST" action = "addForum.asp">
118
119        <p>
120           Forum Name:<br />
121           <input type = "text" size = "40" name = "name"
122              value = "<% =Request( "name" ) %>">
123        </p>
124
125        <p>
126           Forum File Name:<br />
127           <input type = "text" size = "40" name = "filename"
128              value = "<% =Request( "filename" ) %>">
129        </p>
130
131        <p>
132           User:<br />
133           <input type = "text" size = "40" name = "user"
134              value = "<% =Request( "user" ) %>">
135        </p>
136
137        <p>
138           Message Title:<br />
139           <input type = "text" size = "40" name = "title"
140              value = "<% =Request( "title" ) %>">
141        </p>
142
143        <p>
144           Message Text:<br />
145           <textarea name = "text" cols = "40"
146              rows = "4"><% =Request( "text" ) %></textarea>
147        </p>
148
149        <p>
150           <input type = "submit" name = "submit" value = "Submit">
151           <input type = "Reset" value = "Clear">
152        </p>
153
154     </form>
155
156     <p>
157        <a href = "default.asp">Return to Main Page</a>
158     </p>
159
```

Fig. 15.6   Page to add a forum (part 3 of 4).

```
160  </body>
161
162  </html>
```

Fig. 15.6 Page to add a forum (part 4 of 4).

We will now discuss the script logic for the page. Line 10

```
If Request( "submit" ) <> Empty Then
```

checks if the form was submitted by testing the form's **submit** field for a value. If the **submit** field is **Empty**, then the form was not submitted.

Lines 12–16 check the form's fields for values. If any of the fields are **Empty**, the information for the new forum is incomplete, and line 98

```
strError = "ERROR: Invalid input."
```

sets **strError** to **"ERROR: Invalid input."**.

Line 19

```
Call Application.Lock()
```

calls **Application** method **Lock** to prevent another instance of this script from executing simultaneously. Simultaneous execution can occur when one client is executing the script and another client requests the same document. This type of behavior creates problems for scripts that access files.

Lines 27–30 attempt to load the file specified by the user. If the file successfully loads, then the file already exists, so we redirect to **invalid.html**. Remember, we want to add a new forum, not open an existing one.

Line 33

```
Call xmlFile.Load( Server.MapPath( "template.xml" ) )
```

loads the template XML document (i.e., **template.xml**). We will mark up the form's data and add the data to the in-memory representation of **template.xml**.

Lines 39 and 40

```
Call xmlRoot.SetAttribute( "filename", _
    Request( "filename" ) )
```

call method **SetAttribute** to create an attribute node named **filename** that has the value contained in form field **filename**. If the attribute specified does not exist in the document, it is automatically created.

Line 43

```
Set xmlNode = xmlFile.CreateElement( "name" )
```

creates a new element node named **name** using **DOMDocument** method **CreateElement**. New nodes (i.e., elements, attributes, etc.) can be created only by the document root.

Line 44

```
xmlNode.Text = Request( "name" )
```

assigns form field **name**'s value to the element node's (created in line 43) **Text** property.

Line 45

```
Call xmlRoot.AppendChild( xmlNode )
```

uses method **AppendChild** to append the newly created element **name** node to the root element (i.e., **forum**).

Lines 48–50 create and append element **message**, along with attribute **timestamp**, to the root element **forum**. Lines 55–57 create and append element **user** to element **message**. Lines 60–62 create and append element **title**, and lines 65–67 create and append element **text**, to the root element.

Line 69

```
Call xmlFile.Save( strPath ) ' Save the file.
```

saves the XML document to disk by calling method **Save**. Variable **strPath** contains the filename provided by the user in line 22.

Lines 72–92 open, modify and save **forums.xml**. Line 95

```
Call Application.Unlock()
```

unlocks the script so that other pages can execute it.

15.5 Forum XML Documents

This section presents a sample forum (Fig. 15.7) that contains several messages and the XSLT document (Fig. 15.8) that transforms it into HTML.

```
1   <?xml version = "1.0"?>
2
3   <!-- Fig. 15.7 : forum1.xml -->
4
5   <?xml:stylesheet type = "text/xsl" href = "formatting.xsl"?>
6
7   <forum file = "forum1.xml">
8
9      <name>Forum 1 Name</name>
10
11     <message timestamp = "06/28/00 14:22">
12        <user>Person1</user>
13        <title>Title One</title>
14        <text>Text of message of Title One</text>
15     </message>
16
17     <message timestamp = "06/29/00 14:22">
18        <user>Person2</user>
19        <title>Title Two</title>
20        <text>Text of message of Title Two</text>
21     </message>
22
23     <message timestamp = "06/29/00 14:28">
24        <user>Person1</user>
25        <title>Title Three</title>
26        <text>Text of message of Title <em>Three</em></text>
27     </message>
28
29   </forum>
```

Fig. 15.7 Sample forum.

```
1    <?xml version = "1.0"?>
2
3    <!-- Fig. 15.8 : formatting.xsl -->
4
5    <xsl:stylesheet version = "1.0"
6       xmlns:xsl = "http://www.w3.org/TR/WD-xsl">
7
8       <xsl:template match = "/">
9          <html>
10         <xsl:apply-templates select = "*"/>
11         </html>
12      </xsl:template>
13
```

Fig. 15.8 XSLT to transform XML forum document into HTML (part 1 of 3).

```
14     <xsl:template match = "forum">
15
16        <head>
17           <title><xsl:value-of select = "name"/></title>
18           <link rel = "stylesheet" type = "text/css"
19              href = "site.css"/>
20        </head>
21
22        <body>
23
24           <table width = "100%" cellspacing = "0"
25              cellpadding = "2">
26              <tr>
27                 <td class = "forumTitle">
28                    <xsl:value-of select = "name" />
29                 </td>
30              </tr>
31           </table>
32           <xsl:apply-templates select = "message" />
33
34           <p>
35              <a>
36                 <xsl:attribute
37                    name = "href">addPost.asp?file=<xsl:value-of
38                    select = "@file" />
39                    </xsl:attribute>
40                 Post a Message</a><br />
41              <a href = "default.asp">Return to Main Page</a>
42           </p>
43
44        </body>
45
46     </xsl:template>
47
48     <xsl:template match = "message">
49
50        <table width = "100%" cellspacing = "0"
51           cellpadding = "2">
52
53           <tr>
54              <td class = "msgTitle">
55                 <xsl:value-of select = "title"/>
56              </td>
57           </tr>
58
59           <tr>
60              <td class = "msgInfo">
61                 by
62                 <em><xsl:value-of select = "user"/></em>
63                 at
64                 <span class = "date">
65                    <xsl:value-of select = "@timestamp"/>
66                 </span>
```

Fig. 15.8   XSLT to transform XML forum document into HTML (part 2 of 3).

```
67                    </td>
68                 </tr>
69
70                 <tr>
71                    <td class = "msgText">
72                       <xsl:apply-templates select = "text"/>
73                    </td>
74                 </tr>
75
76           </table>
77
78        </xsl:template>
79
80   </xsl:stylesheet>
```

Fig. 15.8   XSLT to transform XML forum document into HTML (part 3 of 3).

Lines 5 and 6 (Fig. 15.8)

```
<xsl:stylesheet version = "1.0"
   xmlns:xsl = "http://www.w3.org/TR/WD-xsl">
```

use a different XSL namespace than the one presented in Chapter 12. Internet Explorer uses the URI **http://www.w3.org/TR/WD-xsl** for processing of XSL documents. We use this namespace because Internet Explorer does not support the newer, XSLT namespace.

Figure 15.9 shows the result of the transformation of **forum1.xml**. Line 67

```
<a href = "addPost.asp?file=forum1.xml">Post a Message</a>
```

```
1    <html>
2
3    <head>
4       <title>Forum 1 Name</title>
5       <link href = "site.css" type = "text/css" rel = "stylesheet">
6    </head>
7
8    <body>
9       <table cellpadding = "2" cellspacing = "0" width = "100%">
10         <tr>
11            <td class = "forumTitle">Forum 1 Name</td>
12         </tr>
13      </table>
14
15      <table cellpadding = "2" cellspacing = "0" width = "100%">
16         <tr>
17            <td class = "msgTitle">Title One</td>
18         </tr>
19         <tr>
```

Fig. 15.9   Output of the transformation of the forum XML document (part 1 of 3).

```
20          <td class = "msgInfo">
21              by
22              <em>Person1</em>
23              at
24              <span class = "date">06/28/00 14:22</span>
25          </td>
26       </tr>
27       <tr>
28          <td class = "msgText">Text of message of Title One</td>
29       </tr>
30    </table>
31
32    <table cellpadding = "2" cellspacing = "0" width = "100%">
33       <tr>
34          <td class = "msgTitle">Title Two</td>
35       </tr>
36       <tr>
37          <td class = "msgInfo">
38              by
39              <em>Person2</em>
40              at
41              <span class = "date">06/29/00 14:22</span>
42          </td>
43       </tr>
44       <tr>
45          <td class = "msgText">Text of message of Title Two</td>
46       </tr>
47    </table>
48
49    <table cellpadding = "2" cellspacing = "0" width = "100%">
50       <tr>
51          <td class = "msgTitle">Title Three</td>
52       </tr>
53       <tr>
54          <td class = "msgInfo">
55              by
56              <em>Person1</em>
57              at
58              <span class = "date">06/29/00 14:28</span>
59          </td>
60       </tr>
61       <tr>
62          <td class = "msgText">Text of message of Title Three</td>
63       </tr>
64    </table>
65
66    <p>
67       <a href = "addPost.asp?file=forum1.xml">Post a Message</a>
68       <br>
69       <a href = "default.asp">Return to Main Page</a>
70    </p>
71  </body>
72
73  </html>
```

Fig. 15.9   Output of the transformation of the forum XML document (part 2 of 3).

Fig. 15.9 Output of the transformation of the forum XML document (part 3 of 3).

provides a link to **addPost.asp**, along with the name of the file to which the new message will be added.

15.6 Posting Messages

In this section, we present the ASP document **addPost.asp** (Fig. 15.10), which posts messages to a forum. This ASP uses much of the same functionality that **addForum.asp** uses.

Lines 25–28 load the forum XML document. Lines 34–36 create a **message** element and an associated **timestamp** attribute. Lines 41–43 create child element **user**; lines 46–48 create child element **title** and lines 51–53 create child element **text** for element **message**. Finally, the forum is saved to disk in line 55.

15.7 Other HTML Documents

In this section, we present two other documents used in the case study. Figure 15.11 lists the HTML document that displays error messages (**invalid.html**).

```
1   <% @LANGUAGE = "VBScript" %>
2   <% Option Explicit %>
3
```

Fig. 15.10 Adding a message to a forum (part 1 of 4).

```
4    <% ' Fig. 15.10 : addPost.asp %>
5
6    <%
7        Dim xmlFile, xmlRoot, xmlNode
8        Dim strTitle, strError, strPath
9
10       If Request( "submit" ) <> Empty Then
11
12          If Request( "file" ) <> Empty And _
13              Request( "user" ) <> Empty And _
14              Request( "title" ) <> Empty And _
15              Request( "text" ) <> Empty Then
16
17              ' Lock application. No modifications but ours.
18              Call Application.Lock()
19
20              strPath = Server.MapPath( Request( "file" ) )
21
22              Set xmlFile = Server.CreateObject( "Microsoft.XMLDOM" )
23              xmlFile.Async = False
24
25              If Not xmlFile.Load( strPath ) Then
26                  Call Application.Unlock()
27                  Call Response.Redirect( "invalid.html" )
28              End If
29
30              ' Get the root node.
31              Set xmlRoot = xmlFile.DocumentElement
32
33              ' Create first message.
34              Set xmlNode = xmlFile.CreateElement( "message" )
35              Call xmlNode.SetAttribute( "timestamp", Now & " EST" )
36              Call xmlRoot.AppendChild( xmlNode )
37
38              Set xmlRoot = xmlNode
39
40              ' Create user node.
41              Set xmlNode = xmlFile.CreateElement( "user" )
42              xmlNode.Text = Request( "user" )
43              Call xmlRoot.AppendChild( xmlNode )
44
45              ' Create title node.
46              Set xmlNode = xmlFile.CreateElement( "title" )
47              xmlNode.Text = Request( "title" )
48              Call xmlRoot.AppendChild( xmlNode )
49
50              ' Create text node.
51              Set xmlNode = xmlFile.CreateElement( "text" )
52              xmlNode.Text = Request( "text" )
53              Call xmlRoot.AppendChild( xmlNode )
54
55              Call xmlFile.Save( strPath ) ' Save the file.
56
```

Fig. 15.10 Adding a message to a forum (part 2 of 4).

```
57                ' Finished processing.
58                Call Application.Unlock()
59                Call Response.Redirect( Request( "file" ) )
60           Else
61                strError = "ERROR: Invalid input."
62           End If
63
64      End If
65   %>
66
67   <!DOCTYPE html
68       PUBLIC "-//W3C//DTD HTML 4.0//EN"
69       "http://www.w3.org/TR/REC-html40/strict.dtd">
70
71   <html>
72   <head>
73      <title>Post a Message</title>
74      <link rel = "stylesheet" type = "text/css" href = "site.css">
75   </head>
76
77   <body>
78      <p><% =strError %></p>
79
80      <form method = "POST" action = "addPost.asp">
81         <p>
82            User:<br />
83            <input type = "text" size = "40" name = "user"
84               value = "<% =Request( "user" ) %>">
85         </p>
86         <p>
87            Message Title:<br />
88            <input type = "text" size = "40" name = "title"
89               value = "<% =Request( "title" ) %>">
90         </p>
91         <p>
92            Message Text:<br />
93            <textarea name = "text" cols = "40"
94               rows = "4"><% =Request( "text" ) %></textarea>
95         </p>
96         <p>
97            <input type = "hidden" name = "file"
98               value = "<% =Request( "file" ) %>">
99            <input type = "submit" name = "submit" value = "Submit">
100           <input type = "Reset" value = "Clear">
101        </p>
102     </form>
103
104     <p>
105        <a href = "<% =Request( "file" ) %>">Return to Forum</a>
106     </p>
107  </body>
108
109  </html>
```

Fig. 15.10 Adding a message to a forum (part 3 of 4).

Fig. 15.10 Adding a message to a forum (part 4 of 4).

Figure 15.12 lists the cascading stylesheet document used to format the HTML documents (**site.css**).

```
1   <!DOCTYPE html
2      PUBLIC "-//W3C//DTD HTML 4.0//EN"
3      "http://www.w3.org/TR/REC-html40/strict.dtd">
4
5   <html>
6
7   <!-- Fig. 15.11 : invalid.html -->
8
9   <head>
10     <title>Deitel Book Organization</title>
11     <link rel = "stylesheet" type = "text/css" href = "site.css">
12   </head>
13
14   <body>
15      <h1>Invalid Request.</h1>
16      <p>
17         <a href = "default.asp">Return to Main Page</a>
18      </p>
19   </body>
20
21   </html>
```

Fig. 15.11 Document showing that an error has occurred.

```
1    /* Fig. 15.12 : site.css */
2
3    BODY
4    {
5       background: white;
6       color: black;
7       font-family: Arial, sans-serif;
8       font-size: 10pt;
9    }
10
11   A
12   {
13      background: transparent;
14      color: blue;
15      text-decoration: none;
16   }
17
18   A:hover
19   {
20      text-decoration: underline;
21   }
22
23   TABLE
24   {
25      border-width: 1px;
26      border-style: solid;
27   }
28
29   .forumTitle
30   {
31      background: lime;
32      color: black;
33      font-size: 12pt;
34      font-weight: bold;
35      text-align: center;
36   }
37
38   .msgTitle
39   {
40      background: silver;
41      color: black;
42      font-size: 10pt;
43      font-weight: bold;
44   }
45
46   .msgInfo
47   {
48      background: silver;
49      color: black;
50      font-size: 10pt;
51   }
52
```

Fig. 15.12 CSS document for HTML pages (part 1 of 2).

```
53   .msgPost
54   {
55      background: silver;
56      color: black;
57      font-size: 8pt;
58   }
59
60   .msgText
61   {
62      font-size: 10pt;
63      padding-left: 10px;
64   }
65
66   .date
67   {
68      font-size: 8pt;
69   }
```

Fig. 15.12 CSS document for HTML pages (part 2 of 2).

15.8 Internet and World Wide Web Resources

**msdn.microsoft.com/workshop/c-frame.htm?/workshop/server/asp/
ASP-over.asp**
This Web site is arguably the best ASP resource on the Web. This page, part of the *Microsoft Developers Network* , provides an introduction to ASP technologies.

msdn.microsoft.com/workshop/server/asp/asptutorial.asp
This site is the starting page of an ASP tutorial provided by the *Microsoft Developers Network* . It is one of the most comprehensive ASP tutorials on the Web.

support.microsoft.com/support/default.asp?SD=SO&PR=asp
This site, located on the *Microsoft Personal Online Support Network* , should be your first stop when you are having trouble or when you are just curious about an aspect of ASP. In addition to providing links to other useful help sites, the site also includes a collection of links to ASP technical resources.

html.about.com/compute/html/msubasp.htm
This page has a listing of links to many ASP-related resources on the Web. The site's links range from FAQs pages to tutorials to descriptions of more advanced aspects of ASP. The page is a good place to start if you are interested in finding out more about specific ASP-related technologies.

www.w3schools.com/asp
This site is the home of a number of comprehensive ASP tutorials. Topic categories range from ASP objects to general syntax usage. The page is a great place to go to if you are unclear on any individual aspect of ASP programming. Examples are provided at this site.

www.w3scripts.com/asp
This site is the home page of an ASP script repository written to teach different aspects of ASP programming. All script example screens are split into two parts: the script being demonstrated and the script's output. It is an extremely useful site for all levels of ASP programmers.

TERMINOLOGY

Application object
Async property

asynchronous
collection

CreateElement method
CreateObject method
DOMDocument object
Load method
Lock method
MapPath method of **Server** object

Request method
Save method
Server object
synchronous
Unlock method

SELF-REVIEW EXERCISES

15.1   What purpose does the **Async** property of a **DOMDocument** object serve?

15.2   To create child element nodes for elements in an XML document, what needs to be done?

ANSWERS TO SELF-REVIEW EXERCISES

15.1   The **Async** property is used to set the execution type of **DOMDocument** methods. If **Async** is set to **True**, methods are performed asynchronously, so execution continues even if the method call was not completed. If **Async** is set to **False**, methods are performed synchronously, so execution waits until the method call is completed.

15.2   To create element nodes, call **DOMDocument** object's method **CreateElement**, with the name of the element to be created as a parameter. Next, method **appendChild** is called on the element to which the new element is to be a child, with the child element as the parameter.

EXERCISES

15.3   Create an Active Server Page to delete messages from a forum. This ASP should take a forum's filename and the timestamp of the message as form arguments. Modify **formatting.xsl** to provide a link to the ASP for each message. [*Hint* : To remove an element's child, use **removeChild**, with the node to remove as a parameter.]

15.4   Create an Active Server Page to delete forums. This ASP should list the available forums and allow the user to select one for deletion.

16

Server-side Java Programming

Objectives

- To understand server-side technologies based on XML.
- To be able to use Cocoon to deliver specialized content to different browsers using XSL.
- To be able to use Extensible Server Pages (XSP) and Java to handle user input.
- To be able to use Java servlets and the DOM to dynamically build XML documents.
- To understand how Java servlets, XML, XSL and Wireless Markup Language (WML) can be used together to create a wireless e-business application.

A deck of cards was built like the purest of hierarchies...
Ely Culbertson

16.1 Introduction

In this chapter we introduce three technologies that take advantage of XML to deliver Web content. We first introduce the Apache Group's Web publishing framework Cocoon. In our first example we take advantage of Cocoon's XSL capabilities to dynamically deliver Web content to different types of clients, including Web browsers, such as Netscape Communicator and Internet Explorer, and wireless devices, such as digital cellular phones. In our second example, we use Cocoon's XML-based scripting technology—Extensible Server Pages (XSP)—to perform a user survey.

Also included in this chapter is a case study in which we build a wireless online bookstore using Java servlets, XML, XSL and wireless markup language (WML). WML is part of the wireless applications protocol (WAP) and is used to deliver Web content to cellular phones and other wireless devices.

16.2 Cocoon

Throughout the history of the Web, delivering content to different Web browsers has been problematic. Because of a lack of adherence to a standard for HTML early on in the Web's development, different Web browsers supported different sets of tags in HTML pages. Web pages that appeared one way in one Web browser would often look very different when displayed in another Web browser. In the past few years there have been a number of standards defined for HTML, however, the most popular Web browsers still differ in a number of respects and often display Web pages differently. To solve the problem of having a Web site appear differently on each browser, Web site developers began detecting which browser was requesting a Web page so that a page with appropriate tags could be delivered. This, of course, meant developing at least two versions of the same content, one for each of the most popular Web browsers.

Cocoon takes advantage of XML technologies to enable content creators and Web developers to deliver the same content to any type of client without the need to create multiple versions of their Web sites. Cocoon separates the Web publishing process into three steps: XML creation, XML processing and XSL rendering. In this framework, the content for a site is marked up using XML. The XML data are then processed and formatted for display using XSL transformations and formatting objects. Each type of client has an associated XSL style sheet, so the XSL transformation is performed based on the type of client that made the request. In older HTML applications, formatting, fonts, colors and other elements of presentation were mixed in with the data. Using XSL to transform and format XML data allows content creators to generate pure content without worrying about presentation.

Cocoon uses Java technologies along with XML and XSL. Notes on installation can be found at **xml.apache.org/cocoon/index.html**. In Fig. 16.1 we show our content marked up with XML. In this example our content consists of the message (line 10)

Welcome to XML!

The processing instruction on line 2 instructs Cocoon to use its XSLT processor to process this document before delivering it to the client. The processing instruction on line 3 specifies **welcome.xsl** as the default style sheet to use with the XSLT processor. This style sheet will be used to transform the document for all clients except those for which a specific style sheet is defined. On lines 4 and 5 we instruct the XSLT processor to use the **welcome-wml.xsl** style sheet for WAP devices.

Figure 16.2 lists the types of clients that Cocoon is pre-configured to detect using the *media* attribute, shown in line 5 of Fig 16.1.

Figure 16.3 lists the default XSL style sheet used to render our content. This style sheet transforms the original XML document into an HTML document for display in a browser.

```
1   <?xml version = "1.0"?>
2   <?cocoon-process type = "xslt"?>
3   <?xml-stylesheet href = "welcome.xsl" type = "text/xsl"?>
4   <?xml-stylesheet href = "welcome-wml.xsl"
5      type = "text/xsl" media = "wap"?>
6
7   <!-- Fig. 16.1 : welcome.xml -->
8
9   <myMessage>
10     <message>Welcome to XML!</message>
11  </myMessage>
```

Fig. 16.1 XML document to be processed by Cocoon.

Media type	Browser
explorer	Microsoft Internet Explorer browser.
opera	Opera browser.
lynx	Lynx browser.
java	Java code using standard URL classes.
wap	Nokia WAP Toolkit browser.
netscape	Netscape Communicator browser.

Fig. 16.2 Cocoon's media types for various browsers.

```
1    <?xml version = "1.0"?>
2
3    <!-- Fig. 16.3 : welcome.xsl -->
4
5    <xsl:stylesheet
6        xmlns:xsl = "http://www.w3.org/1999/XSL/Transform"
7        version = "1.0">
8
9        <xsl:template match = "myMessage">
10           <html>
11               <head>
12                   <title><xsl:value-of select = "message"/></title>
13               </head>
14
15               <body bgcolor = "cyan">
16                   <xsl:apply-templates select = "message"/>
17                   <p>This page has been transformed
18                       from XML into HTML by Cocoon's XSLT processor.
19                   </p>
20               </body>
21
22           </html>
23       </xsl:template>
24
25       <xsl:template match = "message">
26           <h1>
27               <xsl:apply-templates/>
28           </h1>
29       </xsl:template>
30   </xsl:stylesheet>
```

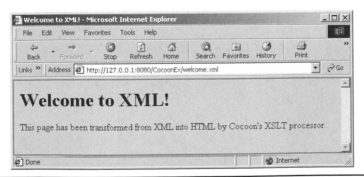

Fig. 16.3 Style sheet to render `welcome.xml`.

In Fig. 16.4 we present the XSL style sheet **welcome-wml.xsl**, which is used to transform the XML content into WML for display on a wireless device, such as a cellular phone. WML places multiple pages of content into a *deck*. Each deck is composed of one or more *cards*, which each contain a page of content. In this example we only have a single page of information, which is contained in the **card** on lines 15–26. On line 17 the **p** element begins a new paragraph, into which we place the text of the **message** element from the original XML document. On lines 21–24 there is another **p** element that contains text describing how the original XML document was transformed. The output from this style sheet is also shown in a wireless device simulator in Fig. 16.4. We will show how to use this simulator for testing wireless applications in the case study later in this chapter.

```
1   <?xml version = "1.0"?>
2
3   <!-- Fig. 16.4 : welcome-wml.xsl -->
4
5   <xsl:stylesheet
6      xmlns:xsl = "http://www.w3.org/1999/XSL/Transform"
7      version = "1.0">
8
9      <xsl:template match = "myMessage">
10         <xsl:processing-instruction name = "cocoon-format">
11            type = "text/wml"
12         </xsl:processing-instruction>
13
14         <wml>
15            <card>
16
17               <p>
18                  <xsl:value-of select = "message"/>
19               </p>
20
21               <p>
22                  This page has been transformed
23                  from XML into WML by Cocoon's XSLT processor.
24               </p>
25
26            </card>
27         </wml>
28      </xsl:template>
29   </xsl:stylesheet>
```

Fig. 16.4 `welcome-wml.xsl`.

16.3 Extensible Server Pages (XSP)

Cocoon also includes a processor for *Extensible Server Page* (XSP), part of the Apache Cocoon Project. XSPs are similar to JavaServer Pages™ and ASP, allowing programming code to be included within markup for processing on the server. Figure 16.5 lists some of the tags available in XSP along with their descriptions.

We present an example that uses XSP to perform a survey. The client is first sent an HTML page with a form asking their favorite color. This HTML page is the result of XSLT processing of **survey.xml** (Fig. 16.6) with style sheet **survey.xsl** (Fig. 16.7). When the client clicks **Submit**, a **POST** request is sent to the server. Figure 16.8 (**response.xml**) is an XSP document used to generate a response to this **POST** request, updating the survey results. The survey results are stored in an XML document on the server—**colors.xml**—containing

```
<colors total = "0">
    <color name = "Red" votes = "0"/>
    <color name = "Blue" votes = "0"/>
    <color name = "Green" votes = "0"/>
    <color name = "Yellow" votes = "0"/>
    <color name = "Purple" votes = "0"/>
</colors>
```

After XSP processing, XML similar to

```
<survey title = "Color survey">
    <total>23</total>
    <color value = "Red" percentage = "26.09%"/>
    <color value = "Blue" percentage = "17.39%"/>
    <color value = "Green" percentage = "30.43%"/>
    <color value = "Yellow" percentage = "8.70%"/>
    <color value = "Purple" percentage = "17.39%"/>
</survey>
```

XSP element	Description
xsp:page	This is the root element for every XSP page; specify the coding language to be used with the **language** attribute. Any tag libraries should be specified within this element as well.
xsp:structure	This element contains program-level code declarations, such as **<xsp:include>**.
xsp:include	This element is used to include a predefined package in a language-dependent manner; for example, if the coding language has been specified as Java, this element **import**s a package.
xsp:logic	Program code in the specified language is included within this element.
xsp:content	Within **<xsp:logic>**, XML content is embedded so that no further nested **<xsp:logic>** elements are needed.
xsp:expr	This element is used to include a program expression.

Fig. 16.5 XSP elements (part 1 of 2).

XSP element	Description
xsp:element	This element dynamically creates an XML element.
xsp:attribute	This element sets an attribute of the enclosing XML element.
xsp:pi	Processing instructions are included with this element.
xsp:comment	This element embeds an XML comment.

Fig. 16.5 XSP elements (part 2 of 2).

is passed to Cocoon to be transformed with style sheet **response.xsl**. Cocoon uses the XSLT processor to send an HTML page containing the results of the survey back to the browser client.

```
1   <?xml version = "1.0"?>
2   <?cocoon-process type = "xslt"?>
3   <?xml-stylesheet href = "survey.xsl" type = "text/xsl"?>
4
5   <!-- Fig. 16.6 : survey.xml -->
6
7   <page title = "Color survey">
8      <color>Red</color>
9      <color>Blue</color>
10     <color>Green</color>
11     <color>Yellow</color>
12     <color>Purple</color>
13  </page>
```

Fig. 16.6 XML document with color choices.

```
14  <?xml version = "1.0"?>
15
16  <!-- Fig. 16.7 : survey.xsl -->
17
18  <xsl:stylesheet
19     xmlns:xsl = "http://www.w3.org/1999/XSL/Transform"
20     version = "1.0">
21
22     <xsl:template match = "page">
23        <html>
24           <head>
25              <title>
26                 <xsl:value-of select = "@title"/>
27              </title>
28           </head>
29           <body bgcolor = "cyan">
30              <h1>
31                 <xsl:value-of select = "@title"/>
32              </h1>
```

Fig. 16.7 Style sheet to present color choices as HTML (part 1 of 2).

```
33                    <b>What is your favorite color?</b>
34                    <form method = "post"
35                        action =
36                            "http://127.0.0.1:8080/CocoonEx/response.xml">
37
38                        <xsl:apply-templates select = "color"/>
39                        <input type = "submit" value = "Submit"/>
40                    </form>
41                </body>
42            </html>
43        </xsl:template>
44
45        <xsl:template match = "color">
46            <input type = "radio" name = "color">
47                <xsl:attribute name = "value">
48                    <xsl:value-of select = "."/>
49                </xsl:attribute>
50            </input>
51            <xsl:value-of select = "."/>
52            <br/>
53        </xsl:template>
54    </xsl:stylesheet>
```

Fig. 16.7   Style sheet to present color choices as HTML (part 2 of 2).

```
55    <?xml version = "1.0"?>
56    <?cocoon-process type = "xsp"?>
57    <?cocoon-process type = "xslt"?>
58    <?xml-stylesheet href = "response.xsl" type = "text/xsl"?>
```

Fig. 16.8   XML document containing the logic to retrieve survey statistics (part 1 of 4).

```
59
60   <!-- Fig. 16.8 : response.xml -->
61
62   <xsp:page language = "java"
63      xmlns:xsp = "http://www.apache.org/1999/XSP/Core">
64
65      <xsp:structure>
66         <xsp:include>java.text.*</xsp:include>
67         <xsp:include>org.apache.xerces.parsers.*</xsp:include>
68         <xsp:include>org.apache.xml.serialize.*</xsp:include>
69      </xsp:structure>
70
71      <xsp:logic>
72         private Document colors = inputColors();
73         private int total = Integer.parseInt(
74            colors.getDocumentElement().getAttribute( "total" ) );
75         NodeList colorElements =
76            colors.getDocumentElement().
77            getElementsByTagName( "color" );
78
79         private Document inputColors()
80         {
81            try {
82               InputSource input =
83                  new InputSource( new FileInputStream(
84                     "../webapps/CocoonEx/colors.xml" ) );
85               DOMParser domParser = new DOMParser();
86
87               domParser.parse( input );
88               return domParser.getDocument();
89            }
90            catch ( Exception e ) {
91               e.printStackTrace();
92               return null;
93            }
94         }
95
96         private Element getColorElement( String color )
97         {
98            for ( int i = 0; i &lt; colorElements.getLength(); i++ ) {
99               Element current = ( Element ) colorElements.item( i );
100
101               if ( current.getAttribute( "name" ).equals( color ) )
102                  return current;
103
104            }
105            return null;
106         }
107
108         private String getPercentage( String color )
109         {
110            if ( total == 0 )
111               return "No entries yet";
```

Fig. 16.8   XML document containing the logic to retrieve survey statistics (part 2 of 4).

```
112            else {
113                int votes = Integer.parseInt(
114                    getColorElement( color ).getAttribute( "votes" ) );
115                double percentage = 100.0 * votes / total;
116
117                return
118                    new DecimalFormat( "#0.00" ).format( percentage )
119                    + "%";
120            }
121        }
122
123        private void updateSurvey( String voteColor )
124        {
125            // update total number of votes
126            ++total;
127            colors.getDocumentElement().setAttribute(
128                "total", Integer.toString( total ) );
129
130            // update number of votes for voted color
131            Element votedColorElement = getColorElement( voteColor );
132            int votes = Integer.parseInt(
133                votedColorElement.getAttribute( "votes" ) ) + 1;
134
135            votedColorElement.setAttribute(
136                "votes", Integer.toString( votes ) );
137
138            // save XML file
139            try {
140                XMLSerializer serializer = new XMLSerializer(
141                    new FileOutputStream(
142                        "../webapps/CocoonEx/colors.xml" ),
143                    null );
144
145                serializer.serialize( colors );
146            }
147            catch ( Exception e ) {
148                e.printStackTrace();
149            }
150        }
151    </xsp:logic>
152
153    <survey title = "Color survey">
154        <xsp:logic>
155            String vote = request.getParameter( "color" );
156            updateSurvey( vote );
157
158            // create total element to hold total number of votes
159            <total><xsp:expr>total</xsp:expr></total>
160
161            // create a new color element for each color
162            for ( int i = 0; i &lt; colorElements.getLength(); i++ ) {
163                Element current = ( Element ) colorElements.item( i );
164                String colorName = current.getAttribute( "name" );
```

Fig. 16.8   XML document containing the logic to retrieve survey statistics (part 3 of 4).

```
165                <color>
166                    <xsp:attribute name = "value">
167                        <xsp:expr>colorName</xsp:expr>
168                    </xsp:attribute>
169                    <xsp:attribute name = "percentage">
170                        <xsp:expr>getPercentage( colorName )</xsp:expr>
171                    </xsp:attribute>
172                </color>
173            }
174        </xsp:logic>
175    </survey>
176 </xsp:page>
```

Fig. 16.8 XML document containing the logic to retrieve survey statistics (part 4 of 4).

XSP page **response.xml** (Fig. 16.8) processes the client's **POST** request. The root element of every XSP page is **xsp:page** (line 62). Attribute **language** specifies that the programming language used is Java. Line 65 uses XSP tag **xsp:structure**. This tag contains top-level code declarations such as **xsp:include**. Lines 66–68 use **xsp:include** tags to **import** Java packages. We **import** packages that allow us to input and output XML documents.

We embed all Java code in the **xsp:logic** element. Note that since this is an XML document, we must use the **<** entity instead of **<** in lines 98 and 162. Within the first **xsp:logic** element (lines 71–151), we define methods to manipulate the XML document storing the results of the survey. Method **inputColors** uses the **DOMParser** object from package **org.apache.xerces.parsers** to parse **colors.xml** and create **Document** object **colors** in memory.

Method **getColorElement** (lines 96–106) **return**s the **color** element corresponding to the parameter **String color**. This method uses a **for** loop to iterate through the **NodeList colorElements**, returning the element whose **name** attribute is **color**.

We use method **getPercentage** to calculate the percentage of votes the specified **color** has received. First, we retrieve the **color** element corresponding to **color** by using method **getColorElement**. We then access the **votes** attribute, which contains the total number of **votes** this **color** has received. Line 115 calculates the **percentage**, and lines 117–119 create an instance of class **DecimalFormat** (from package **java.text**) to **return** the **percentage**, formatted to two decimal places, as a **String**.

Lines 123–150 define method **updateSurvey**, which is used to update **colors.xml** to reflect the client's vote. First we increment variable **total** by **1** (line 126); then we update attribute **total** of root element **colors**. In lines 131 and 132, we access the voted **color** element and its **votes** attribute, incrementing local variable **votes** by **1** on lines 135–136. We then save the XML document, using a new instance of class **XMLSerializer** (from package **org.apache.xml.serialize**).

We create the root element **survey** of the XML document that is the target of XSP processing. Using another **xsp:logic** element, we embed Java code to create the child elements of root element **survey**. First, we retrieve the client's **vote** using the **request** object. The **request** object is Cocoon's wrapper for the **HttpServletRequest** object. We then call method **updateSurvey** to update **colors.xml**. Line 159 creates element **total** to hold the total number of votes. In the **<total>** element, we use the **xsp:expr** element to substitute the value of variable **total**. The **for** loop (lines 162–173) iterates through the **color** elements (stored in **NodeList colorElements**); for each **color** element, we create a new **color** element. Using XSP tag **<xsp:attribute>**, we dynamically set the attributes **value** and **percentage** to **colorName** and the **return**ed value of method **getPercentage**, respectively. After XSP processing, this produces an XML document containing the results of the survey. Combined with the style sheet **response.xsl** (Fig. 16.9), these data are returned to the client as HTML.

```
177   <?xml version = "1.0"?>
178
179   <!-- Fig. 16.09 : response.xsl -->
180
181   <xsl:stylesheet
182       xmlns:xsl = "http://www.w3.org/1999/XSL/Transform"
183       version = "1.0">
184
185       <xsl:template match = "survey">
186           <html>
187               <head>
188                   <title>
189                       <xsl:value-of select = "@title"/>
190                   </title>
191               </head>
192               <body bgcolor = "cyan">
193                   <h1>
194                       <xsl:value-of select = "@title"/>
195                   </h1>
196                   <table border = "1">
197                       <thead>
198                           <td>Color</td>
199                           <td>Percentage</td>
200                       </thead>
201                       <xsl:apply-templates/>
202                   </table>
203               </body>
204           </html>
205       </xsl:template>
206
207       <xsl:template match = "total">
208           <p>Total votes so far:
209               <xsl:value-of select = "."/>
210           </p>
211       </xsl:template>
212
213       <xsl:template match = "color">
214           <tr>
215               <td><xsl:value-of select = "@value"/></td>
216               <td><xsl:value-of select = "@percentage"/></td>
```

Fig. 16.9   response.xsl (part 1 of 2).

```
217              </tr>
218          </xsl:template>
219  </xsl:stylesheet>
```

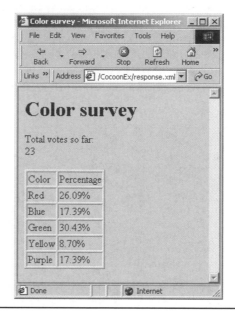

Fig. 16.9 `response.xsl` (part 2 of 2).

16.4 Case Study: A Wireless Online Bookstore

In this section we present a case study that uses XML and XSL with Java servlets and the *Wireless Applications Protocol (WAP)* to build a wireless online bookstore. WAP uses the *Wireless Markup Language (WML)*, which adheres to the XML 1.0 recommendation from the World Wide Web Consortium (W3C). Many digital cellular phones now support WAP for browsing the Web, reading e-mail and shopping online. Using WAP will allow customers to purchase books from our store using these devices.

The wireless bookstore application uses a *multitier application model*. A multitier application—sometimes called an *n*-tier application—is divided into several modular parts (i.e., tiers), each of which may be located on a different physical computer. In the wireless bookstore application, we use the three-tier architecture shown in Fig. 16.10.

The data tier maintains all of the information needed for an application. Most often this information is stored in a database. The database may contain product information, such as a description, price and quantity in stock and customer information, such as a user name, billing and shipping information.

The middle tier of a multitier application acts as a sort of "middleman" between the data in the data tier and users of the application. All user requests for data (e.g., a request to view the product catalog) go through the middle tier before reaching the database. Likewise, responses to requests for data travel back through the middle tier before reaching the user. The middle tier implements *business logic* and *presentation logic* to control interactions between users and data.

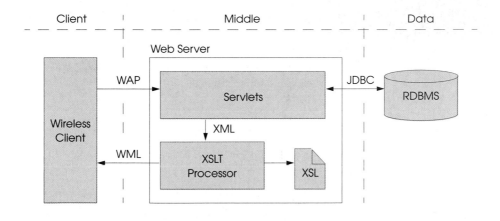

Fig. 16.10 Three-tier architecture for the Deitel wireless bookstore.

Business logic enforces *business rules* and is used to ensure that data are reliable before being updated in the database or retrieved for the user. Business rules dictate how such data can and cannot be accessed and updated. For example, an online store may have a business rule requiring that a customer's credit card is verified with the credit card issuer before the customer's order is shipped. Business logic might implement this business rule by obtaining the credit card number and expiration date from the user and performing the verification. Once this verification is successful, the business logic would update the database to indicate the customer's order may be shipped.

The middle tier is also responsible for presenting data to the user. The middle tier accepts a user request for data, retrieves the data from the data tier, and then transforms the data into a suitable representation for the user. In our application, the middle tier transforms database data into WML documents, which are then presented to the user.

The third tier is the client tier, which provides a user interface for the application. Users interact directly with the client tier through the user interface. For our online bookstore application, the client is a WAP-enabled wireless device, such as a digital cellular phone. The user interface on a wireless phone is text based, so data from our application is presented to the user in the client tier as text. The user also makes requests through the user interface in the client tier. Again, our user interface is text based, so the user makes requests by typing letters and numbers on the phone keypad. Our application uses the familiar shopping cart e-commerce model to make it easy for customers to select and purchase products.

Our online wireless bookstore application consists of a number of different components in each tier. Figure 16.11 lists each of these components along with a short description of the functionality each one provides.

Filename	Description
`index.wml`	Home page for bookstore; allows user to log in or to create a new account.

Fig. 16.11 Client-side documents for wireless bookstore (part 1 of 2).

Filename	Description
login.wml	Login page; asks the user to enter a username and password.
newuser.wml	Page to create a new account; asks the user to enter a username and password. User re-enters password for verification.

Fig. 16.11 Client-side documents for wireless bookstore (part 2 of 2).

Figure 16.12 lists the source code components of this case study along with a brief description of the role of each component.

Filename	Description
Database.java	Class **Database**; used to query and update the database.
ShoppingCart.java	Class **ShoppingCart**; represents the customer's shopping cart.
Book.java	Class **Book**; each **Book** instance represents a book in the bookstore.
XMLCreator.java	Class **XMLCreator**; used to create XML **Document** objects and manipulate the DOM.
Processor.java	Class **Processor**; applies an XSL style sheet to an XML document.
LoginServlet.java	Servlet to handle a log-in and new account requests.
newuser.xsl	Style sheet used to transform XML created by **LoginServlet** into WML.
welcome.xsl	Style sheet used to transform XML created by **LoginServlet** into WML.
GetTechnologyServlet.java	Servlet that generates XML containing technology subjects from the catalog database (**catalog.mdb**).
catalog.xsl	Style sheet used to generate WML to display catalog contents.
GetTitlesServlet.java	Servlet that generates XML containing the book titles in each technology subject from the catalog database (**catalog.mdb**).
titles.xsl	Style sheet used to transform XML containing book titles into WML.
GetDescriptionServlet.java	Servlet that generates XML containing a description of a book.
description.xsl	Style sheet used to transform XML containing book descriptions into WML.

Fig. 16.12 Server-side components for wireless bookstore (part 1 of 2).

Filename	Description
`AddToCartServlet.java`	Servlet for adding a book to the shopping cart.
`ViewCartServlet.java`	Servlet that generates XML containing the contents of the customer's shopping cart.
`viewcart.xsl`	Style sheet used to transform XML containing the contents of the customer's shopping cart into WML.
`UpdateCartServlet.java`	Servlet used to change the quantity of the selected item in the customer's shopping cart.
`login.xsl`	Style sheet to generate WML to display message to user.
`GetShoppingCartServlet.java`	Servlet used retrieve a customer's shopping cart contents from a previous shopping session.
`LogoutServlet.java`	Servlet to log out of the online bookstore.

Fig. 16.12 Server-side components for wireless bookstore (part 2 of 2).

16.5 Jakarta Tomcat Setup

In order to build this wireless application, we will need several different tools. Java servlets execute in a *servlet container* in a Web server. A servlet container is simply part of a Web server in which Java servlets are run so they may respond to requests from clients. The Apache Group has built a reference implementation for Java servlets called Jakarta Tomcat, which we will use in our application. We will also make use of a Microsoft Access database to store user and product information. You will therefore need Microsoft Access 97 or later installed on your computer. To set up your computer to build the wireless online bookstore application, follow these steps:

1. Register the databases **cart.mdb** and **catalog.mdb** as ODBC data sources. The username is **anonymous** and the password is **guest** for both databases.

2. Download and install Java™ 2 SDK, Standard Edition Version 1.3.0 from **www.java.sun.com**.

3. Download Jakarta Tomcat from **jakarta.apache.org/downloads/ binindex.html** and follow the installation instructions in the user's guide. In this example, we assume Jakarta Tomcat is installed in **C:\jakarta-tomcat**.

4. Place the XSL files in the directory **jakarta-tomcat\webapps\chapter16** and the Java class files in the directory **jakarta-tomcat\webapps\chapter16\WEB-INF\classes\cartXML**.

5. Download the Xalan XSLT processor from **xml.apache.org/xalan/index.html**. Place **xalan.jar** and **xerces.jar** in **jakarta-tomcat\webapps\chapter16\WEB-INF\lib**.

6. Download and install the UP.SDK from **www.phone.com/products/upsdk.html**. This includes UP.Simulator, which simulates a wireless phone. We will use this to test the wireless online bookstore.

7. Add the following XML tag in the **ContextManager** element in **\jakarta-tomcat\conf\server.xml**:

```
<Context path = "/chapter16" docBase = "webapps/chapter16"
    debug = "0" reloadable = "true"></Context>
```

8. Add the following XML in the **web-app** element in **jakarta-tomcat\conf\web.xml**:

```
<mime-mapping>
    <extension>wml</extension>
    <mime-type>text/vnd.wap.wml</mime-type>
</mime-mapping>
```

9. Run Jakarta Tomcat by executing **\jakarta-tomcat\bin\startup.bat**.

16.6 WAP and WML: Client-side Documents

The client portion of the bookstore consists of both static and dynamically generated WML documents. In the next section we will see how to dynamically generate WML. In this section we introduce WML and discuss the static WML documents used in the wireless bookstore. The first document presented to the user—**index.wml** (Fig. 16.13)—allows the user to choose to log in to the store with an existing account or to create a new account.

WML is an application of XML, so the XML declaration (line 1) is required. On lines 2 and 3 there are two comments that describe the purpose of this WML document. On lines 4 and 5 we specify the DTD for this document, which is defined by the *WAP Forum*. Line 6 begins the document element **wml**.

```
1   <?xml version = "1.0"?>
2   <!-- Fig. 16.13: index.wml -->
3   <!-- Home page for bookstore -->
4   <!DOCTYPE wml PUBLIC "-//WAPFORUM//DTD WML 1.1//EN"
5       "http://www.wapforum.org/DTD/wml_1.1.xml">
6   <wml>
7       <card>
8           <p>Welcome to Deitel Wireless shopping.</p>
9           <p>
10              <select>
11                  <option onpick = "login.wml">
12                  Log in
13                  </option>
14                  <option onpick = "newuser.wml">
15                  New account
16                  </option>
17              </select>
18          </p>
19      </card>
20  </wml>
```

Fig. 16.13 Code listing for **index.wml**(part 1 of 2).

Fig. 16.13 Web browser rendering WML (part 2 of 2). (Courtesy of Phone.com, Inc.)

Since wireless devices that use WAP and WML have limited Internet connections, WML places multiple pages of content in a single WML document, called a *deck*. This way, several pages worth of data are downloaded at once, reducing the number of times the wireless device needs to connect to the wireless network to download information. Each page is stored in a **card** element (line 7). The WML document in Fig. 16.13 consists of only a single card (lines 7–19). The **p** element (line 8) begins a new paragraph. Here we have an introductory message to the customer. On lines 10–17 we have a **select** element, which is used to present multiple **option**s from which the user can choose. The first **option** element (lines 11–13) allows the user to log in to the application. The *onpick attribute* of the **option** element indicates the action to take when the user "picks" (i.e., selects) this option. For the first option, the user is sent to **login.wml**. The second **option** element (lines 14–16) allows the user to create a new account. When selected, the **onpick** attribute indicates that the user will be sent to **newuser.wml**.

Figure 16.14 shows **login.wml**. This page prompts the user for a username and password and submits this information to **LoginServlet**. Notice that **login.wml** contains multiple cards, the first of which can be found on lines 7–26. In this card the user is prompted to enter a user name.

On lines 8–14 we declare and initialize the variable **param1**, which will be used to store the user's login name. The event enclosed by the **<onevent>** element is executed when this card is requested from a **<go>** element.

```
1   <?xml version = "1.0"?>
2   <!-- Fig. 16.14: login.wml              -->
3   <!-- Prompts for username and password -->
4   <!DOCTYPE wml PUBLIC "-//WAPFORUM//DTD WML 1.1//EN"
5      "http://www.wapforum.org/DTD/wml_1.1.xml">
6   <wml>
7      <card>
8         <onevent type = "onenterforward">
9
10           <refresh>
11              <setvar name = "param1" value = ""/>
12           </refresh>
13
14        </onevent>
15
16        <do type="accept">
17           <go href="#pass" />
18        </do>
19
20        <p>Enter your name and password to login</p>
21        <p>
22           Name:
23           <input name = "param1" format = "mmmmm*m" type = "text"
24              maxlength = "10"/>
25        </p>
26     </card>
27
28     <card id = "pass">
29        <onevent type = "onenterforward">
30
31           <refresh>
32              <setvar name = "param2" value = ""/>
33           </refresh>
34
35         </onevent>
36
37        <do type = "accept">
38           <go href = "cartXML.LoginServlet?action=login"
39             method = "post">
40
41              <postfield name = "param2" value = "$(param2)"/>
42              <postfield name = "param1" value = "$(param1)"/>
43
44           </go>
45        </do>
46           <p>Password:
47
48              <input name = "param2" format = "mmmmm*m"
49                 type = "password" maxlength = "10"/>
50
51           </p>
52     </card>
53  </wml>
```

Fig. 16.14 Code listing for **login.wml** (part 1 of 2).

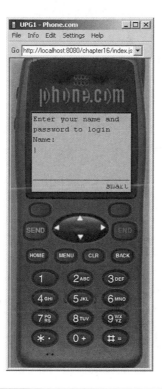

Fig. 16.14 Web browser rendering **login.wml** (part 2 of 2). (Courtesy of Phone.com, Inc.)

Lines 16–18

```
<do type = "accept">
   <go href = "#pass"/>
</do>
```

allow the user to press the **accept** key on the wireless device to continue on to the **pass** card, where the user will be prompted for a password. Element **do** has an optional **label** attribute that specifies the text to be displayed to the user. If no **label** is specified most devices will display the text "**OK**."

Lines 23–24

```
<input name = "param1" format = "mmmmm*m" type = "text"
   maxlength = "10"/>
```

prompt the customer to enter a username. The **format** attribute indicates the format of the text to be entered by the user. The value **mmmmm*m** specifies that the user must enter at least five characters, followed by any number of characters. *Attribute **maxlength** with the value **10** limits the maximum number of characters to 10.*

Once the user has entered a user name and pressed the **accept** key, the user is taken to the **pass** card (lines 28–52). In this card, the user is prompted for a password using an **input** element on line 49. This **input** element has the attribute **type** with the value

password, which prevents the characters from being displayed on the screen, thus adding security. On Lines 38–39

```
<go href = "cartXML.LoginServlet?action=login"
    method = "post">
```

we use a query string to redirect the user to **LoginServlet**, which then reads the username and password from the **param1** and **param2** variables to authenticate the user.

Selecting **option** "New account" from **index.wml** directs the user to **newuser.wml** (Fig. 16.15), which allows a user to create a new account. This WML deck is similar to **login.wml**. The card on lines 9–27 first prompts the user to enter a new username (lines 24 and 25). The card on lines 29–46 then prompts the user to enter a new password. The card on lines 48–73 prompts the user to re-enter the password for verification.

16.7 Java Servlets

Java servlets provide business logic and presentation logic in the middle tier of the wireless bookstore application. Every request that a client makes for data, such as viewing the product catalog, adding an item to a shopping cart and checking out of the store, goes through a servlet, The servlet then processes the request, retrieves data from or updates data to the database and processes the data to be sent back to the client. Using XSL, the servlets transform the XML data built from the database into WML for display on the WAP client.

As business logic components, the servlets in this case study interact directly with the database. Class **Database** (Fig. 16.16) is used to connect to the database and execute queries to retrieve and update data.

```
1   <?xml version = "1.0"?>
2
3   <!-- Fig. 16.15: newuser.wml          -->
4   <!-- Prompts for username and password -->
5
6   <!DOCTYPE wml PUBLIC "-//WAPFORUM//DTD WML 1.1//EN"
7       "http://www.wapforum.org/DTD/wml_1.1.xml">
8   <wml>
9      <card>
10        <onevent type = "onenterforward">
11
12           <refresh>
13              <setvar name = "param1" value = ""/>
14           </refresh>
15
16        </onevent>
17        <do type = "accept">
18        <go href = "#pass1"/>
19        </do>
20        <p>Please enter a name and password to create your
21           account</p>
```

Fig. 16.15 Code listing for **newuser.wml** (part 1 of 3).

```
22          <p>
23              Name(5-10 characters):
24              <input name = "param1" format = "mmmmm*m" type = "text"
25                  maxlength = "10"/>
26          </p>
27      </card>
28
29      <card id = "pass1">
30          <onevent type = "onenterforward">
31
32              <refresh>
33                  <setvar name = "param2" value = ""/>
34              </refresh>
35
36          </onevent>
37
38          <do type = "accept">
39              <go href = "#pass2"/>
40          </do>
41
42          <p>Password(5-10 characters):
43              <input name = "param2" format = "mmmmm*m"
44                  type = "password" maxlength = "10"/>
45          </p>
46      </card>
47
48      <card id = "pass2">
49          <onevent type = "onenterforward">
50
51              <refresh>
52                  <setvar name = "param3" value = ""/>
53              </refresh>
54
55          </onevent>
56          <do type = "accept">
57              <go href=
58                  "cartXML.LoginServlet?action=newuser"
59                  method = "post">
60
61                  <postfield name = "param2" value = "$(param2)"/>
62                  <postfield name = "param1" value = "$(param1)"/>
63                  <postfield name = "param3" value = "$(param3)"/>
64
65              </go>
66          </do>
67          <p>Verify Password:
68
69              <input name = "param3" format = "mmmmm*m"
70                  type = "password" maxlength = "10"/>
71
72          </p>
73      </card>
74  </wml>
```

Fig. 16.15 Code listing for **newuser.wml** (part 2 of 3).

(Courtesy of Phone.com,

Fig. 16.15 Code listing for **newuser.wml** (part 3 of 3).

     The constructor for this class (lines 13–19) takes three arguments. Variable **url** specifies the URL (Uniform Resource Locator) where the database can be located. Remember that in a multitier application each tier may reside on a different computer. The database tier, in this case, could be running on a computer across the network. The **username** and **password** are needed to log into the database. Line 24

```
1   // Fig. 16.16: Database.java
2   // Queries a database
3   package cartXML;
4   import java.sql.*;
5
6   public class Database {
7       private Connection connection;
8       private static String username;
9       private static String password;
10      private static String url;
11      private Statement statement;
12
```

Fig. 16.16 Code listing for **Database.java** (part 1 of 3).

```
13      public Database( String url, String username,
14                      String password )
15      {
16         this.url = url;
17         this.username = username;
18         this.password = password;
19      }
20
21      public boolean connect()
22      {
23         try {
24            Class.forName( "sun.jdbc.odbc.JdbcOdbcDriver" );
25            connection = DriverManager.getConnection( url, username,
26               password );
27            return true;
28         }
29         catch ( Exception ex ) {
30            ex.printStackTrace();
31         }
32
33         return false;
34      }
35
36      public ResultSet get( String query )
37      {
38         try {
39            statement = connection.createStatement();
40            ResultSet rs = statement.executeQuery( query );
41            return rs;
42         }
43         catch ( SQLException sqle ) {
44            return null;
45         }
46      }
47
48      public boolean update( String query )
49      {
50         try {
51            statement = connection.createStatement();
52            statement.executeUpdate( query );
53            return true;
54         }
55         catch ( SQLException sqle ) {
56            return false;
57         }
58      }
59
60      public boolean shutDown()
61      {
62         try {
63            connection.close();
64            return true;
65         }
```

Fig. 16.16 Code listing for **Database.java** (part 2 of 3).

```
66              catch ( SQLException sqlex ) {
67                  return false;
68              }
69          }
70      }
```

Fig. 16.16 Code listing for **Database.java** (part 3 of 3).

```
Class.forName( "sun.jdbc.odbc.JdbcOdbcDriver" );
```

loads the database driver for ODBC databases. This ODBC driver is part of the Java 2 Plat-form and can be used with any ODBC database. In this example we use two Microsoft Ac-cess Databases, each of which is registered as an ODBC database. For more information on JDBC drivers and supported databases, visit the Sun Microsystems JDBC Web site at

```
java.sun.com/products/jdbc
```

Lines 25 and 26

```
connection = DriverManager.getConnection( url, username,
    password );
```

retrieve a connection to the database. This connection will be used to perform queries and updates to the database throughout the application. The **static** method **getConnec-tion** of class **DriverManager** (package **java.sql**) uses **username** and **pass-word** to log into the database specified in **url**.
    Line 39

```
statement = connection.createStatement();
```

invokes the **createStatement** method of object **Connection** to obtain an object that implements the **Statement** interface. The object is used to query the database.
    Line 40

```
ResultSet rs = statement.executeQuery( query );
```

performs the query by calling method **executeQuery** of object **Statement**. When a query is performed on a database, a **ResultSet** object is returned containing the results of the query. It is also possible to insert values into a database. Method **update** is used to accomplish this task. Line 52

```
statement.executeUpdate( query );
```

uses method **executeUpdate** of object **Statement** to update the database with a new record. The method returns a **boolean** that indicates the success or failure of the update operation.
    Class **ShoppingCart** (Fig. 16.17) represents the shopping cart for a user. This class is placed in the session when the user logs in or creates a new account so that its data can be maintained for the entire time the user is browsing the site.
    By implementing the **HttpSessionBindingListener** interface, the user's shopping cart is written to a database when the session ends. This allows the application to retrieve the customers' previous shopping carts when they return to the site.

```
1   // Fig. 16.17: ShoppingCart.java
2   // Shopping cart
3   package cartXML;
4   import javax.servlet.http.*;
5   import java.text.*;
6   import java.io.*;
7   import org.w3c.dom.*;
8   import java.util.*;
9
10  public class ShoppingCart implements HttpSessionBindingListener {
11      private Vector books;
12      private String username;
13      private Database database;
14
15      public ShoppingCart()
16      { books = new Vector( 5 ); }
17
18      public void valueBound( HttpSessionBindingEvent e ) {}
19
20      public void valueUnbound( HttpSessionBindingEvent e )
21      {
22          if ( username == null )   // if username is null, exit
23              return;
24
25          save();
26      }
27
28      public void save()
29      {
30          database = new Database( "jdbc:odbc:cart", "anonymous",
31              "guest" );
32          database.connect();
33          delete( username );
34
35          for ( int i = 0; i < getLength(); i++ ) {
36              Book b = ( Book ) books.elementAt( i );
37              String productID = b.getProductID();
38              int quantity = b.getQuantity();
39
40              insert( username, productID, String.valueOf( quantity ) );
41          }
42
43          database.shutDown();
44      }
45
46      public void delete( String username )
47      {
48          String query = "DELETE * FROM Carts WHERE username = '"
49              + username + "'";
50
51          database.update( query );
52      }
53
```

Fig. 16.17 Code listing for **ShoppingCart.java** (part 1 of 4).

```
54     public void insert( String username, String productID,
55        String quantity )
56     {
57        Date today;
58        String date;
59        DateFormat dateFormatter;
60
61        dateFormatter = DateFormat.getDateInstance(
62           DateFormat.DEFAULT );
63        today = new Date();
64        date = dateFormatter.format(today);
65
66        String query = "INSERT INTO Carts ( username, productID, "
67           + "quantity, dateCreated ) VALUES ('" + username + "',"
68           + productID + "," + quantity + ",'" +  date + "' )";
69
70        database.update( query );
71     }
72
73     public void add( Book b )
74     { books.addElement( b ); }
75
76     public void remove( int i )
77     { books.removeElementAt( i ); }
78
79     public void setQuantity( int i, int quantity )
80     {
81        Book b = ( Book ) books.elementAt( i );
82
83        b.setQuantity( quantity );
84     }
85
86     public String getUsername()
87     { return username; }
88
89     public void setUsername( String s )
90     { username = s; }
91
92     public String[] getDescription( int i )
93     {
94        Book b = ( Book ) books.elementAt( i );
95
96        return b.getDescription();
97     }
98
99     public String getProductID( int i )
100    {
101       Book b = ( Book ) books.elementAt( i );
102
103       return b.getProductID();
104    }
105
```

Fig. 16.17 Code listing for **ShoppingCart.java** (part 2 of 4).

```
106    public int getQuantity( int i )
107    {
108        Book b = ( Book ) books.elementAt( i );
109
110        return b.getQuantity();
111    }
112
113    public double getPrice( int i )
114    {
115        Book b = ( Book ) books.elementAt( i );
116
117        return b.getPrice();
118    }
119
120    public String getFormattedPrice( int i )
121    {
122        Book b = ( Book ) books.elementAt( i );
123        double price = b.getPrice();
124        NumberFormat priceFormatter =
125            NumberFormat.getCurrencyInstance();
126        String formattedPrice = priceFormatter.format( price );
127
128        return formattedPrice;
129    }
130
131    public int getLength()
132    { return books.size(); }
133
134    // returns the index of the vector if productID is found in
135    //   cart, -1 otherwise
136    public int contains( String id )
137    {
138
139        for ( int i = 0; i < getLength(); i++ ) {
140            Book b = ( Book ) books.elementAt( i );
141                String bookID = b.getProductID();
142
143                if ( bookID != null && bookID.equals( id ) )
144                    return i;
145        }
146
147        return -1;
148    }
149
150    public String getTotal()
151    {
152        double total = 0;
153
154        for ( int i = 0; i < getLength(); i++ )
155            total += getPrice( i ) * getQuantity( i );
156
157        NumberFormat priceFormatter =
158            NumberFormat.getCurrencyInstance();
```

Fig. 16.17 Code listing for `ShoppingCart.java` (part 3 of 4).

```
159            String formattedTotal = priceFormatter.format( total );
160
161            return formattedTotal;
162         }
163
164         public Document viewCartXML()
165         {
166            XMLCreator xmlCreator = new XMLCreator();
167            Node cartNode = xmlCreator.initialize( "cart" );
168
169            xmlCreator.addAttribute( cartNode, "numItems",
170               String.valueOf( getLength() ) );
171            xmlCreator.addAttribute( cartNode, "total", getTotal() );
172
173            if ( getLength() != 0 ) {
174
175               for ( int i = 0; i < getLength(); i++ ) {
176                  Node itemNode = xmlCreator.addChild( cartNode,
177                     "item" );
178
179                  xmlCreator.addTextNode( xmlCreator.addChild(
180                     itemNode, "productID" ), getProductID( i ) );
181                  xmlCreator.addTextNode( xmlCreator.addChild(
182                     itemNode, "quantity" ),
183                     String.valueOf( getQuantity( i ) ) );
184                  xmlCreator.addTextNode( xmlCreator.addChild(
185                     itemNode, "price" ), getFormattedPrice( i ) );
186
187                  String description[] = getDescription( i );
188
189                  xmlCreator.addTextNode( xmlCreator.addChild(
190                     itemNode, "title" ), description[ 0 ] );
191                  xmlCreator.addTextNode( xmlCreator.addChild(
192                     itemNode, "author" ), description[ 1 ] );
193                  xmlCreator.addTextNode( xmlCreator.addChild(
194                     itemNode, "isbn" ), description[ 2 ] );
195               }
196
197            }
198
199            return xmlCreator.getDocument();
200         }
201      }
```

Fig. 16.17 Code listing for **ShoppingCart.java** (part 4 of 4).

Lines 66–68

```
String query = "INSERT INTO Carts ( username, productID, "
   + "quantity, dateCreated ) VALUES ('" + username + "',"
   + productID + "," + quantity + ",'" +  date + "' )";
```

insert one item from the user's current shopping cart into table **Carts**. Method **view-CartXML** is called from **ViewCartServlet** when the user requests to view the shopping cart. This method produces XML that describes the shopping cart. We will see how this XML shopping cart is transformed with XSL to create WML.

Each instance of class **Book** (Fig. 16.18) represents a book in our bookstore. Both **set** and **get** methods are provided to give access to the **Book**'s data, such as its price, the quantity of books in the cart, the product ID and a description.

```java
1   // Fig. 16.18: Book.java
2   // Represents a book
3   package cartXML;
4
5   public class Book
6   {
7      private double price;
8      private int quantity;
9      private String productID;
10     private String[] description; //title, author, isbn
11
12     public Book()
13     {
14        description = null;
15        productID = null;
16        quantity = 0;
17        price = 0;
18     }
19
20     public Book( double price, int quantity, String productID )
21     {
22        this.price = price;
23        this.quantity = quantity;
24        this.productID = productID;
25     }
26
27     public Book( double price, int quantity, String productID,
28        String description[] )
29     {
30        this.price = price;
31        this.quantity = quantity;
32        this.productID = productID;
33        this.description = description;
34     }
35
36     public String[] getDescription()
37     { return description; }
38
39     public double getPrice()
40     { return price; }
41
42     public int getQuantity()
43     { return quantity; }
44
45     public String getProductID()
46     { return productID; }
```

Fig. 16.18 Code listing for **Book.java** (part 1 of 2).

```
47
48      public void setDescription( String description[] )
49      { this.description = description; }
50
51      public void setPrice( double d )
52      { price = d; }
53
54      public void setQuantity( int i )
55      { quantity = i; }
56
57      public void setProductID( String s )
58      { productID = s; }
59   }
```

Fig. 16.18 Code listing for **Book.java** (part 2 of 2).

The servlets retrieve data from a database and create XML documents that describe that data. Class **XMLCreator** (Fig. 16.19) is a utility class we use to create XML documents using the Document Object Model (DOM), which we first discussed in Chapter 8.

```
1    // Fig. 16.19: XMLCreator.java
2    // Creates XML
3    package cartXML;
4    import java.io.*;
5    import org.w3c.dom.*;
6    import java.util.*;
7    import javax.xml.parsers.*;
8
9    public class XMLCreator
10   {
11      private Document document;
12
13      public Node initialize( String rootElement )
14      {
15         try {
16            System.setProperty(
17               "javax.xml.parsers.DocumentBuilderFactory",
18               "org.apache.xerces.jaxp.DocumentBuilderFactoryImpl" );
19            System.setProperty(
20               "javax.xml.parsers.SAXParserFactory",
21               "org.apache.xerces.jaxp.SAXParserFactoryImpl" );
22            DocumentBuilderFactory dbf =
23               DocumentBuilderFactory.newInstance();
24            DocumentBuilder db = dbf.newDocumentBuilder();
25
26            document = db.newDocument();
27
28            Node rootNode = document.createElement( rootElement );
29
30            document.appendChild( rootNode );
31            return rootNode;
32         }
```

Fig. 16.19 Code listing for **XMLCreator.java** (part 1 of 2).

```
33              catch ( DOMException domex ) {
34                  domex.printStackTrace();
35              }
36              catch ( ParserConfigurationException pcex ) {
37                  pcex.printStackTrace();
38              }
39
40          return null;
41      }
42
43      public Node addChild( Node parentNode, String element )
44      {
45          parentNode.appendChild( document.createElement(
46              element ) );
47          return parentNode.getLastChild();
48      }
49
50      public void addTextNode( Node parentNode, String element )
51      {
52          parentNode.appendChild( document.createTextNode(
53              element ) );
54      }
55
56      public void addAttribute( Node parentNode, String name,
57          String value )
58      {
59          Element element = ( Element ) parentNode;
60
61          element.setAttribute( name, value );
62      }
63
64      public Document getDocument()
65      {
66          return document;
67      }
68  }
```

Fig. 16.19 Code listing for **XMLCreator.java** (part 2 of 2).

The **static** method **newInstance** of class **DocumentBuilderFactory** creates a new instance of class **DocumentBuilderFactory**. On lines 16–21 we set a system property that instructs **DocumentBuilderFactory** to use the Xerces XML parser. Using a **DocumentBuilderFactory** permits a change of your XML parser implementation without changing how the document is actually built.

Class **Processor** (Fig. 16.20) applies an XSL style sheet to transform an XML document. In this case study the result of the transformation is a WML document that is delivered to the client using the **PrintWriter** object out on line 17. This **PrintWriter** object is used to deliver the resulting WML document to the client.

Class **LoginServlet** (Fig. 16.21) handles user requests to log in to the application. The action taken depends on the value of variable **action**, which **LoginServlet** retrieves from the **request** object. If the value of **action** is **login**, **LoginServlet** attempts to verify the username and password in the database.

```
1   // Figure 16.20: Processor.java
2   // Applies XSL style sheet to XML
3   package cartXML;
4   import org.xml.sax.SAXException;
5   import org.apache.xalan.xslt.XSLTProcessorFactory;
6   import org.apache.xalan.xslt.XSLTInputSource;
7   import org.apache.xalan.xslt.XSLTResultTarget;
8   import org.apache.xalan.xslt.XSLTProcessor;
9   import java.io.*;
10  import java.util.*;
11  import org.xml.sax.InputSource;
12  import org.w3c.dom.*;
13
14  public class Processor
15  {
16     public void process( Node node, String xslFile,
17        PrintWriter out )
18     {
19        try {
20         XSLTProcessor processor = XSLTProcessorFactory.getProcessor(
21              new org.apache.xalan.xpath.xdom.XercesLiaison() );
22          processor.process( new XSLTInputSource( node ),
23              new XSLTInputSource( new InputSource( "file:///"
24              + xslFile ) ), new XSLTResultTarget( out ));
25        }
26        catch( SAXException saxex ) { saxex.printStackTrace(); }
27     }
28  }
```

Fig. 16.20 Code listing for `Processor.java`.

```
1   // Fig. 16.21: LoginServlet.java
2   // Logs user into site and creates new account
3   package cartXML;
4   import java.io.*;
5   import javax.servlet.*;
6   import javax.servlet.http.*;
7   import java.util.*;
8   import java.sql.*;
9   import org.w3c.dom.*;
10
11  public class LoginServlet extends HttpServlet {
12     private Database database;
13
14     public void init( ServletConfig config )
15        throws ServletException
16     {
17        super.init( config );
18        database = new Database( "jdbc:odbc:cart", "anonymous",
19           "guest" );
```

Fig. 16.21 Code listing for `LoginServlet.java` (part 1 of 4).

```
20          database.connect();
21      }
22
23      public void service( HttpServletRequest req,
24          HttpServletResponse res )
25          throws ServletException, IOException
26      {
27          HttpSession session = req.getSession( true );
28          ShoppingCart test = ( ShoppingCart ) session.getAttribute(
29              "cart" );
30          ServletContext sc = getServletConfig().getServletContext();
31
32          if ( test != null ) { // do not allow a user to log in twice
33              sc.getRequestDispatcher(
34                  "/servlet/cartXML.GetTechnologyServlet" )
35                  .forward( req, res );
36              return;
37          }
38
39          ShoppingCart cart = new ShoppingCart();
40          String name = req.getParameter( "param1" );
41          String password = req.getParameter( "param2" );
42          String action = req.getParameter( "action" );
43          XMLCreator xmlCreator = new XMLCreator();
44          Node loginNode = xmlCreator.initialize( "login" );
45          Processor processor = new Processor();
46          res.setContentType( "text/vnd.wap.wml" );
47          PrintWriter output = res.getWriter();
48
49          if ( action.equals( "login" ) ) {
50
51              // send to servlet that retrieves cart
52              if( isValid( name, password ) ) {
53                  cart.setUsername( name );
54                  session.setAttribute( "cart", cart );
55                  sc.getRequestDispatcher(
56                      "/servlet/cartXML.GetShoppingCartServlet" )
57                      .forward( req, res );
58              }
59              else {
60                  Node messageNode = xmlCreator.addChild( loginNode,
61                      "message" );
62
63                  xmlCreator.addTextNode( messageNode,
64                      "You entered an invalid password" );
65                  processor.process( xmlCreator.getDocument(),
66                      "C:/jakarta-tomcat/webapps/chapter16/login.xsl",
67                      output );
68              }
69          }
70          else {
71
```

Fig. 16.21 Code listing for **LoginServlet.java** (part 2 of 4).

```
72          if ( !password.equals( req.getParameter( "param3" ) ) )
73          {
74              xmlCreator.addTextNode( xmlCreator.addChild(
75                  loginNode, "message" ), "You entered two "
76                  + "different passwords. Please try again." );
77              processor.process( xmlCreator.getDocument(),
78                  "C:/jakarta-tomcat/webapps/chapter16/newuser.xsl",
79                  output );
80          }
81          else {
82              boolean created = createUser( name, password );
83
84              if ( created ) {
85                  cart.setUsername( name );
86                  xmlCreator.addTextNode( xmlCreator.addChild(
87                      loginNode, "message" ), "Account created \n "
88                      + "username: " + name + "\n password: "
89                      + password );
90
91                  session.setAttribute( "cart", cart );
92                  processor.process( xmlCreator.getDocument(),
93                      "C:/jakarta-tomcat/webapps/chapter16/welcome.xsl",
94                      output );
95              }
96              else {
97                  xmlCreator.addTextNode( xmlCreator.addChild(
98                      loginNode, "message" ), "That username already "
99                      + "exists. Please try again." );
100                 processor.process( xmlCreator.getDocument(),
101                     "C:/jakarta-tomcat/webapps/chapter16/newuser.xsl",
102                     output );
103             }
104         }
105     }
106 }
107
108 public boolean isValid( String user, String passwd )
109 {
110     try {
111         String query = "SELECT username FROM Users WHERE "
112             + "username = '" + user +  "' and password = '"
113             + passwd + "'";
114         ResultSet rs = database.get( query );
115
116         if ( rs.next() )
117             return true;
118     }
119     catch ( SQLException sqlex ) {
120         sqlex.printStackTrace();
121     }
122
123     return false;
124 }
```

Fig. 16.21 Code listing for **LoginServlet.java** (part 3 of 4).

```
125
126      private boolean found( String user )
127      {
128         try
129         {
130            String query = "SELECT username FROM Users WHERE "
131               + "username= '" + user + "'";
132            ResultSet rs = database.get( query );
133
134            if ( rs.next() )
135               return true;
136         }
137         catch ( SQLException sqlex ) {
138            sqlex.printStackTrace();
139         }
140
141         return false;
142      }
143
144      public boolean createUser( String user, String passwd )
145      {
146         boolean canInsert = found( user );
147
148         if ( !canInsert ) { // if name does not already exist
149            String query = "INSERT INTO Users ( username, "
150               + "password ) VALUES ('" + user + "','"
151               + passwd + "' )";
152            return database.update( query );
153         }
154
155         return false;
156      }
157
158      public void destroy()
159      { database.shutDown(); }
160   }
```

Fig. 16.21 Code listing for **LoginServlet.java** (part 4 of 4).

Lines 27–29

```
HttpSession session = req.getSession( true );
ShoppingCart test = ( ShoppingCart ) session.getAttribute(
   "cart" );
```

retrieve the object named **cart** from the **session**. If no object named **cart** is bound to the **session**, **test** will be **null**. If test is not **null**, lines 33–35 use the **Request-Dispatcher** interface to forward the request to another page; this prevents a user from logging in more than once per session.

If a user is logging in (line 49), line 52 tests for a successful login by invoking method **isValid**. Method **isValid** is defined in lines 108–124; we use an instance of class **Database** to query the **cart.mdb** database. Lines 111–113

```
String query = "SELECT username FROM Users WHERE "
   + "username = '" + user +   "' and password = '"
   + passwd + "'";
```

build an **SQL SELECT** query. This query selects fields **username** and **password** from table **Users**. Lines 114–117

```
ResultSet rs = database.get( query );

if ( rs.next() )
   return true;
```

check to see if the **username** and **password** exist in the **cart** database. Initially, the **ResultSet** is positioned before the first record. **ResultSet** method **next** returns a **boolean** indicating whether the method was able to position to the next record. If the method returns **false**, there are no more records to process (i.e., the **username** and **password** are not in the database).

Lines 60–67 are executed when **isValid** returns **false** (i.e., the user entered an invalid **password** for the specified **username**). Lines 63 and 64

```
xmlCreator.addTextNode( messageNode,
   "You entered an invalid password" );
```

add a text node containing the text **"You entered an invalid password"** to node **messageNode**.

If **action** is not **login** (lines 70–104), the user is creating a new account. First, we test if the user entered the same **password** twice for verification (line 72). If the user entered two different passwords, we create XML indicating so.

If the user entered the same **password** in both fields, we attempt to create a new account. We invoke method **createUser** (lines 144–156). Method **found** is called in line 146 to check if **username** already exists in the **cart.mdb** database; a user can only create an account with a **username** that does not yet exist. If the username does not yet exist, method **createUser** inserts the **username** and **password** into table **Users**. Lines 149–151

```
String query = "INSERT INTO Users ( username, "
   + "password ) VALUES ('" + user + "','"
   + passwd + "' )";
```

build the **INSERT INTO** statement, which indicates the values to be inserted in the **username** and **password** fields in table **Users**. Line 152

```
return database.update( query );
```

inserts the record into table **Users**.

The XML document

```
<login>
   <message>
      You entered two different passwords. Please try again.
   </message>
</login>
```

or the XML document

```
<login>
    <message>
        That username already exists. Please try again.
    </message>
</login>
```

is produced in **LoginServlet** when a user unsuccessfully attempts to create a new account. This XML document—the XSL file **newuser.xsl** (Fig. 16.22)—and the **PrintWriter** object **output** are passed as arguments to class **Processor**'s **process** method. Recall that class **process** applies a style sheet to an XML document. The preceding XML is used with style sheet **newuser.xsl** to generate a WML page for **LoginServlet** to display.

The style sheet **newuser.xsl** (Fig. 16.22) is used when a user attempts to create a new account using a username that has already been taken or when the user enters two different passwords. When this style sheet is applied to the XML generated in **LoginServlet**, a WML document is generated. The **xsl:output** element (lines 7–9)

```
<xsl:output method = "xml" omit-xml-declaration = "no"
    doctype-system = "http://www.wapforum.org/DTD/wml_1.1.xml"
    doctype-public = "-//WAPFORUM//DTD WML 1.1//EN"/>
```

```
1   <xsl:stylesheet xmlns:xsl = "http://www.w3.org/1999/XSL/Transform"
2       version = "1.0">
3
4   <!-- Fig. 16.22 : newuser.xsl              -->
5   <!-- Transforms XML from LoginServlet to WML -->
6
7       <xsl:output method = "xml" omit-xml-declaration = "no"
8           doctype-system = "http://www.wapforum.org/DTD/wml_1.1.xml"
9           doctype-public = "-//WAPFORUM//DTD WML 1.1//EN"/>
10      <xsl:template match = "/">
11          <wml>
12              <card>
13                  <onevent type = "onenterforward">
14
15                      <refresh>
16                          <setvar name = "param1" value = ""/>
17                      </refresh>
18
19                  </onevent>
20
21                  <do type = "accept">
22                      <go href = "#pass1"/>
23                  </do>
24                  <p>
25                      <xsl:value-of select = "//message"/>
26                  </p>
27                  <p>
```

Fig. 16.22 Code listing for **newuser.xsl** (part 1 of 3).

```
28
29                        Name:
30
31                            <input name = "param1" format = "mmmmm*m"
32                                type = "text" maxlength = "10"/>
33                        </p>
34                    </card>
35
36                    <card id = "pass1">
37                        <onevent type = "onenterforward">
38
39                            <refresh>
40                                <setvar name = "param2" value = ""/>
41                            </refresh>
42
43                        </onevent>
44
45                        <do type = "accept">
46                            <go href = "#pass2"/>
47                        </do>
48
49                        <p>Password(5-10chars.):
50                            <input name = "param2" format = "mmmmm*m"
51                                type = "password" maxlength = "10"/>
52                        </p>
53                    </card>
54                    <card id = "pass2">
55                        <onevent type = "onenterforward">
56
57                            <refresh>
58                                <setvar name = "param3" value = ""/>
59                            </refresh>
60
61                        </onevent>
62                        <do type = "accept">
63                            <go href =
64                                "cartXML.LoginServlet?action=newuser"
65                                method = "post">
66
67                                <postfield name = "param2" value = "$(param2)"/>
68                                <postfield name = "param1" value = "$(param1)"/>
69                                <postfield name = "param3" value = "$(param3)"/>
70
71                            </go>
72                        </do>
73                        <p>Password:
74                            <input name = "param3" format = "mmmmm*m"
75                                type = "password" maxlength = "10"/>
76                        </p>
77                    </card>
78                </wml>
79        </xsl:template>
80  </xsl:stylesheet>
```

Fig. 16.22 Code listing for **newuser.xsl** (part 2 of 3).

(Courtesy of Phone.com,
Inc.)

Fig. 16.22 Code listing for **newuser.xsl** (part 3 of 3).

produces the XML declaration and document type definition (DTD)

```
<?xml version = "1.0" encoding = "UTF-8"?>
<!DOCTYPE wml PUBLIC "-//WAPFORUM//DTD WML 1.1//EN"
    "http://www.wapforum.org/DTD/wml_1.1.xml">
```

Line 10

```
<xsl:template match = "/">
```

matches the root node of the XML document. Then the next six lines of WML are written out. Line 25

```
<xsl:value-of select = "//message"/>
```

prints out the value between the **<message>**...**</message>** tags. The two slashes in front of **message** tell the XSL processor to look for this element at any level in the tree.

When a user successfully creates a new account, **LoginServlet** produces the XML

```
<login>
   <message>
       Account created \n username: harvey\n password: deitel
   </message>
</login>
```

The style sheet **welcome.xsl** (Fig. 16.23) is applied to this XML to generate WML

When the user selects the **Shopping** link, servlet **GetTechnologyServlet** (Fig. 16.24) is requested.

Servlet **GetTechnologyServlet** (Fig. 16.24) queries the database **catalog.mdb** for a list of technologies for which books are available. Line 42

```
String query = "SELECT * FROM tech";
```

shows the use of an asterisk (*****) to select all fields from the table **tech**. Once the information has been retrieved, lines 40–54 use class **XMLCreator** to create the XML

```
<catalog>
    <product>
       <techID>1</techID>
       <technology>C</technology>
    </product>
    <product>
       <techID>2</techID>
       <technology>C++</technology>
    </product>
    <product>
       <techID>3</techID>
       <technology>Visual Basic</technology>
    </product>
    <product>
       <techID>4</techID>
       <technology>Java</technology>
    </product>
</catalog>
```

```
1   <xsl:stylesheet xmlns:xsl = "http://www.w3.org/1999/XSL/Transform"
2       version = "1.0">
3
4   <!-- Fig. 16.23 : welcome.xsl          -->
5   <!-- Stylesheet to transform into WML -->
6
7       <xsl:output method = "xml" omit-xml-declaration = "no"
8           doctype-system = "http://www.wapforum.org/DTD/wml_1.1.xml"
9           doctype-public = "-//WAPFORUM//DTD WML 1.1//EN"/>
10
11      <xsl:template match = "/">
12          <wml>
13
```

Fig. 16.23 Code listing for **welcome.xsl** (part 1 of 2).

```
14                    <card>
15                        <do type = "accept" label = "Shopping">
16
17                            <go href =
18                                "cartXML.GetTechnologyServlet"
19                                method = "post"/>
20
21                        </do>
22
23                        <p>
24                            <xsl:value-of select = "//message"/>
25                        </p>
26
27                    </card>
28
29                </wml>
30            </xsl:template>
31    </xsl:stylesheet>
```

(Courtesy of Phone.com,

Fig. 16.23 Code listing for **welcome.xsl** (part 2 of 2).

```
1   // Fig. 16.24: GetTechnologyServlet.java
2   // Retrieves technologies from database
3   package cartXML;
4   import java.io.*;
5   import javax.servlet.*;
6   import javax.servlet.http.*;
7   import java.util.*;
8   import java.sql.*;
9   import org.w3c.dom.*;
10
11  public class GetTechnologyServlet extends HttpServlet {
12     private Database database;
13
14     public void init( ServletConfig config )
15        throws ServletException
16     {
17        super.init( config );
18        database = new Database( "jdbc:odbc:catalog", "anonymous",
19           "guest" );
20        database.connect();
21     }
22
23     public void service( HttpServletRequest req,
24        HttpServletResponse res )
25        throws ServletException, IOException
26     {
27        try {
28           HttpSession session = req.getSession( true );
29           ShoppingCart cart =
30              ( ShoppingCart ) session.getAttribute( "cart" );
31           ServletContext sc = getServletConfig()
32              .getServletContext();
33
34           if ( cart.getUsername() == null ) {
35              sc.getRequestDispatcher( "/index.wml" )
36                 .forward( req, res );
37              return;
38           }
39
40           XMLCreator xmlCreator = new XMLCreator();
41           Node catalogNode = xmlCreator.initialize( "catalog" );
42           String query = "SELECT * FROM tech";
43           ResultSet rs = database.get( query );
44
45           while ( rs.next() ) {
46              Node productNode = xmlCreator.addChild( catalogNode,
47                 "product" );
48              xmlCreator.addTextNode( xmlCreator.addChild(
49                 productNode, "techID" ),
50                 rs.getString( "techID" ) );
51              xmlCreator.addTextNode( xmlCreator.addChild(
52                 productNode, "technology" ),
53                 rs.getString( "technology" ) );
54           }
```

Fig. 16.24 Code listing for **GetTechnologyServlet.java** (part 1 of 2).

```
55
56                res.setContentType( "text/vnd.wap.wml" );
57                PrintWriter output = res.getWriter();
58                Processor processor = new Processor();
59                processor.process( xmlCreator.getDocument(),
60                    "C:/jakarta-tomcat/webapps/chapter16/catalog.xsl",
61                    output );
62            }
63        catch ( SQLException sqlex ) {
64            sqlex.printStackTrace();
65        }
66    }
67
68    public void destroy()
69    {
70        database.shutDown();
71    }
72 }
```

Fig. 16.24 Code listing for **GetTechnologyServlet.java** (part 2 of 2).

GetTechnologyServlet uses class **Processor** to apply style sheet **catalog.xsl** (Fig. 16.25) to the XML.

```
1    <xsl:stylesheet xmlns:xsl =
2        "http://www.w3.org/1999/XSL/Transform" version = "1.0">
3
4    <!-- Fig. 16.25 : catalog.xsl                          -->
5    <!-- Tranforms XML from GetTechnologyServlet to WML -->
6
7        <xsl:output method = "xml"
8            omit-xml-declaration = "no"
9            doctype-system = "http://www.wapforum.org/DTD/wml_1.1.xml"
10           doctype-public = "-//WAPFORUM//DTD WML 1.1//EN"/>
11       <xsl:template match = "/">
12           <wml>
13               <card>
14                   <do type = "options" label = "Logout" >
15                       <go href =
16                           "cartXML.LogoutServlet"/>
17                   </do>
18                   <p> Select a link to view titles </p>
19                   <p>
20                       <select name = "items" ivalue = "1">
21                           <xsl:apply-templates/>
22                       </select>
23                   </p>
24               </card>
25           </wml>
26       </xsl:template>
27       <xsl:template match = "product">
```

Fig. 16.25 Code listing for **catalog.xsl** (part 1 of 2).

```
28        <option onpick=
29           "cartXML.GetTitlesServlet?techID={techID}">
30           <xsl:value-of select = "technology"/>
31        </option>
32     </xsl:template>
33  </xsl:stylesheet>
```

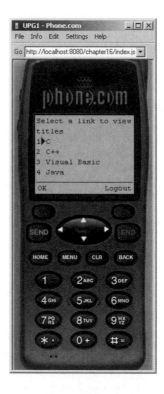

(Courtesy of Phone.com, Inc.)

Fig. 16.25 Code listing for **catalog.xsl** (part 2 of 2).

The user is presented with a list of technologies; selecting a technology requests servlet **GetTitlesServlet** (Fig. 16.26). **GetTitlesServlet** queries the **catalog** data-

```
1   // Fig. 16.26: GetTitlesServlet.java
2   // Retrieves titles from database
3   package cartXML;
4   import java.io.*;
5   import javax.servlet.*;
6   import javax.servlet.http.*;
7   import java.util.*;
8   import java.sql.*;
9   import org.w3c.dom.*;
```

Fig. 16.26 Code listing for **GetTitlesServlet.java** (part 1 of 3).

```
10
11    public class GetTitlesServlet extends HttpServlet {
12        private Database database;
13
14        public void init( ServletConfig config )
15            throws ServletException
16        {
17            super.init( config );
18            database = new Database( "jdbc:odbc:catalog", "anonymous",
19                "guest" );
20            database.connect();
21        }
22
23        public void service( HttpServletRequest req,
24            HttpServletResponse res )
25            throws ServletException, IOException
26        {
27            try {
28                HttpSession session = req.getSession( true );
29                ShoppingCart cart =
30                    ( ShoppingCart ) session.getAttribute( "cart" );
31                ServletContext sc = getServletConfig().
32                    getServletContext();
33
34                if ( cart.getUsername() == null ) {
35                    sc.getRequestDispatcher( "/index.wml" )
36                        .forward( req, res );
37                    return;
38                }
39
40                XMLCreator xmlCreator = new XMLCreator();
41                Node productNode = xmlCreator.initialize( "products" );
42                String techID = req.getParameter( "techID" );
43                String query = "SELECT title, edition, productID FROM "
44                    + "products WHERE techid= " + techID;
45                ResultSet rs = database.get( query );
46
47                while ( rs.next() ) {
48                    Node itemNode = xmlCreator.addChild( productNode,
49                        "item" );
50
51                    xmlCreator.addTextNode( xmlCreator.addChild( itemNode,
52                        "title" ), rs.getString( "title" ) );
53                    xmlCreator.addTextNode( xmlCreator.addChild( itemNode,
54                        "productID" ), rs.getString( "productID" ) );
55                    xmlCreator.addTextNode( xmlCreator.addChild( itemNode,
56                        "techID" ), techID );
57                }
58
59                res.setContentType( "text/vnd.wap.wml" );
60                PrintWriter output = res.getWriter();
61                Processor processor = new Processor();
```

Fig. 16.26 Code listing for **GetTitlesServlet.java** (part 2 of 3).

```
62                 processor.process( xmlCreator.getDocument(),
63                     "C:/jakarta-tomcat/webapps/chapter16/titles.xsl",
64                     output );
65             }
66         catch( SQLException sqlex ){}
67     }
68
69     public void destroy()
70     {
71         database.shutDown();
72     }
73 }
```

Fig. 16.26 Code listing for `GetTitlesServlet.java` (part 3 of 3).

base for a list of titles in a given technology and uses class **XMLCreator** to create XML that contains information obtained from the database. The following XML would be created if the user selected **C** technology:

```
<products>
    <item>
        <title>C: How to Program</title>
        <productID>4</productID>
        <techID>1</techID>
    </item>
</products>
```

GetTitlesServlet uses class **Processor** to transform the passed XML into WML by using style sheet **titles.xsl** (Fig. 16.27).

```
1  <xsl:stylesheet xmlns:xsl = "http://www.w3.org/1999/XSL/Transform"
2     version = "1.0">
3
4  <!-- Fig. 16.27 : titles.xsl                          -->
5  <!-- Tranforms XML from GetTitlesServlet to WML -->
6
7     <xsl:output method = "xml" omit-xml-declaration = "no"
8        doctype-system = "http://www.wapforum.org/DTD/wml_1.1.xml"
9        doctype-public = "-//WAPFORUM//DTD WML 1.1//EN"/>
10
11    <xsl:template match = "/">
12       <wml>
13          <card>
14             <do type = "options" label = "Shopping">
15                <go href =
16                   "cartXML.GetTechnologyServlet"
17                   method = "post"/>
18             </do>
19             <p>Titles</p>
20             <p>
21                <select name = "items" ivalue = "1">
```

Fig. 16.27 Code listing for `titles.xsl` (part 1 of 2).

```
22                          <xsl:apply-templates/>
23                      </select>
24                  </p>
25              </card>
26          </wml>
27  </xsl:template>
28  <xsl:template match = "item">
29      <option title = "Info" onpick =
30          "cartXML.GetDescriptionServlet?productID={produc-
tID}&amp;techID={techID}">
31          <xsl:value-of select = "title"/>
32      </option>
33      </xsl:template>
34  </xsl:stylesheet>
```

(Courtesy of Phone.com, Inc.)

Fig. 16.27 Code listing for `titles.xsl` (part 2 of 2).

The WML generated by applying style sheet **titles.xsl** allows the user to select a title corresponding to the chosen technology. Selecting a title results in the servlet **Get-DescriptionServlet** (Fig. 16.28) being requested.

GetDesriptionServlet also queries the **catalog** database. This servlet looks up a description of a book from the database and generates XML such as

```
1   // Fig. 16.28: GetDescriptionServlet.java
2   // Retrieves description of an item from database
3   package cartXML;
4   import java.io.*;
5   import javax.servlet.*;
6   import javax.servlet.http.*;
7   import java.util.*;
8   import java.text.*;
9   import java.sql.*;
10  import org.w3c.dom.*;
11
12  public class GetDescriptionServlet extends HttpServlet {
13     private Database database;
14
15     public void init( ServletConfig config )
16        throws ServletException
17     {
18        super.init( config );
19        database = new Database( "jdbc:odbc:catalog", "anonymous",
20           "guest" );
21        database.connect();
22     }
23
24     public void service( HttpServletRequest req,
25        HttpServletResponse res )
26        throws ServletException, IOException
27     {
28        try {
29           HttpSession session = req.getSession( true );
30           ShoppingCart cart =
31              ( ShoppingCart ) session.getAttribute( "cart" );
32
33           ServletContext sc = getServletConfig()
34              .getServletContext();
35
36           if ( cart.getUsername() == null ) {
37              sc.getRequestDispatcher( "/index.wml" )
38                 .forward( req, res );
39              return;
40           }
41
42           String productID = req.getParameter( "productID" );
43           String techID = req.getParameter( "techID" );
44           String query = "SELECT * FROM Products, Authors, "
45              + "AuthorList WHERE Products.productID= "
46              + productID + " AND Products.productID = "
```

Fig. 16.28 Code listing for **GetDescriptionServlet.java** (part 1 of 2).

```
47                    + "Authorlist.productid AND Authorlist.authorid = "
48                    + "Authors.authorID";
49
50            ResultSet rs =  database.get( query );
51
52            rs.next();
53
54            double price = rs.getDouble( "price" );
55            String unformattedPrice = String.valueOf( price );
56            NumberFormat priceFormatter =
57               NumberFormat.getCurrencyInstance();
58            String formattedPrice = priceFormatter.format( price );
59
60            XMLCreator xmlCreator = new XMLCreator();
61            Node productNode = xmlCreator.initialize( "product" );
62            Node itemNode  = xmlCreator.addChild(
63               productNode, "item" );
64
65            xmlCreator.addTextNode( xmlCreator.addChild( itemNode,
66               "title" ), rs.getString( "title" ) );
67            xmlCreator.addTextNode( xmlCreator.addChild( itemNode,
68               "edition" ), rs.getString( "edition" ) );
69            xmlCreator.addTextNode( xmlCreator.addChild( itemNode,
70               "pubdate" ), rs.getString( "pubdate" ) );
71            xmlCreator.addTextNode( xmlCreator.addChild( itemNode,
72               "isbn" ), rs.getString( "isbn" ) );
73            xmlCreator.addTextNode( xmlCreator.addChild( itemNode,
74               "author" ), rs.getString( "Name" ) );
75            xmlCreator.addTextNode( xmlCreator.addChild( itemNode,
76               "productID" ), productID );
77            xmlCreator.addTextNode( xmlCreator.addChild( itemNode,
78               "formattedPrice" ), formattedPrice );
79            xmlCreator.addTextNode( xmlCreator.addChild( itemNode,
80               "techID" ), techID );
81
82            res.setContentType( "text/vnd.wap.wml" );
83            PrintWriter output = res.getWriter();
84            Processor processor = new Processor();
85            processor.process( xmlCreator.getDocument(),
86               "C:/jakarta-tomcat/webapps/chapter16/description.xsl",
87               output );
88         }
89      catch ( SQLException sqlex ) {
90          sqlex.printStackTrace();
91      }
92   }
93
94   public void destroy()
95   {
96       database.shutDown();
97   }
98 }
```

Fig. 16.28 Code listing for **GetDescriptionServlet.java** (part 2 of 2).

```
<product>
   <item>
      <title>C: How to Program</title>
      <edition>2</edition>
      <pubdate>1994</pubdate>
      <isbn>0-13-226119-7</isbn>
      <author>Harvey Deitel</author>
      <productID>4</productID>
      <formattedPrice>$50</formattedPrice>
      <unFormattedPrice>50.00</unFormattedPrice>
      <techID>1</techID>
   </item>
</product>
```

containing information for the specified book. This servlet applies style sheet **descrip-tion.xsl** (Fig. 16.29) to the XML generated.

```
1   <!-- Fig. 16.29 : description.xsl -->
2   <!-- Transforms XML from GetDescriptionServlet to WML -->
3   <xsl:stylesheet xmlns:xsl = "http://www.w3.org/1999/XSL/Transform"
4      version = "1.0">
5
6      <xsl:output method = "xml" omit-xml-declaration = "no"
7         doctype-system = "http://www.wapforum.org/DTD/wml_1.1.xml"
8         doctype-public = "-//WAPFORUM//DTD WML 1.1//EN"/>
9
10     <xsl:template match = "/">
11        <wml>
12           <head>
13             <meta http-equiv = "Cache-Control" content = "max-age=0"
14                    forua = "true"/>
15           </head>
16           <card>
17              <xsl:apply-templates/>
18           </card>
19        </wml>
20     </xsl:template>
21
22     <xsl:template match = "item">
23        <do type = "options" label = "Back">
24           <go href =
25              "cartXML.GetTitlesServlet?techID={techID}"
26              method = "post"/>
27        </do>
28        <do type = "accept" label = "Add to cart">
29           <go href =
30              "cartXML.AddToCartServlet"
31              method = "post">
32              <postfield name = "productID" value = "{productID}"/>
33              <postfield name = "title" value = "{title}"/>
34              <postfield name = "author" value = "{author}"/>
35              <postfield name = "isbn" value = "{isbn}"/>
36             <postfield name = "price" value = "{unFormattedPrice}"/>
```

Fig. 16.29 Code listing for **description.xsl** (part 1 of 2).

```
37               </go>
38            </do>
39
40          <p>author: <xsl:value-of select = "author"/></p>
41          <p>price: $<xsl:value-of select = "formattedPrice"/></p>
42          <p>isbn: <xsl:value-of select = "isbn"/></p>
43          <p>edition: <xsl:value-of select = "edition"/></p>
44          <p>published: <xsl:value-of select = "pubdate"/></p>
45       </xsl:template>
46    </xsl:stylesheet>
```

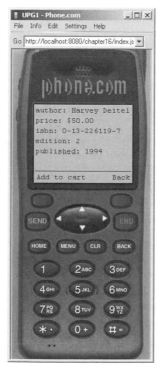

(Courtesy of Phone.com, Inc.)

Fig. 16.29 Code listing for **description.xsl** (part 2 of 2).

If the user selects the **Add to cart** link, servlet **AddToCartServlet** (Fig. 16.30) is requested.

AddToCartServlet (Fig. 16.30) adds one item to the user's shopping cart and forwards the request to **ViewCartServlet** (Fig. 16.31), which displays the user's shopping cart. Line 42

```
int bookElement = cart.contains( productID );
```

checks whether the item is already in the cart. If the book is in the cart, its quantity is increased by one. Otherwise, a new instance of class **Book** (Fig. 16.18) is created and added to the **cart** (line 45).

```
1    // Fig. 16.30: AddToCartServlet.java
2    // Adds an item to shopping cart
3    package cartXML;
4    import java.io.*;
5    import javax.servlet.*;
6    import javax.servlet.http.*;
7    import java.util.*;
8    import java.sql.*;
9
10   public class AddToCartServlet extends HttpServlet {
11
12      public void service( HttpServletRequest req,
13         HttpServletResponse res )
14         throws ServletException, IOException
15      {
16         HttpSession session = req.getSession( true );
17         ShoppingCart cart =
18            ( ShoppingCart ) session.getAttribute( "cart" );
19         ServletContext sc = getServletConfig().getServletContext();
20
21         if ( cart.getUsername() == null ) {
22            sc.getRequestDispatcher( "/index.wml" )
23               .forward( req, res );
24            return;
25         }
26
27         String productID = req.getParameter( "productID" );
28
29         if ( productID == null ) {
30            sc.getRequestDispatcher(
31               "/servlet/cartXML.ViewCartServlet" )
32               .forward( req, res );
33            return;
34         }
35
36         double price = Double.parseDouble(
37            req.getParameter( "price" ) );
38         String title = req.getParameter( "title" );
39         String author = req.getParameter( "author" );
40         String isbn = req.getParameter( "isbn" );
41         String description[] = { title, author, isbn };
42         int bookElement = cart.contains( productID );
43
44         if ( bookElement == -1 )
45            cart.add( new Book( price, 1, productID, description ) );
46         else
47            cart.setQuantity( bookElement, cart.getQuantity (
48               bookElement ) + 1 );
49
50         session.setAttribute( "cart", cart );
51         productID = null;
52         sc.getRequestDispatcher( "/servlet/cartXML.ViewCartServlet" )
53            .forward( req, res );
```

Fig. 16.30 Code listing for **AddToCartServlet.java** (part 1 of 2).

```
54        }
55
56    }
```

Fig. 16.30 Code listing for **AddToCartServlet.java** (part 2 of 2).

The **ShoppingCart** bean is used to create XML because the XML represents what is in the shopping cart. The other servlets used XML that displayed information not belonging to a class. The XML

```xml
<cart numItems = "1" total = "$50">
    <item>
        <productID>4</productID>
        <quantity>1</quantity>
        <price>$50</price>
        <title>C: How to Program</title>
        <author>Harvey Deitel</author>
        <isbn>0-13-226119-7</isbn>
    </item>
</cart>
```

is an example of the XML that could be generated by **ShoppingCart** method **viewCartXML**.

```java
1   // Fig. 16.31: ViewCartServlet.java
2   // displays items in shopping cart
3   package cartXML;
4   import java.io.*;
5   import javax.servlet.*;
6   import javax.servlet.http.*;
7   import java.util.*;
8   import java.sql.*;
9   import org.w3c.dom.*;
10
11  public class ViewCartServlet extends HttpServlet {
12
13     public void service( HttpServletRequest request,
14        HttpServletResponse response )
15        throws ServletException, IOException
16     {
17        HttpSession session = request.getSession( true );
18        ShoppingCart cart = ( ShoppingCart ) session.getAttribute(
19           "cart" );
20        ServletContext sc = getServletConfig()
21           .getServletContext();
22
23        if ( cart.getUsername() == null ) {
24           sc.getRequestDispatcher( "/index.wml" )
25              .forward( request, response );
26           return;
27        }
```

Fig. 16.31 Code listing for **ViewCartServlet.java** (part 1 of 2).

```
28              Document doc = cart.viewCartXML();
29              response.setContentType( "text/vnd.wap.wml" );
30              PrintWriter output = response.getWriter();
31              Processor processor = new Processor();
32              processor.process( doc,
33                 "C:/jakarta-tomcat/webapps/chapter16/viewcart.xsl",
34                 output );
35        }
36  }
```

Fig. 16.31 Code listing for `ViewCartServlet.java` (part 2 of 2).

The document **viewcart.xsl** (Fig. 16.32), the most complicated style sheet in our example, is used to display the user's current shopping cart.

```
1   <xsl:stylesheet xmlns:xsl = "http://www.w3.org/1999/XSL/Transform"
2      version = "1.0">
3
4   <!-- Figure 16.32 : viewcart.xsl            -->
5   <!-- Tranforms XML from ShoppingCart to WML -->
6
7      <xsl:output method = "xml" omit-xml-declaration = "no"
8         doctype-system = "http://www.wapforum.org/DTD/wml_1.1.xml"
9         doctype-public = "-//WAPFORUM//DTD WML 1.1//EN"/>
10
11     <xsl:template match = "/">
12        <wml>
13
14           <head>
15            <meta http-equiv = "Cache-Control" content = "max-age=0"
16                  forua = "true"/>
17           </head>
18
19           <card>
20
21              <do type = "options" label = "Shopping">
22                 <go href =
23                    "cartXML.GetTechnologyServlet"
24                    method = "post"/>
25              </do>
26
27              <xsl:choose>
28                 <xsl:when test = "/cart/@numItems = '0'">
29                    <p>Your cart is empty</p>
30                 </xsl:when>
31                 <xsl:otherwise>  <!-- numItems != 0 -->
32                    <p> Your cart </p>
33                    <p> Total: $<xsl:value-of select =
34                       "/cart/@total"/></p>
35                    <p>
36                       <select name = "items" ivalue = "1">
```

Fig. 16.32 Code listing for **viewcart.xsl** (part 1 of 3).

```
37                          <xsl:for-each select = "/cart/item">
38
39                              <option title = "Info"
40                                 onpick = "#product{productID}">
41                                  <xsl:value-of select = "title"/>
42                              </option>
43
44                          </xsl:for-each>
45                      </select>
46                  </p>
47              </xsl:otherwise>
48          </xsl:choose>
49      </card>
50      <xsl:apply-templates select = "/cart/item"/>
51    </wml>
52   </xsl:template>
53   <xsl:template match = "item">
54
55      <card id = "product{productID}">
56         <p>price: $<xsl:value-of select = "price"/></p>
57         <p>quantity: <xsl:value-of select = "quantity"/></p>
58         <p>author: <xsl:value-of select = "author"/></p>
59         <p>isbn: <xsl:value-of select = "isbn"/></p>
60
61         <do type = "options" label = "change quant">
62            <go href = "#quant{productID}"/>
63         </do>
64
65      </card>
66
67      <card id = "quant{productID}">
68         <onevent type = "onenterforward">
69            <refresh>
70               <setvar name = "quantity" value = ""/>
71            </refresh>
72         </onevent>
73
74         <do type = "accept">
75            <go href =
76               "cartXML.UpdateCartServlet" method = "post">
77              <postfield name = "quantity" value = "$(quantity)"/>
78              <postfield name = "productID" value = "{productID}"/>
79            </go>
80         </do>
81
82         <p>Enter a new quantity</p>
83         <p>
84            <input name = "quantity" emptyok = "false"
85               type = "text" maxlength = "10"/>
86         </p>
87      </card>
88   </xsl:template>
89 </xsl:stylesheet>
```

Fig. 16.32 Code listing for `viewcart.xsl` (part 2 of 3).

(Courtesy of Phone.com, Inc.)

Fig. 16.32 Code listing for **viewcart.xsl** (part 3 of 3).

Lines 14–17

```
<head>
   <meta http-equiv = "Cache-Control" content = "max-age=0"
      forua = "true"/>
</head>
```

delete the cache for this deck. The deck cache is kept by the browser in order to display a page again without requesting it again.

XSL enables document authors to make decisions about what to output, depending on which elements are in an XML document. A common way of doing this is with the **xsl:choose** element. This element selects a condition as specified in the **xsl:when** element. Line 28

```
<xsl:when test = "/cart/@numItems = '0'">
```

is selected when attribute **numItems** of element cart has value 0, and line 31

```
<xsl:otherwise>   <!-- numItems != 0 -->
```

is selected when none of the other **<when>** elements are true (in our example, there is only one **<when>** element). Lines 33 and 34

```
<p> Total: $<xsl:value-of select =
    "/cart/@total"/></p>
```

print out the **total** attribute of element **cart**. The **$** sign escapes the **$** sign contained in the **total** attribute.

There are two ways in XSL to process more than one element. The first way is shown on line 37

```
<xsl:for-each select = "/cart/item">
```

This statement processes all elements of type **item**. Lines 39–42

```
<option title = "Info"
    onpick = "#product{productID}">
    <xsl:value-of select = "title"/>
</option>
```

do not use the **xsl:value-of** element to output a node as previously seen, but use curly braces to display the value of the **productID** element. It is necessary to use this format because it is an error to use the **<** or **>** characters inside an attribute.

The other way of processing multiple elements is by using the **xsl:apply-templates** element. Line 50

```
<xsl:apply-templates select = "/cart/item"/>
```

recursively processes all **item** nodes.

UpdateCartServlet (Fig. 16.33) is requested when the quantity of an item in the user's shopping cart is changed.

```
1   // Fig. 16.33: UpdateCartServlet.java
2   // Changes quantity of an item in shopping cart
3   package cartXML;
4   import java.io.*;
5   import javax.servlet.*;
6   import javax.servlet.http.*;
7   import java.util.*;
8   import java.sql.*;
9
10  public class UpdateCartServlet extends HttpServlet {
11
12      public void service( HttpServletRequest req,
13          HttpServletResponse res )
14          throws ServletException, IOException
15      {
16          HttpSession session = req.getSession( true );
17          ShoppingCart cart = ( ShoppingCart ) session.getAttribute(
18              "cart" );
```

Fig. 16.33 Code listing for **UpdateCartServlet.java** (part 1 of 2).

```
19            ServletContext sc = getServletConfig()
20                .getServletContext();
21
22            if ( cart.getUsername() == null ) {
23                sc.getRequestDispatcher( "/index.wml" )
24                    .forward( req, res );
25                return;
26            }
27
28            String productID =  req.getParameter( "productID" );
29            int bookElement = cart.contains( productID );
30            int quantity = Integer.parseInt( req.getParameter(
31                "quantity" ) );
32
33            if ( quantity == 0 )
34                cart.remove( bookElement );
35            else
36                cart.setQuantity( bookElement, quantity );
37
38            session.setAttribute( "cart", cart );
39           sc.getRequestDispatcher( "/servlet/cartXML.ViewCartServlet" )
40                .forward( req, res );
41        }
42
43    }
```

Fig. 16.33 Code listing for **UpdateCartServlet.java** (part 2 of 2).

Line 34

```
cart.remove( bookElement );
```

removes an item from the cart if the user changes the quantity to zero. Line 36

```
cart.setQuantity( bookElement, quantity );
```

sets the quantity of an item if the **quantity** is changed to a number other than zero.
The file **login.xsl** (Fig. 16.34) uses the XML

```
<login>
    <message>
        You entered an invalid password.
    </message>
</login>
```

created in **LoginServlet** to generate a WML page that displays the message to the user.
If a user logs in successfully, **LoginServlet** requests **GetShoppingCart-Servlet** (Fig. 16.35).

GetShoppingCartServlet (Fig. 16.35) retrieves the user's stored items from database **cart.mdb** and adds the items to the current shopping cart. After the items from the database are added to the shopping cart, line 69

```
session.setAttribute( "cart", cart );
```

adds the shopping cart to the **session**. Finally, when the user decides to log out, servlet **LogoutServlet** (Fig. 16.36) is requested.

Line 27

```
session.invalidate()
```

invalidates the **session**, causing the **valueUnbound** method in class **Shopping-Cart** to be called. The **request** is then forwarded to **index.wml**.

```
1   <xsl:stylesheet xmlns:xsl = "http://www.w3.org/1999/XSL/Transform"
2      version = "1.0">
3
4   <!-- Fig. 16.34 : login.xsl -->
5   <!-- Generate WML page      -->
6
7      <xsl:output method = "xml" omit-xml-declaration = "no"
8         doctype-system = "http://www.wapforum.org/DTD/wml_1.1.xml"
9         doctype-public = "-//WAPFORUM//DTD WML 1.1//EN"/>
10     <xsl:template match = "/">
11        <wml>
12           <card>
13              <do type = "accept">
14                 <go href = "#pass"/>
15              </do>
16              <p>
17                 <xsl:value-of select = "//message"/>
18              </p>
19              <p>
20                 Name:
21                 <input name = "param1" format = "mmmmm*m"
22                    type = "text" maxlength = "10"/>
23              </p>
24           </card>
25           <card id = "pass">
26              <onevent type = "onenterforward">
27                 <refresh>
28                    <setvar name = "param2" value = ""/>
29                 </refresh>
30              </onevent>
31              <do type = "accept">
32                 <go href =
33                    "cartXML.LoginServlet?action=login"
34                    method = "post">
35                    <postfield name = "param2" value = "$(param2)"/>
36                    <postfield name = "param1" value = "$(param1)"/>
37                 </go>
38              </do>
39              <p>Password:
40                 <input name = "param2" format = "mmmmm*m"
41                    type = "password" maxlength = "10"/>
42              </p>
43           </card>
44        </wml>
45     </xsl:template>
46  </xsl:stylesheet>
```

Fig. 16.34 Code listing for **login.xsl** (part 1 of 2).

(Courtesy of Phone.com, Inc.)

Fig. 16.34 Code listing for `login.xsl` (part 2 of 2).

```
1   // Fig. 16.35 : GetShoppingCartServlet.java
2   // Retrieves shopping cart from database
3   package cartXML;
4   import java.io.*;
5   import javax.servlet.*;
6   import javax.servlet.http.*;
7   import java.util.*;
8   import java.sql.*;
9
10  public class GetShoppingCartServlet extends HttpServlet {
11     private Database database1;
12     private Database database2;
13
14     public void init( ServletConfig config )
15        throws ServletException
16     {
17        super.init( config );
```

Fig. 16.35 Code listing for `GetShoppingCartServlet.java` (part 1 of 3).

```
18          database1 = new Database( "jdbc:odbc:cart", "anonymous",
19             "guest" );
20          database1.connect();
21          database2 = new Database( "jdbc:odbc:catalog", "anonymous",
22             "guest" );
23          database2.connect();
24       }
25
26       public void service( HttpServletRequest req,
27          HttpServletResponse res )
28          throws ServletException, IOException
29       {
30
31          HttpSession session = req.getSession( true );
32          ShoppingCart cart =
33             ( ShoppingCart ) session.getAttribute( "cart" );
34          ServletContext sc = getServletConfig()
35                .getServletContext();
36
37          if ( cart.getUsername() == null ) {
38             sc.getRequestDispatcher( "/index.wml" )
39                .forward( req, res );
40             return;
41          }
42
43          ResultSet rs2 = null;
44          ResultSet rs1 = getSavedCart( cart.getUsername() );
45
46          try {
47
48             while ( rs1.next() ) {
49                String productID = rs1.getString( "productID" );
50                int quantity = rs1.getInt( "quantity" );
51
52                rs2 = getBookInfo( productID );
53                rs2.next();
54
55                double price = rs2.getDouble( "price" );
56                Book b = new Book( price, quantity, productID );
57                String[] description = { rs2.getString( "title" ),
58                   rs2.getString( "Name" ), rs2.getString( "isbn" ) };
59
60                b.setDescription( description );
61                cart.add( b );
62             }
63
64          }
65          catch ( SQLException sqlex ) {
66             sqlex.printStackTrace();
67          }
68
69          session.setAttribute( "cart", cart );
```

Fig. 16.35 Code listing for **GetShoppingCartServlet.java** (part 2 of 3).

```
70            sc.getRequestDispatcher( "/servlet/cartXML.ViewCartServlet" )
71               .forward( req, res );
72         }
73
74         public ResultSet getSavedCart( String username )
75         {
76            String query = "SELECT productID, quantity FROM Carts "
77               + "WHERE username= '" + username + "'";
78
79            return database1.get( query );
80         }
81
82         public ResultSet getBookInfo( String s )
83         {
84            String query = "SELECT * FROM Products, Authors, "
85               + "AuthorList  WHERE Products.productID= " + s + " AND "
86               + " Products.productID = Authorlist.productid AND "
87               + "Authorlist.authorid = Authors.authorID";
88
89            return database2.get( query );
90         }
91
92         public void destroy()
93         {
94            database1.shutDown();
95            database2.shutDown();
96         }
97      }
```

Fig. 16.35 Code listing for **GetShoppingCartServlet.java** (part 3 of 3).

```
1    // Fig. 16.36: LogoutServlet.java
2    // Logs user out of site
3    package cartXML;
4    import java.io.*;
5    import javax.servlet.*;
6    import javax.servlet.http.*;
7    import java.util.*;
8
9    public class LogoutServlet extends HttpServlet {
10
11      public void service( HttpServletRequest req,
12         HttpServletResponse res )
13         throws ServletException, IOException
14      {
15         HttpSession session = req.getSession( true );
16         ShoppingCart cart = ( ShoppingCart ) session.getAttribute(
17            "cart" );
18         ServletContext sc = getServletConfig().getServletContext();
19
```

Fig. 16.36 Code listing for **LogoutServlet.java** (part 1 of 2).

```
20          if ( cart.getUsername() == null ) {
21              sc.getRequestDispatcher( "/index.wml" )
22                  .forward( req, res );
23              return;
24          }
25
26          // causes method valueUnbound in ShoppingCart to be called
27          session.invalidate();
28          sc.getRequestDispatcher( " /index.wml" )
29              .forward( req, res );
30      }
31
32  }
```

Fig. 16.36 Code listing for **LogoutServlet.java** (part 2 of 2).

16.8 Internet and World Wide Web Resources

xml.apache.org/cocoon
Home page of the Cocoon Web publishing framework. You can download the latest version of Cocoon with its documentations from this site. Also featured are introductions and explanations of various Cocoon-related technologies and links to useful Java and Cocoon resources on the Web.

www-4.ibm.com/software/developer/education/jsptech
An extensive tutorial for JavaServer Pages. Topics covered include servlets and JavaBeans, in addition to a general comprehensive JSP introduction and tutorial.

java.sun.com/products/jsp/html/jspbasics.fm.html
This is a JSP tutorial from Sun Microsystems. This tutorial provides many code examples and screen shots to demonstrate features and techniques.

java.about.com/compute/java/msubservlet.htm
This page has links to many servlet resources, covering just about all servlet-related topics for which a Web site has been created. This is a great place to start if you would like to get a closer look into current servlet technology.

www.jguru.com/jguru/faq/faqpage.jsp?name=Servlets
The Servlets Frequently Asked Questions page. In addition to providing a good overview of servlets, this site allows you to post your own questions to it.

TERMINOLOGY

Apache Cocoon Project	data sources
application	**Document** object
attribute **class**	**Document** object **colors**
attribute **id**	Document Object Model
attribute **language**	DOM
attribute **scope**	**DOMParser** object
boolean	**Element**
class **DecimalFormat**	explorer
class **Document**	Extensible Server Pages (XSP)
class **XMLSerializer**	**HttpServletRequest** object
Cocoon	**import** packages

INSERT INTO statement

IOException

Java

JavaServer Pages™ (JSP)

JDBC

JDBC drivers

language-dependent manner

lynx

method **executeQuery**

method **executeUpdate**

method **update**

netscape

Node interface

class **Connection**

object **out**

ODBC data sources

opera

package **org.apache.xerces.parsers**

POST request

print methods

PrintWriter class

program-level code declarations

query string

request

request object

RequestDispatcher interface

response

ResultSet

ResultSet object

server

servlet engine

session

SELECT query

Statement interface

supported databases

tag libraries

top-level code declarations

Uniform Resource Locator (URL)

URL (Uniform Resource Locator)

useBean tag

WAP (Wireless Application Protocol)

Web publishing framework

WML (Wireless Markup Language)

wrapper

XSP (Extensible Server Pages)

XSP document

xsp:attribute

xsp:comment

xsp:content

xsp:element

xsp:expr

xsp:include

xsp:logic

xsp:page

xsp:pi

xsp:structure

SELF-REVIEW EXERCISES

16.1   How does Cocoon separate content from presentation for delivering Web content to different types of clients?

16.2   How is processing logic embedded and implemented in an XSP?

16.3   What is the structure of a WML document and how does this benefit wireless device users?

16.4   What is the purpose of the Java servlets in the wireless online bookstore case study?

ANSWERS TO SELF-REVIEW EXERCISES

16.1   Cocoon uses a three-level framework in which content is marked up as XML and then processed and formatted using XSLT. Through XSLT processing the original content is transformed into a specialized presentation for each type of client for which an XSL style sheet is supplied.

16.2   XSP uses the **xsp:logic** element to embed processing logic within an XSP. The processing logic is then implemented in a programming language, such as Java.

16.3   A WML document consists of a deck of cards. Each card contains one page of content to be displayed on the WAP device. Since multiple pages of content are contained in a single WML deck, the overhead of connecting to the network to download each page of content is reduced. This provides quicker response to the user and reduced connection costs.

16.4   In the wireless online bookstore case study, servlets form the middle tier of the three-tier application. Servlets implement all of the business and presentation logic needed to present data to users and receive and process requests from users.

EXERCISES

16.5   Use Cocoon to transform a simple XML file. Create a separate XSL style sheet for four of the browsers listed in Fig. 16.2. After XSL processing, each page should indicate which browser the client is using.

16.6   Create an XSP guestbook that allows users to enter their names, e-mail addresses and comments. The guestbook should ask the user to select a color, which should be used when displaying the user's comments. Once the user has entered information, the server should display all the comments stored in the guestbook, as well as the dates on which the comments were entered; the contents of the guestbook should be stored as an XML file on the server.

16.7   Modify the online bookstore application by creating a WML page that allows the user to search for a book by title and year published. This information should be sent to a servlet that looks up the search string in the database and returns the results, if any. The servlet should create XML containing the search results. The servlet should also process the XSL to generate the results.

17

Perl and XML: A Web-based Message Forums Application

Objectives

- To understand how to use Perl and XML to create a message forum.
- To understand how to use the **XML::Parser** module.
- To understand how to use the **XML::DOM** module.
- To be able to add a new forum.
- To be able to add a message to a forum.
- To understand how to perform XSLT transformations on both the client and server.

If it's a good script I'll do it. And if it's a bad script, and they pay me enough, I'll do it.
George Burns

The Universe is like a safe to which there is a combination. But the combination is locked up in the safe.
Peter De Vries

Comment is free, but facts are sacred.
C. P. Scott

17.1 Introduction

In this chapter, we use XML and many of the technologies presented in the first 14 chapters to create one of the most popular types of Web sites: a *message forum*. Message forums are "virtual" bulletin boards where various topics are discussed. Common features of message forums include discussion groups, questions and answers, and general comments. Many Web sites host message forums. For example,

```
www.egroups.com
web.eesite.com/forums
www.deja.com
```

are popular message forums.

The message forum we create in this chapter uses *Perl (Practical Extraction and Report Language)*. [*Note*: If you are not familiar with Perl or need a review, we have provided an introduction to Perl in Chapter 26.] In this case study, users can post messages and start new forums. We leave the removal of a forum as an exercise for the reader.

17.2 Perl and XML

Perl is well known for its powerful text-processing capabilities, which make it an ideal candidate for XML processing. Support for XML is provided through a large collection of XML libraries, or *modules*, which are freely available. In this chapter, we focus on the two most mature Perl/XML modules, **XML::Parser** and **XML::DOM**, to process and manipulate our XML documents.

17.3 Setup

In this section, we provide the instructions for setting up the software and networks necessary to execute this case study. Perform the following steps:

1. Install Microsoft Personal Web Server (PWS), Microsoft Internet Information Server (IIS) or Apache Web Server. [*Note*: Each of these three servers may be used with Windows.] The Web server must be configured to execute Common Gateway Interface (CGI) scripts. This usually means that the server must be set up

to execute files located in a certain directory (e.g., **cgi-bin**) or with a certain extension (such as **.cgi** or **.pl**). The CGI scripts must be accessible and (on Unix systems) executable by the Web server. From the Chapter 17 examples directory on the CD-ROM that accompanies this book copy the files **default.pl**, **addForum.pl**, **addPost.pl** and **forum.pl** to the **cgi-bin** directory. This directory is at the same level as our Web root directory (e.g., **htdocs** on Apache, **c:\InetPub\Wwwroot** on Windows, etc.). See the Web server's documentation for the specifics of CGI configuration.

2. Install Perl 5. Windows users can download ActivePerl (a Perl 5 implementation for Windows) from **www.activestate.com**. Unix users can download Perl 5 from **www.perl.com**.

3. Install the **XML::Parser** and **XML::DOM** Perl modules. These modules are available at CPAN (**www.cpan.org**) or may be installed with ActivePerl using the PPM (Perl Package Manager).

4. Copy the XML, XSL and CSS files from the Chapter 17 examples directory (on the CD-ROM that accompanies this book) to the directory named **XML**, located in your Web root directory. If this directory does not exist, create it. Each of these files and documents is summarized in Fig. 17.1. We discuss these momentarily.

The main page generated by **default.pl** displays the list of available message forums, which are stored in the XML document **forums.xml**. Hyperlinks are provided to each XML message forum document and to script **addForum.pl**, which adds a forum to **forums.xml** and creates a new XML message forum (e.g., **forum2.xml**) using the message forum template **template.xml**.

Each XML message forum document (e.g., **feedback.xml**) is transformed into an HTML document using XSLT document **formatting.xsl**. The CSS document **site.css** formats the HTML for display. New messages are posted to a forum by **addPost.pl**. If errors occur when the document is processed, **invalid.html** is displayed. Some of the key interactions between documents are illustrated in Fig. 17.2.

Filename	Description
forums.xml	XML document listing all available forums and their filenames.
default.pl	Main page, providing navigational links to the forums.
template.xml	Template for a message forum XML document.
addForum.pl	Adds a forum.
feedback.xml	Sample message forum.
formatting.xsl	Document for transforming message forums into HTML.
addPost.pl	Adds a message to a forum.
invalid.html	Used to display an error message.
site.css	Stylesheet for formatting HTML documents.

Fig. 17.1   Message forum documents.

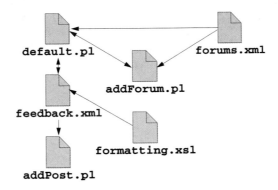

Fig. 17.2 Key interactions between message forum documents.

17.4 Displaying the Forums using `XML::Parser`

This section introduces the documents used for organizing and displaying the message fo rums. For this case study, we provide a sample forum named **feedback.xml** (Fig. 17.3) to show the structure of a form document.

Notice on line 4 the reference to the stylesheet **formatting.xsl**. This XSL document, which we discuss later in the chapter, transforms the forum to HTML for display. Every forum document has root element **forum**, which contains one attribute named **file**. This attribute's value is the name of the forum's XML document. Child elements include **name**, for specifying the title of the forum, and **message**, for marking up the of the message. A message contains a user name, a message title and the message text, which are marked up by elements **user**, **title** and **text**, respectively.

Every message forum name and filename is stored in a document named **forums.xml** (Fig. 17.4). As forums are added, this document is modified to add the new forum names and filenames.

```
1   <?xml version = "1.0"?>
2   <!-- Fig. 17.3: feedback.xml -->
3
4   <?xml:stylesheet type = "text/xsl" href = "../XML/formatting.xsl"?>
5
6   <forum file = "feedback.xml">
7      <name>Feedback</name>
8
9      <message timestamp = "Tue Aug  8 13:18:15 2000">
10         <user>Emily</user>
11         <title>Nice forums!</title>
12         <text>These forums are great! Well done, all.</text>
13      </message>
14
15   </forum>
```

Fig. 17.3 XML document representing a forum containing one message.

```
1   <?xml version = "1.0"?>
2   <!-- Fig. 17.4: forums.xml -->
3
4   <?xml:stylesheet type = "text/xsl" href = "formatting.xsl"?>
5
6   <forums>
7
8      <forum filename = "feedback.xml">
9         <name>Feedback</name>
10     </forum>
11
12  </forums>
```

Fig. 17.4 XML document containing data for all available forums.

Root element **forums** (line 6) contains one or more **forum** child elements. Initially, one forum (i.e., **Feedback**) is provided. Each forum element has attribute **filename** and child element **name**. This forum corresponds to the XML document presented in Fig. 17.3.

Visitors to the message forum are first greeted by the Web page displayed in Fig. 17.5, which displays links to all forums and provides forum management options. Initially, only two links are active—one to the **Feedback** forum and one to create a new forum. The links for modifying and deleting forums are to be created by the reader in chapter exercises and are therefore disabled here. This Perl CGI script **use**s the **XML::Parser** module (line 8) to parse **forums.xml**.

```
1   #!/usr/bin/perl
2   # Fig. 17.5: default.pl
3   # Default page for XML forums
4
5   use warnings;
6   use strict;
7   use CGI qw( :standard );
8   use XML::Parser;
9   use Fcntl qw( :flock );
10
11  my ( $parser, @files, @forums, @items );
12
13  open  XML, "../htdocs/XML/forums.xml" or die "Could not open: $!";
14  flock XML, LOCK_SH;
15  $parser = new XML::Parser( Handlers => { Start => \&startTag,
16                                           Char  => \&text      } );
17  $parser->parse( \*XML );
18  close XML;
19
20  print header, start_html( -title => "Deitel Message Forums",
21                            -style => { -src => "../XML/site.css" } );
22
23  print h1( "Deitel Message Forums" );
24
```

Fig. 17.5 Opening page for message forums (part 1 of 2).

```
25   @items = map { a( { -href => "../XML/$files[ $_ ]" }, $forums[ $_ ])}
26                 ( 0 .. $#files );
27
28   print p( strong( "Available Forums" ), ul( li( \@items ) ) );
29
30   @items = ( a( { -href => "addForum.pl" }, "Add a Forum" ),
31              "Delete a Forum", "Modify a Forum" );
32
33   print p( strong( "Forum Management" ), ul( li( \@items ) ) ),
34         end_html;
35
36   sub startTag
37   {
38      my ( $expat, $element, %attributes ) = @_;
39      push( @files, $attributes{ "filename" } ) if $element eq "forum";
40   }
41
42   sub text
43   {
44      my ( $expat, $string ) = @_;
45      push( @forums, $string ) if $expat->in_element( "name" );
46   }
```

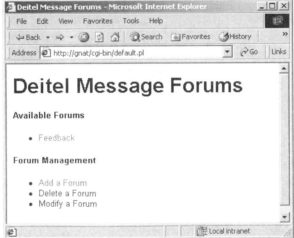

Fig. 17.5   Opening page for message forums (part 2 of 2).

In order to perform the parsing, we open **forums.xml** (line 13) and obtain a *shared lock* on the file (line 14) using **flock**. The first argument to **flock** is a filehandle. The second argument is one of four different lock types. If the second argument is a **1**, it locks the file with a *shared lock* (i.e., more than one script may read from the file at the same time). We use the **Fcntl** module's **:flock** tag (line 9) so that we can use **LOCK_SH** instead of the number **1** (line 14) to specify a shared lock.

Lines 15 and 16

```
$parser = new XML::Parser( Handlers => { Start => \&startTag,
                           Char  => \&text        } );
```

instantiate an event-based parser object. A set of handlers, i.e., references to programmer-defined subroutines, are declared and passed to the **Parser** constructor. For example, the assignment of subroutine **startTag** to handler **Start** indicates that every time the parser encounters a start tag, it invokes subroutine **startTag**. Similarly, every time the parser encounters character data, it invokes subroutine **text**. [*Note*: A *reference* is a scalar whose value is the location of another variable. A reference is created when a variable or subroutine is preceded with a backslash, \.]

Line 17

```
$parser->parse( \*XML );
```

invokes the parser object's ***parse*** method to parse **forums.xml**. We pass this method a reference to a filehandle. Method **parse** creates the arrays of filenames and forum names. Once the parsing is complete, we close **forums.xml** (line 18).

In lines 20–34, we output the HTML shown in Fig. 17.5. We set the attribute **-style** (line 21) in order to use a Cascading Style Sheet to format the page. Lines 25 and 26

```
@items = map { a( { -href => "../XML/$files[ $_ ]" }, $forums[ $_ ] ) }
           ( 0 .. $#files );
```

use ***map*** to create an array (**@items**) containing links to the various forums. To create this array, we call function **a** (i.e., an anchor) to create anchors for the filenames and forum names. One link is created for each element in **@files** (line 26).

After array **@items** is created, we create a reference to it (line 28) and use **li**'s distributive property to output an unordered list (i.e., **ul**) to the page.

We reuse array **@items** in lines 30 and 31 to create an array of links to the forum-management option. These links are written to the client in lines 33 and 34.

Lines 36–46 are the handler subroutines that the parser calls. The parser passes arguments to these subroutines. The first argument passed to all handlers is an ***Expat*** object (defined in the ***XML::Parser::Expat*** *module*) that describes the element encountered. This object is a low-level interface to *expat*, an XML parser written in C by James Clark. We use this **Expat** object in **startTag**, which we discuss momentarily.

The other arguments passed to a handler vary, depending on the handler. A **Start** handler is passed the name of the start tag and an attribute name-value pair list. In line 38, we assign these arguments to the variables **$expat**, **$element** and **%attributes**, respectively. A **Char** handler is passed a string containing the character data, which we assign to variable **$string** in the **text** subroutine in line 44.

In **startTag**, we check if we have encountered the start tag of a **forum** element (line 39). If so, we extract the **filename** attribute from the element and **push** it onto an array of filenames (**@files**). Similarly, in subroutine **text**, we call method ***in_element*** for the object referenced by **$expat** to determine if the text was found within a **name** element. If so, we **push** the found text (**$string**) onto a list of forum names (**@forums**).

17.5 Using **XML::DOM** to Add Forums and Messages

In this section, we discuss the scripts and documents used to add forums and messages. The Perl script that adds a new forum is shown in Fig. 17.6. It uses the **XML::DOM** module to manipulate XML documents in accordance with the W3C DOM recommendation.

```perl
1   #!/usr/bin/perl
2   # Fig. 17.6: addForum.pl
3   # Adds a forum to the list
4
5   use warnings;
6   use strict;
7   use CGI qw( :standard );
8   use XML::DOM;
9   use Fcntl qw( :flock :DEFAULT );
10
11  if ( param ) {
12     my ( $parser, $document, $forums, $forum, $name );
13
14     my ( $file, $newfile ) = ( "forums.xml", param( "filename" ) );
15     $newfile =~ /^\w+\.xml$/ or die "Not a valid file: $!";
16
17     sysopen NEW, "../htdocs/XML/$newfile" , O_WRONLY|O_EXCL|O_CREAT
18        or die "Could not create: $!";
19     open FORUMS, "+< ../htdocs/XML/$file" or die "Could not open: $!";
20     flock FORUMS, LOCK_EX;
21
22     $parser = new XML::DOM::Parser;
23     $document = $parser->parse( \*FORUMS );
24     $forums = $document->getDocumentElement;
25
26     $forum = $document->createElement( "forum" );
27     $forum->setAttribute( "filename", $newfile );
28     $forums->insertBefore( $forum, $forums->getFirstChild );
29
30     $name = $document->createElement( "name" );
31     $name->addText( param( "name" ) );
32     $forum->appendChild( $name );
33
34     seek FORUMS, 0, 0;
35     truncate FORUMS, 0;
36     $document->print( \*FORUMS );
37     close FORUMS;
38
39     $document = $parser->parsefile( "../htdocs/XML/template.xml" );
40     $forum = $document->getDocumentElement;
41     $forum->setAttribute( "file", $newfile );
42
43     $name = $document->createElement( "name" );
44     $name->addText( param( "name" ) );
45     $forum->appendChild( $name );
46
47     $document->print( \*NEW );
48     close NEW;
49     print redirect( "default.pl" );
50
51  }
52  else {
```

Fig. 17.6 Script that adds a new forum to forums.xml (part 1 of 2).

```
53        print header, start_html( -title => "Add a forum",
54                                -style => { -src => "../XML/site.css" } );
55        print start_form,
56            "Forum Name", br,
57            textfield( -name => "name", -size => 40 ), br,
58            "Forum File Name", br,
59            textfield( -name => "filename", -size => 40 ), br,
60            submit( -name => "submit", value => "Submit" ),
61            reset, end_form,
62            a( { -href => "default.pl" }, "Return to Main Page" ),
63            end_html;
64    }
```

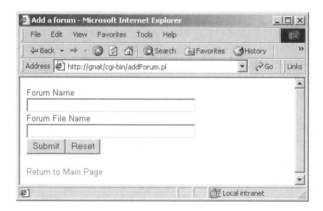

Fig. 17.6   Script that adds a new forum to **forums.xml** (part 2 of 2).

When the script is initially executed, it is not passed any parameters. The **if** statement in line 11 directs program flow immediately to line 52. Lines 52–64 output a simple form that prompts the user for a forum name and a filename for the XML document to be created. When the form is submitted, the script is executed again. This time, **param** returns true, and lines 12–49 are executed.

In line 15, as a security precaution, we examine the filename posted to the script to make sure it contains only alphanumeric characters and ends with **.xml**; if not, the script terminates. This helps prevent the possibility of someone writing to a system file or otherwise gaining unrestricted access to the server. If the filename is valid, we attempt to create the new file in lines 17 and 18 using function **sysopen**. This file is write only (i.e., **O_WRONLY**). The **sysopen** operation will fail if the file already exists, as specified by **O_EXCL**. Constant **O_CREAT** specifies that the file should be created if it does not exist.

In lines 19 and 20, we open file **forums.xml** for reading and writing (**+<**) and obtain an *exclusive lock* (i.e., only this script can access the file's contents), because we will be altering the file. This lock is released when the script terminates.

The **XML::DOM::Parser** object created in line 22 is a derivation of the **XML::Parser** object discussed in Fig. 17.5. Method **parse** creates a DOM representation of the document (a W3C **Document** object), which we assign to variable **$document**. In line 24, we call **getDocumentElement** to access the root element **forums**.

Because we wish to create a new **forum** element within **forums**, we call the **Document** object's method **createElement** in line 26 with the name of the new element (**forum**). We set the **filename** attribute of the newly created element (an **Element** object) by calling **setAttribute** with the name and value of the attribute. Line 28

```
$forums->insertBefore( $forum, $forums->getFirstChild );
```

inserts the new **$forum** before the first child of **$forums** (found with method **getFirstChild**) by calling method **insertBefore**. This way, the most recently added forums appear first in the forum list.

The **forum** element contains only one piece of information—the forum name—which we add in lines 30–32. We first create another new element (line 30). To add character data between the start and end tags of the new element, we call method **addText** in line 31 with the name entered by the user in the form, i.e., **param("name")**. We then add this child element to **$forum** with the method **appendChild** (line 32).

To rewrite over the old file, we **seek** (line 34) to the beginning and delete any existing data (by truncating the file to size 0). We use method **print** to print the updated XML document to filehandle **FORUMS**, and then we close the filehandle (lines 36 and 37).

Line 39 parses file **template.xml** (Fig. 17.7, which is discussed momentarily) by calling method **parsefile** and assigns the new document to **$document**. We again call **getDocumentElement** to get the empty forum (line 40) and then set its **filename** attribute to contain the given filename (line 41). In lines 43–45, we add the **name** element, much as we did earlier in lines 30–32. We output the final result to **NEW** and close the filehandle in lines 47 and 48. The user is returned to the default page in line 49.

After updating **forums.xml** to include the new forum, we must create a new XML document that represents the forum. To simplify things, we provide a template XML document named **template.xml** (Fig. 17.7), which we use for all new forums. The template contains an empty **forums** element, to which we add the forum name and filename.

Figure 17.8 is a script that allows users to add messages. When the documents are rendered using **formatting.xsl** (Fig. 17.9), a link to **addPost.pl** is added to the page, which includes the current forum's filename. This filename is passed as a parameter to **addPost.pl** (e.g., **addPost.pl?file=forum1.xml**) in Fig. 17.8.

If a single parameter (i.e., the filename) is passed, the script execution proceeds to lines 40–57, which, as in Fig. 17.5, output a simple form. The form includes fields for the user name, message title and message text and passes the forum filename as a hidden value (line 51). Note that if no parameters are passed to the script, the script has been accessed in an inappropriate way, and the user is redirected to an error document (line 59).

When the form data are submitted, the posted information is processed, starting by the script starting in line 11. As in the previous example (Fig. 17.6), we validate the filename, open the file and obtain an exclusive lock (lines 15–17). We parse the forum file, create a new message element, set the **timestamp** attribute and append the **timestamp** attribute as a child to the **forum** element (lines 19–25).

In lines 27–31, we create elements representing the **user**, **title** and **text**, and add text based on the values entered in the form (obtained by **param**). We then **seek** and **truncate** to eliminate the old data, and then we write the new XML markup to **FORUM** in lines 33–35, after which the filehandle is closed and the user is **redirect**ed to the newly created XML document.

```
1    <?xml version = "1.0"?>
2
3    <!-- Fig. 17.7 : template.xml -->
4
5    <?xml:stylesheet type = "text/xsl" href = "../XML/formatting.xsl"?>
6    <forum>
7    </forum>
```

Fig. 17.7   XML template used to generate new forums.

```
1    #!/usr/bin/perl
2    # Fig. 17.8: addPost.pl
3    # Adds a posting to a forum
4
5    use warnings;
6    use strict;
7    use CGI qw( :standard );
8    use XML::DOM;
9    use Fcntl qw( :flock );
10
11   if ( param( "submit" ) ) {
12       my ( $parser, $document, $forum, $message, $element );
13
14       my $file = param( "file" );
15       $file =~ /^\w+\.xml$/                or die "Not a valid file: $!";
16       open FORUM, "+< ../htdocs/XML/$file" or die "Could not open: $!";
17       flock FORUM, LOCK_EX;
18
19       $parser = new XML::DOM::Parser;
20       $document = $parser->parse( \*FORUM );
21       $forum = $document->getDocumentElement;
22
23       $message = $document->createElement( "message" );
24       $message->setAttribute( "timestamp", scalar( localtime ) );
25       $forum->appendChild( $message );
26
27       foreach ( qw( user title text ) ) {
28           $element = $document->createElement( $_ );
29           $element->addText( param( $_ ) );
30           $message->appendChild( $element );
31       }
32
33       seek FORUM, 0, 0;
34       truncate FORUM, 0;
35       $document->printToFileHandle( \*FORUM );
36       close FORUM;
37       print redirect( "../XML/$file" );
38
39   }
40   elsif ( param ) {
41       my $file = param( "file" );
```

Fig. 17.8   Script that adds a new message to a forum (part 1 of 2).

```
42       print header, start_html( -title => "Add a posting",
43                            -style => { -src => "../XML/site.css" } );
44       print start_form,
45          "User", br,
46          textfield( -name => "user", -size => 40 ), br,
47          "Message Title", br,
48          textfield( -name => "title", -size => 40 ), br,
49          "Message Text", br,
50          textarea( -name => "text", -cols =>  40, -rows => 5 ), br,
51          hidden(   -name => "file", -value => $file ),
52          submit(   -name => "submit", -value => "Submit" ),
53          reset, end_form,
54          a( { -href => "../XML/$file" }, "Return to Forum" ),
55          end_html;
56
57    }
58    else {
59       print redirect( "error.html" );
60    }
```

Fig. 17.8   Script that adds a new message to a forum (part 2 of 2).

17.6 Alterations for Non-XSL Browsers

The forum system implemented in this case study uses an XSL stylesheet to display XML documents in the client's browser. This XSL file (**formatting.xsl**) is shown in Fig. 17.9. Lines 18–53 contain the template for the **forum** element, and lines 55–84 describe the template for rendering each message element in the forum file.

```
1    <?xml version = "1.0"?>
2
3    <!-- Fig. 17.9 : formatting.xsl -->
4
5    <xsl:stylesheet xmlns:xsl = "http://www.w3.org/TR/WD-xsl">
6
7       <xsl:template match = "*|@*|text()|cdata()|comment()|pi()">
8          <xsl:copy><xsl:apply-templates
9             select = "*|@*|text()|cdata()|comment()|pi()"/></xsl:copy>
10      </xsl:template>
11
12      <xsl:template match = "/">
13         <HTML>
14         <xsl:apply-templates select = "*"/>
15         </HTML>
16      </xsl:template>
17
18      <xsl:template match = "forum">
19         <HEAD>
20            <TITLE><xsl:value-of select = "name"/></TITLE>
21            <LINK REL = "stylesheet" TYPE = "text/css"
22               HREF = "../XML/site.css"/>
23         </HEAD>
24
25         <BODY>
26            <TABLE WIDTH = "100%" CELLSPACING = "0"
27               CELLPADDING = "2">
28               <TR>
29                  <TD CLASS = "forumTitle">
30                     <xsl:value-of select = "name"/>
31                  </TD>
32               </TR>
33            </TABLE>
34
35            <BR/>
36            <xsl:apply-templates select = "message"/>
37            <BR/>
38
39            <CENTER>
40               <A>
41                  <xsl:attribute name = "HREF">
42                     ../cgi-bin/addPost.pl?file=
43                     <xsl:value-of select = "@file"/>
44                  </xsl:attribute>
45                  Post a Message
46               </A>
47               <BR/>
48               <BR/>
49             <A HREF = "../cgi-bin/default.pl">Return to Main Page</A>
50            </CENTER>
51
52         </BODY>
```

Fig. 17.9   XSL stylesheet used to format and display XML forum files (part 1 of 2).

```
53          </xsl:template>
54
55          <xsl:template match = "message">
56             <TABLE WIDTH = "100%" CELLSPACING = "0"
57                CELLPADDING = "2">
58                <TR>
59
60                   <TD CLASS = "msgTitle">
61                      <xsl:value-of select = "title"/>
62                   </TD>
63
64                </TR>
65
66                <TR>
67                   <TD CLASS = "msgInfo">
68                      by
69                      <EM><xsl:value-of select = "user"/></EM>
70                      at
71                      <SPAN CLASS = "date">
72                         <xsl:value-of select = "@timestamp"/>
73                      </SPAN>
74                   </TD>
75                </TR>
76
77                <TR>
78                   <TD CLASS = "msgText">
79                      <xsl:apply-templates select = "text"/>
80                   </TD>
81                </TR>
82
83             </TABLE>
84          </xsl:template>
85
86    </xsl:stylesheet>
```

Fig. 17.9   XSL stylesheet used to format and display XML forum files (part 2 of 2).

However, support for XSL is currently available only for Internet Explorer 5 and higher. This means that our message forum application will send XML documents to some browsers (e.g., Netscape Navigator 4.7) that will not know how to render them. To create a more portable application, we will need to include a server-side XML parser that will translate the forum XML documents into HTML.

There is a module named **XML::XSLT**, written by Geert Josten and Egon Willighagen and available on CPAN, that transforms XML using an XSL stylesheet. However, the module is still in its alpha stages (partly because XSL itself is a W3C Candidate Recommendation). For this example, therefore, we use **XML::Parser** to transform the XML forum files.

We first need to make some minor modifications to the existing code in **default.pl** (Fig. 17.5) and **addPost.pl** (Fig. 17.8). Instead of including links to the XML forum files themselves, we want to direct clients to a CGI script that will parse the XML document and display the appropriate HTML. However, it is more efficient to direct browsers that support XSL straight to the XML. We therefore insert a browser check at line 24 of **default.pl** and line 10 of **addPost.pl**:

```
if ( $ENV{ "HTTP_USER_AGENT" } =~ /MSIE/i ) {
    $prefix = "../XML/";
}
else {
    $prefix = "forum.pl?file=";
}
```

The check sets variable **$prefix** according to whether or not MSIE (Microsoft Internet Explorer) appears in the ***HTTP_USER_AGENT*** environment variable. For simplicity, we assume that Internet Explorer 5 is the only version of MSIE being used and do not test for older versions. Note that **use strict** requires that we declare **$prefix** using **my** earlier in the program.

Once **$prefix** has been set, we may use it to customize the URLs generated by the scripts. For example, in line 25 of **default.pl**, we change

```
a( { -href => "../XML/$files[ $_ ]" }, $forums[ $_ ] )
```

to the more versatile

```
a( { -href => "$prefix$files[ $_ ]" }, $forums[ $_ ] )
```

This change directs Internet Explorer users to **../XML/forum.xml**, as before, but sends users of other browsers to **forum.pl?file=forum.xml**, a CGI script (**forum.pl**) that receives a single parameter (i.e., the filename). Similar changes are made in lines 37 and 53 of **addPost.pl**. [*Note*: These modified files are available in the Chapter 17 examples **XSL** directory on the CD-ROM that accompanies this book. The files are named **default_new.pl** and **addPost_new.pl**. Rename the files to **default.pl** and **addPost.pl**, respectively, and place them in the **cgi-bin** directory.]

Figure 17.10 shows **forum.pl**, which transforms the XML documents to HTML. The figure also includes the rendered HTML output. We use Netscape's Communicator to render the HTML.

```
1   #!/usr/bin/perl
2   # Fig. 17.10: forum.pl
3   # Display forum postings for non-XSL browser
4
5   use warnings;
6   use strict;
7   use CGI qw( :standard *center *table );
8   use XML::Parser;
9   use Fcntl qw( :flock );
10
11  print redirect( "error.html" ) if not param;
12
13  my ( $file, $parser, %info );
14
```

Fig. 17.10 Script that transforms an XML forum file into HTML (part 1 of 3).

```
15   $file = param( "file" );
16   $file  =~ /^\w+\.xml$/                   or die "Not a valid file: $!";
17   open  FORUM, "../htdocs/XML/$file" or die "Could not open: $!";
18   flock FORUM, LOCK_SH;
19
20   $parser = new XML::Parser( Style    => "Subs",
21                                Handlers => { Char => \&text } );
22   $parser->parse( \*FORUM );
23   close FORUM;
24
25   sub forum
26   {
27      print header;
28   }
29
30   sub forum_
31   {
32      print br, start_center,
33
34          a( { -href => "../cgi-bin/addPost.pl?file=$file" },
35              "Post a Message" ),
36          br, br,
37          a( { -href => "../cgi-bin/default.pl" },
38              "Return to Main Page" ),
39          end_center, end_html;
40   }
41
42   sub name_
43   {
44      print start_html( -title => $info{ "name" },
45                         -style => { -src => "../XML/site.css" } ),
46
47            start_table( { -width       => "100%",
48                           -cellspacing => "0",
49                           -cellpadding => "2"    } ),
50
51            Tr( td( { -class => "forumTitle" }, $info{ "name" } ) ),
52
53            end_table, br;
54   }
55
56   sub message
57   {
58      my ( $expat, $element, %attributes ) = @_;
59      $info{ "date" } = $attributes{ "timestamp" };
60   }
61
62   sub message_
63   {
64      print start_table( { -width       => "100%",
65                           -cellspacing => "0",
66                           -cellpadding => "2"    } ),
67
```

Fig. 17.10 Script that transforms an XML forum file into HTML (part 2 of 3).

```
68          Tr( [ td( { -class    => "msgTitle" }, $info{ "title" } ),
69
70              td( { -class   => "msgInfo"  },
71                  " by " . em( $info{ "user" } ) . " at " .
72                  span( { -class => "date" }, $info{ "date" } ) ),
73
74              td( { -class    => "msgText"  }, $info{ "text" } ) ] ),
75
76          end_table;
77  }
78
79  sub text
80  {
81      my ( $expat, $string ) = @_;
82      $info{ $expat->current_element } = $string;
83  }
```

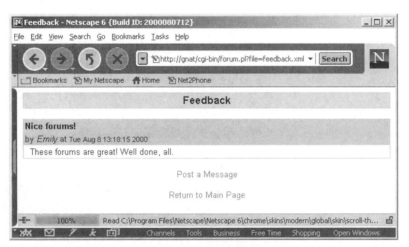

Netscape Communicator browser window© 1999 Netscape Communications
Corporation. Used with permission. Netscape Communications has not authorized,
sponsored, endorsed, or approved this publication and is not responsible for its
content.

Fig. 17.10 Script that transforms an XML forum file into HTML (part 3 of 3).

If no filename is passed to the script, the user is redirected to an error page (Fig. 17.10,
line 11). The basic program procedure (validating the filename, opening, locking, parsing
and closing the XML document) in lines 15–23 is similar to the procedure of the last few
examples. In line 7, we add ***center** and ***table** to import tag **:standard**, thus
instructing **CGI.pm** to create **start_center**, **start_table**, **end_center** and
end_table subroutines for us, which generate the corresponding HTML tags.

One notable change appears in line 20, where we set the parser **Style** attribute to the
value **Subs**. The **XML::Parser Subs** style automatically creates handlers set to subroutines with names derived from the corresponding tag names. For example, every time an
opening **<message>** tag is encountered, subroutine **message** is called. Closing-tag han-

dler subroutines are marked by a trailing underscore; a closing **</message>** tag results in subroutine **message_** being invoked.

Subroutines **forum** and **forum_** (lines 25 and 30) show how the **Subs** style is used. When the opening **<forum>** tag is found, subroutine **forum** outputs the HTTP header (line 27). Its companion closing tag is handled by subroutine **forum_**, which prints two hyperlinks at the bottom of the page, along with the closing HTML tag (lines 32–39).

Note that we declare our own handler for character data (line 21), because the **Subs** style does not automatically create one for us. The handler subroutine **text** is listed in lines 79–83. Because the majority of the data in the XML document we are parsing is represented by character data, we create hash **%info** (line 13) to store these data so they may be used by other handlers. Subroutine **text**, in turn, simply places the encountered string into hash **%info**, using the **current_element** as the key name. For example, text found within **<title>** tags is placed in **$info{ "title" }**.

Because the textual data are placed into **%info** only *after* we encounter the opening tag that contains them, we access the data in the closing-tag handlers (**name_** and **message_**). Thus, in lines 44 and 51 of subroutine **name_**, we can access the forum title, which has been placed into **$info{ "name" }** by subroutine **text**.

Subroutine **message** (lines 56–60) reads the **message** element's value for the time-stamp attribute and (like subroutine **text**) stores the value in hash **%info**. That value, along with the values for **user**, **title** and **text**, are output by subroutine **message_**. Note that in lines 68–74, we use the distributive property of the table-row function **Tr** with an anonymous array (contained in square brackets **[]**) to create three rows, each with one data cell.

17.7 Internet and World Wide Web Resources

www.perl.com
Perl.com is the first place to look for information about Perl. The home page provides up-to-date news on Perl, answers to common questions about Perl and an impressive collection of links to Perl resources of all kinds on the Internet. It includes sites for Perl software, tutorials, user groups and demos.

www.cpan.org
Modules **XML::Parser** and **XML::DOM** can be downloaded at this site, the official central repository for Perl builds and modules.

TERMINOLOGY

addText method	**O_CREAT** constant
appendChild method	**O_EXCL** constant
createElement method	**O_WRONLY** constant
exclusive lock	**parse** method
expat parser	**parsefile** method
getDocumentElement method	Perl modules
getFirstChild method	Perl (Practical Extraction and Report Language)
HTTP_USER_AGENT environment variable	reference
in_element method	**seek** method
insertBefore method	shared lock
map	**Start** handler

Style attribute   XML::DOM module
Subs attribute value   XML::Parser module
Subs style for XML::Parser   XML::XSLT module
sysopen method

SELF-REVIEW EXERCISES

17.1   What is the purpose of the **startTag** and **text** subroutines in Fig. 17.5? What do they do?

17.2   Why must we use **XML::DOM** instead of **XML::Parser** to add forums and messages?

17.3   In Fig. 17.10, why do we output most of the HTML in the closing-tag handlers?

ANSWERS TO SELF-REVIEW EXERCISES

17.1   The **startTag** and **text** subroutines are handlers that are called when the XML parser encounters an opening tag and character data, respectively. Subroutine **startTag** takes the filename attribute of the tag and **push**es its value onto array **@files** (if the tag that triggered the handler was a **<forum>** tag). Subroutine **text push**es the string value encountered onto array **@forums** if the character data are found within a **name** element.

17.2   **XML::DOM** creates a DOM structure representing XML, data which we can then modify and save to a file as XML. This structure allows us to add nodes that represent new forums and messages. **XML::Parser** simply parses XML and thus cannot be used to modify the underlying XML document.

17.3   Because **XML::Parser** is an event-based parser, when we encounter the start tag of an element that contains a child node of character data, the character data have not yet been seen by the parser. Once we reach the end tag, we know that any character data surrounded by the tags have been handled by subroutine **text**, and the necessary information has been stored in hash **%info**.

EXERCISES

17.4   Implement the **Delete a Forum** option in **default.pl**. Selecting this option should display the initial screen, but with each forum name followed by a hyperlink to a script named **delForum.pl**. Your script should remove the given forum from **forums.xml** and delete the underlying XML document. [*Hint*: Look at the **getElementsByTagName** and **removeChild** methods described in the **XML::DOM** documentation.]

17.5   Implement the **Modify a Forum** option in **default.pl** such that individual messages can be deleted. Selecting this option should display the initial screen, but with each forum name followed by a hyperlink to a script named **modForum.pl**. Script **modForum.pl** should display the messages as in **forum.pl**, but each message title should be followed by a link to a script named **delPost.pl**, which removes the given message from the current forum. [*Hint*: Look at the **getElementsByTagName**, **removeChild** and **item** methods described in the **XML::DOM** documentation.]

18

Accessibility

Objectives

- To introduce the World Wide Web Consortium's Web Content Accessibility Guidelines 1.0 (WCAG 1.0).
- To understand how to use the **alt** attribute of the **img** tag to describe images to blind and vision-impaired people, mobile-Web-device users, search engines, etc.
- To understand how to make tables more accessible to page readers by using the **headers** attribute in HTML 4.01.
- To understand how to verify that HTML tags are used properly and to ensure that Web pages are viewable on any type of display or reader.
- To better understand how VoiceXML™ will change the way people with disabilities access information on the Web.

I once was lost, but now am found,
Was blind, but now I see.
John Newton

'Tis the good reader that makes the good book...
Ralph Waldo Emerson

Outline

18.1 Introduction

On April 7, 1997, the World Wide Web Consortium (W3C) launched the *Web Accessibility Initiative* (WAI™). *Accessibility* refers to the level of usability of an application or Web site for people with disabilities. The vast majority of Web sites are considered inaccessible to people with visual, learning or mobility impairments. A high level of accessibility is difficult to achieve, because there are many different disabilities, language barriers, hardware and software inconsistencies, etc. As greater numbers of people with disabilities begin to use the Internet, it is imperative that Web site designers increase the accessibility of their sites. The WAI is an attempt to make the Web more accessible; its mission is described at **www.w3.org/WAI**.

As a member of the World Wide Web Consortium, Deitel & Associates, Inc., is committed to supporting the WAI. This chapter discusses some of the techniques for developing accessible Web sites. The Web Content Accessibility Guidelines 1.0 (**www.w3.org/TR/WCAG10**) are divided into a three-tier structure of checkpoints according to their priority. *Priority-one checkpoints* are goals that must be met in order to ensure accessibility; we focus on these points in this chapter. *Priority-two checkpoints*, though not essential, are highly recommended. *Priority-three checkpoints* slightly improve accessibility. The WAI also presents a supplemental list of *quick tips*, which are suggestions aimed at solving priority-one problems. More information on the WAI Quick Tips can be found at **www.w3.org/WAI/References/Quicktips**.

18.2 Providing Alternatives for Multimedia Content

One important WAI requirement is to ensure that every image, movie and sound used on a Web page is accompanied by a description that clearly defines its purpose. One way of accomplishing this task is to include a description of each item using the **alt** attribute of the **img** and **input** tags. A text equivalent for **object** elements should also be provided, because the elements do not have an **alt** attribute in the HTML 4.01 specification. Figure 18.1 demonstrates use of the **alt** attribute of the **img** tag.

The lack of well-defined **alt** elements increases the difficulty visually impaired users experience in navigating the Web. Specialized *user agent*s, such as *screen readers* (programs that allow users to hear what is being displayed on their screen) and *braille displays* (devices that receive data from screen-reading software and output the data as braille), allow blind and visually impaired people to access text-based information that is normally displayed on the screen. A user agent is an application that interprets Web-page source code and translates it into formatted text and images. Web browsers, such as Microsoft Internet Explorer and Netscape Communicator, and the screen readers mentioned throughout this chapter are examples of user agents.

Web pages with large amounts of multimedia content are difficult for nonvisual user agents to interpret, unless they are designed properly. Images, movies and other non-HTML objects cannot be read by screen readers. Providing multimedia-based information in a variety of ways (i.e., using the **alt** attribute or providing inline descriptions of images) helps maximize the content's accessibility.

Web designers should be sure to provide useful descriptions in the **alt** attribute for use in nonvisual user agents. For example, if the **alt** attribute describes a sales growth chart, it should not describe the data in the chart. Instead, it should specify the chart's title. The chart's data should be included in the Web site's text. Web designers may also use the *longdesc attribute*, which is intended to augment the **alt** attribute's description. The value of the **longdesc** attribute is a URL that links to a Web page describing the image or multimedia content. [*Note:* If an image is used as a hyperlink and the **longdesc** attribute is also used, there is no set standard as to which page is loaded when the image is clicked.]

```
1   <!DOCTYPE HTML PUBLIC "-//W3C//DTD HTML 4.0 Transitional//EN">
2   <html>
3
4   <!-- Fig. 18.1 : altattribute.html                        -->
5   <!-- Using The alt attribute to Make an Image Accessible -->
6
7   <head>
8
9      <title>How To Use the alt Attribute</title>
10
11     <style type = "text/css">
12        body { background: powderblue; }
13        h1 { text-align: center; }
14        p { margin-top: 1em; text-align: center; }
15        p.description { text-align: left; }
16     </style>
17
18  </head>
19
20  <body>
21     <h1>How to use the <strong>alt</strong> attribute</h1>
22
23     <p class = "description">Below we compare two images,
24        one with the <strong>alt</strong> attribute present,
25        and one without. The <strong>alt</strong> appears as
```

Fig. 18.1   Using the **alt** attribute of the **img** tag (part 1 of 3).

```
26          a tool tip in most Web browsers, but, more importantly,
27          will help users who cannot view information conveyed
28          graphically.</p>
29
30      <p>This image has the <strong>alt</strong> attribute</p>
31
32      <p><img width = "182" height = "238"
33          src = "advjhtp1cov.jpg"
34          alt = "This is a picture of the cover of Advanced Java
35                  How to Program">
36      </p>
37
38      <p>
39          This image does not have the <strong>alt</strong> attribute
40      </p>
41
42      <p>
43          <!-- This markup should be changed     -->
44          <!-- to include the alt attribute.     -->
45          <img src = "advjhtp1cov.jpg" width = "182" height = "238">
46      </p>
47
48  </body>
49  </html>
```

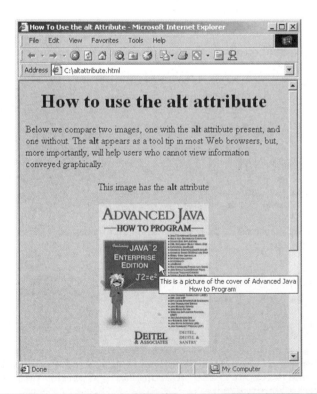

Fig. 18.1 Using the **alt** attribute of the **img** tag (part 2 of 3).

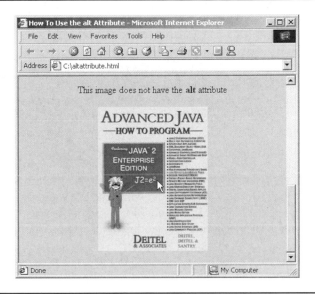

Fig. 18.1   Using the **alt** attribute of the **img** tag (part 3 of 3).

Server-side image maps (images stored on a Web server with areas designated as hyperlinks) are another troublesome technology for some Web users, particularly those who cannot use a mouse. Server-side image maps require clicks of the mouse to initiate their actions. User agents are unable to make server-side image maps accessible to blind people or to users who cannot use a mouse. If equivalent text links are not provided when a server-side image map is used, some users will be unable to navigate the site. User-agent manufacturers will provide accessibility to server-side image maps in the future. Until then, if image maps are used, we recommend using client-side image maps (image maps whose links are designated in the Web page's source and thus can be understood by nongraphical user agents). For an example of the use of client-side image maps, see Fig. 3.7 in Chapter 3, "Introduction to HyperText Markup Language 4: Part II." For more information regarding the use of image maps, visit **www.w3.org/TR/REC-html40/struct/ objects.html#h-13.6**.

Good Programming Practice 18.1

Always provide generous descriptions and corresponding text links for all image maps.

Using a screen reader to navigate a Web site can be time consuming and frustrating, as screen readers are unable to interpret pictures and other graphical content. One method of combatting this problem is to include a link at the top of each Web page that provides easy access to the page's content. Users can use the link to bypass an image map or other inaccessible element, by jumping to another part of the page or to a different page.

18.3 Maximizing Readability by Focusing on Structure

Many Web sites use tags for aesthetic purposes, rather than the purpose for which they were intended. For example, the **h1** heading tag is often erroneously used to make text large and bold. The desired visual effect may be achieved, but it creates a problem for screen readers: When the screen reader software encounters the **h1** tag, it may verbally inform the user that a new section has been reached, which may confuse the user. Only use tags such as **h1** in accordance with their HTML specification (e.g., as headings to introduce important sections of a document). Instead of using **h1** to make text large and bold, use Cascading Style Sheets (discussed in Chapter 4) or XSL (discussed in Chapters 12 and 13) to format and style the text. Please refer to the Web Content Accessibility Guidelines 1.0 at **www.w3.org/TR/WCAG** for further examples. [*Note:* the **strong** tag may also be used to make text bold; however, the inflection with which the text is spoken by screen readers may be affected.]

Another accessibility issue is *readability*. When creating a Web page intended for the general public, it is important to consider the reading level at which it is written. Web site designers can make their site more readable through the use of shorter words, as some users may have difficulty reading long words. In addition, users from other countries may have difficulty understanding slang and other nontraditional language, so these types of words should also be avoided.

The Web Content Accessibility Guidelines 1.0 suggest using a paragraph's first sentence to convey its subject. Immediately stating the point of the paragraph in the first sentence makes finding crucial information much easier and allows readers to bypass unwanted material.

A good way to evaluate a Web site's readability is by using the *Gunning Fog Index*. The Gunning Fog Index is a formula that produces a readability grade when applied to a text sample. For more information on the Gunning Fog Index, see **www.w3.org/TR/ WAI-WEBCONTENT-TECHS**.

18.4 Accessibility in HTML Tables

Complex Web pages often contain tables for formatting content and presenting data. Tables cause problems for many screen readers, which are often incapable of translating tables in an understandable manner unless the tables are designed properly. For example, the *CAST eReader*, a screen reader developed by the Center for Applied Special Technology (**www.cast.org**), starts at the top-left-hand cell and reads, from top to bottom, columns from left to right. This procedure is known as reading a table in a *linearized* manner. The CAST eReader would thus read the table in Fig. 18.2 as follows:

```
Price of Fruit Fruit Price Apple $0.25 Orange $0.50 Banana
$1.00 Pineapple $2.00
```

This reading does not adequately present the content of the table. The Web Content Accessibility Guidelines 1.0 recommend using Cascading Style Sheets (discussed in Chapter 4) instead of tables unless the content in your tables, linearizes in an understandable way.

If the table in Fig. 18.2 were large, the screen reader's linearized reading would be even more confusing to the user. By modifying the **td** tag with the **headers** attribute and modifying *header cells* (cells specified by the **th** tag) with the **id** attribute, you can ensure that a table is read as intended. Figure 18.3 demonstrates how these modifications change the way a table is interpreted.

This table does not appear to be different from a standard HTML table. However, to a person using a screen reader, this table is read in a more intelligent manner. A screen reader would vocalize the data from the table in Fig. 18.3 as follows:

```
1    <!DOCTYPE HTML PUBLIC "-//W3C//DTD HTML 4.0 Transitional//EN">
2
3    <html>
4    <!-- Fig. 18.2 : withoutheaders.html -->
5
6    <head>
7       <title>HTML Table Without Headers</title>
8
9       <style type = "text/css">
10          body { background: #ccffaa;
11                 text-align: center; }
12       </style>
13    </head>
14
15    <body>
16
17       <p>Price of Fruit</p>
18
19       <table border = "1" width = "50%">
20
21          <tr>
22             <td>Fruit</td>
23             <td>Price</td>
24          </tr>
25
26          <tr>
27             <td>Apple</td>
28             <td>$0.25</td>
29          </tr>
30
31          <tr>
32             <td>Orange</td>
33             <td>$0.50</td>
34          </tr>
35
36          <tr>
37             <td>Banana</td>
38             <td>$1.00</td>
39          </tr>
40
41          <tr>
42             <td>Pineapple</td>
43             <td>$2.00</td>
44          </tr>
45
46       </table>
47
48    </body>
49    </html>
```

Fig. 18.2   HTML table without accessibility modifications (part 1 of 2).

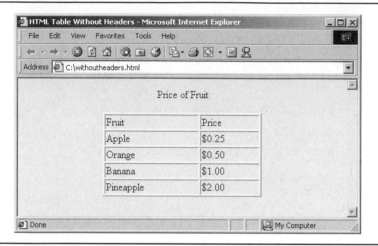

Fig. 18.2   HTML table without accessibility modifications (part 2 of 2).

```
1    <!DOCTYPE HTML PUBLIC "-//W3C//DTD HTML 4.0 Transitional//EN">
2
3    <html>
4    <!-- Fig. 18.3 : withheaders.html -->
5
6    <head>
7       <title>HTML Table With Headers</title>
8
9       <style type = "text/css">
10          body { background: #ccffaa;
11                 text-align: center; }
12       </style>
13    </head>
14
15    <body>
16
17    <!-- This table uses the id and headers attributes to   -->
18    <!-- ensure readability by text-based browsers. It also -->
19    <!-- uses a summary attribute, used screen readers to    -->
20    <!-- describe the table.                                  -->
21
22       <table width = "50%" border = "1"
23          summary = "This table uses th elements and id and headers
24          attributes to make the table readable by screen readers">
25
26          <caption><strong>Price of Fruit</strong></caption>
27
28          <tr>
29             <th id = "fruit">Fruit</th>
30             <th id = "price">Price</th>
31          </tr>
```

Fig. 18.3   Table optimized for screen reading using attribute **headers** (part 1 of 2).

```
32
33        <tr>
34            <td headers = "fruit">Apple</td>
35            <td headers = "price">$0.25</td>
36        </tr>
37
38        <tr>
39            <td headers = "fruit">Orange</td>
40            <td headers = "price">$0.50</td>
41        </tr>
42
43        <tr>
44            <td headers = "fruit">Banana</td>
45            <td headers = "price">$1.00</td>
46        </tr>
47
48        <tr>
49            <td headers = "fruit">Pineapple</td>
50            <td headers = "price">$2.00</td>
51        </tr>
52
53     </table>
54
55   </body>
56   </html>
```

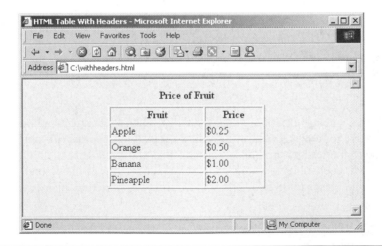

Fig. 18.3 Table optimized for screen reading using attribute **headers** (part 2 of 2).

```
Caption: Price of Fruit
Summary: This table uses th and the id and headers attributes
to make the table readable by screen readers.
Fruit: Apple, Price: $0.25
Fruit: Orange, Price: $0.50
Fruit: Banana, Price: $1.00
Fruit: Pineapple, Price: $2.00
```

Every cell in the table is preceded by its corresponding header when read by the screen reader. This format helps the listener understand the table. The **headers** attribute is specifically intended for tables that hold large amounts of data. Most small tables linearize fairly well as long as the **th** tag is used properly. It also helps to use the **summary** and **caption** attributes.

For more examples demonstrating how to make tables more accessible, visit **www.w3.org/TR/WCAG**.

18.5 Accessibility in HTML Frames

Web designers often use frames to display more than one HTML file in a single browser window. Frames are a convenient way to ensure that certain content is always on screen. Unfortunately, frames often lack proper descriptions, which prevents users with text-based browsers, or users who lack sight, from navigating the Web site.

The most important part of documenting a site with frames is making sure that all of the frames are given a meaningful description in the **title** tag. Examples of good titles are *"Navigation Frame"* and *"Main Content Frame."* Users with text-based browsers, such as Lynx, a UNIX-based Web browser, must choose which frame they want to open, and the use of descriptive titles can make this choice much simpler for them. However, giving titles to frames does not solve all of the navigation problems associated with frames. The **noframes** tag allows Web designers to offer alternative content to users whose browsers do not support frames.

Good Programming Practice 18.2

Always give a text equivalent for frames to ensure that user agents, which do not support frames, are given an alternative.

Good Programming Practice 18.3

*Include a description of each frame's contents within the **noframes** tag.*

The Web Content Accessibility Guidelines 1.0 suggest using Cascading Style Sheets as an alternative to frames, because Cascading Style Sheets can provide similar functionality to that of frames and are highly customizible. Unfortunately, the ability to display multiple HTML documents in a single browser window requires the second generation of Cascading Style Sheets (CSS2), which is not yet fully supported by many user agents.

18.6 Accessibility in XML

Because of the freedom that XML gives developers in creating new markup languages, it is possible that many of these languages might not incorporate accessibility features. To prevent the proliferation of inaccessible languages, the WAI created guidelines for creating accessible XML. The specification focuses only on languages used to mark up data for user-interface rendering, such as the Extensible Hypertext Markup Language (XHTML) discussed in Chapter 19. Accessible DTDs and schemas result in accessible XML documents, so the requirements for accessible DTDs and schemas have been defined. Reuse of existing accessible DTDs and schemas prevents developers from having to reinvent the wheel. In addition, the Guidelines recommend including a text description, similar to HT-

ML's **alt** tag, for each nontext object on a page. XSL, rather than presentational elements, should be used to format XML documents for presentation. To further facilitate accessibility, element types should allow grouping and classification and should identify important content. Without an accessible user interface, other efforts to implement accessibility are much less effective, so it is essential to create stylesheets that can produce multiple outputs, including document outlines. To ensure that hyperlinks are accessible, XLink (discussed in Chapter 14) should be used.

Many XML languages follow the WAI guidelines, including Synchronized Multimedia Integration Language (SMIL) and Scalable Vector Graphics (SVG), which are discussed in Chapter 20. The WAI XML Accessibility Guidelines can be found at **www.w3.org/WAI/PF/xmlgl.htm**.

18.7 Using Voice Synthesis and Recognition with VoiceXML™

A joint effort by AT&T, IBM®, Lucent and Motorola has created an XML application that uses *speech synthesis* to enable the computer to speak to the user. This technology, called *VoiceXML*, has tremendous implications for visually impaired people and for the illiterate. Not only does VoiceXML read Web pages to the user, but it also includes *speech recognition* technology, a technology that enables computers to understand words spoken into a microphone, enabling the computer to interact with the user. An example of a speech recognition tool is IBM's *ViaVoice* (**www-4.ibm.com/software/speech**).

VoiceXML is processed by a VoiceXML interpreter or VoiceXML browser; Web browsers may incorporate these interpreters in the future. When a VoiceXML document is loaded, a *voice server* sends a message to the VoiceXML browser and begins a conversation between the user and the computer.

Voice Server SDK, which was developed by IBM, is a free beta version of a VoiceXML interpreter and can be used for desktop testing of VoiceXML documents. Visit **www.alphaworks.ibm.com** for hardware and software specifications and for more information on Voice Server SDK. Instructions on how to run VoiceXML documents can be obtained along with the software.

Figures 18.4 and 18.5 show examples of VoiceXML for a Web site. The document's text is spoken to the user, and the text embedded within the VoiceXML tags allow for interactivity between the user and the browser. The output included in Fig. 18.5 demonstrates a conversation that might take place between the user and the computer when this document is loaded.

```
1   <?xml version = "1.0"?>
2   <vxml version = "1.0">
3
4   <!-- Fig. 18.4: main.vxml -->
5   <!-- Voice page           -->
6
7   <link next = "#home">
8       <grammar>home</grammar>
9   </link>
10
```

Fig. 18.4 A home page written in VoiceXML (part 1 of 3).

```
11   <link next = "#end">
12      <grammar>exit</grammar>
13   </link>
14
15   <var name = "currentOption" expr = "'home'"/>
16
17   <form>
18      <block>
19         <emp>Welcome</emp> to the voice page of Deitel and
20         Associates. To exit any time say exit.
21         To go to the home page any time say home.
22      </block>
23      <subdialog src = "#home"/>
24   </form>
25
26   <menu id = "home">
27      <prompt count = "1" timeout = "10s">
28         You have just entered the Deitel home page.
29         Please make a selection by speaking one of the
30         following options:
31         <break msecs = "1000 "/>
32         <enumerate/>
33      </prompt>
34
35      <prompt count = "2">
36         Please say one of the following.
37         <break msecs = "1000 "/>
38         <enumerate/>
39      </prompt>
40
41      <choice next = "#about">About us</choice>
42      <choice next = "#directions">Driving directions</choice>
43      <choice next = "publications.vxml">Publications</choice>
44   </menu>
45
46   <form id = "about">
47      <block>
48      About Deitel and Associates, Inc.
49      Deitel and Associates, Inc. is an internationally
50      recognized corporate training and publishing organization,
51      specializing in programming languages, Internet and World
52      Wide Web technology and object technology education.
53      Deitel and Associates, Inc. is a member of the World Wide
54      Web Consortium. The company provides courses on Java, C++,
55      Visual Basic, C, Internet and World Wide Web programming
56      and Object Technology.
57         <assign name = "currentOption" expr = "'about'"/>
58         <goto next = "#repeat"/>
59      </block>
60   </form>
61
62   <form id = "directions">
```

Fig. 18.4   A home page written in VoiceXML (part 2 of 3).

```
63      <block>
64         Directions to Deitel and Associates, Inc.
65         We are located on Route 20 in Sudbury,
66         Massachusetts, equidistant from route
67       <sayas class = "digits">128</sayas> and route
68       <sayas class = "digits">495</sayas>.
69       <assign name = "currentOption" expr = "'directions'"/>
70       <goto next = "#repeat"/>
71      </block>
72   </form>
73
74   <form id = "repeat">
75      <field name = "confirm" type = "boolean">
76         <prompt>
77            To repeat say yes. To go back to home, say no.
78         </prompt>
79
80         <filled>
81            <if cond = "confirm == true">
82               <goto expr = "'#' + currentOption"/>
83            <else/>
84               <goto next = "#home"/>
85            </if>
86         </filled>
87
88      </field>
89   </form>
90
91   <form id = "end">
92      <block>
93         Thank you for visiting Deitel and Associates voice page.
94         Have a nice day.
95         <exit/>
96      </block>
97   </form>
98
99   </vxml>
```

Fig. 18.4   A home page written in VoiceXML (part 3 of 3).

```
100  <?xml version = "1.0"?>
101  <vxml version = "1.0">
102
103  <!-- Fig. 18.5: publications.vxml        -->
104  <!-- Voice page for various publications -->
105
106  <link next = "main.vxml#home">
107     <grammar>home</grammar>
108  </link>
```

Fig. 18.5   Publication page of Deitel's VoiceXML page (part 1 of 4).

```
109  <link next = "main.vxml#end">
110      <grammar>exit</grammar>
111  </link>
112  <link next = "#publication">
113      <grammar>menu</grammar>
114  </link>
115
116  <var name = "currentOption" expr = "'home'"/>
117
118  <menu id = "publication">
119
120      <prompt count = "1" timeout = "12s">
121        Following are some of our publications. For more
122        information visit our web page at www.deitel.com.
123        To repeat the following menu, say menu at any time.
124        Please select by saying one of the following books:
125        <break msecs = "1000 "/>
126        <enumerate/>
127      </prompt>
128
129      <prompt count = "2">
130        Please select from the following books.
131        <break msecs = "1000"/>
132        <enumerate/>
133      </prompt>
134
135      <choice next = "#java">Java.</choice>
136      <choice next = "#c">C.</choice>
137      <choice next = "#cplus">C plus plus.</choice>
138  </menu>
139
140  <form id = "java">
141      <block>
142      Java How to program, third edition.
143      The complete, authoritative introduction to Java.
144      Java is revolutionizing software development with
145      multimedia-intensive, platform-independent,
146      object-oriented code for conventional, Internet,
147      Intranet and Extranet-based applets and applications.
148      This Third Edition of the world's most widely used
149      university-level Java textbook carefully explains
150      Java's extraordinary capabilities.
151        <assign name = "currentOption" expr = "'java'"/>
152        <goto next = "#repeat"/>
153      </block>
154  </form>
155
156  <form id = "c">
157      <block>
158        C How to Program, third edition.
159        This is the long-awaited, thorough revision to the
160        world's best-selling introductory C book! The book's
161        powerful "teach by example" approach is based on
```

Fig. 18.5   Publication page of Deitel's VoiceXML page (part 2 of 4).

```
162           more than 10,000 lines of live code, thoroughly
163           explained and illustrated with screen captures showing
164           detailed output.World-renowned corporate trainers and
165           best-selling authors Harvey and Paul Deitel offer the
166           most comprehensive, practical introduction to C ever
167           published with hundreds of hands-on exercises, more
168           than 250 complete programs written and documented for
169           easy learning, and exceptional insight into good
170           programming practices, maximizing performance, avoiding
171           errors, debugging, and testing. New features include
172           thorough introductions to C++, Java, and object-oriented
173           programming that build directly on the C skills taught
174           in this book; coverage of graphical user interface
175           development and C library functions; and many new,
176           substantial hands-on projects.For anyone who wants to
177           learn C, improve their existing C skills, and understand
178           how C serves as the foundation for C++, Java, and
179           object-oriented development.
180         <assign name = "currentOption" expr = "'c'"/>
181         <goto next = "#repeat"/>
182      </block>
183 </form>
184
185 <form id = "cplus">
186    <block>
187        The C++ how to program, second edition.
188        With nearly 250,000 sold, Harvey and Paul Deitel's C++
189        How to Program is the world's best-selling introduction
190        to C++ programming. Now, this classic has been thoroughly
191        updated! The new, full-color Third Edition has been
192        completely revised to reflect the ANSI C++ standard, add
193        powerful new coverage of object analysis and design with
194        UML, and give beginning C++ developers even better live
195        code examples and real-world projects. The Deitels' C++
196        How to Program is the most comprehensive, practical
197        introduction to C++ ever published with hundreds of
198        hands-on exercises, roughly 250 complete programs written
199        and documented for easy learning, and exceptional insight
200        into good programming practices, maximizing performance,
201        avoiding errors, debugging, and testing. This new Third
202        Edition covers every key concept and technique ANSI C++
203        developers need to master: control structures, functions,
204        arrays, pointers and strings, classes and data
205        abstraction, operator overloading, inheritance, virtual
206        functions, polymorphism, I/O, templates, exception
207        handling, file processing, data structures, and more. It
208        also includes a detailed introduction to Standard
209        Template Library containers, container adapters,
210        algorithms, and iterators.
211      <assign name = "currentOption" expr = "'cplus'"/>
212      <goto next = "#repeat"/>
213   </block>
214 </form>
```

Fig. 18.5   Publication page of Deitel's VoiceXML page (part 3 of 4).

```
215
216  <form id = "repeat">
217     <field name = "confirm" type = "boolean">
218
219        <prompt>
220           To repeat say yes. Say no, to go back to home.
221        </prompt>
222
223        <filled>
224           <if cond = "confirm == true">
225              <goto expr = "'#' + currentOption"/>
226           <else/>
227              <goto next = "#publication"/>
228           </if>
229        </filled>
230     </field>
231  </form>
232  </vxml>
```

Computer:
Welcome to the voice page of Deitel and Associates. To exit any time say exit. To go to the home page any time say home.

User:
Home

Computer:
You have just entered the Deitel home page. Please make a selection by speaking one of the following options: About us, Driving directions, Publications.

User:
Driving directions

Computer:
Directions to Deitel and Associates, Inc.
We are located on Route 20 in Sudbury,
Massachusetts, equidistant from route 128
and route 495.
To repeat say yes. To go back to home, say no.

Fig. 18.5   Publication page of Deitel's VoiceXML page (part 4 of 4).

A VoiceXML document is made up of a series of dialogs and subdialogs, which result in spoken interaction between the user and the computer. The tags that implement the dialogs are the **form** and **menu** tags. A **form** element presents information and gathers data from the user. A **menu** element provides options to the user and transfers control to other dialogs, based on the user's selections.

Lines 7–9

```
<link next = "#home">
   <grammar>home</grammar>
</link>
```

use element *link* to create an active link to the home page. Attribute *next* holds the URI that is navigated to when the link is selected. Element *grammar* provides the text that the user must speak in order to select the link. In this **link** element, we navigate to the element with **id home** when the user says the word **home**. Lines 11–13 use element **link** to create a link to **id end** when the user says the word **exit**.

Lines 17–24 create a form dialog using element *form*, which collects information from the user. Lines 18–22

```
<block>
    <emp>Welcome</emp> to the voice page of Deitel and
    Associates. To exit any time say exit.
    To go to the home page any time say home.
</block>
```

present introductory text to the user. Element **emp** is used to add emphasis to a section of speech.

The **menu** element on line 26 enables the user to select the page to which they would like to link. The **choice** element, which is always part of either a **menu** or a **form**, presents these options to the user. The **next** attribute indicates the page to be loaded when the user makes a selection. The user selects a **choice** element by speaking the words contained in the element into a microphone. In this example, the first and second **choice** elements on lines 41 and 42 transfer control to a *local dialog* (i.e., a location within the same document) when they are selected. The third **choice** element transfers the user to the document **publications.vxml**. Lines 27–33

```
<prompt count = "1" timeout = "10s">
    You have just entered the Deitel home page.
    Please make a selection by speaking one of the
    following options:
    <break msecs = "1000" />
    <enumerate/>
</prompt>
```

use element *prompt* to instruct the user to make a selection. Attribute *count* is used to provide multiple prompts for a task. VoiceXML keeps track of the number of prompts given and matches them to attribute **count**. The closest **prompt** with attribute **count** that is less than the current number of prompts is output. Attribute **timeout** provides a length of time to wait after the output of the prompt. In case the user does not respond before the timeout period expires, lines 35–39 provide a second, shorter prompt to remind the user that a selection is required.

The **publications.vxml** (Fig. 18.5) is loaded into the browser when the user chooses the **publications** option. Lines 106–111 define **link** elements that provide links to **main.vxml**. Lines 112–114 provide links to the **menu** element (lines 118–138), which asks the user to select one of the publications. Java, C and C++ are the three options the user can select. Each of the books on these topics is described in the **form** elements (lines 140–214). Once the browser speaks out the description, the control is transferred to the **form** element with **id** attribute whose value equals **repeat** (lines 216–231).

Figure 18.6 provides a brief description of each of the VoiceXML tags used in the previous example (Fig. 18.5).

VoiceXML Tag	Description
`<assign>`	Assigns a value to a variable.
`<block>`	Presents information to the user without any interaction between the user and the computer (i.e., the computer does not expect any input from the user).
`<break>`	Instructs the computer to pause its speech output for a specified period of time.
`<choice>`	Specifies an option in a **menu** element.
`<enumerate>`	Lists all of the available options to the user.
`<exit>`	Exits the program.
`<filled>`	Contains elements to be executed when the computer receives input for a **form** element from the user.
`<form>`	Gathers information from the user for a set of variables.
`<goto>`	Transfers control from one dialog to another.
`<grammar>`	Specifies grammar for the expected input from the user.
`<if>`, `<else>`, `<elseif>`	Control statements used for making logic decisions.
`<link>`	A transfer of control similar to the **goto** statement, but a **link** can be executed at any time during the program's execution.
`<menu>`	Provides user options and transfers control to other dialogs, based on the selected option.
`<prompt>`	Specifies text to be read to the user when a selection is needed.
`<subdialog>`	Calls another dialog. Control is transferred back to the calling dialog after the subdialog is executed.
`<var>`	Declares a variable.
`<vxml>`	The top-level tag which specifies that the document should be processed by a VoiceXML interpreter.

Fig. 18.6 Elements in VoiceXML.

18.8 JAWS® for Windows

JAWS (Job Access with Sound) is one of the leading screen readers on the market today. It was created by Henter-Joyce, a division of Freedom Scientific™. Freedom Scientific is a company that works to help visually impaired people use technology.

To download a demonstration version of JAWS, visit **www.hj.com/JAWS/JAWS35DemoOp.htm** and select the **JAWS 3.5 FREE Demo** link. The demo will run for 40 minutes, after which it will terminate. The computer must be rebooted before another 40 minute session can be started.

The JAWS demo is fully functional and includes an extensive help system that is highly customizible. The user can select which voice to use, as well as the rate at which text is spoken. Although the demo is in English, the full version of JAWS 3.5 allows the user to choose one of several supported languages.

JAWS also includes special key commands for popular programs, such as Microsoft Internet Explorer and Microsoft Word. For example, when browsing in Internet Explorer, JAWS's capabilities extend beyond just reading the content on the screen. If JAWS is enabled, pressing *Insert + F7* in Internet Explorer opens a **Links List** dialog, which displays all of the links available on a Web page. For more information about JAWS and the other products offered by Henter-Joyce, visit **www.hj.com**.

18.9 Other Accessibility Tools

Most of the accessibility products offered today are aimed at helping hearing and visually impaired users. However, there is also software designed to help people with other types of disabilities. This section describes some accessibility products other than the ones we have already discussed.

One such product, the *braille keyboard*, is similar to a standard keyboard, except that in addition to having each key labeled with the letter it represents, it has the equivalent braille symbol printed on the key. Most often, braille keyboards are combined with a speech synthesizer or a braille display, so users are able to interact with the computer to verify that their typing is correct.

Speech synthesis is another area in which research is being done to help people with disabilities. Speech synthesizers have been used to aid those who are unable to communicate verbally for many years. However, the growing popularity of the Web has prompted a great deal of work in the field of speech synthesis and speech recognition. These technologies are allowing the handicapped to use computers more than ever before. The development of speech synthesizers is also enabling other technologies to improve, such as VoiceXML and *AuralCSS* (**www.w3.org/TR/REC-CSS2/aural.html**). These tools allow visually impaired people and people who cannot read to access Web sites.

Despite the existence of adaptive software and hardware for the visually impaired, the accessibility of computers and the Internet is still hampered by the high costs, rapid obsolescence and unnecessary complexity of current technology. Moreover, almost all software currently available requires installation by a person who can see. *Ocularis* is a project launched in the open-source community to help rectify these problems. Open-source software for the visually impaired already exists, and although it is often superior to its proprietary, closed-source counterparts, it has not yet reached its full potential. Ocularis will ensure that the blind can fully use the Linux operating system by providing an Audio User Interface (AUI). Currently, Ocularis is in the planning stage. Programs to be integrated with Ocularis include a word processor, calculator, basic finance application, Internet browser and e-mail client. A screen reader will also be included for use with programs that have a command-line interface. The official Ocularis Web site is located at **ocularis.sourceforge.net**.

Visually impaired people are not the only beneficiaries of the effort being made to improve markup languages. The deaf also have a great number of tools to help them interpret auditory information delivered over the Web. Hearing-impaired Web users will soon benefit from what is called *Synchronized Multimedia Integration Language* (SMIL™), discussed in Chapter 20. This markup language is designed to add extra *tracks*—layers of content found within a single audio or video file—to multimedia content. The additional tracks may contain data such as closed captioning.

Technologies are also being designed to help severely handicapped persons, such as those with quadriplegia, a form of paralysis that affects the body from the neck down. One such technology, *EagleEyes*, developed by researchers at Boston College (**www.bc.edu/eagleeyes**), is a system that translates eye movements into mouse movements. The user moves the mouse cursor by moving his or her eyes or head and is thereby able to control the computer.

These examples are just a few of the accessibility projects and technologies that currently exist. For more information on Web and general computer accessibility, see the resources provided in the next section.

18.10 Internet and World Wide Web Resources

There are many accessibility resources on the Internet and World Wide Web, and this section lists a variety of them.

www.w3.org/WAI
The World Wide Web Consortium's *Web Accessibility Initiative (WAI)* site promotes design of universally accessible Web sites. This site will help you keep up to date with current guidelines and forthcoming standards for Web accessibility.

www.w3.org/TR/WCAG10
This page is a note published by the WCAG working group. It discusses techniques that can be used to comply with the WAI. This page is a great resource and can be used to find additional information on many of the topics covered in this chapter.

deafness.about.com/health/deafness/msubmenu6.htm
This site is the home page of **deafness.about.com**. It is an excellent resource to find information pertaining to deafness.

www.cast.org
CAST stands for the Center for Applied Special Technology. CAST offers software intended to help individuals with disabilities use a computer, including a valuable accessibility checker—free of charge. The accessibility checker is a Web-based program used to validate the accessibility of Web sites.

www.trainingpost.org/3-2-inst.htm
This site presents a tutorial on the Gunning Fog Index. The Gunning Fog Index is a method of grading text on its readability.

www.w3.org/TR/REC-CSS2/aural.html
This page discusses Aural Style Sheets, outlining the purpose and uses of this new technology.

laurence.canlearn.ca/English/learn/newaccessguide/indie
INDIE is an acronym that stands for "Integrated Network of Disability Information and Education." This site is home to a powerful search engine that helps users find out information about disabilities.

java.sun.com/products/java-media/speech/forDevelopers/JSML
This site outlines the specifications for JSML, Sun Microsystem's Java Speech Markup Language. This language, like VoiceXML, could drastically improve accessibility for visually impaired people.

www.slcc.edu/webguide/lynxit.html
Lynxit is a development tool that allows users to view any Web site just as a text-only browser would. The site's form allows you to enter a URL and returns the Web site in text-only format.

www.trill-home.com/lynx/public_lynx.html
This site allows you to use browse the Web using a Lynx browser. Doing so will allow you to see how your page will load for users without the most current technologies.

www.wgbh.org/wgbh/pages/ncam/accesslinks.html
This site provides links to other accessibility pages across the Web.

ocfo.ed.gov/coninfo/clibrary/software.htm
This page is the U.S. Department of Education's Web site for software accessibility requirements. It is aimed at helping developers produce accessible products.

www.alphaworks.ibm.com
This site is the home page for IBM Alphaworks. It provides information on VoiceXML and offers a download of the beta version of Voice Server SDK.

www-3.ibm.com/able/access.html
This site is the homepage of IBM's accessibility site. It provides information on IBM products and their accessibility and also discusses hardware, software and Web accessibility.

www.microsoft.com/enable/dev/guidelines/software.htm
This Web site presents Microsoft's guidelines for designing accessible software.

www.w3.org/TR/voice-tts-reqs
This page explains the speech synthesis markup requirements for voice markup languages.

deafness.about.com/health/deafness/msubvib.htm
This site provides information on vibrotactile devices. These devices allow deaf people to experience audio in the form of vibrations.

web.ukonline.co.uk/ddmc/software.html
This site provides links to software for people with disabilities.

www.hj.com
Henter-Joyce a division of Freedom Scientific that provides software for blind and visually impaired people. It is the home of JAWS.

www.abledata.com/text2/icg_hear.htm
This page contains a consumer guide that discusses technologies for hearing-impaired people.

www.washington.edu/doit
The University of Washington's DO-IT (Disabilities, Opportunities, Internetworking and Technology) site provides information and Web development resources for creating universally accessible Web sites.

www.webable.com
The WebABLE site contains links to many disability-related Internet resources and is geared towards those looking to develop technologies for people with disabilities.

www.speech.cs.cmu.edu/comp.speech/SpeechLinks.html
The Speech Technology Hyperlinks page has over 500 links to sites related to computer-based speech and speech recognition tools.

www.islandnet.com/~tslemko
The Micro Consulting Limited site contains shareware speech synthesis software.

www.chantinc.com/technology
This page is the Chant Web site, which discusses speech technology and how it works. Chant also provides speech synthesis and speech recognition software.

SUMMARY

- Accessibility refers to the level of usability of an application or Web site for people with disabilities. The vast majority of Web sites are considered inaccessible to people with visual, learning or mobility impairments.

- The WAI is an attempt to make the Web more accessible; its mission is described at **www.w3.org/WAI**.

- Specialized *user agent*s, such as screen readers (programs that allow users to hear what is being displayed on their screen) and braille displays (devices that receive data from screen-reading software and output the data as braille), allow blind and visually impaired people to access text-based information that is normally displayed on the screen.

- Web designers should avoid misuse of the **alt** attribute; it is intended to provide a short description of an HTML object that may not load properly on all user agents.

- The value of the **longdesc** attribute is a text-based URL that is linked to a Web page which describes the image associated with the attribute.

- User agents are unable to make server-side image maps accessible to blind people or to others who cannot use a mouse. If equivalent text links are not provided when a server-side image map is used, some users will be unable to navigate the site.

- When creating a Web page intended for the general public, it is important to consider the reading level at which it is written. Web site designers can make their site more readable through the use of shorter words, as some users may have difficulty reading long words. In addition, users from other countries may have difficulty understanding slang and other nontraditional language, so these types of words should also be avoided.

- Web designers often use frames to display more than one HTML file at a time and are a convenient way to ensure that certain content is always on screen. Unfortunately, frames often lack proper descriptions, which prevents users with text-based browsers, or users who lack sight, from navigating the Web site.

- The **noframes** tag allows the designer to offer alternative content to users whose browsers do not support frames.

- A VoiceXML document is made up of a series of dialogs and subdialogs, which result in spoken interaction between the user and the computer.

- Braille keyboards are similar to standard keyboards, except that in addition to having each key labeled with the letter it represents, braille keyboards have the equivalent braille symbol printed on the key. Most often, braille keyboards are combined with a speech synthesizer or a braille display, so users are able to interact with the computer to verify that their typing is correct.

- Speech synthesis is another area in which research is being done to help people with disabilities.

- Open-source software for the visually impaired already exists and is often superior to most of its proprietary, closed-source counterparts, but it still does not use the Linux OS to its fullest extent.

- Visually impaired people are not the only beneficiaries of the effort being made to improve markup languages. The deaf also have a great number of tools to help them interpret auditory information delivered over the Web.

- EagleEyes, developed by researchers at Boston College (**www.bc.edu/eagleeyes**), is a system that translates eye movements into mouse movements. The user moves the mouse cursor by moving his or her eyes or head and is thereby able to control the computer.

TERMINOLOGY

accessibility

alt attribute

assign tag in VoiceXML

AuralCSS

block tag in VoiceXML

braille display

braille keyboard

break tag in VoiceXML

b tag (bold)

caption

Cascading Style Sheets (CSS)
choice tag in VoiceXML
client-side image map
CSS2
default settings
EagleEyes
enumerate tag in VoiceXML
exit tag in VoiceXML
field variable
filled tag in VoiceXML
form tag in VoiceXML
frames
goto tag in VoiceXML
grammar tag in VoiceXML
Gunning Fog Index
header cells
headers attribute of **td** tag
h1
IBM ViaVoice
id attribute
img tag
JAWS (Job Access With Sound) by Henter-Joyce
a division of Freedom Scientific
linearized reading of a table
link tag in VoiceXML
longdesc attribute
Lynx
markup language
menu tag in VoiceXML
noframes tag
priority 1 checkpoint

priority 2 checkpoint
priority 3 checkpoint
prompt tag in VoiceXML
quick tips
readability
screen reader
server-side image map
speech recognition
speech synthesizer
strong tag
subdialog tag in VoiceXML
summary attribute
Synchronized Multimedia Integration Language
(SMIL)
tables
td tag
text-to-speech
th tag
timeout
title tag
user agent
var tag in VoiceXML
ViaVoice
Voice Server
Voice Server SDK
VoiceXML
vxml tag in VoiceXML
Web Content Accessibility Guidelines 1.0
(WCAG 1.0)
Web Accessibility Initiative (WAI)

SELF-REVIEW EXERCISES

18.1 Spell out the following acronyms:
   a) W3C.
   b) WAI.
   c) JAWS.
   d) SMIL.
   e) CSS.

18.2 Fill in the blanks in each of the following statements.
   a) The highest priority of the Web Accessibility Initiative is to ensure that each _____, _____ and _____ is accompanied by a description that clearly defines its purpose.
   b) Although they can be used as a great layout tool, _____ are difficult for screen readers to interpret and convey clearly to a user.
   c) In order to make your frame accessible to the handicapped, it is important to include _____ tags on your page.
   d) Blind people using computers are often assisted by _____ and _____.

18.3   State whether each of the following is *true* or *false*. If *false*, explain why.
  a) Screen readers have no problem reading and translating images.
  b) Image maps are no problem for screen readers to translate, so long as the programmer has made changes to their code to improve accessibility.
  c) When writing pages for the general public, it is important to consider the reading difficulty level of the text you are writing.
  d) The **alt** tag helps screen readers describe images in a Web page.
  e) Left-handed people have been helped by the improvements made in speech-recognition technology more than any other group of people.
  f) VoiceXML lets users interact with Web content using speech recognition and speech synthesis technologies.

ANSWERS TO SELF-REVIEW EXERCISES

18.1   a) World Wide Web Consortium. b) Web Accessibility Initiative. c) Job Access with Sound. d) Synchronized Multimedia Integration Language. e) Cascading Style Sheets.

18.2   a) image, movie, sound. b) tables. c) **noframes**. d) braille displays, braille keyboards.

18.3   a) False. Screen readers have no way of telling a user what is shown in an image. If the programmer includes an **alt** attribute inside the **img** tag, the screen reader will read this description to the user. b) False. Screen readers have no way of translating image maps, no matter what programming changes are made. The solution to this problem is to include text-based links alongside all image maps. c) True. d) True. e) False. Although left-handed people can use speech-recognition technology as everyone else can, speech-recognition technology has had the largest impact on the blind and on people who have trouble typing. f) True.

EXERCISES

18.4   Insert HTML markup into each segment to make the segment accessible to someone with disabilities. The contents of images and frames should be apparent from the context and filenames.

```
a) <img src = "dogs.jpg" width = "300" height = "250">
b) <table width = "75%">
   <tr><th>Language</th><th>Version</th></tr>
   <tr><td>HTML</td><td>4.01</td></tr>
   <tr><td>Perl</td><td>5.6.0</td></tr>
   <tr><td>Java</td><td>1.3</td></tr>
   </table>
c) <map name = "links">
      <area href = "index.html" shape = "rect"
         coords = "50, 120, 80, 150">
      <area href = "catalog.html" shape = "circle"
         coords = "220, 30">
   </map>
   <img src = "antlinks.gif" width = "300" height = "200"
      usemap = "#links">
```

19

XHTML and XForms

Objectives

- To understand the need for XHTML.
- To understand the differences between XHTML and HTML.
- To understand how XHTML relates to XML.
- To use the three XHTML DTDs.
- To validate an XHTML document.
- To understand the concept of XForms.
- To become familiar with the Extended Forms Architecture (XFA).

This fell sergeant, death,
Is strict in his arrest.
William Shakespeare

Form ever follows function.
Louis Henri Sullivan

19.1 Introduction

This chapter provides a brief introduction to an XML-related technology called *Extensible Hypertext Markup Language (XHTML)*. XHTML is HTML's proposed successor. The current version of XHTML—the XHTML 1.0 W3C Recommendation—includes HTML 4 elements for backwards compatibility and to help Web authors make the transition from HTML to XHTML.

In this chapter, we also discuss a more flexible replacement for HTML forms being developed by the World Wide Web Consortium—called XForms.

Software Engineering Observation 19.1

XHTML is an application of XML and uses the `http://www.w3.org/1999/xhtml` *namespace URI.*

19.2 XHTML

XHTML is better equipped than HTML to represent complex data on the Internet. The majority of existing HTML code is not well formed because browsers do not explicitly check the markup for errors. Most browsers accommodate incorrectly-written HTML documents. The result is that the same document may look different in each Web browser, depending upon how the browser interprets the incorrect HTML code. With the emergence of the wireless Web and Web-enabled appliances, incorrect HTML poses a portability problem. Small devices such as PDAs (personal digital assistants) and digital cellular phones have limited amounts of memory and cannot provide the extra resources required to process incorrectly-written HTML. Documents intended for these devices must be well formed to guarantee uniform processing.

Figure 19.1 shows an HTML document that is not well formed because a closing double quote is missing in line 9. The output shows the document rendered in Internet Explorer 5. Notice that the anchor is displayed as text.

XHTML takes advantage of XML's strict syntax to ensure well-formedness. Although XHTML's elements are almost identical to the elements of HTML, some notable differences exist. All XHTML tags must be in lowercase; a document with uppercase tags is invalid. All XHTML start tags (e.g., `<p>`) must have a corresponding end tag (e.g., `</p>`). Empty tags (i.e., tags that do not have closing tags) must be terminated using the forward slash character (`/`). Therefore, the `<br>` tag in HTML becomes the `<br/>` tag in XHTML.

```
1   <!DOCTYPE html PUBLIC "-//W3C//DTD HTML 4.0 Transitional//EN">
2   <html>
3
4   <!-- Fig. 19.1 : simple.html -->
5   <!-- An ill-formed HTML        -->
6
7      Here is a link to our home page:
8      <br/>
9      <a href = "http://www.deitel.com >www.deitel.com</a>
10
11  </html>
```

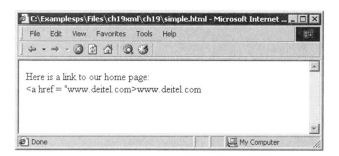

Fig. 19.1   Rendering an ill-formed HTML document.

Portability Tip 19.1

*Adding a space before **/>** in an empty XHTML element (e.g., **
**) improves compatibility with older Web browsers.*

XHTML does not permit overlapping tags. For example, the line

   <font size = "3"><p>This is some text</font></p>

is invalid, because the **<font>** and **<p>** tags overlap. In XHTML, attribute values must appear in quotes and cannot be *minimized*. For example, the **hr** tag has a minimized attribute **noshade**. According to XHTML specifications, the HTML tag **<hr noshade>** must be written as **<hr noshade = "noshade"/>**.

Common Programming Error 19.1

All the elements in an XHTML file must be in lowercase and must have proper open and close tags.

XHTML documents conform to one of three DTDs—*strict, transitional* or *frameset*. The strict DTD is used when the document implements content presentation with cascading style sheets. The transitional DTD is used when the document contains presentational elements (e.g., font and color information) embedded in the XHTML elements. The frameset DTD is used when a browser window is partitioned with HTML frames. The examples in Figs. 19.2–19.7 make use of each of these DTDs.

   Figure 19.2 is an XHTML document that conforms to the frameset DTD. The document defines the frames that contain the remaining documents in this chapter.

Lines 1 and 2 declare the document type and specify the DTD to which this document conforms. Because this document uses frames, we use XHTML's frameset DTD. Line 3 declares the namespace URI for this XHTML document. Because a namespace prefix is not used, elements belong to the default namespace.

The remainder of the document looks almost identical to HTML. All XHTML tags conform to the requirements we described earlier (e.g., the tags are lowercase, all attributes are enclosed in quotes, etc.). XHTML requires the **title** element to appear within the **head** element. The frameset DTD also requires the **body** element to appear within the **noframes** element.

We can validate **xhtmlFrame.html** (Fig. 19.2) using the W3C's validator located at **validator.w3.org**. Figure 19.3 displays the results of validating this document.

Figure 19.4 is the XHTML document that is rendered in the page's **picture** frame. The document displays the Deitel & Associates, Inc. logo that, when clicked, opens the Deitel & Associates, Inc. Web site in a separate browser window. This document uses the transitional DTD because the **target** attribute of tag **<a>** is not defined in the strict DTD.

```
1   <!DOCTYPE html PUBLIC "-//W3C//DTD XHTML 1.0 Frameset//EN"
2      "http://www.w3.org/TR/xhtml1/DTD/frameset.dtd">
3   <html xmlns = "http://www.w3.org/1999/xhtml">
4
5      <!-- Fig. 19.2: xhtmlFrame.html -->
6      <!-- An XHTML example          -->
7
8      <head>
9         <meta name = "keywords" content = "Webpage, design, XHTML,
10        tutorial, personal, help, index, form, contact, feedback,
11        list, links, frame, deitel"/>
12        <meta name = "description" content = "This Web site will
13        help you learn the basics of XHTML and Web page design
14        through the use of interactive examples and
15        instruction."/>
16        <title>Welcome to XHTML</title>
17     </head>
18
19     <frameset rows = "150,*">
20        <frame name = "picture" scrolling = "no"
21           src = "picture.html"/>
22        <frameset cols = "250,*">
23           <frame name = "nav" scrolling = "no" src = "nav.html"/>
24           <frame name = "main" src = "main.html"/>
25        </frameset>
26        <noframes>
27           <body>
28              <p>This page uses frames, but your browser does
29                 not support them.</p>
30
31              <p>Please, <a href = "nav.html">follow this link
32                 to browse our site without frames</a>.</p>
33           </body>
34        </noframes>
```

Fig. 19.2   XHTML frameset document (part 1 of 2).

```
35        </frameset>
36    </html>
```

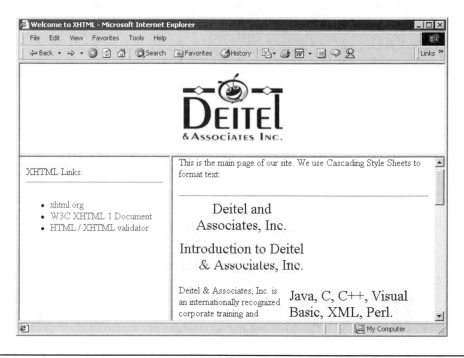

Fig. 19.2   XHTML frameset document (part 2 of 2).

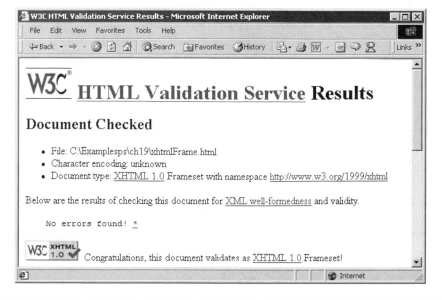

Fig. 19.3   Validating an XHTML document.

```
1   <!DOCTYPE html PUBLIC "-//W3C//DTD XHTML 1.0 Transitional//EN"
2    "http://www.w3c.org/TR/xhtml1/DTD/xhtml1-transitional.dtd">
3   <html xmlns = "http://www.w3.org/1999/xhtml">
4
5      <!-- Fig. 19.4: picture.html         -->
6      <!-- An XHTML  transitional example -->
7
8      <head>
9         <title>Click on our logo to go to deitel.com</title>
10     </head>
11
12     <body>
13        <div style = "text-align: center">
14        <a href = "http://www.deitel.com" target = "_new">
15           <img src = "logotiny.jpg" alt = "deitel.com"
16              border = "0"/>
17        </a></div>
18     </body>
19  </html>
```

Fig. 19.4   XHTML transitional document.

Figure 19.5 is the XHTML document that is rendered in the page's **nav** frame. The document displays a list of links that, when clicked, displays the appropriate page in the main **frame**. Again, we use the transitional DTD because this document makes use of the **target** attribute. In line 10, we import the style sheet **styles.css** (Fig. 19.6).

```
1   <!DOCTYPE html PUBLIC "-//W3C//DTD XHTML 1.0 Transitional//EN"
2    "http://www.w3c.org/TR/xhtml1/DTD/xhtml1-transitional.dtd">
3   <html xmlns = "http://www.w3.org/1999/xhtml">
4
5      <!-- Fig. 19.5: nav.html            -->
6      <!-- An XHTML transitional example -->
7
8      <head>
9         <title>Enter the title of your XHTML document here</title>
10        <link rel = "stylesheet" type = "text/css"
11           href = "styles.css"/>
12     </head>
13
14     <body>
15        XHTML Links: <hr />
16        <ul>
17           <li><a class =  "nodec" href = "http://www.xhtml.org"
18              target = "main">xhtml.org</a></li>
19           <li><a class =  "nodec" target = "main"
20              href = "http://www.w3.org/TR/xhtml1/">
21              W3C XHTML 1 Document</a></li>
22           <li><a class =  "nodec" href = "http://validator.w3.org"
23              target = "main">HTML / XHTML validator</a></li>
24        </ul>
25     </body>
26  </html>
```

Fig. 19.5   XHTML transitional document.

```
1   a.nodec   { text-decoration: none;
2               color: blue }
3   a:hover   { text-decoration: underline;
4               background-color: #FFFF80 }
```

Fig. 19.6 Style sheet used by `nav.html—styles.css`.

Figure 19.7 shows the page displayed (in the **main** frame) when the document is first rendered. This document conforms to the strict DTD. In lines 11–17, we define a style for element **div**. We use this style in the body of the document to format and display some sample text.

```
1   <!DOCTYPE html PUBLIC "-//W3C//DTD XHTML 1.0 Strict//EN"
2     "http://www.w3c.org/TR/xhtml1/DTD/xhtml1-strict.dtd">
3   <html xmlns = "http://www.w3.org/1999/xhtml">
4
5      <!-- Fig. 19.7: main.html   -->
6      <!-- An XHTML / CSS example    -->
7
8      <head>
9         <title>This is the main page</title>
10
11         <style type = "text/css">
12
13            div { background-color: #FFFF80;
14                  margin-bottom: .5em;
15                  font-size: 1.5em;
16                  width: 50% }
17         </style>
18
19      </head>
20
21      <body>
22         <p>This is the main page of our site. We use Cascading
23         Style Sheets to format text:</p><hr />
24
25         <div style = "text-align: center">Deitel and
26            Associates, Inc.</div>
27         <div style = "text-align: right">Introduction to
28            Deitel &amp; Associates, Inc.</div>
29
30         <div style = "float: right; margin: .5em">Java, C, C++,
31            Visual Basic, XML, Perl.</div>
32
33         <p>Deitel &amp; Associates, Inc. is an internationally
34            recognized corporate training and publishing
35            organization specializing in programming languages,
36            Internet/World Wide Web technology and object technology
37            education. Deitel &amp; Associates, Inc. is a member of
38            the World Wide Web Consortium. The company provides
39            courses on Java, C++, Visual Basic, C, Internet
```

Fig. 19.7 XHTML document that conforms to the strict DTD (part 1 of 2).

```
40            and World Wide Web programming, and Object
41            Technology.</p>
42
43        <div style = "float: right; padding: .5em">Our How to
44            Program Series publications in Java, C, C++ and
45            Visual Basic--each published by Prentice Hall
46            (the world&apos;s largest computer science publisher)--
47            are the best-selling college programming language
48            textbooks in their respective fields.
49        </div>
50
51        <div style = "clear: right">The company&apos;s clients include
52            some of the world&apos;s largest computer companies,
53            government agencies, branches of the military and
54            business organizations.
55        </div>
56     </body>
57
58  </html>
```

Fig. 19.7   XHTML document that conforms to the strict DTD (part 2 of 2).

XHTML 1.1, the next version of the XHTML recommendation under development, provides greater extensibility and modularity than XHTML 1.0. Deprecated tags and attributes, most of which are presentation-oriented relics from HTML, will no longer be supported. XHTML will also have a modular framework. Each module will provide specific functionality. For example, there will be modules for frames, stylesheets and hyperlinks. The initial XHTML 1.1 DTD from the W3C is based solely on modules; a similar schema is under development. Content developers will be able to combine and extend modules, as well as integrate tags from other XML languages, such as SMIL. Designers will also be able to specify which features of XHTML are supported by their technologies. This enables software to easily handle XHTML documents by either tailoring content for a device or loading software for processing a particular module. As a result, devices such as cellular phones will be able to render XHTML content more accurately.

19.3 XForms

With the growth of e-commerce, HTML forms have become an essential part of many Web sites for collecting customer data. However, HTML forms suffer from many drawbacks. Forms lack the flexibility that would enable their use by people working on many different platforms. The World Wide Web Consortium is currently developing an XML-based replacement for HTML forms—XForms.

XForms are currently a "work in progress." The information in this section is likely to change as the World Wide Web Consortium continues its work. For the most current information on XForms, visit **www.w3.org/MarkUp/Forms**.

The goal of XForms is to make forms more flexible by separating data from logic and presentation. This separation is accomplished by dividing the form into three portions: data, logic and presentation. The "uncoupling" of data from presentation enables form designers to define different user interfaces for different platforms (e.g., desktops, handhelds, phones, paper, etc.). The data portion defines the structure of the data to be represented in or gathered by the form. The logic portion defines relationships between the fields in the form using a syntax similar to that used in spreadsheet applications. The presentation portion defines how the form looks to users.

The different portions of the form work together to gather data from users and process the data over the Web. The user enters the data through the user interface. The logic portion of the form processes the data entered by the user. The form designer can provide logic, for example, to ensure that the user has entered a telephone number in the proper format or to combine data from different fields. When the form is submitted, the user-entered data is converted to appropriately-formatted XML and sent to the server for further processing. Although much of the functionality provided by XForms can be implemented with a scripting language such as JavaScript, XForms will provide a more flexible architecture for building forms.

19.4 Extended Forms Architecture (XFA)

Extended Forms Architecture (XFA) is a specification developed by JetForm for advanced manipulation of XML forms by both humans and computer systems. It has capabilities for creating, processing, printing, modifying and archiving all types of forms. XFA provides methods for adding interactivity to computer forms, including database query and mathematical functions. In addition, it is optimized for enterprise application integration, enabling form interoperability with different systems.

The specification consists of two parts. The first is the form template, which is a collection of schema and objects that define the rules and intelligence of the form. XFA has flexible formatting capabilities that enable a form to be viewed in many different ways, and multiple presentations can be encoded into one form definition. The data and the form can either be kept separate or merged, depending on the application for which they will be used. The former allows the exchange of data without requiring translation or additional processing, whereas the latter ensures that the data will always be in context. Support for *digital signatures* (i.e., the equivalent of written signatures that authenticates users) is inherent in XFA, which enables signing of the data, the form or the combined document.

The second part of the specification is a scripting language that can be used to perform queries, calculations and other form manipulations. With the combination of XFA templates and scripting, an individual or organization can create unique, customizable forms that are fully interoperable throughout any electronic network.

Further information on XFA can be found at Jetform's official XFA site, **www.xfa.org**.

19.5 Internet and World Wide Web Resources

www.w3.org/TR/xhtml1
This is the W3C's recommendation document for XHTML. The document covers use of the language and provides links to the three XHTML DTDs.

www.w3.org/TR/xforms-datamodel
This is the W3C's draft version of the XForm data-model definition. It contains detailed recommendations and comments on XForm technology design and implementation.

www.w3.org/MarkUp/Forms
This is the W3C's XForms information site.

www.xhtml.org
This Web site is a resource for XHTML users.

validator.w3.org
This site is the W3C's validating tool that can validate XHTML pages.

www.w3schools.com/xhtml
Learn more about XHTML at this site, which features a tutorial and other XHTML resources.

encyclozine.com/WD/XHTML
This site is an introductory article about XHTML. It contains a simple example and links to other informational articles.

wdvl.internet.com/Authoring/Languages/XML/XHTML/dtd.html
This site contains an article on the differences among the three XHTML DTDs.

encyclozine.com/WD/XHTML/dif.html
This site contains an article on the differences between HTML and XHTML.

encyclozine.com/WD/XHTML/dtd.html
This site contains an article about the three XHTML DTDs.

www.xfa.org
Jetform's official Extended Forms Architecture (XFA) Web site.

SUMMARY

- Extensible Hypertext Markup Language (XHTML) is an application of XML and is HTML's proposed successor. The current version of XHTML includes HTML 4 elements to help Web authors make the transition from HTML to XHTML.

- XHTML's design is better equipped than HTML's to represent complex data on the Internet. Browsers can treat poorly written HTML documents differently, requiring browser vendors to write additional features to handle the problem.

- XHTML takes advantage of XML's strict syntax to ensure well-formedness. All XHTML tags must be in lowercase; a document with uppercase tags is invalid. All XHTML opening tags—including empty ones—must have a corresponding closing tag. XHTML does not permit overlapping tags.

- XHTML uses the namespace URI **http://www.w3.org/1999/xhtml**.

- In XHTML, attribute values must appear in quotes and cannot be minimized.

- XHTML documents conform to one of three DTDs—strict, transitional or frameset. The strict DTD is used when the document implements content presentation with cascading style sheets. The transitional DTD is used when the document contains presentational elements embedded in the XHTML elements. The frameset DTD is used when a browser window is partitioned with HTML frames.

- XHTML requires the **title** element to appear within the **head** element. The frameset DTD also requires the **body** element to appear within the **noframes** element.

- The W3C provides a validator that can be used to validate XHTML documents.

- XHTML 1.1, the next version of the XHTML recommendation under development, provides greater extensibility and modularity than XHTML 1.0. Deprecated tags and attributes, most of which are presentation-oriented relics from HTML, will no longer be supported. XHTML will also have a modular framework.

- The World Wide Web Consortium is currently developing XML-based XForms as a more flexible replacement to HTML forms. The goal of XForms is to separate data from presentation. This separation is accomplished by dividing the form into three portions: data, logic and presentation.

- Extended Forms Architecture (XFA) is a specification developed by Jetform technologies for advanced manipulation of XML forms by both users and computer systems. It has capabilities for creating, processing, printing, modifying and archiving all types of forms. XFA provides methods for adding interactivity to computer forms, including database query and mathematical functions. In addition, it is optimized for enterprise application integration, enabling form interoperability with different systems.

TERMINOLOGY

data portion of XForm architecture
document type
Extensible Hypertext Markup Language
    (XHTML)
frameset DTD
HTML 4
in-line style
logic portion of XForm architecture
main **frame**
minimized
nav frame
picture frame
presentation

presentation portion of XForm architecture
presentational elements
strict
strict DTD
target attribute
transitional
transitional DTD
validating an XHTML document
Web-enabled appliances
wireless Web
XForms
XHTML
XML-based XForms

SELF-REVIEW EXERCISES

19.1 State which of the following statements are *true* and which are *false*. If *false*, explain why.
  a) Although the recommendation calls for all XHTML tags to be written in lowercase, an XHTML document with uppercase tags is valid.
  b) Browsers can treat poorly written HTML documents differently.
  c) XHTML tags may optionally have a corresponding closing tag.
  d) XHTML empty tags must be terminated.
  e) XHTML permits overlapping tags.
  f) More than one XForm user interface can be associated with a data representation.
  g) Though XHTML attributes must appear in quotes, they can be minimized like HTML attributes.
  h) HTML forms lack the flexibility that would enable their use by people working on many different platforms.

19.2 Fill in the blanks for each of the following:
  a) XHTML takes advantage of the strict syntax of _____ to ensure well-formedness.
  b) Documents intended for portable devices must be _____ to guarantee uniform processing.
  c) In XHTML, attribute values must appear in _____ and cannot be _____.
  d) XHTML documents conform to one of three types of DTDs: _____, _____ and _____.
  e) The goal of XForms is to separate data from _____.
  f) The XForm architecture is divided into three portions: _____, _____ and _____.

g) All XHTML tags must have corresponding _____ tags.

h) The _____ portion of an XForm defines how the form looks to users.

ANSWERS TO SELF-REVIEW EXERCISES

19.1   a) False. All XHTML tags must be in lowercase. b) True. c) False. All XHTML tags are required to have corresponding closing tags. d) True. e) False. XHTML prohibits overlapping tags. f) True. g) False. XHTML attribute values must appear in quotes and cannot be minimized. h) True.

19.2   a) XML. b) well formed. c) quotes, minimized. d) strict, transitional, frameset. e) presentation. f) data, logic, presentation. g) closing. h) presentation.

EXERCISES

19.3   Write an XHTML document showing the result of a color survey. The document should contain a table showing various colors and corresponding percentage of votes for each color (each row should be displayed in its color). Use attributes to format width, border and cell spacing for the table. The document should also contain a form with radio buttons that allows the users to select their favorite color. One of the colors should be selected as a default. Validate the document against an appropriate XHTML DTD.

19.4   Make changes to Fig. 19.5 so that it conforms to XHTML strict DTD. Validate it using the XHTML validator discussed in Fig. 19.3.

20

Custom Markup Languages: Part I

Objectives

- To understand and be able to use the Mathematical Markup Language (MathML).
- To become familiar with the Chemical Markup Language (CML).
- To understand and be able to use the Wireless Markup Language (WML).
- To understand and be able to use the Synchronized Multimedia Integration Language (SMIL).
- To understand and be able to use the Scalable Vector Graphics (SVG) markup language.
- To become familiar with the Bean Markup Language (BML).
- To become familiar with the Extensible 3D (X3D) language.

What we experience of nature is in models, and all of nature's models are so beautiful.
Richard Buckminster Fuller

Treat nature in terms of the cylinder, the sphere, the cone, all in perspective.
Paul Cezanne

20.1 Introduction

XML is a *metalanguage*—a language for creating other languages. In this and the next chapter, we discuss notable markup languages that have been created using XML.

20.2 Mathematical Markup Language (MathML)

Until recently, mathematical expressions have typically been displayed using images or specialized software packages such as TeX (**www.math.upenn.edu/TeX.html**) and LaTeX (**www.iac.es/galeria/vass/latex/node2.html**). *MathML* was developed by the W3C for describing mathematical notations and expressions using XML syntax. It enables document authors to describe mathematical expressions that can be processed by different applications for different purposes. This flexibility promotes wide reuse of mathematical content over many domains. MathML Version 1.01 is the current W3C Recommendation.

The W3C provides a browser/editing environment called *Amaya*™ to edit, parse and render MathML. The Amaya browser can be downloaded free from

www.w3.org/Amaya/User/BinDist.html

This Web page contains several download links for Windows 95/98/NT, Linux® and Solaris™. Amaya documentation and installation notes are also available at the W3C Web site.

We now take a calculus expression and mark it up with MathML. MathML defines two sets of elements: one set describes mathematical content and the other describes mathematical presentation. Figure 20.1 uses MathML's presentation set to mark up a mathematical expression that contains an integral symbol and a square-root symbol. We embed the MathML content directly into an HTML file by using the HTML **math** *element* (line 8).

```
 1    <html>
 2
 3    <!-- Fig. 20.1 mathml.html            -->
 4    <!-- Calculus example using MathML -->
 5
 6    <body>
 7
 8    <math>
 9        <mrow>
10
11            <msubsup>
12                <mo>&Integral;</mo>
13                <mn> 0 </mn>
14                <mrow>
15                    <mn>1</mn>
16                    <mo>-</mo>
17                    <mi>x</mi>
18                </mrow>
19            </msubsup>
20
21            <msqrt>
22                <mrow>
23                    <mn>4</mn>
24                    <mo>&InvisibleTimes;</mo>
25
26                    <msup>
27                        <mi>x</mi>
28                        <mn>2</mn>
29                    </msup>
30
31                    <mo>+</mo>
32                    <mi>y</mi>
33                </mrow>
34            </msqrt>
35
36            <mo>&delta;</mo>
37            <mi>x</mi>
38        </mrow>
39    </math>
40    </body>
41    </html>
```

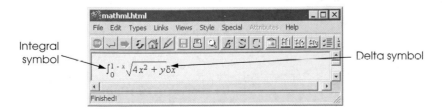

Fig. 20.1   A calculus expression marked up with MathML. (Courtesy of World Wide
Web Consortium)

We use *element* **mrow** (line 9) to group the elements of the mathematical expression. Element **mrow** is a container element that groups related elements. We use *element* **msubsup** to mark up the integral symbol set (lines 10–18). Element **msubsup** requires three child elements: the expression to which the subscript and superscript are applied, the subscript and the superscript. In our example, the integral symbol is the expression portion of element **msubsup**.

The integral symbol is represented by the entity **∫** (line 12). We use tag **<mo>**—the MathML element for marking up mathematical operators—to mark up the integral operator. *Element* **mn** (line 13) marks up the number (i.e., **0**) that represents the subscript. Element **mrow** groups the superscript expression (i.e., **1-x**) in **msubsup**. To mark up variables in MathML, element **mi** (line 17) is used. Collectively, the three child elements within **mrow** (lines 14–18) define the expression **1-x**.

Element **msqrt** (lines 21–34) represents a square-root expression. We use element **mrow** (line 21) to group the expression contained in the square root. Line 24 uses entity **⁢** to specify a multiplication operation without a *symbolic representation* (i.e., a multiplication symbol is not displayed between the **4** and the x^2). Element **msup** (lines 26–29) marks up an expression containing a base and an exponent. This element contains two child elements: the base and the exponent. Although not used in this example, MathML does provide element ***msub*** for marking up an expression that contains a subscript.

Line 36 introduces the entity ***δ*** for representing a delta symbol. Because it is an operator, it is marked up using element **mo**. For information on other operations and symbols provided by MathML visit the resources listed in Fig. 20.2.

URL / Description

www.w3.org/Math
This is the W3C's official Web site for MathML; the site includes a brief introduction and history and links to software and additional documentation.

www.w3.org/TR/MathML2
This document is the current draft standard of MathML 2.0.

www.w3.org/Math/DTD
The MathML DTD can be obtained from this site.

www.oasis-open.org/cover/xml.html#xml-mml
This is a brief overview of MathML.

www.irt.org/articles/js081
This site contains a detailed introduction to MathML. It also contains a comprehensive list of MathML elements.

www.webeq.com/mathml
Use this Web page as a starting point for MathML resources.

www.w3.org/Amaya
This is the main Web site for the Amaya editor/browser.

Fig. 20.2   MathML reference Web sites.

20.3 OpenMath

OpenMath is an emerging standard—developed at **www.openmath.org**—for describing mathematical content. Although MathML does provide a set of semantic elements, it is mostly limited to describing the presentation of mathematical expressions. OpenMath content can be embedded in MathML, synthesizing the description of mathematical content and presentation. See Fig. 20.3 for OpenMath Web resources.

OpenMath represents mathematical expressions with objects that can be exchanged between different software systems, manipulated in databases, displayed by different applications including Internet browsers, used in different contexts and even checked for mathematical correctness. The standard itself includes specifications of binary and XML encoding of OpenMath, extensible libraries of OpenMath objects and libraries defining semantic content.

An OpenMath object has three layers of representation: as an application-specific entity, as an abstract OpenMath object and as a byte stream for communication purposes. The content dictionaries define the meaning of an object so that an application can convert it to an internal representation.

Software is currently being developed to utilize and support OpenMath, as it has great potential in many industries involving manipulation of complex mathematical expressions.

20.4 Chemical Markup Language (CML)

The *Chemical Markup Language (CML)* is an XML-based language for representing molecular and chemical information. Many of the methods previously used to store this type of information (e.g., special file types) inhibited document reuse. CML takes advantage of XML's portability to enable document authors to use and reuse molecular information without corrupting important data in the process. Although many of our readers will not know the chemistry required to fully understand the example in this section, we feel that CML so beautifully illustrates the purpose of XML that we chose to include the example for the readers who wish to see XML "at its best." Document authors can edit and view CML using the *Jumbo browser*, which is available at **www.xml-cml.org**. [*Note:* At the time of this writing, CML documents could not be uploaded to Jumbo for rendering. For illustration purposes, we have created the image shown in Fig. 20.4.]

URL / Description

---

www.openmath.org
This is the official Web site for OpenMath. It contains white papers, specifications and links to more resources.

www.oasis-open.org/cover/openMath.html
This is a listing of articles about OpenMath and other resources.

www.nag.co.uk/projects/OpenMath
This is the Web site of the ESPRIT project, which currently maintains the OpenMath standard and all related documents.

Fig. 20.3 OpenMath reference Web sites (part 1 of 2).

URL / Description

www.naomi.math.ca
This is the Web site of the North American OpenMath Initiative, a coalition of academia and industry working to develop OpenMath and its applications.

www.uni-koeln.de/themen/Computeralgebra/OpenMath/om-obj-jsc/om-obj-jsc.html
This site contains a technological introduction to OpenMath.

www.acm.org/crossroads/xrds6-2/openmath.html
This site contains an introduction to mathematical markup using OpenMath and MathML.

www-sop.inria.fr/safir/OpenMath/papers/Alignment-JHD/align/align.html
This document contains the results of a meeting whose goal was to see how OpenMath and MathML could be more closely aligned.

Fig. 20.3 OpenMath reference Web sites (part 2 of 2).

We now provide an example of marking up the ammonia molecule in Fig. 20.4.

```
1   <?jumbo:namespace ns = "http://www.xml-cml.org"
2       prefix = "C" java = "jumbo.cmlxml.*Node" ?>
3
4   <!-- Fig. 20.4 : ammonia.xml -->
5   <!-- Structure of ammonia      -->
6
7   <C:molecule id = "Ammonia">
8
9      <C:atomArray builtin = "elsym">
10        N H H H
11     </C:atomArray>
12
13     <C:atomArray builtin = "x2" type = "float">
14        1.5 0.0 1.5 3.0
15     </C:atomArray>
16
17     <C:atomArray builtin = "y2" type = "float">
18        1.5 1.5 0.0 1.5
19     </C:atomArray>
20
21     <C:bondArray builtin = "atid1">
22        1 1 1
23     </C:bondArray>
24
25     <C:bondArray builtin = "atid2">
26        2 3 4
27     </C:bondArray>
28
```

Fig. 20.4 CML markup for ammonia molecule (part 1 of 2).

```
29      <C:bondArray builtin = "order" type = "integer">
30         1 1 1
31      </C:bondArray>
32
33   </C:molecule>
```

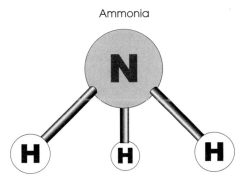

Ammonia

Fig. 20.4   CML markup for ammonia molecule (part 2 of 2).

Lines 1 and 2

```
<?jumbo:namespace ns = "http://www.xml-cml.org"
    prefix = "C" java = "jumbo.cmlxml.*Node" ?>
```

are a processing instruction used by the Jumbo browser that includes a URI, namespace prefix and package information.
Line 7

```
<C:molecule id = "Ammonia">
```

defines an ammonia molecule using element **molecule**. Attribute **id** is used to identify this molecule as **Ammonia**.
Lines 9–11

```
<C:atomArray builtin = "elsym">
   N H H H
</C:atomArray>
```

show element **atomArray** with the attribute **builtin** of value **elsym** that defines this element as containing the atoms of the molecule. Ammonia is composed of one nitrogen atom and three hydrogen atoms, each of which is listed in the element.
Lines 13–15

```
<C:atomArray builtin = "x2" type = "float">
   1.5 0.0 1.5 3.0
</C:atomArray>
```

show element **atomArray** with attribute **builtin** assigned the value **x2** and **type float**. This defines the element as containing a list of floating-point numbers, each of which is the x-coordinate of an atom. The first value (**1.5**) is the x-coordinate of the first atom (nitrogen), the second value (**0.0**) is the *x*-coordinate of the second atom (the first hydrogen atom) and so forth.

Lines 17–19

```
<C:atomArray builtin = "y2" type = "float">
   1.5 1.5 0.0 1.5
</C:atomArray>
```

show element **atomArray** with attribute **builtin** assigned the value **y2** and **type float**. This defines the element as containing a list of values, each being the *y*-coordinate of an atom. The first value (**1.5**) is the *y*-coordinate of the first atom (nitrogen), the second value (**1.5**) is the *y*-coordinate of the second atom (the first hydrogen atom) and so forth.

Lines 21–23

```
<C:bondArray builtin = "atid1">
   1 1 1
</C:bondArray>
```

show element **bondArray** with attribute **builtin** assigned the value **atid1**. Element **bondArray** defines the bonds between atoms. Because this element has a **builtin** value of **atid1**, the values of this element compose the first atom in a pair of atoms. We are defining three bonds, so we specify three values. Each value is a **1**, which denotes the first atom in the **atomArray**, the nitrogen atom.

Lines 25–27

```
<C:bondArray builtin = "atid2">
   2 3 4
</C:bondArray>
```

show element **bondArray** with attribute **builtin** assigned the value **atid2**. The values of this element compose the second atom in a pair of atoms and denote the three hydrogen atoms.

Lines 29–31

```
<C:bondArray builtin = "order" type = "integer">
   1 1 1
</C:bondArray>
```

show element **bondArray** with the attribute **builtin** assigned the value **order** and **type integer**. The values of this element are integers that represent the number of bonds between the pairs of atoms. Thus, the bond between the nitrogen atom and the first hydrogen is a single bond, the bond between the nitrogen atom and the second hydrogen atom is also a single bond and likewise for the third pair.

Figure 20.5 lists several URLs related to CML. The official CML Web site (**www.xml-cml.org**) provides many resources related to CML. One such resource is *ChiMeraL* (Fig. 20.6), which provides several tools for transforming CML documents. The **Molecule Data** combo box provides a selection of CML documents. The **Display Molecules using** combo box provides several style sheets and Java applets. Many of the applets provide animation and/or allow the user to rotate the molecule using the mouse. The **Display Spectra** using combo box provides series of choices for displaying the molecule's spectra. [*Note*: Internet Explorer 5 is required for ChiMeraL.]

URL / Description

www.xml-cml.org
This is the official Web site for CML. Features include a brief introduction and history and links to software and additional documentation.

www.xml-cml.org/dtdschema/index.html
The CML DTD and schema can be obtained from this site.

www.xml-cml.org/jumbo.html
This is the Web page for obtaining Jumbo, a CML authoring environment.

www.xml-cml.org/cmlfaq.html
The xml-cml organization maintains an FAQ document here.

www.xml-cml.org/cmlref.html
This site contains a detailed CML reference.

www.xml-cml.org/chimeral/index.html
This site provides many CML demonstrations that use style sheets and Java applets. A link to the Jumbo browser can also be found here.

Fig. 20.5   CML reference Web sites.

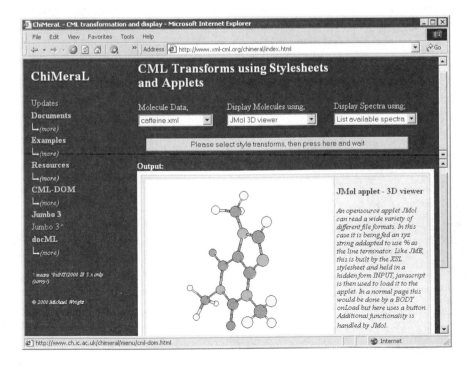

Fig. 20.6   Rendering a CML document using **JMol applet - 3D viewer**. (Courtesy of Prof. Peter Murray-Rust)

ChiMeraL also provides a link in the left frame to the next generation Jumbo browser called *Jumbo 3*. Figure 20.7 shows the Jumbo 3 browser rendering a caffeine molecule. Buttons are provided to manipulate (e.g., rotate, scale, etc.) the rendering of the molecule. [*Note*: Jumbo 3 provides a text field for loading CML documents in Jumbo 3. However, at the time of this writing, this feature was not yet implemented.]

20.5 Wireless Markup Language (WML)

The *Wireless Markup Language* (*WML*) is an XML-based language that allows Web pages to be displayed on wireless devices such as cellular phones and personal digital assistants (PDA). WML also has a companion scripting language, *WMLScript*, which is based on the ECMAScript standard. WML works with the *Wireless Application Protocol* (*WAP*) to deliver this content. WML is similar to HTML but does not require input devices such as a keyboard or mouse for navigation. A WML document is called a *deck* and contains static parts called *cards*. Each card consists of one page of information, providing the WML browser with a small, self-contained document for browsing. This packaging of multiple pages of information is necessary because the devices to which WML is delivered have limited connections to the Internet. WML includes telephone elements so that secure telephone functionality can be implemented with WML/WMLScript. For instance, a voice mail service can have a WML user interface that gives the users choices about their mailbox. WML also has image support for devices that can display bitmapped graphics.

Consider a PDA that requests a Web page on the Internet. A WAP gateway receives the request, translates it to HTTP and sends it to the appropriate Internet server. The server responds by sending the requested WML document, which may be a static WML page or generated dynamically by JavaServer™ Pages, ASP, Perl or some other server-side technology. The gateway then parses the document, sending the proper text to the PDA.

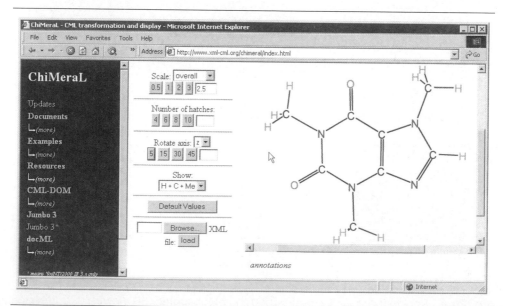

Fig. 20.7   A CML document in Jumbo 3. (Courtesy of Prof. Peter Murray-Rust)

Any WML document will be presented properly on a WAP compliant device, as microbrowsers will automatically tailor the WML presentation to the specific device. For additional information on WAP and WML, visit **www.wapforum.org** or **www.xml.com/pub/Guide/WML**.

Figure 20.8 is an example of a WML document. To be able to view this example, a WML browser and an HTTP server is needed, such as the Nokia WAP Developer Toolkit, which is available free for download from **www.nokia.com/corporate/wap/ sdk.html**. [*Note*: You must register at this Web site before being allowed to download the WAP Developer Toolkit.]

Line 8 contains the **wml** root element, which contains **card** elements. Lines 9–21

```
<card id = "paybill" title = "Welcome">
```

comprise the first **card** element, which has unique identifier **paybill** and title **Welcome**. Lines 10–12

```
<p>
    Welcome to Pay your bill from your cell!
</p>
```

contain a section of text that is denoted by the **p** element.

Line 15

```
<input type = "text" name = "amount" format = "*N"/>
```

shows element **input** with **type** value **text**, marking up a text input box with the identifier **amount**. The format attribute has value ***N**, which sets the input box to take only numerical values.

```
1   <?xml version = "1.0"?>
2   <!DOCTYPE wml PUBLIC "-//WAPFORUM//DTD WML 1.1//EN"
3              "http://www.wapforum.org/DTD/wml_1.1.xml">
4
5   <!-- Fig. 20.8 : payBill.wml -->
6   <!-- Simple WML example      -->
7
8   <wml>
9      <card id = "paybill" title = "Welcome">
10        <p>
11           Welcome to Pay your bill from your cell!
12        </p>
13
14        <p>
15           Enter the amount:
16           <input type = "text" name = "amount" format = "*N"/>
17        </p>
18
19        <do type = "accept" label = "Submit amount">
20           <go href = "#pay"/>
21        </do>
22     </card>
```

Fig. 20.8 WML document for paying a bill (part 1 of 2).

```
23
24      <card id = "pay" title = "PAID">
25         <p>
26            You have paid $$$(amount). Thank you!
27         </p>
28      </card>
29
30   </wml>
```

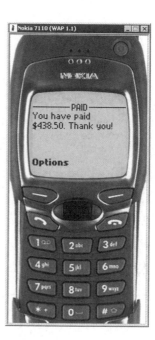

(©2000. Nokia Mobile Phones)

Fig. 20.8   WML document for paying a bill (part 2 of 2).

Lines 19–21

```
<do type = "accept" label = "Submit amount">
   <go href = "#pay"/>
</do>
```

set an action for the page using element **do**. The **accept** value for attribute **type** defines that when the user accepts the data input to the text field—most commonly by pressing a button on a cellular phone—the contents of the **do** element are performed. Element **go** is used to perform hyperlinking to the object in the **href** attribute. In this case, we navigate to the **pay** card. Note that the **pay** card is in the same WML deck as the **paybill** card. The **pay** card is therefore loaded from memory, reducing the number of times the wireless device needs to download information from the Internet.

Line 24

```
<card id = "pay" title = "PAID">
```

is the **pay** card. We display the amount entered into the text box by dereferencing the text box identifier. This is done with the dollar sign (**$**). To display a dollar sign, two dollar signs are needed (i.e., **$$**). So, on line 26

```
You have paid $$$(amount). Thank you!
```

we display a dollar sign, and then output the value entered into the text box with the identifier **amount**. Figure 20.9 lists some WML Web resources.

20.6 Geography Markup Language (GML)

The *Geography Markup Language (GML)* was developed by the *OpenGIS Consortium (OGC)*. GML separates content from presentation. GML describes geographic information for use and reuse by different applications for different purposes. In GML, geographic information is described in terms of *features*. A feature is composed of *properties* and *geometries*. GML properties contain name, type and value elements. Features are geometric entities (e.g., lines, polygons, etc.). Geometries contain the bulk of geographic data, and properties augment that data with descriptive information. Figure 20.10 provides three reference Web sites related to GML.

As a recent markup language, GML is in the early stages of development. Figures 20.11 and 20.12 show an example GML map displayed when the **Experimental GML Viewer** link is selected at **gis.about.com/science/gis/msub30.htm**. This map contains several irregular-shape buildings. The user can zoom, pan and select buildings on the map. Figure 20.12 shows two buildings being selected. The GML markup (Fig. 20.13) for the map is shown at the bottom of the Web page.

URL / Description

www.wapforum.org
This is the official WAP Web site.

www.wapforum.org/DTD/wml_1.1.xml
This is the location of the WML DTD.

allnetdevices.com/faq
This is the WAP/WML FAQ document.

www.oasis-open.org/cover/wap-wml.html
This site contains an extensive list of WML articles and a list of some WML and WAP resources.

webreference.com/js/column61
This site contains an in-depth WML tutorial.

Fig. 20.9   WML reference Web sites (part 1 of 2).

URL / Description

www.wirelessdevnet.com/training/WAP/WML.html
This site contains a WML tutorial.

www.w3scripts.com/wap
A thorough and easy WML tutorial (Requires Internet Explorer 5 or higher).

Fig. 20.9   WML reference Web sites (part 2 of 2).

URL / Description

www.opengis.org
Home page of the OpenGIS Web Consortium, the originators of GML.

www.opengis.org/techno/rfc11info.htm
A draft of the GML recommendation.

gis.about.com/science/gis/msub30.htm
List of GML-related links.

Fig. 20.10 GML reference Web sites.

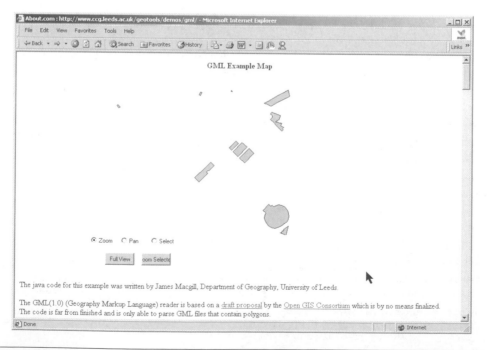

Fig. 20.11 GML example map. (Courtesy of About.com)

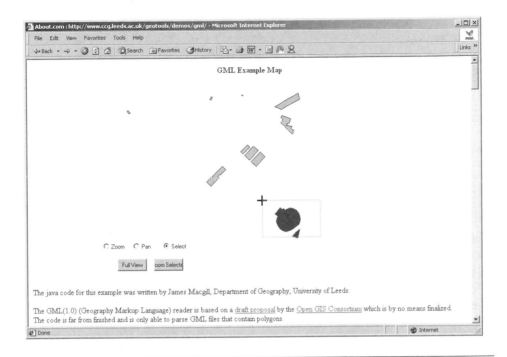

Fig. 20.12 Selecting two buildings in the GML example map. (Courtesy of About.com)

20.7 Synchronized Multimedia Integration Language (SMIL)

The *Synchronized Multimedia Integration Language* (*SMIL*, pronounced "smile") enables Web document authors to coordinate the presentation of a wide range of multimedia elements. A SMIL document specifies the source (i.e., the URL) of multimedia elements and how these elements are presented. In HTML, multimedia elements are autonomous entities that cannot interact without complicated scripts. In SMIL, multimedia elements can work together; this enables document authors to specify when and how these multimedia elements appear in the document. For example, SMIL may be used to produce TV-style content, in which static and dynamic text, audio and video occur simultaneously and sequentially. One way to render SMIL documents is with *RealPlayer*, a multimedia player from Real Networks. This player can be downloaded free from **www.real.com**.

The example in Fig. 20.14 is a SMIL document that displays **.jpg** images for a variety of *Java How to Program* book covers. The images are displayed sequentially, and each image is accompanied by a sound.

Element **head** (lines 5–13) contains all the information for setting up the document. Lines 6–12 show element **layout**, which sets the layout attributes for the document.

Lines 7 and 8

```
<root-layout height = "300" width = "300"
   background-color = "#bbbbee" title = "Example"/>
```

set the document size, color and title using element **root-layout**.

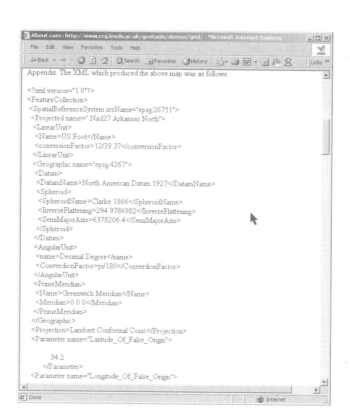

Fig. 20.13 GML markup for the example map. (Courtesy of About.com)

```
1   <smil>
2      <!-- Fig. 20.14 : example1.smil -->
3      <!-- Example SMIL Document       -->
4
5      <head>
6         <layout>
7            <root-layout height = "300" width = "280"
8               background-color = "#bbbbee" title = "Example"/>
9
10           <region id = "image1" width = "177" height = "230"
11              top = "35" left = "50" background-color = "#ffffff"/>
12        </layout>
13     </head>
14     <body>
15        <seq>
16
17           <par>
18              <img src = "book1.jpg" region = "image1"
19                 alt = "book1" dur = "1s" fit = "fill"/>
```

Fig. 20.14 SMIL document with images and sound (part 1 of 2).

```
20                    <audio src = "bounce.au" dur = ".5s"/>
21              </par>
22
23              <par>
24                 <img src = "book2.jpg" region = "image1"
25                     alt = "book2" dur = "1s" fit = "fill"/>
26                 <audio src = "bounce.au" dur = ".5s"/>
27              </par>
28
29              <par>
30                 <img src = "book3.jpg" region = "image1"
31                     alt = "book3" dur = "1s" fit = "fill"/>
32                 <audio src = "bounce.au" dur = ".5s"/>
33              </par>
34
35              <par>
36                 <img src = "book4.jpg" region = "image1"
37                     alt = "book4" dur = "1s" fit = "fill"/>
38                 <audio src = "bounce.au" dur = ".5s"/>
39              </par>
40
41              <par>
42                 <img src = "book5.jpg" region = "image1"
43                     alt = "book5" dur = "1s" fit = "fill"/>
44                 <audio src = "bounce.au" dur = ".5s"/>
45              </par>
46
47              <par>
48                 <img src = "book6.jpg" region = "image1"
49                     alt = "book6" dur = "1s" fit = "fill"/>
50                 <audio src = "bounce.au" dur = ".5s"/>
51              </par>
52           </seq>
53       </body>
54    </smil>
```

Fig. 20.14 SMIL document with images and sound (part 2 of 2).

Lines 10 and 11

```
<region id = "image1" width = "177" height = "230"
    top = "35" left = "50" background-color = "#ffffff"/>
```

set a region for displaying objects (e.g., images) using element **region**. Attribute **id** is a unique identifier for the region. Attributes **width** and **height** specify the size of the region, and attributes **top** and **left** provide the position. Attribute **background-color** sets the color of the region's background.

Line 14 begins the element **body**, which encloses the contents of the document. Line 15 starts element **seq**, which sets its child elements to execute sequentially (i.e., in chronological order), and line 17 starts a **par** element, which sets its child elements to execute in parallel (i.e., at the same time).

Lines 18 and 19

```
<img src = "book1.jpg" region = "image1"
    alt = "book1" dur = "1s" fit = "fill"/>
```

show element **img**, which references an image. Attribute **src** contains the location of the image, and attribute **alt** provides a description of the image. Attribute **region** specifies the region in which the image is to be displayed; a **fit** value of **fill** sets the image to fill the entire region. Attribute **dur** describes how long the image will appear on the screen (e.g., one second). Line 20

```
<audio src = "bounce.au" dur = ".5s"/>
```

shows element **audio**, which references audio file **bounce.au**. The remaining elements in the document (lines 23–51) display a different image and play the audio file.

We can also embed a SMIL document in a Web page. Figure 20.15 uses the *Soja applet* to view our example SMIL document. This applet can be downloaded from **www.helio.org/products/smil**.

```
1   <html>
2
3   <!-- Fig. 20.15 : example1.html   -->
4   <!-- HTML document rendering SMIL -->
5
6   <body>
7      <applet code = "org.helio.soja.SojaApplet.class"
8         archive = "soja.jar" width = "300" height = "300">
9         <param name = "source" value = "example1.smil">
10        <param name = "bgcolor" value = "#FFFFFF">
11     </applet>
12  </body>
13  </html>
```

Fig. 20.15 Using the Soja applet to display a SMIL document.

Lines 7 and 8

```
<applet code = "org.helio.soja.SojaApplet.class"
    archive = "soja.jar" width = "300" height = "300">
```

reference the Soja applet. Line 9

```
<param name = "source" value = "example1.smil">
```

sets the source SMIL document (i.e., the document in Fig. 20.14), and line 10

```
<param name = "bgcolor" value = "#FFFFFF">
```

sets the background color for the applet. Figure 20.16 provides a list of SMIL resources.

20.8 Scalable Vector Graphics (SVG)

The *Scalable Vector Graphics (SVG) markup language* is a way to describe *vector graphics* data for use over the Web. SVG provides considerable advantages over current methods (e.g., the **.jpg**, **.gif** and **.png** formats) for distributing graphics on the Web. The current formats use *bitmaps*, which describe each pixel in the image and may take quite a bit of time to download. Bitmap resolution is fixed, so bitmap images cannot be scaled (i.e., zoomed, panned, etc.) without a loss in image quality, and printed bitmap images often contain low-resolution, jagged lines. Conversely, vector graphics describe graphical information in terms of lines, curves, etc. Not only do images rendered in vector graphics require less bandwidth, but these images also can be easily scaled and printed without producing jagged lines. In addition, because SVG is an application of XML, SVG documents can be scripted, searched and dynamically created.

Both Internet Explorer and Netscape Communicator intend to provide native support for SVG in the near future. Currently, Adobe provides a plug-in for Internet Explorer (version 4.0 or higher for Windows and version 5.0 for Mac) and for Netscape Communicator (version 4.0 or higher for both Windows and Mac) that enables SVG documents to be directly rendered in those browsers. This plug-in is available free of charge from Adobe at **www.adobe.com/svg**.

URL / Description

---

www.w3.org/AudioVideo
The W3C Synchronized Multimedia Integration Language (SMIL) home page.

www.w3.org/TR/REC-smil
The most up-to-date W3C SMIL Specification.

xml.about.com/compute/xml/msubsmil.htm
List of SMIL-related links.

smw.internet.com/smil/smilhome.html
A site dedicated to SMIL with a group of links, resources and definitions.

Fig. 20.16 SMIL Web resources.

Figure 20.17 is an SVG document that displays some simple shapes in a browser. We use the Adobe plug-in to view the document in Internet Explorer.

Line 6

```
<svg viewBox = "0 0 300 300" width = "300" height = "300">
```

```
1   <?xml version="1.0"?>
2
3   <!-- Fig. 20.17 : shapes.svg -->
4   <!-- Simple example of SVG    -->
5
6   <svg viewBox = "0 0 300 300" width = "300" height = "300">
7
8      <!-- Generate a background -->
9      <g>
10        <path style = "fill: #eebb99" d = "M0,0 h300 v300 h-300 z"/>
11     </g>
12
13     <!-- Some shapes and colors -->
14     <g>
15
16        <circle style = "fill: green; fill-opacity: 0.5"
17           cx = "150" cy = "150" r = "50"/>
18
19        <rect style = "fill: blue; stroke: white"
20           x = "50" y = "50" width = "100" height = "100"/>
21
22        <text style = "fill: red; font-size: 24pt"
23           x = "25" y = "250">Welcome to SVG!</text>
24
25     </g>
26  </svg>
```

Fig. 20.17 SVG document example.

is the root element for an SVG document. Attribute **viewBox** sets the viewing area for the document. The first two numbers in the value are the *x*- and *y*-coordinates of the upper-left corner of the viewing area, and the last two numbers are the width and height of the viewing area. Attribute **width** specifies the width of the image, and attribute **height** specifies the height of the image.

Element **g** groups elements of an SVG document. Line 10

```
<path style = "fill: #eebb99" d = "M0,0 h300 v300 h-300 z"/>
```

uses element **path** to create a box. Attribute **style** uses CSS property **fill** to fill the inside of the box with the color **#eebb99**. Attribute **d** defines the points of the box. Property **M** specifies the starting coordinates *(0, 0)* of the path. Property **h** specifies that the next point is horizontal to the current point and spaced 300 pixels to the right of the current point *(300, 0)*. Property **v** specifies that the next point is vertical to the current point and spaced 300 pixels below it *(300, 300)*. Property **h** now places the point to the left by 300 pixels *(0, 300)*. Property **z** sets the **path** to connect the first and last points, thus closing the box.

Lines 14–25 group three elements: a **circle**, a **rect**angle and a **text** element. Lines 16 and 17

```
<circle style = "fill: blue; fill-opacity: 0.5"
    cx = "150" cy = "150" r = "50"/>
```

create a circle with element **circle**. The circle has an *x*-axis center coordinate (attribute **cx**) of 150 pixels, a *y*-axis center coordinate (attribute **cy**) of 150 pixels and a radius (attribute **r**) of 50 pixels. The circle is filled blue, with 50% opacity.

Lines 19 and 20

```
<rect style = "fill: blue; stroke: white"
    x = "50" y = "50" width = "100" height = "100"/>
```

use element **rectangle** to create a rectangle. The rectangle's upper-left corner is set using attributes **x** and **y**. Attribute **width** sets the width of the rectangle, and attribute **height** sets the height of the rectangle.

Lines 22 and 23

```
<text style = "fill: red; font-size: 24pt"
    x = "25" y = "250">Welcome to SVG!</text>
```

create some text with element **text**. The text is placed using attributes **x** and **y**. The format of the text is defined using attribute **style**; in this case, the text is red and has a font size of 24 points.

Figure 20.18 contains a complex SVG image that simulates the Earth and Moon rotating around the Sun. This example uses SVG's animation feature to animate the circles.

```
1   <?xml version = "1.0"?>
2
3   <!-- Figure 20.18 : planet.svg -->
4   <!-- Planetary motion with SVG -->
```

Fig. 20.18 SVG document with animated elements (part 1 of 3).

```
5
6   <svg viewBox = "-500 -500 1000 1000">
7      <g id = "background">
8         <path style = "fill: black"
9            d = "M -2000,-2000 H 2000 V 2000 H -2000 Z"/>
10     </g>
11
12     <circle id = "sun" style = "fill: yellow"
13        cx = "0" cy = "0" r = "100"/>
14
15     <g>
16        <animateTransform attributeName = "transform"
17           type = "rotate" dur = "80s" from = "0" to = "360"
18           repeatCount = "indefinite"/>
19
20        <circle id = "earth" style = "fill: blue"
21           cx = "400" cy = "0" r = "40"/>
22
23        <g transform = "translate( 400 0 )">
24           <circle id = "moon" style = "fill: white"
25              cx = "70" cy = "0" r = "10">
26              <animateTransform attributeName = "transform"
27                 type = "rotate" dur = "20s" from = "360"
28                 to = "0" repeatCount = "indefinite"/>
29           </circle>
30        </g>
31     </g>
32  </svg>
```

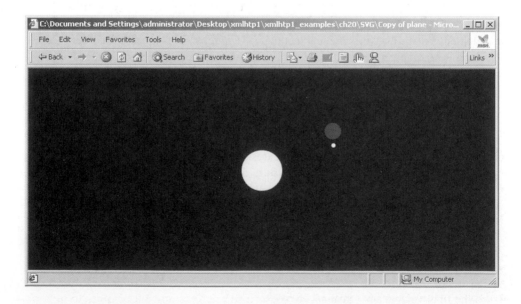

Fig. 20.18 SVG document with animated elements (part 2 of 3).

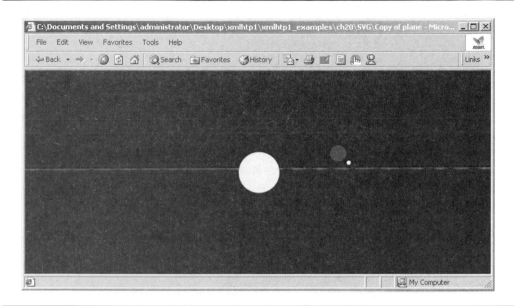

Fig. 20.18 SVG document with animated elements (part 3 of 3).

Lines 8 and 9

```
<path style = "fill: black"
    d = "M -2000,-2000 H 2000 V 2000 H -2000 Z"/>
```

create a box for the background that is much bigger than the viewable size. Attribute **d** has properties **H** and **V** that specify absolute coordinates for the **path**. Thus, the coordinates of the box are: *(-2000, -2000)*, *(2000, -2000)*, *(2000, 2000)* and *(-2000, 2000)*.

Lines 12 and 13

```
<circle id = "sun" style = "fill: yellow"
    cx = "0" cy = "0" r = "100"/>
```

create a yellow circle with a radius of 100 pixels at coordinate *(0, 0)* to represent the Sun.

Line 15 defines element **g**, which groups together the circles representing the Earth and Moon. Lines 16–18

```
<animateTransform attributeName = "transform"
    type = "rotate" dur = "80s" from = "0" to = "360"
    repeatCount = "indefinite"/>
```

use element **animateTransform**, which changes the attribute of the parent element specified in attribute **attributeName**. Attribute **type** defines the property of the attribute that changes. The initial and final values of the transformation are set by attributes **from** and **to**. Attribute **dur** sets the time (i.e., 80 seconds) it takes to change from the initial to the final values, and attribute **repeatCount** sets the amount of times to perform this transformation. In our example, we rotate the group element from 0 degrees to 360 degrees in 80 seconds, repeating the rotation indefinitely (i.e., continuously).

Lines 20 and 21

```
<circle id = "earth" style = "fill: blue"
    cx = "400" cy = "0" r = "40"/>
```

create a blue circle with a radius of 40 pixels at coordinates *(400, 0)*. When the group rotates, this circle's center will stay at a distance of 400 pixels from the origin *(0, 0)*.

Line 23 uses element **g** to group the **circle** element that represents the Moon. This element has attribute **transform**, which **translate**s (shifts) the group element 400 pixels to the right, thus centering the group on the blue circle. For other transformations, see the SVG specification.

The white circle (the Moon) on lines 24 and 25 has a child **animateTransform** element on lines 26–28

```
<animateTransform attributeName = "transform"
    type = "rotate" dur = "20s" from = "360"
    to = "0" repeatCount = "indefinite"/>
```

that rotates the Moon 360 degrees counterclockwise around the Earth every 20 seconds. Figure 20.19 lists SVG-related Web resources.

20.9 Bean Markup Language (BML)

JavaBeans™ (often called *beans*) are software components that can be combined to create Java applications and applets. The *Bean Markup Language (BML)* is an XML-based markup language for describing JavaBeans. BML defines how various beans are interconnected. The BML specification and tools can be downloaded free from **www.alphaworks.ibm.com/aw.nsf/techmain/bml**.

Software Engineering Observation 20.1

BML can be used to manipulate JavaBeans programmatically. For example, an XSLT transformation might create Java code that contains JavaBeans.

URL / Description

---

www.w3.org/TR/SVG
The W3C Scalable Vector Graphics Specification.

www.w3.org/Graphics/SVG
The W3C SVG Home page.

www.irt.org/articles/js176
Good site with overview of SVG accompanied by links and references.

www.adobe.com/svg
Adobe Software's page dedicated to SVG accompanied by tutorials and other resources.

webreview.com/pub/1999/08/13/feature/index4.html
Review of SVG on *Webreview.com* along with useful links.

Fig. 20.19 SVG Web resources.

Figure 20.20 presents an example of a JavaBean that animates a Deitel & Associates, Inc. logo. In Fig. 20.21, we create a BML document that describes this particular JavaBean.

Notice that we added a **package** statement (line 3) to the file for the **LogoAnimator** class. Normally, classes that represent a bean are first placed into a package. You must compile your packaged classes using the **-d** option with the Java compiler as in

```
javac -d . LogoAnimator.java
```

```java
1   // Fig. 20.20 : LogoAnimator.java
2   // Animation bean
3   package logobml;
4
5   import java.awt.*;
6   import java.awt.event.*;
7   import java.io.*;
8   import java.net.*;
9   import javax.swing.*;
10
11  public class LogoAnimator extends JPanel
12         implements ActionListener, Serializable {
13     protected ImageIcon images[];
14     protected int totalImages = 30,
15                   currentImage = 0,
16                   animationDelay = 50; // 50 millisecond delay
17     protected Timer animationTimer;
18
19     public LogoAnimator()
20     {
21        setSize( getPreferredSize() );
22
23        images = new ImageIcon[ totalImages ];
24
25        URL url;
26
27        for ( int i = 0; i < images.length; ++i ) {
28           url = getClass().getResource(
29                    "deitel" + i + ".gif" );
30           images[ i ] = new ImageIcon( url );
31        }
32
33        startAnimation();
34     }
35
36     public void paintComponent( Graphics g )
37     {
38        super.paintComponent( g );
39
40        if ( images[ currentImage ].getImageLoadStatus() ==
41             MediaTracker.COMPLETE ) {
42           images[ currentImage ].paintIcon( this, g, 50, 25 );
43           currentImage = ( currentImage + 1 ) % totalImages;
44        }
45     }
```

Fig. 20.20 Animator bean (part 1 of 2).

```
46
47      public void actionPerformed( ActionEvent e )
48      {
49         repaint();
50      }
51
52      public void startAnimation()
53      {
54         if ( animationTimer == null ) {
55            currentImage = 0;
56            animationTimer = new Timer( animationDelay, this );
57            animationTimer.start();
58         }
59         else  // continue from last image displayed
60            if ( ! animationTimer.isRunning() )
61               animationTimer.restart();
62      }
63
64      public void stopAnimation()
65      {
66         animationTimer.stop();
67      }
68
69      public Dimension getMinimumSize()
70      {
71         return getPreferredSize();
72      }
73
74      public Dimension getPreferredSize()
75      {
76         return new Dimension( 200, 140 );
77      }
78
79      public static void main( String args[] )
80      {
81         LogoAnimator anim = new LogoAnimator();
82
83         JFrame app = new JFrame( "Animator test" );
84         app.getContentPane().add( anim, BorderLayout.CENTER );
85
86         app.addWindowListener(
87            new WindowAdapter() {
88               public void windowClosing( WindowEvent e )
89               {
90                  System.exit( 0 );
91               }
92            }
93         );
94
95         app.setSize( anim.getPreferredSize().width + 10,
96                      anim.getPreferredSize().height + 20 );
97         app.show();
98      }
99   }
```

Fig. 20.20 Animator bean (part 2 of 2).

The first "**.**" represents the directory in which the **logobml** package should be placed ("**.**" represents the current directory, which we use here for simplicity).

Line 12 specifies that the class **implements** interface **Serializable** to support *persistence*—saving a bean object in its current state for future use. Objects of our **Logo-Animator** class can be serialized with **ObjectOutputStream**s and **ObjectInputStream**s. Implementing interface **Serializable** allows programmers using a builder tool to save their customized bean by *serializing* the bean to a file.

Class **LogoAnimator** maintains an array of **ImageIcon**s that are loaded in the constructor. As each **ImageIcon** object is instantiated in the **for** structure at line 30, the **ImageIcon** constructor loads one image for the animation (there are 30 total images) with the statement

```
images[ i ] = new ImageIcon( url );
```

The argument **url** contains a URL assembled from the pieces **"deitel"**, **i** and **".gif"**. Each of the images in the animation is in one of the files "**deitel0.gif**" through "**deitel29.gif**." The value of the control variable in the **for** structure is used to select one of the 30 images.

After loading the images, the constructor calls **startAnimation** (defined at line 52) to begin the animation. The animation is driven by an instance of class ***Timer*** (package **javax.swing**). An object of class **Timer** generates **ActionEvent**s at a fixed interval in milliseconds (normally specified as an argument to the **Timer**'s constructor) and notifies all of its registered **ActionListener**s that the event occurred. Lines 54–58

```
if ( animationTimer == null ) {
   currentImage = 0;
   animationTimer = new Timer( animationDelay, this );
   animationTimer.start();
}
```

determine if the **Timer** reference **animationTimer** is **null**. If so, **currentImage** is set to 0 to indicate that the animation should begin with the image in the first element of array **images**. Line 56 assigns a new **Timer** object to **animationTimer**. The **Timer** constructor receives two arguments—the delay in milliseconds (**animationDelay** is 50 in this example) and the **ActionListener** that will respond to the **Timer**'s **Action-Event**s (**this LogoAnimator** implements **ActionListener** at line 12). Line 57 starts the **Timer** object. Once started, **animationTimer** generates an **ActionEvent** every 50 milliseconds. Lines 59–61

```
else  // continue from last image displayed
   if ( ! animationTimer.isRunning() )
      animationTimer.restart();
```

are for programs that may stop the animation and restart it. For example, to make an animation "browser friendly" in an applet, the animation should be stopped when the user switches Web pages. If the user returns to the Web page with the animation, method **startAnimation** can be called to restart the animation. The **if** condition at line 60 uses **Timer** method **isRunning** to determine if the **Timer** is currently running (i.e., generating events). If it is not running, line 61 calls **Timer** method **restart** to indicate that the **Timer** should start generating events again.

In response to every **Timer** event in this example, method **actionPerformed** (line 47) calls method **repaint**. This results in a call to the **LogoAnimator**'s **paint-Component** method (line 36). The first statement in any **paintComponent** method should be a call to the superclass's **paintComponent** method to ensure that Swing components are displayed correctly. The **if** condition at lines 40 and 41

```
if ( images[ currentImage ].getImageLoadStatus() ==
    MediaTracker.COMPLETE ) {
```

uses *ImageIcon* method *getImageLoadStatus* to determine if the image to display is completely loaded into memory. Only complete images should be displayed to make the animation as smooth as possible. When the image is fully loaded, the method returns *MediaTracker.COMPLETE*. An object of class *MediaTracker* (package **java.awt**) is used by class **ImageIcon** to track the loading of an image.

When loading images into a program, the images can be registered with an object of class **MediaTracker** to enable the program to determine when an image is loaded completely. Class **MediaTracker** also provides the ability to wait for an image or several images to load before allowing a program to continue and to determine if an error occurred while loading an image. We do not need to create a **MediaTracker** directly in this example because class **ImageIcon** does this already. However, when using class **Image**, you may want to create your own **MediaTracker**.

If the image is fully loaded, lines 42 and 43

```
images[ currentImage ].paintIcon( this, g, 50, 25 );
currentImage = ( currentImage + 1 ) % totalImages;
```

paint the **ImageIcon** at element **currentImage** in the array and prepare for the next image to be displayed by incrementing **currentImage** by 1. Notice the modulus calculation to ensure that the value of **currentImage** is set to 0 when it is incremented past 29 (the last element subscript in the array).

Method **stopAnimation** (line 64), stops the animation with line 66

```
animationTimer.stop();
```

which uses **Timer** method *stop* to indicate that the **Timer** should stop generating events. This, in turn, prevents **actionPerformed** from calling **repaint** to initiate the painting of the next image in the array.

Methods **getMinimumSize** (line 69) and **getPreferredSize** (line 74) are overridden to help a layout manager determine the appropriate size of a **LogoAnimator** in a layout. In this example, the images are 200 pixels wide and 140 pixels tall, so method **getPreferredSize** returns a **Dimension** object containing the values **200** and **140**. Method **getMinimumSize** simply calls **getPreferredSize** (a common programming practice). Notice in **main** (line 79) that the size of the application window is set (lines 95 and 96) to the preferred width of the animation plus 10 pixels and the preferred height of the animation plus 20 pixels. This is because a window's width and height specify the outer bounds of the window, not the window's *client area* (the area in which GUI components can be attached). We are now ready to describe the JavaBean (Fig. 20.20) using BML in Fig. 20.21.

```
1    <?xml version = "1.0"?>
2
3    <!-- Fig. 20.21 : logo.bml -->
4    <!-- logo animator bean     -->
5
6    <bean class = "javax.swing.JFrame" id = "mainFrame">
7       <property name = "title" value = "Logo Animator"/>
8
9       <call-method name = "setContentPane">
10
11      <bean class = "javax.swing.JPanel" id = "containerPanel">
12      <property name = "layout">
13         <bean class = "java.awt.BorderLayout"/>
14      </property>
15
16      <add>
17
18         <!-- registering LogoAnimator bean -->
19         <bean class = "logobml.LogoAnimator" id = "Deitel">
20            <call-method name = "startAnimation"/>
21         </bean>
22         <string value = "Center"/>
23      </add>
24
25      <add>
26
27         <!-- adding a panel -->
28         <bean class = "javax.swing.JPanel">
29            <property name = "background" value = "0xff9999"/>
30
31            <add>
32
33               <!-- adding a button to start animation -->
34               <bean class = "javax.swing.JButton">
35                  <property name = "label"
36                     value = "Start Animation"/>
37
38                  <event-binding name = "action">
39                     <script>
40                        <call-method target = "Deitel"
41                           name = "startAnimation"/>
42                     </script>
43                  </event-binding>
44
45               </bean>
46            </add>
47
48            <add>
49
50               <!-- adding a button to stop animation -->
51               <bean class = "javax.swing.JButton">
52                  <property name = "label" value = "Stop Animation"/>
53
```

Fig. 20.21 BML markup for Logo Animator (part 1 of 2).

```
54                     <event-binding name = "action">
55                         <script>
56                             <call-method target = "Deitel"
57                                 name = "stopAnimation"/>
58                         </script>
59                     </event-binding>
60
61                 </bean>
62             </add>
63
64         </bean>
65
66         <string value = "South"/>
67     </add>
68
69     </bean>
70
71     </call-method>
72
73   </bean>
```

Fig. 20.21 BML markup for Logo Animator (part 2 of 2).

Line 6

```
<bean class = "javax.swing.JFrame" id = "mainFrame">
```

creates a bean of class **javax.swing.JFrame** for the application's user interface. Each bean is marked up using element **bean**. Attribute **class** specifies the bean's type, and attribute **id** specifies the bean's name. In this particular case, the bean is a **JFrame** object identified by the name **mainFrame**.

Line 7

```
<property name = "title" value = "Logo Animator"/>
```

sets the **JFrame**'s title using element **property**. Attribute **name** specifies which property or characteristic is to be set, and attribute **value** specifies the value that property will have. In this particular case, the **title** property is assigned **Logo Animator**—which specifies the text displayed in the **JFrame**'s title bar.

Line 9

```
<call-method name = "setContentPane">
```

marks up a call to **JFrame** method **setContentPane**. A method call is marked up using element ***call-method***. Attribute **name** is assigned the name of the method to invoke.

Lines 11–14

```
<bean class = "javax.swing.JPanel" id = "containerPanel">
<property name = "layout">
   <bean class = "java.awt.BorderLayout"/>
</property>
```

mark up a **JPanel** bean named **containerPanel**. This **bean**'s layout manager is set to **BorderLayout**. Notice that each Java class, including **BorderLayout**, is represented as a **bean** element.

Lines 16–23 use element ***add*** to add a bean to the content pane. Lines 19–21

```
<bean class = "logobml.LogoAnimator" id = "Deitel">
   <call-method name = "startAnimation"/>
</bean>
```

create a **logobml.LogoAnimator** bean, the same as the animation bean we created in Fig. 20.20. Element **call-method** calls the method specified in attribute **name**. Therefore, upon instantiation of the **LogoAnimator**, method **startAnimation** is called. Line 22

```
<string value = "Center"/>
```

is an additional argument to the **JFrame** bean. Element ***string*** provides a string value of **Center**, placing the **LogoAnimator** bean in the center region of the **JFrame** bean.

Lines 28–69 add a **JPanel** bean. Within the **JPanel** bean, two **JButton** beans are added.

The first **JButton** bean (lines 34–45) has a label of **Start Animation**. Lines 38–43

```
<event-binding name = "action">
   <script>
      <call-method target = "Deitel"
         name = "startAnimation"/>
   </script>
</event-binding>
```

bind an event to the bean. In this case, when an **action** event occurs, the elements in element **script** are performed. Method **startAnimation** is called on the bean with an **id** of **Deitel** (the **logobml.LogoAnimator** bean in line 19).

The second **JButton** bean (lines 51–61) has a label of **Stop Animation**, which calls method **stopAnimation** on an **action** event.

To execute the BML document, a *BML player* is used. IBM provides a BML player with the BML distribution. To execute this example, follow these instructions:

1. Download and install the Java 2 Platform Standard Edition from **java.sun.com**.

2. Download and install the Bean Markup Language tool kit from **www.alphaworks.ibm.com**.

3. In a command window, modify the **CLASSPATH** to contain **bmlall.jar**, **xml4j_2_0_11.jar**, the BML distribution directory (e.g., **C:\bml-2.4**) and the current directory (i.e., **.**). The JAR files are provided in the BML distribution's **lib** directory.

4. Copy the **20_20** directory from the Chapter 20 examples directory provided on the CD-ROM that accompanies this book onto your computer (e.g., **C:\20_20**).

5. In the **20_20** directory, execute **logo.bml** by typing

```
java demos.driver.PlayerDriver logo.bml
```

Although BML allows the generation of JavaBeans, it does not permit JavaBeans to be saved as serialized objects. *Koala Bean Markup Language (KBML)* was developed to remedy this deficiency. With KBML, which is similar to BML, a JavaBean can be saved as a serialized Java object. KBML determines all of the properties for a JavaBean and saves them to an KBML document. The JavaBean can then be recreated from this KBML document. Figure 20.22 provides a list of BML and KBML resources.

20.10 Extensible 3D Language (X3D)

In 1997, the *Web3D Consortium* recommended the *Virtual Reality Modeling Language* (VRML97) for use on the Internet as a file format for describing interactive 3D objects and worlds. VRML was created with the goal of providing a way to share "virtual worlds" (i.e., three-dimensional objects grouped together in some common way). Fig. 20.23 shows a sample 3D world.

The *Extensible 3D (X3D) language* is the result of the combined efforts of the World Wide Web Consortium and the Web3D Consortium to extend VRML with XML. X3D is the next generation of VRML, and the current version is backwards compatible with VRML97. X3D's XML base enables wide use and extensibility of the VRML standard.

Figure 20.24 contains an X3D document that describes a 3D rocket. The **DOCTYPE** declaration (lines 2–3) specifies the X3D DTD. The root element of an X3D document is the **X3D** element (line 8).

URL / Description

www.alphaworks.ibm.com/aw.nsf/techmain/bml
Home page of BML located at IBM.

www.oasis-open.org/cover/beanML.html
This site contains an extensive list of BML articles and a list of some BML resources.

www-sop.inria.fr/koala/kbml
This is the official site for Koala BML, a variation of BML

Fig. 20.22 BML resources.

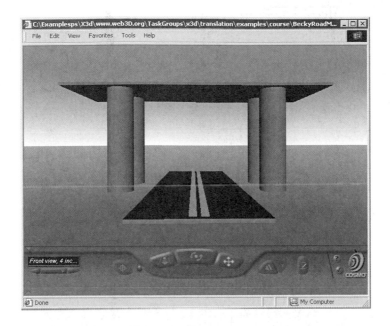

Fig. 20.23 Sample X3D world containing a road under a bridge. (Courtesy of Don Brutzman, Naval Postgraduate School and Web3D Consortium)

```
1   <?xml version = "1.0" encoding = "UTF-8"?>
2   <!DOCTYPE X3D PUBLIC
3     "C:/www.web3D.org/TaskGroups/x3d/translation/x3d-compromise.dtd">
4
5   <!-- Fig. 20.24: rocket.xml -->
6   <!-- Simple example of X3D  -->
7
8   <X3D>
9      <Header>
10        <meta name = 'myrocket' content = 'rocket.xml'/>
11        <meta name = 'description' content = 'simple example'/>
12     </Header>
13
14     <Scene>
15        <NavigationInfo type = '"EXAMINE" "ANY"'/>
16
17        <!-- declare view points for viewing the rocket -->
18        <Viewpoint description = 'Main view' position = '0 0 6'/>
19        <Viewpoint description = '150 Angular' fieldOfView = '2.61'
20           position = '0 3 2'/>
21
22        <Group>
23           <children>
24
```

Fig. 20.24 X3D markup for a rocket (part 1 of 3).

```
25                  <!-- draw a cylinder -->
26                  <Shape>
27                     <appearance>
28                        <Appearance>
29                           <material>
30                              <Material
31                                 diffuseColor = '0 0.75 1'/>
32                           </material>
33                        </Appearance>
34                     </appearance>
35
36                     <geometry>
37                        <Cylinder radius = '0.4' height = '2'/>
38                     </geometry>
39                  </Shape>
40
41                  <Transform translation = '0 -0.5 0'>
42                     <children>
43
44                        <!-- draw the lower part of rocket as cone -->
45                        <Shape>
46
47                           <appearance>
48                              <Appearance>
49                                 <material>
50
51                                    <!-- set the color -->
52                                    <Material
53                                       diffuseColor = '1 1 0'/>
54                                 </material>
55                              </Appearance>
56                           </appearance>
57
58                           <geometry>
59                              <Cone bottomRadius = '0.6'
60                                 height = '1.3'/>
61                           </geometry>
62                        </Shape>
63
64                        <Transform translation = '-3.2 -1.5 0'>
65                           <children>
66                              <Shape>
67                                 <geometry>
68                                    <Text string = 'Welcome to X3D!'/>
69                                 </geometry>
70                              </Shape>
71                           </children>
72                        </Transform>
73                     </children>
74                  </Transform>
75
76                  <Transform translation = '0 1.5 0'>
77                     <children>
```

Fig. 20.24 X3D markup for a rocket (part 2 of 3).

```
78
79                      <!-- draw the head of rocket -->
80                      <Shape>
81
82                          <appearance>
83                              <Appearance>
84                                  <material>
85                                      <Material
86                                          diffuseColor = '0.9 0.9 1'/>
87                                  </material>
88                              </Appearance>
89                          </appearance>
90
91                          <geometry>
92                              <Cone bottomRadius = '0.4'
93                                  height = '1'/>
94                          </geometry>
95                      </Shape>
96                  </children>
97              </Transform>
98
99          </children>
100      </Group>
101   </Scene>
102 </X3D>
```

Fig. 20.24 X3D markup for a rocket (part 3 of 3).

The *Header* element (lines 9–12) contains two *meta* elements that describe the 3D world contained in this document. The *Scene* element (line 14) contains the elements that will be used to describe the 3D elements in this world.

Lines 18 and 19 declare two different **Viewpoint** elements. A **Viewpoint** indicates the position from which a user views a scene. The first **Viewpoint** (line 18) uses the *position* attribute with the value **0 0 6** to place the viewer at *x*-coordinate **0**, *y*-coordinate **0** and *z*-coordinate **6**. The second **Viewpoint** (lines 19 and 20) has a *fieldOfView* attribute with a value of **2.61** *radians* (i.e., a unit of measurement for angles). The **fieldOfView** specifies how much of a scene is visible from a particular viewpoint. The **position** attribute (line 20) places this viewpoint at the coordinate *(0, 3, 2)*. The rendered output in Fig. 20.24 shows the scene from the **Viewpoint** on line 18.

Element *Group* (lines 22–100) groups a collection of 3D objects. The *children* element (line 23) specifies a sub-group of 3D objects. The *Shape* element (lines 26–39) is used to create a *Cylinder* that will form the body of a rocket. The *appearance* element (lines 27–34) contains *Appearance* elements that specify the visual properties of the **Shape** (e.g., its coloring). The *material* element contains *Material* elements that describe the surface of the **Shape**. Attribute *diffuseColor* (line 31) specifies the red, green and blue values used to create the color of the **Material**. The *geometry* element (lines 36–38) creates the cylinder based on the values of the *radius* and **height** attributes.

The *Transform* element (line 41) changes the position at which the next **Shape** will be rendered based on the value of the *translation* attribute. In this case, on line 41 we move down **0.5** units on the *y*-axis for the base of the rocket. The **Shape** element on lines 45–62 creates a *Cone* (line 59) for the base of the rocket. Another **Transform** element (line 64) is used to position the *Text* element with the *string* attribute **Welcome to X3D!** (line 68).

The **Transform** element (line 76) is used to position the remaining **Shape** element for the top of the rocket. The **Cone** element (line 92) is used to create the top of the rocket.

In order to view the example in Fig. 20.24, the following software is required:

1. Java 2 SDK from **java.sun.com**.

2. Virtual Reality Modeling Language (VRML) plug-in from **www.cosmosoftware.com/download** or **www.parallelgraphics.com/cortona**.

3. Xeena (version 1.2EA only) **www.alphaWorks.ibm.com/tech/xeena**. For Windows, download the executable, which is self extracting. For UNIX, download the Xeena 1.2EA for UNIX and follow installation instructions in the downloaded package.

4. WEB3D's X3D-Edit from **www.web3D.org/TaskGroups/x3d/translation/X3D-Edit.zip**.

Figure 20.25 provides a list of X3D Web resources.

20.11 Additional Internet and World Wide Web Resources

In this chapter, we chose to put most of these resources inline in the sections in which their topics were introduced. Here are a few extras.

URL / Description

www.web3d.org/x3d.html
Home page of the *Extensible 3D Task Group* located on the Web3D Consortium Web site.

www.web3d.org/TaskGroups/x3d/faq
The *X3D Frequently Asked Questions* page.

www.web3d.org/news/x3d
Links to documents summarizing the X3D standardization process.

www.shout3d.com/x3d/contents.html
The *Core X3D Specification.*

Fig. 20.25 Extensible 3D Language resources.

www.xml.org/xmlorg_registry
A list of links to custom XML specifications grouped by industry, located on the **XML.org** Web site.

www.oasis-open.org/cover/xml.html#applications
A list of links to proposed XML applications and industry initiatives.

www.xml.com/pub/resourceguide
XML resource guide run by **XML.com**. This page is a great place to start your search into all areas of XML-custom languages.

SUMMARY

- XML is a metalanguage—a language for creating other languages.

- Until recently, mathematical expressions have typically been displayed using images or specialized software packages such as TeX and LaTeX. MathML was developed by the W3C for describing mathematical notations and expressions in an XML-like manner. It enables document authors to describe mathematical expressions that can be processed by different applications for different purposes.

- The W3C provides a browser/editor called Amaya to edit, parse and render MathML.

- MathML content is embedded directly into an HTML document using the HTML **math** element.

- Element **mrow** is a container element that groups related elements.

- Element *msubsup* marks up a subscript and a superscript. Element **msubsup** requires three child elements: the expression to which the subscript and superscript are applied, the subscript and the superscript.

- The integral symbol is represented by the entity **∫**. Element **mo** marks up an operator. Element **mn** marks up a number. Element **mi** marks up an identifier or variable.

- Element **msqrt** represents a square root expression. Entity **⁢** specifies a multiplication operation without a symbolic representation (i.e., a multiplication symbol is not displayed). Element **msup** marks up an expression containing a base and an exponent. This element contains two child elements: the base and the exponent (i.e., the superscript). Element *msub* marks up an expression that contains a subscript.

- Entity **δ** represents a delta symbol, which is marked up using element **mo**.

- OpenMath is an emerging standard for describing mathematical content. Although MathML does provide a set of semantic elements, it is mostly limited to describing the presentation of mathematical expressions. OpenMath content can be embedded in MathML, synthesizing the description of mathematical content and presentation.

- OpenMath represents mathematical expressions with objects that can be exchanged between different software systems, manipulated in databases, displayed by different applications including Internet browsers, used in different contexts and even checked for mathematical correctness. The standard itself includes specifications of binary and XML encoding of OpenMath, extensible libraries of OpenMath objects and libraries defining semantic content.

- An OpenMath object has three layers of representation: as an application-specific entity, as an abstract OpenMath object and as a byte stream for communication purposes. The content dictionaries define the meaning of an object so that an application can convert it to an internal representation.

- The Chemical Markup Language (CML) is an XML-based language for representing molecular and chemical information. CML takes advantage of XML's portability to enable document authors to use and reuse molecular information without corrupting important data in the process. Document authors can edit and view CML using the Jumbo browser.

- The Wireless Markup Language (WML) is an XML-based language that allows text portions of Web pages to be displayed on wireless devices such as cellular phones and personal digital assistants (PDA). WML also has a companion scripting language, WMLScript, which is based on the ECMAScript standard. WML works with the Wireless Application Protocol (WAP) to deliver content.

- WML is similar to HTML but does not require input devices such as a keyboard or mouse for navigation. A WML document is called a deck and contains static parts called cards. Each card consists of one user interaction, providing the WML browser with a small, self-contained document for browsing.

- WML documents have root element **wml**, which contains **card** elements. Text is marked up using element **p**.

- Element **do** sets the action for a document. Element **go** hyperlinks to an object in attribute **href**.

- The Geography Markup Language (GML) was developed by the OpenGIS Consortium (OGC) to describe geographic information. In GML, geographic information is described in terms of features. A feature is composed of properties and geometries. GML properties contain the **name**, **type** and **value** elements common to all XML tags; features are geometric entities (e.g., lines, polygons, etc.). Geometries contain the bulk of geographic data, and properties augment that data to provide a more precise description. As a recent markup language, GML is in the early stages of development.

- The Synchronized Multimedia Integration Language (SMIL, pronounced "smile") enables Web document authors to coordinate the presentation of a wide range of multimedia elements. A SMIL document specifies the source (i.e., the URL) of multimedia elements and how these elements are presented. One way to render SMIL documents is with RealPlayer, a multimedia player from Real Networks.

- A region for displaying objects (e.g., images) is specified using element **region**. Attribute **id** uniquely identifies a region. Attributes **width** and **height** specify the size of the region, and attributes **top** and **left** provide the position. Attribute **background-color** sets the color of the region's background.

- Element **body** encloses the contents of the document. Element **seq** sets child elements to execute sequentially (i.e., in chronological order). A **par** element sets its child elements to execute in parallel (i.e., at the same time).

- Element **img** references an image. Attribute **src** contains the location of the image, and attribute **alt** provides a description of the image. Attribute **region** specifies the region in which the image is to be displayed. Attribute **dur** describes how long the image appears on the screen. Element **audio** references an audio file.

- SMIL documents can also be embedded in Web pages using the *Soja applet.*
- The Scalable Vector Graphics (SVG) markup language describes graphics. SVG provides considerable advantages over current methods (e.g., the **.jpg**, **.gif** and **.png** formats) for distributing graphics on the Web. Vector graphics describe graphical information in terms of lines, curves, etc. Not only do images rendered in vector graphics require less bandwidth, but these images also can be easily scaled and printed. In addition, SVG's XML base enables SVG documents to be scripted, searched and dynamically created.
- Attribute **viewBox** sets the viewing area for the document. Attribute **width** specifies the width of the image, and attribute **height** specifies the height of the image.
- The Bean Markup Language (BML) facilitates the use of JavaBeans. JavaBeans (often called beans) are predefined software components that can be combined to create Java applications and applets. BML defines how various beans are interconnected. To use a BML document, a B*ML player* is required.
- Although BML allows the generation of JavaBeans, it does not permit JavaBeans to be saved. *Koala Bean Markup Language (KBML)* was developed to remedy this deficiency. With KBML, which is similar to BML, a JavaBean can be saved as a class name. KBML also provides a means to serialize JavaBeans in XML.
- The Extensible 3D (X3D) language is the result of the combined efforts of the World Wide Web Consortium and the Web 3D Consortium to extend VRML with XML. X3D is the next generation of VRML, and the current version is backwards compatible. X3D's XML base enables wide use and extensibility of the VRML standard.

TERMINOLOGY SELF-REVIEW EXERCISES

&delta
&Integral
&InvisibleTimes
*N
.gif
.jpg images
.png
<mo>
accept
W3C Amaya Web browser
amount
animateTransform element
attribute alt
attribute attributeName
attribute background-color
attribute cx
attribute cy
attribute d
attribute height
attribute id
attribute r
attribute region
attribute repeatCount

attribute src
attribute style
attribute transform
attribute translates
attribute type
attribute viewBox
attribute width
attribute x
attribute y
attributes from
attributes to
backwards compatible
Bean Markup Language (BML)
bondArray
card elements of WML document
Chemical Markup Language (CML)
child elements
CML
container element
CSS property fill
deck (WML document)
delta symbol
dereferencing the text box identifier

SELF-REVIEW EXERCISES

20.1 State whether each of the following are *true* or *false*. If *false*, explain why.

a) Custom XML languages can only be produced for industries that are involved with com-
    merce or multimedia.

b) The Amaya browser is able to render roughly 50% of all custom XML languages.

c) MathML can be embedded directly into HTML using the **math** element.

d) Before CML, many previous methods for storing molecular information inhibited document reuse.

e) WML requires an input device such as a keyboard or a mouse for navigation.

f) A small, self-contained document for browsing is a requirement for WML because since a wireless device has limited memory resources, it can only load one document at a time.

g) Images rendered in vector graphics require less bandwidth.

h) GML stands for the Grammar Markup Language and is used to dynamically edit grammar in text documents according to specific guidelines.

i) In SMIL, multimedia elements can work together to produce a better looking and more efficient multimedia document.

j) Scalable Vector Graphics (SVG) appear the same when rendered with different dimensions because they are not bitmap images.

20.2   Fill in the blanks in each of the following statements.

a) The _____ browser is provided by the W3C to edit, parse and render MathML.

b) The two sets of elements defined by MathML are _____ and _____.

c) The XML-based language used for representing molecular and chemical information is known as the _____.

d) CML can be edited and viewed using the _____ browser.

e) WML, which stands for _____ uses the _____ Application Protocol (WAP) to deliver its content.

f) A WML document is called a _____, with static parts called _____.

g) In GML, geographic information is described in terms of _____, which are composed of _____ and _____.

h) The Synchronized _____ Language enables Web document authors to coordinate the presentation of a wide range of multimedia elements.

i) _____ graphics describe graphical information in terms of lines, curves and other vector shapes, saving space and allowing complete scalability.

j) Produced by the Web3D Consortium, _____ is an attempt to make VRML 97 more Web capable through the use of XML.

ANSWERS TO SELF-REVIEW EXERCISES

20.1   a) False. Custom XML languages can be produced for any industry. b) False. The Amaya browser, provided by the W3C, is capable of rendering several custom XML languages, including MathML. c) True. d) True. e) False. WML does not require input devices like keyboard or mice for navigation. f) True. g) True. h) False. GML stands for the Geography Markup Language and is used to describe geographic information for use and reuse by different applications. i) True. j) True.

20.2   a) Amaya. b) mathematical content, mathematical presentation. c) Chemical Markup Language (CML). d) Jumbo. e) Wireless Markup Language, Wireless. f) deck, cards. g) features, properties, geometries. h) Multimedia Integration. i) Vector. j) Extensible 3D (X3D).

EXERCISES

20.3   Write a MathML document for the following equations. Use Amaya to render the resulting documents.

a) $\int_{-\frac{1}{2}}^{1} 5y\delta x$

b) $x = \sqrt{2y^{-3}} - 8y + \dfrac{\sqrt{y}}{3}$

20.4   Write a MathML document that represents Schrodinger's wave equation as shown in Fig. 20.26. [*Hint:* Symbol psi can be represented by **Ψ**, and delta by **∇**]

20.5   Write a CML document that displays 2-CycloHexeneCarbonitrile (C_6N). Figure 20.27 shows an example output.

20.6   Write a simple WML document that displays the available books at a bookstore for the user to select. After the user selects a book, the device should accept the user's identification number or code. It should then display both the selected book as well as the ID for confirmation.

20.7   Create an SVG document that simulates a clock with a pendulum (i.e., hour hand, minute hand, pendulum). An example image is shown in Fig. 20.28.

psi

$$ih\frac{\delta\Psi(x,t)}{\delta t} = -\frac{h^2}{2m}\nabla^2\Psi(x,t) + V(x,t)\,\Psi(x,t)$$

Fig. 20.26 Schrodinger's wave equation.

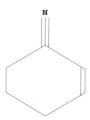

Fig. 20.27 2-CycloHexeneCarbonitrile.

Fig. 20.28 Clock simulation with SVG.

21

Custom Markup Languages: Part II

Objectives

- To become familiar with the Extensible Business Reporting Language (XBRL).
- To become familiar with the Bank Internet Payment System (BIPS).
- To become familiar with Electronic Business XML (ebXML).
- To become familiar with Visa XML Invoice Specification.
- To become familiar with Commerce XML (cXML).
- To become familiar with LegalXML and NewsML.
- To become familiar with the Open eBook Publication Structure.
- To become familiar with Extensible User Interface Language (XUL).

Be a little careful about your library. Do you foresee what you will do with it?...
Ralph Waldo Emerson

It is the huge buildings of commerce and trade which now align the people to attention.
Sean O'Casey

You will come here and get books that will open your eyes, and your ears, and your curiosity...
Ralph Waldo Emerson

Outline

21.1 Introduction

XML languages are being developed for many areas of e-commerce. This chapter discusses some of the prominent e-business languages emerging on the Web. We also present brief introductions and links to a few other, miscellaneous custom markup languages.

21.2 Extensible Business Reporting Language (XBRL)

Development of the *Extensible Business Reporting Language* (*XBRL*) began in 1998, initially under the direction of the American Institute of Certified Public Accountants (AICPA). XBRL captures existing financial and accounting information standards in XML, providing significant advantages over current methods of business information representation and transfer (Fig. 21.1). XBRL's XML origin permits financial information to be reused in a variety of situations (e.g., publishing reports, extracting data for applications, submitting regulatory forms, etc.), thus increasing efficiency and reducing costs and redundancy. Future versions of XBRL will expand to encompass descriptions of information in other areas of business.

Figure 21.2 is a financial statement marked up as XBRL for a fictitious company named ExComp. An XBRL document contains three elements: `group`, `item` and `label`.

Business Process	Relevant Financial Applications
Internal Financial Reporting	Business Event Reporting
External Financial Reporting	Audit Schedules, G/L Journal Entry Reporting
Investment and Lending Analysis	EDGAR Filings, Tax Filings

Fig. 21.1   Business processes to which XBRL applies.

A **group** element groups **item**, **label** and other **group** elements. XBRL documents usually have **group** as the root element. An **item** element represents a single statement. Element **label** provides a caption for **group** and **item** elements.

```
1   <?xml version = "1.0" encoding = "utf-8"?>
2   <!DOCTYPE group SYSTEM "xbrl-core-00-04-04.dtd">
3
4   <!-- Fig. 21.2 : financialHighlights.xml -->
5   <!-- XBRL example                        -->
6
7   <group
8       xmlns = "http://www.xbrl.org/us/aicpa-us-gaap-ci-00-04-04"
9       xmlns:ExComp = "http://www.example-ExComp.org/fHighlights.xml"
10      id = "XXXXXX-X-X-X"
11      entity = "NASDAQ:EXCOMP"
12      period = "2000-12-31"
13      scaleFactor = "3"
14      precision = "3"
15      type = "ExComp:statement.financialHighlights"
16      unit = "ISO4217:USD"
17      decimalPattern = "#,###.###">
18
19     <group id = "1" type = "ExComp:financialHighlights.introduction">
20         <item type = "ExComp:statement.declaration"
21               period = "2000-12-31">
22         ExComp has adopted all standard procedures for accounting.
23         This statement gives a financial highlight summary for the
24         last 4 years.
25         It also gives an account of percentage change in profit
26         for each year, which is useful in measuring the company's
27         performance.
28         </item>
29     </group>
30
31     <group id = "2" type = "ExComp:financialHighlights.statistics">
32         <group id = "21" type = "ExComp:sales.revenue">
33             <item period = "P1Y/2000-12-30">2961.5</item>
34             <item period = "P1Y/1999-12-30">3294.97</item>
35             <item period = "P1Y/1998-12-30">3593.78</item>
36             <item period = "P1Y/1997-12-30">4301.55</item>
37         </group>
38
39         <group id = "22" type = "ExComp:cost.production">
40             <item period = "P1Y/2000-12-30">1834.126</item>
41             <item period = "P1Y/1999-12-30">1923.226</item>
42             <item period = "P1Y/1998-12-30">2872.10</item>
43             <item period = "P1Y/1997-12-30">3101.11</item>
44         </group>
45
46         <group id = "23"
47               type = "ExComp:cost.transportAndMaintenance">
48             <item period = "P1Y/2000-12-30">134.07</item>
```

Fig. 21.2   XBRL example that marks up a company's financial highlights (part 1 of 2).

```
49         <item period = "P1Y/1999-12-30">334.47</item>
50         <item period = "P1Y/1998-12-30">821.59</item>
51         <item period = "P1Y/1997-12-30">1007.12</item>
52      </group>
53
54      <group id = "24" type = "ExComp:net.profit">
55         <item period = "P1Y/2000-12-30">1335.5</item>
56         <item period = "P1Y/1999-12-30">1135.52</item>
57         <item period = "P1Y/1998-12-30">1142.03</item>
58         <item period = "P1Y/1997-12-30">1312.62</item>
59      </group>
60
61      <group id = "25" type = "ExComp:percentageChange.profit">
62         <item period = "P1Y/2000-12-30">18.35</item>
63         <item period = "P1Y/1999-12-30">11.11</item>
64         <item period = "P1Y/1998-12-30">10.25</item>
65         <item period = "P1Y/1997-12-30">24.98</item>
66      </group>
67
68      <!-- Labels -->
69      <label href = "#21">Revenue</label>
70      <label href = "#22">Production cost</label>
71      <label href = "#23">Transport and Maintenance</label>
72      <label href = "#24">Profit</label>
73      <label href = "#25">Percentage Change in profit</label>
74
75   </group>
76
77 </group>
```

ExComp

Financial Highlights Report

Dated : 2000-12-31
Symbol: NASDAQ: EXCOMP

Introduction: ExComp has adopted all standard procedures for accounting. This statement gives a final highlight summary for the last 4 years. It also gives an account of percentage change in profit for each year, which is useful in measuring the company's performance.

Statistics:

Year	Revenue*	Production Cost*	Transportation and Maintenance*	Profit*	Percentage Change in Profit (%)
1997	4301.55	3101.11	1007.12	1312.62	24.98
1998	3593.78	2872.10	821.59	1142.03	10.25
1999	3294.97	1923.23	334.47	1135.52	11.11
2000	2961.50	1834.13	134.07	1335.50	18.35

* All values USD

Chairman
ExComp

Fig. 21.2 XBRL example that marks up a company's financial highlights (part 2 of 2).

Line 2 in Fig. 21.2 is the **DOCTYPE** declaration that specifies the DTD used by XBRL documents (i.e., **xbrl-core-00-04-04.dtd**). Line 7's root element (**group**) contains six other **group** elements and five **label** elements that describe the financial statement. Root element **group** specifies a set of attributes (or properties) that apply to all of its child elements. If a child **group** element specifies an attribute that is the same as the parent's attribute, the child's attribute overrides the parent's attribute within the child element.

Line 8

```
xmlns = "http://www.xbrl.org/us/aicpa-us-gaap-ci-00-04-04"
```

declares a default namespace for the XBRL document through the use of keyword **xmlns** and assigns it a URI.

Line 9 declares a namespace prefix (**ExComp**) for elements specific to the company ExComp. Attribute **id** (line 10) specifies a unique identity for the company. Attribute *entity* (line 11) identifies *business entities*. For example, **entity** value **URI:www.deitel.com** indicates that the company is associated with the URI **www.deitel.com**. Line 11 indicates that ExComp's **NASDAQ** symbol is **EXCOMP**. Attribute **period** (line 12) is used to specify the creation date of the document. Attribute **scalefactor** (line 13) specifies the power of 10 by which a numeric value appearing in the **group** should be multiplied to calculate the actual value; for example, a value of **3** indicates the value should be multiplied by 1000. Attribute **precision** (line 14) indicates the numeric precision of measurement that should be used for calculations; for example, a value of **3** indicates an accuracy of 3 decimal places.

Attribute **type** (line 15) specifies the category of the group. It also differentiates one **group** element from another. Values of the **type** attribute use the "*parent.child*" naming convention, where *parent* represents a category and *child* is its property.

Attribute **unit** (line 16) specifies the unit of currency adopted by the document, and attribute **decimalPattern** (line 17) specifies the format for displaying numeric values, using pound (**#**) symbols as placeholders.

The root element **group** (line 7) contains two **group** child elements. The first **group** element (line 19) gives a brief introduction to the financial highlights statement. Its child element, **item** (line 20), contains the actual description. The **period** attribute (line 21) marks up the declaration date of the statement.

The second **group** element (line 31) contains ExComp's financial statistics (i.e., revenue, cost, profit, etc.,) grouped by their respective categories. This **group** element also contains captions for each of the categories, using *label* elements (lines 69–73). The **id** attribute uniquely identifies a **group** or **item** element. Lines 31–66 declare **group** elements for revenue, cost of production, cost of transportation and maintenance, net profit and percentage change in profit. Each **group** element contains **item** elements that hold values until the time specified by the **group** element's attribute **period**. The period **P1Y/2000-12-30** indicates a year that ends on the 30th of December 2000.

The **label** elements (lines 69–73) give each **group** element a caption. Their attribute **href** contains a reference to the **group** element that they label. The output of Fig. 21.2 shows how this document might be rendered. For example, an XML application may choose to use XSL Formatting Objects to render this XML document. XSL formatting objects are discussed in Chapter 13. Figure 21.3 provides several XBRL Web resources.

URL / Description

www.xbrl.org
This is the Web site for XBRL that contains technical and business information on XBRL.

www.xbrl.org/TR/00-04-06/XBRL-00-04-06.htm
The site contains the XBRL specification.

www.xbrl.org/Core/2000-07-31/default.htm
XBRL DTDs can be obtained from this site.

www.xbrl.org/Overview.htm
An brief introduction to, and highlights of, XBRL can be found at this site.

www.xbrl.org/BriefingRoom.htm
This site posts links to several PowerPoint™ presentations on XBRL.

www.oasis-open.org/cover/xbrl.html
This site contains an introduction to XBRL and several links to XBRL resources and articles.

www.xbrl.org/Faq.htm
This site contains **xbrl.org** FAQs.

www.xbrl.org/Demos/demos.htm
This site contains links to practical XBRL applications.

www.oasis-open.org/cover/xfrml.html
This site contains information on XFRML, the predecessor of XBRL.

www.xbrl.org/Tools.htm
This site lists a few XBRL tools.

www.aicpa.org
This is the home page for the AICPA, the initiators of the XBRL initiative.

Fig. 21.3   XBRL reference Web sites.

21.3 Bank Internet Payment System (BIPS)

Bank Internet Payment System (*BIPS*) facilitates secure electronic transactions over the Internet. Client-server applications can use BIPS to communicate payment instructions over the Internet. This freely distributed XML specification enables BIPS users (e.g., banks, small businesses, etc.) to implement e-business services affordably for their customers. The decision to build the BIPS specification using XML also enables BIPS-formatted data to be easily converted into other business-related XML standards. BIPS transactions can be initiated by either the payer or the payee, and transactions are secured using digital certificate technology. Figure 21.4 lists several BIPS Web resources.

21.4 Electronic Business XML (ebXML)

In September 1999, the United Nations's Center for Trade Facilitation and Electronic Business (UN/CEFACT) and the Organization for the Advancement of Structured Information Standards (OASIS) began a 15- to 18-month project to standardize the global exchange of business information. The result of this project is *Electronic Business XML* (*ebXML*). Currently in draft specification form, ebXML provides a standard infrastructure for global electronic business that enables medium to large businesses to exchange business information.

URL / Description

www.fstc.org/projects/bips
The BIPS official Web site.

www.fstc.org/projects/bips/spec/license.html
The BIPS specification can be downloaded or viewed from this site.

www.fstc.org/projects/bips/spec/summary.html
This site posts a brief introduction to BIPS.

www.fstc.org/projects/bips/public/BIPSFAQ21a.htm
This site contains BIPS FAQs.

Fig. 21.4 BIPS reference Web sites.

The wide reach of two international organizations, coupled with the open nature in which this standard is being developed, ensures a strong user foundation for a single, XML-based, global business framework. The *Global Commerce Initiative*, a coalition of 40 major business, including Kraft Foods and Home Depot, has adopted ebXML as an integral part of its e-commerce framework.

Rather than emphasizing business documents, ebXML emphasizes business processes that describe a series of actions, such as "procure materials." A process contains details of the data exchange and the sequences, or *choreographies*, of messages. Reusable objects called *core components* can be used in messages to represent information such as telephone numbers. Core components give businesses a mechanism to use industry-specific vocabularies, but are semantically neutral themselves, thus forming a common set of data items that can be used across all industries. The connections that identify industry-specific semantics with core components will be stored in distributed data repositories, along with the other models, data and objects that will enable businesses to communicate. Repositories will be accessed with APIs provided by ebXML registries. Businesses can also make contracts electronically with ebXML by using the *trading partner agreement* feature. Figure 21.5 provides links to several ebXML Web resources.

21.5 Visa XML Invoice Specification

VISA International has developed the *VISA XML Invoice Specification* to enable its business customers to exchange credit-card purchase information between businesses over the Internet in a secure and standardized form. The VISA Invoice Specification enables commercial credit-card users to maintain and leverage more detailed information on credit-card purchases. Currently, the specification provides a framework that describes credit-card purchases in the areas of procurement (i.e., business-to-business purchasing) and travel-and-entertainment (T&E) expenses. Future versions of the specification will be expanded to include purchases in the areas of health care, government, temporary services and others. Figure 21.6 provides Visa XML Invoice Specification Web resources.

21.6 Commerce XML (cXML)

Commerce XML (cXML) is an XML-based framework for describing catalog data and performing business-to-business electronic transactions that use the data. Developed by a group of 40 e-commerce companies led by Ariba, Inc., cXML enables businesses and suppliers to conduct transactions over the Internet more efficiently. cXML provides several DTDs that describe data for catalogs, interactive catalogs ("punchouts") and purchase orders. The language also specifies ways in which cXML documents may be requested and posted over the Web.

Figure 21.7 illustrates a sample purchase order a company might use to transact with another business, and Fig. 21.8 lists a cXML document that corresponds to this purchase order. Figure 21.9 lists a sample cXML response.

Lines 6 and 7

```
<!DOCTYPE cXML SYSTEM
    "http://xml.cXML.org/schemas/cXML/1.1.008/cXML.dtd">
```

specify the external DTD to which this cXML document conforms.

Lines 9–11

```
<cXML payloadID = "200.989.2991@myhostname"
    timestamp = "2000-08-14T12:42:19-05:00"
    version = "1.1" xml:lang = "en-US">
```

URL / Description

www.ebxml.org
This is the official ebXML Web site.

www.oasis-open.org/cover/ebXML.html
This site provides the ebXML cover page, which features an understandable overview of the technology, along with references and links.

www.ebxml.org/specindex2.htm
This site contains a list of links to ebXML specifications.

www.ebxml.org/news/pr_20000515.htm
This site is a press release describing developments in the ebXML project.

Fig. 21.5   ebXML reference Web sites.

URL/Description

www.visa.com/xml
This is VISA's Web site for the VISA XML Invoice Specification.

www.visa.com/ut/dnld/spec.ghtml
This site contains information on the Invoice Specification's documentation. Readers must register before downloading or viewing the documentation.

www.oasis-open.org/cover/visaXMLInvoice.html
This site contains an introduction to the Invoice Specification and links to resources and articles.

Fig. 21.6   VISA XML Invoice Specification reference Web sites.

form the cXML envelope—the root element of a cXML document. Attribute **timestamp** provides the time of creation of the document in ISO 8601 format—a standard format for representing a timestamp. Attribute **payloadID** provides a unique ID for the logging of documents.

Lines 12–35 are the header of the document, contained in element **Header**. This section contains the information used to authenticate the document and also provides information about the sender and receiver of the document.

Lines 14–18 show element **From**, which specifies the source from which the document was sent. Lines 15–17 use element **Credential** to set identification and authentication information. Lines 20–24 show element **To**, which specifies where the document was sent.

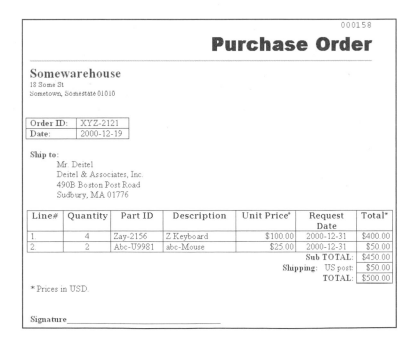

Fig. 21.7   Simple purchase order.

```
1   <?xml version = "1.0"?>
2
3   <!-- Figure 21.8 : cxmlorder.xml   -->
4   <!-- An order request             -->
5
6   <!DOCTYPE cXML SYSTEM
7       "http://xml.cXML.org/schemas/cXML/1.1.008/cXML.dtd">
8
```

Fig. 21.8   Order request using cXML (part 1 of 4).

```
 9   <cXML payloadID = "200.989.2991@myhostname"
10      timestamp = "2000-08-14T12:42:19-05:00"
11      version = "1.1" xml:lang = "en-US">
12      <Header>
13
14         <From>
15            <Credential domain = "DeitelNetworkUserID">
16               <Identity>xyz@deitel.com</Identity>
17            </Credential>
18         </From>
19
20         <To>
21            <Credential domain = "WarehouseNetworkID">
22               <Identity>xyz@somewarehouse.com</Identity>
23            </Credential>
24         </To>
25
26         <Sender>
27
28            <Credential domain = "DeitelNetworkUserID">
29               <Identity>deitel@deitel.com</Identity>
30            </Credential>
31
32            <UserAgent>Deitel cXML v1.0</UserAgent>
33
34         </Sender>
35      </Header>
36
37      <Request deploymentMode = "production">
38         <OrderRequest>
39            <OrderRequestHeader orderID = "xyz-2121"
40                                orderDate = "2000-07-19">
41               <Total>
42                  <Money currency = "USD">500</Money>
43               </Total>
44
45               <ShipTo>
46                  <Address>
47
48                     <Name xml:lang = "en">
49                        Deitel and Associates
50                     </Name>
51
52                     <PostalAddress>
53                        <DeliverTo>Mr. Xyz</DeliverTo>
54                        <Street>490B Boston Post road</Street>
55                        <City>Sudbury</City>
56                        <State>MA</State>
57                        <PostalCode>01776</PostalCode>
58
59                        <Country isoCountryCode = "US">
60                           United States
61                        </Country>
```

Fig. 21.8   Order request using cXML (part 2 of 4).

```
62                          </PostalAddress>
63
64                      </Address>
65                  </ShipTo>
66
67                  <BillTo>
68                      <Address>
69
70                          <Name xml:lang = "en">
71                              Deitel and Associates
72                          </Name>
73
74                          <PostalAddress>
75                              <Street>490B Boston Post road</Street>
76                              <City>Sudbury</City>
77                              <State>MA</State>
78                              <PostalCode>01776</PostalCode>
79                              <Country isoCountryCode = "US">
80                                  United States
81                              </Country>
82                          </PostalAddress>
83
84                      </Address>
85                  </BillTo>
86
87                  <Shipping>
88                      <Money currency = "USD">50</Money>
89
90                      <Description xml:lang = "en-us">
91                          US post
92                      </Description>
93                  </Shipping>
94
95                  <Payment>
96                      <PCard number = "222211113333"
97                             expiration = "2001-08-01"/>
98                  </Payment>
99              </OrderRequestHeader>
100
101             <!-- Products ordered -->
102             <ItemOut quantity = "4"
103                      requestedDeliveryDate = "2000-12-31">
104
105                 <ItemID>
106                     <SupplierPartID>zay-2156</SupplierPartID>
107                 </ItemID>
108
109                 <ItemDetail>
110                     <UnitPrice>
111                         <Money currency = "USD">100</Money>
112                     </UnitPrice>
113
```

Fig. 21.8 Order request using cXML (part 3 of 4).

```
114                    <Description xml:lang = "en">
115                        Z Keyboard
116                    </Description>
117                </ItemDetail>
118            </ItemOut>
119
120            <ItemOut quantity = "2"
121                    requestedDeliveryDate = "2000-08-05">
122
123                <ItemID>
124                    <SupplierPartID>abc-u9981</SupplierPartID>
125                </ItemID>
126
127                <ItemDetail>
128                    <UnitPrice>
129                        <Money currency = "USD">25</Money>
130                    </UnitPrice>
131
132                    <Description xml:lang = "en">
133                        abc-Mouse
134                    </Description>
135                </ItemDetail>
136
137            </ItemOut>
138        </OrderRequest>
139    </Request>
140 </cXML>
```

Fig. 21.8 Order request using cXML (part 4 of 4).

Lines 26–34 show element **Sender**, which specifies the sender of the document. Lines 37–139 are the request portion of the document, contained in element **Request**. For a purchase-order submission, element **OrderRequest** (lines 38–138) is used.

Lines 39–99 make up the header of the purchase order (element **OrderRequest-Header**), providing information about the billing address (element **BillTo**, lines 67–85), shipping address (element **ShipTo**, lines 45–65), shipping method (element **Shipping**, lines 87–93), payment method (element **Payment**) and total amount due (element **Total**, lines 41–43). In addition, the cXML specification defines elements for the amount of tax due, contact information, comments, attachments and more.

Lines 102–108 and lines 120–137 define the items in the purchase order using element **ItemOut**. Each **ItemOut** element describes an item in an order.

Figure 21.9 shows a purchase-order response for the cXML document of Fig. 21.8. The response from the warehouse consists of element **Response**, with child element **Status** announcing that the request was accepted. Figure 21.10 lists some Web sites that provide more information on cXML.

21.7 LegalXML

Currently, all court documents must be filed with a clerk, and information in the documents often must be entered into different document management systems multiple times. *LegalXML* hopes to reduce the redundancy of such management systems. With LegalXML, the information in court documents can be described to enable more efficient processing. Currently, the LegalXML draft proposal contains only elements that mark up data for electronic court filing, and not other legal content. A number of law firms are working to expand LegalXML so it may be used more widely. Figure 21.11 provides some LegalXML Web resources.

21.8 NewsML

News items exist in many different formats and are presented and received through different means. The International Press Telecommunications Council (IPTC) has coordinated the development of *NewsML* to provide news content creators and consumers with a means to maximize news-content potential. NewsML is designed to be media independent, so that all news-content formats (e.g., text, photo, video, etc.) can be described. XML formatting enables news content to be reused and customized for a specific consumer base or platform. Custom news items can be created by excluding or including certain parts of a news item. For example, the content of a television news story can be reused to create audio for a radio news show. Internal relationships between parts of a news item, such as supporting pictures or audio for a text article, can be described. Other relationships, such as "see also" or "related news," can also be specified. NewsML enables tracking and revision of documents over time. It supports different representations and encodings of data as well as different methods of attaching various types of metadata. NewsML can also take advantage of XML communication over the Web to permit various media to be separately stored in remote locations that can be accessed by many clients for use in news content. Because NewsML is an XML language, it can be processed and delivered to many different types of clients, such as Web browsers, cellular phones, pagers, etc. To aid in the management of news data, NewsML provides an envelope structure for transmitting, processing and routing information with news content. Figure 21.12 lists several NewsML Web resources.

```
1   <?xml version = "1.0"?>
2
3   <!-- Fig. 21.9 : cxmlorderResponse.xml      -->
4   <!-- Order response document                -->
5
6   <!DOCTYPE cXML SYSTEM
7            "http://xml.cXML.org/schemas/cXML/1.1.008/cXML.dtd">
8
9   <cXML payloadID = "xyz4@somewarehouse.com"
10     timestamp = "2000-08-15T15:45:19-05:00"
11     version = "1.1" xml:lang = "en-US">
12
13     <Response>
14        <Status code = "201" text = "Accepted"/>
15     </Response>
16
17  </cXML>
```

Fig. 21.9 Response cXML document to an order.

URL / Description

www.cxml.org
This is the official Web site for cXML.

www.cxml.org/files/cxml.zip
This site links to the cXML documentation download.

www.oasis-open.org/cover/cxml.html
This site maintains a brief introduction to cXML and links to resources and articles.

ecommerce.internet.com/outlook/article/0,1467,7761_124921_1,00.html
This page is an older article that provides an introduction to and explains the motivation for cXML.

ecommerce.internet.com/outlook/article/0,1467,7761_128341,00.html
This page begins a detailed summary of the cXML 0.91 specification document.

www.oasis-open.org/cover/aribaCXML.html
This site contains Ariba's press release announcing its adoption of cXML.

Fig. 21.10 cXML reference Web sites.

21.9 Open eBook Publication Structure

In early 2000, several companies dedicated to electronic text publication founded the Open eBook Forum with the goal of developing a standard for describing publishable electronic content. The result of this collaboration is the *Open eBook Publication Structure*, an XML-based language that specifies a file format and describes content elements. The language is designed to be platform independent, but maintains flexibility and permits document authors to embed platform-specific content as long as a platform-independent alternative is provided. The Open eBook Forum hopes that wide adoption of the Open eBook Publication Structure will spur growth in the electronic-publications market. Figure 21.13 lists some Open eBook Publication Structure Web resources.

URL/Description

www.legalxml.org
This is the Web page for the organization devoted to creating and maintaining LegalXML.

www.legalxml.org/DocumentRepository/ProposedStandards/Clear/PS_10001/PS_10001_2000_07_24.htm
This site contains the LegalXML proposed standard. It also contains links to the LegalXML DTDs.

www.legalxml.org/Information/LegalXMLOverview.asp
This site describes the history of LegalXML.

www.legalxml.org/DocumentRepository/UnofficialNotes
This site contains links to several LegalXML issues.

Fig. 21.11 LegalXML reference Web sites (part 1 of 2).

URL/Description

www.wsba.org/c/ec2/xml/1999/eficourt.htm
This page is an article on the topic of electronic court filings.

www.legalxml.org/transcripts/NCRA_Article.pdf
This page is an article on LegalXML in **.pdf** format (requires Adobe Acrobat Reader, which can be downloaded free of charge from **www.adobe.com**).

Fig. 21.11 LegalXML reference Web sites (part 2 of 2).

URL / Description

www.iptc.org/NMLIntro.htm
This site posts the IPTC's NewsML Web page.

www.karben14.com/newsml
This site contains links to the NewsML DTDs.

www.iptc.org/whatisnewsml.htm
This page contains an overview of NewsML.

www.oasis-open.org/cover/newsML.html
This site provides a brief introduction to NewsML and links to resources and articles.

www.iptc.org/iptc/newsmlprel.htm
This page is the press release from IPTC that announces its plan to create NewsML.

www.iptc.org
This is the home page for the IPTC, the organization behind NewsML.

Fig. 21.12 NewsML reference Web sites.

21.10 Extensible User Interface Language (XUL)

XML has proved a valuable catalyst to the field of cross-platform (XP) application development. Projects such as Mozilla (**www.mozilla.org**) work to provide cross-platform development platforms and services for use in a variety of purposes. One challenge facing cross-platform application developers is that each operating system has a unique graphical user interface (GUI). XUL (Extensible User Interface Language) is an XML-based language created by the Mozilla project for describing user interfaces. Cross-platform applications can load the information from an XUL (pronounced "zool") document to create the appropriate user interface. Figure 21.14 lists several Mozilla and XUL Web resources.

21.11 Internet and World Wide Web Resources

In this chapter, we have listed resources within the sections in which their associated topics were introduced. Here are a few extras:

www.oasis-open.org/cover/xml.html#applications
This page links to summaries of many XML-based applications.

www.xml.org/xmlorg_registry/index.shtml
This page provides a list of links to XML-based applications, sorted by category.

www.xml.com/pub/resourceguide/index.html
This page contains a list of XML resources.

SUMMARY

- Development of the Extensible Business Reporting Language (XBRL) began in 1998, initially under the direction of the American Institute of Certified Public Accountants (AICPA). XBRL captures existing financial and accounting information standards in XML, providing significant advantages over current methods of business information representation and transfer.

- An XBRL document contains three elements: **group**, **item** and **label**. A **group** element groups **item**, **label** and other **group** elements. XBRL documents usually have **group** as the root element. An **item** element represents a single statement. Element **label** provides a caption for **group** and **item** elements.

- Attribute *entity* identifies business entities. Attribute **period** specifies the creation date of the document. Attribute **scalefactor** specifies the power of 10 by which a numeric value appearing in the **group** should be multiplied to arrive at the actual value. Attribute **precision** indicates the numeric precision of measurement that should be used for calculations.

- Attribute **type** specifies the category of the group. It also differentiates one **group** element from another. Values of the **type** attribute use the "parent.child" naming convention, where parent represents a category and child is its property. Attribute **unit** specifies the unit of currency adopted by the document and attribute **decimalPattern** specifies the format for displaying numeric values, using pound (**#**) symbols as placeholders. The **period** attribute marks up the declaration date of the statement.

URL / Description

---

www.openebook.org
This is the home page for the Open eBook Forum, the organization that oversees development and maintenance of the Open eBook Publication Structure.

www.openebook.org/oebpsdownload.htm
The Open eBook specification can be obtained from this page in a variety of formats.

www.oasis-open.org/cover/openEbook.html
This page contains an introduction to the Open eBook Publication Structure and links to relevant resources and articles.

www.openebook.org/faq.htm
This is the Open eBook Forum's FAQ page.

www.openebook.org/release011300.htm
This page contains the Open eBook Forum's initial press release.

Fig. 21.13 Open eBook Publication Structure reference Web sites.

URL / Description

www.mozilla.org
This is the Mozilla project home page. XUL was created by Mozilla to manage the user interface for its browser.

www.mozilla.org/xpfe
This site is the home page for Mozilla's cross-platform toolkit project, which includes XUL.

www.mozilla.org/xpfe/languageSpec.html
This site posts the XUL specification document.

www.oasis-open.org/cover/xul.html
This site contains an introduction to XUL and links to relevant resources and articles.

www.webtechniques.com/news/2000/07/powers
This page is an article on developing cross-platform applications with XUL.

www.mozilla.org/xpfe/xptoolkit/xulintro.html
This site contains an introduction to XUL.

www.xulplanet.com/tutorials/xultu/index.html
This site contains a XUL tutorial.

Fig. 21.14 XUL reference Web sites.

- The DTD used by XBRL documents is *xbrl-core-00-04-04.dtd*.

- Bank Internet Payment System (BIPS) facilitates secure electronic transactions over the Internet. It is used by client-server applications to communicate payment instructions. This freely distributed XML specification enables BIPS users (e.g., banks, small businesses, etc.) to implement e-business services affordably for their customers.

- BIPS transactions can be initiated by either the payer or payee, and transactions are secured using digital certificate technology.

- In September 1999, the United Nations's Center for Trade Facilitation and Electronic Business (UN/CEFACT) and the Organization for the Advancement of Structured Information Standards (OASIS) began a project to standardize the global exchange of business information. The result of this project is Electronic Business XML (ebXML).

- ebXML provides a standard infrastructure for global electronic business that enables medium to large businesses to exchange business information. The *Global Commerce Initiative*, a coalition of 40 major business, including Kraft Foods and Home Depot, has adopted ebXML as an integral part of its e-commerce framework.

- ebXML emphasizes business processes that describe a series of actions, such as "procure materials." A process contains details of the data exchange and the sequences, or choreographies, of messages. Reusable objects called core components can be used in messages to represent information such as telephone numbers. Core components give businesses a mechanism with which to use industry-specific vocabularies, but are semantically neutral themselves.

- VISA International has developed the VISA XML Invoice Specification to enable its business customers to exchange credit-card purchase information over the Internet in a secure and standardized form. The VISA Invoice Specification enables commercial credit-card users to maintain and leverage more detailed information on credit-card purchases.

- Commerce XML (cXML) is an XML-based framework for describing catalog data and performing business-to-business electronic transactions that use the data. cXML enables customers and suppliers to conduct transactions over the Internet.

- Attribute **timestamp** provides the time of creation of the document in ISO 8601 format, and attribute **payloadID** provides a unique ID for the logging of documents.

- Element **Header** contains the information used to authenticate the document and also provides information about the sender and receiver of the document.

- Element **From** specifies the source from which the document was sent and element **Credential** sets identification and authentication information. Element **To** specifies where the document was sent.

- Element **Sender** specifies the sender of the document. Element **Request** contains the request portion of the document. Element **OrderRequest** is used for submission of purchase orders.

- Currently, all court documents must be filed with a clerk, and information in these documents often must be entered into different document management systems multiple times. LegalXML hopes to reduce the redundancy of such management systems. With LegalXML, the information in court documents can be described to enable more efficient use.

- News items exist in many different formats and are presented and received through different means. The International Press Telecommunications Council (IPTC) has coordinated the development of NewsML to provide news-content creators and consumers with a means to maximize news content potential. NewsML is designed to be media independent, so that all news-content formats (e.g., text, photo, video, etc.) can be described.

- NewsML enables tracking and revision of documents over time. It supports different representations and encodings of data, as well as different methods of attaching various types of metadata. NewsML can also take advantage of XML communication over the Web to permit various media to be separately stored in remote locations that can be accessed by many clients for use in news content. To aid in the management of news data, NewsML provides an envelope structure for transmitting, processing and routing information with news content.

- In early 2000, several companies dedicated to electronic text publication founded the Open eBook Forum with the goal of developing a standard for describing publishable electronic content. The result of this collaboration is the Open eBook Publication Structure, an XML-based language that specifies a file format and describes content elements. The language is designed to be platform independent, but maintains flexibility and permits document authors to embed platform-specific content as long as a platform-independent alternative is provided.

- XUL (Extensible User Interface Language) is an XML-based language created by the Mozilla project for describing user interfaces. Cross-platform applications can load the information from an XUL document to create the user interface.

TERMINOLOGY

AICPA (American Institute of Certified Public Accountants)

American Institute of Certified Public Accountants (AICPA)

Bank Internet Payment System (BIPS)

BIPS (Bank Internet Payment System)

BIPS-formatted data

Body

Commerce XML (cXML)

cross-platform

custom markup languages

cXML (Commerce XML)

digital certificate technology

DOCTYPE declaration

ebXML (Electronic Business XML)

Electronic Business XML (ebXML)

Extensible Business Reporting Language (XBRL)

Extensible User Interface Language (XUL)

From	**Offers** element
graphical user interface (GUI)	Open eBook Forum
group element	Open eBook Publication Structure
GUI (graphical user interface)	Organization for the Advancement of Structured
handle	Information Standards (OASIS)
id attribute	platform independent
International Press Telecommunications Council	**Route**
(IPTC)	routing information
IPTC (International Press Telecommunications	**To**
Council)	UN/CEFACT (United Nations' Center for Trade
item element	Facilitation and Electronic Business)
label element	United Nations' Center for Trade Facilitation and
LegalXML	Electronic Business (UN/CEFACT)
locationID	VISA International
locationType	VISA XML Invoice Specification
Mozilla	XBRL (Extensible Business Reporting Language)
NewsML	**xbrl** XBRL root element
OASIS (Organization for the Advancement of	XP
Structured Information Standards)	XUL (Extensible User Interface Language)

SELF-REVIEW EXERCISES

21.1 State whether each of the following are *true* or *false*. If *false*, explain why.
   a) XBRL documents usually have **xbrl** as the root element.
   b) XUL is an XML-based language for describing user interfaces.
   c) BIPS facilitates unsecure electronic transactions over the Internet.
   d) cXML enables customers and suppliers to more efficiently conduct transactions over the Internet.
   e) The Open eBook Publication Structure is an XML-based language that specifies a file format and describes content elements.

21.2 Fill in the blanks in each of the following statements.
   a) _____ provides an envelope structure for transmitting processing and routing information with news content.
   b) _____ is an XML-based framework for describing catalog data and performing business-to-business electronic transactions.
   c) XUL is an acronym for _____.
   d) With _____, the information in court documents can be described.
   e) BIPS is an acronym for _____.

ANSWERS TO SELF-REVIEW EXERCISES

21.1 a) False. XBRL documents usually have **group** as the root element. b) True. c) False. BIPS facilitates secure electronic transactions over the Internet. d) True. e) True.

21.2 a) NewsML. b) cXML. c) Extensible User Interface Language. d) LegalXML. e) Bank Internet Payment System.

EXERCISES

21.3 State whether each of the following are *true* or *false*. If *false*, explain why.
   a) The VISA Invoice Specification enables commercial credit-card users to maintain and leverage more detailed information on credit-card purchases.

    b) Client and server applications can use BIPS to communicate payment instructions over the Internet.

    c) cXML is an acronym for Cash XML.

    d) An XBRL document contains three elements: **group**, **items** and **label**.

    e) XUL was created by Microsoft.

21.4 Fill in the blanks in each of the following statements.

    a) _____ XML Invoice Specification enables business customers to exchange credit-card purchase information over the Internet in a secure standardized form.

    b) ebXML is an acronym for _____.

    c) _____ provides a standard infrastructure for global electronic business.

    d) _____ captures existing financial and accounting information standards in XML.

    e) _____ developed the Open eBook Publication Structure.

XML Technologies and Applications

Objectives

- To become familiar with the XML Query Language (XML Query).
- To understand and use the Resource Definition Framework (RDF).
- To understand and use the Channel Definition Format (CDF).
- To become familiar with Rich Site Summary (RSS).
- To become familiar with the Platform for Privacy Preferences (P3P).
- To learn about the Blocks Extensible Exchange Protocol (BXXP).

If there is but little water in the stream, it is the fault, not of the channel, but of the source.
St. Jerome

Private faces in public places
Are wiser and nicer
Than public faces in private places.
W. H. Auden

But what, to serve our private ends,
Forbids the cheating of our friends?
Charles Churchill

22.1 Introduction

Every day, individuals and organizations are discovering new and exciting ways to enhance existing technologies and create entirely new ones with XML. This chapter introduces several emerging XML-related technologies that cover a broad range of industries. In the first half of the chapter, we introduce the *XML Query Language (XML Query),* for searching and retrieving data from XML documents; *Directory Services Markup Language (DSML),* for describing relational data and *metadata* (i.e., information about information; elements are examples of metadata) so that they can be managed by directory services (e.g., software used to manage a company's personnel resources, etc.); *Resource Definition Framework (RDF),* which enables document authors to describe the data in an XML document; an information-mapping technology called *XML Topic Maps (XTM)*; *Channel Definition Format (CDF)* and *Rich Site Summary (RSS),* which provide dynamic content to subscribers; and the *Information and Content Exchange (ICE) Protocol,* which manages content syndication over networks.

In the second half of this chapter, we introduce a specification for describing a Web site's privacy policy called the *Platform for Privacy Preferences (P3P)*; a technology for transferring data over the Internet called the *Blocks Extensible Exchange Protocol (BXXP)*; a W3C recommendation for XML implementation of security and authentication technologies called *XML Digital Signatures*; the *Extensible Rights Markup Language (XrML),* for licensing proprietary digital content and the *XML Metadata Interchange (XMI),* for exchanging program-modeling data.

Although many of our readers will not know the technical details required to fully understand all the technologies presented in this chapter, we feel that this chapter nicely illustrates the wide varieties of applications of XML. Each section introduces an XML technology and provides a list of Web resources for finding additional information about that technology.

22.2 XML Query Language (XML Query)

XML Query (*XML Query Language*) uses the power of XSL patterns to search XML documents for specific data. Just as *SQL* (*Structured Query Language*) searches for data stored in relational databases, XML Query searches for data stored in an XML document. XML Query syntax resembles the path specification in a UNIX environment (e.g., **root/directory/subdirectory**). XML Query was submitted to W3C as a proposal in 1998, and development on the language is ongoing. Figure 22.1 provides XML Query resources.

22.3 Directory Services Markup Language (DSML)

Directory services provide a method for managing relational resources and metadata. Aside from their usual usage for storing records of organizational assets, directory services can be used with XML to dynamically match data across networks. The *Directory Services Markup Language* (*DSML*) is the bridge between directory services and XML. A standard vocabulary and schema provide the means for directory services information to be described in an XML document. With DSML, directories gain the ability to handle distributed Web-based applications, such as those used in e-business, network and supply chain management. DSML is platform independent, requiring only that the data be structured so that they can be manipulated with DSML. Figure 22.2 provides DSML Web resources.

URL / Description

www.w3.org/TandS/QL/QL98/pp/xql.html
This page contains the original XML Query proposal.

www.xml.com/pub/1999/03/quest/index2.html
This site contains a series of articles that summarize the results of the QL'98 conference, which resulted in the submission of XML Query to the W3C.

metalab.unc.edu/xql
This site contains XML Query FAQs.

metalab.unc.edu/xql/xql-tutorial.html
This site contains a brief XML Query tutorial.

www.cuesoft.com/docs/cuexsl_activex/xql_users_guide.htm
This site contains a detailed description of XML Query syntax.

www.w3.org/TR/xmlquery-req
This site contains the W3C requirements for XML Query.

www.w3.org/TR/query-datamodel
This site defines the data model for XML Query.

Fig. 22.1   XML Query reference Web sites.

URL / Description

www.dsml.org
This is the official Web site of the DSML standard.

www.oasis-open.org/cover/dsml.html
This site contains an introduction to DSML and links to relevant resources and articles.

Fig. 22.2   DSML reference Web sites.

22.4 Resource Definition Framework (RDF)

The availability of the Web and the relative ease of creating documents has led to a wealth of information on the Web. Unfortunately, finding information on a specific topic can often be difficult and time consuming. The *Resource Definition Framework* (*RDF*) is an XML-based language for describing information contained in a resource. A resource can be a Web page, an entire Web site or any item on the Web that contains information in some form. RDF's "information about information" (or *metadata*) can be used by search engines or intelligent software agents to list or catalog information on the Web. RDF can also be used to evaluate a Web site for rating purposes or to create digital signatures (i.e., the digital equivalent of a written signature). The Resource Definition Framework Model and Syntax is a W3C Recommendation. The RDF Schema Specification Version 1.0 is currently a W3C Candidate Recommendation. Figure 22.3 presents a simple RDF document that describes the Deitel & Associates, Inc., Web site.

```
1   <?xml version = "1.0"?>
2
3   <!-- Fig 22.3 : simple.rdf -->
4   <!-- Using RDF             -->
5
6   <rdf:RDF
7      xmlns:rdf = "http://www.w3.org/1999/02/22-rdf-syntax-ns#"
8      xmlns:dc = "http://purl.org/dc/elements/1.1/">
9
10      <rdf:Description about = "http://www.deitel.com">
11         <dc:Title>Deitel and Associates, Inc.</dc:Title>
12         <dc:Description>
13            This is the home page of
14            Deitel and Associates, Inc.
15         </dc:Description>
16         <dc:Date>2000-5-24</dc:Date>
17         <dc:Format>text/html</dc:Format>
18         <dc:Language>en</dc:Language>
19         <dc:Creator>Deitel and Associates, Inc.</dc:Creator>
20      </rdf:Description>
21
22   </rdf:RDF>
```

Fig. 22.3   Simple RDF document describing a Web page.

Lines 6–8

```
<rdf:RDF
    xmlns:rdf = "http://www.w3.org/1999/02/22-rdf-syntax-ns#"
    xmlns:dc = "http://purl.org/dc/elements/1.1/">
```

define root element **rdf:RDF**. We declare the namespace prefixes **rdf** and **dc**. Namespace prefix **rdf** is used for RDF elements, and namespace prefix **dc** is used for metadata elements that are defined by the Dublin Core's *Dublin Core Metadata Initiative*. Dublin Core is an organization that is primarily concerned with metadata standards.

Line 10

```
<rdf:Description about = "http://www.deitel.com">
```

uses element **rdf:Description** to describe the resource specified in attribute **about**. In our case, we use the URL **http://www.deitel.com**.

Line 11

```
<dc:Title>Deitel and Associates Inc.</dc:Title>
```

uses element **Title** to mark up the resource's name. Lines 12–20 use other metadata elements to provide further information about the resource.

Figure 22.4 uses a *visualization tool* for RDF—located at **www.w3.org/RDF/ Implementations/SiRPAC**—to parse RDF documents into the RDF data model.

Figure 22.5 presents a more substantial RDF document for describing the entire Deitel & Associates, Inc., Web site.

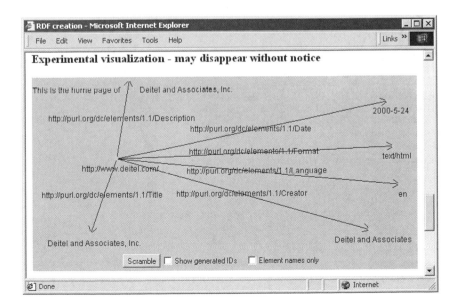

Fig. 22.4 Visualization tool showing **simple.rdf**. (Courtesy of World Wide Web Consortium)

```
1   <?xml version = "1.0"?>
2
3   <!-- Fig. 22.5 : links.rdf      -->
4   <!-- Describing entire Web site -->
5
6   <rdf:RDF xmlns:rdf = "http://www.w3.org/1999/02/22-rdf-syntax-ns#"
7      xmlns:dc = "http://purl.org/dc/elements/1.1/">
8
9   <rdf:Description about = "www.deitel.com">
10     <dc:Title>Home page of Deitel products</dc:Title>
11     <dc:Creator>Deitel and Associates, Inc.</dc:Creator>
12
13     <dc:Subject>
14
15        <rdf:Bag ID = "links_1">
16         <rdf:li resource = "http://www.deitel.com/books/index.htm"/>
17           <rdf:li resource =
18           "http://www.deitel.com/services/training/index.htm"/>
19        </rdf:Bag>
20
21        <rdf:Bag ID = "links_2">
22           <rdf:li resource =
23              "http://www.deitel.com/announcements/contractors.htm"/>
24           <rdf:li resource =
25              "http://www.deitel.com/announcements/internships.htm"/>
26        </rdf:Bag>
27
28        <rdf:Seq ID = "links_3">
29           <rdf:li resource = "http://www.deitel.com/intro.htm"/>
30          <rdf:li resource = "http://www.deitel.com/directions.htm"/>
31        </rdf:Seq>
32
33     </dc:Subject>
34
35  </rdf:Description>
36
37  <!-- description of the common feature of the Bag links_1-->
38  <rdf:Description aboutEach = "#links_1">
39     <dc:Description>About our Products</dc:Description>
40  </rdf:Description>
41
42  <rdf:Description aboutEach = "#links_2">
43
44     <dc:Description>
45        Announcements, Opportunities
46        and Internships at Deitel and Associates, Inc.
47     </dc:Description>
48
49  </rdf:Description>
50
51  <rdf:Description aboutEach = "#links_3">
52     <dc:Description>All about us</dc:Description>
53  </rdf:Description>
```

Fig. 22.5   RDF document describing an entire Web site (part 1 of 2).

```
54
55   <!-- further description of each link -->
56   <rdf:Description about = "http://www.deitel.com/books/index.htm">
57
58
59      <!-- description of page title -->
60      <rdf:Title>
61          Books, Multimedia Cyber Classrooms
62          and Complete Training Courses
63      </rdf:Title>
64
65   </rdf:Description>
66
67   <rdf:Description about =
68      "http://www.deitel.com/services/training/index.htm">
69      <rdf:Title>Corporate Training Courses</rdf:Title>
70   </rdf:Description>
71
72   <rdf:Description about =
73      "http://www.deitel.com/announcements/contractors.htm">
74      <rdf:Title>Looking for Training Contractors</rdf:Title>
75   </rdf:Description>
76
77   <rdf:Description about =
78      "http://www.deitel.com/announcements/internships.htm">
79
80      <rdf:Title>
81          Internships at Deitel and Associates, Inc.
82      </rdf:Title>
83
84   </rdf:Description>
85
86   <rdf:Description about = "http://www.deitel.com/intro.htm">
87
88      <rdf:Title>
89          Introduction to Deitel and Associates, Inc.
90      </rdf:Title>
91
92   </rdf:Description>
93
94   <rdf:Description about = "http://www.deitel.com/directions.htm">
95      <rdf:Title>Our location and how to get there</rdf:Title>
96   </rdf:Description>
97
98   </rdf:RDF>
```

Fig. 22.5 RDF document describing an entire Web site (part 2 of 2).

Lines 15 and 21 use element **rdf:Bag**, which is a container element for an unordered list of resources. Element **Bag** contains **li** elements, which represent individual resources. Element **Seq** is used (line 28) to represent an ordered list of resources.

By using attribute **aboutEach** with element **Description**, we provide a description of each resource. For example, lines 38–40 provide a description of each resource in the unordered list on lines 15–19. Figure 22.6 lists some RDF resources.

URL / Description

`www.w3.org/RDF`
This is the W3C's RDF information site.

`www.w3.org/TR/1999/REC-rdf-syntax-19990222`
This is the RDF specification document.

`www.oasis-open.org/cover/rdf.html`
This site contains an introduction to RDF and links to resources and articles.

`www.ilrt.bris.ac.uk/discovery/rdf/resources`
This site contains an extensive list of RDF resources.

`www.w3.org/RDF/FAQ`
This site contains RDF FAQs.

`www.wdvl.com/Internet/Future/rdf.html`
This site contains a brief article on RDF, including an example.

`www.wdvl.com/Authoring/Languages/RDF.html`
This site contains a brief article on RDF, and includes links to other resources.

`www.w3.org/DesignIssues/RDF-XML.html`
This site is an article on the differences between RDF and XML.

`purl.oclc.org/dc`
Home page of the Dublin Core Metadata Initiative.

Fig. 22.6   RDF reference Web sites.

22.5 XML Topic Maps (XTM)

Topic maps, an International Standards Organization (ISO) standard, are a new model for navigating and linking resources. They can be thought of as a melding of an index, glossary, thesaurus and concept map (i.e., a graphical representation of data). Much as XML separates content from presentation, topic maps separate content from links. Topic maps, like XLink, exist as hypertext layers above, rather than within, an information set. They have many similar linking capabilities, including the ability to independently reference resources.

The *topic*, the basic unit of a topic map, is used to represent a subject and to reference data pertaining to that subject. Each topic is described by other topics that detail its *names*, *occurrences* and *associations*. The occurrences of a topic are the various information resources that relate to it. Each occurrence has a certain *role*, such as "chart" or "article," and a *type* that provides further information on the role. The various relationships between topics are described by using associations of different *types* as well as the *role* that each topic plays within the association. In addition, topic maps incorporate mechanisms that define the *identity* and *scope* of a topic, as well as the *facets*, or properties, of the information it references. Almost every component of a topic map is a topic, enabling the topic map to be self-documenting and self-describing. Indeed, processing instructions, queries and schemas for topic maps can themselves be expressed as topic maps. Depending on its application, a topic map may consider different subjects to be topics and deal with them in different ways. It logically follows that multiple topic maps may be applied to one information set and one topic map can be applied to multiple information sets.

Figure 22.7 lists an example of a topic map. The example lists various topics, their associations (if any) and their occurrences (if any). The listing at the end of code shows an output of the application for some of the commands.Topic map documents contain element **topicmap** (line 6) as the root element. Each topic in a topic map is described by *element* **topic**. Lines 9–72 list six such topics: **light-vehicle** (lines 9–17), **heavy-vehicle** (lines 19–27), **car** (lines 29–45), **earth-mover** (lines 47–60), **make** (lines 62–66) and **product** (lines 68–72). Each topic is identified by the **id** *attribute*, which must be unique. Line 9 declares the identifier **light-vehicle** for one such topic. Lines 11–15 contain a **topname** *element* that describe the characteristics of its parent **topic** element. A **basename** *element* (line 12) gives the topic a name to be used by applications. Every topic must have a **basename** element. The **dispname** *element* (line 13) is used to display the name of the topic (e.g., to a human reader). The **sortname** *element* (line 14) describes a name that is used for sorting purposes by applications. In the absence of **dispname** or **sortname** elements, the **basename** element is used.

Lines 29–35 describe the **car** topic. *Attribute* **types** (line 29) indicates that a **car** is a type of **light-vehicle**. The **car topic** element also contains a **topname** element that further describes **car**.

Occurrences of a topic are described by *element* **occurs** (lines 38–44 and 56–58). The role of the occurrence is specified by the *attribute* **occurl** (line 38) and the *attribute* **loctype** (line 38) specifies the type of the location at which the topic occurs, which in this case is a URL. The **occurs** element on lines 38–44 indicates that the URL **http://www.abcsportscar.com/new** is a **webpage** that has information relating to the topic of cars.

Associations in topic maps are represented by *element* **assoc** (line 75–78). In our case the association between **car** and the company **ABC, Inc.**, can be expressed as—*car is a make of ABC, Inc.* The association is therefore declared as type **make** (line 75). Line 76 declares the topics involved in the association using the *element* **assocrl**. The role of **car** in this association would be that of a **product**. We therefore declare the type as **product** (line 76).

```
1   <?xml version = "1.0"?>
2
3   <!-- Fig. 22.7: vehicles.xml -->
4   <!-- simple topic map        -->
5
6   <topicmap>
7
8      <!-- topics -->
9      <topic id = "light-vehicle">
10
11        <topname>
12           <basename>Light weight vehicles</basename>
13           <dispname>Passenger vehicles</dispname>
14           <sortname>Light weight vehicles</sortname>
15        </topname>
```

Fig. 22.7 Topic map for types of motor vehicles (part 1 of 3).

```
16
17      </topic>
18
19      <topic id = "heavy-vehicle">
20
21          <topname>
22              <basename>Heavy weight vehicles</basename>
23              <dispname>Construction vehicles</dispname>
24              <sortname>Heavy weight vehicles</sortname>
25          </topname>
26
27      </topic>
28
29      <topic id = "car" types = "light-vehicle">
30
31          <topname>
32              <basename>ABC&apos;s car</basename>
33              <dispname>Sports car</dispname>
34              <sortname>car</sortname>
35          </topname>
36
37          <!-- occurrences of topic car -->
38          <occurs occrl = "webpage" loctype = "URL">
39              http://www.abcsportscar.com/new
40          </occurs>
41
42          <occurs occrl = "order-online" loctype = "URL">
43              http://www.abcsportscar.com/outlet
44          </occurs>
45      </topic>
46
47      <topic id = "earth-mover" types = "heavy-vehicle">
48
49          <topname>
50              <basename>ABC&apos;s heavy duty mover</basename>
51              <dispname>Earth movers</dispname>
52              <sortname>Earth mover</sortname>
53          </topname>
54
55          <!-- occurrences of topic earth-mover -->
56          <occurs occrl = "webpage" loctype = "URL">
57              http://www.abcsportscar.com/heavy-vehicles
58          </occurs>
59
60      </topic>
61
62      <topic id = "make">
63          <topname>
64              <basename>ABC, Inc.</basename>
65          </topname>
66      </topic>
67
```

Fig. 22.7   Topic map for types of motor vehicles (part 2 of 3).

```
68      <topic id = "product">
69         <topname>
70             <basename>Product</basename>
71         </topname>
72      </topic>
73
74      <!-- associations -->
75      <assoc type = "make">
76         <assocrl type = "product">car</assocrl>
77         <assocrl type = "product">earth-mover</assocrl>
78      </assoc>
79
80   </topicmap>
```

```
C:\tmproc>c:\Python\python -i tmproc.py vehicles.xml
Starting topic map processing...
Parsing vehicles.xml with xmlproc 0.62
Finished topic map processing...

>>> tm.get_topics()
[<tm.Topic light-vehicle>, <tm.Topic make>, <tm.Topic earth-mover>,
<tm.Topic car>, <tm.Topic product>, <tm.Topic heavy-vehicle>]

>>> tm.get_types_list(tm["car"])
[<tm.Topic light-vehicle>]

>>> tm.is_type(tm["earth-mover"], tm["heavy-vehicle"])
1

>>> tm.get_topics_of_type(tm["heavy-vehicle"])
[<tm.Topic earth-mover>]

>>> topic = tm["car"]
>>> topicname = topic.get_names()[0]
>>> n = topicname.get_basenames()[0]
>>> n.get_name()
"ABC's car"

>>> dispname = topicname.get_dispnames()[0]
>>> dispname.get_name()
'Sports car'

>>> firstOccur = topic.get_occurrences()[0]
>>> firstOccur.get_rolename()
'webpage'
>>> secondOccur = topic.get_occurrences()[1]
>>> secondOccur.get_rolename()
'order-online'

>>> association = tm.get_associations()[0]
>>> association.get_type()
<tm.Topic make>
```

Fig. 22.7 Topic map for types of motor vehicles (part 3 of 3).

Currently, there are several preliminary XML topic-map implementations. For the example in this section, we use an implementation written in the Python programming language. To execute the example in Fig. 22.7, the following software must be installed:

1. Download Python version 1.5.2 from **www.python.org/1.5** and follow the installation instructions.

2. Download **saxlib** Version 1.0 (a Python version of SAX), **driver package** Version 1.01 and **xmlproc** (a validating XML parser) from the links in **www.stud.ifi.uio.no/~lmariusg/download/python/xml**.

3. Unpack all three packages into **Lib** subdirectory, e.g., **c:\Python\Lib**.

4. Download the topic-map implementation **tmproc** from **www.ontopia.net/software/tmproc/index.html**.

5. Decompress **tmproc** to a local directory (e.g., **c:\tmproc**).

The Python implementation for topic maps can used to query the topic map. To run the application, at the command prompt (in **tmproc** subdirectory) enter the command

```
c:\tmproc> c:\Python\python -i tmproc.py <file.xml>
```

This would start an interactive session with the user. Various commands (Fig. 22.8) in the **tmproc** library can be used to query the topic map.

As an ISO standard, topic maps have an SGML specification with a corresponding DTD, which has been translated into several XML DTDs and schema. A standards committee is currently developing a specification for XML Topic Maps (XTM). Figure 22.9 lists Web resources for topic maps.

22.6 Virtual HyperGlossary (VHG)

VHG is a platform-independent specification for terminology. It provides a method of knowledge management that attaches extensive semantic information to structured data, enabling, for instance, human-understandable definitions to be attached to tags. VHG specifies a framework of hyperlinked glossaries, dictionaries and thesauri that provide documents with a terminological environment. Documents can be linked to a glossary, which has an extensive network of internal hyperlinks. VHG takes advantage of the XML DOM to give its glossaries a hierarchical structure that can be easily searched and indexed. In addition, VHG has software tools that give it advanced capabilities, including automatic lexical markup of documents, advanced indexing, concept-map generation, taxonomic manipulation of glossaries and support for multilingual glossaries using translation algorithms. Figure 22.9 provides VHG Web resources.

22.7 Channel Definition Format (CDF)

CDF (*Channel Definition Format*) is a Microsoft XML application that implements a technology—called *push technology*—that automatically sends contents to users. Using CDF, Web authors can define channels that automatically deliver content to subscribed users. For example, a user can subscribe to a financial-information Web site's channel to receive information about certain stocks at a regular interval. Additionally, several related Web sites can use channels to refer users between sites.

Methods	Description
get_topics	Returns all the topics found in the document.
get_types_list	Lists the types of a given topic.
is_type	Determines if a topic is of given type or not.
get_topics_of_type	Returns all the topics for a given type.
get_names	Returns all the names for a topic.
get_basenames	Returns the base names for a given topic.
get_dispnames	Returns the display names for a given topic.
get_occurrences	Returns the occurrence for a topic.
get_rolename	Returns the role an occurrence.
get_associations	Returns all the associations in the document.
get_type	Returns the type of association or occurrence.

Fig. 22.8 Some **tmproc** topic-map processor commands.

URL / Description

www.infoloom.com
Infoloom is developing topic map implementations and is also a member of the XTM authoring group. This site contains XTM resources and topic-map links.

www.oasis-open.org/cover/topicMaps.html
This site provides a brief introduction to topic maps and links to relevant resources and articles.

www.ontopia.com
Ontopia is another topic-map developer. Its site contains extensive articles and papers on topic maps and their relation to XML technologies.

www.topicmaps.com
This site, run by STEP, a topic-map developer, contains an introduction to and background information on topic maps.

Fig. 22.9 XTM Web resources.

URL / Description

www.vhg.org.uk
This is the official VHG site, providing extensive information on VHG.

www.oasis-open.org/cover/vhg.html
This site provides a brief introduction to VHG and links to relevant resources and articles.

Fig. 22.10 VHG Web resources.

> **Software Engineering Observation 22.1**
>
> *Because CDF documents are external documents that are linked, Web sites are easily modified to incorporate them.*

Figure 22.11 lists an HTML document that links to a CDF document. When a user clicks on the hyperlink, the browser (i.e., Internet Explorer) processes the CDF document and sets up the Web sites listed within for information retrieval. A screen capture of Internet Explorer using CDF is shown in Fig. 22.12. Figure 22.13 lists the CDF document.

Root element **`channel`** (line 8) describes the channel for the Web site. Attribute **`href`** references the Web page that will be displayed when the channel is selected. In this particular case, clicking the **Deitel Products** link (Fig. 22.12) directs the user to the home page for Deitel & Associates, Inc. (i.e., **`www.deitel.com`**).

Elements **`title`** and **`abstract`** (lines 10 and 11, respectively) provide a title name for the channel and a description for the channel, respectively. Lines 13 and 14

```
<logo href = "http://www.deitel.com/images/logotiny.gif"
      style = "ICON"/>
```

```
1   <!-- Fig. 22.11 : simple.html   -->
2   <!-- Simple example of CDF       -->
3   <!doctype html public "-//w3c//dtd html 4.0 transitional//en">
4   <html>
5
6     <body>
7       <a href = "simple.cdf">Get a simple channel!!</a>
8     </body>
9
10  </html>
```

Fig. 22.11 HTML document referencing a CDF document.

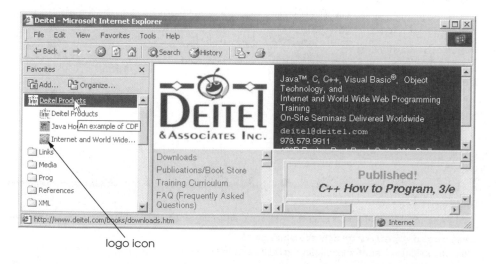

logo icon

Fig. 22.12 Internet Explorer and CDF.

```
1   <?xml version = "1.0"?>
2
3   <!-- Fig. 22.13 : simple.cdf  -->
4   <!-- Simple example of CDF     -->
5
6   <!DOCTYPE channel SYSTEM "cdf.dtd">
7
8   <channel href = "http://www.deitel.com">
9
10     <title>Deitel Products</title>
11     <abstract>An example of CDF</abstract>
12
13     <logo href = "http://www.deitel.com/images/logotiny.gif"
14        style = "ICON"/>
15
16     <item  href =
17        "http://www.deitel.com/books/1999/jhtp3/jhtp3toc.htm">
18        <title>Java How to Program 3rd Edition</title>
19        <logo href =
20           "http://www.deitel.com/images/0130125075_small.jpg"
21           style = "ICON"/>
22     </item>
23
24     <item href =
25        "http://www.deitel.com/books/1999/iw3htp/iw3htp_toc.htm">
26        <title>Internet and World Wide Web How to Program</title>
27        <logo href =
28           "http://www.deitel.com/images/0130161438_small.jpg"
29            style = "ICON"/>
30     </item>
31
32   </channel>
```

Fig. 22.13 CDF document for Deitel products.

define a *logo* for the channel. Attribute **href** references the image, and attribute *style* has value *ICON*—indicating that the resource referenced by **href** is to be used as the icon for the channel.

Each *item* element provides a Web page by using attribute **href**. Element **item** can also contain elements **title**, **abstract** and **logo**.

For more information on Microsoft's CDF implementation, including additional elements and attributes, visit **msdn.microsoft.com/workshop/delivery** or the Web site listed in Fig. 22.14.

URL / Description
www.w3.org/TR/NOTE-CDFsubmit.html This site contains the CDF document submitted to the W3C.

Fig. 22.14 CDF reference Web sites (part 1 of 2).

URL / Description

www.oasis-open.org/cover/gen-apps.html#CDF
This site provides a brief introduction to CDF and links to relevant resources and articles.

www.wdvl.com/Authoring/Languages/CDF.html
This site contains a brief article on CDF, with links to other resources.

msdn.microsoft.com/workshop/delivery/channel/cdf1/cdf1.asp?RLD=363
This site contains a tutorial on creating channel content for the Web using CDF.

msdn.microsoft.com/library/periodic/period97/cutting1297.htm
This is a Microsoft technology article on channel content.

www.techweb.com/se/directlink.cgi?NTG19970601S0049
This article is a reflection on push technology and CDF.

Fig. 22.14 CDF reference Web sites (part 2 of 2).

22.8 Information and Content Exchange (ICE) Protocol

The *Information and Content Exchange Protocol* (*ICE*) was designed to facilitate the redistribution and reuse of Web content. It automates the syndication, transfer and analysis of data, supporting a broad array of software systems and data formats. ICE governs the interaction between a media syndicator and a subscriber after they have entered into a business relationship. Communication with the protocol is based on the request/response model. The subscriber is sent a catalog of subscription offers, and ICE is used to establish and manage any subscriptions that are made. Data is contained in generic *packages*, which are transferred to the subscriber by one of several delivery models defined by ICE. A *sequenced package model* is available for both incremental and full updates, and there are also push and pull models. In addition to data transfer, ICE also provides a structure for exchanging and examining the event logs that keep track of the subscription. ICE also includes functionality for modifying the parameters of the protocol, unsolicited text messaging and querying between the two systems. ICE has been submitted to the W3C for recommendation consideration. For additional information on ICE, consult the Web sites listed in Fig. 22.15.

URL / Description

www.icestandard.org
This is the official site of the ICE standard.

www.w3.org/TR/1998/NOTE-ice-19981026
This site contains the ICE document submitted to the W3C.

www.oasis-open.org/cover/ICE
This site provides a brief introduction to ICE and provides links to resources and articles.

Fig. 22.15 ICE reference Web sites.

22.9 Rich Site Summary (RSS)

Rich Site Summary (*RSS*) is a Netscape technology that implements push technology. Like CDF, RSS can be used to create channels that automatically distribute information to subscribed users. RSS enables Web authors to create a link that visitors can select to receive a specified channel. Figure 22.16 provides several RSS Web resources.

22.10 Platform for Privacy Preferences (P3P)

As Internet and e-commerce use continue to increase, users are becoming more aware of privacy issues. Many Web sites require visitors to divulge personal information in order to receive certain services. More ominously, companies such as DoubleClick have the potential to combine a user's personal information with the user's surfing and shopping preferences. In the last few years, federal and state governments and independent organizations have raised several concerns about privacy.

The W3C is developing the Platform for Privacy Preferences (P3P) recommendation to help Web users manage how their personal information is collected and used on the Internet. A Web site that uses P3P specifies what information the site requests and how the site uses that information. The user's browser then interprets this information and compares the information with user-defined privacy settings. For example, the site may collect visitor information in order to send third-party information to the visitor's home address. If the visitor has specified that personal information should not be used for third-party offers, the visitor's browser could simply prevent access to the Web site or could display a message informing the visitor of the Web site's privacy policy and prompt the user for further action.

URL / Description

my.netscape.com/publish/help/mnn20/quickstart.html
This is a Netscape documentation/tutorial site for RSS.

webreference.com/xml/column13
This site contains a how-to article on creating RSS content for a Web site.

www.webreference.com/authoring/languages/xml/rss/intro/index.html
This site contains a technical introduction to RSS.

webreview.com/pub/1999/10/29/feature/index2a.html
This site is an article that discusses the semantics and prospects of RSS.

webreview.com/pub/1999/10/29/feature/index2b.html
This site contains an article that examines the benefits of RSS.

www.webreference.com/authoring/languages/xml/rss
This site contains an extensive list of RSS resources.

my.netscape.com/publish/help/validate.tmpl
Users can validate their RSS documents at this site.

www.webreference.com/perl/tools
This site lists available RSS tools for Perl.

Fig. 22.16 RSS reference Web sites.

Some privacy advocates contest P3P's viability as a privacy protocol. They assert that the current problem with on-line security arises because users are compelled to settle for less restrictive privacy protection in order to receive the services they desire, or because changing default privacy preferences is too complicated or time consuming. Web companies and users will continue to debate privacy issues as more e-business companies and consumers come on-line. For more information on P3P, visit the Web sites provided in Fig. 22.17.

22.11 Blocks Extensible Exchange Protocol (BXXP)

Blocks Extensible Exchange Protocol (*BXXP*) is an alternative to HTTP for transferring data over the Internet. BXXP was developed by Marshall Rose as a general application protocol on which users can develop more specific protocols. For example, BXXP can be used to develop reusable protocols for instant-messaging, chat or file-transfer applications. BXXP sends "blocks" of XML data over TCP and has the capability to send multiple simultaneous blocks of data. Currently, BXXP is still in development. For more information, refer to the resources in Fig. 22.18.

URL / Description
www.w3.org/TR/P3P This site provides the W3C's P3P specification.
www.w3.org/P3P This site posts an overview of P3P and provides links to resources and previous P3P events.
www.oasis-open.org/cover/p3p.html This site contains an introduction to P3P and provides links to relevant resources and articles.
www.research.att.com/projects/p3p/p3p-www9.ppt This site contains a PowerPoint presentation on privacy and P3P.
www.xml.com/pub/1999/05/p3pdraft.html This site is an article that discusses the development of privacy standards on the Web.
www.w3.org/TR/P3P-for-ecommerce This site contains an article that discusses using P3P in e-commerce.

Fig. 22.17 P3P reference Web sites.

URL/Description
mappa.mundi.net/Internet-Drafts/blocks-protocol.html This site contains the BXXP draft.
mappa.mundi.net/Internet-Drafts/blocks-architecture.html This document describes the architecture of BXXP.

Fig. 22.18 BXXP reference Web sites (part 1 of 2).

URL/Description

`www.nwfusion.com/news/2000/0626bxxp.html?nf`
This site contains an article that discusses BXXP.

`mappa.mundi.net/features/mtr/bxxp.html`
This site contains a brief article that discusses protocol design.

Fig. 22.18 BXXP reference Web sites (part 2 of 2).

22.12 XML Digital Signatures

Because of XML's open nature, there are significant security concerns for an XML-based Web. Externally referenced DTDs and stylesheets could be modified to omit, mangle or otherwise alter information and, even worse, leave large security holes that would enable anybody to access information. Digital signature technology can solve this problem by providing a way to verify documents.

Many security technologies use XML. Most of them are designed specifically for financial transactions, but the most important is the W3C's XML Signature, a general specification for digital signatures. The algorithms used in the specification include the DSS (Digital Signature Standard) public-key algorithm and the SHA-1 (Secure Hash) hash authentication code algorithm (view `csrc.nist.gov/fips/fip180-1.pdf` for information on this algorithm), which is based on the secret-key model. In addition, users can extend XML Signature with their own algorithms and security models. An XML signature can be applied to any type of data, either inside or outside of the XML document containing the signature. The data object is digested and placed, along with other information, inside an XML element that is, in turn, digested and cryptographically signed. The data are canonicalized to avoid any processing-incurred changes from breaking the signature between the signer and verifier. URIs link signatures to data objects. Signed data are either *enveloped* by the signature, *enveloping* the signature or *detached* from the signature.

IBM's XML Security Suite is a program on which the W3C has drawn for its XML Signature specification. It is designed specifically for business-to-business transactions and provides a variety of different technologies, including digital signatures, elementwise encryption and access control, in addition to public-key cryptography and hash authentication. The XML Security Suite is being developed through a joint effort with the Internet Engineering Task Force (IETF). Figure 22.19 provides XML Signature Web resources.

22.13 Extensible Rights Markup Language (XrML)

The *Extensible rights Markup Language (XrML)* is a proprietary application of XML, released by ContentGuard, Inc., on a royalty-free basis, for Digital Rights Management (DRM). Using XrML, providers of electronic content can specify the rights, fees and conditions of usage in a manner that can be both displayed to people and implemented by computers in an invisible manner. XrML licenses, which the user must possess in order to access e-content, are embedded into the content they protect, making tampering more difficult. A different XrML license applies to each right, allowing customizable and extensible combinations. The flexibility of XrML leads to many different usage arrangements for each type of e-content, giving a greater choice to customers. Using DRM with XrML, an e-content provider can specify subscription, rental and even transfer of e-content from one consumer to another. Transactions are made according to these terms of usage and can be triggered by content-specific events such as pressing the play button on a media player. Unlike copyright contracts for physical media, which can often be ignored, digital rights management ensures protection of e-content through automatic enforcement by software. Even if digital content is transferred to physical media, such as CD or print, it can be regulated through watermarking and the exclusive use of trusted delivery systems for printing. However, the terms of a digital contract can be renegotiated if the e-content user desires additional functionality. XrML also provides a framework for professional and legal agreements, certification, risk management and emergency responses to cyberattacks. XrML supports several different server platforms and all of the major operating systems, ensuring that content can be delivered portably. Figure 22.20 provides XrML resources.

22.14 XML Metadata Interchange (XMI)

In a world of heterogeneous applications, it is often difficult for developers to communicate and collaborate with each other. The Object Management Group (OMG) standardized the Unified Modeling Language (UML™), giving developers a common language for designing object, distributed and business models for computing. UML is, in turn, part of a larger model, the *Meta Object Facility (MOF)*, which describes all software modeling environments including itself. The MOF provides a rigorous definition of object-oriented models, technologies, semantics and data interchange formats. To enable the exchange of programming information across a network, UML and MOF were integrated with XML, creating XMI, the OMG standard for sharing and storing object-oriented information. With XMI, developers using different tools and programming in different development environments can collaborate and create compatible distributed applications. XMI is also a *Stream-based Model Interchange Format (SMIF),* which enables the streaming of object data from remote databases as well as from traditional file storage. There are standard XMI DTDs for many widely used object models, and it is possible to automatically generate DTDs for any meta-information model. Figure 22.21 provides a couple of XMI Web resources.

URL/Description

www.w3.org/Signature
This is W3C's main page for its XML Signature initiative.

www.xml.com/pub/Guide/Digital_Signatures
This site contains a listing of links related to digital signature technologies.

www.alphaworks.ibm.com/tech/xmlsecuritysuite
This is the Web site for IBM's XML Security Suite.

Fig. 22.19 XML Signature reference Web sites.

URL/Description

`www.xrml.org`
This is the official XrML page run by ContentGuard, Inc., which contains the white paper, specification and other resources.

`www.oasis-open.org/cover/xrml.html`
OASIS provides a listing of links and articles related to XrML on this Web site.

Fig. 22.20 XrML reference Web sites.

URL/Description

`www.omg.org/technologies/xml`
This is the OMG's XML and XMI Web site. It provides links to XMI specifications and articles.

`www-4.ibm.com/software/ad/standards/xmi.html`
This is IBM's XMI Web site, which provides links to various XMI resources, as well as an explanation of XMI and related technologies.

Fig. 22.21 XMI Web resources.

22.15 W3C's XML Protocol

Responding to a widespread demand for technologies that allow communication between peers in a distributed computing environment, the W3C has begun work on a framework for XML-based messaging. The aim is to design an envelope for interoperable XML encapsulation and transfer, a convention for making remote procedure calls (RPC), a mechanism for serializing nonsyntactic data, such as object graphs, and a method to bind HTTP to XML. The encapsulation language will enable applications to independently, automatically and dynamically introduce new features, as well as support interaction with network intermediaries. Ideas from SOAP (i.e., the Simple Object Access Protocol, which is an XML-based messaging system discussed in Chapter 23) will shape the envelope and serialization technologies, potentially making the new protocols supersets of SOAP. The focus of the entire project is on simplicity, extensibility, modularity and interoperability, as the protocols must operate across all types of software models, platforms and applications. To enable maximum extensibility and flexibility, the protocols will be implemented as a layered system designed to support further, more robust layers of technologies on top of it. As of the time of this writing, XML Protocol is in its planning phase, and more information should be forthcoming as the project moves along. For more information on the XML Protocol, visit **www.w3.org/2000/xp**.

22.16 XAML

As this book was going to press, Sun Microsystems, IBM, Hewlett-Packard and Oracle announced plans to develop a new XML-based specification—named *XAML*—for automating transactions. We expect that this initiative will be significant.

SUMMARY

- XML Query Language (XML Query) uses the power of XSL patterns to search XML documents for specific data. XML Query syntax resembles the path specification in a UNIX environment. XML Query was submitted to W3C as a proposal in 1998, and development on the language is ongoing.

- Directory services provide a method for managing relational resources and metadata. The Directory Services Markup Language (DSML) is the bridge between directory services and XML. A standard vocabulary and schema provide the means for directory services information to be described in an XML document. DSML is platform independent, requiring only that the data be structured so that they can be manipulated with DSML.

- The Resource Definition Framework (RDF) is an XML-based language for describing information contained in a resource. A resource can be a Web page, an entire Web site or any item on the Web that contains information in some form. RDF's metadata can be used by search engines or intelligent software agents to list or catalog information on the Web. The Resource Definition Framework is a W3C recommendation.

- RDF documents have root element **rdf:RDF**. Namespace prefix **rdf** is used for RDF elements, and namespace prefix **dc** is used for metadata elements. Element **rdf:Description** describes the resource specified in attribute **about**.

- Element **Title** marks up a resource's name. Element **rdf:Bag** is a container element for an unordered list of resources. Within **Bag** elements are **li** elements, which represent individual resources. Element **Seq** is used to represent an ordered list of resources.

- *Topic maps*, an International Standards Organization (ISO) standard, are a new model for navigating and linking resources. Just as XML separates content from presentation, topic maps separate content from links. Topic maps, like XLink, exist as hypertext layers above, rather than within, an information set.

- *Virtual HyperGlossary (VHG)* is a platform-independent specification for terminology. It provides a method of knowledge management that attaches extensive semantic information to structured data, enabling, for instance, human-understandable definitions to be attached to tags. VHG specifies a framework of hyperlinked glossaries, dictionaries and thesauri that provide documents with a terminological environment.

- CDF (Channel Definition Format) is a Microsoft XML application that implements a technology—called push technology—that automatically sends contents to users. Using CDF, Web authors can define channels that automatically deliver content to subscribed users.

- CDF documents have root element **channel**, which describes the channel for the Web site. Attribute **href** references the Web page that will be displayed when the channel is selected. Elements **title** and **abstract** provide a title name for the channel and a description for the channel, respectively. Element **logo**'s attribute **href** references an image when attribute **style** has the value **ICON**.

- The Information and Content Exchange Protocol (ICE) was designed to facilitate the redistribution and reuse of Web content. It automates the syndication, transfer and analysis of data, supporting a broad array of software systems and data formats. ICE governs the interaction between a media syndicator and a subscriber after they have entered into a business relationship. Communication with the protocol is based on the request/response model. ICE has been submitted to the W3C for recommendation consideration.

- Rich Site Summary (RSS) is a Netscape technology that implements push technology. Like CDF, RSS can be used to create channels that automatically distribute information to subscribers. RSS enables Web authors to create a link that visitors can click to receive a specified channel.

- The W3C is developing the Platform for Privacy Preferences (P3P) recommendation to help Web users manage how their personal information is collected and used on the Internet. A Web site that uses P3P specifies what information the site requests and how the site uses that information.

- Blocks Extensible Exchange Protocol (BXXP) is an alternative to HTTP for transferring data over the Internet. BXXP was developed by Marshall Rose as a general application protocol on which users can develop more specific protocols.

- Many security technologies use XML. Most of them are designed specifically for financial transactions, but the most important is the W3C's XML Signature, a general specification for digital signatures.

- IBM's XML Security Suite is a program on which the W3C has drawn for its XML Signature specification. It is designed specifically for business-to-business transactions and provides a variety of different technologies, including digital signatures, elementwise encryption and access control, in addition to public-key cryptography and hash authentication.

- The *Extensible rights Markup Language (XrML)* is a proprietary application of XML, released by ContentGuard, Inc., on a royalty-free basis, for Digital Rights Management (DRM). Using XrML, providers of electronic content can specify the rights, fees and conditions of usage in a manner that can be both displayed to people and implemented by computers in an invisible manner. XrML licenses, which the user must possess in order to access e-content, are embedded into the content they protect, making tampering more difficult.

- XrML also provides a framework for professional and legal agreements, certification, risk management and emergency responses to cyberattacks. XrML supports several different server platforms and all of the major operating systems, ensuring that content can be delivered portably.

- The *Meta Object Facility (MOF)* describes all software modeling environments, including itself. The MOF provides a rigorous definition of object-oriented models, technologies, semantics and data interchange formats. To enable the exchange of programming information across a network, the Unified Modeling Language (UML) and MOF were integrated with XML, creating XML Metadata Interchange (XMI), the OMG standard for sharing and storing object-oriented information.

- With XMI, developers using different tools and programming in different development environments can collaborate and create compatible distributed applications. XMI is also a *Stream-based Model Interchange Format (SMIF)*, which enables the streaming of object data from remote databases as well as from traditional file storage.

- The W3C has begun work on a framework for XML-based messaging. The aim is to design an envelope for interoperable XML encapsulation and transfer, a convention for making remote procedure calls (RPC), a mechanism for serializing nonsyntactic data, such as object graphs, and a method to bind HTTP to XML. The encapsulation language will enable applications to independently, automatically and dynamically introduce new features, as well as support interaction with network intermediaries.

TERMINOLOGY

Blocks Extensible Exchange Protocol (BXXP)	dynamic content
BXXP (Blocks Extensible Exchange Protocol)	envelope
CDF (Channel Definition Framework)	metadata
channel	Netscape technology
Channel Definition Framework (CDF)	P3P (Platform for Privacy Preferences)
channel subscriber	path specification
digital signature	Platform for Privacy Preferences (P3P)
distributed application	proprietary data specification

push technology
RDF (Resource Definition Framework)
Remote Procedure Call (RPC)
Resource Definition Framework (RDF)
Rich Site Summary (RSS)
RPC (Remote Procedure Call)
RSS (Rich Site Summary)
Simple Object Access Protocol (SOAP)

SOAP (Simple Object Access Protocol)
SQL (Structured Query Language)
Structured Query Language (SQL)
tree format
XMI (XML Metadata Interchange)
XML Metadata Interchange (XMI)
XML Query (XML Query Language)
XML Query Language (XML Query)

SELF-REVIEW EXERCISES

22.1 State whether the following are *true* or *false*. If *false*, explain why.
  a) XML Query searches for data stored in a tree format.
  b) The W3C is currently developing a technology for XML digital signatures.
  c) XMI is an acronym for XML Metadata Interchange.
  d) Due to the large amount of information available over the Internet, finding information on a specific topic can often be difficult and time consuming.
  e) The Resource Definition Framework can be used to validate a document's markup or for digitally signing documents.
  f) A person using the Channel Definition Format can define channels that automatically deliver content to subscribed users.
  g) Unlike CDF, Rich Site Summary (RSS) cannot be used to create channels that automatically distribute information to subscribed users. This task must be done manually with RSS.
  h) Many Web sites require visitors to divulge personal information in order to receive certain services.
  i) BXXP sends "blocks" of data encoded in scripting languages over TCP.
  j) P3P is an encryption algorithm used with digital signatures.

22.2 Fill in the blanks in each of the following statements.
  a) BXXP is an acronym for _____.
  b) XML _____ Language uses the power of XSL patterns to search XML documents for specific data.
  c) _____ is "information about information."
  d) The _____ Framework is an XML-based language for describing information contained in a resource.
  e) Search engines use RDF's _____ to list or catalog information on the Web.
  f) Channel Definition Format is an XML application that implements _____ technology.
  g) A Web site that uses _____ specifies what information the site requests and how the site uses that information.
  h) A CDF document has root element _____.
  i) BXXP is an alternative to _____ for transferring data over the Internet.
  j) Rich _____ is a Netscape technology that implements push technology.

ANSWERS TO SELF-REVIEW EXERCISES

22.1   a) True. b.) True. c) True. d) True. e) False. The Resource Definition Framework can be used to evaluate a Web site for ratings purposes or to create digital signatures. f) True. g) False. Like CDF, Rich Site Summary can be used to create channels that automatically distribute information to subscribers. h) True. i) False. BXXP sends "blocks" of XML data over TCP. j) False. P3P is a W3C initiative to address privacy issues on the Internet.

22.1   a) Blocks Extensible Exchange Protocol. b) Query. c) Metadata. d) Resource Definition. e) metadata. f) push. g) P3P, or Platform for Privacy Preferences. h) **channel**. i) HTTP. j) Site Summary.

EXERCISES

22.3   Write a simple RDF document for **www.deitel.com**. The RDF document should point to **http://www.deitel.com/toc.html** for a description of **www.deitel.com**. The RDF document should also give a brief description of **toc.html**. Parse the RDF document using SiRPAC's RDF parser and compiler.

22.4   Consider the fictitious HTML page **www.deitel.com/books/index.html**, which describes books in the *How to Program* series and allows on-line shopping. Write an RDF document that describes this page using a **Description** element. The RDF statement should give a brief description of each book using a **Bag** element with **li** elements—for example, Java How to Program, C How to Program, etc.

22.5   Consider a fictitious entertainment company, ExComp. ExComp broadcasts two audio channels over the Internet: an oldies and a pop-music channel. It also has a photo gallery, which is updated on a daily basis. Write a CDF document that, when downloaded, provides access to all of ExComp's services. Create fictitious URLs as needed.

23

Simple Object Access Protocol (SOAP) and Microsoft BizTalk™

Objectives

- To understand the Simple Object Access Protocol and how it uses XML.
- To understand the structure of a SOAP message.
- To be able to write Java to applications that send SOAP messages.
- To understand what BizTalk is and how it works.

Nothing happens until something is sold.
Arthur H. Motley

Men are going to have to learn to be managers in a world where the organization will come close to consisting of all chiefs and one Indian. The Indian, of course, is the computer.
Thomas L. Whisler

Outline

23.1 Introduction

Interoperability, or seamless communication and interaction between different software systems, is a primary goal of many businesses and organizations that rely heavily on computers and electronic networks. Many applications use the Internet to transfer data. Some of these applications are run on client systems with little processing power, so they invoke a method call on a different machine to process their data. Many of the applications use proprietary data specifications, which makes communication between other applications difficult. The majority of these applications also reside behind different *firewalls*, security barriers that restrict data communication to and from applications. The *Simple Object Access Protocol (SOAP)* is a protocol that addresses these problems. Combining the powers of HTTP and XML, it provides a fully extensible mode of communication between software systems.

Microsoft BizTalk, a framework for business messaging and transactions, is designed to overcome barriers to *Enterprise Application Integration (EAI)*—the networking of diverse software systems both within and between organizations—and *business-to-business (B2B)* integration. It relies on the *BizTalk Library* of standardized schema, the *BizTalk Framework* of protocols and the *BizTalk Server*, which is implemented in *Microsoft BizTalk Server 2000* for handling communication between different software systems. SOAP processing capabilities are supported by BizTalk and built into its Framework.

23.2 Simple Object Access Protocol (SOAP)

SOAP was developed and drafted by IBM, Lotus Development Corporation, Microsoft, DevelopMentor and Userland Software, and it is supported by Sun Microsystems. SOAP is an HTTP–XML-based protocol that allows applications to communicate easily over the Internet, by using XML documents called *SOAP messages*. It is compatible with any object model, for it includes only functions and capabilities that are absolutely necessary for defining a communication framework. Thus, SOAP is both platform and software independent, and it can be implemented in any language. SOAP supports transport using almost any conceivable protocol. For example, it can be bound to HTTP and follow the HTTP request–response model. SOAP also supports any method of encoding data.

A SOAP message contains an *envelope*, which describes the content, intended recipient and processing requirements of a message. The optional **header** element of a SOAP message provides a means for additional processing in transit from the sender to the recipient. It can also incorporate routing information. Through the header, more complex protocols can be built onto SOAP. The message can be extended modularly through header entries for purposes such as authentication, transaction management and payment. The body of a SOAP message contains application-specific data for the final intended recipient of the message.

SOAP can be used to make a *Remote Procedure Call* (*RPC*), which is a request made to another machine to run a task. The RPC uses an XML vocabulary to specify the method to be invoked, any parameters the method takes and the URI of the target object. An RPC call naturally maps to an HTTP request, so the message is sent through an HTTP POST. A SOAP-response message is an HTTP response document that contains the results of the method call (e.g., returned values, error messages, etc.). SOAP also supports *asynchronous RPC*, in which the data follow different encoding rules and do not map to the parameters of a specific RPC.

As of the time of publication of this book, SOAP is still under development, and many of the technologies that will build on it are in their planning stages. Before the benefits of SOAP can be realized fully, higher level specifications and standards that use this technology must be established. Nevertheless, SOAP is the leading industry standard for an XML-distributed computing infrastructure, providing previously nonexistent extensibility and interoperability.

Figures 23.1–23.4 show a SOAP example that uses Apache's SOAP implementation API, version 2.0; it can be downloaded from **xml.apache.org/soap**. To run the SOAP RPC, a servlet engine, such as Jakarta-Tomcat (**jakarta.apache.org**), is required. Apache's SOAP API also requires Apache's Xerces parser for Java, which is available at **xml.apache.org/xerces-j/index.html**. Installation instructions for both the server and the client are included in the SOAP documentation (**docs/install/index.html**).

Figure 23.1 shows class **SimpleService**, which resides on the server and contains method **getWelcome**. The Java application presented in Fig. 23.4 will invoke this method using an RPC.

```
1   // Fig. 23.1 : SimpleService.java
2   // implementation for the requested method on the server
3
4   public class SimpleService {
5
6      public String getWelcome( String message ) throws Exception
7      {
8         String text =
9            "Welcome to SOAP!\nHere is your message: " + message;
10
11         return text;   // return text to the request
12      }
13   }
```

Fig. 23.1 Class **SimpleService**.

Method **getWelcome** (lines 6–13) returns a **String** when invoked. To make this method available to clients (i.e., to facilitate RPC), we need to provide the server with the name of the method that must be invoked to process the request. This procedure is called *deploying a service*.

To deploy the service, first copy the **SimpleService.class** file into the **jakarta-tomcat/classes** directory, or, if you have created a Java Archive (JAR) file, copy the JAR file into the **jakarta-tomcat/lib** directory. Create the **classes** or **lib** directories if they do not already exist. Files in these directories are included automatically in the **CLASSPATH** of **Jakarta-Tomcat**.

The service can be deployed using the XML-SOAP administration tool included in the SOAP package (located in the directory **webapps/soap**). To run this application, type the URL **localhost:8080/soap/admin** into a Web browser. Figures 23.2 and 23.3 show the administration tool that allows you to deploy, remove and list services. The **ID** field in Fig. 23.2 contains a URI (**urn:xml-simple-message**) that we created to identify the service to the client. If one service has the same URI as another, the client cannot differentiate between them, and consequently, errors may occur. The **Scope** field specifies the lifetime of the object created (on the server) for serving the SOAP request. The object can exist for the duration of the **Request**, **Session** or **Application**. **Request** denotes that the object will be deleted after the response is sent, **Session** indicates that the object persists for a short time after the end of the server interaction with the client and **Application** signifies that the object is available for successive sessions. The **Methods** field (Fig. 23.2) stipulates the methods that can be invoked upon a SOAP request—in this case, method **getWelcome**. The **Provider Type** field specifies the language in which the service is implemented. Languages supported include Java, JavaScript, Perl and Bean Markup Language (BML). In our case, we use Java. We describe the class providing the service, **SimpleService**, in the **Provider Class** field. There are also other fields, but we do not use them, they and are not shown in Fig. 23.2. Because we are using Java, we do not fill in the **Script Provider** field, which designates the scripting language and the script code. The **Type Mapping** field allows manual type mapping of the objects. When the form is completed, click on the **Deploy** button on the left to deploy the service. In Fig. 23.3, we confirm that the service has been deployed by clicking on the **List** button, which lists the services.

Instructions for other methods of deployment (such as using the command line) are located in **docs\guide\index.html**.

Figure 23.4 lists the client-side code that we use for the RPC. When executed, the program sends a SOAP request to the server, which in our case is the same machine, the local host. The client sends a message as a parameter to the remote method. (This message can be supplied by the user at the command line; by default, the message **Thanks!** is used.) When the method is invoked on the server, it sends back the message

```
Welcome to SOAP!
Here is your message: Thanks!
```

Line 7 **import**s the SOAP package that provides the API for SOAP implementation. The package **org.apache.soap.rpc** in line 8 provides the implementation for RPC over SOAP. Line 13 specifies the encoding style used for the message. SOAP, which has no default encoding style, supports many encoding styles, including XMI, but we use the standard RPC encoding. The **if** statement in lines 16–19 assigns **message** either the **String** input at the command line or the **String** "**Thanks!**". Lines 22 and 23 specify the server-side URL to which **message**'s value is sent, **rpcrouter.jsp**. This document, a JavaServer Page, receives the SOAP envelope through the HTTP POST method. Using the URI specified in the SOAP message, it looks up the services deployed on the server in order to instantiate the appropriate object, in this case a **SimpleService** object.

Objects of class **Call** invoke remote methods. Line 26 instantiates a **Call** object that is assigned to reference **remoteMethod**, and lines 27 and 28 set the URI of the remote method. Line 31 specifies the name of the method to be invoked, **getWelcome**. We then set the encoding style for the message on line 32. Lines 35–37 build the parameters that will be passed to the remote method for processing. Each parameter must be contained in its own object, and the parameters must be contained in a **vector**.

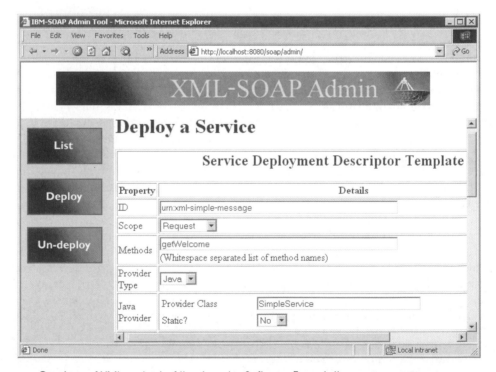

Courtesy of XML project of the Apache Software Foundation; **xml.apache.org**

Fig. 23.2 SOAP Package administration tool.

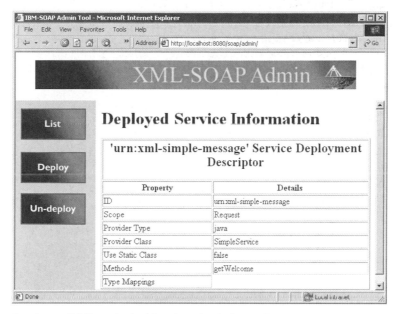

Courtesy of XML project of the Apache Software Foundation; **xml.apache.org**

Fig. 23.3   Description of deployed service.

```
1   // Fig. 23.4 : GetMessage.java
2   // Program that makes a SOAP RPC
3
4   import java.io.*;
5   import java.net.*;
6   import java.util.*;
7   import org.apache.soap.*;
8   import org.apache.soap.rpc.*;
9
10  public class GetMessage {
11
12      public static void main( String args[] ) {
13          String encodingStyleURI = Constants.NS_URI_SOAP_ENC;
14          String message;
15
16          if ( args.length != 0 )
17            message = args[ 0 ];
18          else
19            message = "Thanks!";
20
21          try {
22            URL url = new URL(
23                "http://localhost:8080/soap/servlet/rpcrouter" );
```

Fig. 23.4   Client making a SOAP request (part 1 of 3).

```
24
25              // build the call
26              Call remoteMethod = new Call();
27              remoteMethod.setTargetObjectURI(
28                 "urn:xml-simple-message" );
29
30              // set the name of the remote method to be invoked
31              remoteMethod.setMethodName( "getWelcome" );
32              remoteMethod.setEncodingStyleURI( encodingStyleURI );
33
34              // set the parameters for the remote method
35              Vector parameters = new Vector();
36              parameters.addElement( new Parameter( "message",
37                 String.class, message, null ) );
38              remoteMethod.setParams( parameters );
39              Response response;
40
41              // invoke the remote method
42              response = remoteMethod.invoke( url, "" );
43
44              // get the response
45              if ( response.generatedFault() ) {
46                 Fault fault = response.getFault();
47
48                 System.out.println( "CALL FAILED:\nFault Code = "
49                    + fault.getFaultCode()+ "\nFault String = "
50                    + fault.getFaultString() );
51              }
52              else {
53                 Parameter result = response.getReturnValue();
54
55                 // display the result of call
56                 System.out.println( result.getValue() );
57              }
58           }
59        catch ( MalformedURLException me ) {
60           me.printStackTrace();
61           System.exit( 1 );
62        }
63        catch ( SOAPException se ) {
64           System.err.println( "Error message: " + se.getMessage() );
65           System.exit( 1 );
66        }
67     }
68  }
```

```
java GetMessage
Welcome to SOAP!
Here is your message: Thanks!
```

Fig. 23.4   Client making a SOAP request (part 2 of 3).

```
java GetMessage "my message"
Welcome to SOAP!
Here is your message: my message
```

Fig. 23.4   Client making a SOAP request (part 3 of 3).

On lines 36 and 37,

```
parameters.addElement( new Parameter( "message",
   String.class, message, null ) );
```

we build a new parameter for the method by constructing a **Parameter** object. The first constructor argument is the name of the variable or reference (**message**), the second argument is the class to which the **Parameter** object belongs (**String**), the third argument is the value of the parameter (the object **message**) and the fourth argument specifies the parameter's encoding (**null** specifies the application's default encoding). Method **setParams** in line 38 sets the parameters of the **remoteMethod** object.

We invoke the remote method by calling method **invoke** in line 42. It takes two arguments: the server URL to which the SOAP message is being sent and the value of the SOAPAction Header, which specifies the intent of the request. The second argument can take a null string if a SOAPAction Header is not being used. Method **invoke** throws a **SOAPException** (lines 63–66) if any network error occurs while the SOAP request is being sent. Once the method is invoked on the server, the result is sent back to the client and stored in the **response** object (line 42). The **response** object receives an error message if a server error, such as a failure to locate the appropriate services or an error in the invoked method, occurs. Lines 45–51 determine whether or not the received message is an error message. Lines 53–56 print the output if no error has been received.

23.3 Microsoft BizTalk[1]

Increasingly, companies are using the Internet to exchange data with their business partners in what are called *Business to Business (B2B) transactions*. Because businesses use different platforms, applications and data specifications, exchanging data can be difficult. Business partners therefore establish protocols and data formats to engage in electronic commerce. While electronic commerce allows for more efficient exchange of data among businesses, standards for data formats and protocols have not been implemented widely in industry.

Sharing data electronically can reduce costs and improve efficiency in many industries. The portable and descriptive nature of XML simplifies the packaging of data for sharing among business partners. However, for XML to be useful across industries there must be a common vocabulary of XML schemas. Standards are also needed for transmitting and translating XML documents between business partners. Microsoft developed BizTalk

---

1. At the time of this writing, Microsoft had released only a beta version of Microsoft BizTalk Server 2000. Given the high likelihood of changes in this product, we felt it best to present an overview of BizTalk in this chapter. We will discuss BizTalk extensively in *XML How to Program: Second Edition*. We will also prepare live-code case studies on BizTalk and make them available free for download at **www.deitel.com**.

for the purpose of creating and integrating business processes that may be applied across existing applications and businesses. The BizTalk Framework, which is based on platform-independent messaging protocols, consists of three parts: the BizTalk Framework, the Biz-Talk Server and the BizTalk Schema Library.

23.3.1 BizTalk Framework

The *BizTalk Framework* is a set of guidelines for publishing schemas and using XML messages to integrate software systems. The XML messages in the BizTalk framework are based on SOAP. Anyone can download the framework specifications and implement Biz-Talk schemas, which can then be submitted to the **BizTalk.org** Web site for validation. **BizTalk.org** provides a common repository of XML schemas necessary to enable e-commerce and B2B transactions using XML.

BizTalk schemas follow the *XML Data Reduced (XDR)* format. XDR is a simplified version of *XML Data*, which provides a vocabulary of XML elements for defining schemas. The BizTalk Framework specifies a standard set of tags for use in XML messaging between applications, including an optional set of routing tags. In the BizTalk Framework, the only thing two applications must have in common to communicate is the ability to format, transmit, receive and process an XML message that uses a schema from the **Biz-Talk.org** repository. The BizTalk Framework also allows these XML documents to traverse a network as SOAP messages. Communication can be conducted with a simple HTTP POST or through other protocols.

One of the more powerful methods for exchanging documents is using a *message queuing* technology, such as *Microsoft Message Queuing (MSMQ)*. This loosely coupled approach to distributed computing increases efficiency and scalability by freeing client applications from the "lock-up" of waiting for the server to complete a transaction. A client posts a message to the queue for processing and may be notified when the processing is complete. The BizTalk Framework also enables applications to be more flexible since the client interacts with a messaging system or other standard protocol, rather than a specific, proprietary server application.

23.3.2 BizTalk Server

Although Microsoft started the BizTalk initiative, Microsoft's BizTalk Server is not required by the BizTalk Framework. Because XML and the protocols used by BizTalk are platform and application independent, any BizTalk-Framework-compliant server may be used. A BizTalk Server must be able to parse, translate and route all inbound and outbound XML messages to and from a business or between applications.

As of the time of publication of this book, Microsoft BizTalk Server 2000 is in beta form and is the only implementation of a BizTalk-Framework-compliant server. Biztalk Server 2000 supports a number of protocols, including HTTP, some existing EDI protocols, Simple Mail Transport Protocol (SMTP) and Microsoft Message Queuing (MSMQ). Both synchronous and asynchronous communication is possible using BizTalk Server 2000.

Microsoft BizTalk Server 2000 manages XML messages using a rules-based routing system in which BizTalk examines queued documents in MSMQ and prioritizes them according to routing data contained in the documents. Microsoft BizTalk Server 2000 manages the flow of XML messages through the application. As XML messages flow, transformations are performed using XSLT. These transformations correspond to the *business rules* of the application. For example, an application may require that a telephone number is in a certain format (e.g., (800) 555-1212). This telephone number formatting is a business rule of the application. If an XML message contains a telephone number in some other format (e.g., 800-555-1212), the business rule is applied by transforming the message with XSLT to produce the proper telephone number format. For developers who are not familiar with XSLT, the *BizTalk Mapper*—a translation tool that maps records and fields between data formats—can be used to graphically define the transformations for manipulating the data. These transformations allow applications to receive XML messages in a standard format and then convert the messages to an application-specific format for processing. A tracking utility allows advanced monitoring of documents as they flow through the server. Figure 23.5 illustrates a sample B2B exchange using BizTalk.

In Fig. 23.5, a store sends a purchase order as an XML document to its supplier. This purchase order may be generated by an inventory management system at the store that automatically orders new stock of a certain item when current inventory runs low. Because Biz-Talk uses standard protocols, an HTTP POST can be used to transmit the XML purchase order to the supplier. The XML purchase order is then passed to a messaging queue for processing. From the messaging queue, the message is delivered to a *mapping channel*. As the message passes through the channel, XSLT transformations are applied to enforce the business rules of the application. From the mapping channel, the XML message enters one of two *ports*. In this example, one port is used to deliver the XML message to a warehouse's Web server to check for available stock of items in the purchase order. Another port is used to deliver a confirmation of the order to the originating store. Alternatively, the XML message could be passed through another mapping channel to undergo further transformations, depending on the business rules of the application. Note that each of the business partners in this application may not, in fact, be using BizTalk. However, because the standard HTTP protocol is used for communicating XML messages, the business partners are able to complete the business processes necessary for the transaction to complete.

To manage business relationships, BizTalk Server 2000 includes *Microsoft BizTalk Messaging Manager*. The Messaging Manager provides a Web-based graphical user interface (GUI) for tracking data exchange. *BizTalk Orchestration Designer* is a visual tool for designing business processes. A business analyst can create a chart that describes a particular business process, such as the submission of a purchase order to a supplier for a store. A developer can then use the chart to build the software components that implement the business process in the application. The *BizTalk Editor* tool is provided for editing/creating specifications, including most of the XML schemas in the **BizTalk.org** repository.

BizTalk Orchestration automates the implementation of business processes for generating and processing messages. It facilitates the definition of a process, the subsequent connection of the software components necessary to implement the process, and any modifications or upgrades that need to be made in the future. An XML language called *XLANG* is used to define business processes that can operate dynamically. These business processes may be modified using the Orchestration Designer. Each process is completely separate from its implementation, making the process easier to build, modify and scale. The semantic definition of a process, like the implementation, can be spread across its constituent units, allowing modifications to a unit to be dynamically integrated into the process. BizTalk Orchestration also provides fault tolerance for applications, which enables applications to handle failures in business processes.

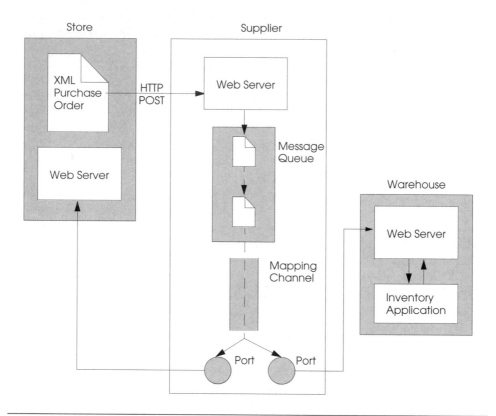

Fig. 23.5 Sample BizTalk interaction between a store, a supplier and a warehouse.

23.3.3 BizTalk Schema Library

The BizTalk Schema Library is a collection of BizTalk Framework schemas that have been validated and agreed upon by organizations using BizTalk. The Library provides a common repository for XML schemas that will be used to validate and standardize documents for exchange through the BizTalk Framework. Businesses can choose among the schemas in the BizTalk Schema Library or design their own schemas and submit them for inclusion in the Library. The Biztalk Schema Library is housed on the **BizTalk.org** Web site.

23.3.4 Microsoft BizTalk Server 2000

To encourage developers to adopt the BizTalk Framework, Microsoft has provided a version of BizTalk Server 2000 for download at **www.microsoft.com/biztalk**. Included in the download is a tutorial on building a BizTalk application using MSMQ and Internet Information Services with ASP.

23.4 Internet and World Wide Web Resources

msdn.microsoft.com/xml/general/soaptemplate.asp
This site provides an introduction to SOAP. It also contains links to examples and other information.

www.oasis-open.org/cover/soap.html
This site provides information on SOAP and XML.

www.develop.com/soap
This site provides downloads and FAQs.

www.whatis.com/soap.htm
This site provides background information about SOAP and links for further information on it.

www.biztalk.org/BizTalk
This site provides an introduction to Biztalk and contains many BizTalk resources.

www.microsoft.com/biztalk
Microsoft's BizTalk Server 2000 site. Provides a beta download of BizTalk Server 2000 as well as documentation and product information.

www.xmlglobal.com/biztalk
This site provides a BizTalk toolkit for Perl.

xml.apache.org/soap
Apache's SOAP implementation can be downloaded from this site, which also provides information and documentation on it.

xml.apache.org/xerces-j/index.html
Apache's Xerces parser for Java can be downloaded from this site, along with documentation.

jakarta.apache.org
This page is the Web site of Apache's Jakarta-Tomcat servlet engine.

SUMMARY

- SOAP is an HTTP–XML-based protocol that allows applications to communicate easily over the Internet, using XML documents called SOAP messages.

- SOAP is both platform and software independent, and can be implemented in any language. SOAP supports transport using almost any conceivable protocol. For example, it can be bound to HTTP and follow the HTTP request–response model.

- A SOAP message contains an envelope, which describes the content, intended recipient and processing requirements of a message. The optional **header** element of a SOAP message provides a means for additional processing in transit from the sender to the recipient.

- Through the header, more complex protocols can be built onto SOAP. The body of a SOAP message contains application-specific data for the final intended recipient of the message.

- SOAP can be used to make a Remote Procedure Call (RPC), which is a request made to another machine to run a task. The RPC uses an XML vocabulary to specify the method to be invoked, any parameters the method takes and the URI of the target object.

- Because businesses use different platforms, applications and data specifications, exchanging data can be difficult. Business partners therefore establish protocols and data formats to engage in electronic commerce.

- For XML to be useful across industries, there must be a common vocabulary of XML schemas. Standards are also needed for transmitting and translating XML documents between business partners.

- The BizTalk Framework, which is based on platform-independent messaging protocols, consists of three parts: the BizTalk Framework, the BizTalk Server and the BizTalk Schema Library.

- The BizTalk Framework is a set of guidelines for publishing schemas and using XML messages to integrate software systems. **BizTalk.org** provides a common repository of XML schemas necessary to enable e-commerce and B2B transactions using XML.

- BizTalk schemas follow the *XML Data Reduced (XDR)* format. XDR is a simplified version of *XML Data*, which provides a vocabulary of XML elements for defining schemas. The BizTalk Framework specifies a standard set of tags for use in XML messaging between applications, including an optional set of routing tags.

- One of the more powerful methods for exchanging documents is using a *message queuing* technology, such as *Microsoft Message Queuing (MSMQ)*. This loosely coupled approach to distributed computing increases efficiency and scalability by freeing client applications from the "lock-up" of waiting for the server to complete a transaction.

- A BizTalk Server must be able to parse, translate and route all inbound and outbound XML messages to and from a business or between applications.

- Microsoft BizTalk Server 2000 manages XML messages using a rules-based routing system in which BizTalk examines queued documents in MSMQ and prioritizes them according to routing data contained in the documents.

- The BizTalk Mapper—a translation tool that maps records and fields between data formats—can be used to graphically define the transformations for manipulating XML Messages. These transformations allow applications to receive XML messages in a standard format and then convert the messages to an application-specific format for processing.

- Microsoft BizTalk Messaging Manager provides a Web-based graphical user interface (GUI) for tracking data exchange. BizTalk Orchestration Designer is a visual tool for designing business processes.

- An XML language called *XLANG* is used to define business processes that can operate dynamically. These business processes may be modified using the Orchestration Designer. Each process is completely separate from its implementation, making the process easier to build, modify and scale.

- The BizTalk Schema Library a common repository for XML schemas that will be used to validate and standardize documents for exchange through the BizTalk Framework. Businesses can choose among the schemas in the BizTalk Schema Library or design their own schemas and submit them for inclusion in the Library.

- To encourage developers to adopt the BizTalk Framework, Microsoft has provided a version of BizTalk Server 2000 for download at **www.microsoft.com/biztalk**.

TERMINOLOGY

application-to-application (A2A) integration	loosely-coupled messaging
asynchronous RPC	messaging
BizTalk Framework	Microsoft Host Integration Server
BizTalk Orchestration	org.apache.soap.rpc
BizTalk Schema Library	Remote Procedure Call (RPC)
BizTalk Server	request–response
deploying a service	schema
distributed object architecture	Simple Object Access Protocol (SOAP)
Enterprise Application Integration (EAI)	synchronous RPC
firewall	throwing an exception
Hypertext Transfer Protocol (HTTP)	

SELF-REVIEW EXERCISES

23.1 State whether each of the following is *true* or *false*. If *false*, explain why.

    a) SOAP is a technology for facilitating data transfer across a network.

    b) SOAP must be bound to HTTP in order to work.

    c) In order to communicate with SOAP, software systems must have the same distributed object architecture.

    d) The body of a SOAP message can contain a Remote Procedure Call.

    e) Anybody can publish a BizTalk Schema.

    f) BizTalk does not support SOAP.

    g) The **body** element in a SOAP document must be a child of the **header** element.

    h) When an intermediary program receives a header element, it must forward it to the next recipient.

    i) A BizTalk Server can process incoming and outgoing BizTalk messages.

    j) The BizTalk Framework specifies a standard tag set for its messages.

23.2   Fill in the blanks in each of the following statements:

    a) A SOAP RPC requires the name of the method being called, its parameters and _____.

    b) The _____ element describes the content, recipient and processing requirements of a SOAP message.

    c) SOAP can pass through most firewalls because _____ is its transport mechanism.

    d) SOAP RPCs use the HTTP _____ model.

    e) The _____ provides a standard tag set for BizTalk messages.

    f) The _____ filters and processes BizTalk messages.

    g) Business processes can be automated using _____.

    h) BizTalk messages can be sent in the form of _____ objects.

    i) The BizTalk Library stores _____.

ANSWERS TO SELF-REVIEW EXERCISES

23.1   a) True. b) False. SOAP can be bound to another protocol, and it does not have to be bound to any protocol. c) False. SOAP is platform independent. d) True. e) True. f) False. g) False. It must be the child of the **envelope** element. h) False. It must not forward it. i) True. j) True.

23.2   a) the processing requirements of the message. b) **envelope**. c) HTTP. d) request–response. e) BizTalk Framework. f) BizTalk Server. g) BizTalk Orchestration. h) SOAP. i) schema.

EXERCISES

23.3   Write a server-side class with two methods that can determine if a number is prime or not and if two given numbers are twin primes or not. Deploy a service that would enable clients to use these methods over SOAP. For the client side, write a Java program that can make SOAP RPC invoke these methods. The user should be able to find out if a given number is prime or not and also if two given numbers are twin primes or not. (*Hint:* To deploy two methods, separate them with a space in the SOAP administration tool.)

23.4   Write a server-side class with a **sort** method that can sort given numbers. Write a client-side program that can make SOAP RPC invoke the **sort** method by sending a set of unsorted numbers. Display the results of sorting on the client side.

23.5   Visit **schemas.biztalk.org/intelisys_com/scf6lunl.xml** to find a BizTalk schema specific to manufacturing firms (developed by Intelisys Electronic Commerce, LLC). The schema can be used to place an order to a supplier. Write an XML document that places an order for a multimedia kit. Validate the document with the BizTalk schema.

24

Bonus Chapter: Introduction to Scripting with VBScript®

Objectives

- To become familiar with the VBScript language.
- To use VBScript keywords, operators and functions to write client-side scripts.
- To be able to write **Sub** and **Function** procedures.
- To be able to create and use arrays and dynamic arrays.
- To be able to use VBScript's string-processing functions.

When they call the roll in the Senate, the senators do not know whether to answer "present" or "not guilty."
Theodore Roosevelt

While I nodded, nearly napping,
suddenly there came a tapping,
As of someone gently rapping, rapping at my chamber door.
Edgar Allan Poe

Basic research is what I am doing when I don't know what I am doing.
Wernher von Braun

A problem is a chance for you to do your best.
Duke Ellington

Everything comes to him who hustles while he waits.
Thomas Alva Edison

24.1 Introduction

[*Note: This Chapter is a bonus chapter that is intended to support the discussion of Active Server Pages in Chapters 15 and 25. We anticipate that a large number of readers are already familiar with HTML and JavaScript, but not with VBScript. In this chapter, we introduce client-side VBScript for use in HTML documents. When possible, we compare VBScript features with JavaScript features. By design, this chapter does not use XML.*]

Visual Basic Script (VBScript) is a subset of Microsoft Visual Basic® used in World Wide Web HTML documents to enhance the functionality of a Web page displayed in a Web browser. Microsoft's Internet Explorer Web browser contains a *VBScript scripting engine* (i.e., an interpreter) that executes VBScript code.

VBScript is particularly valuable when used with Microsoft Web servers to create *Active Server Pages (ASPs)*, a technology that allows a server-side script to create dynamic content that is sent to the client's browser. Although other scripting languages can be used, VBScript is the de facto language for ASP. You will learn about ASP in Chapter 25.

24.2 Operators

VBScript is a case-insensitive language that provides arithmetic operators, logical operators, concatenation operators, comparison operators and relational operators. VBScript's arithmetic operators (Fig. 24.1) are similar to the JavaScript arithmetic operators. Two major differences between them are the *division operator*, \, which returns an integer result, and the *exponentiation operator*, ^, which raises a value to a power. [*Note:* See the Appendix, "Operator Precedence Charts," for a list of VBScript operators and their precedences.]

Figure 24.2 lists VBScript's comparison operators. Only the symbols for the equality operator and the inequality operator are different in JavaScript. In VBScript, these comparison operators may also be used to compare strings.

The VBScript logical operators are **And** (logical AND), **Or** (logical OR), **Not** (logical negation), **Imp** (logical implication), **Xor** (exclusive OR) and **Eqv** (logical equivalence). Figure 24.3 shows truth tables for these logical operators. [*Note:* Despite the mixture of case in keywords, functions, etc., VBScript is not case sensitive: Uppercase and lowercase letters are treated the same, except, as we will see, in *character string constants* (also called *character string literals*).]

VBScript provides the *plus sign*, +, and *ampersand*, **&**, operators for string concatenation as follows:

```
s1 = "Pro"
s2 = "gram"
s3 = s1 & s2
```

or

```
s3 = s1 + s2
```

VBScript operation	Arithmetic operator	Algebraic expression	VBScript expression
Addition	+	$x + y$	`x + y`
Subtraction	–	$z - 8$	`z - 8`
Multiplication	*	yb	`y * b`
Division (floating point)	/	$v \div u$ or $\dfrac{v}{u}$	`v / u`
Division (integer)	\	none	`v \ u`
Exponentiation	^	q^p	`q ^ p`
Negation	–	$-e$	`-e`
Modulus	**Mod**	$q \bmod r$	`q Mod r`

Fig. 24.1   Arithmetic operators.

Standard algebraic equality operator or relational operator	VBScript comparison operator	Example of VBScript condition	Meaning of VBScript condition
=	=	`d = g`	**d** is equal to **g**
≠	<>	`s <> r`	**s** is not equal to **r**
>	>	`y > x`	**y** is greater than **x**
<	<	`p < m`	**p** is less than **m**
≥	>=	`c >= z`	**c** is greater than or equal to **z**
≤	<=	`m <= s`	**m** is less than or equal to **s**

Fig. 24.2   Comparison operators.

Truth tables for VBScript Logical Operators	
Logical And:	*Logical Or:*
`True And True = True`	`True Or True = True`
`True And False = False`	`True Or False = True`
`False And True = False`	`False Or True = True`
`False And False = False`	`False Or False = False`
Logical Imp:	*Logical Eqv:*
`True Imp True = True`	`True Eqv True = True`
`True Imp False = False`	`True Eqv False = False`
`False Imp True = True`	`False Eqv True = False`
`False Imp False = True`	`False Eqv False = True`
Logical Xor:	*Logical Not:*
`True Xor True = False`	`Not True = False`
`True Xor False = True`	`Not False = True`
`False Xor True = True`	
`False Xor False = False`	

Fig. 24.3   Truth tables for VBScript logical operators.

Performance Tip 24.1

VBScript logical operators do not use "short-circuit" evaluation. Both conditions are always evaluated.

The ampersand is more formally called the *string concatenation operator*. The above statements would concatenate (or append) **s2** to the right of **s1** to create an entirely new string, **s3**, containing **"Program"**.

If both operands of the concatenation operator are strings, these two operators can be used interchangeably; however, if the **+** operator is used in an expression consisting of varying data types, there can be a problem. For example, consider the statement

```
s1 = "hello" + 22
```

VBScript first tries to convert the string **"hello"** to a number and then add **22** to it. The string **"hello"** cannot be converted to a number, so a type-mismatch error occurs at runtime. For this reason, the **&** operator should be used for string concatenation.

Testing and Debugging Tip 24.1

*Always use the ampersand (**&**) operator for string concatenation.*

24.3 Data Types and Control Structures

VBScript has only one data type—*variant*—that is capable of storing different types of data (e.g., strings, integers, floating-point numbers, etc.). The data types (or *variant subtypes*) a variant stores are listed in Fig. 24.4. VBScript interprets a variant in a manner that is suitable to the type of data it contains. For example, if a variant contains numeric information, it will be treated as a number; if it contains string information, it will be treated as a string.

Subtype	Range/Description
Boolean	**True** or **False**
Byte	Integer in the range 0 to 255
Currency	–922337203685477.5808 to 922337203685477.5807
Date/Time	1 January 100 to 31 December 9999 0:00:00 to 23:59:59
Double	–1.79769313486232E308 to –4.94065645841247E–324 (negative) 1.79769313486232E308 to 4.94065645841247E–324 (positive)
Empty	Uninitialized. This value is 0 for numeric types (e.g., double), **False** for booleans and the *empty string* (i.e., **""**) for strings.
Integer	–32768 to 32767
Long	–2147483648 to 2147483647
Object	Any object type
Single	–3.402823E38 to –1.401298E–45 (negative) 3.402823E38 to 1.401298E–45 (positive)
String	0 to ~2000000000 characters.

Fig. 24.4 Some VBScript variant subtypes.

Software Engineering Observation 24.1

Because all variables are of type variant, *the programmer does not specify a data type when declaring a variable in VBScript.*

Variable names cannot be keywords and must begin with a letter. The maximum length of a variable name is 255 characters, and the name must contain only letters, digits (0–9) and underscores. Variables can be declared simply by using their name in the VBScript code. The statement **Option Explicit** can be used to force all variables to be declared before they are used.

Common Programming Error 24.1

Attempting to declare a variable name that does not begin with a letter is an error.

Testing and Debugging Tip 24.2

Forcing all variables to be declared, by using **Option Explicit**, *can help eliminate various kinds of subtle errors.*

Common Programming Error 24.2

If a variable name is misspelled (when **Option Explicit** *is not used), a new variable is declared, usually resulting in an error.*

VBScript provides control structures (Fig. 24.5) for controlling program execution. Many of the control structures provide the same capabilities as their JavaScript counterparts. Syntactically, every VBScript control structure ends with one or more keywords (e.g., **End If**, **Loop**, etc.). Keywords, not curly braces (i.e., **{}**, as in JavaScript), delimit a control structure's body.

JavaScript Control Structure	VBScript Control Structure Equivalent
sequence	sequence
if	If/Then/End If
if/else	If/Then/Else/End If
while	While/Wend or Do While/Loop
for	For/Next
do/while	Do/Loop While
switch	Select Case/End Select
none	Do Until/Loop
none	Do/Loop Until

Fig. 24.5   Comparing VBScript control structures with JavaScript control structures.

The **If/Then/End If** and **If/Then/Else/End If** behave identically to their Java-Script counterparts. VBScript's **If/Then/Else/End If** uses a different syntax than JavaScript's version, because it includes keyword **ElseIf** (Fig. 24.6).

Common Programming Error 24.3

*Writing an **If** control structure that does not contain keyword **Then** is an error.*

Notice that VBScript does not use a statement terminator like the semicolon (**;**) in JavaScript. Unlike in JavaScript, placing parentheses around conditions is optional in VBScript. A condition evaluates to **True** if the variant subtype is boolean **True** or if the variant subtype is considered to be nonzero. A condition evaluates to **False** if the variant subtype is boolean **False** or if the variant subtype is considered to be zero.

VBScript's **Select Case/End Select** structure provides all the functionality of JavaScript's **switch** structure, and more (Fig. 24.7).

Notice that the **Select Case/End Select** structure does not require the use of a statement like **break**. One **Case** cannot accidentally run into another. The VBScript **Select Case/End Select** structure is equivalent to VBScript's **If/Then/Else/End If** multiple-selection structure. The only difference is syntax: Any variant subtype can be used with the **Select Case/End Select** structure.

JavaScript	VBScript
1 if (s == t) 2 u = s + t; 3 else if (s > t) 4 u = r; 5 else 6 u = n;	1 If s = t Then 2 u = s + t 3 ElseIf s > t Then 4 u = r 5 Else 6 u = n 7 End If

Fig. 24.6   Comparing JavaScript's **if** structure with VBScript's **If** structure.

JavaScript	VBScript
| ```
1   switch ( x ) {
2      case 1:
3         alert("1");
4         break;
5       case 2:
6          alert("2");
7          break;
8      default:
9          alert("?");
10  }
``` | ```
1   Select Case x
2       Case 1
3          Call MsgBox("1")
4       Case 2
5          Call MsgBox("2")
6       Case Else
7          Call MsgBox("?")
8   End Select
``` |

Fig. 24.7   Comparing JavaScript's **switch** with VBScript's **Select Case**.

VBScript's *While/Wend* repetition structure and *Do While/Loop* behave identically to JavaScript's **while** repetition structure. VBScript's *Do/Loop While* structure behaves identically to JavaScript's **do/while** repetition structure.

VBScript contains two additional repetition structures, *Do Until/Loop* and *Do/Loop Until*, that do not have direct JavaScript equivalents. Figure 24.8 shows the closest equivalent to VBScript's **Do Until/Loop** structure: JavaScript's **while** structure. The **Do Until/Loop** structure loops until its condition becomes **True**. In this example, the loop terminates when **x** becomes 10. We used the condition **! (x == 10)** in JavaScript here, so both control structures have a test to determine whether **x** is **10**. The JavaScript **while** structure loops while **x** is not equal to 10 (i.e., until **x** becomes 10).

Figure 24.9 shows the closest equivalent to VBScript's **Do/Loop Until** structure: JavaScript's **do/while** structure. The **Do/Loop Until** structure loops until its condition becomes **True**. In this example, the loop terminates when **x** becomes 10. Once again, we used the condition **! (x == 10)** in JavaScript here, so both control structures have a test to determine if **x** is **10**. The JavaScript **do/while** structure loops while **x** is not equal to 10 (i.e., until **x** becomes 10).

Notice that these **Do Until** repetition structures iterate until the condition becomes **True**. VBScript's *For* repetition structure behaves differently than JavaScript's **for** repetition structure. Consider the side-by-side comparison in Fig. 24.10.

Unlike JavaScript's **for** repetition structure's condition, VBScript's **For** repetition structure's condition cannot be changed during the loop's iteration. In Fig.24.1, the JavaScript **for** loop would iterate exactly two times, because the condition is evaluated on each iteration. The VBScript **For** loop would iterate exactly eight times, because the condition is fixed as **1 To 8**—even though the value of **x** is changing in the body. VBScript **For** loops may also use the optional **Step** keyword to indicate an increment or decrement. By default, **For** loops increment in units of 1. Figure 24.11 shows a **For** loop that begins at **2** and counts to **20** in **Step**s of **2**.

The *Exit Do* statement, when executed in a **Do While/Loop**, **Do/Loop While**, **Do Until/Loop** or **Do/Loop Until**, causes immediate exit from that structure. The fact that a **Do While/Loop** may contain **Exit Do** is the only difference, other than syntax, between **Do While/Loop** and **While/Wend**. Statement *Exit For* causes immediate exit from the **For/Next** structure. With **Exit Do** and **Exit For**, program execution continues with the first statement after the exited repetition structure.

Common Programming Error 24.4

*Attempting to use **Exit Do** or **Exit For** to exit a **While/Wend** repetition structure is an error.*

Common Programming Error 24.5

*Attempting to use a relational operator in a **For/Next** loop (e.g., **For x = 1 < 10**) is an error.*

Common Programming Error 24.6

*Attempting to place the name of a **For** repetition structures's control variable after **Next** is an error. .*

JavaScript	VBScript
1 while (!(x == 10)) 2 ++x;	1 Do Until x = 10 2 x = x + 1 3 Loop

Fig. 24.8   Comparing JavaScript's **while** with VBScript's **Do Until**.

JavaScript	VBScript
1 do { 2 ++x; 3 } while (!(x == 10));	1 Do 2 x = x + 1 3 Loop Until x = 10

Fig. 24.9   Comparing JavaScript's **do/while** with VBScript's **Do Loop/Until**.

JavaScript	VBScript
1 x = 8; 2 for (y = 1; y < x; y++) 3 x /= 2;	1 x = 8 2 For y = 1 To x 3 x = x \ 2 4 Next

Fig. 24.10 Comparing JavaScript's **for** with VBScript's **For**.

```
1   ' VBScript
2   For y = 2 To 20 Step 2
3       Call MsgBox( "y = " & y )
4   Next
```

Fig. 24.11 Using keyword **Step** in VBScript's **For** repetition structure.

24.4 VBScript Functions

VBScript provides several functions, many of which are summarized in this section. We provide an overview of variant functions, math functions, functions for interacting with the user, formatting functions and functions for obtaining information about the interpreter.

Figure 24.12 summarizes several functions that allow the programmer to determine which subtype is currently stored in a variant. VBScript provides function *IsEmpty* to determine if the variant has ever been initialized by the programmer. If **IsEmpty** returns **True**, the variant has not been initialized by the programmer.

VBScript math functions allow the programmer to perform common mathematical calculations. Figure 24.13 summarizes some VBScript math functions. Note that trigonometric functions, such as **Cos**, **Sin**, etc., take arguments expressed in radians. To convert from degrees to radians, use the formula *radians = (degrees × π) / 180*.

VBScript provides two functions, *InputBox* and *MsgBox*, for interacting with the user. Function **InputBox** displays a dialog in which the user can input data. For example, the statement

```
intValue = InputBox( "Enter an integer", "Input Box", , _
                     1000, 1000 )
```

displays an *input dialog* (as shown in Fig. 24.15) containing the prompt **"Enter an integer"** and the caption **"Input Box"** at position *(1000, 1000)* on the screen. VBScript coordinates are measured in units of *twips* (1440 twips equal 1 inch). Position *(1000, 1000)* is relative to the upper-left corner of the screen, which is position *(0, 0)*. On the screen, *x* coordinates increase from left to right, and *y* coordinates increase from top to bottom.

VBScript functions often take *optional arguments* (i.e., arguments that programmers can pass if they wish or that can be omitted). Notice, in the preceding call to **InputBox**, the consecutive commas (between **"Input Box"** and **1000**). These commas indicate that an optional argument is being omitted. In this particular case, the optional argument corresponds to a filename for a help file—a feature we do not wish to use in this particular call to **InputBox**. Before using a VBScript function, check the VBScript documentation:

Function	Variant subtype returned	Description
IsArray	Boolean	Returns **True** if the variant subtype is an array, and **False** otherwise.
IsDate	Boolean	Returns **True** if the variant subtype is a date or time, and **False** otherwise.
IsEmpty	Boolean	Returns **True** if the variant subtype is **Empty** (i.e., the variant has not been explicitly initialized by the programmer), and **False** otherwise.
IsNumeric	Boolean	Returns **True** if the variant subtype is numeric, and **False** otherwise.

Fig. 24.12 Some variant functions (part 1 of 2).

Function	Variant subtype returned	Description
IsObject	Boolean	Returns **True** if the variant subtype is an object, and **False** otherwise.
TypeName	String	Returns a string that provides subtype information. Some strings returned are **"Byte"**, **"Integer"**, **"Long"**, **"Single"**, **"Double"**, **"Date"**, **"Currency"**, **"String"**, **"Boolean"** and **"Empty"**.
VarType	Integer	Returns a value indicating the subtype (e.g., **0** for **Empty**, **2** for integer, **3** for long, **4** for single, **5** for double, **6** for currency, **7** for date/time, **8** for string, **9** for object, etc.).

Fig. 24.12 Some variant functions (part 2 of 2).

Function	Description	Example
Abs(x)	Absolute value of **x**	**Abs(-7)** is **7** **Abs(0)** is **0** **Abs(76)** is **76**
Atn(x)	Trigonometric arctangent of **x** (in radians)	**Atn(1)*4** is **3.14159265358979**
Cos(x)	Trigonometric cosine of **x** (in radians)	**Cos(0)** is **1**
Exp(x)	Exponential function e^x	**Exp(1.0)** is **2.71828** **Exp(2.0)** is **7.38906**
Int(x)	Returns the whole-number part of **x**. **Int** rounds to the next smallest number.	**Int(-5.3)** is **-6** **Int(0.893)** is **0** **Int(76.45)** is **76**
Fix(x)	Returns the whole-number part of **x**. (*Note*: **Fix** and **Int** are different. When **x** is negative, **Int** rounds to the next-smallest number, while **Fix** rounds to the next-largest number.)	**Fix(-5.3)** is **-5** **Fix(0.893)** is **0** **Fix(76.45)** is **76**
Log(x)	Natural logarithm of **x** (base e)	**Log(2.718282)** is **1.0** **Log(7.389056)** is **2.0**
Rnd()	Returns a pseudorandom floating-point number in the range **0 ≤ Rnd < 1**. Call function ***Randomize*** once before calling **Rnd** to get a different sequence of random numbers each time the program is run.	**Call Randomize** **...** **z = Rnd()**

Fig. 24.13 VBScript math functions (part 1 of 2).

Function	Description	Example
Round(x, y)	Rounds **x** to **y** decimal places. If **y** is omitted, **x** is returned as an **Integer**.	Round(4.844) is 5 Round(5.7839, 2) is 5.78
Sgn(x)	Sign of **x**	Sgn(-1988) is –1 Sgn(0) is 0 Sgn(3.3) is 1
Sin(x)	Trigonometric sine of **x** (in radians)	Sin(0) is 0
Sqr(x)	Square root of **x**	Sqr(900.0) is 30.0 Sqr(9.0) is 3.0
Tan(x)	Trigonometric tangent of **x** (in radians)	Tan(0) is 0

Fig. 24.13 VBScript math functions (part 2 of 2).

msdn.microsoft.com/scripting/default.htm?/scripting/vbscript

to determine whether the function allows for optional arguments.

The *underscore character*, _, is VBScript's *line-continuation character*. A statement cannot extend beyond the current line without using this character. A statement may use as many line-continuation characters as necessary.

Common Programming Error 24.7

Splitting a statement over several lines without the line-continuation character is an error.

Common Programming Error 24.8

Placing anything, including comments, after a line-continuation character is an error.

When called, function **MsgBox** displays a *message dialog* (a sample of which is shown in Fig. 24.15). For example, the statement

```
Call MsgBox( "VBScript is fun!", , "Results" )
```

displays a message dialog containing the string **"VBScript is fun!"**, with **"Results"** in the title bar. Although not used here, the optional argument allows the programmer to customize the **MsgBox**'s buttons (e.g., **OK**, **Yes**, etc.) and icon (e.g., question mark, exclamation point, etc.); see the VBScript documentation for more information on these features. The preceding statement could also have been written as

```
MsgBox "VBScript is fun!", , "Results"
```

which behaves identically to the version of the statement that explicitly uses **Call**. In VBScript, function calls that wrap arguments in parentheses must be preceded with keyword *Call*, unless the function call is assigning a value to a variable, as in

```
a = Abs( z )
```

We prefer the more formal syntax that uses **Call** and parentheses to clearly indicate a function call.

VBScript provides formatting functions for currency values, dates, times, numbers and percentages. Figure 24.14 summarizes these formatting functions.

Although they are not discussed in this chapter, VBScript provides many functions for manipulating dates and times. Such manipulations include adding dates, subtracting dates and parsing dates. Consult the VBScript documentation for a list of these functions.

VBScript also provides functions for getting information about the scripting engine (i.e., the VBScript interpreter). These functions are ***ScriptEngine*** (which returns "***JScript***", "***VBScript***" or "***VBA***"), ***ScriptEngineBuildVersion*** (which returns the current *build version*—i.e., the identification number for the current release), ***ScriptEngineMajorVersion*** (which returns the major version number for the script engine) and ***ScriptEngineMinorVersion*** (which returns the minor release number). For example, the expression

```
ScriptEngine() & ", " & ScriptEngineBuildVersion() & ", " _
& ScriptEngineMajorVersion() & ", " & _
ScriptEngineMajorVersion()
```

evaluates to **"VBScript, 5207, 5, 5"** (where the numbers are the build version, major version and minor version, respectively, of the script engine at the time of this writing).

Testing and Debugging Tip 24.3

*VBScript functions **ScriptEngine**, **ScriptEngineBuildVersion**, **Script-EngineMajorVersion** and **ScriptEngineMinorVersion** are useful if you are experiencing difficulty with the scripting engine and need to report information about the scripting engine to Microsoft.*

Portability Tip 24.1

*VBScript functions **ScriptEngine**, **ScriptEngineBuildVersion**, **Script-EngineMajorVersion** and **ScriptEngineMinorVersion** can be used to determine whether the browser's version of the script engine is different from the version of the script engine you used to develop the page. Older script engines do not support the latest VB-Script features.*

24.5 VBScript Example Programs

In this section, we present several complete VBScript "live-code" programs and show the screen inputs and outputs produced as the programs execute. The HTML document of Fig. 24.15 includes VBScript code that enables users to click on a button to display an input dialog in which they can type an integer to be added into a running total. When the input dialog's **OK** button is clicked on, a message dialog is displayed with a message indicating the number that was entered and the total of all the numbers entered so far.

In Line 8, the HTML tag **script** sets the **language** attribute to **VBScript**. This tag tells the browser to use its built-in VBScript interpreter to interpret the script code. Notice the HTML comment tags on lines 9, and 22 which appear to "comment out" the VBScript code.

If the browser understands VBScript, these HTML comments are ignored, and the VBScript is interpreted. If the browser does not understand VBScript, the HTML comments prevent the VBScript code from being displayed as text.

Function	Description
`FormatCurrency`	Returns a string formatted according to the local machine's currency **Regional Settings** (in the **Control Panel**). For example, the call `FormatCurrency("-1234.789")` returns `"($1,234.79)"`, and the call `FormatCurrency(123456.789)` returns `"$123,456.79"`. Note the rounding to the right of the decimal place.
`FormatDateTime`	Returns a string formatted according to the local machine's date/time **Regional Settings** (in the **Control Panel**). For example, the call `FormatDateTime(Now, vbLongDate)` returns the current date in the format `"Wednesday, September 01, 1999"`, and the call `FormatDateTime(Now, vbShortTime)` returns the current time in the format `"17:26"`. Function *Now* returns the local machine's time and date. Constant *vbLongDate* indicates that the day of the week, month, day and year is displayed. Constant *vbShortTime* indicates that the time is displayed in 24-hour format. Consult the VBScript documentation for additional constants that specify other date and time formats.
`FormatNumber`	Returns a string formatted according to the number **Regional Settings** (in the **Control Panel**) on the local machine. For example, the call `FormatNumber("3472435")` returns `"3,472,435.00"`, and the call `FormatNumber(-123456.789)` returns `"-123,456.79"`. Note the rounding to the right of the decimal place.
`FormatPercent`	Returns a string formatted as a percentage. For example, the call `FormatPercent(".789")` returns `"78.90%"`, and the call `FormatPercent(0.45)` returns `"45.00%"`.

Fig. 24.14 Some VBScript formatting functions.

```
1   <!DOCTYPE HTML PUBLIC "-//W3C//DTD HTML 4.0 Transitional//EN">
2   <html>
3   <!--Fig. 24.15: addition.html -->
4
5   <head>
6   <title>Our first VBScript</title>
7
8   <script language = "VBScript">
9   <!--
10     Option Explicit
11     Dim intTotal
12
13     Sub cmdAdd_OnClick()
14         Dim intValue
15
16         intValue = InputBox("Enter an integer", "Input Box", , _
17                         1000, 1000)
```

Fig. 24.15 Adding integers on a Web page using VBScript (part 1 of 2).

```
18              intTotal = CInt( intTotal ) + CInt( intValue )
19              Call MsgBox("You entered " & intValue & _
20                          "; total so far is " & intTotal, , "Results")
21          End Sub
22      -->
23      </script>
24      </head>
25
26      <body>
27      Click the button to add an integer to the total.
28          <hr />
29          <form>
30              <input name = "cmdAdd" type = "BUTTON"
31                      value = "Click Here to Add to the Total">
32          </form>
33      </body>
34      </html>
```

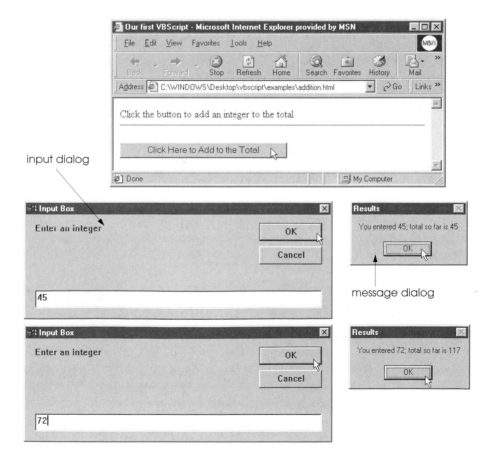

input dialog

message dialog

Fig. 24.15 Adding integers on a Web page using VBScript (part 2 of 2).

Portability Tip 24.2

Always place client-side VBScript code inside HTML comments to prevent the code from being displayed as text in browsers that do not understand VBScript.

Line 10 uses the **Option Explicit** statement to force all variables in the VBScript code to be declared. Statement **Option Explicit**, if present, must be the first statement in the VBScript code. Line 11 declares variant variable **intTotal**, which is visible to all procedures within the script. Variables declared outside of procedures are called *script variables*.

Common Programming Error 24.9

*Placing VBScript code before the **Option Explicit** statement is an error.*

Lines 13–21 define a *procedure* (i.e., VBScript's equivalent of a function in JavaScript) called **OnClick** for the **cmdAdd** button. VBScript procedures that do not return a value begin with the keyword **Sub** (line 13) and end with the keywords **End Sub** (line 21). We will discuss VBScript procedures that return values later in this chapter. Line 14 declares the *local variable* **intValue**. Variables declared within a VBScript procedure are visible only within that procedure's body. Procedures that perform event handling (such as the **cmdAdd_OnClick** procedure in lines 13–21) are more properly called *event procedures*.

Line 16 calls the function **InputBox** to display an input dialog. The value entered into the input dialog is assigned to the **intValue** variable and is treated by VBScript as a string subtype. When using variants, conversion functions are often necessary to ensure that you are using the proper type. Line 18 calls VBScript function **CInt** twice to convert from the string subtype to the integer subtype. VBScript also provides conversion functions **CBool**, for converting to the boolean subtype; **CByte**, for converting to the byte subtype; **CCur**, for converting to the currency subtype; **CDate**, for converting to the date/time subtype; **CDbl**, for converting to the double subtype; **CLng**, for converting to the long subtype; **CSng**, for converting to the single subtype, and **CStr**, for converting to the string subtype. Lines 19 and 20 display a message dialog indicating the last value input and the running total.

VBScript provides many predefined constants for use in your VBScript code. The constant categories include color constants, comparison constants (to specify how values are compared), date/time constants, date format constants, drive type constants, file attribute constants, file I/O constants, **MsgBox** constants, special folder constants, string constants, **VarType** constants (to help determine the type stored in a variable) and miscellaneous, other constants. VBScript constants usually begin with the prefix **vb**. For a list of VBScript constants, see the VBScript documentation. You can also create your own constants by using keyword **Const**, as in

```
Const PI = 3.14159
```

Figure 24.16 provides another VBScript example. The HTML form provides a **SELECT** component, to allow the user to select a Web site from a list of sites. When the selection is made, the new Web site is displayed in the browser. Lines 30–35

```
<script for = "SiteSelector" event = "ONCHANGE"
        language = "VBScript">
<!--
    Document.Location = Document.Forms( 0 ).SiteSelector.Value
-->
</script>
```

specify a VBScript. In such code, the **<script>** tag's **for** attribute indicates the HTML component on which the script operates (**SiteSelector**), attribute **event** indicates the event to which the script responds (**OnChange**, which occurs when the user makes a selection) and attribute **language** specifies the scripting language (**VBScript**). Line 33

```
Document.Location = Document.Forms( 0 ).SiteSelector.Value
```

causes the browser to change to the selected location. This line uses Internet Explorer's **Document** object to change the location. The **Document** object's *Location* property specifies the URL of the page to display. The expression **SiteSelector.Value** gets the **value** of the selected **option** in the **select**. When the assignment is performed, Internet Explorer automatically loads and displays the Web page for the selected location.

```
1   <!DOCTYPE HTML PUBLIC "-//W3C//DTD HTML 4.0 Transitional//EN">
2   <html>
3   <!-- Fig. 24.16: site.html -->
4
5   <head>
6      <title>Select a site to browse</title>
7   </head>
8
9   <body>
10  Select a site to browse<P>
11  <hr />
12  <form>
13  <select name = "SiteSelector" size = "1">
14
15     <option value = "http://www.deitel.com">
16        Deitel & Associates, Inc.
17     </option>
18
19     <option value = "http://www.prenhall.com">
20        Prentice Hall
21     </option>
22
23     <option value = "http://www.phptr.com/phptrinteractive">
24        Prentice Hall Interactive
25     </option>
26
27  </select>
28
29  <!-- VBScript code -->
30  <script for = "SiteSelector" event = "ONCHANGE"
31          language = "VBScript">
```

Fig. 24.16 Using VBScript code to respond to an event (part 1 of 2).

```
32   <!--
33       Document.Location = Document.Forms( 0 ).SiteSelector.Value
34   -->
35   </script>
36   </form>
37   </body>
38   </html>
```

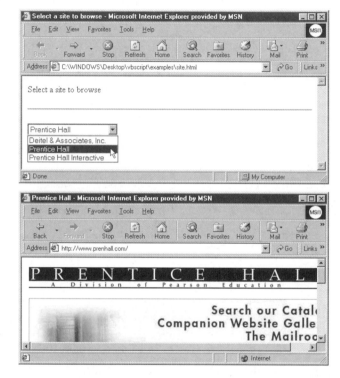

Fig. 24.16 Using VBScript code to respond to an event (part 2 of 2).

Fig. 24.17 uses two procedures: **Minimum**, to determine the smallest of three numbers; and **OddEven**, to determine if the smallest number is odd or even.

Lines 12–13 are VBScript single-line comments. Comments are placed in VBScript code by using either a single quote (**'**) or the keyword **Rem** (for *remark*) before the comment. [*Note*: Keyword **Rem** can be used only at the beginning of a line of VBScript code.]

```
1    <!DOCTYPE HTML PUBLIC "-//W3C//DTD HTML 4.0 Transitional//EN">
2    <html>
3    <!--Fig. 24.17: minimum.html -->
4
5    <head>
6    <title>Using VBScript Procedures</title>
7
8    <script language = "VBScript">
```

Fig. 24.17 Program that determines the smallest of three numbers (part 1 of 3).

```
9    <!--
10      Option Explicit
11
12      ' Find the minimum value. Assume that first value is
13      ' the smallest.
14      Function Minimum( min, a, b )
15
16         If a < min Then
17            min = a
18         End If
19
20         If b < min Then
21            min = b
22         End If
23
24         Minimum = min      ' Return value
25      End Function
26
27      Sub OddEven( n )
28         If n Mod 2 = 0 Then
29            Call MsgBox( n & " is the smallest and is even" )
30         Else
31            Call MsgBox( n & " is the smallest and is odd" )
32         End If
33      End Sub
34
35      Sub cmdButton_OnClick()
36         Dim number1, number2, number3, smallest
37
38         ' Convert each input to Long subtype
39         number1 = CLng( Document.Forms( 0 ).txtBox1.Value )
40         number2 = CLng( Document.Forms( 0 ).txtBox2.Value )
41         number3 = CLng( Document.Forms( 0 ).txtBox3.Value )
42
43         smallest = Minimum( number1, number2, number3 )
44         Call OddEven( smallest )
45      End Sub
46    -->
47    </script>
48    </head>
49
50    <body>
51    <form><p>Enter a number
52    <input type = "text" name = "txtBox1" size = "5" value = "0"></p>
53    <p>Enter a number
54    <input type = "text" name = "txtBox2" size = "5" value = "0"></p>
55    <p>Enter a number
56    <input type = "text" name = "txtBox3" size = "5" value = "0"></p>
57    <br /><input type = "BUTTON" name = "cmdButton" value = "Enter">
58
59    </form>
60    </body>
61    </html>
```

Fig. 24.17 Program that determines the smallest of three numbers (part 2 of 3).

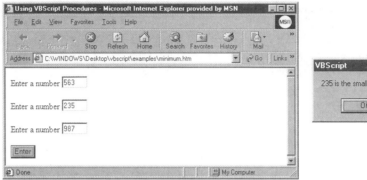

Fig. 24.17 Program that determines the smallest of three numbers (part 3 of 3).

Good Programming Practice 24.1

*VBScript programmers use the single-quote character for comments. The use of **Rem** is considered archaic.*

Lines 14–25 define the programmer-defined procedure **Minimum**. VBScript procedures that return a value are delimited with the keywords ***Function*** (line 14) and ***End Function*** (line 25). **Minimum** determines the smallest of its three arguments by using **If/Then/Else** structures. A value is returned from a **Function** procedure by assigning a value to the **Function** procedure name (line 24). A **Function** procedure can return only one value.

Procedure **OddEven** (lines 27–33) takes one argument and displays a message dialog indicating the smallest value and whether or not it is odd or even. The modulus operator **Mod** is used to determine whether the number is odd or even. Because the data stored in the variant variable can be viewed as a number, VBScript performs any conversions between subtypes implicitly before performing the modulus operation. The advantage of placing these procedures in the **HEAD** is that other VBScripts can call them.

Lines 35–45 define an event procedure for handling **cmdButton**'s **OnClick** event. The statement

```
smallest = Minimum( number1, number2, number3 )
```

calls **Minimum**, passing **number1**, **number2** and **number3** to it as arguments. Parameters **min**, **a** and **b** are declared in **Minimum** to receive the values of **number1**, **number2** and **number3**, respectively. Procedure **OddEven** is passed the smallest number, on line 44.

Common Programming Error 24.10

Declaring a variable in a procedure body with the same name as a parameter variable is an error.

One last word about procedures: VBScript provides statements **Exit Sub** and **Exit Function** for exiting **Sub** procedures and **Function** procedures, respectively. Control is returned to the caller, and the next statement in sequence after the call is executed.

24.6 Arrays

Arrays are data structures consisting of related data items of the same type. A *fixed-size array*'s size does not change during program execution; a *dynamic array*'s size can change during execution. A dynamic array is also called a *redimmable array* (short for a "redimensionable" array). Individual array elements are referred to by giving the array name followed by the element's position number in parentheses, ( ). The first array element is at position zero.

The position number contained within parentheses is more formally called an *index*. An index must be in the range 0 to 2,147,483,648. (Any floating-point number is rounded to the nearest whole number.)

The declaration

```
Dim numbers(2)
```

instructs the interpreter to reserve three elements for array **numbers**. The value **2** defines the *upper bound* (i.e., the highest valid index) of **numbers**. The *lower bound* (the lowest valid index) of **numbers** is **0**. When an upper bound is specified in the declaration, a fixed-size array is created.

Common Programming Error 24.11

Attempting to access an index that is less than the lower bound or greater than the upper bound is an error.

The programmer can explicitly initialize an array with assignment statements. For example, the lines

```
numbers(0)  = 77
numbers(1)  = 68
numbers(2)  = 55
```

initialize **numbers**. Repetition statements can also be used to initialize arrays. For example, the statements

```
Dim h( 11 ), x, i
For x = 0 To 30 Step 3
   h(i) = CInt( x )
   i = CInt( i ) + 1
Next
```

initialize the elements of **h** to the values 0, 3, 6, 9, …, 30.

The program in Fig. 24.18 declares, initializes and prints three arrays. Two of the arrays are fixed-size arrays, and one of the arrays is a dynamic array. The program introduces function **UBound**, which returns the upper bound of the array (i.e., the highest numbered index). [*Note:* VBScript does provide function **LBound**, for determining the lowest numbered index. However, the current version of VBScript does not permit the lowest numbered index to be nonzero.]

Testing and Debugging Tip 24.4

*Arrays' upper bounds can vary. Use function **UBound** to ensure that each index is in range (i.e., within the bounds of the array).*

Lines 12–21 define **Sub** procedure **DisplayArray**. VBScript procedures are *Public* by default; therefore, they are accessible to scripts on other Web pages. Keyword **Public** can be used explicitly to indicate that a procedure is public. A procedure can be marked as *Private* to indicate that the procedure can be called only from the HTML document in which it is defined.

```
1   <!DOCTYPE HTML PUBLIC "-//W3C//DTD HTML 4.0 Transitional//EN">
2   <html>
3   <!--Fig. 24.18: arrays.html -->
4
5   <head>
6   <title>Using VBScript Arrays</title>
7
8   <script language = "VBScript">
9   <!--
10     Option Explicit
11
12     Public Sub DisplayArray( x, s )
13        Dim j
14
15        Document.Write( s & ": " )
16        For j = 0 To UBound( x )
17           Document.Write( x( j ) & " " )
18        Next
19
20        Document.Write( "<BR>" )
21     End Sub
22
23     Dim fixedSize( 3 ), fixedArray, dynamic(), k
24
25     ReDim dynamic( 3 )   ' Dynamically size array
26     fixedArray = Array( "A", "B", "C" )
27
28     ' Populate arrays with values
29     For k = 0 to UBound( fixedSize )
30        fixedSize( k ) = 50 - k
31        dynamic( k ) = Chr( 75 + k )
32     Next
33
34     ' Display contents of arrays
35     Call DisplayArray( fixedSize, "fixedSize" )
36     Call DisplayArray( fixedArray, "fixedArray" )
37     Call DisplayArray( dynamic, "dynamic" )
38
39     ' Resize dynamic, preserve current values
40     ReDim Preserve dynamic( 5 )
41     dynamic( 3 ) = 3.343
42     dynamic( 4 ) = 77.37443
43
44     Call DisplayArray( dynamic, _
45                        "dynamic after ReDim Preserve" )
46   -->
```

Fig. 24.18 Using VBScript arrays (part 1 of 2).

```
47    </script>
48    </head>
49    </html>
```

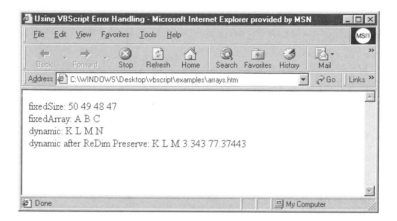

Fig. 24.18 Using VBScript arrays (part 2 of 2).

Procedure **DisplayArray** receives arguments **x** and **s** and declares local variable **j**. Parameter **x** receives an array, and parameter **s** receives a string. The **For** header (line 16) calls function **UBound** to get the upper bound of **x**. The **Document** object's **Write** method is used to print each element of **x**.

The declaration at line 23

```
Dim fixedSize( 3 ), fixedArray, dynamic(), k
```

declares a four-element fixed-sized array named **fixedSize** (the value in parentheses indicates the highest index in the array, and the array has a starting index of 0), variants **fixedArray** and **k** and dynamic array **dynamic**.

Statement *ReDim* (line 25) allocates memory for array **dynamic** (four elements, in this example). All dynamic-array memory must be allocated via **ReDim**. Dynamic arrays are more flexible than fixed-sized arrays, because they can be resized anytime, by using **ReDim**, to accommodate new data.

Performance Tip 24.2
Dynamic arrays allow the programmer to manage memory more efficiently than do fixed-size arrays.

Performance Tip 24.3
Resizing dynamic arrays consumes processor time and can slow a program's execution speed.

Common Programming Error 24.12
*Attempting to use **ReDim** on a fixed-size array is an error.*

Line 26

```
fixedArray = Array( "A", "B", "C" )
```

creates an array containing three elements and assigns it to **fixedArray**. VBScript function **Array** takes any number of arguments and returns an array containing those arguments. Lines 35–37 pass the three arrays and three strings to **DisplayArray**. Line 40

```
ReDim Preserve dynamic( 5 )
```

reallocates **dynamic**'s memory to five elements. When keyword **Preserve** is used with **ReDim**, VBScript maintains the current values in the array; otherwise, all values in the array are lost when the **ReDim** operation occurs.

Common Programming Error 24.13

*Using **ReDim** without **Preserve** and assuming that the array still contains previous values is a logic error.*

Testing and Debugging Tip 24.5

*Failure to **Preserve** array data can result in unexpected loss of data at runtime. Always double check every array **ReDim** statement to determine whether **Preserve** is needed.*

If **ReDim Preserve** creates a larger array, every element in the original array is preserved. If **ReDim Preserve** creates a smaller array, every element up to (and including) the new upper bound is preserved (e.g., if there were 10 elements in the original array and the new array contains 5 elements, the first 5 elements of the original array are preserved). Lines 41 and 42 assign values to the new elements. Procedure **DisplayArray** is called to display array **dynamic**.

Arrays can have multiple dimensions. VBScript supports at least 60 array dimensions, but most programmers will need to use only two- or three-dimensional arrays.

Common Programming Error 24.14

*Referencing a two-dimensional array element **u(x, y)** as **u(x)(y)** is an error.*

A multidimensional array is declared much like a one-dimensional array. For example, consider the declarations

```
Dim b(2, 2), tripleArray(100, 8, 15)
```

which declare **b** as a two-dimensional array and **tripleArray** as a three-dimensional array. Functions **UBound** and **LBound** can also be used with multidimensional arrays. When calling **UBound** or **LBound**, the dimension to which the function should be applied is passed as the second argument. Array dimensions always begin at 1. If a dimension is not provided, the default dimension, 1, is used. For example, the **For** header

```
For x = 0 To UBound(tripleArray, 3)
```

would increment **x** from the third dimension's lower bound, **0**, to the third dimension's upper bound, **15**.

Multidimensional arrays can also be created dynamically. Consider the declaration

```
Dim threeD()
```

which declares a dynamic array **threeD**. The number of dimensions is not set until the first time **ReDim** is used. Once the number of dimensions is set, the number of dimensions cannot be changed by **ReDim** (e.g., if the array is a two-dimensional array, it cannot become a three-dimensional array). The statement

```
ReDim threeD(11, 8, 1)
```

allocates memory for **threeD** and sets the number of dimensions at 3.

Common Programming Error 24.15

*Attempting to change the total number of dimensions in an array using **ReDim** is an error.*

Common Programming Error 24.16

*Attempting to change the upper bound for any dimension except the last dimension in a dynamic multidimensional array (when using **ReDim Preserve**) is an error.*

Memory allocated for dynamic arrays can be *deallocated* (*released*) at runtime by using the keyword **Erase**. A dynamic array that has been deallocated must be redimensioned with **ReDim** before it can be used again. **Erase** can also be used with fixed-sized arrays to initialize all the array elements to the empty string. For example, the statement

```
Erase mDynamic
```

releases **mDynamic**'s memory.

Common Programming Error 24.17

Accessing a dynamic array that has been deallocated is an error.

24.7 String Manipulation

One of VBScript's most powerful features is its string-manipulation functions, some of which are summarized in Fig. 24.19. For a complete list, consult the VBScript documentation. VBScript strings are case sensitive. The first character in a string has index 1 (as opposed to arrays, which begin at index 0). [*Note*: Almost all VBScript string-manipulation functions do not modify their string argument(s); rather, they return new strings containing the results. Most VBScript string-manipulation functions take optional arguments.]

We now present a VBScript program that converts a line of text into its pig Latin equivalent (Fig. 24.20). Pig Latin is a form of coded language often used for amusement. Many variations exist in the methods used to form pig Latin phrases. For simplicity, we use the following algorithm:

> *To form a pig Latin phrase from an English language phrase, the translation proceeds one word at a time. To translate an English word into a pig Latin word, place the first letter of the English word (if it is not a vowel) at the end of the English word and add the letters "**ay**." If the first letter of the English word is a vowel, place it at the end of the word and add "**y**." Thus, the word "**jump**" becomes "**umpjay**," the word "**the**" becomes "**hetay**," and the word "**ace**" becomes "**ceay**." Blanks between words remain as*

blanks. Make the following assumptions: The English phrase consists of words separated by blanks, there are no punctuation marks and all words have two or more letters.

Function	Description
Asc	Returns the ASCII numeric value of a character. For example, **Asc("x")** returns **120**.
Chr	Returns the character representation for an ASCII value. For example, the call **Chr(120)** returns "**x**." The argument passed must be in the range 0 to 255, inclusive; otherwise, an error occurs.
InStr	Searches a string (i.e., the first argument) for a substring (i.e., the second argument). Searching is performed from left to right. If the substring is found, the index of the found substring in the search string is returned. For example, the call **Instr("sparrow","arrow")** returns **3**, and the call **Instr("japan","wax")** returns **0**.
Len	Returns the number of characters in a string. For example, the call **Len("hello")** returns **5**.
LCase	Returns a lowercase string. For example, the call **LCase("HELLO@97[")** returns "**hello@97[**."
UCase	Returns an uppercase string. For example, the call **UCase("hello@97[")** returns "**HELLO@97[**."
Left	Returns a string containing characters from the left side of a string argument. For example, the call **Left("Web",2)** returns "**We**."
Mid	Function **Mid** returns a string containing a range of characters from a string. For example, the call **Mid("abcd",2,3)** returns "**bcd**."
Right	Returns a string containing characters from the right side of a string argument. For example, the call **Right("Web",2)** returns "**eb**."
Space	Returns a string of spaces. For example, the call **Space(4)** returns a string containing four spaces.
StrComp	Compares two strings for equality. Returns **1** if the first string is greater than the second string, returns **-1** if the first string is less than the second string and returns **0** if the strings are equivalent. The default is a binary comparison (i.e., case sensitive). An optional third argument of **vbTextCompare** indicates a case-insensitive comparison. For example the call **StrComp("bcd", "BCD")** returns **1**, the call **StrComp("BCD", "bcd")** returns **-1**, the call **StrComp("bcd", "bcd")** returns **0** and the call **StrComp("bcd", "BCD", vbTextCompare)** returns **0**.
String	Returns a string containing a repeated character. For example, the call **String(4,"u")** returns "**uuuu**."
Trim	Returns a string that does not contain leading or trailing space characters. For example the call **Trim(" hi ")** returns "**hi**."
LTrim	Returns a string that does not contain any leading space characters. For example, the call **LTrim(" yes")** returns "**yes**."

Fig. 24.19 Some string-manipulation functions (part 1 of 2).

Function	Description
RTrim	Returns a string that does not contain any trailing space characters. For example, the call **RTrim("no ")** returns "**no**".
Filter	Returns an array of strings containing the result of the **Filter** operation. For example, the call **Filter(Array("A","S","D","F","G","D"),"D")** returns a two-element array containing **"D"** and **"D"**, and the call **Filter(Array("A","S","D","F","G","D"),"D",False)** returns an array containing **"A"** , **"S"**, **"F"** and **"G"**.
Join	Returns a string containing the concatenation of array elements separated by a delimiter. For example, the call **Join(Array("one","two","three"))** returns "**one two three**." The default delimiter is a space, which can be changed by passing a delimiter string as the second argument. For example, the call **Join(Array("one","two","three"),"$^")** returns "**one$^two$^three**."
Replace	Returns a string containing the results of a **Replace** operation. Function **Replace** requires three string arguments: the string in which characters will be replaced, the substring to search for and the replacement string. For example, **Replace("It's Sunday and the sun is out","sun","moon")** returns "**It's Sunday and the moon is out**." Note the case-sensitive replacement.
Split	Returns an array containing substrings. The default delimiter for **Split** is a space character. For example, the call **Split("I met a traveller")** returns an array containing elements **"I"**, **"met"**, **"a"** and **"traveller"**, and **Split("red,white,and blue", ",")** returns an array containing elements **"red"**, **"white"** and **"and blue"**. The optional second argument changes the delimiter.
StrReverse	Returns a string in reverse order. For example, the call **StrReverse("deer")** returns "**reed**."
InStrRev	Searches a string (i.e., the first argument) for a substring (i.e., the second argument). Searching is performed from right to left. If the substring is found, the index of the found substring in the search string is returned. For example, the call **InstrRev("sparrow","arrow")** returns **3**, the call **InstrRev("japan","wax")** returns **0** and the call **InstrRev("to be or not to be","to be")** returns **14**.

Fig. 24.19 Some string-manipulation functions (part 2 of 2).

Lines 12–38 define the **Function** procedure **TranslateToPigLatin**, which translates the string input by the user from English to pig Latin. Line 18 calls function **Split** to extract each word in the sentence. By default, **Split** uses spaces as delimiters. The condition (line 22)

```
InStr( 1, "aeiou", _
       LCase( Left( words( k ), 1 ) ) )
```

calls functions **InStr**, **LCase** and **Left** to determine whether the first letter of a word is
a vowel. Function **Left** is called to retrieve the first letter in **words(k)**, which is then
converted to lowercase using **LCase**. Function **InStr** is called to search the string
"aeiou" for the string returned by **LCase**. The starting index in every string is **1**, and
this position is where **Instr** begins searching.

```
1    <!DOCTYPE HTML PUBLIC "-//W3C//DTD HTML 4.0 Transitional//EN">
2    <html>
3    <!--Fig. 24.20: piglatin.html -->
4
5    <head>
6    <title>Using VBScript String Functions</title>
7
8    <script language = "VBScript">
9    <!--
10      Option Explicit
11
12      Public Function TranslateToPigLatin( englishPhrase )
13         Dim words        ' Stores each individual word
14         Dim k, suffix
15
16         ' Get each word and store in words the
17         ' default delimiter for Split is a space
18         words = Split( englishPhrase )
19
20         For k = 0 to UBound( words )
21            ' Check if first letter is a vowel
22            If InStr( 1, "aeiou", _
23                       LCase( Left( words( k ), 1 ) ) ) Then
24               suffix = "y"
25            Else
26               suffix = "ay"
27            End If
28
29            ' Convert the word to pig Latin
30            words( k ) = Right( words( k ), _
31                         Len( words( k ) ) - 1 ) & _
32                         Left( words( k ), 1 ) & suffix
33      Next
34
35         ' Return translated phrase, each word
36         ' is separated by spaces
37         TranslateToPigLatin = Join( words )
38      End Function
39
40      Sub cmdButton_OnClick()
41         Dim phrase
42
43         phrase = Document.Forms( 0 ).txtInput.Value
44
45         Document.forms( 0 ).txtPigLatin.Value = _
46            TranslateToPigLatin( phrase )
47      End Sub
```

Fig. 24.20 Using VBScript string-processing functions (part 1 of 2).

```
48    -->
49    </script>
50    </head>
51
52    <body>
53    <form><p>Enter a sentence
54    <input type = "text" name = "txtInput" size = "50"></p>
55    <p>Pig Latin
56    <input type = "text" name = "txtPigLatin" size = "70"></p><p>
57    <input type = "button" name = "cmdButton" value = "Translate"></p>
58    </script>
59    </form>
60    </body>
61    </html>
```

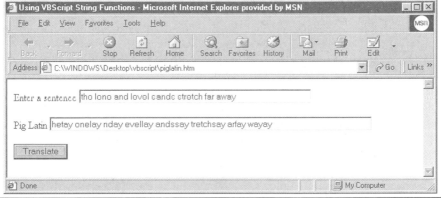

Fig. 24.20 Using VBScript string-processing functions (part 2 of 2).

Lines 30–33

```
words( k ) = Right( words( k ), _
                    Len( words( k ) ) - 1 ) & _
                    Left( words( k ), 1 ) & suffix
```

translate an individual word to pig Latin. Function **Len** is called to get the number of characters in **words(k)**. The value returned by **Len** is decreased by 1, to ensure that the first letter in **words(k)** is not included in the string returned by **Right**. Function **Left** is called to get the first letter of **words(k)**, which is then concatenated to the string returned by **Right**. Finally, the contents of **suffix** (either **"ay"** or **"y"**) and a space are concatenated.

Lines 40–47 define an event procedure for **cmdButton**'s **OnClick** event. Line 46 calls function **TranslateToPigLatin**, passing the string input by the user. The pig Latin sentence returned by **TranslateToPigLatin** is displayed in a text box (line 45).

24.8 Internet and World Wide Web Resources

Although the VBScript language contains far more features than can be presented in one chapter, there are many Web resources available that are related to VBScript. Visit the following sites for additional information:

`msdn.microsoft.com/scripting/VBScript/doc/vbstutor.htm`
The *VBScript tutorial* contains a short tutorial on VBScript.

`msdn.microsoft.com/scripting/VBScript/doc/vbstoc.htm`
The *VBScript language reference* contains links for constants, keywords, functions, etc.

`www.msdn.microsoft.com/vbasic/technical/Documentation.asp`
Visual Basic 6 documentation. Use the Visual Basic 6 documentation to get additional information on functions, constants, etc. VBScript is a subset of Visual Basic.

SUMMARY

- Visual Basic Script (VBScript) is a case-insensitive subset of Microsoft Visual Basic® used in World Wide Web HTML documents to enhance the functionality of a Web page displayed in a Web browser (such as Microsoft's Internet Explorer) that contains a VBScript scripting engine (i.e., interpreter). It is also used on servers to enhance the functionality of server-side applications.

- VBScript's arithmetic operators are similar to JavaScript's arithmetic operators. Two major differences between them are the division operator, \, which returns an integer result, and the exponentiation operator, ^, which raises a value to a power. VBScript operator precedence differs from that of JavaScript.

- VBScript's symbols for the equality operator and inequality operators are different from JavaScript's symbols. VBScript comparison operators may also be used to compare strings.

- VBScript provides the following logical operators: **And** (logical AND), **Or** (logical Or), **Not** (logical negation), **Imp** (logical implication), **Xor** (exclusive Or) and **Eqv** (logical equivalence).

- Despite the mixture of case in keywords, functions, etc., VBScript is not case sensitive: Uppercase and lowercase letters are treated the same.

- VBScript provides the plus sign, **+**, the and ampersand, **&**, operators for string concatenation. The ampersand is more formally called the string concatenation operator. If both operands of the concatenation operator are strings, the two operators can be used interchangeably. However, if the **+** operator is used in an expression consisting of varying data types, there can be a problem.

- Comments are placed in VBScript code by using either a single quote (**'**) or the keyword **Rem** before the comment. As with JavaScript's two forward slashes, **//**, VBScript comments are single-line comments.

- Like JavaScript, VBScript has only one data type—variant—and it is capable of storing different types of data (e.g., strings, integers, floating-point numbers, etc.). A variant is interpreted by VBScript in a manner that is suitable to the type of data it contains.

- Variable names cannot be keywords and must begin with a letter. The maximum length of a variable name is 255 characters, and the name may contain only letters, numbers and underscores. Variables can be declared simply by using their name in the VBScript code. Statement **Option Explicit** can be used to force all variables to be declared before they are used.

- VBScript provides nine control structures for controlling program execution. Many of the control structures provide the same capabilities as their JavaScript counterparts. Syntactically, every VBScript control structure ends with one or more keywords (e.g., **End If**, **Loop**, etc.). Keywords, not curly braces (i.e., **{}**), delimit a control structure's body.

- The **If/Then/End If** and **If/Then/Else/End If** control structures behave identically to their JavaScript counterparts. VBScript's multiple-selection version of **If/Then/Else/End If** uses a different syntax from JavaScript's version, because it includes keyword **ElseIf**.

- VBScript does not use a statement terminator (e.g., a semicolon, **;**). Unlike in JavaScript, placing parentheses around conditions in VBScript is optional. A condition evaluates to **True** if the variant subtype is boolean **True** or if the variant subtype is considered to be nonzero. A condition evaluates to **False** if the variant subtype is boolean **False** or if the variant subtype is considered to be zero.

- VBScript's **Select Case/End Select** structure provides the same functionality as JavaScript's **switch** structure, and more. The **Select Case/End Select** structure does not require the use of a statement such as **break**. One **Case** cannot accidently run into another. The VBScript **Select Case/End Select** structure is equivalent to VBScript's **If/Then/Else/End If** multiple-selection structure. The only difference between them is syntactical. Any variant subtype can be used with the **Select Case/End Select** structure.

- VBScript's **While/Wend** repetition structure and **Do While/Loop** behave identically to JavaScript's **while** repetition structure. VBScript's **Do/Loop While** structure behaves identically to JavaScript's **do/while** repetition structure. VBScript contains two additional repetition structures, **Do Until/Loop** and **Do/Loop Until**, that do not have direct JavaScript equivalents. These **Do Until** repetition structures iterate until the condition becomes **True**.

- The **Exit Do** statement, when executed in a **Do While/Loop**, **Do/Loop While**, **Do Until/Loop** or **Do/Loop Until**, causes immediate exit from that structure, and execution continues with the next statement in sequence. The fact that a **Do While/Loop** may contain **Exit Do** is the only difference, other than syntax, between **Do While/Loop** and **While/Wend**. Statement **Exit For** causes immediate exit from the **For/Next** structure.

- Function **IsEmpty** determines whether the variant has ever been initialized by the programmer. If **IsEmpty** returns **True**, the variant has not been initialized by the programmer.

- VBScript's math functions allow the programmer to perform common mathematical calculations. Trigonometric functions, such as **Cos**, **Sin**, etc., take arguments that are expressed in radians. To convert from degrees to radians, use the formula *radians = (degrees × π) / 180.*

- Function **InputBox** displays a dialog in which the user can input data.

- VBScript coordinates are measured in units of twips (1440 twips equals 1 inch). Coordinates are relative to the upper-left corner of the screen, which is position *(0, 0)*. *x* coordinates increase from left to right, and *y* coordinates increase from top to bottom.

- Many VBScript functions often take optional arguments.

- The underscore character, _, is VBScript's line-continuation character. A statement cannot extend beyond the current line without using this character. A statement may use as many line-continuation characters as necessary.

- Function **MsgBox** displays a message dialog.

- In VBScript, function calls that wrap arguments in parentheses must be preceded with keyword **Call**, unless the function call is assigning a value to a variable.

- VBScript provides functions for getting information about the scripting engine (i.e., the interpreter). These functions are **ScriptEngine**, which returns either **"JScript"**, **"VBScript"** or **"VBA"**; **ScriptEngineBuildVersion**, which returns the current build version; **ScriptEngineMajorVersion**, which returns the major version number for the script engine, and **ScriptEngineMinorVersion**, which returns the minor release number.

- HTML comment tags comment out the VBScript code. If the browser understands VBScript, these tags are ignored and the VBScript is interpreted. If the browser does not understand VBScript, the HTML comment prevents the VBScript code from being displayed as text.

- Procedures that do not return a value begin with keyword **Sub** and end with keywords **End Sub**.

- Variables declared within a VBScript procedure are visible only within the procedure body. Procedures that perform event handling are more properly called event procedures.

- VBScript provides functions **CBool**, **CByte**, **CCur**, **CDate**, **CDbl**, **CInt**, **CLng**, **CSng** and **CStr** for converting between variant subtypes.
- Programmer-defined constants are created by using keyword **Const**.
- Because the **HEAD** section of an HTML document is decoded first by the browser, VBScript code is normally placed there, so it can be decoded before it is invoked in the document.
- VBScript procedures that return a value are delimited with keywords **Function** and **End Function**. A value is returned from a **Function** procedure by assigning a value to the procedure name. As in JavaScript, a **Function** procedure can return only one value at a time.
- VBScript provides statements **Exit Sub** and **Exit Function** for exiting **Sub** procedures and **Function** procedures, respectively. Control is returned to the caller, and the next statement in sequence after the call is executed.
- A fixed-size array's size does not change during program execution; a dynamic array's size can change during execution. A dynamic array is also called a redimmable array. Array elements may be referred to by giving the array name followed by the element's position number in parentheses, **()**. The first array element is at index 0.
- Function **UBound** returns the upper bound (i.e., the highest numbered index), and function **LBound** returns the lowest numbered index (i.e., 0).
- Keyword **Public** explicitly indicates that a procedure is public. A procedure may also be marked as **Private**, to indicate that only scripts on the same Web page may call the procedure.
- Statement **ReDim** allocates memory for a dynamic array. All dynamic arrays must receive memory via **ReDim**. Dynamic arrays are more flexible than fixed-sized arrays, because they can be resized anytime, using **ReDim**, to accommodate new data.
- Function **Array** takes any number of arguments and returns an array containing those arguments.
- Keyword **Preserve** may be used with **ReDim** to maintain the current values in the array. When **ReDim** is executed without **Preserve**, all values contained in the array are lost.
- Arrays can have multiple dimensions. VBScript supports at least 60 array dimensions, but most programmers will need to use only two- or three-dimensional arrays. Multidimensional arrays can also be created dynamically.
- Memory allocated for dynamic arrays can be deallocated (released) at runtime by using keyword **Erase**. A dynamic array that has been deallocated must be redimensioned with **ReDim** before it can be used again. **Erase** can also be used with fixed-sized arrays to initialize all the array elements to the empty string.
- VBScript strings are case sensitive and begin with an index of 1.

TERMINOLOGY

Abs function	byte subtype
Active Server Pages (ASPs)	**CBool** function
addition operator, **+**	**CByte** function
And logical operator	**CCur** function
Array function	**CDate** function
Asc function	**CDbl** function
Atn function	**Chr** function
attribute	**CInt** function
behavior	client
boolean subtype	**CLng** function
build version	comment character, **'**

25

Bonus Chapter: Introduction to Active Server Pages (ASP)

Objectives

- To be able to program Active Server Pages using VBScript.
- To understand how Active Server Pages work.
- To understand the differences between client-side scripting and server-side scripting.
- To be able to pass data between Web pages.
- To be able to use server-side include statements.
- To be able to use server-side ActiveX components.
- To be able to create sessions.
- To be able to use cookies.
- To be able to use ActiveX Data Objects (ADO) to access a database.

A client is to me a mere unit, a factor in a problem.
Sir Arthur Conan Doyle

Rule One: Our client is always right.
Rule Two: If you think our client is wrong, see Rule One.
Anonymous

Protocol is everything.
Francoise Giuliani

25.1 Introduction

[*Note: This Chapter is a bonus chapter that is intended to support the discussion of Active Server Pages in Chapters 15. By design, this chapter does not use XML.*]

In this chapter, we discuss server-side scripting, which is essential to e-commerce applications. We use server-side text files called *Active Server Pages* (*ASP*) that are processed in response to a client (e.g., browser) request. These pages are processed by an *ActiveX component* (i.e., a server-side ActiveX control) called a *scripting engine*. An ASP file has the file extension `.asp` and contains HTML tags and scripting code. Although other languages, like JavaScript, can be used for ASP scripting, VBScript is the most widely used language for ASP scripting. If you are not familiar with VBScript, please read Chapter 24, "VBScript," before reading this chapter.

Software Engineering Observation 25.1

Some independent software vendors (ISVs) provide scripting engines for use with ASP that support languages other than VBScript and JavaScript.

Server-side scripting uses information sent by clients, information stored on the server, information stored in the server's memory and information from the Internet to dynamically create Web pages. The examples in this chapter illustrate how Active Server Pages use server and client information to send dynamic Web pages to clients. We present a clock, advertisement rotator, guest book, Web-page creator and user verification system.

25.2 How Active Server Pages Work

The Active Server Pages in this chapter demonstrate communication between clients and servers via the HTTP of the World Wide Web. When a server receives a client's HTTP request, the server loads the document (or page) requested by the client. HTML documents are *static documents*—that is, all clients see the same content when requesting an HTML document. ASP is a Microsoft technology for sending to the client dynamic Web content, which includes HTML, Dynamic HTML, ActiveX controls, client-side scripts and *Java applets* (i.e., client-side Java programs that are embedded in a Web page). The Active Server Page processes the request (which often includes interacting with a database) and returns the results to the client. The results are normally returned in the form of an HTML document, but other data formats (e.g., images, binary data, etc.) can also be returned.

The two most common *HTTP request types* (also known as *request methods*) are **GET** and **POST**. These requests are frequently used to send client form data to a Web server. Although **GET** and **POST** both send information to the server, their methods of sending the information are different. A **GET** request sends form content as part of the URL (e.g., **www.searchsomething.com/search?query=userquery**). A **POST** request *posts* form contents to the end of an HTTP request. An HTTP request contains information about the server, client, connection, authorization, etc.

Software Engineering Observation 25.2

*The data sent in a **POST** request are not part of the URL and cannot be seen by the user. Forms that contain many fields are most often submitted by a **POST** request. Sensitive form fields, such as passwords, are usually sent using this request type.*

An HTTP request is often used to post data to a server-side form handler that processes the data. For example, when the user responds to a Web-based survey, a request sends the Web server the information specified in the HTML form.

Browsers often *cache* (i.e., save on disk) Web pages for quick reloading. This speeds up the user's browsing experience by reducing the amount of data downloaded to view a Web page. Browsers typically do not cache the server's response to a **POST** request, because the next **POST** request may not contain the same information. For example, several users might request the same Web page to participate in a survey. Each user's response changes the overall results of the survey.

When a Web-based search engine is used, a **GET** request normally supplies the search engine with the information specified in the HTML form. The search engine then performs the search and returns the results as a Web page. These pages are often cached in the event that the user performs the same search again.

When a client requests an ASP document, it is loaded into memory and parsed (top to bottom) by a scripting engine named **asp.dll**. Script code is interpreted as it is encountered.

Portability Tip 25.1

Because browsers are capable of rendering HTML, an ASP page that generates pure HTML can be rendered on any client browser, regardless of the fact that the page requested ends in **.asp**.

Software Engineering Observation 25.3

*To take advantage of Active Server Page technology, a Web server must provide a component such as **asp.dll** to support ASP.*

Software Engineering Observation 25.4

Server-side scripts are not visible to the client; only HTML (plus any client-side scripts) is sent to the client.

25.3 Client-side Scripting versus Server-side Scripting

In previous chapters, we focused on client-side scripting with JavaScript and VBScript. Client-side scripting is often used for validation, interactivity, accessing the browser and enhancing a Web page with ActiveX controls, Dynamic HTML and Java applets. Client-side validation reduces the number of requests the server receives and therefore reduces the amount of work the server must perform. Interactivity allows the user to make decisions, click on buttons, play games, etc., activities that are often more interesting than just reading text. ActiveX controls, Dynamic HTML and Java applets enhance a Web page's appearance by providing richer functionality than that provided by HTML. Client-side scripts can access the browser, use features specific to that browser and manipulate browser documents.

Client-side scripting does have limitations, however, such as browser dependency, where the browser or *scripting host* must support the scripting language. Another limitation is that client-side scripts are viewable (e.g., using the **View** menu's **Source** command in Internet Explorer) to the client. Some Web developers do not like this feature, because people can easily steal their scripting code.

Software Engineering Observation 25.5

JavaScript is the most popular client-side scripting language and is supported by both Microsoft Internet Explorer and Netscape Communicator.

Performance Tip 25.1

To conserve server resources, perform as much processing as possible on the client side.

Because server-side scripts reside on the server, programmers have greater flexibility—especially when accessing databases. Scripts executed on the server usually generate custom responses for clients. For example, a client might connect to an airline's Web server and request a list of all flights from Boston to Dallas between September 18th and November 5th. The script queries the database, dynamically generates HTML content containing the flight list and sends the HTML to the client. A client who connects to the airline's Web server always gets the most current database information.

Server-side scripts also have access to server-side *ActiveX components* that extend scripting language functionality. We discuss some of these components later in this chapter.

An HTML document can contain both client-side script (e.g., JavaScript) and server-side script (e.g., VBScript).

Portability Tip 25.2

Server-side scripts run exclusively on the server; therefore, cross-platform issues are not a concern.

25.4 Using Personal Web Server and Internet Information Server

This chapter contains several examples that require Personal Web Server (PWS) 4.0 or *Internet Information Server* (*IIS*) 4.0 or higher to execute. Before attempting to execute any example, you should make sure that PWS or IIS is running. For help installing and running

PWS, see the "Web Server Installation" document on the CD that accompanies this book for instructions on how to install and set up a Web server.

[*Note*: Do not confuse Internet Information Server 4.0 (IIS 4.0) with *Internet Information Services 5.0* (*IIS 5.0*). IIS 5.0 is integrated into Windows 2000 and is similar to PWS. For more information on Internet Information Services 5.0, visit the following Web site: **www.microsoft.com/windows2000/guide/server/features/web.asp**.]

If you are going to execute the chapter examples, we recommend that you create a subdirectory beneath **C:\Webshare\Wwwroot** or **C:\Inetpub\Wwwroot** named **Deitel**. Copy all the **.asp** files from the Chapter 25 examples directory (included on the book's CD) to this directory. Create two other directories beneath **C:\Webshare\Wwwroot** named **includes** and **images**. Copy all **.shtml** files from the CD to **includes** and all **.gif** (or any other graphic file extension) files to **images**. [*Note*: you will need to modify some of the paths in the **.asp** files to reflect these directories.]

To execute a particular example, type **http://**machineName**/Deitel/**name**.asp** into the Web browser's **Address** field and press the *Enter* key. For example, to execute **clock.asp** on a machine named **viper**, type

```
http://viper/Deitel/clock.asp
```

into the Web browser's **Address** field and press the *Enter* key. To determine the name of the machine, in Windows 98, right-click **Network Neighborhood** and select **Properties** from the context menu to display the **Network** dialog. In the **Network** dialog, click on the **Identification** tab. The computer name is displayed in the **Computer name:** field. Click on **Cancel** to close the **Network** dialog.

In Windows 2000, right click on **My Network Places** and select **Properties** from the context menu to display the **Network and Dialup Connections** explorer. In the explorer, click on **Network Identification**. The computer name is displayed in the **Full Computer Name:** field in the **System Properties** window. Click **Cancel** to close the **System Properties** window.

Several examples access a database. The database files (e.g., **.mdb** files) can be copied into any directory on your system. Before executing these examples, you must set up a System Data Source Name (DSN). See the "Setting up a System Data Source Name" document on the CD that accompanies this book for instructions on how to create a DSN.

25.5 Active Server Page Objects

Active Server Pages provide several built-in objects to offer programmers straightforward methods for communicating with a Web browser, gathering data sent by an HTTP request and distinguishing between users. Figure 25.1 provides a short description of the most commonly used ASP objects.

The **Request** *object* is commonly used to access the information passed by a **GET** or **POST** request. This information usually consists of data provided by the user in an HTML form. The **Request** object provides access to information, such as "cookies", that are stored on a client's machine. This object can also access binary information (e.g., a file upload) as well. The **Response** object sends information (e.g., HTML/text) to the client.

Object Name	Description
Request	Used to access information passed by an HTTP request.
Response	Used to control the information sent to the user.
Server	Used to access methods and properties on the server.

Fig. 25.1 Some built-in ASP objects.

The **Server** *object* provides access to methods and properties on the server. The **Server** object provides a method (**CreateObject**) to instantiate other objects. We can create instances of built-in objects, ActiveX components, etc.

25.6 A Simple ASP Example

In this section, we present a simple ASP example (Fig. 25.2) that represents a clock. Every 60 seconds, the page is updated with the server's time.

Notice the *scripting delimiters*, **<%** and **%>**, wrapped around the VBScript code. These characters indicate that the scripting code is executed on the server, not the client. Nothing enclosed in scripting delimiters is sent to the client; the code inside the delimiters is processed by the scripting engine. However, the scripting code inside the delimiters can generate information that is sent to the client. Everything outside of **<%** and **%>** is simply written to the client. The client's browser then interprets and renders the Web page (e.g., HTML sent to the client).

```
1   <% @LANGUAGE = VBScript %>
2   <% Option Explicit %>
3   <% ' Fig. 25.2 : clock.asp %>
4
5   <!DOCTYPE HTML PUBLIC "-//W3C//DTD HTML 4.0 Transitional//EN">
6   <HTML>
7   <HEAD>
8   <TITLE>A Simple ASP Example</TITLE>
9   <META HTTP-EQUIV = "REFRESH" CONTENT = "60; URL=CLOCK.ASP">
10  </HEAD>
11  <BODY>
12
13  <FONT FACE = "Arial" SIZE = "4"><STRONG>Simple ASP Example</STRONG>
14  </FONT><P>
15     <TABLE BORDER = "6">
16     <TR>
17     <TD BGCOLOR = "#000000">
18        <FONT FACE = "Arial" COLOR = "#00FF00" SIZE = "4">
19           <% =Time() %>
20        </FONT>
21     </TD>
22     </TR>
23     </TABLE>
```

Fig. 25.2 A simple Active Server Page (part 1 of 2).

```
24    </BODY>
25    </HTML>
```

Fig. 25.2   A simple Active Server Page (part 2 of 2).

 Common Programming Error 25.1

Leaving out the opening delimiter, <%, or the closing delimiter, %>, or both for a server-side scripting statement is an error.

Line 1

```
<% @LANGUAGE = "VBScript" %>
```

uses the optional **@LANGUAGE** *processing directive* to specify VBScript as the scripting language. This code indicates that the scripting engine needed to interpret the scripting code. In this chapter, we use VBScript exclusively to develop our Active Server Pages, although other scripting languages, such as JavaScript, may be used as well. If the **@LANGUAGE** processing directive is not used, VBScript is the default.

 Good Programming Practice 25.1

*When using VBScript code in an Active Server Page, use the **@LANGUAGE** statement for clarity.*

 Common Programming Error 25.2

*When using the **@LANGUAGE** tag, not placing it inside the first statement in an ASP file is an error.*

Line 2 uses **Option Explicit** to indicate that the programmer must explicitly declare all VBScript variables. Remember that by simply mentioning a new name, VBScript variables are implicitly declared. This can lead to subtle errors. When used, the **Option Explicit** statement must be the first VBScript scripting statement after the **@LANGUAGE** statement. In this particular example, we do not declare any variables, but we include the **Option Explicit** statement as an example of good programming practice.

 Testing and Debugging Tip 25.1

*Always include **Option Explicit**, even if you are not declaring any VBScript variables. As a script evolves over time, you may need to declare variables, and the presence of the **Option Explicit** statement can help eliminate subtle errors.*

We use the **META** tag on line 9 to set the refresh interval for the page. The **CONTENT** attribute specifies the number of seconds (**60**) until the **URL** attribute's value (**clock.asp**) is requested. Refreshing occurs every minute.

Line 19

```
<% =Time() %>
```

calls VBScript function *Time* to get the current time on the server. Function **Time** returns the time in the format *hh:mm:ss*. This statement is short for

```
<% Call Response.Write( Time() ) %>
```

which calls the **Response** method *Write* to send the time as text to the client. One of the key points of this example is that the ASP indirectly requests itself. The **URL** attribute requests that the page reload itself every 60 seconds. This procedure is perfectly valid and is often done in ASP programming.

25.7 Server-side ActiveX Components

Server-side script functionality is extended with server-side ActiveX components—ActiveX controls that typically reside on the Web server and do not have a graphical user interface. These components make powerful features accessible to the ASP author. Figure 25.3 summarizes some of the ActiveX components included with Internet Information Server (IIS), Internet Information Services and Personal Web Server (PWS).

Component Name	Description
MSWC.BrowserType	ActiveX component for gathering information about the client's browser (e.g., type, version, etc.).
MSWC.AdRotator	ActiveX component for rotating advertisements on a Web page.
MSWC.NextLink	ActiveX component for linking Web pages together.
MSWC.ContentRotator	ActiveX component for rotating HTML content on a Web page.
MSWC.PageCounter	ActiveX component for storing the number of times a Web page has been requested.
MSWC.Counters	ActiveX components that provide general-purpose persistent counters.
MSWC.MyInfo	ActiveX component that provides information about a Web site (e.g., owner name, owner address, etc.).

Fig. 25.3   Some server-side ActiveX components included with IIS and PWS.

Component Name	Description
`Scripting.FileSystemObject`	ActiveX component that provides an object library for accessing files on the server or on the server's network.
ActiveX Data Objects (ADO) Data Access Components	ActiveX components that provide an object library for accessing databases.

Fig. 25.3   Some server-side ActiveX components included with IIS and PWS.

Software Engineering Observation 25.6

If the scripting language you are using in an Active Server Page does not support a certain feature, an ActiveX server component can be created using Visual C++, Visual Basic, Delphi, etc., to provide that feature.

Performance Tip 25.2

Server-side ActiveX components usually execute faster than their scripting language equivalents.

Many Web sites sell advertising space, especially Web sites with large numbers of hits. In Fig. 25.4, we demonstrate the *AdRotator ActiveX component* for rotating advertisements on a Web page. Each time a client requests this Active Server Page, the AdRotator component randomly displays one of several advertisements—in this example, one of five flag images. When the user clicks on a country's flag image, the country's corresponding Central Intelligence Agency (CIA) Factbook Web page is displayed. [*Note:* This is the first of several examples that consist of multiple files. When a file is part of the same example, we continue the line numbering from the last line number in the previous listing. We do this for discussion purposes and to connect all of the example parts.] Line 20

```
Set flagChanger = Server.CreateObject( "MSWC.AdRotator" )
```

```
1   <% @LANGUAGE = VBScript %>
2   <% Option Explicit %>
3   <% ' Fig. 25.4 : rotate.asp %>
4
5   <!DOCTYPE HTML PUBLIC "-//W3C//DTD HTML 4.0 Transitional//EN">
6   <HTML>
7   <HEAD>
8   <TITLE>AdRotator Example</TITLE>
9   </HEAD>
10
11  <BODY>
12  <FONT FACE = "Arial" SIZE = "4">
13  <STRONG>AdRotator Example</STRONG>
14  </FONT><P>
```

Fig. 25.4   Demonstrating AdRotator ActiveX component (part 1 of 2).

```
15   <%
16      ' Declare flagChanger
17      Dim flagChanger
18
19      ' Create an AdRotator object
20      Set flagChanger = Server.CreateObject( "MSWC.AdRotator" )
21
22      ' Use config.txt to send an advertisement to the client
23      Call Response.Write( _
24         flagChanger.GetAdvertisement( "config.txt" ) )
25   %>
26   </BODY>
27   </HTML>
```

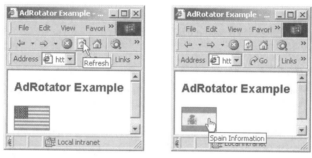

Fig. 25.4   Demonstrating AdRotator ActiveX component (part 2 of 2).

creates an instance of an AdRotator component and assigns it to reference **flagChanger**. Server-side ActiveX components are instantiated by passing the name of the component as a string to the **Server** object's method *CreateObject*.

Lines 23 and 24

```
Call Response.Write( _
    flagChanger.GetAdvertisement( "config.txt" ) )
```

call the **Response** object's **Write** method to send the advertisement as HTML to the client. Method **GetAdvertisement** is called using reference **flagChanger** to get the advertisements from the file **config.txt** (Fig. 25.5).

Software Engineering Observation 25.7

The AdRotator ActiveX component allows the page author to minimize the amount of space on a Web page committed to advertisements, while at the same time to maximize the number of advertisements to be displayed.

Portability Tip 25.3

Because the AdRotator ActiveX component is executed on the server, clients do not directly interact with the component and therefore do not have to support ActiveX technologies

The file's header (lines 28–31) includes the URL of the **REDIRECT** file, **redirect.asp** (discussed momentarily), the image **HEIGHT**, the image **WIDTH** and the image **BORDER** width. The asterisk (line 32) separates the header from the advertisements. Lines 33–36

```
/images/us.gif
http://www.odci.gov/cia/publications/factbook/us.html
United States Information
20
```

describe the first advertisement by providing the image's URL, the destination URL for redirection upon clicking the ad, a value for the **ALT** tag (browsers that cannot display graphics display the specified text) and a number (between 0 and 1000) representing the ratio of time this particular image appears. The ratios must be numbers between 0 and 10,000. For example, if four ads have the ratios 6, 9, 12 and 3, then the time ratios are calculated as 20% (6/30), 30% (9/30), 40% (12/30) and 10% (3/30), respectively. Lines 37–52 list the other four advertisements. [Note: If you are executing this example, copy **config.txt** to the **Deitel** directory you created in Section 25.4.]

```
28   REDIRECT redirect.asp
29   WIDTH 54
30   HEIGHT 36
31   BORDER 1
32   *
33   /images/us.gif
34   http://www.odci.gov/cia/publications/factbook/us.html
35   United States Information
36   20
37   /images/france.gif
38   http://www.odci.gov/cia/publications/factbook/fr.html
39   France Information
```

Fig. 25.5 File **config.txt** that describes the advertisements (part 1 of 2).

```
40  20
41  /images/germany.gif
42  http://www.odci.gov/cia/publications/factbook/gm.html
43  Germany Information
44  20
45  /images/italy.gif
46  http://www.odci.gov/cia/publications/factbook/it.html
47  Italy Information
48  20
49  /images/spain.gif
50  http://www.odci.gov/cia/publications/factbook/sp.html
51  Spain Information
52  20
```

Fig. 25.5   File **config.txt** that describes the advertisements (part 2 of 2).

File **redirect.asp** contains exactly one line:

```
<% Call Response.Redirect( Request( "url" ) ) %>
```

This line redirects the user to the country page when the ad is clicked on. Each time the ad is clicked on, the document **redirect.asp** is requested and a *query string* is sent with the request. The query string contains an attribute **url** that is equal to the destination URL found in **config.txt** for this ad. For example, if you click on the U.S. flag, the result is the same as that of typing

```
http://localhost/Deitel/redirect.asp?url=http://www.odci.gov/
cia/publications/factbook/us.html
```

in the browser's **Address** field.

We arbitrarily chose the names **config.txt** and **redirect.asp**. You may choose any name you prefer. The redirect file loads (into the browser) the page referenced by the ad's URL. These files can be placed anywhere in the publishing directory (i.e., they do not have to be under the same directory as **rotate.asp**). For example, if you put **config.txt** under directory **X** in the publishing directory, then lines 23 and 24 would read

```
Call Response.Write( _
    flagChanger.GetAdvertisement( "/X/config.txt" ) )
```

Note that **GetAdvertisement** is passed a URL, not a physical disk path, hence the use of the forward slash. Also note that **/X/config.txt** is short for **http://local-host/X/config.txt**. (The server is **localhost**, and the publishing directory is **C:\Webshare\Wwwroot**.) You can replace **localhost** by the IP address **127.0.0.1**, which also refers to the local machine.

Figure 25.6 shows the HTML sent by **rotate.asp**. [*Note*: This file has been edited for presentation (e.g., the HTML **HEAD** and **BODY** tags have been omitted).]

25.8 File System Objects

File System Objects (*FSOs*) provide the programmer with the ability to manipulate files, directories and drives. FSOs also allow the programmer to read and write text and are an essential element for Active Server Pages that persist data. We first provide an overview of FSO features and then provide a "live-code" example that uses FSOs.

FSOs are objects in the *Microsoft Scripting Runtime Library*. Five types of FSO exist: **FileSystemObject**, **File**, **Folder**, **Drive** and **TextStream**. Each type is summarized in Fig. 25.7.

The programmer can use **FileSystemObject**s to create directories, move files, determine whether a **Drive** exists, etc. Figure 25.8 summarizes some common methods of **FileSystemObject**.

The **File** object allows the programmer to gather information about files, manipulate files and open files. Figure 25.9 lists some common **File** properties and methods.

```
53    <A HREF = "redirect.asp?url=http://www.odci.gov/cia/publications/
54       factbook/us.html&image=/images/us.gif">
55    <IMG SRC = "/images/us.gif" ALT = "United States Information"
56       WIDTH = "54" HEIGHT = "36" BORDER = "1"></A>
```

Fig. 25.6 HTML sent to the client by **rotate.asp** for the USA advertisement.

Object type	Description
FileSystemObject	Allows the programmer to interact with **File**s, **Folder**s and **Drive**s.
File	Allows the programmer to manipulate **File**s of any type.
Folder	Allows the programmer to manipulate **Folder**s (i.e., directories).
Drive	Allows the programmer to gather information about **Drive**s (hard disks; RAM disks, which are computer memory used as a substitute for hard disks to allow high-speed file operations; CD-ROMs, etc.). **Drive**s can be local or remote.
TextStream	Allows the programmer to read and write text files.

Fig. 25.7 File System Objects (FSOs).

Methods	Description
CopyFile	Copies an existing **File**.
CopyFolder	Copies an existing **Folder**.
CreateFolder	Creates and returns a **Folder**.

Fig. 25.8 **FileSystemObject** methods (part 1 of 2).

Methods	Description
CreateTextFile	Creates and returns a text **File**.
DeleteFile	Deletes a **File**.
DeleteFolder	Deletes a **Folder**.
DriveExists	Tests whether or not a **Drive** exists. Returns a boolean.
FileExists	Tests whether or not a **File** exists. Returns a boolean.
FolderExists	Tests whether or not a **Folder** exists. Returns a boolean.
GetAbsolutePathName	Returns the absolute path as a string.
GetDrive	Returns the specified **Drive**.
GetDriveName	Returns the **Drive** drive name.
GetFile	Returns the specified **File**.
GetFileName	Returns the **File** filename.
GetFolder	Returns the specified **Folder**.
GetParentFolderName	Returns a string representing the parent folder name.
GetTempName	Creates and returns a string representing a filename.
MoveFile	Moves a **File**.
MoveFolder	Moves a **Folder**.
OpenTextFile	Opens an existing text **File**. Returns a **TextStream**.

Fig. 25.8   FileSystemObject methods (part 2 of 2).

Property/method	Description
Properties	
DateCreated	Date. The date the **File** was created.
DateLastAccessed	Date. The date the **File** was last accessed.
DateLastModified	Date. The date the **File** was last modified.
Drive	Drive object. The **Drive** where the file is located.
Name	String. The **File** name.
ParentFolder	String. The **File**'s parent folder name.
Path	String. The **File**'s path.
ShortName	String. The **File**'s name expressed as a short name.
Size	Variant. The size of the **File**, in bytes.
Methods	
Copy	Copy the **File**. Same as **CopyFile** of **FileSystemObject**.
Delete	Delete the **File**. Same as **DeleteFile** of **FileSystemObject**.

Fig. 25.9   Some common **File** properties and methods (part 1 of 2).

Property/method	Description
Move	Move the **File**. Same as **MoveFile** of **FileSystemObject**.
OpenAsTextStream	Opens an existing **File** as a text **File**. Returns **TextStream**.

Fig. 25.9 Some common **File** properties and methods (part 2 of 2).

Property **Path** contains the **File**'s path in *long-name format*. (The operating system does not abbreviate the name when it exceeds the 8.3 format.) Property **ShortName** contains, if applicable, the filename in *short-name format*. (A filename exceeding the 8.3 format is abbreviated.) For example, a filename in long-name format might be "**ABCD EFG HIJ.doc**." That same filename in short-name format might be abbreviated as "**ABCDEF~1.doc**."

The **Folder** object allows the programmer to manipulate and gather information about directories. Figure 25.10 lists some common **Folder** properties and methods.

Property **IsRootFolder** indicates whether the folder is the *root folder* for the **Drive** (i.e., the folder that contains everything on the drive). If the folder is not the root folder, method **ParentFolder** may be called to get the folder's *parent folder* (i.e., the folder in which the selected folder is contained). Method **Size** returns the total number of bytes the folder contains. The size includes the size of *subfolders* (i.e., folders inside the selected folder) and files.

Property/method	Description
Properties	
Attributes	Integer. Value indicating **Folder**'s attributes (read only, hidden, etc.).
DateCreated	Date. The date the folder was created.
DateLastAccessed	Date. The date the folder was last accessed.
DateLastModified	Date. The date the folder was last modified.
Drive	Drive object. The **Drive** where the folder is located.
IsRootFolder	Boolean. Indicates whether or not a **Folder** is the root folder.
Name	String. The **Folder**'s name.
ParentFolder	Folder object. The **Folder**'s parent folder.
Path	String. The **Folder**'s path.
ShortName	String. The **Folder**'s name expressed as a short name.
ShortPath	String. The **Folder**'s path expressed as a short path.
Size	Variant. The total size in bytes of all subfolders and files.
Type	String. The **Folder** type.

Fig. 25.10 Some **Folder** properties and methods (part 1 of 2).

Property/method	Description
Methods	
Delete	Delete the **Folder**. Same as **DeleteFolder** of **FileSystemObject**.
Move	Move the **Folder**. Same as **MoveFolder** of **FileSystemObject**.
Copy	Copy the **Folder**. Same as **CopyFolder** of **FileSystemObject**.

Fig. 25.10 Some **Folder** properties and methods (part 2 of 2).

The **Drive** object allows the programmer to gather information about drives. Figure 25.11 lists some common **Drive** properties. Property **DriveLetter** contains the **Drive**'s letter. Property **SerialNumber** contains the **Drive**'s serial number. Property **FreeSpace** contains the number of bytes available.

Figure 25.12 is an Active Server Page for a guest book that allows the visitors to the site to enter their name, e-mail address and comments. We use file system objects to write the visitor information to a file on the server.

Property	Description
AvailableSpace	Variant. The amount of available **Drive** space in bytes.
DriveLetter	String. The letter assigned to the **Drive** (e.g., "C").
DriveType	Integer. The **Drive** type. Constants **Unknown**, **Removable**, **Fixed**, **Remote**, **CDRom** and **RamDisk** represent **Drive** types and have the values 0–5, respectively.
FileSystem	String. The file system **Drive** description (FAT, FAT32, NTFS, etc.).
FreeSpace	Variant. Same as **AvailableSpace**.
IsReady	Boolean. Indicates whether or not a **Drive** is ready for use.
Path	String. The **Drive**'s path.
RootFolder	Folder object. The **Drive**'s root **Folder**.
SerialNumber	Long. The **Drive** serial number.
TotalSize	Variant. The total **Drive** size, in bytes.
VolumeName	String. The **Drive** volume name.

Fig. 25.11 **Drive** properties.

```
1   <% @LANGUAGE = VBScript %>
2   <% Option Explicit %>
3
```

Fig. 25.12 Guest book Active Server Page (part 1 of 4).

```
4    <% ' Fig. 25.12 : guestbook.asp %>
5
6    <!DOCTYPE HTML PUBLIC "-//W3C//DTD HTML 4.0 Transitional//EN">
7    <HTML>
8    <HEAD>
9    <TITLE>GuestBook Example</TITLE>
10   <BODY>
11   <FONT SIZE = "4" FACE = "Arial" COLOR = "blue">
12
13   <%
14       Dim fileObject, textFile, guestBook, mailtoUrl
15
16       ' If user has made an entry and thus the page is
17       ' reloading, then process this entry
18       If Request( "entry" ) = "true" Then
19
20          ' Print a thank you
21          Call Response.Write( "Thanks for your entry, " )
22          Call Response.Write( Request( "name" ) & "!" )
23   %>
24   <HR COLOR = "blue" SIZE = "1">
25   <%       ' Instantiate a FileSystemObject
26          Set fileObject = Server.CreateObject( _
27             "Scripting.FileSystemObject" )
28
29          ' Guestbook path must be modified to reflect the file
30          ' structure of the server.
31          guestBook = "c:\Inetpub\Wwwroot\Deitel\" & "guestbook.txt"
32
33          ' Check if the file exists. If not, create it.
34          If fileObject.FileExists( guestbook ) <> True Then
35             Call fileObject.CreateTextFile( guestBook )
36          End If
37
38          ' Guestbook must be open for writing.
39          ' Open the guestbook, 8 is for appending
40          Set textFile = fileObject.OpenTextFile( guestbook, 8, True )
41
42          ' Build the mailtoUrl
43          mailtoUrl = Date() & " <A HREF = " & Chr( 34 ) _
44             & "mailto:" & Request( "email" ) & Chr( 34 ) _
45             & ">" & Request( "name" ) & "</A>:   "
46
47          ' Write data to guestbook.txt
48          Call textFile.WriteLine( "<HR COLOR = " & Chr( 34 ) _
49             & "blue" & Chr( 34 ) & " SIZE = " & Chr( 34 ) _
50             & "1" & Chr( 34 ) & ">" )
51          Call textFile.WriteLine( mailtoUrl )
52          Call textFile.WriteLine( Request( "comment" ) )
53          Call textFile.Close()
54       End If
55   %>
56
```

Fig. 25.12 Guest book Active Server Page (part 2 of 4).

```
57    Please leave a message in our guestbook.
58
59    </FONT>
60    <FORM ACTION = "guestbook.asp?entry=true" METHOD = "POST">
61    <CENTER>
62    <TABLE>
63    <TR>
64    <TD><FONT FACE = "Arial" SIZE = "2">Your Name:   </FONT></TD>
65    <TD><INPUT TYPE = "text" FACE = "Arial"
66        SIZE = "60" NAME = "name"></TD>
67    </TR>
68    <TR>
69    <TD><FONT FACE = "Arial" SIZE = "2">Your email address:
70    </FONT></TD>
71    <TD><INPUT TYPE = "text" FACE = "Arial" SIZE = "60"
72        NAME = "email" VALUE = "user@isp.com"></TD>
73    </TR>
74    <TR>
75    <TD><FONT FACE = "Arial" SIZE = "2">Tell the world:   </FONT>
76    </TD>
77    <TD><TEXTAREA NAME = "comment" ROWS = "3" COLS = "50">
78    Replace this text with the information
79    you would like to post.
80    </TEXTAREA></TD>
81    </TR>
82    </TABLE>
83    <INPUT TYPE = "submit" VALUE = "SUBMIT">
84    <INPUT TYPE = "reset" VALUE = "CLEAR">
85    </CENTER>
86    </FORM>
87
88    <%
89       Dim fileObject2, textFile2
90
91         ' Instantiate a FileSystemObject
92         Set fileObject2 = Server.CreateObject( _
93            "Scripting.FileSystemObject" )
94
95         ' Guestbook path must be modified to reflect
96         ' the file structure of the server.
97         guestBook = "c:\Inetpub\wwwroot\Deitel\" & "guestbook.txt"
98
99         ' Check if the file exists. If not, create it.
100        If fileObject2.FileExists( guestBook ) = True Then
101
102           ' Guestbook must be open for writing.
103           ' Open the guestbook, "1" is for reading.
104           Set textFile2 = fileObject2.OpenTextFile( guestbook, 1 )
105
106           ' Read the entries from the file and write them to
107           ' the client.
108           Call Response.Write( "Guestbook Entries:<BR>" )
109           Call Response.Write( textFile2.ReadAll() )
```

Fig. 25.12 Guest book Active Server Page (part 3 of 4).

```
110            Call textFile2.Close()
111        End If
112 %>
113
114 </BODY>
115 </HTML>
```

Fig. 25.12 Guest book Active Server Page (part 4 of 4).

The guest book page displayed in the browser consists of a form (to be filled in by the user) and a list of guest book entries (initially, there are no entries in this list). We begin by discussing the form (lines 60–86). The form contains three text fields used to input the name, e-mail account and user comments.

Line 60

```
<FORM ACTION = "guestbook.asp?entry=true" METHOD = "POST">
```

indicates that a **POST** request occurs upon form submission. The action for the form requests the same ASP page in which the form is contained—**guestbook.asp**. As we demonstrated earlier, this is perfectly valid; a form's action is not required to request a different document. When the form is submitted, **guestbook.asp** is requested from the server. Notice that the form passes **guestbook.asp** a parameter in the URL. Passing parameters in a page's name simulates an HTTP **GET** request. We send the parameters in the page's name by appending a question mark to the page's URL, followed by a list of parameters and values, separated by ampersands:

```
SomeURL?param1=value1&param2=value2& ... paramN=valueN
```

Our form passes one parameter named **entry**:

```
guestbook.asp?entry=true
```

This URL is a "virtual path" for

```
http://localhost/Deitel/guestbook.asp?entry=true
```

Upon submission, **guestbook.asp** is requested and passed parameter **entry**, which is assigned **"true"**. [*Note*: **"true"** is a string, and not a boolean value.] The name **entry** is programmer defined; you, of course, may choose any name you prefer. We use this technique to determine whether this ASP page is being requested by a form submitted from **guestbook.asp**.

We want only lines 21–53 to execute when the page is loaded with a **POST** request. Line 18

```
If Request( "entry" ) = "true" Then
```

uses the **Request** object to get **entry**'s value and test it against the string **"true"**. When this page is requested by a client for the first time, **entry** has the value **""** (an empty string), and lines 21–53 are not executed. Variable **entry** is passed **"true"** only during the **POST** operation (line 60). When **entry** is **"true"**, lines 21–53 are executed.

Lines 21 and 22

```
Call Response.Write( "Thanks for your entry, " )
Call Response.Write( Request( "name" ) & "!" )
```

print **Thanks for your entry,** followed by the user's name. Notice that the **Request** object is used to get the value posted in the **name** text field of the submitted form.

Lines 26 and 27

```
Set fileObject = Server.CreateObject( _
   "Scripting.FileSystemObject" )
```

create an FSO instance (i.e., an object) and assign it to reference **fileObject**. When assigning an object to a reference in VBScript, keyword **Set** is required. We specify the location of the file that stores guest book information in line 31. *You may need to modify this path to conform to the directory structure on your machine.*

Before writing data to the guest book, we call **FileExists** in line 34 to determine if **guestbook.txt** exists. If it does not, method **CreateTextFile** is called to create the file.

Line 40

```
Set textFile = fileObject.OpenTextFile( guestbook, 8, True )
```

calls method **OpenTextFile** to get a **TextStream** object for accessing the text file **guestbook.txt**. The constant value **8** indicates *append mode* (writing to the end of the file), and **True** indicates that the file will be created if it does not already exist. Opening for read or write is specified with constant values **1** and **2**, respectively. The user's submitted name and e-mail address are combined with HTML tags and assigned to string **mailtoUrl** (lines 43–45). This string, when displayed in the browser, shows the submitted name as a *mailto link*. Clicking on this link opens an e-mail message editor with the person's name in the **To:** field. Line 43 calls VBScript function **Date** to assign the current server date to the beginning of **mailtoUrl**. The **Request** object is used to retrieve the values from the **email** field (line 44) and the **name** field (line 45). We pass the value **34** to the VBScript function **Chr** to get a double-quote (**"**) character. We store HTML tags in **mailtoUrl**. We choose to be formal and include quotations around HTML values. For example, we use **<FONT FACE="Arial">** instead of **<FONT FACE=Arial>**. Because the interpreter would treat a double quote as the end of the **mailtoUrl** string, we use function **Chr** to return a double quote.

Lines 48–52 write text to **guestbook.txt** using the **TextStream** method **WriteLine**. After writing the text to the file, **TextStream** method **Close** is called in line 53 to close the file.

Every time a client requests this Active Server Page, lines 89–111 execute. This VBScript code displays a list of all the users who have made guest book entries. If the **guestbook.txt** file exists, it is opened for reading in line 104. Lines 108 and 109 write HTML/text to the client. The entire contents of **guestbook.txt** are read by calling **TextStream** method **ReadAll**. The text is written to the client using **Response.Write**. Because the text contains HTML markup, it is rendered in the client browser.

25.9 Session Tracking and Cookies

HTTP does not support persistent information that could help a Web server distinguish between clients. In this section, we will introduce two related technologies that enable a Web server to distinguish between clients: session tracking and cookies.

Many Web sites provide custom Web pages and/or functionality on a client-by-client basis. For example, some Web sites allow you to customize their home page to suit your needs. An excellent example of this type of site is the *Yahoo!* Web site (**my.yahoo.com**), which allows you to customize how the Yahoo! site appears. [*Note:* You need to get a free Yahoo! ID first.]

Another example of a service that is customized on a client-by-client basis is a *shopping cart* for shopping on the Web. Obviously, the server must distinguish between clients so the business can assign the proper items and charge each client the proper amount.

A third example of customizing on a client-by-client basis lies in marketing. Companies often track the pages you visit so they can display advertisements based upon your browsing trends. Many people consider tracking to be an invasion of their privacy, and thus tracking is an increasingly sensitive issue in our information-based society.

There are a number of popular techniques for uniquely identifying clients. For the purposes of this chapter, we introduce two techniques to track clients individually: *session tracking* and *cookies*.

The server handles session tracking. The first time a client connects to the server, the server assigns the user a unique *session ID*. When the client makes additional requests, the client's session ID is compared with the session IDs stored in the server's memory. Active Server Pages use the **Session** object to manage sessions. The **Session** object's **Timeout** property specifies the number of minutes that a session exists before it expires. The default value for property **Timeout** is 20 minutes. Calling **Session** method **Abandon** can also terminate an individual session.

We are now ready to present an example that uses session tracking. Figure 25.13 is an ASP page generator. Users who are not familiar with ASP can input their information in a form and submit the form, and the ASP page generator does all the work of creating the user's ASP page. This example consists of two Active Server Pages linked to each other through HTTP **POST** requests. We use session variables in this example to maintain a state between the two ASP pages. Multiple Active Server Pages connected in this manner are sometimes called an *ASP application*.

The first page, **instantpage.asp** (Fig. 25.13), consists of a form that requests information from the user. When submitted, the form is **POST**ed to **process.asp** (Fig. 25.17). If there are no errors, **process.asp** creates the user's ASP page. Otherwise, **process.asp** redirects the user back to **instantpage.asp**, passing it parameter **error=yes**. Also, **process.asp** stores a "welcome back" message in a session variable. Each time a user submits the form, **process.asp** stores a new "welcome back" message in the session variable. If a filename is not provided, **process.asp** returns an error to **instantpage.asp** (Fig. 25.14).

Line 15

```
<!-- #include virtual = "/includes/mgtheader.shtml" -->
```

is a *server-side include* (*SSI*) statement that incorporates the contents of **mgtheader.shtml** (Fig. 25.15) into the ASP file. Server-side includes are commands embedded in HTML documents that add dynamic content. The SSI statement in line 15 is replaced with the contents of the file **mgtheader.shtml**. Not all Web servers support the available SSI commands. Therefore, SSI commands are written as HTML comments. SSI statements always execute before any scripting code executes.

We also use an SSI in line 69 to include **mgtfooter.shtml** (Fig. 25.16). The word **virtual** in the SSI refers to the include file's path as it appears below the server's root directory. This path is often referred to as a *virtual path*. SSIs can also use **file**, instead of **virtual**, to indicate a *physical path* on the server. For example, line 15 could be rewritten as

```
<!-- #include file = "C:\Webshare\Wwwroot\includes\
mgtheader.shtml"-->
```

which assumes that **mgtheader.shtml** is in the directory **C:\Webshare\Wwwroot\includes** on the server.

Software Engineering Observation 25.8

Virtual paths hide the server's internal file structure.

```
1   <% @LANGUAGE = VBScript %>
2   <% Option Explicit %>
3
4   <% ' Fig. 25.13 : instantpage.asp %>
5
6   <!DOCTYPE HTML PUBLIC "-//W3C//DTD HTML 4.0 Transitional//EN">
7   <HTML>
8   <HEAD>
9   <TITLE>Instant Page Content Builder</TITLE>
10  </HEAD>
11
12  <BODY>
13
14  <% ' Include the header %>
15  <!-- #include virtual = "/includes/mgtheader.shtml" -->
16  <FONT FACE = "Arial" SIZE = "2">
17  <H2>Instant Page Content Builder</H2>
18
19  <% ' If process.asp signaled an error, print the error
20     ' message.
21     If Request( "error" ) = "yes" Then
22        Call Response.Write( Session( "errorMessage" ) )
23     ' Otherwise, print the welcome back message, if any.
24     Else
25        Call Response.Write( Session( "welcomeBack" ) )
26     End If
27
28     ' A form to get the information from the user.
29  %>
30  <FORM ACTION = "process.asp" METHOD = "POST">
31
32  <CENTER>
33
34  <TABLE>
35  <TR>
36  <TD><FONT FACE = "Arial" SIZE = "2">Your Name:
37  </FONT><BR></TD>
38  <TD><INPUT TYPE = "text" FACE = "Arial" SIZE = "60"
39              NAME = "name"><BR></TD>
40  </TR>
41  <TR>
42  <TD><FONT FACE = "Arial" SIZE = "2">Enter the Filename:
43  </FONT><BR></TD>
```

Fig. 25.13 Listing for **instantpage.asp** (part 1 of 2).

```
44  <TD><INPUT TYPE = "text" FACE = "Arial" SIZE = "60"
45            NAME = "filename" VALUE = "YourFileName.asp"><BR>
46  </TD>
47  </TR>
48  <TR>
49  <TD><FONT FACE = "Arial" SIZE = "2">Enter the Title:
50  </FONT><BR></TD>
51  <TD><INPUT TYPE = "text" FACE = "Arial" SIZE = "60"
52            NAME = "doctitle" VALUE = "Document Title"><BR>
53  </TD>
54  </TR>
55  <TR>
56  <TD><FONT FACE = "Arial" SIZE = "2">Enter the Content:
57  </FONT><BR></TD>
58  <TD><TEXTAREA NAME = "content" ROWS = "3" COLS = "50">
59  Replace this text with the
60  information you would like to post.
61  </TEXTAREA><BR></TD>
62  </TR>
63  </TABLE>
64  <INPUT TYPE = "submit" VALUE = "SUBMIT">
65  <INPUT TYPE = "reset" VALUE = "CLEAR">
66  </CENTER>
67  </FORM>
68
69  <!-- #include virtual = "/includes/mgtfooter.shtml" -->
70  </FONT>
71  </BODY>
72  </HTML>
```

Fig. 25.13 Listing for **instantpage.asp** (part 2 of 2).

Fig. 25.14 Error message returned by `instantpage.asp`.

The session variables used in this example are **errorMessage**, for the error message, and **welcomeBack**, for the user's "welcome back" message. The **If** statement on lines 21–26

```
If Request( "error" ) = "yes" Then
  Call Response.Write( Session( "errorMessage" ) )
' Otherwise, print the welcome back message, if any.
Else
  Call Response.Write( Session( "welcomeBack" ) )
End If
```

```
73  <HR SIZE = "1" COLOR = "blue">
74  <IMG HEIGHT = "100" SRC = "/images/mgheader.gif">
75  <HR SIZE = "1" COLOR = "blue">
```

Fig. 25.15 File listing for `mgtheader.shtml`.

```
76  <HR COLOR = "blue" SIZE = "1">
77  <CENTER>
78  <A HREF = "mailto:orders">Ordering Information</A> -
79  <A HREF = "mailto:editor">Contact the Editor</A><BR>
80  <HR COLOR = "blue" SIZE = "1">
81  </CENTER>
```

Fig. 25.16 File listing for `mgtfooter.shtml`.

test if the value of **error** is **"yes"**. If the **If** statement returns a value of true, the value of session variable **errorMessage** is written to the client. Otherwise, **welcomeBack**'s value is written to the client. A session variable's value is set and retrieved using the **Session** object. Note that **Request("error")** never equals **"yes"** unless **process.asp** passes **error=yes** as a parameter to **instantpage.asp**. Otherwise, **Request("error")** contains an empty string. A session variable that has not been explicitly given a value contains an empty string. When **instantpage.asp** is requested for the first time, **Request("error")** is equal to an empty string and the "welcome back" message is not written.

Line 30

```
<FORM ACTION = "process.asp" METHOD = "POST">
```

requests Active Server Page **process.asp** when the form is posted. The remainder of **instantpage.asp** is HTML that defines the form input items and the page footer.

Software Engineering Observation 25.9

Server-side includes may include any type of information. Text files and HTML files are two of the most common server-side include files.

Software Engineering Observation 25.10

Server-side includes are performed before any scripting code is interpreted. An Active Server Page cannot dynamically decide which server-side includes are used and which are not. Through scripting, an ASP can determine which SSI block is sent to the client.

Testing and Debugging Tip 25.2

Server-side includes that contain scripting code should enclose the scripting code in **<SCRIPT>** *tags or in* **<% %>** *delimiters to prevent one block of scripting code from running into another block of scripting code.*

Software Engineering Observation 25.11

By convention, server-side include (SSI) files end with the **.shtml** *extension.*

Software Engineering Observation 25.12

Server-side includes are an excellent technique for reusing HTML, Dynamic HTML, scripts and other programming elements.

The document **process.asp** (Fig. 25.17) creates the user's ASP document and presents a link to the user's page. This page is requested by **instantpage.asp** (line 30).

The **If** statement in line 91 validates the contents of field **Enter the Filename**. If the text box is empty or contains the default string **YourFileName.asp**, HTML text containing an error message is assigned to the session variable **errorMessage**:

```
Session( "errorMessage" ) = "<FONT COLOR = " & q _
    & "red" & q & " SIZE = " & q & "4" & q & ">" _
    & "Please enter a filename." & "</FONT>" & "<BR>"
```

Then, line 96

```
Call Response.Redirect( "instantpage.asp?error=yes" )
```

calls **Response** method *Redirect* to request **instantpage.asp** and pass it **error=yes**. ASP **instantpage.asp** was presented in Fig. 25.13.

```
82   <% @LANGUAGE = VBScript %>
83   <% Option Explicit %>
84
85   <% ' Fig. 25.17 : process.asp %>
86
87   <%  Dim q
88        q = Chr( 34 )
89
90        ' Check to make sure that they have entered a filename
91        If Request( "filename" ) = "YourFileName.asp" Or _
92           Request( "filename" ) = "" Then
93           Session( "errorMessage" ) = "<FONT COLOR = " & q _
94              & "red" & q & " SIZE = " & q & "4" & q & ">" _
95              & "Please enter a filename." & "</FONT>" & "<BR>"
96           Call Response.Redirect( "instantpage.asp?error=yes" )
97        End If
98
99        Dim directoryPath, filePath, fileObject
100
101       ' Create a FileSystem Object
102       Set fileObject = Server.CreateObject( _
103          "Scripting.FileSystemObject" )
104
105       ' directoryPath must be modified to reflect the file
106       ' structure of your server
107       directoryPath = "c:\Inetpub\Wwwroot\userpages\"
108
109       ' See if the directory exists. If not, create it.
110       If Not fileObject.FolderExists( directoryPath ) Then
111          Call fileObject.CreateFolder( directoryPath )
112       End If
113
114       ' Build path for text file.
115       filePath = directoryPath & Request( "filename" )
116
117       ' Check if the file already exists
118       If fileObject.FileExists( filePath ) Then
119          Session( "errorMessage" ) = "<FONT COLOR = " & q _
120             & "red" & q & " SIZE = " & q & "4" & q & ">" _
121             & "This filename is in use. " _
122             & "Please enter another filename." & "</FONT>" _
123             & "<BR>"
124          Call Response.Redirect( "instantpage.asp?error=yes" )
125       End If
126
127       ' Save HTML for the welcome back message
128       ' in a session variable
129       Session( "welcomeBack" )= "<FONT COLOR = " _
130          & q & "blue" & q & " SIZE = " _
131          & q & "4" & q & ">" _
```

Fig. 25.17 Listing for **process.asp** (part 1 of 3).

```
132              & "Welcome Back, " & Request( "name" ) & "!</FONT>" _
133              & "<BR>"
134
135      Dim header, footer, textFile, openMark, closeMark
136      openMark = "<" & "%"
137      closeMark = "%" & ">"
138
139      ' Build the header.
140      ' vbCrLf inserts a carriage return/linefeed into the text
141      ' string which makes the HTML code more readable
142      header = openMark & " @LANGUAGE = VBScript " & closeMark _
143          & vbCrLf & openMark & " ' " & Request( "filename" ) _
144          & " " & closeMark & vbCrLf & vbCrLf _
145          & "<!DOCTYPE HTML PUBLIC " & q _
146          & "-//W3C//DTD HTML 4.0 Transitional//EN" & q & ">" _
147          & vbCrLf & "<HTML>" & vbCrLf & "<HEAD>" & vbCrLf _
148          & "<META NAME = " & q & "author" & q & " CONTENT = " _
149          & q & Request( "name" ) & q & ">" & vbCrLf _
150          & "<META NAME = " & q & "pubdate" & q _
151          & " CONTENT = " & q & Date() & q & ">" & vbCrLf _
152          & "<TITLE>" & Request( "doctitle" ) & "</TITLE>" _
153          & vbCrLf & "</HEAD>" & vbCrLf & "<BODY>" & vbCrLf _
154          & "<FONT FACE = " & q & "arial" & q & " SIZE = " & q _
155          & "3" & q & " >" & vbCrLf _
156          & "<!-- #include virtual = " & q _
157          & "/includes/mgtheader.shtml" & q & " -->" & vbCrLf _
158          & "<CENTER><U><H2>" & Request( "doctitle" ) _
159          & "</H2></U>" & vbCrLf & "<BR>" & vbCrLf
160
161      ' Build the footer using a different style for
162      ' building the string
163      footer = vbCrLf & "</CENTER><BR><BR><BR>" & vbCrLf
164      footer = footer & "You have requested this page on "
165      footer = footer & openMark & " =Date() " & closeMark & ","
166      footer = footer & vbCrLf & "at " & openMark & " =Time() "
167      footer = footer & closeMark & "." & vbCrLf
168      footer = footer & "<!-- #include virtual = " & q
169      footer = footer & "/includes/mgtfooter.shtml" & q
170      footer = footer & " -->" & vbCrLf & "</FONT>"
171      footer = footer & vbCrLf & "</BODY>" & vbCrLf & "</HTML>"
172
173      ' Create the html file
174      Set textFile = fileObject.CreateTextFile( filePath, False )
175      Call textFile.WriteLine( header )
176      Call textFile.WriteLine( Request( "content" ) )
177      Call textFile.Write( footer )
178      Call textFile.Close
179  %>
180  <!DOCTYPE HTML PUBLIC "-//W3C//DTD HTML 4.0 Transitional//EN">
181  <HTML>
182  <HEAD>
183
184  <% ' Use the title given by the user %>
```

Fig. 25.17 Listing for **process.asp** (part 2 of 3).

```
185   <TITLE>File Generated: <% =Request( "filename" ) %></TITLE>
186   </HEAD>
187
188   <BODY>
189
190   <!-- #include virtual = "/includes/mgtheader.shtml" -->
191
192   <FONT FACE = "Arial" SIZE = "3">
193   <CENTER><U><H2>
194      File Generated: <% =Request( "filename" ) %>
195   </H2></U></CENTER><BR>
196   <% ' Provide a link to the generated page %>
197   Your file is ready:
198   <A HREF = "/userpages/<% =Request( "filename" ) %>">
199   <% =Request( "doctitle" ) %></A>
200
201   <!-- #include virtual = "/includes/mgtfooter.shtml" -->
202
203   </FONT>
204   </BODY>
205   </HTML>
```

Fig. 25.17 Listing for **process.asp** (part 3 of 3).

If the user has entered a valid filename, an FSO object is created in lines 102 and 103 and assigned to reference **fileObject**. Line 107 specifies the path on the server where the ASP file will eventually be written. We have chosen to store all the user pages in a directory that we created called **userpages** (beneath the publishing directory, **C:\Inetpub\Wwwroot**). *You will need to either create this directory or modify this path on your machine.*

The **If** statement in line 110 tests for the existence of the **C:\Inetpub\Wwwroot\userpages** folder by calling FSO method **FolderEx-**

ists to determine if the directory specified in line 107 exists. If the folder does not exist, FSO method **CreateFolder** is called to create it in line 111.

Line 115 builds the file path by concatenating the filename to the directory path. This **filePath** is passed to FSO method **FileExists**, which is called in line 118 to determine if the file exists. If it does exist, another user has already created an ASP document with the same filename. In this case, HTML containing an error message is saved to the session variable **errorMessage**. On line 124, **error=yes** is passed to **instantpage.asp**, indicating that an error has occurred.

Lines 129–133 assign HTML for the "welcome back" message to session variable **welcomeBack**. The format of the message is

```
Welcome back, X!
```

where **X** is the current user's name, obtained from the form's **name** field.

Lines 136 and 137 assign the ASP scripting delimiters to string variables **openMark** and **closeMark**. We use two strings instead of one to represent the opening and closing delimiters (i.e., **"<" & "%"**) because the interpreter treats the single string **"<%"** as a scripting delimiter.

Next, we build the user's ASP file. For clarity, we divide the file into three parts: a header, a footer and the content (provided by the user in the form's **content** field).

Lines 142–159 construct HTML for the header and assign it to string **header**. VBScript constant **vbCrLf** is used to insert a carriage-return line-feed combination. The form's values are retrieved using the **Request** object. Note that character variable **q** is assigned the value **Chr(34)** in line 88, where **34** is the decimal ASCII code for the double-quote character. For more on ASCII characters, see Appendix C. Lines 163–171 create the page's footer and assign it to variable **footer**.

Lines 174–178 write **header**, text area **content**'s text and **footer** to the text file before closing it. Lines 180–205 send HTML to the client that contains a link to the created page. Figure 25.18 lists a sample ASP file—named **test.asp**—created by Active Server Page **process.asp**. [*Note*: We added line 2 for presentation purposes.] The first screen capture in Fig. 25.19 contains shows the message that is displayed when the user returns back to **instantpage.asp**. The second screen capture shows the error message generated when the user does not change the default filename in the **Enter the Filename** textfield.

```
1   <% @LANGUAGE = VBScript %>
2   <% ' Fig. 25.18 : test.asp %>
3
4   <!DOCTYPE HTML PUBLIC "-//W3C//DTD HTML 4.0 Transitional//EN">
5   <HTML>
6   <HEAD>
7   <META NAME = "author" CONTENT = "Test User">
8   <META NAME = "pubdate" CONTENT = "5/29/2000">
9   <TITLE>My Personal Page</TITLE>
10  </HEAD>
11  <BODY>
```

Fig. 25.18 Listing for **test.asp** (part 1 of 2).

```
12   <FONT FACE = "Arial" SIZE = "3">
13   <!-- #include virtual = "/includes/mgtheader.shtml" -->
14   <CENTER><U><H2>My Personal Page</H2></U>
15   <BR>
16
17   My personal page is under construction. Come again soon.
18
19   </CENTER><BR><BR><BR>
20   You have requested this page on <% =Date() %>,
21   at <% =Time() %>.
22   <!-- #include virtual = "/includes/mgtfooter.shtml" -->
23   </FONT>
24   </BODY>
25   </HTML>
```

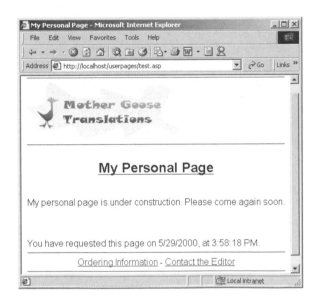

Fig. 25.18 Listing for **test.asp** (part 2 of 2).

Another popular way to customize Web pages is via *cookies*. Cookies can store information on the client's computer for retrieval later in the same browsing session or in future browsing sessions. For example, cookies could be used in a shopping application to keep track of the client's shopping-cart items.

Cookies are small files sent by an ASP (or similar technology, such as Perl, discussed in Chapter 26) as part of a response to a client. Every HTTP-based interaction between a client and a server includes a *header* that contains information about either the request (when the communication is from the client to the server) or the response (when the communication is from the server to the client). When an Active Server Page receives a request, the header includes information such as the request type (e.g., **GET** or **POST**) and cookies stored on the client machine by the server. When the server formulates its response, the header information includes any cookies the server wants to store on the client computer.

Software Engineering Observation 25.13

Some clients do not allow cookies to be written on their machine. A refusal to accept cookies may prevent the client from being able to properly use the Web site that attempted to write the cookies.

Depending on the *maximum age* of a cookie, the Web browser either maintains the cookie for the duration of the browsing session (i.e., until the user closes the Web browser) or stores the cookie on the client computer for future use. When the browser makes a request to a server, cookies previously sent to the client by that server are returned to the server (if the cookies have not expired) as part of the request formulated by the browser. Cookies are automatically deleted when they *expire* (i.e., reach their maximum age). We use cookies in Section 25.11 to store user IDs.

25.10 Databases, SQL, Microsoft UDA and ADO

A *database* is an integrated collection of data. A *database management system (DBMS)* involves the data itself and the software that controls the storage and retrieval of data. Database management systems provide mechanisms for storing and organizing data in a manner that facilitates satisfying sophisticated queries and manipulations of the data.

The most popular database systems in use today are *relational databases*. A language called *Structured Query Language* (*SQL*—pronounced "sequel") is almost universally used with relational database systems to make *queries* (i.e., to request information that satisfies given criteria) and manipulate data. Some popular enterprise-level relational database systems include Microsoft SQL Server, Oracle, Sybase, DB2 and Informix. Enterprise-level database systems are used for large-scale database access. A popular personal relational database is Microsoft Access, which we use for simplicity in our examples. *Universal Data Access (UDA) is* a Microsoft architecture that provides data access to many data sources. We first discuss database structure and how to query a database using SQL and then briefly discuss the UDA architecture.

A relational database is composed of *tables*, which in turn are composed of *columns* (or *fields*). Figure 25.20 shows the table relationships in a database named **catalog.mdb**. The database contains four tables: **products**, **authorlist**, **authors** and **technologies**. Within each of these tables are multiple fields. For example, the **technologies** table has **technologyID** and **technology** fields. The *records* (or *rows*) of the **technologies** table are also shown in Fig. 25.20. The **technologyID** field is the *primary key*. A primary key is a unique field that is used to identify a record. The records of the **technologies** table are ordered by a primary key. The first record has **technologyID** "1" and **technology** "C".

A line between two tables in Fig. 25.20 represents a relationship between those tables. Consider the line between the **products** and **technologies** tables. On the **technologies** end of the line, there is a **1**; on the **products** end, there is an infinity symbol. This indicates that every technology in the **technologies** table corresponds to an arbitrary number of products in the **products** table—a *one-to-many relationship*. The **products** and **technologies** tables are linked by their **technologyID** fields.

Different database users are often interested in different data and different relationships between those data. SQL statements are commonly used to specify which data to *select* from a table. SQL provides a complete set of keywords (including **SELECT**) that enable programmers to define complex queries for retrieving data from a table. Query results are commonly called *result sets* (or *record sets*).

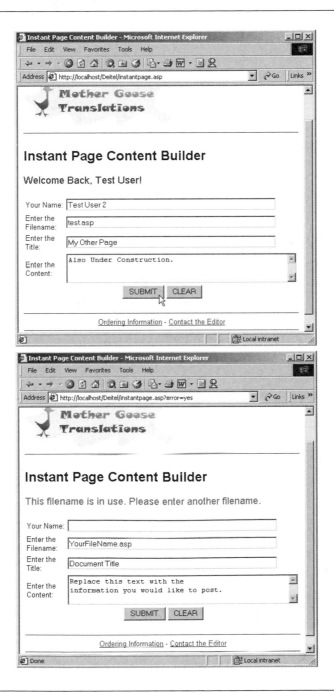

Fig. 25.19 Output from `instantpage.asp`.

Figure 25.21 lists some SQL keywords for querying a database, inserting records into a database and updating existing records in a database. For more information on SQL keywords, visit **www.aspin.com/home/references/database/sql**.

A typical SQL query selects information from one or more tables in a database. Such selections are performed by **SELECT** *queries*. The simplest form of a **SELECT** query is

> **SELECT * FROM** *TableName*

In the preceding query, the asterisk (*****) indicates that all rows and columns (fields) from table *TableName* should be selected. To select specific fields from a table, replace the asterisk (*****) with a comma-separated list of the field names to select. For example,

> **SELECT** *FieldName1,* *FieldName2,* **FROM** *TableName*

selects all the *FieldName1* and *FieldName2* fields from the records in the *TableName* table.

Software Engineering Observation 25.14

For most SQL statements, the asterisk (*****) should not be used to specify field names to select from a table (or several tables). In general, programmers process result sets by knowing in advance the order of the fields in the result set.

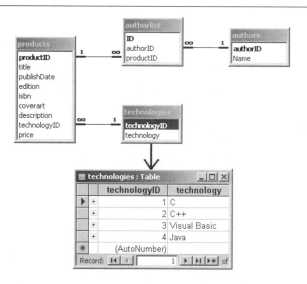

Fig. 25.20 Table relationships in **catalog.mbd**.

SQL keyword	Description
SELECT	Select (retrieve) fields from one or more tables.
FROM	Tables from which to get fields. Required in every **SELECT**.

Fig. 25.21 Some SQL query keywords (part 1 of 2).

SQL keyword	Description
WHERE	Criteria for selection that determine the rows to be retrieved.
ORDER BY	Criteria for ordering (sorting) of records.
INSERT INTO	Insert values into one or more tables. [*Note:* Some databases do not require the SQL keyword **INTO**.]
UPDATE	Update existing data in one or more tables.

Fig. 25.21 Some SQL query keywords (part 2 of 2).

Software Engineering Observation 25.15

Specifying the actual field names to select from a table (or several tables) guarantees that the fields are always returned in the same order, even if the actual order of the fields in the database table(s) changes.

Common Programming Error 25.3

When composing an SQL statement using the asterisk (*) to select fields, assuming that the fields in the result set of the query are always returned in the same order may result in incorrect processing of the data in the application receiving the result set. If the order of the fields in the database table(s) changes, the order of the fields in the result set changes accordingly.

Common Programming Error 25.4

In a query, forgetting to enclose a field name containing spaces in square brackets ([]) is an error.

Often it is necessary to identify records in a database that satisfy only certain *selection criteria*. SQL provides the optional ***WHERE*** *clause* in a **SELECT** query to specify the selection criteria for a query. The simplest form of a **SELECT** query with selection criteria is

> **SELECT** *fieldName1*, *fieldName2*, ... **FROM** *TableName* **WHERE** *criteria*

The **WHERE** clause condition can contain operators such as **<**, **>**, **<=**, **>=**, **=**, **<>** and **LIKE**. Operator **LIKE** is used for *pattern matching* with wildcard characters *asterisk (*)* and *question mark (?)*. Pattern matching allows SQL to search for similar strings to the pattern provided." An asterisk (*****) in the pattern indicates any number of (i.e., zero or more) characters in a row at the asterisk's location in the pattern. [*Note:* Many databases use the **%** character in place of the ***** character in a **LIKE** expression.]

It may be necessary to merge data from multiple tables into a single report for analysis purposes. This is accomplished using a join condition—a condition that joins, merges or extracts data from more than one table. For example, to extract all of the Visual Basic products from the database in Fig. 25.20, we would use

> **SELECT * FROM products, technologies WHERE technologyID = 3**

This command returns the **technologyID**, **technology** name and all of the **products** associated with the **technologyID** for Visual Basic ("**3**") in a record set.

The query results can be sorted into ascending or descending order by using the optional **ORDER BY** *clause*. The simplest forms of an **ORDER BY** clause are

SELECT *field1*, *field2*, ... **FROM** *TableName* **ORDER BY** *fieldName* **ASC**
SELECT *field1*, *field2*, ... **FROM** *TableName* **ORDER BY** *fieldName* **DESC**

where **ASC** specifies ascending (lowest to highest) order, **DESC** specifies descending (highest to lowest) order and *fieldName* represents the field (the column of the table) that is used for sorting purposes.

Often, it is necessary to insert data into a table (i.e., add a new record). This task is accomplished by using the **INSERT INTO** keywords. The simplest form for an **INSERT INTO** statement is

INSERT INTO *TableName* (*fieldName1*, *fieldName2*, ..., *fieldNameN*)
    VALUES (*value1*, *value2*, ..., *valueN*)

where *TableName* is the table into which the record will be inserted. The *TableName* is followed by a comma-separated list of field names in parentheses. (This list is not required if the **INSERT INTO** operation fills a complete row in the table.) The list of field names is followed by the SQL keyword **VALUES** and a comma-separated list of values in parentheses.

It is also often necessary to modify data in a table (i.e., update a record). This is accomplished by using an **UPDATE** operation. The simplest form for an **UPDATE** statement is

UPDATE *TableName*
    SET *fieldName1* = *value1*, *fieldName2* = *value2*, ..., *fieldNameN* = *valueN*
    WHERE *criteria*

where *TableName* is the table in which the record will be updated. The *TableName* is followed by the **SET** keyword and a comma-separated list of field name/value pairs in the format *fieldName* = *value*. The **WHERE** clause specifies the criteria used to determine which record(s) to update.

To execute an SQL query, a program must be able to access a database. Many different database vendors exist, each one potentially providing different database manipulation methods. Microsoft developed the *Open Database Connectivity (ODBC) Application Programming Interface (API)* to allow Windows applications to communicate in a uniform manner with disparate relational databases. Database vendors write a piece of software, called an *ODBC driver*, using the ODBC API to provide uniform access to the database (i.e., database programmers do not have to learn vendor-specific database implementations).

Microsoft *Universal Data Access* (*UDA*) is an architecture that is designed for high-performance data access to relational data sources, nonrelational data sources and mainframe/legacy data sources. The UDA architecture (Fig. 25.22) consists of three primary components: *OLE DB*, the core of the UDA architecture that provides low-level access to any data source; *Open Database Connectivity* (*ODBC*), a C programming-language library that uses SQL to access data, and *ActiveX Data Objects* (*ADO*), a simple object model that provides uniform access to any data source by interacting with OLE DB. [*Note:* OLE DB is required to implement a minimum set of data access services that can be used by ADO.]

More specifically, the *ADO object model* provides objects and *collections* (i.e., containers that hold one or more objects of a specific type). Figure 25.23 briefly describes some ADO objects and collections. Visit

www.microsoft.com/data/ado/adords15

to access the ADO documentation and view a complete list of methods, properties and events for these ADO objects.

25.11 Accessing a Database from an Active Server Page

As discussed in the previous section, Active Server Pages can communicate with databases through ADO (ActiveX Data Objects). ADO provides a uniform way for a program to connect with a variety of databases in a general manner without having to deal with the specifics of those database systems.

Web applications are typically *three-tier distributed applications,* consisting of a *user interface*, *business logic* and *database access*. The user interface in such an application is often created using HTML, Dynamic HTML or XML. The user interface, can of course, contain ActiveX controls and client-side scripts. In some cases, Java applets are also used for this tier. HTML is the preferred mechanism for representing the user interface in systems for which portability is a concern. Because all browsers support HTML, designing the user interface to be accessed through a Web browser guarantees portability across all browser platforms. The user interface can communicate directly with the middle-tier business logic by using the networking provided automatically by the browser. The middle tier can then access the database to manipulate the data. All three tiers may reside on separate computers that are connected to a network or on a single machine.

In multitier architectures, Web servers are increasingly used to build the middle tier. They provide the business logic that manipulates data from databases and that communicates with client Web browsers. Active Server Pages, through ADO, can interact with popular database systems. Developers do not need to be familiar with the specifics of each database system. Rather, developers use SQL-based queries, and ADO handles the specifics of interacting with each database system through OLE DB.

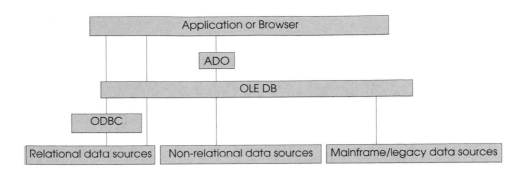

Fig. 25.22 Microsoft's UDA architecture.

Object/Collection	Description
Connection object	The connection to the data source.
Command object	Contains the query that interacts with the database (the *data source*) to manipulate data.
Parameter object	Contains information needed by a **Command** object to query the data source.
Parameters collection	Contains one or more **Parameter** objects.
Error object	Created when an error occurs while data is being accessed.
Errors collection	Contains one or more **Error** objects.
Recordset object	Contains zero or more records that match the database query. Collectively, this group of records is called a *record set*.
Field object	Contains the value (and other attributes) of one data source field.
Fields collection	Contains one or more **Field** objects.

Fig. 25.23 Some ADO object and collection types.

Databases can enhance applications by providing a data source that can be used to dynamically generate Web pages. Figure 25.13 (**instantpage.asp**) puts the power of Web page creation into the hands of individuals who are not familiar with HTML and ASP. However, we may want only a certain subset of preapproved users to be able to access **instantpage.asp**. We can use password protection to restrict access. In Fig. 25.24, we provide an Active Server Page named **login.asp** that prompts the user for a login name and password. The login names and passwords are stored in an Access database.

This example uses cookies to identify users, which must be enabled by the browser before executing this example. If cookies are disabled, the browser will not permit the example to write a cookie to the client machine, and the example will not be able to properly identify the user. To enable cookies in Internet Explorer 5, select Internet Options from the Tools menu to display the Internet Options dialog. Click on the **Security** tab at the top of the dialog to view the current security settings. Click on the **Custom Level...** button, scroll down and find **Cookies**. Click on **Enable** for both cookie options.

The Active Server Page **login.asp** prompts the user for a login ID and a password, while **submitlogin.asp** is responsible for validating the user's login. Both **submitlogin.asp** and **login.asp** use session variable **loginFailure**. If login is successful, **loginFailure** is set to **False** and the client is redirected to **instantpage.asp**. If login is unsuccessful, the variable is set to **True** and the client is redirected back to **login.asp**. Because **login.asp** has access to session variable **loginFailure**, the page recognizes that there was an error in **submitlogin.asp** and displays the error message.

```
1    <% @LANGUAGE = VBScript %>
2    <% Option Explicit %>
3
```

Fig. 25.24 Listing for **login.asp** (part 1 of 5).

```
4   <% ' Fig. 25.24 : login.asp %>
5
6   <% Dim connection, query, loginData
7
8      Set connection = Server.CreateObject( "ADODB.Connection" )
9      Call connection.Open( "login" )
10
11     ' Create the SQL query
12     query = "SELECT loginID FROM Users"
13
14     ' Create the record set
15     Set loginData = Server.CreateObject( "ADODB.Recordset" )
16     Call loginData.Open( query, connection )
17
18     ' If an error occurs, ignore it
19     On Error Resume Next
20  %>
21
22  <!DOCTYPE HTML PUBLIC "-//W3C//DTD HTML 4.0 Transitional//EN">
23  <HTML>
24  <HEAD><TITLE>Login Page</TITLE></HEAD>
25
26  <BODY>
27
28  <!-- #include virtual="/includes/mgtheader.shtml" -->
29
30  <%
31     ' If this is a return after a failed attempt,
32     ' print an error
33     If Session( "loginFailure" ) = True Then %>
34  <FONT SIZE = "4" COLOR = "red"> Login attempt failed,
35  please try again <P></FONT>
36  <% End If
37
38     ' Begin the form %>
39  <FONT FACE = "Arial" SIZE = "2">
40  Please select your name and enter
41  your password to login:<BR>
42  </FONT>
43  <FORM ACTION = "submitlogin.asp" METHOD = "POST">
44
45  <% ' Format the form using a table %>
46  <TABLE BORDER = "0">
47  <TR>
48  <TD><FONT FACE = "Arial" SIZE = "2">Name:</FONT></TD>
49  <TD><SELECT NAME = "loginID">
50  <OPTION VALUE = "noSelection">Select your name
51
52  <% ' If the loginID cookie is an empty string then there is
53     ' no need to consider the returning case
54     If Request.Cookies( "loginID" ) <> "" Then
55        Call BuildReturning()
```

Fig. 25.24 Listing for **login.asp** (part 2 of 5).

```
56       Else
57          Call BuildNewUser()
58       End If
59    %>
60
61    </SELECT>
62    </TD>
63    </TR>   .
64
65    <TR>
66    <TD><FONT FACE = "Arial" SIZE = "2">Password:</FONT></TD>
67    <TD><INPUT TYPE = "password" NAME = "password"></TD>
68    </TR>
69    <TR>
70    <TD> </TD>
71    <TD ALIGN = "left">
72       <INPUT TYPE = "submit" VALUE = "Log Me In">
73    </TD>
74    </TR>
75    </TABLE>
76    </FORM>
77    </FONT>
78
79    <!-- #include virtual="/includes/mgtfooter.shtml" -->
80
81    </BODY>
82    </HTML>
83
84    <% ' Builds the OPTION items for loginIDs and writes
85       ' selected for the loginID of the returning user
86       Sub BuildReturning()
87          Dim found
88
89          ' Pull user names from the record set to populate the
90          ' dropdown list
91          found = False
92          While Not loginData.EOF
93             ' Create this record's dropdown entry
94    %>       <OPTION
95    <%       ' If we did not write SELECTED for any OPTION
96             ' before
97             If ( Not found ) Then
98
99                ' If the current record's loginID is equal to
100               ' the loginID cookie, then it is the loginID of
101               ' the returning user, and thus we need to write
102               ' SELECTED for this option; in this case we also
103               ' need to signal that we have written SELECTED
104               ' for an OPTION by setting found to True.
105               If Request.Cookies( "loginID" ) _
106                  = loginData( "loginID" ) _
107               Then
108                  Call Response.Write( "SELECTED" )
```

Fig. 25.24 Listing for `login.asp` (part 3 of 5).

```
109                          found = True
110                  End If
111              End If
112 %>           VALUE = "<% =loginData( "loginID" ) %>">
113              <% =loginData( "loginID" ) %>
114 <%           Call loginData.MoveNext()
115          Wend
116      End Sub
117
118      ' Builds the OPTION items for loginIDs without writing
119      ' SELECTED for any loginID
120      Sub BuildNewUser()
121
122          ' Pull user names from the record set to populate the
123          ' dropdown list
124          While Not loginData.EOF
125              ' Create this record's dropdown entry
126 %>           <OPTION VALUE = "<% =loginData( "loginID" ) %>">
127              <% =loginData( "loginID" ) %>
128 <%           Call loginData.MoveNext()
129          Wend
130      End Sub
131 %>
```

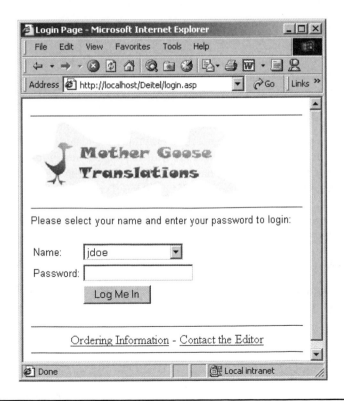

Fig. 25.24 Listing for **login.asp** (part 4 of 5).

Fig. 25.24 Listing for `login.asp` (part 5 of 5).

The `loginID` and `password` fields are stored in table `Users` inside an Access database named `login.mdb`. For this particular example, all users have the same password (i.e., `password`). Before executing this example, an ODBC System DSN for this database must be created. See the "Setting up a System Data Source Name" document on the CD that accompanies this book for instructions on how to create a DSN.

Users select their `loginID` from a drop-down list populated from the `Users` table. Note that `submitlogin.asp` also accesses the database to verify login information.

To recognize returning users and have their `loginID` displayed in the drop-down list, `submitlogin.asp` writes a cookie (named `loginID`) to the client containing the user's `loginID` string. When the user returns, `login.asp` reads the cookie and selects the user's login name from the drop-down list.

Line 8

```
Set connection = Server.CreateObject( "ADODB.Connection" )
```

calls `Server` method `CreateObject` to create an `ADODB.Connection` object and `Set`s it to reference `connection`. An `ADODB.Connection` object encapsulates the functionality necessary to connect to a data source.

Line 9

```
Call connection.Open( "login" )
```

calls method *Open* to open the database referred to by the specified ODBC System DSN (i.e., `login`).

Line 12

```
query = "SELECT loginID FROM Users"
```

assigns the SQL query that **SELECT**s all the **loginID**s **FROM** the **Users** table.
Lines 15 and 16

```
Set loginData = Server.CreateObject( "ADODB.Recordset" )
Call loginData.Open( query, connection )
```

Set reference **loginData** to an **ADODB.Recordset** object and call method **Open** to execute the query (from line 12) against the database referenced by **connection**. Method **Open** is passed a string containing the SQL query and the **ADODB.Connection** object that **connection** references. When **Open** finishes executing, the **ADODB.Recordset** object referenced by **loginData** contains all records that match the SQL query and points to either the first record or *end of file* (*EOF*) if no records were found.

For simplicity, if an error occurs while the records are being retrieved, we choose to ignore it. Line 19

```
On Error Resume Next
```

specifies that any error caused by a statement from this point onward is ignored, and control is transferred to the statement immediately following the statement that caused the error.

Lines 33–36 determine whether or not the session variable **loginFailure** is **True**, indicating that **submitlogin.asp** has detected an invalid login. If it is **True**, a message is displayed informing the client that the login attempt failed and prompting for another login.

Next, we use the HTML **SELECT** structure to build the drop-down list of **loginID**s. Line 50 writes the first **OPTION** that displays **Select your name**. If no other **OPTION** is marked as **SELECTED**, this **OPTION** is displayed when the page is loaded. The next **OPTION**s are the **loginID**s retrieved from the database. If the user is a returning user, we want to display the user's **loginID** as **SELECTED**.

Line 54 requests the **loginID** cookie. If it is the user's first visit, or if the cookie has expired, **Cookie** returns an empty string. [*Note*: It is possible for a cookie to store an empty string. If this is the case, **Cookie** returns the contents of the cookie, which is an empty string.] Otherwise, the user's **loginID** is returned. Lines 54–58

```
If Request.Cookies( "loginID" ) <> "" Then
   Call BuildReturning()
Else
   Call BuildNewUser()
End If
```

call procedure **BuildReturning** if **loginID** contains a login ID, and call procedure **BuildNewUser** otherwise. Both **BuildReturning** and **BuildNewUser** build the login ID **OPTION**s. However, **BuildReturning** selects the returning user's login ID **OPTION**, while **BuildNewUser** does not.

BuildReturning's **While** loop (lines 92–115) iterates through **loginData**'s records. Recall that **loginData** contains the **loginID** column (field) of the **Users** table and points either to the first record or to **EOF**. Line 92

```
While Not loginData.EOF
```

tests for the end of the record set, indicating that there are no further records. Line 114

```
Call loginData.MoveNext()
```

increments the record set pointer to the next record.

Each iteration of the **While** loop builds an **OPTION** item for the current record. Line 94 simply writes the opening of the **OPTION** item. Next, we test whether or not this **OPTION** needs to be **SELECTED** with the **If** statement in lines 105–110. Note that once we have written **SELECTED** for an **OPTION**, there is no need to perform this check in further iterations; **SELECTED** is written for one and only one **OPTION**. The code that writes **SELECTED** for an option is thus wrapped in another **If** statement (lines 97–111). Variable **found** is set to **False** before the loop, in line 91. Once **SELECTED** is written for an **OPTION**, **found** is assigned the value **True**. Line 97 prevents the code that writes **SELECTED** for an option from being executed unnecessarily after an **OPTION** is already selected. Lines 105 and 106

```
If Request.Cookies( "loginID" ) _
   = loginData( "loginID" ) _
```

determine whether or not the current record's **loginID** field is equal to the value of the **loginID** cookie. If so, lines 108 and 109 write **SELECTED** and set **found** to **True**.

Line 112 sets the **VALUE** for the **OPTION** to the current **loginID**. Finally, line 113 writes the display of this **OPTION** as the current **loginID**.

Active Server Page **submitlogin.asp** (Fig. 25.25) takes the values passed to it by **login.asp** and checks the values against the **Users** table in the database. If a match is found, the user is redirected to **instantpage.asp**. If no match is found, the user is redirected back to **login.asp**. The user never sees or knows about **submitlogin.asp**, because the page is pure scripting code (i.e., its entire contents are enclosed in scripting delimiters).

```
132  <% @LANGUAGE = VBScript %>
133  <% Option Explicit %>
134
135  <% ' Fig. 25.25 : submitlogin.asp %>
136
137  <% ' First, make sure that a user name and a password were
138     ' entered. If not, redirect back to the login page.
139
140     If Request( "password" ) = "" Or _
141        Request( "loginID" ) = "noSelection" _
142     Then
143        Session( "loginFailure" ) = True
144        Call Response.Redirect( "login.asp" )
145     End If
146
147     Dim connection, query, loginData
148
```

Fig. 25.25 Listing for **submitlogin.asp** (part 1 of 2).

```
149      Set connection = Server.CreateObject( "ADODB.Connection" )
150      Call connection.Open( "login" )
151
152      ' Create the SQL query
153      query = "SELECT * FROM Users WHERE loginID = '" _
154                  & Request( "loginID" ) & "'"
155
156      ' Create the record set
157      Set loginData = Server.CreateObject( "ADODB.Recordset" )
158      Call loginData.Open( query, connection )
159
160      ' If an error occurs, ignore it
161      On Error Resume Next
162
163      If Request( "password" ) = loginData( "password" ) Then
164
165         ' Password is OK, adjust loginFailure
166         Session( "loginFailure" ) = False
167
168         ' Write a cookie to recognize them the next time they
169         ' go to login.asp
170         Response.Cookies( "loginID" ) = Request( "loginID" )
171
172         ' Give it three days to expire
173         Response.Cookies( "loginID" ).Expires = Date() + 3
174
175         ' Send them on to the next page
176         Call Response.Redirect( "instantpage.asp" )
177      Else
178         Session( "loginFailure" ) = True
179         Call Response.Redirect( "login.asp" )
180      End If
181   %>
```

Fig. 25.25 Listing for **submitlogin.asp** (part 2 of 2).

Lines 140–145 check whether the form's **password** field is empty or if the **loginID** field was submitted with the default value. If so, session variable **loginFailure** is set to **True** and the client is redirected to **login.asp**.

Lines 153 and 154

```
query = "SELECT * FROM Users WHERE loginID = '" _
            & Request( "loginID" ) & "'"
```

select all the fields from the table. The **WHERE** clause in this SQL statement specifies a condition on which records are selected: Only the record(s) whose **loginID** field has the same value as the form's **loginID** field is (are) selected. Also, note that this SQL statement always finds a record, because the form's **loginID** values are retrieved from the **Users**'s **loginID** field. For example, if **loginID jdoe** is selected, then **query** contains

```
SELECT * FROM Users WHERE loginID = 'jdoe'
```

Line 163 checks the password against the password from the record set. Note that the submitted **loginID** is a valid login ID that was selected from the drop-down list. Thus, we only need to check the password here to validate a login. If the password is correct, then line 170

```
Response.Cookies( "loginID" ) = Request( "loginID" )
```

writes the form's **loginID** value as a cookie named **loginID**.

Line 173

```
Response.Cookies( "loginID" ).Expires = Date() + 3
```

sets the expiration date of this cookie to the current date plus three days. If we do not set an expiration date for the cookie when we create it, it is treated as a session cookie (i.e., it is destroyed when the browser is closed). [*Note*: If an existing cookie's content is updated, then the expiration date needs to be set again. Otherwise, the cookie is destroyed at the end of the session regardless of the expiration date it had before the update.] The cookie remains on the client's machine until it expires, at which time the browser deletes it.

Next, line 176 calls method **Redirect** to redirect the client to **instantpage.asp**. Otherwise, the session variable **loginFailure** is set to **True**, and the client is redirected back to **login.asp** (lines 178 and 179).

25.12 Internet and World Wide Web Resources

www.microsoft.com
Microsoft's home page. This site provides a link to search Microsoft's entire Web-based information structure. Check this site first for answers. Some information is provided on a subscribers-only basis.

www.tcp-ip.com
The *ASP Toolbox* home page is an excellent source for ASP information and resources. The site contains numerous links to free components and other resources helpful in Web development using Active Server Pages. The site tutorials include an overview of Active Server technology, as well as helpful hints and demos with source code provided. Other features of this page include ASP discussion forums and resources.

www.4guysfromrolla.com/webtech/index_asp.shtml
Contains FAQs, ASP-related articles, coding tips, message boards, etc.

www.aspin.com/index
Contains ASP resources, including applications, books, forums, references, examples and tutorials, links, etc.

www.kamath.com/default.asp
Contains downloads, FAQs, tutorials, book excerpts, columns, etc.

www.aspwatch.com/
Contains ASP-related articles and examples of code.

www.developer.com
Great source of information for developers. The ASP section contains working code, troubleshooting techniques and advice.

www.paessler.com/tools/ASPBeautify
Home of a tool that formats ASP pages for readability.

SUMMARY

- Active Server Pages (ASP) are processed in response to a client (e.g., browser) request. An ASP file—which has file extension **.asp**—contains HTML and scripting code. Although other languages, such as JavaScript, can be used for ASP scripting, VBScript is the de facto language for ASP scripting.

- ASP is a Microsoft-developed technology for generating dynamic Web content—which includes HTML, Dynamic HTML, ActiveX controls, client-side scripts and Java applets (i.e., client-side Java programs that are embedded in a Web page).

- The two most common HTTP request types (also known as request methods) are **GET** and **POST**. These requests are frequently used to send client form data to a Web server.

- A **GET** request sends form content as part of the URL. A **POST** request posts form content inside the HTTP request. The post data are appended to the end of an HTTP request.

- Browsers often cache (save on disk) Web pages so they can quickly reload the pages. There are no changes between the last version stored in the cache and the current version on the Web. Browsers typically do not cache the server's response to a **POST** request, because the next **POST** may not return the same result.

- When a client requests an ASP file, the ASP file is parsed (top to bottom) by an ActiveX component named **asp.dll**. Scripting code is executed as it is encountered.

- The **@LANGUAGE** statement is used by the programmer to specify which scripting engine is needed to interpret the scripting code. If **@LANGUAGE** is not used, VBScript is assumed to be the default. As the script is interpreted, HTML (plus any client-side scripts) is sent to the client.

- Client-side scripting is often used for validation; interactivity, enhancing a Web page with ActiveX controls, Dynamic HTML and Java applets and accessing the browser.

- Client-side scripting is browser dependent—that is, the scripting language must be supported by the browser or scripting host. Because Microsoft Internet Explorer and Netscape Communicator both support JavaScript, JavaScript has become the de facto scripting language on the client side.

- Because server-side scripts reside on the server, programmers have greater flexibility, especially with respect to database access. Scripts executed on the server usually generate custom responses for clients.

- Server-side scripts have access to ActiveX server components, which extend scripting language functionality. Server-side ActiveX components typically do not have a GUI. Many ActiveX components are included with Internet Information Server (IIS) and Personal Web Server (PWS).

- Scripting delimiters **<%** and **%>** indicate that the scripting code is to be executed on the server—not the client. Scripting code enclosed in a scripting delimiter is never sent to the client.

- Function **Time** returns the server's current time in the format *hh:mm:ss*.

- The **Response** object provides functionality for sending information to the client.

- The AdRotator ActiveX component rotates advertisements on a Web page.

- Server-side ActiveX components are instantiated by passing the name of the component as a string to **Server** object method **CreateObject**. The **Server** object represents the Web server.

- **Response** object method **Write** writes text to the client.

- File System Objects (FSOs) provide the programmer with the ability to manipulate files, directories and drives. FSOs also allow the programmer to read and write text to sequential files. FSOs are an essential element for Active Server Pages with persistent data.

- FSOs are objects in the Microsoft Scripting Runtime Library. Five FSO types exist: **FileSystemObject**, **File**, **Folder**, **Drive** and **TextStream**.

- Type **FileSystemObject** allows the programmer to interact with **File**s, **Folder**s and **Drive**s. The programmer can use **FileSystemObject**s to create directories, move files, determine whether or not a **Drive** exists, etc. **File**s allow the programmer to gather information about files, manipulate files and open files. **Folder** objects allow the programmer to gather information about directories and to manipulate directories. **Drive** objects allow the programmer to gather information about drives.

- Many Web sites today provide custom Web pages and/or functionality on a client-by-client basis. HTTP does not support persistent information that could help a Web server determine that a request is from a particular client. As far as a Web server is concerned, every request could be from the same client, or every request could be from a different client.

- Session tracking is handled by the server. The first time a client connects to the server, it is assigned a unique session ID by the server. When the client makes additional requests, the client's session ID is compared with the session IDs stored in the server's memory. Active Server Pages use the **Session** object to manage sessions. The **Session** object's **Timeout** property specifies the number of minutes for which a session exists before it expires. The default value for property **Timeout** is 20 minutes. An individual session can also be terminated, by calling **Session** method **Abandon**.

- Cookies can store information on the client's computer for retrieval later in the same browsing session or in future browsing sessions. Cookies are files that are sent by an Active Server Page as part of a response to a client. Every HTTP-based interaction between a client and a server includes a header that contains information about the request or information about the response. When an Active Server Page receives a request, the header includes information such as the request type and cookies stored on the client machine by the server. When the server formulates its response, the header information includes any cookies the server wants to store on the client computer.

- Server-side include (SSI) statements are always executed before any scripting code is executed. The word **virtual** in the SSI refers to the include file's path as it appears below the server root directory. This path is often referred to as a virtual path. SSIs can also use **file**, instead of **virtual**, to indicate a physical path on the server.

- VBScript constant **vbCrLf** is used to insert a carriage-return line-feed combination.

- Method **Redirect** redirects the client to another Web page.

- A *database* is an integrated collection of data. A *database management system (DBMS)* involves the data themselves and the software that controls the storage and retrieval of data.

- Database management systems provide mechanisms for storing and organizing data in a manner that facilitates satisfying sophisticated queries and manipulations of the data.

- A language called *Structured Query Language (SQL)* is almost universally used with relational database systems to make *queries* (i.e., to request information that satisfies given criteria) and manipulate data.

- *Universal Data Access (UDA) is* a Microsoft architecture that provides data access to many data sources.

- A relational database is composed of tables, which in turn are composed of columns (or fields).

- A primary key is a unique field that is used to identify a record.

- SQL provides a complete set of keywords that enable programmers to define complex queries for retrieving data from a table.

- Query results are commonly called *result sets* (or *record sets*).

- **SELECT** queries select information from one or more tables in a database.

- An asterisk (*****) indicates that all rows and columns (fields) from a table should be selected.

- SQL provides the optional **WHERE** *clause* in a **SELECT** query to specify the selection criteria for a query. The **WHERE** clause condition can contain operators such as **<, >, <=, >=, =, <>** and **LIKE**.
- Operator **LIKE** is used for *pattern matching* with wildcard characters *asterisk (*)* and *question mark (?)*.
- An asterisk (*****) in a pattern indicates any number of (i.e., zero or more) characters in a row at the asterisk's location in the pattern.
- Query results can be sorted into ascending (**ASC**) or descending (**DESC**) order using the optional **ORDER BY** clause.
- The **INSERT INTO** keywords insert data into a table.
- The **UPDATE/SET** keywords modify data in a table.
- Microsoft developed the Open Database Connectivity (ODBC) Application Programming Interface (API) to allow Windows applications to communicate in a uniform manner with disparate relational databases.
- Web applications are three-tier distributed applications, consisting of a user interface (UI), business logic and database access. The UI in such an application is often created using HTML, Dynamic HTML or XML. All three tiers may reside on separate computers that are connected to a network, or all three tiers may reside on a single machine.
- In multitier architectures, Web servers are increasingly used to build the middle tier. They provide the business logic that manipulates data from databases and that communicates with client Web browsers.
- Method **Open** opens a connection to the data source.
- Method **Execute** executes a query against the data source.
- **ADODB.Recordset** method **MoveFirst** moves to the first record in a record set.
- **ADODB.RecordSet** constant **EOF** represents a record set's end-of-file marker.

TERMINOLOGY

#include	**Close** method
%> closing scripting delimiter	columns
.asp file	**CommandText** property
.mdb file	**CommandType** property
.shtml file	configuration file
@LANGUAGE directive	cookie
<% opening script delimiter	cookie expiration
Abandon method of **Session**	**CreateObject** method
ActiveConnection property	**CreateTextFile** method
ActiveX Data Objects (ADO)	database
ADODB.Command object	database access
ADODB.Connection object	database management system (DBMS)
ADODB.RecordSet object	**Drive**
AdRotator ActiveX Control	**EOF** constant
appending to a file	**Execute** method
asp.dll	expiration of a cookie
business logic	fields
cache Web pages	**File**
Chr method	file system object
client-side scripting	**FileExists** method

FileSystemObject
Folder
GET HTTP request
GetAdvertisement method
guest book application
header
join condition
mailto link
maximum age of a cookie
MoveFirst method
MoveNext method
On Error Resume Next statement
one-to-many relationship
Open Database Connectivity (ODBC) Application
Programming Interface (API)
Open method
OpenTextFile method
Option Explicit statement
physical path
POST HTTP request
primary key
ReadAll method
record
record set
Redirect method of **Response**
relational database
Request object
Response object

result set
script engine
script host
SELECT query
selection criteria
Server object
server-side ActiveX component
server-side include (SSI)
server-side scripting
session
session ID
Session object
session tracking
Set keyword
shopping-cart application
short-name format
Structured Query Language (SQL)
table
TextStream
three-tier distributed application
Timeout property of **Session**
Universal Data Access (UDA)
user interface
vbCrLf constant
VBScript
virtual path
Write method
WriteLine method

26

Bonus Chapter: Introduction to Perl Programming

Objectives

- To understand the Common Gateway Interface.
- To understand string processing and regular expressions in Perl.
- To be able to read and write client data using cookies.
- To construct programs that interact with databases.

This is the common air that bathes the globe.
Walt Whitman

The longest part of the journey is said to be the passing of the gate.
Marcus Terentius Varro

Railway termini... are our gates to the glorious and unknown. Through them we pass out into adventure and sunshine, to them, alas! we return.
E.M. Forster

There comes a time in a man's life when to get where he has to go—if there are no doors or windows—he walks through a wall.
Bernard Malamud

You ought to be able to show that you can do it a good deal better than anyone else with the regular tools before you have a license to bring in your own improvements.
Ernest Hemingway

26.1 Introduction

In this chapter, we provide a concise introduction to the *Practical Extraction and Report Language (Perl)*—one of the most widely used languages for Web programming. This chapter is included for our readers who do not know Perl or who would like a basic review of Perl before studying Chapter 17. We do not present any XML in this chapter.

Larry Wall began developing this high-level programming language in 1987 while working at Unisys. His initial intent was to create a programming language to monitor large software projects and generate reports. Wall wanted to create a language that would be more powerful than shell scripting and more flexible than C, a language with rich text-processing capabilities and, most of all, a language that would make common programming tasks straightforward and easy. In this chapter, we discuss Perl 5 and examine several practical examples using Perl for electronic commerce on the Internet.

Common Gateway Interface (CGI) is a standard protocol through which applications interact with Web servers. Thus, CGI provides a way for clients (e.g., Web browsers) to indirectly interface with applications on the Web server. Because CGI is an interface, it cannot be directly programmed—a script or executable program (commonly called a *CGI script*) must be executed to interact with it. While CGI scripts can be written in many different programming languages, Perl is commonly used due to its power and flexibility.

Figure 26.1 illustrates the interaction between client and server when the client requests a document that references a CGI script. Often CGI scripts utilize and process information (e.g., a search-engine query, a credit-card number, etc.) gathered from a form. For example, a CGI script could verify credit-card information and notify the client of the results (i.e., accepted or rejected). Permission is granted within the Web server (usually by the *Webmaster* or the author of the Web site) to allow specific programs on the server to be executed. These programs are typically either designated with a certain filename extension (such as `.cgi` or `.pl`) or located within a special directory (such as `/cgi-bin`). After the application output is sent to the server through CGI, the results may be sent to the client. Information received by the client is usually an HTML document, but may contain images, streaming audio, Macromedia Flash files, etc.

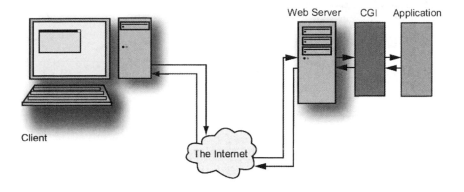

Fig. 26.1   Data path of a typical CGI-based application.

Applications typically interact with the user through *standard input* and *standard output*. Standard input is the stream of information received by a program from a user, typically through the keyboard, but also possibly from a file or another input device. Standard output is the information stream presented to the user by an application; it is typically displayed on the screen but may be printed by a printer, written to a file, etc.

For CGI scripts, the standard output is redirected (or *piped*) through the Common Gateway Interface to the server and then sent over the Internet to a Web browser for rendering. If the server-side script is correctly programmed, output will be readable to the client. Usually, that means that the output is a HTML document which can be viewed using a Web browser.

26.2 Perl

With the advent of the World Wide Web and Web browsers, the Internet gained tremendous popularity. This greatly increased the volume of requests users made for information from Web servers. It became evident that the degree of interactivity between the user and the server would be crucial. The power of the Web resides not only in serving content to users, but also in responding to requests from users and generating dynamic content. The framework for such communication already existed through CGI. Because most of the information users send to servers is text, Perl was a logical choice for programming the server side of interactive Web-based applications, due to its simple, yet powerful, text processing capabilities. It is arguably the most popular CGI scripting language. The Perl community, headed by Wall (who currently works for O'Reilly & Associates as a Perl developer and researcher) continuously works to evolve the language, keeping it competitive with newer server-side technologies such as Microsoft's Active Server Pages (see Chapter 25).

Figure 26.2 presents a simple Perl program that writes the text **"Welcome to Perl!"** to the screen. Because the program does not interact with the Common Gateway Interface, it is not a CGI script. Our first examples in Perl will be command-line programs to help explain the basics of the language. See Fig. 26.11 for our first CGI example.

```
1   #!perl
2   # Fig. 26.2: first.pl
3   # A first program in Perl.
4
5   print "Welcome to Perl!\n";
```

```
Welcome to Perl!
```

Fig. 26.2   A simple program in Perl.

Lines 2–3 use the Perl *comment character* (#) to instruct the interpreter to ignore everything on the current line following the #. This syntax allows programmers to write descriptive comments inside their programs. The exception to this rule is the *"shebang" construct* (#!) in line 1. On Unix systems, it indicates the path to the Perl interpreter (such as #!/usr/bin/perl). On other systems (e.g., Windows), the line may be ignored or it may indicate to the server (e.g., Apache) that a Perl program follows the statement.

The comment on line 2 indicates that the filename of the program is **first.pl**. Perl scripts file names typically end with the **.pl** extension. The program can be executed by running the Perl interpreter from the command-line prompt (e.g., DOS prompt in Windows).

In order to run the Perl script, Perl must first be installed on the system. Windows users, see the "ActiveState Perl Installation" document on the CD that accompanies this book for instructions on how to install ActivePerl, the standard Perl implementation for Windows. For installation on other platforms visit **www.perl.com**.

To run **first.pl** type

```
perl first.pl
```

where **perl** is the interpreter and **first.pl** is the perl script. Alternatively, we could type

```
perl -w first.pl
```

which instructs the Perl interpreter to output warnings to the screen if it finds possible bugs in your code.

Testing and Debugging Tip 26.1

*When running a Perl script from the command line, always use the **-w** option. The program may seem to execute correctly when there is actually something wrong with the source code. The **-w** option displays warnings encountered while executing a Perl program.*

On Windows systems, a Perl script may also be executed by double-clicking its programs icon. The program window closes automatically once the script terminates and any screen output is lost. For this reason, it is usually better to run a script from the DOS prompt.

Line 5 calls function **print** to write text to the screen. Note that since Perl is case-sensitive, writing **Print** or **PRINT** instead of **print** would yield an error. The text, **"Welcome to Perl!\n"**, is surrounded in quotes and called a *string*. The last portion of the string—the newline *escape sequence* **\n**—moves the cursor to the next line. The semicolon (;) at the end of line 5 is always used to terminate Perl statements.

Common Programming Error 26.1

Forgetting to terminate a statement with a ; is a syntax error.

Good Programming Practice 26.1

While not all servers require the "shebang" construct (# !) it is good practice to include it for program portability.

Like other programming languages, Perl has built-in data types (Fig. 26.3) that represent the different kinds of data. Notice that each variable name has a specific character (i.e., **$**, **@** and **%**) preceding it. For example, the **$** character specifies that the variable contains a *scalar* value (i.e., strings, integer numbers and floating-point numbers). The script **variable.pl** (Fig. 26.4) demonstrates manipulation of scalar variables.

Common Programming Error 26.2

Failure to place a preceding $ character before a scalar variable name is a syntax error.

Data type	Format for variable names of this type	Description
Scalar	*$scalarname*	Can be a string, an integer number or a floating-point number.
Array	*@arrayname*	An ordered list of scalar variables which can be accessed using integer indices.
Hash	*%hashname*	An unordered set of scalar variables whose values are accessed using unique scalar values (i.e., strings) called keys.

Fig. 26.3 Perl data types.

```
1   #!perl
2   # Fig. 26.4: variable.pl
3   # Program to illustrate the use of scalar variables.
4
5   $a = 5;
6   print "The value of variable a is: $a\n";
7
8   $a = $a + 5;
9   print "Variable a after adding 5 is: $a\n";
10
11  $a *= 2;
12  print "Variable a after multiplying by 2 is: $a\n";
13
14  # using an uninitialized variable in the context of a string
15  print "Using a variable before initializing: $var\n";
16
```

Fig. 26.4 Using scalar variables (part 1 of 2).

```
17   # using an uninitialized variable in a numeric context
18   $test = $num + 5;
19   print "Adding uninitialized variable \$num to 5 yields: $test.\n";
20
21   # using strings in numeric contexts
22   $str = "A string value";
23   $a = $a + $str;
24   print "Adding a string to an integer yields: $a\n";
25
26   $strnum = "15charactersand1";
27   $c = $a + $strnum;
28   print "Adding $a to string \"$strnum\" yields: $c\n";
```

```
The value of variable a is: 5
Variable a after adding 5 is: 10
Variable a after multiplying by 2 is: 20
Using a variable before initializing:
Adding uninitialized variable $num to 5 yields: 5.
Adding a string to an integer yields: 20
Adding 20 to string "15charactersand1" yields: 35
```

Fig. 26.4   Using scalar variables (part 2 of 2).

In Perl, a variable is created automatically the first time it is encountered by the interpreter. Line 5 creates a variable with name **$a** and sets its value to **5**. Line 8 adds the integer **5** to **$a**. Line 9 calls function **print** to write text followed by the value of **$a**. Notice that the actual value of **$a** is printed, not "**$a**". When a variable is encountered inside a double quoted (**" "**) string, Perl uses a process called *interpolation* to replace the variable with its associated data. Line 11 uses an *assignment operator* ***=** to yield an expression equivalent to **$a = $a * 2** (thus assigning **$a** the value **20**). These assignment operators (i.e., **+=, -=, *=** and **/=**) are syntactical shortcuts.

Testing and Debugging Tip 26.2

*Function **print** can be used to display the value of a variable at a particular point during a program's execution. This is often helpful in debugging a program.*

In Perl, uninitialized variables have the value **undef**, which can evaluate to different things depending on context. When **undef** is found in a numeric context (e.g., **$num** in line 18), it evaluates to **0**. In contrast, when it is interpreted in a string context (such as **$var** in line 15), **undef** evaluates to the empty string (**" "**).

Lines 22–28 show the results of evaluating strings in numeric context. Unless a string begins with a digit it is evaluated as **undef** in a numeric context. If it does begin with a digit, every character up to (but not including) the first non-digit character is evaluated as a number and the remaining characters are ignored. For example, the string **"A string value"** (line 23) does not begin with a digit and therefore evaluates to **undef**. Because **undef** evaluates to **0**, variable **$a**'s value is unchanged. The string **"15charactersand1"** (line 27) begins with a digit and is therefore interpolated as **15**. The character **1** on the end is ignored because there are non-digit characters preceding it. Evaluating a string in numeric context does not actually change the value of the string. This is shown by line 28's output, which prints the **"15charactersand1"**.

Notice that the programmer does not need to differentiate between numeric and string data types because the interpreter evaluates scalar variables depending on the context in which they are used.

Common Programming Error 26.3

Using an uninitialized variable might make a numerical calculation incorrect. For example, multiplying a number by an uninitialized variable results in **0**.

Testing and Debugging Tip 26.3

While it is not always necessary to initialize variables before using them, errors can be avoided by doing so.

Perl provides the capability to store data in arrays. Arrays are divided into *elements* that each contain a scalar value. The script **arrays.pl** (Fig. 26.5) demonstrates some techniques for array initialization and manipulation.

Line 5 initializes array **@array** to contain the strings **"Bill"**, **"Bobby"**, **"Sue"** and **"Michelle"**. Note that in Perl, all array variable names must be preceded by the **@** symbol. Parentheses are necessary to group the strings in the array assignment; this group of elements surrounded by parentheses is called a *list* in Perl. In assigning the list to **@array**, each person's name is stored in an individual array element with a unique integer index value starting at 0.

When **print**ing an array inside double quotes (line 7), the array element values are printed with only one space separating them. If the array name is not enclosed in double quotes when it is **print**ed (line 8), the interpreter prints the element values without separating them with spaces.

```
1   #!perl
2   # Fig. 26.5: arrays.pl
3   # Program to demonstrate arrays in Perl
4
5   @array = ( "Bill", "Bobby", "Sue", "Michelle" );
6
7   print "The array contains: @array\n";
8   print "Printing array outside of quotes: ", @array, "\n\n";
9
10  print "Third element: $array[ 2 ]\n";
11
12  $number = 3;
13  print "Fourth element: $array[ $number ]\n\n";
14
15  @array2 = ( A..Z );
16  print "The range operator is used to create a list of\n";
17  print "all letters from capital A to Z:\n";
18  print "@array2 \n\n";
19
20  $array3[ 3 ] = "4th";
21  print "@array3 \n\n";
22
23  print 'Printing literal using single quotes: @array and \n', "\n";
24  print "Printing literal using backslashes: \@array and \\n\n";
```

Fig. 26.5   Using arrays (part 1 of 2).

```
The array contains: Bill Bobby Sue Michelle
Printing array outside of quotes: BillBobbySueMichelle

Third element: Sue
Fourth element: Michelle

The range operator is used to create a list of
all letters from capital A to Z:
A B C D E F G H I J K L M N O P Q R S T U V W X Y Z

   4th

Printing literal using single quotes: @array and \n
Printing literal using backslashes: @array and \n
```

Fig. 26.5   Using arrays (part 2 of 2).

Line 10 demonstrates how individual array elements are accessed using braces (**[]**). As mentioned above, if we use the **@** character followed by the array name we reference the array as a whole. But if the array name is prefaced by the **$** character and followed by an index number in square brackets (as in line 10), it refers instead to an individual array element, which is a scalar value. Line 13 demonstrates how a scalar variable can be used as an index. The value of **$number** (3) is used to get the value of the fourth array element.

Line 15 initializes array **@array2** to contain the capital letters from **A** to **Z** inclusive. The *range operator* (**..**), specifies that all values between uppercase **A** and uppercase **Z** be placed in the array. The range operator (**..**) can be used to create any consecutive series of values such as **1** through **15** or **a** through **z**.

The Perl interpreter handles memory management automatically. Therefore, it is not necessary to specify an array's size. If a value is assigned to a position outside the range of the array or to an uninitialized array, the interpreter automatically extends the array range to include the new element. Elements that are added by the interpreter during an adjustment of the range are initialized to the **undef** value. Lines 20 and 21 assign a value to the fourth element in the uninitialized array **@array3**. The interpreter recognizes that memory has not been allocated for this array and creates new memory for the array. The interpreter then sets the value of first three elements to **undef** and the value of the fourth element to the string **"4th"**. When the array is printed, the first three **undef** values are treated as empty strings and printed with a space between each one. This accounts for the three extra spaces in the output before the string **"4th"**.

In order to print special characters like **** and **@** and **"** and not have the interpreter treat them as an escape sequence or array, Perl provides two choices. The first is to *print* (line 23) the characters as a literal string (i.e., a string enclosed in single quotes). When strings are inside single quotes, the interpreter treats the string literally and does not attempt to interpret any escape sequence or variable substitution. The second choice is to use the backslash character (line 24) to *escape* special characters.

26.3 String Processing and Regular Expressions

One of Perl's most powerful capabilities is its ability to process textual data easily and efficiently, allowing for straightforward searching, substitution, extraction and concatenation of strings. Text manipulation in Perl is usually done with *regular expressions*—a series of characters that serve as pattern-matching templates (or search criteria) in strings, text files and databases. This feature allows complicated searching and string processing to be performed using relatively simple expressions.

Many string processing tasks can be accomplished by using Perl's *equality* and *comparison* operators (Fig. 26.6, **equals.pl**). Line 5 declares and initializes array **@fruits**. Operator **qw** ("quote word") takes the contents inside the parentheses and creates a comma-separated list with each element wrapped in double quotes. In this example, **qw(apple orange banana)** is equivalent to **("apple", "orange", "banana")**.

Lines 7–28 demonstrate our first examples of Perl *control structures*. The **foreach** loop beginning in line 7 iterates sequentially through the elements in the **@fruits** array. The value of each element is assigned in turn to variable **$item** and the body of the **foreach** is executed once for each array element. Notice that a semicolon does not terminate the **foreach**.

Line 9 introduces another control structure—the **if** statement. Parentheses surround the condition being tested and required curly braces surround the block of code that is executed when the condition is true. In Perl, anything except the number **0** and the empty string is defined as true. In our example, when the **$item**'s content is tested against **"banana"** (line 9) for equality, the condition evaluates to true, and the **print** command (line 11) is executed.

```perl
1   #!perl
2   # Fig. 26.6: equals.pl
3   # Program to demonstrate the eq, ne, lt, gt operators
4
5   @fruits = qw( apple orange banana );
6
7   foreach $item ( @fruits )
8   {
9      if ( $item eq "banana" )
10     {
11        print "String '$item' matches string 'banana'\n";
12     }
13
14     if ( $item ne "banana" )
15     {
16        print "String '$item' does not match string 'banana'\n";
17     }
18
19     if ( $item lt "banana" )
20     {
21        print "String '$item' is less than string 'banana'\n";
22     }
23
24     if ( $item gt "banana" )
25     {
26        print "String '$item' is greater than string 'banana'\n";
27     }
28  }
```

Fig. 26.6 Using the **eq, ne, lt, gt**, operators (part 1 of 2).

```
String 'apple' does not match string 'banana'
String 'apple' is less than string 'banana'
String 'orange' does not match string 'banana'
String 'orange' is greater than string 'banana'
String 'banana' matches string 'banana'
```

Fig. 26.6   Using the **eq**, **ne**, **lt**, **gt**, operators (part 2 of 2).

The remaining **if** statements (lines 14, 19 and 24) demonstrate the other string comparison operators. Operators **ne**, **lt**, and **gt** test strings for equality, less than, and greater than, respectively. These operators are only used with strings. When comparing numeric values, operators **==**, **!=**, **<**, **<=**, **>** and **>=** are used.

For more powerful string comparisons, Perl provides the *match operator (**m//**)*, which uses regular expressions to search a string for a specified pattern. Figure 26.7 uses the match operator to perform a variety of regular expression tests.

```
1   #!perl
2   # Fig 26.7: expression.pl
3   # searches using the matching operator and regular expressions
4
5   $search = "Now is is the time";
6   print "Test string is: '$search'\n\n";
7
8   if ( $search =~ /Now/ )
9   {
10      print "String 'Now' was found.\n";
11  }
12
13  if ( $search =~ /^Now/ )
14  {
15      print "String 'Now' was found at the beginning of the line.\n";
16  }
17
18  if ( $search =~ /Now$/ )
19  {
20      print "String 'Now' was found at the end of the line.\n";
21  }
22
23  if ( $search =~ /\b ( \w+ ow ) \b/x )
24  {
25      print "Word found ending in 'ow': $1 \n";
26  }
27
28  if ( $search =~ /\b ( \w+ ) \s ( \1 ) \b/x )
29  {
30      print "Repeated words found: $1 $2\n";
31  }
32
33  @matches = ( $search =~ / \b ( t \w+ ) \b /gx );
34  print "Words beginning with 't' found: @matches\n";
```

Fig. 26.7   Using the match operator. (part 1 of 2)

```
String 'Now' was found.
String 'Now' was found at the beginning of the line.
Word found ending in 'ow': Now
Repeated words found: is is
Words beginning with 't' found: the time
```

Fig. 26.7   Using the match operator. (part 2 of 2)

Common Programming Error 26.4

*Using == for string comparisons and **ne** for numerical comparisons can result in errors in the program.*

Common Programming Error 26.5

*While the number **0** and even the string **"0"** evaluate to false in Perl **if** statements, other string values that may look like zero (such as **"0.0"**) evaluate to true.*

We begin by assigning the string **"Now is is the time"** to variable **$search** (line 5). The expression

```
$search =~ /Now/
```

(line 8) uses the **m//** match operator to search for the *literal characters* **Now** inside variable **$search**. Note that the **m** character preceding the slashes of the **m//** operator is optional in most cases, and is thus omitted here.

The match operator takes two operands. The first of these is the regular expression pattern to search for (**Now**), which is placed between the slashes of the **m//** operator. The second operand is the string to search within, which is assigned to the match operator using the **=~** operator. This **=~** operator is sometimes called a binding operator, since it binds whatever is on its left side to a regular expression operator on the right.

In our example, the pattern **Now** is found in the string **"Now is is the time"**, the match operator returns true, and the body of the **if** statement is executed. In addition to literal characters like **Now** which match only themselves, regular expressions can include special characters called *metacharacters* which can specify patterns or contexts that cannot be defined using literal characters. For example, the caret metacharacter (^) matches the beginning of a string. The next regular expression (Line 13)

```
$search =~ /^Now/
```

uses this metacharacter to search the beginning of **$search** for the pattern **Now**.

The **$** metacharacter searches the end of a string for a pattern (line 18). Because the pattern **Now** is not found at the end of **$search**, the body of the **if** statement (line 20) is not executed. Note that **Now$** is not a variable, it is a search pattern that uses **$** to search specifically for **Now** at the end of a string.

The next condition (line 23),

```
$search =~ /\b ( \w+ ow ) \b/x
```

searches (from left to right) for the first word ending with the letters **ow**. As is in strings, backslashes are used in regular expressions to escape characters with special significance.

For example, the **\b** expression does not match the literal characters "**\b**". Instead, the expression matches any *word boundary* (generally, a boundary between an *alphanumeric character*—**0–9**, **a–z**, **A–Z** and the underscore character—and something that is not an alphanumeric character). Between the **\b** characters is a set of parentheses; these will be explained momentarily.

The expression inside the parentheses, **\w+ ow**, indicates that we are looking for patterns ending in **ow**. The first part, **\w+**, is a combination of **\w** (an escape sequence which matches a single *alphanumeric character*) and the **+** *modifier*, which is a *quantifier* that instructs Perl to match the preceding character one or more times. Thus, **\w+** matches one or more alphanumeric characters. The characters **ow** are taken literally. Collectively, the whole expression **/\b (\w+ ow) \b/** matches one or more alphanumeric characters ending with **ow**, with word boundaries at the beginning and end. See Fig. 26.8 for a description of several other Perl regular expression quantifiers and Fig. 26.9 for a list of some regular expression metacharacters.

Parentheses indicate that the text matching the pattern is to be saved in a special Perl variable (e.g., **$1**, etc.). The parentheses in line 23 result in **Now** being stored in variable **$1**. Multiple sets of parentheses may be used in regular expressions, where each match results in a new Perl variable (**$1**, **$2**, **$3**, etc.) being created.

Quantifier	Matches
{n}	Exactly **n** times
{m,n}	Between **m** and **n** times inclusive
{n,}	**n** or more times
+	One or more times (same as **{1,}**)
*	Zero or more times (same as **{0,}**)
?	One or zero times (same as **{0,1}**)

Fig. 26.8   Some of Perl's quantifiers.

Symbol	Matches	Symbol	Matches
^	Beginning of line	**\d**	Digit (i.e., **0** to **9**)
$	End of line	**\D**	Non-digit
\b	Word boundary	**\s**	Whitespace
\B	Non-word boundary	**\S**	Non-whitespace
\w	Word (alphanumeric) character	**\n**	Newline
\W	Non-word character	**\t**	Tab

Fig. 26.9   Some of Perl's metacharacters.

Adding *modifying characters* after a regular expression refines the pattern matching process. Modifying characters (Fig. 26.10) placed to the right of the forward slash that delimits the regular expression instruct the interpreter to treat the preceding expression in different ways. For example, the **i** after the regular expression

```
/computer/i
```

tells the interpreter to ignore case when searching, thus matching **computer**, **COMPUTER**, **Computer** and **CoMputER**.

When added to the end of a regular expression, the **x** modifying character indicates that whitespace characters are to be ignored. This allows programmers to add space characters to their regular expressions for readability without affecting the search. If the expression was written

```
$search =~ /\b ( \w+ ow ) \b/
```

without the **x** modifying character, then the script would be searching for a word boundary, two spaces, one or more alphanumeric characters, one space, the characters **ow**, two spaces and a word boundary. The expression would not match **$search**'s value.

The condition (line 28)

```
$search =~ /\b ( \w+ ) \s ( \1 ) \b/x
```

shows how the memory function of parentheses can be used in the regular expression itself. The first parenthetical expression matches any string containing one or more alphanumeric characters. The expression **\1** then evaluates to the word that was matched in the first parenthetical expression. The regular expression searches for two identical, consecutive words, separated by a whitespace character (**\s**)—in this case "**is is**".

Line 33's condition

```
$search =~ / \b ( t \w+ ) \b /gx
```

searches for words beginning with the letter **t** in the string **$search**. Modifying character **g** indicates a global search—one which does not stop after the first match is found. The array **@matches** is then assigned the value of a list of all matching words (line 33).

26.4 Viewing Client/Server Environment Variables

Knowing information about a client's execution environment can be useful to system administrators by allowing them to provide client-specific information. *Environment variables* contain information about the execution environment a script is being run in, such as the type of Web browser being used, the HTTP host and the HTTP connection. This information might be used by a server to send one Web page to a client using Microsoft Internet Explorer and a different Web page to a client using Netscape Communicator.

Until now, we have written simple Perl applications which output to the local user's screen. Through the use of CGI we can communicate with the Web server and its clients, allowing us to utilize the Internet as a method of input and output for our Perl applications. Note that in order to run Perl scripts as CGI applications, a Web server must first be installed and configured appropriately for your system. See the "Web Server Installation" document on the CD that accompanies this book for detailed information on how to install and set up a Web server.

Modifying Character	Purpose
g	Perform a global search; find and return all matches, not just the first one found.
i	Ignores the case of the search string (case insensitive).
m	The string is evaluated as if it had multiple lines of text (i.e., newline characters are not ignored).
s	Ignore the newline character and treat it as whitespace. The text is seen as a single line.
x	All whitespace characters are ignored when searching the string.

Fig. 26.10 Some of Perl's modifying characters.

Figure 26.11 generates an HTML table that displays the values of the clients' environment variables. The **use** *statement* (line 5) directs Perl programs to include the contents (e.g., functions, etc.) of predefined packages called *modules*. The **CGI** *module*, for example, contains many useful functions for CGI scripting in Perl, including functions that return strings representing HTML tags and HTTP headers. With the **use** statement we can specify which functions we would like to import from a particular module. In line 5, we use the *import tag* **:standard** to import a predefined set of standard functions.

```perl
1   #!perl
2   # Fig. 26.11: environment.pl
3   # Program to display CGI environment variables
4
5   use CGI qw( :standard );
6
7   print header;
8   print <<End_Begin;
9   <HTML>
10     <HEAD>
11        <TITLE>Environment Variables...</TITLE>
12     </HEAD>
13     <BODY TEXT = "BLACK" BGCOLOR = "WHITE">
14     <TABLE BORDER = "0" CELLPADDING = "2" CELLSPACING = "0"
15       WIDTH = 100%>
16  End_Begin
17
18  foreach $variable ( sort( keys( %ENV ) ) )
19  {
20     print <<End_Row;
21     <TR>
22     <TD BGCOLOR = "#11BBFF"><STRONG>$variable</STRONG></TD>
23     <TD><FONT COLOR = "BLACK" SIZE = "2">$ENV{$variable}
24     </FONT></TD>
25     </TR>
```

Fig. 26.11 Displaying CGI environment variables (part 1 of 2).

```
26   End_Row
27   }
28
29   print <<End_Finish;
30      </TABLE>
31      </BODY>
32   </HTML>
33   End_Finish
34   # Must include newline after End_Finish!
```

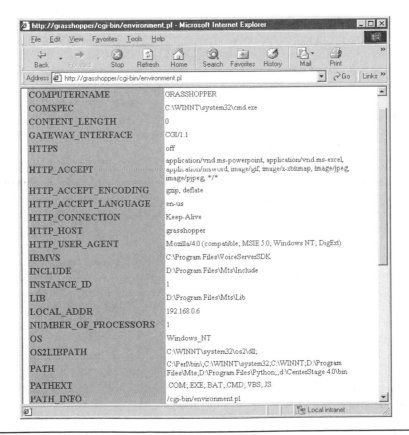

Fig. 26.11 Displaying CGI environment variables (part 2 of 2).

Line 7 directs the Perl program to **print** a valid *HTTP header* using function **header** from the **CGI** library. Browsers use HTTP headers to determine how to handle incoming data. The **header** function returns the string "**Content-type: text/ html\n\n**", indicating to the client that what follows is HTML. The **text/html** portion of the header indicates that the browser must display the returned information as an HTML document. Because standard output is redirected when a CGI script is run, the function **print** outputs to the user's Web browser.

Lines 8–16 write HTML to the client. Line 8

```
print <<End_Begin;
```

instructs the Perl interpreter to print the subsequent lines verbatim (after variable interpolation) until it reaches the **End_Begin** label. This label consists simply of the identifier **End_Begin**, placed at the beginning of a line by itself, with no whitespace characters preceding it, and followed immediately with a newline. This syntax is called a *here document*, and is often used in CGI programs to eliminate the need to repeatedly call function **print**.

The **%ENV** *hash* is a built-in table in Perl that contains the names and values of all the environment variables. The *hash* data type is designated by the **%** character, and basically represents an unordered set of scalar-value pairs. Unlike an array, which accesses elements through integer subscripts (e.g., **$array[2]**), each element in a hash is accessed using a unique string *key* which is associated with that element's value. For this reason, hashes are also known as *associative arrays*, since the keys and values are associated in pairs. Hash values are accessed using the syntax **$hashName{keyName}**. In this example, each key in hash **%ENV** is the name of an environment variable (such as **HTTP_HOST**) which can be used to access the value of each environment variable (**$ENV{"HTTP_HOST"}**).

Function **keys** returns an array of all the keys in the **%ENV** hash (line 18) in no specific order, because hash elements have no defined order. We use function **sort** to order the array of keys alphabetically. Finally, the **foreach** loop iterates sequentially through the array returned by **sort**, repeatedly assigning the current key's value to scalar **$variable**. Lines 20 to 26 are executed for each element in the array of key values. Line 22 prints the key **$variable** (the name of the environment variable) in one column of the HTML table. Line 23 prints **$ENV{$variable}** in the other column, thus displaying the environment variable values associated with each key in hash **%ENV**.

26.5 Form Processing and Business Logic

HTML forms enable Web pages to collect data from users and send it to a Web server for processing by server-side programs and scripts, thus enabling users to purchase products, send and receive Web-based email, participate in a political poll, perform online paging or any number of other tasks. This type of Web communication allows users to interact with the server and is vital to electronic commerce.

Figure 26.12 uses an HTML **FORM** to collect information about users before adding them to a mailing list. This type of registration form could be used (for example) by a software company to get profile information for a company database before allowing the user to download software.

Except for line 16, the HTML code in Fig. 26.12 should look familiar. The **FORM** element (line 16) indicates that, when the user clicks **Register**, the form information is **POST**ed to the server. The statement **ACTION = "cgi-bin/form.pl"** directs the server to execute the **form.pl** Perl script (located in the **cgi-bin** directory) to process the posted form data. We assign a unique name (e.g., **EMAIL**) to each of the form's input fields. When **Register** is clicked, each field's **NAME** and **VALUE** is sent to the **form.pl** script, which can then access the submitted value for each specific field.

```
1   <!DOCTYPE html PUBLIC "-//W3C//DTD HTML 4.0 Transitional//EN">
2   <!-- Fig. 26.12: form.html -->
3
```

Fig. 26.12 User entering a valid phone number (part 1 of 3).

```
4   <HTML>
5   <HEAD>
6   <TITLE>Sample FORM to take user input in HTML</TITLE>
7   </HEAD>
8
9   <FONT FACE = "ARIAL,SANS-SERIF" SIZE = "2">
10
11     <FONT SIZE = "+2">
12        <STRONG>This is a sample registration form.</STRONG>
13     </FONT><BR>
14     Please fill in all fields and click Register.
15
16     <FORM METHOD = "POST" ACTION = "/cgi-bin/form.pl">
17        <IMG SRC = "images/user.gif"><BR>
18        <FONT COLOR = "BLUE">
19           Please fill out the fields below.<BR>
20        </FONT>
21
22        <IMG SRC = "images/fname.gif">
23        <INPUT TYPE = "TEXT" NAME = "FNAME"><BR>
24        <IMG SRC = "images/lname.gif">
25        <INPUT TYPE = "TEXT" NAME = "LNAME"><BR>
26        <IMG SRC = "images/email.gif">
27        <INPUT TYPE = "TEXT" NAME = "EMAIL"><BR>
28        <IMG SRC = "images/phone.gif">
29        <INPUT TYPE = "TEXT" NAME = "PHONE"><BR>
30
31        <FONT SIZE = "-2">
32           Must be in the form (555)555-5555<BR><BR>
33        </FONT>
34
35        <IMG SRC = "images/downloads.gif"><BR>
36        <FONT COLOR = "BLUE">
37           Which book would you like information about?<BR>
38        </FONT>
39
40        <SELECT NAME = "BOOK">
41           <OPTION>Internet and WWW How to Program 1e
42           <OPTION>C++ How to Program 2e
43           <OPTION>Java How to Program 3e
44           <OPTION>Visual Basic How to Program 1e
45        </SELECT>
46        <BR><BR>
47
48        <IMG SRC = "images/os.gif"><BR>
49        <FONT COLOR = "BLUE">
50           Which operating system are you
51           currently using?<BR>
52        </FONT>
53
54        <INPUT TYPE = "RADIO" NAME = "OS" VALUE = "Windows NT"
55        CHECKED>
56        Windows NT
```

Fig. 26.12 User entering a valid phone number (part 2 of 3).

```
57          <INPUT TYPE = "RADIO" NAME = "OS" VALUE = "Windows 2000">
58          Windows 2000
59          <INPUT TYPE = "RADIO" NAME = "OS" VALUE = "Windows 98">
60          Windows 98<BR>
61          <INPUT TYPE = "RADIO" NAME = "OS" VALUE = "Linux">
62          Linux
63          <INPUT TYPE = "RADIO" NAME = "OS" VALUE = "Other">
64          Other<BR>
65          <INPUT TYPE = "SUBMIT" VALUE = "Register">
66       </FORM>
67    </BODY>
68    </HTML>
```

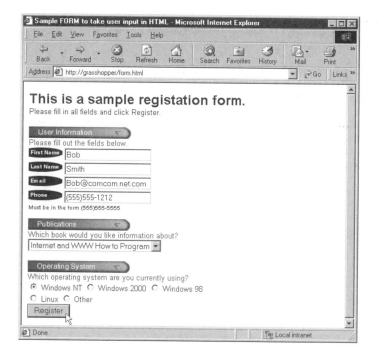

Fig. 26.12 User entering a valid phone number (part 3 of 3).

 Good Programming Practice 26.2

*Use meaningful HTML object names for input fields. This makes Perl programs easier to un-
derstand when retrieving FORM data.*

Figure 26.13 (**form.pl**) processes the data posted by **form.html** and sends a Web
page response back to the client. Function **param** (lines 8–13) is part of the Perl **CGI** module
and is used to retrieve values for the form field elements and assign them to scalar variables.
For example, in line 27 of Fig. 26.12, an HTML form text field is created with the name
EMAIL; later, in line 11 of **form.pl**, we access the value that the user entered for that field
by calling **param("EMAIL")**, and assign the value returned to scalar **$email**.

```perl
1   #!perl
2   # Fig. 26.13: form.pl
3   # Program to read information sent to the server
4   # from the FORM in the form.html document.
5
6   use CGI qw( :standard );
7
8   $os = param( "OS" );
9   $firstName  = param( "FNAME" );
10  $lastName   = param( "LNAME" );
11  $email  = param( "EMAIL" );
12  $phone  = param( "PHONE" );
13  $book   = param( "BOOK" );
14
15  print header;
16  print "<BODY BACKGROUND = \"images/back.gif\">";
17  print "<BASEFONT FACE = \"ARIAL,SANS-SERIF\" SIZE = \"3\">";
18
19  if ( $phone =~ / ^ \( \d{3} \) \d{3} - \d{4} $ /x )
20  {
21      print <<End_Success;
22          Hi <FONT COLOR = "BLUE"><B>$firstName</B></FONT>.
23          Thank you for completing the survey.<BR>
24          You have been added to the
25          <FONT COLOR = "BLUE"><STRONG>$book</STRONG></FONT>
26          mailing list.<BR><BR>
27          <STRONG>The following information has been saved
28          in our database:</STRONG><BR>
29          <TABLE BORDER = "0" CELLPADDING = "0"
30              CELLSPACING = "10">
31          <TR><TD BGCOLOR = #FFFFAA>Name </TD>
32              <TD BGCOLOR = #FFFFBB>Email</TD>
33              <TD BGCOLOR = #FFFFCC>Phone</TD>
34              <TD BGCOLOR = #FFFFDD>OS</TD></TR>
35          <TR><TD>$firstName $lastName</TD><TD>$email</TD>
36              <TD>$phone</TD><TD>$os</TD></TR>
37          </TABLE>
38          <BR><BR><BR>
39          <CENTER><FONT SIZE = "-3">
40          This is only a sample form.
41          You have not been added to a mailing list.
42          </FONT></CENTER>
43  End_Success
44  }
45  else
46  {
47      print <<End_Failure;
48          <FONT COLOR = "RED" SIZE = "+2">
49          INVALID PHONE NUMBER</FONT><BR>
50          A valid phone number must be in the form
51          <STRONG>(555)555-5555</STRONG>
52          <FONT COLOR = "BLUE"> Click the Back button,
53          enter a valid phone number and resubmit.<BR><BR>
```

Fig. 26.13 Script to process user data from `form.html` (part 1 of 2).

```
54          Thank You.
55   End_Failure
56   }
```

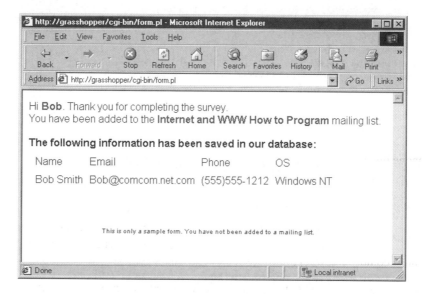

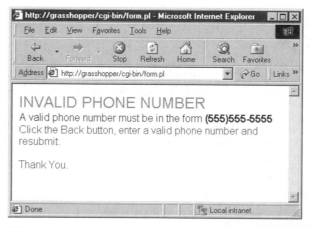

Fig. 26.13 Script to process user data from `form.html` (part 2 of 2).

In line 19, we determine whether the phone number entered by the user is valid. In this case, the format *(555)555-5555* is the only acceptable format. Validating information is crucial when you are maintaining a database or mailing list. For example, validation ensures that data is stored in the proper format in a database, that credit card numbers contain the proper number of digits before encrypting them for submission to a merchant, etc. The design of verifying information is called *business logic* (also called *business rules*).

Good Programming Practice 26.3

Use business logic to ensure that invalid information is not stored in databases.

Line 19's **if** condition

```
( $phone =~ / ^ \( \d{3} \) \d{3} - \d{4} $ /x )
```

uses a regular expression to validate the phone number. The expression **\ (** matches the opening parenthesis of the phone number. Because we want to match the literal character **(**, we must escape its normal meaning by using the **** character. This must be followed by three digits (**\d{3}**), a closing parenthesis, three digits, a literal hyphen, and finally four more digits. Note that we use the **^** and **$** symbols to ensure that there are no extra characters at either end of the string.

If the regular expression is matched, then the phone number is valid and a Web page is sent to the client thanking the user for completing the form. If the user posts an invalid phone number, the **else** clause (lines 46–56) is executed, instructing the user to enter a valid phone number.

26.6 Server-Side Includes

Dynamic content greatly improves the look and feel of a Web page. Pages that include the current date or time, rotating banners or advertisements, a daily message or special offer, or the latest company news will always look new. Clients see new information upon every visit and thus will likely revisit the site in the future.

Server-side includes (SSIs) are commands embedded in HTML documents to allow simple dynamic content creation. SSI commands like **ECHO** and **INCLUDE** allow Web pages to include content that is constantly changing (like the current time) or information stored in a database. The command **EXEC** can be used to run CGI scripts and embed their output directly into a Web page.

Not all Web servers support the available SSI commands. Therefore, SSI commands are written as HTML comments (e.g., **<!--#ECHO VAR="DOCUMENT_NAME" -->**). Servers that do not recognize these commands will simply treat them as comments.

A document containing SSI commands is typically given the **.SHTML** file extension (the extra **S** at the front of the extension stands for server). The **.SHTML** files are parsed by the server. The server executes the SSI commands and writes any output to the client.

Figure 26.14 implements a *Web page hit counter*. Each time a client requests the document, the counter is incremented by one. Perl script **counter.pl** (Fig. 26.15) manipulates the counter.

Performance Tip 26.1

Parsing HTML documents on a server can dramatically increase the load on that server. To increase the performance of a heavily loaded server try to limit the use of Server Side Includes.

```
1   <!DOCTYPE html PUBLIC "-//W3C//DTD HTML 4.0 Transitional//EN">
2   <!-- Fig. 26.14: counter.shtml -->
3
```

Fig. 26.14 Incorporating a Web-page hit counter and displaying environment variables (part 1 of 3).

```
4   <HTML>
5      <HEAD>
6         <TITLE>Using Server Side Includes</TITLE>
7      </HEAD>
8
9   <BODY>
10     <CENTER>
11        <H3>Using Server Side Includes</H3>
12     </CENTER>
13
14     <!--#EXEC CGI="/cgi-bin/counter.pl" --><BR>
15
16     The Greenwich Mean Time is
17     <FONT COLOR = "BLUE">
18     <!--#ECHO VAR="DATE_GMT" -->.
19     </FONT><BR>
20
21     The name of this document is
22     <FONT COLOR = "BLUE">
23     <!--#ECHO VAR="DOCUMENT_NAME" -->
24     </FONT><BR>
25
26     The local date is
27     <FONT COLOR = "BLUE">
28     <!--#ECHO VAR="DATE_LOCAL" -->
29     </FONT><BR>
30
31     This document was last modified on
32     <FONT COLOR = "BLUE">
33     <!--#ECHO VAR="LAST_MODIFIED" -->
34     </FONT><BR>
35
36     Your current IP Address is
37     <FONT COLOR = "BLUE">
38     <!--#ECHO VAR="REMOTE_ADDR" -->
39     </FONT><BR>
40
41     My server name is
42     <FONT COLOR = "BLUE">
43     <!--#ECHO VAR="SERVER_NAME" -->
44     </FONT><BR>
45
46     And I am using the
47     <FONT COLOR = "BLUE">
48     <!--#ECHO VAR="SERVER_SOFTWARE" -->
49     Web Server.</FONT><BR>
50
51     You are using
52     <FONT COLOR = "BLUE">
53     <!--#ECHO VAR="HTTP_USER_AGENT" -->.
54     </FONT><BR>
55
```

Fig. 26.14 Incorporating a Web-page hit counter and displaying environment variables (part 2 of 3).

```
56     This server is using
57     <FONT COLOR = "BLUE">
58     <!--#ECHO VAR="GATEWAY_INTERFACE" -->.
59     </FONT><BR>
60
61     <BR><BR>
62     <CENTER>
63     <HR>
64     <FONT SIZE = -5>This document was last modified on
65     <!--#ECHO VAR="LAST_MODIFIED" --></FONT>
66     </CENTER>
67  </BODY>
68  </HTML>
```

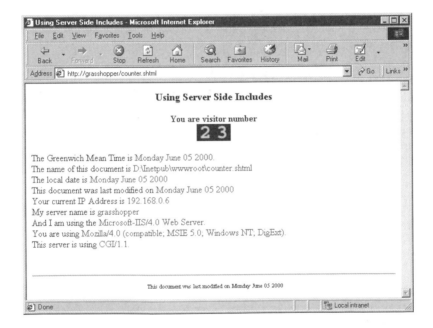

Fig. 26.14 Incorporating a Web-page hit counter and displaying environment variables (part 3 of 3).

Line 14 of the **counter.shtml** script executes the **counter.pl** script using the **EXEC** command. Before the HTML document is sent to the client, the SSI command is executed and any script output is sent to the client. This technique can increase the load on the server tremendously, depending on how many times the script has to be parsed and the size and work load of the scripts.

Line 18 uses the **ECHO** *command* to display variable information. The **ECHO** command is followed by the *keyword* **VAR** and the variable's name. For example, *variable* **DATE_GMT** contains the current date and time in Greenwich Mean Time (GMT). In line 23, the name of the current document is included in the HTML page with the **DOCUMENT_NAME** *variable*. The **DATE_LOCAL** *variable* inserts the date in line 28 (in local format—different formats are used around the world).

Figure 26.15 (**counter.pl**) introduces file input and output in Perl. Line 7 opens (for input) the file **counter.dat**, which contains the number of hits to date for the **counter.shtml** Web page. Function **open** is called to create a *filehandle* to refer to the file during the execution of the script. In this example, the file opened is assigned a filehandle named **COUNTREAD** (line 7). Line 8

```
$data = <COUNTREAD>;
```

uses the *diamond operator* **<>** to read one line of the file referred to by filehandle **COUNTREAD** and assign it to the variable **$data**. When the diamond operator is used in a scalar context, only one line is read. If assigned to an array, each line from the file is assigned to a successive array element. Because the file **counter.dat** contains only one line (in this case only one number), the variable **$data** is assigned the value of that number in line 8. Line 9 then increments **$data** by one.

Now that the counter has been incremented for this hit, we write the counter back to the **counter.dat** file. In line 12

```
open( COUNTWRITE, ">counter.dat" );
```

we open the **counter.dat** file for writing by preceding the file name with a **>** *character*. This immediately truncates (i.e., discards) any data in that file. If the file does not exist, Perl creates a new file with the specified name. Perl also provides an *append* mode (**>>**) for appending to the end of a file.

```
1   #!perl
2   # Fig. 26.15: counter.pl
3   # Program to track the number of times a web page has been accessed.
4
5   use CGI qw( :standard );
6
7   open( COUNTREAD, "counter.dat" );
8       $data = <COUNTREAD>;
9       $data++;
10  close( COUNTREAD );
11
12  open( COUNTWRITE, ">counter.dat" );
13      print COUNTWRITE $data;
14  close( COUNTWRITE );
15
16  print header;
17  print "<CENTER>";
18  print "<STRONG>You are visitor number</STRONG><BR>";
19
20  for ( $count = 0; $count < length( $data ); $count++ )
21  {
22      $number = substr( $data, $count, 1 );
23      print "<IMG SRC = \"images/counter/$number.jpg\">";
24  }
25
26  print "</CENTER>";
```

Fig. 26.15 Perl script for counting Web page hits

After line 12 is executed, data can be written to the file **counter.dat**. Line 13

```
print COUNTWRITE $data;
```

writes the counter number back to the file **counter.dat**. The first argument to **print** (**COUNTWRITE**) simply specifies the filehandle that refers to the file where data is written. If no filehandle is specified, **print** writes to standard out (**STDOUT**). In line 14, the connection to **counter.dat** is terminated by calling function **close**.

Good Programming Practice 26.4

When opening a text file to read its contents, open the file in read-only mode. Opening the file in other modes makes it possible to accidentally overwrite the data.

Good Programming Practice 26.5

Always close files as soon as you are finished with them.

Lines 20–24

```
for ( $count = 0; $count < length( $data ); $count++ )
{
    $number = substr( $data, $count, 1 ) ;
    print "<IMG SRC=\"images/counter/$number.jpg\">";
}
```

use a **for** loop to iterate through each digit of the number scalar **$data**. The **for** loop syntax consists of three semicolon-separated statements in parentheses followed by a body delimited by curly braces. In our example, we loop until **$count** is equal to **length($data)**. Because function **length** returns the length of a character string, the **for** iterates once for each digit in **$data**.

For each iteration, we obtain the current digit by calling function **substr**. The first parameter passed to function **substr** specifies the string from which to obtain a substring. The second parameter specifies the offset, in characters, from the beginning of the string, so an offset of 0 returns the first character, 1 returns the second, and so forth. The third argument specifies the length of the substring to be obtained (just one character in this case). The **for** loop, then, assigns each digit (possibly from a multiple-digit number) to the scalar variable **$number** in turn. Each digit's corresponding image is displayed using an HTML **IMG** tag (line 23).

26.7 Verifying a Username and Password

It is often desirable to have a *private Web site*—one that is visible only to certain people. Implementing privacy generally involves username and password verification. Figure 26.16 presents an example of an HTML form which queries the user for a username and a password to be verified. It posts the fields **USERNAME** and **PASSWORD** to the Perl script **password.pl** upon submission of the form. Note that for simplicity, this example does not encrypt the data before sending it to the server.

```
1   <!DOCTYPE html PUBLIC "-//W3C//DTD HTML 4.0 Transitional//EN">
2   <!-- Fig. 26.16: password.html -->
3
4   <HTML>
5   <HEAD>
6   <TITLE>Verifying a username and a password.</TITLE>
7   </HEAD>
8
9   <BODY>
10     <P>
11        <FONT FACE = "ARIAL">
12        Type in your username and password below.
13        </FONT><BR>
14        <FONT COLOR = "#0000FF" FACE = "ARIAL" SIZE = 1>
15        <STRONG>
16        Note that password will be sent as plain text
17        </STRONG>
18        </FONT>
19     </P>
20
21     <FORM ACTION = "/cgi-bin/password.pl" METHOD = "POST">
22     <BR>
23
24     <TABLE BORDER = "0" CELLSPACING = "0" STYLE = "HEIGHT: 90px;
25         WIDTH: 123px" CELLPADING = "0">
26     <TR>
27        <TD BGCOLOR = "#DDDDDD" COLSPAN = "3">
28        <FONT FACE = "ARIAL" SIZE = "2">
29        <STRONG>Username:</STRONG>
30        </FONT>
31        </TD>
32     </TR>
33     <TR>
34        <TD BGCOLOR = "#DDDDDD" COLSPAN = "3">
35        <INPUT SIZE = "40" NAME = "USERNAME"
36              STYLE = "HEIGHT: 22px; WIDTH: 115px">
37        </TD>
38     </TR>
39     <TR>
40        <TD BGCOLOR = "#DDDDDD" COLSPAN = "3">
41        <FONT FACE = "ARIAL" SIZE = "2">
42        <STRONG>Password:</STRONG>
43        </FONT></TD>
44     </TR>
45     <TR>
46        <TD BGCOLOR = "#DDDDDD" COLSPAN = "3">
47        <INPUT SIZE = "40" NAME = "PASSWORD"
48              STYLE = "HEIGHT: 22px; WIDTH: 115px"
49              TYPE = "PASSWORD">
50        <BR></TD>
51     </TR>
52     <TR>
53        <TD COLSPAN = "3">
```

Fig. 26.16 Entering a username and password (part 1 of 3).

```
54                     <INPUT TYPE = "SUBMIT" VALUE = "Enter"
55                        STYLE = "HEIGHT: 23px; WIDTH: 47px">
56               </TD>
57            </TR>
58         </TABLE>
59         </FORM>
60    </BODY>
61    </HTML>
```

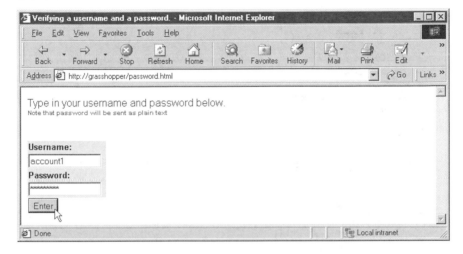

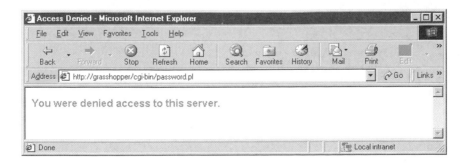

Fig. 26.16 Entering a username and password (part 2 of 3)

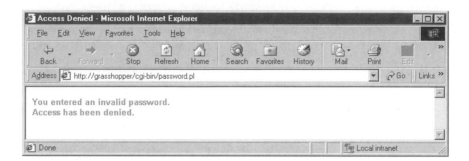

Fig. 26.16 Entering a username and password (part 3 of 3)

The script **password.pl** (Fig. 26.17) is responsible for verifying the username and password of the client by crosschecking against values from a database. The database list of valid users and their passwords is a simple text file: **password.txt** (Fig. 26.18).

```
1   #!perl
2   # Fig. 26.17: password.pl
3   # Program to search a database for usernames and passwords.
4
5   use CGI qw(:standard);
6
7   $testUsername = param( "USERNAME" );
8   $testPassword = param( "PASSWORD" );
9
10  open ( FILE, "password.txt" ) ||
11     die "The database could not be opened";
12
13  while ( $line = <FILE> )
14  {
15     chomp $line;
16     ( $username, $password ) = split( ",", $line );
17
18     if ( $testUsername eq $username )
19     {
20        $userVerified = 1;
21        if ( $testPassword eq $password )
22        {
23           $passwordVerified = 1;
24           last;
25        }
26     }
27  }
28
29  close( FILE );
30  print header;
31
```

Fig. 26.17 Contents of **password.pl** Perl script (part 1 of 2).

```perl
32    if ( $userVerified && $passwordVerified )
33    {
34       accessGranted();
35    }
36    elsif ( $userVerified && !$passwordVerified )
37    {
38       wrongPassword();
39    }
40    else
41    {
42       accessDenied();
43    }
44
45    sub accessGranted
46    {
47       print "<TITLE>Thank You</TITLE>";
48       print "<FONT FACE = \"ARIAL\" SIZE = 2 COLOR = \"BLUE\">";
49       print "<STRONG>Permission has been granted, $username.";
50       print "<BR>Enjoy the site.</STRONG></FONT>";
51    }
52
53    sub wrongPassword
54    {
55       print "<TITLE>Access Denied</TITLE>";
56       print "<FONT FACE = \"ARIAL\" SIZE =2 COLOR=\"RED\"><STRONG>";
57       print "You entered an invalid password.<BR>";
58       print "Access has been denied.</STRONG></FONT>";
59    }
60
61    sub accessDenied
62    {
63       print "<TITLE>Access Denied</TITLE>";
64       print "<FONT FACE = \"ARIAL\" SIZE = 3 COLOR =\"RED\"><STRONG>";
65       print "You were denied access to this server.";
66       print "</STRONG></FONT>";
67    }
```

Fig. 26.17 Contents of **password.pl** Perl script (part 2 of 2).

```
1    account1,password1
2    account2,password2
3    account3,password3
4    account4,password4
5    account5,password5
6    account6,password6
7    account7,password7
8    account8,password8
9    account9,password9
10   account10,password10
```

Fig. 26.18 Database **password.txt** containing user names and passwords.

Line 10 opens the file **password.txt** for reading, assigning it the filehandle **FILE**. To verify that the file was opened successfully, a test is performed using the *logical OR operator* (||). Operator OR returns true if either the left condition or the right condition. If the condition on the left evaluates to true, then the condition on the right is not evaluated. In this case the *die* executes only if **open** returns false, indicating that the file did not open properly. If this happens, **die** displays an error message and the program terminates.

The *while* loop in line 13 is another control structure which repeatedly executes the code enclosed in curly braces (lines 14–27) until the test condition in parentheses returns false. In this case, the test condition assigns the next unread line of **password.txt** to **$line**, and evaluates to true as long as a line from the file was successfully read. When the end of the file is reached, **<FILE>** returns false and the loop terminates.

Each line in **password.txt** consists of an account name and password pair, separated by a comma, and followed with a newline character. For each line read, function *chomp* is called (line 15) to remove the newline character at the end of the line. Then, *split* is called to divide the string into substrings at the specified separator or *delimiter* (in this case, a comma). For example, the **split** of the first line in **password.txt** returns the list **("account1", "password1")**. The syntax

```
( $username, $password ) = split( ",", $line );
```

sets **$username** and **$password** to the first and second elements returned by **split** (**account1** and **password1**), respectively.

If the username is equivalent to the one we have read from the text file, the conditional in line 18 returns true. The **$userVerified** variable is then set to **1**. Next, the value of **$testPassword** is tested against the value in the **$password** variable. If the password matches, the **$passwordVerified** variable is set to **1**. In this case, because a successful username-password match has been found, the *last* statement is used in line 24 to immediately exit the **while** loop. The **last** statement is often used to short-circuit a loop structure once a desired condition has been satisfied. Because we are now finished reading from **password.txt** we **close** it on line 29. Line 32 checks if both the username and password were verified. Using, the Perl *logical AND operator*, **&&** . If both conditions are true (that is, if both variables evaluate to nonzero values), then the function **accessGranted** is called, which sends a Web page to the client indicating a successful login.

If the **if** statement returns false, the condition in the following **elsif** statement is then tested. Line 36, tests if the user was verified, but the password was not. In this case, the function **wrongPassword** is called. The unary *logical negation operator* **!** is used in line 36 to negate the value of **$passwordVerified** and thus test if it is false. If the user was not recognized at all, function **accessDenied** is called, and a message indicating that permission has been denied is sent to the client (line 42).

Perl allows programmers to define their own functions or *subroutines*. Keyword **sub** begins a function definition and curly braces delimit the function body (lines 45, 53 and 61). To call a function, use the function name followed by parentheses (line 34, 38 and 42).

26.8 Using ODBC to Connect to a Database

Database connectivity allows system administrators to maintain information on things such as user accounts, passwords, credit card information, mailing lists and product inventory.

Databases allow companies to enter the world of electronic commerce and maintain crucial data. The Perl module **Win32::ODBC** installed with Perl 5.6 (or higher) provides an interface for Perl programs to connect to **Windows ODBC (Open Database Connectivity)** data sources. To do interact with a database, a data source must first be defined with the Data Source Administrator in Microsoft Windows (see the "Setting up a System Data Source Name" document on the CD that accompanies this book). From a Web browser, the client enters an SQL query string that is sent to the Web server. The Perl script is then executed, querying the database and sending a record set in the form of an HTML document back to the client. This SQL query string is written following the rules and syntax discussed earlier in Chapter 25.

Figure 26.19 (**data.html**) is a Web page that **POST**s a form containing an SQL query to the server. Perl script **data.pl** (Fig. 26.20) processes the form data.

```
1   <!DOCTYPE html PUBLIC "-//W3C//DTD HTML 4.0 Transitional//EN">
2   <!-- Fig. 26.19: data.html -->
3
4   <HTML>
5   <HEAD>
6   <TITLE>Sample Database Query</TITLE>
7   </HEAD>
8
9   <BODY>
10  <FONT FACE = "ARIAL, SANS-SERIF" SIZE = "2">
11
12     <FONT SIZE = "+2">
13        <STRONG>Querying an ODBC database.</STRONG>
14     </FONT><BR>
15
16     <FORM METHOD = "POST" ACTION = "cgi-bin/data.pl">
17        <INPUT TYPE = "TEXT" NAME = "QUERY" SIZE = "40"
18               VALUE = "SELECT * FROM Authors"><BR><BR>
19        <INPUT TYPE = "SUBMIT" VALUE = "Send Query">
20     </FORM>
21  </BODY>
22  </HTML>
```

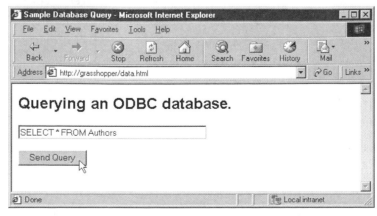

Fig. 26.19 Source code and output of the **data.html** document.

Line 16 creates an HTML **FORM**, indicating that the data submitted from the **FORM** will be sent to the Web server via the **POST METHOD** and the **ACTION** is to execute **data.pl** (Fig. 26.20). Line 17 adds a text field to the **FORM**, setting its name to **QUERY** and its **VALUE** to a default SQL query string. This query specifies that all records (**SELECT ***) are to be retrieved **FROM** the **Authors** table inside the **perl.mdb** database (for this example, we gave it the DSN **Products**. See the "Setting up a ODBC System Data Source Name" document on the CD that accompanies this book for instructions on how to create a DSN.

```perl
1    #!perl
2    # Fig. 26.20: data.pl
3    # Program to query a database and send results to the client.
4
5    use Win32::ODBC;
6    use CGI qw( :standard );
7
8    $queryString = param( "QUERY" );
9    $dataSourceName = "Products";
10
11   print header, start_html( "Search Results" );
12
13   if ( !( $data = new Win32::ODBC( $dataSourceName ) ) )
14   {
15      print "Error connecting to $dataSourceName: ";
16      print Win32::ODBC::Error();
17      exit;
18   }
19
20   if ( $data->Sql( $queryString ) )
21   {
22      print "SQL failed. Error: ", $data->Error();
23      $data->Close();
24      exit;
25   }
26
27   print "<FONT FACE = \"ARIAL,SANS-SERIF\" SIZE = 3>";
28   print "<FONT COLOR = \"BLUE\" SIZE = 4>Search Results</FONT>";
29   print "<TABLE BORDER = 0 CELLPADDING = 5 CELLSPACING = 0>";
30
31   for ( $counter = 0; $data->FetchRow(); $counter++ )
32   {
33      %rowHash = $data->DataHash();
34
35      print <<End_Row;
36      <TR BGCOLOR = "#9999CC">
37      <TD>$rowHash{'ID'}</TD>
38      <TD>$rowHash{'FirstName'}</TD>
39      <TD>$rowHash{'LastName'}</TD>
40      <TD>$rowHash{'Phone'}</TD>
41      </TR>
42   End_Row
43   }
```

Fig. 26.20 Contents of **data.pl** Perl script (part 1 of 2).

```
44
45   print <<End_Results;
46   </TABLE>
47   <BR>Your search yielded <B>$counter</B> results.<BR><BR>
48   <FONT SIZE = "2">
49   Please email comments to
50   <A href = "mailto:deitel\@deitel.com">
51   Deitel and Associates, Inc.</A>.
52   End_Results
53
54   print end_html;
55   $data->Close();
```

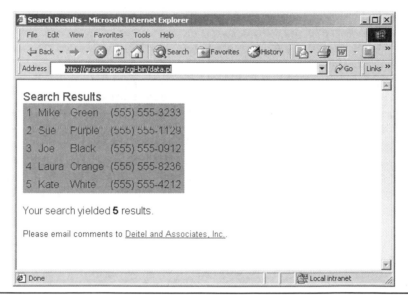

Fig. 26.20 Contents of **data.pl** Perl script (part 2 of 2).

Look-and-Feel Observation 26.1

Using tables to output fields in a database organizes information neatly into rows and columns

The **data.pl** script is responsible for taking the SQL query string and sending it on to the database management system. Line 5 imports the ***Win32::ODBC*** package to allow interaction with ODBC databases. In line 8, function **param** accesses the user input from the text field **QUERY**, and assigns the returned value to variable **$queryString**. Line 9 creates scalar variable **$dataSourceName** and assigns it the string **"Products"**.

Function ***start_html*** (line 11) from the CGI module prints the opening HTML tags, including the page's title, **Search Results**. Line 13 connects to the ODBC data source by passing the Data Source Name to the ***new*** constructor function for the **Win32::ODBC** object, which creates a new instance of the object. Specifically, the program uses Windows ODBC to look for and connect to the database named **Products**, and the variable **$data** becomes a reference to the object representing the Perl connection to that database. If the database cannot be accessed for any reason, the condition in line 13 is—

false and lines 14–18 are executed, reporting the error and terminating the script with function **exit**. Function **Win32::ODBC::Error** is called to return a string describing why the database could not be accessed.

Method **Sql** in line 20 executes the SQL query on the database, as specified by **$queryString**. The database object referenced by **$data** now contains the record set generated by the query on the database. If the query is successful, **Sql** returns an undefined value which is interpreted as false by the **if** statement in line 20. Otherwise, SQL returns a number representing an error code (which evaluates to true) and lines 21–25 are executed. The connection to the database is **Close**d on line 23.

Line 31 uses a **for** loop to iterate through each record in the record set. The loop condition uses function **FetchRow**, which either returns true and sets **$data** to return the next record in the set, or returns **undef** (false) indicating that the end of the record set has been reached. For each record retrieved, variable **$counter** is incremented by one.

Line 33 retrieves the fields from the current record using function **DataHash** and places this data into the hash **%rowHash**. The data can then be accessed using the field names (as specified in the **perl.mdb** database file) as keys. For example, **$rowHash{'Phone'}** yields the phone number of the current record.

In lines 37–40, the document accesses the values of certain fields for the current record using their keys and prints these values into table cells and rows. If a key is not contained in **%rowHash**, the corresponding table cell is simply left empty.

After all rows of the record set have been displayed, the **for** loop condition fails and the table's closing tag is written (line 46). The number of results contained in **$counter** is printed in line 47. Line 54 uses the CGI module's **end_html** in place of the closing HTML tag, and line 55 closes the connection to the database.

26.9 Cookies and Perl

Cookies maintain *state* information for a particular client that uses a Web browser. Preserving this information allows data and settings to be retained even after execution of a CGI script has ended. Cookies are often used to record user preferences (or other information) for the next time a client visits a Web site. For example, many Web sites use cookies to store a client's postal zip code. The zip code is used when the client requests a Web page to send current weather information or news updates for the client's region. On the server side, cookies may be used to help track information about client activity, to determine, for example, which sites are visited most frequently or how effective certain advertisements and products are.

Microsoft Internet Explorer stores cookies as small text files saved on the client's hard drive. The data stored in the cookie is sent back to the Web server that placed it there whenever the user requests a Web page from that particular server. The server can then serve up HTML content to the client that is specific to the information stored in the cookie.

Figure 26.21 uses a script to write a cookie to the client's machine. The **cookies.html** file is used to display an HTML **FORM** that allows a user to enter a name, height and favorite color. When the user clicks the **Write Cookie** button, the **cookies.pl** script (Fig. 26.22) is executed.

```
1   <!DOCTYPE html PUBLIC "-//W3C//DTD HTML 4.0 Transitional//EN">
2   <!-- Fig. 26.21: cookies.html -->
3
4   <HTML>
5      <HEAD>
6         <TITLE>Writing a cookie to the client computer</TITLE>
7      </HEAD>
8
9   <BODY>
10  <FONT FACE = "ARIAL,SANS-SERIF" SIZE = "2">
11
12     <FONT SIZE = "+2">
13        <B>Click Write Cookie to save your cookie data.</B>
14     </FONT><BR>
15
16     <FORM METHOD = "POST" ACTION = "cgi-bin/cookies.pl">
17        <STRONG>Name:</STRONG><BR>
18        <INPUT TYPE = "TEXT" NAME = "NAME"><BR>
19        <STRONG>Height:</STRONG><BR>
20        <INPUT TYPE = "TEXT" NAME = "HEIGHT"><BR>
21        <STRONG>Favorite Color</STRONG><BR>
22        <INPUT TYPE = "TEXT" NAME = "COLOR"><BR>
23        <INPUT TYPE = "SUBMIT" VALUE = "Write Cookie">
24     </FORM>
25  </BODY>
26  </HTML>
```

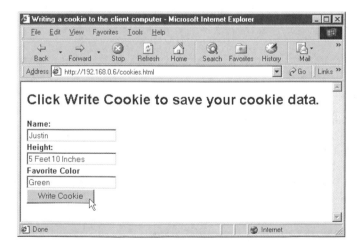

Fig. 26.21 Source for **cookies.html** Web page.

```
1   #!perl
2   # Fig. 26.22: cookies.pl
3   # Program to write a cookie to a client's machine
4
```

Fig. 26.22 Writing a cookie to the client (part 1 of 2).

```
5   use CGI qw( :standard );
6
7   $name = param( NAME );
8   $height = param( HEIGHT );
9   $color = param( COLOR );
10
11  $expires = "Tuesday, 05-JUL-05 16:00:00 GMT";
12
13  print "Set-Cookie: Name=$name; expires=$expires; path=\n";
14  print "Set-Cookie: Height=$height; expires=$expires; path=\n";
15  print "Set-Cookie: Color=$color; expires=$expires; path=\n";
16
17  print header, start_html( "Cookie Saved" );
18
19  print <<End_Data;
20  <FONT FACE = "ARIAL,SANS-SERIF" SIZE = "3">
21  The cookie has been set with the folowing data:<BR><BR>
22  <FONT COLOR = "BLUE">Name:</FONT> $name<BR>
23  <FONT COLOR = "BLUE">Height:</FONT> $height<BR>
24  <FONT COLOR = "BLUE">Favorite Color:</FONT>
25  <FONT COLOR = $color> $color<BR></FONT>
26  <BR>Click <A HREF = "readCookies.pl">here</A> to read saved cookie.
27  End_Data
28
29  print end_html;
```

Fig. 26.22 Writing a cookie to the client (part 2 of 2).

Good Programming Practice 26.6

Critical information such as credit card or password information should not be stored using cookies. Cookies cannot be used to retrieve information such as email addresses or data on the hard drive from a client's computer.

The **cookies.pl** script reads the data sent from the client on lines 7–9. Line 11 declares and initializes variable **$expires** to contain the *expiration date of the cookie*. The browser deletes a cookie after it expires. Lines 13–15 call function **print** to output the cookie information. They use the ***Set-Cookie:*** *header* to indicate that the browser should store the incoming data in a cookie. They set three attributes for each cookie: a name-value pair containing the data to be stored, the expiration date and the URL path of the server domain over which the cookie is valid. For this example, no path is given, making the cookie readable from anywhere within the server's domain. Lines 17–29 send a Web page indicating that the cookie has been written to the client.

If the client is Internet Explorer, cookies are stored in the **Temporary Internet Files** directory on the client's machine. Figure 26.23 shows the contents of this directory prior to the execution of **cookies.pl**. After the cookie is written, a text file is added to this list. The file **Cookie:justin@196.168.0.6** can be seen in the **Temporary Internet Files** directory in Fig. 26.24. The IP address **196.168.0.6** is the domain for which the cookie is valid. The username **justin**, however, is just part of the filename Internet Explorer uses for cookies and is not actually a part of the cookie itself. A remote server, therefore, cannot access the username.

Figure 26.25 (**readCookies.pl**) reads the cookie written in Fig. 26.22 and displays the information in a table.

Environment variable **'HTTP_COOKIE'** contains the client's cookies. Line 12 calls subroutine **readCookies** and places the returned value into hash **%cookies**. The user-defined subroutine **readCookies** splits the environment variable containing the cookie information into separate cookies (using **split**) and stores these as distinct elements in **@cookieArray** (line 29). For each cookie in **@cookieArray**, we call **split** again to obtain the original name-value pair, which in turn is stored in **%cookieHash** in line 33.

Note that the **split** function in line 32 makes reference to a variable named **$_**. The special Perl variable **$_** is used as a default for many Perl functions. In this case, because no variable was provided in the **foreach** loop (line 30), so **$_** is used by default. Thus, in this example, **$_** is assigned the value of the current element of **@cookieArray** as **foreach** loops though it.

Once **%cookieHash** has been created, it is **return**ed in line 36, and **%cookies** is assigned its value (line 12). The **foreach** (line 17) then iterates through the hash with the given key names, printing the key and value for the data from the cookie in an HTML table.

Fig. 26.23 Temporary Internet Files directory before a cookie is written.

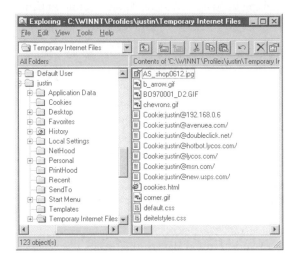

Fig. 26.24 Temporary Internet Files directory after a cookie is written.

```perl
1   #!perl
2   # Fig. 26.25: readCookies.pl
3   # Program to read cookies from the client's computer
4
5   use CGI qw( :standard );
6
7   print header, start_html( "Read cookies" );
8   print "<FONT FACE = \"ARIAL,SANS-SERIF\" SIZE = 3>";
9   print "<STRONG>The folowing data is saved in a cookie on your ";
10  print "computer.<STRONG><BR><BR>";
11
12  %cookies = readCookies();
13
14  print "<TABLE BORDER = \"5\" CELLSPACING = \"0\" ";
15  print "CELLPADDING = \"10\">";
16
17  foreach $cookieName ( "Name", "Height", "Color" )
18  {
19     print "<TR>";
20     print "   <TD BGCOLOR=#AAAAFF>$cookieName</TD>";
21     print "   <TD BGCOLOR=#AAAAAA>$cookies{ $cookieName }</TD>";
22     print "</TR>";
23  }
24  print "</TABLE>";
25  print end_html;
26
27  sub readCookies
28  {
29     @cookieArray = split( "; ", $ENV{ 'HTTP_COOKIE' } );
```

Fig. 26.25 Output displaying the cookie's content (part 1 of 2).

```
30      foreach ( @cookieArray )
31      {
32          ( $cookieName, $cookieValue ) = split ( "=", $_ );
33          $cookieHash{ $cookieName } = $cookieValue;
34      }
35
36      return %cookieHash;
37  }
```

Fig. 26.25 Output displaying the cookie's content (part 2 of 2).

26.10 Internet and World Wide Web Resources

There is a strong established Perl community online that has made available a wealth of information on the Perl language, Perl modules, CGI scripting, etc.

www.perl.com
Perl.com is the first place to look for information about Perl. The homepage provides up-to-date news on Perl, answers to common questions about Perl, and an impressive collection of links to Perl resources of all kinds on the Internet. It includes sites for Perl software, tutorials, user groups and demos.

www.activestate.com
From this site you can download ActivePerl—the Perl 5 implementation for Windows.

www.perl.com/CPAN/README.html
The "Comprehensive Perl Archive Network" is exactly what the name suggests. Here you will find an extensive listing of Perl related information.

www.perl.com/CPAN/scripts/index.html
This is the scripts index from the CPAN archive. Here you will find a wealth of scripts written in Perl.

www.pm.org
This is the homepage of Perl Mongers, a group dedicated to supporting the Perl community. This site is helpful in finding others in the Perl community to converse with; Perl Mongers has established Perl user groups around the globe.

www.speakeasy.org/~cgires
This is a collection of tutorials and scripts that can provide a thorough understanding of CGI and of how it is used.

www.cgi101.com
CGI 101 is a site for those looking to improve their programming ability through familiarity with CGI. The site contains a six-chapter class outlining techniques for CGI programming in the Perl language. The class includes both basics and more sophisticated scripts, with working examples. Also included in the site are script libraries and links to other helpful sources.

www.jmarshall.com/easy/cgi
A good, brief explanation of CGI for those with programming experience.

wdvl.internet.com/Authoring/Languages/Perl/Resources.html
This site contains many links to Perl resources.

wdvl.internet.com/Authoring/CGI
The *Web Developer's Virtual Library* provides tutorials for learning both CGI and Perl, the language most commonly used in developing CGI applications.

www.perlmonth.com
Perlmonth is a monthly online periodical devoted to Perl, with featured articles from professional programmers. This is a good source for those who use Perl frequently and wish to keep up on the latest developments involving Perl.

www.itknowledge.com/tpj
The Perl Journal is a large magazine dedicated to Perl. Subscribers are provided with up-to-date Perl news and articles, on the Internet as well as in printed form.

home.t-online.de/home/wahls/perlnet.html
This page provides a brief tutorial on Perl network programming for those who already know the language. The tutorial uses code examples to explain the basics of network communication.

www.w3.org/CGI
The World Wide Web Consortium page on CGI is concerned with security issues involving the Common Gateway Interface. This page provides links concerning CGI specifications, as indicated by the National Center for Super computing Applications (NCSA).

SUMMARY

- Practical Extraction and Report Language (Perl), developed by Larry Wall, is one of the most widely-used languages for Web programming today.

- Common Gateway Interface (CGI) is a standard protocol through which applications interact with Web servers.

- Permission is granted within the Web server *to* allow CGI scripts to be executed. They are typically either designated by filename extension (such as **.cgi** or **.pl**) or located within a special directory (such as **/cgi-bin**).

- For CGI scripts, standard output is redirected through the Common Gateway Interface to the server and then sent over the Internet to a Web browser for rendering.

- The Perl comment character (**#**) instructs the interpreter to ignore everything on the current line following the **#**.

- The "shebang" syntax (**#!**) indicates the path to the Perl interpreter or may indicate to the server (e.g., Apache) that a Perl program follows the statement.

- The **$** character specifies that the variable contains a *scalar* value (i.e., strings, integer numbers and floating-point numbers).
- In Perl, variables are created automatically the first time they are encountered by the interpreter.
- When a variable is encountered inside a double-quoted (**" "**) string, Perl uses a process called interpolation to replace the variable with its associated data.
- In Perl, uninitialized variables have the value **undef**, which evaluates to **0** or the empty string (**" "**), depending on context.
- Perl does not need to differentiate between numeric and string data types because the interpreter evaluates scalar variables depending on the context in which they are used.
- Perl arrays are named lists of elements, indexed by integer.
- Perl array variable names must be preceded by the **@** symbol.
- An array name prefixed by the **$** character and followed by an index number in square brackets accesses individual array elements.
- The range operator (**..**) creates a consecutive series of values in a list or array.
- The Perl interpreter automatically handles memory management.
- The backslash character (****) is used in Perl to escape special characters.
- One of Perl's most powerful capabilities is its ability to process textual data easily and efficiently, allowing for straightforward searching, substitution, extraction and concatenation of strings.
- Text manipulation in Perl is usually done with a regular expression—a series of characters that serves as a pattern-matching template (or search criteria) in strings, text files and databases.
- Perl has a collection of string operators used to compare and test strings for equality.
- A **foreach** loop iterates sequentially through the elements in a list or array.
- The match operator (**m//**) uses a regular expression to search a string for a specified pattern.
- The **=~** operator (or binding operator) assigns to the match operator a string to search.
- Regular expressions can include special characters called metacharacters which specify patterns or contexts that cannot be defined using literal characters.
- Parentheses in a regular expression indicate that the text matching the pattern is to be saved in special Perl variables **$1**, **$2**, **$3**, etc.
- Modifying characters following the match operator indicate additional search options.
- Environment variables contain information about the script's execution environment.
- In order to run Perl scripts as CGI applications, a Web server must first be installed and configured appropriately.
- The **use** statement directs Perl programs to include the contents (e.g., functions, etc.) of predefined packages called modules.
- The **CGI** module contains many functions for CGI scripting in Perl.
- Functions **header**, **start_html** and **end_html** in the CGI module return strings representing certain HTTP headers and HTML tags.
- The here document syntax is often used in CGI programs to eliminate the need to repeatedly call function **print**.
- The *hash* data type (or associative array), designated by the **%** character, represents an unordered set of scalar-value pairs.
- Elements in a hash are accessed using unique string *keys* which are associated with the elements' values: **$hashName{keyName}**.

- The **%ENV** hash is a built-in hash in Perl that contains the names and values of all environment variables.

- Function ***keys*** returns a list of all keys in a hash.

- Function ***sort*** orders an array of elements alphabetically.

- The design of verifying information entered into a database is called business logic or busin*ess rules*.

- Server-side includes (SSIs) are commands embedded in HTML documents for simple dynamic content creation.

- Function ***open*** creates *filehandles through which Perl scripts can read and write to files.*

- The diamond operator **<>** reads information from a filehandle line by line.

- Function **print** writes to a filehandle.

- Function **die** displays an error message and terminates program execution.

- Function ***chomp*** removes the newline character at the end of a string.

- Function ***split*** divides a string into substrings at the specified separator or *delimiter*.

- The ***last*** statement short-circuits a loop structure once a desired condition is satisfied.

- Keyword **sub** begins a definition for a user-defined subroutine or function.

- Perl module ***Win32::ODBC*** provides an interface for Perl programs to connect to **Windows ODBC (Open Database Connectivity)** data sources.

- Cookies are used to maintain state information for a particular client that uses a Web browser.

- The ***Set-Cookie:*** *HTTP header* indicates that the browser should store the incoming data in a cookie.

TERMINOLOGY

! logical negation operator
comment character
$_ variable in Perl
%ENV hash in Perl
&& logical AND operator
.pl extension for Perl programs
.SHTML file extension
@_ variable in Perl
\n newline character
{} braces denoting a block of code
|| logical OR operator
=~ operator
== numerical equality operator
ActivePerl
alphanumeric character
assignment operators
associative array
business logic
business rules
CGI environment variables
CGI module
cgi-bin directory
chomp function

client
command-line switches in Perl
Common Gateway Interface (CGI)
cookies
CPAN (Comprehensive Perl Archive Network)
Data Source Name (DSN)
DATE_GMT variable
DATE_LOCAL variable
delimiter
diamond operator (**<>**)
DOCUMENT_NAME variable
ECHO SSI command
elements (of an array)
end_html function from **CGI** module
environment variables
eq operator in Perl
escape character
EXEC SSI command
exit function
expiration date of a cookie
FLASTMOD SSI command
for statement in Perl
foreach statement in Perl

27

Bonus Chapter: Introduction to Java 2 Programming

Objectives

- To create command-line and windowed applications.
- To be able to process graphical user interface (GUI) events for a variety of GUI components.
- To be able to arrange GUI components with layout managers.
- To be able to manipulate collections of data with arrays and **Vector**s.
- To understand how to create, manage and destroy threads.
- To implement Java networking applications using streams-based sockets.
- To be able to enhance Web server functionality with a servlet that connects to a database.

Classes struggle, some classes triumph, others are eliminated.
Mao Zedong

I never forget a face, but in your case I'll make an exception.
Groucho (Julius Henry) Marx

The most general definition of beauty...Multeity in Unity.
Samuel Taylor Coleridge

The spider's touch, how exquisitely fine!
Feels at each thread, and lives along the line.
Alexander Pope

Outline

27.1 Introduction

This bonus chapter on Java programming is provided to support the earlier chapters in this book that use Java programming. Our intent here is not to present complete coverage of the Java programming language, which is much too large to be covered in a small amount of space. Rather, this chapter provides examples that are targeted to the areas of Java used throughout this text. This chapter assumes that you are already a programmer familiar with object-oriented programming concepts. If you are interested in pursuing a more in-depth Java learning experience, please consider our textbook *Java How to Program, Third Edition* and our forthcoming textbook *Advanced Java How to Program*.

Java is a powerful object-oriented language that is fun to use for novices but also appropriate for experienced programmers building substantial information systems. Java provides procedural, object-based and object-oriented programming capabilities. The object-based programming paradigm (with classes, encapsulation and objects) and the object-oriented programming paradigm (with inheritance and polymorphism) are crucial for developing elegant, robust and maintainable software systems.

Java is certain to become the language of choice in the new millennium for implementing Internet-based and Intranet-based applications as well as software for devices that communicate over networks (such as cellular phones, pagers and personal digital assistants). Do not be surprised when your new stereo and other devices in your home will be networked together using Java technology!

An implementation of Java and the Java documentation are available for free download from the Sun Microsystems Web site

java.sun.com/j2se/1.3

This chapter is based on Sun's most recent Java release—the *Java 2 Platform*. Sun provides an implementation of the *Java 2 Platform* called the *Java 2 Software Development Kit (J2SDK)* that includes the tools you need to write software in Java. Because of Java's extraordinary portability, the programs in this book should work correctly with any version of the J2SDK. We tested these programs using the most recent release of the J2SDK at the time of this publication—Version 1.3. The J2SDK is a command-line environment—you compile and run your programs from a Command Prompt on Windows (or a shell in UNIX). If you prefer to use a complete development environment, Sun also provides Forté for Java Community Edition free for download at

www.sun.com/forte/ffj/ce/index.html

This robust environment requires that the J2SDK be installed first. Please read the download and installation instructions Sun provides for both the J2SDK and Forté carefully before installing the products.

27.2 Java Keywords, Primitive Data Types and Class Libraries

This section presents several tables introducing Java's keywords, primitive data types, allowed primitive type promotions and a small portion of Java's library of reusable data types.

The table of Fig. 27.1 contains the keywords of the Java programming language. Keywords (or *reserved words*) are reserved for use by Java and are always spelled with all lowercase letters. These keywords should not be used as identifiers in Java programs.

The table of Fig. 27.2 shows Java's eight primitive data types—the fundamental building blocks of all types in Java. Each type is shown with its size in bytes and its value ranges.

Java Keywords				
abstract	boolean	break	byte	case
catch	char	class	continue	default
do	double	else	extends	false
final	finally	float	for	if
implements	import	instanceof	int	interface
long	native	new	null	package
private	protected	public	return	short
static	super	switch	synchro-nized	this
throw	throws	transient	true	try
void	volatile	while		

Keywords that are reserved but not used by Java

const	goto

Fig. 27.1 Java keywords.

Type	Size in bits	Values	Standard
boolean	8	**true** or **false**	
char	16	**'\u0000'** to **'\uFFFF'** (i.e., 0 through 65,535)	(ISO Unicode character set)
byte	8	–128 to +127	
short	16	–32,768 to +32,767	
int	32	–2,147,483,648 to +2,147,483,647	
long	64	–9,223,372,036,854,775,808 to +9,223,372,036,854,775,807	
float	32	*Negative range:* -3.4028234663852886E+38 to -1.1754943508222875E-38 *Positive range:* 1.1754943508222875E-38 to 3.4028234663852886E+38	(IEEE 754 floating point)

Fig. 27.2 The Java primitive data types (part 1 of 2).

Type	Size in bits	Values	Standard
double	64	*Negative range:* -1.7976931348623157E+308 to -2.2250738585072014E-308 *Positive range:* 2.2250738585072014E-308 to 1.7976931348623157E+308	(IEEE 754 floating point)

Fig. 27.2   The Java primitive data types (part 2 of 2).

When writing Java applications, there will be cases where a method (i.e., a function) expects to receive one primitive type, but it passed a different primitive type. Some programming languages are flexible in performing type promotions and demotions. For example, in C++ a method that expects to receive an **int** can be passed a **double** and C++ will truncate the floating-point part of the **double** value (i.e., demote the **double** to an **int**). Similarly, C++ allows a method that expects to receive a **double** to be passed an **int** and C++ will promote the **int** value to a **double**. Java is more strict when processing type conversions of primitive types—it allows only type promotions, not type demotions. Fig. 27.3 shows the allowed type promotions for Java primitive types.

Java programmers rely heavily on *class libraries* (sets of reusable software components) to build programs rapidly and reliably. Java's preexisting class libraries are organized into *packages* of related reusable types known as *classes* and *interfaces*. The table of Fig. 27.4 describes some of the Java packages used in the Java programs from this book. For a complete list of Java packages and their contents, please refer to the online HTML-based Java documentation, which is downloadable from the Sun Microsystems Java Web site **java.sun.com**.

Type	Allowed promotions
double	None
float	double
long	float or double
int	long, float or double
char	int, long, float or double
short	int, long, float or double
byte	short, int, long, float or double
boolean	None (boolean values are not considered to be numbers in Java)

Fig. 27.3   Allowed promotions for primitive data types.

Package	Description
`java.awt`	*The Java Abstract Windowing Toolkit Package.* This package contains the classes and interfaces required to create and manipulate graphical user interfaces (GUIs) in Java 1.0 and 1.1. In Java 2, these classes can still be used, but the *Swing GUI components* of the `javax.swing` packages are often used instead. There are several classes and interfaces in this package which are frequently used in Swing GUI programming.
`java.awt.event`	*The Java Abstract Windowing Toolkit Event Package.* This package contains classes and interfaces that enable event handling for GUI components in both the java.awt and javax.swing packages.
`java.io`	*The Java Input/Output Package.* This package contains classes that enable programs to input and output data using streams. The classes of this package can be used with file processing and networking, as well as with other types of I/O.
`java.lang`	*The Java Language Package.* This package contains classes and interfaces required by many Java programs and is automatically imported by the Java compiler into all programs. These classes and interfaces are considered to be fundamental to Java programming.
`java.net`	*The Java Networking Package.* This package contains classes that enable programs to communicate via networks using streams of bytes or packets of data. The classes in this package provide the foundation for other higher-level networking capabilities in Java.
`java.sql`	*The Java Database Connectivity Package.* This package contain classes and interfaces that enable a Java program to interact with a database.
`java.text`	*The Java Text Package.* This package contains classes and interfaces that enable a Java program to manipulate numbers, dates, characters and strings. This package provides many of Java's internationalization capabilities—features that enable a program to be customized to a specific locale (e.g., an application used around the world may display strings in many languages).
`java.util`	*The Java Utilities Package.* This package contains utility classes and interfaces including: date and time manipulations, random number processing capabilities (**Random**), breaking strings into smaller pieces called tokens (**StringTokenizer**) and other capabilities. All of Java's predefined data structures are defined in this package.

Fig. 27.4 Some packages of the Java API (part 1 of 2).

Package	Description
`javax.swing`	*The Java Swing GUI Components Package.* This package contains classes and interfaces for Java's Swing GUI components that provide support for portable GUIs.
`javax.swing.event`	*The Java Swing Event Package.* This package contains classes and interfaces that enable event handling for GUI components in the `javax.swing` package.
`javax.swing.table`	*The Java Swing Table Package.* This package contains classes and interfaces for creating and manipulating spreadsheet-like tables.

Fig. 27.4   Some packages of the Java API (part 2 of 2).

27.3 Command-Line Java Applications

This section provides an introduction to command-line applications in Java. The applications shown here are executed from a command prompt on Windows or a shell on UNIX/Linux.

27.3.1 Printing a Line of Text at the Command Line

We begin by considering a simple Java *application* that displays a line of text in your command prompt/shell. An application is a program that executes using the **java** interpreter. We will first discuss the program, then discuss how to compile and execute the program. The program (**Welcome1.java**) and its output are shown in Fig. 27.5.

This program illustrates several important features of the Java language. We consider each line of the program in detail. Each program has line numbers for the reader's convenience; those line numbers are not part of Java programs. Line 7 does the "real work" of the program, namely displaying the phrase **Welcome to Java Programming!** on the screen. But let us consider each line in order. Line 1

```
1   // Fig. 27.5: Welcome1.java
2   // A first program in Java
3
4   public class Welcome1 {
5      public static void main( String args[] )
6      {
7         System.out.println( "Welcome to Java Programming!" );
8      }
9   }
```

```
Welcome to Java Programming!
```

Fig. 27.5   A first program in Java.

```
// Fig. 27.2: Welcome1.java
```

begins with **//**, indicating that the remainder of the line is a *comment*. To help you locate the programs on the CD, we begin every program with a comment indicating figure number and file name. A comment that begins with **//** is called a *single-line comment* because the comment terminates at the end of the current line. Java also supports multiple-line comments (delimited with **/*** and ***/**). A similar form of comment called a *documentation comment* is delimited with **/**** and ***/**.

Common Programming Error 27.1

Forgetting one of the delimiters of a multiple-line comment is a syntax error.

Java programmers generally use single-line comments in preference to multiple-line comments. We use single-line comments. Java introduced the documentation comment syntax to enable programmers to highlight portions of programs that the **javadoc** utility program (provided by Sun Microsystems with the Java 2 Software Development Kit) can read and use to prepare documentation for your program automatically. There are subtle issues to using **javadoc**-style comments properly in a program. We do not use **javadoc**-style comments in-line in this chapter.

Line 4

```
public class Welcome1 {
```

begins a *class definition* for class **Welcome1**. Every program in Java consists of at least one class definition that is defined by you—the programmer. These classes are known as *programmer-defined classes* or *user-defined classes*. In Section 27.7, we discuss a program that contains two programmer-defined classes. The **class** keyword introduces a class definition in Java and is immediately followed by the *class name* (**Welcome1** in this program). By convention, all class names in Java begin with a capital first letter and have a capital first letter for every word in the class name (e.g., **SampleClassName**). The name of the class is called an *identifier*. An identifier is a series of characters consisting of letters, digits, underscores (**_**) and dollar signs (**$**) that does not begin with a digit and does not contain any spaces. Some valid identifiers are **Welcome1**, **$value**, **_value**, **m_inputField1** and **button7**. The name **7button** is not a valid identifier because it begins with a digit, and the name **input field** is not a valid identifier because it contains a space. Java is *case sensitive*—uppercase and lowercase letters are different, so **a1** and **A1** are different identifiers.

Common Programming Error 27.2

Java is case sensitive. Not using the proper uppercase and lowercase letters for an identifier is normally a syntax error.

Good Programming Practice 27.1

By convention, you should always begin a class name with a capital first letter.

Good Programming Practice 27.2

When reading a Java program, look for identifiers that start with capital first letters. These normally represent Java classes.

Software Engineering Observation 27.1

Avoid using identifiers containing dollar signs ($) as these are often used by the compiler to create indentifier names.

Most classes we define begin with the ***public*** *keyword* to indicate that the class is potentially a reusable class. When you save a **public** class definition in a file, the class name must be used as the base part of the file name. For our application, the file name is **Welcome1.java**. All Java class definitions are stored in files ending with the "**.java**" file name extension.

Common Programming Error 27.3

*For a **public** class, it is an error if the file name is not identical to the class name in both spelling and capitalization. Therefore, it is also an error for a file to contain two or more **public** classes.*

Common Programming Error 27.4

It is an error not to end a file name with the **.java** *extension for a file containing a class definition. The Java compiler will not be able to compile the class definition.*

A *left brace* (at the end of line 4 in this program), **{**, begins the *body* of every class definition. A corresponding *right brace* (at line 9 in this program), **}**, must end each class definition. Notice that lines 5–8 are indented. This is a spacing convention used to make programs more readable. We define each spacing convention as a *Good Programming Practice*.

Common Programming Error 27.5

If braces do not occur in matching pairs, the compiler indicates an error.

Good Programming Practice 27.3

*Whenever you type an opening left brace, **{**, in your program, immediately type the closing right brace, **}**, then reposition the cursor between the braces to begin typing the body. This helps prevent missing braces.*

Good Programming Practice 27.4

*Indent the entire body of each class definition one "level" of indentation between the left brace, **{**, and the right brace, **}**, that define the body of the class. This emphasizes the structure of the class definition and helps make the class definition easier to read.*

Good Programming Practice 27.5

Set a convention for the indent size you prefer and then uniformly apply that convention. The Tab key may be used to create indents, but tab stops may vary between editors. We recommend using either 1/4-inch tab stops or (preferably) three spaces to form a level of indent.

Line 5

```
public static void main( String args[] )
```

is a part of every Java application. Java applications automatically begin executing at **main**. The parentheses after **main** indicate that **main** is a *method*, or what a C or C++ programmer would call a function. Java class definitions normally contain one or more methods. For a Java application class, exactly one of those methods must be called **main** and must be defined as shown on line 5; otherwise, the **java** interpreter will not execute the application. Methods are able to perform tasks and return information when they complete their tasks. The ***void*** keyword indicates that this method will perform a task (displaying a line of text in this program), but will not return any information when it completes its task. We will see that many methods return information when they complete their task. The keyword **static** specifies that **main** is a class method. Class methods are special in that they are available to be called as soon as the class is loaded into memory at execution time. We will discuss this issue further at the end of this discussion when we show you how to execute the program.

The left brace, **{**, on line 6 begins the *body of the method definition*. A corresponding right brace, **}**, must end the method definition's body (line 8 of the program).

Line 7

```
System.out.println( "Welcome to Java Programming!" );
```

instructs the computer to print the *string* of characters contained between the double quotation marks. Although the Java compiler normally ignores whites-pace characters used to format a program, white-space characters in strings are not ignored by the compiler.

System.out is known as the *standard output object*. **System.out** allows Java applications to display strings and other types of information in the *command window* from which the Java application is executed. On Microsoft Windows 95/98, the command window is the *MS-DOS prompt*. On Microsoft Windows NT/2000, the command window is the *Command Prompt*. On UNIX, the command window is normally called a *command window*, a *command tool*, a *shell tool* or a *shell*. On computers running an operating system that does not have a command window (such as a Macintosh), the **java** interpreter normally displays a window containing the information displayed by the program.

Method ***System.out.println*** displays (or prints) a line of text in the command window. When **System.out.println** completes its task, it automatically positions the *output cursor* (the location where the next character will be displayed) to the beginning of the next line in the command window (this is similar to you pressing the *Enter* key when typing in a text editor—the cursor is repositioned at the beginning of the next line in your file).

The entire line, including **System.out.println**, its *argument* in the parentheses (the string) and the *semicolon* (**;**), is called a *statement*. Every statement must end with a semicolon (also known as the *statement terminator*). When this statement executes, it displays the message **Welcome to Java Programming!** in the command window.

Common Programming Error 27.6

Omitting the semicolon at the end of a statement is a syntax error.

Testing and Debugging Tip 27.1

When the compiler reports a syntax error, the error may not be on the line indicated by the error messages. First, check the line where the error was reported. If that line does not contain syntax errors, check the preceding several lines in the program.

We are now ready to compile and execute our program. You can copy the **Welcome1.java** file from the CD that accompanies this book to your hard drive or you can simply input the program into a text editor and save it as **Welcome1.java**.

Testing and Debugging Tip 27.2

Some text editors automatically add file name extensions such as `.txt` *to the end of a file name. Be sure that the name of the file ends with* `.java` *after you save it.*

To compile the program, we open a command window, change to the directory where the program is stored and type

```
javac Welcome1.java
```

The **javac** command above translates the Java source code stored in **Welcome1.java** into Java bytecodes. If the program contains no syntax errors, the preceding command creates a new file called **Welcome1.class** containing the Java bytecodes that represent our application. These bytecodes will be interpreted by the **java** interpreter when we tell it to execute the program by typing the command

```
java Welcome1
```

which launches the java interpreter. The interpreter automatically looks for a file ending with a "**.class**" extension (in this case, **Welcome1.class**) in the current directory. Note that the "**.class**" file name extension is omitted from the preceding command; otherwise the interpreter will not execute the program. After the preceding command loads **Welcome.class** into memory, the interpreter calls method **main** to begin program execution. The only methods that are available to be called at the time the class is loaded are the **static** methods of the class. To start the program's execution, the interpreter must be able to call method **main**. This is the reason that main was declared **static** on line 5 of the program. Next, the statement at line 7 of **main** displays "**Welcome to Java Programming!**" Figure 27.6 shows the execution of the application in a Microsoft Windows 2000 **Command Prompt** window.

27.3.2 Using a Dialog Box from a Command-Line Application

Although the program of Fig. 27.5 displays output in the command window, most Java applications that display output use windows or *dialog boxes* to display output. For example, World Wide Web browsers such as Netscape Communicator or Microsoft Internet Explorer display Web pages in their own windows. Email programs typically allow you to type messages in a window provided by the email program or read messages you receive in a window provided by the email program.

Fig. 27.6   Executing the **Welcome1** application in a Microsoft Windows 2000 **Command Prompt**.

Dialog boxes are windows that typically are used to display important messages to the user of an application. Java 2 already includes class **JOptionPane** that allows you to easily display a dialog box containing information. The program of Fig. 27.7 is a command-line application, which displays a similar string to the one shown in Fig. 27.5 in a predefined dialog box called a *message dialog*. Notice that this new version of the program also makes use of the C-style "**\n**" *escape sequence* to insert newline characters into the string.

One of the great strengths of Java is its rich set of predefined classes that programmers can reuse rather than "reinventing the wheel." We use a variety of these classes in this book. Java's many predefined classes are grouped into categories of related classes called *packages*. The packages are referred to collectively as the *Java class library* or the *Java applications programming interface (Java API)*. Class **JOptionPane** is defined for us in a package called **javax.swing**.

Line 3

```
import javax.swing.JOptionPane;
```

is an **import** statement. The compiler uses **import** statements to identify and load classes required to compile a Java program. When you use classes from the Java API, the compiler attempts to ensure that you use them correctly. The **import** statements help the compiler locate the classes you intend to use. Each piece of the package name is a directory (or folder) on disk. All the packages in the Java API are stored in the directory **java** or **javax** that contain many subdirectories including **swing** (a subdirectory of **javax**).

```
1   // Fig. 27.7: Welcome2.java
2   // Printing multiple lines in a dialog box
3   import javax.swing.JOptionPane;   // import class JOptionPane
4
5   public class Welcome2 {
6      public static void main( String args[] )
7      {
8         JOptionPane.showMessageDialog(
9            null, "Welcome\nto\nJava\nProgramming!" );
10
11        System.exit( 0 );  // terminate the program
12     }
13  }
```

Fig. 27.7   Displaying multiple lines in a dialog box.

The preceding line tells the compiler to load the **JOptionPane** class from the **javax.swing** package. This package contains many classes that help Java programmers define *graphical user interfaces (GUIs)* for their application. *GUI components* facilitate data entry by the user of your program, and formatting or presenting data outputs to the user. For example, Fig. 27.8 contains a Microsoft Internet Explorer browser window. In the window, there is a bar containing *menus* (**File**, **Edit**, **View**, etc.). Below the menu bar there is a set of *buttons* that each have a defined task in Internet Explorer. Below the buttons there is a *text field* in which the user can type the name of the World Wide Web site to visit. To the left of the text field is a *label* that indicates the purpose of the text field. The menus, buttons, text fields and labels are part of Internet Explorer's GUI. They enable you to interact with the Web browser program. Java contains classes that implement the GUI components described here and many others.

In **main**, lines 8 and 9

```
JOptionPane.showMessageDialog(
    null, "Welcome\nto\nJava\nProgramming!" );
```

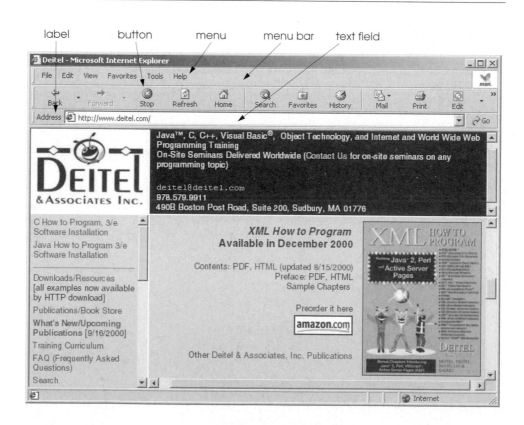

Fig. 27.8   A sample Internet Explorer window with GUI components.

indicate a call to method ***showMessageDialog*** of class **JOptionPane**. The method requires two arguments. When a method requires multiple arguments, the arguments are separated with *commas* (**,**). Until we discuss **JOptionPane** in a windowed application (rather than a command-line application), the first argument will be the keyword ***null***. The second argument is the string to display.

Method **JOptionPane.showMessageDialog** is a special method of the class **JOptionPane** called a ***static*** method. Such methods are always called using their class name followed by a dot operator (**.**) and the method name. Remember that static methods are special in that they are available to be called as soon as the class is loaded at execution time. When a program uses multiple classes, the Java interpreter is responsible for loading each of those classes.

Executing the statement on lines 8 and 9 displays the dialog box in Fig. 27.9. The *title bar* of the dialog contains the string **Message** to indicate that the dialog is presenting a message to the user. The dialog box automatically includes an **OK** button that allows the user to *dismiss (hide) the dialog* by pressing the button. This is accomplished by positioning the *mouse cursor* (also called the *mouse pointer*) over the **OK** button and clicking the mouse.

Note that Java allows large statements to be split over many lines. However, you cannot split a statement in the middle of an identifier or in the middle of a string.

Common Programming Error 27.7

Splitting a statement in the middle of an identifier or a string is a syntax error.

Line 11

```
System.exit( 0 );   // terminate the program
```

uses **static** method ***exit*** of class **System** to terminate the application. This line is required in any application that displays a graphical user interface to terminate the application. Notice once again the syntax used to call the method—the class name (**System**), a dot (**.**) and the method name (**exit**). Remember that identifiers starting with capital first letters normally represent class names. So, you can assume that **System** is a class. The argument **0** to method **exit** indicates that the application terminated successfully (a non-zero value normally indicates that an error occurred). This value is passed to the command window that executed the program. This is useful if the program is executed from a batch file (on Windows 95/98/NT systems) or a shell script (on UNIX systems). Batch files and shell scripts are typically used to execute several programs in sequence such that when the first program ends, the next program begins execution automatically. For more information on batch files or shell scripts, see your operating system's documentation.

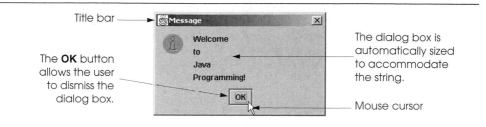

Fig. 27.9   Dialog box produced by the program of Fig. 27.7.

Class **System** is part of the package *java.lang*. Notice that class **System** is not imported with an **import** statement at the beginning of the program. Package **java.lang** is imported automatically in every Java program.

Common Programming Error 27.8

*Forgetting to call **System.exit** in an application that displays a graphical user interface prevents the program from terminating properly. This normally results in the command window preventing you from typing any other commands.*

27.3.3 Another Java Application: Adding Integers

Our next application inputs two integers (whole numbers) typed by a user at the keyboard, computes the sum of these values and displays the result. As the user types each integer and presses the *Enter* key, the integer is read into the program and added to the total.

This program uses another predefined dialog box from class **JOptionPane** called an *input dialog* that allows the user to input a value for use in the program. The program also uses a message dialog to display the results of the addition. Figure 27.10 shows the application and sample screen captures.

Line 4

```
import javax.swing.JOptionPane;   // import class JOptionPane
```

specifies to the compiler where to locate class **JOptionPane** for use in this application.

```
1   // Fig. 27.10: Addition.java
2   // An addition program
3
4   import javax.swing.JOptionPane;   // import class JOptionPane
5
6   public class Addition {
7      public static void main( String args[] )
8      {
9         String firstNumber,      // first string entered by user
10                secondNumber;     // second string entered by user
11         int number1,            // first number to add
12             number2,            // second number to add
13             sum;                // sum of number1 and number2
14
15         // read in first number from user as a string
16         firstNumber =
17            JOptionPane.showInputDialog( "Enter first integer" );
18
19         // read in second number from user as a string
20         secondNumber =
21            JOptionPane.showInputDialog( "Enter second integer" );
22
23         // convert numbers from type String to type int
24         number1 = Integer.parseInt( firstNumber );
25         number2 = Integer.parseInt( secondNumber );
26
```

Fig. 27.10 An addition program "in action" (part 1 of 2).

```
27          // add the numbers
28          sum = number1 + number2;
29
30          // display the results
31          JOptionPane.showMessageDialog(
32             null, "The sum is " + sum, "Results",
33             JOptionPane.PLAIN_MESSAGE );
34
35          System.exit( 0 );    // terminate the program
36       }
37    }
```

Fig. 27.10 An addition program "in action" (part 2 of 2).

As stated earlier, every Java program consists of at least one class definition. Line 6

```
public class Addition {
```

begins the definitions of class **Addition**. The file name for this **public** class must be **Addition.java**. Remember that all class definitions start with an opening left brace (end of line 6), **{**, and end with a closing right brace, **}** (line 37).

Every application begins execution with method **main** (line 7). The left brace (line 8) marks the beginning of **main**'s body and the corresponding right brace (line 36) marks the end of **main**.

Lines 9 and 10

```
String firstNumber,    // first string entered by user
       secondNumber;   // second string entered by user
```

are a *declaration*. The words **firstNumber** and **secondNumber** are the names of *variables*. All variables must be declared with a name and a data type before they can be used in a program. This declaration specifies that the variables **firstNumber** and **secondNumber** are data of type *String* (from package **java.lang**), which means that these variables will hold strings. A variable name can be any valid identifier. Declarations end with a semicolon (**;**) and can be split over several lines with each variable in the declaration separated by a comma (i.e., a *comma-separated list* of variable names). Several variables of the same type may be declared in one declaration or in multiple declarations. We could have written two declarations, one for each variable, but the preceding declaration is more concise. Notice the single-line comments at the end of each line. This is a common syntax used by programmers to indicate the purpose of each variable in the program.

Good Programming Practice 27.6

Choosing meaningful variable names helps a program to be "self-documenting" (i.e., it becomes easier to understand a program simply by reading it rather than having to read manuals or use excessive comments).

Good Programming Practice 27.7

By convention, variable name identifiers begin with a lowercase first letter. As with class names every word in the name after the first word should begin with a capital first letter. For example, identifier **firstNumber** *has a capital* **N** *in its second word* **Number**.

Good Programming Practice 27.8

Some programmers prefer to declare each variable on a separate line. This format allows for easy insertion of a descriptive comment next to each declaration.

Lines 11–13

```
int number1,        // first number to add
    number2,        // second number to add
    sum;            // sum of number1 and number2
```

declare that variables **number1**, **number2** and **sum** are data of type **int**. As an important aside, there are actually two types of variables in Java—*primitive data type variables* (normally called *variables*) and *reference variables* (normally called *references*). The identifiers **firstNumber** and **secondNumber** are actually references—names that are used to *refer to objects* in the program. Such references actually contain the location in the computer's memory of an object such as a **String** in this program.

Lines 15–17

```
// read in first number from user as a string
firstNumber =
    JOptionPane.showInputDialog( "Enter first integer" );
```

read from the user a **String** representing the first of the two integers that will be added. Method **JOptionPane.showInputDialog** displays the input dialog in Fig. 27.11. The argument to **showInputDialog** tells the user what to do in the text field. This message is called a *prompt* because it directs the user to take a specific action. The user types characters in the text field, then clicks the **OK** button to return the string to the program. [*Note:* Unfortunately, Java does not provide a simple form of input that is analogous to displaying output with **System.out.println**. For this reason, we normally receive input from a user through a GUI component such as the input dialog in this program].

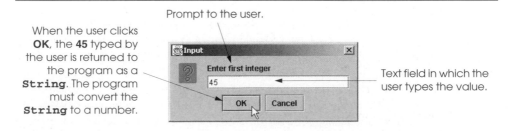

Fig. 27.11 Input dialog displayed to input a value from the user of Fig. 27.10.

Technically, the user can type anything in the text field of the input. For this program, if the user either types a non-integer value or clicks the **Cancel** button, a run-time logic error will occur.

The result of the call to **JOptionPane.showInputDialog** (a **String** containing the characters typed by the user) is given to variable **firstNumber** with the *assignment operator* **=**. The statement is read as, "**firstNumber** *gets* the value of **JOptionPane.showInputDialog("Enter first integer")**." The **=** operator is a *binary operator* because it has two *operands*—**firstNumber** and the result of the expression **JOptionPane.showInputDialog("Enter first integer")**. This whole statement is called an *assignment statement* because it assigns a value to a variable. The expression to the right side of the assignment operator **=** is always evaluated first.

Lines 19–21

```
// read in second number from user as a string
secondNumber =
   JOptionPane.showInputDialog( "Enter second integer" );
```

displays an input dialog in which the user types a **String** representing the second of the two integers that will be added.

Lines 23–25

```
// convert numbers from type String to type int
number1 = Integer.parseInt( firstNumber );
number2 = Integer.parseInt( secondNumber );
```

convert the two strings input by the user to **int** values that can be used in a calculation. Method *Integer.parseInt* (a **static** method of class **Integer**) converts its **String** argument to an integer. Class **Integer** is part of the package **java.lang**. The integer returned by **Integer.parseInt** in line 24 is assigned to variable **number1**. Any subsequent references to **number1** in the program use this same integer value. The integer returned by **Integer.parseInt** in line 25 is assigned to variable **number2**. Any subsequent references to **number2** in the program use this same integer value.

The assignment statement at line 28

```
sum = number1 + number2;
```

calculates the sum of the variables **number1** and **number2**, and assigns the result to variable **sum** using the assignment operator **=**. The statement is read as, "**sum** *gets* the value of **number1 + number2**." Most calculations are performed in assignment statements.

Good Programming Practice 27.9

Place spaces on either side of a binary operator. This makes the operator stand out and makes the program more readable.

After performing the calculation, lines 31–33

```
JOptionPane.showMessageDialog(
   null, "The sum is " + sum, "Results",
   JOptionPane.PLAIN_MESSAGE );
```

use another version of method **JOptionPane.showMessageDialog** to display the result of the addition. The expression

```
"The sum is " + sum
```

from the preceding statement uses the operator **+** to "add" a string (the literal **"The sum is "**) and **sum** (the **int** variable containing the result of the addition on line 28). Java has a version of the **+** operator for *string concatenation* that enables a string and a value of another data type (including another string) to be concatenated—the result of this operation is a new string. If we assume **sum** contains the value **117**, the expression evaluates as follows: Java determines that the two operands of the **+** operator (the string **"The sum is "** and the integer **sum**) are different types and one of them is a string. Next, Java converts **sum** to a string and concatenates it with **"The sum is "**, which results in the string **"The sum is 117"**. This string is displayed in the dialog box. Note that the automatic conversion of integer **sum** only occurs because it is concatenated with the string literal **"The sum is "**. Also note that the space between **is** and **117** is part of the string **"The sum is "**.

Common Programming Error 27.9

*Confusing the + operator used for string concatenation with the + operator used for addition can lead to strange results. For example, assuming integer variable **y** has the value **5**, the expression **"y + 2 = " + y + 2** results in the string **"y + 2 = 52"**, not **"y + 2 = 7"**, because first the value of **y** is concatenated with the string **"y + 2 = "**, then the value **2** is concatenated with the new larger string **"y + 2 = 5"**. The expression **"y + 2 = " + (y + 2)** produces the desired result.*

The version of method **showMessageDialog** used in Fig. 27.10 is different from the one discussed in Fig. 27.7 in that it requires four arguments. The message dialog box in Fig. 27.12 illustrates two of the four arguments. As with the first version, the first argument will be **null** until we discuss using class **JOptionPane** in a windowed application. The second argument is the message to display. The third argument is the string to display in the title bar of the dialog. The fourth argument (**JOptionPane.PLAIN_MESSAGE**) is a value indicating the type of message dialog to display—this type of message dialog does not display an icon to the left of the message.

The message dialog types are shown in Fig. 27.13. All message dialog types except **PLAIN_MESSAGE** dialogs display an icon to the user indicating the type of message.

27.4 Arrays

This section serves as an introduction to the important topic of data structures. *Arrays* are data structures consisting of related data items of the same type. Arrays are "static" entities in that they remain the same size once they are created, although an array reference may be reassigned to a new array of a different size. Section 27.5 discusses class **Vector**, which is an array-like class whose objects can grow and shrink in response to a Java program's changing storage requirements.

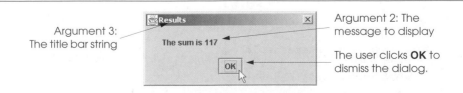

Argument 3:
The title bar string

Argument 2: The message to display

The user clicks **OK** to dismiss the dialog.

Fig. 27.12 Message dialog displayed by the program of Fig. 27.10.

Message dialog type	Icon	Description
JOptionPane.ERROR_MESSAGE		Displays a dialog that indicates an error to the application user.
JOptionPane.INFORMATION_MESSAGE		Displays a dialog with an informational message to the application user—the user can simply dismiss the dialog.
JOptionPane.WARNING_MESSAGE		Displays a dialog that warns the application user of a potential problem.
JOptionPane.QUESTION_MESSAGE		Displays a dialog that poses a question to the application user. This normally requires a response such as clicking a **Yes** or **No** button.
JOptionPane.PLAIN_MESSAGE	no icon	Displays a dialog that simply contains a message with no icon.

Fig. 27.13 JOptionPane constants for message dialogs.

An array is a group of contiguous memory locations that all have the same name and the same type. To refer to a particular location or element in the array, we specify the name of the array and the *position number* of the particular element in the array.

Consider a 12-element integer array called **c**. Any one of these elements may be referred to by giving the name of the array followed by the position number of the particular element in square brackets (**[]**). The first element in every array is the *zeroth element*. Thus, the first element of array **c** is referred to as **c[0]**, the second element of array **c** is referred to as **c[1]**, the seventh element of array **c** is referred to as **c[6]**, and, in general, the *i*th element of array **c** is referred to as **c[i - 1]**. The array **c**'s 12 elements are referred to as **c[0], c[1], c[2], ..., c[11]**. Array names follow the same conventions as other variable names.

The position number in square brackets is more formally called a *subscript* (or an index). A subscript must be an integer or an integer expression. If a program uses an expression as a subscript, the expression is evaluated first to determine the subscript. For example, if we assume that variable **a** is equal to **5** and that variable **b** is equal to **6**, then the statement

        c[a + b] += 2;

adds 2 to array element **c[11]**. Note that a subscripted array name is an *lvalue*—it can be used on the left side of an assignment to place a new value into an array element. The preceding statement is equivalent to

        c[11] = c[11] + 2;

Java provides several assignment operators for abbreviating assignment expressions. For example, the statement

        number = number + 3;

can be abbreviated with the *addition assignment operator* **+=** as

```
number += 3;
```

The += operator adds the value of the expression on the right of the operator to the value of the variable on the left of the operator and stores the result in the variable on the left of the operator. Any arithmetic statement of the form

   variable = *variable operator expression;*

where *operator* is one of the binary operators +, -, *, / or %, can be written in the form

   variable operator= expression;

Thus the assignment **number += 3** adds **3** to **number**.

Every array in Java *knows* its own length. The *length* of the array is determined by the following expression:

```
c.length
```

Common Programming Error 27.10

It is important to note the difference between the "seventh element of the array" and "array element seven." Because array subscripts begin at 0, the "seventh element of the array" has a subscript of 6, while "array element seven" has a subscript of 7 and is actually the eighth element of the array. This confusion is a source of "off-by-one" errors.

The brackets used to enclose the subscript of an array are an operator in Java. Brackets have the same level of precedence as parentheses. The operator precedence chart for Java in Appendix D shows the precedence and associativity of the Java operators. They are shown top to bottom in decreasing order of precedence with their associativity and type.

Arrays occupy space in memory. The programmer specifies the type of the elements and uses operator ***new*** to dynamically allocate the number of elements required by each array. Arrays are allocated with **new** because arrays are considered to be objects and all objects must be created with **new**. To allocate 12 elements for integer array **c**, the declaration

```
int c[] = new int[ 12 ];
```

is used. The preceding statement can also be performed in two steps as follows:

```
int c[];                // declares the array
c = new int[ 12 ];      // allocates the array
```

When arrays are allocated, the elements are automatically initialized to zero for the numeric primitive-data-type variables, to **false** for **boolean** variables or to **null** for references (any nonprimitive type).

Common Programming Error 27.11

*Unlike C or C++ the number of elements in the array is never specified in the square brackets after the array name in a declaration. The declaration **int c[12];** causes a syntax error.*

Memory may be reserved for several arrays with a single declaration. The following **String** declaration reserves 100 elements for array **b** and 27 elements for array **x**:

```
String b[] = new String[ 100 ],
       x[] = new String[ 27 ];
```

When declaring an array, the type of the array and the square brackets can be combined at the beginning of the declaration to indicate that all identifiers in the declaration represent arrays, as in

```
double[] array1, array2;
```

which declares both **array1** and **array2** as arrays of **double** values. As shown previously, the declaration and initialization of the array can be combined in the declaration. The following declaration reserves 10 elements for **array1** and 20 elements for **array2**:

```
double[] array1 = new double[ 10 ],
         array2 = new double[ 20 ];
```

Arrays may be declared to contain any data type. It is important to remember that in an array of primitive data type elements, every element of the array contains one value of the declared data type of the array. For example, every element of an **int** array is an **int** value. However, in an array of a nonprimitive type, every element of the array is a reference to an object of the data type of the array. For example, every element of a **String** array is a reference to a **String** that has the value **null** by default.

The application of Fig. 27.14 uses the **new** operator to dynamically allocate an array of 10 elements which are initially zero, then it prints the array in tabular format.

```
1   // Fig. 27.14: InitArray.java
2   // initializing an array
3   import javax.swing.*;
4
5   public class InitArray {
6      public static void main( String args[] )
7      {
8         String output = "";
9         int n[];                 // declare reference to an array
10
11        n = new int[ 10 ];   // dynamically allocate array
12
13        output += "Subscript\tValue\n";
14
15        for ( int i = 0; i < n.length; i++ )
16           output += i + "\t" + n[ i ] + "\n";
17
18        JTextArea outputArea = new JTextArea( 11, 10 );
19        outputArea.setText( output );
20
21        JOptionPane.showMessageDialog( null, outputArea,
22           "Initializing an Array of int Values",
23           JOptionPane.INFORMATION_MESSAGE );
24
25        System.exit( 0 );
26     }
27  }
```

Fig. 27.14 Initializing the elements of an array to zeros (part 1 of 2).

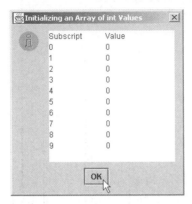

Fig. 27.14 Initializing the elements of an array to zeros (part 2 of 2).

Line 9 declares **n** as a reference capable of referring to array of integers. Line 11 allocates the 10 elements of the array with **new** and initializes the reference. Line 13 appends to the **String output** the headings for the columns of output displayed by the program.
Lines 15 and 16

```
for ( int i = 0; i < n.length; i++ )
    output += i + "\t" + n[ i ] + "\n";
```

uses a **for** *repetition structure* to build the **output** string that will be displayed in a new GUI component called a **JTextArea**, which we will use as the "message" in a message dialog. The **for** repetition structure is frequently used to perform *counter-controlled repetition*. When the **for** structure begins executing, the *control variable* **i** is initialized to **0**. Control variable **i** is known only in the **for** structure's body because it is declared inside the **for**. Next, the *loop-continuation condition* **i < n.length** is checked—while this condition remains true, the loop continues executing. In this example, if the value of **i** is less than **n.length** (i.e., 10), the loop performs the body statement

```
output += i + "\t" + n[ i ] + "\n";
```

Variable **i** is then incremented in the expression **i++**, and the loop continues its execution with the loop-continuation test. This process continues until the control variable **i** is incremented to **n.length** (10)—this causes the loop-continuation test to fail and repetition terminates. The program continues by performing the first statement after the **for** structure (in this case, line 18).

Note the use of zero-based counting (remember, array subscripts start at 0) so the loop can access every element of the array. Also, note the expression **n.length** in the **for** structure condition to determine the length of the array. In this example, the length of the array is 10, so the loop continues executing as long as the value of control variable **i** is less than 10. For a 10-element array, the subscript values are 0 through 9, so using the less than operator **<** guarantees that the loop does not attempt to access an element beyond the end of the array.
Line 18

```
JTextArea outputArea = new JTextArea();
```

declares **JTextArea** reference **outputArea** and initializes it with a new object of class **JTextArea** (from package **javax.swing**). A **JTextArea** is a GUI component that is capable of displaying many *rows* and *columns* of text. One of the many methods for placing text in a **JTextArea** is *setText*. Line 19

```
outputArea.setText( output );
```

uses **JTextArea** method **setText** to specify the **String** the **JTextArea** will display. Initially, a **JTextArea** contains an empty **String** (a **String** with no characters in it). The preceding statement specifies the **String** to which **output** refers as the **String** to display. Note in the message dialog displayed by this program that each **\t** character in **output** tabs to the next column in the **JTextArea** and each **\n** in output creates a new line of text in the **JTextArea**.

The **JOptionPane.showMessageDialog** method call at lines 21–23 uses the reference outputArea as its second argument (i.e., the message to be displayed). Method **showMessageDialog** is flexible in that it can be used to display a **String** or a GUI component such as a **JTextArea**. When the **JTextArea** is displayed on the message dialog, the current text in the **JTextArea** automatically appears in the white area that represents the **JTextArea**.

The elements of an array can be allocated and initialized in the array declaration by following the declaration with an equal sign and a comma-separated *initializer list* enclosed in braces (**{** and **}**). In this case, the array size is determined by the number of elements in the initializer list. For example, the statement

```
int n[] = { 10, 20, 30, 40, 50 };
```

creates a five-element array with subscripts of **0**, **1**, **2**, **3** and **4**. Note that the preceding declaration does not require the **new** operator to create the array object—this is provided automatically by the compiler when it encounters an array declaration that includes an initializer list.

The application of Fig. 27.15 initializes an integer array with 10 values (line 12) and displays the array in tabular format in a **JTextArea** on a message dialog.

```
1   // Fig. 27.15: InitArray2.java
2   // initializing an array with a declaration
3   import javax.swing.*;
4
5   public class InitArray2 {
6      public static void main( String args[] )
7      {
8         String output = "";
9
10        // Initializer list specifies number of elements and
11        // value for each element.
12        int n[] = { 32, 27, 64, 18, 95, 14, 90, 70, 60, 37 };
13
14        output += "Subscript\tValue\n";
15
```

Fig. 27.15 Initializing the elements of an array with a declaration (part 1 of 2).

```
16          for ( int i = 0; i < n.length; i++ )
17              output += i + "\t" + n[ i ] + "\n";
18
19          JTextArea outputArea = new JTextArea();
20          outputArea.setText( output );
21
22          JOptionPane.showMessageDialog( null, outputArea,
23              "Initializing an Array with a Declaration",
24              JOptionPane.INFORMATION_MESSAGE );
25
26          System.exit( 0 );
27      }
28  }
```

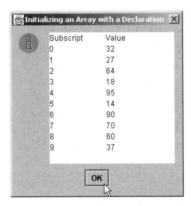

Fig. 27.15 Initializing the elements of an array with a declaration (part 2 of 2).

Testing and Debugging Tip 27.3

When a Java program is executed, the Java interpreter checks array element subscripts to be sure they are valid (i.e., all subscripts must be greater than or equal to 0 and less than the length of the array). If there is an invalid subscript, Java generates an exception.

Testing and Debugging Tip 27.4

Exceptions are used to indicate that an error occurred in a program. They enable the programmer to recover from an error and continue execution of the program instead of abnormally terminating the program. When an invalid array reference is made, an **ArrayIndexOutOfBoundsException** *is generated. We discuss exception handling in the example of Section 27.11.*

Common Programming Error 27.12

Referring to an element outside the array bounds is a logic error.

Testing and Debugging Tip 27.5

When looping through an array, the array subscript should never go below 0 and should always be less than the total number of elements in the array (one less than the size of the array). Make sure the loop terminating condition prevents accessing elements outside this range.

Testing and Debugging Tip 27.6

*Programs should validate the correctness of all input values to prevent erroneous infor-
mation from affecting a program's calculations.*

27.5 Class Vector

In the previous section we discussed Java's array data structure. Arrays work well when
you know in advance exactly the number of elements your program is required to store. For
cases in which your program requires more flexibility, Java provides class **Vector** (from
package **java.util**)—a dynamically resizable array like data structure. Figure 27.16
demonstrates class **Vector**.

Line 9 creates an object of type **Vector**. Lines 10 and 11 create references of type
Object and **String**, respectively. Each refers to a **String** object. Class **Object** is the
fundamental data type on which all other classes in Java are based. A reference of type
Object is special in that it can refer to any type of object in Java. We discuss class
Object more in Section 27.7.

```
1   // Fig. 27.16: VectorDemo.java
2   // This program demonstrates class Vector.
3   import javax.swing.*;
4   import java.util.*;
5
6   public class VectorDemo {
7      public static void main( String args[] )
8      {
9         Vector v = new Vector();
10        Object o = "hello!";
11        String s = "good bye";
12
13        v.addElement( o );
14        v.addElement( s );
15        v.addElement( new Boolean( true ) );
16        v.addElement( new Character( 'Z' ) );
17        v.addElement( new Integer( 7 ) );
18        v.addElement( new Long( 10000000 ) );
19        v.addElement( new Float( 2.5f ) );
20        v.addElement( new Double( 3.333 ) );
21
22        System.out.println( "Vector v contains:" );
23
24        for ( int j = 0; j < v.size(); j++ )
25           System.out.print( v.elementAt( j ) );
26     }
27  }
```

```
hello!good byetrueZ7100000002.53.333
```

Fig. 27.16 Class **Vector**.

Software Engineering Observation 27.2

*Instances of the primitive types such as **int** and **double** are not considered to be objects. However, the **java.lang** package provides classes (such as **Integer** and **Double**) that can be used to create objects which contain values of the primitive data types.*

Lines 13–20 add various objects to **Vector v** using the method ***addElement***. Each element in a **Vector** is actually a reference of type **Object**. The **for** loop (lines 24 and 25) iterates over the elements in the **Vector**. Method **size** (line 26) returns the size of the **Vector**. The program outputs the string value of each object on the command line with **System.out.print**. The primary difference between **print** and **println** is that **println** outputs a newline character automatically and **print** does not. Note that every object in Java has a string representation. Methods **print** and **println** can output any object using that object's own string representation.

27.6 Graphical User Interfaces: A Windowed Application with JFrames and Event Handling

The application of Fig. 27.17 is our first windowed application. We use class **JFrame** from package **javax.swing** to create our own type of window in which we will place GUI components with which the user can interact to drive the program.

This program also introduces class **StringTokenizer** (package **java.util**). When you read a sentence, your mind breaks the sentence into individual words, or *tokens,* each of which conveys meaning to you. Compilers also perform tokenization. They break up statements into individual pieces like keywords, identifiers, operators and other elements of a programming language. Class **StringTokenizer** breaks a string into its component tokens. Tokens are separated from one another by delimiters, typically whitespace characters such as blank, tab, newline and carriage return. Other characters may also be used as delimiters to separate tokens.

```
1   // Fig. 27.17: TokenTest.java
2   // Testing the StringTokenizer class of the java.util package.
3   import javax.swing.*;
4   import java.util.*;
5   import java.awt.*;
6   import java.awt.event.*;
7
8   public class TokenTest extends JFrame
9                          implements ActionListener {
10      private JLabel prompt;
11      private JTextField input;
12      private JTextArea output;
13
14      public TokenTest()
15      {
16          super( "Testing Class StringTokenizer" );
17
18          Container c = getContentPane();
19          c.setLayout( new FlowLayout() );
```

Fig. 27.17 A JFrame-based windowed application with event handling (part 1 of 2).

```
20
21          prompt = new JLabel( "Enter a sentence and press Enter" );
22          c.add( prompt );
23
24          input = new JTextField( 25 );
25          c.add( input );
26          input.addActionListener( this );
27
28          output = new JTextArea( 10, 25 );
29          output.setEditable( false );
30          c.add( new JScrollPane( output ) );
31
32          setSize( 300, 260 );   // set the window size
33          show();                // show the window
34       }
35
36       public void actionPerformed( ActionEvent e )
37       {
38          String stringToTokenize = e.getActionCommand();
39          StringTokenizer tokens =
40             new StringTokenizer( stringToTokenize );
41
42          output.setText( "Number of elements: " +
43             tokens.countTokens() + "\nThe tokens are:\n" );
44
45          while ( tokens.hasMoreTokens() )
46             output.append( tokens.nextToken() + "\n" );
47       }
48
49       // Method main to begin program execution by creating an
50       // object of class TokenTest.
51       public static void main( String args[] )
52       {
53          TokenTest app = new TokenTest();
54
55          app.setDefaultCloseOperation( JFrame.EXIT_ON_CLOSE );
56       }
57    }
```

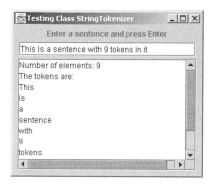

Fig. 27.17 A JFrame-based windowed application with event handling (part 2 of 2).

Until now, all user interactions with applications have been through either an input dialog (in which the user could type an input value for the program) or a message dialog (in which a message was displayed to the user and the user could click **OK** to dismiss the dialog). Although these are valid ways to receive input from a user and display output in a Java program, they are fairly limited in their capabilities—an input dialog can obtain only one value at a time from the user and a message dialog can display only one message. It is much more common to receive multiple inputs from the user at once (such as the user entering name and address information) or display many pieces of data at once. To begin our introduction to more elaborate user interfaces, this program illustrates two new graphical user interface concepts—attaching several GUI components to an application window and graphical user interface *event handling*.

Lines 3 through 6

```
import javax.swing.*;
import java.util.*;
import java.awt.*;
import java.awt.event.*;
```

specify to the compiler where to locate the classes used in this application. The first **import** statement specifies that the program uses classes from package **javax.swing** (specifically, classes **JFrame**, **JLabel**, **JScrollPane**, **JTextField** and **JTextArea**). The second **import** statement specifies that the program uses classes from package **java.util** (specifically, class **StringTokenizer**). The third **import** specifies that the program uses classes from package **java.awt** (specifically, classes **Container** and **FlowLayout**). The last **import** specifies that the program uses classes from package **java.awt.event**. This package contains many data types that enable a program to process a user's interactions with a program's GUI. In this program, we use the **ActionListener** and **ActionEvent** data types from package **java.awt.event**.

Every Java program is based on at least one class definition that extends and enhances an existing class definition via inheritance. Lines 8 and 9

```
public class TokenTest extends JFrame
                        implements ActionListener {
```

indicates that class **TokenTest** inherits from (**extends**) class **JFrame** and *implements ActionListener*. A class can inherit existing attributes and behaviors (data and methods) from another class specified to the right of keyword **extends** in the class definition. By extending class **JFrame**, we create class **TokenTest** as a new type of window. In the extends relationship, **JFrame** is known as the *superclass* (or *base class*) and **TokenTest** is known as the *subclass* (or *derived class*). Using inheritance here results in a new class definition that has the *attributes* (data) and *behaviors* (methods) of the **JFrame** class as well as the new features we are adding in our **TokenTest** class definition (specifically, the ability break a sentence input by the user into tokens).

A key benefit of extending class **JFrame** is that someone else has already defined "what it means to be a window." Programmers do not need to define all these capabilities on their own (again programmers do not need to "reinvent the wheel"). In fact, windows require hundreds of different methods to be defined. In our programs to this point, we have defined one method in every program. If we had to define hundreds of methods just to perform a simple task, we would probably never create a window! By simply using **extends** to inherit from class **JFrame**, all the methods of **JFrame** are now part of our **TokenTest** class.

The inheritance mechanism is easy to use; the programmer does not need to know every detail of class **JFrame** or any other class from which new classes are inherited. The programmer needs to know only that class **JFrame** has already defined the capabilities required to create the minimum window. To make the best use of any class, however, the programmer should study all the capabilities of the class that is extended.

Good Programming Practice 27.10

Investigate the capabilities of any class in the Java API documentation carefully before inheriting a subclass from it. This helps ensure that the programmer does not unintentionally redefine a capability that is already provided.

Classes are used as "templates" or "blueprints" to *instantiate* (or *create*) *objects* for use in a program. An object (or *instance*) resides in the computer's memory and contains information used by the program. The term object normally implies that attributes (data) and behaviors (methods) are associated with the object. The object's methods use the attributes to provide useful services to the *client of the object* (i.e., the code that calls the methods). We create an object of class **TokenTest** to control this program from **main** (discussed later).

In addition to extending one class, a class can implement one or more *interfaces*. An interface specifies one or more behaviors (i.e., methods) *that you must define* in your class definition. The interface **ActionListener** specifies that this class *must define a method* with the first line

```
public void actionPerformed( ActionEvent e )
```

This method's task is to process a user's interaction with the **JTextField** in this example. When the user types a sentence and presses the *Enter* key, this method will be called automatically in response to the user interaction. This process is called *event handling*. The *event* is the user interaction (pressing the *Enter* key). The *event handler* is the **actionPerformed** method, which is called automatically in response to the event. We discuss the details of this interaction and method **actionPerformed** shortly.

Lines 10–12

```
private JLabel prompt;
private JTextField input;
private JTextArea output;
```

declare references to the GUI components used in this application's graphical user interface. Reference **prompt** will refer to a **JLabel** object. A **JLabel** contains a string of characters to display on the screen. Normally, a **JLabel** indicates the purpose of another graphical user interface element on the screen. In the screen capture of Fig. 27.17, the **JLabel** object appears at the top of the user interface as the prompt that tells the user what to do. Reference **input** will refer to the **JTextField** in which the user will input a sentence. **JTextField**s are used to get a single line of information from the user at the keyboard or to display information on the screen. In the screen capture of Fig. 27.17, the **JTextField** object is the rectangle below the **JLabel**. Reference **output** will refer to the **JTextArea** in which the results will be displayed.

Note that the three references declared in lines 10–12 are also *instance variable declarations*—every instance (object) of class **TokenTest** contains its own copy of each instance variable. An important benefit of instance variables is that their identifiers can be used throughout the class definition (i.e., in all methods of the class). Until now, we declared all variables in an application's **main** method. Variables defined in the body of a method are known as *local variables* and can only be used in the body of the method in which they are defined. Another distinction between instance variables and local variables is that instance variables are always assigned a default value by the compiler and local variables are not. The default value for these references is **null** (i.e., the GUI components do not exist yet).

Lines 14–34 define the *constructor* method for class **TokenTest**. This method is called automatically when an object (instance) of class **TokenTest** is created with operator **new**. Line 16

```
super( "Testing Class StringTokenizer" );
```

calls the constructor of class **JFrame** and passes it a string. This string becomes the text that will be displayed in the window's title bar when the **TokenTest** window is displayed on the screen.

The **TokenTest** constructor also creates the GUI component objects and attaches them to the user interface. Line 18

```
Container c = getContentPane();
```

declares **Container** reference **c** and assigns it the result of a call to method **getContentPane**. Method **getContentPane** returns a reference to the window's *content pane*—the object to which we must attach the GUI components so they appear properly in the user interface.

Line 19

```
c.setLayout( new FlowLayout() );
```

uses **Container** method *setLayout* to define the *layout manager* for the **TokenTest** window's user interface. Layout managers are provided to arrange GUI components on a **Container** (package **java.awt**) for presentation purposes. The layout managers determine the position and size of every GUI component attached to the container. This enables the programmer to concentrate on the basic "look and feel" and lets the layout managers process most of the layout details. **FlowLayout** (package **java.awt**) is the most basic layout manager. GUI components are placed on a **Container** from left to right in the order in which they are attached to the **Container** with method **add**. When the edge of the container is reached, components are continued on the next line. The preceding statement creates a new object of class **FlowLayout** and passes it immediately to method **setLayout**. Normally, the layout is set before any GUI components are added to a **Container**.

[Note: Each **Container** can have only one layout manager at a time (separate **Container**s in the same program can have different layout managers). Most Java programming environments provide GUI design tools that help a programmer graphically design a GUI, then automatically write Java code to create the GUI. Some of these GUI designers also allow the programmer to use the layout managers. Section 27.9 discusses two additional layout managers that allow more precise control over the layout of the GUI components.]

Line 21

```
prompt = new JLabel( "Enter a sentence and press Enter" );
```

create a new **JLabel** object, initialize it (i.e., call its constructor) with the string **"Enter a sentence and press Enter"** and assign the object to reference **prompt**. This labels the **JTextField input** in the user interface so the user can determine the purpose of that text field. Line 22 attaches the **JLabel** to which **prompt** refers to the content pane of the window with method **add**.

Line 24

```
input = new JTextField( 25 );
```

creates a new **JTextField** object, initializes it to be **25** characters wide and assigns the object to reference **input**. This **JTextField** receive the input from the user of the program. Line 25 attaches the **JTextField** to which **input** refers to the content pane of the window. We revisit line 26 shortly.

Lines 28 through 30 create a **JTextArea** and add it to the content pane. The **JTextArea** in this case has 10 rows and 25 columns of text. Line 29 specifies that the **JTextArea** should be uneditable (i.e., the user cannot type in this text area). Line 30

```
c.add( new JScrollPane( output ) );
```

attaches the text area to a **JScrollPane** object, which is added to the user interface. Class **JScrollPane** provides scrollbars that can be used to scroll through the text in a text area. The scrollbars are not visible until the text in the text area is too wide or too tall to fit entirely in the text area. At that point, the scrollbars are displayed automatically.

Lines 32 and 33 set the size of the window and display the window. If you do not call methods **setSize** and **show**, the window will not be displayed on the screen.

Line 53

```
input.addActionListener( this );
```

specifies that *this* application should *listen* for events from the **JTextField** called **input**. The **this** keyword enables an object of class **TokenTest** to refer to itself. When the user interacts with the **input** text field an *event* is sent to the application. The event is a message indicating that the user of the program pressed the *Enter* key in the text field. This indicates to the application that *an action was performed* by the user on the **JTextField** and automatically calls method **actionPerformed** to process the user's interaction.

This style of programming is known as *event-driven programming*—the user interacts with a GUI component, the program is notified of the event and the program processes the event. The user's interaction with the GUI "drives" the program. The methods that are called when an event occurs are also known as *event handling methods*. When a GUI event occurs in a program, Java creates an object containing information about the event that occurred and *automatically calls* an appropriate event handling method. Before any event can be processed, each GUI component must know which object in the program defines the event handling method that will be called when an event occurs. In line 25, **JTextField** method *addActionListener* is used to tell **input** that the **TokenTest** application (**this**) can *listen* for *action events* and defines method **actionPerformed**. This is called *registering the event handler* with the GUI component (we also like to call it the *start listening* line because the application is now listening for events from the text field). To respond to an action event, we must define a class that **implements ActionListener** (this requires that the class also define method **actionPerformed**) and we must register the event handler with the GUI component.

Method **actionPerformed** (line 36–47) is one of several methods that process interactions between the user and GUI components. The first line of the method

```
public void actionPerformed( ActionEvent e )
```

indicates that **actionPerformed** is a **public** method that returns nothing (**void**) when it completes its task. Method **actionPerformed** receives one argument—an **ActionEvent**—when it is called automatically in response to an action performed on a GUI component by the user. The **ActionEvent** argument contains information about the action that occurred.

When the user types a sentence in a **JTextField** and presses the *Enter* key, the **actionPerformed** method (line 36) is invoked. Line 38 uses the argument to **actionPerformed** to obtain the string the user typed in the text field with method **getActionCommand**. Lines 39 and 40 create a **StringTokenizer** object (**tokens**) and pass its constructor the string obtained on line 38.

Lines 33 through 35

```
output.setText( "Number of elements: " +
    tokens.countTokens() + "\nThe tokens are:\n" );
```

use the **JTextArea** method **setText** to display the concatenated **String** specified as its argument in the **JTextArea**. In the preceding statement, the expression

```
tokens.countTokens()
```

uses the **StringTokenizer** method **countTokens** to determine the number of tokens in the **String** to be tokenized.

The **while** structure at lines 45 and 46

```
while ( tokens.hasMoreTokens() )
    output.append( tokens.nextToken() + "\n" );
```

uses the condition **tokens.hasMoreTokens()** to determine if there are more tokens in the **String** being tokenized. If so, the **append** method is invoked for the **JTextArea** called **output** to append the next token to the **String** currently in the **JTextArea**. The next token is obtained with a call to **tokens.nextToken()** that returns a **String** object. The token is output followed by a newline character so subsequent tokens appear on separate lines.

If you would like to change the delimiter **String** while tokenizing a **String**, you may do so by specifying a new delimiter string in a **nextToken** call as follows:

```
tokens.nextToken( newDelimiterString );
```

This feature is not demonstrated in the program.

Method **main** (lines 51–55) launches the program's execution by creating an instance of class **TokenTest**. This object acts as the main application window. When line 53 executes, it calls the constructor at line 14 to create the window and display it. Line 55 uses the **JFrame** method **setDefaultCloseOperation** to specify that the program should exit when the window is closed (i.e., the program should be terminated). You can close the window by clicking its *close box* in the upper-right corner of the window.

27.7 Graphical User Interfaces: Event Handling with Inner Classes

All the class definitions discussed to this point were defined one class per file. Java provides a facility called *inner classes* in which classes can be defined inside other classes. Such classes can be complete class definitions or *anonymous inner class* definitions (classes without a name).

Our next example (Fig. 27.18) creates a user-defined type **Time** and uses it in a windowed application that allows the user of the program to set the time by specifying values individually for the hour, minute and second. As the time is modified through the GUI, the current value of the time is displayed in a separate GUI component. After discussing class Time, we demonstrate inner class definitions and discuss the application windowing class called **TimeTestWindow**.

The application of Fig. 27.18 consists of classes **Time** and **TimeTestWindow**. Class **Time** is defined in file **Time.java** (specified in the comment at line 1). Class **TimeTestWindow** is defined in file **TimeTestWindow.java** (specified in the comment at line 59). [Normally, each program in this book that contains more than one file begins the file with a comment indicating the figure number and file name.] Although these two classes are defined in separate files, we number the lines in the program consecutively across both files for discussion purposes in the text. It is important to note that these classes *must* be defined in separate files.

Common Programming Error 27.13

*Defining more than one **public** class in the same file is a syntax error.*

```
1   // Fig. 27.18: Time.java
2   // Time class definition
3   import java.text.DecimalFormat;   // used for number formatting
4
5   // This class maintains the time in 24-hour format
6   public class Time extends Object {
7      private int hour;      // 0 - 23
8      private int minute;    // 0 - 59
9      private int second;    // 0 - 59
10
11     // Time constructor initializes each instance variable
12     // to zero. Ensures that Time object starts in a
13     // consistent state.
14     public Time() { setTime( 0, 0, 0 ); }
15
```

Fig. 27.18 GUI event handling with inner classes—**Time.java** (part 1 of 2).

```
16        // Set a new time value using universal time. Perform
17        // validity checks on the data. Set invalid values to zero.
18        public void setTime( int h, int m, int s )
19        {
20           setHour( h );     // set the hour
21           setMinute( m );   // set the minute
22           setSecond( s );   // set the second
23        }
24
25        // set the hour
26        public void setHour( int h )
27           { hour = ( ( h >= 0 && h < 24 ) ? h : 0 ); }
28
29        // set the minute
30        public void setMinute( int m )
31           { minute = ( ( m >= 0 && m < 60 ) ? m : 0 ); }
32
33        // set the second
34        public void setSecond( int s )
35           { second = ( ( s >= 0 && s < 60 ) ? s : 0 ); }
36
37        // get the hour
38        public int getHour() { return hour; }
39
40        // get the minute
41        public int getMinute() { return minute; }
42
43        // get the second
44        public int getSecond() { return second; }
45
46        // Convert to String in standard-time format
47        public String toString()
48        {
49           DecimalFormat twoDigits = new DecimalFormat( "00" );
50
51           int h = getHour();
52
53           return ( ( h == 12 || h == 0 ) ? 12 : h % 12 ) + ":" +
54                  twoDigits.format( getMinute() ) + ":" +
55                  twoDigits.format( getSecond() ) +
56                  ( h < 12 ? " AM" : " PM" );
57        }
58  }
```

Fig. 27.18 GUI event handling with inner classes—**Time.java** (part 2 of 2).

```
59  // Fig. 27.18: TimeTestWindow.java
60  // Demonstrating the Time class set and get methods
61  import java.awt.*;
62  import java.awt.event.*;
63  import javax.swing.*;
```

Fig. 27.18 GUI event handling with inner classes—**TimeTestWindow.java** (part 1 of 4).

```
64
65  public class TimeTestWindow extends JFrame {
66      private Time t;
67      private JLabel hourLabel, minuteLabel, secondLabel;
68      private JTextField hourField, minuteField,
69                          secondField, display;
70
71      public TimeTestWindow()
72      {
73          super( "Inner Class Demonstration" );
74
75          t = new Time();
76
77          Container c = getContentPane();
78          c.setLayout( new FlowLayout() );
79
80          hourLabel = new JLabel( "Set Hour" );
81          hourField = new JTextField( 10 );
82          hourField.addActionListener(
83              new ActionListener() {  // anonymous inner class
84                  public void actionPerformed( ActionEvent e )
85                  {
86                      t.setHour(
87                          Integer.parseInt( e.getActionCommand() ) );
88                      hourField.setText( "" );
89                      displayTime();
90                  }
91              }
92          );
93          c.add( hourLabel );
94          c.add( hourField );
95
96          minuteLabel = new JLabel( "Set minute" );
97          minuteField = new JTextField( 10 );
98          minuteField.addActionListener(
99              new ActionListener() {  // anonymous inner class
100                 public void actionPerformed( ActionEvent e )
101                 {
102                     t.setMinute(
103                         Integer.parseInt( e.getActionCommand() ) );
104                     minuteField.setText( "" );
105                     displayTime();
106                 }
107             }
108         );
109         c.add( minuteLabel );
110         c.add( minuteField );
111
112         secondLabel = new JLabel( "Set Second" );
113         secondField = new JTextField( 10 );
```

Fig. 27.18 GUI event handling with inner classes—**TimeTestWindow.java** (part 2 of 4).

```
114            secondField.addActionListener(
115               new ActionListener() {   // anonymous inner class
116                  public void actionPerformed( ActionEvent e )
117                  {
118                     t.setSecond(
119                        Integer.parseInt( e.getActionCommand() ) );
120                     secondField.setText( "" );
121                     displayTime();
122                  }
123               }
124            );
125            c.add( secondLabel );
126            c.add( secondField );
127
128            display = new JTextField( 30 );
129            display.setEditable( false );
130            c.add( display );
131         }
132
133         public void displayTime()
134         {
135            display.setText( "The time is: " + t );
136         }
137
138         public static void main( String args[] )
139         {
140            TimeTestWindow window = new TimeTestWindow();
141
142            window.addWindowListener(
143               new WindowAdapter() {
144                  public void windowClosing( WindowEvent e )
145                  {
146                     System.exit( 0 );
147                  }
148               }
149            );
150
151            window.setSize( 400, 120 );
152            window.show();
153         }
154      }
```

Fig. 27.18 GUI event handling with inner classes—**TimeTestWindow.java** (part 3 of 4).

Fig. 27.18 GUI event handling with inner classes—`TimeTestWindow.java` (part 4 of 4).

Figure 27.18 contains a simple definition for class **Time**. Our **Time** class definition begins with line 6

```
public class Time extends Object {
```

indicating that class **Time extends** class *Object* (from package **java.lang**). In Java, you never really create a class definition "from scratch." In fact, when you create a class definition, you always use pieces of an existing class definition. Java uses inheritance to create new classes from existing class definitions. In this inheritance relationship, **Object** is called the superclass or base class and **Time** is called the subclass or derived class. Using inheritance results in a new class definition that has the attributes and behaviors of class **Object** as well as new features we add in our **Time** class definition. Every class in Java is a subclass of **Object**. Therefore, every class inherits the 11 methods defined by class **Object**. One important **Object** method is *toString*, discussed later in this section. Other methods of class **Object** are discussed as they are needed throughout the text.

Software Engineering Observation 27.3

Every class defined in Java must extend another class. If a class does not explicitly use keyword **extends** *in its definition, the class implicitly* **extends Object**. *See the online HTML-based Java documentation for a detailed description of class* **Object**.

Class **Time** contains three integer instance variables—**hour**, **minute** and **second**—that represent the time in *universal-time* format (*24-hour clock* format).

Keywords *public* and *private* are *member access modifiers*. Instance variables or methods declared with member access modifier **public** are accessible wherever the program has a reference to a **Time** object. Instance variables or methods declared with member access modifier **private** are accessible *only* to methods of the class. Every instance variable or method definition should be preceded by a member access modifier. Member access modifiers can appear multiple times and in any order in a class definition.

Good Programming Practice 27.11

Group members by member access modifier in a class definition for clarity and readability.

The three integer instance variables **hour**, **minute** and **second** are each declared (lines 7 through 9) with member access modifier **private**. This indicates that these instance variables of the class are only accessible to methods of the class. When an object of the class is instantiated (created), such instance variables are encapsulated in the object and can be accessed only through methods of that object's class (normally through the class's **public** methods). Instance variables are normally declared **private** and methods are normally declared **public**. It is possible to have **private** methods and

public data, as we will see later. The **private** methods are often called *utility methods* or *helper methods* because they can only be called by other methods of that class and are used to support the operation of those methods. Using **public** data is uncommon and is a dangerous programming practice.

Software Engineering Observation 27.4

Methods tend to fall into a number of different categories: methods that get the values of ***private*** *instance variables; methods that set the values of* ***private*** *instance variables; methods that implement the services of the class; and methods that perform various mechanical chores for the class, such as initializing class objects, assigning class objects, and converting between classes and built-in types or between classes and other classes.*

Class **Time** contains the following **public** methods—**Time** (line 14), **setTime** (line 18), **setHour** (line 26), **setMinute** (line 30), **setSecond** (line 34), **getHour** (line 38), **getMinute** (line 41), **getSecond** (line 44) and **toString** (line 47). These are the ***public*** *methods*, ***public*** *services* or ***public*** *interface* of the class. These methods are used by *clients* (i.e., portions of a program that are users of a class) of the class to manipulate the data stored in objects of the class.

The clients of a class use references to interact with an object of the class. For example, in the program of Fig. 27.16 we used a **Vector** reference to interact with a **Vector** object.

Notice the method with the same name as the class (line 14); it is the *constructor* method of that class. A constructor is a special method that initializes the instance variables of a class object. A class's constructor method is called automatically when an object of that class is instantiated with operator **new**. This constructor simply calls the class's method **setTime** with hour, minute and second values specified as 0.

Common Programming Error 27.14

Attempting to declare a return type for a constructor and/or attempting to ***return*** *a value from a constructor is a logic error. Java allows other methods of the class to have the same name as the class and to specify return types. Such methods are not constructors and will not be called when an object of the class is instantiated.*

Classes often provide **public** methods to allow clients of the class to *set* (i.e., assign values to) or *get* (i.e., obtain the values of) **private** instance variables. These methods need not be called *set* and *get*, but they often are. *Get* methods are also commonly called *accessor methods* or *query methods*. *Set* methods are also commonly called *mutator methods* (because they typically change a value).

Method **setTime** (line 18) is a **public** method that receives three integer arguments and uses them to set the time. Each argument is passed to a corresponding *set* method (lines 26, 30 and 34). The *set* method tests the value it receives in a conditional expression and determines if the value is in range. For example, the **hour** value must be greater than or equal to 0 and less than 24 (tested on line 27) because we represent the time in universal time format (0–23 for the hour, 0–59 for the minute and 0–59 for the second). Any value outside this range is an invalid value and is set to zero—ensuring that a **Time** object always contains valid data. This is also known as *keeping the object in a consistent state*.

Good Programming Practice 27.12

Always define a class so its instance variables are maintained in a consistent state.

Each *get* method (lines 38, 41 and 44) simply returns a copy of one of class **Time**'s instance variables. It would seem that providing *set* and *get* capabilities is essentially the same as making the instance variables **public**. However, if an instance variable is **public**, the instance variable may be read or written at will by any method in the program. If an instance variable is **private**, a **public** *get* method certainly seems to allow other methods to read the data at will but the *get* method controls the formatting and display of the data. A **public** *set* method can carefully scrutinize attempts to modify the instance variable's value. This ensures that the new value is appropriate for that data item. So, although *set* and *get* methods may provide access to **private** data, the access is restricted by the programmer's implementation of the methods.

Method **toString** (line 47) takes no arguments and returns a **String**. This method produces a standard-time-format string consisting of the **hour**, **minute** and **second** values separated by colons and an AM or PM indicator as in **1:27:06 PM**. Line 49

```
DecimalFormat twoDigits = new DecimalFormat( "00" );
```

creates an instance of class **DecimalFormat** (from package **java.text** imported at line 3) to help format the time. Object **twoDigits** is initialized with the *format control string* **"00"**, which indicates that the number format should consist of two digits—each **0** is a placeholder for a digit. If the number being formatted is a single digit, it is automatically preceded by a leading **0** (i.e., **8** is formatted as **08**). The **return** statement at lines 53–56

```
return ( ( h == 12 || h == 0 ) ? 12 : h % 12 ) + ":" +
        twoDigits.format( getMinute() ) + ":" +
        twoDigits.format( getSecond() ) +
        ( h < 12 ? " AM" : " PM" );
```

uses method **format** (that returns a formatted **String** containing the number) from object **twoDigits** to format the **minute** and **second** values into two-digit strings. Those strings are concatenated with the **+** operator (separated by colons) and returned from method **toString**.

Method **toString** is special in that we inherited from class **Object** a **toString** method with exactly the same first line as our **toString** on line 47. The original **toString** method of class **Object** is a generic version that is used mainly as a placeholder that can be redefined by a subclass. Our version replaces the version we inherited to provide a **toString** method that is more appropriate for our class. This is known as *overriding* the original method definition.

We now discuss class **TimeTestWindow** (lines 59–154). Line 65

```
public class TimeTestWindow extends JFrame {
```

indicates that class **TimeTestWindow** extends class **JFrame**. Superclass **JFrame** provides the basic attributes and behaviors of a window—a *title bar* and buttons to *minimize*, *maximize* and *close* the window (all labeled in the first screen capture). The user can set the hour, minute or second value by typing a value in the appropriate **JTextField** and pressing the *Enter* key.

The constructor (line 71–131) creates the window's GUI components as the application begins executing. Method **main** (line 138) creates a **new** object of class **TimeTestWindow** that results in a call to the constructor. As we build the GUI in the constructor we define *anonymous inner classes* that will handle the events in the GUI.

Because an anonymous inner class has no name, one object of the anonymous inner class must be created at the point where the class is defined in the program. We demonstrate anonymous inner classes two ways in this example. First, we use separate anonymous inner classes that implement an interface (**ActionListener**) to create event handlers for each of the three **JTextField**s **hourField**, **minuteField** and **secondField**. We also demonstrate how to define your own event handling that responds when the user clicks the close box on the window. The event handler is defined as an anonymous inner class that extends a class (**WindowAdapter**).

Each of the three **JTextField**s that generate events in this program has a similar anonymous inner class to handle its events, so we discuss only the anonymous inner class for **hourField** here. Lines 82–92

```
hourField.addActionListener(
    new ActionListener() {  // anonymous inner class
        public void actionPerformed( ActionEvent e )
        {
            t.setHour(
                Integer.parseInt( e.getActionCommand() ) );
            hourField.setText( "" );
            displayTime();
        }
    }
);
```

are a call to **hourField**'s **addActionListener** method. The argument to this method must be an object that *is an* **ActionListener** (i.e., any object of a class that implements the **ActionListener** interface). Lines 83–91 use special Java syntax to define an anonymous inner class and create one object of that class that is passed as the argument to **addActionListener**. Line 83

```
new ActionListener() {  // anonymous inner class
```

uses operator **new** to create an object. The syntax **ActionListener()** begins the definition of an anonymous inner class that implements interface **ActionListener**. This is similar to beginning a class definition with

```
public class MyHandler implements ActionListener {
```

The parentheses after **ActionListener** indicate a call to the default constructor of the anonymous inner class. Because the anonymous class implements **ActionListener**, every object of this class *is an* **ActionListener**. The requirement that **addAction-Listener** be passed an object of type **ActionListener** is satisfied! The *is a* relationship is used extensively in the GUI event handling mechanism.

The opening left brace (**{**) at the end of line 83 and the closing right brace (**}**) at line 91 define the body of the class. Lines 84–90 define the one method—**actionPerformed**—that is required in any class that implements **ActionListener**. Method **actionPer-formed** is called when the user presses *Enter* while typing in **hourField**. In response to the event, **actionPerformed** calls the **Time** object **t**'s **setHour** function and passes it the int value of the **String** the user input. Next, the text field is cleared by setting its text to the empty string. Then, the time is displayed with a call to method **displayTime**.

An inner class object has a special relationship with the outer class object that creates it. The inner class object is allowed to access directly all the instance variables and methods of the outer class object. The **actionPerformed** method (line 84) does just that. In the method, instance variables **t** and **hourField**, and method **displayTime** are used.

Software Engineering Observation 27.5

An inner class object is allowed to access directly all the instance variables and methods of the outer class object that defined it.

Software Engineering Observation 27.6

When an anonymous inner class implements an interface, the class must define every method in the interface.

Method **main** creates one instance of class **TimeTestWindow** (line 140), sizes the window (line 151) and displays the window (line 152).

Windows generate a variety of events. For this example we discuss the one event generated when the user clicks the window's close box—a *window closing event*. Lines 142–149

```
window.addWindowListener(
    new WindowAdapter() {
        public void windowClosing( WindowEvent e )
        {
            System.exit( 0 );
        }
    }
);
```

enable the user to terminate the application by clicking the window's close box (labeled in the first screen capture. Method ***addWindowListener*** registers a window event listener. The argument to **addWindowListener** must be a reference to an object that *is a* ***WindowListener*** (package **java.awt.event**) (i.e., any object of a class that implements **WindowListener**). However, there are seven different methods that must be defined in every class that implements **WindowListener** and we only need one in this example—***windowClosing***. For event handling interfaces with more than one method, Java provides a corresponding class (called an *adapter class*) that already implements all the methods in the interface for you. All you need to do is extend the adapter class and override the methods you require in your program.

Common Programming Error 27.15

Extending an adapter class and misspelling the name of the method you are overriding is a logic error and will not generate a compiler error.

Lines 143–148 use special Java syntax to define an anonymous inner class and create one object of that class that is passed as the argument to **addWindowListener**. Line 143

```
new WindowAdapter() {
```

uses operator **new** to create an object. The syntax **WindowAdapter()** begins the definition of an anonymous inner class that extends class **WindowAdapter**. This is similar to beginning a class definition with

```
public class MyHandler extends WindowAdapter {
```

The parentheses after **WindowAdapter** indicate a call to the default constructor of the anonymous inner class. Class **WindowAdapter** implements interface **WindowListener**, so every **WindowAdapter** object *is a* **WindowListener**—the exact type required for the argument to **addWindowListener**.

The opening left brace (**{**) at the end of line 143 and the closing right brace (**}**) at line 148 define the body of the class. Lines 144–147 override the one method of **WindowAdapter**—**windowClosing**—that is called when the user clicks the window's close box. In this example, **windowClosing** terminates the application with a call to **System.exit(0)**.

27.8 Graphical User Interfaces: Miscellaneous Components

In the next two subsections, we present the **JComboBox** and **JList** GUI components and demonstrate how to handle their events.

27.8.1 Class **JComboBox**

A *combo box* (sometimes called a *drop-down list*) provides a list of items from which the user can make a selection. Combo boxes are implemented with class **JComboBox**, which inherits from class **JComponent**. **JComboBox**es generate **ActionEvent**s in response to user interactions.

The application of Fig. 27.19 uses a **JComboBox** to provide a list of four image file names. When an image file name is selected, the corresponding image is displayed as an **Icon** on a **JLabel**. The screen captures for this program show the **JComboBox** list after the selection was made to illustrate which image file name was selected.

```
1   // Fig. 27.19: ComboBoxTest.java
2   // Using a JComboBox to select an image to display.
3   import java.awt.*;
4   import java.awt.event.*;
5   import javax.swing.*;
6
7   public class ComboBoxTest extends JFrame {
8       private JComboBox images;
9       private JLabel label;
10      private String names[] =
11          { "bug1.gif", "bug2.gif",
12            "travelbug.gif", "buganim.gif" };
13      private Icon icons[] =
14          { new ImageIcon( names[ 0 ] ),
15            new ImageIcon( names[ 1 ] ),
16            new ImageIcon( names[ 2 ] ),
17            new ImageIcon( names[ 3 ] ) };
18
19      public ComboBoxTest()
20      {
21          super( "Testing JComboBox" );
22
23          Container c = getContentPane();
```

Fig. 27.19 Program that uses a **JComboBox** to select an icon (part 1 of 2).

```
24              c.setLayout( new FlowLayout() );
25
26              images = new JComboBox( names );
27              images.setMaximumRowCount( 3 );
28
29              images.addActionListener(
30                 new ActionListener() {
31                    public void actionPerformed( ActionEvent e )
32                    {
33                       label.setIcon(
34                          icons[ images.getSelectedIndex() ] );
35                    }
36                 }
37              );
38
39              c.add( images );
40
41              label = new JLabel( icons[ 0 ] );
42              c.add( label );
43
44              setSize( 350, 100 );
45              show();
46           }
47
48           public static void main( String args[] )
49           {
50              ComboBoxTest app = new ComboBoxTest();
51
52              app.setDefaultCloseOperation( JFrame.EXIT_ON_CLOSE );
53           }
54        }
```

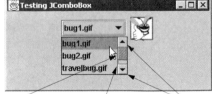

scroll thumb   A *scrollbar* scrolls through   scroll arrows
the items in the list.

Fig. 27.19 Program that uses a **JComboBox** to select an icon (part 2 of 2).

Lines 13–17

```
private Icon icons[] =
   { new ImageIcon( names[ 0 ] ),
     new ImageIcon( names[ 1 ] ),
     new ImageIcon( names[ 2 ] ),
     new ImageIcon( names[ 3 ] ) };
```

declare and initialize array icons with four new **ImageIcon** objects. **String** array **names** (defined on lines 10–12) contains the names of the four image files that are stored in the same directory as the application.

Line 26

```
images = new JComboBox( names );
```

creates a **JComboBox** object using the **String**s in array **names** as the elements in the list. A numeric *index* keeps track of the ordering of items in the **JComboBox**. The first item is added at index 0; the next item is added at index 1, and so forth. The first item added to a **JComboBox** appears as the currently selected item when the **JComboBox** is displayed. Other items are selected by clicking the **JComboBox**. When clicked, the **JComboBox** expands into a list from which the user can make a selection. Line 27

```
images.setMaximumRowCount( 3 );
```

uses **JComboBox** method *setMaximumRowCount* to set the maximum number of elements that are displayed when the user clicks the **JComboBox**. If there are more items in the **JComboBox** than the maximum number of elements that are displayed, the **JCombo-Box** automatically provides a *scrollbar* (see the first screen capture) that allows the user to view all the elements in the list. The user can click the *scroll arrows* at the top and bottom of the scrollbar to move up and down through the list one element at a time, or the user can drag the *scroll thumb* in the middle of the scrollbar up and down to move through the list. To drag the scroll thumb, hold the mouse button down with the mouse cursor on the scroll box and move the mouse.

Look-and-Feel Observation 27.1

*Set the maximum row count for a **JComboBox** to a number of rows that prevents the list from expanding outside the bounds of the window in which it is used. This will ensure that the list displays correctly when it is expanded by the user.*

Lines 29–37

```
images.addActionListener(
    new ActionListener() {
        public void actionPerformed( ActionEvent e )
        {
            label.setIcon(
                icons[ images.getSelectedIndex() ] );
        }
    }
);
```

register an instance of an anonymous inner class that implements **ActionListener** as the listener for **JComboBox images**. When the user makes a selection from **images**, method **actionPerformed** (line 31) sets the **Icon** for **label**. The **Icon** is selected from array **icons** by determining the index number of the selected item in the **JCombo-Box** with method *getSelectedIndex* in line 34.

27.8.2 JList

A *list* displays a series of items from which the user may select one or more items. Lists are created with class **JList**, which inherits from class **JComponent**. Class **JList** supports *single-selection lists* (i.e., lists that allow only one item to be selected at a time) and *multiple-selection lists* (lists that allow any number of items to be selected). In this section, we discuss single-selection lists.

The application of Fig. 27.20 creates a **JList** of 13 colors. When a color name is clicked in the **JList**, a *ListSelectionEvent* occurs and the application window content pane's background color changes.

```
1   // Fig. 27.20: ListTest.java
2   // Selecting colors from a JList.
3   import java.awt.*;
4   import java.awt.event.*;
5   import javax.swing.*;
6   import javax.swing.event.*;
7
8   public class ListTest extends JFrame {
9       private JList colorList;
10      private Container c;
11
12      private String colorNames[] =
13          { "Black", "Blue", "Cyan", "Dark Gray", "Gray", "Green",
14            "Light Gray", "Magenta", "Orange", "Pink", "Red",
15            "White", "Yellow" };
16
17      private Color colors[] =
18          { Color.black, Color.blue, Color.cyan, Color.darkGray,
19            Color.gray, Color.green, Color.lightGray,
20            Color.magenta, Color.orange, Color.pink, Color.red,
21            Color.white, Color.yellow };
22
23      public ListTest()
24      {
25          super( "List Test" );
26
27          c = getContentPane();
28          c.setLayout( new FlowLayout() );
29
30          // create a list with the items in the colorNames array
31          colorList = new JList( colorNames );
32          colorList.setVisibleRowCount( 5 );
33
34          // do not allow multiple selections
35          colorList.setSelectionMode(
36              ListSelectionModel.SINGLE_SELECTION );
37
38          // add a JScrollPane containing the JList
39          // to the content pane
40          c.add( new JScrollPane( colorList ) );
41
42          // set up event handler
43          colorList.addListSelectionListener(
44              new ListSelectionListener() {
45                  public void valueChanged( ListSelectionEvent e )
46                  {
47                      c.setBackground(
48                          colors[ colorList.getSelectedIndex() ] );
```

Fig. 27.20 Selecting colors from a **JList** (part 1 of 2).

```
49                      }
50                  }
51              );
52
53          setSize( 350, 150 );
54          show();
55      }
56
57      public static void main( String args[] )
58      {
59          ListTest app = new ListTest();
60
61          app.setDefaultCloseOperation( JFrame.EXIT_ON_CLOSE );
62      }
63  }
```

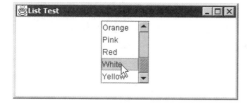 

Fig. 27.20 Selecting colors from a **JList** (part 2 of 2).

A **JList** object is instantiated at line 31

```
colorList = new JList( colorNames );
```

and assigned to reference **colorList** in the constructor. The argument to the **JList** constructor is the array of **Object**s (in this case **String**s) to display in the list. Line 32

```
colorList.setVisibleRowCount( 5 );
```

uses **JList** method ***setVisibleRowCount*** to determine the number of items that are visible in the list. Lines 35 and 36

```
colorList.setSelectionMode(
    ListSelectionModel.SINGLE_SELECTION );
```

use **JList** method ***setSelectionMode*** to specify the *selection mode* for the list. Class ***ListSelectionModel*** (package **javax.swing**) defines three constants to specify a **JList**'s selection mode—***SINGLE_SELECTION***, ***SINGLE_INTERVAL_SELECTION*** and ***MULTIPLE_INTERVAL_SELECTION***. A **SINGLE_SELECTION** list allows only one item to be selected at a time. A **SINGLE_INTERVAL_SELECTION** list is a multiple-selection list that allows several items in a contiguous range in the list to be selected. A **MULTIPLE_INTERVAL_SELECTION** list is a multiple-selection list that does not restrict the items that can be selected.

Class **JList** *does not* automatically provide a scrollbar if there are more items in the list than the number of visible rows. In this case, a ***JScrollPane*** object is used to provide the automatic scrolling capability for the **JList**. Line 40

```
c.add( new JScrollPane( colorList ) );
```

adds a new instance of class **JScrollPane** to the content pane. The **JScrollPane** constructor receives as its argument the **JComponent** for which it will provide automatic scrolling functionality (in this case **JList colorList**). Notice in the screen captures that a scrollbar created by the **JScrollPane** appears at the right side of the **JList**. The scrollbar only appears when the number of items in the **JList** exceeds the number of visible items.

Lines 43–51

```
colorList.addListSelectionListener(
   new ListSelectionListener() {
      public void valueChanged( ListSelectionEvent e )
      {
         c.setBackground(
            colors[ colorList.getSelectedIndex() ] );
      }
   }
);
```

use **JList** method ***addListSelectionListener*** to register an instance of an anonymous inner class that implements ***ListSelectionListener*** (defined in package **javax.swing.event**) as the listener for **JList colorList**. When the user makes a selection from **colorList**, method ***valueChanged*** (line 45) executes and sets the background color of the content pane with method ***setBackground*** (inherited from class **Component** into class **Container**). The color is selected from the array **colors** with the selected item's index in the list that is returned by **JList** method **getSelectedIndex**.

27.9 Graphical User Interfaces: Layout Managers

Layout managers are provided to arrange GUI components on a container for presentation purposes. The layout managers provide basic layout capabilities that are easier to use than determining the exact position and size of every GUI component. This enables the programmer to concentrate on the basic "look and feel" and lets the layout managers process most of the layout details. Some GUI designer tools also allow the programmer to use the layout managers described here.

Look-and-Feel Observation 27.2

Most Java programming environments provide GUI design tools that help a programmer graphically design a GUI, then automatically write Java code to create the GUI.

Most previous application examples in which we created our own GUI used layout manager ***FlowLayout***. Class ***FlowLayout*** inherits from class **Object** and implements interface ***LayoutManager***, which defines the methods a layout manager uses to arrange and size GUI components on a container.

27.9.1 BorderLayout

The ***BorderLayout*** layout manager (the default layout manager for the content pane) arranges components into five regions: *North, South, East, West and Center* (North corresponds to the top of the container). Class **BorderLayout** inherits from **Object** and implements interface ***LayoutManager2***.

Up to five components can be added directly to a **BorderLayout**—one for each region. The components placed in the North and South regions extend horizontally to the sides of the container and are as tall as the components placed in those regions. The East and West regions expand vertically between the North and South regions and are as wide as the components placed in those regions. The component placed in the Center region expands to take all remaining space in the layout (this is the reason the **JTextArea** in Figure 27.21 occupies the entire window). If all five regions are occupied, the entire container's space is covered by GUI components. If the North or South region is not occupied, the GUI components in the East, Center and West regions expand vertically to fill the remaining space. If the East or West region is not occupied, the GUI component in the Center region expands horizontally to fill the remaining space. If the Center region is not occupied, the area is left empty—the other GUI components do not expand to fill the remaining space.

The application of Fig. 27.21 demonstrates the **BorderLayout** layout manager using five **JButton**s, which produce **ActionEvent**s.

```
1   // Fig. 27.21: BorderLayoutDemo.java
2   // Demonstrating BorderLayout.
3   import java.awt.*;
4   import java.awt.event.*;
5   import javax.swing.*;
6
7   public class BorderLayoutDemo extends JFrame
8                                 implements ActionListener {
9      private JButton b[];
10     private String names[] =
11        { "Hide North", "Hide South", "Hide East",
12          "Hide West", "Hide Center" };
13     private BorderLayout layout;
14
15     public BorderLayoutDemo()
16     {
17        super( "BorderLayout Demo" );
18
19        layout = new BorderLayout( 5, 5 );
20
21        Container c = getContentPane();
22        c.setLayout( layout );
23
24        // instantiate button objects
25        b = new JButton[ names.length ];
26
27        for ( int i = 0; i < names.length; i++ ) {
28           b[ i ] = new JButton( names[ i ] );
29           b[ i ].addActionListener( this );
30        }
31
32        // order not important
33        c.add( b[ 0 ], BorderLayout.NORTH );   // North position
34        c.add( b[ 1 ], BorderLayout.SOUTH );   // South position
```

Fig. 27.21 Demonstrating components in **BorderLayout** (part 1 of 3).

```
35          c.add( b[ 2 ], BorderLayout.EAST );    // East position
36          c.add( b[ 3 ], BorderLayout.WEST );    // West position
37          c.add( b[ 4 ], BorderLayout.CENTER );  // Center position
38
39          setSize( 300, 200 );
40          show();
41       }
42
43       public void actionPerformed( ActionEvent e )
44       {
45          for ( int i = 0; i < b.length; i++ )
46             if ( e.getSource() == b[ i ] )
47                b[ i ].setVisible( false );
48             else
49                b[ i ].setVisible( true );
50
51          // re-layout the content pane
52          layout.layoutContainer( getContentPane() );
53       }
54
55       public static void main( String args[] )
56       {
57          BorderLayoutDemo app = new BorderLayoutDemo();
58
59          app.setDefaultCloseOperation( JFrame.EXIT_ON_CLOSE );
60       }
61    }
```

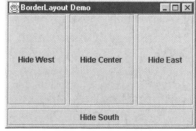

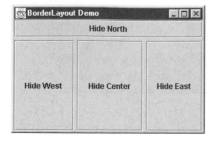

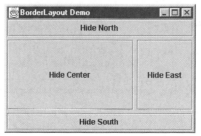

Fig. 27.21 Demonstrating components in **BorderLayout** (part 2 of 3).

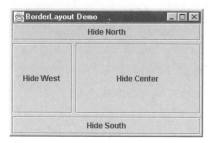 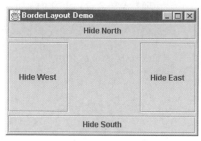

Fig. 27.21 Demonstrating components in **BorderLayout** (part 3 of 3).

Line 19 in the constructor

```
layout = new BorderLayout( 5, 5 );
```

defines a **BorderLayout**. The arguments specify the number of pixels between components that are arranged horizontally (*horizontal gap space*) and the number of pixels between components that are arranged vertically (*vertical gap space*), respectively. The default **BorderLayout** constructor supplies 0 pixels of gap space horizontally and vertically. Line 22 uses method **setLayout** to set the content pane's layout to **layout**.

Adding **Component**s to a **BorderLayout** requires a different add method from class **Container**, which takes two arguments—the **Component** to add and the region in which the **Component** will be placed. For example, line 33

```
add( b[ 0 ], BorderLayout.NORTH );   // North position
```

specifies that the **b[0]** is to be placed in the **NORTH** position. The components can be added in any order, but only one component can be added to each region.

 ### Look-and-Feel Observation 27.3

*If no region is specified when adding a **Component** to a **BorderLayout**, it is assumed that the **Component** should be added to region **BorderLayout.CENTER**.*

Common Programming Error 27.16

*Adding more than one component to a particular region in a **BorderLayout** results in only the last component added being displayed. There is no error message to indicate this problem.*

When the user clicks a particular **JButton** in the layout, method **actionPerformed** (line 43) is called. The **for** loop at line 46 uses the following **if/else** structure:

```
if ( e.getSource() == b[ i ] )
   b[ i ].setVisible( false );
else
   b[ i ].setVisible( true );
```

to hide the particular **JButton** that generated the event. Method *setVisible* (inherited into **JButton** from class **Component**) is called with a **false** argument to hide the **JButton**. If the current **JButton** in the array is not the one that generated the event, method **setVisible** is called with a **true** argument to ensure that the **JButton** is displayed on the screen. Line 52

```
            layout.layoutContainer( getContentPane() );
```

uses **LayoutManager** method **layoutContainer** to recalculate the layout of the content pane. Notice in the screen captures of Fig. 27.21 that certain regions in the **Bor-derLayout** change shape as **JButton**s are hidden and displayed in other regions. Try resizing the application window to see how the various regions resize based on the width and height of the window.

27.9.2 GridLayout

The *GridLayout* layout manager divides the container into a grid so that components can be placed in rows and columns. Class **GridLayout** inherits directly from class **Object** and implements interface **LayoutManager**. Every **Component** in a **GridLayout** has the same width and height. Components are added to a **GridLayout** starting at the top-left cell of the grid and proceeding left-to-right until the row is full. Then the process continues left-to-right on the next row of the grid, etc. Figure 27.23 demonstrates the **Grid-Layout** layout manager using six **JButton**s.

```
1   // Fig. 27.22: GridLayoutDemo.java
2   // Demonstrating GridLayout.
3   import java.awt.*;
4   import java.awt.event.*;
5   import javax.swing.*;
6
7   public class GridLayoutDemo extends JFrame
8                               implements ActionListener {
9      private JButton b[];
10     private String names[] =
11        { "one", "two", "three", "four", "five", "six" };
12     private boolean toggle = true;
13     private Container c;
14     private GridLayout grid1, grid2;
15
16     public GridLayoutDemo()
17     {
18        super( "GridLayout Demo" );
19
20        grid1 = new GridLayout( 2, 3, 5, 5 );
21        grid2 = new GridLayout( 3, 2 );
22
23        c = getContentPane();
24        c.setLayout( grid1 );
25
26        // create and add buttons
27        b = new JButton[ names.length ];
28
29        for ( int i = 0; i < names.length; i++ ) {
30           b[ i ] = new JButton( names[ i ] );
31           b[ i ].addActionListener( this );
32           c.add( b[ i ] );
33        }
```

Fig. 27.22 Program that demonstrates components in **GridLayout** (part 1 of 2).

```
34
35          setSize( 300, 150 );
36          show();
37       }
38
39       public void actionPerformed( ActionEvent e )
40       {
41          if ( toggle )
42             c.setLayout( grid2 );
43          else
44             c.setLayout( grid1 );
45
46          toggle = !toggle;
47          c.validate();
48       }
49
50       public static void main( String args[] )
51       {
52          GridLayoutDemo app = new GridLayoutDemo();
53
54          app.setDefaultCloseOperation( JFrame.EXIT_ON_CLOSE );
55       }
56    }
```

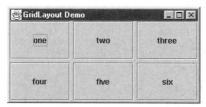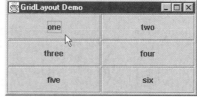

Fig. 27.22 Program that demonstrates components in **GridLayout** (part 2 of 2).

Lines 20 and 21 in the constructor

```
grid1 = new GridLayout( 2, 3, 5, 5 );
grid2 = new GridLayout( 3, 2 );
```

define two **GridLayout** objects. The **GridLayout** constructor used at line 20 specifies a **GridLayout** with **2** rows, **3** columns, **5** pixels of horizontal-gap space between **Component**s in the grid and **5** pixels of vertical-gap space between **Component**s in the grid. The **GridLayout** constructor used at line 21 specifies a **GridLayout** with **3** rows, **2** columns and no gap space.

The JButton objects in this example initially are arranged using **grid1** (set for the content pane at line 24 with method **setLayout**). The first component is added to the first column of the first row. The next component is added to the second column of the first row, etc. When a **JButton** is pressed, method **actionPerformed** (line 39) is called. Every call to **actionPerformed** toggles the layout between **grid2** and **grid1**.

Line 47

```
c.validate();
```

illustrates another way to re-layout a container for which the layout has changed. **Container** method ***validate*** recomputes the container's layout based on the current layout manager for the **Container** and the current set of displayed GUI components.

27.10 Graphical User Interfaces: Customizing a Component and Introducing Graphics

Complex GUIs require that each component be placed in an exact location. They often consist of multiple *panels* with each panel's components arranged in a specific layout. Panels are created with class **JPanel**—a subclass of **JComponent**. Class **JComponent** inherits from class **java.awt.Container**, so every **JPanel** is a **Container**. Thus **JPanel**s may have components, including other panels, added to them.

A **JPanel** can be used as a *dedicated drawing area* that can receive mouse events and is often extended to create new components. In earlier exercises you may have noticed that combining Swing GUI components and drawing in one window often leads to improper display of the GUI components or the graphics. This is because Swing GUI components are displayed using the same graphics techniques as the drawings and are displayed in the same area as the drawings. The order in which the GUI components are displayed and the drawing is performed may result in drawing over the GUI components or GUI components obscuring the graphics. To fix this problem, we can separate the GUI and the graphics by creating dedicated drawing areas as subclasses of **JPanel**.

Look-and-Feel Observation 27.4

*Combining graphics and Swing GUI components may lead to incorrect display of the graphics, the GUI components or both. Using **JPanel**s for drawing can eliminate this problem by providing a dedicated area for graphics.*

Swing components that inherit from class **JComponent** contain method ***paintComponent*** that helps them draw properly in the context of a Swing GUI. When customizing a **JPanel** for use as a dedicated drawing area, method **paintComponent** should be overridden as follows:

```
public void paintComponent( Graphics g )
{
   super.paintComponent( g );

   // your additional drawing code
}
```

Notice the call to the superclass version of **paintComponent** appears as the first statement in the body of the overridden method. This ensures that painting occurs in the proper order and that Swing's painting mechanism remains intact. If the superclass version of **paintComponent** is not called, typically the customized GUI component (the subclass of **JPanel** in this case) will not be displayed properly on the user interface. Also, if the superclass version is called after performing the customized drawing statements, the results will typically be erased.

Look-and-Feel Observation 27.5

*When overriding a **JComponent**'s **paintComponent** method, the first statement in the body should always be a call to the superclass's original version of the method.*

Common Programming Error 27.17

*When overriding a **JComponent**'s **paintComponent** method, not calling the super-class's original version of **paintComponent** prevents the GUI component from displaying properly on the GUI.*

Common Programming Error 27.18

*When overriding a **JComponent**'s **paintComponent** method, calling the superclass's version of **paintComponent** after other drawing is performed erases the other drawings.*

Class **JFrame** is not a subclass of **JComponent**; so, it does not contain method **paintComponent**. To draw directly on a subclass of **JFrame**, override method **paint**.

Look-and-Feel Observation 27.6

*Calling **repaint** for a Swing GUI component indicates that the component should be painted as soon as possible. The background of the GUI component is cleared only if the component is opaque. Most Swing components are transparent by default. **JComponent** method **setOpaque** can be passed a **boolean** argument indicating if the component is opaque (**true**) or transparent (**false**). The GUI components of package **java.awt** are different from Swing components in that **repaint** results in a call to **Component** method **update** (which clears the component's background) and **update** calls method **paint** (rather than **paintComponent**).*

Figure 27.23 demonstrates a customized subclass of **JPanel**. Class **CustomPanel** has its own **paintComponent** method that draws a circle or a square depending on the value passed to its **draw** method.

```java
1   // Fig. 27.23: CustomPanel.java
2   // A customized JPanel class.
3   import java.awt.*;
4   import javax.swing.*;
5
6   public class CustomPanel extends JPanel {
7      public final static int CIRCLE = 1, SQUARE = 2;
8      private int shape;
9
10     public void paintComponent( Graphics g )
11     {
12        super.paintComponent( g );
13
14        if ( shape == CIRCLE )
15           g.fillOval( 50, 10, 60, 60 );
16        else if ( shape == SQUARE )
17           g.fillRect( 50, 10, 60, 60 );
18     }
19
20     public void draw( int s )
21     {
22        shape = s;
23        repaint();
24     }
25  }
```

Fig. 27.23 Extending class **JPanel**—**CustomPanel.java**.

```java
1   // Fig. 27.23: CustomPanelTest.java
2   // Using a customized Panel object.
3   import java.awt.*;
4   import java.awt.event.*;
5   import javax.swing.*;
6
7   public class CustomPanelTest extends JFrame {
8       private JPanel buttonPanel;
9       private CustomPanel myPanel;
10      private JButton circle, square;
11
12      public CustomPanelTest()
13      {
14          super( "CustomPanel Test" );
15
16          myPanel = new CustomPanel();   // instantiate canvas
17          myPanel.setBackground( Color.green );
18
19          square = new JButton( "Square" );
20          square.addActionListener(
21             new ActionListener() {
22                public void actionPerformed( ActionEvent e )
23                {
24                   myPanel.draw( CustomPanel.SQUARE );
25                }
26             }
27          );
28
29          circle = new JButton( "Circle" );
30          circle.addActionListener(
31             new ActionListener() {
32                public void actionPerformed( ActionEvent e )
33                {
34                   myPanel.draw( CustomPanel.CIRCLE );
35                }
36             }
37          );
38
39          buttonPanel = new JPanel();
40          buttonPanel.setLayout( new GridLayout( 1, 2 ) );
41          buttonPanel.add( circle );
42          buttonPanel.add( square );
43
44          Container c = getContentPane();
45          c.add( myPanel, BorderLayout.CENTER );
46          c.add( buttonPanel, BorderLayout.SOUTH );
47
48          setSize( 300, 150 );
49          show();
50      }
51
52      public static void main( String args[] )
53      {
```

Fig. 27.23 Extending class **JPanel—CustomPanelTest.java** (part 1 of 2).

```
54              CustomPanelTest app = new CustomPanelTest();
55
56              app.setDefaultCloseOperation( JFrame.EXIT_ON_CLOSE );
57          }
58      }
```

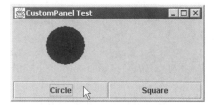 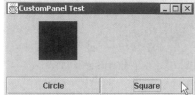

Fig. 27.23 Extending class **JPanel**—**CustomPanelTest.java** (part 2 of 2).

For this purpose, **CustomPanel** line 7

```
public final static int CIRCLE = 1, SQUARE = 2;
```

defines constants that are used to specify the shape a **CustomPanel** draws on itself with each call to its **paintComponent** method. The application consists of two classes— **CustomPanel** to draw the chosen shape and **CustomPanelTest** to run the application. Variables **CIRCLE** and **SQUARE** are declared *final* so they cannot be modified. Also, these variables are declared *static* so that only one copy of each variable exists in memory. Such static variables are shared by all objects of a given class.

Class **CustomPanel** (lines 6–25) contains one instance variable **shape** that keeps track of the shape to be drawn. Method **paintComponent** (line 10) is overridden in class **CustomPanel** to draw a shape on the panel. If **shape** is **CIRCLE**, **Graphics** method **fillOval** draws a solid circle. If **shape** is **SQUARE**, **Graphics** method **fillRect** draws a solid square. Method **draw** (line 20) sets instance variable **shape** and calls **repaint** to refresh the **CustomPanel** object. Note that calling **repaint** (which is really **this.repaint()**) for the **CustomPanel** schedules a repaint operation for the **CustomPanel**. Method **paintComponent** will be called to repaint the **Custom-Panel**. When **paintComponent** is called, the appropriate shape is drawn on the panel.

The constructor (line 37) of class **CustomPanelTest** instantiates a **Custom-Panel** object and sets its background color to green so the **CustomPanel** area is visible on the application. Next, **JButton** objects **circle** and **square** are instantiated. Lines 45–52 define an anonymous inner class to handle the **square**'s **ActionEvent**. Lines 55–62 define an anonymous inner class to handle the **circle**'s **ActionEvent**. Lines 49 and 59 each call method **draw** of **CustomPanel myPanel**. In each case, the appropriate constant (**CustomPanel.CIRCLE** or **CustomPanel.SQUARE**) is passed as an argument to indicate which shape to draw.

For layout of the buttons, **JPanel buttonPanel** is created with a **GridLayout** of one row and two columns and the buttons are added to **buttonPanel** with lines 39–42

```
buttonPanel = new JPanel();
buttonPanel.setLayout( new GridLayout( 1, 2 ) );
buttonPanel.add( circle );
buttonPanel.add( square );
```

Note the use of **setLayout** to set **buttonPanel**'s layout. Each container can have its own layout manager. Finally, **myPanel** is added to the center region and **buttonPanel** is added to the south region of the content pane's **BorderLayout**. Note that the **BorderLayout** automatically expands the **myPanel** to fill the center region.

27.11 Multithreading

It would be nice if we could "do one thing at a time" and "do it well," but that is simply not how the world works. The human body performs a great variety of operations *in parallel,* or as we will say throughout this chapter, *concurrently.* Respiration, blood circulation and digestion, for example, can occur concurrently. All of the senses—seeing, touching, smelling, tasting and hearing—can occur concurrently. An automobile can be accelerating, turning, air conditioning and playing music concurrently. Computers, too, perform operations concurrently. It is common today for desktop personal computers to be compiling a program, printing a file and receiving electronic mail messages over a network concurrently.

Java is unique among popular general-purpose programming languages in that it makes concurrency primitives available to the applications programmer. The programmer specifies that applications contain threads of execution, each thread designating a portion of a program that may execute concurrently with other threads. This capability, called *multithreading,* gives the Java programmer powerful capabilities not available in C and C++, the languages on which Java is based. C and C++ are called single-threaded languages.

An example of multithreading is Java's automatic garbage collection. C and C++ place with the programmer the responsibility for reclaiming dynamically allocated memory. Java provides a garbage collector thread that automatically reclaims dynamically allocated memory that is no longer needed. Java's garbage collector runs as a low-priority thread. When Java determines that there are no longer any references to an object, it marks the object for eventual garbage collection. The garbage collector thread runs when processor time is available and when there are no higher-priority runnable threads. The garbage collector will, however, run immediately when the system is out of memory.

Performance Tip 27.1

Java's garbage collection is not as efficient as the dynamic memory management code C and C++ programmers write, but it is relatively efficient and much safer for the programmer.

Performance Tip 27.2

*Setting an object reference to **null** marks that object for eventual garbage collection (if there are no other references to the object). This can help conserve memory in a system in which an automatic object is not going out of scope because the method it is in will execute for a lengthy period.*

27.11.1 Class **Thread**: An Overview of the **Thread** Methods

In this section we overview the various thread-related methods in the Java API. We use many of these methods in live-code examples throughout the chapter. The reader should refer to the Java API directly for more details on using each method, especially the exceptions thrown by each method.

Class **Thread** (package **java.lang**) has several constructors. The constructor

```
public Thread( String threadName )
```

constructs a **Thread** object whose name is **threadName**. The constructor

```
public Thread()
```

constructs a **Thread** whose name is **"Thread-"** concatenated with a number, like **Thread-1**, **Thread-2**, and so on.

The code that "does the real work" of a thread is placed in its *run* method. The **run** method can be overridden in a subclass of **Thread** or it may be overridden in an object that implements the **Runnable** interface.

A program launches a thread's execution by calling the thread's *start* method, which, in turn, calls the **run** method. After **start** launches the thread, **start** returns to its caller immediately. The caller then executes concurrently with the launched thread. The **start** method throws an **IllegalThreadStateException** if the thread it is trying to start has already been started.

The **static** method *sleep* is called with an argument specifying how long the currently executing thread should sleep (in milliseconds); while a thread sleeps, it does not contend for the processor, so other threads can execute. This can give lower-priority threads a chance to run.

The *interrupt* method is called to interrupt a thread. The **static** method *interrupted* returns **true** if the current thread has been interrupted and **false** otherwise. Method call *isInterrupted* (a non-**static** method) is sent to some other thread to determine if that thread has been interrupted.

Method *isAlive* returns **true** if **start** has been called for a given thread and the thread is not dead (i.e., its controlling **run** method has not completed execution).

We will discuss the *yield* method in detail after we have considered thread priorities and thread scheduling.

Method *setName* sets a **Thread**'s name. Method *getName* returns the name of the **Thread**. Method *toString* returns a **String** consisting of the name of the thread, the priority of the thread and the thread's **ThreadGroup**.

The **static** method *currentThread* returns a reference to the currently executing **Thread**.

Method *join* waits for the **Thread** to which the message is sent to die before the calling **Thread** can proceed; no argument or an argument of 0 milliseconds this method indicates that the current **Thread** will wait forever for the target **Thread** to die before proceeding. Such waiting can be dangerous; it can lead to two particularly serious problems called deadlock and indefinite postponement. We will discuss these momentarily.

Testing and Debugging Tip 27.7

*Method **dumpStack** is useful for debugging multithreaded applications. A program calls **static** method **dumpStack** to print a method-call stack trace for the current **Thread**.*

27.11.2 Thread States: Life Cycle of a Thread

At any time, a thread is said to be in one of several *thread states* (illustrated in Fig. 27.24). Let us say that a thread that was just created is in the *born* state. The thread remains in this state until the thread's **start** method is called; this causes the thread to enter the *ready* state (also known as the *runnable* state). The highest-priority *ready* thread enters the *running state* when the system assigns a processor to the thread (i.e., the thread begins executing). A thread enters the *dead* state when its **run** method completes or terminates for any reason—a *dead* thread will eventually be disposed of by the system.

One common way for a *running* thread to enter the blocked state is when the thread issues an input/output (I/O) request. In this case, a blocked thread becomes ready when the I/O it is waiting for completes. A blocked thread cannot use a processor even if one is available.

When a **sleep** method is called in a running thread, that thread enters the sleeping state. A sleeping thread becomes ready after the designated sleep time expires. A sleeping thread cannot use a processor even if one is available.

When a running thread calls **wait** the thread enters a waiting state for the particular object on which **wait** was called. One thread in the waiting state for a particular object becomes ready on a call to **notify** issued by another thread associated with that object. Every thread in the waiting state for a given object becomes ready on a call to **notifyAll** by another thread associated with that object.

A thread enters the *dead state* when its **run** method either completes or throws an uncaught exception.

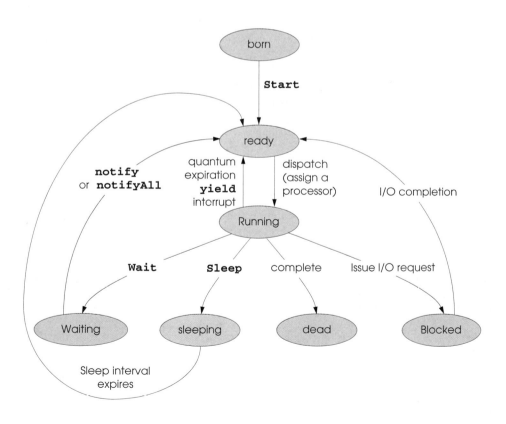

Fig. 27.24 Life cycle of a thread.

27.11.3 Thread Priorities and Thread Scheduling

Every Java application is multithreaded. Every Java thread has a priority in the range **Thread.MIN_PRIORITY** (a constant of 1) and **Thread.MAX_PRIORITY** (a constant of 10). By default, each thread is given priority **Thread.NORM_PRIORITY** (a constant of 5). Each new thread inherits the priority of the thread that creates it.

Some Java platforms support a concept called *timeslicing* and some do not. Without timeslicing, each thread in a set of equal-priority threads runs to completion (unless the thread leaves the running state) before that thread's peers get a chance to execute. With timeslicing, each thread receives a brief burst of processor time called a *quantum* during which that thread can execute. At quantum completion, even if that thread has not completed, the processor is taken away from that thread and given to the next thread of equal priority if one is available.

The job of the Java scheduler is to keep a highest-priority thread running at all times, and if timeslicing is available, to ensure that several equally high-priority threads each execute for a quantum in round-robin fashion. Figure 27.25 illustrates Java's multilevel priority queue for threads. In the figure, threads A and B each execute for a quantum in round-robin fashion until both threads complete execution. Next, thread C runs to completion. Then, threads D, E and F each execute in round-robin fashion until they all complete execution. This process continues until all threads run to completion. Note that new higher-priority threads could postpone—possibly indefinitely—the execution of lower-priority threads. Such *indefinite postponement* is often referred to more colorfully as *starvation*.

A thread's priority can be adjusted with method *setPriority*, which takes an **int** argument. If the argument is not in the range 1 through 10, **setPriority** throws an **IllegalArgumentException**. Method *getPriority* returns the thread's priority.

A thread can call the **yield** method to give other threads a chance to execute. Actually, whenever a higher-priority thread becomes ready, the current thread is preempted. Thus, a thread cannot **yield** to a higher-priority thread because the first thread will have been preempted when the higher-priority thread became ready. Similarly, **yield** always allows the highest-priority *ready* thread to run, so if only lower-priority threads are ready at the time of a **yield** call, the current thread will be the highest-priority thread and will continue executing. Therefore, a thread **yield**s to give threads of an equal priority a chance to run. On a timesliced system this is unnecessary because threads of equal priority will each execute for their quantum (or until they lose the processor for some other reason) and other threads of equal priority will execute in round-robin fashion. Thus **yield** is appropriate for non-timesliced systems in which a thread would ordinarily run to completion before another thread of equal priority would have an opportunity to run.

Performance Tip 27.3

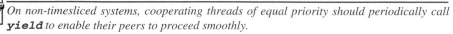

On non-timesliced systems, cooperating threads of equal priority should periodically call **yield** *to enable their peers to proceed smoothly.*

A thread executes unless it dies, it becomes blocked for input/output (or some other reason), it calls **sleep**, it calls **wait**, it calls **yield**, it is preempted by a thread of higher priority or its quantum expires. A thread with a higher priority than the running thread can become ready (and hence preempt the running thread) if a sleeping thread finishes sleeping, if I/O completes for a thread waiting for that I/O or if either **notify** or **notifyAll** is called on a thread that called **wait**.

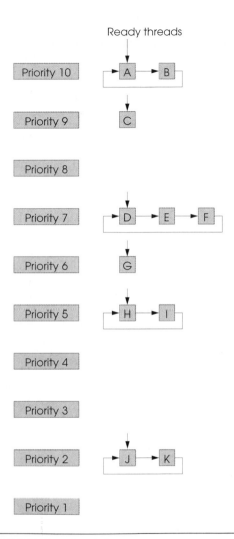

Fig. 27.25 Java thread priority scheduling.

27.11.4 Creating Threads in an Application

The application of Fig. 27.26 demonstrates basic threading techniques, including creation of a class derived from **Thread**, construction of a **Thread** and using the **Thread** class **sleep** method. Each thread of execution we create in the program displays its name after sleeping for a random amount of time between 0 and 5 seconds. The program consists of two classes—**ThreadTester** and **PrintThread**.

```
1   // Fig. 27.26: ThreadTester.java
2   // Show multiple threads printing at different intervals.
3
```

Fig. 27.26 Multiple threads printing at random intervals (part 1 of 3).

```java
4   public class ThreadTester {
5      public static void main( String args[] )
6      {
7         PrintThread thread1, thread2, thread3, thread4;
8
9         thread1 = new PrintThread( "thread1" );
10        thread2 = new PrintThread( "thread2" );
11        thread3 = new PrintThread( "thread3" );
12        thread4 = new PrintThread( "thread4" );
13
14        System.err.println( "\nStarting threads" );
15
16        thread1.start();
17        thread2.start();
18        thread3.start();
19        thread4.start();
20
21        System.err.println( "Threads started\n" );
22     }
23  }
24
25  class PrintThread extends Thread {
26     private int sleepTime;
27
28     // PrintThread constructor assigns name to thread
29     // by calling Thread constructor
30     public PrintThread( String name )
31     {
32        super( name );
33
34        // sleep between 0 and 5 seconds
35        sleepTime = (int) ( Math.random() * 5000 );
36
37        System.err.println( "Name: " + getName() +
38                            ";  sleep: " + sleepTime );
39     }
40
41     // execute the thread
42     public void run()
43     {
44        // put thread to sleep for a random interval
45        try {
46           System.err.println( getName() + " going to sleep" );
47           Thread.sleep( sleepTime );
48        }
49        catch ( InterruptedException exception ) {
50           System.err.println( exception.toString() );
51        }
52
53        // print thread name
54        System.err.println( getName() + " done sleeping" );
55     }
56  }
```

Fig. 27.26 Multiple threads printing at random intervals (part 2 of 3).

```
Name: thread1;   sleep: 1653
Name: thread2;   sleep: 2910
Name: thread3;   sleep: 4436
Name: thread4;   sleep: 201

Starting threads
Threads started

thread1 going to sleep
thread2 going to sleep
thread3 going to sleep
thread4 going to sleep
thread4 done sleeping
thread1 done sleeping
thread2 done sleeping
thread3 done sleeping
```

```
Name: thread1;   sleep: 3876
Name: thread2;   sleep: 64
Name: thread3;   sleep: 1752
Name: thread4;   sleep: 3120

Starting threads
Threads started

thread2 going to sleep
thread4 going to sleep
thread1 going to sleep
thread3 going to sleep
thread2 done sleeping
thread3 done sleeping
thread4 done sleeping
thread1 done sleeping
```

Fig. 27.26 Multiple threads printing at random intervals (part 3 of 3).

Class **PrintThread**—which inherits from **Thread** so each object of the class can execute in parallel—consists of instance variable **sleepTime**, a constructor and a **run** method. Variable **sleepTime** stores a random integer value chosen when a **Print-Thread** object is constructed. Each **PrintThread** object sleeps for the amount of time specified by **sleepTime** then outputs its name.

The **PrintThread** constructor (line 30) initializes **sleepTime** to a random integer between 0 and 4999 (0 to 4.999 seconds). Then, the name of the thread and the value of **sleepTime** are output to show the values for the particular **PrintThread** being constructed. The name of each thread is specified as a **String** argument to the **Print-Thread** constructor and is passed to the superclass constructor at line 32. *Note:* It is possible to allow class **Thread** to choose a name for your thread by using the **Thread** class's default constructor.

When a **PrintThread**'s **start** method (inherited from **Thread**) is invoked, the **PrintThread** object enters the *ready* state. When the system assigns a processor to the

PrintThread object, it enters the *running* state and its **run** method begins execution. Method **run** prints a **String** in the command window indicating that the thread is going to sleep then invokes the **sleep** method (line 47) to immediately put the thread into a *sleeping* state. When the thread awakens, it is placed into a *ready* state again until it is assigned a processor. When the **PrintThread** object enters the *running* state again, it outputs its name (indicating that the thread is done sleeping), its **run** method terminates and the thread object enters the *dead* state. Note that the **sleep** method can throw a checked **InterruptedException** (if another thread invokes the sleeping thread's **interrupt** method), therefore **sleep** must be called in a **try** block (in this example, we simply output the **String** representation of the exception if one occurs). Exception handling enables us to make this program more robust.

Lines 45–51 use ***try*** and ***catch*** blocks to test for the possibility of an exception. In the **try** block, we place any code that might cause a problem at execution time. If the code in the **try** block executes properly, the corresponding **catch** block is ignored. If the code in the **try** block causes an exception, the **try** block terminates immediately. Then, the exception-handling mechanism jumps to the first **catch** block (there may be several following a **try**) and attempts to locate a **catch** block that handles the type of exception that occurred. If the type of exception thrown matches the type of exception specified in the **catch** block's parentheses, that **catch** block's body executes to handle the exception. Note that in this program, the try/catch mechanism is required because an **InterruptedException** is a *checked exception*—the compiler checks that we catch this problem if it occurs. Java also has *unchecked exceptions*, which are ignored by the compiler. You can distinguish between exception types with class ***RuntimeException***. If the type of the exception is a subclass of **RuntimeException**, the exception is an unchecked exception.

Class **ThreadTester**'s **main** method (line 5) instantiates four **PrintThread** objects and invokes the **Thread** class **start** method on each one to place all four **PrintThread** objects in a *ready* state. Note that the program terminates execution when the last **PrintThread** awakens and prints its name. Also note that the **main** method terminates after starting the four **PrintThread**s, but the application does not terminate until the last thread dies.

27.12 Networking with Sockets and Streams

There is much excitement over the Internet and the World Wide Web. The Internet ties the "information world" together. The World Wide Web makes the Internet easy to use and gives it the flair and sizzle of multimedia. Organizations see the Internet and the Web as crucial to their information systems strategies. Java provides a number of built-in networking capabilities that make it easy to develop Internet-based and Web-based applications. Not only can Java specify parallelism through multithreading, but it can enable programs to search the world for information and to collaborate with programs running on other computers internationally, nationally or just within an organization. Java can even enable applets and applications running on the same computer to communicate with one another, subject to security constraints.

Java's networking capabilities are grouped into several packages. The fundamental networking capabilities are defined by classes and interfaces of package ***java.net***, through which Java offers *socket-based communications* that enable applications to view networking as streams of data—a program can read from a *socket* or write to a socket as simply as reading from a file or writing to a file.

This section introduces Java's socket-based communications. We show how to create and manipulate sockets. Java's *stream sockets* enable a process to establish a *connection* to another process. While the connection is in place, data flows between the processes in continuous *streams*. Stream sockets are said to provide a *connection-oriented service*. The protocol used for transmission is the popular *TCP (Transmission Control Protocol)*.

27.12.1 Establishing a Simple Server (Using Stream Sockets)

Establishing a simple server in Java requires five steps. Step 1 is to create a *Server-Socket* object. A call to the *ServerSocket* constructor such as

```
ServerSocket s = new ServerSocket( port, queueLength );
```

registers an available *port* number and specifies a maximum number of clients that can request connections to the server (i.e., the *queueLength*). If the queue is full, client connections are automatically refused. The preceding statement establishes the port where the server waits for connections from clients (also known as *binding the server to the port*). Each client will ask to connect to the server on this *port*.

Each client connection is managed with a *Socket* object. Once the **ServerSocket** is established (Step 2), the server listens indefinitely (or *blocks*) for an attempt by a client to connect. This is accomplished with a call to the **ServerSocket accept** method as in

```
Socket connection = s.accept();
```

which returns a **Socket** object when a connection is established.

Step 3 is to get the *OutputStream* and *InputStream* objects that enable the server to communicate with the client. The server sends information to the client via an **OutputStream** object. The server receives information from the client via an **Input-Stream** object. To obtain the streams, the server invokes method **getOutputStream** on the **Socket** to get a reference to the **OutputStream** associated with the **Socket** and invokes method **getInputStream** on the **Socket** to get a reference to the **Input-Stream** associated with the **Socket**.

The **OutputStream** and **InputStream** objects can be used to send or receive individual bytes or sets of bytes with the **OutputStream** method **write** and the **Input-Stream** method **read**, respectively. Often it is useful to send or receive values of primitive data types (such as **int** and **double**) or class data types (such as **String** and **Employee**) rather than sending bytes. In our example, we will use a common technique to *chain* other stream types (such as *ObjectOutputStream* and *ObjectInputStream*) to the **Out-putStream** and **InputStream** associated with the **Socket**. For example,

```
ObjectInputStream input =
    new ObjectInputStream( connection.getInputStream() );

ObjectOutputStream output =
    new ObjectOutputStream( connection.getOutputStream() );
```

The beauty of establishing these relationships is that whatever the server writes to the **Ob-jectOutputStream** is sent via the **OutputStream** and is available at the client's

InputStream and whatever the client writes to its **OutputStream** (with a corresponding **ObjectOutputStream**) is available via the server's **InputStream**.

Step 4 is the processing phase in which the server and the client communicate via the **InputStream** and **OutputStream** objects. In Step 5, when the transmission is complete, the server closes the connection by invoking the **close** method on the **Socket**.

Software Engineering Observation 27.7

With sockets, network I/O appears to Java programs to be identical to sequential file I/O. Sockets hide much of the complexity of network programming from the programmer.

Software Engineering Observation 27.8

With Java's multithreading, we can easily create multithreaded servers that can manage many simultaneous connections with many clients; this multithreaded-server architecture is precisely what is used in popular UNIX, Windows NT and OS/2 network servers.

Software Engineering Observation 27.9

*A multithreaded server can be implemented to take the **Socket** returned by each call to **accept** and create a new thread that would manage network I/O across that **Socket**, or a multithreaded server can be implemented to maintain a pool of threads ready to manage network I/O across the new **Socket**s as they are created.*

Performance Tip 27.4

*In high-performance systems in which memory is abundant, a multithreaded server can be implemented to create a pool of threads that can be assigned quickly to handle network I/O across each new **Socket** as it is created. Thus, when a connection is received, the server need not incur the overhead of thread creation.*

27.12.2 Establishing a Simple Client (Using Stream Sockets)

Establishing a simple client in Java requires four steps. In Step 1, we create a **Socket** to connect to the server. The connection to the server is established using a call to the Socket constructor with two arguments—the server's Internet address and the port number—as in

```
Socket connection = new Socket( serverAddress, port );
```

If the connection attempt is successful, this statement returns a **Socket**. A connection attempt that fails throws an instance of a subclass of **IOException**, so many programs simply catch **IOException**.

Common Programming Error 27.19

*An **UnknownHostException** is thrown when a server address indicated by a client cannot be resolved. A **ConnectException** is thrown when an error occurs while attempting to connect to a server.*

In Step 2, **Socket** methods **getInputStream** and **getOutputStream** are used to get references to the **Socket**'s associated **InputStream** and **OutputStream**, respectively. **InputStream** method **read** can be used to input individual bytes or sets of bytes from the server. **OutputStream** method **write** can be used to output individual bytes or sets of bytes to the server. As we mentioned in the preceding section, often it is useful to send or receive values of primitive data types (such as **int** and **double**) or class data types (such as **String** and **Employee**) rather than sending bytes. If the server is sending information in the form of actual data types, the client should receive the information in the same format. Thus, if the server sends values with an **ObjectOutput-Stream**, the client should read those values with an **ObjectInputStream**.

Step 3 is the processing phase in which the client and the server communicate via the **InputStream** and **OutputStream** objects. In Step 4 when the transmission is complete, the client closes the connection by invoking the **close** method on the **Socket**. When processing information sent by a server, the client must determine when the server is done sending information so the client can call **close** to close the **Socket** connection. For example, the **InputStream** method **read** returns –1 when end-of-stream (also called EOF—end-of-file) is detected. If an **ObjectInputStream** is used to read information from the server, an **EOFException** is generated when the client attempts to read a value from a stream on which end-of-stream is detected.

When the client closes the **Socket**, an **IOException** may be thrown. The **getInputStream** and **getOutputStream** methods may also throw **IOException**s.

27.12.3 Client/Server Interaction with Stream Socket Connections

The applications of Fig. 27.27 and Fig. 27.28 use *stream sockets* to demonstrate a simple *client/server chat application*. The server waits for a client connection attempt. When a client application connects to the server, the server application sends a **String** object indicating that the connection was successful to the client and the client displays the message. Both the client and the server applications contain **JTextField**s, which allow the user to type a message and send it to the other application. When the client or the server sends the **String** "**TERMINATE**", the connection between the client and the server terminates. Then, the server waits for the next client to connect. The definition of class **Server** is given in Fig. 27.27. The definition of class **Client** is given in Fig. 27.28. The screen captures showing the execution between the client and the server are shown as part of Fig. 27.28.

Class **Server**'s constructor creates the GUI of the application (a **JTextField** and a **JTextArea**). The **Server** object displays its output in a **JTextArea**. When the **main** method (line 121) executes, it creates an instance of class **Server**, registers a **WindowListener** to terminate the program when the user clicks the window's close box and calls method **runServer** (defined at line 43).

```
1   // Fig. 27.27: Server.java
2   // Set up a Server that will receive a connection
3   // from a client, send a string to the client,
4   // and close the connection.
5   import java.io.*;
6   import java.net.*;
7   import java.awt.*;
8   import java.awt.event.*;
9   import javax.swing.*;
10
11  public class Server extends JFrame {
12      private JTextField enter;
13      private JTextArea display;
14      private ObjectOutputStream output;
```

Fig. 27.27 Server portion of a client/server stream socket connection (part 1 of 4).

```
15       private ObjectInputStream input;
16
17       public Server()
18       {
19          super( "Server" );
20
21          Container c = getContentPane();
22
23          enter = new JTextField();
24          enter.setEnabled( false );
25          enter.addActionListener(
26             new ActionListener() {
27                public void actionPerformed( ActionEvent e )
28                {
29                   sendData( e.getActionCommand() );
30                }
31             }
32          );
33          c.add( enter, BorderLayout.NORTH );
34
35          display = new JTextArea();
36          c.add( new JScrollPane( display ),
37                 BorderLayout.CENTER );
38
39          setSize( 300, 150 );
40          show();
41       }
42
43       public void runServer()
44       {
45          ServerSocket server;
46          Socket connection;
47          int counter = 1;
48
49          try {
50             // Step 1: Create a ServerSocket.
51             server = new ServerSocket( 5000, 100 );
52
53             while ( true ) {
54                // Step 2: Wait for a connection.
55                display.setText( "Waiting for connection\n" );
56                connection = server.accept();
57
58                display.append( "Connection " + counter +
59                   " received from: " +
60                   connection.getInetAddress().getHostName() );
61
62                // Step 3: Get input and output streams.
63                output = new ObjectOutputStream(
64                         connection.getOutputStream() );
65                output.flush();
66                input = new ObjectInputStream(
67                         connection.getInputStream() );
```

Fig. 27.27 Server portion of a client/server stream socket connection (part 2 of 4).

```
68                   display.append( "\nGot I/O streams\n" );
69
70                   // Step 4: Process connection.
71                   String message =
72                      "SERVER>>> Connection successful";
73                   output.writeObject( message );
74                   output.flush();
75                   enter.setEnabled( true );
76
77                   do {
78                      try {
79                         message = (String) input.readObject();
80                         display.append( "\n" + message );
81                         display.setCaretPosition(
82                            display.getText().length() );
83                      }
84                      catch ( ClassNotFoundException cnfex ) {
85                         display.append(
86                            "\nUnknown object type received" );
87                      }
88                   } while ( !message.equals( "CLIENT>>> TERMINATE" ) );
89
90                   // Step 5: Close connection.
91                   display.append( "\nUser terminated connection" );
92                   enter.setEnabled( false );
93                   output.close();
94                   input.close();
95                   connection.close();
96
97                   ++counter;
98                }
99             }
100            catch ( EOFException eof ) {
101               System.out.println( "Client terminated connection" );
102            }
103            catch ( IOException io ) {
104               io.printStackTrace();
105            }
106         }
107
108         private void sendData( String s )
109         {
110            try {
111               output.writeObject( "SERVER>>> " + s );
112               output.flush();
113               display.append( "\nSERVER>>>" + s );
114            }
115            catch ( IOException cnfex ) {
116               display.append(
117                  "\nError writing object" );
118            }
119         }
120
```

Fig. 27.27 Server portion of a client/server stream socket connection (part 3 of 4).

```
121        public static void main( String args[] )
122        {
123            Server app = new Server();
124
125            app.setDefaultCloseOperation( JFrame.EXIT_ON_CLOSE );
126            app.runServer();
127        }
128    }
```

Fig. 27.27 Server portion of a client/server stream socket connection (part 4 of 4).

Method **runServer** does the work of setting up the server to receive a connection and processing the connection when it is received. The method declares a **Server-Socket** called **server** (line 45) to wait for connections, a **Socket** called **connection** (line 46) to process the connection from a client and an integer **counter** to keep track of the total number of connections processed.

In the **try** block (line 49), the **ServerSocket** is set up (line 51) to listen for a connection from a client at port **5000**. The second argument to the constructor is the number of connections that can wait in a queue to connect to the server (**100** in this example). If the queue is full when a connection is attempted, the connection is refused.

Software Engineering Observation 27.10

Port numbers can be between 0 and 65535. Many operating systems reserve port numbers below 1024 for system services (such as email and World Wide Web servers). Generally, these ports should not be specified as connection ports in user programs. In fact, some operating systems require special access privileges to use port numbers below 1024.

In the infinite **while** loop (line 53), line 56

```
connection = server.accept();
```

uses **ServerSocket** method **accept** to listen for a connection from a client. This method blocks until a connection is received (i.e., the thread in which **accept** is called stops executing until a connection is received). Once a connection is received, **connection** is assigned a **Socket** object that will be used to manage the connection. Lines 58–60 append text to the **JTextArea**, indicating that a connection was received. The expression

```
connection.getInetAddress().getHostName()
```

uses **Socket** method **getInetAddress** to obtain the Internet address of the client computer that connected to this server. This method returns an *InetAddress* reference, which is used in a chained method call to invoke **InetAddress** method **getHostName**, which returns the client computer's host name. For example, if the Internet address of the computer is **127.0.0.1**, the corresponding host name would be **localhost**.

Lines 63–67

```
output = new ObjectOutputStream(
            connection.getOutputStream() );
output.flush();
input = new ObjectInputStream(
            connection.getInputStream() );
```

create the **ObjectOutputStream** and **ObjectInputStream** objects that send and receive **Object**s between the server and the client. These objects are connected to the **OutputStream** returned by **Socket** method **getOutputStream** and the **Input-Stream** returned by **Socket** method **getInputStream**, respectively. Notice the call to **ObjectOutputStream** method **flush** at line 65. This statement causes the **ObjectOutputStream** on the server to send a *stream header* to the corresponding client's **ObjectInputStream**. The stream header contains information such as the version of object serialization being used to send objects. This information is required by the **ObjectInputStream** so it can prepare to receive those objects correctly.

Software Engineering Observation 27.11

*When using an **ObjectOutputStream** and **ObjectInputStream** to send and receive objects over a network connection, always create the **ObjectOutputStream** first and **flush** the stream so the client's **ObjectInputStream** can prepare to receive the data.*

Line 73

```
output.writeObject( message );
```

uses **ObjectOutputStream** method **writeObject** to send the string "**SERVER>>> Connection successful**" to the client. Line 74 flushes the output stream to ensure that the object is sent immediately; otherwise, the object may be held in an output buffer until more information is available to send.

Performance Tip 27.5

Output buffers are typically used to increase the efficiency of an application by sending larger amounts of data fewer times. The input and output components of a computer are typically much slower than the memory of the computer.

The **do/while** structure at lines 77–88 loops until the server receives the message "**CLIENT>>> TERMINATE**". Line 79

```
message = (String) input.readObject();
```

uses **ObjectInputStream** method **readObject** to read a **String** from the client. Line 80 displays the message in the **JTextArea**. Lines 81 and 82 use **JTextComponent** method *setCaretPosition* to position the input cursor in the **JTextArea** after the last character in the **JTextArea**. This allows the **JTextArea** to scroll as text is appended to it.

When the transmission is complete, the streams and the **Socket** are closed with lines 93–95

```
output.close();
input.close();
connection.close();
```

Next, the server awaits the next connection attempt from a client by continuing with line 56 at the beginning of the **while** loop.

When the user of the server application enters a **String** in the **JTextField** and presses the *Enter* key, method **actionPerformed** (line 27) reads the **String** from the **JTextField** and calls utility method **sendData** (defined at line 108). Method **send-**

Data sends the **String** object to the client, flushes the output buffer and appends the same **String** to the **JTextArea** in the server window.

Notice that the **Server** receives a connection, processes the connection, closes the connection and waits for the next connection. A more likely scenario would be a **Server** that receives a connection, sets up that connection to be processed as a separate thread of execution, then waits for new connections. The separate threads that process existing connections can continue to execute while the **Server** concentrates on new connection requests.

Like class **Server**, class **Client**'s (Fig. 27.28) constructor creates the GUI of the application (a **JTextField** and a **JTextArea**). The **Client** object displays its output in a **JTextArea**. When the **main** method (line 108) executes, it creates an instance of class **Client**, registers a **WindowListener** to terminate the program when the user clicks the window's close box and calls method **runClient** (defined at line 43).

```
1   // Fig. 27.28: Client.java
2   // Set up a Client that will read information sent
3   // from a Server and display the information.
4   import java.io.*;
5   import java.net.*;
6   import java.awt.*;
7   import java.awt.event.*;
8   import javax.swing.*;
9
10  public class Client extends JFrame {
11     private JTextField enter;
12     private JTextArea display;
13     private ObjectOutputStream output;
14     private ObjectInputStream input;
15     private String message = "";
16
17     public Client()
18     {
19        super( "Client" );
20
21        Container c = getContentPane();
22
23        enter = new JTextField();
24        enter.setEnabled( false );
25        enter.addActionListener(
26           new ActionListener() {
27              public void actionPerformed( ActionEvent e )
28              {
29                 sendData( e.getActionCommand() );
30              }
31           }
32        );
33        c.add( enter, BorderLayout.NORTH );
34
35        display = new JTextArea();
36        c.add( new JScrollPane( display ),
37              BorderLayout.CENTER );
```

Fig. 27.28 Demonstrating the client portion of a stream socket connection between a client and a server (part 1 of 4).

```
38
39          setSize( 300, 150 );
40          show();
41       }
42
43       public void runClient()
44       {
45          Socket client;
46
47          try {
48             // Step 1: Create a Socket to make connection.
49             display.setText( "Attempting connection\n" );
50             client = new Socket(
51                InetAddress.getByName( "127.0.0.1" ), 5000 );
52
53             display.append( "Connected to: " +
54                client.getInetAddress().getHostName() );
55
56             // Step 2: Get the input and output streams.
57             output = new ObjectOutputStream(
58                       client.getOutputStream() );
59             output.flush();
60             input = new ObjectInputStream(
61                       client.getInputStream() );
62             display.append( "\nGot I/O streams\n" );
63
64             // Step 3: Process connection.
65             enter.setEnabled( true );
66
67             do {
68                try {
69                   message = (String) input.readObject();
70                   display.append( "\n" + message );
71                   display.setCaretPosition(
72                      display.getText().length() );
73                }
74                catch ( ClassNotFoundException cnfex ) {
75                   display.append(
76                      "\nUnknown object type received" );
77                }
78             } while ( !message.equals( "SERVER>>> TERMINATE" ) );
79
80             // Step 4: Close connection.
81             display.append( "Closing connection.\n" );
82             input.close();
83             output.close();
84             client.close();
85          }
86          catch ( EOFException eof ) {
87             System.out.println( "Server terminated connection" );
88          }
```

Fig. 27.28 Demonstrating the client portion of a stream socket connection between a client and a server (part 2 of 4).

```
89                catch ( IOException e ) {
90                   e.printStackTrace();
91                }
92             }
93
94             private void sendData( String s )
95             {
96                try {
97                   message = s;
98                   output.writeObject( "CLIENT>>> " + s );
99                   output.flush();
100                  display.append( "\nCLIENT>>>" + s );
101               }
102               catch ( IOException cnfex ) {
103                  display.append(
104                     "\nError writing object" );
105               }
106            }
107
108            public static void main( String args[] )
109            {
110               Client app = new Client();
111
112               app.setDefaultCloseOperation( JFrame.EXIT_ON_CLOSE );
113               app.runClient();
114            }
115         }
```

Client	Server	
Attempting connection Connected to: 127.0.0.1 Got I/O streams SERVER>>> Connection successful	Waiting for connection Connection 1 received from: 127.0.0.1 Got I/O streams	The **Server** and **Client** windows after the **Client** connects to the **Server**
Client — Hello server Attempting connection Connected to: 127.0.0.1 Got I/O streams SERVER>>> Connection successful CLIENT>>>Hello server	Server Waiting for connection Connection 1 received from: 127.0.0.1 Got I/O streams CLIENT>>> Hello server	The **Server** and **Client** windows after the **Client** sends a message to the **Server**
Client — Hello server Connected to: 127.0.0.1 Got I/O streams SERVER>>> Connection successful CLIENT>>>Hello server SERVER>>> How are you doing?	Server — How are you doing? Waiting for connection Connection 1 received from: 127.0.0.1 Got I/O streams CLIENT>>> Hello server SERVER>>>How are you doing?	The **Server** and **Client** windows after the **Server** sends a message to the **Client**

Fig. 27.28 Demonstrating the client portion of a stream socket connection between a client and a server (part 3 of 4).

The **Server** and **Client** windows after the **Client** terminates the connection

Fig. 27.28 Demonstrating the client portion of a stream socket connection between a client and a server (part 4 of 4).

Client method **runClient** performs the work necessary to connect to the **Server**, to receive data from the **Server** and to send data to the **Server**. The method declares a **Socket** called **client** (line 45) to establish a connection. The **Client** will use an **ObjectOutputStream** to send data to the server and an **ObjectInput-Stream** to receive data from the server. In the **try** block, lines 50 and 51

```
client = new Socket(
    InetAddress.getByName( "127.0.0.1" ), 5000 );
```

create a **Socket** with two arguments to the constructor—the Internet address of the server computer and the port number (5000) where that computer is awaiting client connections. The call to **InetAddress** method **getByName** in the first argument returns an **Inet-Address** object containing the Internet address **127.0.0.1** (i.e., **localhost**). Method **getByName** can receive a **String** containing either the actual Internet address or the host name of the server. The first argument also could have been written other ways:

```
InetAddress.getByName( "localhost" )
```

or

```
InetAddress.getLocalHost()
```

Also, there are versions of the **Socket** constructor that receive a **String** for the Internet address or host name. The first argument could have been specified as **"127.0.0.1"** or **"localhost"**. *[Note: We chose to demonstrate the client/server relationship by connecting between programs executing on the same computer (**localhost**). Normally, this first argument would be the Internet address of another computer. The **InetAddress** object for another computer can be obtained by specifying the Internet address or host name of the other computer as the **String** argument to **InetAddress.getByName.**]*

The **Socket** constructor's second argument is the server port number. This number must match the port number at which the server is waiting for connections (called the *handshake point*). Once the connection is made, a message is displayed in the **JTextArea** (lines 53 and 54) indicating the name of the server computer to which the client connected. Lines 57–61

```
output = new ObjectOutputStream(
            client.getOutputStream() );
output.flush();
input = new ObjectInputStream(
            client.getInputStream() );
```

create the **ObjectOutputStream** and **ObjectInputStream** objects that are connected to the **OutputStream** and **InputStream** objects associated with **client**.

The **do/while** structure at lines 67–78 loops until the client receives the message "**SERVER>>> TERMINATE**." Line 69

```
message = (String) input.readObject();
```

uses **ObjectInputStream** method **readObject** to read a **String** from the server. Line 70 displays the message in the **JTextArea**. Lines 71 and 72 use **JTextComponent** method **setCaretPosition** to position the input cursor in the **JTextArea** after the last character in the **JTextArea**.

When the transmission is complete, the streams and the **Socket** are closed with lines 82–84

```
output.close();
input.close();
connection.close();
```

When the user of the client application enters a **String** in the **JTextField** and presses the *Enter* key, method **actionPerformed** (line 27) reads the **String** from the **JTextField** and calls utility method **sendData** (defined at line 94). Method **sendData** sends the **String** object to server client, flushes the output buffer and appends the same **String** to the **JTextArea** in the client window.

27.13 Enhancing a Web Server with Servlets

We now continue our discussion of networking. Here focus on both sides of a *client-server relationship*. The *client* requests that some action be performed and the *server* performs the action and responds to the client. This request-response model of communication is the foundation for the highest-level view of networking in Java—*servlets*. A servlet extends the functionality of a server. The ***javax.servlet*** package and the ***javax.servlet.http*** package provide the classes and interfaces to define servlets.

A common implementation of the request-response model is between World Wide Web browsers and World Wide Web servers. When a user selects a Web site to browse through their browser (the client application), a request is sent to the appropriate Web server (the server application). The server normally responds to the client by sending the appropriate HTML Web page.

Servlet technology today is primarily designed for use with the HTTP protocol of the Web, but servlets are being developed for other technologies. Servlets are effective for developing Web-based solutions that help provide secure access to a Web site, that interact with databases on behalf of a client, that dynamically generate custom HTML documents to be displayed by browsers and that maintain unique session information for each client.

Many developers feel that servlets are the right solution for database-intensive applications that communicate with so-called thin clients—applications that require minimal client-side support. The server is responsible for the database access. Clients connect to the server using standard protocols available on all client platforms. Thus, the logic code can be written once and reside on the server for access by clients.

Our servlet example will make use of JDBC (Java Database Connectivity) database facilities to build a multi-tier client-server application that access a database.

The Servlet APIs are now developed by the Apache group (**www.apache.org**). Before you can program with servlets, you must download and install the Apache group's implementation of servlets called *Tomcat*. You may download Tomcat at no charge from Sun Microsystems at the Web site

    java.sun.com/products/jsp/tomcat

After downloading Tomcat, install it on your system and carefully read the **readme** file supplied in the **doc** directory. It explains how to set up Tomcat and discusses how to start the *server* that can be used to test servlets if you do not have a Web server that supports servlets. To develop servlets, you also need to copy the **servlet.jar** file containing the servlet class files from the installation directory to your JDK extensions directory (the directory **c:\jdk1.3\jre\lib\ext** on Windows or the directory **~/jdk1.3/jre/ lib/ext** on UNIX).

The *World Wide Web Consortium (W3C)* is a multinational organization dedicated to developing common protocols for the World Wide Web that "promote its evolution and ensure its interoperability." To that end, W3C provides *Open Source software*—a main benefit of such software is that it is free for anyone to use. W3C provides through their Open Source license a Web server called *Jigsaw* that is written completely in Java and fully supports servlets. Jigsaw and its documentation can be downloaded from

    www.w3.org/Jigsaw

For more information on the Open Source license, visit the site

    www.opensource.org

27.13.1 Overview of Servlet Technology

The Internet offers many *protocols*. The *HTTP protocol (HyperText Transfer Protocol)* that forms the basis of the World Wide Web uses URLs (*Uniform Resource Locators*, also called *Universal Resource Locators*) to locate data on the Internet. Common URLs represent files or directories and can represent complex tasks such as database lookups and Internet searches. For more information on URL formats visit

    www.ncsa.uiuc.edu/demoweb/url-primer.html

For more information on the *HTTP* protocol visit

    www.w3.org/Protocols/HTTP/

For general information on a variety of World Wide Web topics visit

    www.w3.org

Servlets are the analog on the server side to applets on the client side. Servlets are normally executed as part of a Web server. In fact, servlets have become so popular that they are now supported by most major Web servers, including the Netscape Web servers, Microsoft's Internet Information Server (IIS), the World Wide Web Consortium's Jigsaw Web server and the popular Apache Web server.

The servlets in this chapter demonstrate communication between clients and servers via the HTTP protocol of the World Wide Web. A client sends an HTTP request to the server. The server receives the request and directs it to be processed by appropriate servlets. The servlets do their processing (which often includes interacting with a database), then return their results to the client—normally in the form of HTML documents to display in a browser, but other data formats, such as images and binary data, can be returned.

27.13.2 The Servlet API

In this section we discuss at a high level the servlet-related classes, methods and exceptions. Architecturally, all servlets must implement the **Servlet** interface. The methods of interface **Servlet** are invoked automatically (by the server on which the servlet is installed). This interface defines five methods described in Fig. 27.29.

Software Engineering Observation 27.12

*All servlets must implement the **javax.servlet.Servlet** interface.*

The servlet packages define two **abstract** classes that implement the interface **Servlet**—class **GenericServlet** (from the package **javax.servlet**) and class **HttpServlet** (from the package **javax.servlet.http**). These classes provide default implementations of all the **Servlet** methods. Most servlets extend either **GenericServlet** or **HttpServlet** and override some or all of their methods with appropriate customized behaviors.

Method	Description
void init(ServletConfig config)	This method is automatically called once during a servlet's execution cycle to initialize the servlet. The **ServletConfig** argument is supplied automatically by the server that executes the servlet.
ServletConfig getServletConfig()	This method returns a reference to an object that implements interface **ServletConfig**. This object provides access to the servlet's configuration information such as initialization parameters and the servlet's **ServletContext**, which provides the servlet with access to its environment (i.e., the server in which the servlet is executing).
void service(ServletRequest request, ServletResponse response)	This is the first method called on every servlet to respond to a client request.
String getServletInfo()	This method is defined by a servlet programmer to return a **String** containing servlet information such as the servlet's author and version.
void destroy()	This "cleanup" method is called when a servlet is terminated by the server on which it is executing. This is a good method to use to deallocate a resource used by the servlet (such as an open file or an open database connection).

Fig. 27.29 Methods of interface **Servlet**.

The example we present extends class **HttpServlet**, which defines enhanced processing capabilities for servlets that extend the functionality of a Web server. The key method in every servlet is method **service**, which receives both a *ServletRequest* object and a *ServletResponse* object. These objects provide access to input and output streams that allow the servlet to read data from the client and send data to the client. These streams can be either byte-based streams or character-based streams. If problems occur during the execution of a servlet, either **ServletException**s or **IOException**s are thrown to indicate the problem.

27.13.3 **HttpServlet** Class

Web-based servlets typically extend class **HttpServlet**. Class **HttpServlet** overrides method **service** to distinguish between the typical requests received from a client Web browser. The two most common HTTP *request types* (also known as *request methods*) are *get* and *post*. A *get* request *gets* (or *retrieves*) information from the server. Common uses of *get* requests are to retrieve an HTML document or an image. A **post** request posts (or sends) data to the server. Common uses of **post** requests are to send the server information from an *HTML form* in which the client enters data, to send the server information so it can search the Internet or query a database for the client, to send authentication information to the server, etc.

Class **HttpServlet** defines methods *doGet* and *doPost* to respond to **get** and **post** requests from a client, respectively. These methods are called by the **Http-Servlet** class's **service** method, which is called when a request arrives at the server. Method **service** first determines the request type, then calls the appropriate method. Other less common request types are available, but these are beyond the scope of this book. For more information on the HTTP protocol visit the site

> **www.w3.org/Protocols**

Methods **doGet** and **doPost** receive as arguments an **HttpServletRequest** object and an **HttpServletResponse** object that enable interaction between the client and the server. The methods of **HttpServletRequest** make it easy to access the data supplied as part of the request. The **HttpServletResponse** methods make it easy to return the servlet's results in HTML format to the Web client. Interfaces **HttpServlet-Request** and **HttpServletResponse** are discussed in the next two sections.

27.13.4 **HttpServletRequest** Interface

Every call to **doGet** or **doPost** for an **HttpServlet** receives an object that implements interface **HttpServletRequest**. The Web server that executes the servlet creates an **HttpServletRequest** object and passes this to the servlet's **service** method (which, in turn, passes it to **doGet** or **doPost**). This object contains the request from the client. A variety of methods are provided to enable the servlet to process the client's request. Some of these methods are from interface *ServletRequest*—the interface that **HttpServletRequest** extends. A few key methods used in this chapter are presented in Fig. 27.30.

Method	Description

String getParameter(String name)

Returns the value associated with a parameter sent to the servlet as part of a **GET** or **POST** request. The **name** argument represents the parameter name.

Enumeration getParameterNames()

Returns the names of all the parameters sent to the servlet as part of a **POST** request.

String[] getParameterValues(String name)

Returns a **String** array containing the values for a specified servlet parameter.

Cookie[] getCookies()

Returns an array of **Cookie** objects stored on the client by the server. **Cookie**s can be used to uniquely identify clients to the servlet.

HttpSession getSession(boolean create)

Returns an **HttpSession** object associated with the client's current browsing session. An **HttpSession** object can be created by this method (**true** argument) if an **HttpSession** object does not already exist for the client. **HttpSession** objects can be used in similar ways to **Cookie**s for uniquely identifying clients.

Fig. 27.30 Important methods of interface **HttpServletRequest**.

27.13.5 HttpServletResponse Interface

Every call to **doGet** or **doPost** for an **HttpServlet** receives an object that implements interface **HttpServletResponse**. The Web server that executes the servlet creates an **HttpServletResponse** object and passes this to the servlet's **service** method (which, in turn, passes it to **doGet** or **doPost**). This object contains the response to the client. A variety of methods are provided to enable the servlet to formulate the response to the client. Some of these methods are from interface *ServletResponse*—the interface that **HttpServletResponse** extends. A few key methods used in this chapter are presented in Fig. 27.31.

Method	Description

void addCookie(Cookie cookie)

Used to add a **Cookie** to the header of the response to the client. The **Cookie**'s maximum age and whether the client allows **Cookie**s to be saved determine whether or not **Cookie**s will be stored on the client.

ServletOutputStream getOutputStream()

Obtains a byte-based output stream enabling binary data to be sent to the client.

Fig. 27.31 Important methods of **HttpServletResponse** (part 1 of 2).

Method	Description

PrintWriter getWriter()

      Obtains a character-based output stream enabling text data to be sent to the client.

void setContentType(String type)

      Specifies the MIME type of the response to the browser. The MIME type helps the browser determine how to display the data (or possibly what other application to execute to process the data). For example, MIME type **"text/html"** indicates that the response is an HTML document, so the browser displays the HTML page.

Fig. 27.31 Important methods of **HttpServletResponse** (part 2 of 2).

27.13.6 Multi-tier Client/Server Application with Servlets

Servlets can communicate with databases via JDBC (Java Database Connectivity). JDBC provides a uniform way for a Java program to connect with a variety of databases in a general manner without having to deal with the specifics of those database systems.

Many of today's applications are *three-tier distributed applications,* consisting of a *user interface*, *business logic* and *database access*. The user interface in such an application is often created using HTML (as shown in this chapter) or Dynamic HTML. In some cases, Java applets are also used for this tier. HTML is the preferred mechanism for representing the user interface in systems where portability is a concern. Because HTML is supported by all browsers, designing the user interface to be accessed through a Web browser guarantees portability across all platforms that have browsers. Using the networking provided automatically by the browser, the user interface can communicate with the middle-tier business logic. The middle tier can then access the database to manipulate the data. All three tiers may reside on separate computers that are connected to a network.

In multi-tier architectures, Web servers are increasingly used to build the middle tier. They provide the business logic that manipulates data from databases and that communicates with client Web browsers. Servlets, through JDBC, can interact with popular database systems. Developers do not need to be familiar with the specifics of each database system. Rather, developers use SQL-based queries and the JDBC driver handles the specifics of interacting with each database system.

The servlet of Fig. 27.32 and the HTML document of Fig. 27.33 demonstrate a three-tier distributed application that displays the user interface in a browser using HTML. The middle tier is a Java servlet that handles requests from the client browser and provides access to the third tier—a Microsoft Access database (set up as an ODBC data source) accessed via JDBC. The servlet in this example is a guest book servlet that allows the user to register for several different mailing lists. When the servlet receives a **post** request from the HTML document of Fig. 27.33, it ensures that the required data fields are present, then stores the data in the database and sends a confirmation page to the client.

Class **GuestBookServlet** extends class **HttpServlet** (line 9) so it is capable of responding to **GET** and **POST** requests. Servlets are initialized by overriding method **init** (line 14). Method **init** is called exactly once in a servlet's lifetime and is guaranteed to complete before any client requests are accepted. Method **init** takes a ***Servlet-***

Config argument and throws a **ServletException**. The argument provides the servlet with information about its *initialization parameters* (i.e., parameters not associated with a request, but passed to the servlet for initializing servlet variables).

```
1   // Fig. 27.32: GuestBookServlet.java
2   // Three-Tier Example
3   import java.io.*;
4   import javax.servlet.*;
5   import javax.servlet.http.*;
6   import java.util.*;
7   import java.sql.*;
8
9   public class GuestBookServlet extends HttpServlet {
10      private PreparedStatement statement = null;
11      private Connection connection = null;
12      private String URL = "jdbc:odbc:Guests";
13
14      public void init( ServletConfig config )
15         throws ServletException
16      {
17         super.init( config );
18
19         try {
20            Class.forName( "sun.jdbc.odbc.JdbcOdbcDriver" );
21            connection =
22               DriverManager.getConnection( URL, "", "" );
23            statement = connection.prepareStatement(
24               "INSERT INTO Guests values ( " +
25                  "?, ?, ?, ?, ?, ?, ?, ? );" );
26         }
27         catch ( Exception e ) {
28            e.printStackTrace();
29            connection = null;
30         }
31      }
32
33      public void doPost( HttpServletRequest req,
34                          HttpServletResponse res )
35         throws ServletException, IOException
36      {
37         String email = req.getParameter( "Email" ),
38                firstName = req.getParameter( "FirstName" ),
39                lastName = req.getParameter( "LastName" );
40
41         PrintWriter output = res.getWriter();
42         res.setContentType( "text/html" );
43
44         if ( email.equals( "" ) || firstName.equals( "" ) ||
45              lastName.equals( "" ) ) {
46            output.println( "<H3> Please click the back " +
47               "button and fill in all fields.</H3>" );
```

Fig. 27.32 GuestBookServlet, which allows client to register for mailing lists (part 1 of 2).

```
48              output.close();
49              return;
50          }
51
52          // set parameters before performing insert
53          try {
54              statement.setString( 1, email );
55              statement.setString( 2, firstName );
56              statement.setString( 3, lastName );
57              statement.setString( 4, req.getParameter("Company") );
58              statement.setString( 5,
59                  req.getParameter( "c_cpp" ) != null ? "yes":"no" );
60              statement.setString( 6,
61                  req.getParameter( "java" ) != null ? "yes":"no"  );
62              statement.setString( 7,
63                  req.getParameter( "vb" ) != null ? "yes":"no" );
64              statement.setString( 8,
65                  req.getParameter( "iwww" ) != null ? "yes":"no" );
66              statement.executeUpdate();
67              statement.close();
68              output.print( "<H2>Thank you " + firstName +
69                              " for registering.</H2>" );
70          }
71          catch ( Exception e ) {
72              System.err.println(
73                  "ERROR: Problems with adding new entry" );
74              e.printStackTrace();
75              output.print( "<H2>An error occurred. " +
76                              "Please try again later.</H2>" );
77          }
78          finally {
79              output.close();
80          }
81      }
82
83      public void destroy()
84      {
85          try {
86              connection.close();
87          }
88          catch( Exception e ) {
89              System.err.println( "Problem closing the database" );
90          }
91      }
92  }
```

Fig. 27.32 GuestBookServlet, which allows client to register for mailing lists (part 2 of 2).

In this example, the servlet's **init** method performs the connection to the Microsoft Access database. The method loads the **JdbcOdbcDriver** at line 20 with

```
Class.forName( "sun.jdbc.odbc.JdbcOdbcDriver" );
```

Lines 21 and 22

```
connection =
    DriverManager.getConnection( URL, "", "" );
```

attempt to open a connection to the **Guests** database. The string **jdbc:odbc:Guests** stored in **URL** specifies the database *URL (Uniform Resource Locator)* that helps the program locate the database (possibly on a network or in the local file system of the computer). The URL specifies the *protocol* for communication (***jdbc***), the *subprotocol* for communication (***odbc***) and the name of the database (**Guests**). The subprotocol **odbc** indicates that the program will be using **jdbc** to connect to a *Microsoft ODBC data source* (see appendix H for information on setting up an ODBC data source). ODBC is a technology developed by Microsoft to allow generic access to disparate database systems on the Windows platform (and some UNIX platforms). The Java 2 Software Development Kit (J2SDK) comes with the *JDBC-to-ODBC-bridge database driver* to allow any Java program to access any ODBC data source. The driver is defined by class ***JdbcOdbcDriver*** in package ***sun.jdbc.odbc***. The second and third arguments to **getConnection** represent the username and password (in this example the database does not have a username and password).

Lines 23–25

```
statement = connection.prepareStatement(
    "INSERT INTO Guests values ( " +
        "?, ?, ?, ?, ?, ?, ?, ? );" );
```

create a **PreparedStatement** that will be used to insert a record into the database. The question mark characters in the string represent the placeholders for values that will be inserted. These values are specified with **PreparedStatement** *set* method calls before executing the insert operation. The eight placeholders in this example represent the user's email address, first name, last name, company and the four mailing lists the user would like to register to receive.

When a **post** request is received from the HTML document in Fig. 27.33, method **doPost** (line 33) responds by reading the HTML form field values from the **post** request, setting the parameters for the **INSERT INTO** operation on the database (lines 54–65) and executing the insert operation (line 66). Line 67 closes the **statement** to ensure that the insert operation is committed to the database

The **if** structure at lines 44–50 determines if the email, first name or last name parameters are empty **String**s. If so, the servlet response asks the user to return to the HTML form and enter those fields.

Line 83 defines method **destroy** to ensure that the database connection is closed before the servlet terminates.

Figure 27.33 defines the HTML document that presents the guest book form to the user and **POST**s the information to the servlet of Fig. 27.32.

```
1   <!-- Fig. 27.33: GuestBookForm.html -->
2   <html>
3   <head><title>Deitel Guest Book Form</title></head>
```

Fig. 27.33 HTML that invokes the **GuestBookServlet** (part 1 of 3).

```
4
5   <body>
6      <h1>Guest Book</h1>
7      <form action = http://localhost:8080/servlet/GuestBookServlet
8            method = "post"><pre>
9         * Email address: <input type = "text" name = "Email">
10        * First Name:    <input type = "text" name = "FirstName">
11        * Last name:     <input type = "text" name = "LastName">
12        Company:         <input type = "text" name = "Company">
13                         * fields are required</pre>
14        <p>Select mailing lists from which you want
15        to receive information<br>
16        <input type = "checkbox" name = "c_cpp" name = "c_cpp">
17           C++ How to Program & C How to Program<br>
18        <input type = "checkbox" name = "java" name = "java">
19           Java How to Program<br>
20        <input type = "checkbox" name = "vb" name = "vb">
21           Visual Basic How to Program<br>
22        <input type = "checkbox" name = "iwww" name = "iwww">
23           Internet and World Wide Web How to Program<br>
24        </p>
25        <input type = "submit" value = "Submit">
26     </form>
27  </body>
28  </html>
```

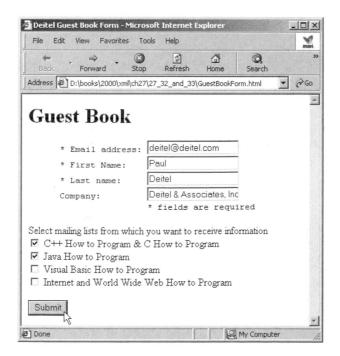

Fig. 27.33 HTML that invokes the **GuestBookServlet** (part 2 of 3).

Fig. 27.33 HTML that invokes the **GuestBookServlet** (part 3 of 3).

Lines 9–11 specify that the form's **action** is to **post** information to the **Guest-BookServlet**. The screen captures show the form filled with one set of information (the first screen) and the confirmation Web page that was sent back to the client as the response to the **post** request.

27.14 Internet and World Wide Web Resources

There is a bounty of Java information on the World Wide Web. Many people are experimenting with Java and sharing their thoughts, discoveries, ideas and source code with each other via the Internet.

General Resources

java.sun.com
The *Sun Microsystems, Inc. Java Web site* is an essential stop when searching the web for Java information. Go to this site to download the Java 2 Software Development Kit. This site is also a complete resource with news, information, on-line support, code samples and more.

developer.earthweb.com
Visit EarthWeb's *Developer.com* Web site for a wide variety of information on Java and Internet-related topics. The Java directory page contains links to thousands of Java applets and other Java resources.

www.jars.com
JARS—originally called the *Java Applet Rating Service* calls itself the "#1 Java Review Service." This site originally was a large Java repository for applets. Its benefit was that it rated every applet registered at the site as top 1%, top 5% and top 25%, so you could immediately view the best applets on the Web. Early in the development of the Java language, having your applet rated here was a great way to demonstrate your Java programming abilities. JARS is now another all-around resource for Java programmers. Many of the resources for this site and Developer.com, are now shared as these sites are both owned by EarthWeb.

developer.java.sun.com/developer/
On the Sun Microsystems Java Web site, visit the *Java Developer Connection*. This free site has close to one million members. The site includes technical support, discussion forums, on-line training courses, technical articles, resources, announcements of new Java features, early access to new Java technologies, and links to other important Java Web sites. Even though the site is free, you must register to use it.

www.jguru.com

The *jGuru* Web site is an all around Java resource for Java professionals. The site also contains FAQs on most Java topics.

www.java-zone.com/

The Development Exchange Java Zone site includes Java discussion groups, and "ask the Java Pro" section and some recent Java news.

dir.yahoo.com/Computers_and_Internet/Programming_Languages/Java/

Yahoo, a popular World Wide Web search engine, provides a complete Java resource. You can initiate a search using key words or explore the categories listed at the site including games, contests, events, tutorials and documentation, mailing lists, security and more.

www.ibm.com/developer/java/

The *IBM Developers Java Technology Zone* site lists the latest news, tools, code, case studies and events related to IBM and Java.

FAQs

java.sun.com/products/jdbc/faq.html

This is the *Sun JDBC FAQ*.

www.nikos.com/javatoys/

The *Java Toys* web site includes links to the latest Java news, Java User Groups (JUGs), FAQs, tools, Java-related mailing lists, books and white papers.

www.java-zone.com/

The *Development Exchange Java Zone* site includes Java discussion groups, and "ask the Java Pro" section and some recent Java news.

www.sunsite.unc.edu/javafaq

This site provides the latest Java news. It also has some helpful Java resources including the following: the Java FAQ List, a tutorial called Brewing Java, Java User Groups, Java Links, the Java Book List, Java Trade Shows, Java Training and Exercises.

Tutorial

java.sun.com/docs/books/tutorial/

The *Java Tutorial Site* has a number of tutorials, including sections on JavaBeans, JDBC, RMI, Servlets, Collections and Java Native Interface.

Magazines

www.javaworld.com

The *JavaWorld* on-line magazine is an excellent resource for current Java information. You will find news clips, conference information and links to Java-related web sites.

www.sys-con.com/java/

Catch up with the latest Java news at the *Java Developer's Journal* site. This magazine is one of the premier resources for Java news.

www.javareport.com/

The *Java Report* is a great resource for Java Developers. You will find the latest industry news, sample code, event listings, products and jobs.

www.Sun.COM/sunworldonline/

SunWorld is the on-line magazine "for the Sun community." You will find some news and information related to Java.

www.intelligence.com/java/default.asp
Intelligence.com is a great resource for Java news and information. You will find a collection of the latest articles, book reviews, interviews and case studies from various trade publications.

Servlets and Server-Side Java Programming

java.sun.com/products/servlet/index.html
The servlet page at the Sun Microsystems, Inc. Java Web site provides access to the latest servlet information, servlet resources and the Java Servlet Development Kit (JSDK).

theserverside.com/home/index.jsp
This Web site is an excellent resource for anyone doing server-side Java development and development with the Java 2 Enterprise Edition.

www.servlets.com
This is the Web site for the book *Java Servlet Programming* published by O'Reilly. The book provides a variety of resources. This book is an excellent resource for programmers who are learning servlets.

www.servletcentral.com
Servlet Central is an online magazine for server-side Java programmers. This includes technical articles and columns, news and "Ask the Experts." Resources include: books, servlet documentation links on the Web, a servlet archive, a list of servlet-enabled applications and servers and servlet development tools.

www.servletsource.com
ServletSource.com is a general servlet resource site containing code, tips, tutorials and links to many other Web sites with information on servlets.

www.cookiecentral.com
A good all-around resource site for cookies.

www.purpletech.com/java/servlet-faq/
The *Purple Servlet FAQ* is a great resource with dozens of links to tutorials, other servlet FAQs, mailing lists and newsgroups, articles, web servers, whitepapers and Java e-mail resources.

www.servletforum.com/
Servletforum.com is an on-line newsgroup dedicated to Java Servlets. Post your own questions or check out the archived list of previously asked questions.

www.enhydra.org/
Enhydra is an open source Java/XML application server and development environment available for free download.

www.locomotive.org/locolink/disp?home
The *Locomotive Project* is an open source, servlet-compatible, web application server available for free download.

www.servlet.com/srvpages/srvdev.html
The *Servlet, Inc. Servlet Developer's Forum* has links to numerous web resources, examples, products that use servlets and server-enabled web servers.

Newsgroups

news:comp.lamg.java

news:comp.lang.java.advocacy

news:comp.lang.java.announce

news:comp.lang.java.databases

```
news:comp.lang.java.gui
news:comp.lang.java.help
news:comp.lang.java.programmer
```

SUMMARY

- Java provides procedural, object-based and object-oriented programming capabilities. The object-based programming paradigm (with classes, encapsulation and objects) and the object-oriented programming paradigm (with inheritance and polymorphism) are crucial for developing elegant, robust and maintainable software systems.

- Keywords (or reserved words) are reserved for use by Java and are always spelled with all lower-case letters. These keywords should not be used as identifiers in Java programs.

- Java's eight primitive data types are the fundamental building blocks of all types in Java.

- Java allows only primitive type promotions, not type demotions.

- Java programmers rely on class libraries to build programs rapidly and reliably. Java's preexisting libraries are organized into packages of related reusable types known as classes and interfaces.

- A line that begins with **//** indicates that the remainder of the line is a comment. A comment that begins with **//** is called a single-line comment because the comment terminates at the end of the current line. Java also supports multiple-line comment (delimited with **/*** and ***/**). A similar form of comment called a documentation comment is delimited with **/**** and ***/**.

- Every program in Java consists of at least one class definition that is defined by you—the programmer. These classes are known as programmer-defined classes or user-defined classes.

- The **class** keyword introduces a class definition in Java and is immediately followed by the class name. By convention, all class names in Java begin with a capital first letter and have a capital first letter for every word in the class name.

- The name of the class is called an identifier. An identifier is a series of characters consisting of letters, digits, underscores (**_**) and dollar signs (**$**) that does not begin with a digit and does not contain any spaces.

- Java is case sensitive—uppercase and lowercase letters are different.

- Most classes we define begin with the **public** keyword to indicate that the class is potentially a reusable class. When you save a **public** class definition in a file, the class name must be used as the base part of the file name.

- A left brace, **{**, begins the body of every class definition. A corresponding right brace, **}**, must end each class definition.

- Java applications automatically begin executing at **main**.

- Java class definitions normally contain one or more methods. For a Java application class, exactly one of those methods must be called **main**.

- The **void** keyword indicates that a method will perform a task, but will not return any information when it completes its task.

- Class methods (**static** methods) are special in that they are available to be called as soon as the class to which they belong is loaded into memory at execution time.

- A left brace, **{**, begins the body of a method definition. A corresponding right brace, **}**, must end the method definition's body.

- **System.out** is known as the standard output object. **System.out** allows Java applications to display strings and other types of information in the command window from which the Java application is executed.

- Method **System.out.println** displays (or prints) a line of text in the command window. When **System.out.println** completes its task, it automatically positions the output cursor to the beginning of the next line in the command window.

- Use the **javac** command to compile a program. The **javac** command translates Java source code into Java bytecodes.

- Bytecodes are interpreted by the **java** interpreter. The interpreter calls method **main** to begin program execution.

- Most Java applications that display output use windows or dialog boxes. Dialog boxes are windows that typically are used to display important messages to the user of an application.

- Class **JOptionPane** allows you to display a dialog box containing information.

- One of the great strengths of Java is its rich set of predefined classes that programmers can reuse rather than "reinventing the wheel." Java's many predefined classes are grouped into categories of related classes called packages. The packages are referred to collectively as the Java class library or the Java applications programming interface (Java API).

- The compiler uses **import** statements to identify and load classes required to compile a program.

- GUI components facilitate data entry by the user of your program and formatting or presenting data outputs to the user of your program.

- Method **JOptionPane.showMessageDialog** is a special method of the class **JOptionPane** called a **static** method. Such methods are always called using their class name followed by a dot operator (**.**) and the method name.

- The **static** method **exit** of class **System** terminates an application. This line is required in any application that displays a graphical user interface to terminate the application.

- Class **System** is part of the package **java.lang**. Package **java.lang** is imported automatically in every Java program.

- All variables must be declared with a name and a data type before they can be used in a program.

- There are two types of variables in Java—primitive data type variables (normally called variables) and reference variables (normally called references). References are used to refer to objects in the program. Such references actually contain the location in the computer's memory of an object.

- Method **JOptionPane.showInputDialog** displays an input dialog.

- **Integer.parseInt** (a **static** method of class **Integer**) converts its **String** argument to an integer. Class **Integer** is part of the package **java.lang**.

- Java has a version of the **+** operator for string concatenation that enables a string and a value of any other data type to be concatenated—the result of this operation is a new string.

- An array is a group of contiguous memory locations that all have the same name and the same type. To refer to a particular location or element in the array, we specify the name of the array and the position number of the particular element in the array.

- The position number in square brackets is more formally called a subscript (or an index). A subscript must be an integer or an integer expression.

- The **+=** operator adds the value of the expression on the right of the operator to the value of the variable on the left of the operator and stores the result in the variable on the left of the operator. Any arithmetic statement of the form

    variable **=** *variable operator expression***;**

where operator is one of the binary operators **+**, **-**, *****, **/** or **%**, can be written in the form

    *variable operator***=** *expression***;**

- Every array in Java knows its own length via its **length** instance variable.

- Arrays occupy space in memory. The programmer specifies the type of the elements and uses operator **new** to allocate the number of elements required by each array. Arrays are allocated with **new** because arrays are considered to be objects and all objects must be created with **new**.

- When arrays are allocated, the elements are automatically initialized to zero for the numeric primitive-data-type variables, to **false** for **boolean** variables or to **null** for references (any non-primitive type).

- The **for** repetition structure is frequently used to perform counter-controlled repetition.

- A **JTextArea** is a GUI component that is capable of displaying many rows and columns of text.

- **JTextArea** method **setText** specifies the **String** the **JTextArea** will display.

- Class **Vector** is a dynamically resizable array-like data structure.

- Class **Object** is the fundamental data type on which all other classes in Java are based. A reference of type **Object** is special in that it can refer to any type of object in Java.

- **Vector** method **size** returns the size of the **Vector**.

- Class **StringTokenizer** breaks a string into its component tokens. Tokens are separated from one another by delimiters, typically white-space characters.

- Every Java program is based on at least one class definition that extends and enhances an existing class definition via inheritance.

- A class (the subclass) can inherit existing attributes and behaviors (data and methods) from another class (the superclass) specified to the right of keyword **extends** in the class definition.

- Using inheritance results in a new class definition that has the attributes (data) and behaviors (methods) of the superclass.

- Classes are used as "templates" or "blueprints" to instantiate objects for use in a program. An object (or instance) resides in the computer's memory and contains information used by the program.

- The term object normally implies that attributes and behaviors are associated with the object. The object's methods use the attributes to provide useful services to the client of the object.

- In addition to extending one class, a class can implement one or more interfaces. An interface specifies one or more behaviors (i.e., methods) that you must define in your class definition.

- When a user interacts with a GUI component and the program responds, this process is called event handling. The event is the user interaction (pressing the button). An event handler is called automatically in response to the event.

- Every instance (object) of a class contains one copy of each of its instance variables. An important benefit of instance variables is that their identifiers can be used throughout the class definition.

- Variables defined in the body of a method are known as local variables and can be used only in the body of the method in which they are defined.

- Instance variables are always assigned a default value and local variables are not.

- The constructor method of a class is called automatically when an object (instance) of the class is created with operator **new**.

- **Container** method **getContentPane** returns a reference to the window's content pane—the object to which we must attach the GUI components so they appear properly in the user interface.

- **Container** method **setLayout** sets the layout manager for a window's user interface. Layout managers are provided to arrange GUI components on a **Container** for presentation purposes.

- The layout managers determine the position and size of every GUI component attached to the container. This enables the programmer to concentrate on the basic "look and feel" and lets the layout managers process most of the layout details.

- Each **Container** can have only one layout manager at a time.

- In event-driven programming, the user interacts with a GUI component, the program is notified of the event and the program processes the event. The user's interaction "drives" the program.

- The methods that are called when an event occurs are also known as event handling methods. When a GUI event occurs in a program, Java creates an object containing information about the event that occurred and automatically calls an appropriate event handling method.

- Before any event can be processed, each GUI component must know which object in the program defines the event handling method that will be called when an event occurs. The is accomplished by registering the event handler.

- **JFrame** method **setDefaultCloseOperation** specifies the default action to take when a window is closed.

- Java provides a facility called inner classes in which classes can be defined inside other classes. Such classes can be complete class definitions or anonymous inner class definitions.

- Every class in Java is a subclass of **Object**. Therefore, every class inherits the 11 methods defined by class **Object**. One important **Object** method is **toString**.

- Keywords **public** and **private** are member access modifiers. Class members declared with member access modifier **public** are accessible to clients of the code. Class members declared with member access modifier **private** are accessible only to methods of the class.

- The **public** methods of a class are often called the class's **public** services or **public** interface. These methods are used by clients of the class to manipulate objects of the class.

- The method with the same name as the class is the constructor method of that class. A constructor is a special method that initializes the instance variables of a class object. A class's constructor method is called automatically when an object of that class is instantiated with operator **new**.

- Classes often provide **public** methods to allow clients of the class to set or get **private** instance variables. These methods need not be called set and get, but they often are. Get methods are also commonly called accessor methods or query methods. Set methods are also commonly called mutator methods (because they typically change a value).

- Creating a new version of an inherited method is known as method overriding.

- Because an anonymous inner class has no name, one object of the anonymous inner class must be created at the point where the class is defined in the program.

- An object of a class that implements **ActionListener** is an **ActionListener**.

- An inner class object has a special relationship with the outer class object that creates it. The inner class object is allowed to access directly all the members of the outer class object.

- For event handling interfaces with more than one method, Java provides a corresponding adapter class that implements all the methods in the interface for you. All you need to do is extend the adapter class and override the methods you require in your program.

- A **JComboBox** provides a list of items from which the user can make a selection. A numeric index keeps track of the ordering of items in the **JComboBox**. The first item is added at index 0; the next item is added at index 1, and so forth.

- A **JList** displays a series of items from which the user may select one or more items. Class **JList** supports single-selection lists and multiple-selection lists.

- **JList** method **setSelectionMode** specifies the selection mode for the list.

- Class **JList** does not automatically provide a scrollbar if there are more items in the list than the number of visible rows. A **JScrollPane** is used to provide scrolling capability for the **JList**.

- The **BorderLayout** layout manager (the default layout manager for the content pane) arranges components into five regions: North, South, East, West and Center.

- Up to five components can be added directly to a **BorderLayout**—one for each region.

- **GridLayout** divides the container into a grid so that components can be placed in rows and columns. Every **Component** in a **GridLayout** has the same width and height. Components are added to a **GridLayout** starting at the top-left cell of the grid and proceeding left-to-right until the row is full. Then the process continues left-to-right on the next row of the grid, etc.

- Panels are created with class **JPanel**—a subclass of **JComponent**. Class **JComponent** inherits from class **java.awt.Container**, so every **JPanel** is a **Container**. Thus **JPanel**s may have components, including other panels, added to them.

- A **JPanel** can be used as a dedicated drawing area that can receive mouse events and is often extended to create new components.

- Swing components that inherit from class **JComponent** contain method **paintComponent** that helps them draw properly in the context of a Swing GUI.

- Java is unique among popular general-purpose programming languages in that it makes concurrency primitives available to the applications programmer. The programmer specifies that applications contain threads of execution, each thread designating a portion of a program that may execute concurrently with other threads. This capability is called multithreading.

- The highest-priority ready thread enters the running state when the system assigns a processor to the thread. A thread enters the dead state when its **run** method completes or terminates for any reason a dead thread will eventually be disposed of by the system.

- A sleeping thread becomes ready after the designated sleep time expires. A sleeping thread cannot use a processor even if one is available.

- Every Java application is multithreaded.

- When a thread's **start** method is invoked, the thread enters the ready state.

- When the system assigns a processor to a thread for the first time, the thread enters the running state and its **run** method begins execution.

- Java's stream sockets enable a process to establish a connection to another process. While the connection is in place, data flows between the processes in continuous streams. Stream sockets are said to provide a connection-oriented service. The protocol used for transmission is the popular TCP (Transmission Control Protocol).

- The request-response model of communication is the foundation for the highest-level view of networking in Java—servlets. A servlet extends the functionality of a server.

- The **javax.servlet** package and the **javax.servlet.http** package provide the classes and interfaces to define servlets.

- A common implementation of the request-response model is between World Wide Web browsers and World Wide Web servers. When a user selects a Web site to browse through their browser (the client application), a request is sent to the appropriate Web server (the server application). The server normally responds to the client by sending the appropriate HTML Web page.

- All servlets must implement the **Servlet** interface. The methods of interface **Servlet** are invoked automatically (by the server on which the servlet is installed).

- An **HttpServlet** defines enhanced processing capabilities for servlets that extend the functionality of a Web server.

- Class **HttpServlet** overrides method **service** to distinguish between the typical requests received from a client Web browser. The two most common HTTP request types (also known as request methods) are **get** and **post**.

- Class **HttpServlet** defines methods **doGet** and **doPost** to respond to **get** and **post** requests from a client, respectively.

- Servlets can communicate with databases via JDBC (Java Database Connectivity). JDBC provides a uniform way for a Java program to connect with a variety of databases in a general manner without having to deal with the specifics of those database systems.

- To connect to a database, you must first load the database driver, then connect to the database with class **DriverManager**'s **getConnection** method.

- The URL to connect to a database specifies the protocol for communication, the subprotocol for communication and the name of the database.

- The subprotocol **odbc** indicates that the program will be using **jdbc** to connect to a Microsoft ODBC data source. ODBC is a technology developed by Microsoft to allow generic access to disparate database systems on the Windows platform (and some UNIX platforms).

- A **PreparedStatement** creates an SQL statement that will be executed at a later time. The parameters to the **PreparedStatement** are specified with set method calls before executing the **PreparedStatement**.

TERMINOLOGY

accessor method
ActionListener
ActionListener interface
actionPerformed method
adapter class
addActionListener
addElement method of class **Vector**
addListSelectionListener
addWindowListener
anonymous inner class,
array bounds
array declaration
arrays as objects
assignment statement
associativity of operators
attributes (data)
automatic garbage collection
base class
binding the server to the port
body of the method definition
BorderLayout layout manager
bytecodes
case sensitive
checked exception
class definition
.class file
class keyword
class name
class **Object**
class **System**
classes defined inside other classes
client/server
command window
comment (**//**)

compile a program
concatenation
connect to a server
consistent state
Container
content pane
control variable
convert numbers from **String** to **int**
converting between classes and built-in types
database
DecimalFormat class
dedicated drawing area
derived class
dialog box
event-driven programming
event handling
extends keyword
fillOval method of **Graphics**
fillRect method of **Graphics**
FlowLayout class
format
garbage collector
get method
getContentPane method of **JFrame**
graphical user interface (GUI)
GridLayout class
GUI component
GUI event-handling mechanism
HTTP request
HttpServlet class
HttpServletRequest interface
HyperText Transfer Protocol (HTTP)
identifier
implements keyword

HTML Special
Characters

The table of A.1 shows many commonly used HTML special characters—called *character entity references* by the World Wide Web Consortium. For a complete list of character entity references, see the site

http://www.w3.org/TR/REC-html40/sgml/entities.html

Character	HTML encoding	Character	HTML encoding
non-breaking space		ê	&#234;
§	&#167;	ì	&#236;
©	&#169;	í	&#237;
®	&#174;	î	&#238;
π	&#188;	ñ	&#241;
∫	&#189;	ò	&#242;
Ω	&#190;	ó	&#243;
à	&#224;	ô	&#244;
á	&#225;	õ	&#245;
â	&#226;	÷	&#247;
ã	&#227;	ù	&#249;
å	&#229;	ú	&#250;
ç	&#231;	û	&#251;
è	&#232;	•	&#8226;
é	&#233;	™	&#8482;

Fig. A.1 HTML special characters.

HTML Colors

Colors may be specified by using a standard name (such as **aqua**) or a hexadecimal RGB value (such as **#00FFFF** for aqua). Of the six hexadecimal digits in an RGB value, the first two represent the amount of red in the color, the middle two represent the amount of green in the color, and the last two represent the amount of blue in the color. For example, **black** is the absence of color and is defined by **#000000**, whereas **white** is the maximum amount of red, green and blue and is defined by **#FFFFFF**. Pure **red** is **#FF0000**, pure green (which the standard calls **lime**) is **#00FF00** and pure **blue** is **#00FFFF**. Note that **green** in the standard is defined as **#008000**. Figure B.1 contains the HTML standard color set. Figure B.2 contains the HTML extended color set.

Color name	Value	Color name	Value
aqua	#00FFFF	navy	#000080
black	#000000	olive	#808000
blue	#0000FF	purple	#800080
fuchsia	#FF00FF	red	#FF0000
gray	#808080	silver	#C0C0C0
green	#008000	teal	#008080
lime	#00FF00	yellow	#FFFF00
maroon	#800000	white	#FFFFFF

Fig. B.1 HTML standard colors and hexadecimal RGB values.

Color name	Value	Color name	Value
aliceblue	#F0F8FF	dodgerblue	#1E90FF
antiquewhite	#FAEBD7	firebrick	#B22222
aquamarine	#7FFFD4	floralwhite	#FFFAF0
azure	#F0FFFF	forestgreen	#228B22
beige	#F5F5DC	gainsboro	#DCDCDC
bisque	#FFE4C4	ghostwhite	#F8F8FF
blanchedalmond	#FFEBCD	gold	#FFD700
blueviolet	#8A2BE2	goldenrod	#DAA520
brown	#A52A2A	greenyellow	#ADFF2F
burlywood	#DEB887	honeydew	#F0FFF0
cadetblue	#5F9EA0	hotpink	#FF69B4
chartreuse	#7FFF00	indianred	#CD5C5C
chocolate	#D2691E	indigo	#4B0082
coral	#FF7F50	ivory	#FFFFF0
cornflowerblue	#6495ED	khaki	#F0E68C
cornsilk	#FFF8DC	lavender	#E6E6FA
crimson	#DC1436	lavenderblush	#FFF0F5
cyan	#00FFFF	lawngreen	#7CFC00
darkblue	#00008B	lemonchiffon	#FFFACD
darkcyan	#008B8B	lightblue	#ADD8E6
darkgoldenrod	#B8860B	lightcoral	#F08080
darkgray	#A9A9A9	lightcyan	#E0FFFF
darkgreen	#006400	lightgoldenrodyellow	#FAFAD2
darkkhaki	#BDB76B	lightgreen	#90EE90
darkmagenta	#8B008B	lightgrey	#D3D3D3
darkolivegreen	#556B2F	lightpink	#FFB6C1
darkorange	#FF8C00	lightsalmon	#FFA07A
darkorchid	#9932CC	lightseagreen	#20B2AA
darkred	#8B0000	lightskyblue	#87CEFA
darksalmon	#E9967A	lightslategray	#778899
darkseagreen	#8FBC8F	lightsteelblue	#B0C4DE
darkslateblue	#483D8B	lightyellow	#FFFFE0
darkslategray	#2F4F4F	limegreen	#32CD32
darkturquoise	#00CED1	linen	#FAF0E6
darkviolet	#9400D3	magenta	#FF00FF

Fig. B.2   HTML extended colors and hexadecimal RGB values (part 1 of 2).

Color name	Value	Color name	Value
deeppink	#FF1493	mediumaquamarine	#66CDAA
deepskyblue	#00BFFF	mediumblue	#0000CD
dimgray	#696969	mediumorchid	#BA55D3
mediumpurple	#9370DB	plum	#DDA0DD
mediumseagreen	#3CB371	powderblue	#B0E0E6
mediumslateblue	#7B68EE	rosybrown	#BC8F8F
mediumspringgreen	#00FA9A	royalblue	#4169E1
mediumturquoise	#48D1CC	saddlebrown	#8B4513
mediumvioletred	#C71585	salmon	#FA8072
midnightblue	#191970	sandybrown	#F4A460
mintcream	#F5FFFA	seagreen	#2E8B57
mistyrose	#FFE4E1	seashell	#FFF5EE
moccasin	#FFE4B5	sienna	#A0522D
navajowhite	#FFDEAD	skyblue	#87CEEB
oldlace	#FDF5E6	slateblue	#6A5ACD
olivedrab	#6B8E23	slategray	#708090
orange	#FFA500	snow	#FFFAFA
orangered	#FF4500	springgreen	#00FF7F
orchid	#DA70D6	steelblue	#4682B4
palegoldenrod	#EEE8AA	tan	#D2B48C
palegreen	#98FB98	thistle	#D8BFD8
paleturquoise	#AFEEEE	tomato	#FF6347
palevioletred	#DB7093	turquoise	#40E0D0
papayawhip	#FFEFD5	violet	#EE82EE
peachpuff	#FFDAB9	wheat	#F5DEB3
peru	#CD853F	whitesmoke	#F5F5F5
pink	#FFC0CB	yellowgreen	#9ACD32

Fig. B.2   HTML extended colors and hexadecimal RGB values (part 2 of 2).

ASCII Character Set

ASCII character set									
	0	**1**	**2**	**3**	**4**	**5**	**6**	**7**	**8**	**9**
0	nul	soh	stx	etx	eot	enq	ack	bel	bs	ht
1	nl	vt	ff	cr	so	si	dle	dc1	dc2	dc3
2	dc4	nak	syn	etb	can	em	sub	esc	fs	gs
3	rs	us	sp	!	"	#	$	%	&	`
4	(	)	*	+	,	-	.	/	0	1
5	2	3	4	5	6	7	8	9	:	;
6	<	=	>	?	@	A	B	C	D	E
7	F	G	H	I	J	K	L	M	N	O
8	P	Q	R	S	T	U	V	W	X	Y
9	Z	[	\	]	^	_	'	a	b	c
10	d	e	f	g	h	i	j	k	l	m
11	n	o	p	q	r	s	t	u	v	w
12	x	y	z	{	|	}	~	del		

Fig. C.1   ASCII Character Set.

The digits at the left of the table are the left digits of the decimal equivalent (0-127) of the character code, and the digits at the top of the table are the right digits of the character code. For example, the character code for "**F**" is 70, and the character code for "**&**" is 38. *Note:* Most users of this book are interested in the ASCII character set used to represent English characters on many computers. The ASCII character set is a subset of the Unicode character set used by XML to represent characters from most of the world's languages. For more information on the Unicode character set, visit the World Wide Web site **unicode.org**.

Operator Precedence Charts

This appendix contains the operator precedence charts for JavaScript/JScript/ECMAScript (Fig. D.1), VBScript (Fig. D.2), Perl (Fig. D.3) and Java (Fig. D.4). In each figure, the operators are shown in decreasing order of precedence from top to bottom.

Operator	Type	Associativity
.	member access	left to right
[]	array indexing	
()	function calls	
++	increment	right to left
--	decrement	
-	unary minus	
~	bitwise complement	
!	logical NOT	
delete	delete an array element or object property	
new	create a new object	
typeof	returns the data type of its argument	
void	prevents an expression from returning a value	
*	multiplication	left to right
/	division	
%	modulus	
+	addition	left to right
-	subtraction	
+	string concatenation	

Fig. D.1 JavaScript/JScript/ECMAScript operator precedence and associativity (part 1 of 2).

Operator	Type	Associativity

`<<`
`>>`
`>>>`
	left shift
	right shift with sign extension
	right shift with zero extension
		left to right

`<`
`<=`
`>`
`>=`
`instanceof`
	less than
	less than or equal
	greater than
	greater than or equal
	type comparison
		left to right

`==`
`!=`
`===`
`!==`
	equality
	inequality
	identity
	nonidentity
		left to right

`&`	bitwise AND	left to right
`^`	bitwise XOR	left to right
`|`	bitwise OR	left to right
`&&`	logical AND	left to right
`||`	logical OR	left to right
`?:`	conditional	left to right

`=`
`+=`
`-=`
`*=`
`/=`
`%=`
`&=`
`^=`
`|=`
`<<=`
`>>=`
`>>>=`
	assignment
	addition assignment
	subtraction assignment
	multiplication assignment
	division assignment
	modulus assignment
	bitwise AND assignment
	bitwise exclusive OR assignment
	bitwise inclusive OR assignment
	bitwise left shift assignment
	bitwise right shift with sign extension assignment
	bitwise right shift with zero extension assignment
		right to left

Fig. D.1   JavaScript/JScript/ECMAScript operator precedence and associativity (part 2 of 2).

Operator	Type	Associativity
( )	parentheses	left to right
^	exponentiation	left to right
–	unary minus	left to right
* / \	multiplication division integer division	left to right
Mod	modulus	left to right
+ –	addition subtraction	left to right
&	string concatenation	left to right
= <> < <= > >= Is	equality inequality less than less than or equal greater than greater than or equal object equivalence	left to right
Not	logical NOT	left to right
And	logical AND	left to right
Or	logical OR	left to right
Xor	logical exclusive OR	left to right
Eqv	logical equivalence	left to right
Imp	logical implication	left to right

Fig. D.2   VBScript operator precedence chart.

Operator	Type	Associativity
terms and list operators	**print @array** or **sort (4, 2, 7)**	left to right
->	member access	left to right
++ --	increment decrement	none
**	exponentiation	right to left
! ~ \ + -	logical NOT bitwise one's complement reference unary plus unary minus	right to left
=~ !~	matching negated match	left to right
* / % x	multiplication division modulus repetition	left to right
+ - .	addition subtraction string concatenation	left to right
<< >>	left shift right shift	left to right
named unary operators	unary operators, e.g. -e (filetest)	none
< > <= >= lt gt le ge	numerical less than numerical greater than numerical less than or equal numerical greater than or equal string less than string greater than string less than or equal string greater than or equal	none
== != <=> eq ne cmp	numerical equality numerical inequality numerical comparison (returns -1, 0 or 1) string equality string inequality string comparison (returns -1, 0 or 1)	none
&	bitwise AND	left to right

Fig. D.3   Perl operator precedence chart (part 1 of 2).

Operator	Type	Associativity
| ^	bitwise inclusive OR bitwise exclusive OR	left to right
&&	logical AND	left to right
||	logical OR	left to right
..	range operator	none
?:	conditional operator	right to left
= += -= *= /= %= **= .= x= &= |= ^= <<= >>= &&= ||=	assignment addition assignment subtraction assignment multiplication assignment division assignment modulus assignment exponentiation assignment string concatenation assignment repetition assignment bitwise AND assignment bitwise inclusive OR assignment bitwise exclusive OR assignment left shift assignment right shift assignment logical AND assignment logical OR assignment	right to left
, =>	expression separator; returns value of last expression expression separator; groups two expressions	left to right
not	logical NOT	right to left
and	logical AND	left to right
or xor	logical OR logical exclusive OR	left to right

Fig. D.3   Perl operator precedence chart (part 2 of 2).

Operator	Type	Associativity
( )	parentheses	left to right
[ ]	array subscript	
.	member selection	
++	unary postincrement	right to left
--	unary postdecrement	
++	unary preincrement	right to left
--	unary predecrement	
+	unary plus	
-	unary minus	
!	unary logical negation	
~	unary bitwise complement	
(*type*)	unary cast	
*	multiplication	left to right
/	division	
%	modulus	
+	addition	left to right
-	subtraction	
<<	bitwise left shift	left to right
>>	bitwise right shift with sign extension	
>>>	bitwise right shift with zero extension	
<	relational less than	left to right
<=	relational less than or equal to	
>	relational greater than	
>=	relational greater than or equal to	
instanceof	type comparison	
==	relational is equal to	left to right
!=	relational is not equal to	
&	bitwise AND	left to right
^	bitwise exclusive OR	left to right
	boolean logical exclusive OR	
|	bitwise inclusive OR	left to right
	boolean logical inclusive OR	
&&	logical AND	left to right
||	logical OR	left to right
?:	ternary conditional	right to left

Fig. D.4   Java operator precedence chart (part 1 of 2).

Operator	Type	Associativity
=	assignment	right to left
+=	addition assignment	
-=	subtraction assignment	
*=	multiplication assignment	
/=	division assignment	
%=	modulus assignment	
&=	bitwise AND assignment	
^=	bitwise exclusive OR assignment	
|=	bitwise inclusive OR assignment	
<<=	bitwise left shift assignment	
>>=	bitwise right shift with sign extension assignment	
>>>=	bitwise right shift with zero extension assignment	

Fig. D.4   Java operator precedence chart (part 2 of 2).

Number Systems

Objectives

- To understand basic number systems concepts such as base, positional value, and symbol value.
- To understand how to work with numbers represented in the binary, octal, and hexadecimal number systems
- To be able to abbreviate binary numbers as octal numbers or hexadecimal numbers.
- To be able to convert octal numbers and hexadecimal numbers to binary numbers.
- To be able to covert back and forth between decimal numbers and their binary, octal, and hexadecimal equivalents.
- To understand binary arithmetic, and how negative binary numbers are represented using two's complement notation.

Here are only numbers ratified.
William Shakespeare

Nature has some sort of arithmetic-geometrical coordinate system, because nature has all kinds of models. What we experience of nature is in models, and all of nature's models are so beautiful.
It struck me that nature's system must be a real beauty, because in chemistry we find that the associations are always in beautiful whole numbers—there are no fractions.
Richard Buckminster Fuller

Outline

E.1 Introduction

In this appendix, we introduce the key number systems that programmers use, especially when they are working on software projects that require close interaction with "machine-level" hardware. Projects like this include operating systems, computer networking software, compilers, database systems, and applications requiring high performance.

When we write an integer such as 227 or -63 in a program, the number is assumed to be in the *decimal (base 10) number system*. The *digits* in the decimal number system are 0, 1, 2, 3, 4, 5, 6, 7, 8, and 9. The lowest digit is 0 and the highest digit is 9—one less than the *base* of 10. Internally, computers use the *binary (base 2) number system*. The binary number system has only two digits, namely 0 and 1. Its lowest digit is 0 and its highest digit is 1—one less than the base of 2. Fig. E.1 summarizes the digits used in the binary, octal, decimal and hexadecimal number systems.

As we will see, binary numbers tend to be much longer than their decimal equivalents. Programmers who work in assembly languages and in high-level languages that enable programmers to reach down to the "machine level," find it cumbersome to work with binary numbers. So two other number systems the *octal number system (base 8)* and the *hexadecimal number system (base 16)*—are popular primarily because they make it convenient to abbreviate binary numbers.

In the octal number system, the digits range from 0 to 7. Because both the binary number system and the octal number system have fewer digits than the decimal number system, their digits are the same as the corresponding digits in decimal.

The hexadecimal number system poses a problem because it requires sixteen digits—a lowest digit of 0 and a highest digit with a value equivalent to decimal 15 (one less than the base of 16). By convention, we use the letters A through F to represent the hexadecimal digits corresponding to decimal values 10 through 15. Thus in hexadecimal we can have numbers like 876 consisting solely of decimal-like digits, numbers like 8A55F consisting of digits and letters, and numbers like FFE consisting solely of letters. Occasionally, a hexadecimal number spells a common word such as FACE or FEED—this can appear strange to programmers accustomed to working with numbers. Fig. E.2 summarizes each of the number systems.

Each of these number systems uses *positional notation*—each position in which a digit is written has a different *positional value*. For example, in the decimal number 937 (the 9, the 3, and the 7 are referred to as *symbol values*), we say that the 7 is written in the *ones position*, the 3 is written in the *tens position*, and the 9 is written in the *hundreds position*. Notice that each of these positions is a power of the base (base 10), and that these powers begin at 0 and increase by 1 as we move left in the number (Fig. E.3).

Binary digit	Octal digit	Decimal digit	Hexadecimal digit
0	0	0	0
1	1	1	1
	2	2	2
	3	3	3
	4	4	4
	5	5	5
	6	6	6
	7	7	7
		8	8
		9	9
			A (decimal value of 10)
			B (decimal value of 11)
			C (decimal value of 12)
			D (decimal value of 13)
			E (decimal value of 14)
			F (decimal value of 15)

Fig. E.1 Digits of the binary, octal, decimal and hexadecimal number systems.

Attribute	Binary	Octal	Decimal	Hexadecimal
Base	2	8	10	16
Lowest digit	0	0	0	0
Highest digit	1	7	9	F

Fig. E.2 Comparison of the binary, octal, decimal and hexadecimal number systems.

Positional values in the decimal number system			
Decimal digit	9	3	7
Position name	Hundreds	Tens	Ones
Positional value	100	10	1
Positional value as a power of the base (10)	10^2	10^1	10^0

Fig. E.3 Positional values in the decimal number system.

For longer decimal numbers, the next positions to the left would be the *thousands position* (10 to the 3rd power), the *ten-thousands position* (10 to the 4th power), the *hundred-thousands position* (10 to the 5th power), the *millions position* (10 to the 6th power), the *ten-millions position* (10 to the 7th power), and so on.

In the binary number 101, we say that the rightmost 1 is written in the *ones position* , the 0 is written in the *twos position* , and the leftmost 1 is written in the *fours position* . Notice that each of these positions is a power of the base (base 2), and that these powers begin at 0 and increase by 1 as we move left in the number (Fig. E.4).

For longer binary numbers, the next positions to the left would be the *eights position* (2 to the 3rd power), the *sixteens position* (2 to the 4th power), the *thirty-twos position* (2 to the 5th power), the *sixty-fours position* (2 to the 6th power), and so on.

In the octal number 425, we say that the 5 is written in the *ones position* , the 2 is written in the *eights position* , and the 4 is written in the *sixty-fours position* . Notice that each of these positions is a power of the base (base 8), and that these powers begin at 0 and increase by 1 as we move left in the number (Fig. E.5).

For longer octal numbers, the next positions to the left would be the *five-hundred-and-twelves position* (8 to the 3rd power), the *four-thousand-and-ninety-sixes position* (8 to the 4th power), the *thirty-two-thousand-seven-hundred-and-sixty eights position* (8 to the 5th power), and so on.

In the hexadecimal number 3DA, we say that the A is written in the *ones position* , the D is written in the *sixteens position* , and the 3 is written in the *two-hundred-and-fifty-sixes position* . Notice that each of these positions is a power of the base (base 16), and that these powers begin at 0 and increase by 1 as we move left in the number (Fig. E.6).

For longer hexadecimal numbers, the next positions to the left would be the *four-thousand-and-ninety-sixes position* (16 to the 3rd power), the *sixty-five-thousand-five-hundred-and-thirty-six position* (16 to the 4th power), and so on.

Positional values in the binary number system			
Binary digit	1	0	1
Position name	Fours	Twos	Ones
Positional value	4	2	1
Positional value as a power of the base (2)	2^2	2^1	2^0

Fig. E.4 Positional values in the binary number system.

Positional values in the octal number system			
Decimal digit	4	2	5
Position name	Sixty-fours	Eights	Ones
Positional value	64	8	1
Positional value as a power of the base (8)	8^2	8^1	8^0

Fig. E.5 Positional values in the octal number system.

Positional values in the hexadecimal number system			
Decimal digit	**3**	**D**	**A**
Position name	Two-hundred-and-fifty-sixes	Sixteens	Ones
Positional value	**256**	**16**	**1**
Positional value as a power of the base (16)	16^2	16^1	16^0

Fig. E.6 Positional values in the hexadecimal number system.

E.2 Abbreviating Binary Numbers as Octal Numbers and Hexadecimal Numbers

The main use for octal and hexadecimal numbers in computing is for abbreviating lengthy binary representations. Fig. E.7 highlights the fact that lengthy binary numbers can be expressed concisely in number systems with higher bases than the binary number system.

Decimal number	Binary representation	Octal representation	Hexadecimal representation
0	0	0	0
1	1	1	1
2	10	2	2
3	11	3	3
4	100	4	4
5	101	5	5
6	110	6	6
7	111	7	7
8	1000	10	8
9	1001	11	9
10	1010	12	A
11	1011	13	B
12	1100	14	C
13	1101	15	D
14	1110	16	E
15	1111	17	F
16	10000	20	10

Fig. E.7 Decimal, binary, octal, and hexadecimal equivalents.

A particularly important relationship that both the octal number system and the hexadecimal number system have to the binary system is that the bases of octal and hexadecimal (8 and 16 respectively) are powers of the base of the binary number system (base 2). Consider the following 12-digit binary number and its octal and hexadecimal equivalents. See if you can determine how this relationship makes it convenient to abbreviate binary numbers in octal or hexadecimal. The answer follows the numbers.

Binary Number	Octal equivalent	Hexadecimal equivalent
100011010001	**4321**	**8D1**

To see how the binary number converts easily to octal, simply break the 12-digit binary number into groups of three consecutive bits each, and write those groups over the corresponding digits of the octal number as follows

```
100     011     010     001
4       3       2       1
```

Notice that the octal digit you have written under each group of thee bits corresponds precisely to the octal equivalent of that 3-digit binary number as shown in Fig. E.7.

The same kind of relationship may be observed in converting numbers from binary to hexadecimal. In particular, break the 12-digit binary number into groups of four consecutive bits each and write those groups over the corresponding digits of the hexadecimal number as follows

```
1000    1101    0001
8       D       1
```

Notice that the hexadecimal digit you wrote under each group of four bits corresponds precisely to the hexadecimal equivalent of that 4-digit binary number as shown in Fig. E.7.

E.3 Converting Octal Numbers and Hexadecimal Numbers to Binary Numbers

In the previous section, we saw how to convert binary numbers to their octal and hexadecimal equivalents by forming groups of binary digits and simply rewriting these groups as their equivalent octal digit values or hexadecimal digit values. This process may be used in reverse to produce the binary equivalent of a given octal or hexadecimal number.

For example, the octal number 653 is converted to binary simply by writing the 6 as its 3-digit binary equivalent 110, the 5 as its 3-digit binary equivalent 101, and the 3 as its 3-digit binary equivalent 011 to form the 9-digit binary number 110101011.

The hexadecimal number FAD5 is converted to binary simply by writing the F as its 4-digit binary equivalent 1111, the A as its 4-digit binary equivalent 1010, the D as its 4-digit binary equivalent 1101, and the 5 as its 4-digit binary equivalent 0101 to form the 16-digit 1111101011010101.

E.4 Converting from Binary, Octal, or Hexadecimal to Decimal

Because we are accustomed to working in decimal, it is often convenient to convert a binary, octal, or hexadecimal number to decimal to get a sense of what the number is "really" worth. Our diagrams in Section D.1 express the positional values in decimal. To convert a number to decimal from another base, multiply the decimal equivalent of each digit by its positional value, and sum these products. For example, the binary number 110101 is converted to decimal 53 as shown in Fig. E.8.

To convert octal 7614 to decimal 3980, we use the same technique, this time using appropriate octal positional values as shown in Fig. E.9.

To convert hexadecimal AD3B to decimal 44347, we use the same technique, this time using appropriate hexadecimal positional values as shown in Fig. E.10.

Converting a binary number to decimal					
Positional values:	32	16	8	4	2	1
Symbol values:	1	1	0	1	0	1
Products:	1*32=32	1*16=16	0*8=0	1*4=4	0*2=0	1*1=1
Sum:	= 32 + 16 + 0 + 4 + 0 + 1 = 53					

Fig. E.8 Converting a binary number to decimal.

Converting an octal number to decimal				
Positional values:	512	64	8	1
Symbol values:	7	6	1	4
Products	7*512=3584	6*64=384	1*8=8	4*1=4
Sum:	= 3584 + 384 + 8 + 4 = 3980			

Fig. E.9 Converting an octal number to decimal.

Converting a hexadecimal number to decimal				
Positional values:	4096	256	16	1
Symbol values:	A	D	3	B
Products	A*4096=40960	D*256=3328	3*16=48	B*1=11
Sum:	= 40960 + 3328 + 48 + 11 = 44347			

Fig. E.10 Converting a hexadecimal number to decimal.

E.5 Converting from Decimal to Binary, Octal, or Hexadecimal

The conversions of the previous section follow naturally from the positional notation conventions. Converting from decimal to binary, octal, or hexadecimal also follows these conventions.

Suppose we wish to convert decimal 57 to binary. We begin by writing the positional values of the columns right to left until we reach a column whose positional value is greater than the decimal number. We do not need that column, so we discard it. Thus, we first write:

Positional values: **64   32   16   8   4   2   1**

Then we discard the column with positional value 64 leaving:

Positional values: **32   16   8   4   2   1**

Next we work from the leftmost column to the right. We divide 32 into 57 and observe that there is one 32 in 57 with a remainder of 25, so we write 1 in the 32 column. We divide 16 into 25 and observe that there is one 16 in 25 with a remainder of 9 and write 1 in the 16 column. We divide 8 into 9 and observe that there is one 8 in 9 with a remainder of 1. The next two columns each produce quotients of zero when their positional values are divided into 1 so we write 0s in the 4 and 2 columns. Finally, 1 into 1 is 1 so we write 1 in the 1 column. This yields:

Positional values:	32	16	8	4	2	1
Symbol values:	1	1	1	0	0	1

and thus decimal 57 is equivalent to binary 111001.

To convert decimal 103 to octal, we begin by writing the positional values of the columns until we reach a column whose positional value is greater than the decimal number. We do not need that column, so we discard it. Thus, we first write:

Positional values: **512   64   8   1**

Then we discard the column with positional value 512, yielding:

Positional values: **64   8   1**

Next we work from the leftmost column to the right. We divide 64 into 103 and observe that there is one 64 in 103 with a remainder of 39, so we write 1 in the 64 column. We divide 8 into 39 and observe that there are four 8s in 39 with a remainder of 7 and write 4 in the 8 column. Finally, we divide 1 into 7 and observe that there are seven 1s in 7 with no remainder so we write 7 in the 1 column. This yields:

Positional values:	64	8	1
Symbol values:	1	4	7

and thus decimal 103 is equivalent to octal 147.

To convert decimal 375 to hexadecimal, we begin by writing the positional values of the columns until we reach a column whose positional value is greater than the decimal number. We do not need that column, so we discard it. Thus, we first write

Positional values: **4096 256   16   1**

Then we discard the column with positional value 4096, yielding:

Positional values: **256   16   1**

Next we work from the leftmost column to the right. We divide 256 into 375 and observe that there is one 256 in 375 with a remainder of 119, so we write 1 in the 256 column. We divide 16 into 119 and observe that there are seven 16s in 119 with a remainder of 7 and write 7 in the 16 column. Finally, we divide 1 into 7 and observe that there are seven 1s in 7 with no remainder so we write 7 in the 1 column. This yields:

Positional values:	256	16	1
Symbol values:	1	7	7

and thus decimal 375 is equivalent to hexadecimal 177.

E.6 Negative Binary Numbers: Two's Complement Notation

The discussion in this appendix has been focussed on positive numbers. In this section, we explain how computers represent negative numbers using *two's complement notation*. First we explain how the two's complement of a binary number is formed, and then we show why it represents the negative value of the given binary number.

Consider a machine with 32-bit integers. Suppose

```
var value = 13;
```

The 32-bit representation of **value** is

```
00000000 00000000 00000000 00001101
```

To form the negative of **value** we first form its *one's complement* by applying JavaScript's bitwise complement operator (~), which is also called the *bitwise NOT operator* :

```
onesComplementOfValue = ~value;
```

Internally, ~value is now value with each of its bits reversed—ones become zeros and zeros become ones as follows:

```
value:
00000000 00000000 00000000 00001101
```

```
~value  (i.e., value's ones complement):
11111111 11111111 11111111 11110010
```

To form the two's complement of **value** we simply add one to **value**'s one's complement. Thus

```
Two's complement of value:
11111111 11111111 11111111 11110011
```

Now if this is in fact equal to -13, we should be able to add it to binary 13 and obtain a result of 0. Let us try this:

```
  00000000 00000000 00000000 00001101
+11111111 11111111 11111111 11110011
-------------------------------------
  00000000 00000000 00000000 00000000
```

The carry bit coming out of the leftmost column is discarded and we indeed get zero as a result. If we add the one's complement of a number to the number, the result would be all 1s. The key to getting a result of all zeros is that the twos complement is 1 more than the one's complement. The addition of 1 causes each column to add to 0 with a carry of 1. The carry keeps moving leftward until it is discarded from the leftmost bit, and hence the resulting number is all zeros.

Computers actually perform a subtraction such as

```
x = a - value;
```

by adding the two's complement of **value** to **a** as follows:

```
x = a + ( ~value + 1 );
```

Suppose **a** is 27 and **value** is 13 as before. If the two's complement of **value** is actually the negative of **value**, then adding the two's complement of value to a should produce the result 14. Let us try this:

```
a (i.e., 27) 00000000 00000000 00000000 00011011
+(~value + 1)+11111111 11111111 11111111 11110011
             -------------------------------------
             00000000 00000000 00000000 00001110
```

which is indeed equal to 14.

SUMMARY

- When we write an integer such as 19 or 227 or -63 in a program, the number is automatically assumed to be in the decimal (base 10) number system. The digits in the decimal number system are 0, 1, 2, 3, 4, 5, 6, 7, 8, and 9. The lowest digit is 0 and the highest digit is 9—one less than the base of 10.

- Internally, computers use the binary (base 2) number system. The binary number system has only two digits, namely 0 and 1. Its lowest digit is 0 and its highest digit is 1—one less than the base of 2.

- The octal number system (base 8) and the hexadecimal number system (base 16) are popular primarily because they make it convenient to abbreviate binary numbers.

- The digits of the octal number system range from 0 to 7.

- The hexadecimal number system poses a problem because it requires sixteen digits—a lowest digit of 0 and a highest digit with a value equivalent to decimal 15 (one less than the base of 16). By convention, we use the letters A through F to represent the hexadecimal digits corresponding to decimal values 10 through 15.

- Each number system uses positional notation—each position in which a digit is written has a different positional value.

- A particularly important relationship that both the octal number system and the hexadecimal number system have to the binary system is that the bases of octal and hexadecimal (8 and 16 respectively) are powers of the base of the binary number system (base 2).

- To convert an octal number to a binary number, simply replace each octal digit with its three-digit binary equivalent.

- To convert a hexadecimal number to a binary number, simply replace each hexadecimal digit with its four-digit binary equivalent.

- Because we are accustomed to working in decimal, it is convenient to convert a binary, octal or hexadecimal number to decimal to get a sense of the number's "real" worth.

- To convert a number to decimal from another base, multiply the decimal equivalent of each digit by its positional value, and sum these products.

- Computers represent negative numbers using two's complement notation.

- To form the negative of a value in binary, first form its one's complement by applying JavaScript's bitwise complement operator (~). This reverses the bits of the value. To form the two's complement of a value, simply add one to the value's one's complement.

TERMINOLOGY

base	digit
base 2 number system	hexadecimal number system
base 8 number system	negative value
base 10 number system	octal number system
base 16 number system	one's complement notation
binary number system	positional notation
bitwise complement operator (~)	positional value
conversions	symbol value
decimal number system	two's complement notation

SELF-REVIEW EXERCISES

E.1   The bases of the decimal, binary, octal, and hexadecimal number systems are _____, _____, _____, and _____ respectively.

E.2   In general, the decimal, octal, and hexadecimal representations of a given binary number contain (more/fewer) digits than the binary number contains.

E.3   (True/False) A popular reason for using the decimal number system is that it forms a convenient notation for abbreviating binary numbers simply by substituting one decimal digit per group of four binary bits.

E.4   The (octal / hexadecimal / decimal) representation of a large binary value is the most concise (of the given alternatives).

E.5   (True/False) The highest digit in any base is one more than the base.

E.6   (True/False) The lowest digit in any base is one less than the base.

E.7   The positional value of the rightmost digit of any number in either binary, octal, decimal, or hexadecimal is always _____.

E.8   The positional value of the digit to the left of the rightmost digit of any number in binary, octal, decimal, or hexadecimal is always equal to _____.

E.9   Fill in the missing values in this chart of positional values for the rightmost four positions in each of the indicated number systems:

```
decimal     1000100 10 1
hexadecimal ...256......
binary      ............
octal       512 64 8 1
```

E.10   Convert binary **110101011000** to octal and to hexadecimal.

E.11   Convert hexadecimal **FACE** to binary.

E.12   Convert octal **7316** to binary.

E.13   Convert hexadecimal **4FEC** to octal. (Hint: First convert 4FEC to binary then convert that binary number to octal.)

E.14   Convert binary **1101110** to decimal.

E.15   Convert octal **317** to decimal.

E.16   Convert hexadecimal **EFD4** to decimal.

E.17   Convert decimal **177** to binary, to octal, and to hexadecimal.

E.18   Show the binary representation of decimal **417**. Then show the one's complement of **417**, and the two's complement of **417**.

E.19   What is the result when the one's complement of a number is added to itself?

SELF-REVIEW ANSWERS

E.1   **10, 2, 8, 16**.

E.2   Fewer.

E.3   False.

E.4   Hexadecimal.

E.5   False. The highest digit in any base is one less than the base.

E.6   False. The lowest digit in any base is zero.

E.7   **1** (the base raised to the zero power).

E.8   The base of the number system.

E.9   Fill in the missing values in this chart of positional values for the rightmost four positions in each of the indicated number systems:

```
decimal     1000100101
hexadecimal4096256161
binary         8    4 21
octal        512 64 81
```

E.10   Octal **6530**; Hexadecimal **D58**.

E.11   Binary **1111 1010 1100 1110**.

E.12   Binary **111 011 001 110**.

E.13   Binary **0 100 111 111 101 100; Octal 47754**.

E.14   Decimal **2+4+8+32+64=110**.

E.15   Decimal **7+1*8+3*64=7+8+192=207**.

E.16   Decimal **4+13*16+15*256+14*4096=61396**.

E.17   Decimal **177**
to binary:

```
256 128 64 32 16 8 4 2 1
128 64 32 16 8 4 2 1
(1*128)+(0*64)+(1*32)+(1*16)+(0*8)+(0*4)+(0*2)+(1*1)
10110001
```

to octal:

```
512 64 8 1
64 8 1
(2*64)+(6*8)+(1*1)
261
```

to hexadecimal:

```
256 16 1
16 1
(11*16)+(1*1)
(B*16)+(1*1)
B1
```

E.18   Binary:

```
512 256 128 64 32 16 8 4 2 1
256 128 64 32 16 8 4 2 1
(1*256)+(1*128)+(0*64)+(1*32)+(0*16)+(0*8)+(0*4)+(0*2)+
(1*1)
110100001
```

One's complement: **001011110**
Two's complement: **001011111**
Check: Original binary number + its two's complement

```
110100001
001011111
---------
000000000
```

E.19   Zero.

EXERCISES

E.20   Some people argue that many of our calculations would be easier in the base **12** number system because **12** is divisible by so many more numbers than **10** (for base **10**). What is the lowest digit in base **12**? What might the highest symbol for the digit in base **12** be? What are the positional values of the rightmost four positions of any number in the base **12** number system?

E.21   How is the highest symbol value in the number systems we discussed related to the positional value of the first digit to the left of the rightmost digit of any number in these number systems?

E.22   Complete the following chart of positional values for the rightmost four positions in each of the indicated number systems:

decimal	**1000**	**100**	**10**	**1**
base 6	...	...	**6**	...
base 13	...	**169**	...	...
base 3	**27**	...	...	...

E.1   Convert binary **100101111010** to octal and to hexadecimal.

E.2   Convert hexadecimal **3A7D** to binary.

E.3   Convert hexadecimal **765F** to octal. (Hint: First convert **765F** to binary, then convert that binary number to octal.)

E.4   Convert binary **1011110** to decimal.

E.5   Convert octal **426** to decimal.

E.6   Convert hexadecimal **FFFF** to decimal.

E.7   Convert decimal **299** to binary, to octal, and to hexadecimal.

E.8   Show the binary representation of decimal **779**. Then show the one's complement of **779**, and the two's complement of **779**.

E.9   What is the result when the two's complement of a number is added to itself?

E.10   Show the two's complement of integer value **−1** on a machine with 32-bit integers.

Career Resources

Objectives

- To explore the various on-line career services.
- To examine the advantages and disadvantages of posting and finding jobs on-line.
- To review the major on-line career services Web sites available to the job seeker.
- To explore the various on-line services available to employers seeking to build their workforce.

I found Rome a city of bricks and left it a city of marble.
Augustus Caesar

People don't choose their careers; they are engulfed by them.
John Dos Passos

What is the city but the people?
William Shakespeare

A great city is that which has the greatest men and women, If it be a few ragged huts it is still the greatest city in the whole world.
Walt Whitman

Outline

F.1 Introduction

The Internet provides worldwide access to a vast number of job opportunities. *Entry-level positions*, or positions commonly sought by individuals who are entering a specific field or the job market for the first time; contracting positions; executive-level positions and middle-management-level positions are all available on the Web. Job seekers can learn how to write a resume and cover letter, post them on-line and search through job listings to find the jobs that best suit their needs. Employers can post jobs that can be searched by an enormous pool of applicants. On-line interviews, testing services and other resources also expedite the recruiting process. [*Note*: The unemployment rate in the United States is at its lowest point in 30 years.[1]]

Applying for a position on-line is a relatively new method of exploring career opportunities. By allowing the majority of the job search to be conducted from the desktop, on-line recruiting services streamline the process and allow job seekers to concentrate their energies in careers that are of interest to them. Job seekers can explore opportunities according to geographic location, position, salary or benefits package.

Storing and distributing resumes digitally, e-mail notification of possible positions, salary and relocation calculators, job coaches and self-assessment tools are among the resources job seekers can find on-line to help them in their career searches. These sites also provide information on continuing education.

XML is one of the hottest technologies in industry today and many XML-related job opportunities exist. In this appendix, we examine some of the career services and related resources available on the Web. Web sites such as `xmlhack.com`, `www.eccnet.com`

and **prescottgroup.com** list many XML-related employment opportunities. Many of the other Web sites we discuss in this appendix provide similar resources.

F.2 On-line Career Services

There are approximately 40,000 career-advancement services on the Internet today.[2] These services include large, comprehensive job sites, such as **monster.com** (see the upcoming feature), as well as interest-specific job sites such as **xmlhack.com/jobs.php**. In this section, we will explore some of the resources available to employers and job seekers and address some of the advantages and disadvantages of on-line career services.

Finding a job on-line can greatly reduce the amount of time spent applying for a position. Instead of searching through newspapers and mailing resumes, job seekers can request a specific position in a specific industry through a search engine. Resumes can be stored digitally, customized quickly to meet job requirements and e-mailed instantaneously. Potential candidates can also learn more about a company by visiting its Web site. Most sites are free to job seekers. These sites typically generate their revenues by charging employers for posting job opportunities and by selling advertising space on their Web pages.

Career services, such as **FlipDog.com**, search a list of employer job sites to find positions. By searching links to employer Web sites, FlipDog is able to identify positions from companies of all sizes. This feature enables job seekers to find jobs that employers may not have posted outside the corporation's Web site.

Job seekers can visit **FlipDog.com** and choose, by state, the area in which they are looking for a position. Applicants can also conduct worldwide searches. After a user selects a region, FlipDog requests the user to specify a job category containing several specific positions. The user's choice causes a list of local employers to appear. The user can choose a specific employer or request that FlipDog search the employment databases for jobs offered by all employers.

Other services, such as employment networks, also help job seekers in their search. Sites such as **Vault.com** (see the upcoming feature) and **WetFeet.com** allow job seekers to post questions about employers and positions in designated chat rooms and bulletin boards.

The large number of applicants presents a challenge to both job seekers and employers. On many recruitment sites, matching resumes to positions is conducted by *resume-filtering software*. The software scans a pool of resumes for keywords that match the job description. While this software increases the number of resumes that receive some attention, it is not a foolproof system. For example, the resume-filtering software might overlook someone with similar skills to those listed in the job description, or someone whose current abilities would enable them to learn the skills required for the position. Other shortcomings include digital transmission and including catchy keywords.

Confidentiality is another disadvantage of on-line career services. In many cases, a job candidate will want to search for job opportunities anonymously. This reduces the possibility of offending the candidate's current employer. Posting a resume on the Web increases the likelihood that the candidate's employer might come across it when recruiting new employees. The traditional method of mailing resumes and cover letters to potential employers does not impose the same risk.

Monster.com

Super Bowl ads and effective marketing have made **Monster.com** one of the most recognizable on-line brands. In fact, in the 24 hours following Super Bowl XXXIV, 5 million job searches occurred on **Monster.com**.[3] The site allows people looking for jobs to post their resumes, search job listings, read advice and information about the job-search process and take proactive steps to improve their careers. These services are free to job seekers. Employers can post job listings, search resume databases and become featured employers.

Posting your resume at **Monster.com** is simple and free. **Monster.com** has a resume builder that allows you to post a resume to its site in 15–30 minutes. You can store up to 5 resumes and cover letters on the **Monster.com** server. Some companies offer their employment applications directly through the **Monster.com** site. **Monster.com** has job postings in every state and all major categories. You can limit access to your personal identification information. As one of the leading recruiting sites on the Web, **Monster.com** is a good place to start your job search or to find out more about the search process.

Vault.com[4]

Vault.com allows potential employees to seek out additional, third-party information for over 3000 companies. By visiting the *Insider Research* page, Web users have access to a profile on the company of their choice, as long as it exists in **Vault.com**'s database. In addition to **Vault.com**'s profile, there is also a link to additional commentary by company employees. Most often anonymous, these messages can provide prospective employees with potentially valuable, decision-making information. However, users must also consider the integrity of the source. For example, a disgruntled employee may leave a posting that is not a good representation of the corporate culture of his or her company.

The **Vault.com** *Electronic Watercooler*™ is a message board that allows visitors to post stories, questions and concerns and to advise employees and job seekers. In addition, the site provides e-newsletters and feature stories designed to help job seekers in their search. Individuals seeking information on the best business, law and graduate schools can also find information on **Vault.com**.

Job-posting and career-advancement services for the job seeker are also featured on **Vault.com**. These services include *VaultMatch*, a career service that e-mails job postings as requested, and *Salary Wizard*™, which helps job seekers determine what they are worth. Online guides to with advice for fulfilling your career ambitions are also available.

Employers can also use the site. *HR Vault*, a feature of **Vault.com**, provides employers with a free job-posting site. It also features career-management advice, employer-to-employee relationship management and recruiting resources. HR Vault can be visited directly at **vault.com/hr_channel/index.cfm?object-group_id=302**.

According to recent studies, the number of individuals researching employment positions through other means, such as referrals, newspapers and temporary agencies, far outweighs the number of job seekers researching positions through the Internet.[5] Optimists feel, however, that this disparity is largely due to the early stages of e-business development. Given time, on-line career services will become more refined in their posting and searching capabilities, decreasing the amount of time it takes for a job seeker to find jobs and employers to fill positions.

F.3 Career Opportunities for Employees

In this section, we will explore a variety of career services Web sites. We will include sites that provide opportunities for technically trained individuals, independent contractors, students and young professionals and executives.

F.3.1 Comprehensive Career Sites

As mentioned previously, there are many sites on the Web that provide job seekers with career opportunities in multiple fields. **monster.com** is the largest of these sites, attracting the largest number of unique visitors per month. Other popular on-line recruiting sites include **JobsOnline.com**, **HotJobs.com** and **Headhunter.net**.

Searching for a job on-line can be a conducted in a few steps. For example, during an initial visit to **JobsOnline.com**, a user is required to fill out a registration form. The form requests basic information, such as name, address and area of interest. After registering, members can search through job postings according to such criteria as the number of days posted, category and location. Contact information is provided for additional communication. Registered members are offered access to XDrive™ (**www.xdrive.com**), which provides 25 MB of storage space for resumes, cover letters and additional communication. Stored files can be shared through any Web browser or Wireless Application Protocol (WAP) enabled device.[6] **Driveway.com** offers a similar service, allowing individuals to store, share and organize files on-line. An on-line demonstration of the service can be found at **www.driveway.com**. The animated demo walks the user through the features offered by the service. **Driveway.com** offers 100 MB of space, and the service is free.[7]

Other sites, such as Cruel World (see the upcoming feature), allow you to store and send your resume directly.

F.3.2 Technical Positions

The amount of time for an employer to fill a technical position can be greatly reduced by using an industry-specific site. Career sites designed for individuals seeking technical positions are among the most popular on-line career sites. In this section, we review several sites that offer recruiting and hiring opportunities for technical positions.

Dice.com (**www.dice.com**) is a recruiting Web site that focuses on technical fields. Fees to companies are based on the number of jobs they post and the frequency with which the postings are updated. Job seekers can post their resumes and search the job database for free.

JustComputerJobs.com directs job seekers toward 39 specific computer technologies for their job search. Language-specific sites include **JustJavaJobs.com**,

JustCJobs.com and **JustPerlJobs.com**. Hardware, software and communications technology sites are also available.

Other technology recruiting sites include **Bid4Geeks.com**, **HotDispatch.com** and **www.cmpnet.com/careerdirect**.

F.3.3 Contracting On-line

The Internet also serves as a forum for job seekers to find employment on a project-by-project basis. On-line contracting services allow businesses to post positions for which they want to hire outside resources, and individuals can identify projects that best suit their interests, schedules and skills. [*Note*: Approximately six percent of America's workforce falls into the category of independent contractor.[9]]

Guru.com (**www.guru.com**) is a recruiting site for contract employees. Independent contractors, private consultants and trainers use **guru.com** to find short-term and long-term contract assignments. Tips, articles and advice are available for contractors who wish to learn more about their industry. Other sections of the site teach you how to manage your business, buy the best equipment and deal with legal issues. **Guru.com** includes an on-line store where you can buy products associated with small-business management, such as printing services and office supplies. Companies wishing to hire contractors need to register, but individuals seeking contract assignments do not.

Monster.com's Talent Market™ offers online auction-style career services to free agents. Interested users design a profile, listing their qualifications. After establishing a profile, free agents "Go Live" to start the bidding on their services. The bidding lasts for five days during which users can view the incoming bids. At the close of five days, the user can choose the job of their choice. The service is free for users, bidding employers pay a commission on completed transactions.

Cruel World[8]

Cruel World is a free, on-line career advancement service for job seekers. After becoming a registered member, your information is matched with available positions in the Cruel World database. When an available job matches your criteria, *JobCast*®, a feature of Cruel World, sends an e-mail alerting you of the available position. If you are interested, you can send your resume to the employer that posted the position, customized to the job's requirements. If you do not wish to continue your search, you can simply send a negative response via e-mail.

The client list, or the list of companies seeking new employees through Cruel World, can be viewed at **www.cruelworld.com/corporate/aboutus.asp** Additional features on the site include hints for salary negotiation; a self-assessment link to **CareerLeader.com**, where, for a small fee, members can reassess their career goals under the advisement of career counselors, and a relocation calculator, for job seekers who are considering changing location.

Employers seeking to hire new talent can post opportunities through Cruel World. posting positions requires a fee. A demonstration of the service can be viewed at **www.cruelworld.com/clients/quicktour1.asp**. The demonstration is a three-step slide of JobCast.

---

eLance.com is another site where individuals can find contracting work. Interested applicants can search eLance's database by category, including business, finance and marketing. These projects, or *requests for proposals* (RFPs), are posted by companies worldwide. When you find a project for which you feel you are qualified, you submit a bid on the project. Your bid will contain your required payment, a statement detailing your skills and a feedback rating drawn from other projects on which you have worked. If your bid is accepted, you are given the project, and the work is conducted over eLance's file-sharing system, enabling both the contractor and the employer to contact one another quickly and easily. For an on-line demonstration, visit **www.elance.com** and click on the **demonstration** icon.

FreeAgent (**www.freeagent.com**) is another site designed for contracting projects. Candidates create an *e.portfolio* that provides an introductory "snapshot" of their skills, a biography, a list of their experience and references. An interview section of the portfolio lists questions and the applicant's answers. Examples of e.portfolios can be found at **www.freeagent.com/splash/models.asp**. Free Agent's *e.office* offers a benefits package to outside contractors, including health insurance, a retirement plan and reimbursement for business-related expenses, among other features.

Other Web sites that provide contractors with projects and information include eWork® Exchange (**www.ework.com**), **MBAFreeAgent.com**, **Aquent.com**, **WorkingSolo.com**.

F.3.4 Executive Positions

The Internet provides career opportunities ranging from entry-level positions to senior level positions. Executive career advancement sites usually include many of the features that you might find on a comprehensive job-search site. In this section, we discuss the challenges of and opportunities for finding an executive position on-line.

Searching for an executive position on-line differs from finding an entry-level position on-line. The Internet allows individuals to continually survey the job market. However, candidates for executive-level positions must exercise a higher level of confidentiality when determining who is able to view their resume. Applying for an executive position on-line is an extensive process. Because of the high level of scrutiny passed on a candidate during the hiring process, the initial criteria presented by an executive level candidate are often more specific than the criteria presented by the first-time job seeker. Executive positions are often difficult to fill, due to the high demands and large amount of experience required for the jobs.

SixFigureJobs (**www.sixfigurejobs.com**) is a recruitment site designed for experienced executives. Resume posting and job searching is free to job seekers.Other sites designed for helping executives find positions include **www.execunet.com** and **www.nationjob.com**.

F.3.5 Students and Young Professionals

The Internet provides students and young professionals with many tools to get them started in the job market. Individuals still in school and seeking internships, individuals who are just graduating and individuals who have been in the workforce for a few years make up the target market. Additional tools specifically designed for this *demographic*, or a population defined by a specific characteristic, are also available. For example, journals kept by previous interns provide prospective interns with information regarding what to look for in an internship, what to expect and what to avoid. Many of these sites will provide information to start young professionals in the right direction, such as matching positions to college or university major.

Experience.com is a career services Web site geared toward the younger population. Members can search for positions according to specific criteria, such as geographic location, job category, keywords, commitment (i.e. full time, part time, internship), amount of vacation and amount of travel time. After applicants register, they can send their resumes directly to the companies posting on the site. In addition to the resume, candidates also provide a personal statement, a list of applicable skills and their language proficiency. Registered members also receive access to the site's *Job Agent*. Members can set up to three Job Agents. The agents search for available positions, based on the criteria posted by the member. If a match is made, the site contacts the candidate via e-mail.[10,11]

Internshipprograms.com helps students find internships. In addition to posting a resume and searching for an internship, students can also use the relocation calculator and read through information and tips on building resumes and writing essays. The *City Intern* program provides travel, housing, entertainment and guides to interns interviewing or accepting a position in an unfamiliar city, making them feel more at home in a new location.

In addition to its internship locators, undergraduate, graduate, law school, medical school and business school services, the Princeton Review's Web site (**www.review.com**) offers career services to graduating students. While searching for a job, students and young professionals can also read through the site's news reports or even increase their vocabulary by visiting the "word for the day."

Other Web sites geared toward the younger population include **campuscareercenter.com**, **brassringcampus.com** and **collegegrads.com**.

F.3.6 Other On-line Career Services

In addition to Web sites that help you find and post jobs on-line, there are a number of Web sites that offer features that will enhance your search, prepare you for searching on-line, help you design your resume or help you calculate the cost of relocating.

Salary.com helps job seekers gauge their expected income, based on position, level of responsibility and years of experience. The search requires job category, ZIP code and specific job title. Based on this information, the site will return an estimated salary for an individual living in the specified area, and employed in the position described. Estimates are returned based on the average level of income for that position.

In addition to being a resource for finding employment, **www.careerpower.com** also provides individuals with tests that will help them realize their strengths, weaknesses, values, skills and personality traits. Based on the results, which can be up to 10–12 pages per test, users can best decide what job category they are best qualified for and what career choice will be best suited to their personal ambitions. The service is available for a fee.

InterviewSmart™ is another service offered through CareerPower that prepares job seekers of all levels for the interviewing process. The service can be downloaded for a minimal fee or can be used on the Web for free. Both versions are available at **www.careerpower.com/CareerPerfect/interviewing.htm#is.start.anchor**.

Additional services will help you find a position that meets your unique needs, or design your resume to attract the attention of employers. **Dogfriendly.com**, organized by geographic location, helps job seekers find opportunities that allow them to bring their pets to work, and **cooljobs.com** is a searchable database of unique job opportunities.

F.4 On-line Opportunities for Employers

Recruiting on the Internet provides several benefits over traditional recruiting. For example, Web recruiting reaches a much larger audience than posting an advertisement in a local newspaper. Given the breadth of the services provided on most on-line career services Web sites, the cost of posting on-line can be considerably less expensive than posting positions through traditional means. Generally, jobs posted on-line are viewed by a larger number of job seekers than jobs posted through traditional means. However, it is important not to overlook the benefits of combining these efforts with human-to-human interaction. There are many job seekers who are not yet comfortable with the process of finding a job on-line. Often, on-line recruiting is used as a means of freeing up a recruiter's time for the interviewing process and final selection.

F.4.1 Posting Jobs On-line

When searching for job candidates on-line, there are many things employers need to consider. The Internet is a valuable tool for recruiting, but one that takes careful planning to get the best results. It provides a good supplementary tool, but should not be considered the complete solution for filling positions. On-line services, such as WebHire (**www.webhire.com**), enhance a company's on-line employment search (see the upcoming feature).

WebHire™ [12]

Designed specifically for recruiters and employers, WebHire is a multifaceted service that provides employers with end-to-end recruiting solutions. The service offers job-posting services as well as candidate searches. The most comprehensive of the services, *WebHire™ Enterprise*, locates and ranks candidates found through resume-scanning mechanisms. Clients will also receive a report indicating the best resources for their search. Other services, available through the *WebHire™ Employment Services Network*, include preemployment screening, tools for assessing employees' skill levels and information on compensation packages. An employment law advisor helps organizations design interview questions.

WebHire™ Agent is an intelligent agent that searches for qualified applicants, based on your job specifications. When WebHire Agent identifies a potential candidate, an e-mail is automatically sent to that candidate to generate interest. WebHire Agent then ranks applicants according to the skills information it gains from the Web search; the information is stored, so that new applicants are distinguished from those who have already received an e-mail from the site.

Yahoo!® Resumes, a feature of WebHire, allows recruiters to find potential employees by typing in keywords to the Yahoo! Resumes search engine. Employers can purchase a year's membership to the recruiting solution for a flat fee; there are no per-use charges.

There are a variety of sites that allow employers to post jobs on-line. Some of these sites require a fee, which generally runs between $100–$200. Postings typically remain on the Web site for 30–60 days. Employers should be careful to post to sites that are most likely to be visited by eligible candidates. As we discovered in the previous section, there are a variety of on-line career services focused on specific industries, and many of the larger, more comprehensive sites have categorized their database by job category.

When designing a posting, the recruiter should also consider the vast number of postings already on the Web. Defining what makes your position unique, including information such as benefits and salary, might convince a qualified candidate to further investigate the position.[13]

Boston Herald *Job Find* (**www.jobfind.com**) also charges employers to post on its site. The initial fee entitles the employer to post up to three listings. Employers have no limitations on the length of their postings.

HotJobs.com career postings are cross-listed on a variety of other sites, thus increasing the number of potential employees that see the job listings. Like **monster.com** and **jobfind.com**, **hotjobs.com** requires a fee per listing. Employers also have the option of becoming **HotJob.com** members. Employers also receive access to HotJob's *Private Label Job Board*s (private corporate employment sites), on-line recruiting technology and on-line career fairs.

Other Web sites providing employers with employee recruitment services include **CareerPath.com**, America's Job Bank (**www.ajb.dni.us/employer**), CareerWeb (**www.cweb.com**), **Jobs.com** and **Career.com**..

F.4.2 Diversity in the Workplace

Every workplace inevitably develops its own culture. Responsibilities, schedules, deadlines and projects all contribute to a working environment. However, perhaps the most defining elements of a *corporate culture* are the employees. For example, if all employees were to have the same skills and the same ideas, then the workplace would lack diversity. It might also lack creativity and enthusiasm. One way to increase the dynamics of an organization is to employee people of all backgrounds and cultures.

The Internet hosts demographic-specific sites for employers seeking to increase diversity in the workplace. Increasing diversity enhances organizations in many ways. By recruiting people from different backgrounds, new ideas and perspectives are brought forth, helping businesses meet the needs of a larger, more diverse target audience.[14]

Blackvoices.com and **hirediversity.com** are demographic-specific Web sites. BlackVoices™, which functions primarily as a portal, features job searching capabilities and the ability for prospective employees to post resumes. HireDiversity is divided into several categories, including African American, Hispanic and opportunities for women. Other on-line recruiting services place banner advertisements on ethnic Web sites for companies seeking diverse workforces.

The Diversity Directory (**www.mindexchange.com**) offers international career-searching capabilities. Users selecting the **Diversity** site can find job opportunities, information and additional resources to help them in their career search. The site can be searched according to demographics (African American, Hispanic, alternative lifestyle, etc.) or by subject (employer, position, etc.) through hundreds of links. Featured sites include **BilingualJobs.com**, *Latin World* and *American Society for Female Entrepreneurs*.

The Internet also provides people with disabilities opportunities for career advancement. Many sites have sections dedicated to job seekers with disabilities. In addition to providing job-searching capabilities, these sites include additional resources, such as equal opportunity documents and message boards. The *National Business and Disability Council* (*NBDC*) provides employers with information on employing people with disabilities, such as integration and accessibility, as well as opportunities for job seekers.

F.4.3 Recruiting Services

There are many services on the Internet that help employers match individuals to positions. The time saved by conducting preliminary searches on the Internet can then be dedicated to interviewing qualified candidates and making the best matches possible.

Advantage Hiring, Inc. (**www.advantagehiring.com**) provides employers with a resume-screening service. When a prospective employee submits a resume for a particular position, Advantage Hiring, Inc., presents *Net-Interview™*, a small questionnaire to supplement the information presented on the resume. The site also offers *SiteBuilder*, a service that helps employers build an employee recruitment site. An on-line demonstration can be found at **www.advantagehiring.com**. The demonstration walks the user through the Net-Interview software, as well as a number of the other services offered by Advantage Hiring.

Recruitsoft.com is an application service provider (ASP) that offers companies recruiting software on a *pay-per-hire* basis; that is, Recruitsoft receives a commission on hires made via its service. *Recruiter WebTop™* is the company's on-line recruiting software. It includes a host of features, such as Web-site hosting, an employee-referral program, skill-based resume screening, applicant-tracking capabilities and job-board posting capabilities. A demonstration of Recruiter WebTop's *Corporate Recruiting Solutions* can be found at **www.recruitsoft.com/process**. The demonstration shows how recruiting solutions find and rank potential candidates. More information about Recruitsoft's solution can be viewed in a *QuickTime* media player demonstration, found at **www.recruitsoft.com/corpoVideo**.[15]

RecruitingSolutions (**www.recruitingsoftware.com**) provides Web-based solutions for the on-line recruiting process. *RecruitingCenter™* allows companies to integrate career services on their Web sites.

Peoplescape.com is an on-line service that help employers recruit employees and maintain a positive work environment once the employee has been hired. In addition to searches for potential candidates, Peoplescape also offers *PayCheck™*, *LegalCheck™* and *PeopleCheck™*. These services help to ensure that compensation offers are adequate, legal guidelines are met during the hiring process and in the workplace and candidates have provided accurate information both on their resume and during the hiring process.

For job seekers, Peoplescape offers searching capabilities, insights to career transitions, a job compensation calculator that takes benefits and bonuses into consideration when exploring a new job possibility and a series of regularly posted articles relevant to the job search.[16]

To further assist companies in their recruiting process, Web sites such as **Refer.com** reward visitors for successful job referrals. Highly sought-after positions can earn thousands of dollars. If you refer a friend or a family member and they are hired, you receive a commission.

Other on-line recruiting services include **Hire.com**, **MorganWorks.com** and **Futurestep.com**™.

F.4.4 Testing Potential Employees On-line

The Internet has also provided employers with a cost-effective means of testing their prospective employees in such categories as decision making, problem solving and personality. Services such *eTest* help to reduce the cost of in-house testing and to make the interview process more effectively. Test results, given in paragraph form, present the interested individual's strengths and weaknesses. Based on these results, the report suggests interview methods, such as asking open-ended questions, or questions that require more than a "yes" or "no" response. Sample reports and a free-trial test can be found at **www.etest.net**.

Employers and Job seekers can also find career placement exercises at **www.advisorteam.net/AT/User/kcs.asp**. Some of these services require a fee. The tests ask several questions regarding the individual's interests and working style. Results help candidates to determine the best career for their skills and interests.

F.5 Internet and World Wide Web Resources

Information Technology (IT) Career Sites

www.dice.com
Dice.com is a recruiting Web site that focuses on the computer industry.

www.peoplescape.com
This site provides career advancement services for both employers and job seekers. Its services include PayCheck™, LegalCheck™ and PeopleCheck™, to assist employers in the hiring process.
www.guru.com
This is a recruiting site for contract employees. Independent contractors, private consultants and trainers can use **guru.com** to find short-term and long-term work.

www.hallkinion.com
This is a Web recruiting service for individuals seeking IT positions.

www.techrepublic.com
This site provides employers and job seekers with recruiting capabilities and information regarding developing technology.

www.justcomputerjobs.com
This site serves as a portal with access to language-specific sites, including Java, Perl, C and C++.

www.bid4geeks.com
This career services site is geared toward the technical professional.

www.hotdispatch.com
This forum provides software developers with an opportunity to share projects, discuss code and ask questions.

Career Sites

www.careerbuilder.com
A network of career sites, including IT Careers, *USA Today* and MSN, CareerBuilder attracts 3 million unique job seekers per month. This site also provides resume-builder and job-searching agents.

www.recruitek.com
This free site caters to jobs seekers, employers and contractors.

`www.monster.com`

This site, the largest of the on-line career sites, allows people looking for jobs to post their resumes, search job listings and read advice and information about the job-search process. It also provides a variety of recruitment services for employers.

`www.jobsonline.com`

Similar to `monster.com`, this site provides opportunities for job seekers and employers.

`www.hotjobs.com`

This on-line recruiting site offers cross-listing possibilities on additional sites.

`www.jobfind.com`

This job site is an example of locally targeted job-search resources. `JobFind.com` targets the Boston area.

`www.flipdog.com`

This site allows on-line job candidates to search for career opportunities. It employs intelligent agents to scour the Web and return jobs matching the candidate's request.

`www.cooljobs.com`

This site highlights unique job opportunities.

Other Career Web Sites

The following sites provide job opportunities and information and employer services:

`www.careerpath.com`

`www.cweb.com`

`www.career.com`

`www.jobs.com`

`www.careerpower.com`

`www.careermag.com`

Executive Positions

`www.sixfigurejobs.com`

This is a recruitment site designed for experienced executives.

`www.leadersonline.com`

This career services Web site offers confidential job searches for mid-level professionals. Potential job matches are e-mailed to job candidates.

Diversity

`www.latpro.com`

This site is designed for Spanish- and Portuguese-speaking job seekers. In addition to provide resume-posting services, the site enables job seekers to receive matching positions via e-mail. Advice and information services are also available.

`www.blackvoices.com`

This site hosts a career center designed to match African American job seekers with job opportunities.

`www.hirediversity.com`

This site targets a variety of demographics. In addition to services for searching for and posting positions, resume-building and up-dating services are also available. Specialized groups include African Americans, Asian Americans, people with disabilities, women and Latin Americans.

People with Disabilities

www.halftheplanet.com

This site represents people with disabilities. The site is large and includes many different resources and information services. A special section is dedicated to job seekers and employers.

www.wemedia.com

This site is designed to meet the needs of people with disabilities. It also includes a section for job seekers and employers.

www.disabilities.com

This site provides users with a host of links to information resources on career opportunities.

www.rileyguide.com

This site includes a section with opportunities for people with disabilities, which can be viewed at **www.dbm.com/jobguide/vets.html#abled**.

www.mindexchange.com

The diversity section of this site provides users with several links to additional resources regarding people with disabilities and employment.

www.usdoj.gov/crt/ada/adahom1.htm

This is the Americans with Disabilities Act home page.

www.abanet.org/disability/home.html

This is the Web site for The Commission on Mental and Physical Disability Law.

janweb.icdi.wvu.edu

The Job Accommodation Web site offers consulting services to employers regarding the integration of people with disabilities in the workplace.

General Resources

www.vault.com

This site provides potential employees with inside information on over 3000 companies. In addition, job seekers can search through available positions and post and answer questions on the message board.

www.wetfeet.com

Similar to **vault.com**, this site allows visitors to ask questions and receive "insider information" on companies that are hiring.

Free Services

www.sleuth.com

On this site job seekers can fill out a form that indicates their desired field of employment. Job Sleuth™ searches the Internet and returns potential matches to the user's inbox. The service is free.

www.refer.com

This site rewards visitors for successful job referrals. If you refer a friend or family member and they are hired, you receive a commission.

www.ajb.org

America's Job Bank is an on-line recruiting service provided through the Department of Labor and the state employment service. Searching and for posting positions on the site are free.

www.xdrive.com

This free site provides members with 25 MB of storage space for housing documents. XDrive is able to communicate with all browser types and has wireless capabilities.

www.driveway.com
Similar to **XDrive.com**, this Web site provides users with 100 MB of storage space. Users can back up, share and organize the information. **Driveway.com** works on all platforms.

Special Interest

www.eharvest.com/careers/index.cfm
This site provides job seekers interested in agricultural positions with online career services capabilities.

www.opportunitynocs.org
This career services Web site is for both employers and job seekers interested in nonprofit opportunitites.

www.experience.com
This Web site is designed specifically for young professionals and students seeking full-time, part-time and internship positions.

www.internshipprograms.com
Students seeking internships can search job listings on this site. It also features City Intern, to help new interns become acquainted with a new location.

www.brassringcampus.com
This site provides college graduates and young professionals with less than five years of experience with job opportunities. Additional features help users buy a car or find an apartment.

On-line Contracting

www.ework.com
This on-line recruiting site matches outside contractors with companies needing project specialists. Other services provided through eWork include links to on-line training sites, benefits packages and payment services and on-line meeting and management resources.

www.elance.com
Similar to **eWork.com**, eLance matches outside contractors with projects.

www.freeagent.com
Similar to other sites in this category, Freeagent matches contractors with projects.

MBAFreeAgent.com
This site is designed to match MBAs with contracting opportunities.

Aquent.com
This site provides access to technical contracting positions.

WorkingSolo.com
This site helps contractors start working for themselves.

Recruiting Services

www.advantagehiring.com
This site helps employers screen resumes.

www.morganworks.com
MorganWorks.com is an on-line recruiting-services provider.Its services include outsourced recruiting, searchable candidate databases, career-site-building services, career-searching capabilities and international executive searches.

www.etest.net
This site provides employers with testing services to assess the strengths and weaknesses of prospective employees. Acquired information can be used for better hiring strategies.

`www.hire.com`
`Hire.com`'s eRecruiter is an application service provider that helps organizations streamline their Web-recruiting process.

`www.futurestep.com`
Executives can register confidentially at **`Futurestep.com`** to be considered for senior executive positions. The site connects registered individuals to positions. It also offers career management services.

`www.webhire.com`
This site provides employers with end-to-end recruiting solutions.

XML-Specific Job Resources

`xmlhack.com/jobs.php`
This page provides a search engine for finding XML-related jobs.

`www.eccnet.com/sgmlug/sgmljobs.html`
This site lists SGML/XML jobs in the Washington DC area.

`www.prescottgroup.com`
This site lists many SGML/XML jobs across the country.

SUMMARY

- The Internet can improve your ability to recruit employees and find career opportunities from around the world.

- Job seekers can learn how to write a resume and cover letter, post them on-line and search through job listings to find the jobs that best suit their needs.

- Employers can post jobs that can be searched by an enormous pool of applicants.

- Storing and distributing resumes digitally, e-mail notification of possible positions, salary and relocation calculators, job coaches and self-assessment tools are among the resources that job seekers can find on-line to help them in their career searches.

- There are approximately 40,000 career-advancement services on the Internet today.

- Finding a job on-line can greatly reduce the amount of time spent applying for a position. Potential candidates can also learn more about a company by visiting its Web site.

- Most sites are free to job seekers. These sites typically generate their revenues by charging employers to post their job opportunities and by selling advertising space on their Web pages.

- Sites such as **`Vault.com`** and **`WetFeet.com`** allow job seekers to post questions about employers and positions in designated chat rooms and bulletin boards.

- On many recruitment sites, the match of a resume to a position is conducted by *resume filtering software*.

- Confidentiality is disadvantage of on-line career services.

- According to recent studies, the number of individuals researching employment positions through means other than the Internet, such as referrals, newspapers and temporary agencies, far outweighs the number of Internet job seekers.

- Career sites designed for individuals seeking a technical position are among the most popular on-line career sites.

- On-line contracting services allow businesses to post positions for which they want to hire outside resources, and individuals can identify projects that best suit their interests, schedules and skills.

- The Internet provides students and young professionals with some of the necessary tools to get them started in the job market. The target market is made up of individuals still in school and seeking internships, individuals that are just graduating and individuals who have been in the workforce for a few years.

- There are a number of Web sites that offer features that will enhance your job search, prepare you for searching online, help design your resume or help you calculate the cost of relocating.

- Web recruiting reaches a larger audience than posting an advertisement in the local newspaper.

- Given the breadth of the services provided on most on-line career services Web sites, the cost of posting on-line is considerably less expensive than posting positions through traditional means.

- There are a variety of sites that allow employers to post jobs on-line. Some of these sites require a fee, which generally runs between $100–$200. Postings remain on the Web site for approximately 30–60 days.

- Employers should try to post to sites that are most likely to be visited by eligible candidates.

- When designing a job posting, defining what makes your position unique and including information such as benefits and salary might convince a qualified candidate to further investigate the position.

- The Internet hosts demographic-specific sites for employers seeking to increase diversity in the workplace.

- The Internet has also provided employers with a cost-effective means of testing their prospective employees in such categories as decision making, problem solving and personality.

WORKS CITED

1. C. Wilde, "Recruiters Discover Diverse Value In Web Sites," *Information Week*   7 February 2000: 144.

2. J. Gaskin, "Web Job Sites Face Tough Job," *Inter@ctive Week*   14 August 2000: 50.

3. J. Gaskin, "Web Job Sites Face Tough Job," *Inter@ctive Week*   14 August 2000: 50.

4. *www.vault.com*

5. J. Gaskin, "Web Job Sites Face Tough Job," *Inter@ctive Week*   14 August 2000: 50.

6. <www.jobsonline.com>

7. <www.driveway.com>

8. *www.cruelworld.com*

9. D. Lewis, "Hired! By the Highest Bidder," *The Boston Globe*   9 July 2000: G1.

10. <www.experience.com>

11. M. French, "Experience, Inc., e-recruiting for jobs for college students," *Mass High Tech*   7 February - 13 February 2000: 29.

12. *www.webhire.com*

13. M. Feffer, "Posting Jobs on the Internet," <www.webhire.com/hr/spotlight.asp> 18 August 2000.

14. C. Wilde, "Recruiters Discover Diverse Value in Web Sites," *Information Week*   7 February 2000: 144.

15. <www.recruitsoft.com>

16. <www.peoplescape.com>

Bibliography

A., Fabio Arciniegas, "What is XLink?" <http://www.xml.com/pub/2000/09/xlink/index.html> 18 September 2000.

Boumphrey, F.; Direnzo, O.; and et. al., *XML Applications*. USA: Wrox Press, 1998.

Boumphrey, F.; Greer, C.; and et. al., *Beginning XHTML*. USA: Wrox Press. 2000.

Ceponkus, A., and Hoodbhoy, F., *Applied XML: A Toolkit for Programmers*. United States: John Wiley & Sons, 1999.

Chang, D., and Harkey, D., *Client/Server Data Access with Java and XML*. United States: John Wiley & Sons, 1998.

Chen, A., "Getting to XML: The new B2B lingua Franca will need to live with EDI. Here's how to mix the two." *eWeek* <http://www.zdnet.com/eweek/stories/general/0,11011,2610043,00.html> 7 August 2000.

Dick, K., *XML A Manager's Guide*. Reading, MA: Addison-Wesley, 2000.

Didie, M. "Getting into i-Mode." <http://www.xml.com/pub/2000/09/20/wireless/imode.html> 20 September 2000.

Dodds, L., "Gentrifying the Web: Taking a look at XHTML, the *XML-Deviant* finds that although the W3C HTML Activity is moving forward, the rest of the web is still lagging behind." <http://www.xml.com/pub/2000/09/13/xhtml/index.html> 13 September 2000.

Dodds, L., "Schema Round-up." <http://www.xml.com/pub/2000/09/06/deviant.html> 6 September 2000.

Ducharme, B., *XML The Annotated Specification*. Upper Saddle River, NJ: Prentice Hall, 1999.

Eddy, S.E., *XML in Plain English*. Foster City, CA: IDG Books Worldwide, 1998.

Floyd, M., *Building Web Sites with XML*. Upper Saddle River, NJ: Prentice Hall, 2000.

Goldfarb, C.F., and Prescod, P., *The XML Handbook*.Upper Saddle River, NJ: Prentice Hall, 1998.

Goldfarb, C.F., and Prescod, P., *The XML Handbook: Second Edition*. Upper Saddle River, NJ: Prentice Hall, 2000.

Harold, E.R., *XML Bible*. Foster City, CA: IDG Books Worldwide, 1999.

Holland, R., "More and more, XML diving into the 'stream.'" *eWeek* <http://www.zdnet.com/eweek/stories/general/0,11011,2608541,00.html> 27 July 2000.

Holland, R., "XML bridges e-apps." eWeek <http://www.zdnet.com/eweek/stories/general/0,11011,2585447,00.html> 12 June 2000.

Holland, R., "XML takes on graphics: Vector-based spec promises to deliver flexible, high resolution images." *eWeek* <http://www.zdnet.com/eweek/stories/general/0,11011,2612024,00.html> 7 August 2000.

Hollander, J., "Netscape Sees XML in Its E-Commerce Future." *E-Commerce Times* <http://www.ecommercetimes.com/news/articles/990309-2.shtml> 9 March 1999.

Jelliffe, R., *The XML & SGML Cookbook*. Upper Saddle River, NJ: Prentice Hall, 1998.

Kay, M., *XSLT Programmer's Reference*. USA: Wrox Press, 2000.

Kropag, B., and et. al., *Professional ASP XML*. Canada: Wrox Press, Inc.,

Leventhal, M.; Lewis, D.; and Fuchs, M., *Designing XML Internet Applications*. Upper Saddle River, NJ: Prentice Hall, 1998.

Matranga, J.,*Understanding BizTalk*. Indianapolis, Indiana: Sams, 2000.

McGrath, S., *XML By Example*. Upper Saddle River, NJ: Prentice Hall, 1998.

McLaughlin, B., *Java and XML*. Sebastopol, CA: O'Reilly & Associates, 2000.

Megginson, D., *Structuring XML Documents*. Upper Saddle River, NJ: Prentice Hall, 1998.

Mohr, S., *Designing Distributed Applications With XML, ASP, IE5, LDAP and MSMQ*. USA: Wrox Press, 1999.

Morgenthal, JP and La Forge, B. *Enterprise Application Integration with XML and Java*. Upper Saddle River, NJ: Prentice Hall, 2001.

Moultis, N.P., and Kirk, C., *XML Black Book*. Scottsdale, AZ: The Coriolis Group, 1999.

Scribner, K., *Understanding SOAP*. Indianapolis, Indiana, 2000: Sams, 2000.

Tittel, E.; Mikula, N.; and Chandak, R., *XML for Dummies*. Foster City, CA: IDG Books Worldwide, 1998.

Travis, B., *XML and SOAP Programming for BizTalk Servers*, Redmond, Washington, 2000: Microsoft Press, 2000.

Walsh, N. "A Technical Introduction to XML." <http://www.xml.com/pub/98/10/guide0.html> 3 October 1998.

Index

License Agreement and Limited Warranty

READ THE FOLLOWING TERMS AND CONDITIONS CAREFULLY BEFORE OPENING THIS SOFTWARE PACKAGE. THIS LEGAL DOCUMENT IS AN AGREEMENT BETWEEN YOU AND PRENTICE-HALL, INC. (THE "COMPANY"). BY OPENING THIS SEALED SOFTWARE PACKAGE, YOU ARE AGREEING TO BE BOUND BY THESE TERMS AND CONDITIONS. IF YOU DO NOT AGREE WITH THESE TERMS AND CONDITIONS, DO NOT OPEN THE SOFTWARE PACKAGE. PROMPTLY RETURN THE UNOPENED SOFTWARE PACKAGE AND ALL ACCOMPANYING ITEMS TO THE PLACE YOU OBTAINED THEM FOR A FULL REFUND OF ANY SUMS YOU HAVE PAID.

1. GRANT OF LICENSE: In consideration of your purchase of this book, and your agreement to abide by the terms and conditions of this Agreement, the Company grants to you a nonexclusive right to use and display the copy of the enclosed software program (hereinafter the "SOFTWARE") on a single computer (i.e., with a single CPU) at a single location so long as you comply with the terms of this Agreement. The Company reserves all rights not expressly granted to you under this Agreement.

2. OWNERSHIP OF SOFTWARE: You own only the magnetic or physical media (the enclosed media) on which the SOFTWARE is recorded or fixed, but the Company and the software developers retain all the rights, title, and ownership to the SOFTWARE recorded on the original media copy(ies) and all subsequent copies of the SOFTWARE, regardless of the form or media on which the original or other copies may exist. This license is not a sale of the original SOFTWARE or any copy to you.

3. COPY RESTRICTIONS: This SOFTWARE and the accompanying printed materials and user manual (the "Documentation") are the subject of copyright. The individual programs on the media are copyrighted by the authors of each program. Some of the programs on the media include separate licensing agreements. If you intend to use one of these programs, you must read and follow its accompanying license

agreement. You may not copy the Documentation or the SOFTWARE, except that you may make a single copy of the SOFTWARE for backup or archival purposes only. You may be held legally responsible for any copying or copyright infringement which is caused or encouraged by your failure to abide by the terms of this restriction.

4. USE RESTRICTIONS: You may not network the SOFTWARE or otherwise use it on more than one computer or computer terminal at the same time. You may physically transfer the SOFTWARE from one computer to another provided that the SOFTWARE is used on only one computer at a time. You may not distribute copies of the SOFTWARE or Documentation to others. You may not reverse engineer, disassemble, decompile, modify, adapt, translate, or create derivative works based on the SOFTWARE or the Documentation without the prior written consent of the Company.

5. TRANSFER RESTRICTIONS: The enclosed SOFTWARE is licensed only to you and may not be transferred to any one else without the prior written consent of the Company. Any unauthorized transfer of the SOFTWARE shall result in the immediate termination of this Agreement.

6. TERMINATION: This license is effective until terminated. This license will terminate automatically without notice from the Company and become null and void if you fail to comply with any provisions or limitations of this license. Upon termination, you shall destroy the Documentation and all copies of the SOFTWARE. All provisions of this Agreement as to warranties, limitation of liability, remedies or damages, and our ownership rights shall survive termination.

7. MISCELLANEOUS: This Agreement shall be construed in accordance with the laws of the United States of America and the State of New York and shall benefit the Company, its affiliates, and assignees.

8. LIMITED WARRANTY AND DISCLAIMER OF WARRANTY: The Company warrants that the SOFTWARE, when properly used in accordance with the Documentation, will operate in substantial conformity with the description of the SOFTWARE set forth in the Documentation. The Company does not warrant that the SOFTWARE will meet your requirements or that the operation of the SOFTWARE will be uninterrupted or error-free. The Company warrants that the media on which the SOFTWARE is delivered shall be free from defects in materials and workmanship under normal use for a period of thirty (30) days from the date of your purchase. Your only remedy and the Company's only obligation under these limited warranties is, at the Company's option, return of the warranted item for a refund of any amounts paid by you or replacement of the item. Any replacement of SOFTWARE or media under the warranties shall not extend the original warranty period. The limited warranty set forth above shall not apply to any SOFTWARE which the Company determines in good faith has been subject to misuse, neglect, improper installation, repair, alteration, or damage by you. EXCEPT FOR THE EXPRESSED WARRANTIES SET FORTH ABOVE, THE COMPANY DISCLAIMS ALL WARRANTIES, EXPRESS OR IMPLIED, INCLUDING WITHOUT LIMITATION, THE IMPLIED WARRANTIES OF MERCHANTABILITY AND FITNESS FOR A PARTICULAR PURPOSE. EXCEPT FOR THE EXPRESS WARRANTY SET

FORTH ABOVE, THE COMPANY DOES NOT WARRANT, GUARANTEE, OR MAKE ANY REPRESENTATION REGARDING THE USE OR THE RESULTS OF THE USE OF THE SOFTWARE IN TERMS OF ITS CORRECTNESS, ACCURACY, RELIABILITY, CURRENTNESS, OR OTHERWISE.

IN NO EVENT, SHALL THE COMPANY OR ITS EMPLOYEES, AGENTS, SUPPLIERS, OR CONTRACTORS BE LIABLE FOR ANY INCIDENTAL, INDIRECT, SPECIAL, OR CONSEQUENTIAL DAMAGES ARISING OUT OF OR IN CONNECTION WITH THE LICENSE GRANTED UNDER THIS AGREEMENT, OR FOR LOSS OF USE, LOSS OF DATA, LOSS OF INCOME OR PROFIT, OR OTHER LOSSES, SUSTAINED AS A RESULT OF INJURY TO ANY PERSON, OR LOSS OF OR DAMAGE TO PROPERTY, OR CLAIMS OF THIRD PARTIES, EVEN IF THE COMPANY OR AN AUTHORIZED REPRESENTATIVE OF THE COMPANY HAS BEEN ADVISED OF THE POSSIBILITY OF SUCH DAMAGES. IN NO EVENT SHALL LIABILITY OF THE COMPANY FOR DAMAGES WITH RESPECT TO THE SOFTWARE EXCEED THE AMOUNTS ACTUALLY PAID BY YOU, IF ANY, FOR THE SOFTWARE.

SOME JURISDICTIONS DO NOT ALLOW THE LIMITATION OF IMPLIED WARRANTIES OR LIABILITY FOR INCIDENTAL, INDIRECT, SPECIAL, OR CONSEQUENTIAL DAMAGES, SO THE ABOVE LIMITATIONS MAY NOT ALWAYS APPLY. THE WARRANTIES IN THIS AGREEMENT GIVE YOU SPECIFIC LEGAL RIGHTS AND YOU MAY ALSO HAVE OTHER RIGHTS WHICH VARY IN ACCORDANCE WITH LOCAL LAW.

ACKNOWLEDGMENT

YOU ACKNOWLEDGE THAT YOU HAVE READ THIS AGREEMENT, UNDERSTAND IT, AND AGREE TO BE BOUND BY ITS TERMS AND CONDITIONS. YOU ALSO AGREE THAT THIS AGREEMENT IS THE COMPLETE AND EXCLUSIVE STATEMENT OF THE AGREEMENT BETWEEN YOU AND THE COMPANY AND SUPERSEDES ALL PROPOSALS OR PRIOR AGREEMENTS, ORAL, OR WRITTEN, AND ANY OTHER COMMUNICATIONS BETWEEN YOU AND THE COMPANY OR ANY REPRESENTATIVE OF THE COMPANY RELATING TO THE SUBJECT MATTER OF THIS AGREEMENT.

Should you have any questions concerning this Agreement or if you wish to contact the Company for any reason, please contact in writing at the address below.

Robin Short
Prentice Hall PTR
One Lake Street
Upper Saddle River, New Jersey 07458

End-User License Agreement for Microsoft Software

IMPORTANT-READ CAREFULLY: This Microsoft End-User License Agreement ("EULA") is a legal agreement between you (either an individual or a single entity) and Microsoft Corporation for the Microsoft software products included in this package, which includes computer software and may include associated media, printed materials, and "on-line" or electronic documentation ("SOFTWARE PRODUCT"). The SOFTWARE PRODUCT also includes any updates and supplements to the original SOFTWARE PRODUCT provided to you by Microsoft. By installing, copying, downloading, accessing or otherwise using the SOFTWARE PRODUCT, you agree to be bound by the terms of this EULA. If you do not agree to the terms of this EULA, do not install, copy, or otherwise use the SOFTWARE PRODUCT.

SOFTWARE PRODUCT LICENSE

The SOFTWARE PRODUCT is protected by copyright laws and international copyright treaties, as well as other intellectual property laws and treaties. The SOFTWARE PRODUCT is licensed, not sold.

1. GRANT OF LICENSE. This EULA grants you the following rights:

    1.1 License Grant. Microsoft grants to you as an individual, a personal nonexclusive license to make and use copies of the SOFTWARE PRODUCT for the sole purposes of evaluating and learning how to use the SOFTWARE PRODUCT, as may be instructed in accompanying publications or documentation. You may install the software on an unlimited number of computers provided that you are the only individual using the SOFTWARE PRODUCT.

    1.2 Academic Use. You must be a "Qualified Educational User" to use the SOFTWARE PRODUCT in the manner described in this section. To determine whether you are a Qualified Educational User, please contact the Microsoft Sales Information Center/One Microsoft Way/Redmond, WA 98052-6399 or the Microsoft subsidiary serving your country. If you are a Qualified Educational User, you may either:

(i) exercise the rights granted in Section 1.1, OR

(ii) if you intend to use the SOFTWARE PRODUCT solely for instructional purposes in connection with a class or other educational program, this EULA grants you the following alternative license models:

(A) Per Computer Model. For every valid license you have acquired for the SOFTWARE PRODUCT, you may install a single copy of the SOFTWARE PRODUCT on a single computer for access and use by an unlimited number of student end users at your educational institution, provided that all such end users comply with all other terms of this EULA, OR

(B) Per License Model. If you have multiple licenses for the SOFTWARE PRODUCT, then at any time you may have as many copies of the SOFTWARE PRODUCT in use as you have licenses, provided that such use is limited to student or faculty end users at your educational institution and provided that all such end users comply with all other terms of this EULA. For purposes of this subsection, the SOFTWARE PRODUCT is "in use" on a computer when it is loaded into the temporary memory (i.e., RAM) or installed into the permanent memory (e.g., hard disk, CD ROM, or other storage device) of that computer, except that a copy installed on a network server for the sole purpose of distribution to other computers is not "in use". If the anticipated number of users of the SOFTWARE PRODUCT will exceed the number of applicable licenses, then you must have a reasonable mechanism or process in place to ensure that the number of persons using the SOFTWARE PRODUCT concurrently does not exceed the number of licenses.

2. DESCRIPTION OF OTHER RIGHTS AND LIMITATIONS.

- Limitations on Reverse Engineering, Decompilation, and Disassembly. You may not reverse engineer, decompile, or disassemble the SOFTWARE PRODUCT, except and only to the extent that such activity is expressly permitted by applicable law notwithstanding this limitation.

- Separation of Components. The SOFTWARE PRODUCT is licensed as a single product. Its component parts may not be separated for use on more than one computer.

- Rental. You may not rent, lease or lend the SOFTWARE PRODUCT.

- Trademarks. This EULA does not grant you any rights in connection with any trademarks or service marks of Microsoft.

- Software Transfer. The initial user of the SOFTWARE PRODUCT may make a one-time permanent transfer of this EULA and SOFTWARE PRODUCT only directly to an end user. This transfer must include all of the SOFTWARE PRODUCT (including all component parts, the media and printed materials, any upgrades, this EULA, and, if applicable, the Certificate of Authenticity). Such transfer may not be by way of consignment or any other indirect transfer. The transferee of such one-time transfer must agree to comply with the terms of this EULA, including the obligation not to further transfer this EULA and SOFTWARE PRODUCT.

- No Support. Microsoft shall have no obligation to provide any product support for the SOFTWARE PRODUCT.

- Termination. Without prejudice to any other rights, Microsoft may terminate this EULA if you fail to comply with the terms and conditions of this EULA. In such event, you must destroy all copies of the SOFTWARE PRODUCT and all of its component parts.

3.   COPYRIGHT. All title and intellectual property rights in and to the SOFTWARE PRODUCT (including but not limited to any images, photographs, animations, video, audio, music, text, and "applets" incorporated into the SOFTWARE PROD-UCT), the accompanying printed materials, and any copies of the SOFTWARE PRODUCT are owned by Microsoft or its suppliers. All title and intellectual property rights in and to the content which may be accessed through use of the SOFT-WARE PRODUCT is the property of the respective content owner and may be protected by applicable copyright or other intellectual property laws and treaties. This EULA grants you no rights to use such content. All rights not expressly granted are reserved by Microsoft.

4.   BACKUP COPY. After installation of one copy of the SOFTWARE PROD-UCT pursuant to this EULA, you may keep the original media on which the SOFTWARE PRODUCT was provided by Microsoft solely for backup or archival purposes. If the original media is required to use the SOFTWARE PRODUCT on the COMPUTER, you may make one copy of the SOFTWARE PRODUCT solely for backup or archival purposes. Except as expressly pro-vided in this EULA, you may not otherwise make copies of the SOFTWARE PRODUCT or the printed materials accompanying the SOFTWARE PROD-UCT.

5.   U.S. GOVERNMENT RESTRICTED RIGHTS. The SOFTWARE PROD-UCT and documentation are provided with RESTRICTED RIGHTS. Use, duplication, or disclosure by the Government is subject to restrictions as set forth in subparagraph (c)(1)(ii) of the Rights in Technical Data and Computer Software clause at DFARS 252.227-7013 or subparagraphs (c)(1) and (2) of the Commercial Computer Software-Restricted Rights at 48 CFR 52.227-19, as applicable. Manufacturer is Microsoft Corporation/One Microsoft Way/ Redmond, WA 98052-6399.

6.   EXPORT RESTRICTIONS. You agree that you will not export or re-export the SOFTWARE PRODUCT, any part thereof, or any process or service that is the direct product of the SOFTWARE PRODUCT (the foregoing collectively referred to as the "Restricted Components"), to any country, person, entity or end user subject to U.S. export restrictions. You specifically agree not to export or re-export any of the Restricted Components (i) to any country to which the U.S. has embargoed or restricted the export of goods or services, which currently include, but are not necessarily limited to Cuba, Iran, Iraq, Libya, North Korea, Sudan and Syria, or to any national of any such country, wherever located, who intends to transmit or transport the Restricted Compo-nents back to such country; (ii) to any end-user who you know or have reason to know will utilize the Restricted Components in the design, development or

production of nuclear, chemical or biological weapons; or (iii) to any end-user who has been prohibited from participating in U.S. export transactions by any federal agency of the U.S. government. You warrant and represent that neither the BXA nor any other U.S. federal agency has suspended, revoked, or denied your export privileges.

7. NOTE ON JAVA SUPPORT. THE SOFTWARE PRODUCT MAY CONTAIN SUPPORT FOR PROGRAMS WRITTEN IN JAVA. JAVA TECHNOLOGY IS NOT FAULT TOLERANT AND IS NOT DESIGNED, MANUFAC-TURED, OR INTENDED FOR USE OR RESALE AS ON-LINE CONTROL EQUIPMENT IN HAZARDOUS ENVIRONMENTS REQUIRING FAIL-SAFE PERFORMANCE, SUCH AS IN THE OPERATION OF NUCLEAR FACILITIES, AIRCRAFT NAVIGATION OR COMMUNICATION SYS-TEMS, AIR TRAFFIC CONTROL, DIRECT LIFE SUPPORT MACHINES, OR WEAPONS SYSTEMS, IN WHICH THE FAILURE OF JAVA TECH-NOLOGY COULD LEAD DIRECTLY TO DEATH, PERSONAL INJURY, OR SEVERE PHYSICAL OR ENVIRONMENTAL DAMAGE.

MISCELLANEOUS

If you acquired this product in the United States, this EULA is governed by the laws of the State of Washington.

If you acquired this product in Canada, this EULA is governed by the laws of the Province of Ontario, Canada. Each of the parties hereto irrevocably attorns to the jurisdiction of the courts of the Province of Ontario and further agrees to commence any litigation which may arise hereunder in the courts located in the Judicial District of York, Province of Ontario.

If this product was acquired outside the United States, then local law may apply.

Should you have any questions concerning this EULA, or if you desire to contact Microsoft for any reason, please contact

Microsoft, or write: Microsoft Sales Information Center/One Microsoft Way/Redmond, WA 98052-6399.

LIMITED WARRANTY

LIMITED WARRANTY. Microsoft warrants that (a) the SOFTWARE PRODUCT will perform substantially in accordance with the accompanying written materials for a period of ninety (90) days from the date of receipt, and (b) any Support Services provided by Microsoft shall be substantially as described in applicable written materials provided to you by Microsoft, and Microsoft support engineers will make commercially reasonable efforts to solve any problem. To the extent allowed by applicable law, implied warranties on the SOFTWARE PRODUCT, if any, are limited to ninety (90) days. Some states/jurisdictions do not allow limitations on duration of an implied warranty, so the above limitation may not apply to you.

CUSTOMER REMEDIES. Microsoft's and its suppliers' entire liability and your exclusive remedy shall be, at Microsoft's option, either (a) return of the price paid, if any, or (b) repair or replacement of the SOFTWARE PRODUCT that does not meet Microsoft's Limited Warranty and that is returned to Microsoft with a copy of your receipt. This Limited Warranty is void if failure of the SOFTWARE PRODUCT has resulted from accident, abuse, or misapplication. Any replacement SOFTWARE PRODUCT will be warranted for the remainder of the original warranty period or thirty (30) days, whichever is longer. Outside the United States, neither these remedies nor any product support services offered by Microsoft are available without proof of purchase from an authorized international source.

NO OTHER WARRANTIES. TO THE MAXIMUM EXTENT PERMITTED BY APPLICABLE LAW, MICROSOFT AND ITS SUPPLIERS DISCLAIM ALL OTHER WARRANTIES AND CONDITIONS, EITHER EXPRESS OR IMPLIED, INCLUDING, BUT NOT LIMITED TO, IMPLIED WARRANTIES OR CONDITIONS OF MER-CHANTABILITY, FITNESS FOR A PARTICULAR PURPOSE, TITLE AND NON-INFRINGEMENT, WITH REGARD TO THE SOFTWARE PRODUCT, AND THE PROVISION OF OR FAILURE TO PROVIDE SUPPORT SERVICES. THIS LIMITED WARRANTY GIVES YOU SPECIFIC LEGAL RIGHTS. YOU MAY HAVE OTHERS, WHICH VARY FROM STATE/JURISDICTION TO STATE/JURISDICTION.

LIMITATION OF LIABILITY. TO THE MAXIMUM EXTENT PERMITTED BY APPLICABLE LAW, IN NO EVENT SHALL MICROSOFT OR ITS SUPPLIERS BE LIABLE FOR ANY SPECIAL, INCIDENTAL, INDIRECT, OR CONSEQUENTIAL DAMAGES WHATSOEVER (INCLUDING, WITHOUT LIMITATION, DAMAGES FOR LOSS OF BUSINESS PROFITS, BUSINESS INTERRUPTION, LOSS OF BUSI-NESS INFORMATION, OR ANY OTHER PECUNIARY LOSS) ARISING OUT OF THE USE OF OR INABILITY TO USE THE SOFTWARE PRODUCT OR THE FAILURE TO PROVIDE SUPPORT SERVICES, EVEN IF MICROSOFT HAS BEEN ADVISED OF THE POSSIBILITY OF SUCH DAMAGES. IN ANY CASE, MICROSOFT'S ENTIRE LIABILITY UNDER ANY PROVISION OF THIS EULA SHALL BE LIMITED TO THE GREATER OF THE AMOUNT ACTUALLY PAID BY YOU FOR THE SOFTWARE PRODUCT OR U.S.$5.00; PROVIDED, HOWEVER, IF YOU HAVE ENTERED INTO A MICROSOFT SUPPORT SERVICES AGREEMENT, MICROSOFT'S ENTIRE LIABILITY REGARDING SUPPORT SERVICES SHALL BE GOVERNED BY THE TERMS OF THAT AGREEMENT. BECAUSE SOME STATES/JURISDICTIONS DO NOT ALLOW THE EXCLUSION OR LIMITATION OF LIA-BILITY, THE ABOVE LIMITATION MAY NOT APPLY TO YOU.

0495 Part No. 64358

The DEITEL & DEITEL Suite of Products...

C# How to Program

BOOK / CD-ROM

*©2002, 1400 pp., paper
(0-13-062221-4)*

An exciting new addition to the *How to Program* series, *C# How to Program* provides a comprehensive introduction to Microsoft's new object-oriented language. C# builds on the skills already mastered by countless C++ and Java programmers, enabling them to create powerful Web applications and components—ranging from XML-based Web services on Microsoft's .NET platform to middle-tier business objects and system-level applications. *C# How to Program* begins with a strong foundation in the introductory and intermediate programming principles students will need in industry. It then explores such essential topics as object-oriented programming and exception handling. Graphical user interfaces are extensively covered, giving readers the tools to build compelling and fully interactive programs. Internet technologies such as XML, ADO .NET and Web services are also covered as well as topics including regular expressions, multithreading, networking, databases, files and data structures.

Visual Basic .NET How to Program
Second Edition

BOOK / CD-ROM

*©2002, 1400 pp., paper
(0-13-029363-6)*

Teach Visual Basic .NET programming from the ground up! This introduction of Microsoft's .NET Framework marks the beginning of major revisions to all of Microsoft's programming languages. This book provides a comprehensive introduction to the next version of Visual Basic—Visual Basic .NET—featuring extensive updates and increased functionality. *Visual Basic .NET How to Program, Second Edition* covers introductory programming techniques as well as more advanced topics, featuring enhanced treatment of developing Web-based applications. Other topics discussed include an extensive treatment of XML and wireless applications, databases, SQL and ADO .NET, Web forms, Web services and ASP .NET.

Also coming soon in the Deitels' *.NET Series:*
• *Visual C++ .NET How to Program*

C How to Program
Third Edition

BOOK / CD-ROM

*©2001, 1253 pp., paper
(0-13-089572-5)*

Highly practical in approach, the Third Edition of the world's best-selling C text introduces the fundamentals of structured programming and software engineering and gets up to speed quickly. This comprehensive book not only covers the full C language, but also reviews library functions and introduces object-based and object-oriented programming in C++ and Java. The Third Edition includes a new 346-page introduction to Java 2 and the basics of GUIs, and the 298-page introduction to C++ has been updated to be consistent with the most current ANSI/ISO C++ standards. Plus, icons throughout the book point out valuable programming tips such as Common Programming Errors, Portability Tips and Testing and Debugging Tips.

C++ How to Program
Third Edition

BOOK / CD-ROM

*©2001, 1168 pp., paper
(0-13-089571-7)*

The world's best-selling C++ text teaches programming by emphasizing object-oriented programming, software reuse and component-oriented software construction. This comprehensive book uses the Deitels' signature LIVE-CODE™ Approach, presenting every concept in the context of a complete, working C++ program followed by a screen capture showing the program's output. It also includes a rich collection of exercises and valuable insights in its set of Common Programming Errors, Software Engineering Observations, Portability Tips and Testing and Debugging Tips. The Third Edition features an extensive treatment of the Standard Template Library and includes a new case study that focuses on object-oriented design with the UML, illustrating the entire process of object-oriented design from conception to implementation. In addition, it adheres to the latest ANSI/ISO C++ standards. The accompanying CD-ROM contains Microsoft® Visual C++™ 6.0 Introductory Edition software, source code for all examples in the text and hyperlinks to C++ demos and Internet resources.

Getting Started with Microsoft® Visual C++™ 6 with an Introduction to MFC

BOOK / CD-ROM

©2000, 163 pp., paper (0-13-016147-0)

Internet & World Wide Web How to Program, Second Edition

BOOK / CD-ROM

©2002, 1428 pp., paper
(0-13-030897-8)

The revision of this groundbreaking book in the Deitels' *How to Program* series offers a thorough treatment of programming concepts that yield visible or audible results in Web pages and Web-based applications. This book discusses effective Web-based design, server- and client-side scripting, multitier Web-based applications development, ActiveX® controls and electronic commerce essentials. This book offers an alternative to traditional programming courses using markup languages (such as XHTML, Dynamic HTML and XML) and scripting languages (such as JavaScript, VBScript, Perl/CGI, Python and PHP) to teach the fundamentals of programming "wrapped in the metaphor of the Web." Updated material on **www.deitel.com** and **www.prenhall.com/deitel** provides additional resources for instructors who want to cover Microsoft® or non-Microsoft technologies. The Web site includes an extensive treatment of Netscape® 6 and alternate versions of the code from the Dynamic HTML chapters that will work with non-Microsoft environments as well.

Python How to Program

BOOK / CD-ROM

©2002, 1400 pp., paper
(0-13-092361-3)

This exciting new book provides a comprehensive introduction to Python—a powerful object-oriented programming language with clear syntax and the ability to bring together various technologies quickly and easily. This book covers introductory-programming techniques and more advanced topics such as graphical user interfaces, databases, wireless Internet programming, networking, security, process management, multithreading, XHTML, CSS, PSP and multimedia. Readers will learn principles that are applicable to both systems development and Web programming. The book features the consistent and applied pedagogy that the *How to Program* series is known for, including the Deitels' signature LIVE-CODE™ Approach, with thousands of lines of code in hundreds of working programs; hundreds of valuable programming tips identified with icons throughout the text; an extensive set of exercises, projects and case studies; two-color four-way syntax coloring and much more.

Wireless Internet & Mobile Business How to Program

©2002, 1327 pp., paper
(0-13-062226-5)

While the rapid expansion of wireless technologies, such as cell phones, pagers and personal digital assistants (PDAs), offers many new opportunities for businesses and programmers, it also presents numerous challenges related to issues such as security and standardization. This book offers a thorough treatment of both the management and technical aspects of this growing area, including coverage of current practices and future trends. The first half explores the business issues surrounding wireless technology and mobile business, including an overview of existing and developing communication technologies and the application of business principles to wireless devices. It also discusses location-based services and location-identifying technologies, a topic that is revisited throughout the book. Wireless payment, security, legal and social issues, international communications and more are also discussed. The book then turns to programming for the wireless Internet, exploring topics such as WAP (including 2.0), WML, WMLScript, XML, XHTML™, wireless Java programming (J2ME), Web Clipping and more. Other topics covered include career resources, wireless marketing, accessibility, Palm™, PocketPC, Windows CE, i-mode, Bluetooth, MIDP, MIDlets, ASP, Microsoft .NET Mobile Framework, BREW™, multimedia, Flash and VBScript.

e-Business & e-Commerce for Managers

©2001, 794 pp., cloth
(0-13-032364-0)

This comprehensive overview of building and managing e-businesses explores topics such as the decision to bring a business online, choosing a business model, accepting payments, marketing strategies and security, as well as many other important issues (such as career resources). The book features Web resources and online demonstrations that supplement the text and direct readers to additional materials. The book also includes an appendix that develops a complete Web-based shopping-cart application using HTML, JavaScript, VBScript, Active Server Pages, ADO, SQL, HTTP, XML and XSL. Plus, company-specific sections provide "real-world" examples of the concepts presented in the book.

XML How to Program

BOOK / CD-ROM

©2001, 934 pp., paper (0-13-028417-3)

This book is a comprehensive guide to programming in XML. It teaches how to use XML to create customized tags and includes chapters that address standard custom-markup languages for science and technology, multimedia, commerce and many other fields. Concise introductions to Java, JavaServer Pages, VBScript, Active Server Pages and Perl/CGI provide readers with the essentials of these programming languages and server-side development technologies to enable them to work effectively with XML. The book also covers cutting-edge topics such as XSL, DOM™ and SAX, plus a real-world e-commerce case study and a complete chapter on Web accessibility that addresses Voice XML. It includes tips such as Common Programming Errors, Software Engineering Observations, Portability Tips and Debugging Hints. Other topics covered include XHTML, CSS, DTD, schema, parsers, XPath, XLink, namespaces, XBase, XInclude, XPointer, XSLT, XSL Formatting Objects, JavaServer Pages, XForms, topic maps, X3D, MathML, OpenMath, CML, BML, CDF, RDF, SVG, Cocoon, WML, XBRL, and BizTalk™ and SOAP™ Web resources.

Perl How to Program

BOOK / CD-ROM

©2001, 1057 pp., paper (0-13-028418-1)

This comprehensive guide to Perl programming emphasizes the use of the Common Gateway Interface (CGI) with Perl to create powerful, dynamic multi-tier Web-based client/server applications. The book begins with a clear and careful introduction to programming concepts at a level suitable for beginners, and proceeds through advanced topics such as references and complex data structures. Key Perl topics such as regular expressions and string manipulation are covered in detail. The authors address important and topical issues such as object-oriented programming, the Perl database interface (DBI), graphics and security. Also included is a treatment of XML, a bonus chapter introducing the Python programming language, supplemental material on career resources and a complete chapter on Web accessibility. The text includes tips such as Common Programming Errors, Software Engineering Observations, Portability Tips and Debugging Hints.

e-Business & e-Commerce How to Program

BOOK / CD-ROM

©2001, 1254 pp., paper (0-13-028419-X)

This innovative book explores programming technologies for developing Web-based e-business and e-commerce solutions, and covers e-business and e-commerce models and business issues. Readers learn a full range of options, from "build-your-own" to turnkey solutions. The book examines scores of the top e-businesses (examples include Amazon, eBay, Priceline, Travelocity, etc.), explaining the technical details of building successful e-business and e-commerce sites and their underlying business premises. Learn how to implement the dominant e-commerce models—shopping carts, auctions, name-your-own-price, comparison shopping and bots/ intelligent agents—by using markup languages (HTML, Dynamic HTML and XML), scripting languages (JavaScript, VBScript and Perl), server-side technologies (Active Server Pages and Perl/CGI) and database (SQL and ADO), security and online payment technologies. Updates are regularly posted to **www.deitel.com** and the book includes a CD-ROM with software tools, source code and live links.

ORDER INFORMATION

SINGLE COPY SALES:
Visa, Master Card, American Express, Checks, or Money Orders only
Toll-Free: 800-643-5506; Fax: 800-835-5327

GOVERNMENT AGENCIES:
Prentice Hall Customer Service
(#GS-02F-8023A)
Phone: 201-767-5994; Fax: 800-445-6991

COLLEGE PROFESSORS:
For desk or review copies, please visit us on the World Wide Web at www.prenhall.com

CORPORATE ACCOUNTS:
Quantity, Bulk Orders totaling 10 or more books. Purchase orders only — No credit cards.
Tel: 201-236-7156; Fax: 201-236-7141
Toll-Free: 800-382-3419

CANADA:
Pearson Education Canada
26 Prince Andrew Place
Don Mills, ON M3C 2T8 Canada
Tel: 416 447 5101; Fax: 416 443 0948
E-mail: phcinfo.pubcanada@pearsoned.com

UK/IRELAND:
Pearson Education
Edinburgh Gate
Harlow, Essex CM20 2JE UK
Tel: 01279 623928; Fax: 01279 414130
E-mail: enq.orders@pearsoned-ema.com

EUROPE, MIDDLE EAST & AFRICA:
Pearson Education
P.O. Box 75598
1070 AN Amsterdam, The Netherlands
Tel: 31 20 5755 800; Fax: 31 20 664 5334
E-mail: amsterdam@pearsoned-ema.com

ASIA:
Pearson Education Asia
317 Alexandra Road #04-01
IKEA Building
Singapore 159965
Tel: 65 476 4688; Fax: 65 378 0370

JAPAN:
Pearson Education
Nishi-Shinjuku, KF Building 101
8-14-24 Nishi-Shinjuku, Shinjuku-ku
Tokyo, Japan 160-0023
Tel: 81 3 3365 9001; Fax: 81 3 3365 9009

INDIA:
Pearson Education Indian Liaison Office
90 New Raidhani Enclave, Ground Floor
Delhi 110 092, India
Tel: 91 11 2059850 & 2059851
Fax: 91 11 2059852

AUSTRALIA:
Pearson Education Australia
Unit 4, Level 2
14 Aquatic Drive
Frenchs Forest, NSW 2086, Australia
Tel: 61 2 9454 2200; Fax: 61 2 9453 0089
E-mail: marketing@pearsoned.com.au

NEW ZEALAND/FIJI:
Pearson Education
46 Hillside Road
Auckland 10, New Zealand
Tel: 649 444 4968; Fax: 649 444 4957
E-mail: sales@pearsoned.co.nz

SOUTH AFRICA:
Pearson Education
P.O. Box 12122
Mill Street
Cape Town 8010 South Africa
Tel: 27 21 686 6356; Fax: 27 21 686 4590

LATIN AMERICA:
Pearson Education Latinoamerica
815 NW 57th Street Suite 484
Miami, FL 33158
Tel: 305 264 8344; Fax: 305 264 7933

Complete Training Courses

Each complete package includes the corresponding *How to Program Series* book and interactive multimedia CD-ROM. *Complete Training Courses* are perfect for anyone interested in learning Java, C++, Visual Basic, XML, Perl, Internet/World Wide Web and e-commerce programming. They are exceptional and affordable resources for college students and professionals learning programming for the first time or reinforcing their knowledge.

Each *Complete Training Course* is compatible with Windows 95, Windows 98, Windows NT and Windows 2000 and includes the following features:

Intuitive Browser-Based Interface

Whether you choose the Web-based *Complete Training Course* or the CD-ROM, you'll love the new browser-based interface, designed to be easy and accessible to anyone who's ever used a Web browser. Every *Complete Training Course* features the full text, illustrations and program listings of its corresponding *How to Program* book—all in full color—with full-text searching and hyperlinking.

Further Enhancements to the Deitels' Signature Live-Code™ Approach

Every code sample from the main text can be found in the interactive, multimedia, CD-ROM-based *Cyber Classrooms* included in the *Complete Training Courses*. Syntax coloring of code is included for the *How to Program* books that are published in full color. Even the recent two-color books use effective four-way syntax coloring. The *Cyber Classroom* software is provided in full color for all the Deitel books.

Audio Annotations

Hours of detailed, expert audio descriptions of thousands of lines of code help reinforce concepts.

Easily Executable Code

With one click of the mouse, you can execute the code or save it to your hard drive to manipulate using the programming environment of your choice. With selected *Complete Training Courses*, you can also load all of the code into a development environment such as Microsoft® Visual C++™, enabling you to modify and execute the programs with ease.

Abundant Self-Assessment Material

Practice exams test your understanding with hundreds of text questions and answers in addition to those found in the main text. Hundreds of self-review questions, all with answers, are drawn from the text; as are hundreds of programming exercises, half with answers.

Announcing New Web-Based Versions of the Deitels' *Complete Training Courses!*

The same highly acclaimed material found on the *Cyber Classroom* CD-ROMs is now available at the same price via the World Wide Web! When you order the Web-based version of a *Complete Training Course,* you receive the corresponding *How to Program* book with a URL and password that give you six months of access to the *Cyber Classroom* software via the Web.

To explore a demo of this new option, please visit
http://ptgtraining.com

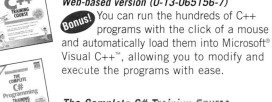

www.InformIT.com/deitel

Deitel & Associates, Inc. is partnering with Prentice Hall's parent company, Pearson PLC, and its information technology Web site, InformIT (www.informit.com) to launch the Deitel InformIT site at www.InformIT.com/deitel. The Deitel InformIT kiosk will be up and running in Q1 2002 with information on the continuum of Deitel products, including:

 • **Free informational articles**

 • **Deitel e-Matter**

• **Books and new e-Books**

• **Instructor-led training**
• **Web-based training**
• *Complete Training Courses/Cyber Classrooms*

Deitel will contribute to a weekly column in the popular InformIT newsletter, currently subscribed to by more than 800,000 IT professionals worldwide (for opt-in registration, see www.informit.com). This column will provide information on topics including:

• Deitel publications and products including the complete Deitel Catalog for product ordering information and updates
• Resources and articles on leading-edge technologies and IT issues

• WBT and e-learning updates
• Instructor-led training information
• Programming tips and methods
• Progress reports on forthcoming publications
• Deitel research and development activities

Web-Based Tutorials

Deitel is committed to continuous research and development in e-learning and is enhancing its series of self-paced CD-ROM and Web-based tutorials using content from the Deitel *How to Program Series* textbooks. The tutorials are appropriate for distance education and on-campus courses. Our instructional designers are currently developing features that include:
• Interactive Macromedia® Flash™ animations demonstrating key programming concepts.
• Interactive Questions (with answers) relating to specific lines of code.
• Dynamic Glossary linking designated keywords or phrases to small windows containing definitions.
• More abundant audio, including some examples with animated, interactive code walk-throughs highlighting each section of code as it is mentioned.

A Sneak Peek at the Interactive Animation in the *Java Multimedia Cyber Classroom 4/e*

1. When the animation starts a ball is dropped into a bucket signifying that the flow through the flowchart has begun. The ball continues through the flowchart stopping three times along the way.

2. First, the loop-continuation condition is checked; next, a line is drawn in a simulated output window...

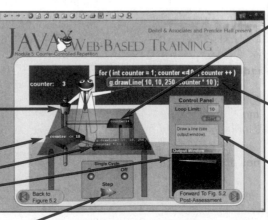

3. ...then the value of the conditional variable is incremented.

4. At each step, the appropriate code is highlighted...

5. ...and a short description of that step is given on the control panel.

If the user misses something in the animation, it can be repeated as needed. The animation may also be switched to "single-cycle" mode, allowing the student to step through the code manually one action at a time.

WHAT'S COMING FROM THE DEITELS

Future Publications

Here are some new titles we are considering for 2002/2003 release:

Computer Science Series: *Theory and Principles of Operating Systems: a Simulation Approach, Data Structures in C++, Data Structures in Java, Theory and Principles of Database Systems.*

Database Series: *Oracle How to Program, SQL Server How to Program, MySQL How to Program.*

Internet and Web Programming Series: *Open Source Software Development: Apache, Linux, MySQL and PHP How to Program, Perl 6 How to Program 2/e.*

Programming Series: *Flash™ How to Program, Multimedia How to Program.*

.NET Programming Series: *Advanced C# .NET How to Program, Advanced Visual Basic .NET How to Program, Visual C++ .NET™ How to Program, Advanced Visual C++ .NET How to Program, ASP .NET How to Program.*

Object Technology Series: *OOAD with the UML, Design Patterns, Java and XML.*

Advanced Java Series: *JDBC How to Program, Enterprise JavaBeans How to Program, Java Media Framework (JMF) How to Program, Java Security and Java Cryptography (JCE) How to Program, Java Servlets How to Program, Java2D and Java3D How to Program, JavaServer Pages (JSP) How to Program, JINI How to Program, Java 2 Micro Edition (J2ME) How to Program.*

Deitel Newsletter

Deitel and Associates, Inc. is launching a free, opt-in newsletter that will include:

- Updates and commentary on industry trends and developments
- Resources and links to articles from our published books and upcoming publications.
- Information on the Deitel publishing plans, including future publications and product-release schedules

To sign up for the Deitel Newsletter, visit www.deitel.com.

E-Books

We are committed to providing our content in traditional print formats and in emerging electronic formats, such as e-books, to fulfill our customers' needs. We are currently exploring several solutions. Visit www.deitel.com for periodic updates.

E-Learning

(Cyber Classrooms, Web-Based Training and Course Management Systems)

Deitel is committed to continuous research and development in e-Learning. On the page to the left, we provide a sneak peek at our plans for Web-based training, including a five-way Macromedia® Flash™ animation of a `for` loop in Java. We are pleased to announce that we have incorporated this example into the *Java 2 Multimedia Cyber Classroom, 4/e* (which is included in *The Complete Java 2 Training Course, 4/e*). Our instructional designers and Flash animation team are developing additional simulations that demonstrate key programming concepts. We are enhancing the *Multimedia Cyber Classroom* products to include more audio, pre- and post-assessment questions and Web-based labs with solutions for the benefit of professors and students alike. In addition, our *Multimedia Cyber Classroom* products, available in both CD and Web-based formats, are being ported to Pearson's CourseCompass course-management system—a powerful e-platform for teaching and learning.

Turn the page to find out more about Deitel & Associates!

License Agreement and Limited Warranty

Using the CD-ROM

Microsoft Windows users may access the contents of this CD through the interface provided in the file **AUTORUN.EXE**. If a startup screen does not pop up automatically when you insert the CD into your computer, double click on the icon for **AUTORUN.EXE** to launch the program or launch the file **WELCOME.HTM** in your browser. Linux users should launch **WELCOME.HTM** in a browser to get started.

Contents of the CD-ROM

- Microsoft® Internet Explorer 5 (for Windows only)
- W3C ® Amaya™ 3.2.1
- The following software developed by the Apache Software Foundation (www.apache.org),
  - Xalan 1.2
  - FOP 0.14,
  - Xerces 1.2.0
  - Crimson 1.0
- Live links to websites mentioned in the book *XML How to Program*
- Live code examples from the book *XML How to Program*

Software and Hardware System Requirements

- Intel Pentium 133 MHz or faster processor (200 MHz recommended)
- Microsoft Windows 95 or later, or
- Microsoft Windows NT 4.0 (or later) or
- Red Hat Linux 6.0 (or later)
- 32 Mb (48 MB recommended)
- CD-ROM drive
- Internet connection